Readings in Nonmonotonic Reasoning

Readings in Nonmonotonic Reasoning

Edited by
Matthew L. Ginsberg
Stanford University

MORGAN KAUFMANN PUBLISHERS, INC.
LOS ALTOS, CALIFORNIA

Editor and President *Michael B. Morgan*
Production Manager *Jennifer Ballentine*
Production and Permissions Editor *Todd R. Armstrong*
Design *Beverly Kennon-Kelley*
Composition and Typesetting *Arthur Ogawa*
Pasteup and Cover Design *Earlywine Design*
Copy Editor *Lyn Dupré*

Library of Congress Cataloging-in-Publication Data

Readings in nonmonotonic reasoning / edited by Matthew L. Ginsberg.
p. cm.
Bibliography: p.
Includes index.
ISBN 0-934613-45-1
1. Artificial intelligence. 2. Reasoning. 3. Logic, Symbolic and mathematical I. Ginsberg, Matthew L. 1955–
Q335.R433 1987
006.3--dc19 87-24144
CIP

Morgan Kaufmann Publishers, Inc.
95 First Street, Los Altos, California 94022

Printed in the United States of America

91 90 89 88 87 5 4 3 2 1

Acknowledgments

The editor would like to thank the publishers and authors for permission to reprint copyrighted material in this volume.

J. McCarthy and P. J. Hayes, "Some philosophical problems from the standpoint of artificial intelligence," in B. Meltzer and D. Mitchie (eds.), *Machine Intelligence 4*, Edinburgh University Press, pp. 463-502, 1969. © 1969, Edinburgh University Press. Reprinted with permission of the publisher and the authors.

J. McCarthy, "Epistemological problems of artificial intelligence," *Proceedings of the Fifth International Joint Conference on Artificial Intelligence*, Cambridge, MA, pp. 1038–1044, 1977. © 1977, IJCAI. Used by permission of the International Joint Conferences on Artificial Intelligence, Inc., and of the author; copies of the Proceedings are available from Morgan Kaufmann Publishers, Inc., 95 First Street, Los Altos, CA 94022 USA.

D. J. Israel, "What's wrong with non-monotonic logic?" *Proccedings of the First Annual National Conference on Artificial Intelligence*, Stanford, CA, pp. 99-101, 1980. © 1980, American Association for Artificial Intelligence. All rights reserved. Used by permission of AAAI and the author; copies of the Proceedings are available from Morgan Kaufmann Publishers, Inc., 95 First Street, Los Altos, CA 94022 USA.

D. Perlis, "On the consistency of commonsense reasoning," *Computational Intelligence*, 2:180–190, 1986. © 1986, National Research Council of Canada. Reproduced by permission of the National Research Council of Canada and the author.

R. Reiter, "A logic for default reasoning," *Artificial Intelligence*, 13:81–132, 1980. © 1980, North–Holland. Reprinted with permission of the editor-in-chief, Daniel Bobrow, and of the publisher, North–Holland, Amsterdam, and of the author.

R. Reiter and G. Criscuolo, "On interacting defaults," *Proceedings of the Seventh International Joint Conference on Artificial Intelligence*, Vancouver, British Columbia, Canada, pp. 270–276, 1981. © 1981, IJCAI. Used by permission of the International Joint Conferences on Artificial Intelligence, Inc., and of the authors; copies of the Proceedings are available from Morgan Kaufmann Publishers, Inc., 95 First Street, Los Altos, CA 94022 USA.

D. W. Etherington and R. Reiter, "On inheritance hierarchies with exceptions," *Proceedings of the Third National Conference on Artificial Intelligence*, Washington, DC, pp. 104–108, 1983. © 1983, American Association for Artificial Intelligence. All rights reserved. Used by permission of AAAI and the authors; copies of the Proceedings are available from Morgan Kaufmann Publishers, Inc., 95 First Street, Los Altos, CA 94022 USA.

D. S. Touretzky, "Implicit ordering of defaults in inheritance systems," *Proceedings of the Fifth National Conference on Artificial Intelligence*, Austin, TX, pp. 322–325, 1984. © 1984, American Association for Artificial Intelligence. All rights reserved. Used by permission of AAAI and the author; copies of the Proceedings are available from Morgan Kaufmann Publishers, Inc., 95 First Street, Los Altos, CA 94022 USA.

D. McDermott and J. Doyle, "Non-monotonic logic I," *Artificial Intelligence*, 13:41–72, 1980. © 1980, North-Holland. Reprinted with permission of the editor-in-chief, Daniel Bobrow, and of the publisher, North-Holland, Amsterdam, and of the authors.

R. C. Moore, "Semantical considerations on nonmonotonic logic," *Artificial Intelligence*, 25:75–94, 1985. © 1985, North-Holland. Reprinted with permission of the editor-in-chief, Daniel Bobrow, and of the publisher, North-Holland, Amsterdam, and of the author.

R. C. Moore, "Possible-world semantics for autoepistemic logic," *Proceedings 1984 Non-monotonic Reasoning Workshop*, New Paltz, NY, pp. 344–354, 1984. © 1984, American Association for Artificial Intelligence. Reprinted with permission of AAAI and the author.

J. McCarthy, "Circumscription—a form of non-monotonic reasoning," *Artificial Intelligence*, 13:27–39, 171–172, 1980. © 1980, North-Holland. Reprinted with permission of the editor-in-chief, Daniel Bobrow, and of the publisher, North–Holland, Amsterdam, and of the author.

J. McCarthy, "Applications of circumscription to formalizing common sense knowledge," *Artificial Intelligence*, 28:89–116, 1986. © 1986, North–Holland. Reprinted with permission of the editor-in-chief, Daniel Bobrow, and of the publisher, North–Holland, Amsterdam, and of the author.

V. Lifschitz, "Computing circumscription," *Proceedings of the Ninth International Joint Conference on Artificial Intelligence*, Los Angeles, CA, pp. 121–127, 1985. © 1985, IJCAI.

Used by permission of the International Joint Conferences on Artificial Intelligence, Inc., and of the author; copies of the Proceedings are available from Morgan Kaufmann Publishers, Inc., 95 First Street, Los Altos, CA 94022 USA.

D. W. Etherington, R. E. Mercer, and R. Reiter, "On the adequacy of predicate circumscription for closed-world reasoning," *Computational Intelligence*, 1:11–15, 1985. © 1985, National Research Council of Canada. Reproduced by permission of the National Research Council of Canada and the authors.

V. Lifschitz, *Pointwise Circumscription*, Stanford preprint, 1987. © 1987, Vladimir Lifschitz. Reprinted with permission of the author.

K. Konolige, *On the Relation Between Default and Autoepistemic Logic*, SRI preprint, 1987. © 1987, Kurt Konolige. Reprinted with permission of the author.

Y. Shoham, "A semantical approach to nonmonotonic logics," *Proceedings of the Tenth International Joint Conference on Artificial Intelligence*, Milan, Italy, pp. 388–392, 1987. © 1987, IJCAI. Used by permission of the International Joint Conferences on Artificial Intelligence, Inc., and of the authors; copies of the Proceedings are available from Morgan Kaufmann Publishers, Inc., 95 First Street, Los Altos, CA 94022 USA.

M. L. Ginsberg, "Multi-valued logics," *Proceedings of the Fifth National Conference on Artificial Intelligence*, Philadelphia, PA, pp. 243–247, 1986. © 1986, American Association for Artificial Intelligence. All rights reserved. Used by permission of AAAI and the author; copies of the Proceedings are available from Morgan Kaufmann Publishers, Inc., 95 First Street, Los Altos, CA 94022 USA.

J. Doyle, "A truth maintenance system," *Artificial Intelligence*, 12:231–272, 1979. © 1979, North–Holland. Reprinted with permission of the editor-in-chief, Daniel Bobrow, and of the publisher, North–Holland, Amsterdam, and of the author.

J. de Kleer, "An assumption-based TMS," *Artificial Intelligence*, 28:127–162, 1986. © 1986, North–Holland. Reprinted with permission of the editor-in-chief, Daniel Bobrow, and of the publisher, North–Holland, Amsterdam, and of the author.

R. Reiter, "On closed world data bases," in H. Gallaire and J. Minker (eds.), *Logic and Data Bases*, pp. 119–140, Plenum, New York, 1978. © 1978, Plenum Publishing Corporation. Reprinted with permission of the publisher and the author.

K. L. Clark, "Negation as failure," in H. Gallaire and J. Minker (eds.), *Logic and Data Bases*, pp. 293–322, Plenum, New York, 1978. © 1978, Plenum Publishing Corporation. Reprinted with permission of the publisher and the author.

V. Lifschitz, "Closed-world databases and circumscription," *Artificial Intelligence*, 27:229–235, 1985. © 1985, North–Holland. Reprinted with permission of the editor-in-chief, Daniel Bobrow, and of the publisher, North–Holland, Amsterdam, and of the author.

V. Lifschitz, "On the declarative semantics of logic programs with negation," in J. Minker (ed.), *Foundations of Deductive Databases and Logic Programming*, Morgan Kaufmann Publishers, Inc., Los Altos, CA, 1987. © 1987, Morgan Kaufmann Publishers, Inc. Reprinted with permission of the publisher and the author.

R. Reiter, "A theory of diagnosis from first principles," *Artificial Intelligence*, 32:57–95, 1987. © 1987, North–Holland. Reprinted with permission of the editor-in-chief, Daniel Bobrow, and of the publisher, North–Holland, Amsterdam, and of the author.

J. de Kleer and B. C. Williams, "Diagnosing multiple faults," *Artificial Intelligence*, 32:97–130, 1987. © 1987, North–Holland. Reprinted with permission of the editor-in-chief, Daniel Bobrow, and of the publisher, North–Holland, Amsterdam, and of the authors.

S. Hanks and D. McDermott, "Default reasoning, nonmonotonic logics, and the frame problem," *Proceedings of the Fifth National Conference on Artificial Intelligence*, Philadelphia, PA, pp. 328–333, 1986. © 1986, American Association for Artificial Intelligence. All rights reserved. Used by permission of AAAI and the authors; copies of the Proceedings are available from Morgan Kaufmann Publishers, Inc., 95 First Street, Los Altos, CA 94022 USA.

Y. Shoham, "Chronological ignorance," *Proceedings of the Fifth National Conference on Artificial Intelligence*, Philadelphia, PA, pp. 389–393, 1986. © 1986, American Association for Artificial Intelligence. All rights reserved. Used by permission of AAAI and the author; copies of the Proceedings are available from Morgan Kaufmann Publishers, Inc., 95 First Street, Los Altos, CA 94022 USA.

V. Lifschitz, "Formal theories of action," in F. Brown (ed.), *The Frame Problem in Artificial Intelligence: Proceedings of the 1987 Workshop*, pp. 35–58, Morgan Kaufmann Publishers, Inc., Los Altos, CA, 1987. © 1987, Morgan Kaufmann Publishers, Inc. Reprinted with permission of the publisher and the author.

M. L. Ginsberg and D. E. Smith, "Reasoning about action I: A possible worlds approach," in F. Brown (ed.), *The Frame Problem in Artificial Intelligence: Proceedings of the 1987 Workshop*, pp. 233–258, Morgan Kaufmann Publishers, Inc., Los Altos, CA, 1987. © 1987, Morgan Kaufmann Publishers, Inc. Reprinted with permission of the publisher and the authors.

D. Perlis, "Bibliography of literature on non-monotonic reasoning," *Proceedings 1984 Non-monotonic Reasoning Workshop*, New Paltz, NY, pp. 396–401, 1984. © 1984, American Association for Artificial Intelligence. Reprinted with permission of AAAI and the author.

The editor wishes to thank Angus Andrews for suggesting the Sidney Harris drawing that appears on the cover. The drawing appears in Sidney Harris, *What's So Funny about Science*, William Kaufmann, Inc., Los Altos, CA, 1977. © 1977, Sidney Harris. Used by permission of the artist.

Contents

Chapter 1

Introduction

1.1 Overview

"Nothing is certain," wrote Benjamin Franklin in 1789, "but death and taxes."

The view that Franklin was expressing is that virtually every conclusion we draw is an uncertain one. We all believe that the sun will rise tomorrow, but no one has a real proof of it. I believe that I have no brother, since if I did have one, I'd know about it. But it is still possible that, unbeknownst to me, I have a brother after all.

You believe that the rest of this book is written in English. But some of the articles that follow may have originally been written in a foreign language, and it is possible that no translation is supplied. Even *my* belief that the book is in English depends on unproven assumptions about the steps to be taken by the publisher between the time the manuscript is submitted and the time the book reaches print.

This sort of reasoning in the face of uncertainty is ubiquitous. It has also proven to be remarkably difficult to formalize. The papers in this collection represent our best efforts to understand this sort of commonsense reasoning; as will be apparent, many questions remain to be answered.

It is perhaps somewhat misleading to describe your conclusion that the papers in this collection are all written in English as "uncertain." The actions you took prior to purchasing the book (or withdrawing it from the library, or whatever) don't reflect any uncertainty. Did you check to make sure that none of the articles is written in Serbo-Croatian? Of course not, although the book will be substantially less useful to you if one is.

Rather than describe your belief that the book is in English as uncertain, perhaps it is better to describe it as "defeasible," or capable of being defeated. Certainly, if the book happens to fall open to page 238, and page 238 happens to contain text written entirely in French, you will retract your conclusion about the book being written in English. (Until you realize that the text on page 238 is merely a computerized translation into French of the English text on page 237, of course.)

A key property of intelligence—whether exhibited by man or by machine—is *flexibility.* This flexibility is intimately connected with the defeasible nature of commonsense inference described in the previous paragraph; we are all capable of drawing conclusions, acting on them, and then retracting them if necessary in the face of new evidence. If our computer programs are to act intelligently, they will need to be similarly flexible.

A large portion of the work in artificial intelligence (AI) on reasoning or deduction involves the development of formal systems that describe this process. Thus, for example, if you know that all men are mortal, and that Socrates was a man, you can conclude that Socrates was mortal. This sort of syllogistic reasoning is well understood mathematically, and this understanding has led to the development of computer programs capable of reasoning in this fashion.[1]

Unfortunately, the mathematical work on inference has only recently become concerned with flexible inference of the sort we are discussing. Conventional deductive inference has a property known as *monotonicity*: As your set of beliefs grows, so does the set of conclusions that can be drawn from those beliefs.

[1] Of course, it is not the case that *all* reasoning programs have solid formal underpinnings. In Section 1.3.1, we discuss the reasons why most work on nonmonotonic reasoning is of a fairly formal nature.

Consider the syllogism example in which we concluded that Socrates was mortal from the facts that he was a man and that all men are mortal. If we add some new facts to our premises, the conclusion that Socrates was mortal will remain valid; short of *removing* one of the premises that underlies it, there is nothing we can do to invalidate the argument. Even if we were to add the fact that Socrates could leap the Parthenon in a single bound, we would still conclude that he was mortal: Physical prowess notwithstanding, he was still a man.

Our conclusion about Socrates' mortality remains valid because the rule, "All men are mortal," is universally quantified. There are no exceptions, not even implicit ones. *All* men are mortal, including those capable of jumping over the Parthenon or those possessing other extraordinary qualities.

This is to be contrasted with, for example, a statement such as, "Birds fly." It is not the case that *all* birds fly, but only that *typically* birds fly. Now if I tell you that Tweety is a bird, it is reasonable for you to conclude that Tweety can fly, since you have no evidence that Tweety is atypical. But there is a crucial difference here: You based your conclusion that Tweety could fly on an *absence* of information about Tweety's atypicality. On learning something new about Tweety (such as that he has a foot set in concrete), you will need to flexibly revise your conclusion that he can fly.

The inference here is *non*monotonic: On learning a new fact (that Tweety has a foot set in concrete), you were forced to retract your conclusion that he could fly. This original conclusion didn't follow logically from the facts that birds typically fly and that Tweety is a bird; it followed from these facts together with the *assumption* that Tweety is a typical bird. When we learn more about Tweety, we may discover that this assumption is unjustified.

What justified the assumption in the first place? Answering this question has proved to be far more difficult than we would expect; many of the papers in this collection are simply a discussion of possible answers to it. The most natural approach would be to say that we assume Tweety to be a typical bird in the absence of information to the contrary. This idea underlies much of the work in nonmonotonic reasoning, but is somewhat circular. As we will see in Section 1.4.1, this circularity can lead to interesting and difficult problems.

In addition to applications to the understanding of commonsense reasoning, nonmonotonic reasoning also has been shown to be important in other areas. There are applications to logic programming, to planning and reasoning about action, and to automated diagnosis. As the formal work matures, increasing effort is being devoted to applying our improved understanding to the solution of practical problems.

It is in response to the increasing understanding of nonmonotonic reasoning and its applications throughout AI that this collection has been assembled. Members of the AI community—be they researchers or knowledge engineers—will need to understand both the formal ideas underlying work in nonmonotonic reasoning and the applicability of these ideas to their own areas of interest. This collection of papers will begin to address their needs.

This book contains a fairly complete and representative collection of the work in nonmonotonic reasoning. Be warned, however, that a great many of the papers in this collection are quite formal, and you must have a degree of formal sophistication in order to understand them.

A good background in classical logic should enable you to understand most, if not all, of the papers that follow. If you are comfortable with logic at the level used in Nilsson's *Principles of Artificial Intelligence* [Nilsson, 1980] or the more recent *Logical Foundations of Artificial Intelligence* [Genesereth, Nilsson, 1987], that should do it. If you know what's in Enderton's *A Mathematical Introduction to Logic* [Enderton, 1972] or an equivalent text, so much the better.

Technically, the most difficult papers in the collection are those on circumscription, in Section 3.3. The effort needed to understand them probably is worth it, because, among the various competing approaches, circumscription appears to have the most advocates. The papers themselves are discussed at greater length in Section 1.7 of this introduction, which suggests a variety of paths through the book, depending on your reasons for reading it. The discussion in the introduction is deliberately informal and nontechnical; once again, be warned that this is very much in contrast with the papers that follow.

1.2 Uses of nonmonotonic reasoning

Rather than dive straight into the formal details of the various approaches to nonmonotonic reasoning, let us first discuss the better-known applications of these ideas.

1.2.1 Inheritance hierarchies

The most usual example of a nonmonotonic inference—what Reiter has called the "canonical" example in [Reiter, 1987a]—is the flying birds example presented in the last section.

Tweety, we are told, is a bird. From this, and the fact that birds fly, we conclude that Tweety can fly, since birds, by and large, do indeed fly. This conclusion, however, is defeasible: Tweety may be an ostrich, a penguin, a bird with a broken wing, or a bird whose feet have been set in concrete. (The exceptions grow increasingly macabre as the work on nonmonotonic inference matures.)

In the absence of information to the contrary, we assume that Tweety is a typical bird, and therefore can fly. It is precisely this "absence of information to the contrary" that makes the inference nonmonotonic, or defeasible—contrary information may be just around the corner.

This example can be extended to deal with hierarchies of defaults. Birds, by and large, fly. Ostriches are a special sort of bird that, by and large, do not fly. Ostriches from the planet Krypton are a special sort of ostrich that, by and large, do fly. We can extend the hierarchy in the other direction, as well:

Animals, by and large, don't fly. Birds, however, are a special sort of animal that, by and large, do.

The reason a hierarchy such as this one is of interest is that it has very attractive computational properties. Suppose, for example, that we are told that Fred is an ostrich, and we want to know whether Fred flies. Since we have an explicit statement to the effect that ostriches don't fly, we can conclude immediately that Fred cannot, either.

Now suppose that we want to know whether Fred has feathers. Our database might well tell us that animals in general do not have feathers, but that birds are a special type of animal that do. Nothing is said explicitly about ostriches having feathers, but they can inherit this property from the class of birds (since ostriches are birds). To determine whether or not Fred has feathers, we need simply work our way up the hierarchy, returning the first answer found. If we want to know whether Fred can bark, we will have to work all the way up to the class of all animals (the root of the inheritance hierarchy in this example). Since animals do not in general bark (dogs are an exception), we conclude that Fred also does not bark.

The notion of inheriting properties by default is due to Minsky [Minsky, 1975], who made it a cornerstone of the concept of *frames*. A frame is essentially an attribute-and-value data structure in which attributes can have default values or inherit values based on the values of other attributes. Data structures such as these can underlie extremely efficient representations of the sorts of default rules that appear in inheritance hierarchies with exceptions.

1.2.2 Closed-world databases

Suppose that you want to travel from Oshkosh to Minsk. You call your travel agent, and are told that there are no direct flights. (This is probably not a surprise.) How does your travel agent know that there are no direct flights from Oshkosh to Minsk?

The bottom line is that he doesn't. All he really knows is that there is no information in his database indicating that there *is* such a flight. Given this, he draws a default conclusion that no such flight exists. Once again, the inference is defeasible; it will be defeated if he learns of a direct flight on the route in question.

This example is Reiter's. In general, he explains this sort of inference using what he calls the *closed-world assumption* **[Reiter, 1978]**.[2] Informally, it is possible to assume that all commercially available flights are listed in the travel agent's database. If there is no information concerning a flight from Oshkosh to Minsk, then no such flight exists.

This has the same flavor as the inheritance examples of the last section: In the absence of information to the contrary, we assume that there is no flight from Oshkosh to Minsk. But here there is another useful way to think of things: Our database tells us of a variety of scheduled flights. Given this knowledge, we assume that there are no *additional* flights. Alternatively, the set of scheduled flights is as small as it could be, given the explicit information in our database.

This is how the closed-world assumption works in general. Given a relational database such as:

flight(New-York, Athens, Pan-Am-233)
flight(New-York, Paris, Air-France-22)

and so on, we try to minimize the extent of the predicate "flight": If we do not know of a flight from a to b, we assume there isn't one. By "minimize" we mean that we assume that the set of arguments for which the predicate is true is as small as possible: if we don't *know* that the predicate "flight" (for example) holds for some fixed pair of cities c and d and some flight number f, we assume that flight(c, d, f) is false.

Another example involves a database describing the connections among various components in an electronic circuit. Here, we minimize whatever predicate describes the existence of the specific connections, so that two components are assumed unconnected in the absence of a statement to the contrary.

Suppose that we consider this electronic example in a little more detail. Imagine that there is an entry in our database telling us that the transformer is connected to the power supply. Is the power supply connected to the transformer?

The answer, of course, is yes, since the connection predicate should be symmetric:

$$\text{connects}(a, b) \Rightarrow \text{connects}(b, a)$$

How are we to reconcile this with the closed-world assumption? Since it is not stated in our database that the power supply *is* connected to the transformer, aren't we likely to conclude that it isn't, contradicting the symmetry of the connection relation?

The answer, of course, is that our database *does* state that the power supply is connected to the transformer. The statement is simply implicit, as opposed to explicit, since the connection can be *derived* from information in the database, even though it does not appear directly.

We see that the predicate minimization that is captured by the closed world assumption should be relative not to what appears explicitly in the database, but rather to what can be *derived* from what appears explicitly in the database. When we asked our travel agent about flights from Oshkosh to Minsk, he told us not only that no such flight was mentioned in his airline database, but also that he could not prove the existence of such a flight from the information available to him. Negation is treated as a "failure to prove".

This interpretation of negation dates back to the **thnot** operator used by Hewitt in his PLANNER system [Hewitt, 1972]. It also underlies the treatment of negation in many logic programming languages, such as PROLOG. So here is another application of nonmonotonic reasoning—in the description of what a PROLOG program actually does.

[2] Citations set in boldface type refer to papers in this collection.

1.2.3 Diagnosis

Suppose we return to our electronic example, but instead of asking whether the transformer is connected to the power supply, we ask whether the two sides of the power supply are connected to each other. (Let's hope not, since a short across the power supply is hardly good news for the rest of the device.)

In light of the discussion of the previous section, answering this question is straightforward. We have no information to the effect that the two sides of the power supply are shorted together, and cannot prove that they are from other information in our database. We therefore conclude that no, the two sides of the power supply are not wired together.

Bear in mind, however, that this is a *defeasible* conclusion. Suppose that, while working with the gadget in question, we notice that whenever we turn it on, there is a loud bang, and the fuse that controls the current to the power supply blows. Now what?

Well, there's a short in the power supply, that's what. The reversal of the default conclusion that there was *not* a short is, remarkably enough, exactly what is needed to diagnose the source of the problem.

Once again, this is a special case of a general idea. Every time we use a piece of equipment, we do so without being able to *prove* that it will work. We might be able to prove that it would work if all of its component pieces were working and were correctly connected, but we generally will not have a proof that the components are working. So we know only by default that the device in question is functioning when we turn it on.

By and large, we turn it on anyway; and, by and large, it works. In many cases where it does *not* work, however, we can examine the symptoms, and determine precisely which of our assumptions about the functionality of the internal components was in error. A good understanding of nonmonotonic reasoning turns out to be closely related to this ability to diagnose failures based on an understanding of how a particular device is designed to work.

1.2.4 Reasoning about action

Yet another way to think about our electronic example is in terms of *qualification*. We know that our assumption that there is no short across the power supply is only a default one, and we have already noticed that, even though we can't *prove* that the device is going to function, we turn it on anyway.

If we wanted to be sure that there was no short in the power supply, we could check this explicitly before turning on the device—but we don't. We also don't check all the other things that could go wrong and keep the machine from functioning. The switch to turn it on might be broken, for example, or the socket it's plugged into might not be getting power (either because the socket is broken or because there has been a power failure). Any of these things (or others) could potentially cause the device not to function.

Once again, this is a special instance of a general situation. Whenever an action is performed, there are many "hidden" preconditions that would prevent the action from succeeding. We know about these preconditions, since we understand that, if they *were* to happen, our intended action would be blocked. But we assume, in a nonmonotonic way, that they are not relevant to the particular situation in which we find ourselves.

This general issue is known as the *qualification problem*, so named by McCarthy [**McCarthy, 1977**]. McCarthy's best-known example involves starting your car in the morning. Before turning the key in the ignition, do you check to make sure that no one has stuck a potato in the tailpipe? Surely not, even though you have no *proof* that there is no potato, and even though the car won't start if there is one.

Before turning to other matters, suppose for a moment that we decide to check the power supply before turning on our device. Ignoring the manufacturer's warnings, we remove the cover and connect some sort of resistance-measuring device across the terminals of the power supply, discovering that there is no short.[3] Satisfied, we replace the cover and prepare to throw the switch.

But wait a minute! We know there was no short before we replaced the cover, but how do we know that the act of replacing the cover didn't cause one?

The answer, of course, is that we do *not* know. We simply have a default rule saying that the action of replacing the cover does not change things like whether or not the power supply is shorted.

The difficulties involved in formalizing this sort of notion make up the *frame problem*. Frame axioms tell us that, by and large, things do not change mysteriously as actions are performed. Covering the power supply does not cause it to become shorted. Moving a block won't change either its color or the color of some other block. Your car won't start working again just because you drive it to the mechanic.

In short, we assume that actions change only what they are known to change. This nonmonotonic description of the frame problem can be thought of, as usual, either in terms of consistency (anything true before the action occurs will be true afterward, provided that this is consistent with the known effects of the action), or in terms of a minimization (as little as possible changes when an action occurs).

1.2.5 Other applications

All the application areas discussed so far are treated extensively by papers in this collection. The work on inheritance is discussed specifically in many of the papers in Section 3.1 (default theories), and is used to provide motivation by a variety of other papers. Logic programming applications, diagnosis,

[3] Assuming, of course, that our measuring tool is working. But that gets us back to the qualification problem.

and reasoning about action are the three application areas investigated in Chapter 5.

Before turning to a more general discussion of nonmonotonic inference itself, however, we should touch on a few more areas where the ideas appear applicable.

The first is vision. Minsky's original frames paper was principally directed at solving problems arising in vision; loosely speaking, when we see part of a scene, we draw default conclusions about the rest of the scene, how it would look from another angle, and so on. We then test our understanding of the content of the visual image by comparing our default conclusions with the actual observations they predict.

A similar story can be told in natural language processing. When reading (or listening), we draw default conclusions about the content of a sentence before the sentence itself is complete. In addition, McCarthy has suggested that default reasoning is used quite broadly as a communication convention; he argues that when we describe a situation, we communicate information about only those default rules that are violated in it [**McCarthy, 1986**]. Finally, Perrault has investigated the interaction between default logic and speech acts [Perrault, 1987].

The last area we will mention is that of temporal logic. Because of the close connection between the understanding of actions and a formalization of time, it is important that any formal description of time be able to express conveniently the frame problem and some sort of nonmonotonic solution to it. Typical here is work such as Kowalski and Sergot's paper, "A logic-based calculus of events" [Kowalski, Sergot, 1986].

Papers describing these applications have not been included in this collection. Although these papers discuss nonmonotonic reasoning and its applications, their main emphasis is *not* on nonmonotonic reasoning per se, since they involve many issues that have little or nothing to do with formal inference methods. Pointers to these and other papers can be found in Perlis's bibliography of the nonmonotonic literature [**Perlis, 1984**], which appears at the end of this book.

1.3 Approaches to nonmonotonic inference

1.3.1 The rules of the game

Having mentioned a variety of uses to which nonmonotonic reasoning can be put, let us now go on to describe in broad terms the theoretical work that has been done on it.

Before discussing any of the approaches themselves, we should say something about the field as a whole. With a few exceptions, all the papers in this collection are cut from much the same cloth: The ideas vary (and conflict, to some extent), and some of the formalisms have matured since their introduction, but the *methodology* that underlies the work is much the same. The scientists working in this area hold common assumptions about what constitutes progress, and understanding those assumptions is a necessary precursor to understanding and appreciating the papers themselves.

Classical logic is insufficient

The first assumption made is that conventional, first-order logic is, in itself, insufficient to solve effectively the sorts of problems discussed in Section 1.2. The key word here is *effectively*. It is well known that classical logic is descriptively universal: Anything that can be expressed in any language can be expressed (somehow) in classical logic.

The problem is that a description using classical logic may be extremely unwieldy. Consider the frame problem, for example. There is an attractive conciseness about the simple default rule that, "Everything that can stay the same, does stay the same." Although making this vague statement more precise is formally very difficult, the belief of the nonmonotonic community is that the effort is worth it, since this default really does capture the essence of the solution to the frame problem.

This is to be contrasted with a solution using monotonic reasoning, which would need to indicate explicitly under what circumstances various things change or stay the same. If moving an object never changes its color, we need to say so explicitly. We also need to state explicitly that moving an object never changes the location of another object, and that painting an object doesn't change the colors or the positions of other objects, and so on.

There are a variety of problems with this sort of approach. The first is simply that the collection of monotonic frame axioms is enormous. Reasoning with them is likely to be computationally intractable.[4]

Another problem is that the generation of the monotonic axioms can be very difficult. Consider the example in which we remarked that moving an object never changes the location of another object. What if the two objects are connected? A description suitable for monotonic reasoning will need to list the exceptions explicitly: If two objects are unconnected, *then* moving the first will never change the location of the second. The same problem occurs for the remark that moving an object never causes it to change color; imagine moving your car into the path of a spray paint gun. Cameras work because moving one object (the shutter) causes *another* object to change color (the film). In *principle*, it is always possible to describe any particular domain in a fashion that allows us to reason about it monotonically; in *practice*, this may not be the case.

An additional difficulty is that monotonic reasoning tends to be inflexible. If some fact (such as whether or not Tweety is an ostrich) bears on a monotonic rule (such as a rule saying that birds that are not ostriches can fly), then, to apply the rule, we have to know that Tweety is not an ostrich—it's not enough for us *not* to know that Tweety *is* an ostrich. Thus, we are forced

[4] A detailed examination of this point can be found in [**Ginsberg, Smith, 1987a**].

to include in our database the results of applying the closed-world assumption (or something like it) to every predicate in our world description. As soon as we do this, the world description becomes completely inflexible and incapable of incorporating new information.

For all these reasons, there is a general consensus that some nonmonotonic extension to first-order reasoning is needed. Some people, however, disagree with this view. Both Levesque [Levesque, 1987] and Nutter [Nutter, 1983] have proposed monotonic approaches to default reasoning, and Georgeff [Georgeff, 1987] has suggested a monotonic solution to the frame problem. These monotonic suggestions seem to lack the power of their nonmonotonic counterparts, but they are still worthy of consideration. Finally, several authors ([Kramosil, 1975] is typical) have suggested that the monotonic approach should be salvaged because the idea of a nonmonotonic formalism is fundamentally flawed. We will turn to their arguments in Section 1.3.4, once we have sketched the details of the nonmonotonic approaches themselves.

Declarativism

A second assumption made by the authors of the papers in this collection is that the problems of nonmonotonic inference need a *declarative* solution. By this I mean that an eventual description of nonmonotonic inference should be clear and precise, with a sharply defined syntax and semantics, and also that the objects being analyzed should be sentences in some formal language.[5]

The advantage of a precisely defined syntax and semantics is that it makes it possible to determine exactly what the consequences of a given theory are. As an alternative, suppose that we defined nonmonotonic inference in terms of the output of some particular implementation of PROLOG; it would be all too easy to overlook some property of nonmonotonic reasoning that was not an obvious consequence of the implementation being considered.

Rather than making this argument at an abstract level, let us examine an example of this phenomenon. Suppose we return to our canonical sort of default rule, but instead of birds flying, consider the following situation:[6]

1. Normally, Quakers are pacifists.
2. Normally, Republicans are not pacifists.

Nixon is both a Republican and a Quaker. Is he a pacifist? The problem is that we have two conflicting default rules, and we don't know which to apply.

Suppose that we rewrite the above two rules as the following:

1. Any Quaker who is not known to be a hawk is a pacifist.
2. Any Republican who is not known to be a pacifist is a hawk.

Encoding these default rules as a PROLOG program, we obtain

```
pacifist(x) :- Quaker(x),not(hawk(x)).
hawk(x) :- Republican(x),not(pacifist(x)).
Quaker(Nixon).
Republican(Nixon).
```

Now, when we provide the program with the query `pacifist(Nixon)`, it will probably fail to return an answer because of the recursive nature of the first two rules above. If it does return an answer, the nature of the answer will be a function of the method used to break the recursion.

This is an important and subtle problem, and is apparent in any of the declarative approaches.[7] An approach based on an implementation may obscure the difficulty.

The advantages of the declarativists' assumption that the description refers to sentences in some formal language are fairly well known. McCarthy described them as early as 1960 [McCarthy, 1960]; here is a comment from [Genesereth, Ginsberg, 1985]:

> There are several advantages to this [assumption]. Chief among these is incremental development. As new information about an application area is discovered (or perhaps just discovered to be important to the problem the program is designed to solve), that information can be added to the program's knowledge base and so incorporated into the program itself. There is no need for algorithm development or revision. [Genesereth, Ginsberg, 1985, page 933]

As with the assumption in the previous section, not everyone is an adherent of the view that a declarative approach should be taken to nonmonotonic inference. One principal objector these days is McDermott, who suggests that procedural approaches by and large work well, and there is therefore no need to address the difficult formal issues faced by the declarativists [McDermott, 1987b].

Numeric approaches

The final assumption made in the papers in this collection is that the approach taken to nonmonotonic reasoning should be symbolic as opposed to numeric.

Whether or not AI needs a quantitative approach to defeasible reasoning is the topic of a long-standing debate in the AI

[5] Declarativism also assumes that the terms in the formal theory being used correspond to objects in the agent's world. This is a much less controversial point, however.

[6] This example is due to Reiter [Reiter, Criscuolo, 1981].

[7] In terms of terminology to be introduced in Section 1.3.2, default logic and modal approaches admit multiple extensions and fixed points; circumscriptive theories need to deal with nonunique minimal models.

community. McCarthy argues that nonmonotonic logic can offer help in situations where probabilistic reasoning is of no use [**McCarthy, 1986**]; I myself argue that numeric methods are of interest [Ginsberg, 1985]. As time has passed, I have found McCarthy's arguments increasingly compelling, especially in light of Shortliffe's observation that the results of some expert systems are fairly insensitive to the specific values of their numeric data [Shortliffe, 1976].

Editorial bias would be slim reason for excluding the numeric literature from this collection, however. The actual reason this has been done is simply that the probabilistic community has a well-established literature of its own. Of specific interest to AI are the proceedings of the workshops on uncertainty in AI [Uncertainty workshop, 1985; Uncertainty workshop, 1986].

1.3.2 Formal approaches to nonmonotonic inference

As described in Section 1.2, it is possible to think of nonmonotonic inference in two distinct ways. In one, we draw default conclusions in the absence of information to the contrary. This is the approach we took when discussing inheritance hierarchies and reasoning about action, for example.

In the other approach, we try to minimize the extent of some predicate or relation. This is the approach we took when analyzing the closed-world assumption and related database applications. It also is reasonable in diagnostic applications, where we generally try to minimize the set of suspected failures. Why worry whether the picture tube is broken if it does not appear to be malfunctioning?

This distinction has an analog in first-order logic.[8] Here, entailment is defined in terms of models: we say that p entails q if q holds in all the models in which p holds; this is written $p \models q$. Proof procedures to determine whether or not p entails q, however, work not by enumerating all the models in which p holds, but by seeing whether q can be obtained from p as a result of applying some set of operators to the facts in p. If q can be derived in this fashion, we write $p \vdash q$.

The description of default conclusions as drawn in the absence of information to the contrary is similar to this latter notion of derivability. Loosely speaking, we try to find a proof for the negation of any particular default conclusion; if none exists, the default conclusion is consistent, and we assume it to be true.

The minimization approach that underlies circumscription is similar to the model-theoretic notion $p \models q$. Indeed, one way to define circumscription is to say that p *circumscriptively* entails q if q holds in all *minimal* models of p (where one model M is "smaller" than another model N if the extent of the predicate being minimized is smaller in M than in N). This notion is implicit in all the circumscription work (and explicit in some of it, such as Lifschitz' [**Lifschitz, 1985b; Lifschitz, 1987b**]). Shoham also discusses this idea at length [**Shoham, 1987**].

Just as the two first-order notions of entailment and derivability are closely related, the two approaches to default reasoning are as well. Predicate minimization must be done in a way that preserves the overall consistency of the database, for example. Nevertheless, the various formal approaches to nonmonotonic reasoning can be usefully distinguished by considering which of these two distinct—but related—ideas of default inference any particular scheme is trying to capture.

Proof-based approaches

The approaches based directly on consistency are probably somewhat more natural than are those based on minimization, so let us consider them first. The general idea is to describe a rule such as, "Birds fly," by formalizing the following restatement of it:

> If Tweety is a bird, and it is *consistent* that Tweety can fly, then Tweety does fly.

Default logic Suppose that we denote the statement, "Tweety is a bird," by b, and the statement that he can fly by f. Reiter's default logic [**Reiter, 1980**] would now encode the above default rule as

$$\frac{b : f}{f} \tag{1.1}$$

If b is true, and it is consistent that f is true, then assume f is true.

In general, a default rule is an expression such as

$$\frac{\alpha : \beta}{\gamma}$$

where α is the precondition to the rule, β is the clause that is checked for consistency with the database, and γ is added to the database if β is consistent. A rule such as (1.1), where $\beta = \gamma$, is called a *normal* default rule.

Default rules in Reiter's logic are not part of the logical language as such. Instead, they are better thought of as rules of inference, like modus ponens. Reiter's default rules describe modifications to be made to a database when drawing a default conclusion, just as modus ponens describes a modification commonly made in conventional first-order systems:

$$\frac{\alpha, \alpha \rightarrow \beta}{\beta}$$

Now suppose that we have a logical theory, together with a set of default rules. Reiter defines an *extension* of this theory to be a new logical theory such that

[8] This analogy is due to Vladimir Lifschitz (personal communication).

1. None of the default rules can be consistently applied to obtain a conclusion not already in the extension.
2. The extension is minimal subject to the first condition.

The first condition guarantees that we have drawn all the default conclusions we consistently can, and the second ensures that we haven't added anything to our logical theory without reason.

Suppose we look at this definition a bit more abstractly. Imagine that we had some operator Δ_D that took a formal theory, say E, and produced a new formal theory in which the default rules in some set D had been applied in a fashion consistent with the facts in E. Now the first condition is simply telling us that, if E is to be an extension, this application of the default rules must have no effect. More succinctly, we should have that

$$E = \Delta_D(E) \qquad (1.2)$$

In other words, *extensions are fixed points of the Δ_D operator.* The second condition is simply that E be minimal subject to the first condition, so that extensions in default logic are minimal fixed points of Δ_D.

Modal approaches The first attempt to use modal logic to describe nonmonotonic inference was made by McDermott and Doyle [**McDermott, Doyle, 1980**]; their paper is in Section 3.2 of this collection.

McDermott and Doyle augmented first-order logic with a modal operator M, so that, if p were some sentence in first-order logic, then Mp would be a sentence in the modal logic. The intention was that Mp would mean, "maybe p," or, "p is consistent with everything else that is known." A default rule such as (1.1) can now be expressed as:

$$b \wedge Mf \rightarrow f \qquad (1.3)$$

The advantage of this approach is that, since the default rule is now itself a sentence of the logic, it is possible to express easily within the logic facts about default rules, default rules about default rules, and so on.

The disadvantage is that the semantics of the M operator turned out to be quite elusive. The first completely satisfactory description was *autoepistemic logic*, introduced by Moore [**Moore, 1985**]. Moore's description can be stated somewhat more succinctly if, instead of using a "possibly" modal operator M, we use a "necessarily" modal operator L. (We also might think of Lp as meaning that p is known or believed.) Note that p is possible if and only if $\neg p$ is not *necessary*, so Mp is equivalent to $\neg L \neg p$. Now (1.3) becomes

$$b \wedge \neg L \neg f \rightarrow f$$

If Tweety is a bird, and it is not believed that Tweety *cannot* fly, then Tweety can fly.

Now suppose we denote by $th(E)$ the set of logical consequences of some set E of sentences.[9] Moore looked for solutions to the equation

$$T = th\{A \cup LT \cup \neg L\overline{T}\} \qquad (1.4)$$

where LT is the set of sentences Lp for the various $p \in T$, and $\neg L\overline{T}$ is the set of sentences $\neg Lp$ for those p that are *not* in T. A here is the set of initial axioms in our theory. As in the default approach, extensions (Moore calls them *expansions*) are described as fixed points, with (1.4) replacing the earlier fixed-point equation (1.2).

The intuition here is that the facts in T should be those that can be derived from those in A, together with some sort of "introspection" on T itself: Anything in T is believed to be in T (corresponding to facts of the form Lp for some p in T), and anything not in T is not believed to be in T (corresponding to the term $\neg L\overline{T}$ in (1.4)).

As an example, suppose we consider $A = \{b, b \wedge \neg L \neg f \rightarrow f\}$. This theory says that Tweety is a bird (b), and that, if Tweety is a bird, and it is not believed that Tweety cannot fly, then Tweety can fly.

What we would like to show is that Tweety can fly—in other words, that f will be in any solution to (1.4). To see this, first note that we surely cannot conclude with certainty that Tweety cannot fly, since $\neg f$ can never follow from the facts in A together with any collection of "modal" facts of the form Lp or $\neg Lp$. Therefore, $\neg f \in \overline{T}$, and it follows that $\neg L \neg f \in T$: Since we can't prove that Tweety can't fly, we don't believe that Tweety can't fly.

We conclude from this that T is the logical closure of a superset of $\{b, b \wedge \neg L \neg f \rightarrow f, \neg L \neg f\}$, and it follows that $f \in T$. Of course, were we to add $\neg f$ to A (stating with certainty that Tweety cannot fly), this argument would break down; herein lies the nonmonotonicity of the modal approach.

Minimization approaches

The other formal approaches to default inference proceed by attempting to describe directly the notion of minimization that underlies, for example, the closed-world assumption.

This idea was originally due to McCarthy [**McCarthy, 1980**], who described default rules in terms of "abnormality".[10] For example, a bird will fly, unless it is abnormal in some way. McCarthy's formalization, *circumscription*, proceeds by attempting to minimize abnormality.

[9] $th(E)$ stands for "the set of theorems of E."

[10] The description of defaults using minimization appears in [McCarthy, 1980]. The explicit use of abnormality in circumscription did not appear until [McCarthy, 1986], however; Levesque also discusses abnormality in [Levesque, 1982].

There are two steps to the formalization. The first is straightforward, and involves simply expressing the default as a sentence of first-order logic:

$$b(x) \wedge \neg \mathbf{ab}_1(x) \rightarrow f(x) \qquad (1.5)$$

In other words, if x is a bird and x is not abnormal, then x can fly. The subscript on the abnormality predicate **ab** reflects the fact that we may want to deal with a variety of default rules, each with its own abnormality predicate.

The more difficult issue in this formalism is that of deciding what's abnormal. The idea, of course, is to minimize the number of abnormal objects, accepting as abnormal only those things that are *known* to be abnormal. McCarthy formalized this notion as follows. Initially, we have some axiomatization A that mentions the abnormality predicate **ab**; suppose we make this explicit by calling our initial axiomatization $A(\mathbf{ab})$. Now, we can replace **ab** in this theory with any other predicate, obtaining perhaps $A(p)$. McCarthy minimized **ab** by assuming that **ab** was the *smallest* predicate p for which $A(p)$ held. In other words,

$$A(\mathbf{ab}) \wedge \forall p. \neg [A(p) \wedge p < \mathbf{ab}] \qquad (1.6)$$

where $p < \mathbf{ab}$ means that the extent of p is properly contained in that of **ab**. Formally, $p < \mathbf{ab}$ is shorthand for

$$\forall x.[p(x) \rightarrow \mathbf{ab}(x)] \wedge \neg \forall x.[\mathbf{ab}(x) \rightarrow p(x)]$$

It follows in our example that only those birds that are provably abnormal cannot fly. (Ostriches are abnormal, for example.) The reason is that, if any birds were unnecessarily believed to be abnormal, we could take p to be a predicate describing minimal abnormality and get a contradiction with (1.6).

Probably the most attractive feature of the circumscriptive approach is that it proceeds simply by adjoining the formula (1.6) to the original theory. No fixed-point equations need to be solved, as in the consistency-based approaches. This tends to make the semantics of this approach cleaner than that of the others.

Because of this, circumscription has been studied more extensively than the other approaches, and this examination has shown that there are still some problems with it. As shown by Etherington and colleagues, there are some cases where the circumscription axiom (1.6) is inconsistent with the original theory [**Etherington, Mercer, Reiter, 1985**]. In other examples, the authors show that circumscription does not give the intended (i.e., intuitively correct) results. This has led to the introduction of a variety of circumscriptive theories, and articles describing what appear to be the most powerful approaches can be found in Section 3.3. The approach as a whole is still evolving, as are the consistency-based ideas of the previous section.

A more serious difficulty is that the circumscription axiom itself involves a quantification over predicates, and is therefore a formula in second-order logic. Little is known about automated deduction using second-order formulae. In some special cases [**Lifschitz, 1985b; Lifschitz, 1987b**], the second-order axiom can be shown to be equivalent to a first-order formula; in many situations, however, the question of the existence of such a first-order formula remains open.

Unifications

Three of the most recent papers in this collection (those in Section 3.4) discuss newly found connections among these various approaches, and between them and other work on inference. Konolige shows that the two consistency-based approaches (default logic and autoepistemic logic) are formally identical [**Konolige, 1987**].

Shoham argues that all the existing approaches to nonmonotonic reasoning can be understood by introducing a partial order on entire *models*, instead of minimizing the extent of a predicate such as **ab** [**Shoham, 1987**].

Finally, my own work on multi-valued logics shows that much of the work on nonmonotonic inference can be unified formally with the work on truth maintenance in Section IV [**Ginsberg, 1986b**; Ginsberg, 1987b]. The advantage of the unification is that, as discussed in Section 1.5.2, ideas from the work on reason maintenance appear to be critical to the construction of efficient implementations of any of the nonmonotonic formalisms.[11]

1.3.3 The nature of nonmonotonic inference

As we have already remarked, the key distinction between defeasible and indefeasible inference is that of monotonicity: Defeasible conclusions may need to be retracted in the presence of additional information.

This distinction manifests itself in a variety of ways. Our aim in this section is to use the formal material in Section 1.3.2 to examine the differences between material implications such as $p \rightarrow q$ and default rules such as, "From p, conclude q by default."

Strengthening the antecedent As an example, it is always possible to strengthen the antecedent of a material implication: From $p \rightarrow q$, we can derive $p \wedge r \rightarrow q$. Is it possible to strengthen the antecedent of a default rule?

This question makes sense because all the formalisms for default inference identify default rules such as, "From p, conclude q by default," with specific mathematical expressions. The circumscriptive approach identifies the default rule with

$$p \wedge \neg \mathbf{ab} \rightarrow q \qquad (1.7)$$

[11] We use the terms *reason maintenance* and *truth maintenace* interchangably. The latter is Doyle's original name for the approach; the former is a more recent (and more accurate) description. Both expressions are in wide use.

for example. The default rule with the antecedent strengthened would be

$$(p \wedge r) \wedge \neg \mathbf{ab} \rightarrow q \tag{1.8}$$

What we want to know is whether (1.8) follows from (1.7). When can one default rule be generated from another?[12]

It is clear that, in the circumscriptive approach, we can indeed strengthen the antecedents of default rules, since (1.8) is a logical consequence of (1.7).

The consistency-based approaches are similar. Consider a default rule in modal logic:

$$p \wedge Mq \rightarrow q$$

Once again, the antecedent clearly can be strengthened to give $(p \wedge r) \wedge Mq \rightarrow q$.

The fact that default rules can have their antecedents strengthened distinguishes default logic from other forms of uncertain inference, such as that based on probabilities: If the probability of a randomly selected bird being able to fly is greater than 0.9 (say), it clearly does *not* follow that the probability of a randomly selected *red* bird being able to fly also is greater than 0.9.

The fact that default rules allow their antecedents to be strengthened also has some counterintuitive consequences. For example, it is possible to strengthen (1.7) to get

$$p \wedge \neg q \wedge \neg \mathbf{ab} \rightarrow q$$

so that q follows by default from $\neg q$! The point, of course, is that the premise $p \wedge \neg q$ already implies $\mathbf{ab}$ because of (1.7), so the premise of this particular default rule will never hold.

Transitivity Another property of material implication is that it is *transitive*: If $a \rightarrow b$ and $b \rightarrow c$, then $a \rightarrow c$. Given a, we conclude b. Then from b, we can conclude c. Can default rules be composed similarly?

As an example, robins are birds, and birds fly (by default). Does it follow by default that robins fly?

It does in circumscription, because from

$$r \rightarrow b$$
$$b \wedge \neg \mathbf{ab} \rightarrow f$$

we *can* legitimately conclude that

$$r \wedge \neg \mathbf{ab} \rightarrow f$$

Note that we can similarly conclude that *ostriches* fly by default: $o \wedge \neg \mathbf{ab} \rightarrow f$. The difficulty here, as in the strengthening of antecedents example, is that we already know $o \rightarrow \mathbf{ab}$ (ostriches are abnormal), so the default rule is blocked.

In general, a pair of default rules would be represented as

$$p \wedge \neg \mathbf{ab}_1 \rightarrow q$$
$$q \wedge \neg \mathbf{ab}_2 \rightarrow r$$

from which it is possible to conclude

$$p \wedge \neg(\mathbf{ab}_1 \vee \mathbf{ab}_2) \rightarrow r \tag{1.9}$$

Thus in the circumscriptive description, we can, roughly speaking, compose default rules.[13]

The modal case is quite different. Here we have

$$p \wedge Mq \rightarrow q$$
$$q \wedge Mr \rightarrow r$$

leading to

$$p \wedge Mq \wedge Mr \rightarrow r$$

The appearance of the new term Mq makes it much more difficult to think of this as a default rule than to consider the circumscriptive version (1.9) in this fashion. This is because the modal operators above refer explicitly to the predicate in the conclusion of the default rule. This is in contrast with the abnormality predicate used by circumscription.

Contraposition The difference between the two approaches is even clearer when we consider contraposition. Given a material implication $p \rightarrow q$, we can conclude $\neg q \rightarrow \neg p$. Given a rule allowing us to conclude q by default from p, should we be able to conclude $\neg p$ by default from $\neg q$? Should nonflyers, by default, not be birds?

The answer given by circumscription appears to be yes, because from

$$b \wedge \neg \mathbf{ab} \rightarrow f$$

we clearly can obtain

$$\neg f \wedge \neg \mathbf{ab} \rightarrow \neg b$$

Given that Tweety cannot fly, Tweety shouldn't be a bird, because if Tweety *were* a bird, he would be an abnormal one.[14]

The answer given by the modal approach appears to be *no*, however. From

$$b \wedge Mf \rightarrow f \tag{1.10}$$

[12] Note that this is *not* the same question as asking whether or not an additional assumption can be added to a nonmonotonic derivation (it cannot be). This is a consequence of the fact that the modified default rule (1.8) may be blocked for some reason.

[13] But *only* roughly speaking, since minimizing ab_1 and ab_2 separately may not be the same as minimizing their disjunction.

[14] The situation is unfortunately not quite so simple. In more recent versions of circumscription **[Lifschitz, 1987b; McCarthy, 1986]**, it is possible to minimize ab while varying f but keeping b fixed. In this case, we would conclude that Tweety can fly, but could not conclude that an arbitrary nonflyer is not a bird.

all we get is

$$\neg f \land Mf \rightarrow \neg b$$

which is of no use whatsoever. Given that Tweety can't fly, the modal approach tells us that there is no real evidence that Tweety isn't a bird—just that, whether Tweety is a bird or not, the default rule (1.10) should not be applied to him.[15]

1.3.4 Objections to nonmonotonic inference

This overall description of the existing work on nonmonotonic inference would be incomplete if we did not discuss the view that all the formal work is a waste of time.

There are at least four sorts of objections to work on nonmonotonic logic. Israel remarks that the endeavor could do with some better terminology **[Israel, 1980]**: Logic is, by its very definition, monotonic, and the notion of "nonmonotonic logic" is a contradiction in terms. Probabilists, meanwhile, argue that probability theory is much better understood than the nonnumeric methods; why not just use that?

We have little to say about these two objections. Perhaps, back in the late 1970s when the first papers on default inference appeared, a more suitable name could have been chosen.[16] As far as the probabilists are concerned, the debate (which we touched on in Section 1.3.1) seems far from settled.

The other two objections are far more serious. The first, which is discussed by Israel **[Israel, 1980]**, but which was first recognized as a problem by Reiter **[Reiter, 1980]**, is that the formal approaches to nonmonotonic inference are in general *non-semidecidable*.[17]

Suppose we ask a machine a question, and the machine has some algorithm that it uses to produce a correct answer. If the machine is guaranteed eventually to stop and to give us an answer (yes or no, let us suppose), then the problem is called *decidable*. If the machine definitely will stop and tell us if the answer is yes, but might run forever if the answer is no, then the problem is *semidecidable*. The general question of entailment in first-order logic, for example, is semidecidable: If we want to know whether or not some sentence follows from a first-order theory, there are algorithms that are guaranteed always to terminate (with success) if it does, but may run forever if it does not. There can be no algorithm that is guaranteed always to terminate with a correct answer in both cases.

The problem, from the standpoint of nonmonotonic logic, is that applying a default rule requires checking for the consistency of the conclusion—in other words, we have to show that any attempt to prove the negation of the conclusion would fail. There is no uniform way of doing this, and, as a result, problems in nonmonotonic logic are not semidecidable.

This conclusion has two consequences. The first is that implementations of nonmonotonic reasoning systems (and there are very few) tend to be excruciatingly slow because of the repeated need for consistency checking.[18] We will return to this point in Section 1.5.2, where we discuss potential implementations of the theoretical work in default inference.

The second consequence of the non-semidecidability of nonmonotonic inference is that any system that uses a nonmonotonic approach will necessarily make mistakes from time to time (or loop forever, which is probably worse). Israel discusses this problem **[Israel, 1980]**, and his arguments are extended by Perlis **[Perlis, 1986]**. Essentially, these authors argue that the eventual inconsistency of the set of beliefs of a nonmonotonic reasoning system will make it difficult (if not impossible) for such a system to interact effectively with a first-order theorem prover.

This is a serious difficulty, and it remains largely unaddressed in the formal literature. One possible solution, suggested by Perlis and implicit in the work on multi-valued logics **[Ginsberg, 1986b]**, is to label tentative conclusions as such, so that no problem need arise if these conclusions are subsequently found to conflict with information elsewhere in the database.

The final objection we will discuss is due to Kramosil [Kramosil, 1975]. He notes that one of the reasons first-order inference "works" is that the intersection of two deductively closed sets also is deductively closed. Thus, for example, it is possible to define the closure of some set S of logical formulae as the intersection of all the deductively closed supersets of S, and this intersection will itself be deductively closed.

Now suppose we use this approach to find a minimal solution to a fixed-point equation such as (1.2) of Section 1.3.2. The problem is that the intersection of two solutions to this equation need *not* be a solution itself, and it follows that (1.2) may not have a *unique* minimal solution.

Kramosil attempted to argue from this that it is impossible for nonmonotonic logic to have a well-defined semantics, but this view seems overly pessimistic. Rather, it turns out that this "multiple-extension" problem has led to some of the most interesting theoretical questions associated with nonmonotonic reasoning. Sufficiently interesting and important, in fact, that the issue merits a section of its own.

1.4 The multiple-extension problem

The extensions mentioned at the end of the previous section were, informally speaking, collections of sentences to which

[15] Once again, the situation is not quite this simple. Myers has remarked that it is possible to express defaults in a fashion that admits contraposition, writing perhaps $b \land \neg L\phi \rightarrow f$, corresponding to the (nonnormal) default rule $b : \phi / f$. In [Konolige, Myers, 1987], she and Konolige suggest writing default rules in the noncontraposing form $Lb \land \neg L\phi \rightarrow f$.

[16] But perhaps not. After all, much of the nonmonotonic literature is concerned with things like "nonflying birds". Perhaps "nonmonotonic logic" is exactly the *right* name.

[17] In some cases **[Lifschitz, 1985b; Lifschitz, 1987b]**, circumscription reduces to a first-order axiom, and therefore is semidecidable.

[18] In *practice*, they are merely slow. In *theory*, they might not return any answer at all to a given query.

no more default rules could be applied without obtaining a contradiction. A *minimal* extension is one that is obtained without making any "unnecessary" modifications to the database. Thus, in the simple case where we have a fact b and a default rule $b \wedge Mf \rightarrow f$, there is a single minimal extension containing the facts b and f, where f is derived by default from b.

If we add another default rule, say $b \wedge Mg \rightarrow g$, there is still a single extension, which now contains b, f, and g as well. But what if the default rule we add is $b \wedge M\neg f \rightarrow \neg f$?

Now there are two extensions. One contains b and f, whereas the other contains b and $\neg f$; having applied one default rule, we cannot apply the other. The intersection of the two extensions, however, which contains b only, is *not* an extension, since we can apply either default rule in this situation.

1.4.1 Examples

We have in fact already seen an example of this problem in Section 1.3.1. There, we considered the two default rules $q \wedge Mp \rightarrow p$ (Quakers are pacifists) and $r \wedge M\neg p \rightarrow \neg p$ (Republicans are not pacifists). Nixon is a Quaker and a Republican: $q \wedge r$. Is he a pacifist? In one extension, he is; in the other, he is not.

This problem of conflicting default rules is ubiquitous in work on nonmonotonic logic. Before discussing possible solutions to it, let us work through each of the uses of nonmonotonic inference from Section 1.2, showing ways in which this problem can arise.

The Nixon example we have already seen involves inheritance hierarchies. With regard to logic programming and the closed world assumption, suppose we are told that Pan Am is starting a new low-fare service from San Francisco to the East Coast, but has not yet decided whether the destination will be New York or Washington:

flight(San-Fran, New-York, Pan-Am-000)
$\vee$ flight(San-Fran, Washington, Pan-Am-000) (1.11)

The closed-world assumption now tells us that

$\neg$flight(San-Fran, New-York, Pan-Am-000)

since this fact cannot be proven from (1.11). Similarly, we can derive

$\neg$flight(San-Fran, Washington, Pan-Am-000)

Unfortunately, these two facts are collectively in contradiction with the original assumption (1.11). What is happening there is that the "negation as failure" rule is effectively applying *all* the default rules, ignoring the possibility that they conflict with each other.

If the database in question consists only of Horn clauses,[19] it turns out that this problem cannot arise. We shall touch on this point briefly in Section 1.4.2; a much more complete treatment is given in **[Reiter, 1978]** and in the other papers in Section 5.1 of this collection.

Let us continue with the examples. In the diagnostic domain, suppose that we have observed a failure in our usual hi-tech device, and that the failure can be caused by a fault in either the power supply or the transformer. If we denote the first fault by $\neg p$ (the power supply is not working), and the second by $\neg t$, then since one of the two is faulted, we have

$$\neg p \vee \neg t \tag{1.12}$$

We also have the rules stating that, by default, everything is working:

$$Mp \rightarrow p$$
$$Mt \rightarrow t$$

Once again, because of (1.12), we can apply either one of the default rules, but not both. In this case, the two extensions correspond to the two possible diagnoses of the failure—is it the power supply or the transformer that is faulty?

Finally, consider the planning domain. The inevitable appearance of multiple extensions here was quite a surprise, and was first discovered by Hanks and McDermott in 1986 **[Hanks, McDermott, 1986]**; a similar example was discovered independently by McCarthy **[McCarthy, 1986]**.[20]

Perhaps the simplest form of the Hanks-McDermott problem is the following: Suppose that we are reasoning about actions in some domain, and that there is an action a in this domain. We will write $\mathtt{holds}(p, s)$ to indicate that some fact p holds in some situation s, and use $\mathtt{do}(a, s)$ to denote the situation that results if we perform the action a in s. Thus p's holding after the execution of the action would be written as

$$\mathtt{holds}(p, \mathtt{do}(a, s))$$

Now suppose that the result of the action is to make p false. That is, unless a is qualified in some particular situation s, p will not hold after a is executed:

$$M[\neg\mathtt{holds}(p, \mathtt{do}(a, s))] \rightarrow \neg\mathtt{holds}(p, \mathtt{do}(a, s)) \tag{1.13}$$

This is a default rule because it is possible for the action to be qualified for some reason. However, (1.13) is *not* a frame axiom, since it describes the result of the action a, as opposed

[19] A Horn clause is one that can be expressed in disjunctive normal form using at most one nonnegated literal. Thus, $a(x) \wedge b(x) \rightarrow c(x)$ is Horn, since the disjunctive normal form of this expression is $\neg a(x) \vee \neg b(x) \vee c(x)$. But $\neg a(x) \rightarrow c(x)$, which rewrites to $a(x) \vee c(x)$, is not Horn; neither is (1.11).

[20] Hanks and McDermott had circulated their result widely before its presentation at the national AI conference in 1986; by the time of their talk describing the problem, at least three other authors [Kautz, 1986; Lifschitz, 1986c; **Shoham, 1986**] had already proposed solutions to it!

to the persistence of the fact $\neg p$. Specifically, $\neg\mathtt{holds}(p, s)$ is not part of the premise in (1.13).

On the other hand, the frame axiom, applied to p, tells us that

$$\mathtt{holds}(p, s) \wedge M[\mathtt{holds}(p, \mathtt{do}(a, s))] \rightarrow \mathtt{holds}(p, \mathtt{do}(a, s)) \quad (1.14)$$

In any situation where p holds (i.e., any s with $\mathtt{holds}(p, s)$), (1.14) will be in conflict with (1.13), and we will get two extensions as a result. In one, the action takes place as expected, and the frame axiom fails for p. In the other, the frame axiom is satisfied and p is preserved, but the action is qualified.

The example given by Hanks and McDermott involves firing a gun at someone (who is generally referred to as Fred). By and large, doing so will cause Fred to die, and (1.13) becomes

$$M[\neg\mathtt{holds}(\mathtt{alive}, \mathtt{do}(\mathtt{shoot}, s))] \rightarrow \neg\mathtt{holds}(\mathtt{alive}, \mathtt{do}(\mathtt{shoot}, s)) \quad (1.15)$$

Once again, this is a default rule because the shooting action may be qualified (in Hanks and McDermott's example, the gun may have become unloaded for some reason). The frame axiom, meanwhile, tells us that living things tend to continue living:

$$\mathtt{holds}(\mathtt{alive}, s) \wedge M[\mathtt{holds}(\mathtt{alive}, \mathtt{do}(\mathtt{shoot}, s))] \rightarrow \mathtt{holds}(\mathtt{alive}, \mathtt{do}(\mathtt{shoot}, s)) \quad (1.16)$$

When we fire the gun, we get two extensions. In one, Fred dies as expected. In the other, the shooting action is qualified and Fred lives on.

1.4.2 Prioritization and stratification

Wait a minute! It is clear why Fred should die if the action succeeds. After all, the firing of the gun causes his death. But what possible cause is there for the action being qualified? Does it make sense for the gun to become unloaded (thereby qualifying the shooting action) simply to avoid the mathematical unpleasantness of violating the frame axiom (1.14)?

Of course not. It is reasonable for a car to fail to start because of the presence of a potato in the tailpipe (or something else the owner has not thought of). It is *not* reasonable for the car to fail to start in order to avoid violating the frame axiom.

In these examples, there should *not* be two extensions. The action should succeed, and the frame axiom for p should fail. From a formal point of view, however, it is not clear how to represent this.

This sort of problem also can arise in some of the other examples we have seen. Perhaps the transformer is far more likely to fail than is the power supply. Perhaps the evidence that Quakers are pacifists is stronger than the evidence that Republicans are not. How are we to capture formally the notion that one default rule may be more important than another?

A great deal of the recent work in nonmonotonic inference has been aimed at precisely this issue. Etherington and Reiter discuss the properties of inheritance hierarchies with exceptions [**Etherington, Reiter, 1983**], work that was extended by Touretzky [**Touretzky, 1984**]. More recently, Etherington himself has extended these results further in [Etherington, 1987].

Work on circumscription also has addressed this issue. McCarthy introduces a notion of prioritized circumscription in [**McCarthy, 1980**], and this idea is generalized by Lifschitz in his work on *pointwise* circumscription [**Lifschitz, 1987b**].

Loosely speaking, all this work assumes that there is some partial order on the collection of default rules being considered, and the various authors show how to incorporate formally the sense of the partial order into the description of nonmonotonic logic they are considering. Unaddressed, however, is the question of where the partial order comes from in the first place.

Here also, some answers are beginning to emerge. Shoham has examined the Hanks-McDermott problem, and concluded that when reasoning about action, default rules about early times should take precedence over those about later times [**Shoham, 1986**].

Some results have also been found for PROLOG programs describing non-Horn databases. Consider the following PROLOG fragment, taken from [**Lifschitz, 1986a**]:

$$\begin{array}{l} p(1) \\ q(2) \\ r(x) :- \neg q(x) \end{array} \quad (1.17)$$

Expressed with the negation-as-failure default rules explicit, this becomes:

$$\begin{array}{ll} p(1) & \\ q(2) & \\ q(x) \vee r(x) & (1.18) \\ M\neg p(x) \rightarrow \neg p(x) & \\ M\neg q(x) \rightarrow \neg q(x) & (1.19) \\ M\neg r(x) \rightarrow \neg r(x) & (1.20) \end{array}$$

The three default rules tell us, for example, that, if $\neg p(x)$ is possible, then $\neg p(x)$ should be assumed. The last two defaults, (1.19) and (1.20), are in conflict because of the non-Horn clause (1.18).

The solution, dating back at least to Clark [**Clark, 1978**], is to realize that the PROLOG rule (1.17) makes a syntactic distinction between the predicates q and r. In some sense, the rule is "about" r, and not about q. So we should use this rule to prove things about r, but should not let it affect what we conclude about q. In other words, the default rule (1.19) should be applied preferentially to the rule (1.20).

This notion has been investigated by Poole [Poole, 1984], and has been formalized both by Apt and colleagues [Apt,

Blair, Walker, 1986] and independently by Van Gelder [Van Gelder, 1986]. These authors define a logic program to be *stratified* if the associated dependency graph (e.g., r depends on q because of (1.17), but not vice versa) does not contain any cycles. The dependency graph is constructed only from the *non-Horn* clauses in the database, since the semantics of the Horn part of the database are well-defined. Lifschitz goes on to show that pointwise circumscription can be used to give a well-defined semantics to any stratified PROLOG program [**Lifschitz, 1986a**].

1.4.3 Valor and caution

Unfortunately, not every logic program is stratified. Consider our database example from Section 1.4.1, which contained the clause,

$$\text{flight(San-Fran, New-York, Pan-Am-000)} \vee \text{flight(San-Fran, Washington, Pan-Am-000)} \quad (1.21)$$

or, in PROLOG form:

$$\text{flight(San-Fran, New-York, Pan-Am-000)} :- \neg\text{flight(San-Fran, Washington, Pan-Am-000)} \quad (1.22)$$

This is of the form

$$f(a) :- \neg f(b) \quad (1.23)$$

for constants a and b; since f is in a non-Horn rule about f itself, it is clear that a logic program containing an expression such as (1.23) can never be stratified.

This should not be a surprise. One extension has the Pan Am flight going to New York; the other has it going to Washington. There is really no reason to prefer one of these extensions over the other.

Surprisingly, the two approaches to default reasoning (consistency-based vs. circumscriptive) take very different approaches at this point. The circumscriptive approach is "cautious"—a result will follow after circumscribing the flight predicate if and only if it holds in *all* of the associated extensions. Default logic, on the other hand, is "brave"—the proof theory given by Reiter [**Reiter, 1980**] will sanction a conclusion that is valid in *any* of the extensions. This terminology is due to McDermott [McDermott, 1982].

Each approach seems to have advantages. It certainly would be a mistake for a travel agent to assume that the Pan Am flight goes to New York (assuming that is the intended destination), and to tell a client that he should avoid making another reservation because Pan Am is about to introduce an inexpensive flight on this route. Caution is called for here.

The argument for bravery is one of efficiency. Reiter's resolution-like algorithm determines whether a given conclusion holds in some extension of a default theory [**Reiter, 1980**]. More recently, Przymusinski has constructed a similar but cautious algorithm that determines whether a conclusion holds in *every* extension of a default theory [Przymusinski, 1986]. Needless to say, the brave algorithm is far more computationally effective than is its cautious counterpart, since Reiter needs to examine only one extension (and can focus the construction on the proposition in question), whereas Przymusinski must examine all of them. This is no small matter—the number of extensions easily can grow exponentially with the number of default rules in any particular default theory. We will consider the question of the effective implementation of nonmonotonic formalisms at greater length in Section 1.5.2.

1.5 Practical import

1.5.1 Useful applications

When we described the various examples of Section 1.2, the intention was principally to provide some foundation for the discussion of the formalisms that followed. In this section, we return to these examples, describing briefly the influence that the work on nonmonotonic reasoning can be expected to have in areas of practical interest.

Logic programming The most immediate applications of nonmonotonic reasoning are in the widespread use of logic programs that draw default conclusions. Logic programming is becoming an increasingly popular approach to all sorts of programming problems, ranging from operating systems to knowledge engineering applications. By logic programming here, we mean not so much PROLOG, but any declarative approach to programming.

Of course, the use of nonmonotonic techniques by logic programmers predates the formal work on them. Nonetheless, it seems likely that the logic programming community will directly benefit from this work for the following reasons:

1. Formal work on stratification [Apt, Blair, Walker, 1986; **Lifschitz, 1986a**; Van Gelder, 1986] will lead to a sharper understanding of the results returned by logic programming systems working with non-Horn databases.
2. It appears that effective implementations of nonmonotonic inference systems will depend on theoretical progress in understanding the formalisms themselves; we will return to this point in Section 1.5.2.

Diagnosis The growing use of computer assistance in the design and support of high-technology devices also promises to benefit greatly from the use of nonmonotonic techniques. Applying nonmonotonic logic to diagnostic tasks is discussed in [**de Kleer, Williams, 1987**; Ginsberg, 1986a; Poole, Aleliunas, Goebel, 1985; **Reiter, 1987b**]; two of these papers are included in this collection.

The use of logic in diagnosis appears to stem from work by Genesereth on the DART project [Genesereth, 1985]. Genesereth's key observation is that failures can be viewed not as *device* failures (the device is, after all, continuing to obey the laws of physics), but as *design* failures, in that the design has stopped describing the device in question. The diagnostic task then becomes one of determining what modifications must be made to the design in order to get it to correspond to the device exhibiting the apparent misfunction.

Genesereth's ideas have been implemented as part of the HELIOS project, a computer-aided design (CAD) tool being developed at Stanford [Singh, 1987]. HELIOS has been used in diagnostic tasks involving the IBM PC printer adapter card and the Intel 80286 microprocessor.

The diagnostic ideas will also be applicable in the area of design debugging. In principle, diagnostic and debugging tasks are nearly identical—the behavior associated with a particular design is incorrect (either because it does not match the behavior of the physical device, or because it does not match the intentions of the designer), and we would like to modify the design in a way that will lead to the desired behavior. As the papers in this collection demonstrate, this is a problem that can be attacked effectively using nonmonotonic reasoning.

Commonsense reasoning The final application we consider is that of commonsense reasoning, both in terms of property inheritance as in Section 1.2.1, and in domains involving planning and reasoning about action.

Formal work in nonmonotonic inference in these areas seems unlikely to lead to any immediate advances. The principal reason is that the contribution to be made by nonmonotonic techniques is in the area of *weak methods*—general-purpose algorithms capable of solving a wide range of planning or other problems.

AI generally seems insufficiently mature for weak methods to be of much practical import in planning (for example). Planning problems are simply too difficult for general-purpose solutions to be practical—yet. As time passes, we can expect this to change. For the time being, however, the "applications" section describing reasoning about action (5.3) should be taken in a different light from Sections 5.1 and 5.2.

1.5.2 Implementation considerations

Of course, none of these proposed applications will amount to much in the absence of an effectively implemented nonmonotonic reasoning system.

The difficulty in developing such an implementation is that none of the formal descriptions provides a constructive definition of a valid nonmonotonic derivation. The consistency-based approaches require solving a particular fixed-point equation; there are no known general-purpose techniques for this. Circumscription, meanwhile, uses a second-order axiom; once again, there are no complete proof procedures for second-order theories.[21]

Some progress is being made here. Reiter, in his original paper [**Reiter, 1980**], gave an algorithm for default logic. (The algorithm is brave, in the sense of Section 1.4.3, and applies to normal default theories only.) Przymusinski has developed a similar but cautious algorithm for circumscription [Przymusinski, 1986]. Lifschitz has discovered a variety of situations in which the usual circumscription formula is provably equivalent to a first-order axiom [**Lifschitz, 1985b; Lifschitz, 1987b**].

Although a step forward, these algorithms probably are still insufficient in the long run. The reason, as discussed in Section 1.3.4, and as argued by Israel [**Israel, 1980**] and by Perlis [**Perlis, 1986**], is that the nonmonotonic reasoning task is simply too difficult. An effective system will need to draw a default conclusion *without* doing a complete consistency check. If the conclusion subsequently turns out to be wrong, it will need to be retracted.

A similar view is expressed by Etherington, who discusses the open problem of updating databases that include nonmonotonic rules or conclusions [Etherington, 1986]. Etherington remarks that justification information is needed if a nonmonotonic conclusion is to be retracted, since the *consequences* of that conclusion also will need to be withdrawn. This will be true of any system that draws default conclusions and works with them before performing the consistency check. (In practice, it may be necessary to defer or abandon a consistency check if an answer is needed quickly—recall the nonsemidecidability of the problem.) If a deferred consistency check subsequently shows the original default conclusion to have been drawn in error, database modifications made because of that conclusion also will have to be retracted.

Consider once again our canonical example, but suppose that we add to our database the fact that flying things are not afraid of heights. If Opus is a bird, is Opus afraid of heights?

Apparently not, since Opus can supposedly fly. So suppose that we therefore add to our database the facts that Opus can fly and that he is not afraid of heights, marking each as defeasible if new information arrives.

New information does arrive; as is fairly well known, Opus is a penguin. He therefore cannot fly, and this conclusion must be removed from our database. Now we must *also* remove the conclusion that he is not acrophobic. Even though this conclusion is still consistent, it has become unsupported. If we are to avoid the need to reevaluate *all* our default conclusions when we learn that Opus cannot fly, we will need to have marked the conclusion that he is unafraid of heights as depending on the belief that he could fly. Alternatively, we can record, with the fact that Opus can fly, a list of the consequences of this conclusion. Either way, we need the information somewhere.

[21] And there won't be, since second-order logic is provably incomplete. I am indebted to David Israel for pointing this out to me.

1.6 Organization and contents

Organizing the papers in this collection turned out to be a surprisingly difficult task. The reason is simply that the field of nonmonotonic reasoning is still young and small enough that it has not split into subfields in any coherent way. A paper discussing the application of default logic to diagnosis is quite likely to refer to another paper on circumscription.

This is an editor's nightmare. The only way to avoid having papers refer to work that appears later in the collection is simply to order them chronologically. (Even that turns out not to be enough, since authors generally know what work is in progress, and often refer to that.)

The organization that has been used arranges the papers loosely by topic, and orders both the topics and the papers within each topic chronologically. Thus, the first section contains papers that give motivation for the work that has followed (or in some cases, papers that present arguments *against* the following work).

After that, the book is basically divided into two large parts. The first discusses formalisms, first presenting the consistency -based approaches, and following with papers on circumscription and work on unifications between the approaches. The second major part discusses applications, and contains papers discussing logic programming, diagnosis, and reasoning about action. Finally, you'll find an updated version of Don Perlis' bibliography of the nonmonotonic literature [**Perlis, 1984**].

1.6.1 The papers included in this collection

Within each of these topic areas are those papers that are generally recognized as the most significant or noteworthy.

Also included are all the "landmark" papers in nonmonotonic reasoning. These include the original papers on default logic [**Reiter, 1980**], the modal approach [**McDermott, Doyle, 1980**], and circumscription [**McCarthy, 1980**]. In the section on truth maintenance, you'll find Doyle's original paper describing the idea [**Doyle, 1979**]. McDermott and Doyle's paper [**McDermott, Doyle, 1980**] has a variety of technical problems, and is difficult to read as well; if your interest in the material is anything other than historical, you may not wish to read it. Doyle's original TMS paper is also difficult to understand in spots.

The decision to include a section on truth maintenance was a difficult one. In the end, there were three reasons for doing so:

1. As discussed in Section 1.5.2, any effective implementation of a nonmonotonic reasoning system apparently will depend on the inclusion of truth maintenance information.
2. The work on multi-valued logics [**Ginsberg, 1986b**] indicates be subsumed under a uniform framework. It seems likely from this that a better understanding of one may lead to better insights with regard to the other.
3. DeKleer's work on diagnosis[**de Kleer, Williams, 1987**] is formally closely related to Reiter's [**Reiter, 1987b**]. DeKleer uses an assumption-based truth maintenance system [**de Kleer, 1986a**], whereas Reiter uses an explicitly nonmonotonic approach; once again, we see the close link between these ideas.

In the end, one must admit that the inclusion of this section reflects an editorial bias toward the view that improved understanding of truth and reason maintenance is crucial to continued progress in the nonmonotonic work.

As mentioned in Section 1.5, the application areas of logic programming tools and diagnostic systems are very different from the application to commonsense reasoning. The first two are much more practical than the third, with practical systems either already in existence or well on the way. The reason the final section has been included is that, at least at the time of this writing, this application is clearly the hottest research area in nonmonotonic reasoning. We have already discussed the frame and qualification problems, as well as the Hanks-McDermott problem (which is also known as the *temporal projection* problem). A final difficulty is that of dealing with an action's indirect consequences, or *ramifications* [Finger, 1987; **Ginsberg, Smith, 1987a**]. No completely satisfactory solution exists to this suite of difficulties, although the work in Section 5.3 is a start. So the story on the applications section is that if you're looking to develop a practical application, Sections 5.1 and 5.2 are relevant; if you're looking for a thesis topic, 5.3 may well be the place to start.

1.6.2 The papers omitted from this collection

We remarked in Section 1.3.1 that there were rules to the nonmonotonic game. By and large, papers that broke the rules have not been included in this collection.

So, you won't find work here discussing "informal" approaches to nonmonotonic reasoning. Much of the early work on frames was of this sort, loosely describing inheritance and defaults in terms of "natural kinds". Fahlman's work on NETL [Fahlman, 1979] and Brachman's more recent work on inheritance [Brachman, 1985] extend these ideas.

This is important work, and perhaps should have been included. But the papers didn't seem to fit within the formal framework that has become accepted in the nonmonotonic community.

As already remarked, papers on numeric approaches also have been omitted, as the numericists have a literature of their own [Uncertainty workshop, 1985; Uncertainty workshop, 1986]. There have been a few papers discussing connections between numeric and nonnumeric approaches [Ginsberg, 1984; Grosof, 1986; Rich, 1983]; those have been omitted, as well.

You also will find very little from the negation-as-failure literature. Clark's original paper is here [**Clark, 1978**], although principally for historical reasons. The difficulty with much of this material is that it tends to discuss negation as failure *with respect to a specific inference procedure*. As a result, work such as Shepherdson's [Shepherdson, 1984; Shepherdson, 1985] tends to be very "algorithmic," often depending on the exact details of the inference procedure being considered. A notable exception is Lifschitz' recent work [**Lifschitz, 1986a**], and that paper is included.

There are other papers the technical content of which merit inclusion, but that have yet to appear in a polished form. These include Przymusinski's work on mechanizing circumscription [Przymusinski, 1986], Gelfond's recent work on the connection between autoepistemic logic and circumscription [Gelfond, 1986], and de Kleer and Reiter's formalization of ATMSs [Reiter, de Kleer, 1987]. We hope that new versions of these papers will appear in the literature soon.

1.6.3 Other sources

We conclude this section by describing the principal other sources of papers on nonmonotonic reasoning.

The best is probably the bibliography at the end of this volume, coupled with a good library. There also are a few places where material on nonmonotonic logic has already been collected:

1. The 1980 special issue of *Artificial Intelligence* [Bobrow, 1980]. Although principally of historical interest at this point, this volume contains the landmark papers by McCarthy, McDermott and Doyle, and Reiter [**McCarthy, 1980; McDermott, Doyle, 1980; Reiter, 1980**], as well as a few others [Davis, 1980; Weyhrauch, 1980; Winograd, 1980].
2. The proceedings of the 1984 Workshop on Nonmonotonic Reasoning, which was held in New Paltz, New York [Nonmonotonic workshop, 1984].
3. The proceedings of the 1987 Workshop on the Frame Problem in Artificial Intelligence, which was held in Lawrence, Kansas [Frame problem workshop, 1987].
4. A recent survey paper by Reiter [Reiter, 1987a].
5. Finally, interesting remarks can be found in the interview paper, "Artificial intelligence—where are we?" that appeared in the AI Journal in 1985 [Bobrow, Hayes, 1985]. Bobrow and Hayes discuss the (then) current state of the art with a variety of researchers in the field; remarks bearing on nonmonotonic logic can be found between pages 380 and 395 of the AI Journal article.

1.7 How to read this book

How you should read this book depends on what you want to get out of it. Let us assume that the readers of this book fall into three principal groups:

1. People looking for a general introduction to the field of nonmonotonic reasoning
2. People intending to apply nonmonotonic ideas to problems of practical interest
3. People looking for a potential thesis topic or research area to explore within nonmonotonic reasoning

1.7.1 As an introduction to nonmonotonic reasoning

If you're interested in an overview of the field, you probably should read a paper on each of the main approaches, but first read something to put them in perspective. You might start with McCarthy's epistemology paper [**McCarthy, 1977**], on page 46, and then Sections 3–9 of the revised circumscription paper [**McCarthy, 1986**], on page 153; save the rest of this second paper for later. Perlis' paper [**Perlis, 1986**], on page 56, is also worth looking at.

Next, read Reiter's paper on the closed-world assumption [**Reiter, 1978**], on page 300. It's an early paper, with a lot of motivation, and is fairly independent of the rest of the work in the field. Then go back to his paper on default logic [**Reiter, 1980**], on page 68, but don't worry about the material in Sections 4 and later, which tends to be quite technical. A quick look at Section 6 (revision of belief) might be in order.

The clearest paper on a modal approach is probably Moore's original paper on autoepistemic logic [**Moore, 1985**], on page 127; the circumscriptive work is more difficult. The first thing to look at might well be Sections 1–4 of Lifschitz' paper on computing circumscription, [**Lifschitz, 1985b**], on page 167; then try the rest of McCarthy's 1986 paper [**McCarthy, 1986**], on page 153, and also Lifschitz' paper on pointwise circumscription [**Lifschitz, 1987b**], on page 179. By and large, Lifschitz is the clearest of the authors who have published results on circumscription, but the material appears to be inherently difficult.

Definitely have a look at the Hanks-McDermott paper [**Hanks, McDermott, 1986**], on page 390; it's clearly written and is especially interesting in light of the fact that McDermott was one of the originators of the field. If you still have energy at this point, try one of the papers on unifications, either Shoham's paper on nonmonotonic theories generally [**Shoham, 1987**], on page 227, or the work on multi-valued logics [**Ginsberg, 1986b**], on page 251.

1.7.2 Applications

Logic programming

If your interest is in applications to logic programming, Reiter's paper on the closed-world assumption [**Reiter, 1978**], on page 300, is probably the best place to start. Sections 3–9 of McCarthy's 1986 paper also are likely to be worthwhile.

At this point, go back and have a look at Reiter's paper on default logic [**Reiter, 1980**], on page 68; it's probably worth the effort to work your way through the material on proof theory. Then try Minker's paper on the generalized closed-world assumption [**Minker, 1984**], on page 326, and Clark's original negation as failure work [**Clark, 1978**], on page 311.

Lifschitz' formal work in this area, [**Lifschitz, 1986a**], on page 337, is the logical next step. If you can understand it without appealing to the circumscription papers directly, so much the better. If not, the pointwise circumscription paper [**Lifschitz, 1987b**], on page 179, is probably the best place to turn for help.

Diagnosis

Diagnosis is rather a different matter. You may actually want to start with Genesereth's DART paper [Genesereth, 1985], or his coauthored introduction to logic programming [Genesereth, Ginsberg, 1985], which covers much of the same material.

Now have a look at Reiter's default logic paper [**Reiter, 1980**], on page 68; Sections 1–3 should give you all you need. After this, read his paper on diagnosis itself [**Reiter, 1987b**], on page 352.

After looking at the explicitly nonmonotonic work, turn to deKleer's paper on truth maintenance [**de Kleer, 1986a**], on page 280, and then to his paper with Williams on diagnosing multiple faults [**de Kleer, Williams, 1987**], on page 372.

1.7.3 Research problems

If you're looking to make a research contribution, start out by covering the field as a whole, as described in Section 1.7.1. Now the path you take depends on what area of nonmonotonic reasoning you're interested in.[22]

Reasoning about action One option is to jump into the discussion concerning the Hanks-McDermott problem and reasoning about action. After you read Hanks and McDermott's paper [**Hanks, McDermott, 1986**], on page 390, have a look at Shoham's general paper [**Shoham, 1987**], on page 227, before trying his work on chronological ignorance [**Shoham, 1986**], on page 396. The Ginsberg and Smith paper on reasoning about action [**Ginsberg, Smith, 1987a**], on page 433, is probably a bit easier to understand than is Lifschitz' paper [**Lifschitz, 1987a**], on page 410, so you may want to read them in that order instead of as they appear in the collection. Lifschitz' pointwise circumscription paper [**Lifschitz, 1987b**], on page 179, also discusses the Hanks-McDermott problem. You also may want to read Kautz' paper on persistence [Kautz, 1986], Haugh's paper addressing this question [Haugh, 1987], and the papers presented at the Workshop on the Frame Problem in Artificial Intelligence [Frame problem workshop, 1987].

Unifications Alternatively, you may want to explore the possibility of unifying some (or all?) of the approaches to nonmonotonic inference. Look at the papers in Section 3.4 to see what suggestions have been made; Etherington also discusses this issue in his thesis [Etherington, 1986].

Now you're pretty much on your own. You might try reading the material on diagnosis, however, as discussed in Section 1.7.2. Are the two approaches really the same? If so, what does this tell us about the connection between reason maintenance and nonmonotonic inference generally? DeKleer and Reiter's paper describing the formal properties of ATMSs [Reiter, de Kleer, 1987] is probably relevant here.

Implementations Effective computational procedures probably are needed more than anything else is by the nonmonotonic community. Unfortunately, too much of the formal work simply has not been reduced to practice at this point.

Of the papers mentioned in the overview section 1.7.1, only Reiter's original paper on default reasoning [**Reiter, 1980**], on page 68, presents an inference algorithm based on the formal construction being investigated. Lifschitz [**Lifschitz, 1985b**], on page 167, discusses some of the problems involved in constructing an effective implementation for circumscription, and a fairly general (but computationally extremely expensive) algorithm can be found in [Przymusinski, 1986]. Shoham presents an alogrithm for chronological ignorance (a form of nonmonotonic reasoning) in [**Shoham, 1986**], on page 396, and one can also be found for the possible worlds construction proposed in [**Ginsberg, Smith, 1987a**], on page 433. Some situations in which the work on multi-valued logics in [**Ginsberg, 1986b**], on page 251, can be expected to lead to a tractable algorithm are discussed in [Ginsberg, 1987c; Ginsberg, 1987d], and the development of a circumscriptive theorem prover based on these ideas is discussed in [Ginsberg, 1987a]. Only a few of these algorithms has actually been reduced to code,[23] so substantial work remains to be done.

Theory Considered as a whole, the papers in this collection seem to be telling us two things: that default reasoning can be effectively thought of as a minimization of some sort, and that the multiple extension problem can be tackled by introducing a partial order on the default rules causing the trouble.

Perhaps your intention in reading this collection is to add a third principle to these two. Well, that would be terrific. I suggest you do the following:

[22] Needless to say, the following suggestions reflect the biases of the editor. Other researchers would make different proposals.

[23] Several efforts are under way, however. Rabinov, working with McCarthy at Stanford, has implemented some of the results of Lifschitz' work on separable formulas from [**Lifschitz, 1985b**], on page 167, and multi-valued logics have been incorporated into the MRS expert system shell [Genesereth, 1983; Russell, 1985]. There are undoubtedly similar projects at other institutions as well.

1. Put the book aside for at least a month, and think about default reasoning *before* you get polluted by what other people have done.
2. Read the book from cover to cover.
3. Repeat the first two steps, probably more than once.

Good luck!

Acknowledgments

Many people have helped this collection come about, and I would like to take this opportunity to thank them. Most important are the authors and publishers who have been kind enough to contribute their work, and Mike Morgan at Morgan Kaufmann, who encouraged me with the entire project. Thanks also to those people who reviewed my selection of papers and the material in the introduction.

I owe thanks specifically to Ron Brachman, Benjamin Grosof, Haym Hirsh, David Israel, Kurt Konolige, Vladimir Lifschitz, Jock Mackinlay, Karen Myers, Nils Nilsson, Don Perlis, Ray Reiter, Narinder Singh, and Dave Smith for their comments and suggestions. Of course, any errors remaining in the editorial material reflect my oversights, rather than theirs.

Finally, I would like to thank two people who have helped to enrich my life over the course of the past few years. The first is my stepfather, Ken Riggs, who, sadly, did not live to see this book appear. The second already knows who she is.

Matt Ginsberg
Palo Alto, California
July, 1987

Bibliography

[Frame problem workshop, 1987] *Workshop on the Frame Problem in Artificial Intelligence*, Lawrence, KS, 1987. Published as F. Brown (ed.), *The Frame Problem in Artificial Intelligence: Proceedings of the 1987 Workshop*, Morgan Kaufmann Publishers, Los Altos, CA, 1987.

[Nonmonotonic workshop, 1984] *Non-Monotonic Reasoning Workshop*, New Paltz, NY, 1984.

[Uncertainty workshop, 1985] *Workshop on Uncertainty and Probability in Artificial Intelligence*, UCLA, Los Angeles, California, 1985.

[Uncertainty workshop, 1986] *Workshop on Uncertainty in Artificial Intelligence*, University of Pennsylvania, Philadelphia, PA, 1986.

[Apt, Blair, Walker, 1986] K. Apt, H. Blair, and A. Walker. "Towards a theory of declarative knowledge." In *Proceedings of the 1986 Workshop on Foundations of Deductive Databases and Logic Programming*, 1986.

[Bobrow, 1980] D. G. Bobrow (ed.). Special issue on nonmonotonic logic. *Artificial Intelligence*, 13:1–174, 1980.

[Bobrow, Hayes, 1985] D. G. Bobrow and P. J. Hayes. "Artificial intelligence—Where are we?" *Artificial Intelligence*, 24:375–415, 1985.

[Bossu, Siegel, 1985] G. Bossu and P. Siegel. "Saturation, nonmonotonic reasoning and the closed-world assumption." *Artificial Intelligence*, 25:13–63, 1985.

[Brachman, 1985] R. J. Brachman. " 'I lied about the trees' or, defaults and definitions in knowledge representation." *AI Magazine*, 6:80–93, 1985.

[Clark, 1978] K. L. Clark. "Negation as failure." In H. Gallaire and J. Minker (eds.), *Logic and Data Bases*, pp. 293–322, Plenum, New York, 1978.

[Davis, 1980] M. Davis. "The mathematics of non-monotonic reasoning." *Artificial Intelligence*, 13:73–80, 1980.

[de Kleer, 1984] J. de Kleer. "Choices without backtracking." In *Proceedings of the Fourth National Conference on Artificial Intelligence*, pp. 79–85, 1984.

[de Kleer, 1986a] J. de Kleer. "An assumption-based TMS." *Artificial Intelligence*, 28:127–162, 1986.

[de Kleer, 1986b] J. de Kleer. "Extending the ATMS." *Artificial Intelligence*, 28:163–196, 1986.

[de Kleer, 1986c] J. de Kleer. "Problem solving with the ATMS." *Artificial Intelligence*, 28:197–224, 1986.

[de Kleer, Williams, 1987] J. de Kleer and B. C. Williams. "Diagnosing multiple faults." *Artificial Intelligence*, 32:97–130, 1987.

[Doyle, 1979] J. Doyle. "A truth maintenance system." *Artificial Intelligence*, 12:231–272, 1979.

[Doyle, 1982] J. Doyle. *Some Theories of Reasoned Assumptions: An Essay in Rational Psychology*. Technical Report, Department of Computer Science, Carnegie-Mellon University, 1982.

[Doyle, 1983] J. Doyle. "The ins and outs of reason maintenance." In *Proceedings of the Eigth International Joint Conference on Artificial Intelligence*, pp. 349–351, 1983.

[Doyle, 1984] J. Doyle. "Circumscription and implicit definability." In *Proceedings 1984 Non-monotonic Reasoning Workshop*, pp. 57–69, American Association for Artificial Intelligence, New Paltz, NY, 1984.

[Doyle, 1985] J. Doyle. "Reasoned assumptions and Pareto optimality." In *Proceedings of the Ninth International Joint Conference on Artificial Intelligence*, pp. 87–90, 1985.

[Enderton, 1972] H. B. Enderton. *A Mathematical Introduction to Logic*. Academic Press, New York, 1972.

[Etherington, 1986] D. W. Etherington. *Reasoning with Incomplete Information: Investigations of Non-Monotonic Reasoning*. PhD thesis, University of British Columbia, Vancouver, Canada, 1986.

[Etherington, 1987] D. W. Etherington. "Formalizing nonmonotonic reasoning systems." *Artificial Intelligence*, 31:41–85, 1987.

[Etherington, Mercer, Reiter, 1985] D. W. Etherington, R. E. Mercer, and R. Reiter. "On the adequacy of predicate circumscription for closed-world reasoning." *Computational Intelligence*, 1:11–15, 1985.

[Etherington, Reiter, 1983] D. W. Etherington and R. Reiter. "On inheritance hierarchies with exceptions." In *Proceedings of the Third National Conference on Artificial Intelligence*, pp. 104–108, 1983.

[Fahlman, 1979] S. E. Fahlman. NETL: *A System for Representing and Using Real-World Knowledge*. MIT Press, Cambridge, MA, 1979.

[Fikes, Nilsson, 1971] R. Fikes and N. J. Nilsson. "STRIPS: A new approach to the application of theorem proving to problem solving." *Artificial Intelligence*, 2:189–208, 1971.

[Finger, 1987] J. J. Finger. *Exploiting Constraints in Design Synthesis*. PhD thesis, Stanford University, Stanford, CA, 1987.

[Gelfond, 1986] M. Gelfond. *On Stratified Autoepistemic Theories*. Technical Report, Department of Computer Science, University of Texas at El Paso, 1986.

[Gelfond, 1987] M. Gelfond and H. Przymusinska. "Negation as failure: Careful closure procedure." *Artificial Intelligence*, 1987.

[Gelfond, Przymusinska, 1986] M. Gelfond and H. Przymusinska. *On the Relationship between Autoepistemic Logic and Parallel Circumscription*. Technical Report, Department of Computer Science, University of Texas at El Paso, 1986.

[Gelfond, Przymusinska, Prsymusinski, 1986] M. Gelfond, H. Przymusinska, and T. Przymusinski. "The extended closed world assumption and its relationship to parallel circumscription." In *Proceedings of ACM SIGACT-SIGMOD Symposium on Principles of Database Systems*, pp. 133–139, 1986.

[Genesereth, 1983] M. R. Genesereth. "An overview of meta-level architecture." In *Proceedings of the Third National Conference on Artificial Intelligence*, pp. 119–124, 1983.

[Genesereth, 1985] M. R. Genesereth. "The use of design descriptions in automated diagnosis." *Artificial Intelligence*, 24:411–436, 1985.

[Genesereth, Ginsberg, 1985] M. R. Genesereth and M. L. Ginsberg. "Logic programming." *Commun. ACM*, 28:933–941, 1985.

[Genesereth, Nilsson, 1987] M. R. Genesereth and N. J. Nilsson. *Logical Foundations of Artificial Intelligence*. Morgan Kaufmann Publishers, Los Altos, CA, 1987.

[Georgeff, 1987] M. P. Georgeff. "Many agents are better than one." In F. Brown (ed.), *The Frame Problem in Artificial Intelligence: Proceedings of the 1987 Workshop*, pp. 59–75, Morgan Kaufmann Publishers, Los Altos, CA, 1987.

[Ginsberg, 1984] M. L. Ginsberg. "Non-monotonic reasoning using Dempster's rule." In *Proceedings of the Fourth National Conference on Artificial Intelligence*, pp. 126–129, 1984.

[Ginsberg, 1985] M. L. Ginsberg. "Does probability have a place in non-monotonic reasoning?" In *Proceedings of the Ninth International Joint Conference on Artificial Intelligence*, pp. 107–110, 1985.

[Ginsberg, 1986a] M. L. Ginsberg. "Counterfactuals." *Artificial Intelligence*, 30:35–79, 1986.

[Ginsberg, 1986b] M. L. Ginsberg. "Multi-valued logics." In *Proceedings of the Fifth National Conference on Artificial Intelligence*, pp. 243–247, 1986.

[Ginsberg, 1987a] M. L. Ginsberg. *A Circumscriptive Theorem Prover*. Technical Report 87-8, Logic Group, Stanford University, Stanford, CA, 1987.

[Ginsberg, 1987b] M. L. Ginsberg. *Multi-valued Logics I: Formal Description*. Technical Report 87-4, Logic Group, Stanford University, Stanford, CA, 1987.

[Ginsberg, 1987c] M. L. Ginsberg. *Multi-valued Logics II: Inference*. Technical Report 87-5, Logic Group, Stanford University, Stanford, CA, 1987.

[Ginsberg, 1987d] M. L. Ginsberg. *Multi-valued Logics III: Applications*. Technical Report 87-6, Logic Group, Stanford University, Stanford, CA, 1987.

[Ginsberg, Smith, 1987a] M. L. Ginsberg and D. E. Smith. "Reasoning about action I: A possible worlds approach." In F. Brown (ed.), *The Frame Problem in Artificial Intelligence: Proceedings of the 1987 Workshop*, pp. 233–258, Morgan Kaufmann Publishers, Los Altos, CA, 1987.

[Ginsberg, Smith, 1987b] M. L. Ginsberg and D. E. Smith. "Reasoning about action II: The qualification problem." In F. Brown (ed.), *The Frame Problem in Artificial Intelligence: Proceedings of the 1987 Workshop*, pp. 259–287, Morgan Kaufmann Publishers, Los Altos, CA, 1987.

[Goodwin, 1987] J. W. Goodwin. *A Theory and System for Non-Monotonic Reasoning*. PhD thesis, Linkoping University, Linkoping, Sweden, 1987.

[Grosof, 1986] B. N. Grosof. "Non-monotonicity in probabilistic reasoning." In *Proceedings 1986 Workshop on Uncertainty in Artificial Intelligence*, pp. 91–98, Philadelphia, PA, 1986.

[Halpern, Moses, 1984] J. Y. Halpern and Y. Moses. "Towards a theory of knowledge and ignorance." In *Proceedings 1984 Non-monotonic Reasoning Workshop*, pp. 165–193, American Association for Artificial Intelligence, New Paltz, NY, 1984.

[Hanks, McDermott, 1986] S. Hanks and D. McDermott. "Default reasoning, nonmonotonic logics, and the frame problem." In *Proceedings of the Fifth National Conference on Artificial Intelligence*, pp. 328–333, 1986.

[Haugh, 1987] B. Haugh. "Simple causal minimizations for temporal persistance and projection." In *Proceedings of the Sixth National Conference on Artificial Intelligence*, pp. 218–223, 1987.

[Hewitt, 1972] C. E. Hewitt. *Description and Theoretical Analysis (using schemata) of* PLANNER*: A Language for Proving Theorems and Manipulating Models in a Robot*. Technical Report TR-258, AI Laboratory, Massachusetts Institute of Technology, Cambridge, MA, 1972.

[Imielinski, 1987] T. Imielinski. "Results on translating defaults to circumscription." *Artificial Intelligence*, 32:131–146, 1987.

[Israel, 1980] D. J. Israel. "What's wrong with non-monotonic logic?" In *Proceedings of the First Annual National Conference on Artificial Intelligence*, pp. 99–101, 1980.

[Jaeger, 1986] G. Jaeger. "Some contributions to the logical analysis of circumscription." In *Eigth International Conference on Automated Deduction*, pp. 154–171, Oxford, England, 1986.

[Kautz, 1986] H. A. Kautz. "The logic of persistence." In *Proceedings of the Fifth National Conference on Artificial Intelligence*, pp. 401–405, 1986.

[Konolige, 1987] K. Konolige. "On the relation between default theories and autoepistemic logic." Technical Report, SRI International, Menlo Park, CA, 1987.

[Konolige, Myers, 1987] K. Konolige and K. L. Myers. *Representing defaults with epistemic concepts*. Technical Report, SRI International, Menlo Park, CA, 1987.

[Kowalski, Sergot, 1986] R. Kowalski and M. Sergot. "A logic-based calculus of events." *New Generation Computing*, 4:67–95, 1986.

[Kramosil, 1975] I. Kramosil. "A note on deduction rules with negative premises." In *Proceedings of the Fourth International Joint Conference on Artificial Intelligence*, pp. 53–56, 1975.

[Kripke, 1971] S. A. Kripke. "Semantical considerations on modal logic." In L. Linsky (ed.), *Reference and Modality*, pp. 63–72, Oxford University Press, London, 1971.

[Levesque, 1982] H. J. Levesque. *A Formal Treatment of Incomplete Knowledge*. Technical Report 3, Fairchild Laboratory for AI Research, Palo Alto, CA, 1982.

[Levesque, 1987] H. J. Levesque. "All I know: A preliminary report." In *Proceedings of the Sixth National Conference on Artificial Intelligence*, pp. 426–431, 1987.

[Lewis, 1973] D. Lewis. *Counterfactuals*. Harvard University Press, Cambridge, 1973.

[Lifschitz, 1985a] V. Lifschitz. "Closed-world databases and circumscription." *Artificial Intelligence*, 27:229–235, 1985.

[Lifschitz, 1985b] V. Lifschitz. "Computing circumscription." In *Proceedings of the Ninth International Joint Conference on Artificial Intelligence*, pp. 121–127, 1985.

[Lifschitz, 1986a] V. Lifschitz. "On the declarative semantics of logic programs with negation." In J. Minker (ed.), *Foundations of Deductive Databases and Logic Programming*, Morgan Kaufmann Publishers, Los Altos, CA, 1987.

[Lifschitz, 1986b] V. Lifschitz. "On the satisfiability of circumscription." *Artificial Intelligence*, 28:17–27, 1986.

[Lifschitz, 1986c] V. Lifschitz. "Pointwise circumscripton: preliminary report." In *Proceedings of the Fifth National Conference on Artificial Intelligence*, pp. 406–410, 1986.

[Lifschitz, 1987a] V. Lifschitz. "Formal theories of action." In F. Brown (ed.), *The Frame Problem in Artificial Intelligence: Proceedings of the 1987 Workshop*, pp. 35–58, Morgan Kaufmann Publishers, Los Altos, CA, 1987.

[Lifschitz, 1987b] V. Lifschitz. *Pointwise Circumscription*. Technical Report, Stanford University, Stanford, CA, 1987.

[Lukaszewicz, 1984] V. Lukaszewicz. "Considerations on default logic." In *Proceedings 1984 Non-monotonic Reasoning Workshop*, pp. 165–193, American Association for Artificial Intelligence, New Paltz, NY, 1984.

[Martins, Shapiro, 1983] J. P. Martins and S. C. Shapiro. "Reasoning in multiple belief spaces." In *Proceedings of the Eigth International Joint Conference on Artificial Intelligence*, pp. 370–373, 1983.

[Martins, Shapiro, 1984] J. P. Martins and S. C. Shapiro. "A model for belief revision." In *Proceedings 1984 Non-monotonic Reasoning Workshop*, pp. 241–294, American Association for Artificial Intelligence, New Paltz, NY, 1984.

[McCarthy, 1960] J. McCarthy. "Programs with commmon sense." In M. Minsky, editor, *Semantic Information Processing*, pp. 403–418, MIT Press, Cambridge, MA, 1960.

[McCarthy, 1977] J. McCarthy. "Epistemological problems of artificial intelligence." In *Proceedings of the Fifth International Joint Conference on Artificial Intelligence*, pp. 1038–1044, Cambridge, MA, 1977.

[McCarthy, 1980] J. McCarthy. "Circumscription—a form of non-monotonic reasoning." *Artificial Intelligence*, 13:27–39, 171–172, 1980.

[McCarthy, 1986] J. McCarthy. "Applications of circumscription to formalizing common-sense knowledge." *Artificial Intelligence*, 28:89–116, 1986.

[McCarthy, Hayes, 1969] J. McCarthy and P. J. Hayes. "Some philosophical problems from the standpoint of artificial intelligence." In B. Meltzer and D. Mitchie (eds.), *Machine Intelligence 4*, pp. 463–502, Edinburgh University Press, 1969.

[McDermott, 1982] D. McDermott. "Non-monotonic logic II." *Journal ACM*, 29:33–57, 1982.

[McDermott, 1987a] D. McDermott. "AI, logic, and the frame problem." In F. Brown (ed.), *The Frame Problem in Artificial Intelligence: Proceedings of the 1987 Workshop*, pp. 105–118, Morgan Kaufmann Publishers, Los Altos, CA, 1987.

[McDermott, 1987b] D. McDermott. "A critique of pure reason." *Computational Intelligence*, 1987.

[McDermott, Doyle, 1980] D. McDermott and J. Doyle. "Nonmonotonic logic I." *Artificial Intelligence*, 13:41–72, 1980.

[Minker, 1984] J. Minker. "On indefinite databases and the closed world assumption." In *Sixth International Conference on Automated Deduction*, pp. 292–308, 1982.

[Minker, Perlis, 1984] J. Minker and D. Perlis. "Protected circumscription." In *Proceedings 1984 Non-monotonic Reasoning Workshop*, pp. 337–343, American Association for Artificial Intelligence, New Paltz, NY, 1984.

[Minsky, 1975] M. Minsky. "A framework for representing knowledge." In P. Winston (ed.), *The Psychology of Computer Vision*, pp. 211–277, McGraw-Hill, 1975.

[Moore, 1984] R. C. Moore. "Possible worlds semantics for autoepistemic logic." In *Proceedings 1984 Non-monotonic Reasoning Workshop*, pp. 344–354, American Association for Artificial Intelligence, New Paltz, NY, 1984.

[Moore, 1985] R. C. Moore. "Semantical considerations on nonmonotonic logic." *Artificial Intelligence*, 25:75–94, 1985.

[Nilsson, 1980] N. J. Nilsson. *Principles of Artificial Intelligence.* Morgan Kaufmann Publishers, Los Altos, CA, 1980.

[Nutter, 1983] J. Nutter. "Default reasoning using monotonic logic: A modest proposal." In *Proceedings of the Third National Conference on Artificial Intelligence*, pp. 297–300, 1983.

[Perlis, 1984] D. Perlis. "Bibliography of literature on nonmonotonic reasoning." In *Proceedings 1984 Non-monotonic Reasoning Workshop*, pp. 396–401, American Association for Artificial Intelligence, New Paltz, NY, 1984.

[Perlis, 1986] D. Perlis. "On the consistency of commonsense reasoning." *Computational Intelligence*, 2:180–190, 1986.

[Perlis, Minker, 1986] D. Perlis and J. Minker. "Completeness results for circumscription." *Artificial Intelligence*, 28:29–42, 1986.

[Perrault, 1987] R. Perrault. *An Application of Default Logic to Speech Act Theory.* Technical Report, SRI International, Menlo Park, CA, 1987.

[Poole, 1984] D. Poole. "A logical system for default reasoning." In *Proceedings 1984 Non-monotonic Reasoning Workshop*, pp. 373–384, American Association for Artificial Intelligence, New Paltz, NY, 1984.

[Poole, Aleliunas, Goebel, 1985] D. Poole, R. Aleliunas, and R. Goebel. *THEORIST: A Logical Reasoning System for Defaults and Diagnosis.* Technical Report, Depratment of Computer Science, University of Waterloo, Waterloo, Canada, 1985.

[Przymusinski, 1986] T. C. Przymusinski. "Query-answering in circumscriptive and closed-world theories." In *Proceedings of the Fifth National Conference on Artificial Intelligence*, pp. 186–190, 1986.

[Reiter, 1978] R. Reiter. "On closed world data bases." In H. Gallaire and J. Minker (eds.), *Logic and Data Bases*, pp. 119–140, Plenum, New York, 1978.

[Reiter, 1980] R. Reiter. "A logic for default reasoning." *Artificial Intelligence*, 13:81–132, 1980.

[Reiter, 1987a] R. Reiter. "Nonmonotonic reasoning." *Annual Reviews of Computer Science*, 2:147–187, 1987.

[Reiter, 1987b] R. Reiter. "A theory of diagnosis from first principles." *Artificial Intelligence*, 32:57–95, 1987.

[Reiter, Criscuolo, 1981] R. Reiter and G. Criscuolo. "On interacting defaults." In *Proceedings of the Seventh International Joint Conference on Artificial Intelligence*, pp. 270–276, 1981.

[Reiter, de Kleer, 1987] R. Reiter and J. de Kleer. "Foundations of assumption-based truth maintenance systems: Preliminary report." In *Proceedings of the Sixth National Conference on Artificial Intelligence*, pp. 183–188, 1987.

[Rich, 1983] E. Rich. "Default reasoning as likelihood reasoning." In *Proceedings of the Third National Conference on Artificial Intelligence*, pp. 348–351, 1983.

[Russell, 1985] S. Russell. *The Compleat Guide to* MRS. Technical Report STAN-CS-85-1080, Stanford University, Stanford, CA, June 1985.

[Schlipf, 1986] J. S. Schlipf. "How uncomputable is general circumscription? (extended abstract)." In *IEEE 1986 Symposium on Logic in Computer Science*, pp. 92–95, 1986.

[Shepherdson, 1984] J. C. Shepherdson. "Negation as failure: A comparison of Clark's completed data base and Reiter's closed world assumption." *Journal of Logic Programming*, 1:51–79, 1984.

[Shepherdson, 1985] J. C. Shepherdson. "Negation as failure II." *Journal of Logic Programming*, 3:185–202, 1985.

[Shoham, 1986] Y. Shoham. "Chronological ignorance." In *Proceedings of the Fifth National Conference on Artificial Intelligence*, pp. 389–393, 1986.

[Shoham, 1987] Y. Shoham. "A semantical approach to nonmonotonic logics." In *Proceedings of the Tenth International Joint Conference on Artificial Intelligence*, pp. 388–392, 1987.

[Shortliffe, 1976] E. H. Shortliffe. *Computer-Based Medical Consultations:* MYCIN. American Elsevier, New York, 1976.

[Singh, 1987] N. P. Singh. *An Artificial Intelligence Approach to Test Generation.* Kluwer, Norwell, MA, 1987.

[Touretzky, 1984] D. S. Touretzky. "Implicit ordering of defaults in inheritance systems." In *Proceedings of the Fifth National Conference on Artificial Intelligence*, pp. 322–325, 1984.

[Van Gelder, 1986] A. Van Gelder. "Negation as failure using tight derivations for general logic programs." In J. Minker (ed.), *Proceedings of the Workshop on the Foundations of Deductive Databases and Logic Programming*, pp. 420–432, Morgan Kaufmann Publishers, Los Altos, CA, 1987.

[Weyhrauch, 1980] R. W. Weyhrauch. "Prolegomena to a theory of mechanized formal reasoning." *Artificial Intelligence*, 13:133–170, 1980.

[Winograd, 1980] T. Winograd. "Extended inference modes in reasoning by computer systems." *Artificial Intelligence*, 13:5–26, 1980.

[Yahya, Henschen, 1985] A. Yahya and L. J. Henschen. "Deduction in non-Horn databases." *Journal of Automated Reasoning*, 1:141–160, 1985.

Chapter 2

Background and Historical Papers

This first group of four papers contains two giving insight into the introduction of nonmonotonic issues into the AI field as a whole, and two more recent papers arguing that the current approaches are sadly lacking in one way or another.

McCarthy's early work focusses on planning as an applications domain, and reflects his bias toward formal solutions to AI problems. In the first of these papers, "Some philosophical problems from the standpoint of artificial intelligence," he and Hayes touch on a wide range of issues. The situation calculus is introduced in Section 2, and the frame problem appears (for the first time) at the end of this section.

McCarthy and Hayes go on to draw connections between this problem of "defeasible" inference and other work in the formal community. At the end of Section 3, they mention (and dismiss) a probabilistic approach; a modal approach is considered in some depth in Section 4. The use of a modal approach in investigating a logic of knowledge also is discussed.

McCarthy's ideas had crystallized substantially by the time "Epistemological problems of artificial intelligence" appeared eight years later. McCarthy is still considering the planning domain, and has identified the qualification problem in addition to the frame difficulty; he recognizes that the monotonicity of logical inference is causing the problem. This paper also contains the first appearance of the circumscription axiom, although the ideas are not yet worked out and McCarthy points us to a forthcoming paper for them. The closed world assumption also is discussed, although not by that name.

The only other paper of comparable importance in the development of nonmonotonic formalism is Minsky's original frame paper [Minsky, 1975].[1] Unfortunately, this paper is rather long and stresses many issues unrelated to nonmonotonic reasoning, and therefore is not included in this collection.

The other two papers appearing in this section are Israel's, "What's wrong with nonmonotonic logic?" and Perlis', "On the consistency of commonsense reasoning." Both of these papers were discussed in Section 1.3.4 of the introduction; we review our comments on them only briefly.

Israel raises two prinicpal objections. The first is simply that "nonmonotonic logic" is a contradiction in terms; the second—and far more substantial—is that the nonmonotonic reasoning schemes are tackling a roblem that is non-semidecidable and, as such, may not *ever* yield a formally satisfactory solution.

Perlis extends Israel's arguments considerably. Specifically, he investigates the fact that the non-semidecidability of nonmonotonic databases will inevitably cause them to draw conclusions in error, and they may in some cases need to acknowledge the possibility of such a mistake.

Consider the lottery paradox. Imagine that there are one million entrants in some lottery; surely we should have a default rule that, in the absence of information to the contrary, any particular individual should be assumed not to be the winner. But we also know, from the nature of lotteries, that *some* person *will* win. In other words, we know that one of our default conclusions is wrong. Perlis shows from this that many nonmonotonic databases are necessarily either self-inconsistent or incapable of drawing the intended default conclusions.

[1] All references are to papers in the bibliography at the end of the introduction.

Some Philosophical Problems from the Standpoint of Artificial Intelligence

J. McCarthy
Computer Science Department
Stanford University

P. J. Hayes
Metamathematics Unit
University of Edinburgh

Abstract

A computer program capable of acting intelligently in the world must have a general representation of the world in terms of which its inputs are interpreted. Designing such a program requires commitments about what knowledge is and how it is obtained. Thus, some of the major traditional problems of philosophy arise in artificial intelligence.

More specifically, we want a computer program that decides what to do by inferring in a formal language that a certain strategy will achieve its assigned goal. This requires formalizing concepts of causality, ability, and knowledge. Such formalisms are also considered in philosophical logic.

The first part of the paper begins with a philosophical point of view that seems to arise naturally once we take seriously the idea of actually making an intelligent machine. We go on to the notions of metaphysically and epistemologically adequate representations of the world and then to an explanation of *can*, *causes*, and *knows* in terms of a representation of the world by a system of interacting automata. A proposed resolution of the problem of freewill in a deterministic universe and of counterfactual conditional sentences is presented.

The second part is mainly concerned with formalisms within which it can be proved that a strategy will achieve a goal. Concepts of situation, fluent, future operator, action, strategy, result of a strategy and knowledge are formalized. A method is given of constructing a sentence of first-order logic which will be true in all models of certain axioms if and only if a certain strategy will achieve a certain goal.

The formalism of this paper represents an advance over McCarthy (1963) and Green (1969) in that it permits proof of the correctness of strategies that contain loops and strategies that involve the acquisition of knowledge; and it is also somewhat more concise.

The third part discusses open problems in extending the formalism of part 2.

The fourth part is a review of work in philosophical logic in relation to problems of artificial intelligence and a discussion of previous efforts to program 'general intelligence' from the point of view of this paper.

1. PHILOSOPHICAL QUESTIONS

Why artificial intelligence needs philosophy

The idea of an intelligent machine is old, but serious work on the problem of artificial intelligence or even serious understanding of what the problem is awaited the stored-program computer. We may regard the subject of artificial intelligence as beginning with Turing's article 'Computing Machinery and Intelligence' (Turing 1950) and with Shannon's (1950) discussion of how a machine might be programmed to play chess.

Since that time, progress in artificial intelligence has been mainly along the following lines. Programs have been written to solve a class of problems that give humans intellectual difficulty: examples are playing chess or checkers, proving mathematical theorems, transforming one symbolic expression into another by given rules, integrating expressions composed of elementary functions, determining chemical compounds consistent with mass-spectrographic and other data. In the course of designing these programs intellectual mechanisms of greater or lesser generality are identified sometimes by introspection, sometimes by mathematical analysis, and sometimes by experiments with human subjects. Testing the programs sometimes leads to better understanding of the intellectual mechanisms and the identification of new ones.

An alternative approach is to start with the intellectual mechanisms (for example, memory, decision-making by comparisons of scores made up of weighted sums of sub-criteria, learning, tree search, extrapolation) and make up problems that exercise these mechanisms.

In our opinion the best of this work has led to increased understanding of intellectual mechanisms and this is essential for the development of artificial intelligence even though few investigators have tried to place their particular mechanism in the general context of artificial intelligence. Sometimes this is because the investigator identifies his particular problem with the field as a whole; he thinks he sees the woods when in fact he is looking at a tree. An old but not yet superseded discussion on intellectual mechanisms is in Minsky (1961); see also Newell's (1965) review of the state of artificial intelligence.

There have been several attempts to design a general intelligence with the same kind of flexibility as that of a human. This has meant different things to different investigators, but none has met with much success even in the sense of general intelligence used by the investigator in question. Since our criticism of this work will be that it does not face the philosophical problems discussed in this paper we shall postpone discussing it until a concluding section.

However, we are obliged at this point to present our notion of general intelligence.

It is not difficult to give sufficient conditions for general intelligence. Turing's idea that the machine should successfully pretend to a sophisticated observer to be a human being for half an hour will do. However, if we direct our efforts towards such a goal our attention is distracted by certain superficial aspects of human behaviour that have to be imitated. Turing excluded some of these by specifying that the human to be imitated is at the end of a teletype line, so that voice, appearance, smell, etc., do not have to be considered. Turing did allow himself to be distracted into discussing the imitation of human fallibility in arithmetic, laziness, and the ability to use the English language.

However, work on artificial intelligence, expecially general intelligence, will be improved by a clearer idea of what intelligence is. One way is to give a purely behavioural or black-box definition. In this case we have to say that a machine is intelligent if it solves certain classes of problems requiring intelligence in humans, or survives in an intellectually demanding environment. This definition seems vague; perhaps it can be made somewhat more precise without departing from behavioural terms, but we shall not try to do so.

Instead, we shall use in our definition certain structures apparent to introspection, such as knowledge of facts. The risk is twofold: in the first place we might be mistaken in our introspective views of our own mental structure; we may only think we use facts. In the second place there might be entities which satisfy behaviourist criteria of intelligence but are not organized in this way. However, we regard the construction of intelligent machines as fact manipulators as being the best bet both for constructing artificial intelligence and understanding natural intelligence.

We shall, therefore, be interested in an intelligent entity that is equipped with a representation or model of the world. On the basis of this representation a certain class of internally posed questions can be answered, not always correctly. Such questions are

1. What will happen next in a certain aspect of the situation?
2. What will happen if I do a certain action?
3. What is 3+3?
4. What does he want?
5. Can I figure out how to do this or must I get information from someone else or something else?

The above are not a fully representative set of questions and we do not have such a set yet.

On this basis we shall say that an entity is intelligent if it has an adequate model of the world (including the intellectual world of mathematics, understanding of its own goals and other mental processes), if it is clever enough to answer a wide variety of questions on the basis of this model, if it can get additional information from the external world when required, and can perform such tasks in the external world as its goals demand and its physical abilities permit.

According to this definition intelligence has two parts, which we shall call the epistemological and the heuristic. The epistemological part is the representation of the world in such a form that the solution of problems follows from the facts expressed in the representation. The heuristic part is the mechanism that on the basis of the information solves the problem and decides what to do. Most of the work in artificial intelligence so far can be regarded as devoted to the heuristic part of the problem. This paper, however, is entirely devoted to the epistemological part.

Given this notion of intelligence the following kinds of problems arise in constructing the epistemological part of an artificial intelligence:

1. What kind of general representation of the world will allow the incorporation of specific observations and new scientific laws as they are discovered?
2. Besides the representation of the physical world what other kind of entities have to be provided for? For example, mathematical systems, goals, states of knowledge.
3. How are observations to be used to get knowledge about the world, and how are the other kinds of knowledge to be obtained? In particular what kinds of knowledge about the system's own state of mind are to be provided for?
4. In what kind of internal notation is the system's knowledge to be expressed?

These questions are identical with or at least correspond to some traditional questions of philosophy, especially in metaphysics, epistemology and philosophic logic. Therefore, it is important for the research worker in artificial intelligence to consider what the philosophers have had to say.

Since the philosophers have not really come to an agreement in 2500 years it might seem that artificial intelligence is in a rather hopeless state if it is to depend on getting concrete enough information out of philosophy to write computer programs. Fortunately, merely undertaking to embody the philosophy in a computer program involves making enough philosophical presuppositions to exclude most philosophy as irrelevant. Undertaking to construct a general intelligent computer program seems to entail the following presuppositions:

1. The physical world exists and already contains some intelligent machines called people.
2. Information about this world is obtainable through the senses and is expressible internally.
3. Our common-sense view of the world is approximately correct and so is our scientific view.

4. The right way to think about the general problems of metaphysics and epistemology is not to attempt to clear one's own mind of all knowledge and start with 'Cogito ergo sum' and build up from there. Instead, we propose to use all of our own knowledge to construct a computer program that knows. The correctness of our philosophical system will be tested by numerous comparisons between the beliefs of the program and our own observations and knowledge. (This point of view corresponds to the presently dominant attitude towards the foundations of mathematics. We study the structure of mathematical systems–from the outside as it were–using whatever metamathematical tools seem useful instead of assuming as little as possible and building up axiom by axiom and rule by rule within a system.)
5. We must undertake to construct a rather comprehensive philosophical system, contrary to the present tendency to study problems separately and not try to put the results together.
6. The criterion for definiteness of the system becomes much stronger. Unless, for example, a system of epistemology allows us, at least in principle, to construct a computer program to seek knowledge in accordance with it, it must be rejected as too vague.
7. The problem of 'free will' assumes an acute but concrete form. Namely, in common-sense reasoning, a person often decides what to do by evaluating the results of the different actions he can do. An intelligent program must use this same process, but using an exact formal sense of of *can*, must be able to show that it has these alternatives without denying that it is a deterministic machine.
8. The first task is to define even a naïve, common-sense view of the world precisely enough to program a computer to act accordingly. This is a very difficult task in itself.

We must mention that there is one possible way of getting an artificial intelligence without having to understand it or solve the related philosophical problems. This is to make a computer simulation of natural selection in which intelligence evolves by mutating computer programs in a suitably demanding environment. This method has had no substantial success so far, perhaps due to inadequate models of the world and of the evolutionary process, but it might succeed. It would seem to be a dangerous procedure, for a program that was intelligent in a way its designer did not understand might get out of control. In any case, the approach of trying to make an artificial intelligence through understanding what intelligence is, is more congenial to the present authors and seems likely to succeed sooner.

Reasoning programs and the Missouri program

The philosophical problems that have to be solved will be clearer in connection with a particular kind of proposed intelligent program, called a reasoning program or RP for short. RP interacts with the world through input and output devices some of which may be general sensory and motor organs (for example, television cameras, microphones, artificial arms) and others of which are communication devices (for example, teletypes or keyboard-display consoles). Internally, RP may represent information in a variety of ways. For example, pictures may be represented as dot arrays or a lists of regions and edges with classifications and adjacency relations. Scenes may be represented as lists of bodies with positions, shapes, and rates of motion. Situations may be represented by symbolic expressions with allowed rules of transformation. Utterances may be represented by digitized functions of time, by sequences of phonemes, and parsings of sentences.

However, one representation plays a dominant role and in simpler systems may be the only representation present. This is a representation by sets of sentences in a suitable formal logical language, for example *w*-order logic with function symbols, description operator, conditional expressions, sets, etc. Whether we must include modal operators with their referential opacity is undecided. This representation dominates in the following sense:

1. All other data structures have linguistic descriptions that give the relations between the structures and what they tell about the world.
2. The subroutines have linguistic descriptions that tell what they do, either internally manipulating data, or externally manipulating the world.
3. The rules that express RP's beliefs about how the world behaves and that give the consequences of strategies are expressed linguistically.
4. RP's goals, as given by the experimenter, its devised subgoals, its opinion on its state of progress are all linguistically expressed.
5. We shall say that RP's information is adequate to solve a problem if it is a logical consequence of all these sentences that a certain strategy of action will solve it.
6. RP is a deduction program that tries to find strategies of action that it can prove will solve a problem; on finding one, it executes it.
7. Strategies may involve subgoals which are to be solved by RP, and part or all of a strategy may be purely intellectual, that is, may involve the search for a strategy, a proof, or some other intellectual object that satisfies some criteria.

Such a program was first discussed in McCarthy (1959) and was called the Advice Taker. In McCarthy (1963) a preliminary approach to the required formalism, now superseded by this paper, was presented. This paper is in part an answer to Y. Bar-Hillel's comment, when the original paper was presented at the 1958 Symposium on the Mechanization of Thought Processes, that the paper involved some philosophical presuppositions.

Constructing RP involves both the epistemological and the heuristic parts of the artificial intelligence problem: that is, the information in memory must be adequate to determine a strategy for achieving the goal (this strategy may involve the acquisition of further information) and RP must be clever enough to find the strategy and the proof of its correctness. Of course, these problems interact, but since this paper is focused on the epistemological part, we mention the Missouri program (MP) that involves only this part.

The Missouri program (its motto is, 'Show me') does not try to find strategies or proofs that the strategies achieve a goal. Instead, it allows the experimenter to present it proof steps and checks their correctness. Moreover, when it is 'convinced' that it ought to perform an action or execute a strategy it does so. We may regard this paper as being concerned with the construction of a Missouri program that can be persuaded to achieve goals.

Representations of the world

The first step in the design of RP or MP is to decide what structure the world is to be regarded as having, and how information about the world and its laws of change are to be represented in the machine. This decision turns out to depend on whether one is talking about the expression of general laws or specific facts. Thus, our understanding of gas dynamics depends on the representation of a gas as a very large number of particles moving in space; this representation plays an essential rôle in deriving the mechanical, thermal electrical and optical properties of gases. The state of the gas at a given instant is regarded as determined by the position, velocity and excitation states of each particle. However, we never actually determine the position, velocity or excitation of even a single molecule. Our practical knowledge of a particular sample of gas is expressed by parameters like the pressure, temperature and velocity fields or even more grossly by average pressures and temperatures. From our philosophical point of view this is entirely normal, and we are not inclined to deny existence to entities we cannot see, or to be so anthropocentric as to imagine that the world must be so constructed that we have direct or even indirect access to all of it.

From the artificial intelligence point of view we can then define three kinds of adequacy for representations of the world.

A representation is called metaphysically adequate if the world could have that form without contradicting the facts of the aspect of reality that interests us. Examples of metaphysically adequate representations for different aspects of reality are:

1. The representation of the world as a collection of particles interacting through forces between each pair of particles.
2. Representation of the world as a giant quantum-mechanical wave function.
3. Representation as a system of interacting discrete automata. We shall make use of this representation.

Metaphysically adequate representations are mainly useful for constructing general theories. Deriving observable consequences from the theory is a further step.

A representation is called epistemologically adequate for a person or machine if it can be used practically to express the facts that one actually has about the aspect of the world. Thus none of the above-mentioned representations are adequate to express facts like 'John is at home' or 'dogs chase cats' or 'John's telephone number is 321–7580'. Ordinary language is obviously adequate to express the facts that people communicate to each other in ordinary language. It is not, for instance, adequate to express what people know about how to recognize a particular face. The second part of this paper is concerned with an epistemologically adequate formal representation of common-sense facts of causality, ability and knowledge.

A representation is called heuristically adequate if the reasoning processes actually gone through in solving a problem are expressible in the language. We shall not treat this somewhat tentatively proposed concept further in this paper except to point out later that one particular representation seems epistemologically but not heuristically adequate.

In the remaining sections of the first part of the paper we shall use the representations of the world as a system of interacting automata to explicate notions of causality, ability and knowledge (including self-knowledge).

The automaton representation and the notion of 'can'

Let S be a system of interacting discrete finite automata such as that shown in figure 1

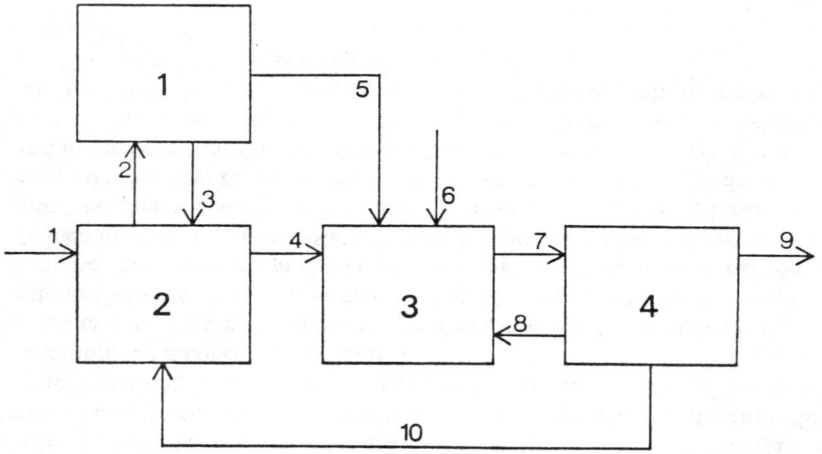

Figure 1

Each box represents a subautomaton and each line represents a signal. Time takes on integer values and the dynamic behaviour of the whole automaton is given by the equations:

$$(1)\ a_1(t+1)=A_1(a_1(t),\ s_3(t))$$
$$a_2(t+1)=A_2(a_2(t),\ s_1(t),\ s_2(t),\ s_{10}(t))$$
$$a_3(t+1)=A_3(a_3(t),\ s_4(t),\ s_5(t),\ s_6(t))$$
$$a_4(t+1)=A_4(a_4(t),\ s_7(t))$$
$$(2)\ s_2(t)=S_2(a_1(t))$$
$$s_3(t)=S_3(a_2(t))$$
$$s_4(t)=S_4(a_2(t))$$
$$s_5(t)=S_5(a_1(t))$$
$$s_7(t)=S_7(a_4(t))$$
$$s_8(t)=S_8(a_4(t))$$
$$s_9(t)=S_9(a_4(t))$$
$$s_{10}(t)=S_{10}(a_4(t))$$

The interpretation of these equations is that the state of any automaton at time $t+1$ is determined by its state at time t and by the signals received at time t. The value of a particular signal at time t is determined by the state at time t of the automaton from which it comes. Signals without a source automaton represent inputs from the outside and signals without a destination represent outputs.

Finite automata are the simplest examples of systems that interact over time. They are completely deterministic; if we know the initial states of all the automata and if we know the inputs as a function of time, the behaviour of the system is completely determined by equations (1) and (2) for all future time.

The automaton representation consists in regarding the world as a system of interacting subautomata. For example, we might regard each person in the room as a subautomaton and the environment as consisting of one or more additional subautomata. As we shall see, this representation has many of the qualitative properties of interactions among things and persons. However, if we take the representation too seriously and attempt to represent particular situations by systems of interacting automata we encounter the following difficulties:

1. The number of states required in the subautomata is very large, for example $2^{10^{10}}$, if we try to represent someone's knowledge. Automata this large have to be represented by computer programs, or in some other way that does not involve mentioning states individually.
2. Geometric information is hard to represent. Consider, for example, the location of a multi-jointed object such as a person or a matter of even more difficulty – the shape of a lump of clay.
3. The system of fixed interconnections is inadequate. Since a person may handle any object in the room, an adequate automaton representation would require signal lines connecting him with every object.
4. The most serious objection, however, is that (in our terminology) the automaton representation is epistemologically inadequate. Namely, we do not ever know a person well enough to list his internal states. The kind of information we do have about him needs to be expressed in some other way.

Nevertheless, we may use the automaton representation for concepts of *can*, *causes*, some kinds of counterfactual statements ('If I had struck this match yesterday it would have lit') and, with some elaboration of the representation, for a concept of *believes*.

Let us consider the notion of *can*. Let S be a system of subautomata without external inputs such as that of figure 2. Let p be one of the subautomata, and suppose that there are m signal lines coming out of p. What p can do is defined in terms of a new system S_p, which is obtained from the system S by disconnecting the m signal lines coming from p and replacing them by m external input lines to the system. In figure 2, subautomaton 1 has one output, and in the system S_1 this is replaced by an external input. The new system S_p always has the same set of states as the system S. Now let π be a condition on the state such as, 'a_2 is even' or '$a_2=a_3$'. (In the applications π may be a condition like 'The box is under the bananas'.)

We shall write

$$can(p,\pi,s)$$

which is read, 'The subautomaton p *can* bring about the condition π in the situation s' if there is a sequence of outputs from the automaton S_p that will eventually put S into a state a' that satisfies $\pi(a')$. In other words, in determining what p can achieve, we consider the effects of sequences of its actions, quite apart from the conditions that determine what it actually will do.

In figure 2, let us consider the initial state a to be one in which all subautomata are initially in state 0. Then the reader will easily verify the following propositions:

1. Subautomaton 2 *will* never be in state 1.
2. Subautomaton 1 *can* put subautomaton 2 in state 1.
3. Subautomaton 3 *cannot* put subautomaton 2 in state 1.

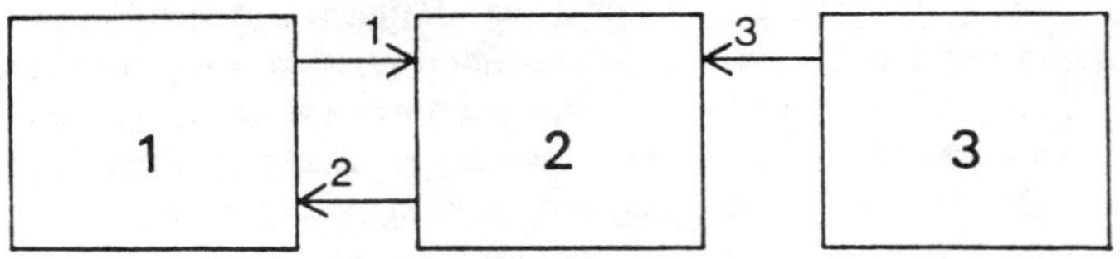

Figure 2. System S

$$a_1(t+1)=a_1(t)+s_2(t)$$
$$a_2(t+1)=a_2(t)+s_1(t)+2s_3(t)$$
$$a_3(t+1)=\textbf{if}\ a_3(t)=0\ \textbf{then}\ 0\ \textbf{else}\ a_3(t)+1$$

$s_1(t) = \textbf{if } a_1(t) = 0 \textbf{ then } 2 \textbf{ else } 1$
$s_2(t) = 1$
$s_3(t) = \textbf{if } a_3(t) = 0 \textbf{ then } 0 \textbf{ else } 1$

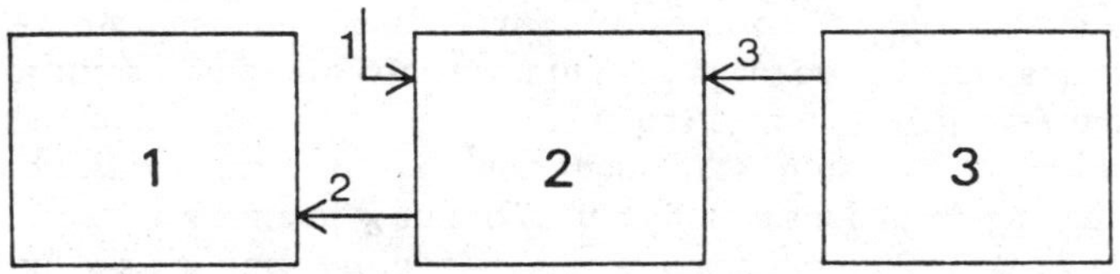

System S_1

We claim that this notion of *can* is, to a first approximation, the appropriate one for an automaton to use internally in deciding what to do by reasoning. We also claim that it corresponds in many cases to the common sense notion of *can* used in everyday speech.

In the first place, suppose we have an automaton that decides what to do by reasoning, for example suppose it is a computer using an RP. Then its output is determined by the decisions it makes in the resoning process. It does not know (has not computed) in advance what it will do, and, therefore, it is appropriate that it considers that it can do anything that can be achieved by some sequence of its outputs. Common-sense reasoning seems to operate in the same way.

The above rather simple notion of *can* requires some elaboration both to represent adequately the commonsense notion and for practical purposes in the reasoning program.

First, suppose that the system of automata admits external inputs. There are two ways of defining *can* in this case. One way is to assert $can(p,\pi,s)$ if p can achieve π regardless of what signals appear on the external inputs. Thus, instead of requiring the existence of a sequence of outputs of p that achieves the goal we shall require the existence of a strategy where the output at any time is allowed to depend on the sequence of external inputs so far received by the system. Note that in this definition of *can* we are not requiring that p have any way of knowing what the external inputs were. An alternative definition requires the outputs to depend on the inputs of p. This is equivalent to saying that p can achieve a goal provided the goal would be achieved for arbitrary inputs by some automaton put in place of p. With either of these definitions *can* becomes a function of the place of the subautomaton in the system rather than of the subautomaton itself. We do not know which of these treatments is preferable, and so we shall call the first concept *cana* and the second *canb*.

The idea that what a person can do depends on his position rather than on his characteristics is somewhat counter-intuitive. This impression can be mitigated as follows: Imagine the person to be made up of several sub-automata; the output of the outer subautomaton is the motion of the joints. If we break the connection to the world at that point we can answer questions like, 'Can he fit through a given hole?' We shall get some counter-intuitive answers, however, such as that he can run at top speed for an hour or can jump over a building, since there are sequences of motions of his joints that would achieve these results.

The next step, however, is to consider a subautomaton that receives the nerve impulses from the spinal cord and transmits them to the muscles. If we break at the input to this automaton, we shall no longer say that he can jump over a building or run long at top speed since the limitations of the muscles will be taken into account. We shall, however, say that he can ride a unicycle since appropriate nerve signals would achieve this result.

The notion of *can* corresponding to the intuitive notion in the largest number of cases might be obtained by hypothesizing an 'organ of will', which makes decisions to do things and transmits these decisions to the main part of the brain that tries to carry them out and contains all the knowledge of particular facts. If we make the break at this point we shall be able to say that so-and-so cannot dial the President's secret and private telephone number because he does not know it, even though if the question were asked could he dial that particular number, the answer would be yes. However, even this break would not give the statement, 'I cannot go without saying goodbye, because this would hurt the child's feelings'.

On the basis of these examples, one might try to postulate a sequence of narrower and narrower notions of *can* terminating in a notion according to which a person can do only what he actually does. This notion would then be superfluous. Actually, one should not look for a single best notion of *can*; each of the above-mentioned notions is useful and is actually used in some circumstances. Sometimes, more than one notion is used in a single sentence, when two different levels of constraint are mentioned.

Besides its use in explicating the notion of *can*, the automaton representation of the world is very suited for defining notions of causality. For, we may say that subautomaton p caused the condition π in state s, if changing the output of p would prevent π. In fact the whole idea of a system of interacting automata is just a formalization of the commonsense notion of causality.

Moreover, the automaton representation can be used to explicate certain counterfactual conditional sentences. For example, we have the sentence, 'If I had struck this match yesterday at this time it would have lit'. In a suitable automaton representation, we have a certain state of the system yesterday at that time, and we imagine a break made where the nerves lead from my head or perhaps at the output of my 'decision box', and the appropriate signals to strike the match having been made. Then it is a definite and decidable question about the system S_p, whether the match lights or not, depending on whether it is wet, etc. This interpretation of this kind of counterfactual sentence seems to be what is needed for RP to learn from its mistakes, by accepting or generating sentences of the form, 'had I done thus-and-so I would have been successful, so I should alter my procedures in some way that would have produced the correct action in that case'.

In the foregoing we have taken the representation of the situation as a system of interacting subautomata for granted. However, a given overall situation might be represented as a system of interacting subautomata in a number of ways, and different representations might yield different results about what a given subautomaton can achieve, what would have happened if some subautomaton had acted differently, or what caused what. Indeed, in a different representation, the same or corresponding subautomata might not be identifiable. Therefore, these notions depend on the representation chosen.

For example, suppose a pair of Martians observe the situation in a room. One Martian analyses it as a collection of interacting people as we do, but the second Martian groups all the heads together into one subautomaton and all the bodies into another. (A creature from momentum space would regard the Fourier components of the distribution of matter as the separate interacting subautomata.) How is the first Martian to convince the second that his representation is to be preferred? Roughly speaking, he would argue that the interaction between the heads and bodies of the same person is closer than the interaction between the different heads, and so more of an analysis has been achieved from 'the primordial muddle' with the conventional representation. He will be especially convincing when he points out that when the meeting is over the heads will stop interacting with each other, but will continue to interact with their respective bodies.

We can express this kind of argument formally in terms of automata as follows: Suppose we have an autonomous automaton A, that is an automaton without inputs, and let it have k states. Further, let m and n be two integers such that $m,n \geqslant k$. Now label k points of an m-by-n array with the states of A. This can be done in $\binom{mn}{k}!$ ways. For each of these ways we have a representation of the automaton A as a system of an m-state automaton B interacting with an n-state automaton C. Namely, corresponding to each row of the array we have a state of B and to each column a state of C. The signals are in 1–1 correspondence with the states themselves; thus each subautomaton has just as many values of its output as it has states. Now it may happen that two of these signals are equivalent in their effect on the other subautomaton, and we use this equivalence relation to form equivalence classes of signals. We may then regard the equivalence classes as the signals themselves. Suppose then that there are now r signals from B to C and s signals from C to B. We ask how small r and s can be taken in general compared to m and n. The answer may be obtained by counting the number of inequivalent automata with k states and comparing it with the number of systems of two automata with m and n states respectively and r and s signals going in the respective directions. The result is not worth working out in detail, but tells us that only a few of the k state automata admit such a decomposition with r and s small compared to m and n. Therefore, if an automaton happens to admit such a decomposition it is very unusual for it to admit a second such decomposition that is not equivalent to the first with respect to some renaming of states. Applying this argument to the real world, we may say that it is overwhelmingly probable that our customary decomposition of the world automaton into separate people and things has a unique, objective and usually preferred status. Therefore, the notions of *can*, of causality, and of counterfactual associated with this decomposition also have a preferred status.

In our opinion, this explains some of the difficulty philosophers have had in analysing counterfactuals and causality. For example, the sentence, 'If I had struck this match yesterday, it would have lit' is meaningful only in terms of a rather complicated model of the world, which, however, has an objective preferred status. However, the preferred status of this model depends on its correspondence with a large number of facts. For this reason, it is probably not fruitful to treat an individual counterfactual conditional sentence in isolation.

It is also possible to treat notions of belief and knowledge in terms of the automaton representation. We have not worked this out very far, and the ideas presented here should be regarded as tentative. We would like to be able to give conditions under which we may say that a subautomaton p believes a certain proposition. We shall not try to do this directly but only relative to a predicate $B_p(s,w)$. Here s is the state of the automaton p and w is a proposition; $B_p(s,w)$ is true if p is to be regarded as believing w when in state s and is false otherwise. With respect to such a predicate B we may ask the following questions:

1. Are p's beliefs consistent? Are they correct?
2. Does p reason? That is, do new beliefs arise that are logical consequences of previous beliefs?
3. Does p observe? That is, do true propositions about automata connected to p cause p to believe them?
4. Does p behave rationally? That is, when p believes a sentence asserting that it should do something, does p do it?
5. Does p communicate in language L? That is, regarding the content of a certain input or ouput signal line as a text in language L, does this line transmit beliefs to or from p?
6. Is p self-conscious? That is, does it have a fair variety of correct beliefs about its own beliefs and the processes that change them?

It is only with respect to the predicate B_p that all these questions can be asked. However, if questions 1 thru 4 are answered affirmatively for some predicate B_p, this is certainly remarkable, and we would feel fully entitled to consider B_p a reasonable notion of belief.

In one important respect the situation with regard to belief or knowledge is the same as it was for counterfactual conditional statements: no way is provided to assign a meaning to a single statement of belief or knowledge, since for any single statement a suitable B_p can easily be constructed. Individual statements about belief or knowledge are made on the basis of a larger system which must be validated as a whole.

2. FORMALISM

In part 1 we showed how the concepts of ability and belief could be given formal definition in the metaphysically adequate automaton model and indicated the correspondence between these formal concepts and the corresponding commonsense concepts. We emphasized, however, that practical systems require epistemologically adequate systems in which those facts which are actually ascertainable can be expressed.

In this part we begin the construction of an epistemologically adequate system. Instead of giving formal definitions, however, we shall introduce the formal notions by informal natural-language descriptions and give examples of their use to describe situations and the possibilities for action they present. The formalism presented is intended to supersede that of McCarthy (1963).

Situations

A situation s is the complete state of the universe at an instant of time. We denote by *Sit* the set of all situations. Since the universe is too large for complete description, we shall never completely describe a situation; we shall only give facts about situations. These facts will be used to deduce further facts about that situation, about future situations and about situations that persons can bring about from that situation.

This requires that we consider not only situations that actually occur, but also hypothetical situations such as the situation that would arise if Mr Smith sold his car to a certain person who has offered $250 for it. Since he is not going to sell the car for that price, the hypothetical situation is not completely defined; for example, it is not determined what Smith's mental state would be and therefore it is also undetermined how quickly he would return to his office, etc. Nevertheless, the representation of reality is adequate to determine some facts about this situation, enough at least to make him decide not to sell the car.

We shall further assume that the laws of motion determine, given a situation, all future situations.*

In order to give partial information about situations we introduce the notion of fluent.

* This assumption is difficult to reconcile with quantum mechanics, and relativity tells us that any assignment of simultaneity to events in different places is arbitrary. However, we are proceeding on the basis that modern physics is irrelevant to common sense in deciding what to do, and in particular is irrelevant to solving the 'free will problem'.

Fluents

A *fluent* is a function whose domain is the space *Sit* of situations. If the range of the function is (*true*, *false*), then it is called a *propositional fluent*. If its range is *Sit*, then it is called a *situational fluent*.

Fluents are often the values of functions. Thus $raining(x)$ is a fluent such that $raining(x)(s)$ is true if and only if it is raining at the place x in the situation s. We can also write this assertion as $raining(x,s)$ making use of the well-known equivalence between a function of two variables and a function of the first variable whose value is a function of the second variable.

Suppose we wish to assert about a situation s that person p is in place x and that it is raining in place x. We may write this in several ways each of which has its uses:

1. $at(p,x)(s) \wedge raining(x)(s)$. This corresponds to the definition given.
2. $at(p,x,s) \wedge raining(x,s)$. This is more conventional mathematically and a bit shorter.
3. $[at(p,x) \wedge raining(x)](s)$. Here we are introducing a convention that operators applied to fluents give fluents whose values are computed by applying the logical operators to the values of the operand fluents, that is, if f and g are fluents then

   $$(f \mathbf{\ op\ } g)(s) = f(s) \mathbf{\ op\ } g(s)$$

4. $[\lambda s' . at(p,x,s') \wedge raining(x,s')](s)$. Here we have formed the composite fluent by λ-abstraction.

Here are some examples of fluents and expressions involving them:

1. $time(s)$. This is the time associated with the situation s. It is essential to consider time as dependent on the situation as we shall sometimes wish to consider several different situations having the same time value, for example, the results of alternative courses of actions.
2. $in(x,y,s)$. This asserts that x is in the location y in situation s. The fluent *in* may be taken as satisfying a kind of transitive law, namely:

   $$\forall x . \forall y . \forall z . \forall s . in(x,y,s) \wedge in(y,z,s) \supset in(x,z,s)$$

   We can also write this law

   $$\forall x . \forall y . \forall z . \forall . in(x,y) \wedge in(y,z) \supset in(x,z)$$

   where we have adopted the convention that a quantifier without a variable is applied to an implicit situation variable which is the (suppressed) argument of a propositional fluent that follows. Suppressing situation arguments in this way corresponds to the natural language convention of writing sentences like, 'John was at home' or 'John is at home' leaving understood the situations to which these assertions apply.
3. $has(Monkey,Bananas,s)$. Here we introduce the convention that capitalized words denote proper names, for example, 'Monkey' is the

name of a particular individual. That the individual is a monkey is not asserted, so that the expression *monkey(Monkey)* may have to appear among the premisses of an argument. Needless to say, the reader has a right to feel that he has been given a hint that the individual Monkey will turn out to be a monkey. The above expression is to be taken as asserting that in the situation s the individual *Monkey* has the object *Bananas*. We shall, in the examples below, sometimes omit premisses such as *monkey(Monkey)*, but in a complete system they would have to appear.

Causality

We shall make assertions of causality by means of a fluent $F(\pi)$ where π is itself a propositional fluent. $F(\pi,s)$ asserts that the situation s will be followed (after an unspecified time) by a situation that satisfies the fluent π.

We may use F to assert that if a person is out in the rain he will get wet, by writing:

$$\forall x\,.\,\forall p\,.\,\forall s\,.\,raining(x,s) \wedge at(p,x,s) \wedge outside(p,s) \supset F(\lambda s'\,.\,wet(p,s'),s)$$

Suppressing explicit mention of situations gives:

$$\forall x\,.\,\forall p\,.\,\forall\,.\,raining(x) \wedge at(p,x) \wedge outside(p) \supset F(wet(p)).$$

In this case suppressing situations simplifies the statement.

F can also be used to express physical laws. Consider the law of falling bodies which is often written

$$h = h_0 + v_0\,.\,(t-t_0) - \tfrac{1}{2}g\,.\,(t-t_0)^2$$

together with some prose identifying the variables. Since we need a formal system for machine reasoning we cannot have any prose. Therefore, we write:

$$\forall b\,.\,\forall t\,.\,\forall s\,.\,falling(b,s) \wedge t \geqslant 0 \wedge height(b,s) + velocity(b,s)\,.\,t - \tfrac{1}{2}gt^2 > 0$$
$$\supset$$
$$F(\lambda s'\,.\,time(s') = time(s) + t \wedge falling(b,s') \wedge height(b,s') = height(b,s) + velocity(b,s)\,.\,t - \tfrac{1}{2}gt^2, s)$$

Suppressing explicit mention of situations in this case requires the introduction of real auxiliary quantities v, h and τ so that the sentence takes the following form

$$\forall b\,.\,\forall t\,.\,\forall \tau\,.\,\forall v\,.\,\forall h.$$
$$falling(b) \wedge t \geqslant 0 \wedge h = height(b) \wedge v = velocity(b) \wedge h + vt - \tfrac{1}{2}gt^2 > 0 \wedge time = \tau \supset F(time = t + \tau \wedge falling(b) \wedge height = h + vt - \tfrac{1}{2}gt^2)$$

There has to be a convention (or declarations) so that it is determined that *height(b)*, *velocity(b)* and *time* are fluents, whereas t, v, τ and h denote ordinary real numbers.

$F(\pi,s)$ as introduced here corresponds to A.N. Prior's (1957, 1968) expression $F\pi$.

The use of situation variables is analogous to the use of time-instants in the calculi of world-states which Prior (1968) calls *U-T* calculi. Prior provides many interesting correspondences between his *U-T* calculi and various axiomatizations of the modal tense-logics (that is, using this F-operator: see part 4). However, the situation calculus is richer than any of the tense-logics Prior considers.

Besides F he introduces three other operators which we also find useful; we thus have:

1. $F(\pi,s)$. For some situation s' in the future of s, $\pi(s')$ holds.
2. $G(\pi,s)$. For all situations s' in the future of s, $\pi(s')$ holds.
3. $P(\pi,s)$. For some situations s' in the past of s, $\pi(s')$ holds.
4. $H(\pi,s)$. For all situations s' in the past of s, $\pi(s')$ holds.

It seems also useful to define a situational fluent $next(\pi)$ as the next situation s' in the future of s for which $\pi(s')$ holds. If there is no such situation, that is, if $\neg F(\pi,s)$, then $next(\pi,s)$ is considered undefined. For example, we may translate the sentence 'By the time John gets home, Henry will be home too' as *at(Henry,home(Henry),next(at(John,home(John)),s))*. Also the phrase 'when John gets home' translates into *time(next(at(John,home(John)),s))*.

Though $\text{next}(\pi,s)$ will never actually be computed since situations are too rich to be specified completely, the values of fluents applied to $\text{next}(\pi,s)$ will be computed.

Actions

A fundamental rôle in our study of actions is played by the situational fluent

$$result(p,\sigma,s)$$

Here, p is a person, σ is an action or more generally a strategy, and s is a situation. The value of $result(p,\sigma,s)$ is the situation that results when p carries out σ, starting in the situation s. If the action or strategy does not terminate, $result(p,\sigma,s)$ is considered undefined.

With the aid of *result* we can express certain laws of ability. For example:

$$has(p,k,s) \wedge fits(k,sf) \wedge at(p,sf,s) \supset open(sf,result(p,opens(sf,k),s))$$

This formula is to be regarded as an axiom schema asserting that if in a situation s a person p has a key k that fits the safe sf, then in the situation resulting from his performing the action $opens(sf,k)$, that is, opening the safe sf with the key k, the safe is open. The assertion $fits(k,sf)$ carries the information that k is a key and sf a safe. Later we shall be concerned with combination safes that require p to *know* the combination.

Strategies

Actions can be combined into strategies. The simplest combination is a finite sequence of actions. We shall combine actions as though they were

ALGOL statements, that is, procedure calls. Thus, the sequence of actions, ('move the box under the bananas', 'climb onto the box', and 'reach for the bananas') may be written:

begin *move*(*Box,Under-Bananas*); *climb*(*Box*); *reach-for*(*Bananas*) **end**;

A strategy in general will be an ALGOL-like compound statement containing actions written in the form of procedure calling assignment statements, and conditional **go to**'s. We shall not include any declarations in the program since they can be included in the much larger collection of declarative sentences that determine the effect of the strategy.

Consider for example the strategy that consists of walking 17 blocks south, turning right and then walking till you come to Chestnut Street. This strategy may be written as follows:

```
begin
      face(South);
      n:=0;
   b: if n=17 then go to a;
      walk-a-block, n:=n+1;
      go to b;
   a: turn-right;
   c: walk-a-block;
      if name-on-street-sign≠'Chestnut Street' then go to c
end;
```

In the above program the external actions are represented by procedure calls. Variables to which values are assigned have a purely internal significance (we may even call it mental significance) and so do the statement labels and the **go to** statements.

For the purpose of applying the mathematical theory of computation we shall write the program differently: namely, each occurrence of an action α is to be replaced by an assignment statement $s := result(p,\alpha,s)$. Thus the above program becomes

```
begin
      s:=result(p,face(South),s);
      n:=0;
   b: if n=17 then go to a;
      s:=result(p,walk-a-block,s);
      n:=n+1;
      go to b;
   a: s:=result(p,turn-right,s);
   c: s:=result(p,walk-a-block,s);
      if name-on-street-sign(s)≠'Chestnut Street' then go to c.
end;
```

Suppose we wish to show that by carrying out this strategy John can go home provided he is initially at his office. Then according to the methods of Zohar Manna (1968a, 1968b), we may derive from this program together with the initial condition *at*(*John,office*(*John*),s_0) and the final condition *at*(*John,home* (*John*),*s*), a sentence *W* of first-order logic. Proving *W* will show that the procedure terminates in a finite number of steps and that when it terminates *s* will satisfy *at*(*John,home*(*John*),*s*).

According to Manna's theory we must prove the following collection of sentences inconsistent for arbitrary interpretations of the predicates q_1 and q_2 and the particular interpretations of the other functions and predicates in the program:

$$at(John,office(John),s_0),$$
$$q_1(0,result(John,face(South),s_0)),$$
$$\forall n\,.\,\forall s\,.\,q_1(n,s) \supset \textbf{if } n=17 \textbf{ then } q_2(result(John,walk\text{-}a\text{-}block,result(John,turn\text{-}right,s))) \textbf{ else } q_1(n+1,result(John,walk\text{-}a\text{-}block,s)),$$
$$\forall s\,.\,q_2(s) \supset \textbf{if } name\text{-}on\text{-}street\text{-}sign(s) \neq \text{`}Chestnut\ Street\text{'} \textbf{ then } q_2(result(John,walk\text{-}a\text{-}block,s)) \textbf{ else } \neg at(John,home(John),s)$$

Therefore the formula that has to be proved may be written

$$\exists s_0 \{at(John,office(John),s_0) \wedge q_1(0,result(John,face(South),s_0))\}$$
$$\supset$$
$$\exists n\,.\,\exists s\,.\,\{q_1(n,s) \wedge \textbf{if } n=17 \textbf{ then } \wedge q_2(result(John,walk\text{-}a\text{-}block,result(John,turn\text{-}right,s))) \textbf{ else } \neg q_1(n+1,result(John,walk\text{-}a\text{-}block,s))\}$$
$$\vee$$
$$\exists s\,.\,\{q_2(s) \wedge \textbf{if } name\text{-}on\text{-}street\text{-}sign(s) \neq \text{`}Chestnut\ Street\text{'} \textbf{ then } \neg q_2(result(John,walk\text{-}a\text{-}block,s)) \textbf{ else } at(John,home(John),s)\}$$

In order to prove this sentence we would have to use the following kinds of facts expressed as sentences or sentence schemas of first-order logic:

1. Facts of geography. The initial street stretches at least 17 blocks to the south, and intersects a street which in turn intersects Chestnut Street a number of blocks to the right; the location of John's home and office.
2. The fact that the fluent name-on-street-sign will have the value 'Chestnut Street' at that point.
3. Facts giving the effects of action α expressed as predicates about *result*(p,α,s) deducible from sentences about *s*.
4. An axiom schema of induction that allows us to deduce that the loop of walking 17 blocks will terminate.

5. A fact that says that Chestnut Street is a finite number of blocks to the right after going 17 blocks south. This fact has nothing to do with the possibility of walking. It may also have to be expressed as a sentence schema or even as a sentence of second-order logic.

When we consider making a computer carry out the strategy, we must distinguish the variable s from the other variables in the second form of the program. The other variables are stored in the memory of the computer and the assignments may be executed in the normal way. The variable s represents the state of the world and the computer makes an assignment to it by performing an action. Likewise the fluent name-on-street-sign requires an action, of observation.

Knowledge and ability

In order to discuss the rôle of knowledge in one's ability to achieve goals let us return to the example of the safe. There we had

1. $\mathit{has}(p,k,s) \wedge \mathit{fits}(k,sf) \wedge \mathit{at}(p,sf,s) \supset \mathit{open}(sf,\mathit{result}(p,\mathit{opens}(sf,k),s))$,

which expressed sufficient conditions for the ability of a person to open a safe with a key. Now suppose we have a combination safe with a combination c. Then we may write:

2. $\mathit{fits2}(c,sf) \wedge \mathit{at}(p,sf,s) \supset \mathit{open}(sf,\mathit{result}(p,\mathit{opens2}(sf,c),s))$,

where we have used the predicate *fits*2 and the action *opens*2 to express the distinction between a key fitting a safe and a combination fitting it, and also the distinction between the acts of opening a safe with a key and a combination. In particular, $\mathit{opens2}(sf,c)$ is the act of manipulating the safe in accordance with the combination c. We have left out a sentence of the form $\mathit{has2}(p,c,s)$ for two reasons. In the first place it is unnecessary: if you manipulate a safe in accordance with its combination it will open; there is no need to have anything. In the second place it is not clear what $\mathit{has2}(p,c,s)$ means. Suppose, for example, that the combination of a particular safe sf is the number 34125, then $\mathit{fits}(34125, sf)$ makes sense and so does the act $\mathit{opens2}(sf, 34125)$. (We assume that $\mathit{open}(sf,\mathit{result}(p,\mathit{opens2}(sf,34111),s))$ would not be true.) But what could $\mathit{has}(p,34125,s)$ mean? Thus, a direct parallel between the rules for opening a safe with a key and opening it with a combination seems impossible.

Nevertheless, we need some way of expressing the fact that one has to know the combination of a safe in order to open it. First we introduce the function $\mathit{combination}(sf)$ and rewrite 2 as

3. $\mathit{at}(p,sf,s) \wedge \mathit{csafe}(sf) \supset \mathit{open}(sf,\mathit{result}(p,\mathit{opens2}(sf,\mathit{combination}(sf),s)))$

where $\mathit{csafe}(sf)$ asserts that sf is a combination safe and $\mathit{combination}(sf)$ denotes the combination of sf. (We could not write $\mathit{key}(sf)$ in the other case unless we wished to restrict ourselves to the case of safes with only one key.)

Next we introduce the notion of a feasible strategy for a person. The idea is that a strategy that would achieve a certain goal might not be feasible for a person because he lacks certain knowledge or abilities.

Our first approach is to regard the action $\mathit{opens2}(sf,\mathit{combination}(sf))$ as infeasible because p might not know the combination. Therefore, we introduce a new function $\mathit{idea\text{-}of\text{-}combination}(p,sf,s)$ which stands for person p's idea of the combination of sf in situation s. The action $\mathit{opens2}(sf,\mathit{idea\text{-}of\text{-}combination}(p,sf,s))$ is regarded as feasible for p, since p is assumed to know his idea of the combination if this is defined. However, we leave sentence 3 as it is so we cannot yet prove $\mathit{open}(sf,\mathit{result}(p,\mathit{opens2}(sf,\mathit{idea\text{-}of\text{-}combination}(p,sf,s)),s))$. The assertion that p knows the combination of sf can now be expressed as

5. $\mathit{idea\text{-}of\text{-}combination}(p,sf,s) = \mathit{combination}(sf)$

and with this, the possibility of opening the safe can be proved.

Another example of this approach is given by the following formalization of getting into conversation with someone by looking up his number in the telephone book and then dialling it.

The strategy for p in the first form is

begin
  lookup(*q*,*Phone-book*);
  dial(*idea-of-phone-number*(*q*,*p*))
end;

or in the second form

begin
  $s := \mathit{result}(p,\mathit{lookup}(q,\mathit{Phone\text{-}book}),s_0)$;
  $s := \mathit{result}(p,\mathit{dial}(\mathit{idea\text{-}of\text{-}phone\text{-}number}(q,p,s)),s)$
end;

The premisses to write down appear to be

1. $\mathit{has}(p,\mathit{Phone\text{-}book},s_0)$
2. $\mathit{listed}(q,\mathit{Phone\text{-}book},s_0)$
3. $\forall s . \forall p . \forall q . \mathit{has}(p,\mathit{Phone\text{-}book},s) \wedge \mathit{listed}(q,\mathit{Phone\text{-}book},s) \supset \mathit{phone\text{-}number}(q) = \mathit{idea\text{-}of\text{-}phone\text{-}number}(p,q,\mathit{result}(p,\mathit{lookup}(q,\mathit{Phone\text{-}book}),s))$
4. $\forall s . \forall p . \forall q . \forall x . \mathit{at}(q,\mathit{home}(q),s) \wedge \mathit{has}(p,x,s) \wedge \mathit{telephone}(x) \supset \mathit{in\text{-}conversation}(p,q,\mathit{result}(p,\mathit{dial}(\mathit{phone\text{-}number}(q)),s))$
5. $\mathit{at}(q,\mathit{home}(q),s_0)$
6. $\mathit{telephone}(\mathit{Telephone})$
7. $\mathit{has}(p,\mathit{Telephone},s_0)$

Unfortunately, these premisses are not sufficient to allow one to conclude that

$\mathit{in\text{-}conversation}(p,q,\mathit{result}(p,\mathbf{begin}\ \mathit{lookup}(q,\mathit{Phone\text{-}book});\ \mathit{dial}(\mathit{idea\text{-}of\text{-}phone\text{-}number}(q,p))\ \mathbf{end};, s_0))$.

The trouble is that one cannot show that the fluents $at(q,home(q))$ and $has(p,Telephone)$ still apply to the situation $result(p,lookup(q,Phone\text{-}book),s_0)$. To make it come out right we shall revise the third hypothesis to read:

$$\forall s . \forall p . \forall q . \forall x . \forall y . at(q,y,s) \wedge has(p,x,s) \wedge has(p,Phone\text{-}book,s) \wedge listed(q,Phone\text{-}book) \supset [\lambda r . at(q,y,r) \wedge has(p,x,r) \wedge phone\text{-}number(q) = idea\text{-}of\text{-}phone\text{-}number(p,q,r)]\ (result(p,lookup(q,Phone\text{-}book),s)).$$

This works, but the additional hypotheses about what remains unchanged when p looks up a telephone number are quite *ad hoc*. We shall treat this problem in a later section.

The present approach has a major technical advantage for which, however, we pay a high price. The advantage is that we preserve the ability to replace any expression by an equal one in any expression of our language. Thus if $phone\text{-}number(John) = 3217580$, any true statement of our language that contains 3217580 or $phone\text{-}number(John)$ will remain true if we replace one by the other. This desirable property is termed referential transparency.

The price we pay for referential transparency is that we have to introduce $idea\text{-}of\text{-}phone\text{-}number(p,q,s)$ as a separate *ad hoc* entity and cannot use the more natural $idea\text{-}of(p,phone\text{-}number(q),s)$ where $idea\text{-}of(p,\phi,s)$ is some kind of operator applicable to the concept ϕ. Namely, the sentence $idea\text{-}of(p,phone\text{-}number(q),s) = phone\text{-}number(q)$ would be supposed to express that p knows q's phone-number, but $idea\text{-}of(p,3217580,s) = 3217580$ expresses only that p understands that number. Yet with transparency and the fact that $phone\text{-}number(q) = 3217580$ we could derive the former statement from the latter.

A further consequence of our approach is that feasibility of a strategy is a referentially opaque concept since a strategy containing $idea\text{-}of\text{-}phone\text{-}number(p,q,s)$ is regarded as feasible while one containing $phone\text{-}number(q)$ is not, even though these quantities may be equal in a particular case. Even so, our language is still referentially transparent since feasibility is a concept of the metalanguage.

A classical poser for the reader who wants to solve these difficulties to ponder is, 'George IV wondered whether the author of the Waverley novels was Walter Scott' and 'Walter Scott is the author of the Waverley novels', from which we do not wish to deduce, 'George IV wondered whether Walter Scott was Walter Scott'. This example and others are discussed in the first chapter of Church's *Introduction to Mathematical Logic* (1956).

In the long run it seems that we shall have to use a formalism with referential opacity and formulate precisely the necessary restrictions on replacement of equals by equals; the program must be able to reason about the feasibility of its strategies, and users of natural language handle referential opacity without disaster. In part 4 we give a brief account of the partly successful approach to problems of referential opacity in modal logic.

3. REMARKS AND OPEN PROBLEMS

The formalism presented in part 2 is, we think, an advance on previous attempts, but it is far from epistemological adequacy. In the following sections we discuss a number of problems that it raises. For some of them we have proposals that might lead to solutions.

The approximate character of *result* (p, σ, s).

Using the situational fluent $result(p,\sigma,s)$ in formulating the conditions under which strategies have given effects has two advantages over the $can(p,\pi,s)$ of part 1. It permits more compact and transparent sentences, and it lends itself to the application of the mathematical theory of computation to prove that certain strategies achieve certain goals.

However, we must recognize that it is only an approximation to say that an action, other than that which will actually occur, leads to a definite situation. Thus if someone is asked, 'How would you feel tonight if you challenged him to a duel tomorrow morning and he accepted?' he might well reply, 'I can't imagine the mental state in which I would do it; if the words inexplicably popped out of my mouth as though my voice were under someone else's control that would be one thing; if you gave me a long-lasting belligerence drug that would be another'.

From this we see that $result(p,\sigma,s)$ should not be regarded as being defined in the world itself, but only in certain representations of the world; albeit in representations that may have a preferred character as discussed in part 1.

We regard this as a blemish on the smoothness of interpretation of the formalism, which may also lead to difficulties in the formal development. Perhaps another device can be found which has the advantages of *result* without the disadvantages.

Possible meanings of 'can' for a computer program

A computer program can readily be given much more powerful means of introspection than a person has, for we may make it inspect the whole of its memory including program and data to answer certain introspective questions, and it can even simulate (slowly) what it would do with given initial data. It is interesting to list various notions of $can(Program,\pi)$ for a program.

1. There is a sub-program σ and room for it in memory which would achieve π if it were in memory, and control were transferred to σ. No assertion is made that *Program* knows σ or even knows that σ exists.
2. σ exists as above and that σ will achieve π follows from information in memory according to a proof that *Program* is capable of checking.
3. *Program*'s standard problem-solving procedure will find σ if achieving π is ever accepted as a subgoal.

The frame problem

In the last section of part 2, in proving that one person could get into conversation with another, we were obliged to add the hypothesis that if a person has a telephone he still has it after looking up a number in the telephone book. If we had a number of actions to be performed in sequence, we would have quite a number of conditions to write down that certain actions do not change the values of certain fluents. In fact with n actions and m fluents we might have to write down mn such conditions.

We see two ways out of this difficulty. The first is to introduce the notion of frame, like the state vector in McCarthy (1962). A number of fluents are declared as attached to the frame and the effect of an action is described by telling which fluents are changed, all others being presumed unchanged.

This can be formalized by making use of yet more ALGOL notation, perhaps in a somewhat generalized form. Consider a strategy in which p performs the action of going from x to y. In the first form of writing strategies we have $go(x,y)$ as a program step. In the second form we have $s := result(p, go(x,y), s)$. Now we may write

$location(p) := tryfor(y,x)$

and the fact that other variables are unchanged by this action follows from the general properties of assignment statements. Among the conditions for successful execution of the program will be sentences that enable us to show that when this statement is executed, $tryfor(y,x) = y$. If we were willing to consider that p could go anywhere we could write the assignment statement simply as

$location(p) := y.$

The point of using *tryfor* here is that a program using this simpler assignment is, on the face of it, not possible to execute, since p may be unable to go to y. We may cover this case in the more complex assignment by agreeing that when p is barred from y, $tryfor(y,x) = x$.

In general, restrictions on what could appear on the right side of an assignment to a component of the situation would be included in the conditions for the feasibility of the strategy. Since components of the situation that change independently in some circumstances are dependent in others, it may be worthwhile to make use of the block structure of ALGOL. We shall not explore this approach further in this paper.

Another approach to the frame problem may follow from the methods of the next section; and in part 4 we mention a third approach which may be useful, although we have not investigated it at all fully.

Formal literatures

In this section we introduce the notion of formal literature which is to be contrasted with the well-known notion of formal language. We shall mention some possible applications of this concept in constructing an epistemologically adequate system.

A formal literature is like a formal language with a history: we imagine that up to a certain time a certain sequence of sentences have been said. The literature then determines what sentences may be said next. The formal definition is as follows.

Let A be a set of potential sentences, for example, the set of all finite strings in some alphabet. Let $Seq(A)$ be the set of finite sequences of elements of A and let $L: Seq(A) \rightarrow \{\mathbf{true}, \mathbf{false}\}$ be such that if $\sigma \in Seq(A)$ and $L(\sigma)$, that is, $L(\sigma) = \mathbf{true}$, and σ_1 is an initial segment of σ then $L(\sigma_1)$. The pair (A,L) is termed a *literature*. The interpretation is that a_n may be said after $a_1, \ldots, a_{n-1}$, provided $L((a_1, \ldots, a_n))$. We shall also write $\sigma \in L$ and refer to σ as a string of the literature L.

From a literature L and a string $\sigma \in L$ we introduce the derived literature L_σ. Namely, $\tau \in L_\sigma$ if and only if $\sigma * \tau \in L$, where $\sigma * \tau$ denotes the concatenation of σ and τ.

We shall say that the language L is universal for the class Φ of literatures if for every literature $M \in \Phi$ there is a string $\sigma(M) \in L$ such that $M = L_{\sigma(M)}$; that is, $\tau \in M$ if and only if $\sigma(M) * \tau \in L$.

We shall call a literature computable if its strings form a recursively enumerable set. It is easy to see that there is a computable literature U_C that is universal with respect to the set C of computable literatures. Namely, let e be a computable literature and let c be the representation of the Gödel number of the recursively enumerable set of e as a string of elements of A. Then, we say $c * \tau \in U_C$ if and only if $\tau \in e$.

It may be more convenient to describe natural languages as formal literatures than as formal languages: if we allow the definition of new terms and require that new terms be used in accordance with their definitions, then we have restrictions on sentences that depend on what sentences have previously been uttered. In a programming language, the restriction that an identifier not be used until it has been declared, and then only consistently with the declaration, is of this form.

Any natural language may be regarded as universal with respect to the set of natural languages in the approximate sense that we might define French in terms of English and then say 'From now on we shall speak only French'.

All the above is purely syntactic. The applications we envisage to artificial intelligence come from a certain kind of interpreted literature. We are not able to describe precisely the class of literatures that may prove useful, only to sketch a class of examples.

Suppose we have an interpreted language such as first-order logic perhaps including some modal operators. We introduce three additional operators: $consistent(\phi)$, $normally(\phi)$, and $probably(\phi)$. We start with a list of sentences as hypotheses. A new sentence may be added to a string σ of sentences according to the following rules:

1. Any consequence of sentences of σ may be added.
2. If a sentence ϕ is consistent with σ, then *consistent*(ϕ) may be added. Of course, this is a non-computable rule. It may be weakened to say that *consistent*(ϕ) may be added provided ϕ can be shown to be consistent with σ by some particular proof procedure.
3. *normally*(ϕ), *consistent*$(\phi) \vdash$ *probably*(ϕ).
4. $\phi \vdash$ *probably*(ϕ) is a possible deduction.
5. If $\phi_1, \phi_2, \ldots, \phi_n \vdash \phi$ is a possible deduction then *probably*$(\phi_1), \ldots,$ *probably*$(\phi_n) \vdash$ *probably*(ϕ) is also a possible deduction.

The intended application to our formalism is as follows:

In part 2 we considered the example of one person telephoning another, and in this example we assumed that if p looks up q's phone-number in the book, he will know it, and if he dials the number he will come into conversation with q. It is not hard to think of possible exceptions to these statements such as:

1. The page with q's number may be torn out.
2. p may be blind.
3. Someone may have deliberately inked out q's number.
4. The telephone company may have made the entry incorrectly.
5. q may have got the telephone only recently.
6. The phone system may be out of order.
7. q may be incapacitated suddenly.

For each of these possibilities it is possible to add a term excluding the difficulty in question to the condition on the result of performing the action. But we can think of as many additional difficulties as we wish, so it is impractical to exclude each difficulty separately.

We hope to get out of this difficulty by writing such sentences as

$$\forall p\,.\,\forall q\,.\,\forall s.\ at(q,home(q),s) \supset normally(in\text{-}conversation(p,q, result(p,dials(phone\text{-}number(q)),s)))$$

We would then be able to deduce

$$probably(in\text{-}conversation(p,q,result(p,dials(phone\text{-}number(q)),s_0)))$$

provided there were no statements like

$$kaput(Phone\text{-}system,s_0)$$

and

$$\forall s.\ kaput(Phone\text{-}system,s) \supset \neg in\text{-}conversation(p,q,result(p,dials(phone\text{-}number(q)),s))$$

present in the system.

Many of the problems that give rise to the introduction of frames might be handled in a similar way.

The operators *normally*, *consistent* and *probably* are all modal and referentially opaque. We envisage systems in which *probably*(π) and *probably*$(\neg\pi)$ and therefore *probably*(**false**) will arise. Such an event should give rise to a search for a contradiction.

We hereby warn the reader, if it is not already clear to him, that these ideas are very tentative and may prove useless, especially in their present form. However, the problem they are intended to deal with, namely the impossibility of naming every conceivable thing that may go wrong, is an important one for artificial intelligence, and some formalism has to be developed to deal with it.

Probabilities

On numerous occasions it has been suggested that the formalism take uncertainty into account by attaching probabilities to its sentences. We agree that the formalism will eventually have to allow statements about the probabilities of events, but attaching probabilities to all statements has the following objections:

1. It is not clear how to attach probabilities to statements containing quantifiers in a way that corresponds to the amount of conviction people have.
2. The information necessary to assign numerical probabilities is not ordinarily available. Therefore, a formalism that required numerical probabilities would be epistemologically inadequate.

Parallel processing

Besides describing strategies by ALGOL-like programs we may also want to describe the laws of change of the situation by such programs. In doing so we must take into account the fact that many processes are going on simultaneously and that the single-activity-at-a-time ALGOL-like programs will have to be replaced by programs in which processes take place in parallel, in order to get an epistemologically adequate description. This suggests examining the so-called simulation languages; but a quick survey indicates that they are rather restricted in the kinds of processes they allow to take place in parallel and in the types of interaction allowed. Moreover, at present there is no developed formalism that allows proofs of the correctness of parallel programs.

4. DISCUSSION OF LITERATURE

The plan for achieving a generally intelligent program outlined in this paper will clearly be difficult to carry out. Therefore, it is natural to ask if some simpler scheme will work, and we shall devote this section to criticising some simpler schemes that have been proposed.

1. L. Fogel (1966) proposes to evolve intelligent automata by altering their state transition diagrams so that they perform better on tasks of greater

and greater complexity. The experiments described by Fogel involve machines with less than 10 states being evolved to predict the next symbol of a quite simple sequence. We do not think this approach has much chance of achieving interesting results because it seems limited to automata with small numbers of states, say less than 100, whereas computer programs regarded as automata have 2^{10^5} to 2^{10^7} states. This is a reflection of the fact that, while the representation of behaviours by finite automata is metaphysically adequate – in principle every behaviour of which a human or machine is capable can be so represented – this representation is not epistemologically adequate; that is, conditions we might wish to impose on a behaviour, or what is learned from an experience, are not readily expressible as changes in the state diagram of an automaton.

2. A number of investigators (Galanter 1956, Pivar and Finkelstein 1964) have taken the view that intelligence may be regarded as the ability to predict the future of a sequence from observation of its past. Presumably, the idea is that the experience of a person can be regarded as a sequence of discrete events and that intelligent people can predict the future. Artificial intelligence is then studied by writing programs to predict sequences formed according to some simple class of laws (sometimes probabilistic laws). Again the model is metaphysically adequate but epistemologically inadequate.

In other words, what we know about the world is divided into knowledge about many aspects of it, taken separately and with rather weak interaction. A machine that worked with the undifferentiated encoding of experience into a sequence would first have to solve the encoding, a task more difficult than any the sequence extrapolators are prepared to undertake. Moreover, our knowledge is not usable to predict exact sequences of experience. Imagine a person who is correctly predicting the course of a football game he is watching; he is not predicting each visual sensation (the play of light and shadow, the exact movements of the players and the crowd). Instead his prediction is on the level of: team A is getting tired; they should start to fumble or have their passes intercepted.

3. Friedberg (1958, 1959) has experimented with representing behaviour by a computer program and evolving a program by random mutations to perform a task. The epistemological inadequacy of the representation is expressed by the fact that desired changes in behaviour are often not representable by small changes in the machine language form of the program. In particular, the effect on a reasoning program of learning a new fact is not so representable.

4. Newell and Simon worked for a number of years with a program called the General Problem Solver (Newell *et al.* 1959, Newell and Simon 1961). This program represents problems as the task of transforming one symbolic expression into another using a fixed set of transformation rules. They succeeded in putting a fair variety of problems into this form, but for a number of problems the representation was awkward enough so that GPS could only do small examples. The task of improving GPS was studied as a GPS task, but we believe it was finally abandoned. The name, General Problem Solver, suggests that its authors at one time believed that most problems could be put in its terms, but their more recent publications have indicated other points of view.

It is interesting to compare the point of view of the present paper with that expressed in Newell and Ernst (1965) from which we quote the second paragraph:

> We may consider a problem solver to be a process that takes a problem as input and provides (when successful) the solution as output. The problem consists of the problem statement, or what is immediately given; and auxiliary information, which is potentially relevant to the problem but available only as the result of processing. The problem solver has available certain methods for attempting to solve the problem. These are to be applied to an internal representation of the problem. For the problem solver to be able to work on a problem it must first transform the problem statement from its external form into the internal representation. Thus (roughly), the class of problems the problem solver can convert into its internal representation determines how broad or general it is; and its success in obtaining solutions to problems in internal form determines its power. Whether or not universal, such a decomposition fits well the structure of present problem solving programs.

In a very approximate way their division of the problem solver into the input program that converts problems into internal representation and the problem solver proper corresponds to our division into the epistemological and heuristic parts of the artificial intelligence problem. The difference is that we are more concerned with the suitability of the internal representation itself.

Newell (1965) poses the problem of how to get what we call heuristically adequate representations of problems, and Simon (1966) discusses the concept of 'can' in a way that should be compared with the present approach.

Modal logic

It is difficult to give a concise definition of modal logic. It was originally invented by Lewis (1918) in an attempt to avoid the 'paradoxes' of implication (a false proposition implies any proposition). The idea was to distinguish two sorts of truth: *necessary* truth and mere *contingent* truth. A contingently true proposition is one which, though true, could be false. This is formalized by introducing the modal operator $\Box$ (read 'necessarily') which forms propositions from propositions. Then *p*'s being a necessary truth is expressed by $\Box p$'s being true. More recently, modal logic has become a much-used tool for analysing the logic of such various propositional operators as belief, knowledge and tense.

There are very many possible axiomatizations of the logic of $\Box$, none of which seem more intuitively plausible than many others. A full account of the main classical systems is given by Feys (1965), who also includes an excellent bibliography. We shall give here an axiomatization of a fairly simple modal logic, the system M of Feys-Von Wright. One adds to any full axiomatization of propositional calculus the following:

$Ax.\ 1$: $\Box p \supset p$

$Ax.\ 2$: $\Box(p \supset p) \supset (\Box p \supset \Box q)$

Rule 1: from p and $p \supset q$, infer q

Rule 2: from p, infer $\Box p$.

(This axiomatization is due to Gödel).

There is also a dual modal operator $\Diamond$, defined as $\neg\Box\neg$. Its intuitive meaning is 'possibly': $\Diamond p$ is true when p is at least possible, although p may be in fact false (or true). The reader will be able to see the intuitive correspondence between $\neg\Diamond p$ – p is impossible, and $\Box \sim p$ – that is, p is necessarily false.

M is a fairly weak modal logic. One can strengthen it by adding axioms, for example, adding $Ax.\ 3$: $\Box p \supset \Box\Box p$ yields the system called $S4$; adding $Ax.\ 4$: $\Diamond p \supset \Box\Diamond p$ yields $S5$; and other additions are possible. However, one can also weaken all these systems in various ways, for instance by changing $Ax.\ 1$ to $Ax.\ 1'$:$\Box p \supset \Diamond p$. One easily sees that $Ax.\ 1$ implies $Ax.\ 1'$, but the converse is not true. The systems obtained in this way are known as the *deontic* versions of the systems. These modifications will be useful later when we come to consider tense-logics as modal logics.

One should note that the truth or falsity of $\Box p$ is not decided by p's being true. Thus $\Box$ is not a truth-functional operator (unlike the usual logical connectives, for instance) and so there is no direct way of using truth-tables to analyse propositions containing modal operators. In fact the decision problem for modal propositional calculi has been quite nontrivial. It is just this property which makes modal calculi so useful, as belief, tense, etc., when interpreted as propositional operators, are all nontruthfunctional.

The proliferation of modal propositional calculi, with no clear means of comparison, we shall call the *first problem* of modal logic. Other difficulties arise when we consider modal predicate calculi, that is, when we attempt to introduce quantifiers. This was first done by Barcan-Marcus (1946).

Unfortunately, all the early attempts at modal predicate calculi had unintuitive theorems (*see* for instance Kripke 1963a), and, moreover, all of them met with difficulties connected with the failure of Leibniz' law of identity, which we shall try to outline.

Leibniz' law is

L: $\forall x\ .\ \forall y.\ x=y \supset (\Phi(x) \equiv \Phi(y))$

where Φ is any open sentence. Now this law fails in modal contexts. For instance, consider this instance of L:

L_1: $\forall x\ .\ \forall y.\ x=y \supset (\Box(x=x) \equiv \Box(x=y))$

By rule 2 of M (which is present in almost all modal logics), since $x=x$ is a theorem, so is $\Box(x=x)$. Thus L_1 yields

L_2: $\forall x\ .\ \forall y.\ x=y \supset \Box(x=y)$

But, the argument goes, this is counterintuitive. For instance the morning star is in fact the same individual as the evening star (the planet Venus). However, they are not *necessarily* equal: one can easily imagine that they might be distinct. This famous example is known as the 'morning star paradox'.

This and related difficulties compel one to abandon Leibniz' law in modal predicate calculi, or else to modify the laws of quantification (so that it is impossible to obtain the undesirable instances of universal sentences such as L_2). This solves the purely formal problem, but leads to severe difficulties in interpreting these calculi, as Quine has urged in several papers (cf. Quine 1964).

The difficulty is this. A sentence $\Phi(a)$ is usually thought of as ascribing some property to a certain individual a. Now consider the morning star; clearly, the morning star is necessarily equal to the morning star. However, the evening star is not necessarily equal to the morning star. Thus, this one individual – the planet Venus – both has and does not have the property of being necessarily equal to the morning star. Even if we abandon proper names the difficulty does not disappear: for how are we to interpret a statement like $\exists x\ .\ \exists y(x=y \land \Phi(x) \land \neg\Phi(y))$?

Barcan-Marcus has urged an unconventional reading of the quantifiers to avoid this problem. The discussion between her and Quine in Barcan-Marcus (1963) is very illuminating. However, this raises some difficulties – see Belnap and Dunn (1968) – and the recent semantic theory of modal logic provides a more satisfactory method of interpreting modal sentences.

This theory was developed by several authors (Hintikka 1963, 1967a; Kanger 1957; Kripke 1963a, 1963b, 1965), but chiefly by Kripke. We shall try to give an outline of this theory, but if the reader finds it inadequate he should consult Kripke (1963a).

The idea is that modal calculi describe several *possible worlds* at once, instead of just one. Statements are not assigned a single truth-value, but rather a spectrum of truth-values, one in each possible world. Now, a statement is necessary when it is true in *all* possible worlds – more or less. Actually, in order to get different modal logics (and even then not all of them) one has to be a bit more subtle, and have a binary relation on the set of possible worlds – the alternativeness relation. Then a statement is necessary in a world when it is true in all alternatives to that world. Now it turns out that many common axioms of modal propositional logics correspond directly to conditions on this relation of alternativeness. Thus for instance in the system M above, $Ax.\ 1$ corresponds to the reflexiveness of the alternativeness relation; $Ax.\ 3(\Box p \supset \Box\Box p)$ corresponds to its transitivity. If we make the alternativeness relation into an equivalence relation, then this is just like not having one at all; and it corresponds to the axiom: $\Diamond p \supset \Box\Diamond p$.

This semantic theory already provides an answer to the first problem of modal logic: a rational method is available for classifying the multitude of propositional modal logics. More importantly, it also provides an intelligible interpretation for modal predicate calculi. One has to imagine each possible world as having a set of individuals and an assignment of individuals to names of the language. Then each statement takes on its truthvalue in a world s according to the particular set of individuals and assignment associated with s. Thus, a possible world is an interpretation of the calculus, in the usual sense.

Now, the failure of Leibniz' law is no longer puzzling, for in one world the morning star – for instance – may be equal to (the same individual as) the evening star, but in another the two may be distinct.

There are still difficulties, both formal – the quantification rules have to be modified to avoid unintuitive theorems (see Kripke, 1963a, for the details) – and interpretative: it is not obvious what it means to have the *same* individual existing in *different* worlds.

It is possible to gain the expressive power of modal logic without using modal operators by constructing an ordinary truth-functional logic which describes the multiple-world semantics of modal logic directly. To do this we give every predicate an extra argument (the world-variable; or in our terminology the situation-variable) and instead of writing '$\Box\,\Phi$', we write

$$\forall t\,.\,A(s,t) \supset \Phi(t),$$

where A is the alternativeness relation between situations. Of course we must provide appropriate axioms for A.

The resulting theory will be expressed in the notation of the situation calculus; the proposition Φ has become a propositional fluent $\lambda s\,.\,\Phi(s)$, and the 'possible worlds' of the modal semantics are precisely the situations. Notice, however, that the theory we get is weaker than what would have been obtained by adding modal operators directly to the situation calculus, for we can give no translation of assertions such as $\Box\pi(s)$, where s is a situation, which this enriched situation calculus would contain.

It is possible, in this way, to reconstruct within the situation calculus subtheories corresponding to the tense-logics of Prior and to the knowledge-logics of Hintikka, as we shall explain below. However, there is a qualification here: so far we have only explained how to translate the propositional modal logics into the situation calculus. In order to translate quantified modal logic, with its difficulties of referential opacity, we must complicate the situation calculus to a degree which makes it rather clumsy. There is a special predicate on individuals and situation – $exists(i,s)$ – which is regarded as true when i names an individual existing in the situation s. This is necessary because situations may contain different individuals. Then quantified assertions of the modal logic are translated according to the following scheme:

$$\forall x\,.\,\Phi(x) \rightarrow \forall x\,.\,exists(x,s) \supset \Phi(x,s)$$

where s is the introduced situation variable.

We shall not go into the details of this extra translation in the examples below, but shall be content to define the translations of the propositional tense and knowledge logics into the situation calculus.

Logic of knowledge

The logic of knowledge was first investigated as a modal logic by Hintikka in his book *Knowledge and belief* (1962). We shall only describe the knowledge calculus. He introduces the modal operator Ka (read 'a knows that'), and its dual Pa, defined as $\neg Ka \neg$. The semantics is obtained by the analogous reading of Ka as: 'it is true in all possible worlds compatible with a's knowledge that'. The propositional logic of Ka (similar to $\Box$) turns out to be $S4$, that is, $M + Ax\,.\,3$; but there are some complexities over quantification. (The last chapter of the book contains another excellent account of the overall problem of quantification in modal contexts.) This analysis of knowledge has been criticized in various ways (Chisholm 1963, Follesdal 1967) and Hintikka has replied in several important papers (1967b, 1967c, 1969). The last paper contains a review of the different senses of 'know' and the extent to which they have been adequately formalized. It appears that two senses have resisted capture. First, the idea of 'knowing how', which appears related to our 'can'; and secondly, the concept of knowing a person (place, etc.), when this means 'being acquainted with' as opposed to simply knowing *who* a person *is*.

In order to translate the (propositional) knowledge calculus into 'situation' language, we introduce a three-place predicate into the situation calculus termed 'shrug'. $Shrug(p,s_1,s_2)$, where p is a person and s_1 and s_2 are situations, is true when, if p is in fact in situation s_2, then for all he knows he might be in situation s_1. That is to say, s_1 is an *epistemic alternative* to s_2, as far as the individual p is concerned – this is Hintikka's term for his alternative worlds (he calls them model-sets).

Then we translate $K_p q$, where q is a proposition of Hintikka's calculus, as $\forall t\,.\,shrug(p,t,s) \supset q(t)$, where $\lambda s\,.\,q(s)$ is the fluent which translates q. Of course we have to supply axioms for *shrug*, and in fact so far as the pure knowledge-calculus is concerned, the only two necessary are

$$K1\colon \forall s\,.\,\forall p\,.\,shrug(p,s,s)$$

and $K2\colon \forall p\,.\,\forall s\,.\,\forall t\,.\,\forall r\,.\,(shrug(p,t,s) \wedge shrug(p,r,t)) \supset shrug(p,r,s)$

that is, reflexivity and transitivity.

Others of course may be needed when we add tenses and other machinery to the situation calculus, in order to relate knowledge to them.

Tense logics

This is one of the largest and most active areas of philosophic logic. Prior's book *Past, present and future* (1968) is an extremely thorough and lucid account of what has been done in the field. We have already mentioned the four propositional operators *F, G, P, H* which Prior discusses. He regards these as modal operators; then the alternativeness relation of the semantic theory is simply the time-ordering relation. Various axiomatizations are given, corresponding to deterministic and nondeterministic tenses, ending and nonending times, etc; and the problems of quantification turn up again here with renewed intensity. To attempt a summary of Prior's book is a hopeless task, and we simply urge the reader to consult it. More recently several papers have appeared (see, for instance, Bull 1968) which illustrate the technical sophistication tense-logic has reached, in that full completeness proofs for various axiom systems are now available.

As indicated above, the situation calculus contains a tense-logic (or rather several tense-logics), in that we can define Prior's four operators in our system and by suitable axioms reconstruct various axiomatizations of these four operators (in particular, all the axioms in Bull (1968) can be translated into the situation calculus).

Only one extra nonlogical predicate is necessary to do this: it is a binary predicate of situations called *cohistorical*, and is intuitively meant to assert of its arguments that one is in the other's future. This is necessary because we want to consider some pairs of situations as being not temporally related at all. We now define F(for instance) thus:

$$F(\pi,s) \equiv \exists t\,.\, cohistorical(t,s) \wedge time(t) > time(s) \wedge \pi(t).$$

The other operators are defined analogously.

Of course we have to supply axioms for 'cohistorical' and time: this is not difficult. For instance, consider one of Bull's axioms, say $Gp \supset GGp$, which is better (for us) expressed in the form $FFp \supset Fp$. Using the definition, this translates into:

$$(\exists t\,.\, cohistorical(t,s) \wedge time(t) > time(s) \wedge \exists r\,.\, cohistorical(r,t)$$
$$\wedge\, time(r) > time(t) \wedge \pi(r)) \supset (\exists r\,.\, cohistorical(r,s)$$
$$\wedge\, time(r) > time(s) \wedge \pi(r))$$

which simplifies (using the transitivity of '>') to

$$\forall t\,.\,\forall r\,.\,(cohistorical(r,t) \wedge cohistorical(t,s)) \supset cohistorical(r,s)$$

that is, the transitivity of 'cohistorical'. This axiom is precisely analogous to the $S4$ axiom $\Box p \supset \Box\Box p$, which corresponded to transitivity of the alternativeness relation in the modal semantics. Bull's other axioms translate into conditions on 'cohistorical' and time in a similar way; we shall not bother here with the rather tedious details.

Rather more interesting would be axioms relating 'shrug' to 'cohistorical' and time; unfortunately we have been unable to think of any intuitively plausible ones. Thus, if two situations are epistemic alternatives (that is, $shrug(p,s_1,s_2)$) then they may or may not have the same time value (since we want to allow that p may not know what the time is), and they may or may not be cohistorical.

Logics and theories of actions

The most fully developed theory in this area is von Wright's action logic described in his book *Norm and Action* (1963). Von Wright builds his logic on a rather unusual tense-logic of his own. The basis is a binary modal connective T, so that pTq, where p and q are propositions, means '*p,then q*'. Thus the action, for instance, of opening the window is: (*the window is closed*)T(*the window is open*). The formal development of the calculus was taken a long way in the book cited above, but some problems of interpretation remained as Castañeda points out in his review (1965). In a more recent paper von Wright (1967) has altered and extended his formalism so as to answer these and other criticisms, and also has provided a sort of semantic theory based on the notion of a life-tree.

We know of no other attempts at constructing a single theory of actions which have reached such a degree of development, but there are several discussions of difficulties and surveys which seem important. Rescher (1967) discusses several topics very neatly, and Davidson (1967) also makes some cogent points. Davidson's main thesis is that, in order to translate statements involving actions into the predicate calculus, it appears necessary to allow actions as values of bound variables, that is (by Quine's test) as real individuals. The situation calculus of course follows this advice in that we allow quantification over strategies, which have actions as a special case. Also important are Simon's papers (1965, 1967) on command-logics. Simon's main purpose is to show that a special logic of commands is unnecessary, ordinary logic serving as the only deductive machinery; but this need not detain us here. He makes several points, most notably perhaps that agents are most of the time not performing actions, and that in fact they only stir to action when forced to by some outside interference. He has the particularly interesting example of a serial processor operating in a parallel-demand environment, and the resulting need for interrupts. Action logics such as von Wright's and ours do not distinguish between action and inaction, and we are not aware of any action-logic which has reached a stage of sophistication adequate to meet Simon's implied criticism.

There is a large body of purely philosophical writings on action, time, determinism, etc., most of which is irrelevant for present purposes. However, we mention two which have recently appeared and which seem interesting: a paper by Chisholm (1967) and another paper by Evans (1967), summarizing the recent discussion on the distinctions between states, performances and activities.

Other topics

There are two other areas where some analysis of actions has been necessary: command-logics and logics and theories of obligation. For the former the best reference is Rescher's book (1966) which has an excellent bibliography. Note also Simon's counterarguments to some of Rescher's theses (Simon 1965, 1967). Simon proposes that no special logic of commands is necessary, commands being analysed in the form 'bring it about that p!' for some proposition p, or, more generally, in the form 'bring it about that $P(x)$ by changing x!', where x is a *command* variable, that is, under the agent's control. The translations between commands and statements take place only in the context of a 'complete model', which specifies environmental constraints and defines the command variables. Rescher argues that these schemas for commands are inadequate to handle the *conditional command* 'when p, do q', which becomes 'bring it about that $(p \supset q)$!': this, unlike the former, is satisfied by making p false.

There are many papers on the logic of obligation and permission. Von Wright's work is oriented in this direction; Castañeda has many papers on the subject and Anderson also has written extensively (his early influential report (1956) is especially worth reading). The review pages of the *Journal of Symbolic Logic* provide many other references. Until fairly recently these theories did not seem of very much relevance to logics of action, but in their new maturity they are beginning to be so.

Counterfactuals

There is, of course, a large literature on this ancient philosophical problem, almost none of which seems directly relevant to us. However, there is one recent theory, developed by Rescher (1964), which may be of use. Rescher's book is so clearly written that we shall not attempt a description of his theory here. The reader should be aware of Sosa's critical review (1967) which suggests some minor alterations.

The importance of this theory for us is that it suggests an alternative approach to the difficulty which we have referred to as the frame problem. In outline, this is as follows. One assumes, as a rule of procedure (or perhaps as a rule of inference), that when actions are performed, *all* propositional fluents which applied to the previous situation also apply to the new situation. This will often yield an inconsistent set of statements about the new situation; Rescher's theory provides a mechanism for restoring consistency in a rational way, and giving as a by-product those fluents which change in value as a result of performing the action. However, we have not investigated this in detail.

The communication process

We have not considered the problems of formally describing the process of communication in this paper, but it seems clear that they will have to be tackled eventually. Philosophical logicians have been spontaneously active here. The major work is Harrah's book (1963); Cresswell has written several papers on 'the logic of interrogatives', see for instance Cresswell (1965). Among other authors we may mention Åqvist (1965) and Belnap (1963); again the review pages of the *Journal of Symbolic Logic* will provide other references.

Acknowledgements

The research reported here was supported in part by the Advanced Research Projects Agency of the Office of the Secretary of Defense (SD-183), and in part by the Science Research Council (B/SR/2299)

REFERENCES

Anderson, A.R. (1956) The formal analysis of normative systems. Reprinted in *The Logic of decision and action* (ed. Rescher, N.). Pittsburgh: University of Pittsburgh Press.

Åqvist, L. (1965) *A new approach to the logical theory of interrogatives, part I.* Uppsala: Uppsala Philosophical Association.

Barcan-Marcus, R.C. (1946) A functional calculus of the first order based on strict implication. *Journal of Symbolic Logic*, **11**, 1–16.

Barcan-Marcus, R.C. (1963) Modalities and intensional languages. *Boston studies in the Philosophy of Science.* (ed. Wartofsky, W.). Dordrecht, Holland.

Belnap, N.D. (1963) *An analysis of questions.* Santa Monica.

Belnap, N.D. & Dunn, J.M. (1968) The substitution interpretation of the quantifiers. *Noûs*, **2**, 177–85.

Bull, R.A. (1968) An algebraic study of tense logics with linear time. *Journal of Symbolic Logic*, **33**, 27–39

Castañeda, H.N. (1965) The logic of change, action and norms. *Journal of Philosophy*, **62**, 333–4.

Chisholm, R.M. (1963) The logic of knowing. *Journal of Philosophy*, **60**, 773–95.

Chisholm, R.M. (1967) He could have done otherwise. *Journal of Philosophy*, **64**, 409–17.

Church, A. (1956) *Introduction to Mathematical Logic.* Princeton: Princeton University Press.

Cresswell, M.J. (1965). The logic of interrogatives.' *Formal systems and recursive functions.* (ed. Crossley, J.N. & Dummett, M.A.E.). Amsterdam: North-Holland.

Davidson, D. (1967) The logical form of action sentences. *The logic of decision and action.* (ed. Rescher, N.). Pittsburgh: University of Pittsburgh Press.

Evans, C.O. (1967) States, activities and performances. *Australasian Journal of Philosophy*, **45**, 293–308.

Feys, R. (1965) *Modal Logics.* (ed. Dopp, J.). Louvain: Coll. de Logique Math. série B.

Fogel, L.J., Owens, A.J. & Walsh, M.J. (1966) *Artificial Intelligence through simulated evolution.* New York: John Wiley.

Føllesdal, D. (1967) Knowledge, identity and existence. *Theoria*, **33**, 1–27.

Friedberg, R.M. (1958) A learning machine, part I. *IBM J. Res. Dev.*, **2**, 2–13.

Friedberg, R.M., Dunham, B., & North, J.H. (1959) A learning machine, part II. *IBM J. Res. Dev.*, **3**, 282–7.

Galanter, E. & Gerstenhaber, M. (1956). On thought: the extrinsic theory. *Psychological Review*, **63**, 218–27

Green, C. (1969) Theorem-proving by resolution as a basis for question-answering systems. *Machine Intelligence 4*, pp.183–205 (eds Meltzer, B. & Michie, D.). Edinburgh: Edinburgh University Press.

Harrah, D. (1963) *Communication: a logical model.* Cambridge, Massachusetts: MIT press.
Hintikka, J. (1962) *Knowledge and belief: an introduction to the logic of the two notions.* New York: Cornell University Press.
Hintikka, J. (1963) The modes of modality. *Acta Philosophica Fennica*, **16**, 65–82.
Hintikka, J. (1967a) A program and a set of concepts for philosophical logic. *The Monist*, **51**, 69–72.
Hintikka, J. (1967b) Existence and identity in epistemic contexts. *Theoria*, **32**, 138–47.
Hintikka, J. (1967c) Individuals, possible worlds and epistemic logic. *Noûs*, **1**, 33–62.
Hintikka, J. (1969) Alternative constructions in terms of the basic epistemological attitudes *Contemporary philosophy in Scandinavia* (ed. Olsen, R. E.) (to appear).
Kanger, S. (1957) A note on quantification and modalities. *Theoria*, **23**, 133–4.
Kripke, S. (1963a) Semantical considerations on modal logic. *Acta Philosophica Fennica*, **16**, 83–94.
Kripke, S. (1963b) Semantical analysis of modal logic I. *Zeitschrift für math. Logik und Grundlagen der Mathematik*, **9**, 67–96.
Kripke, S. (1965) Semantical analysis of modal logic II. *The theory of models* (eds Addison, Henkin & Tarski). Amsterdam: North-Holland.
Lewis, C.I. (1918) *A survey of symbolic logic.* Berkeley: University of California Press.
Manna, Z. (1968a) *Termination of algorithms.* Ph.D Thesis, Carnegie-Mellon University.
Manna, Z. (1968b) *Formalization of properties of programs.* Stanford Artificial Intelligence Report: Project Memo AI-64.
McCarthy, J. (1959) Programs with common sense. *Mechanization of thought processes*, Vol. I. London: HMSO
McCarthy, J. (1962) Towards a mathematical science of computation. *Proc. IFIP Congress* 62. Amsterdam: North-Holland Press.
McCarthy, J. (1963) *Situations, actions and causal laws.* Stanford Artificial Intelligence Project: Memo 2.
Minsky, M. (1961) Steps towards artificial intelligence. *Proceedings of the I.R.E.*, **49**, 8–30.
Newell, A., Shaw, V.C. & Simon, H.A. (1959) Report on a general problem-solving program. *Proceedings ICIP.* Paris: UNESCO House.
Newell, A. & Simon H.A. (1961) GPS – a program that simulates human problem-solving. *Proceedings of a conference in learning automata.* Munich: Oldenbourgh.
Newell, A. (1965) Limitations of the current stock of ideas about problem-solving. *Proceedings of a conference on Electronic Information Handling*, pp. 195–208 (eds Kent, A. & Taulbee, O.). New York: Spartan.
Newell, A. & Ernst, C. (1965) The search for generality. *Proc. IFIP Congress* 65.
Pivar, M. & Finkelstein, M. (1964). *The Programming Language LISP: its operation and applications* (eds Berkely, E.C. & Bobrow, D.G.). Cambridge, Massachusetts: MIT Press.
Prior, A.N. (1957) *Time and modality.* Oxford: Clarenden Press.
Prior, A.N. (1968) *Past, present and future.* Oxford: Clarendon Press.
Quine, W.V.O. (1964) Reference and modality. *From a logical point of view.* Cambridge, Massachusetts: Harvard University Press.
Rescher, N. (1964) *Hypothetical reasoning.* Amsterdam: North-Holland.
Rescher, N. (1966) *The logic of commands.* London: Routledge.
Rescher, N. (1967) Aspects of action. *The logic of decision and action* (ed. Rescher, N.). Pittsburgh: University of Pittsburgh Press.
Shannon, C. (1950) Programming a computer for playing chess. *Philosophical Magazine*, **41.**
Simon, H.A. (1965) The logic of rational decision. *British Journal for the Philosophy of Science*, **16**, 169–86.
Simon, H.A. (1966) *On Reasoning about actions.* Carnegie Institute of Technology: Complex Information Processing Paper 87.
Simon, H.A. (1967) The logic of heuristic decision making. *The logic of decision and action* (ed. Rescher, N.). Pittsburgh: University of Pittsburgh Press.
Sosa, E. (1967) Hypothetical reasoning. *Journal of Philosophy*, **64**, 293–305.
Turing, A.M. (1950) Computing machinery and intelligence. *Mind*, **59**, 433–60.
von Wright, C.H. (1963) *Norm and action: a logical enquiry.* London: Routledge.
von Wright, C.H. (1967) The Logic of Action – a sketch. *The logic of decision and action* (ed. Rescher, N.). Pittsburgh: University of Pittsburgh Press.

EPISTEMOLOGICAL PROBLEMS OF ARTIFICIAL INTELLIGENCE

John McCarthy
Computer Science Department
Stanford University
Stanford, California 94305

Introduction

In (McCarthy and Hayes 1969), we proposed dividing the artificial intelligence problem into two parts - an epistemological part and a heuristic part. This lecture further explains this division, explains some of the epistemological problems, and presents some new results and approaches.

The epistemological part of AI studies what kinds of facts about the world are available to an observer with given opportunities to observe, how these facts can be represented in the memory of a computer, and what rules permit legitimate conclusions to be drawn from these facts. It leaves aside the heuristic problems of how to search spaces of possibilities and how to match patterns.

Considering epistemological problems separately has the following advantages:

1. The same problems of what information is available to an observer and what conclusions can be drawn from information arise in connection with a variety of problem solving tasks.

2. A single solution of the epistemological problems can support a wide variety of heuristic approaches to a problem.

3. AI is a very difficult scientific problem, so there are great advantages in finding parts of the problem that can be separated out and separately attacked.

4. As the reader will see from the examples in the next section, it is quite difficult to formalize the facts of common knowledge. Existing programs that manipulate facts in some of the domains are confined to special cases and don't face the difficulties that must be overcome to achieve very intelligent behavior.

We have found first order logic to provide suitable languages for expressing facts about the world for epistemological research. Recently we have found that introducing concepts as individuals makes possible a first order logic expression of facts usually expressed in modal logic but with important advantages over modal logic - and so far no disadvantages.

In AI literature, the term *predicate calculus* is usually extended to cover the whole of first order logic. While predicate calculus includes just formulas built up from variables using predicate symbols, logical connectives, and quantifiers, first order logic also allows the use of function symbols to form terms and in its semantics interprets the equality symbol as standing for identity. Our first order systems further use conditional expressions (non-recursive) to form terms and λ-expressions with individuaal variables to form new function symbols. All these extensions are logically inessential, because every formula that includes them can be replaced by a formula of pure predicate calculus whose validity is equivalent to it. The extensions are heuristically non-trivial, because the equivalent predicate calculus may be much longer and is usually much more difficult to understand - for man or machine.

The use of first order logic in epistemological research is a separate issue from whether first order sentences are appropriate data structures for representing information within a program. As to the latter, sentences in logic are at one end of a spectrum of representations; they are easy to communicate, have logical consequences and can be logical consequences, and they can be meaningful in a wide context. Taking action on the basis of information stored as sentences, is slow and they are not the most compact representation of information. The opposite extreme is to build the information into hardware, next comes building it into machine language program, then a language like LISP, and then a language like MICROPLANNER, and then perhaps productions. Compiling or hardware building or "automatic programming" or just planning takes information from a more context independent form to a faster but more context dependent form. A clear expression of this is the transition from first order logic to MICROPLANNER, where much information is represented similarly but with a specification of how the information is to be used. A large AI system should represent some information as first order logic sentences and other information should be compiled. In fact, it will often be necessary to represent the same information in several ways. Thus a ball player habit of keeping his eye on the ball is built into his "program", but it is also explicitly represented as a sentence so that the advice can be communicated.

Whether first order logic makes a good programming language is yet another issue. So far it seems to have the qualities Samuel Johnson ascribed to a woman preaching or a dog walking on its hind legs - one is sufficiently impressed by seeing it done at all that one doesn't demand it be done well.

Suppose we have a theory of a certain class of phenomena axiomatized in (say) first order logic. We regard the theory as adequate for describing the epistemological aspects of a goal seeking process involving these phenomena provided the following criterion is satisfied:

Imagine a robot such that its inputs become sentences of the theory stored in the robot's data-base, and such that whenever a sentence of the form "*I should emit output X now*" appears in its data base, the robot emits output X. Suppose that new sentences appear in its data base only as logical consequences of sentences already in the data base. The deduction of these sentences also use general sentences stored in the data base at the beginning constituting the theory being tested. Usually a data-base of sentences permits many different deductions to be made so that a deduction program would have to choose which deduction to make. If there was no program that could achieve the goal by making deductions allowed by the theory no matter how fast the program ran, we would have to say that the theory was epistemologically inadequate. A theory that was epistemologically adequate would be considered heuristically inadequate if no program running at a reasonable speed with any representation of the facts expressed by the data could do the job. We believe that most present AI formalisms are epistemologically inadequate for general intelligence; i.e. they wouldn't achieve enough goals requiring general intelligence no matter how fast they were allowed to run. This is because the epistemological problems discussed in the following sections haven't even been attacked yet.

The word "epistemology" is used in this paper substantially as many philosophers use it, but the problems considered have a different emphasis. Philosophers emphasize what is potentially knowable with maximal opportunities to observe and compute, whereas AI must take into account what is knowable with available observational and computational facilities. Even so, many of the same formalizations have both philosophical and AI interest.

The subsequent sections of this paper list some epistemological problems, discuss some first order formalizations, introduce concepts as objects and use them to express facts about knowledge, describe a new mode of reasoning called circumscription, and place the AI problem in a philosphical setting.

Epistemological problems

We will discuss what facts a person or robot must take into account in order to achieve a goal by some strategy of action. We will ignore the question of how these facts are represented, e.g., whether they are represented by sentences from which deductions are made or whether they are built into the program. We start with great generality, so there many difficulties. We obtain successively easier problems by assuming that the difficulties we have recognized don't occur until we get to a class of problems we think we can solve.

1. We begin by asking whether solving the problem requires the co-operation of other people or overcoming their opposition. If either is true, there are two subcases. In the first subcase, the other people's desires and goals must be taken into account, and the actions they will take in given circumstances predicted on the hypothesis that they will try to achieve their goals, which may have to be discovered. The problem is even more difficult if bargaining is involved, because then the problems and indeterminacies of game theory are relevant. Even if bargaining is not involved, the robot still must "put himself in the place of the other people with whom he interacts". Facts like a person wanting a thing or a person disliking another must be described.

The second subcase makes the assumption that the other people can be regarded as machines with known input-output behavior. This is often a good assumption, e.g., one assumes that a clerk in a store will sell the goods in exchange for their price and that a professor will assign a grade in accordance with the quality of the work done. Neither the goals of the clerk or the professor need be taken into account; either might well regard an attempt to use them to optimize the interaction as an invasion of privacy. In such circumstances, man usually prefers to be regarded as a machine.

Let us now suppose that either other people are not involved in the problem or that the information available about their actions takes the form of input-output relations and does not involve understanding their goals.

2. The second question is whether the strategy involves the acquisition of knowledge. Even if we can treat other people as machines, we still may have to reason about what they know. Thus an airline clerk knows what airplanes fly from here to there and when, although he will tell you when asked without your having to motivate him. One must also consider information in books and in tables. The latter information is described by other information.

The second subcase of knowledge is according to whether the information obtained can be simply plugged into a program or whether it enters in a more complex way. Thus if the robot must telephone someone, its program can simply dial the number obtained, but it might have to ask a question, "*How can I get in touch with Mike?*" and reason about how to use the resulting information in conjunction with other information. The general distinction may be according to whether new sentences are generated or whether values are just assigned to variables.

An example worth considering is that a sophisticated air traveler rarely asks how he will get from the arriving flight to the departing flight at an airport where he must change planes. He is confident that the information will be available in a form he can understand at the time he will need it.

If the strategy is embodied in a program that branches on an environmental condition or reads a numerical parameter from the environment, we can regard it as obtaining knowledge, but this is obviously an easier case than those we have discussed.

3. A problem is more difficult if it involves concurrent events and actions. To me this seems to be the most difficult unsolved epistemological problem for AI - how to express rules that give the effects of actions and events when they occur concurrently. We may contrast this with the sequential case treated in (McCarthy and Hayes 1969). In the sequential case we can write

1) $s' = result(e, s)$

where s' is the situation that results when event e occurs in situation s. The effects of e can be described by sentences relating s', e and s. One can attempt a similar formalism giving a *partial situation* that results from an event in another partial situation, but it is difficult to see how to apply this to cases in which other events may affect with the occurrence.

When events are concurrent, it is usually necessary to regard time as continuous. We have events like *raining until the reservoir overflows* and questions like *Where was his train when we wanted to call him?*.

Computer science has recently begun to formalize parallel processes so that it is sometimes possible to prove that a system of parallel processes will meet its specifications. However, the knowledge available to a robot of the other processes going on in the world will rarely take the form of a Petri net or any of the other formalisms used in engineering or computer science. In fact, anyone who wishes to prove correct an airline reservation system or an air traffic control system must use information about the behavior of the external world that is less specific than a program. Nevertheless, the formalisms for expressing facts about parallel and indeterminate programs provide a start for axiomatizing concurrent action.

4. A robot must be able to express knowledge about space, and the locations, shapes and layouts of objects in space. Present

programs treat only very special cases. Usually locations are discrete - block A may be on block B but the formalisms do not allow anything to be said about where on block B it is, and what shape space is left on block B for placing other blocks or whether block A could be moved to project out a bit in order to place another block. A few are more sophisticated, but the objects must have simple geometric shapes. A formalism capable of representing the geometric information people get from seeing and handling objects has not, to my knowledge, been approached.

The difficulty in expressing such facts is indicated by the limitations of English in expressing human visual knowledge. We can describe regular geometric shapes precisely in English (fortified by mathematics), but the information we use for recognizing another person's face cannot ordinarily be transmitted in words. We can answer many more questions in the presence of a scene than we can from memory.

5. The relation between three dimensional objects and their two dimensional retinal or camera images is mostly untreated. Contrary to some philosophical positions, the three dimensional object is treated by our minds as distinct from its appearances. People blind from birth can still communicate in the same language as sighted people about three dimensional objects. We need a formalism that treats three dimensional objects as instances of patterns and their two dimensional appearances as projections of these patterns modified by lighting and occlusion.

6. Objects can be made by shaping materials and by combining other objects. They can also be taken apart, cut apart or destroyed in various ways. What people know about the relations between materials and objects remains to be described.

7. Modal concepts like *event e1 caused event e2* and *person e can do action a* are needed. (McCarthy and Hayes 1969) regards ability as a function of a person's position in a causal system and not at all as a function of his internal structure. This still seems correct, but that treatment is only metaphysically adequate, because it doesn't provide for expressing the information about ability that people actually have.

8. Suppose now that the problem can be formalized in terms of a single state that is changed by events. In interesting cases, the set of components of the state depends on the problem, but common general knowledge is usually expressed in terms of the effect of an action on one or a few components of the state. However, it cannot always be assumed that the other components are unchanged, especially because the state can be described in a variety of co-ordinate systems and the meaning of changing a single co-ordinate depends on the co-ordinate system. The problem of expressing information about what remains unchanged by an event was called *the frame problem* in (McCarthy and Hayes 1969). Minsky subsequently confused matters by using the word "frame" for patterns into which situations may fit. (His hypothesis seems to have been that almost all situations encountered in human problem solving fit into a small number of previously known patterns of situation and goal. I regard this as unlikely in difficult problems).

9. The *frame problem* may be a subcase of what we call the *qualification problem*, and a good solution of the qualification problem may solve the frame problem also. In the *missionaries and cannibals* problem, a boat holding two people is stated to be available. In the statement of the problem, nothing is said about how boats are used to cross rivers, so obviously this information must come from common knowledge, and a computer program capable of solving the problem from an English description or from a translation of this description into logic must have the requisite common knowledge. The simplest statement about the use of boats says something like, "*If a boat is at one point on the shore of a body of water, and a set of things enter the boat, and the boat is propelled to the another point on the shore, and the things exit the boat, then they will be at the second point on the shore*". However, this statement is too rigid to be true, because anyone will admit that if the boat is a rowboat and has a leak or no oars, the action may not achieve its intended result. One might try amending the common knowledge statement about boats, but this encounters difficulties when a critic demands a qualification that the vertical exhaust stack of a diesel boat must not be struck square by a cow turd dropped by a passing hawk or some other event that no-one has previously thought of. We need to be able to say that the boat can be used as a vehicle for crossing a body of water unless something prevents it. However, since we are not willing to delimit in advance possible circumstances that may prevent the use of the boat, there is still a problem of proving or at least conjecturing that nothing prevents the use of the boat. A method of reasoning called *circumscription*, described in a subsequent section of this paper, is a candidate for solving the qualification problem. The reduction of the frame problem to the qualification problem has not been fully carried out, however.

Circumscription - a way of jumping to conclusions

There is an intuition that not all human reasoning can be translated into deduction in some formal system of mathematical logic, and therefore mathematical logic should be rejected as a formalism for expressing what a robot should know about the world. The intuition in itself doesn't carry a convincing idea of what is lacking and how it might be supplied.

We can confirm part of the intuition by describing a previously unformalized mode of reasoning called *circumscription*, which we can show does not correspond to deduction in a mathematical system. The conclusions it yields are just conjectures and sometimes even introduce inconsistency. We will argue that humans often use circumscription, and robots must too. The second part of the intuition - the rejection of mathematical logic - is not confirmed; the new mode of reasoning is best understood and used within a mathematical logical framework and co-ordinates well with mathematical logical deduction. We think *circumscription* accounts for some of the successes and some of the errors of human reasoning.

The intuitive idea of *circumscription* is as follows: We know some objects in a given class and we have some ways of generating more. We jump to the conclusion that this gives all the objects in the class. Thus we *circumscribe* the class to the objects we know how to generate.

For example, suppose that objects a, b and c satisfy the predicate P and that the functions $f(x)$ and $g(x,y)$ take arguments satisfying P into values also satisfying P. The first order logic expression of these facts is

2) $P(a) \wedge P(b) \wedge P(c) \wedge (\forall x)(P(x) \supset P(f(x))) \wedge (\forall x\ y)(P(x) \wedge P(y) \supset P(g(x,y)))$.

The conjecture that everything satisfying P is generated from a, b and c by repeated application of the functions f and g is expressed by the sentence schema

3) $\Phi(a) \wedge \Phi(b) \wedge \Phi(c) \wedge (\forall x)(\Phi(x) \supset \Phi(f(x))) \wedge (\forall x\ y)(\Phi(x) \wedge \Phi(y) \supset \Phi(g(x,y))) \supset (\forall x)(\Phi(x) \supset P(x))$,

where Φ is a free predicate variable for which any predicate may be substituted.

It is only a conjecture, because there might be an object d such that $P(d)$ which is not generated in this way. (3) is one way of writing *the circumscription* of (2). The heuristics of circumscription - when one can plausibly conjecture that the objects generated in known ways are all there are - are completely unstudied.

Circumscription is not deduction in disguise, because every form of deduction has two properties that circumscription lacks - transitivity and what we may call *monotonicity*. Transitivity says that if $p \vdash r$ and $r \vdash s$, then $p \vdash s$. Monotonicity says that if $A \vdash p$ (where A is a set of sentences) and $A \subset B$, then $B \vdash p$ for deduction. Intuitively, circumscription should not be monotonic, since it is the conjecture that the ways we know of generating P's are all there are. An enlarged set B of sentences may contain a new way of generating P's.

If we use second order logic or the language of set theory, then circumscription can be expressed as a sentence rather than as a schema. In set theory it becomes.

3') $(\forall\Phi)(a \in \Phi \wedge b \in \Phi \wedge c \in \Phi \wedge (\forall x)(x \in \Phi \supset f(x) \in \Phi) \wedge (\forall x\ y)(x \in \Phi \wedge y \in \Phi \supset g(x,y) \in \Phi)) \supset P \subset \Phi)$,

but then we will still use the comprehension schema to form the set to be substituted for the set variable Φ.

The axiom schema of induction in arithmetic is the result of applying circumscription to the constant 0 and the successor operation.

There is a way of applying circumscription to an arbitrary sentence of predicate calculus. Let p be such a sentence and let Φ be a predicate symbol. The *relativization* of p with respect to Φ (written p^Φ) is defined (as in some logic texts) as the sentence that results from replacing every quantification $(\forall x)E$ that occurs in p by $(\forall x)(\Phi(x) \supset E)$ and every quantification $(\exists x)E$ that occurs in p by $(\exists x)(\Phi(x) \wedge E)$. The circumscription of p is then the sentence

4) $p^\Phi \supset (\forall x)(P(x) \supset \Phi(x))$.

This form is correct only if neither constants nor function symbols occur in p. If they do, it is necessary to conjoin $\Phi(c)$ for each constant c and $(\forall x)(\Phi(x) \supset \Phi(f(x)))$ for each single argument function symbol f to the premiss of (4). Corresponding sentences must be conjoined if there are function symbols of two or more arguments. The intuitive meaning of (4) is that the only objects satisfying P that exist are those that the sentence p forces to exist.

Applying the circumscription schema requires inventing a suitable predicate to substitute for the symbol Φ (inventing a suitable set in the set-theoretic formulation). In this it resembles mathematical induction; in order to get the conclusion, we must invent a predicate for which the premiss is true.

There is also a semantic way of looking at applying circumscription. Namely, a sentence that can be proved from a sentence p by circumscription is true in all minimal models of p, where a deduction from p is true in all models of p. Minimality is defined with respect to a containment relation $\leq$. We write that $M1 \leq M2$ if every element of the domain of $M1$ is a member of the domain of $M2$ and on the common members all predicates have the same truth value. It is not always true that a sentence true in all minimal models can be proved by circumscription. Indeed the minimal model of Peano's axioms is the standard model of arithmetic, and Gödel's theorem is the assertion that not all true sentences are theorems. Minimal models don't always exist, and when they exist, they aren't always unique.

(McCarthy 1977a) treats circumscription in more detail.

Concepts as objects

We shall begin by discussing how to express such facts as "*Pat knows the combination of the safe*", although the idea of treating a concept as an object has application beyond the discussion of knowledge.

We shall use the symbol *safe*1 for the safe, and *combination*(s) is our notation for the combination of an arbitrary safe s. We aren't much interested in the domain of combinations, and we shall take them to be strings of digits with dashes in the right place, and, since a combination is a string, we will write it in quotes. Thus we can write

5) *combination*(*safe*1) = "45-25-17"

as a formalization of the English "*The combination of the safe is* 45-25-17". Let us suppose that the combination of *safe*2 is, co-incidentally, also 45-25-17, so we can also write

6) *combination*(*safe*2) = "45-25-17".

Now we want to translate "*Pat knows the combination of the safe*". If we were to express it as

7) **knows*(*pat*, *combination*(*safe*1)),

the inference rule that allows replacing a term by an equal term in first order logic would let us conclude

8) **knows*(*pat*, *combination*(*safe*2)),

which mightn't be true.

This problem was already recognized in 1879 by Frege, the founder of modern predicate logic, who distinguished between direct and indirect occurrences of expressions and would consider the occurrence of *combination*(*safe*1) in (7) to be indirect and not subject to replacement of equals by equals. The modern way of stating the problem is to call *Pat knows* a referentially opaque operator.

The way out of this difficulty currently most popular is to treat *Pat knows* as a *modal operator*. This involves changing the logic so that replacement of an expression by an equal expression is not allowed in opaque contexts. Knowledge is not the only operator that admits modal treatment. There is also belief, wanting, and logical or physical necessity. For AI purposes, we would need all the above modal operators and many more in the same system. This would make the semantic discussion of the resulting modal logic extremely complex. For this reason, and because we want functions from material objects to concepts of them, we have followed a different path - introducing concepts as individual objects. This has not been popular in philosophy, although I suppose no-one would doubt that it could be done.

Our approach is to introduce the symbol *Safe1* as a name for the concept of safe1 and the function *Combination* which takes a concept of a safe into a concept of its combination. The second operand of the function *knows* is now required to be a concept, and we can write

9) *knows(pat, Combination(Safe1))*

to assert that Pat knows the combination of safe1. The previous trouble is avoided so long as we can assert

10) *Combination(Safe1) ≠ Combination(Safe2),*

which is quite reasonable, since we do not consider the concept of the combination of *safe1* to be the same as the concept of the combination of *safe2*, even if the combinations themselves are the same.

We write

11) *denotes(Safe1, safe1)*

and say that *safe1* is the denotation of *Safe1*. We can say that Pegasus doesn't exist by writing

12) $\neg(\exists x)(denotes(Pegasus, x))$

still admitting *Pegasus* as a perfectly good concept. If we only admit concepts with denotations (or admit partial functions into our system), we can regard denotation as a function from concepts to objects - including other concepts. We can then write

13) *safe1 = den(Safe1).*

The functions *combination* and *Combination* are related in a way that we may call extensional, namely

14) $(\forall S)(combination(den(S)) = den(Combination(S)),$

and we can also write this relation in terms of *Combination* alone as

15) $(\forall S1\ S2)(den(S1) = den(S2) \supset den(Combination(S1)) = den(Combination(S2))),$

or, in terms of the denotation predicate,

16) $(\forall S1\ S2\ s\ c)(denotes(S1, s) \wedge denotes(S2, s) \wedge denotes(Combination(S1), c) \supset denotes(Combination(S2), c)).$

It is precisely this property of extensionality that the above-mentioned *knows* predicate lacks in its second argument; it is extensional in its first argument.

Suppose we now want to say *"Pat knows that Mike knows the combination of safe1"*. We cannot use *knows(mike, Combination(Safe1))* as an operand of another *knows* function for two reasons. First, the value of *knows(person, Concept)* is a truth value, and there are only two truth values, so we would either have Pat knowing all true statements or none. Second, English treats knowledge of propositions differently from the way it treats knowledge of the value of a term. To know a proposition is to know that it is true, whereas the analog of knowing a combination would be knowing whether the proposition is true.

We solve the first problem by introducing a new knowledge function *Knows(Personconcept, Concept)*. *Knows(Mike, Combination(Safe1))* is not a truth value but a *proposition*, and there can be distinct true propositions. We now need a predicate *true(proposition)*, so we can assert

17) *true(Knows(Mike, Combination(Safe1))*

which is equivalent to our old-style assertion

18) *knows(mike, Combination(Safe1)).*

We now write

19) *true(Knows(Pat, Knows(Mike, Combination(Safe1))))*

to assert that Pat knows *whether* Mike knows the combination of safe1. We define

20) $(\forall\ Person, Proposition)(K(Person, Proposition) = true(Proposition)\ and\ Knows(Person, Proposition)),$

which forms the proposition *that* a person knows a proposition from the truth of the proposition and that he knows whether the proposition holds. Note that it is necessary to have new connectives to combine propositions and that an equality sign rather than an equivalence sign is used. As far as our first order logic is concerned, (20) is an assertion of the equality of two terms. These matters are discussed thoroughly in (McCarthy 1977b).

While a concept denotes at most one object, the same object can be denoted by many concepts. Nevertheless, there are often useful functions from objects to concepts that denote them. Numbers may conveniently be regarded has having *standard concepts*, and an object may have a distinguished concept relative to a particular person. (McCarthy 1977b) illustrates the use of functions from objects to concepts in formalizing such chestnuts as Russell's, *"I thought your yacht was longer than it is"*.

The most immediate AI problem that requires concepts for its successful formalism may be the relation between knowledge and ability. We would like to connect Mike's ability to open safe1 with his knowledge of the combination. The proper formalization of the notion of *can* that involves knowledge rather than just physical possibility hasn't been done yet. Moore (1977) discusses the relation between knowledge and action from a similar point of view, and the final version of (McCarthy 1977b) will contain some ideas about this.

There are obviously some esthetic disadvantages to a theory that has both *mike* and *Mike*. Moreover, natural language doesn't make such distinctions in its vocabulary, but in rather roundabout ways when necessary. Perhaps we could manage with just *Mike* (the concept), since the *denotation* function will be available for referring to *mike* (the person himself). It makes some sentences longer, and we have to use and equivalence relation which we may call *eqdenot* and say *"Mike eqdenot Brother(Mary)"* rather than write *"mike = brother(mary)"*, reserving the equality sign for equal concepts. Since many AI programs don't make much use of replacement of equals by equals, their notation may admit either interpretation, i.e., the formulas may stand for either objects or concepts. The biggest objection is that the semantics of reasoning about objects is more complicated if one refers to them only via concepts.

I believe that circumscription will turn out to be the key to inferring non-knowledge. Unfortunately, an adequate formalism has not yet been developed, so we can only give some ideas of why establishing non-knowledge is important for AI and how circumscription can contribute to it.

If the robot can reason that it cannot open safe1, because it doesn't know the combination, it can decide that its next task is to find the combination. However, if it has merely failed to determine the combination by reasoning, more thinking might solve the problem. If it can safely conclude that the combination cannot be determined by reasoning, it can look for the information externally.

As another example, suppose someone asks you whether the President is standing, sitting or lying down at the moment you read the paper. Normally you will answer that you don't know and will not respond to a suggestion that you think harder. You conclude that no matter how hard you think, the information isn't to be found. If you really want to know, you must look for an external source of information. How do you know you can't solve the problem? The intuitive answer is that any answer is consistent with your other knowledge. However, you certainly don't construct a model of all your beliefs to establish this. Since you undoubtedly have some contradictory beliefs somewhere, you can't construct the required models anyway.

The process has two steps. The first is deciding what knowledge is relevant. This is a conjectural process, so its outcome is not guaranteed to be correct. It might be carried out by some kind of keyword retrieval from property lists, but there should be a less arbitrary method.

The second process uses the set of "relevant" sentences found by the first process and constructs models or circumscription predicates that allow for both outcomes if what is to be shown unknown is a proposition. If what is to be shown unknown has many possible values like a safe combination, then something more sophisticated is necessary. A parameter called the value of the combination is introduced, and a "model" or circumscription predicate is found in which this parameter occurs free. We used quotes, because a one parameter family of models is found rather than a single model.

We conclude with just one example of a circumscription schema dealing with knowledge. It is formalization of the assertion that all Mike knows is a consequence of propositions P and Q.

21) $$\Phi(P0) \wedge \Phi(Q0) \wedge (\forall P\ Q)(\Phi(P) \wedge \Phi(P\ implies\ Q) \supset \Phi(Q)) \supset (\forall P)(knows(Mike, P) \supset \Phi(P)).$$

Philosophical Notes

Philosophy has a more direct relation to artificial intelligence than it has to other sciences. Both subjects require the formalization of common sense knowledge and repair of its deficiencies. Since a robot with general intelligence requires some general view of the world, deficiencies in the programmers' introspection of their own world-views can result in operational weaknesses in the program. Thus many programs, including Winograd's SHRDLU, regard the history of their world as a sequence of situations each of which is produced by an event occuring in a previous situation of the sequence. To handle concurrent events, such programs must be rebuilt and not just provided with more facts.

This section is organized as a collection of disconnected remarks some of which have a direct technical character, while others concern the general structure of knowledge of the world. Some of them simply give sophisticated justifications for some things that programmers are inclined to do anyway, so some people may regard them as superfluous.

1. Building a view of the world into the structure of a program does not in itself give the program the ability to state the view explicitly. Thus, none of the programs that presuppose history as a sequence of situations can make the assertion "*History is a sequence of situations*". Indeed, for a human to make his presuppositions explicit is often beyond his individual capabilities, and the sciences of psychology and philosophy still have unsolved problems in doing so.

2. Common sense requires scientific formulation. Both AI and philosophy require it, and philosophy might even be regarded as an attempt to make common sense into a science.

3. AI and philosophy both suffer from the following dilemma. Both need precise formalizations, but the fundamental structure of the world has not yet been discovered, so imprecise and even inconsistent formulations need to be used. If the imprecision merely concerned the values to be given to numerical constants, there wouldn't be great difficulty, but there is a need to use theories which are grossly wrong in general within domains where they are valid. The above-mentioned *history-as-a-sequence-of-situations* is such a theory. The sense in which this theory is an approximation to a more sophisticated theory hasn't been examined.

4. (McCarthy 1977c) discusses the need to use concepts that are meaningful only in an approximate theory. Relative to a Cartesian product co-ordinatization of situations, counterfactual sentences of the form "*If co-ordinate x had the value c and the other co-ordinates retained their values, then p would be true*" can be meaningful. Thus, within a suitable theory, the assertion "*The skier wouldn't have fallen if he had put his weight on his downhill ski*" is meaningful and perhaps true, but it is hard to give it meaning as a statement about the world of atoms and wave functions, because it is not clear what different wave functions are specified by "*if he had put his weight on his downhill ski*". We need an AI formalism that can use such statements but can go beyond them to the next level of approximation when possible and necessary. I now think that circumscription is a tool that will allow drawing conclusions from a given approximate theory for use in given circumstances without a total commitment to the theory.

5. One can imagine constructing programs either as empiricists or as realists. An empiricist program would build only theories connecting its sense data with its actions. A realist program would try to find facts about a world that existed independently of the program and would not suppose that the only reality is what might somehow interact with the program.

I favor building realist programs with the following example in mind. It has been shown that the Life two dimensional cellular automaton is universal as a computer and as a constructor. Therefore, there could be configurations of Life cells acting as self-reproducing computers with sensory and motor capabilities with respect to the rest of the Life plane. The program in such a computer could study the physics of its world by making theories and experiments to test them and might eventually come up with the theory that its fundamental physics is that of the Life cellular automaton.

We can test our theories of epistemology and common sense reasoning by asking if they would permit the Life-world computer to conclude, on the basis of experiments, that its physics was that of Life. If our epistemology isn't adequate for such a simple universe, it surely isn't good enough for our much more complicated universe. This example is one of the reasons for preferring to build realist rather than empiricist programs. The empiricist program, if it was smart enough, would only end up with a statement that "*my experiences are best organized as if there were a Life cellular automaton and events isomorphic to my thoughts occurred in a certain subconfiguration of it*". Thus it would get a result equivalent to that of the realist program but more complicated and with less certainty.

More generally, we can imagine a *metaphilosophy* that has the same relation to philosophy that metamathematics has to mathematics. Metaphilosophy would study mathematical systems consisting of an "epistemologist" seeking knowledge in accordance with the epistemology to be tested and interacting with a "world". It would study what information about the world a given philosophy would obtain. This would depend also on the structure of the world and the "epistemologist"'s opportunities to interact.

AI could benefit from building some very simple systems of this kind, and so might philosophy.

References

McCarthy, J. and Hayes, P.J. (1969) Some Philosophical Problems from the Standpoint of Artificial Intelligence. *Machine Intelligence* 4, pp. 463-502 (eds Meltzer, B. and Michie, D.). Edinburgh: Edinburgh University Press.

McCarthy, J. (1977a) Minimal Inference - A New Way of Jumping to Conclusions (to be published).

McCarthy, J. (1977b) First Order Theories of Individual Concepts (to be published).

McCarthy, J. (1977c) Ascribing Mental Qualities to Machines (to be published).

Moore, Robert C. (1977) Reasoning about Knowledge and Action, 1977 *IJCAI Proceedings*.

WHAT'S WRONG WITH NON-MONOTONIC LOGIC?

David J. Israel

Bolt Beranek and Newman Inc.
50 Moulton St.
Cambridge, Mass. 02238

ABSTRACT

In this paper, I ask, and attempt to answer, the following question: What's Wrong with Non-Monotonic Logic? The answer, briefly, is that the motivation behind the wonderfully impressive work involved in its development is based on a confusion of proof-theoretic with epistemological issues.

- - - - - - - - - - - -

What's wrong with non-monotonic logic (and for that matter, with the logic of default reasoning)?*

The first question we should ask is: What's supposed to be wrong with "standard", monotonic logic? In recent - and extremely impressive - work, Doyle and McDermott [1], McDermott [2], and Reiter [3] have argued that classical logic - in virtue of its monotonicity - is incapable of adequately capturing or representing certain crucial features of real live reasoning and inference. In particular, they note that our knowledge is always incomplete, and is almost always known to be so; that, in pursuing our goals - both practical and theoretical - we are forced to make assumptions or to draw conclusions on the basis of incomplete evidence; conclusions and assumptions which we may have to withdraw in the light of either new evidence or further cogitation on what we already believe. An essential point here is that new evidence or new inference may lead us to reject previously held beliefs, especially those that we knew to be inadequately supported or merely presumptively assumed. In sum, our theories of the world are revisable; and thus our attitudes towards at least some our beliefs must likewise be revisable.

Now what has all this to do with logic and its monotonicity? Both Reiter and Doyle-McDermott characterize the monotonicity of standard logic in syntactic or proof-theoretic terms. If A and B are two theories, and A is a subset of B, then the theorems of A (the set of sentences p such that p is a syntactic consequence of A) is a subset of the theorems of B. (If one keeps in mind that in standard logical theory, a theory is identified with a set of sentences closed under syntactic consequence, that is with its theorems, one can see how unsurprising "syntactic monotonicity" is.) A slightly more interesting property is "semantic monotonicity", that is the monotonicity of the (functional) relation of semantic consequence or entailment. A set of sentences A entails a sentence p iff every model of A is a model of p; that is, iff every interpretation under which every sentence in A is true is an interpretation under which p is true also. If this relation holds for some A and some p, it holds between any set of sentences which properly includes A and that same p. Roughly speaking, embedding A in a larger set cannot alter the fact that if all the sentences in A were true, p would have to be true too. Thus Doyle and McDermott: "Monotonic logics lack the phenomenon of new information leading to a revision of old conclusions". [1]

To remedy this lack, Doyle and McDermott introduce into an otherwise standard first order language a modal operator "M" which, they say, is to be read as "It is consistent with everything that is believed that..." (Reiter's "M", which is not a symbol of the object language, is also supposed to be read "It is consistent to assume that..". I think there is some unclarity on Reiter's part about his "M". He speaks of it in ways conducive to interpreting it as a metalinguistic predicate on sentences of the object language; and hence not as an operator at all, either object-language or metalanguage. So his default rules are expressed in a language whose object-language contains sentences of the form "Mp", i.e., in a language which, relative to the original first-order object language, is a meta-meta-language.) Now in fact this reading isn't quite right.** The suggested reading doesn't capture the notion Doyle-McDermott and Reiter seem to have in mind. What they have in mind is, to put it non-linguistically (and hence, of course, non-syntactically): that property that a belief has just in case it is both compatible with everything a given subject believes at a given time and remains so when the subject's belief set undergoes certain kinds of changes under the pressure of both new information and further thought, and where those changes are the result of rational epistemic policies.

*The research reported in this paper was supported in part by the Advanced Research Projects Agency, and was monitored by ONR under Contract No. N00014-77-C-0378.

I've put the notion in this very epistemologically oriented way precisely to hone in on what I take to be the basic misconception underlying the work on non-monotonic logic and the logic of default reasoning. The researchers in question seem to believe that logic - deductive logic, for there is no other kind - is centrally and crucially involved in the fixation and revision of belief. Or to put it more poignantly, they mistake so-called deductive rules of inference for real, honest-to-goodness rules of inference. Real rules of inference are precisely rules of belief fixation and revision; deductive rules of transformation are precisely not. Consider that old favorite: modus (ponendo) ponens. It is not a rule that should be understood as enjoining us as follows: whenever you believe that p and believe that if p then q, then believe that q. This, after all, is one lousy policy. What if you have overwhelmingly good reasons for rejecting the belief that q? All logic tells you is that you had best reconsider your belief that p and/or your belief that if p then q (or, to be fair, your previously settled beliefs on the basis of which you were convinced that not-q); it is perforce silent on how to revise your set of beliefs so as to .. to what? Surely, to come up with a good theory that fits the evidence, is coherent, simple, of general applicability, reliable, fruitful of further testable hypotheses, etc. Nor is it the case that if one is justified in believing that p and justified in believing that if p then q (or even justified in believing that p entails q), is one justified in believing (inferring) that q. Unless, of course, one has no other relevant beliefs. But one always does.

The rule of modus ponens is, first and foremost, a rule that permits one to perform certain kinds of syntactical transformations on (sets of) formally characterized syntactic entities. (Actually, first and foremost, it is not really a rule at all; it is "really" just a two-place relation between on the one hand an ordered pair of wffs., and on the other, a wff.) It is an important fact about it that, relative to any one of a family of interpretations of the conditional, the rule is provably sound, that is truth (in an interpretation)-preserving. The crucial point here, though, is that adherence to a set of deductive rules of transformation is not a sufficient condition for rational belief; it is sufficient (and necessary) only for producing derivations in some formal system or other. Real rules of inference are rules (better: policies) guiding belief fixation and revision. Indeed, if one is sufficiently simple-minded, one can even substitute for the phrase "good rules of inference", the phrase "(rules of) scientific procedure" or even "scientific method". And, of course, there is no clear sense to the phrase "good rules of transformation". (Unless "good" here means "complete" - but with respect to what? Truth?)

Given this conception of the problem to which Doyle-McDermott and Reiter are addressing themselves, certain of the strange properties of, on the one hand, non-monotonic logic and on the other, the logic of default reasoning, are only to be expected. In particular, the fact that the proof relation is not in general decidable. The way the "M" operator is understood, we believers are represented as follows: to make an assumption that p or to put forth a presumption that p is to believe a proposition to the effect that p is consistent with everything that is presently believed and that it will remain so even as my beliefs undergo certain kinds of revisions. And in general we can prove that p only if we can prove at least that p is consistent with everything we now believe. But, of course, by Church's theorem there is no uniform decision procedure for settling the question of the consistency of a set of first-order formulae. (Never mind that the problem of determining the consistency of arbitrary sets of formulae of the sentential calculus is NP-complete.) This is surely wrong-headed: assumptions or hypotheses or presumptions are not propositions we accept only after deciding that they are compatible with everything else we believe, not to speak of having to establish that they won't be discredited by future evidence or further reasoning. When we assume p, it is just p that we assume, not some complicated proposition about the semantic relations in which it stands to all our other beliefs, and certainly not some complicated belief about the syntactic relations any one of its linguistic expressions has to the sentences which express all those other beliefs. (Indeed, there is a problem with respect to the consistency requirement, especially if we allow beliefs about beliefs. Surely, any rational subject will believe that s/he has some false beliefs, or more to the point, any such subject will be disposed to accept that belief upon reflection. By doing so, however, the subject guarantees itself an inconsistent belief-set; there is no possible interpretation under which all of its beliefs are true. Should this fact by itself worry it (or us?).)

After Reiter has proved that the problem of determining whether an arbitrary sentence is in an extension for a given default theory is undecidable, he comments:

**Nor is it quite clear. By "consistent" are we to mean syntactically consistent in the standard monotonic sense of syntactic derivability or in the to-be-explicated non-monotonic sense? Or is it semantic consistency of one brand or another that is in question? This unclarity is fairly quickly remedied. We are to understand by "consistency" standard syntactic consistency, which in standard systems can be understood either as follows: A theory is syntactically consistent iff there is no formula p of its language such that both p and its negation are theorems, or as follows: iff there is at least one sentence of its language which is not a theorem. There are otherwise standard, that is, monotonic, systems for which the equivalence of these two notions does not hold; and note that the first applies only to a theory whose language includes a negation operator.

> (A)ny proof theory whatever for... default theories must somehow appeal to some inherently non semi-decidable process. [That is, the proof-relation, not just the proof predicate, is non recursive; the proofs, not just the theorems, are not recursively enumerable. Why such a beast is to be called a logic is somewhat beyond me - DI.] This extremely pessimistic result forces the conclusion that any computational treatment of defaults must necessarily have an heuristic component and will, on occasion, lead to mistaken beliefs. Given the faulty nature of human common sense reasoning, this is perhaps the best one could hope for in any event.

Now once again substitute in the above "(scientific or common sense) reasoning" for "default(s)" and then reflect on how odd it is to think that there could be a purely proof-theoretic treatment of scientific reasoning. A heuristic treatment, that is a treatment in terms of rational epistemic policies, is not just the best we could hope for. It is the only thing that makes sense. (Of course, if we are very fortunate, we may be able to develop a "syntactic" encoding of these policies; but we certainly mustn't expect to come up with rules for rational belief fixation that are actually provably truth-preserving. Once again, the only thing that makes sense is to hope to formulate a set of rules which, from within our current theory of the world and of ourselves as both objects within and inquirers about that world, can be argued to embody rational policies for extending our admittedly imperfect grasp of things.)

Inference (reasoning) is non-monotonic: New information (evidence) and further reasoning on old beliefs (including, but by no means limited to, reasoning about the semantic relationships - e.g., of entailment - among beliefs) can and does lead to the revision of our theories and, of course, to revision by "subtraction" as well as by "addition". Entailment and derivability are monotonic. That is, logic - the logic we have, know, and - if we understand its place in the scheme of things - have every reason to love, is monotonic.

BRIEF POSTSCRIPT

I've been told that the tone of this paper is overly critical; or rather, that it lacks constructive content. A brief postscript is not the appropriate locus for correcting this defect; but it may be an appropriate place for casting my vote for a suggestion made by John McCarthy. In his "Epistemological Problems of Artificial Intelligence" [4], McCarthy characterizes the epistemological part of "the AI problem" as follows: "(it) studies what kinds of facts about the world are available to an observer with given opportunities to observe, how these facts can be represented in the memory of a computer, and what rules permit legitimate conclusions to be drawn from these facts." [Emphasis added.] This, though brief, is just about right, except for a perhaps studied ambiguity in that final clause. Are the conclusions legitimate because they are entailed by the facts? (Are the rules provably sound rules of transformation?) Or are the conclusions legitimate because they constitute essential (non-redundant) parts of the best of the competing explanatory accounts of the original data; the best by our own, no doubt somewhat dim, lights? (Are the rules arguably rules of rational acceptance?) At the conclusion of his paper, McCarthy disambiguates and opts for the right reading. In the context of an imaginative discussion of the Game of Life cellular automaton, he notes that "the program in such a computer could study the physics of its world by making theories and experiments to test them and might eventually come up with the theory that its fundamental physics is that of the Life cellular automaton. We can test our theories of epistemology and common sense reasoning by asking if they would permit the Life-world computer to conclude, on the basis of its experiments, that its physics was that of Life." McCarthy continues:

> More generally, we can imagine a metaphilosophy that has the same relation to philosophy that metamathematics has to mathematics. Metaphilosophy would study mathematical (? - D.I.) systems consisting of an "epistemologist" seeking knowledge in accordance with the epistemology to be tested and interacting with a "world". It would study what information about the world a given philosophy would obtain. This would depend also on the structure of the world and the "epistemologist's" opportunities to interact. AI could benefit from building some very simple systems of this kind, and so might philosophy.

Amen; but might I note that such a metaphilosophy does exist. Do some substituting again: for "philosophy" (except in its last occurrence), substitute "science"; for "epistemologist", "scientist"; for "epistemology", either "philosophy of science" or "scientific methodology". The moral is, I hope, clear. Here is my constructive proposal: AI researchers interested in "the epistemological problem" should look, neither to formal semantics nor to proof-theory; but to - of all things - the philosophy of science and epistemology.

REFERENCES

[1] McDermott, D., Doyle, J. "Non-Monotonic Logic I", AI Memo 486, MIT Artificial Intelligence Laboratory, Cambridge, Mass., August 1978.

[2] McDermott, D. "Non-Monotonic Logic II", Research Report 174, Yale University Department of Computer Science, New Haven, Conn., February 1980.

[3] Reiter, R. "A Logic for Default Reasoning", Technical Report 79-8, University of British Columbia Department of Computer Science, Vancouver, B.C., July 1979.

[4] McCarthy, J. "Epistemological Problems of Artificial Intelligence", In Proc. IJCAI-77. Cambridge, Mass., August, 1977, pp. 1038-1044.

On the consistency of commonsense reasoning

DONALD PERLIS
University of Maryland, Department of Computer Science, College Park, MD 20742, U.S.A.

Received March 14, 1986
Revision accepted August 25, 1986

Default reasoning is analyzed as consisting (implicitly) of at least three further aspects—oracles, jumps, and fixes—which in turn are related to the notion of a belief. Beliefs are then discussed in terms of their use in a reasoning agent. Next an idea of Israel is embellished to show that certain desiderata regarding these aspects of default reasoning lead to inconsistent belief sets, and that as a consequence the handling of inconsistencies must be taken as central to commonsense reasoning. Finally, these results are applied to standard cases of default reasoning formalisms in the literature (circumscription, default logic, and nonmonotonic logic), where it turns out that even weaker hypotheses lead to failure to achieve commonsense default conclusions.

Key words: beliefs, consistency, introspection, knowledge representation, defaults, circumscription, nonmonotonic logic, commonsense reasoning, ornithology.

Le raisonnement par défaut est analysé comme consistant (implicitement) de trois autres aspects que nous appelons oracles, sauts et fixations, qui sont à leur tour reliés à la notion de croyance. Nous discutons ensuite des croyances en fonction de leur utilisation par un agent qui raisonne. Puis nous relevons une idée de David Israel pour montrer que certains desiderata concernants ces aspects du raisonnement par défaut conduisent à des ensembles inconsistants de croyances et que par conséquent le traitement des inconsistances doit être considéré comme central dans le raisonnement de sens commun. Enfin ces résultats sont appliqués à des cas standards de formalismes de raisonnement par défaut que l'on retrouve dans la littérature (circonscription, logique par défaut, logique non monotone), où il apparaît que même des hypothèses plus faibles ne permettent pas d'obtenir des conclusions de défaut selon le sens commun.

Mots clés: croyances, consistance, introspection, représentation de connaissances, défauts, circonscription, logique non monotone, raisonnement de sens commun.

[Traduit par la revue]

Comput. Intell. 2, 180–190 (1986)

1. Introduction

Much of the present paper will focus on default reasoning. We will primarily consider a stylized form of default reasoning that appears to be current in the literature, and try to isolate aspects of this stylization that need modification if deeper modelling of commonsense reasoning is to succeed. Specifically, we will show that default reasoning, as has been studied in particular by McCarthy (1980, 1986), McDermott and Doyle (1980), and Reiter (1980) in their respective formalisms (circumscription, nonmonotonic logic, and default logic), will lead to inconsistency under rather natural conditions that we call *Socratic* and *recollective* reasoning. Roughly, a Socratic reasoner is one that believes its default conclusions in general to be error-prone, and a recollective reasoner is one that can recall at least certain kinds of its previous default conclusions. We will show that the standard approaches, based on what we term *jumps* (as in *jumping to a conclusion*), are inconsistent with these desiderata.[1]

This is not to say that research into these formalisms has been misguided, or that their authors have assumed that they were adequate for all contexts. On the contrary, these studies have been essential first steps into an area of high complexity demanding a "spiralling" approach of more and more realistic settings. Here then we hope to show one further stage of development that is called for. In fact, elsewhere (Drapkin *et al.* 1986) we have argued that inconsistency is a somewhat normal state of affairs in commonsense reasoning, and that mechanisms are needed for reasoning effectively in the presence of inconsistency.

Note that there are at least two general frameworks in which such formal studies can proceed: We can seek a specification of formal relations that might hold between axioms and inferences in a supposed default reasoner (the "spec" approach), or we can seek to identify specific actions that constitute the process of drawing default conclusions (the "process" approach). That these are related is no surprise. In effect, the first is a more abstract study of the second, aimed at providing a characterization of what sort of things we are talking about in our study of defaults. However, there is a hidden further difference, namely that in pursuing the former, one is naturally led to consider idealized situations in which features irrelevant to the particular phenomenon at hand are deliberately left out of consideration. Such an approach has been customary in research in commonsense reasoning, most conspicuously in the assumption of logical omniscience: that an agent knows (and even instantly) all logical consequences of its beliefs, generally regarded as part of the notion of epistemological adequacy. That is, although no one believes that agents *actually* can reason this way, it has seemed to be a convenient test-bed for ideas about what reasoning is *like*, apart from the "noise" of the real world.

While this has come under criticism lately, and while authors of default formalisms acknowledge the importance *to their very topic* of the process nature of defaults,[2] still the latter has remained conspicuously absent from the continuing development of such formalisms. Here we argue that the very essence of

[1]"Jumping to conclusion can lead to unpleasant landing." Chinese fortune cookie, 1986.

[2]At least regarding their context of an overall process of reasoning going on over time within a changing environment of inputs. For example, McDermott and Doyle (1980, p. 41) speak of "... modelling the beliefs of active processes which, acting in the presence of incomplete information, must make and subsequently revise assumptions in light of new observations." Reiter (1980, p. 86) mentions "... the need for some kind of mechanism for *revising beliefs* [his emphasis] in the presence of new information. What this amounts to is the need to record, with each derived belief, the default assumptions made in deriving that belief. Should subsequent observations invalidate the default assumptions supporting some belief, then it must be removed from the data base."

default reasoning, and of commonsense reasoning in general, derives from its being embedded in the real world, and in agents evolved to deal with such by means of an appropriately introspective view of their own fallibility and corrigibility over time. This in turn will be seen to pose problems for logical omniscience. We refer to the "spec" view of an ideal thinker, which we are critiquing, as that of an "omnithinker" (or OT for short).

To facilitate this discussion, we first present an extended illustration of default reasoning along lines found in the literature. Reasoning by default involves reaching a conclusion C on the basis of lack of information that might rule out C.[3] For example, given that Tweety is a bird and no more, one might, if prompted, conclude (at least tentatively) that Tweety can fly.[4] Here C is the statement that Tweety can fly. Such a conclusion may be appropriate when "typical" elements of a given category (in this case, birds) have the property under consideration (ability to fly).

In the bird example, additional information, such as that Tweety is an ostrich or that Tweety has a broken wing, should block the conclusion that Tweety can fly. Just how it is to be determined that the conclusion is or is not to be blocked is still a matter of debate. Nonetheless, we can usefully discuss the phenomenon of default reasoning in the form of a sequence of steps in a suitable formal deduction as follows: We simply list the "beliefs" that a reasoning agent may consider in drawing the default conclusion. This will be done first in a very sparse form, and then in a more amplified form. The following list is intended to be in temporal order as our reasoner "thinks" first one thought (belief) and then another. Step (2) is the usual default conclusion, given belief (1), and steps (3) and (4) illustrate the apparent nonmonotonicity in which additional data (3) can seemingly block or contradict an earlier conclusion.

(1) Bird(Tweety) [this simply comes to mind, or is told to the agent]
(2) Flies(Tweety) [this "default" comes to mind, perhaps prompted by a question]
(3) Ostrich(Tweety) [observed, remembered, or told to the agent]
(4) ¬Flies(Tweety) [this comes to mind]

Now, the above sketch of reasoning steps ignores several crucial points. In particular, the direct passage from (1) to (2) obscures several possible underlying events,[5] namely, (a) a recognition that it is not known that Tweety cannot fly (i.e., Tweety is not known to be atypical regarding flying), (b) an axiom to the effect that flying is indeed typical for birds (so that if a bird can be consistently assumed typical, it is likely that it can fly, and therefore a reasonable tentative assumption), and (c) the willingness to go ahead and use the tentative assumption as if it were true.[6]

Similarly, the passage from (3) to (4) obscures the necessary information that ostriches cannot fly. Finally, (4) leaves unsaid the implicit conclusions that (a) Tweety must be atypical and (b) the assertion that Tweety can fly is to be suppressed. The following sequence illustrates this more explicit description.[7] Certain of the new steps have been labelled with the terms *oracle*, *jump*, and *fix*. For the moment, we limit ourselves to the following brief remarks (later we will elaborate on them). Oracles are what make default reasoning computationally difficult and also what make it nonmonotonic; jumps are what make it shaky (unsound); and fixes keep it stable. Only the work of McCarthy (1980, 1986) has seriously addressed the oracle problem; McDermott and Doyle (1980) and to some extent Reiter (1980) have characterized jumps; and Doyle (1979) has the only work on fixes.

(1) Bird(Tweety) [axiom]
(1*a*) Unknown(¬Flies(Tweety)) [oracle]
(1*b*) Unknown(¬Flies(x)) & Bird(x) .→ Tentative(Flies(x)) [default]
(1*c*) Tentative(Flies(x)) → Flies(x) [jump]
(2) Flies(Tweety) [consequence of 1, 1*a*, 1*b*, 1*c*]
(3) Ostrich(Tweety) [new axiom]
(3*a*) Ostrich(x) → ¬Flies(x) [axiom]
(4) ¬Flies(Tweety) [consequence of 3, 3*a*]
(4*a*) Flies(x) & ¬Flies(x) .→. Suppress(Flies(x)) & Atypical(x) [fix]
(4*b*) Atypical(Tweety) [consequence of 2, 4, 4*a*]
(4*c*) Suppress(Flies(Tweety)) [consequence of 2, 4, 4*a*]

To restate quickly (and a bit oversimply) our aims in this paper, we will argue that any mechanism for default reasoning that utilizes jumps will be inconsistent if it also is Socratic (believes it can make mistakes) and recollective (recalls its past conclusions). Moreover, the above expanded scenario with fixes strongly suggests the need for precisely these kinds of additional features (Socratic and recollective).

It is now time to turn to an extended look at the nature of beliefs, since the cursory treatment of defaults above should make clear that beliefs are the stuff that defaults are made of, and that if we do not know what beliefs are, at least in rough form, then we will remain in the dark about defaults as well. More specifically, addressing the issue of *consistency* of an agent's set of beliefs makes it essential to decide, at least informally, what counts as a belief.

2. A preliminary analysis of beliefs

Much AI literature purports to be about the beliefs of reasoning agents, e.g., Moore (1977), Perlis (1981), and Konolige (1984). Yet little in this literature has been said as to what actually makes something a belief.[8] While it is acknowledged that the ontological character of beliefs is unclear, and that at least two approaches are worth considering (the syntactic and the propositional), not much attention has been given to the issue of what distinguishes a statement or proposition that is a belief from one that is not. Agents are endowed with a fairly arbitrary set *Bel*, subject perhaps to the requirements of being

[3]Doyle (1983, 1985) has presented interesting views on this phenomenon, relating it to group decision making.

[4]Tentativity is the obvious key, which all default formalisms are designed to capture, as opposed to other more robust kinds of inferences. And it is this that our analysis will focus on most.

[5]Here emphasis is placed on "possible." It is not claimed that these events must occur; but we will argue that for certain commonsense situations they are appropriate.

[6]Note that Nutter (1982, 1983*a*) in effect cautions against careless use of this latter step. To an extent the present paper can be construed as illustrating how badly things can go wrong if Nutter's warning goes unheeded.

[7]Here we are relaxing the "spec" approach a bit; but still it fits the philosophy for an omnithinker: no claims are being made regarding actual implementations, and the new sequence corresponds to technical features of the three standard formalisms, as will be pointed out later. Thus we have a kind of meta-example of the spec approach.

[8]Among philosophers, Dennett (1978) and Harman (1973, 1986) have studied this question in ways congenial to our approach.

internally consistent and deductively closed, and that is that. It is as if any statement whatever may count as a belief. For our purposes, this is insufficient; therefore we shall spend some time discussing this matter, and especially how it relates to the issues of consistency and tentativity in commonsense reasoning.

In everyday language, the word "believe" is used in several rather different ways. For instance, one might hear any of the following statements: "I believe you are right," "I believe Canada and Mexico are the only countries bordering the United States," "I believe this is the greatest country in the world," and "I believe gravity causes things to fall." These seem not to employ the same sense of the word "believe." Moreover, "two plus two equals four" can be regarded as a statement believed by whoever asserts it, and yet "I believe two plus two equals four" seems to convey a sense of less assurance than the bald assertion of the believed statement without the self-conscious attention to the fact that it is believed. An especially thorny aspect of this is that even when the statement of belief seems unambiguous, what is it that makes it true (or false)? That is, I may claim to believe x, but how do I mean this? That x is "in my head" seems both the obvious answer and yet completely misguided, for many things can be in my head without my believing them. That $2+2=5$ is surely in my head now as I write it, yet as something I *don't* believe. So it is a special "mark" of belief that makes certain things in the head beliefs. What "mark" is this, and what has it to do with reasoning?

We need then a definition of beliefs, so that we can make precise claims and attempt to defend them. Unfortunately, a precise definition will not be forthcoming here; it is a subject of considerable difficulty. However, a tentative but useful answer may be as follows: Certain things in the head (or within a reasoning system) may be *used in reasoning* as steps in drawing conclusions as to plans of action; let us call these *use-beliefs*. In effect, use-beliefs are simply potential steps in proofs of plans. (Note that these must be *genuine* steps, not convenient hypotheses, as in a natural deduction case argument, which later are discharged. That is, any such step must itself be a possible terminal step, i.e., a theorem.) Such entities would seem to form an interesting class of objects, relevant to the topic of commonsense reasoning. It is not offered as a matter of contention or empirical verification, but rather as an aspect of reasoning worth study. The main issue we wish to address then is the mutual consistency of use-beliefs in a commonsense reasoning system. For somewhat greater definiteness, we codify our "definition" below:

Definition

α is *(use-)believed* by agent g, if g is willing to use α as a step in reasoning when drawing conclusions as to plans of action.[9]

Whether an assertion A is to be a use-belief may depend on the context in which it is to be used. Thus in some contexts one and the same assertion "I believe X" may correspond to the presence of a belief X in our sense, and in another not, depending on the speaker's willingness to use X in planning and acting. Roughly speaking, the word "belief" will be used to refer to any strong notion that the agent is willing to trust, and does trust and use in planning and acting, "as if it were true." Now, this is not without its murky aspects. Many assertions can be sincerely doubted and sincerely taken as plausible at the same time (see Nutter (1982, 1983*a,b*) for a well-argued point of view on this). Instead of attempting to provide a foolproof analysis of beliefs by defining precisely the words "willing," "conclusion," "plan," etc. in the above definition, we will rely on examples.

Consider the following: That my car is still where I last parked it seems very likely, and I may well behave as if I regarded this to be the case, and yet I also recognize it is merely highly probable. Our proposal is to take such a statement to be a belief *if* I am prepared to use it as if it is true, and not otherwise. That is, if I regard it as highly probable but also hedge my bets by checking to see whether a bus will pass by in case the car is missing, then I do not have the belief that my car is where I last parked it; rather I may have the belief that *the probability is high* that my car is where I last parked it. However, if I ignore the possibility that my car may not be where I last parked it and *base my actions* on the assumption that it is still there, then even though I may admit that I am not certain where it is, I have the belief that it is where I last parked it. That is, we are defining the word "belief" in this manner (which incidentally seems consistent with one fairly common usage: one might very well say, "I realize my car may somehow have moved, but I nonetheless believe it has not").

Another example illustrating the difficulties in pinning down use-beliefs is the following (due to Michael Miller): Individual X believes (or so we wish to say) that smoking is dangerous to one's health, yet X does not give up smoking. Can we fairly say X is using that "belief" in planning and acting? I think that the answer is yes, but in a qualified sense. X will make use of Dangerous(smoking) as a fact to reason with, but this need not mean going along with (putting into action) the conclusion that X "should" give up smoking. (Compare Newell's principle of rationality (Newell 1981) in which "action P causes Q" and "Want Q" lead to "Do P.") What we need to do is to create (perhaps only as a thought experiment) a "neutral" or *ceteris paribus* ("other things being equal") situation in which X's actions can be supposed to be influenced only by the relevant "beliefs" we are testing. We are not in any way taking the view that X's behavior is determined only by a set of formulas in X's head (rather than by, say, stubbornness or competing concerns).

In other words, there may be many competing use-beliefs in one agent; this is not to be construed as all of them leading independently to given actions. Only in rarefied circumstances will this be the case. For instance, we may imagine a situation in which the belief that smoking is unhealthy would lead to a direct action in the given agent. For instance, if the agent's 12-year-old niece wishes to begin smoking, and if the agent is very concerned about her health, and if the agent lives thousands of miles away and would derive no comfort from another smoker in the family, and so on, *then* the given belief will lead to action to discourage the niece from smoking. Of course, the trick here is the "and so on." The definition then serves a purpose in being suggestive rather than definitive. What we need is a far deeper understanding of "what is in the head," perhaps something along the lines of Levesque's[10] notion of "vividness."

Are there situations where a more definitive kind of belief is available? Perhaps in the realm of scientific law, one can have beliefs that are held to be certain. It is worth exploring further examples. For instance, a belief in the actuality of gravity. As a physical theory, this is well supported, and yet most physicists

[9]An anonymous referee suggested the friendly amendment: "agent A believes that p in case, if A desires e, A is disposed to act in a way that will produce e given that p is true." I regard this as in the spirit I am aiming for; however, see below on *ceteris paribus* conditions.

[10]Levesque, H. 1985. Ninth International Joint Conference on Artificial Intelligence, Los Angeles, CA. Unpublished address.

reasoning and analyze it more carefully. The expanded sequence of steps given in Sect. 1 was as follows:

(1) Bird(Tweety) [axiom]
(1*a*) Unknown(¬Flies(Tweety)) [oracle]
(1*b*) Unknown(¬Flies(*x*)) & Bird(*x*) .→ Tentative(Flies(*x*)) [default]
(1*c*) Tentative(Flies(*x*)) → Flies(*x*) [jump]
(2) Flies(Tweety) [consequence of 1, 1*a*, 1*b*, 1*c*]
(3) Ostrich(Tweety) [new axiom]
(3*a*) Ostrich(*x*) → ¬Flies(*x*) [axiom]
(4) ¬Flies(Tweety) [consequence of 3, 3*a*]
(4*a*) Flies(*x*) & ¬Flies(*x*) .→. Suppress(Flies(*x*)) & Atypical(*x*) [fix]
(4*b*) Atypical(Tweety) [consequence of 2, 4, 4*a*]
(4*c*) Suppress(Flies(Tweety)) [consequence of 2, 4, 4*a*]

The fact that *in order to take advantage of the absence of information to the contrary, that absence must be recognized*[13] is codified in step (1*a*). This recognition in general is not decidable,[14] and so appeal is made to an outside source of wisdom, an "oracle," which tells us that a given proposition (e.g., Flies(Tweety)) is consistent with what we know. In the nonmonotonic logic (NML) of McDermott and Doyle (1980) and the default logic (DL) of Reiter (1980), such an oracle is explicitly represented, although in significantly different ways: NML presents an axiom including a modal operator M (for consistency), whereas DL uses M as a meta-symbol in a rule of inference. In McCarthy's circumscriptive logic (CL), a "weak" oracle appears in the form of the circumscriptive axiomatization itself, which is a source of both advantage and disadvantage: it is computationally more tractable and less prone than NML to suffer inconsistency of certain sorts (as we will see later), but also fails to recognize certain typical situations for the same reason.

Note that (1*b*) and (1*c*) are combined into a single default axiom or rule in NML and DL. We have drawn out the presumed underlying notions to focus attention on (1*c*) in particular—the *jump*. That is, up to that point, the reasoning is fairly clearcut; but at the jump, something that is only tentative is treated as if it were outright true. Herein is the source of the familiar unsoundness of nonmonotonic forms of reasoning. The agent whose reasoning is being stylized in the above sequence has jumped to a (firm) conclusion, albeit with plausible grounds to do so; but in the very jump is the possibility of error. This can be regarded as the point at which tentative conclusions are elevated into use-beliefs. However, the earlier discussion of use-beliefs indicates that even tentative beliefs (unelevated into "truths") can be use-beliefs.

In step (4*a*) recognition is made of the fact that an earlier conclusion has been contradicted and that the situation must be fixed. Actually, much more than what has been recorded in (4*a*) is necessary to thoroughly deal with the clash, but for now we will leave it as that.

We then arrive at the following preliminary characterization of default reasoning: it is a sequence of steps involving, in its most general form, oracles, jumps, and fixes. That is, it is error-prone reasoning owing to convenient but unsound guesses (jumps), in which therefore fixes are necessary to preserve (or re-establish) consistency, and which makes the mentioned guesses by means of appeals to undecidable properties (oracles). We will make use of this characterization in what follows. The general thrust of our line of argument will be that contradictions (such as between Flies and ¬Flies) generate the need for fixes, and that both then are necessary for the evolution of self-reflective reasoning. That is, we claim that a kind of temporary inconsistency pervades commonsense reasoning, and is one of its principal drivers.

[13]This is not to say that such recognition need be conscious, but merely that some mechanism or other must perform it.

[14]By *any* deterministic mechanism, of a logical stripe or not.

4. Israel's argument

Israel (1980) offers an argument for the inconsistency of commonsense reasoning. Recall that we use the intials "OT" to stand for "omnithinker," i.e., an idealized reasoning agent that is intended to be able to carry out an appropriate form of default reasoning and other desiderata as will be specified later. Israel begins by stating that OT will have some false beliefs and will have reason to believe that is the case, i.e., OT will believe what we shall designate as *Israel's sentence, IS*:

$$(\exists x)[\mathrm{Bel}(x)\ \&\ \mathrm{False}(x)]$$

where Bel refers in the intended interpretation to the very set of OT's beliefs, i.e., Bel(*x*) means that *x* is a belief of OT. (Note that *IS*, if it is to be a belief itself, requires that beliefs be representable as terms, e.g., quoted wffs, and that a certain amount of self-reference is then at least implicit in whatever language is used.)

Now, if *IS* is true in the intended interpretation, it follows that OT has a belief that is not true, namely, one of the *other* beliefs. On the other hand, if all the other beliefs are true in the intended interpretation, then *IS* is paradoxical in the sense that, in this interpretation, it is equivalent to its own denial. However, this does not force OT's belief set to be inconsistent, for the intended interpretation is not the only possible one. Moreover, *IS* may well be true there, i.e., other beliefs of OT may be false, and indeed this is the much more likely situation, and apparently the one Israel has in mind.

One might think (and Israel suggests) that even when *IS* is true, more is forthcoming, namely that since OT believes all OT's beliefs (i.e., OT believes them to be true) and yet also believes one of them not to be true, then OT believes contradictory statements and therefore has an inconsistent set of beliefs. However, for interesting reasons, this does not follow. The hitch is in the necessity of pinning down all OT's beliefs (or at least a suitable subset containing the supposedly false belief). That is, the phrases "all OT's beliefs" and "one of them not to be true" do not refer directly, in OT's asserting them, to the same things.

For example, suppose OT has three beliefs: α, β, and *IS*, and let us further suppose α is false. To follow the above suggestion for deriving a contradiction, we would like to argue as follows. OT believes one of α, β, and *IS* to be false: ¬(α & β & *IS*). Also OT believes α and β and *IS*, hence believes (α & β & *IS*). But these are contradictory. However, this argument makes exactly the oracle fallacy that many (including Israel) have inveighed against. For OT to conclude False(α & β & *IS*) from *IS* (i.e., from (∃*x*)[Bel(*x*) & False(*x*)]), OT must believe, in addition to α, β, and *IS*, that these are OT's only beliefs. But this would be another belief! Of course, a clever encoding of α might allow it to state that it itself along with β and *IS* are OT's only beliefs, thereby avoiding the trouble of an extra belief unaccounted for. (Alternatively, OT may mistakenly believe the aforementioned three to be its only beliefs.) But this does not resolve the difficulty at hand, for it is not plausible to argue in will likely say that any theory of gravity is after all only an approximation that will almost surely be replaced by a better theory in the future, and indeed perhaps a theory in which gravity as such does not figure at all. Now, gravity may become a derived notion in such a future theory, but then it plays the role of naming a class of macroscopic phenomena such as "when I release a cup I have been holding, it will drop." But in what way is this a belief? Surely in the same sense as any everyday claim. That is, we expect the cup to drop, but do not regard it as absolutely beyond question. It may stick to our fingers, someone may catch it, a gust of wind may carry it upwards, and so on. If we try to eliminate "extraneous" factors such as these, we simply end up with the familiar qualification problem. It is not clear that any assertions of a general nature having practical consequences can be stated with certainty outside the realm of basic science where extraneous factors can be stipulated in full (at least relative to the theory one is using), and this lies far outside the realm of commonsense reasoning. Moreover, even in basic science, as we have illustrated, the so-called laws are usually taken to be tentative.

We can envision someone saying, "I definitely believe this cup will fall when I release my hold on it." And yet that same person will certainly grant our exceptional cases above, perhaps however protesting that these aren't what he or she had in mind. But that's just the point of the frame problem: We do not, and cannot, have in mind all the appropriate qualifications. We take the statement as asserted (the cup will fall when released) to be (or represent) the belief. Perhaps such thinking is more in the form of visual imagery than explicit statements to oneself, and perhaps visual imagery allows a certain loose notion of generic situations appropriate to commonsense reasoning. Be that as it may, people are often willing to assert boldly, even when questioned, that they believe such-and-such, and yet afterwards will agree that it is not so certain after all.

However, the "bare" unqualified assertions in Bel, by their definition as use-beliefs, are in fact significant as elements of thought, and it is also significant whether two or more elements of Bel conflict *in and of themselves*. To illustrate this, consider Reiter and Criscuolo's (1983) example of interacting defaults for Quakers and Republicans. Quakers (typically) are pacifists; Republicans (typically) are not. Nixon is a Quaker and a Republican. One might then tentatively conclude that Nixon is a pacifist, and also that he is not. Now, there is a sense in which this is quite reasonable: It does appear appropriate to consider that, on the one hand, Nixon might very well be a pacifist since he is a Quaker and, on the other hand, he might very well not be a pacifist since he is a Republican. That is, speculation about the origins and influences on this status regarding pacifism may be of interest for a given concern.

However, it will not do to entertain both that he is and that he is not a pacifist in one and the same planned sequence of actions. If one is using the assumption that Nixon is a pacifist, then one is not simultaneously willing to use the assumption that he is not a pacifist. That is, even though the expanded statements—that there is some evidence that Nixon might be a pacifist and some evidence that he might not—are not contradictory, nonetheless one would not be willing to assume, even for the sake of a very tentative kind of planning, that he both is and is not a pacifist. Moreover, if probabilities are used so that, let us suppose, Quakers have a 99% chance of being pacifists and Republicans a 90% chance of not being pacifists, then the recognition that these should not both be used separately to form tentative conclusions as to Nixon's pacifism depends on noting that such unexpanded conclusions—Nixon is a pacifist and Nixon is not a pacifist—indeed do conflict.

Consider again the released cup that may or may not fall. The speaker who claimed it would fall may enact a plan to cause the cup to fall, by releasing the cup. But if there is honey on the edge of the cup so that when released it remains stuck to the fingers, this plan will not be effective. However, when the honey is pointed out, thereby creating a belief that the cup will not fall when released, the direct contradiction with the earlier claim becomes important for the correct forming of a new plan. Now one must remove the honey or use more force in separating the cup from fingers, etc. However, if the original claim were to be qualified so that it accounted for the possible presence of honey, then the original plan of releasing the cup is not so easily accounted for. The point is that we do try to keep our unexpanded (use-)beliefs consistent, even though we may recognize that they are not strictly justified. A plan involves a package of tentative beliefs which are intended to be internally consistent, so that they can be enacted. Thus even if the planning agent may not firmly believe, say, the cup will definitely fall when released, still, his willingness to act as if he so believed appears to mandate his *not* believing, even tentatively, that the cup will also *rise* when released.

The point we are illustrating is that we usually do not tolerate direct[11] contradictions in the use-beliefs that enter into any one plan. If we decide to take a statement A as an assumption for purposes of a certain tentative line of reasoning, we ordinarily will not allow ourselves to also assume some other statement B that contradicts A in that same line of reasoning, even if we realize that both A and B are merely possibilities. Nonetheless, we shall argue below that contradictions do arise within our use-beliefs. Our previous arguments about the undesirability of contradictions among use-beliefs are intended to show that the presence of such a contradiction cannot be taken lightly. Once we have presented the form of contradiction we have in mind, we then will discuss its significance for formalizing commonsense reasoning.

The notion of use-beliefs has been described here at considerable length. This may have seemed overkill, especially on a topic that remains quite befuddled even as we come to the end of this section. Nonetheless, it has been a necessary exercise, for we wish to offset a possible objection to the analysis of default reasoning we will now pursue. In particular, we intend to analyze defaults in terms of beliefs. Now, it can be argued that the consequences of default reasoning, such as that Tweety can fly, are more properly regarded as tentative notions *that are not actual beliefs* (see Nutter (1982, 1983*a*)). However, the discussion of use-beliefs was intended to show that even tentative conclusions of this sort, if they are potentially *used* in any significant way in planning activity, should be treated much as if they were simply asserted flatly without qualification of tentativity.[12] That is, in particular, inconsistencies among such beliefs is a serious matter, more so than would be suggested by treating them as "shielded" by a "Tentative" modality. So we contend that, far from believing very little, commonsense reasoners will have very many use-beliefs.

3. A preliminary analysis of defaults

We now return to our earlier extended example of default

[11]More on this later.

[12]Much as if, bu· not wholly as if. This distinction will be brought out more later.

general that OT will at any given moment have a belief such as this, unless a means is presented by which OT can deduce such a belief. This is exactly where oracles come into the picture. OT must know that it doesn't know (or believe) anything other than the three stated beliefs.

Now if OT refers to its beliefs by means of a term *S* for the set of these beliefs, then OT may have a belief such as $(\exists x)[x \in S \,\&$ False$(x)]$ as well as $(\forall x)[x \in S \leftrightarrow$ Bel$(x)]$. But this is not contradictory, for OT will presumably not believe Bel$(x) \rightarrow$ True(x), given that OT believes *IS*. For each belief *x* of OT, indeed OT believes *x* (to be true). But that is not the same as believing the conjunction of these beliefs to be true. This is a peculiar situation. OT indeed uses full deductive logic, but cannot prove the conjunction of its beliefs (axioms), not because of deductive limitations so much as descriptive power: OT has no name that is tied formally to its actual set of beliefs. If a superfancy brand of oracle is invoked to present such a name and the assertion that all elements named by that term are true, then indeed a contradiction follows. But there is no obvious argument that such an oracle is a part of commonsense reasoning.

Another way to state this is that getting OT's hands on its *set* of beliefs is not trivial, if this is to be done in a way that makes OT's term for that set correspond effectively to the elements (and no others) of that actual set.

(An interesting counterpoint is that the *negation* of *IS*, namely, $(\forall x)($Bel$(x) \rightarrow$ True$(x))$, when coupled with a relatively uncontroversial rule of inference (from *x* infer Bel(x), i.e., OT may infer that it believes *x*, if it has already inferred *x*), often *does* produce inconsistency! Essentially, if T is a suitable first-order theory subsuming the mentioned rule, then *IS* is a *theorem* of T, quite the opposite of contradicting T. See Perlis (to appear) for details on this and related results.)

Nevertheless, we shall presently see that Israel's argument can be revised in such a way as to bear significantly on formalisms for default reasoning. To address this, we return now to our analysis of default reasoning.

5. Default reasoning and commonsense

The current breed of formal default reasoning tends to ignore the eventuality of errors cropping up in the course of reasoning, attention having focussed more on the semantics of getting the right initial default conclusion. But it is clear that if this can be done, then a mechanism is required to "undo" such a conclusion in the light of further evidence, as our example with Tweety indicates. Indeed, to deny information about errors to OT amounts to allowing OT the following kind of clumsy reasoning hardly suitable for an ideal reasoner:

> Tweety is a bird; so (perhaps in Reiter's or McCarthy's version) Tweety can fly. Why do I think Tweety can fly? I do not know. But Tweety turns out to be an Ostrich, so Tweety can't fly. Did I say Tweety could fly? I do not know why I said that. Do I think any bird can fly unless known otherwise? No, I do not think that.

While this may contain no inconsistency, it also seems not to be a very impressive instance of commonsense. We are not here trying to poke fun at proposals in the literature, but rather simply to illustrate how far indeed they are from the ideal of commonsense that apparently motivates their study. This will not be news, but it is nonetheless worthwhile to draw the boundaries to see where to go next. A slightly more commonsensical version is as follows:

> Tweety is a bird; so (because I do not know otherwise, perhaps in McDermott and Doyle's version) Tweety can fly: Bird(x) & $\neg$ Known($\neg$Flies(x)) $. \rightarrow \neg$.Flies(x), and also $\neg$Known($\neg$Flies(Tweety)); but Tweety is an Ostrich, so Tweety can't fly. Did I say Tweety could fly? I do not know why I said that, for I believe birds fly if I do not know otherwise, but in Tweety's case I know otherwise. Did I say $\neg$Known($\neg$Flies(Tweety))? I wonder why, for it's not true.

A still smarter version, one that appears to deal with errors appropriately and keeps track of its reasoning over time, is

> Tweety is a bird; so (I may as well assume) Tweety can fly; but Tweety is an Ostrich and so cannot fly after all; my belief that Tweety could fly was false, and arose from my acceptance of a plausible hypothesis. Do all birds that may fly (as far as I know) in fact fly? No, that's just a convenient rule of thumb.

Note that here too a contradiction (between past and present) arises, but out of an explicit recognition that the default rule leads to other beliefs some of which are false. Which are the "real" facts? OT must be able to stand back from (some of) its beliefs to question their relative accuracy, temporarily suspending judgement on certain matters so they can be assessed, without thereby giving up other beliefs (such as general rules of reason) which may be needed to assess the ones in question.

Now the above scenarios strongly suggest that for OT to be capable of appropriate commonsense reasoning, it must be able to reflect on its past errors, indeed, on its potential future errors. This observation will form the basis of our next section, in which we consider "Socratic" reasoners, i.e., ones that know something of their own limitations, and in particular the fallibility of their use of defaults.

6. Israel's argument revisited

There is a way to make Israel's argument good after all, by reformulating *IS* into a version, say, *IS'*, to make it refer to a particular proscribed set, indeed a finite one that can be listed. It is not essential at all for *IS'* to refer to all beliefs of OT, nor even to itself. It is sufficient that *IS'* refer to a finite set *S* of beliefs of OT that OT can explicitly conjoin into a single formula; this will then produce a contradiction if OT has the full deductive power of logic and if *IS'* is a belief of OT that states that at least one of the elements of *S* is false. Now, what reason can be given for OT having such a belief as *IS'*? Why would an intelligent reasoner such as OT concede that some subset *S* of its beliefs holds an error, especially since it is not just *some* subset, and not just a finite one, but one that can be explicitly divulged.

Our answer to this is that it is precisely default reasoning, i.e., reasoning by guess, uncertainty, or jumps that makes such a concession inevitable. For OT, to be truly intelligent, must realize that its default beliefs are just that: error-prone and therefore at times just plain wrong. Indeed, the very necessity of making fixes blatantly exposes the error-prone quality of default reasoning. Now we can get an explicit formal contradiction, for we can argue that *IS'* will reasonably be believed by OT. All OT needs is a handle on its own past, e.g., that it has judged many instances of a default to be positive (such as 1000 birds to fly).

For the purpose of the following definitions, we consider OT to be a "reasoning system," i.e., some version of a formal theory (actually, a sequence of such theories) that varies over time as it interacts with new information. Thus in our earlier example, at the point at which it is learned that Tweety is an ostrich, the reasoning system is considered to have evolved into another formal state. However, as will be seen below, time and the elements of defaults (oracles, jumps, and fixes) serve only a motivational role, not needed for the formal treatment. We work then within an appropriate first-order theory, supplemented with names for wffs to allow quotation and unquotation as in Perlis (1985).

Definition

A reasoning system OT is *quandaried* (at a given time) if it has an axiom (belief) that says not all of an explicitly specified finite set of its beliefs are true.

Theorem 1

No quandaried reasoner can be consistent.

Proof

Let OT be a quandaried reasoner, for which the explicitly specified set of beliefs is $\{B_1, \ldots, B_n\}$, and having in addition the axiom (belief) $\neg(B_1 \,\&\, \ldots \,\&\, B_n)$. The result follows immediately.

Now while theorem 1 may seem trivial, it does hold an interesting lesson. For any reasoner that has perfect recall of its past reasoning will be able to explicitly specify its past default conclusions, and in particular those that have not been revoked (fixed). If it then also believes on general principles that one or more of *these* beliefs is false, it will be quandaried and hence inconsistent. We presently codify this in further definitions and a theorem. Note, however, that theorem 1 does not necessarily spell despair for quandaried reasoners. For the spirit of the Tweety example, which has motivated much of our discussion, is precisely that an inconsistency giving rise to a fix that restores consistency. That is, it is to be expected that OT may fluctuate between quandaried and nonquandaried states, as it finds and corrects its errors.

Definition

OT is *recollective* if at any time t it contains the belief

$$(\forall x)(\mathrm{Dflt}(x) \leftrightarrow x = b_1 \vee \ldots \vee x = b_n)$$

where $b_1, \ldots, b_n$ are (names of) all the beliefs $B_1, \ldots, B_n$ derived by default prior to t (i.e., b_i = "B_i"), and if for each i either OT retains the belief B_i as well as $\mathrm{Bel}(b_i)$, or else B_i has been revoked (e.g., by a fix) and then it contains the belief $\neg\mathrm{Bel}(b_i)$.

Definition

OT is *Socratic* if it has the belief $(\exists x)(\mathrm{Dflt}(x) \,\&\, \mathrm{Bel}(x) \,\&\, \mathrm{False}(x))$ as well as the beliefs $\mathrm{False}(``\alpha") \rightarrow \neg\alpha$ for all wffs α.

Theorem 2

No recollective Socratic reasoner can be consistent.

Proof

Any such reasoner OT will be quandaried and so by theorem 1 will be inconsistent. To see that OT will indeed be quandaried, simply observe that in being Socratic and recollective, OT will believe

(i) $(\exists x)((x = b_1 \vee \ldots \vee x = b_n) \,\&\, \mathrm{Bel}(x) \,\&\, \mathrm{False}(x))$

But also (in being recollective) OT will believe either

(ii) $B_i \,\&\, \mathrm{Bel}(b_i)$

or

(iii) $\neg\mathrm{Bel}(b_i)$

for each b_i. Now consider those b_i such that $\mathrm{Bel}(b_i)$ is believed (i.e., is a theorem of OT), say, $b_{i_1}, \ldots, b_{i_k}$. Since OT believes $\neg\mathrm{Bel}(b_i)$ for the *other* beliefs among $b_1, \ldots, b_n$, then by (i) OT believes one of $b_{i_1}, \ldots, b_{i_k}$ to be false, yet each is believed; so OT is quandaried. (It is also not hard to form a direct contradiction without exploiting the notion of a quandary; we have pursued this route simply to illustrate the application of Israel's (modified) argument.)

As an example, OT may believe a rule such as that "typically birds can fly," and operationalize it with a (second) rule such as that given $\mathrm{Bird}(x)$ and if $\mathrm{Flies}(x)$ is consistent with OT's beliefs, then $\mathrm{Flies}(x)$ is true. But OT will also believe (since it is smart enough to know what defaults are about) that this very procedure is error-prone, and sometimes $\mathrm{Flies}(x)$ will be consistent with its beliefs and yet be false. Indeed, it will reasonably believe that one of its *past* (and yet still believed) default conclusions is such an exception, and these it can enumerate (suppose it has reasoned about 1000 birds) and yet it will also believe of each of them that it is true! So OT is inconsistent. Of course, the very realization of the clash (which OT also should be capable of noticing) should generate a fix which calls the separate default conclusions into question, perhaps to be relegated again to their more accurate status of tentativity. We will see in the next section how these results relate to the standard default formalisms in the literature.

It is necessary here to address the possible objection that OT will not be able to enumerate its past defaults and so will refer to them only generically, defusing the contradiction as we did with Israel's original argument. However, it is not at all unreasonable to suppose that OT keeps a list of its defaults, especially in certain settings. For instance, if OT works as a zookeeper and keeps a written record of the animals there, 1000 North American (i.e., "flying") birds may have been recorded by OT as in good health (and so able to fly), and OT may continue to defend these judgements even while granting that some of them will be errors. More will be said on this in the following section. (Readers may recognize this as a version of the Paradoxes of the Preface or of the Lottery.[15] See Stalnaker (1984).)

7. Analysis of three formalisms

We are now in a position to present rather striking examples of the situation that has been dealt with in the earlier sections. We will show that major weakenings occur when the standard "epistemological adequacy" approaches to commonsense reasoning are combined with a recollective *or* Socratic treatment of use-beliefs. We will examine McCarthy's circumscription (CL), McDermott and Doyle's nonmonotonic logic (NML), and Reiter's default logic (DL). Recall (theorem 2) that any Socratic *and* recollective default reasoner is inconsistent. This of course applies as well to CL, NML, and DL; that is, if any of these is endowed with Socratic and recollective powers, it will become inconsistent. This already is unfortunate, in that it seems to suggest that quite a different sort of formalism will be required to handle defaults "realistically." But even more damaging observations can be made, namely, relaxing in various ways the Socratic and recollective hypotheses still produces undesired results in these formalisms.

We begin by reviewing the extent to which our three default "keys" (oracles, jumps, and fixes) come into these treatments. The case of circumscription, or CL, is slightly complicated by the fact that the predicate "Unknown" (that is, Unknown($\neg\mathrm{Flies}(x)$) in our example) is not explicit, and indeed, CL does

[15]McDermott (1982) mentions this paradox as one giving trouble for monotonic logics; here we see that it is also problematic for nonmonotonic logics.

not quite test fully for whether Flies(x) is already entailed by the given axioms, but rather uses a substitute (known as the method of inner models). This has the advantage of being semidecidable (i.e., the oracle is actually represented somewhat algorithmically, in the form of a second-order axiom schema), though it has the disadvantage of being incomplete (Davis 1980; Perlis and Minker 1986). Thus steps 1a, 1b, and 1c are implicit in CL, whereas in NML and DL step 1a is implicit (with an ineffective oracle used to supply full consistency information for Unknown) and steps 1b and 1c are combined into a single step (an axiom of NML and in inference rule of DL) stating directly (in the case of our example) that if Tweety is a bird and if it is consistent to assume Tweety flies, then Tweety does fly. In other respects, however, the three approaches are much the same. Steps 4a, 4b, and 4c are simply not present in any form in any of them, since once Ostrich(Tweety) is added as a new axiom, the previous axiomatization is no longer under consideration and it and its conclusions (e.g., Flies(Tweety)) are ignored.

It is clear then that to address the issues urged here, these approaches must be supplemented, and in particular with "histories" of their conclusions. More generally, far greater explicitness of world knowledge and of their own processes is required. But we have seen that when such information is allowed in a default reasoner, it has a high chance of becoming inconsistent. In particular, if it can represent the fact that it is using default rules, and that some of its default conclusions will therefore be erroneous, and if it can recall its default conclusions, then it is recollective and Socratic and so falls prey to theorem 2 and will be inconsistent. However, the particular features of CL, NML, and DL are such that simpler means exist to derive implausible conclusions within an intuitively commonsense framework. This is most easily illustrated in the case of NML because, of the three formalisms mentioned already, it alone has enough apparatus present to express the required concept of default fallibility directly.[16]

In NML, the Tweety example might be handled as follows. We could specify the axiom

$$(\forall x)((\mathrm{Bird}(x)\ \&\ \mathrm{MFlies}(x))\ .\!\rightarrow \mathrm{Flies}(x))$$

where M is a modal operator interpreted as meaning that the wff following it is consistent with the axioms of the formalism itself. Since this involves an apparent circularity, McDermott and Doyle go to some lengths to specify a semantics for M. However, for our purposes, it is not essential to follow them in such details; we can form a "Socratic" version of *IS'* easily for this case:

$$(\exists x)(\mathrm{Bird}(x)\ \&\ \mathrm{MFlies}(x)\ \&\ \neg\,\mathrm{Flies}(x))$$

This at least partly expresses that, for some bird, NML has the needed hypotheses to infer by default that the bird flies, and yet it will not fly. One could hardly ask for a more direct statement of the fallibility of defaults. Yet now NML is in trouble; it will immediately find the following direct contradiction:

$$(\exists x)(\mathrm{Flies}(x)\ \&\ \neg\,\mathrm{Flies}(x))$$

Note that here we do not need the recollective hypothesis since a Socratic[17] extension of NML is already inconsistent. (Nutter (1982) and Moore (1983) have pointed out that the formalization of NML seems to commit an error of representation vis-a-vis intuitive semantics, and it is this in effect that we are exploiting here.)

Even though, as we have seen above, in NML it is possible to express a Socratic-type axiom that some *default* conclusion has gone awry, thereby producing inconsistency, one can make an even (apparently) weaker assumption and still achieve distressing results. In all three formalisms, a simple additional "counter-example" axiom seems to undermine the ability of the reasoning system to make appropriate default conclusions consistently, surrendering the full Socratic condition but (for DL and NML) employing the recollective condition.

For instance, given the zookeeper axiom

$$(\exists x)(\mathrm{Bird}(x)\ \&\ \neg\,\mathrm{Flies}(x)\ \&\ x = b_1 \vee \ldots \vee x = b_{1000})$$

Reiter's DL "sanctions" the conclusion Flies(b_i) for each bird b_i separately. Now a problem arises: How are we to interpret these sanctions? Reiter apparently intends that any wffs entailed by *all* default extensions are to be treated as default conclusions, and that others *may* be so treated if we are careful not to mix such from distinct extensions. In any case, we are stuck, because we need the zookeeper to make a sequence of such conclusions that do *not* fall into any one extension. That is, DL augmented by sufficient axioms to specify all the (finitely many) birds in the zoo might conclude of each one by one that (it is "ok" to suppose that) it flies, up until the last one, and since it also has the belief that one of them does not, it will be forced to conclude of the last that *it* is the culprit that does not fly. Therefore, DL (so construed) is prey to the "paradox of the zookeeper" in that, although avoiding inconsistency, its ability to derive the intuitive default conclusions is compromised.[18] The same arguments apply to NML and counter-example axioms. Alternatively, if the time sequence is finessed, these formal specifications of default reasoning can be viewed as producing the conclusion that precisely one bird of the 1000 does not fly, without committing themselves to even a single default conclusion about any individual bird. This, however, amounts to avoiding drawing any atomic defaults, largely defeating the prime motivation for such reasoning.[19] This will arise even more dramatically when we examine CL below.

Here our earlier treatment of use-beliefs comes in handy. For we can argue that the zookeeper "really" believes that each separate bird at the zoo can fly, that he is highly unwilling to leave any of their cage doors open, and that he is also unwilling

[16]And this is its downfall regarding our present discussion. In effect, NML makes an axiom out of DL's rule. Thus DL's ability to refuse to believe the rule as a truth is not available to NML. Of course, this is indulging in an introspectivist fantasy, for neither formalism represents reasons for its conclusions. But this fantasy does, I think, accurately pinpoint the critical distinction that allows DL to survive the threat of inconsistency in the present example.

[17]We use the term "Socratic" somewhat loosely here, since it is not precisely the same as the formal definition given earlier. However, intuitively it still expresses the idea of self-error.

[18]That is, the zookeeper concludes of *no* bird that it does not fly; only the existence of such is believed. I grant that, to get DL, NML, and CL to take the job of zookeeper, I am stretching them in unintended ways and making arbitrary choices in the process. But that is the point: We must devise formalisms that do lend themselves to introspection; and when we do, there will be difficulties of the sorts described here.

[19]It also seems related to Reiter's suggestion that DL has a representation of the notion of "few" or "many." However, the actual inferences sanctioned by DL (or by NML or CL, for that matter) seem to miss much of the import of these terms, in that a strict minimum is determined. For example, that most birds fly, when represented as a default, leads to the conclusion that *all* birds fly if no counter examples are known, and that *all but* known counter examples fly in other cases. But there is an intended indefiniteness in the words "few" and "many." See our discussion of CL below.

to call any one of them to the attention of the zoo veterinarian. Yet, he is also very concerned at the veterinarian's failure to arrive for work at the usual hour, because the zookeeper also believes that *some* (unspecified) birds in the zoo *are* ill (and unable to fly).

There is an intuitive appeal to this, in that a zookeeper might very well defend each separate conclusion of the form Flies(b_i), and yet not agree to the statement that all the birds fly. Indeed, the zookeeper has *use-beliefs* Flies(b_i) for each i as well as the use-belief $(\exists x)(\neg \text{Flies}(x) \ \& \ x = b_1 \ v ... v \ x = b_{1000})$. The problem is that whereas the zookeeper may refuse to apply an inference rule to form the conjunction of given beliefs (recognizing, in effect, that there is a contradiction afoot and that his beliefs are tentative), DL and NML are formal extensions of first-order logic and will have such conjunctions as theorems, with no means to control the usual disastrous consequences of this in logically closed formalisms. That is, zookeepers and other commonsensical beings are perhaps not obedient to slavish rules of formal logic regarding their use-beliefs.[20]

One might seek to alter the logic as a way around this, for instance by not allowing arbitrary conjunctions of theorems. Such alternatives have been raised in connection with the lottery and preface paradoxes (Stalnaker 1984). However, this does not affect our conclusion that the beliefs of any agent fully in the zookeeper's shoes would in fact be mutually (but not directly) contradictory, whether or not there are mechanisms in place to keep the contradiction from being deduced. Moreover, an intelligent agent should be able to recognize the contradiction and conclude, perhaps, that its conclusions of the form Flies(x) were after all only tentative (that is, undo the "jump"). For this, a record must be kept of the origin of conclusions, a point utilized in Doyle (1979) and emphasized in Nutter (1983*a*).

It is worth contrasting the zookeeper scenario with another, the "detective" scenario. Here there are, say, 10 suspects in a murder case, each of whom has an alibi and is apparently a very nice person. Yet instead of concluding separately of each that he or she is (tentatively) innocent, our detective tentatively suspects each (separately) of being guility. But if there were 1000 or more suspects (e.g., if relatively little at all existed in the form of clues, so that *anyone* may have been the murderer), then it is no longer reasonable to tentatively treat each individual as guilty. That is, in the case of 10 suspects, it may be life-preserving to be wary of all 10, but in the case of 1000, it surely is counter productive. This seems to say that raw numbers do (should) affect the course of default reasoning, a matter we will not pursue further here.

The case of CL is still more interesting. Here, the defaults are not as explicitly represented as in NML (or even DL).[21] So, following the cue of our additional axiom above, we say simply that there is a bird that does not fly, as well as circumscribing nonflying birds. Thus

$$\{\text{Bird(Tweety)}, (\exists x)(\text{Bird}(x) \ \& \ \neg \text{Flies}(x))\}$$

when circumscribed with respect to ¬Flies (letting Flies be a "variable" circumscriptive predicate), instead of providing the expected and usual (when the second axiom is not present) conclusion that Tweety flies, allows us no conclusion at all about Tweety not already contained in the axioms before circumscribing.[22] That is, from Bird(Tweety) *alone* circumscription of ¬Flies produces Flies(Tweety), as desired. Yet with the additional axiom present, this no longer is the case. This is easily seen, for the above axiom set has a minimal model in which Tweety is precisely the claimed exceptional bird. Here we do not even need the recollective condition.

We wish to regard Tweety as a typical bird, since nothing else is known explicitly about Tweety; however, the additional axiom raises the possibility that Tweety may not fly, i.e., Tweety may be the intransigent nonflying bird that is asserted to exist. The result is that *no* birds will be shown (even tentatively) to fly by circumscribing in such a conext. Clearly this is not what we wish of a default reasoner. In terms of our analysis of default reasoning, CL does not perform step 1*a*; the circumscriptive schema (oracle), when faced with a weak Socratic axiom, no longer recognizes the "typical" case. The result claimed above is formalized below.

Theorem 3

The set

$$T = \{P(c), (\exists x)(P(x) \ \& \ \neg Q(x))\}$$

when circumscribed with respect to $\neg Q$, does not have $Q(c)$ as theorem, even in formula circumscription with P and Q allowed as variable predicates.

Proof

By the soundness theorem for circumscription[23] (see McCarthy (1980) and Perlis and Minker (1986)), if $Q(c)$ were a theorem of Circum(T, $\neg Q$), then $Q(c)$ would hold in all minimal models of T (with respect to $\neg Q$). But this is not so. There are minimal models of T in which $\neg Q(c)$ holds, namely, ones in which c is the only P-entity. (Intuitively, c = Tweety is the only bird (P) that does not fly (Q).)

One might try to "disconnect" Tweety from the existentially asserted nonflying bird, for instance, by Skolemizing the additional axiom as

$$\text{Bird}(c) \ \& \ \neg \text{Flies}(c)$$

However, this will not work either. We still cannot prove Flies(Tweety) by circumscription, unless we adopt the further axiom that Tweety $\neq c$. But to do this amounts to begging the question, i.e., to assuming we already know (before we circumscribe) that Tweety is not to be exceptional in regard to

[20]We might say the zookeeper is *quasi-consistent* (and *quasi-inconsistent*), that is, his belief set B *entails* a contradiction X & ¬X, but does not *contain* one directly (X and ¬X are not both elements of B). It follows that such an agent cannot be logically omniscient, but in a way that is no weakness at all. The entailed contradiction need not be *missed* out of logical ignorance, but rather can be deliberately rejected *on the basis* of having been duly (and logically) noted and judged impossible and attributed to an error.

[21]Although *formula* circumscription does provide at least part of a mechanism for expressing within the logic the fact of self-error, and if this is teased out by means of suitable metalogical devices, then in close analogy with the following treatment commonsense is compromised.

[22]That is, about Tweety in isolation. As seen above with NML and DL, shotgun results about the whole set of birds may be derivable, such as that there is only one nonflying bird, but no conclusion specific to any particular bird follows. Indeed, the easily proved circumscriptive result that there is only one bird that does not fly (also derivable in NML and DL when interpreted as in our earlier discussion in the recollective case for zoo birds) runs counter to intuition: the existence of a nonflying bird suggests "few," not "only one." It would be much more satisfactory if there were a way to remain noncommittal on the exact number.

[23]Etherington, D. 1984. Week on logic and AI. University of Maryland. Private communication.

flying. Moreover, we can then simply consider the wff $\neg$Flies(x) & $x \neq c$ instead, and assert (reasonably) that some bird satisfies *this*. For if c were the only nonflying bird, then we would not need defaults in the first place. The whole point is that even among those birds that seem typical as far as we can tell, still there lurk exceptions.

This can be seen in a more dramatic form by postulating that $b_1, \ldots, b_n$ are *all* the birds in the world (where n is some large known integer, say, 100 billion, and distinct b_i's may or may not represent distinct birds). Then the axiom $(\exists x)$(Bird(x) & $\neg$Flies(x)) cannot be Skolemized with a constant that is also assumed to have a distinct reference from every b_i. Note that this is similar to Reiter's unique names hypothesis (1980) that likewise is not handled directly by circumscription. We suggest that a solution to one of these problems may harbor a solution to the other. Note, however, that even if names are introduced into CL in such a way that one can circumscriptively prove $\neg$Flies(Tweety) (i.e., so that jumps are reinstated), then CL immediately falls prey to inconsistency if it is also recollective. (See Etherington *et al.* (1985) for the crucial role of existential quantifiers in circumscriptive consistency.)

What we have found, then, regarding "realistic" default reasoning and three standard formalisms in the literature, can be represented in the following table:

Hypotheses	Formalism		
	CL	DL	NML
Socratic	compromised	—	inconsistent
Recollective	—	—	—
Socratic–recollective	inconsistent	inconsistent	inconsistent
Counter example	compromised	—	—
Counter example–recollective	compromised	compromised	compromised

Here "compromised" means that the formalism in question will not produce the intuitively correct commonsense default conclusions, and "—" means that no apparent difficulties arise. So we see that any of the three formalisms can be made recollective without upsetting the intended usage. On the other hand, the Socratic or counter-example conditions, which are what express the *tentativity* (i.e., the default-hood) of defaults, tend to spell trouble. It is of interest that Reiter's version, DL, comes out "best" of the three: it suffers the least affront to its default integrity as a specification for an omnithinker.

Finally, in no case can the "ideal" of a Socratic recollective default reasoner be achieved within the framework of the epistemological adequacy approach, since that approach is based on the assumption of a consistent, logically closed axiomatization. This is of course relative to our definition of use-beliefs; that is, the inconsistency may lie hidden inside tentativity predicates, as Nutter (1983*b*) urges. But the three formalisms discussed in this section all employ jumps, i.e., they baldly assert their default conclusions, and therefore the implicit use-belief inconsistency that will arise when they are endowed with Socratic-recollective features will become an explicit logical inconsistency.

8. Conclusions

We need formalisms adequate to the task of capturing "introspective" default reasoning. This is essential to performing certain kinds of fixes. Furthermore, the latter often cannot be done at all without sacrificing consistency in favour of a kind of quasi-consistency.

The thrust of our remarks has been that desiderata underlying commonsense reasoning simply are inconsistent, and that we now must devise and study systems having such characteristics. Specifically, the "jump" phenomenon, so central to most work on default reasoning (and, notably, attacked by Nutter (1982)), will not withstand simultaneous admission of fallibility implicit in a "fix." On the other hand, dealing with inconsistent formalisms seems to force us toward deeper analysis of processes of memory, inference, and focus over time. These are the topics of work in progress (Drapkin *et al.* 1986; Drapkin and Perlis 1986). Nutter (1983*b*) prefers to avoid jumps and seeks other means of utilizing default conclusions such as relevance logic. The extent to which the term "logic" is appropriate at all for such an undertaking is also a matter of debate (see Doyle (1983, 1985) and Harman (1986)). It will be interesting to see whether any of these approaches bear fruit.

Acknowledgements

I wish to thank James Allen, Jennifer Drapkin, Jerry Feldman, Rosalie Hall, Jim Hendler, Hector Levesque, Vladimir Lifschitz, Ron Loui, Michael Miller, Jack Minker, Dana Nau, Rich Pelavin, Jim des Rivieres, John Schlipf, and Jay Weber for useful discussion on the topic of this paper. Special thanks to Pat Hayes and Ray Reiter, who challenged me to write down and clarify my spoken claims.

This research has been supported in part by the U.S. Army Research Office (DAAG29-85-K-0177) and the Martin Marietta Corporation.

Davis, M. 1980. The mathematics of non-monotonic reasoning. Artificial Intelligence, **13**, pp. 73–80.

Dennett, D. 1978. Brainstorms. Bradford Books, Montgomery, VT. pp. 300–309.

Doyle, J. 1979. A truth maintenance system. Artificial Intelligence, **12**, pp. 41–72.

——— 1983. A society of mind. Proceedings of the Eighth International Joint Conference on Artificial Intelligence, Karlsruhe, West Germany, pp. 309–313.

——— 1985. Reasoned assumptions and Pareto optimality. Proceedings of the Ninth International Joint Conference on Artificial Intelligence, Los Angeles, CA, pp. 87–90.

Drapkin, J., and Perlis, D. 1986. Step-logics: an alternative approach to limited reasoning. Proceedings, Seventh European Conference on Artificial Intelligence, Brighton, England.

Drapkin, J., Miller, M., and Perlis, D. 1986. A memory model for real-time default reasoning. University of Maryland, College Park, MD, Technical Report.

Etherington, D., Mercer, R., and Reiter, R. 1985. On the adequacy of predicate circumscription for closed-world reasoning. Computational Intelligence, **1**, pp. 11–15.

Harman, G. 1973. Thought. Princeton University Press, Princeton, NJ.

——— 1986. Change in view. MIT Press, Cambridge, MA.

Israel, D. 1980. What's wrong with non-monotonic logic? Proceedings of the First National Conference on Artificial Intelligence, Standford, CA, pp. 99–101.

Konolige, K. 1984. Belief and incompleteness. SRI International, Menlo Park, CA, Technical Note 319.

McCarthy, J. 1980. Circumscription—a form of non-monotonic reasoning. Artificial Intelligence, **13**, pp. 27–39.

——— 1986. Applications of circumscription to formalizing commonsense knowledge. Artificial Intelligence, **28**, pp. 89–116.

COMPUT. INTELL. VOL. 2, 1986

McDermott, D. 1982. Non-monotonic logic. II. Journal of the Association for Computing Machinery, **29**, pp. 33–57.
McDermott, J., and Doyle, J. 1980. Non-monotonic logic I. Artificial Intelligence, **13**, pp. 41–72.
Moore, R. 1977. Reasoning about knowledge and action. Proceedings of the Fifth International Joint Conference on Artificial Intelligence, Cambridge, MA, pp. 223–227.
——— 1983. Semantical considerations on non-monotonic logic. Proceedings of the Eighth International Joint Conference on Artificial Intelligence, Karlsruhe, West Germany, pp. 272–279.
Newell, A. 1981. The knowledge level. AI Magazine, **2**, pp. 1–20.
Nutter, J. T. 1982. Defaults revisited, or "Tell me if you're guessing". Proceedings, Fourth Conference of the Cognitive Science Society, Ann Arbor, MI, pp. 67–69.
——— 1983*a*. What else is wrong with non-monotonic logic? Proceedings, Fifth Conference of the Cognitive Science Society, Rochester, NY.
——— 1983*b*. Default reasoning using monotonic logic: a modest proposal. Proceedings of the International Joint Conference on Artificial Intelligence, Washington, D.C., pp. 297–300.
Perlis, D. 1981. Language, computation, and reality. Ph.D. thesis, University of Rochester, Rochester, NY.
——— 1985. Languages with self-reference I: foundations. Artificial Intelligence, **25**, pp. 301–322.
——— 1986. Languages with self-reference II: knowledge, belief, and modality. Artificial Intelligence, to appear.
Perlis, D., and Minker, J. 1986. Completeness results for circumscription. Artificial Intelligence, **28**, pp. 29–42.
Reiter, R. 1980. A logic for default reasoning. Artificial Intelligence, **13**, pp. 81–132.
Reiter, R., and Criscuolo, G. 1983. Some representational issues in default reasoning. International Journal of Computers and Mathematics (Special issue on computational linguistics), **9**(1), pp. 15–27.
Stalnaker, R. 1984. Inquiry. MIT Press, Cambridge, MA, pp. 90–92.

Chapter 3

Formalizations of Nonmonotonic Reasoning

3.1 Default Theories

Of all the approaches to nonmonotonic reasoning, Reiter's default logic appears to be the most stable: almost without exception, the articles that have appeared after Reiter's original one focus on applying Reiter's ideas as opposed to modifying them. (The single exception is Lukaszewicz' suggestion of a slight modification in [Lukaszewicz, 1984].)

Reiter's original paper begins (as all the early papers do) with motivational material on nonmonotonic reasoning generally; his formal description of extensions as fixed points appears in Section 2. We have already remarked that default theories are brave; he discusses this point specifically at the end of this section.

Normal defaults (of the form $\alpha : \beta / \beta$) are introduced in Section 3, and a proof theory for the propositional case (no quantified default rules, essentially) is presented in Section 4, which also discusses the non-semidecidability of default inference. Inference in the more general (i.e., quantified) case is delayed until Section 7. Reiter also discusses the use of a resolution theorem prover in default inference (Section 5), and briefly mentions the problem of belief revision (Section 6).

The next three papers present an increasingly focussed investigation of the multiple-extension problem in default logic. The problem is identified in Reiter's paper with Criscuolo; the Nixon-Quaker-Republican example appears here.

A more general investigation of the properties of inheritance hierarchies with exceptions is the subject of the next paper. Etherington and Reiter show that, in general, the description of inheritance hierarchies of this sort involves the use of *seminormal* default rules. Their description requires the explicit mention of some exceptions within the default rules themselves; this results in descriptive unwieldiness when large problems are considered.

Etherington and Reiter also discuss the possible use of a parallel algorithm to propagate information through default inheritance hierarchies, extending work done by Fahlman in NETL [Fahlman, 1979]. This extension is only partially successful; Etherington deals with this subject at much greater length in [Etherington, 1987].

Touretzky's paper notices that Etherington and Reiter's use of seminormal defaults is really an attempt to sidestep the multiple-extension problem when there is enough information in the inheritance net to guarantee a preference of one extension over another. Touretzky argues that a more natural approach to this problem is to prioritize the default rules based on a concept he calls "inferential distance." The essential idea is that default rules about subclasses should override default rules about the superclasses that contain them; Touretzky argues that inferential distance is formally correct (in that the corresponding prioritized default system captures the intent of the network) while retaining the conceptual simplicity of the shortest-path heuristic used by Fahlman in NETL.

A Logic for Default Reasoning

R. Reiter

Department of Computer Science, University of British Columbia, Vancouver, B.C., Canada

Recommended by Patrick J. Hayes

ABSTRACT

The need to make default assumptions is frequently encountered in reasoning about incompletely specified worlds. Inferences sanctioned by default are best viewed as beliefs which may well be modified or rejected by subsequent observations. It is this property which leads to the non-monotonicity of any logic of defaults.

In this paper we propose a logic for default reasoning. We then specialize our treatment to a very large class of commonly occurring defaults. For this class we develop a complete proof theory and show how to interface it with a top down resolution theorem prover. Finally, we provide criteria under which the revision of derived beliefs must be effected.

The gods did not reveal, from the beginning,
All things to us, but in the course of time
Through seeking we may learn and know things better.
But as for certain truth, no man has known it,
Nor shall he know it, neither of the gods
Nor yet of all the things of which I speak.
For even if by chance he were to utter
The final truth, he would himself not know it:
For all is but a woven web of guesses.

Xenophanes

1. Introduction and Motivation

Various forms of default reasoning commonly arise in Artificial Intelligence. Such reasoning corresponds to the process of deriving conclusions based upon patterns of inference of the form "in the absence of any information to the contrary, assume ...". Reasoning patterns of this kind represent a form of plausible inference and are typically required whenever conclusions must be drawn despite the absence of total knowledge about a world.

In order to fix some of these ideas, we begin by surveying a number of instances of default reasoning as they often occur in the Artificial Intelligence literature. Most of the examples are adapted from those in Reiter (1978a).

1.1. Some examples of default reasoning

1.1.1. *Defaults and exceptions*

A good deal of what we know about a world is 'almost always' true, with a few exceptions. Such facts usually assume the form "Most P's are Q's" or "Most P's have property Q". For example most birds fly except for penguins, ostriches, the Maltese falcon etc. Given a particular bird, we will conclude that it flies unless we happen to know that it satisfies one of these exceptions. How is the fact that most birds fly to be represented? The natural first order representation explicitly lists the exceptions to flying:

$$(x).\mathrm{BIRD}(x) \wedge \neg\mathrm{PENGUIN}(x) \wedge \neg\mathrm{OSTRICH}(x) \wedge \cdots \supset \mathrm{FLY}(x).$$

But with this representation one cannot conclude of a 'general' bird that it can fly. To see why, consider an attempt to prove FLY(tweety) where all we know of tweety is that it is a bird. Then we must establish the subgoal

$$\neg\mathrm{PENGUIN(tweety)} \wedge \neg\mathrm{OSTRICH(tweety)} \wedge \cdots$$

which is impossible given that there is no further information about tweety. We are blocked from concluding that tweety can fly even though intuitively we want to deduce just that.

What is required is somehow to allow tweety to fly *by default*. How is this default to be interpreted? We take it to mean something like "If x is a bird, then in the absence of any information to the contrary, infer that x can fly". The problem then is to interpret the phrase "in the absence of any information to the contrary". The interpretation we adopt is "It is consistent to assume that x can fly". Thus "If x is a bird and it is consistent to assume that x can fly, then infer that x can fly". We represent this more formally as the following *default rule*:

$$\frac{\mathrm{BIRD}(x) : \mathrm{MFLY}(x)}{\mathrm{FLY(x)}}.^{1} \qquad (1.1)$$

Here M is to be read as "it is consistent to assume". The exceptions to flight are then given a standard first order representation.

$$(x).\mathrm{PENGUIN}(x) \supset \neg\mathrm{FLY}(x)$$
$$(x).\mathrm{OSTRICH}(x) \supset \neg\mathrm{FLY}(x)$$
etc.

Notice that if FLY(tweety) is inferred by default then the assertion FLY(tweety) has the status of a *belief*; it is subject to change, say by the subsequent discovery

[1] In plain text we use the notation BIRD(x) : MFLY(x) / FLY(x).

that tweety is a penguin. We can then reinterpret the default rule (1.1) as saying "If x is a bird and it is consistent to believe that x can fly then one may believe that x can fly".

There still remains a problem of interpretation. For exactly what is meant by the consistency requirement associated with a default? Consistent with what? Providing an appropriate formal definition of this consistency requirement is perhaps the thorniest issue in defining a logic for default reasoning, and we defer this question to Section 2. For the time being a good intuitive interpretation is to view this consistency requirement with respect to all of the first order facts about the world, together with all of the other beliefs sanctioned by all of the other default rules in force.

Notice that we have provided a representation for the 'fuzzy' quantifier 'most' or 'almost all' in terms of defaults, without appealing to frequency distributions or fuzzy logics.

Notice also that the dual 'fuzzy' quantifier 'few' has a dual representation as a default. For example "Few Americans are socialists" has the representation

$$\frac{\mathrm{AMERICAN}(x) : \mathsf{M}\, \neg \mathrm{SOCIALIST}(x)}{\neg \mathrm{SOCIALIST}(x)} .$$

1.1.2. *Frames, knowledge representation languages and defaults*

Default reasoning plays a prominent role in the influential frames proposal of Minsky (1975). See also Hayes (1977). At least two knowledge representation languages, FRL (Roberts and Goldstein (1977)), and KRL (Bobrow and Winograd (1977)) have been designed as attempts, in part, to computationally represent some of Minsky's proposals. Not surprisingly, both FRL and KRL provide for default assignments. For example, in KRL the unit for a person in an airline travel system has the form:

```
[Person UNIT Basic
        :
<hometown{(a City) Palo Alto; DEFAULT}>
        :].
```

This declaration can be regarded as an instruction to the KRL interpreter to proceed as follows:

Whenever x is a person, then in the absence of any information to the contrary assume hometown(x) = Palo Alto.

In view of the previous discussion, this can be represented by the following default rule:

$$\frac{\mathrm{PERSON}(x) : \mathsf{M}\, \mathrm{hometown}(x) = \text{Palo Alto}}{\mathrm{hometown}(x) = \text{Palo Alto}}$$

1.1.3. *The closed world assumption*

Deductive question–answering systems often implicitly appeal to a particular form of default reasoning in the process of answering queries. As an illustration of the default involved, consider a data base representing an airline flight schedule, and the query "Does Air Canada flight 113 connect Vancouver with New York?" A deductive question–answering system will typically treat the data base together with some general knowledge about the flight domain as a set of premises from which it will attempt to prove CONNECT(AC113,Van,NY). If this proof succeeds, then the system responds "yes". The interesting case is when this proof fails, for then such a system will typically respond "no", i.e. it will conclude ¬CONNECT (AC113,Van,NY). Failure to find a proof has sanctioned an inference. Now CONNECT(AC113,Van,NY) is not provable iff ¬CONNECT(AC113,Van,NY) is consistent with the data base so that the derivation of ¬CONNECT(AC113, Van,NY) by failing to prove CONNECT(AC113,Van,NY) is justified by the following closed world default rule:

$$\frac{: \mathsf{M}\, \neg \mathrm{CONNECT}(x,y,z)}{\neg \mathrm{CONNECT}(x,y,z)} .$$

In general, if R is an n-ary relation, then the following is a *closed world default* for R:

$$\frac{: \mathsf{M}\, \neg R(x_1, \ldots, x_n)}{\neg R(x_1, \ldots, x_n)} .$$

If this default is in force for all relations R of some domain, then reasoning is being done under the *closed world assumption* (Reiter (1978b)). In effect, the closed world assumption says that for any relation R, and any individuals $x_1, \ldots, x_n$ one can assume $\neg R(x_1, \ldots, x_n)$ whenever it is consistent to do so.

Reasoning about a world under the closed world assumption considerably simplifies the representation of that world. In effect, only positive information about the world need be explicitly represented in the data base. Negative information is not so represented, but is inferred by default. Since in general the amount of negative knowledge about a world vastly exceeds the positive things known about it, there is a considerable computational and representational advantage to reasoning under the closed world assumption. For example, in the airline data base we would not have to represent the facts that AC113 does not connect London and Bombay, or Toronto and Boston, or New York and Paris, etc.

There are a number of other settings in Artificial Intelligence where the closed world assumption is made. Reiter (1978a) discusses two of these in some detail, specifically blocks world problem-solving, and reasoning about taxonomies (IS-A hierarchies).

1.1.4. *The frame default*

The frame problem (Raphael (1971)) arises in the representation of dynamic worlds. The problem stems from the need to represent those aspects of the world which remain invariant under certain state changes. For example, moving a particular object or switching on a light will not change the colours of any objects in the world. In a first order representation of such worlds, it is necessary to explicitly represent all of the invariants under all state changes. These are referred to as the frame axioms for the world being modelled. Thus, to represent the fact that painting an object does not alter the locations of objects would require, in the situational calculus of McCarthy and Hayes (1969) a frame axiom something like

$$(x\,y\,z\,s\,c)\text{LOCATION}(x,y,s) \supset \text{LOCATION}(x,y,\text{paint}(z,c,s)),$$

where s is a state variable, x and z are objects, c is a colour, and y is some location.

The problem is that in general a vast number of such axioms will be required, e.g. object locations also remain invariant when lights are switched on, when it thunders, when someone speaks, etc. so there is a major difficulty in even articulating a deductively adequate set of frame axioms for a given world.

A solution to the frame problem is a representation of the world coupled with appropriate rules of inference such that the frame axioms are neither explicitly represented nor explicitly used in reasoning about the world. We will focus on a proposed solution in Sandewall (1972). A related approach is described in Hayes (1973). Sandewall proposes a modal operator, UNLESS, which takes a first order formula as argument. The intended interpretation of UNLESS(W) is "W can not be proved" or in terms of consistency, "$\neg W$ is consistent." Sandewall proposes a single 'frame inference rule' which, in our notation for defaults, can be paraphrased as a default schema: For all relations R which take a state variable as an argument, and for all state transition functions f

$$\frac{R(\mathrm{x},s) : \mathsf{M}R(\mathrm{x},f(\mathrm{x},s))}{R(\mathrm{x},f(\mathrm{x},s))}.$$

Intuitively this default schema formalizes the so-called 'STRIPS assumption' (Waldinger (1975)): Every action (state change) is assumed to leave every relation unaffected unless it is possible to deduce otherwise.

1.2. The non monotonic character of default reasoning

A fundamental feature of first order logic is that it is *monotonic*, i.e. if A and B are sets of first order formulae and $A \vdash w$ then $A \cup B \vdash w$. What was valid in the presence of information A remains valid when new information B is discovered. In contrast, any logic which presumes to formalize default reasoning must be non-monotonic. To see why consider a simple theory consisting of the single default $: \mathsf{M}A/B$. Thus B may be believed. If subsequently $\neg A$ is discovered to hold (say through some observation) we then have the new theory $: \mathsf{M}A/B, \neg A$ in which B cannot be believed. One extremely interesting approach to the formalization of a non-monotonic logic of beliefs is described in McDermott and Doyle (1978).

This last example also demonstrates the need for some kind of mechanism for *revising beliefs* in the presence of new information. What this amounts to is the need to record, with each derived belief, the default assumptions made in deriving that belief. Should subsequent observations invalidates the default assumptions supporting some belief, then it must be removed from the data base. The Truth Maintenance System of Doyle (1978) is an heuristic implementations of just such a system for belief revision.

1.3. Defaults and incomplete knowledge

Consider the following natural pair of defaults which should be capable of peaceful co-existence:

"Assume a person's hometown is that of his/her spouse."

$$\frac{\text{SPOUSE}(x,y) \wedge \text{hometown}(y) = z : \mathsf{M}\ \text{hometown}(x) = z}{\text{hometown}(x) = z}$$

"Assume a person's hometown is where his/her employer is located."

$$\frac{\text{EMPLOYER}(x,y) \wedge \text{location}(y) = z : \mathsf{M}\ \text{hometown}(x) = z}{\text{hometown}(x) = z}$$

Suppose Mary's spouse lives in Toronto while her employer is located in Vancouver. By the first default, Mary's hometown is Toronto, and by the second it is Vancouver. To believe both is inconsistent since hometown is a function. If first we derive Toronto, we are then blocked from deriving Vancouver. On the other hand if we first derive Vancouver then the derivation of Toronto is blocked. We can derive one or the other, but not both simultaneously. From the point of view of conventional logical systems this is a perplexing, seemingly incoherent situation. From our intuitive perspective that default assumptions lead to beliefs, the example makes perfect sense; one can choose to believe that Mary's hometown is Toronto or that it is Vancouver, but not both.[2] It would seem that defaults can sanction different sets of beliefs about a world.

Now a point of view that begins to make formal sense of this example is the following:

Imagine a first order formalization of what it is we know about any reasonably complex world. Since we cannot know everything about that world—there will be gaps in our knowledge—this first order theory will be incomplete. Nevertheless, there will arise situations in which it is necessary to act, to draw some inferences,

[2] There is another possibility, which is to believe the proposition hometown(Mary) = Toronto $\vee$ hometown(Mary) = Vancouver. In terms of the theory which we develop in the remainder of this paper, this possibility amounts to refusing to choose between the Toronto extension and the Vancouver extension. See the following discussion.

despite the incompleteness of the knowledge base. That role of a default is to fill in some of the gaps in the knowledge base, i.e. to further complete the underlying incomplete first order theory, so as to permit the inferences necessary to act. Defaults therefore function somewhat like meta-rules; they are instructions about how to create an *extension* of this incomplete theory. Those formulae sanctioned by the defaults and which extend the theory can then be viewed as beliefs about the world. Now in general there are many different ways of extending an incomplete theory, which suggests that the default rules may be nondeterministic. Different applications of the defaults yield different extensions and hence different sets of beliefs about the world.

As an example of this point of view, consider the closed world assumption. This fully completes the underlying first order theory. Thus, the theory $p \vee q$ under the closed world defaults $: \mathrm{M}\neg p/\neg p$ and $: \mathrm{M}\neg q/\neg q$ has two different complete extensions, $\{p, \neg q\}$ and $\{\neg p, q\}$. In the first we choose to believe $\neg q$ by invoking the second default, whence we are forced to believe p. In the second we choose to believe $\neg p$ by invoking the first default.

It is this point of view—that defaults are rules for extending an underlying incomplete first order theory—which is adopted in this paper, and which motivates the subsequent development. The rest of this paper is devoted to articulating a logic for default reasoning. We see a two-fold task for such a logic:

(1) To provide a formal definition of the extensions to an underlying first order theory induced by a set of defaults.

(2) To provide a proof theory in the form of a procedure which, given a formula w, determines whether w can be believed, i.e., whether there is an extension induced by the defaults which contains w.

In this paper we propose a definition for the first task. The second will turn out to be intractable for default theories in general. However, by focusing upon a special class of defaults called normal defaults, we can provide a proof theory. Fortunately the class of normal defaults embraces a broad spectrum of naturally occurring defaults, for instance all of the examples of this section. In addition to providing a proof theory for normal defaults, we obtain the pessimistic result that in general the beliefs of a theory are not recursively enumerable. Finally, we determine conditions under which it is necessary to revise a set of derived beliefs when confronted with some new observations about a world.

2. Default Theories and their Extensions

In this section we provide a precise notion of a default theory, and then proceed to formally define the concept of an extension for such a theory. In view of the discussion of Section 1.3 these extensions are meant to formally specify the set of beliefs induced by a set of defaults, as a way of further completing some underlying incomplete collection of facts about a world.

2.1. Formal preliminaries

We shall be dealing with a first order language L_A consisting of the usual well formed formulae (wffs) over an alphabet A of variables, function and predicate letters, logical constants, and suitable punctuation signs. 0-ary function letters will sometimes be called constant letters. More specifically, L_A is the set of first order wffs which can be formed using an alphabet A consisting of countably many variables $x, y, z, x_1, y_1, z_1, \ldots$, countably many function letters $a, b, c, f, g, h, \ldots$, countably many predicate letters $P, Q, R, \ldots$, the usual punctuation signs, and the standard logical constants $\neg$ (not), $\wedge$ (and), $\vee$ (or), $\supset$ (implies) and quantifiers (x) (for all x), $(\mathrm{E}x)$ (there exists an x). As the alphabet A will usually remain fixed throughout this paper, we will generally write L instead of L_A for the first order language.

As usual, a wff is said to be *closed* iff it contains no free variables. For any set of closed wffs S, and any closed wff w, $S \vdash w$ means that w is first order provable from premises S. For any set of closed wffs $S \subseteq L$, define $\mathrm{Th}_L(S) = \{w \mid w \in L,$ w is closed, and $S \vdash w\}$.

A *default* is any expression of the form

$$\frac{\alpha(\mathbf{x}) : \mathrm{M}\beta_1(\mathbf{x}), \ldots, \mathrm{M}\beta_m(\mathbf{x})}{w(\mathbf{x})},$$

where $\alpha(\mathbf{x}), \beta_1(\mathbf{x}), \ldots, \beta_m(\mathbf{x}), w(\mathbf{x})$ are wffs whose free variables are among those of $\mathbf{x} = x_1, \ldots, x_n$. $\alpha(\mathbf{x})$ is called the *prerequisite* of the default, and $w(\mathbf{x})$ is its *consequent*. A default is *closed* iff none of $\alpha, \beta_1, \ldots, \beta_m, w$ contains a free variable. None of the defaults of Section 1 is closed. An (artificial) example of a closed default is

$$\frac{(x)(P(x) \vee Q(x)) : \mathrm{M}(\mathrm{E}y)(z)R(y,z) \wedge P(y), M(\mathrm{E}y)Q(y)}{(x)(\mathrm{E}y)R(x,y) \wedge P(x)}.$$

A *default theory* is a pair (D, W) where D is a set of defaults and W a set of closed wffs. Notice that D and/or W need not be finite; they will be at most countably infinite however, in view of the countability of L. A default theory (D, W) is *closed* iff every default of D is closed.

2.2. The extensions of a closed default theory

We begin by defining the concept of an extension for closed default theories only. Later, in Section 7, we shall suitably generalize this notion for arbitrary theories.

The intuitive idea which must be captured is that of a set of defaults D inducing an extension of some underlying incomplete set of first order wffs W. In view of the discussion in Section 1.3 we cannot expect this extension to be unique. Any such extension will be interpreted as an acceptable set of beliefs that one may hold about the incompletely specified world W. There are three properties which can reasonably be expected of such an extension E:

(1) It should contain W; $W \subseteq E$.

(2) It should be deductively closed; $\mathrm{Th}_L(E) = E$.

(3) Suppose $(\alpha : \mathsf{M}\beta_1, \ldots, \mathsf{M}\beta_m/w)$ is a default. If $\alpha \in E$ and $\neg\beta_1, \ldots, \neg\beta_m \notin E$ (so that each of $\beta_1, \ldots, \beta_m$ is consistent with E) then $w \in E$. Thus, if α is believed, and if each of $\beta_1, \ldots, \beta_m$ can be consistently believed, then w is believed.

This motivates the following definition:

Definition 1. Let $\Delta = (D,W)$ be a closed default theory, so that every default of D has the form $(\alpha : \mathsf{M}\beta_1, \ldots, \mathsf{M}\beta_m/w)$ where $\alpha, \beta_1, \ldots, \beta_m, w$ are all closed wffs of L. For any set of closed wffs $S \subseteq L$ let $\Gamma(S)$ be the smallest set satisfying the following three properties:

D1. $W \subseteq \Gamma(S)$

D2. $\mathrm{Th}_L(\Gamma(S)) = \Gamma(S)$

D3. If $(\alpha : \mathsf{M}\beta_1, \ldots, \mathsf{M}\beta_m/w) \in D$ and $\alpha \in \Gamma(S)$, and $\neg\beta_1, \ldots, \neg\beta_m \notin S$ then $w \in \Gamma(S)$.

A set of closed wffs $E \subseteq L$ is an *extension* for Δ iff $\Gamma(E) = E$, i.e. iff E is a fixed point of the operator Γ.

The next theorem provides a more intuitive characterization of extensions.

Theorem 2.1. *Let $E \subseteq L$ be a set of closed wffs, and let $\Delta = (D,W)$ be a closed default theory. Define*

$$E_0 = W$$

and for $i \geqslant 0$

$$E_{i+1} = \mathrm{Th}_L(E_i) \cup \left\{ w \;\middle|\; \frac{\alpha : \mathsf{M}\beta_1, \ldots, \mathsf{M}\beta_m}{w} \in D \text{ where } \alpha \in E_i \text{ and } \neg\beta_1, \ldots, \neg\beta_m \notin E \right\}^{1}.$$

Then E is an extension for Δ iff

$$E = \bigcup_{i=0}^{\infty} E_i.$$

Proof. We begin by observing that $\bigcup_{i=0}^{\infty} E_i$ enjoys the following properties:

D1′. $W \subseteq \bigcup_{i=0}^{\infty} E_i$

D2′. $\mathrm{Th}_L\left(\bigcup_{i=0}^{\infty} E_i\right) = \bigcup_{i=0}^{\infty} E_i$

D3′. If $\dfrac{\alpha : \mathsf{M}\beta_1, \ldots, \mathsf{M}\beta_m}{w} \in D$ and $\alpha \in \bigcup_{i=0}^{\infty} E_i$ and $\neg\beta_1, \ldots, \neg\beta_m \notin E$, then $w \in \bigcup_{i=0}^{\infty} E_i$.

[1] Note the occurrence of E in the definition of E_{i+1}.

Hence, by the minimality of $\Gamma(E)$, we have

$$\Gamma(E) \subseteq \bigcup_{i=0}^{\infty} E_i. \tag{2.1}$$

($\Rightarrow$) We inductively prove $E_i \subseteq E$ for all $i \geqslant 0$, whence $\bigcup_{i=0}^{\infty} E_i \subseteq E$. Clearly, since $E = \Gamma(E)$, $E_0 \subseteq E$. Assume $E_i \subseteq E$ and consider $w \in E_{i+1}$. If $w \in \mathrm{Th}_L(E_i)$, then since $E_i \subseteq E$ we have $w \in \mathrm{Th}_L(E) = E$. Otherwise there is a default $(\alpha : \mathsf{M}\beta_1, \ldots, \mathsf{M}\beta_m/w) \in D$, where $\alpha \in E_i$ and $\neg\beta_1, \ldots, \neg\beta_m \notin E$. Then since $E_i \subseteq E$, $\alpha \in E = \Gamma(E)$. Hence $w \in \Gamma(E)$ by D3 of Definition 1 and since $\Gamma(E) = E$, we have $w \in E$.

Thus $\bigcup_{i=0}^{\infty} E_i \subseteq E$. By (2.1) and the fact that $E = \Gamma(E)$ we have $E = \bigcup_{i=0}^{\infty} E_i$.

($\Leftarrow$) We inductively prove $E_i \subseteq \Gamma(E)$ for all $i \geqslant 0$, whence $E = \bigcup_{i=0}^{\infty} E_i \subseteq \Gamma(E)$. By invoking (2.1) we will then have $E = \Gamma(E)$ whence E is an extension for Δ.

Clearly $E_0 \subseteq \Gamma(E)$, so assume $E_i \subseteq \Gamma(E)$ and consider $w \in E_{i+1}$. If $w \in \mathrm{Th}_L(E_i)$, then since $E_i \subseteq \Gamma(E)$ we have $w \in \mathrm{Th}_L(\Gamma(E)) = \Gamma(E)$. Otherwise there is a default $(\alpha : \mathsf{M}\beta_1, \ldots, \mathsf{M}\beta_m/w) \in D$ where $\alpha \in E_i$ and $\neg\beta_1, \ldots, \neg\beta_m \notin E$. Then since $E_i \subseteq \Gamma(E)$, $\alpha \in \Gamma(E)$. Hence $w \in \Gamma(E)$ by D3 of Definition 1. Hence $E_{i+1} \subseteq \Gamma(E)$.

Example 2.1.

$$D = \left\{\frac{:\mathsf{M}A}{A}, \frac{:\mathsf{M}B}{B}, \frac{:\mathsf{M}C}{C}\right\} \qquad W = \{B \supset \neg A \wedge \neg C\}$$

This has two extensions given by

$E_1 = \mathrm{Th}(W \cup \{A, C\}) \qquad E_2 = \mathrm{Th}(W \cup \{B\})$.

Example 2.2.

$$D = \left\{\frac{:\mathsf{M}C}{\neg D}, \frac{:\mathsf{M}D}{\neg E}, \frac{:\mathsf{M}E}{\neg F}\right\} \qquad W = \emptyset.$$

This is example (26) of McDermott and Doyle (1978) which is a variant of an example in Sandewall (1972). This theory has one extension given by

$E = \mathrm{Th}(\{\neg D, \neg F\})$

Example 2.3.

$$D = \left\{\frac{:\mathsf{M}C}{\neg D}, \frac{:\mathsf{M}D}{\neg C}\right\} \qquad W = \emptyset$$

This is example (27) of McDermott and Doyle (1978). This theory has two extensions:

$E_1 = \mathrm{Th}(\{\neg C\}) \qquad E_2 = \mathrm{Th}(\{\neg D\})$.

Example 2.4.

$$D = \left\{ \frac{:\mathsf{M}A}{A}, \frac{B:\mathsf{M}C}{C}, \frac{D \wedge A:\mathsf{M}E}{E}, \frac{C \wedge E:\mathsf{M}\neg A, \mathsf{M}(D \vee A)}{F} \right\}$$

$W = \{B, C \supset D \vee A, A \wedge C \supset \neg E\}$

This has three extensions:

$E_1 = \mathrm{Th}(W \cup \{A,C\})$ $\quad E_2 = \mathrm{Th}(W \cup \{A,E\})$ $\quad E_3 = \mathrm{Th}(W \cup \{C, E, F\})$.

Example 2.5.

$$D = \left\{ \frac{A:\mathsf{M}(\mathrm{E}x)P(x)}{(\mathrm{E}x)P(x)}, \frac{:\mathsf{M}A}{A}, \frac{:\mathsf{M}\neg A}{\neg A} \right\} \qquad W = \emptyset$$

This has two extensions:

$E_1 = \mathrm{Th}(\{\neg A\})$ $\quad E_2 = \mathrm{Th}(\{A, (\mathrm{E}x)P(x)\})$.

What is interesting about this example is that in the second extension, the existence of some individual is believed, while this belief is not held in the first extension. *Different extensions for the same default theory can support different ontologies.* Defaults leading to an ontological commitment of some kind are quite common For example, "Most American adults have a car".

$$\frac{\mathrm{AMERICAN}(x) \wedge \mathrm{ADULT}(x) : \mathsf{M}(\mathrm{E}y)\mathrm{CAR}(y) \wedge \mathrm{OWNS}(x,y)}{(\mathrm{E}y)\mathrm{CAR}(y) \wedge \mathrm{OWNS}(x,y)}$$

Unfortunately, there are default theories with no extensions.

Example 2.6.

$$D = \left\{ \frac{:\mathsf{M}A}{\neg A} \right\} \qquad W = \emptyset$$

This theory has no extension.

It is easy to see that in general default theories are *non-monotonic*. By this we mean that if $\Delta = (D,W)$ is a default theory with an extension E, D' is a set of defaults and W' is a set of first order wffs then $\Delta' = (D \cup D', W \cup W')$ may have no extension E' such that $E \subseteq E'$.

We shall say that a closed default theory has an *inconsistent extension* iff one of its extensions is the set of all closed wffs of L. As immediate corollaries of Theorem 2.1 we have:

Corollary 2.2. *A closed default theory (D, W) has an inconsistent extension iff W is inconsistent.*

Corollary 2.3. *If a closed default theory has an inconsistent extension then this is its only extension.*

A closed default theory is *consistent* iff it has a consistent extension. By Corollary 2.2 if (D,W) is consistent then W is consistent.

Theorem 2.4 (Minimality of Extensions). *If E and F are extensions for a closed default theory (D,W) and if $E \subseteq F$, then $E = F$.*

Proof. By Theorem 2.1, $E = \bigcup_{i=0}^{\infty} E_i$, $F = \bigcup_{i=0}^{\infty} F_i$. We inductively prove $F_i \subseteq E_i$ for all $i \geqslant 0$, whence $F \subseteq E$ whence $E = F$.

Trivially $F_0 \subseteq E_0$. Assume $F_i \subseteq E_i$ and consider $w \in F_{i+1}$. If $w \in \mathrm{Th}_L(F_i)$ then, since $F_i \subseteq E_i$, $w \in \mathrm{Th}_L(E_i) \subseteq E_{i+1}$. Otherwise there is a default $(\alpha : \mathsf{M}\beta_1, \ldots, \mathsf{M}\beta_m)/w) \in D$ where $\alpha \in F_i$ and $\neg\beta_1, \ldots, \neg\beta_m \notin F$. Since $F_i \subseteq E_i$ and $E \subseteq F$ we have $\alpha \in E_i$ and $\neg\beta_1, \ldots, \neg\beta_m \notin E$. Hence $w \in E_{i+1}$.

Definition 2. Suppose $\Delta = (D,W)$ is a closed default theory and E is an extension for Δ. The set of *generating defaults* for E with respect to Δ is defined to be

$$\mathrm{GD}(E, \Delta) = \left\{ \frac{\alpha : \mathsf{M}\beta_1, \ldots, \mathsf{M}\beta_m}{w} \in D \,\middle|\, \alpha \in E \text{ and } \neg\beta_1, \ldots, \neg\beta_m \notin E \right\}.$$

If D is any set of defaults (not necessarily closed) then

$$\mathrm{CONSEQUENTS}(D) = \left\{ w(\mathbf{x}) \,\middle|\, \frac{\alpha(\mathbf{x}) : \mathsf{M}\beta_1(\mathbf{x}), \ldots, \mathsf{M}\beta_m(\mathbf{x})}{w(\mathbf{x})} \in D \right\},$$

i.e., it is the set of consequents of the defaults of D.

The next theorem justifies the terminology of 'generating default'.

Theorem 2.5. *Suppose E is an extension for a closed default theory $\Delta = (D,W)$. Then*

$$E = \mathrm{Th}_L(W \cup \mathrm{CONSEQUENTS}(\mathrm{GD}(E, \Delta)))$$

Proof. Using Theorem 2.1 we inductively prove that $E_i \subseteq \mathrm{RHS}$ for all $i \geqslant 0$, whence $E = \bigcup_{i=0}^{\infty} E_i \subseteq \mathrm{RHS}$. Trivially $E_0 \subseteq \mathrm{RHS}$. Assume $E_i \subseteq \mathrm{RHS}$ and let $\theta \in E_{i+1}$. If $\theta \in \mathrm{Th}_L(E_i)$ then since $\mathrm{Th}_L(E_i) \subseteq \mathrm{RHS}$, $\theta \in \mathrm{RHS}$. Otherwise θ is w where $(\alpha : \mathsf{M}\beta_1, \ldots, \mathsf{M}\beta_m/w) \in D$, $\alpha \in E_i$ and $\neg\beta_1, \ldots, \neg\beta_m \notin E$. Since $\alpha \in E_i, \alpha \in E$. Hence $(\alpha : \mathsf{M}\beta_1, \ldots, \mathsf{M}\beta_m/w) \in \mathrm{GD}(E,\Delta)$ so that

$\theta \in \mathrm{CONSEQUENTS}(\mathrm{GD}(E,\Delta)) \subseteq \mathrm{RHS}$.

Next we prove $\mathrm{RHS} \subseteq E$. It is clearly sufficient to prove

$W \cup \mathrm{CONSEQUENTS}(\mathrm{GD}(E,\Delta)) \subseteq E$ since $\mathrm{Th}_L(E) = E$.

Obviously $W \subseteq E$ so it is sufficient to prove $\mathrm{CONSEQUENTS}(\mathrm{GD}(E,\Delta)) \subseteq E$. If $w \in \mathrm{CONSEQUENTS}(\mathrm{GD}(E,\Delta))$ then there is a default $(\alpha : \mathsf{M}\beta_1, \ldots, \mathsf{M}\beta_m/w) \in D$ such that $\alpha \in E$ and $\neg\beta_1, \ldots, \neg\beta_m \notin E$. Since, by Theorem 2.1, $E = \bigcup_{i=0}^{\infty} E_i$ then $\alpha \in E_i$ for some i which means $w \in E_{i+1} \subseteq E$.

We shall later require the following result:

Theorem 2.6. *Suppose that E is an extension for a closed default theory (D, W), and that $B \subseteq E$. Then E is also an extension for $(D,W \cup B)$.*

Proof. By Theorem 2.1, $E = \bigcup_{i=0}^{\infty} E_i$. Let $F_0 = W \cup B$ and for $i \geqslant 0$

$$F_{i+1} = \mathrm{Th}_L(F_i) \cup \left\{ w \,\middle|\, \frac{\alpha : \mathsf{M}\beta_1, \ldots, \mathsf{M}\beta_m}{w} \in D, \right.$$

$$\left. \text{where } \alpha \in F_i \text{ and } \neg\beta_1, \ldots, \neg\beta_m \notin E \right\}.$$

We prove that $\bigcup_{i=0}^{\infty} F_i = E$ whence E will be an extension for $(D, W \cup B)$. An easy inductive proof establishes that $E_i \subseteq F_i$ for all $i \geqslant 0$ so that $E \subseteq \bigcup_{i=0}^{\infty} F_i$. To prove $\bigcup_{i=0}^{\infty} F_i \subseteq E$ we inductively prove that for each $i \geqslant 0$ there is a $k \geqslant 0$ such that $F_i \subseteq E_k$. Now $B \subseteq E = \bigcup_{i=0}^{\infty} E_i$ so $B \subseteq E_k$ for some k. Since $W \subseteq E_j$ for all $j \geqslant 0$, $F_0 = W \cup B \subseteq E_k$. The inductive step is straightforward.

There are a number of close parallels between default logic and the non-monotonic logic of McDermott and Doyle (1978). The necessary translation from our logic to theirs is to map a default $\alpha(x) : \mathsf{M}\beta_1(x), \ldots, \mathsf{M}\beta_m(x)/w(x)$ into the modalized formula

$$(x).\alpha(x) \wedge \mathsf{M}\beta_1(x) \wedge \ldots \wedge \mathsf{M}\beta_m(x) \supset w(x). \tag{2.2}$$

Default theories thus map into a special class of non-monotonic theories, namely those non-monotonic theories whose modalized formulae all have the form (2.2). The approach of McDermott and Doyle is therefore far more general than ours, since they admit arbitrary modalized formulae into their theory. However, when relativized to formulae of the form (2.2) non-monotonic logic has many similarities with default logic. The extensions of a default theory obviously correspond to the fixed points of a non-monotonic theory. Both admit theories with no extensions and fixed points respectively. Corollaries 2.2 and 2.3, and Theorem 2.4 have their anologues in non-monotonic logic.

A major distinction between the two approaches arises from the different ways that extensions and non-monotonic fixed points are defined. While both are defined to be fixed points of certain operators, these operators differ significantly. As a result there are default theories whose extensions differ from the fixed points of the corresponding non-monotonic theories, even when the modalized elements of the latter are ignored. As an example, consider the default theory $\Delta = (\{A : \mathsf{M}B/B,\ C : \mathsf{M}D/D\}, \{A \vee C\})$. This has the unique extension $\mathrm{Th}(\{A \vee C\})$. The corresponding non-monotonic theory is $\{A \wedge \mathsf{M}B \supset B, C \wedge \mathsf{M}D \supset D, A \vee C\}$ and this has a unique fixed point which contains $B \vee D$. In some instances there are default theories which have an extension while the corresponding non-monotonic theory has no fixed point. An example is given following the proof of Theorem 3.1 below.

There are also some significant differences in emphasis between our two approaches. We avoid modal logic or any modal concepts entirely and work only within a first order framework. For us defaults function as meta-rules whose role it is to further complete an underlying incomplete first order theory whereas for McDermott and Doyle defaults are formulae of a modal logic. In addition they introduce the notion of the theorems of a non-monotonic theory as the intersection of all of the fixed points of that theory and they proceed to give a proof theory for the sentential case. While we could analogously define the theorems of a default theory as the intersection of its extensions, we choose not to pursue this point of view. Instead our position is that the purpose of default reasoning is to determine *one* consistent set of beliefs about a world, i.e. *one* extension, and to reason within this extension until such time as the evidence at hand forces a revision of those beliefs, in which case a switch to a new extension may be called for. This seems also to be the point of view of the Truth Maintenance System of Doyle (1978). Accordingly, the proof theory developed in the next few sections, is not for theoremhood but for 'believability'. By this we mean a proof theory which, given a wff β, determines whether or not there is an extension containing β, rather than determining whether β is in all extensions.

In general the relationship between default and non-monotonic logics appears to be complex. A few results relating the two will be contained in a forthcoming paper (Reiter (1980)).

In an attempt to formalize the ideas in Sandewall (1972), Kramosil postulated a logic which admits deduction rules with 'negative premises' (Kramosil (1975)). In their intended interpretation these deduction rules correspond in a straightforward way to our closed defaults. Unfortunately, Kramosil's notion of theoremhood for his logic fails to capture a suitable intuitive interpretation of a default rule with the result that he is lead to the conclusion that either the default rules are irrelevant, or the resulting theory is meaningless.

3. Normal Default Theories

The fact that some default theories have no extension is not very encouraging for a general theory of default reasoning. In view of this, it is natural to seek out restricted default theories for which extensions can be proved to exist. Fortunately, a very large and natural class of such default theories immediately presents itself. To emphasize the common pattern which defines this class we review the examples of Section 1.

The Closed World Default:

$$\frac{: \mathsf{M}\neg R(x_1, \ldots, x_n)}{\neg R(x_1, \ldots, x_n)}$$

for each n-ary relation R of the data base.

Exceptions:

$$\frac{\mathrm{BIRD}(x) : \mathrm{MFLY}(x)}{\mathrm{FLY}(x)}$$

The Frame Default Schema:

$$\frac{R(\mathbf{x},s) : \mathsf{M}R(\mathbf{x},f(\mathbf{x},s))}{R(\mathbf{x},f(\mathbf{x},s))}$$

for each relation R and state transition function f.

KRL's Palo Alto Default:

$$\frac{\text{PERSON}(x) : \mathsf{M}\text{hometown}(x) = \text{Palo Alto}}{\text{hometown}(x) = \text{Palo Alto}}$$

The Hometown Example:

$$\frac{\text{SPOUSE}(x,y) \wedge \text{hometown}(y) = z : \mathsf{M}\text{hometown}(x) = z}{\text{hometown}(x) = z}$$

$$\frac{\text{EMPLOYER}(x,y) \wedge \text{location}(y,z) : \mathsf{M}\text{hometown}(x) = z}{\text{hometown}(x) = z}$$

All of these examples share a common pattern; they all have the form $\alpha(\mathbf{x}) : \mathsf{M}w(\mathbf{x})/w(\mathbf{x})$. In fact I know of no naturally occurring default which cannot be represented in this form. Accordingly, we propose to focus attention on such defaults. A *normal* default is one which has the above form for wffs $\alpha(\mathbf{x})$, $w(\mathbf{x}) \in L$. Notice that, although in each of the examples the wff $w(\mathbf{x})$ is a literal, we are adopting a more general point of view in which $w(\mathbf{x})$ is any wff, possibly involving quantifiers, whose free variables are among $\mathbf{x}$. Similarly, $\alpha(\mathbf{x})$ is arbitrary. A default theory (D,W) is *normal* iff every default of D is normal.

The rest of this section deals with properties of closed normal default theories, i.e. theories all of whose defaults have the form $\alpha : \mathsf{M}w/w$ for closed wffs α and w. Although this seems not to be a very interesting class, (None of the examples of Section 1 is closed.) the results which are derived for it will all generalize in Section 7.

3.1. Closed normal default theories

In this section we derive a variety of results about closed normal default theories which will provide some insight into their structure. The most important such result is the following:

Theorem 3.1. *Every closed normal default theory has an extension.*

Proof. Let $\Delta = (D,W)$ be a closed normal default theory. If W is inconsistent then by Corollary 2.2, Δ has an (inconsistent) extension. Hence assume W is consistent. We construct an extension for Δ as follows: Let $E_0 = W$. For $i \geqslant 0$ let T_i be a maximal set of closed wffs such that

(1) $E_i \cup T_i$ is consistent, and

(2) If $u \in T_i$ then for some $(\alpha : \mathsf{M}w/w) \in D$, u is w, where $\alpha \in E_i$.

Define $E_{i+1} = \text{Th}_L(E_i) \cup T_i$ and $E = \bigcup_{i=0}^{\infty} E_i$. We prove E is an extension for Δ by proving that

$$T_i = \left\{ w \;\middle|\; \frac{\alpha : \mathsf{M}w}{w} \in D, \text{ where } \alpha \in E_i \text{ and } \neg w \notin E \right\}$$

and invoking Theorem 2.1.

Clearly $T_i \subseteq$ RHS. Assume $T_i \neq$ RHS so there is a wff $u \in \text{RHS} - T_i$. By the maximality of T_i we must have that $E_i \cup T_i \cup \{u\}$ is inconsistent, i.e. $\text{Th}_L(E_i) \cup T_i \cup \{u\}$ is inconsistent, i.e. $E_{i+1} \cup \{u\}$ is inconsistent, and, since $E_{i+1} \subseteq E$, $E \cup \{u\}$ is inconsistent. Since clearly $\text{Th}_L(E) = E$ we must have $\neg u \in E$ which contradicts the fact that $u \in$ RHS.

For the benefit of those familiar with the non-monotonic logic of McDermott and Doyle (1978) it is worth pointing out that Theorem 3.1 does not hold for their logic in the sense that there are 'normal non-monotonic theories' with no fixed point. The simplest counterexample I know of is the following:

$$\left.\frac{\alpha_1 : \mathsf{M}w_1}{w_1} \quad \frac{\alpha_2 : \mathsf{M}w_2}{w_2} \quad \frac{\alpha_3 : \mathsf{M}w_3}{w_3}\right\} D$$

$$\left.\begin{array}{lll} w_1 \supset \alpha_2 & w_2 \supset \alpha_3 & w_3 \supset \alpha_1 \\ w_1 \supset \neg w_2 & w_2 \supset \neg w_3 & w_3 \supset \neg w_1 \end{array}\right\} W$$

This closed normal default theory has the unique extension $\text{Th}(W)$. The corresponding non-monotonic logic would represent the defaults by

$$\alpha_1 \wedge \mathsf{M}w_1 \supset w_1 \qquad \alpha_2 \wedge \mathsf{M}w_2 \supset w_2 \qquad \alpha_3 \wedge \mathsf{M}w_3 \supset w_3$$

and these together with W define a non-monotonic theory with no fixed point.

Theorem 3.2. (Semi-monotonicity). *Suppose D and D' are sets of closed normal defaults with $D' \subseteq D$. Let E' be an extension for the closed normal default theory $\Delta' = (D',W)$ and let $\Delta = (D,W)$. Then Δ has an extension E such that*

(1) $E' \subseteq E$ and

(2) $\text{GD}(E',\Delta') \subseteq \text{GD}(E,\Delta)$.

Proof. If W is inconsistent then by Corollaries 2.2 and 2.3 E' is inconsistent and we can take $E = E'$. In this case the theorem trivially holds. Hence, assume W is consistent, whence E' is consistent.

By Corollary 2.2, (D,E') has a consistent extension E. Trivially, $E' \subseteq E$ so if we prove that E is an extension for Δ then the first half of the theorem will be established.

Towards that end, define $F_0 = W$ and for $i \geqslant 0$

$$F_{i+1} = \text{Th}_L(F_i) \cup \left\{ w \;\middle|\; \frac{\alpha : \mathsf{M}w}{w} \in D, \text{ where } \alpha \in F_i \text{ and } \neg w \notin E \right\}$$

We shall prove that $E = \bigcup_{i=0}^{\infty} F_i$ in which case by Theorem 2.1 E will be an extension for Δ. First, however, we prove that $E' \subseteq \bigcup_{i=0}^{\infty} F_i$. Since E' is an extension for (D',W), then by Theorem 2.1, $E' = \bigcup_{i=0}^{\infty} E'_i$ where $E'_0 = W$ and for $i \geqslant 0$

$$E'_{i+1} = \mathrm{Th}_L(E'_i) \cup \left\{ w \;\middle|\; \frac{\alpha : \mathsf{M}w}{w} \in D', \text{ where } \alpha \in E_i \text{ and } \neg w \notin E' \right\}.$$

We inductively prove that $E'_i \subseteq F_i$ for all $i \geqslant 0$. Trivially, $E'_0 \subseteq F_0$. Assume $E'_i \subseteq F_i$ and consider $w \in E'_{i+1}$. If $w \in \mathrm{Th}_L(E'_i)$ then, since $E'_i \subseteq F_i$, $w \in \mathrm{Th}_L(F_i) \subseteq F_{i+1}$. Otherwise, for some $(\alpha : \mathsf{M}w/w) \in D'$, $\alpha \in E'_i$ and $\neg w \notin E'$. Since $D' \subseteq D$ and $E'_i \subseteq F_i$ then $\alpha \in F_i$ and $(\alpha : \mathsf{M}w/w) \in D$. We prove $\neg w \notin E$ whence $w \in F_{i+1}$. For if $\neg w \in E$, then since $w \in E'_{i+1} \subseteq E' \subseteq E$, E would be inconsistent, a contradiction.

Hence $E' \subseteq \bigcup_{i=0}^{\infty} F_i$. We now prove $E = \bigcup_{i=0}^{\infty} F_i$. Since E is an extension for (D,E') then by Theorem 2.1, $E = \bigcup_{i=0}^{\infty} E_i$, where $E_0 = E'$ and for $i \geqslant 0$

$$E_{i+1} = \mathrm{Th}_L(E_i) \cup \left\{ w \;\middle|\; \frac{\alpha : \mathsf{M}w}{w} \in D, \text{ where } \alpha \in E_i \text{ and } \neg w \notin E \right\}.$$

We first inductively prove that for all $i \geqslant 0$ $E_i \subseteq \bigcup_{i=0}^{\infty} F_i$, whence $E = \bigcup_{i=0}^{\infty} E_i \subseteq \bigcup_{i=0}^{\infty} F_i$. We have already proved that $E_0 = E' \subseteq \bigcup_{i=0}^{\infty} F_i$. Assume $E_j \subseteq \bigcup_{i=0}^{\infty} F_i$ and consider $w \in E_{j+1}$. If $w \in \mathrm{Th}_L(E_j)$ then since $\bigcup_{i=0}^{\infty} F_i$ is closed under Th_L, $w \in \bigcup_{i=0}^{\infty} F_i$. Otherwise, for some $(\alpha : \mathsf{M}w/w) \in D$, $\alpha \in E_j$ and $\neg w \notin E$. Hence $\alpha \in \bigcup_{i=0}^{\infty} F_i$ so that $\alpha \in F_i$ for some i. Since $\neg w \notin E$, $w \in F_{i+1} \subseteq \bigcup_{i=0}^{\infty} F_i$.

Hence $E \subseteq \bigcup_{i=0}^{\infty} F_i$. The opposite inclusion, $\bigcup_{i=0}^{\infty} F_i \subseteq E$ has a simple inductive proof based upon $F_i \subseteq E_i$ for all $i \geqslant 0$.

There remains to prove $\mathrm{GD}(E',\Delta') \subseteq \mathrm{GD}(E,\Delta)$. To that end, suppose $(\alpha : \mathsf{M}w/w) \in \mathrm{GD}(E',\Delta')$. Then $(\alpha : \mathsf{M}w/w) \in D'$, $\alpha \in E'$ and $\neg w \notin E'$. Since $D' \subseteq D$ and $E' \subseteq E$, $(\alpha : \mathsf{M}w/w) \in D$ and $\alpha \in E$. It remains only to prove that $\neg w \notin E$. Now by Theorem 2.5,

$$E' = \mathrm{Th}_L(W \cup \mathrm{CONSEQUENTS}(\mathrm{GD}(E',\Delta'))).$$

Hence $w \in E'$. Since $E' \subseteq E$ and since E is consistent, $\neg w \notin E$.

Theorem 3.2 is a surprising and fortuitous result, one which of course is not true for arbitrary default theories. As we shall see in Section 4, it makes possible a proof theory which is local with respect to the defaults entering into the proof. To see what is meant by this, consider the usual first order proof theory. If A is some set of first order axioms, and if we determine a proof of some wff T using only a subset A' of A then we know that T is a theorem of the first order theory A. This of course is nothing else but a restatement of the monotonicity property of first order logic. It is precisely this property which admits a local proof theory for first order logic, local in the sense that one need not necessarily compute on all of the axioms in A to determine a proof of T.

Now default theories (D,W) in general are non-monotonic in both D and W, i.e. by augmenting either D or W we can so change the extensions of (D, W) that none of these is a subset of any extension of the augmented theory. This means that any proof procedure for general default theories must necessarily compute on all of the defaults of D and all of the wffs of W—no locality is possible. Indeed, the sentential non-monotonic proof theory of McDermott and Doyle (1978) has precisely this global characteristic; every axiom must be taken into account before an attempted proof can succeed.

What Theorem 3.2 tells us is that for closed normal default theories there is a proof procedure which is local with respect to the defaults so that proofs can be constructed which ignore some of the defaults. Indeed, the proof procedure of Section 4 and its refinement in Section 5 have just this property. In view of the large number of defaults which are likely to be in force in the representation of any interesting domain of knowledge this is a very real computational advantage. Of course this kind of locality cannot be expected with respect to W for otherwise closed normal default theories would be monotonic. And in fact the proof theory of Section 4 requires a satisfiability test involving all of W, which is precisely the kind of global property on W one would expect.

The following theorem tells us that one can attempt to simultaneously hold beliefs in two distinct extensions only at the risk of inconsistency.

Theorem 3.3 (Orthogonality of Extensions). *If a closed normal default theory (D,W) has distinct extensions E and F then $E \cup F$ is inconsistent.*

Proof. By Theorem 2.1, $E = \bigcup_{i=0}^{\infty} E_i$ and $F = \bigcup_{i=0}^{\infty} F_i$ where $E_0 = W$ and for $i \geqslant 0$

$$E_{i+1} = \mathrm{Th}_L(E_i) \cup \left\{ w \;\middle|\; \frac{\alpha : \mathsf{M}w}{w} \in D, \text{ where } \alpha \in E_i \text{ and } \neg w \notin E \right\}$$

Similarly for the F_i.

Since E and F are distinct, there is a least integer i such that $E_{i+1} \neq F_{i+1}$ in which case $E_i = F_i$. Hence for some $(\alpha : \mathsf{M}w/w) \in D$ it is the case that $\alpha \in E_i = F_i$, $\neg w \notin E$ and $w \in E_{i+1}$ but $w \notin F_{i+1}$. But if $\alpha \in F_i$ and $w \notin F_{i+1}$ then $\neg w \in F$. Hence $w \in E$ and $\neg w \in F$ so $E \cup F$ is inconsistent.

Corollary 3.4. *Suppose $\Delta = (D,W)$ is a closed normal default theory such that $W \cup \mathrm{CONSEQUENTS}(D)$ is consistent. Then Δ has a unique extension.*

Proof. Suppose on the contrary that Δ has two distinct extensions E_1 and E_2. By Theorem 2.5,

$$E_i = \mathrm{Th}_L(W \cup \mathrm{CONSEQUENTS}(\mathrm{GD}(E_i,\Delta))) \quad \text{for } i = 1,2.$$

By Theorem 3.3, $E_1 \cup E_2$ is inconsistent. Now

$$E_i \subseteq \mathrm{Th}_L(W \cup \mathrm{CONSEQUENTS}(D)) \quad \text{for } i = 1,2$$

since $\mathrm{GD}(E_i,\Delta) \subseteq D$. Hence

$$E_1 \cup E_2 \subseteq \mathrm{Th}_L(W \cup \mathrm{CONSEQUENTS}(D))$$

But $W \cup$ CONSEQUENTS(D) is consistent, by hypothesis, and this contradicts the inconsistency of $E_1 \cup E_2$.

Theorem 3.5. *Suppose $\Delta = (D,W)$ is a closed normal default theory, and that $D' \subseteq D$. Suppose further that E_1' and E_2' are distinct extensions of (D',W). Then Δ has distinct extensions E_1 and E_2 such that $E_1' \subseteq E_1$ and $E_2' \subseteq E_2$.*

Remark. This theorem has the interesting interpretation that the addition of new closed normal defaults to a closed normal default theory (D',W) can never lead to a default theory (D,W) with fewer extensions than the original. *The number of extensions of a closed normal default theory is monotone non-decreasing under the addition of closed normal defaults.*

Proof. By Theorem 3.2 there are extensions E_1 and E_2 for Δ such that $E_1' \subseteq E_1$ and $E_2' \subseteq E_2$. Suppose that $E_1 = E_2$. Then $E_1' \cup E_2' \subseteq E_1$. But by Theorem 3.3, $E_1' \cup E_2'$ is inconsistent. Hence E_1 is inconsistent so by Corollary 2.2 W is inconsistent. But this contradicts the fact that (D',W) has distinct extensions E_1 and E_2, by Corollary 2.3.

4. Proof Theory: Closed Normal Default Theories

In this section we provide a proof theory for closed normal default theories. By a proof theory here we mean a method for answering the question "Given β, can β be believed?". We interpret this as the following formal task:

> Given a closed normal default theory Δ and a closed wff $\beta \in L$, determine whether Δ has an extension E such that $\beta \in E$.

Having devised such a proof theory we shall discover that no procedure exists which, for every Δ and β such that β is a legitimate belief with respect to Δ, will determine a proof of β, i.e. in general beliefs are not recursively enumerable.

4.1. Default proofs

We shall require the following notation: If D is a finite set of closed normal defaults, define PREREQUISITES$(D) = \wedge\, \alpha$ where the conjunction is taken over all wffs α such that $(\alpha : \mathsf{M}w/w) \in D$. Thus PREREQUISITES$(D)$ is the conjunction of all of the prerequisites of the defaults of D.

Definition 3. Let $\Delta = (D,W)$ be a closed normal default theory, and $\beta \in L$ a closed wff. A finite sequence $D_0, \ldots, D_k$ of finite subsets of D is a *default proof of β* with respect to Δ iff

P1. $W \cup$ CONSEQUENTS$(D_0) \vdash \beta$

P2. For $1 \leqslant i \leqslant k$
$W \cup$ CONSEQUENTS$(D_i) \vdash$ PREREQUISITES(D_{i-1}).

P3. $D_k = \emptyset$

P4. $W \cup \bigcup_{i=0}^{k}$ CONSEQUENTS(D_i) is satisfiable.

Example 4.1. $\Delta = (D,W)$ has defaults

$$\delta_1 = \frac{E \vee F : \mathsf{M}(A \wedge F)}{A \wedge F} \qquad \delta_2 = \frac{A : \mathsf{M}B}{B}$$

$$\delta_3 = \frac{A \wedge E : \mathsf{M}C}{C} \qquad \delta_4 = \frac{: \mathsf{M}\neg E}{\neg E}$$

$$W = \{C \supset D,\ A \wedge B \supset E,\ E \vee D,\ D \supset F\}$$

Then $\{\delta_3\}, \{\delta_1,\delta_2\}, \{\delta_1\}, \{\ \}$ is a default proof of D with respect to Δ. So is $\{\delta_4\}, \{\ \}$. Notice that $\{\delta_3,\delta_4\}, \{\delta_1,\delta_2\}, \{\ \}$ is not a default proof of $D \wedge \neg E$, for, while it satisfies conditions P1–P3, it fails to satisfy P4.

The notion of a default proof does not actually provide a proof procedure in the conventional sense of that term. For it gives no method for determining the D_i, not does it specify a first order proof procedure for verifying P1 or P2. Nor for that matter does it specify how to verify condition P4. In fact most readers will have already balked at P4 given that the first order satisfiable wffs are not recursively enumerable. The best way to view this definition is as a bare bones set of conditions on a sequence of default sets $D_0, \ldots, D_k$. As we shall see, whenever these conditions are satisfied the wff β can be believed. Conversely, as we shall also see, whenever β can be believed then some sequence of defaults will satisfy these conditions. Once this completeness result has been established, we will proceed to fill in some of the obvious computational gaps in this computationally spare notion of a default proof.

Accordingly, we now proceed to prove the completeness of default proofs for closed normal default theories.

Lemma 4.1. *Suppose (D,W) is a closed normal default theory with $(\beta : \mathsf{M}v/v) \in D$. If $W \vdash \beta$ and $W \cup \{v\}$ is consistent, then any extension for the default theory $(D, W \cup \{v\})$ is also an extension for (D,W).*

Proof. Suppose $(D, W \cup \{v\})$ has an extension E. By Theorem 2.1, $E = \bigcup_{i=0}^{\infty} E_i$, where $E_0 = W \cup \{v\}$ and for $i \geqslant 0$

$$E_{i+1} = \mathrm{Th}_L(E_i) \cup \left\{ w \,\middle|\, \frac{\alpha : \mathsf{M}w}{w} \in D, \text{ where } \alpha \in E_i \text{ and } \neg w \notin E \right\}$$

Define $F_0 = W$ and for $i \geqslant 0$

$$F_{i+1} = \mathrm{Th}_L(F_i) \cup \left\{ w \,\middle|\, \frac{\alpha : \mathsf{M}w}{w} \in D, \text{ where } \alpha \in F_i \text{ and } \neg w \notin E \right\}.$$

We prove $E = \bigcup_{i=0}^{\infty} F_i$ whence by Theorem 2.1 E is an extension for (D,W).

Clearly, $F_i \subseteq E_i$ for all $i \geqslant 0$, so that $\bigcup_{i=0}^{\infty} F_i \subseteq \bigcup_{i=0}^{\infty} E_i = E$. We inductively prove that for all i, $E_i \subseteq F_{i+2}$ whence $\bigcup_{i=0}^{\infty} E_i \subseteq \bigcup_{i=0}^{\infty} F_i$.

To prove $E_0 \subseteq F_2$ it is obviously sufficient to prove $v \in F_2$. Since $W \vdash \beta$, $\beta \in \mathrm{Th}_L(F_0) \subseteq F_1$. Since $W \cup \{v\}$ is consistent, and since E is an extension for $(D, W \cup \{v\})$, then by Corollary 2.2, E is consistent. Since $v \in E$, $\neg v \notin E$. Hence $\beta \in F_1$, $\neg v \notin E$ so $v \in F_2$.

For the inductive step, assume $E_i \subseteq F_{i+2}$ and consider $w \in E_{i+1}$. If $w \in \mathrm{Th}_L(E_i)$ then $w \in \mathrm{Th}_L(F_{i+2}) \subseteq F_{i+3}$. Otherwise for some $(\alpha : \mathsf{M}w/w) \in D$, $\alpha \in E_i$ and $\neg w \notin E$ so that $\alpha \in F_{i+2}$ and $\neg w \notin E$ whence $w \in F_{i+3}$.

Corollary 4.2. *Suppose (D, W) is a closed normal default theory, and that $D' \subseteq D$ such that $W \cup$ CONSEQUENTS(D') is consistent and such that $W \vdash$ PREREQUISITES(D'). Then any extension for the default theory $(D, W \cup$ CONSEQUENTS$(D'))$ is also an extension for (D, W).*

The next theorem provides one half of the completeness result we seek for default proofs.

Theorem 4.3. *Let $\Delta = (D, W)$ be a closed normal default theory, and let $\beta \in L$ be a closed wff. If β has a default proof $D_0, \ldots, D_k$ with respect to Δ, then Δ has an extension E such that $\beta \in E$.*

Proof. Consider the closed normal default theory $\Delta' = (\bigcup_{i=0}^{k} D_i, W)$. We prove that Δ' has an extension E' such that $\beta \in E'$. Since $\bigcup_{i=0}^{k} D_i \subseteq D$, then by semi-monotonicity (Theorem 3.2) we will be assured that Δ has an extension E such that $E' \subseteq E$, from which the theorem will then follow.

Now by property P2 of default proofs $W \cup$ CONSEQUENTS$(D_k) \vdash$ PREREQUISITES(D_{k-1}) and since $D_k = \emptyset$, $W \vdash$ PREREQUISITES(D_{k-1}). Also, from property P4 of default proofs it follows that $W \cup$ CONSEQUENTS(D_{k-1}) is consistent. Hence by Corollary 4.2, any extension for $\Delta'_1 = (\bigcup_{i=0}^{k} D_i, W \cup$ CONSEQUENTS$(D_{k-1}))$ is also an extension for Δ', and since Δ'_1 is a closed normal default theory it has such an extension, by Theorem 3.1.

Again by property P2 of default proofs $W \cup$ CONSEQUENTS$(D_{k-1}) \vdash$ PREREQUISITES(D_{k-2}) and by property P4 $W \cup$ CONSEQUENTS$(D_{k-1}) \cup$ CONSEQUENTS(D_{k-2}) is consistent so again by Corollary 4.2:

$$\Delta'_2 = \left(\bigcup_{i=0}^{k} D_i, W \cup \mathrm{CONSEQUENTS}(D_{k-1}) \cup \mathrm{CONSEQUENTS}(D_{k-2})\right)$$

has an extension which is also an extension for Δ'_1 and hence which is also an extension for Δ'.

We can continue in this way, finally arriving at a default theory

$$\Delta'_k = \left(\bigcup_{i=0}^{k} D_i, W \cup \bigcup_{i=1}^{k} \mathrm{CONSEQUENTS}(D_{k-i})\right),$$

which has an extension E' which is also an extension for Δ'. Since clearly $W \cup$ CONSEQUENTS$(D_0) \subseteq E'$ and since $W \cup$ CONSEQUENTS$(D_0) \vdash \beta$, then $\beta \in E'$.

Suppose that β has a default proof $P_\beta = D_0, \ldots, D_k$. Then the *default support* of this proof is defined to be $\mathrm{DS}(P_\beta) = \bigcup_{i=0}^{k} D_i$. The default support of a proof is simply the set of all default rules which are invoked in that proof. Notice that condition P4 in the definition of a default proof P_β is the same as the requirement that $W \cup$ CONSEQUENTS$(\mathrm{DS}(P_\beta))$ be satisfiable.

Lemma 4.4. *Suppose that $\Delta = (D, W)$ is a closed normal default theory, and that $\beta', \beta'' \in L$ are closed wffs. Then $\beta' \wedge \beta''$ has a default proof with respect to Δ, iff β' and β'' have default proofs $P_{\beta'}$ and $P_{\beta''}$ respectively with respect to Δ, such that $W \cup$ CONSEQUENTS$(\mathrm{DS}(P_{\beta'}) \cup \mathrm{DS}(P_{\beta''}))$ is satisfiable.*

Proof ($\Rightarrow$). Suppose P is a default proof of $\beta' \wedge \beta''$ with respect to Δ. Then trivially P is also a default proof of β' and of β'' and the result immediately follows.

($\Leftarrow$). Assume $P_{\beta'} = D'_0, \ldots, D'_m$ and $P_{\beta''} = D''_0, \ldots, D''_n$ and suppose $n \geqslant m$, Then clearly

$$P = D'_0 \cup D''_0, \ldots, D'_m \cup D''_m, D''_{m+1}, \ldots, D''_n$$

is a default proof of $\beta' \wedge \beta''$ with respect to Δ.

Corollary 4.5. *Suppose that $\Delta = (D, W)$ is a closed normal default theory, and that $\theta_1, \ldots, \theta_r$ have default proofs $P_{\theta_1}, \ldots, P_{\theta_r}$ respectively with respect to Δ. Suppose further that $W \cup$ CONSEQUENTS $(\bigcup_{i=1}^{r} \mathrm{DS}(P_{\theta_i}))$ is satisfiable. Then $\theta_1 \wedge \cdots \wedge \theta_r$ has a default proof P with respect to Δ, such that $\mathrm{DS}(P) = \bigcup_{i=1}^{r} \mathrm{DS}(P_{\theta_i})$.*

Proof. Notice that, in the proof of the $\Leftarrow$ half of Lemma 4.4, the default proof P of $\beta' \wedge \beta''$ has the property that $\mathrm{DS}(P) = \mathrm{DS}(P_{\beta'}) \cup \mathrm{DS}(P_{\beta''})$. The corollary easily follows from this.

Lemma 4.6. *Suppose α has a default proof P_α with respect to a closed normal default theory $\Delta = (D, W)$. Suppose further that the wff $\alpha \supset \beta$ is valid. Then P_α is also a default proof of β with respect to Δ.*

Proof. Suppose $P_\alpha = D_0, \ldots, D_k$. Then $W \cup$ CONSEQUENTS$(D_0) \vdash \alpha$. Since $\alpha \supset \beta$ is valid, $\vdash \alpha \supset \beta$ so trivially $W \cup$ CONSEQUENTS$(D_0) \vdash \alpha \supset \beta$. Hence by modus ponens, $W \cup$ CONSEQUENTS$(D_0) \vdash \beta$ so that P_α is also a default proof of β.

The next theorem provides the remaining half of the completeness result for default proofs.

Theorem 4.7. *Suppose that E is an extension for a consistent closed normal default theory $\Delta = (D, W)$, and that $\beta \in E$. Then β has a default proof with respect to Δ.*

Proof. By Theorem 2.1, $E = \bigcup_{i=0}^{\infty} E_i$, where $E_0 = W$ and for $i \geqslant 0$.

$$E_{i+1} = \mathrm{Th}_L(E_i) \cup \left\{ w \,\middle|\, \frac{\alpha : \mathsf{M}w}{w} \in D, \text{ where } \alpha \in E_i \text{ and } \neg w \notin E \right\}.$$

Since $\beta \in E$, $\beta \in E_i$ for some i. We shall inductively prove the following result, for all $i \geqslant 0$:

> If $\theta \in E_i$, then there is a default proof P_θ of θ with respect to Δ such that $\mathrm{DS}(P_\theta) \subseteq \mathrm{GD}(E,\Delta)$.

The case $i = 0$ is trivial; if $\theta \in E_0$ then since W is consistent (Corollary 2.2), $P_\theta = \emptyset$ is a definite proof of θ with $\mathrm{DS}(P_\theta) = \emptyset$.

Now assume the induction hypothesis for all wffs of E_i and consider $\theta \in E_{i+1}$.

Case 1. $\theta \in \mathrm{Th}_L(E_i)$

Then there exist finitely many wffs $\theta_1, \ldots, \theta_r \in E_i$ such that $\{\theta_1, \ldots, \theta_r\} \vdash \theta$. By the induction hypothesis, each θ_j has a default proof P_{θ_j} such that $\mathrm{DS}(P_{\theta_j}) \subseteq \mathrm{GD}(E,\Delta)$. Hence $\bigcup_{j=1}^{r} \mathrm{DS}(P_{\theta_j}) \subseteq \mathrm{GD}(E,\Delta)$. By Theorem 2.5

$E = \mathrm{Th}_L(W \cup \mathrm{CONSEQUENTS}(\mathrm{GD}(E, \Delta)))$

and since E is consistent so is $W \cup \mathrm{CONSEQUENTS}(\mathrm{GD}(E,\Delta))$. Hence, so is

$$W \cup \mathrm{CONSEQUENTS}\left(\bigcup_{j=1}^{r} \mathrm{DS}(P_{\theta_j})\right)$$

so by Corollary 4.5, $\theta_1 \wedge \cdots \wedge \theta_r$ has a default proof P such that

$$\mathrm{DS}(P) = \bigcup_{j=1}^{r} \mathrm{DS}(P_{\theta_j}) \subseteq \mathrm{GD}(E, \Delta). \qquad (4.1)$$

Since $\{\theta_1, \ldots, \theta_r\} \vdash \theta$, $\theta_1 \wedge \cdots \wedge \theta_r \supset \theta$ is valid. Hence by Lemma 4.6 P is also a default proof of θ, and by (4.1) $\mathrm{DS}(P) \subseteq \mathrm{GD}(E,\Delta)$.

Case 2. θ is w where $(\alpha : \mathrm{M}w/w) \in D$, $\alpha \in E_i$ and $\neg w \notin E$.

By the induction hypothesis, α has a default proof $P_\alpha = D_0, \ldots, D_k$ and $\mathrm{DS}(P_\alpha) \subseteq \mathrm{GD}(E,\Delta)$. Consider the sequence $P_w = \{\alpha : \mathrm{M}w/w\}, D_0, \ldots, D_k$. This clearly satisfies conditions P1–P3 of the definition of a default proof of w. Now $(\alpha : \mathrm{M}w/w) \in \mathrm{GD}(E,\Delta)$, and since $\mathrm{DS}(P_\alpha) \subseteq \mathrm{GD}(E,\Delta)$, then $\mathrm{DS}(P_w) \subseteq \mathrm{GD}(E,\Delta)$. Moreover, by the same argument as in Case 1, we have that $W \cup \mathrm{CONSEQUENTS}(\mathrm{DS}(P_w))$ is consistent. Hence P_w satisfies property P4 so that P_w is a default proof of w.

By combining Theorems 4.3 and 4.7 we obtain the following completeness result:

Theorem 4.8. *Let $\beta \in L$ be a closed wff. A consistent closed normal default theory Δ has an extension E such that $\beta \in E$ iff β has a default proof with respect to Δ.*

While this completeness result is gratifying we still have no computationally reasonable way of deriving default proofs. We shall defer this question to Section 5. In the interim we show that in a very real sense, default proofs cannot always be derived, even when they exist.

4.2. The extension membership problem

It is known that there is no decision procedure for the validity problem of first order logic (Church (1936)). What this amounts to is that there is no algorithm which, when presented with a closed first order wff, will determine whether or not that wff is valid. The validity problem is, however, semidecidable, i.e. there is a procedure (namely first order proof theory) which will confirm the validity of a closed wff (by finding a proof for it) if that wff is valid, but which fails to terminate on some non-valid wffs. Another way of expressing this state of affairs is by saying that the closed valid wffs are recursively enumerable, but that there is no recursive enumeration of the closed non-valid wffs. From this it follows that the set of closed satisfiable wffs is not recursively enumerable.

Now the definition of a default proof appeals, in condition P4, to a test for the satisfiability of some set of first order wffs. In view of the fact that the closed satisfiable first order wffs are not recursively enumerable, this suggests that there may not be a recursive enumeration of the set of beliefs of an arbitrary closed normal default theory, i.e. that the extension membership problem is not even semi-decidable. By the *extension membership problem* we mean the following:

> Given a closed default theory Δ and a closed wff $\beta \in L$, is there an extension for Δ which contains β?

We now confirm this intuition that the extension membership problem for closed normal default theories is not semi-decidable, or what amounts to the same thing, that the union of the extensions of an arbitrary closed normal default theory is not recursively enumerable.

Given a default theory Δ, let $B(\Delta) = \cup E$ where the union is taken over all extensions E of Δ. Let $w_1, w_2, \ldots$, be a recursive enumeration of the closed wffs of L. For $i = 1, 2, \ldots$, let Δ_i be the closed normal default theory $(\{: \mathrm{M}w_i/w_i\}, \emptyset)$ so that Δ_i has the single default rule $: \mathrm{M}w_i/w_i$, and no first order axioms. Then clearly Δ_i has a unique extension E_i. E_i and therefore $B(\Delta_i)$ is empty if w_i is unsatisfiable, and is $\mathrm{Th}_L(\{w_i\})$ if w_i is satisfiable. Hence $\bigcup_{i=1}^{\infty} E_i = \bigcup_{i=1}^{\infty} B(\Delta_i)$ is the set of closed satisfiable wffs of L.

We shall argue that there is no recursive enumeration of $B(\Delta)$ for arbitrary closed normal default theories Δ. For if there were, then there is a recursive function $f(\Delta,i)$, defined on closed normal default theories Δ and nonnegative integers i, such that $\mathrm{range}(f(\Delta,\cdot)) = B(\Delta)$. In particular, $\mathrm{range}(f(\Delta_j,\cdot)) = B(\Delta_j)$. Then it is known (see e.g. Rogers 1967)) that there is a recursive function $g(i)$ defined on the nonnegative integers i such that $\mathrm{range}(g) = \bigcup_{j=1}^{\infty} B(\Delta_j)$, i.e. $\bigcup_{j=1}^{\infty} B(\Delta_j)$, the set of closed satisfiable wffs of L, is recursively enumerable, a contradiction.

Theorem 4.9. *The extension membership problem for closed normal default theories is not semi-decidable.*

This result assures us that the appeal to satisfiability in condition P4 of the definition of a default proof is not merely an accidental feature of our particular brand of proof theory. Rather, any proof theory whatever for closed normal default theories must somehow appeal to some inherently non-semi-decidable process. This extremely pessimistic result forces the conclusion that any computational treatment of defaults must necessarily have an heuristic component and will, on occasion, lead to mistaken beliefs. Given the faulty nature of human common sense reasoning, this is perhaps the best one could hope for in any event.

Of course there are decidable subcases of the extension membership problem. It is not difficult to see from the definition of a default proof that provided

$$W \cup \left\{\alpha \;\middle|\; \frac{\alpha : Mw}{w} \in D\right\} \cup \left\{w \;\middle|\; \frac{\alpha : Mw}{w} \in D\right\}$$

belongs to a decision class for first order provability then the extension membership problem will be decidable. In particular then, this problem is decidable for the sentential case, i.e. when each α and w and each formula of W is a sentential wff. It is also decidable in the monadic case, i.e. when each of these is a formula of the monadic predicate calculus.

It is also of some interest to contrast Theorem 4.9 with the corresponding result for first order theories. It is well known that the set of theorems of any first order theory is recursively enumerable. If the elements of the extensions of a default theory are viewed as the 'theorems' of that theory, then Theorem 4.9 tells us that the 'theorems' of an arbitrary default theory are not recursively enumerable. This then provides another major distinction between default logic and first order logic, in addition to that of the non-monotonicity of default logic.

5. Top Down Default Proofs: Interface with a Resolution Theorem Prover

The definition of a default proof naturally admits both top down and bottom up search procedures. The top down approach can be loosely described as follows: given β, determine a subset D_0 of the defaults such that $W \cup$ CONSEQUENTS $(D_0) \vdash \beta$. For $i \geqslant 1$, if D_{i-1} has been determined, then determine a subset D_i of the defaults such that

$W \cup$ CONSEQUENTS$(D_i) \vdash$ PREREQUISITES(D_{i-1}).

If, for some k, $W \vdash$ PREREQUISITES(D_{k-1}) and if $W \bigcup_{i=0}^{k-1}$ CONSEQUENTS (D_i) is satisfiable, then a proof of β has been found.

The bottom up approach is as follows: given β, determine whether $W \vdash \beta$. If so, and if W is satisfiable return success. Otherwise, determine a subset D_0 of the defaults such that $W \vdash$ PREREQUISITES(D_0). If $W \cup$ CONSEQUENTS(D_0) $\vdash \beta$ and if $W \cup$ CONSEQUENTS(D_0) is satisfiable, return success. Otherwise, for $i \geqslant 1$, assuming that D_{i-1} has been determined, determine a subset D_i of the defaults such that $W \cup \bigcup_{j=0}^{i-1}$ CONSEQUENTS$(D_j) \vdash$ PREREQUISITES(D_i). If $W \cup \bigcup_{j=0}^{i}$ CONSEQUENTS$(D_j) \vdash \beta$ and if $W \cup \bigcup_{j=0}^{i}$ CONSEQUENTS(D_j) is satisfiable, return success.[4]

The bottom up search procedure does not appear to be computationally very promising. We shall focus instead on the top down approach. At first blush this does not look too promising either. How, for example, are we to determine a D_0 such that $W \cup$ CONSEQUENTS$(D_0) \vdash \beta$? Are we to simply randomly select subsets D_0 of D and try each in turn? The solution lies with the appropriate choice of a first order proof procedure. For if a top down theorem prover is used, then the goal wff β can help to select out a suitable subset D_0 of D.

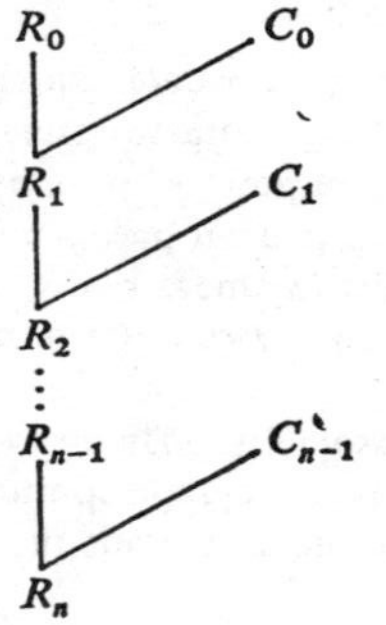

FIG. 1. A linear resolution proof.

Linear resolution (Loveland (1970), Luckham (1970)) provides just such a top down theorem prover. A *linear resolution proof of* β from some set of clauses S has the form of Fig. 1, where

(1) The *top clause*, R_0, is a clause of $\neg\beta$.

(2) For $1 \leqslant i \leqslant n$, R_i is a resolvent of R_{i-1} and C_{i-1}.

(3) For $0 \leqslant i \leqslant n-1$, $C_i \in S$ or C_i is a clause of $\neg\beta$ or C_i is R_j for some $j < i$.

(4) $R_n = \square$, the empty clause.

Linear resolution is known to be complete. It is also a suitable generalization of conventional incomplete back-chaining (subgoaling) proof procedures which reason backward from a goal β until a suitable set of premises is reached.

Now the idea is to use linear resolution to allow the goal wff β to help select out a suitable subset D_0 of D. To do this requires an appropriate representation of a closed normal default theory (D, W). Specifically, assume with no loss of generality that W is a set of clauses. In addition we shall require a special clausal form of the consequents of each default of D. If $\delta = (\alpha : Mw/w) \in D$, suppose $C_1, \ldots, C_r$

[4] This bottom up approach is not immediately apparent from the definition of a default proof. It can be shown to follow from that definition. We omit the details.

are all of the clauses of w. Then for $1 \leqslant i \leqslant r$ the ordered pair $(C_i, \{\delta\})$ is called a *consequent clause* of the default δ. In effect, a consequent clause of δ will function as an ordinary clause of w indexed by the name of the default giving rise to that clause.

Example 5.1. Consider a closed normal default theory $\Delta = (D,W)$ with defaults

$$\delta_1 = \frac{:\mathrm{M}A}{A} \qquad \delta_2 = \frac{(\mathrm{E}x)(\mathrm{E}y)B(x,y):\mathrm{M}C}{C}$$

$$\delta_3 = \frac{D \vee A:\mathrm{M}E}{E} \qquad \delta_4 = \frac{C \wedge E:\mathrm{M}(\mathrm{E}x)(y)F(x,y) \wedge G(x)}{(\mathrm{E}x)(y)F(x,y) \wedge G(x)}.$$

Suppose the clausal form of W is

$C_1 = B(x,f(x)) \qquad C_2 = \neg C \vee D \vee A \qquad C_3 = \neg C \vee \neg E \vee \neg A.$

The consequent clauses are:

$(A,\{\delta_1\}) \qquad (C,\{\delta_2\}) \qquad (E,\{\delta_3\})$

$(F(a,y),\{\delta_4\}), (G(a),\{\delta_4\});$

a is a Skolem constant introduced in forming the clausal form of the consequent of δ_4.

If $\Delta = (D,W)$ is a closed normal default theory, where W is a set of (ordinary) clauses, define

$$\mathrm{CLAUSES}(\Delta) = \{(C,\{\delta\}) \mid \delta \in D \text{ and } (C,\{\delta\}) \text{ is a consequent clause of } \delta\} \cup \{(C,\{\ \}) \mid C \in W\}.$$

In general, we shall refer to an ordered pair (C,D) where C is a clause and D a set of defaults as an *indexed clause*; C will be said to be *indexed by* D. Thus the elements of CLAUSES(Δ) are all indexed clauses, where each clause is indexed by the default which gave rise to it. In what follows, we shall usually not distinguish between $(C,\{\ \})$ i.e. a clause C indexed by the empty set of defaults, and C itself.

Now we propose to invoke linear resolution as the first order theorem proving component of a default theorem prover. The representation of Δ to be used by the linear resolution theorem prover will be CLAUSES(Δ), i.e. a set of indexed clauses. Hence the notion of a resolvent of two indexed clauses must be defined. If (C_1,D_1) and (C_2,D_2) are indexed clauses, and if R is a usual resolvent of C_1 and C_2, then $(R, D_1 \cup D_2)$ is a *resolvent* of the indexed clauses (C_1,D_1) and (C_2,D_2). Then a linear resolution proof of a wff β from some set S of indexed clauses is the same as that using ordinary (non-indexed clauses) except that all of the clauses in the proof are indexed, i.e. it has the form of Fig. 1, where

(1) The top clause, R_0, is a clause of $\neg\beta$.

(2) For $1 \leqslant i \leqslant n$, R_{i-1} and C_{i-1} are indexed clauses and R_i is a resolvent of these indexed clauses.

(3) For $0 \leqslant i \leqslant n-1$, $C_i \in S$ or C_i is a clause of $\neg\beta$ or C_i is R_j for some $j < i$.

(4) $R_n = (\square, D)$ for some set of defaults D.

We shall say that such a linear resolution proof of β *returns* D.

Now recall the original problem: Given β and a closed normal default theory $\Delta = (D,W)$ how are we to determine a D_0 such that $W \cup \mathrm{CONSEQUENTS}(D_0) \vdash \beta$? Suppose we can determine a linear resolution proof of β from the set of indexed clauses CLAUSES(Δ), and that this proof returns D_0. Then it is immediately apparent that $W \cup \mathrm{CONSEQUENTS}(D_0) \vdash \beta$.

Now having determined D_0, there will in general be the problem of determining D_1 such that $W \cup \mathrm{CONSEQUENTS}(D_1) \vdash \mathrm{PREREQUISITES}(D_0)$. Again, we can proceed in a top down fashion by determining a linear resolution proof of PREREQUISITES(D_0) from CLAUSES(Δ) and this proof will return the required D_1. And so on.

These considerations motivate the following definition:

Definition 4. A *top down default proof* of β with respect to a closed normal default theory $\Delta = (D,W)$ is a sequence of linear resolution proofs $L_0, \ldots, L_k$ such that

(1) L_0 is a linear resolution proof of β from CLAUSES(Δ).

(2) For $0 \leqslant i \leqslant k$, L_i returns D_i.

(3) For $1 \leqslant i \leqslant k$, L_i is a linear resolution proof of PREREQUISITES(D_{i-1}) from CLAUSES (Δ).

(4) $D_k = \emptyset$.

(5) $W \cup \bigcup_{i=0}^{k} \mathrm{CONSEQUENTS}(D_i)$ is satisfiable.

Example 5.2. This is the closed normal default theory of Example 4.1, which has two extensions given by

$$E_1 = \mathrm{Th}(W \cup \{A \wedge F, B, C\})$$

$$E_2 = \mathrm{Th}(W \cup \{A \wedge F, \neg E\}),$$

both of which contain D. Figure 2(a) gives a top down default proof of D as an element of E_2, and Fig. 2(b) is a proof of D as an element of E_1.

Example 5.3. This is the default theory of Example 5.1. It has three extensions:

$$E_1 = \mathrm{Th}(W \cup \{A,C\}),$$

$$E_2 = \mathrm{Th}(W \cup \{A,E\}),$$

$$E_3 = \mathrm{Th}(W \cup \{C,E,(\mathrm{E}x)(y)F(x,y) \wedge G(x)\}).$$

Clearly, $(\mathrm{E}x)G(x) \in E_3$. Figure 3(a) represents a top down default proof of $(\mathrm{E}x)G(x)$. This does indeed represent a default proof since δ_2, δ_3 and δ_4 are all of the defaults which enter into the proof and $W \cup \mathrm{CONSEQUENTS}(\{\delta_2,\delta_3,\delta_4\}) = W \cup \{C,E,(\mathrm{E}x)(y)F(x,y) \wedge G(x)\}$ is satisfiable.

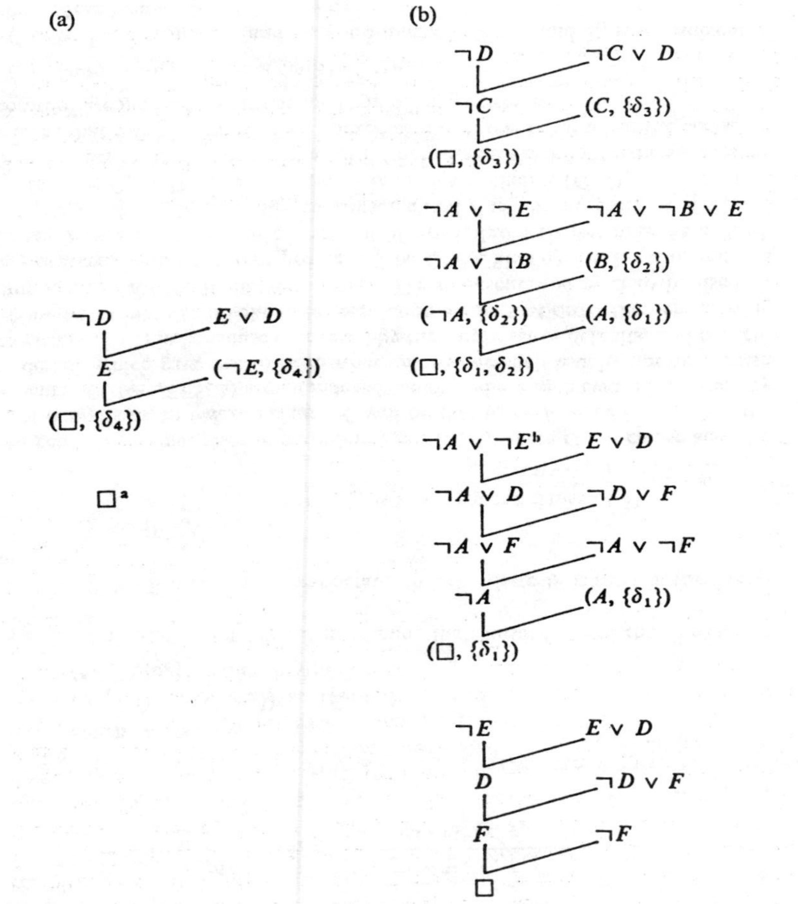

FIG. 2.

[a] Since the prerequisite of δ_4 is T, the identically true clause, its negation is □, which completes the proof.
[b] This is one of the clauses of the negation of PREREQUISITES $(\{\delta_1, \delta_2\}) = A \wedge (E \vee F)$.
[c] This is the other clause of the negation of PREREQUISITES $(\{\delta_1, \delta_2\})$.

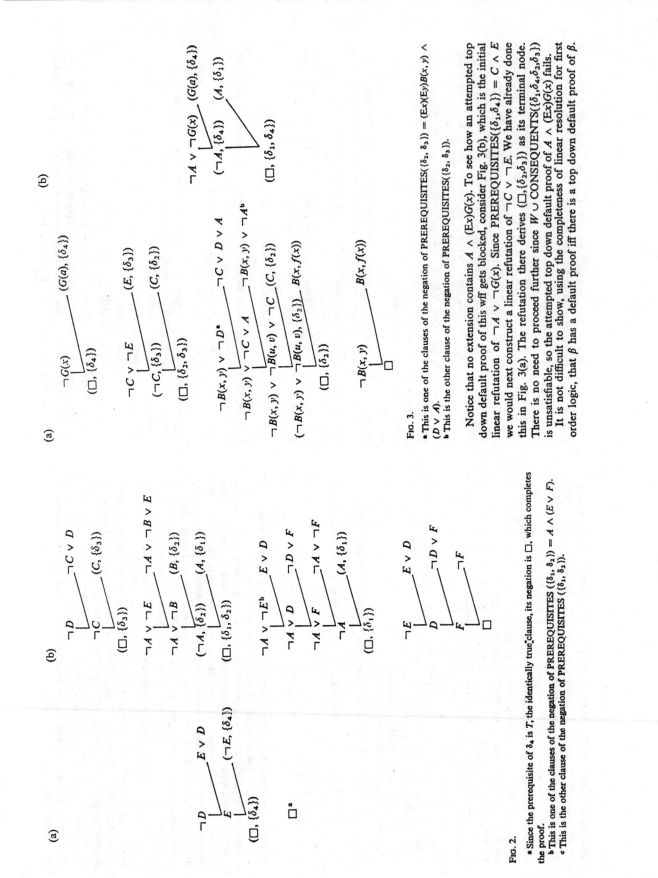

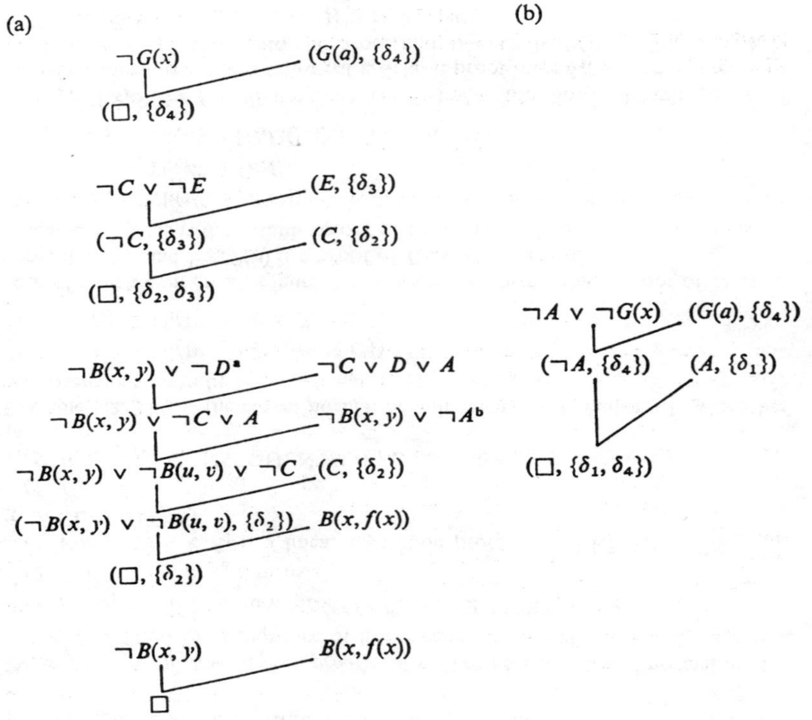

FIG. 3.

[a] This is one of the clauses of the negation of PREREQUISITES$(\{\delta_2, \delta_3\}) = (Ex)(Ey)B(x, y) \wedge (D \vee A)$.
[b] This is the other clause of the negation of PREREQUISITES$(\{\delta_2, \delta_3\})$.

Notice that no extension contains $A \wedge (Ex)G(x)$. To see how an attempted top down default proof of this wff gets blocked, consider Fig. 3(b), which is the initial linear refutation of $\neg A \vee \neg G(x)$. Since PREREQUISITES$(\{\delta_1,\delta_4\}) = C \wedge E$ we would next construct a linear refutation of $\neg C \vee \neg E$. We have already done this in Fig. 3(a). The refutation there derives $(\square, \{\delta_2, \delta_3\})$ as its terminal node. There is no need to proceed further since $W \cup$ CONSEQUENTS$(\{\delta_1,\delta_4,\delta_2,\delta_3\})$ is unsatisfiable, so the attempted top down default proof of $A \wedge (Ex)G(x)$ fails.

It is not difficult to show, using the completeness of linear resolution for first order logic, that β has a default proof iff there is a top down default proof of β.

This result, when coupled with the completeness of default proofs (Theorem 4.8) yields the following:

Theorem 5.1 (Completeness of Top Down Default Proofs). *Let $\Delta = (D,W)$ be a consistent closed normal default theory and let $\beta \in L$ be a closed wff. Then Δ has an extension containing β iff there is a top down default proof of β with respect to Δ.*

This result is of some computational importance. Top down default proofs provide a coherent method for determining the necessary defaults to invoke in establishing a wff β. Moreover, at each stage the current goal (i.e. β or PRE-REQUISITES(D_{i-1})) provides guidance in a top down fashion in the selection of the defaults necessary for establishing that goal. Another important feature of top down default proofs is that they can be implemented in such a way as to favour 'default free' proofs of β, i.e. the linear proof L_0 can seek first to establish β using W alone, only introducing consequent clauses when this fails. Such wffs β, free of default assumptions, have a much firmer status than those which rest upon one or more default assumptions. For example they have a monotonic character in the sense that they need never be retracted under the addition of new first order facts about the world. And they need never take part in the process of belief revision which is required whenever inconsistencies arise. (See Section 6 for a discussion of this issue).) Finally, top down default proofs may invoke any of a variety of complete linear resolution strategies, among which some quite restrictive methods are known e.g. *C*-ordered linear resolution (Reiter (1971)) and SL resolution (Kowalski and Kuehner (1971)).

It is of some interest to reflect upon the nature of top down default proofs in view of the discussion following the proof of Theorem 3.2. For one can see quite clearly how it is that the top down linear resolution proofs L_i select out a subset of all of the defaults. Any default not selected out in this way is irrelevant to the proof and need not be further considered. This is precisely the property of locality with respect to the defaults referred to in that discussion. We also pointed out there that no such locality principle can be expected with respect to W. This expectation is realized in the final defining property of top down default proofs, namely that $W \cup \bigcup_{i=0}^{k}$ CONSEQUENTS(D_i) be satisfiable, for satisfiability is clearly a global property.

6. Closed Normal Default Theories and the Revision of Beliefs

The point of view of this section is that the role of a default reasoning program is to successively derive new beliefs in response to some task at hand. Now an extension specifies one coherent view of an incompletely specified world; moreover many such coherent views are possible, one for each extension of the default theory. We are free to choose any one of these extensions as our current view of the world; the particular choice made will usually be conditioned by some overall objective, e.g. some task to be performed, some decision to be made, etc.

From this perspective, the default reasoner cannot entertain just any set of derived beliefs; they must all belong to some common extension. This requirement gives rise to a variety of problems:

(1) How can one determine when a set of derived beliefs is a subset of some extension?

(2) Suppose given a set B of derived beliefs all of which belong to some common extension of (D,W). Now imagine updating W with some new facts (observations, perhaps) about the world. How can one determine whether B is a subset of some extension of this new default theory? That is can we continue to entertain our previously held beliefs in the presence of new information about the world?

(3) This is the same as (2), except that D is updated rather than W. Can we continue to entertain our previously held beliefs in the presence of new defaults?

It is the purpose of this section to provide answers to these questions.

6.1. Derived beliefs: maintaining a common extension

We envisage a default reasoning program as functioning in the following way:

Initially, some closed normal default theory $\Delta_0 = (D,W)$ is specified. The default reasoner then determines some default proof P_{β_0} with respect to Δ_0. Now that β_0 has been derived, it should be made available as a premise for future derivations, i.e. the 'current default theory' becomes $\Delta_1 = (D, W \cup \{\beta_0\})$. If now a default proof P_{β_1} is determined with respect to Δ_1 then both derived beliefs β_0 and β_1 should be available as premises for future derivations so that the 'current default theory' becomes $\Delta_2 = (D, W \cup \{\beta_0, \beta_1\})$. And so on. In effect, we want to view derived beliefs as lemmas to be subsequently used in the derivation of new beliefs. What is required is that the default reasoner, by proceeding in this way, will be generating 'an approximation' to some extension for the original default theory Δ_0, i.e. the set of derived beliefs $\{\beta_0, \beta_1, \ldots,\}$ must be a subset of some extension for Δ_0. The following example demonstrates that this requirement is not always fulfilled:

Example 6.1.

$$\Delta_0 = \left(\left\{\frac{:\mathsf{M}A}{A}, \frac{B:\mathsf{M}\neg A}{\neg A}\right\}, \{A \supset B\}\right).$$

Then $\beta_0 = B$ is a derived belief of Δ_0. Also $\beta_1 = \neg A$ is a derived belief of

$$\Delta_1 = \left(\left\{\frac{:\mathsf{M}A}{A}, \frac{B:\mathsf{M}\neg A}{\neg A}\right\}, \{A \supset B, B\}\right),$$

yet β_1 is not in any extension for the original default theory Δ_0.

Some care must therefore be exercised in using derived beliefs as lemmas. The following theorem provides a sufficient condition for the proper use of derived beliefs as lemmas in the derivation of new beliefs.

Theorem 6.1. *Let $\Delta_0 = (D,W)$ be a closed normal default theory. In general, suppose Δ_i has been determined and that P_{β_i} is a default proof of β_i with respect to Δ_i. Let $\Delta_{i+1} = (D, W \cup \{\beta_0, \ldots, \beta_i\})$. For any $n \geqslant 0$, if*

$$W \cup \bigcup_{i=0}^{n} \text{CONSEQUENTS}(\text{DS}(P_{\beta_i})) \text{ is consistent} \tag{6.1}$$

then Δ_0 has an extension E_0 such that $\{\beta_0, \ldots, \beta_n\} \subseteq E_0$.

Proof. Let

$$\Delta_0' = \left(\bigcup_{j=0}^{n} \text{DS}(P_{\beta_j}), W\right)$$

and

$$\Delta_i' = \left(\bigcup_{j=0}^{n} \text{DS}(P_{\beta_j}), W \cup \{\beta_0, \ldots, \beta_{i-1}\}\right) \qquad \text{for } 1 \leqslant i \leqslant n.$$

We first inductively prove that for $0 \leqslant i \leqslant n$

$$W \cup \{\beta_0, \ldots, \beta_{i-1}\} \cup \bigcup_{j=0}^{n} \text{CONSEQUENTS}(\text{DS}(P_{\beta_j})) \text{ is consistent.}$$

The case $i = 0$ is simply the hypothesis (6.1). Assume the result for i and consider

$$W \cup \{\beta_0, \ldots, \beta_i\} \cup \bigcup_{j=0}^{n} \text{CONSEQUENTS}(\text{DS}(P_{\beta_j})) \tag{6.2}$$

Now P_{β_i} is a default proof of β_i with respect to Δ_i. Hence

$$W \cup \{\beta_0, \ldots, \beta_{i-1}\} \cup \text{CONSEQUENTS}(\text{DS}(P_{\beta_i})) \vdash \beta_i.$$

Thus, the consistency of (6.2) reduces to that of the induction hypothesis.

This result coupled with Corollary 3.4 assures us that for $0 \leqslant i \leqslant n$ Δ_i' has a unique extension E_i'. Since P_{β_i} is a default proof of β_i with respect to Δ_i it is also a default proof of β_i with respect to Δ_i' and since E_i' is the unique extension for Δ_i', $\beta_i \in E_i'$. Hence $\beta_0 \in E_0'$, so by Theorem 2.6 E_0' is an extension for Δ_1'. Since Δ_1' has a unique extension E_1' then $E_0' = E_1'$. Since $\beta_1' \in E_1'$ we can apply Theorem 2.6 again to conclude that E_1' is an extension for Δ_2' and again by uniqueness $E_1' = E_2'$. We can continue in this way to obtain $E_0' = E_1' = \cdots = E_n'$ and since, for $0 \leqslant i \leqslant n$, $\beta_i \in E_i'$ we have $\{\beta_0, \ldots, \beta_n\} \subseteq E_0'$.

Finally, since $\bigcup_{j=0}^{n} \text{DS}(P_{\beta_j}) \subseteq D$, then by Theorem 3.2, $\Delta_0 = (D,W)$ has an extension E_0 such that $E_0' \subseteq E_0$.

This last theorem provides a mechanism by which a default reasoning program can be assured that all of its current beliefs have a common extension: Let B be the current set of derived beliefs. For each $\beta \in B$ let P_β be the default proof of β. P_β may invoke other β's of B as lemmas. Then the members of B all share a common extension if $W \cup \bigcup_{\beta \in B} \text{DS}(P_\beta)$ is consistent.

The question arises "How does the default reasoner proceed in the event its derived beliefs B do not satisfy this consistency property?" This raises some quite complex issues which we do not address in this paper. However, the basic flavour of the required approach is clear. To restore the consistency property, the system must initiate a process of *belief revision* as follows:

(1) Attempt to rederive some minimal subset of the derived beliefs B in order that the resulting new set of default proofs has the consistency property.

(2) Failing this, reject some minimal subset of B.

This process of belief revision is one of the tasks performed by the Truth Maintenance System of Doyle (1978).

6.2. Derived beliefs and the assimilation of new information

Section 1.2 noted the need for belief revision in the event that a belief depends upon some default assumptions which are subsequently violated by new first order facts about a world. Our purpose now is to make this idea precise, and to formulate a condition under which belief revision will not be necessary.

Theorem 6.2. *Let $\Delta_0 = (D,W)$ be a closed normal default theory, and let $\{\beta_0, \ldots, \beta_n\}$ be a set of derived beliefs determined as in the statement of Theorem 6.1. Suppose further that $F \subseteq L$ is a set of closed wffs. If*

$$W \cup F \cup \bigcup_{i=0}^{n} \text{CONSEQUENTS}(\text{DS}(P_{\beta_i})) \text{ is consistent} \tag{6.3}$$

then $(D, W \cup F)$ has an extension E such that $\{\beta_0, \ldots, \beta_n\} \subseteq E$.

Proof. Let

$$\Delta_0' = (D, W \cup F)$$

and

$$\Delta_i' = (D, W \cup F \cup \{\beta_0, \ldots, \beta_{i-1}\}) \qquad \text{for } 1 \leqslant i \leqslant n.$$

Now P_{β_i} is a default proof of β_i with respect to Δ_i. By the consistency property (6.3), $W \cup F \cup \text{CONSEQUENTS}(\text{DS}(P_{\beta_i}))$ is consistent so that P_{β_i} is also a default proof of β_i with respect to Δ_i'. Hence, by Theorem 6.1, $\Delta_0' = (D, W \cup F)$ has an extension E such that $\{\beta_0, \ldots, \beta_n\} \subseteq E$.

Theorem 6.2 provides a mechanism with which a default reasoning program can be assured that all of its current beliefs $\{\beta_0, \ldots, \beta_n\}$ with respect to a theory (D,W) have a common extension in the theory $(D, W \cup F)$ obtained by updating W with some new facts F about the world. Again, the problem of belief revision arises whenever the consistency property (6.3) fails to hold.

6.3. Derived beliefs and the assimilation of new defaults

We consider here the problem of updating a closed normal default theory with new defaults, and how this may influence our confidence in some set of previously derived beliefs.

Theorem 6.3. *Let $\Delta_0 = (D,W)$ be a closed normal default theory, and let $\{\beta_0, \ldots, \beta_n\}$ be a set of derived beliefs determined as in the statement of Theorem 6.1. Suppose further that D' is a set of closed normal defaults. If (D,W) has an extension E such that $\{\beta_0, \ldots, \beta_n\} \subseteq E$ then $(D \cup D',W)$ has an extension E' such that $\{\beta_0, \ldots, \beta_n\} \subseteq E'$.*

Proof. The proof is a simple consequence of semi-monotonicity (Theorem 3.2).

Theorem 6.3 provides the only truly comforting result *vis à vis* belief revision. It guarantees that provided the derived beliefs $\beta_0, \ldots, \beta_n$ have a common extension in (D,W) then they will continue to have a common extension in $(D \cup D',W)$. Updating a closed normal default theory with new defaults cannot affect old beliefs.

7. Arbitrary Default Theories

The technical results of the previous sections have been derived for closed default theories, i.e. theories all of whose defaults have the form $\alpha : M\beta_1, \ldots, M\beta_m / w$, where $\alpha, \beta_1, \ldots, \beta_m, w$ are all closed first order wffs. In view of the examples of Section 1, none of which is a closed default, the genuinely interesting cases involve open defaults. An *open* default has the form $\alpha(\mathbf{x}) : M\beta_1(\mathbf{x}), \ldots, M\beta_m(\mathbf{x}) / w(\mathbf{x})$ where at least one of $\alpha(\mathbf{x}), \beta_1(\mathbf{x}), \ldots, \beta_m(\mathbf{x}), w(\mathbf{x})$ contains free variables in $\mathbf{x}$. The purpose of this section is to generalize our earlier results on closed default theories to the case of open defaults. We do this by first defining the notion of an extension for default theories with open defaults. Then we focus upon normal default theories and generalize the proof theory of Section 5 for this case. Finally, the results of Section 6 on belief revision are suitably generalized.

7.1. The extensions for arbitrary default theories

The first task at hand is to suitably generalize the concept of an extension from closed default theories to arbitrary theories. Intuitively, we want to interpret the open default $\alpha(\mathbf{x}) : M\beta_1(\mathbf{x}), \ldots, M\beta_m(\mathbf{x}) / w(\mathbf{x})$ as saying something like: "For all individuals $x_1, \ldots, x_n$, if $\alpha(\mathbf{x})$ is believed and each of $\beta_1(\mathbf{x}), \ldots, \beta_m(\mathbf{x})$ can be consistently believed, then one is permitted to believe $w(\mathbf{x})$." The initial problem then is to specify exactly what are the individuals of a default theory.

To begin with a default theory is defined over the language L_A whose alphabet is A. If $F \subseteq A$ is the set of all function letters of A (including the 0-ary function letters, or constant letters) then any term constructable using the function letters of F should count as an individual of the default theory, so that the free variables of an open default should at least be seen as ranging over these terms. This seems fine with respect to these explicitly nameable individuals. However, there will generally be implicitly defined individuals which are introduced via existential quantifiers. For example, the theory

$$\frac{: MP(x)}{P(x)} \qquad (Ex)Q(x) \qquad \neg P(a)$$

has an explicitly named individual a, together with an implicitly defined individual which satisfies Q. Intuitively one would expect of this implicitly defined individual that it satisfy P in the extension for this theory. In order to accommodate this intuition, we introduce a new constant letter α distinct from any element of F to denote this implicitly defined individual and replace $(Ex)Q(x)$ by $Q(\alpha)$. This immediately yields $P(\alpha)$ in the extension whence $(Ex).Q(x) \wedge P(x)$ is in the extension.[5]

What the previous discussion amounts to is the suggestion that each wff of W be replaced by its Skolemized form. If Σ is the set of Skolem functions so introduced, then we would like to view the individuals constructable from the elements of $F \cup \Sigma$ as the individuals of the default theory, and the free variables of an open default as ranging over these individuals.

While this feels closer to the truth, there still remains the problem of implicitly defined individuals which may be introduced by default. For example, in the theory

$$\frac{: M(Ex)P(x)}{(Ex)P(x)} \qquad \frac{: MQ(x)}{Q(x)}$$

there is an implicitly defined individual which is introduced by the first default, and which satisfies P. One would expect, by the second default, that this individual will also satisfy Q, i.e. one would expect $(Ex).P(x) \wedge Q(x)$ to be in the extension. As before, we introduce a new constant letter α to denote this individual, and represent the first default by its Skolemized form $: MP(\alpha)/P(\alpha)$. This immediately yields $P(\alpha)$ in the extension and then, by the second default, $Q(\alpha)$ is in the extension, and hence so is $(Ex).P(x) \wedge Q(x)$.

In general then, if Σ is the set of Skolem functions introduced by Skolemizing W as well as all of the defaults, then we shall view the individuals constructable from the elements of $F \cup \Sigma$ as the individuals of the default theory, and the free variables of an open default as ranging over these individuals. We proceed to make these ideas precise.

Let w be a closed wff of L_A. With no loss in generality assume w is in prenex form. Then the *Skolemized form* of w is obtained as follows (Robinson (1965)): replace each existentially quantified variable y of w by $\sigma(x_1, \ldots, x_n)$ where $(x_1), \ldots, (x_n)$ are all of the universal quantifiers preceding (Ey) in the prefix of w. σ must be a new function letter distinct from any in the alphabet A and distinct from any other such function letters previously introduced. Do this for all existentially quantified variables of w, and then delete all of w's quantifiers. The result is a quantifier free formula. The new function letters σ so introduced are called *Skolem functions*.

[5] It would appear from the definition of a fixed point in McDermott and Doyle (1978) that $(Ex) . Q(x) \wedge P(x)$ is not in the fixed point of this theory, which suggests some fundamental differences between default logic and their non-monotonic logic.

We also require the notion of the *Skolemized form* of a default

$$\frac{\alpha(x) : M\beta_1(x), \ldots, M\beta_m(x)}{w(x)}.$$

This is obtained by replacing the wff $w(x)$ by the Skolemized form of $(x)w(x)$. For example the Skolemized form of

$$\frac{(Ey)(z)P(x,y,z) : M(Ey)Q(x,y)}{(Ey)(z)(Ew)R(x,y,z,w)}$$

is

$$\frac{(Ey)(z)P(x,y,z) : M(Ey)Q(x,y)}{R(x,f(x),z,g(x,z))},$$

where f and g are Skolem functions. Notice that the 'top half' of a default remains unchanged in converting it to its Skolemized form.

A default theory (D,W) is in *Skolemized form* iff all of the defaults of D, and all of the wffs of W are in Skolemized form.

Let G be a set of function letters. Then $H(G)$ is the smallest set of terms such that $a \in H(G)$ for all constant letters $a \in G$, and if $t_1, \ldots, t_n \in H(G)$ and $g \in G$ is an n-ary function letter then $g(t_1, \ldots, t_n) \in H(G)$. $H(G)$ is simply the set of all terms constructable using the function letters of G.

Suppose $\Delta = (D,W)$ is a Skolemized default theory (not necessarily normal). Suppose further that Σ is the set of Skolem functions of Δ, and that F is the set of function letters of the alphabet A. Define

$$\text{CLOSED-DEFAULTS}(\Delta) = \{\delta(\mathbf{g}) \mid \delta(\mathbf{x}) \in D \text{ and } \mathbf{g} \text{ is a tuple of ground terms of } H(F \cup \Sigma)\}$$

Thus CLOSED-DEFAULTS(Δ) is the set of all ground instances over $H(F \cup \Sigma)$ of the defaults of D. Notice that each such ground instance of a default is a closed default. The extensions for a general (not necessarily closed) default theory can now be defined as follows:

Definition 5. E is an *extension* for $\Delta = (D,W)$ iff E is an extension for the closed default theory CLOSED(Δ) = (CLOSED-DEFAULTS(Δ), W).

There are several points worth noting about this definition:

(1) The set CLOSED-DEFAULTS(Δ) will in general be countably infinite so that CLOSED(Δ) is a closed default theory with countably infinitely many defaults. Since the entire preceding development for closed default theories (Sections 2–6) makes no finiteness assumption about the number of defaults, these results apply equally to CLOSED(Δ). In particular then, the definition of an extension for Δ as being that for CLOSED(Δ) makes sense.

(2) Initially we began with an unskolemized default theory defined over a first order language L_A whose alphabet A contains a set of function letters F. In Skolemizing this theory, we introduced a new set of function letters Σ, the Skolem functions of the theory, and CLOSED(Δ) is a closed default theory over the first order language $L_{A \cup \Sigma}$. Thus the extensions for Δ consist of closed wffs of the extended language $L_{A \cup \Sigma}$, not of the original language L_A.

(3) In view of the observation in (2), the notion of an extension for a general default theory Δ is not quite a generalization of this notion for closed default theories. For if Δ is closed to begin with, then its extensions will be subsets of $L_{A \cup \Sigma}$ whereas in the definition of an extension for closed theories given in Section 2 these extensions are subsets of L_A. This is not a substantive issue, however. We can easily modify the definition of extension given in Section 2 so that these are subsets of $L_{A \cup \Sigma}$ rather than of L_A, without affecting the subsequent theory. The effect of this modification is merely to admit into extensions certain wffs containing Skolem terms of the original closed default theory.

7.2. Normal default theories: proof theory

Before defining a proof procedure for general normal default theories we shall modify the top down default proofs for closed normal theories of Section 5 to a form that is more appropriate for generalization to the case of open normal defaults. The principal change is that we shall require the notion of a linear resolution proof of an arbitrary wff where this wff is indexed by some set of defaults.

Definition 6. *A linear resolution proof of* (β, D_0') from some set S of indexed clauses has the form of Fig. 4, where

(1) The *top indexed clause* (R_0, D_0') is such that R_0 is a clause of $\neg\beta$.

(2) For $1 \leqslant i \leqslant n$, (R_i, D_i') is a resolvent of the indexed clauses (R_{i-1}, D_{i-1}') and (C_{i-1}, D_{i-1}).

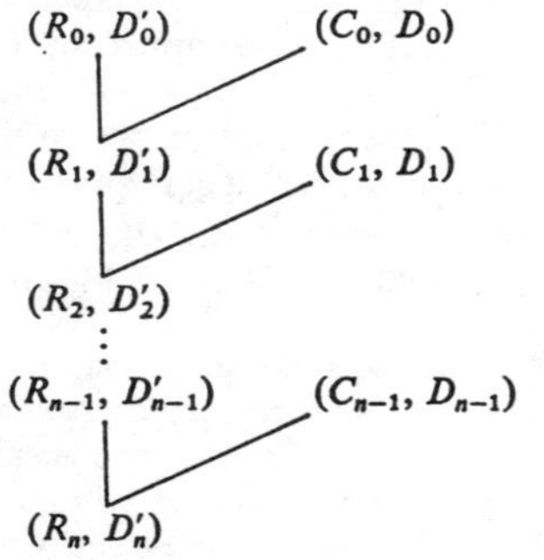

FIG. 4.

(3) For $0 \leq i \leq n-1$, $(C_i, D_i) \in S$ or C_i is a clause of $\neg \beta$ and $D_i = D'_0$, or (C_i, D_i) is (R_j, D'_j) for some $j < i$.

(4) $R_n = \square$.

As before, we say that such a proof *returns* D_n. The clauses (C_i, D_i) are called the *side* clauses of the proof. For $1 \leq i \leq n$, the clauses (R_i, D'_i) are called *centre* clauses.

Suppose L is a linear resolution proof from CLAUSES(Δ). If $(C, \{\delta\}) \in$ CLAUSES(Δ) is a side clause of L, then the default δ is said to have been *introduced into* L.

Definition 7. A *top down default proof* of β with respect to a closed normal default theory $\Delta = (D, W)$ is a sequence of linear resolution proofs $L_0, \ldots, L_k$ such that

(1) L_0 is a linear resolution proof of $(\beta, \{ \})$ from CLAUSES(Δ),

(2) For $0 \leq i \leq k$, L_i returns D_i,

(3) For $1 \leq i \leq k$, let $D^{(i-1)}$ be the set of defaults introduced into L_{i-1}. Then L_i is a linear resolution proof of (PREREQUISITES($D^{(i-1)}$), D_{i-1}) from CLAUSES(Δ).

(4) The set of defaults introduced into L_k is empty.

(5) $W \cup$ CONSEQUENTS(D_k) is satisfiable.

Example 7.1. In Example 5.2, Fig. 2(b) represented a top down default proof of D. Fig. 5 is the corresponding proof under the current modified notion of a top down default proof.

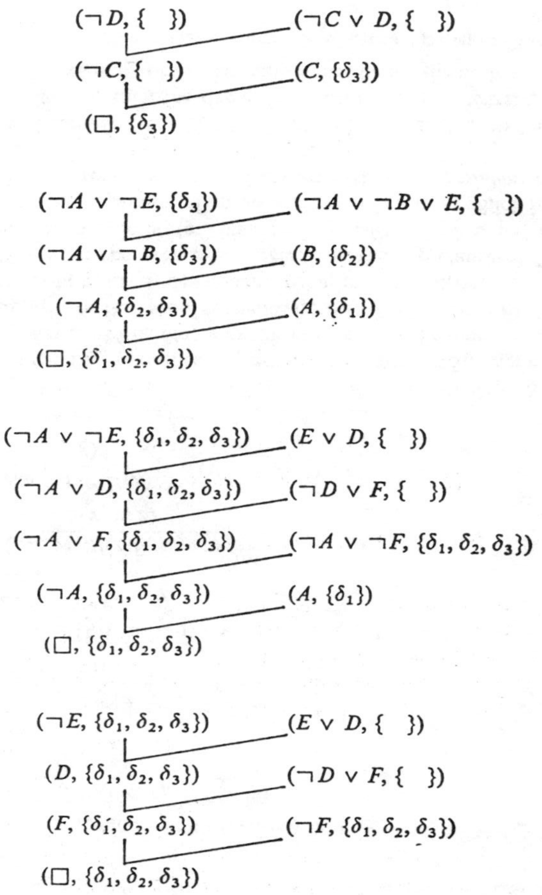

Example 7.1 should make it clear that there is no essential difference between the present notion of a top down default proof and that of Section 5. The only distinction is that in the current notion, each subproof L_i carries along with it all of the defaults introduced into the subproofs $L_0, \ldots, L_{i-1}$, so that the final subproof L_k returns D_k, the set of all of the defaults introduced into all of the subproofs. For closed default theories this modified notion is of no consequence. In fact the earlier notion of Section 5 was rather more transparent. However, for the purpose of generalizing a proof theory to the case of open normal defaults, the modified version of top down default proofs is just what is needed. We now proceed with this generalization.

Let $\Delta = (D, W)$ be a normal default theory, assumed Skolemized. With no loss in generality, assume W is a set of clauses. If $\delta(x) = (\alpha(x) : M_w(x)/w(x)) \in D$, suppose $C_1(x), \ldots, C_r(x)$ are all of the clauses of $w(x)$. Then for $1 \leq i \leq r$ the ordered pair $(C_i(x), \{\delta(x)\})$ is called a *consequent clause* of the default $\delta(x)$. Define

$$\text{CLAUSES}(\Delta) = \{(C(x), \{\delta(x)\}) \mid \delta(x) \in D \text{ and } (C(x), \{\delta(x)\}) \text{ is a} \atop \text{consequent clause of } \delta(x)\} \cup \{(C, \{ \}) \mid C \in W\}$$

$(\neg D, \{ \})$ $(\neg C \lor D, \{ \})$
_____
$(\neg C, \{ \})$ $(C, \{\delta_3\})$
_____
$(\square, \{\delta_3\})$

$(\neg A \lor \neg E, \{\delta_3\})$ $(\neg A \lor \neg B \lor E, \{ \})$
_____
$(\neg A \lor \neg B, \{\delta_3\})$ $(B, \{\delta_2\})$
_____
$(\neg A, \{\delta_2, \delta_3\})$ $(A, \{\delta_1\})$
_____
$(\square, \{\delta_1, \delta_2, \delta_3\})$

$(\neg A \lor \neg E, \{\delta_1, \delta_2, \delta_3\})$ $(E \lor D, \{ \})$
_____
$(\neg A \lor D, \{\delta_1, \delta_2, \delta_3\})$ $(\neg D \lor F, \{ \})$
_____
$(\neg A \lor F, \{\delta_1, \delta_2, \delta_3\})$ $(\neg A \lor \neg F, \{\delta_1, \delta_2, \delta_3\})$
_____
$(\neg A, \{\delta_1, \delta_2, \delta_3\})$ $(A, \{\delta_1\})$
_____
$(\square, \{\delta_1, \delta_2, \delta_3\})$

$(\neg E, \{\delta_1, \delta_2, \delta_3\})$ $(E \lor D, \{ \})$
_____
$(D, \{\delta_1, \delta_2, \delta_3\})$ $(\neg D \lor F, \{ \})$
_____
$(F, \{\delta_1, \delta_2, \delta_3\})$ $(\neg F, \{\delta_1, \delta_2, \delta_3\})$
_____
$(\square, \{\delta_1, \delta_2, \delta_3\})$

Fig. 5.

As before, an ordered pair (C,D) where C is a clause and D a set of defaults is called an *indexed clause*. If (C_1,D_1) and (C_2,D_2) are indexed clauses, define their resolvent as follows:

Let (C_1',D_1') and (C_2',D_2') be obtained by uniform renamings[6] of the variables occurring in (C_1,D_1) and (C_2,D_2) respectively such that (C_1',D_1') has no variable in common with (C_2',D_2'). Suppose R is an ordinary resolvent of C_1' and C_2' under most general unifier (mgu) σ. Then $(R,(D_1' \cup D_2')\sigma)$ is a *resolvent* of the indexed clauses (C_1,D_1) and (C_2,D_2).

With this notion of the resolvent of two indexed clauses the definition of a linear resolution proof of (β,D_0') from a set S of indexed clauses is the same as before. The only difference is that here the defaults taking part in the proof have free variables and these will become instantiated during the course of the proof.

Consider a linear resolution proof of the form of Fig. 4. Assume that (R_i,D_i') and (C_i,D_i) are variable disjoint, and that their resolvent (R_{i+1},D_{i+1}') is formed under mgu σ, so that $D_{i+1}' = (D_i' \cup D_i)\sigma$. If $\delta(\mathbf{t}) \in D_i'$ for some terms $\mathbf{t}$, then $\delta(\mathbf{t})\,\sigma \in D_{i+1}'$. This occurrence of $\delta(\mathbf{t})\sigma$ in D_{i+1}' is said to be a *descendant* of the occurrence of $\delta(\mathbf{t})$ in D_i'. Similarly, if $\delta(\mathbf{t}) \in D_i$, then again $\delta(\mathbf{t})\sigma \in D_{i+1}'$ and this occurrence of $\delta(\mathbf{t})\sigma$ in D_{i+1}' is a *descendant* of the occurrence of $\delta(\mathbf{t})$ in D_i. Finally, for $i < j < k$, if an occurrence of $\delta(\mathbf{t})$ in D_k' is a descendant of an occurrence of $\delta(\mathbf{s})$ in D_j' which in turn is a descendant of an occurrence of $\delta(\mathbf{r})$ in D_i' or in D_i, then $\delta(\mathbf{t})$ is a *descendant* of the occurrence of $\delta(\mathbf{r})$ in D_i' or D_i.

The descendants of an occurrence of a default in the tree of Fig. 4 are simply the successive instances of that default created under successive resolution operations. If a default occurs at node (C_i,D_i), then it will have descendants at each successor node $(R_{i+1},D_{i+1}'),\ldots,(R_n,R_n')$. Likewise if a default occurs at node (R_i,D_i').

We are now almost in a position to propose the necessary generalization to open defaults of the top down default proofs for closed normal default theories. The following notion comes very close to what is needed.

Definition 8. Let $\Delta = (D,W)$ be a normal default theory, assumed Skolemized, and suppose Σ is the set of Skolem functions of Δ. A sequence of linear resolution proofs $L_0,\ldots,L_k$ is an *admissible proof sequence* for β with respect to Δ iff

(1) L_0 is a linear resolution proof of $(\beta,\{\ \})$ from CLAUSES(Δ).

(2) For $0 \leqslant i \leqslant k$, L_i returns D_i.

(3) For $1 \leqslant i \leqslant k$, let $D^{(i-1)}$ be the set of those defaults in D_{i-1} which are descendants of the defaults introduced into L_{i-1}. Then L_i is a linear resolution proof of (PREREQUISITES($D^{(i-1)}$),D_{i-1}) from CLAUSES(Δ).

(4) The set of defaults introduced into L_k is empty.

(5) There is a ground substitution γ over $H(F \cup \Sigma)$ such that $D_k\gamma$ has the following two properties:

(i) Each default instance occurring in $D_k\gamma$ is a ground instance over $H(F \cup \Sigma)$, i.e. if $\delta(\mathbf{g}) \in D_k\gamma$, then each component g_i of the tuple of ground terms $\mathbf{g}$ is an element of $H(F \cup \Sigma)$.[7]

(ii) $W \cup$ CONSEQUENTS($D_k\gamma$) is satisfiable.

We call the set of ground defaults $D_k\gamma$ the *default support* of the admissible proof sequence. Notice that by footnote 7 the default support is a subset of CLOSED-DEFAULTS(Δ).

Example 7.2. Consider the normal default theory Δ with defaults

$$\delta_1(x) = \frac{P(x):\mathrm{M}(\mathrm{E}y)Q(x,y) \wedge R(x,y)}{(\mathrm{E}y)Q(x,y) \wedge R(x,y)}$$

or, in Skolemized form,

$$\delta_1(x) = \frac{P(x):\mathrm{M}(\mathrm{E}y)Q(x,y) \wedge R(x,y)}{Q(x,f(x)) \wedge R(x,f(x))};$$

$$\delta_2(x,y) = \frac{Q(x,y):\mathrm{M}(z)S(x,y,z)}{(z)S(x,y,z)}$$

or, in Skolemized form,

$$\delta_2(x,y) = \frac{Q(x,y):\mathrm{M}(z)S(x,y,z)}{S(x,y,z)};$$

$$\delta_3(x,y) = \frac{R(x,y):\mathrm{M}U(x)}{U(x)}; \qquad W = \{P(a)\}.$$

Fig. 6(a) is an admissible proof sequence for $(\mathrm{E}x)(\mathrm{E}y)(z).S(x,y,z) \wedge U(x)$. The negation of this is $(x)(y)(\mathrm{E}z).\neg S(x,y,z) \vee \neg U(x)$ which, after introducing a Skolem function g for the existentially quantified z, leads to the clause $\neg S(x,y,g(x,y)) \vee \neg U(x)$. This is the top clause of Fig. 6(a). For this example γ is the empty substitution so the default support for this proof sequence is $\{\delta_3(a,f(a)), \delta_2(a,f(a)), \delta_1(a)\}$.

Let us extend the notion of a descendant to admissible proof sequences $L_0,\ldots,L_k$. For $1 \leqslant i \leqslant k$ an occurrence of a default in the top clause of L_i is a *descendant* of its occurrence in the bottom clause of L_{i-1}. And for $h \leqslant i \leqslant j$ if an occurrence of $\delta(\mathbf{t})$ in L_j is a descendant of an occurrence of $\delta(\mathbf{s})$ in L_i which in turn is a descendant of an occurrence of $\delta(\mathbf{r})$ in L_h, then $\delta(\mathbf{t})$ is a *descendant* of the occurrence of $\delta(\mathbf{r})$ in L_h.

If one imagines the successive trees $L_0,\ldots,L_k$ placed vertically, each beneath its predecessor, as in Fig. 6(a) then the descendants of a default occurrence are simply its successive instances in all of the left hand nodes below the node in which

[6] By a uniform renaming of the variables of (C, D) we mean that if x is renamed as y, then every occurrence of x in C as well as in D is replaced by y.

[7] Notice that by this property $\delta(\mathbf{g})$ is a closed normal default, and that $\delta(\mathbf{g}) \in$ CLOSED-DEFAULTS(Δ).

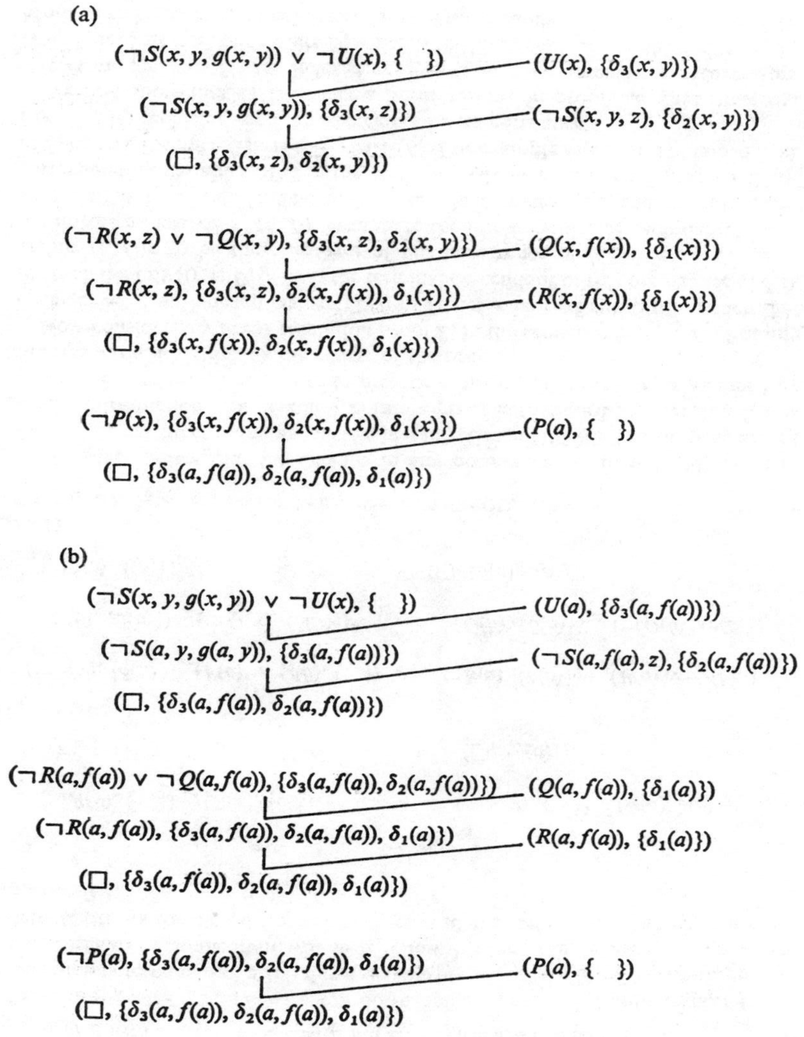

(a)

$(\neg S(x, y, g(x, y)) \vee \neg U(x), \{\ \})$ — $(U(x), \{\delta_3(x, y)\})$

$(\neg S(x, y, g(x, y)), \{\delta_3(x, z)\})$ — $(\neg S(x, y, z), \{\delta_2(x, y)\})$

$(\Box, \{\delta_3(x, z), \delta_2(x, y)\})$

$(\neg R(x, z) \vee \neg Q(x, y), \{\delta_3(x, z), \delta_2(x, y)\})$ — $(Q(x, f(x)), \{\delta_1(x)\})$

$(\neg R(x, z), \{\delta_3(x, z), \delta_2(x, f(x)), \delta_1(x)\})$ — $(R(x, f(x)), \{\delta_1(x)\})$

$(\Box, \{\delta_3(x, f(x)), \delta_2(x, f(x)), \delta_1(x)\})$

$(\neg P(x), \{\delta_3(x, f(x)), \delta_2(x, f(x)), \delta_1(x)\})$ — $(P(a), \{\ \})$

$(\Box, \{\delta_3(a, f(a)), \delta_2(a, f(a)), \delta_1(a)\})$

(b)

$(\neg S(x, y, g(x, y)) \vee \neg U(x), \{\ \})$ — $(U(a), \{\delta_3(a, f(a))\})$

$(\neg S(a, y, g(a, y)), \{\delta_3(a, f(a))\})$ — $(\neg S(a, f(a), z), \{\delta_2(a, f(a))\})$

$(\Box, \{\delta_3(a, f(a)), \delta_2(a, f(a))\})$

$(\neg R(a, f(a)) \vee \neg Q(a, f(a)), \{\delta_3(a, f(a)), \delta_2(a, f(a))\})$ — $(Q(a, f(a)), \{\delta_1(a)\})$

$(\neg R(a, f(a)), \{\delta_3(a, f(a)), \delta_2(a, f(a)), \delta_1(a)\})$ — $(R(a, f(a)), \{\delta_1(a)\})$

$(\Box, \{\delta_3(a, f(a)), \delta_2(a, f(a)), \delta_1(a)\})$

$(\neg P(a), \{\delta_3(a, f(a)), \delta_2(a, f(a)), \delta_1(a)\})$ — $(P(a), \{\ \})$

$(\Box, \{\delta_3(a, f(a)), \delta_2(a, f(a)), \delta_1(a)\})$

FIG. 6.

it occurs. It follows that if $L_0, \ldots, L_k$ is an admissible proof sequence then every default occurrence has a descendant in $(\Box, D_k)$, the bottom clause of L_k. Suppose $\delta(t)$ is a default occurrence whose descendant in D_k is $\delta(s)$. Then $\delta(s)\gamma \in D_k\gamma$, the default support of the admissible proof sequence. We call $\delta(s)\gamma$ the *terminal descendant* of the default occurrence $\delta(t)$. By the nature of γ (see footnote 7 associated with the Definition 8) this terminal descendant is a ground instance of $\delta(t)$ and is an element of CLOSED-DEFAULTS(Δ).

Example 7.2 (continued). Suppose, in the admissible proof sequence for $(Ex)(Ey)(z)S(x,y,z) \wedge U(x)$ of Fig. 6(a) we do the following to each indexed clause (C,D): if $\delta \in D$, instantiate the variables of δ so that it becomes identical with its terminal descendant, and instantiate the corresponding variables of C in the same way. The result is Fig. 6(b), which is a top down default proof of $(Ex)(Ey)(z)S(x,y,z) \wedge U(x)$ with respect to CLOSED(Δ), i.e. $(Ex)(Ey)(z)S(x,y,z) \wedge U(x)$ is in some extension for CLOSED(Δ) and hence by definition is in an extension for Δ.

This example indicates the basic intuition behind the notion of an admissible proof sequence. Unfortunately, this notion does not quite give us what we want.

Example 7.3. Δ has one default

$$\delta(x) = \frac{P(x) \vee Q(x) : MR(x)}{R(x)} \qquad W = \{P(a) \vee Q(b)\}$$

Fig. 7(a) is an admissible proof sequence for $(Ey)R(y)$. But the only extension for this theory is Th(W) and this does not contain $(Ey)R(y)$. Notice however that if we replace each default occurrence of Fig. 7(a) by its terminal descendant, as we did for Example 7.2, we obtain Fig. 7(b) which is not a top down default proof of $(Ey)R(y)$ with respect to CLOSED(Δ). The basic reason for this is that the terminal descendant of the occurrence of $\delta(x)$ in the clause $(\neg P(x), \{\delta(x)\})$ in Fig. 7(a) is $\delta(a)$, and this is different than $\delta(b)$, the terminal descendant of $\delta(x)$ in $(\neg Q(x), \{\delta(x)\})$ despite the fact that $\neg P(x)$ and $\neg Q(x)$ are both of the clauses of $\neg$PREREQUISITES($\{\delta(x)\}$).

To obtain a proof theory for open defaults it is necessary to restrict the class of admissible proof sequences in order to exclude situations like that of Example 7.3.

Definition 9. An admissible proof sequence $L_0, \ldots, L_k$ for β with respect to a normal default theory Δ is a *top down default proof* of β with respect to Δ iff:

(1) Suppose, for $1 \leqslant i \leqslant k$, that L_i has top clause (C, D_{i-1}) and a side clause (C', D_{i-1}) where C and C' are both clauses of the negation of PREREQUISITES $(D^{(i-1)})$. Then the terminal descendants of the defaults of D_{i-1} in the top clause are identical with the terminal descendants of the defaults of D_{i-1} in the side clause.

(2) Suppose, for $0 \leqslant i \leqslant k$, that (C,D) is a centre clause of L_i which also occurs as a side clause of L_i. Then the terminal descendants of the defaults of D in the centre clause are identical with the terminal descendants of the defaults of D in the side clause.

Theorem 7.1. *Let $\Delta = (D,W)$ be a normal default theory, and let $\beta \in L_{A \cup \Sigma}$ be a closed wff where Σ is the set of Skolem functions of Δ. If there is a top down default proof of β with respect to Δ, then Δ has an extension which contains β.*

Proof. Suppose $L_0, \ldots, L_k$ is a top down default proof of β with respect to Δ. Our plan is to construct a top down default proof $L'_0, \ldots, L'_k$ of β with respect to CLOSED(Δ). The theorem will then follow by the completeness of top down default proofs for closed normal theories, and the definition of an extension of Section 7.1.

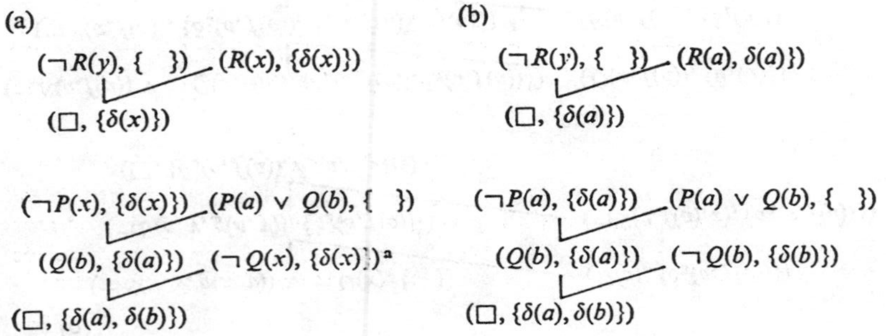
(a)
(b)
$(\neg R(y), \{\ \})$
$(R(x), \{\delta(x)\})$
$(\square, \{\delta(x)\})$
$(\neg R(y), \{\ \})$
$(R(a), \delta(a)\})$
$(\square, \{\delta(a)\})$
$(\neg P(x), \{\delta(x)\})$
$(P(a) \vee Q(b), \{\ \})$
$(Q(b), \{\delta(a)\})$
$(\neg Q(x), \{\delta(x)\})^a$
$(\square, \{\delta(a), \delta(b)\})$
$(\neg P(a), \{\delta(a)\})$
$(P(a) \vee Q(b), \{\ \})$
$(Q(b), \{\delta(a)\})$
$(\neg Q(b), \{\delta(b)\})$
$(\square, \{\delta(a), \delta(b)\})$

FIG. 7.

[a] $\neg Q(x)$ is the other clause of the negation of PREREQUISITES($\{\delta(x)\}$).

To begin, notice that the defaults in any occurrence of an indexed clause in $L_0, \ldots, L_k$ are functioning as 'answer literals' (Green (1969)). The purpose served by the introduction of a default $\delta(x)$ into a proof is to record the fact that $\delta(x)$ is required in the proof, as well as to provide a history of the instances assumed by the free variables x during the course of the proof.

Now consider any linear resolution proof L_i in the sequence $L_0, \ldots, L_k$. For any occurrence of an indexed clause (C,D) in L_i, let σ be that substitution such that for each default $\delta(t) \in D$, $\delta(t)\sigma$ is the terminal descendant of this occurrence of $\delta(t)$. Define $(C,D)\sigma$ to be the *g-instance* of this occurrence of (C,D) in L_i. (Thus to obtain the g-instance of (C,D), instantiate the free variables of each default of D such that it becomes identical with its terminal descendant, and instantiate the corresponding variables of C in the same way.) Now replace each indexed clause of L_i by its g-instance. The result is a tree L'_i. For example Fig. 6(b) is obtained from Fig. 6(a) by replacing each indexed clause by its g-instance.

We first show that L'_i is in fact a linear resolution proof, i.e. that successive clauses in the tree L'_i are indexed resolvents of their immediate predecessors. Now L_i returns a set of defaults D_i which is the 'answer clause' of the deduction L_i. Moreover, the set of terminal descendants of the defaults of D_i is an instance of D_i, i.e. this set is an instance of the 'answer clause' of L_i. It then follows from the results in Luckham and Nilsson (1971) that the tree L'_i represents a linear resolution proof.

To prove that $L'_0, \ldots, L'_k$ is a top down default proof of β with respect to CLOSED(Δ) it is necessary to prove:

(1) L'_0 is a linear resolution proof of $(\beta,\{\ \})$ from CLAUSES(CLOSED(Δ)).

(2) For $0 \leqslant i \leqslant k-1$, if $D^{(i)'}$ is the set of defaults introduced into L'_i and if L'_i returns D'_i then L'_{i+1} is a linear resolution proof of (PREREQUISITES($D^{(i)'}$), D'_i) from CLAUSES(CLOSED(Δ)).

(3) The set of defaults introduced into L'_k is empty.

(4) If L'_k returns D'_k then $W \cup$ CONSEQUENTS(D'_k) is satisfiable.

Property (3) follows immediately from the corresponding property for L_k. To prove (4) notice that by the construction of $L'_0, \ldots, L'_k$ it is the case that D'_k is precisely the default support of the admissible proof sequence $L_0, \ldots, L_k$ so by the definition of an admissible proof sequence, $W \cup$ CONSEQUENTS(D'_k) is satisfiable.

We now prove (1). We begin by proving that L'_0 is a linear resolution proof of $(\beta,\{\ \})$ from CLAUSES(CLOSED(Δ)). We know that L'_0 is a linear resolution proof of $(\beta,\{\ \})$ from CLAUSES(Δ) and L'_0 is obtained from L_0 by replacing each indexed clause by its g-instance. If, for some clause C_β of $\neg\beta$ $(C_\beta,\{\ \})$ is a top or side clause of L_0, then it is its own g-instance and $(C_\beta,\{\ \})$ is the corresponding top or side clause of L'_0. Similarly, if $(C,\{\ \}) \in$ CLAUSES(Δ) (so that $C \in W$) is a side clause of L_0 then it is a side clause of L'_0 and $(C,\{\ \}) \in$ CLAUSES (CLOSED(Δ)). Suppose $(C(x),\{\delta(x)\}) \in$ CLAUSES(Δ) (so that $C(x)$ is a clause of the consequent of $\delta(x)$) is a side clause of L_0. Then if $\delta(g)$ is the terminal descendant of this occurrence of $\delta(x)$, then $(C(g),\{\delta(g)\})$ is the g-instance of $(C(x),\{\delta(x)\})$ and this is the corresponding side clause of L'_0; clearly $(C(g),\{\delta(g)\}) \in$ CLAUSES (CLOSED(Δ)). Finally, suppose (C,D) is a side clause of L_0 which is also a centre clause of L_0. Then in L'_0 the corresponding side clause is $(C,D)\sigma$, the g-instance of the occurrence of (C,D) as a side clause of L_0. Also, in L'_0 the corresponding centre clause is $(C,D)\sigma'$, the g-instance of the occurrence of (C,D) as a centre clause of L_0. But by condition (2) of Definition g, $\sigma = \sigma'$ so that in L'_0 the side clause $(C,D)\sigma$ is also a centre clause. This completes the proof of (1).

It remains to prove (2), i.e. that L'_{i+1} is a linear resolution proof of (PREREQUISITES($D^{(i)'}$), D'_i) from CLAUSES(CLOSED(Δ)). We already know that L'_{i+1} is a linear resolution proof. Hence it is sufficient to prove:

(a) Whenever $(C(x),\{\ \}) \in$ CLAUSES(Δ) is a side clause of L_{i+1} then its g-instance, which is identical to itself, is in CLAUSES(CLOSED(Δ)). This is immediate.

(b) Whenever $(C(x),\{\delta(x)\}) \in$ CLAUSES(Δ) is a side clause of L_{i+1} then its g-instance $(C(g),\{\delta(g)\})$ is in CLAUSES(CLOSED(Δ)). This is immediate.

(c) Whenever (C,D) is a side clause of L_{i+1} which is also a centre clause of L_{i+1} then the g-instance of its occurrence as a side clause in L_{i+1} is identical to the g-instance of its occurrence as a centre clause in L_{i+1}. The proof of this is the same as for L_0.

(d) Whenever (C,D_i) occurs in L_{i+1}, either as the top clause or as a side clause, where C is a clause of $\neg$PREREQUISITES($D^{(i)}$), then its g-instance $(C\sigma,D_i\sigma)$ is such that $C\sigma$ is a clause of $\neg$PREREQUISITES($D^{(i)\prime}$) and $D_i\sigma = D_i'$.

To prove (d) we distinguish two cases:

Case 1. (C,D_i) is the top clause of L_{i+1}.

Now $D_i\sigma$ is the set of terminal descendants of the default occurrences in (C,D_i), the top clause of L_{i+1}. But these are the same as the terminal descendants of the default occurrences in $(\Box,D_i)$, the bottom clause of L_i. Since L_i' returns D_i', this latter clause has g-instance $(\Box,D_i')$. Hence $D_i\sigma = D_i'$. Moreover, $D^{(i)}\sigma$ is the set of terminal descendants of the defaults introduced into L_i and by the construction of L_i', this is the same as the set of defaults introduced into L_i', i.e. $D^{(i)}\sigma = D^{(i)\prime}$. Hence

PREREQUISITES($D^{(i)}$)σ = PREREQUISITES($D^{(i)}\sigma$) = PREREQUISITES($D^{(i)\prime}$). Since C is a clause of $\neg$PREREQUISITES($D^{(i)}$), $C\sigma$ is a clause of $\neg$PREREQUISITES($D^{(i)\prime}$).

Case 2. (C,D_i) is a side clause of L_{i+1}.

Then if (B,D_i) is the top clause of L_{i+1}, and $(B\sigma',D_i\sigma')$ its g-instance, then by condition (1) of Definition g $\sigma = \sigma'$ so that $D_i\sigma = D_i\sigma'$. By Case 1, $D_i\sigma' = D_i'$ so $D_i\sigma = D_i'$. By the same argument as in Case 1 $C\sigma$ is a clause of $\neg$PREREQUISITES($D^{(i)\prime}$).

We shall say, as we did for closed theories, that a default theory is *consistent* iff it has a consistent extension.

Theorem 7.2. *Let $\Delta = (D,W)$ be a consistent normal default theory. If Δ has an extension which contains β then there is a top down default proof of β with respect to Δ.*

Proof. We shall merely sketch a proof. Since Δ has an extension E containing β then E is an extension for the closed normal default theory CLOSED(Δ) = (CLOSED-DEFAULTS(Δ),W). CLOSED(Δ) is consistent since Δ is. Then by the completeness of top down default proofs for closed normal default theories (Theorem 5.1), there is a top down default proof $L_0', \ldots, L_k'$ of β with respect to CLOSED(Δ). By using standard lifting techniques from resolution theory (Robinson (1965)) we can lift this proof $L_0', \ldots, L_k'$ to a top down default proof $L_0, \ldots, L_k$ of β with respect to Δ. Essentially this is done by first lifting L_0' to L_0 by replacing, in L_0', each clause $(C(\mathrm{g}),\{\delta(\mathrm{g})\}) \in$ CLAUSES(CLOSED(Δ)) by its uninstantiated general clause $(C(\mathrm{x}),\{\delta(\mathrm{x})\}) \in$ CLAUSES(Δ) and using this general clause to form the resulting resolvent. In the case of a side clause of L_0' which is also a centre clause, this centre clause will already have been lifted and it is this lifted clause which replaces the side clause. In general then, assume $L_0', \ldots, L_i'$ have been lifted to $L_0, \ldots, L_i$ respectively. Assume L_i' and L_i return D_i' and D_i respectively, and that $D^{(i)\prime}$ and $D^{(i)}$ are the defaults introduced into L_i' and L_i respectively. Now to lift L_{i+1}' to L_{i+1} first lift its top clause (C',D_i'). C' is a clause of $\neg$PREREQUISITES($D^{(i)\prime}$). Now D_i' is an instance of D_i so that (C',D_i') is an instance of a clause (C,D_i) where C is a clause of $\neg$PREREQUISITES($D^{(i)}$). Replace (C',D_i') in L_{i+1}' by (C,D_i). Similarly, if (C',D_i') is a side clause of L_{i+1}' replace it by (C,D_i). To lift the remaining side clauses of L_{i+1}' proceed as for L_0'.

The resulting lifted proofs $L_0, \ldots, L_k$ have the following properties:

(1) L_0 is a linear resolution proof of (β,{ }) from CLAUSES(Δ).

(2) For $1 \leqslant i \leqslant k$, L_i is a linear resolution proof of (PREREQUISITES($D^{(i-1)}$),D_{i-1}) from CLAUSES(Δ).

(3) The set of defaults introduced into L_k is empty.

Moreover, since $L_0', \ldots, L_k'$ is a top down default proof of β with respect to CLOSED(Δ), $D_k' \subseteq$ CLOSED-DEFAULTS(Δ). Since D_k' is a ground instance of D_k there is a ground substitution γ over $H(F \cup \Sigma)$, where Σ is the set of Skolem functions of Δ, such that $D_k' = D_k\gamma$. Finally, since $W \cup$ CONSEQUENTS(D_k') is satisfiable, so is $W \cup$ CONSEQUENTS($D_k\gamma$). We have proved that $L_0, \ldots, L_k$ is an admissible proof sequence for β with respect to Δ.

To see that $L_0, \ldots, L_k$ is a top down default proof of β, notice that if (C',D') is a clause of L' which was lifted to a clause (C,D) of L_i, then the terminal descendants of the defaults of D are precisely the defaults of D'. From this the result follows.

The combination of Theorems 7.1 and 7.2 yields the following:

Theorem 7.3 (Completeness of top down default proofs). *Let Δ be a consistent normal default theory and Σ the set of Skolem functions of Δ. Suppose $\beta \in L_{A \cup \Sigma}$ is a closed wff. Then Δ has an extension containing β iff β has a top down default proof with respect to Δ.*

7.3. Open defaults: other generalizations

In view of the definition of an extension for default theories with open defaults, all of the results of Section 3 continue to hold for normal default theories in general. In particular then, any such theory always has an extension, its extensions are orthogonal, it will be semi-monotonic, and the addition of new normal defaults cannot decrease the number of its extensions.

To generalize the results of Section 6 on belief revision requires only defining. for a top down default proof P_β of β, DS(P_β) to be the default support of P_β, i.e, with reference to Definition 8 in Section 7.2, DS(P_β) is defined to be $D_k\gamma$. In the case of closed normal default theories DS(P_β) is the set of all of the defaults which enter into the proof P_β. In the case of normal default theories in general, the defaults entering into the proof P_β become instantiated during the course of the proof. DS(P_β) is the set of all of the final instances of these defaults or, in the unlikely event that these final instances still contain variables, DS(P_β) is obtained from these final instances by suitably substituting ground terms of $H(F \cup \Sigma)$ for these variables in such a way that $W \cup$ CONSEQUENTS(DS(P_β)) is satisfiable. With this notion of DS(P_β) all of the results on belief revision of Section 6 continue to hold for normal default theories in general.

8 Discussion and Further Problems

Many interesting problems related to default logic remain to be explored. The most obvious formal omission in the previous sections is a model theory; the concept of an extension is defined proof theoretically. What one would like is a model theoretic characterization of the extensions of a default theory (D,W) in the following sense:

We want some way of viewing the defaults of D as restricting the models of W such that any resulting restricted set of models of W satisfies all and only the wffs of an extension for (D,W); and conversely, any extension for (D,W) will be the set of wffs satisfied by some such restricted set of models of W.

An interesting proposal which involves non-monotonic reasoning is the method of circumscription described in McCarthy (1977). Briefly circumscription is a formalization of the notion of reasoning within the minimal models of some set of first order axioms. There appears to be some relationship between circumscription and default logic. What can be proved is that the minimal models for a sentential set of wffs coincide with the models of the extensions induced on these wffs by the closed world assumption. This result suggests some deeper relationship between closed world default theories and the method of circumscription although I have been unable to discover just what this might be.

We have elsewhere (Reiter (1978a)) discussed some relationship between defaults and the 'negation' operator of Artificial Intelligence programming languages like PROLOG (Roussel (1975), Kowalski (1979)) and PLANNER (Hewitt (1972)). As implemented in these languages, NOT(⟨wff⟩) succeeds iff ⟨wff⟩ is not provable. It turns out that there are a number of difficulties with this notion of a procedural negation (Clark (1978)), not the least of which is specifying just what 'not provable' means in this setting. Accordingly, it might be of some interest to view the proof theory of Section 7 for normal default theories as a possible basis for defining the semantics of negation in such languages.

A major computational problem stems from the ubiquitous satisfiability tests required in the proof theory as well as in the conditions for belief revision. These all have the form of a satisfiability requirement on $W \cup$ CONSEQUENTS(D') for some set of defaults $D' \subseteq D$. While no algorithm exists for this, a variety of heuristics are possible. One such heuristic would be to begin with the wffs of CONSEQUENTS(D') and use these as a basis for successive 'forward chaining' or bottom up deductions into W, in order to derive new consequences of these. If, after some time bound or forward chaining level bound has been exceeded, no contradiction has been derived then one might assume satisfiability of the original set of wffs. While this appears to be the most general such heuristic it is also apt to be the most computationally expensive. Clever schemes should be possible. One such might involve extensive indexing of the wffs of W, perhaps along the lines of Kowalski (1974). Accessibility links in this index scheme could in some instances provide rapid tests for the satisfiability of W with respect to CONSEQUENTS(D'). The whole question of heuristics for testing satisfiability appears to be totally unexplored.

An important pragmatic problem is the specification of techniques for choosing between two or more competing extensions. In the hometown example of Section 1.3 we were faced with choosing between extensions, one in which Mary's hometown is Toronto because her spouse lives there, the other in which her hometown is Vancouver because her employer is located there.

One general heuristic would be to rank order conflicting defaults of this kind in order of their intuitive plausibility, selecting the highest priority default first in attempting a proof for some wff. Only during a process of belief revision would lower priority defaults be invoked. While some such static priority scheme might well be useful in certain settings, it seems not to work for the example of Mary's hometown. There appears to me to be no a priori reason for preferring Toronto over Vancouver, or vice versa here. Instead, what seems to be required is some dynamic scheme for *rationalizing* the apparent discrepancy. For example, having discovered that Mary's hometown might be both Vancouver and Toronto a default reasoning program should seek ways of resolving the conflict by searching out suitable detailed information about Mary. Is she separated from her spouse? If so, opt for her employer's location. Is she some sort of area representative for her employer? Is that area near Toronto? If so, choose her spouse's hometown. This view of extension selection as a process of rationalizing discrepancies has the nice property of avoiding the introduction of fine details, such as the possibility of Mary being an area representative, into the default reasoning process itself. Such details are taken into consideration only if the default reasoner discovers a discrepancy in its derivation of a belief. One can imagine a similar need for rationalization whenever belief revision is called for.

Only one same reason is shared by all of us:
we wish to create worlds as real as,
but other than the world that is.

John Fowles, *The French Lieutenant's Woman*

ACKNOWLEDGEMENTS

Keith Clark and Bob Kowalski patiently entertained the many incarnations of my ideas on default reasoning, and often asked the right question at the right time. Alan Bundy and David Warren provided valuable insights into the relationship between default proofs and PROLOG. Susan Frykberg through her speculative metaphysics prevented the enterprise from taking itself too seriously.

I am indebted to the University of British Columbia for granting me the sabbatical leave during which much of this work was done, and to Imperial College, London, and Bob Kowalski in particular, for making available to me the facilities of the Department of Computing and Controls. This paper was written and typed with the financial support of the National Research Council of Canada under grant A7642.

REFERENCES

Bobrow, D. G. and Winograd, T., An overview of KRL-O, a knowledge representation language, *Cognitive Science* **1** (1) (January 1977).

Church, A., An unsolvable problem of number theory, *Amer. J. Math.* **58** (1936) 345–363.

Clark, K., Negation as failure, in: H. Gallaire and J. Minker (Eds.), *Logic and Data Base*. (Plenum Press, New York, 1978) 293–322.

Doyle, J., *Truth Maintenance Systems for Problem Solving*, MIT Artificial Intelligence Laboratory, Report AI-TR-419 (January 1978).

Green, C., Application of theorem proving to problem solving, *Proc. First IJCAI* (1969) 219–239.

Hayes, P. J., The frame problem and related problems in artificial intelligence, in: A. Elithorn and D. Jones (Eds.), *Artificial and Human Thinking* (Jossey-Bass, San Francisco, 1973) 45–49.

Hayes, P. J., *The Logic of Frames*, Technical Report, Dept. of Computer Science, Univ. of Essex (November 1977).

Hewitt, C., *Description and Theoretical Analysis* (*Using Schemata*) *of PLANNER: A Language for Proving Theorems and Manipulating Models in a Robot*, A.I. Memo No. 251, MIT Project MAC, Cambridge, MA (April 1972).

Kowalski, R. A., A Proof procedure using connection graphs, *J. ACM* **22** (October 1974) 572–595.

Kowalski, R. A., *Logic for Problem Solving* (North-Holland Elsevier, New York, 1979).

Kowalski, R. A. and Kuehner, D., Linear resolution with selection function, *Artificial Intelligence* **2** (1971) 221–260.

Kramosil, I., A note on deduction rules with negative premises, *Proc. Fourth IJCAI* (1975) 53–56.

Loveland, D. W., A linear format for resolution, *Proc. IRIA Symp. Automatic Demonstration*, Versailles, France, 1968 (Springer-Verlag, New York, 1970) 147–162.

Luckham, D., Refinements in resolution theory, *Proc. IRIA Symp. Automatic Demonstration*, Versailles, France, 1968 (Springer-Verlag, New York, 1970) 163–190.

Luckham, D. and Nilsson, N. J., Extracting information from resolution proof trees, *Artificial Intelligence* **2** (1971) 27–54.

McCarthy, J., Epistemological problems of Artificial Intelligence, *Proc. Fifth IJCAI* (1977) 1038–1044.

McCarthy, J. and Hayes, P. J., Some philosophical problems from the standpoint of artificial intelligence, in: B. Meltzer and D. Michie (Eds.), *Machine Intelligence* 4 (Edinburgh University Press, Edinburgh, 1969) 463–502.

McDermott, D. and Doyle, J., Non-monotonic Logic I, MIT AI Memo 486 (August 1978).

Minsky, M., A framework for representing knowledge, in: P. Winston (Ed.), *The Psychology of Computer Vision* (McGraw–Hill, New York, 1975).

Raphael, B., The frame problem in problem-solving systems, in: N. V. Findler and B. Meltzer (Eds.), *Artificial Intelligence and Heuristic Programming* (Edinburgh University Press, Edinburgh, 1971).

Reiter, R., Two results on ordering for resolution with merging and linear format, *J. ACM* **18** (4) (1971) 630–646.

Reiter, R., On reasoning by default, *Proc. Second Symp. on Theoretical Issues in Natural Language Processing*, Urbana, Illinois, July 25–27, 1978a

Reiter, R., On closed world data bases, in: H. Gaillaire and J. Minker (Eds.), *Logic and Data Bases* (Plenum Press, New York, 1978b) 55–76.

Reiter, R., Some results on default logics, Technical Report, Dept. of Computer Science, Univ. of British Columbia. Forthcoming.

Roberts, R. B. and Goldstein, I., *The FRL Manual*, A.I. Memo No. 409, MIT, Cambridge, MA, 1977.

Robinson, J. A., A machine oriented logic based on the resolution principle, *J. ACM* **12** (1965) 25–41.

Rogers, H., *Theory of Recursive Functions and Effective Computability* (McGraw–Hill, New York, 1967).

Roussel, P., *PROLOG, Manuel de Reference et d'Utilisation*, Group d'Intelligence Artificielle, U.E.R. de Marseille, France, 1975.

Sandewall, E., An approach to the frame problem and its implementation, in: B. Meltzer and D. Michie (Eds.), *Machine Intelligence* **7** (Edinburgh University Press, Edinburgh, 1972) 195–204.

Waldinger, R., *Achieving Several Goals Simultaneously*, Artificial Intelligence Center Technical Note 107, Stanford Research Institute, Menlo Park, CA, 1975.

ON INTERACTING DEFAULTS

Raymond Reiter and Giovanni Criscuolo

Department of Computer Science
The University of British Columbia

Istituto di Fisica Teorica
University of Naples

ABSTRACT

Although most commonly occurring default rules are normal when viewed in isolation, they can interact with each other in ways that lead to the derivation of anomalous default assumptions. In order to deal with such anomalies it is necessary to re-represent these rules, in some cases by introducing non-normal defaults. The need to consider such potential interactions leads to a new concept of integrity, distinct from the conventional integrity issues of first order data bases.

The non-normal default rules required to deal with default interactions all have a common pattern. Default theories conforming to this pattern are considerably more complex than normal default theories. For example, they need not have extensions, and they lack the property of semi-monotonicity.

I INTRODUCTION

In an earlier paper [Reiter 1980a] one of us proposed a logic for default reasoning. The objective there was to provide a representation for, among other things, common sense facts of the form "Most A's are B's", and to articulate an appropriate logic to characterize correct reasoning using such facts.* One such form of reasoning is the derivation of default assumptions: Given a particular A, conclude that "This particular A is a B". Because some A's are not B's this conclusion must be treated as a default assumption or belief about the world since subsequent observations in the world may yield that "This particular A is not a B". The derivation of the belief that "This particular A is a B" is a form of plausible reasoning which is typically required whenever conclusions must be drawn from incomplete information about a world.

It is important to note that not all senses of the word "most" lead to default assumptions. One can distinguish two such senses:

1. A purely statistical connotation, as in "Most voters refer Carter." Here, "most" is being used exclusively in the sense of "the majority of". This setting does not lead to default assumptions: given that Maureen is a voter one would not want to assume that Maureen prefers Carter. Default logic makes no attempt to represent or reason with such statistical facts.

2. A prototypical sense, as in "Most birds fly." There is a statistical connotation here - the majority of birds do fly - but there is also the sense that a characteristic of a prototypical or normal bird is being described. Given a bird Polly, one is prepared to assume that it flies unless one has reasons to the contrary.* It is towards such prototypical settings that default logic is addressed.

The concept of a prototypical situation is central to the frames proposal of [Minsky 1975] and is realized in such frame inspired knowledge representation languages as KRL [Bobrow and Winograd 1977] and FRL [Roberts and Goldstein 1977]. That these are alternative representations for some underlying logic has been convincingly argued in [Hayes 1977]. Default logic presumes to provide a formalization of this underlying logic.

The approach taken by default logic is to distinguish between prototypical facts, such as "Typically mammals give birth to live young", and "hard" facts about the world such as "All dogs are mammals." The former are viewed as rules of inference, called <u>default rules</u>, which apply to the latter "hard" facts. The point of view is that the set of all "hard" facts will fail to completely specify the world - there will be gaps in our knowledge - and that the default rules serve to help fill in those gaps with plausible but not infallible conclusions. A <u>default theory</u> then is a pair (D,W) where D is a set of default rules applying to some world being modelled, and W is a set of "hard" facts about that world. Formally, W is a

---

This paper was written with the financial support of the National Science and Engineering Research Council of Canada under grant A7642.

* Other closely related work with much the same motivation is described in [McCarthy 1980], [McDermott 1980] and [McDermott and Doyle 1980].

* One way of distinguishing between these two senses of "most" is by replacing its setting using the word "typically". Thus, "Typically voters prefer Carter" sounds inappropriate, whereas "Typically birds fly" seems more accurate. In the rest of this paper we shall use "typically" whenever we are referring to a prototypical situation.

set of first order formulae while a typical default rule of D is denoted

$$\frac{\alpha(\vec{x}) : M\beta_1(\vec{x}),\ldots,M\beta_n(\vec{x})}{w(\vec{x})}$$

where $\alpha(\vec{x})$, $\beta_1(\vec{x}),\ldots,\beta_n(\vec{x})$, $w(\vec{x})$ are all first order formulae whose free variables are among those of $\vec{x} = x_1,\ldots,x_m$. Intuitively, this default rule is interpreted as saying "For all individuals $x_1,\ldots,x_m$, if $\alpha(\vec{x})$ is believed and if each of $\beta_1(\vec{x}),\ldots,\beta_n(\vec{x})$ is consistent with our beliefs, then $w(\vec{x})$ may be believed." The set(s) of beliefs sanctioned by a default theory is precisely defined by a fixed point construction in [Reiter 1980a]. Any such set is called an extension for the default theory in question, and is interpreted as an acceptable set of beliefs that one may entertain about the world being represented.

It turns out that the general class of default theories is mathematically intractable. Accordingly, many of the results in [Reiter 1980a] (e.g. that extensions always exist, a proof theory, conditions for belief revision) were obtained only for the class of so-called normal default theories, namely theories all of whose defaults have the form

$$\frac{\alpha(\vec{x}) : Mw(\vec{x})}{w(\vec{x})} .$$

Such defaults are extremely common; for example "Typically dogs bark.:

$$\frac{DOG(x) : M\ BARK(x)}{BARK(x)}$$

"Typically American adults own a car.":

$$\frac{AMERICAN(x) \wedge ADULT(x) : M((Ey).CAR(y) \wedge OWNS(x,y))}{(Ey).CAR(y) \wedge OWNS(x,y)}$$

Many more examples of such normal defaults are described in [Reiter 1980a]. Indeed, the claim was made there that all naturally occurring defaults are normal. Alas, this claim appears to be true only when interactions involving default rules are ignored. For normal default theories such interactions can lead to anomalous conclusions.

It is the purpose of this paper to describe a variety of settings in which interactions involving defaults are important, and to uniformly generalize the notion of a normal default theory so as to correctly treat these interactions. The resulting semi-normal default theories will then be seen to lack some important properties: for example they need not have extensions, and they lack the semi-monotonicity property which all normal theories enjoy. We shall also see that the interactions introduced by default rules lead to a new concept of data base integrity, distinct from the integrity issues arising in first order data bases.

This paper is an abridged version of [Reiter and Criscuolo 1980].

II INTERACTING NORMAL DEFAULTS

In this section we present a number of examples of default rules which, in isolation, are most naturally represented as normal defaults but whose interaction with other defaults or first order formulae leads to counterintuitive results. In each case we show how to "patch" the representation in order to restore the intended interpretation. The resulting "patches" all have a uniform character, which will lead us in Section IIIB to introduce the notion of a semi-normal default theory.

A. "Typically" is not Necessarily Transitive

Consider:

"Typically A's are B's":

$$\frac{A(x) : MB(x)}{B(x)} \qquad (2.1)$$

"Typically B's are C's":

$$\frac{B(x) : MC(x)}{C(x)} \qquad (2.2)$$

These are both normal defaults. Default logic then admits the conclusion that "Typically A's are C's" in the following sense: If a is an individual for which A(a) is known or believed, and if $\neg B(a)$ and $\neg C(a)$ are not known or believed, then C(a) may be derived. In other words, normal default theories impose transitivity of "typically". But this need not be transitive, for example:

"Typically high school dropouts are adults."
"Typically adults are employed." } (2.3)

From these one would not want to conclude that "Typically high school dropouts are employed."*
Transitivity must be blocked. This can be done in general by replacing the normal default (2.2) by the non-normal default

$$\frac{B(x) : M(\neg A(x) \wedge C(x))}{C(x)} \qquad (2.4)$$

To see why this works, consider a prototypical individual a which is an A i.e. A(a) is given. By (2.1) B(a) can be derived. But B(a) cannot be used in conjunction with (2.4) to derive C(a) since the consistency condition $\neg A(a) \wedge C(a)$ of (2.4) is violated by the given A(a). On the other hand, for a prototypical individual b which is a B (i.e. B(b) is given) (2.4) can be used to derive C(b) since presumably nothing is known about b's A-ness - we do not know that A(b) - so that the consistency condition of (2.4) is satisfied.

The introduction of non-normal defaults like (2.4) is a particularly unpleasant solution to the transitivity problem, for as we shall see in Section IIIB, the resulting non-normal default theories lack most of the desirable properties that normal theories enjoy. For example, they sometimes fail to have an extension, they lack semi-monotonicity, and their proof theory appears to be considerably more complex than that for normal theories. Accordingly, to the extent that it can be done, we would prefer to keep our representations "as normal as possible." Fortunately transitivity can be blocked using normal defaults whenever it is the case that in addition to (2.1) and (2.2) we have "Typically B's are not A's". This is the case for example (2.3): "Typically adults are not high school dropouts". Under this circumstance, the following normal representation blocks transitivity:

$$\frac{A(x) : MB(x)}{B(x)} \qquad (2.5)$$

$$\frac{B(x) : M \neg A(x)}{\neg A(x)} \qquad (2.6)$$

----

* Nor would we want to conclude that "Typically high school dropouts are not employed." Rather we would remain agnostic about the employment status of a typical high school dropout.

$$\frac{B(x) \wedge \sim A(x) \;:\; MC(x)}{C(x)} \qquad (2.7)$$

Notice how, whem given that B(a), a simple back-chaining interpreter would establish the goal C(a). Back-chaining into (2.7) yields the subgoal B(a) ∧ ~ A(a). This splits into the subgoal B(a), which is given and hence solved, and the subgoal ~ A(a). This latter back-chains into (2.6) yielding the subgoal B(a) which is solved. There remains only to verify the consistency requirements associated with the defaults (2.6) and (2.7) entering into the proof i.e. to verify that {C(a), ~ A(a)} is consistent with all of the first order formulae in force. Such a back-chaining default reasoner is an incomplete realization of the complete proof procedure of [Reiter 1980a]. The reader might find it instructive to simulate this back-chaining interpreter for the case that A(a) is given, in order to see how a derivation of C(a) is prevented.

Notice also that the representation (2.5), (2.6) and (2.7) yields a very interesting prediction. Given an individual a which is simultaneously an instance of A and B, nothing can be concluded about its C-ness. This prediction is confirmed with respect to example (2.3): Given that John is both a high school dropout and an adult, we do not want to assume that John is employed. Notice that the non-normal representation (2.1) and (2.4) yields the same prediction. We shall have more to say about defaults with common instances of their prerequisites in Section IIC.*

A somewhat different need for blocking transitivity arises when it is the case that "Typically A's are not C's" i.e. in addition to (2.1) and (2.2) we have

$$\frac{A(x) \;:\; M \sim C(x)}{\sim C(x)} \qquad (2.8)$$

For example,

"Typically university students are adults."
"Typically adults are employed."
"Typically university students are not employed." (2.9)

Under these circumstances, consider a prototypical instance a of A. By (2.1) and (2.2) C(a) can be derived. But by (2.8) ~ C(a) can be derived. This means that the individual a gives rise to two different extensions for the fragment default theory (2.1), (2.2) and (2.8). One of these extensions - the one containing C(a) - is intuitively unacceptable; only the other extension - the one containing ~ C(a) - is admissible. But a fundamental premise of default logic is that <u>any</u> extension provides an acceptable set of beliefs about a world. The problem then is to eliminate the extension containing C(a). This can be done by replacing the normal default (2.2) by the non-normal (2.4), exactly as we did earlier in order to block the transitivity of "typically". Now, given A(a), B(a) can be derived from (2.1), and ~ C(a) from (2.8). C(a) cannot be derived using (2.4) since its consistency requirement is violated. On the other hand, given a prototypical instance b of B, C(b) can be derived using (2.4).

Once again a non-normal default has been introduced, something we would prefer to avoid. As before, a normal representation can be found whenever it is the case that "Typically B's are not A's". This is the case for example (2.9): "Typically adults are not university students". Under this circumstance the following normal representation will do:

$$\frac{A(x) \;:\; MB(x)}{B(x)}$$

$$\frac{B(x) \;:\; M \sim A(x)}{\sim A(x)}$$

$$\frac{B(x) \wedge \sim A(x) \;:\; MC(x)}{C(x)}$$

$$\frac{A(x) \;:\; M \sim C(x)}{\sim C(x)}$$

Notice that this representation predicts that any individual which is simultaneously an instance of A and B will be an instance of not C, rather than an instance of C. This is the case for example (2.9): Given that Maureen is both a university student and an adult one wants to assume that Maureen is not employed.

Figure 2.1 summarizes and extends the various cases discussed in this section. The first three entries of this table are unproblematic cases which were not discussed, and are included only for completeness.

---

* If $\frac{\alpha(\vec{x}) \;:\; M\beta_1(\vec{x}),\ldots,M\beta_n(\vec{x})}{w(\vec{x})}$ is a default rule then $\alpha(\vec{x})$ is its <u>prerequisite</u>.

Typically A's are B's. Typically B's are C's.	Default Representation
No A is a C.	$(x) \, . \, A(x) \supset \sim C(x)$ $\frac{A(x) \, : \, MB(x)}{B(x)}$ $\frac{B(x) \, : \, MC(x)}{C(x)}$
All A's are C's.	$(x) \, . \, A(x) \supset C(x)$ $\frac{A(x) \, : \, MB(x)}{B(x)}$ $\frac{B(x) \, : \, MC(x)}{C(x)}$
Typically A's are C's.	$\frac{A(x) \, : \, MB(x)}{B(x)}$ $\frac{B(x) \, : \, MC(x)}{C(x)}$
It is not the case that A's are typically C's. Transitivity must be blocked.	$\frac{A(x) \, : \, MB(x)}{B(x)}$ $\frac{B(x) \, : \, M(\sim A(x) \wedge C(x))}{C(x)}$
Typically B's are not A's. It is not the case that A's are typically C's. Transitivity must be blocked.	$\frac{A(x) \, : \, MB(x)}{B(x)}$ $\frac{B(x) \, : \, M \sim A(x)}{\sim A(x)}$ $\frac{B(x) \wedge \sim A(x) \, : \, MC(x)}{C(x)}$
Typically A's are not C's.	$\frac{A(x) \, : \, MB(x)}{B(x)}$ $\frac{B(x) \, : \, M(\sim A(x) \wedge C(x))}{C(x)}$ $\frac{A(x) \, : \, M \sim C(x)}{\sim C(x)}$
Typically B's are not A's. Typically A's are not C's.	$\frac{A(x) \, : \, MB(x)}{B(x)}$ $\frac{B(x) \, : \, M \sim A(x)}{\sim A(x)}$ $\frac{B(x) \wedge \sim A(x) \, : \, MC(x)}{C(x)}$ $\frac{A(x) \, : \, M \sim C(x)}{\sim C(x)}$

Figure 2.1

B. Interactions Between "All" and "Typically"

Phenomena closely related to those stemming from the non-transitivity of "typically" arise from interactions between normal defaults and certain universally quantified first order formulae. Consider

"All A's are B's". $(x).A(x) \supset B(x)$ (2.10)

"Typically B's are C's". $\frac{B(x) \, : \, MC(x)}{C(x)}$ (2.11)

Default logic forces the conclusion that "Typically A's are C's" in the sense that if a is a prototypical A then it will also be a C. But this conclusion is not always warranted, for example:

"All 21 year olds are adults."
"Typically adults are married." (2.12)

Given that John is a 21 year old, we would not want to conclude that he is married. To block the unwarranted derivation, replace (2.11) by

$$\frac{B(x) \, : \, M(\sim A(x) \wedge C(x))}{C(x)} \quad (2.13)$$

As was the case in Section IIA the introduction of this non-normal default can be avoided whenever it is the case that "Typically B's are not A's"* by means of the representation (2.10) together with

$$\frac{B(x) \, : \, M \sim A(x)}{\sim A(x)} \qquad \frac{B(x) \wedge \sim A(x) \, : \, MC(x)}{C(x)} \quad (2.14)$$

Notice that this representation, as well as the representation (2.10) and (2.13) predicts that no conclusion is warranted about the C-ness of any given common instance of A and B.

A related problem arises when it is the case that "Typically A's are not C's" so that, in addition to (2.10) and (2.11) we have

$$\frac{A(x) \, : \, M \sim C(x)}{\sim C(x)} \quad (2.15)$$

For example:
"All Quebecois are Canadians."
"Typically Canadians are native English speakers."
"Typically Quebecois are not native English speakers."

As in Section IIA, a prototypical instance a of A will give rise to two extensions for the theory (2.10), (2.11) and (2.15), one containing C(a); the other containing ~ C(a). To eliminate the extension containing C(a), replace (2.11) by (2.13).

As before, the introduction of the non-normal default (2.13) can be avoided whenever it is the case that "Typically B's are not A's", by means of the representation (2.10), (2.14) and (2.15).

Figure 2.2 summarizes the cases discussed in this section. The first three entries of this table are unproblematic cases which were not discussed, and are included only for completeness.

C. Conflicting Default Assumptions: Prerequisites with Common Instances

In this section we discuss the following pattern, in which a pair of defaults have contradictory consequents but whose prerequisites may share common

----

* Note that example (2.12) seems not to have this character. One is unlikely to include that "Typically adults are not 21 years old" in any representation of a world.

instances*:

$$\left.\begin{array}{l}\dfrac{A(x) : M\sim C(x)}{\sim C(x)}\\[1ex] \dfrac{B(x) : MC(x)}{C(x)}\end{array}\right\} \qquad (2.16)$$

The problem here is which default assumption (if any) should be made when given an instance a of both A and B i.e. should C(a) be assumed, or ~ C(a) or neither? Two cases have already been considered:

1. If it is the case that all A's are B's, then row 6 and possibly row 7 of Figure 2.2 provide representations; in both ~ C(a) is derivable whenever A(a) and B(a) are simultaneously given.
2. If it is the case that "Typically A's are B's" then row 6 and possibly row 7 of Figure 2.1 provide representations in both of which ~ C(a) is derivable given A(a) and B(a).

All A's are B's. Typically B's are C's.	Default Representation
No A is a C.	$(x) . A(x) \supset \sim C(x)$ $(x) . A(x) \supset B(x)$ $\frac{B(x) : MC(x)}{C(x)}$
All A's are C's.	$(x) . A(x) \supset C(x)$ $(x) . A(x) \supset B(x)$ $\frac{B(x) : MC(x)}{C(x)}$
Typically A's are C's.	$(x) . A(x) \supset B(x)$ $\frac{B(x) : MC(x)}{C(x)}$
It is not the case that A's are typically C's Transitivity must be blocked.	$(x) . A(x) \supset B(x)$ $\frac{B(x) : M(\sim A(x) \wedge C(x))}{C(x)}$
Typically B's are not A's. It is not the case that A's are typically C's. Transitivity must be blocked.	$(x) . A(x) \supset B(x)$ $\frac{B(x) : M\sim A(x)}{\sim A(x)}$ $\frac{B(x) \wedge \sim A(x) : MC(x)}{C(x)}$
Typically A's are not C's.	$(x) . A(x) \supset B(x)$ $\frac{B(x) : M(\sim A(x) \wedge C(x))}{C(x)}$ $\frac{A(x) : M\sim C(x)}{\sim C(x)}$
Typically B's are not A's. Typically A's are not C's.	$(x) . A(x) \supset B(x)$ $\frac{B(x) : M\sim A(x)}{\sim A(x)}$ $\frac{B(x) \wedge \sim A(x) : MC(x)}{C(x)}$ $\frac{A(x) : M\sim C(x)}{\sim C(x)}$

Figure 2.2

The problematic setting is when there is no entailment relationship between A and B. For example:

"Typically Republicans are not pacifists." }
"Typically Quakers are pacifists." } (2.17)

Now, given that John is both a Quaker and a Republican, we intuitively want to make no assumptions about his warlike nature. This can be done in the general case by replacing the representation (2.16) by the non-normal defaults

$$\left.\begin{array}{l}\dfrac{A(x) : M(\sim B(x) \wedge \sim C(x))}{\sim C(x)}\\[1ex] \dfrac{B(x) : M(\sim A(x) \quad C(x))}{C(x)}\end{array}\right\} \qquad (2.18)$$

This representation admits that a typical A is not a C, a typical B is a C, but a typical A which is also a B leads to no conclusion.

When it is the case that "Typically A's are not B's" and "Typically B's are not A's" the non-normal defaults (2.18) can be replaced by the following normal ones:

$$\frac{A(x) : M\sim B(x)}{\sim B(x)}$$

$$\frac{B(x) : M\sim A(x)}{\sim A(x)}$$

$$\frac{A(x) \wedge \sim B(x) : M\sim C(x)}{\sim C(x)}$$

$$\frac{B(x) \wedge \sim A(x) : MC(x)}{C(x)}$$

This appears to be the case for example (2.17):

"Typically, Republicans are not Quakers."
"Typically, Quakers are not Republicans."

It is not always the case that the pattern (2.16) should lead to no default assumptions for common instances of A and B. Consider:

"Typically full time students are not employed."
"Typically adults are employed."

Suppose that John is an adult full time student. One would want to assume that he is not employed. So in general, given the setting (2.16) for which the default assumption ~ C is preferred for common instances of A and B, use the following non-normal representation:

$$\frac{A(x) : M\sim C(x)}{\sim C(x)}$$

$$\frac{B(x) : M(\sim A(x) \wedge C(x))}{C(x)}$$

Whenever, in addition, it is the case that "Typically B's are not A's", use the following normal representation:

$$\frac{A(x) : M\sim C(x)}{\sim C(x)}$$

$$\frac{B(x) : M\sim A(x)}{\sim A(x)}$$

$$\frac{B(x) \wedge \sim A(x) : MC(x)}{C(x)}$$

----

* If $\dfrac{\alpha(\vec{x}) : M\beta_1(\vec{x}),\ldots,M\beta_n(\vec{x})}{w(\vec{x})}$ is a default rule, then $\alpha(\vec{x})$ is its <u>prerequisite</u> and $w(\vec{x})$ its <u>consequent</u>.

III DISCUSSION

In this section we discuss some issues raised by the previous results of this paper. Specifically, we address the question of data base integrity arising from default interactions, as well as some of the formal problems associated with the non-normal default rules introduced to correctly represent these interactions. We conclude with a brief discussion of semantic network representations for default reasoning.

A. Integrity of Default Theories

A very nice feature of first order logic as an Artificial Intelligence representation language is the extensibility of any theory expressed in this language. That is, provided that some axiomatization of a world has that world as a model (so that the axiomatization faithfully represents certain aspects of that world) then the result of adding a new axiom about the world is still a faithful representation. It is true that specialized deduction mechanisms may be sensitive to such updates (e.g. adding a new "theorem" to a PLANNER-like data base); but semantically there is no problem. Unfortunately, as we have seen, default theories lack this semantic extensibility; the addition of a new default rule may create interactions leading to unwarranted conclusions, even though in isolation this rule appears perfectly correct.

This observation leads to a new concept of data base integrity, one with quite a different character than the integrity issues arising in data base management systems [Hammer and McLeod 1975] or in first order data bases [Nicolas and Yazdanian 1978, Reiter 1980b]. For such systems an integrity constraint specifies some invariant property which every state of the data base must satisfy. For example, a typical integrity constraint might specify that an employee's age must lie in the range 16 to 99 years. Any attempt to update the data base with an employee age of 100 would violate this constraint. Formally one can say that a data base satisfies some set of integrity constraints if the data base is logically consistent with the constraints. The role of integrity constraints is to restrict the class of models of a data base to include as a model the particular world being represented. Now the objective of the default representations of Section II had precisely this character; we sought representations which would rule out unwarranted default assumptions so as to guarantee a faithful representation of real world common sense reasoning. But notice that there was no notion of an integrity constraint with which the representation was to be consistent. Indeed, consistency of the representation cannot be an issue at all since any default theory will be consistent provided its first order facts are [Reiter 1980a, Corollary 2.2]. It follows that, while there is an integrity issue lurking here, it has a different nature than that of classical data base theory.

We are thus led to the need for some form of integrity maintenance mechanism as an aid in the design of large default data bases. The natural initial data base design would involve representing all default rules as normal defaults, thereby ignoring those potential interactions of the kind analyzed in Section II. An integrity maintenance system would then seek out possible sources of integrity violations and query the user as to the appropriate default assumptions to be made in this setting. Once the correct interpretation has been determined, the system would appropriately re-represent the offending normal default rules. For example, when confronted with a pair of default rules of the form (2.16), the system would first attempt to prove that A and B can have no common instance i.e. that $W \cup \{(Ex).A(x) \wedge B(x)\}$ is inconsistent, where W is the set of first order facts. If so, this pair of defaults can lead to no integrity violation. Otherwise the system would ask whether a common instance of A and B is typically a C, a ~ C, or neither, and depending on the response would suitably re-represent the pair (2.16), if necessary by non-normal default rules.

B. Semi-Normal Default Theories

In Section II we had occasion to introduce certain non-normal default rules in order, for example, to block the transitivity of "typically". Inspection of the representations of that section will reveal that all such non-normal default rules share a common pattern; they all have the form

$$\frac{A(x) : M(\sim B(x) \wedge C(x))}{C(x)} .$$

Accordingly, it is natural to define a default rule to be semi-normal iff it has the form

$$\frac{\alpha(\vec{x}) : M(\beta(\vec{x}) \wedge w(\vec{x}))}{w(\vec{x})}$$

where α, β and w are formulae of first order logic with free variables among $\vec{x} = x_1,\ldots,x_m$. A default theory is semi-normal iff all of its default rules are semi-normal. Normal default rules are a special case of semi-normal, in which $\beta(\vec{x})$ is the identically true proposition.

[Reiter 1980a] investigates the properties of normal default theories. Among the results obtained there are the following:

1. Every normal theory has an extension.
2. Normal theories are semi-monotonic i.e. if D_1 and D_2 are sets of normal default rules and if E_1 is an extension for the theory (D_1, W), then the theory $(D_1 \cup D_2, W)$ has an extension E_2 such that $E_1 \subseteq E_2$.

One consequence of semi-monotonicity is that one can continue to maintain one's old beliefs whenever a normal theory is updated with new normal defaults. Another is a reasonably clean proof theory.

Unfortunately, semi-normal default theories enjoy none of these nice properties. For example, the following theory has no extension:

$$\frac{: M(A \wedge \sim B)}{\sim B} \qquad \frac{: M(B \wedge \sim C)}{\sim C} \qquad \frac{: M(C \wedge \sim A)}{\sim A}$$

To see that semi-monotonicity may fail to hold for semi-normal theories consider the theory

$$\frac{: M(A \wedge B)}{B}$$

This has unique extension Th({B}) where, in general, Th(S) is the closure of the set of formulae S under first order theoremhood. If the new default rule

$\frac{: M \sim A}{\sim A}$ is added to this theory a new theory is obtained with unique extension Th({~ A}) and this does not contain Th({B}).

Most of the formal properties of semi-normal default theories remain unexplored. Two problems in particular require solutions: Under what conditions are extensions guaranteed to exist, and what is an appropriate proof theory?

C. Default Inheritance in Hierarchies: Network Representations

In Section II we focused on certain fairly simple patterns of default rules. Our choice of these patterns was conditioned by their frequent occurrence in common sense reasoning, and by the fact that they are typical of the kinds of default knowledge which various "semantic" network schemes presume to represent and reason with. Most such networks are designed to exploit the natural hierarchical organization of much of our knowledge about the world and rely heavily for their inferencing power upon the inheritance of properties associated with a general class "down the hierarchy" to more restricted classes.

Space limitations prevent a thorough discussion of the relationship between the considerations of this paper and network representations for default reasoning. Instead we summarize various conclusions which are argued at length in [Reiter and Criscuolo 1980]:

1. Except in the simplest of settings, network interpreters fail to reason correctly with defaults.
2. Network representations are best viewed as indexing schemes for logical formulae. An important role of indexing is the provision of an efficient path tracing heuristic for the consistency checks required by default reasoning.
3. Such consistency checks are examples of the kind of resource limited computations required in common sense reasoning [Winograd 1980].

IV CONCLUSIONS

Default theories are complicated. Unlike theories represented in first order logic, default theories lack extensibility. Whenever a new default rule is to be added to a representation its potential interactions with the other default rules must be analyzed. This can lead to a re-representation of some of these defaults in order to block certain unwarranted derivations. All of which leads to a new concept of data base integrity, distinct from the integrity issues arising in first order data bases. These observations also suggest the need for a default integrity maintenance system as a tool for aiding in the design of large default data bases. Such a system would seek out potentially interacting defaults during the data base design phase and query the designer about the consequences of these interactions.

Semi-normal default theories are complicated. They have none of the nice properties that make normal theories so appealing. Most of their formal properties are totally unexplored. At the very least a proof theory is needed, as well as conditions under which extensions are guaranteed to exist.

ACKNOWLEDGEMENTS

Many of the results and examples of this paper were inspired by a conversation that one of us (R.R.) had with N. Sridharan one afternoon in Vancouver. It was he who first pointed out to us the need for non-normal defaults in common sense reasoning.

This work was done with the financial assistance of the National Science and Engineering Research Council of Canada grant A7642. G. Criscuolo was sponsored by the Council for a six month research position with the Department of Computer Science at the University of British Columbia.

REFERENCES

[1] Bobrow, D.G. and Winograd, T. (1977), An overview of KRL-0, a knowledge representation language, Cognitive Science 1 (1) (January).

[2] Hammer, M.M. and McLeod, D.J. (1975), Semantic integrity in a relational data base system, PROC. of the Int. Conf. on Very Large Data Bases, Framington, Mass., Sept., 25-47.

[3] Hayes, P.J. (1977), the logic of frames, Technical Report, Dept. of Computer Science, University of Essex, Colchester, UK.

[4] McCarthy, J. (1980), Circumscription - a form of non-monotonic reasoning, Artificial Intelligence 13, 27-39.

[5] McDermott, D. (1980), Non-monotonic logic II, Research Report No. 174, Dept. of Computer Science, Yale University, New Haven, Conn.

[6] McDermott, D. and Doyle, J. (1980), Non-monotonic logic I, Artificial Intelligence 13. 41-72.

[7] Minsky, M. (1975), A framework for representing knowledge, in: P. Winston (Ed.), The Psychology of Computer Vision (McGraw-Hill, New York).

[8] Nicolas, J.M. and Yazdanian, K. (1978), Integrity checking in deductive data bases, in: H. Gallaire and J. Minker (Eds.), Logic and Data Bases (Plenum Press, New York).

[9] Reiter, R. (1980a), A logic for default reasoning, Artificial Intelligence 13, 81-132.

[10] Reiter, R. (1980b), Data bases: a logical perspective, ACM SIGART, SIGMOD, SIGPLAN Proc. Workshop on Data Abstraction, Data Bases and Conceptual Modelling, Pingree Park, Colorado, June 23-26, to appear.

[11] Reiter, R. and Criscuolo, G. (1980), Some representational issues in default reasoning, Tech. Report 80-7, Dept. of Computer Science, The University of British Columbia, Vancouver, B.C., Canada.

[12] Roberts, R.B. and Goldstein, I. (1977), The FRL Manual, A.I. Memo No. 409, MIT, Cambridge, MA.

[13] Winograd, T. (1980), Extended inference modes in reasoning by computer systems, Artificial Intelligence 13, 5-26.

On Inheritance Hierarchies With Exceptions

David W. Etherington[1]
University of British Columbia

Raymond Reiter[2]
University of British Columbia
Rutgers University

Abstract

Using default logic, we formalize NETL-like inheritance hierarchies with exceptions. This provides a number of benefits:

(1) A precise semantics for such hierarchies.

(2) A provably correct (with respect to the proof theory of default logic) inference algorithm for acyclic networks.

(3) A guarantee that acyclic networks have extensions.

(4) A provably correct quasi-parallel inference algorithm for such networks.

1. Introduction

Semantic network formalisms have been widely adopted as a representational notation by researchers in AI. Schubert [1976] and Hayes [1977] have argued that such structures correspond quite naturally to certain theories of first-order logic. Such a correspondence can be viewed as providing the semantics which "semantic" networks had previously lacked [Woods 1975].

More recent work has considered the effects of allowing exceptions to inheritance within networks [Brachman 1982, Fahlman 1979, Fahlman et al 1981, Touretzky 1982, Winograd 1980]. Such exceptions represent either implicit or explicit cancellation of the normal property inheritance which IS-A hierarchies enjoy.

In this paper, we establish a correspondence between such hierarchies and suitable theories in Default Logic [Reiter 1980]. This correspondence provides a formal semantics for networks with exceptions in the same spirit as the work of Schubert and Hayes for networks without exceptions. Having established this correspondence, we identify the notion of correct inference in such hierarchies with that of derivability in the corresponding default theory, and give a provably correct algorithm for drawing these inferences. As a corollary of the correctness of this algorithm, the default theories which formalize inheritance hierarchies with exceptions can be seen to be coherent, in a sense which we will define.

We conclude, unfortunately, on a pessimistic note. Our results suggest the unfeasibility of completely general massively parallel architectures for dealing with inheritance structures with cancellation (c.f. NETL [Fahlman 1979]). We do observe, however, that limited parallelism may have some applications, but that these appear to be severely restricted in general.

2. Motivation

In the absence of exceptions, an inheritance hierarchy is a taxonomy organized by the usual IS-A relation, as in Figure 1.

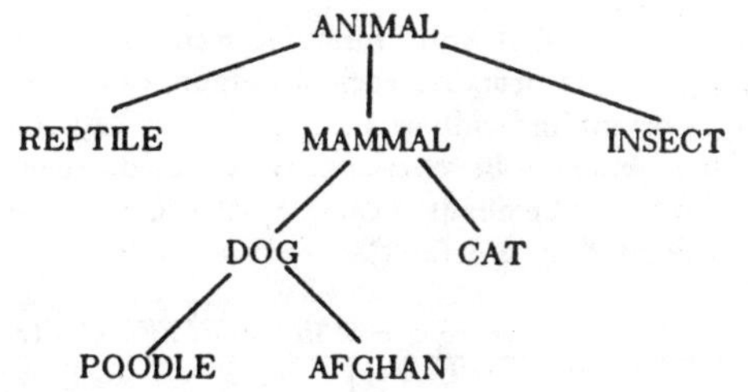

Figure 1 — Fragment of a Taxonomy

The *semantics* of such diagrams can be specified by a collection of first order formulae, such as:

$(x).POODLE(x) \supset DOG(x)$
$(x).DOG(x) \supset MAMMAL(x)$
$(x).MAMMAL(x) \supset ANIMAL(x)$
etc.

If, as is usually the case, the convention is that the immediate subclasses of a node are mutually disjoint, then this too can be specified by first order formulae:

$(x).MAMMAL(x) \supset \neg REPTILE(x)$
$(x).MAMMAL(x) \supset \neg INSECT(x)$
etc.

The significant features of such hierarchies are these:

(1) Inheritance is a logical property of the representation. Given that $POODLE(Fido)$, $MAMMAL(Fido)$ is provable from the given formulae. Inheritance is simply the repeated application of modus ponens.

(2) Formally, the node labels of such a hierarchy are unary predicates: e.g. $DOG(*)$, $ANIMAL(*)$.

(3) No exceptions to inheritance are possible. Given that Fido is a poodle, Fido must be an animal, regardless of what other properties he enjoys.

The logical properties of such hierarchies change dramatically when exceptions are permitted; non-monotonicity can arise. For example, consider the following facts about

[1] This research was supported in part by I.W. Killam Predoctoral and NSERC Postgraduate Scholarships.

[2] This research was supported in part by the Natural Science and Engineering Research Council of Canada grant A7642, and in part by the National Science Foundation grant MCS-8203954.

elephants:

(1) Elephants are gray, except for albino elephants.

(2) All albino elephants are elephants.

It is a feature of our common sense reasoning about prototypes like "elephant" that, when given an individual elephant, say Fred, not known to be an albino, we can infer that he is gray. If we subsequently discover — perhaps by observation — that Fred is an albino elephant, we must retract our conclusion about his grayness. Thus, common sense reasoning about exceptions is non-monotonic, in the sense that new information can invalidate previously derived facts. It is this feature which precludes first order representations, like those used for taxonomies, from formalizing exceptions.

In recent years, there have been several proposed formalisms for such non-monotonic reasoning (See e.g. [AI 1980]). For the purpose of formalizing inheritance hierarchies with exceptions, we shall focus on one such proposal — Default Logic [Reiter 1980]. A default theory consists of a set, W, of ordinary first order formulae, together with a set, D, of rules of inference called *defaults*. In general, defaults have the form:

$$\frac{\alpha(x_1,...,x_n) : \beta(x_1,...,x_n)}{\gamma(x_1,...,x_n)}$$

where α, β, and γ are first order formulae whose free variables are among $x_1,...,x_n$. Informally, such a default can be understood to say: For any individuals $x_1,...,x_n$, if $\alpha(x_1,...,x_n)$ is inferrable and $\beta(x_1,...,x_n)$ can be consistently assumed, then infer $\gamma(x_1,...,x_n)$. For our elephant example, the first statement would be represented by a default:

$$\frac{ELEPHANT(x) : GRAY(x)\ \&\ \neg ALBINO\text{-}ELEPHANT(x)}{GRAY(x)}$$

From the informal reading of this default, one can see that when given only ELEPHANT(Fred), GRAY(Fred) & ¬ALBINO-ELEPHANT(Fred) is consistent with this; hence GRAY(Fred) may be inferred. On the other hand, given ALBINO-ELEPHANT(Fred) one can conclude ELEPHANT(Fred) using the first order fact (x).ALBINO-ELEPHANT(x) ⊃ ELEPHANT(x), but ALBINO-ELEPHANT(Fred) "blocks" the default, thereby preventing the derivation of GRAY(Fred), as required.

The formal details of Default Logic are beyond the scope of this paper. Roughly speaking, however, for a default theory, (D,W), we think of the defaults of D as extending the first order theory given by W. Such an *extension* contains W and is closed under the defaults of D as well as first order theoremhood. It is then natural to think of an extension as defining the "theorems" of a default theory; these are the conclusions sanctioned by the theory. However, these extensions need not be unique [Reiter 1980]. For a default theory with more than one extension, any one of its extensions is interpreted as an acceptable set of beliefs that one may entertain about the world represented by that theory.

In the next section, we show how inheritance hierarchies with exceptions can be formalized as default theories. Default Logic will then be seen to provide a formal semantics for such hierarchies, just as first order logic does for IS-A hierarchies. As was the case for IS-A hierarchies, inheritance will emerge as a logical feature of the representation. Those properties, $P_1, \ldots, P_n$, which an individual, b, inherits will be precisely those for which $P_1(b)$, ..., $P_n(b)$ all belong to a common extension of the corresponding default theory. Should the theory have multiple extensions — an undesirable feature, as we shall see — then b may inherit different sets of properties depending on which extension is chosen.

3. A Semantics for Inheritance Hierarchies With Exceptions

We now show that Default Logic can provide a formal semantics for inheritance structures with exceptions. We adopt a network representation with five link types. Although other approaches to inheritance may omit one or more of these, our formalism subsumes these as special cases. The five link types,[3] with their translations to default logic, are:

(1) Strict IS-A: A.———▶.B: A's are always B's.
Since this is universally true, we identify it with the first order formula: (x).A(x) ⊃ B(x).

(2) Strict ISN'T-A: A.++++++▶.B: A's are never B's.
Again, this is a universal statement, identified with: (x).A(x) ⊃ ¬B(x).

(3) Default IS-A: A.———>.B: Normally A's are B's, but there may be exceptions.
To provide for exceptions, we identify this with a default:

$$\frac{A(x) : B(x)}{B(x)}$$

(4) Default ISN'T-A: A.++++++>.B: Normally A's are not B's, but exceptions are allowed.
Identified with:

$$\frac{A(x) : \neg B(x)}{\neg B(x)}$$

(5) Exception: A.------>
The exception link has no independent semantics; rather, it serves only to make explicit the exceptions, if any, to the above default links. There must always be a default link at the head of an exception link; the exception then alters the semantics of that default link. There are two types of default links with exceptions; their graphical structures and translations are:

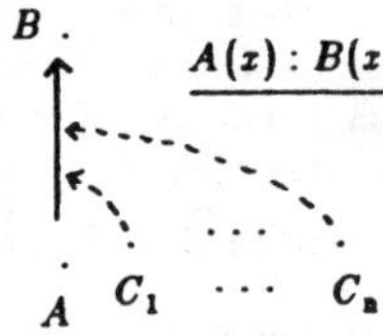

$$\frac{A(x) : B(x)\ \&\ \neg C_1(x)\ \&\ldots\&\ \neg C_n(x)}{B(x)}$$

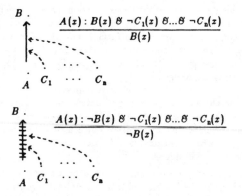

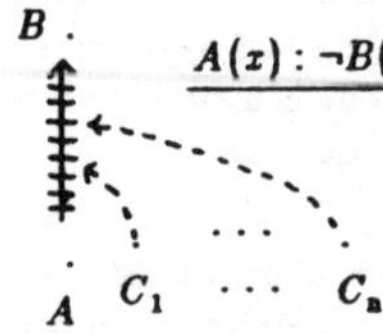

$$\frac{A(x) : \neg B(x)\ \&\ \neg C_1(x)\ \&\ldots\&\ \neg C_n(x)}{\neg B(x)}$$

We illustrate with an example from [Fahlman et al 1981].

> Molluscs are normally shell-bearers.
> Cephalopods must be Molluscs but normally are *not* shell-bearers.
> Nautili must be Cephalopods and must be shell-bearers.

---

[3] Note that strict and default links are distinguished by solid and open arrowheads, respectively.

Our network representation of these facts is given in Figure 2.

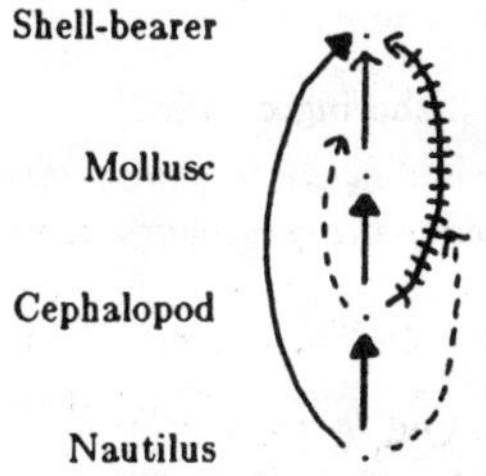

Figure 2 — Network representation of our knowledge about Molluscs.

The corresponding default theory is:

$$\{\frac{M(x) : Sb(x) \,\&\, \neg C(x)}{Sb(x)},\ (x).C(x) \supset M(x),\ (x).N(x) \supset C(x),$$

$$\frac{C(x) : \neg Sb(x) \,\&\, \neg N(x)}{\neg Sb(x)},\ (x).N(x) \supset Sb(x)\}.$$

Given a particular Nautilus, this theory has a unique extension in which it is also a Cephalopod, a Mollusc, and a Shell-bearer. A Cephalopod not known to be a Nautilus will turn out to be a Mollusc with no shell.

It is instructive to compare our network representations with those of NETL [Fahlman et al 1981]. A basic difference is that in NETL there are no strict links; all IS-A and ISN'T-A links are potentially cancellable and hence are defaults. Moreover, NETL allows exception (*UNCANCEL) links only for ISN'T-A (*CANCEL) links. If we restrict the graph of Figure 2 to NETL-like links, we get Figure 3,

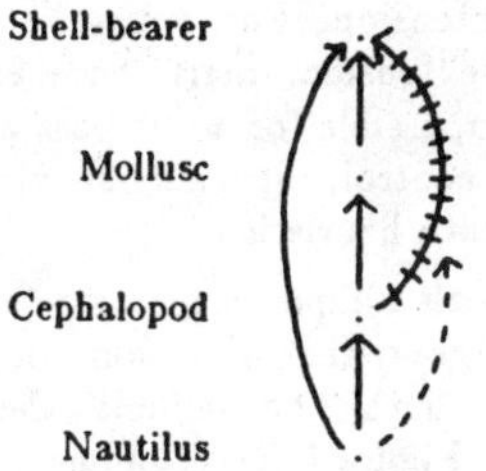

Figure 3 — NETL-like network representation of our knowledge about Molluscs.

which is essentially the graph given by Fahlman. This network corresponds to the theory:

$$\{\frac{M(x) : Sb(x)}{Sb(x)},\ \frac{C(x) : M(x)}{M(x)},\ \frac{N(x) : C(x)}{C(x)},$$

$$\frac{C(x) : \neg Sb(x) \,\&\, \neg N(x)}{\neg Sb(x)},\ \frac{N(x) : Sb(x)}{Sb(x)}\}.$$

As before, a given Nautilus will also be a Cephalopod, a Mollusc, and a Shell-bearer. A Cephalopod not known to be a Nautilus, however, gives rise to *two* extensions, corresponding to an ambivalence about whether or not it has a shell. While counter-intuitive, this merely indicates that an exception to shell-bearing, namely being a Cephalopod, has not been explicitly represented in the network. Default Logic resolves the ambiguity by making the exception explicit, as in Figure 2. NETL, on the other hand, cannot make this exception explicit in the graphical representation, since it does not permit exception links to point to IS-A links.

How then does NETL conclude that a Cephalopod is not a Shell-bearer, without also concluding that it is a Shell-bearer? NETL resolves such ambiguities by means of an inference procedure which prefers shortest paths. Interpreted in terms of default logic, this "shortest path heuristic" is intended to favour one extension of the default theory. Thus, in the example above, the path from Cephalopod to ¬Shell-bearer is shorter than that to Shell-bearer so that, for NETL, the former wins. Unfortunately, this heuristic is not sufficient to replace the excluded exception type in all cases. Reiter and Criscuolo [1983] and Etherington [1982] show that it can lead to conclusions which are unintuitive or even invalid — i.e. not in any extension. Fahlman et al [1981] and Touretzky [1981, 1982] have also observed that such shortest path algorithms can lead to anomalous conclusions and they describe attempts to restrict the form of networks to exclude structures which admit such problems. From the perspective of default logic, these restrictions are intended to yield default theories with unique extensions.

An inference algorithm for network structures is correct only if it can be shown to derive conclusions all of which lie within a single extension of the underlying default theory. This criterion rules out shortest path inference for unrestricted networks. In the next section, we present a correct inference algorithm.

4. Correct Inference

The correspondence between networks and default theories requires defaults all of which have the form:

$$\frac{\alpha(x_1, \cdots, x_n) : \beta(x_1, \cdots, x_n) \,\&\, \gamma(x_1, \cdots, x_n)}{\beta(x_1, \cdots, x_n)}.^4$$

Such defaults are called *semi-normal*, and can be contrasted with *normal* defaults, in which $\gamma(x_1, \ldots, x_n)$ is a tautology. Our criterion for the correctness of a network inference algorithm requires that it derive conclusions all of which lie within a single extension of the underlying default theory. Until recently, the only known methods for determining extensions were restricted to theories involving only normal defaults [Reiter 1980]. Etherington [1982] has developed a more general procedure, which involves a relaxation style constraint propagation technique. This procedure takes as input a default theory, (D,W), where D is a finite set of closed defaults,[5] and W is a finite set of first order formulae. In the presentation of this procedure, below, the following notation is used:

S $\vdash \omega$ means formula ω is first order provable from premises S.
S $\nvdash \omega$ means that ω is not first order provable from S.
$CONSEQUENT(\frac{\alpha : \beta}{\gamma})$ is defined to be γ.

---

[4] $\alpha(x_1, \cdots, x_n)$ and $(\beta(x_1, \cdots, x_n) \,\&\, \gamma(x_1, \cdots, x_n))$ are called the *prerequisite* and *justification* of the default, respectively.

[5] A default, $\frac{\alpha : \beta}{\gamma}$, is *closed* iff α, β, and γ contain no free variables.

$H_0 \leftarrow W;\ j \leftarrow 0;$
repeat
  $j \leftarrow j + 1;\ h_0 \leftarrow W;\ GD_0 \leftarrow \{\ \};\ i \leftarrow 0;$
  repeat
    $D_i \leftarrow \{ \frac{\alpha : \beta}{\gamma} \in D \mid (h_i \vdash \alpha), (h_i \not\vdash \neg\beta), (H_{j-1} \not\vdash \neg\beta) \};$
    if $\neg null(D_i - GD_i)$ **then**
      choose δ **from** $(D_i - GD_i)$;
      $GD_{i+1} \leftarrow GD_i \cup \{\delta\};$
      $h_{i+1} \leftarrow h_i \cup \{CONSEQUENT(\delta)\};$ **endif**;
    $i \leftarrow i + 1;$
  until $null(D_{i-1} - GD_{i-1})$;
  $H_j = h_{i-1}$
until $H_j = H_{j-1}$

Extensions are constructed by a series of successive approximations. Each approximation, H_j, is built up from any first-order components by applying defaults, one at a time. At each step, the default to be applied is chosen from those, not yet applied, whose prerequisites are "known" and whose justifications are consistent with both the previous approximation and the current approximation. When no more defaults are applicable, the procedure proceeds to the next approximation. If two successive approximations are the same, the procedure is said to *converge*.

The choice of which default to apply at each step of the inner loop may introduce a degree of non-determinism. Generality requires this non-determinism, however, since extensions are not necessarily unique. Deterministic procedures can be constructed for theories which have unique extensions, or if full generality is not required.

Notice that there are appeals to *non-provability* in this procedure. In general, such tests are not computable, since arbitrary first order formulae are involved. Fortunately, such difficulties disappear for default theories corresponding to inheritance hierarchies. For these theories, all predicates are unary. Moreover, for such theories, we are concerned with the following problem: Given an individual, b, which is an instance of a predicate, P, determine all other predicates which b inherits — i.e. given $P(b)$ determine all predicates, $P_1, \ldots, P_n$, such that $P(b), P_1(b), \ldots, P_n(b)$, belong to a common extension. For this problem it is clear that predicate arguments can be ignored; the appropriate default theory becomes purely propositional. For propositional logic, non-provability is computable.

Example

Consider the network of Figure 4. Given an instance of A, the corresponding default theory has a unique extension in which A's instance is also an instance of B, C, and D. When the procedure is applied to this theory, it generates the approximations shown. (The formulae in each approximation are listed in the order in which they are derived.) ¬D occurs in H_1 since it can be inferred *before* C.

The following result is proved in [Etherington 1983]:

> *For default theories corresponding to acyclic inheritance networks with exceptions, the procedure always converges on an extension.*

As a simple corollary we have:

> *The default theory corresponding to an acyclic inheritance network with exceptions has at least one extension.*

The latter result is comforting. It says that such networks are always coherent, in the sense that they define at least one acceptable set of beliefs about the world represented by the network.

5. Parallel Inference Algorithms

The computational complexity of inheritance problems, combined with some encouraging examples, has sparked interest in the possibility of performing inferences in parallel. Fahlman [1979] has proposed a massively parallel machine architecture, NETL. NETL assigns one processor to each predicate in the knowledge base. "Inferencing" is performed by nodes passing "markers" to adjacent nodes in response to both their own states and those of their immediate neighbours. Fahlman suggests that such architectures could achieve logarithmic speed improvements over traditional serial machines.

The formalization of such networks as default theories suggests, however, that there might be severe limitations to this approach. For example, correct inference requires that all conclusions share a common extension. For networks with more than one extension, inter-extension interference effects must be prevented. This seems impossible for a one pass parallel algorithm under purely local control, especially in view of the inadequacies of the shortest path heuristic.

Even in knowledge bases with unique extensions, structures requiring an arbitrarily large radius of communication can be created. For example, both the default theories corresponding to the networks in Figure 5 have unique extensions. A network inference algorithm must reach F before propagating through B in the first network and conversely in the second. The salient distinctions between the two networks are not local; hence they cannot be utilized to guide a purely local inference mechanism to the correct choices. Similar networks can be constructed which defeat marker passing algorithms with any fixed radius.

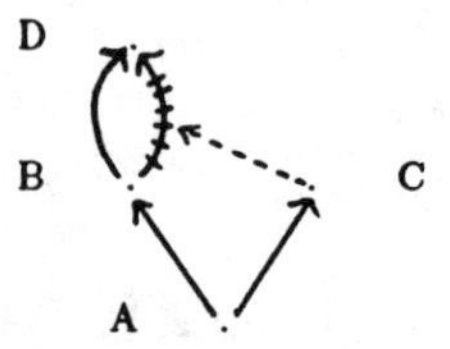

$H_0 = \{ A \}$

$H_1 = \{ A, B, \neg D, C \}$

$H_2 = \{ A, B, C \}$

$H_3 = H_4 = \{ A, B, D, C \}$

Figure 4 — Example of Procedure Behaviour

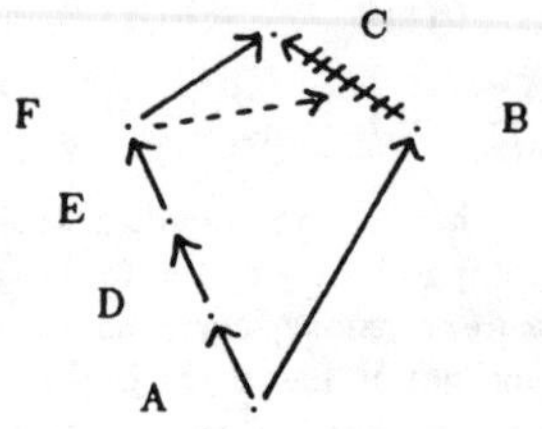

Figure 5a

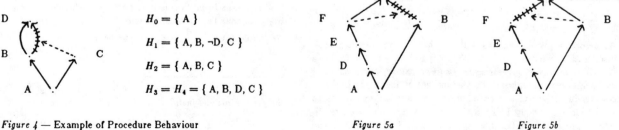

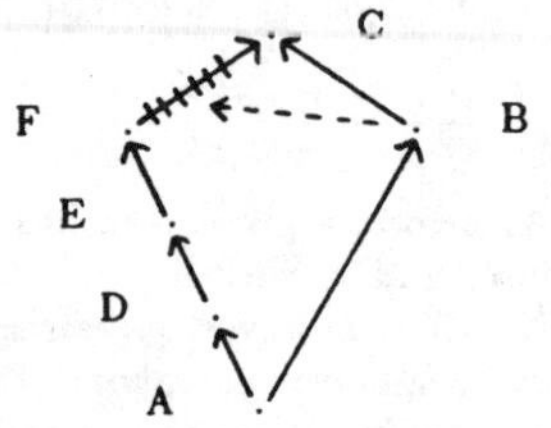

Figure 5b

Touretzky [1981] has observed such behaviour and has developed restrictions on network structures which admit parallel inferencing algorithms. In part, such restrictions appear to have the effect of limiting the corresponding default theory to one extension. Unfortunately, it is unclear how these restrictions affect the expressive power of the resulting networks. Moreover, Touretzky has observed that it is not possible to determine in parallel whether a network satisfies these restrictions.

A form of limited parallelism can be achieved by partitioning a network into a hierarchy of subnetworks, using an algorithm given in [Etherington 1983]. A parallel algorithm can then be applied to the individual subnets, in turn. The number of subnets which must be processed is bounded by the number of exception links in the network. Unfortunately, it can be shown that this technique may exclude some extensions of the theory. We have not yet characterized the biases which this induces in a reasoner.

6. Conclusions

By formalizing inheritance hierarchies with exceptions using default logic we have provided them with a precise semantics. This in turn allowed us to identify the notion of correct inference in such a hierarchy with that of derivability within a single extension of the corresponding default theory. We then provided an inference algorithm for acyclic inheritance hierarchies with exceptions which is provably correct with respect to this concept of derivability.

Our formalization suggests that *for unrestricted hierarchies,* it may not be possible to realize massively parallel marker passing hardware of the kind envisaged by NETL. Fortunately, this pessimistic observation does not preclude parallel architectures for suitably restricted hierarchies. This raises several open problems:

1a) Determine a natural class of inheritance hierarchies with exceptions which admits a parallel inference algorithm yet does not preclude the representation of our commonsense knowledge about taxonomies.

1b) Define such a parallel algorithm and prove its correctness with respect to the derivability relation of default logic.

2) In connection with (1a), notice that it is natural to restrict attention to those hierarchies whose corresponding default theories have unique extensions. Characterize such hierarchies.

7. Acknowledgments

We would like to thank Robert Mercer and David Touretzky for their valuable comments on earlier drafts of this paper.

8. References

AI (1980), Special issue on non-monotonic logic, *Artificial Intelligence 13 (1,2)*, April.

Brachman, R. (1982), "What 'IS-A' Is and Isn't", *Proc. Canadian Soc. for Computational Studies of Intelligence-82*, Saskatoon, Sask., May 17-19, pp 212-220.

Etherington, D.W. (1982), *Finite Default Theories*, M.Sc. Thesis, Dept. Computer Science, University of British Columbia.

Etherington, D.W. (1983), *Formalizing Non-monotonic Reasoning Systems*, TR-83-1, Dept. Computer Science, University of B.C. (To appear).

Fahlman, S.E. (1979), *NETL: A System For Representing and Using Real-World Knowledge*, MIT Press, Cambridge, Mass.

Fahlman, S.E., Touretzky, D.S., and van Roggen, W. (1981), "Cancellation in a Parallel Semantic Network", *Proc. IJCAI-81*, Vancouver, B.C., Aug. 24-28, pp 257-263.

Hayes, P.J. (1977), "In Defense of Logic", *Proc. IJCAI-77*, Cambridge, Mass., pp 559-565.

Reiter, R. (1980), "A Logic for Default Reasoning", *Artificial Intelligence 13*, (April) pp 81-132.

Reiter, R., and Criscuolo, G. (1983), "Some Representational Issues in Default Reasoning", *Int. J. Computers and Mathematics*, (Special Issue on Computational Linguistics), to appear.

Schubert, L.K. (1976), "Extending the Expressive Power of Semantic Networks", *Artificial Intelligence 7(2)*, pp 163-198.

Touretzky, D.S. (1981), Personal Communication.

Touretzky, D.S. (1982), "Exceptions in an Inheritance Hierarchy", Unpublished Manuscript.

Winograd, T. (1980), "Extended Inference Modes in Reasoning", *Artificial Intelligence 13*, (April), pp 5-26.

Woods, W.A. (1975), "What's In A Link?", *Representation and Understanding*, Academic Press, pp 35-82.

Implicit Ordering of Defaults in Inheritance Systems

David S. Touretzky

Computer Science Department
Carnegie-Mellon University
Pittsburgh, PA 15213

Abstract

There is a natural partial ordering of defaults in inheritance systems that resolves ambiguities in an intuitive way. This is not the shortest-path ordering used by most existing inheritance reasoners. The flaws of the shortest-path ordering become apparent when we consider multiple inheritance. We define the correct partial ordering to use in inheritance and show how it applies to semantic network systems. Use of this ordering also simplifies the representation of inheritance in default logic.

1. Introduction

There is a natural partial ordering of defaults in inheritance systems that resolves ambiguities in an intuitive way. This ordering is defined implicitly by the hierarchical structure of the inheritance graph. Surprisingly, it is not the shortest-path ordering used by most existing inheritance systems, such as FRL [1] or NETL [2]. We define the correct ordering, called inferential distance, and show how its use results in more reasonable inheritance behavior than that of either FRL or NETL. We go on to represent inheritance systems in default logic, following the example of Etherington and Reiter [3]. Although exceptions must normally be treated explicitly in default logic, use of inferential distance allows us to handle them implicitly, which has several advantages.

2. The Inferential Distance Ordering

The intuition underlying all inheritance systems is that subclasses should override superclasses. Where inferential distance differs from the shortest-path ordering is in determining subclass/superclass relationships. The inferential distance ordering says that A is a subclass of B iff there is an inheritance path from A to B. In single (as opposed to multiple) inheritance systems, the shortest inference path always contains the inference from the most specific subclass. But under multiple inheritance, there are two cases where the shortest-path ordering disagrees with inferential distance. One involves the presence of true but redundant statements; the other involves ambiguous networks.

3. Handling True But Redundant Statements

Figure 1 illustrates a problem caused by the presence of redundant links in an inheritance graph. Let us start with the following set of assertions: "elephants are typically gray; royal elephants are elephants but are typically not gray; circus elephants are royal elephants; Clyde is a circus elephant." If subclasses override superclasses, then Clyde is not gray. But what happens when we add the explicit statement that Clyde is an elephant, as shown in figure 1? This is a redundant statement because Clyde is indisputably an elephant; he was one before we added this statement; in fact, this is one of the inferences we expect an inheritance reasoner to generate. Yet when we make the fact explicit it causes problems. In FRL Clyde will inherit properties through both Circus.Elephant and Elephant, so FRL will conclude that he both is and is not gray. In NETL, the redundant statement that Clyde is an elephant contributes an inference path to gray that is shorter than either of the two paths (one to gray, one to not-gray) which go through Circus.Elephant. NETL will therefore conclude that Clyde is gray, which contradicts the (correct) conclusion it would reach without the redundant link present.

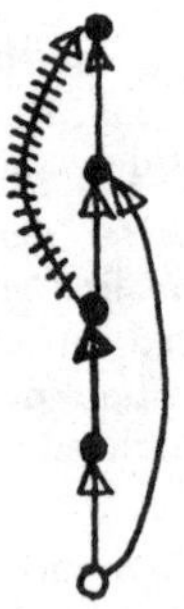

Figure 1.

Inferential distance is unaffected by redundant links. Clyde could either inherit grayness, a property of Elephant, or non-grayness, a property of Royal.Elephant. Since the network contains an inheritance path from Royal.Elephant to Elephant, according to the inferential distance ordering Royal.Elephant is a subclass of Elephant; the direct link from Clyde to Elephant does not alter this relationship. Therefore we conclude that Clyde should inherit non-grayness from Royal.Elephant rather than grayness from Elephant.

4. Ambiguous Inheritance Networks

Consider the following set of assertions, shown in NETL notation in figure 2. "Quakers are typically pacifists; pro-defense people are typically not pacifists; Republicans are typically pro-defense, Nixon is both a Quaker and a Republican." This network is ambiguous: it has two valid extensions. (An extension is the nonmonotonic or default logic equivalent of a theory [4].) In one extension Nixon is a pacifist; in the other he is not.

Most existing inheritance reasoners would not recognize this ambiguity. If pacifism were a slot that could be filled with either

This research was sponsored by the Defense Advanced Research Projects Agency (DOD), ARPA Order No. 3597, monitored by the Air Force Avionics Laboratory Under Contract F33615-81-K-1539. The author was partially supported by a fellowship from the Fannie and John Hertz Foundation. The views and conclusions contained in this document are those of the author and should not be interpreted as representing the official policies, either expressed or implied, of the Defense Advanced Research Projects Agency or the US Government.

"yes" or "no." FRL would simply return both values, with no notice of the inconsistency. NETL would conclude that Nixon was a pacifist simply because the inference path to that conclusion is shorter than the path to the opposite conclusion. Yet the fact that one path is shorter than the other is irrelevant.

Nixon can inherit either pacifism, a property of Quaker, or non-pacifism, a property of Pro.Defense. Since there is no inheritance path from Quaker to Pro.Defense, nor vice versa, the inferential distance ordering provides no justification for viewing either class as a subclass of the other. Thus an inheritance reasoner based on inferential distance would be forced to recognize the ambiguity with regard to Nixon's pacifism.

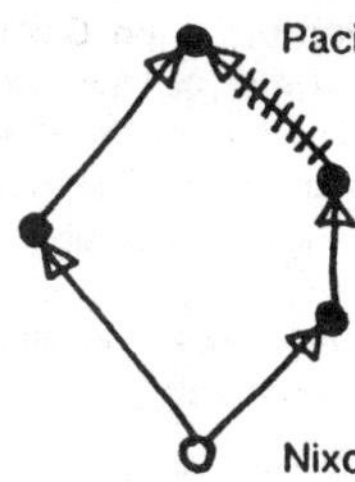

Figure 2.

5. Inferential Distance in Semantic Networks

TINA (for Topological Inheritance Architecture) is a recently implemented inheritance reasoner based on inferential distance [5]. TINA constructs the extensions of unambiguous inheritance networks by incrementally generating inheritance paths and weeding out those that violate the inferential distance ordering. This method also allows TINA to detect and report ambiguities in networks with multiple extensions. Since TINA does not use the shortest-path approach to inheritance, it is not misled by redundant links in the inheritance graph.

Another part of TINA, called the *conditioner*, can be used to correct certain problems with inheritance in NETL reported in [6]. These problems are due to NETL's implementation as a set of parallel marker propagation algorithms based on shortest-path reasoning. TINA's conditioner modifies the topology of a NETL network (after the extension has been computed) so as to force marker propagation scans to produce results in agreement with the correct extension, as defined by inferential distance. This technique can also be applied to other semantic network systems (incuding parallel systems) to speed up their inheritance search, since once a network has been conditioned we can search it using a shortest-path inheritance algorithm. Shortest-path algorithms are simpler and more effcient than inferential distance algorithms. One drawback is that any changes to the network will require at least a portion of it to be reconditioned.

6. Representing Inheritance in Default Logic

In default logic, a default inference rule is written in the form

$$\frac{\alpha(x) : \beta(x)}{\gamma(x)}$$

where $\alpha(x)$, $\beta(x)$, and $\gamma(x)$ are well-formed formulae called the *prerequisite*, the *justification*, and the *consequent* of the default, respectively [7]. The interpretation of this rule is: if $\alpha(x)$ is known, and $\beta(x)$ is consistent with what is known, then $\gamma(x)$ may be concluded. A default is said to be *normal* if the consequent is the entire justification, *i.e.* $\beta(x)$ and $\gamma(x)$ are identical. A default is said to be *semi-normal* if it is of form

$$\frac{\alpha(x) : \beta(x) \wedge \gamma(x)}{\beta(x)}$$

Etherington and Reiter use semi-normal defaults to represent inheritance systems in default logic [3]. To see why semi-normal defaults are necessary, consider the example in figure 3.

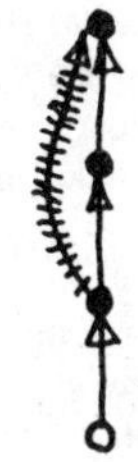

Figure 3.

This figure could be represented as the set of normal defaults D1-D3 below, plus the assertion Ostrich(Henry). We represent "ostriches are birds" (rule D2) in this example as a default rather than as a strict implication mainly for uniformity; this decision is not critical to the example. Another reason, though, is that in NETL, which we are trying to model, all statements are defeasible.

(D1) $$\frac{\text{Bird}(x) : \text{Can.Fly}(x)}{\text{Can.Fly}(x)}$$

(D2) $$\frac{\text{Ostrich}(x) : \text{Bird}(x)}{\text{Bird}(x)}$$

(D3) $$\frac{\text{Ostrich}(x) : \neg\text{Can.Fly}(x)}{\neg\text{Can.Fly}(x)}$$

Ostrich(Henry)

Using D1-D3, the assertion Ostrich(Henry) generates not one but two extensions. In one extension, Henry can't fly because he is an ostrich. But in the other, Henry can fly because he is a bird. This problem of "interacting defaults" was noted by Reiter and Criscuolo [8]. To solve it, they would replace the normal default D1 with the semi-normal version D1':

(D1') $$\frac{\text{Bird}(x) : \neg\text{Ostrich}(x) \wedge \text{Can.Fly}(x)}{\text{Can.Fly}(x)}$$

In D1', the restriction that ostriches should not be inferred to fly is incorporated into the default rule that birds fly. If we add two more types of non-flying birds, say penguins and dodos, then D1' would have to be replaced by another default that mentions all three exceptions.

There are three problems with handling exceptions explicitly using semi-normal defaults. First, as information is added to a knowledge base, existing default rules must continually be replaced with new ones that take the new exceptions into account. Second, the complexity of each individual default increases as the knowledge base grows, because more exceptions must be mentioned. Third, in any given inheritance network, the translation of one link cannot be determined independently of that of the others. For example, an IS-A link between Bird and Can.Fly might be represented as the normal default D1, yet in some networks the exact same link must be represented by D1'. Syntactically, every link in an inheritance network is a normal default, since the network formalism makes no explicit reference to exceptions. The problem with representing inheritance assertions as *semi*-normal defaults can be summarized by saying that it lacks what Woods calls "notational efficacy," a term that encompasses such properties as conciseness of representation and ease of modification [9].

Etherington and Reiter suggest that NETL treats some types of exceptions explicitly (*i.e.* its rules are semi-normal) because two types of exception link were proposed in [6]. These links were to be added to the network automatically, in a preprocessing step, to force NETL's marker propagation algorithms to produce the desired results. In order to add these exception links one must have a specification for the correct interpretation of the network. When one creates a NETL network, then, the meaning must already be determined, whether or not the network is subsequently annotated with exception links. The NETL formalism itself does not require that exceptions be treated explicitly. Exception links were later abandoned as a marker propagation device.

In FRL, an explicit mechanism for noting exceptions has never even been proposed. If we wish to translate inheritance networks into default logic using semi-normal rules, how are we to derive these rules from the syntactically normal ones the inheritance system contains? This question was left unanswered by earlier work on nonmonotonic inheritance. The inferential distance ordering provides an answer.

7. A Formal Analysis of Inferential Distance

By representing inheritance in default logic, Etherington and Reiter were able to give a formal semantics to inheritance systems along with a provably correct inference procedure. However, since their representation does not include the notion that subclasses should override superclasses, it does not fully express the meaning of inheritance. In [5] I present a formal analysis of inheritance under the inferential distance ordering. Some of the major theorems are:

- Every acyclic inheritance network has a constructible extension. (A similar result was proved in [7].)
- Every extension of an acyclic inheritance network is finite.
- An extension is inconsistent iff the network itself is inconsistent. (We use an expanded notion of inconsistency in which the rules "typically birds can fly" and "typically birds cannot fly" are mutually inconsistent. They would not be in default logic.)
- The union of any two distinct extensions is inconsistent.
- A network is ambiguous (has multiple extensions) iff it has an unstable extension. Instability is a property defined in [5]. A necessary condition for instability is that the network contain a subgraph of the form shown in figure 4.
- Every extension of an ambiguous network is unstable. Corollary: we can determine whether a network is ambiguous by constructing one of its extensions and checking it for stability.

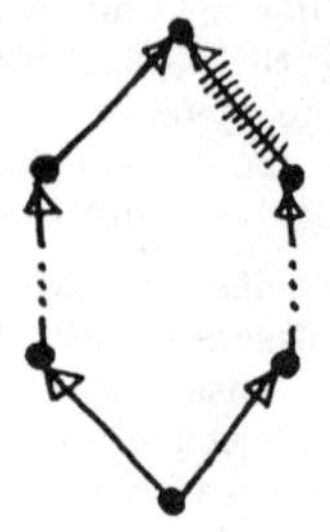

Figure 4.

- Every inheritance network is conditionable. That is, given a network and one of its extensions, we can always adjust the topology of the network so that a shortest path reasoner will produce results in agreement with the chosen extension.
- Additive conditioning (*i.e.* adding but never subtracting links) is sufficient.

8. Implementing Inferential Distance in Default Logic

Consider a subset of default logic corresponding to a family of acyclic inheritance graphs. We can represent an IS-A or IS-NOT-A link between a class P and a class Q as a normal default in the obvious way, *viz.*:

$$\frac{P(x) : Q(x)}{Q(x)} \qquad \frac{P(x) : \neg Q(x)}{\neg Q(x)}$$

Let P(x) be the prerequisite of a rule Di and Q(x) the prerequisite of a rule Dj. We define Di < Dj to mean that either there exists a default with prerequisite P(x) and conclusion Q(x), or there exists a default Dk such that Di < Dk and Dk < Dj. Returning to the ostrich example, note that D3 < D1 and D2 < D1 by this definition. D2 and D3 are unordered with respect to each other since their prerequisites are the same. The < relation is clearly a partial ordering.

The equivalent of an inheritance path in default logic is a proof sequence. The example involving Henry the ostrich, when represented by the normal defaults D1-D3, generates a pair of conflicting proof sequences S1 and S2. The arrows in these sequences indicate the defaults that justify each inference.

(S1) Ostrich(Henry) --D3--> ¬Can.Fly(Henry)

(S2) Ostrich(Henry) --D2--> Bird(Henry)
--D1--> Can.Fly(Henry)

Note that if Di precedes Dj in some proof sequence, then Di < Dj. If we order proof sequences by comparing the ordering of the maximal rules used in each proof, we see that S1 < S2 because D3 < D1. To apply inferential distance to default logic, we use the ordering on proof sequences as a filter over the set of possible extensions. (This idea was suggested by David Etherington.) Basically, we reject as invalid any extension in which a conclusion depends on a proof sequence Si such that there is a contradictory sequence Sj < Si. Thus, the extension in which Henry can fly would be rejected, since that conclusion depends on proof sequence S2 but there is a contradictory proof sequence S1 < S2.

Now let us try expressing figure 2 in default logic:

(D4) $$\frac{Quaker(x) : Pacifist(x)}{Pacifist(x)}$$

(D5) $$\frac{Republican(x) : Pro.Defense(x)}{Pro.Defense(x)}$$

(D6) $$\frac{Pro.Defense(x) : \neg Pacifist(x)}{\neg Pacifist(x)}$$

$$Quaker(Nixon) \wedge Republican(Nixon)$$

The inference paths we generate about Nixon are:

(S3) Quaker(Nixon) **--D4-->** Pacifist(Nixon)

(S4) Republican(Nixon) **--D5-->** Pro.Defense(Nixon) **--D6-->** ¬Pacifist(Nixon)

The only ordering relation among these defaults is D5 < D6. Since D4 and D6 are unordered, the proof sequences S3 and S4 are unordered, so of the two extensions we obtain, one relying on S3 and one on S4, neither is to be preferred over the other.

At this point the reader should have no trouble translating figure 1 into a set of normal defaults and verifying that under the inferential distance ordering, only the desired extension is produced.

9. The Significance of Hierarchy

Brachman, in his discussion of what IS-A is and isn't, suggests that "to the extent inheritance is a useful property, it is strictly implementational and bears no weight in any discussion of the expressive or communicative superiority of semantic nets" [10]. When an inheritance system is devoid of exceptions he is clearly right. But in nonmonotonic inheritance systems, which provide for a simple form of default reasoning, the basic assumption that classes are structured hierarchically makes implicit handling of exceptions possible. In contrast, exceptions must normally be handled *ex*plicitly in default logic, since default logic contains no notion of hierarchy.

Implicit handling of exceptions is possible when we are restricted to hierarchical domains with simple forms of defaults, but default logic admits more intricate sorts of theories. Unrestricted semi-normal theories cannot be represented by normal ones using the ordering defined here. Default logic is clearly a more powerful formalism than inheritance for representing knowledge, but the latter remains important due to its conceptual simplicity and efficient inference algorithms.

10. Conclusions

The intuition underlying all inheritance systems is that subclasses should override superclasses. Inferential distance is a partial ordering on defaults that implements this intuition. The inferential distance ordering differs from the shortest-path ordering used by most inheritance reasoners in cases where the network is ambiguous or contains true but redundant statements. In these cases, the shortest-path ordering fails to ensure that subclasses (and only subclasses) override superclasses.

Applying inferential distance to the default logic representation of inheritance systems allows us to faithfully represent these systems with no loss of notational efficacy. Under inferential distance, default rules need not be discarded as more information is added to the knowledge base; individual rules do not become more complex as exceptions accumulate; and the translation of any one link in an inheritance network into a default is independent of that of any other.

Acknowledgements

I am grateful to David Etherington, Jon Doyle, and Scott Fahlman for many insightful discussions, and to the referees for sugggestions which led to the restructuring of this paper.

References

[1] Roberts, R. B., and I. P. Goldstein. *The FRL Manual.* MIT AI Memo 409, MIT, Cambridge, MA, 1977.

[2] Fahlman, S. E. *NETL: A System for Representing and Using Real-World Knowledege.* MIT Press, Cambridge, MA, 1979.

[3] Etherington, D. W., and R. Reiter. "On Inheritance Hierarchies With Exceptions," *Proc. AAAI-83*, August, 1983, pp. 104-108.

[4] Reiter, R. "A Logic for Default Reasoning," *Artificial Intelligence* Vol. 13, No. 1-2, April 1980, pp. 81-132.

[5] Touretzky, D. S. *The Mathematics of Inheritance Systems.* Doctoral dissertation, Computer Science Dept., Carnegie-Mellon University, Pittsburgh, PA, 1984.

[6] Fahlman, S. E., D. S. Touretzky, and W. van Roggen. "Cancellation in a Parallel Semantic Network," *Proc. IJCAI-81*, August, 1981, pp. 257-263.

[7] Etherington, D. W. *Formalizing Non-Monotonic Reasoning Systems.* Technical report 83-1, Dept. of Computer Science, University of British Columbia, Vancouver, BC, Canada, 1983.

[8] Reiter, R., and G. Criscuolo. "On Interacting Defaults," *Proc. IJCAI-81*, August, 1981, pp. 270-276.

[9] Woods, W. A. "What's Important About Knowledge Representation?" *Computer*, Vol. 16, No. 10, October 1983, pp. 22-27.

[10] Brachman, R. J. "What IS-A Is and Isn't," *Computer*, Vol 16, No. 10, October, 1983, pp. 30-36.

3.2 Modal Approaches

The modal approach to nonmonotonic inference is probably the least explored of the three principal formalisms. The reasons, I suspect, are that the papers describing the work often have been difficult to understand, and the formal work itself has been somewhat unsatisfactory until recently.

The first paper to try this approach is McDermott and Doyle's 1980 paper, "Nonmonotonic logic I." Motivational material is presented in the first three sections, after which the authors turn to the formalities of the modal approach.

Unfortunately, the formalism they present is too weak to be of much use. As McDermott himself remarks in the sequel [McDermott, 1982], "There was not actually any relation between the truth values of p and Lp." McDermott attempted to patch this by using a modal theory based on one of the modal logics T, $S4$ or $S5$. Unfortunately, these approaches also are flawed, since only the logic $S5$ is strong enough to capture the notions McDermott is trying to formalize, but nonmonotonic $S5$ in fact collapses to a monotonic theory. So something else is needed.

Moore supplies the something else in autoepistemic logic, introduced in "Semantical considerations on nonmonotonic logic." He also begins with a variety of motivational material before turning to formal matters in Section 3. The paper is extremely clearly written, although the proofs of many formal results were missing until the appearance of his next paper on the subject, "Possible-world semantics for autoepistemic logic."

In this second paper, Moore draws a connection between autoepistemic logic and a Kripke-style approach to modal logic based on possible worlds [Kripke, 1971]. Because of the fairly constructive nature of Kripke's approach, Moore is able to prove a variety of claims made in the earlier paper about (for example) the existence of multiple extensions in certain cases. He remarks that Halpern and Moses [Halpern, Moses, 1984] obtained similar results independently; more recently, Levesque [Levesque, 1987] has explored these ideas as well.

Non-Monotonic Logic I *

Drew McDermott

Department of Computer Science, Yale University, New Haven, CT 06520, U.S.A.

Jon Doyle

Artificial Intelligence Laboratory, Massachusetts Institute of Technology, Cambridge, MA 02139, U.S.A.

Recommended by Nils Nilsson

ABSTRACT

'Non-monotonic' logical systems are logics in which the introduction of new axioms can invalidate old theorems. Such logics are very important in modeling the beliefs of active processes which, acting in the presence of incomplete information, must make and subsequently revise assumptions in light of new observations. We present the motivation and history of such logics. We develop model and proof theories, a proof procedure, and applications for one non-monotonic logic. In particular, we prove the completeness of the non-monotonic predicate calculus and the decidability of the non-monotonic sentential calculus. We also discuss characteristic properties of this logic and its relationship to stronger logics, logics of incomplete information, and truth maintenance systems.

1. Introduction

'Non-monotonic' logical systems are logics in which the introduction of new axioms can invalidate old theorems. Such logics are very important in modeling the beliefs of active processes which, acting in the presence of incomplete information, must make and subsequently revise assumptions in light of new observations. We present the motivation and history of such logics. We develop model and proof theories, a proof procedure, and applications for one non-monotonic logic. In particular, we prove the completeness of the non-monotonic predicate calculus and the decidability of the non-monotonic sentential calculus. We also discuss characteristic properties of this logic and its relationship to stronger logics, logics of incomplete information, and truth maintenance systems.

* This research was conducted at the Artificial Intelligence Laboratory of the Massachusetts Institute of Technology. Support for the Laboratory's artificial intelligence research is provided in part by the Advanced Research Projects Agency of the Department of Defense under Office of Naval Research contract number N00014–75–C–0643, and in part by NSF Grant MCS77–04828.

2. The Problem of Incomplete Knowledge

The relation between formal logic and the operation of the mind has always been unclear. On one hand, logic was originally the study of the 'laws of thought,' and has remained at least in principle a prescriptive theory of the operation of the 'ideal' mind. On the other hand, many logicians have often been unduly uninterested in ordinary 'non-ideal' mental phenomena. Some of the more striking differences between properties of formal logics and mental phenomenology occur in situations dealing with perception, ambiguity, common sense, causality and prediction. One common feature of these problems is that they seem to involve working with incomplete knowledge. Perception must account for the noticing of overlooked features, common sense ignores myriad special exceptions, assigners of blame can be misled, and plans for the future must consider never-to-be-realized contingencies. It is this apparently unavoidable making of mistakes in these cases that leads to some of the deepest problems of the formal analysis of mind.

Some studies of these problems occur in the philosophical literature, the most relevant here being Rescher's [36] analysis of counterfactual conditionals and belief-contravening hypotheses. In artificial intelligence, studies of perception, ambiguity and common sense have led to knowledge representations which explicitly and implicitly embody much information about typical cases, defaults, and methods for handling mistakes [28, 35]. Studies of problem-solving and acting have attempted representing predictive and causal knowledge so that decisions to act require only limited contemplation, and that actions, their variations, and their effects can be conveniently described and computed [6, 9, 10, 11]. Indeed, one of the original names applied to these efforts, 'heuristic programming,' stems from efficiency requirements forcing the use of methods which occasionally are wrong or which fail. The possibility of failure means that formalizations of reasoning in these areas must capture the process of revisions of perceptions, predictions, deductions, and other beliefs.

In fact, the need to revise beliefs also occurs in certain implementations of deductive systems working within traditional logics. Much work has been done on mechanized proof techniques for the first-order predicate calculus [29, 30, 38]. Incomplete information is represented in these systems as disjunctions of the several possibilities where the individual disjuncts may be independent of the axioms being used, that is, cannot be proven or contradicted by arguments from the axioms. Thus, proof procedures engage in *case-splitting*, in which disjuncts are considered in a case-by-case fashion. At any given time, the proof procedure will have some set of current assumptions, from which the current set of formulas has been derived. If failures in the proof attempt lead to investigating new splits, and so change the set of current assumptions, the current set of derived formulas must also be updated, for it is the current set of formulas on which the proof procedure bases its actions.

Classical symbolic logic lacks tools for describing how to revise a formal theory to deal with inconsistencies caused by new information. This lack is due to a recognition that the general problem of finding and selecting among alternate revisions is very hard. (For an attack on this problem, see Rescher [36]. Quine and Ullian [33] survey the complexities.) Although logicians have been able to ignore this problem, philosophers and researchers in artificial intelligence have been forced to face it because humans and computational models are subject to a continuous flow of new information. One important insight gained through computational experience is that there are at least two different problems involved, what might be called 'routine revision' and 'world-model reorganization.'

World-model reorganization is the very hard problem of revising a complex model of a situation when it turns out to be wrong. Much of the complexity of such models usually stems from parts of the model relying on descriptions of other parts of the model, such as inductive hypotheses, testimony, analogy, and intuition. An example of such large-scale reorganization would be the revision of a Newtonian cosmology to account for perturbations in Mercury's orbit. Less grand examples are children's revisions of their world-models as discovered by Piaget, and the revision of one's opinion of a friend upon discovering his dishonesty.

Routine revision, on the other hand, is the problem of maintaining a set of facts which, although expressed as universally true, have exceptions. For example, a program may have the belief that all animals with beaks are birds. Telling this program about a platypus will cause a contradiction, but intuitively not as serious a contradiction as those requiring total reorganization. The relative simplicity of this type of revision problem stems from the statement itself expressing what revisions are appropriate by referring to possible exceptions. Such relatively easy cases include many forms of inferences, default assumptions, and observations.

Classical logics, by lumping all contradictions together, has overlooked the possibility of handling the easy ones by expanding the notation in which rules are stated. That is, we could have avoided this problem by stating the belief as 'If something is an animal with a beak, then *unless proven otherwise*, it is a bird.' If we allow statements of this kind, the problem becomes how to coordinate sets of such rules. Each such statement may be seen as providing a piece of advice about belief revision; for this approach to make sense, all the little pieces of advice must determine a unique revision. This is the subject of this paper. Of course, if we are successful, the world-model reorganization problem will still be unsolved. But we hope factoring out the routine revision problem will make the more difficult problem clearer.

3. Approaches to Non-Monotonic Logic and the Semantical Difficulties

The study of the problem of formalizing the process of revision of beliefs has been almost completely confined to the practical side of artificial intelligence research, where much work has been done [6, 12, 26, 42]. Theoretical foundations for this work have been lacking. This paper studies the foundations of these forms of reasoning with revisions, which we term *non-monotonic* logic.

Traditional logics are called *monotonic* because the theorems of a theory are always a subset of the theorems of any extension of the theory. (This name for this property of classical logics was used, after a suggestion by Pratt, in Minsky's [28] discussion. Hayes [11] has called this the 'extension' property.) In this paper, by *theory* we will mean a set of axioms. A more precise statement of monotonicity is this: If A and B are two theories, and $A \subseteq B$, then $\mathrm{Th}(A) \subseteq \mathrm{Th}(B)$, where $\mathrm{Th}(S) = \{p: S \vdash p\}$ is the set of theorems of S. We will be even more precise about the definition of $\vdash$ in Section 5.

Monotonic logics lack the phenomenon of new information leading to a revision of old conclusions. We obtain non-monotonic logics from classical logics by extending them with a modality ('consistent') well-known in artificial intelligence circles, and show that the resulting logics have well-founded, if unusual, model and proof theories. We introduce the proposition-forming modality M (read 'consistent'). Informally, Mp is to mean that p is consistent with everything believed. (See [24].) Thus one small theory employing this modality would be

(1) noon $\wedge$ M[sun-shining] $\supset$ sun-shining
(2) noon
(3) eclipse $\supset$ $\neg$sun-shining,

in which we can prove

(4) sun-shining.

If we add the axiom

(5) eclipse

then (4) is inconsistent, so, by (1), (4) is not a theorem of the extended theory.

The use of non-monotonic techniques has some history, but until recently the intuitions underlying these techniques were inadequate and led to difficulties involving the semantics of non-monotonic inference rules in certain cases. We mention some of the guises in which non-monotonic reasoning methods and belief revising processes have appeared.

Scriven [40, 41] proposed that explanations, and in particular historical explanations of rational actions or decisions, are based not on universal or statistical laws, but rather on truisms or more generally, what he terms 'normic' statements. Normic statements include such statements as "In delicate circumstances, rational men act cautiously," or "All murders are committed from motives of revenge, lust, jealously, hate, greed, or fear." Such statements frequently involve terms such as 'naturally,' 'normally,' 'typically,' 'tendency,' 'ought,' 'should,' and others. Normic statements provide plausible explanations of actions or situations, explanations which may be invalidated by providing exceptions, special cases, or other mediating circumstances; that is, instances of normic statements are *defeasible*. In this way, normic statements seem closely related to statements expressible in non-monotonic logic. Scriven pointed out that while in some cases normic statements could imply statistical statements and so have some predictive power, in other cases normic statements can only supply coherent explanations, cannot rule out alternative coherent arguments, and thus fail to have predictive power. De Kleer [4] amplifies this point in considering explanations of the behavior of designed artifacts. As we shall see in this paper, this circumstance is also highly suggestive of non-monotonic logic.

In PLANNER [12], a programming language based on a negationless calculus, the THNOT primitive formed the basis of non-monotonic reasoning. THNOT, as a goal, succeeded only if its argument failed, and failed otherwise. Thus if the argument to THNOT was a formula to be proved, the THNOT would succeed only if the attempt to prove the embedded formula failed. In addition to the non-monotonic primitive THNOT, PLANNER employed antecedent and erasing procedures to update the data base of statements of beliefs when new deductions were made or actions taken. Unfortunately, it was up to the user of these procedures to make sure that there were no circular dependencies or mutual proofs between beliefs. Such circularities could lead to, for example, errors of groundless belief (due to two mutually supporting beliefs) or non-terminating programs (a more technical but no less irritating problem).

Two related forms of non-monotonic deductive systems are those described by McCarthy and Hayes [24] and Sandewall [39]. McCarthy and Hayes give some indications of how actions might be described using modal operators like 'normally' and 'consistent,' but present no detailed guidelines on how such operators might be carefully defined. Sandewall, in a deductive system applied to the frame problem (which is basically the problem of efficiently representing the effects of actions; see [11]) used a deductive representation of non-monotonic rules based on a primitive called UNLESS. This was used to deduce conditions of situations resulting from actions except in those cases where properties of the action changed the extant conditions. Thus one might say that things retain their color unless painted.

Sandewall's interpretation of UNLESS was in accord with then current intuitions: UNLESS (p) is true if p is not deducible from the axioms using the classical first-order inference rules. Unfortunately, this definition has several problems, as pointed out by Sandewall. One problem is that it can happen that both p and UNLESS (p) are deducible, since from a rule like "from UNLESS(C) infer D," D can be inferred, but at the same time UNLESS(D) is also deducible since D is not deducible by classical rules. These problems are partly due to the dependence of the notion of 'deducible' on the intention of deduction rules based on 'not deducible.' This question-begging definition leads to perplexing questions of beliefs when complicated relations between UNLESS statements are present. For example, given the axioms

$$A$$
$$A \wedge \text{UNLESS}(B) \supset C$$
$$A \wedge \text{UNLESS}(C) \supset B,$$

we are faced with the somewhat paradoxical situation that either B or C can be deduced, but not both simultaneously. On the other hand, in the axiom system

$$A$$
$$A \wedge \text{UNLESS}(B) \supset C$$
$$A \wedge \text{UNLESS}(C) \supset D$$
$$A \wedge \text{UNLESS}(D) \supset E,$$

one would expect to see A, C and E believed, and B and D not believed.

One might be tempted to dismiss these anomalous cases as uninteresting. In fact, such cases are not perverse; rather, they occur naturally in many applications. The common way they are introduced is by employing assumptions which require further assumptions to be made.

Spurred by Sandewall's presentation of the problems arising through such non-monotonic inference rules, Kramosil [17] considered sets of inference rules of the form

"From $\vdash p$, $\nvdash q$, infer $\vdash r$",

where $\vdash$ and $\nvdash$ are tokens of the meta-language and the number of antecedents can be arbitrary. Kramosil defined the set of theorems in such a system as the intersection of all subsets of the language closed under the inference rules. He noted that this set may not itself be closed under the inference rules, and showed that in the special case in which the inference rules preserve truth values (that is, are effectively monotonic) that if the set of theorems of the monotonic inference rules alone is also closed with respect to the non-monotonic inference rules, then this set is the set of non-monotonic theorems. Kramosil's conclusion was that a set of inference rules defines a formalized theory (one in which all formulas have a well-defined truth value) if and only if this same theory is that of the monotonic inference rules alone, which he interprets to mean that the non-monotonic rules are either useless or meaningless.

As we will show in this paper, Kramosil's interpretation was too pessimistic with regard to the possibility of formalizing such rules and their unusual properties. As we have argued above, the purpose of non-monotonic inference rules is not to add certain knowledge where there is none, but rather to guide the selection of tentatively held beliefs in the hope that fruitful investigations and good guesses will result. This means that one should not *a priori* expect non-monotonic rules to derive valid conclusions independent of the monotonic rules. Rather one should expect to be led to a set of beliefs which while perhaps eventually shown incorrect will meanwhile coherently guide investigations.

Non-monotonic inference rules need not appear in the explicit forms discussed by Kramosil. Many authors have described artificial intelligence programs which exhibit non-monotonic behavior only implicitly. Non-monotonicity in these systems stems typically from extra-logical devices. For example, one can effect changes in beliefs (as opposed to inferences) by using extra-logical STRIPS-like [8] operators.

Conflict resolution strategies, which use production-rule orderings and specificity criteria to determine the next system action, also induce non-monotonic behavior. ([15] and [31] in fact term this property of their systems 'non-monotonicity'.)

One class of non-monotonic inferences consists of what might be called 'minimal' inferences, in which a minimal model for some set of beliefs is assumed by assuming the set of beliefs to be a complete description of a state of affairs. Joshi and Rosenschein [16] describe a partial-matching procedure based on the operation of taking least upper bounds in a lattice of sets of beliefs. This has the effect of assuming just enough additional information to allow a desired partial match to succeed. McCarthy [25] outlines a procedure called 'circumscription', in which the current partial extension of some predicate is assumed to be the complete extension. Of course, new examples of the predication can invalidate previous completeness assumptions. Reiter [34] analyzes the related technique of assuming false all elementary predications not explicitly known true. He outlines some conditions under which data bases remain consistent under this 'closed world assumption,' and shows certain forms of data bases to be naturally consistent with this assumption. However, the closed world assumption does not seem to allow for any locality of definition of defaults, since it applies this assumption to all primitive predicates, and does not allow defaults applied to defined predicates. Circumscription, on the other hand, would seem to be applicable to any predicate whatever. Although they describe tools for non-monotonic reasoning, none of these authors discuss the problem of revision of beliefs.

These problems were mostly resolved in the Truth Maintenance System (TMS) of Doyle [6] and related systems [21, 23] in which each statement has an associated set of justifications, each of which represents a reason for holding the statement as a belief. These justifications are used to determine the set of current beliefs by examining the recorded justifications to find well-founded support (non-circular proofs) whenever possible for each belief. When hypotheses change, these justifications are again examined to update the set of current beliefs. This scheme provides a more accurate version of antecedent and erasing procedures of PLANNER without the need to explicitly check for circular proofs. The non-monotonic capability appears as a type of justification which is the static analogue of the PLANNER THNOT primitive. Part of the justification of a belief can be the lack of valid justifications for some other possible program belief. This allows, for example, belief in a statement to be justified whenever no proof of the negation of the statement is known. This representation of non-monotonic justifications, in combination with the belief revision algorithms, produced the first system capable of performing the routine revision of apparently inconsistent theories into consistent theories. Part of this revision process is a backtracking scheme called dependency-directed backtracking [42]. We will analyze this system in more detail in Section 10, but first we provide some theoretical foundations for this work.

Weyhrauch [46] presents a formal system organized about a theory/metatheory distinction in which non-monotonic rules (among many others) can be expressed. This system also makes the self-referential nature of such rules clear by allowing explicit self-reference, so that the formal system has a name for itself, and can draw conclusions about itself in the theory of itself taken as an object. However, the system is its own model of itself, so these conclusions can change the referent of its name for itself. This means that new derivations can affect old conclusions drawn from previous observations of the system's state. Much work remains to be done along these lines, one detail of which would be a formal comparison of Weyhrauch's system with non-monotonic logic.

In outline, our analysis of non-monotonic logic will proceed as follows. We first define a standard language of discourse including the non-monotonic modality M ('consistent'). The semantics of the language is based on models constructed from *fixed points* of a formalized non-monotonic proof operator. Provability in this system is then defined, and a proof of completeness for this system is presented. This is augmented by a proof procedure for a restricted class of theories and an analysis of some of the structure of models of non-monotonic theories.

4. Linguistic Preliminaries

We settle on a language $\mathcal{L}$ which will be the language of all theories mentioned in the following. $\mathcal{L}$ has an infinite number of constant letters, variable letters, predicate letters, and propositional constant letters. The formation rules of the language are as follows:

The *atomic formulas* of $\mathcal{L}$ are the propositional constant letters and the strings of the form $g(x_1, \ldots, x_n)$ for predicate letter g and variables or constants $x_1, \ldots, x_n$. The *formulas* of $\mathcal{L}$ are either atomic formulas or, for formulas p, q and variable letter x, strings of the form $\mathsf{M}p$, $\neg p$, $p \supset q$, and $\forall xp$. We use the usual abbreviations of $p \wedge q$ for $\neg[p \supset \neg q]$, $p \vee q$ for $\neg p \supset q$, $\exists xp$ for $\neg \forall x \neg p$, and abbreviate $\neg \mathsf{M} \neg p$ as $\mathsf{L}p$. A *statement* is a formula with no free variables. The usual criteria for determining free variables apply (see [27]). In addition, a variable x is free in $\mathsf{M}p$ if and only if x is free in p.

In this paper, the letters C, D, E and F will be used as syntactic variables ranging over propositional constant letters. The letters p, q and r will be used for formulas. Implicit quasi-quotation is used throughout. That is, if p and q are formulas, $p \supset q$ is the formula obtained by concatenating p, the implication symbol and q. This notation extends to handle finite sets of formulas in the following way: if Q is a finite set of formulas, and Q appears in a quasi-quoted context, it always stands for the conjunction of its elements. For example, $Q \supset p$ means the formula obtained by conjoining all the elements of Q and following the result with the implication symbol and p. (If Q is empty, it stands for $C \vee \neg C$). Since syntax is not a pre-occupation of this paper, the presentation is not rigorous in specifying the number of arguments of predicate letters, parenthesization, etc.

The inferential system used defines a first-order theory to be a set of axioms including the following infinite class of axioms:

For all formulas p, q and r:

(6) (i) $p \supset [q \supset p]$

(ii) $[p \supset [q \supset r]] \supset [[p \supset q] \supset [q \supset r]]$

(iii) $[\neg q \supset \neg p] \supset [[\neg q \supset p] \supset q]$

(iv) $\forall x p(x) \supset p(t)$

where $p(x)$ is a formula and t is a constant or a variable free for x in $p(x)$ and $p(t)$ denotes the result of substituting t for every free occurrence of x in $p(x)$, and

(v) $\forall x[p \supset q] \supset [p \supset \forall x q]$

if p is a formula containing no free occurrence of x. (These axioms are from [27].) These are the *logical* axioms. All other axioms are called *proper*, or non-logical axioms. (This terminology is misleading for axioms which are logical consequences of the logical axioms, but we will ignore this inelegance.) The theory with no proper axioms is called the *predicate calculus* (PC). (Note that this theory also contains strings containing the letter M, so it is actually not strict PC.) The *sentential calculus* (SC) consists of axioms which are instances of (i), (ii) and (iii) only. A theory consisting only of the sentential calculus plus a finite number of statements is called a statement theory.

In this paper, the letters A and B will be used to stand for theories.

5. Proof-Theoretic Operators

The monotonic rules of inference we will use (also from [27]) are

(7) Modus Ponens: from p and $p \supset q$, infer q
Generalization: from p, infer $\forall x p$.

If S is a set of formulas, and p follows from S and the axioms of A by the rules (7), we say $S \vdash_A p$. We abbreviate $\vdash_{PC}$ by $\vdash$ alone. We define $\mathrm{Th}(S) = \{p: S \vdash p\}$.

The particular inference rules (7) are not very important. Later in the paper, when we concentrate on statement theories, the rule of generalization will be dropped without much fanfare. All that is important is that the operator Th have the following properties, which together are called *monotonicity*:

(8) (i) $A \subseteq \mathrm{Th}(A)$

(ii) If $A \subseteq B$, then $\mathrm{Th}(A) \subseteq \mathrm{Th}(B)$,

and the property (9) of *idempotence*

(9) $\mathrm{Th}(\mathrm{Th}(A)) = \mathrm{Th}(A)$.

Clearly, any classical inference system satisfies these conditions. Condition (9) can also be viewed as a fixed point equation, stating that the set of theorems monotonically derivable from a theory is a fixed point of the operator which computes the closure of a set of formulas under the monotonic inference rules. A well-known property of the monotonic inference rules is that $\mathrm{Th}(A)$ is the smallest fixed point of this closing process; in fact, that $\mathrm{Th}(A)$ is the intersection of all S such that $A \subseteq S$ and $\mathrm{Th}(S) = S$.

In order to deal with non-monotonic logic, we need a new inference rule like this one (which we will take back immediately):

(10) "If $\nvdash_A \neg p$, then $\vdash_A \mathrm{M}p$."

That is, if a formula's negation is not derivable, it may be inferred to be consistent. As it stands, however, this rule is of no value because it is circular. 'Derivable' means 'derivable from axioms by inference rules', so we cannot define an inference rule in terms of derivability so casually.

Instead, we retain the definition of $\vdash$ as meaning monotonic derivability, and define the operator NM as follows: for any first-order theory A and any set of formulas $S \subseteq \mathscr{L}$ ($\mathscr{L}$, recall, is the entire language), let

(11) $\mathrm{NM}_A(S) = \mathrm{Th}(A \cup \mathrm{As}_A(S))$,

where $\mathrm{As}_A(S)$, the set of *assumptions* from S, is given by

(12) $\mathrm{As}_A(S) = \{\mathrm{M}q: q \in \mathscr{L} \text{ and } \neg q \notin S\} - \mathrm{Th}(A)$.

Notice that theorems of A of the form $\mathrm{M}q$ are never counted as assumptions. NM_A takes a set S and produces a new set which includes $\mathrm{Th}(A)$ but also includes much more: everything provable from the enlarged set of axioms and assumptions which is the original theory together with all assumptions not ruled out by S.

We would like to define $\mathrm{TH}(A)$, the set of theorems non-monotonically derivable from A, by analogy with the monotonic case as

(13) "$\mathrm{TH}(A)$ = the smallest fixed point of NM_A."

This 'definition' tries to capture the idea of adding the non-monotonic inference rule (10) to a first-order theory A. This is plausible, since it demands a set such that all of its elements may be proven from axioms and assumptions not wiped out by the proofs. Such fixed points $S = \mathrm{NM}_A(S)$ might be depicted as in Fig. 1. Unfortunately, there is in general no appropriate fixed point of NM_A. It can happen that a theory has no fixed point under the operator NM_A. Even if there are fixed points, there need not be a smallest fixed point.

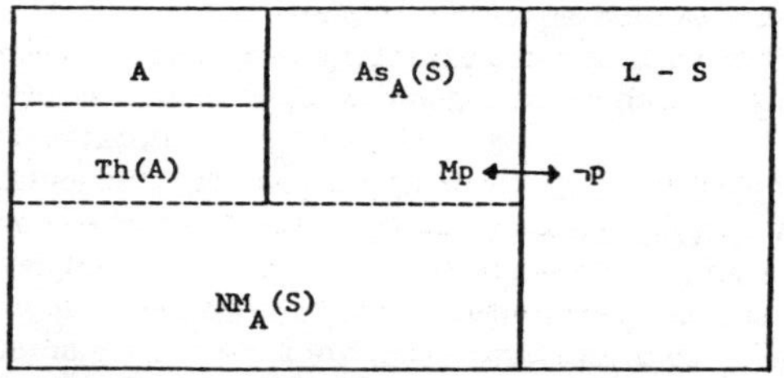

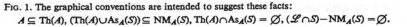

FIG. 1. The graphical conventions are intended to suggest these facts:
$A \subseteq \mathrm{Th}(A)$, $(\mathrm{Th}(A) \cup \mathrm{As}_A(S)) \subseteq \mathrm{NM}_A(S)$, $\mathrm{Th}(A) \cap \mathrm{As}_A(S) = \varnothing$, $(\mathscr{L} \cap S) - \mathrm{NM}_A(S) = \varnothing$.

For example, consider the theory T1 obtained as

(14) $\mathrm{T1} = \mathrm{PC} \cup \{ \mathsf{M}C \supset \neg D,\ \mathsf{M}D \supset \neg C\}$,

where C and D are propositional constants. $\mathrm{NM}_{\mathrm{T1}}$ has two fixed points, which can be called F_1 and F_2. F_1 contains $\neg C$ but not $\neg D$, and F_2 contains $\neg D$ but not $\neg C$. Since $\neg D$ is not in F_1, $\mathsf{M}D$ is in F_1, and so $\neg C$ is in F_1. Similarly, the presence of $\neg D$ in F_2 keeps $\neg C$ out and $\mathsf{M}C$ in F_2. The problem is that neither $F_1 \cap F_2$ nor $F_1 \cup F_2$ is a fixed point of $\mathrm{NM}_{\mathrm{T1}}$. Since neither $\neg C$ nor $\neg D$ is in $\mathrm{F}_1 \cap \mathrm{F}_2$, $\mathsf{M}C$ and $\mathsf{M}D$ are both in $\mathrm{NM}_{\mathrm{T1}}(\mathrm{F}_1 \cap \mathrm{F}_2)$, so $\neg C$ and $\neg D$ are in $\mathrm{NM}_{\mathrm{T1}}(\mathrm{F}_1 \cap \mathrm{F}_2)$, so $\mathrm{F}_1 \cap \mathrm{F}_2 \neq \mathrm{NM}_{\mathrm{T1}}(\mathrm{F}_1 \cap \mathrm{F}_2)$. Similarly, both $\neg C$ and $\neg D$ are in $\mathrm{NM}_{\mathrm{T1}}(\mathrm{F}_1 \cup \mathrm{F}_2)$, so applying $\mathrm{NM}_{\mathrm{T1}}$ to the union results in a smaller set. So in this case there is no natural status for $\neg C$ and $\neg D$.

An example of a theory with no fixed point of the corresponding operator is the theory T2 obtained as

(15) $\mathrm{T2} = \mathrm{PC} \cup \{ \mathsf{M}C \supset \neg C\}$.

In this case, $\mathrm{NM}_{\mathrm{T2}}$ has no fixed point, since alternate applications of the operator to any set produce new sets in which either both $\mathsf{M}C$ and $\neg C$ exist or neither exist.

Therefore, we must accept a somewhat less elegant definition of TH. Let us define TH as follows:

(16) $\mathrm{TH}(A) = \bigcap(\{\mathcal{L}\} \cup \{S\colon \mathrm{NM}_A(S) = S\})$.

That is, the set of provable formulas is the intersection of all fixed points of NM_A, or the entire language if there are no fixed points. We will use the abbreviation $A \mid\!\sim p$ to indicate that $p \in \mathrm{TH}(A)$. With this definition, neither $\mathsf{M}C$ nor $\mathsf{M}D$ is a theorem of T1 in (14), but $\mathsf{M}C \vee \mathsf{M}D$ is. In the following, we will abbreviate $\{S\colon \mathrm{NM}_A(S) = S\}$ as $\mathrm{FP}(A)$, and (somewhat abusing the terms) call the elements of this set *fixed points* of the theory A.

This definition of the provable statements is quite similar in some respects to the definition of compatibility-restricted entailment given by Rescher [36]. In that system, a set S of formulas is said to CR-entail a formula p if p follows in the standard fashion from each of one or more 'preferred' maximal consistent subsets of S. In the present case, we obtain the preferred subsets of formulas as fixed points of the operator NM_A (the 'compatible subsets'), but in contrast to normal deducibility where the empty set always suffices, there need not be any such subsets. This case produces the entire language as the set of provable formulas by vacuous fulfilment of the condition of derivability.

One unusual consequence of this definition of provability is that the deduction theorem does not hold for non-monotonic logic. For example, while $\{C\} \mid\!\sim \mathsf{ML}C$ it is not true that $\mid\!\sim C \supset \mathsf{ML}C$. This failure of the deduction theorem is to be expected, however, since the non-monotonic provability of a formula depends on the completeness of the set of hypotheses, that is, on the fact that no other axioms are available. The deduction theorem, however, would if valid produce implications valid no matter what other axioms were added to the system, even if these axioms would invalidate the completeness condition used in the derivation of the implication. One should note that although the deduction theorem does not hold in general in non-monotonic logic, there are many particular cases in which it does hold. For instance, if some conclusion follows classically from some hypotheses, then the expected implication will also hold. In addition, not all properly non-monotonic theories are such that the deduction theorem fails. It is an interesting open problem to characterize the precise cases in which the deduction theorem is valid in non-monotonic theories.

So far, we have defined 'provability' without defining 'proof'. For a formula to be provable in a theory, it must have a standard proof from axioms and assumptions in each fixed point of the theory, and, as yet, we have no way of enumerating fixed points or even of describing one. It is worth note that when a theory has more than one fixed point, the fixed points are inaccessible in the sense that the sequence $\mathrm{Th}(A)$, $\mathrm{NM}_A(\mathrm{Th}(A))$, $\mathrm{NM}_A(\mathrm{NM}_A(\mathrm{Th}(A)))$, ... does not converge to a fixed point. We have a proof, which we do not present here, that if NM_A has exactly one fixed point, then the fixed point is the limit of successive applications of NM_A to the sequence of sets starting with A. We will eventually attend to defining non-monotonic proof, but first we turn our attention to the topic of semantics.

6. Model Theory

The semantics of non-monotonic logic is built on the notion of model, just like the semantics of classical logic. In fact, the definition of model for a non-monotonic theory depends directly on the usual definition.

An *interpretation* V of formulas over a language $\mathcal{L}$ is a pair $\langle X, U\rangle$, where X is a nonempty set, and U is a function which associates relations and values over the domain X with each predicate, variable, constant and propositional constant letter in the usual fashion. That is, for each n-ary predicate letter P, $U(P) \subseteq X^n$; for each variable or constant x, $U(x) \in X$; and for each propositional constant letter, C, $U(C) \in \{0, 1\}$. Using this mapping function U we define the value $V(p)$ of a formula p in the interpretation V to be an element of $\{0, 1\}$ satisfying the following conditions: For an atomic formula $p(x_1, \ldots, x_n)$, the value is 1 if $\langle U(x_1), \ldots, U(x_n)\rangle \in U(p)$, and is 0 otherwise. $V(\neg p) = 1$ if $V(p) = 0$, and is 0 otherwise. $V(p \supset q) = 1$ if either $V(p) = 0$ or $V(q) = 1$, and is 0 otherwise. $V(\forall xp) = 1$ if for all $y \in X$, $V'(p) = 1$, where $V' = \langle X, [y/x]U\rangle$, where $[y/x]U$ is the mapping derived from U by changing its value at the point x to the value y. $V(\forall xp) = 0$ otherwise. If $V(p) = 1$, we say that V *satisfies* p, and write $V \vDash p$.

A *monotonic model* of a set of formulas $S \subseteq \mathcal{L}$ is an interpretation V which satisfies each formula in S, that is, $V(p) = 1$ for each formula $p \in S$. A *non-monotonic model* of a theory A is a pair $\langle V, S\rangle$, where V is a monotonic model of S, and $S \in \mathrm{FP}(A)$. When the context makes the intended meaning clear, we will use the term *model* of A to mean either a non-monotonic model, a monotonic model, or an element of $\mathrm{FP}(A)$ for the theory A.

Although unorthodox, this definition provides a meaning for formulas Mp which reflects the proof-theoretic property that 'p is consistent with what is believed.' This notion is made precise by including in the model a set of 'current assumptions' (namely, $\mathrm{As}_A(S)$). A model for a theory must assign 1 to all of these assumptions, so the effect is that Mp is assigned 1 in a model if $\neg p$ is not derivable and $\neg$ Mp is not derivable from the current assumptions and the original theory, that is, if p is consistent with what is 'believed' in the model. Unfortunately, Mp may be assigned 1 in some model even when $\neg p$ is derivable (for example, when no axiom mentions Mp at all). This indicates that the logic is too weak.

We view the weakness of this semantics as the worst defect of our logic. We think we can improve it, but it appears that the semantics of non-monotonic systems will always be somewhat unorthodox. The problem is the failure of a kind of locality in semantic definitions. In conventional logics, the meaning of a composite expression can always be defined in terms of the meanings of its parts, even if these meanings are infinite things like functions on sets of possible worlds. In non-monotonic logic, this is impossible. The meaning of Mp can never be purely a function of the meaning of p, because it depends on the available axioms as well. This 'holistic' property seems inescapable. The best we can do is to try to express this dependence semantically, in terms of models of p plus the axioms. In the semantics just presented, this is not achieved, but we have hope that it can be achieved for a slightly stronger logic.

With this definition of model, we can justify the definition of provability.

Theorem 1 (Soundness). *If $A \mid\!\sim p$, then $V \models p$ for all models $\langle V, S\rangle$ of A.*

Proof. Assume $A \mid\!\sim p$. If there are no models of A, the theorem follows trivially. Otherwise, p is a member of every fixed point of A. But since every model of A is a monotonic model of a fixed point of A, every model assigns 1 to p.

Theorem 2 (Completeness). *If $V \models p$ for all models $\langle V, S\rangle$ of A, then $A \mid\!\sim p$.*

Proof. Assume that it is not true that $A \mid\!\sim p$. Thus there is a fixed point S of NM_A which does not contain p. Now $\mathrm{Th}(S) = S$ by idempotence, so $S \nvdash p$. But the predicate calculus is complete, so some monotonic model V of S has $V(p) = 0$.

It is not surprising that we have completeness, since the definition of truth makes reference to provability. The proof was for first-order theories, but it can easily be generalized to any complete formal logic. For example, if we take care not to confuse M with the S5 operator 'possibly,' we can easily get a complete non-monotonic extension of S5. However, none of these observations are very interesting unless we have some assurance that provability is decidable. We will shortly present a proof procedure for non-monotonic statement theories.

7. Fixed Points of Theories

This section will try to analyze the structure of fixed points for non-monotonic theories. We investigate the number of fixed points of theories, and their relation to the provable statements.

Non-monotonic theories may have varying number of fixed points. Classically inconsistent theories have just one fixed point (the entire language $\mathcal{L}$) and thus no models. The theory T2 in (15) also has no models due to the lack of a fixed point. Theories formulated in strictly classical language have exactly one fixed point, as does the theory

(17) $\mathrm{T3} = \mathrm{PC} \cup \{ \mathrm{M}C \supset C\}$.

Some theories have several fixed points, e.g. T1 in (14). It is also possible for a theory to have an infinite number of fixed points. This is exemplified (we assume equality and an infinite domain of unequal constants) by

(18) $\mathrm{T4} = \mathrm{PC} \cup \{\forall x[\,\mathrm{M}p(x) \supset [p(x) \wedge \forall y[x \neq y \supset \neg p(y)]]]\}$.

Even in theories having only one fixed point, the non-monotonically provable statements need not coincide with the classically provable statements. Theory T3 above is an example, for $C \in \mathrm{TH(T3)}$, but $C \notin \mathrm{Th(T3)}$. Some statements will be provable in theories with multiple fixed points, but will have different proofs in each fixed point. For example, $\mathrm{M}C \vee \mathrm{M}D \in \mathrm{TH(T1)}$ and $\exists x\, \mathrm{M}p(x) \in \mathrm{TH(T4)}$.

The classical results concerning truth and provability for logical languages are that, for a given theory A, a formula is *valid* in A (true in all models of A) if and only if it is *provable* in A, and that the theory has a model if and only if it is *consistent* (cannot be used to derive a contradiction). In non-monotonic logic, somewhat different circumstances obtain. As Theorems 1 and 2 have shown, validity in a theory remains equivalent to provability. However, from the definition of models of non-monotonic theories, it follows that a non-monotonic theory A has a model only if the operator NM_A has a classically consistent fixed point. Non-monotonic theories can lack fixed points (e.g. the theory T1), but we have defined such theories to be inconsistent.

The basic structure theorem states that all fixed points of a non-monotonic theory A are (set inclusion-) minimal fixed points.

Theorem 3. *If $S_1, S_2 \in \mathrm{FP}(A)$ and $S_1 \subseteq S_2$, then $S_1 = S_2$.*

Proof. If $S_1 \subseteq S_2$, then $\mathrm{As}_A(S_2) \subseteq \mathrm{As}_A(S_1)$, so by the monotonicity of Th, $\mathrm{NM}_A(S_2) \subseteq \mathrm{NM}_A(S_1)$. But since S_1 and S_2 are fixed points of this operator, $S_2 \subseteq S_1$, so $S_1 = S_2$.

This result suggests that strict set-theoretic minimality is not a particularly interesting distinction among fixed points. In the following sections we will make steps towards more interesting classifications, but without a fully satisfactory solution. Important applications of this theorem are the following two corollaries.

Corollary 4. *If $\mathcal{L}$ is a fixed point of A, then it is the only fixed point of A.*

Proof. If $S \in \mathrm{FP}(A)$, then $S \subseteq \mathcal{L}$, so $S = \mathcal{L}$ by Theorem 3.

Note that if $\mathcal{L}$ is a fixed point of A, then A is classically inconsistent, that is, $\mathrm{Th}(A) = \mathcal{L}$.

Corollary 5. *If p, $\neg p \in \text{TH}(A)$, then* $\text{TH}(A) = \mathscr{L}$.

Proof. If A has no fixed points, the theorem follows by definition. If both p and $\neg p$ are members of a fixed point S of A, then since fixed points are closed under monotonic deduction, $S = \mathscr{L}$. But then $\text{FP}(A) = \{\mathscr{L}\}$, so $\text{TH}(A) = \mathscr{L}$.

With these results, we can study the notion dual to provability in non-monotonic theories. We say that a formula p is *arguable* from A if $p \in \cup\,\text{FP}(A)$, that is, if some fixed point of A contains p. Clearly, all provable formulas are arguable. Our next theorem shows that in consistent theories, provability and arguability are almost dual notions.

Theorem 6. *If A is consistent and p is provable in A, then $\neg p$ is not arguable.*

Proof. If p is provable in a consistent theory A, then any $S \in \text{FP}(A)$ containing $\neg p$ would be inconsistent, which is impossible by Corollary 4.

Unfortunately, the converse of this theorem is not true. For example, in the theory with no proper axioms, $\neg C$ is not arguable, but C is not provable. We will term the notion dual to provability *conceivability*, so that C is conceivable if it is not provably false. Thus all arguable formulas are conceivable, but not vice versa. We say *doubtless p* if and only if $\neg p$ is not arguable. In PC, C is doubtless yet not arguable, and in the theory

(19) $\text{T5} = \text{PC} \cup \{ \text{M}C \supset C,\ \text{M}\neg C \supset \neg C\}$

C is arguable yet not doubtless. Fig. 2 summarizes these classifications.

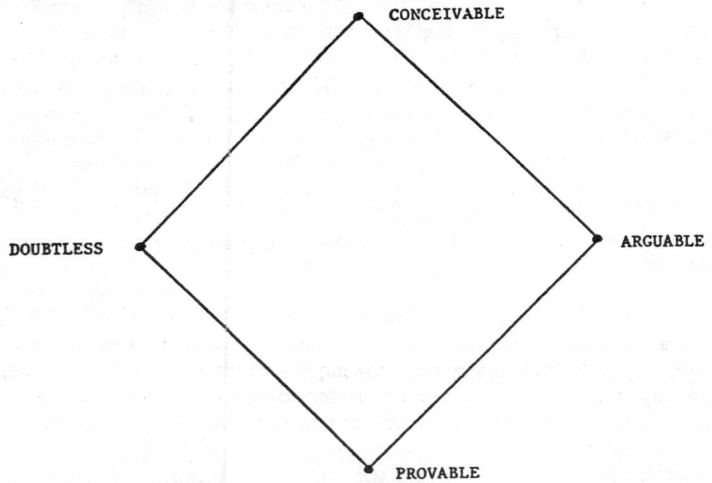

FIG. 2. Diagram of four classifications of formulas. Each line connects a set of formulas with a superset. Incomparable sets are not connected in this way.

It is worthy of note that the provable and arguable statements of a consistent theory cannot be classified as the monotonic theorems of the theory augmented by some set of assumptions. That is, the set of arguable statements may be inconsistent yet not sum to the entire language $\mathscr{L}$, and the set of provable statements may involve assumptions that vary from fixed point to fixed point, as in the theory T2 above, where neither the assumption $\text{M}C$ nor the assumption $\text{M}D$ is present in both fixed points.

Another natural classification is that of 'decision'. We say that p is *decided* by a consistent theory A if and only if for all $S \in \text{FP}(A)$, either $p \in S$ or $\neg p \in S$. The dual to this notion is just its negation. In this case we say that A is *ambivalent* about p if p is not decided by A.

Corollary 7. *If p is doubtless yet decided by A, p is provable.*

Proof. For each $S \in \text{FP}(A)$, either $p \in S$ or $\neg p \in S$; yet $\neg p \notin S$, so $p \in S$.

8. The Evolution of Theories

We now turn to analyzing inter-theory relationships. These are important in describing the effects of incremental changes in the set of axioms, and this is the task of practical systems like the TMS [6], which has the task of maintaining a description of a model of a changing set of axioms. As we shall see, there are many unusual phenomena which occur when theories change. The most striking result shows that the analogue of the compactness theorem of classical model theory does not hold for non-monotonic theories. This has important repercussions on the methods useful in constructing 'models' of theories incrementally.

Theorem 8. *There exists a consistent theory with an inconsistent subtheory.*

Proof. Consider the consistent theory

(20) $\text{T6} = \text{PC} \cup \{ \text{M}C \supset \neg C, \neg C\}$.

The subtheory $\text{PC} \cup \{ \text{M}C \supset \neg C\}$ is inconsistent.

Note, however, that the theory T6 in (20) has as a thesis the formula $\neg\,\text{M}C$, which makes it quite different than some previously considered theories. We will comment further on this type of theory in Section 11.

In many cases, the changes in fixed points induced by changes in theories is less drastic than those apparent in the previous theorem. The simplest cases are as follows.

Theorem 9. *If A is consistent, and p is arguable in A, then $A' = A \cup \{p\}$ is consistent, and* $\text{FP}(A') \cap \text{FP}(A) \neq \varnothing$.

Proof. Since p is arguable, there is some $S \in \text{FP}(A)$ such that $p \in S$. But clearly, S is then also a fixed point $\text{NM}_{A'}$.

Unfortunately, this theorem cannot be strengthened to conclude that FP(A') is contained in FP(A), since in the theory

(21) $\quad T7 = PC \cup \{ MC \supset \neg D,\ MD \supset \neg C,\ \neg C \supset E\}$

there are two fixed points, call them F_1 and F_2, with $\neg C \in F_1$, $E \in F_1$ and $\neg D \in F_2$, $E \notin F_2$. Extending this theory by adding the axiom E produces a theory also with two fixed points, one of which is F_1, but the other fixed point F_3 differs from F_2 in that $E \in F_3$ and $M\neg E \notin F_3$.

Theorem 10. *If A and $A' = A \cup \{p\}$ are consistent and* $FP(A) \cap FP(A') \neq \varnothing$, *then p is arguable in A.*

Proof. Since $p \in A'$, $p \in S$ for every $S \in FP(A')$. Thus $p \in S$ for some $S \in FP(A)$.

Theorem 11. *If A and $A' = A \cup \{p\}$ are consistent, then p is provable in A if and only if* $FP(A') = FP(A)$.

Proof. If p is provable in A, $p \in S$ for every $S \in FP(A)$, so each member of FP(A) is also a member of FP(A'). If $FP(A) = FP(A')$, then since $p \in S$ for each $S \in FP(A')$, $p \in S$ for each $S \in FP(A)$, so p is provable in A.

The import of these theorems is that if a new axiom is already implicit in the current axioms, either no change of fixed point is necessary, or a simple shift to a different fixed point of the previous axioms is allowable. When considering changes which delete axioms from theories, the basic problem is the non-compactness result mentioned above. Other interesting questions are of the form 'how few axioms must be added or removed to remove p.' Answers to these questions will in general depend on the specific theory in question.

Another important phenomenon is the 'hierarchy of assumptions' [6], in which some non-monotonic choices depend on others. This manifests itself in terms of fixed points as the addition of new axioms increasing the number of fixed points of the theory. For example, adding the axiom E to the theory

(22) $\quad T8 = PC \cup \{[E \wedge MC] \supset \neg D, [E \wedge MD] \supset \neg C\}$

increases the number of fixed points from one to two. In this case, E can be interpreted as the reason for choosing between $\neg C$ and $\neg D$. Since E itself might have been an assumption, there might therefore be a hierarchical structure of assumptions in each fixed point.

To get a global view of theory evolution, we consider the set of all consistent theories containing a consistent theory A as a subtheory. For a formula p, we can consider the evolution of the properties of p of being arguable, provable, or decided over sequences of extensions of the theory A. The evolution of arguability is mainly a question of control structures; this is the point of the encoding of control primitives in non-monotonic dependency relationships given by Doyle [6]. We have at present no way of describing the evolution of decision. However, analysis of the relationships between the theories and their extensions will shed light on how our semantics for Mp matches the intuitive notion of 'p can be added consistently to the theory.'

We say that p is *assumable* in a consistent theory A if the theory $A \cup \{p\}$ is also consistent. We name the dual notion by saying that p is *uncontroversial* in a theory if $\neg p$ is not assumable in the theory. The matching of the semantics of non-monotonic logic with this more standard notion of consistency will be apparent upon examining the correlation between assumability of p and the arguability of Mp in a theory, since this latter condition would seem to say there is a coherent interpretation of the axioms in which p is consistent. Our logic is weak, however, and so this correlation is weak. As an approximation, we note that Mp is arguable if p is arguable, and so instead attempt to correlate arguability of p with assumability of p. This correlation is as follows. By Theorem 9 the assumable formulas include the arguable formulas, but not vice versa since C is assumable but not arguable in PC. The assumable formulas are incomparable with the conceivable formulas, since C is conceivable but not assumable in

(23) $\quad T9 = PC \cup \{C \supset [D \wedge [MD \supset \neg D]]\}$,

and $\neg C$ is assumable but not conceivable in the theory T3 of (17). Also, the assumable formulas are incomparable with the uncontroversial formulas, since C is assumable but not uncontroversial in PC, and C is uncontroversial but not assumable in

(24) $\quad T10 = PC \cup \{C \supset [D \wedge [MD \supset \neg D]], \neg C \supset [E \wedge [ME \supset \neg E]]\}$.

We specify another classification by saying that a formula p is *safe* in a consistent theory A if and only if $p \in TH(A')$ for all consistent A' such that $A \subseteq A'$, and that p is *forseeable* if and only if $\neg p$ is not safe. Let $Safe(A) = \{p: p \text{ is safe in } A\}$. We then can characterize the set Safe(A) as follows.

Theorem 12. *If A is consistent, then* Safe(A) *is the least set such that the following three conditions hold:*

(i) $A \subseteq Safe(A)$

(ii) $Th(Safe(A)) = Safe(A)$

(iii) *If* $p \in Safe(A)$, *then* $Mp \in Safe(A)$.

Proof. The first two cases are correct because all formulas classically deducible from safe formulas (in particular the axioms) will remain classically deducible when the set of axioms is enlarged. The case of interest is (iii), which declares that 'covered' assumptions are safe. That is, if $p \in Safe(A)$, then $\neg p$ cannot be a member of any consistent extension of A, so Mp will be a member of every consistent extension; thus Mp is safe.

It is clear that all safe formulas are both assumable and uncontroversial, and that these inclusions are proper. Elementary considerations show further that the forseeable formulas include the assumable and uncontroversial formulas, but again, not vice versa. Also, the provable formulas properly include the safe formulas with theory T3 in (17) as the example, and the forseeable formulas properly include the conceivable formulas via the same example.

A weakened version of assumability is produced by saying that p is *realizable* in a consistent theory A if there is some consistent theory A' such that $A \subseteq A'$ and $p \in A'$. We also say that p is *undeniable* if and only if $\neg p$ is not realizable. Clearly, the realizable formulas include the assumable formulas, but the converse does not hold as $MC \supset \neg C$ is not assumable in PC but is an axiom of the consistent theory T6 in (20). The forseeable formulas obviously include the realizable formulas, but not vice versa since C is forseeable but not realizable in the theory T9 of (23). Also, the realizable formulas are incomparable with the conceivable formulas, since C is conceivable but not realizable in T9 of (23), and $\neg C$ is realizable but not conceivable in T3 of (17). The example of T10 in (24) provides an example of what following Kripke might be called the *paradoxical* formulas of a theory, formulas (in this case C) such that neither they nor their negations are realizable. The example of T9 in (23) provides an example of what might be called the *intrinsic* formulas of a theory, formulas (in this case $\neg C$) which are realizable and undeniable.

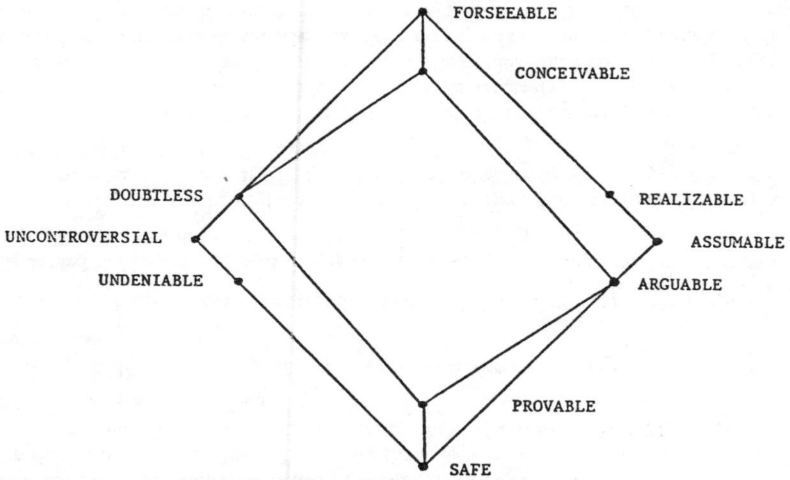

FIG. 3. Diagram of the classifications of formulas. Each line connects a set of formulas with a superset.

Figure 3 summarizes all these observations. These results illustrate the distinction between arguability and assumability, that arguability does not completely capture the notion of assumability. This is probably to be expected from the Gödel–Tarski results on the indescribability of consistency within consistent theories. It would be interesting to see a more careful analysis of this situation. One goal of such an analysis might be to connect the logic of incomplete information implicit in non-monotonic logic to other logics of incomplete information, such as the S4 interpretation of the intuitionistic predicate calculus [13, 18], Kripke's theory of truth [19; cf. 22, 44], and Lipski's theory of incomplete models [20; cf. 37, 45]. The S4 interpretation of IPC tries to describe the gradual accumulation of mathematical truths, and seems closely related to our notion of safety. Kripke's theory of truth has strong similarities to the current theory, for it develops models for the truth of self-referential and theory-referential statements which are fixed points of a certain operator on partially defined truth-predicates. Since the acceptable models of truth are restricted to be fixed points of this operator, there can be never-decided paradoxical statements. The logic of the natural notions of possibility and necessity thus are not dual, but instead form a diamond relationship similar to the case for non-monotonic assumability and safety. Lipski's theory of incomplete models is considerably simpler and stronger than either Kripke's theory or non-monotonic logic, for his incomplete models can be constructed from any partial extensions of the predicates of the language, thus producing a certain completeness in the set of possible models. This logic is particularly interesting in that it allows for the truth value of formulas to change arbitrarily often upon successive extensions of models.

In the above we have been concerned only with ways of describing the evolution of theories upon the addition of new axioms. One might also define descriptors for the case of removing axioms, or for the past history of provability. For example, assuming that all subtheories of A are consistent, we might say that p is *untested* if p is conveivable in every subtheory of A (cf. [13, p. 115]. Are there other interesting descriptors of this kind? If so, what are their properties? We have not investigated these questions, but suspect they may be fruitful.

9. A Proof Procedure for Non-Monotonic Statement Theories

In this section, we demonstrate a proof procedure for the non-monotonic statement logic. This procedure is based on the semantic tableau method for the ordinary sentential calculus [1]. In this method, a systematic attempt is made to find a falsifying interpretation for a formula under test. The formula is labeled 'false' or '0', and semantic rules guide further labeling in an obvious way. For example, to show

$$[C \supset D] \supset [\neg C \vee D],$$

start by labeling the formula false:

$$\underset{0}{[C \supset D] \supset [\neg C \vee D]}$$

For it to be false, its antecedent must be true and its consequent false:

```
[C ⊃ D] ⊃ [¬C ∨ D]
    1    0      0
```

and similarly for disjunction and negation. In order to proceed further, the tableau must split into two cases to handle the embedded implication:

```
Case 1. [C ⊃ D] ⊃ [¬C ∨ D]
         0 1     0 0 1 0

Case 2. [C ⊃ D] ⊃ [¬C ∨ D]
         1 1 1   0 0 1 0 0
```

In case 1, *C* is labeled both 1 and 0: In case 2, *D* is labeled both 1 and 0. Thus there is no falsifying model, and the formula is valid.

On the other hand, consider the tableau for $[C \vee D] \supset [C \wedge D]$:

```
(25) [C ∨ D] ⊃ [C ∧ D]
         1    0    0

       [C ∨ D] ⊃ [C ∧ D]
        1 1    0    0

         [C ∨ D] ⊃ [C ∧ D]   CLOSED
          1 1     0 0 0

         [C ∨ D] ⊃ [C ∧ D]   OPEN
          1 1 0  0 1 0 0

       [C ∨ D] ⊃ [C ∧ D]
          1 1 0     0

         [C ∨ D] ⊃ [C ∧ D]   OPEN
          0 1 1  0 0 0 1

         [C ∨ D] ⊃ [C ∧ D]   CLOSED
          1 1 1  0 1 0 0
```

This tableau has been split twice, for a total of four *branches*. Two branches are *closed* as before, that is, some formula is labeled both true (1) and false (0). But two are *open*, that is, there is an exhaustive consistent labeling of formulas. This means that there are two falsifying models, so the formula is not valid. (Notice that we could have been more clever in labeling the lines of this tableau. In the second line, for instance, we could have labeled both *C*'s at once, forcing the *D*'s to be labeled 0, and arriving at an open branch immediately.)

We will extend this procedure to handle non-monotonic statement theories. Without going into details, we assume an implementation of the algorithm just alluded to, which takes a *goal* and generates the complete tableau for it. (E.g., the goal of (25) is $[C \vee D] \supset [C \wedge D]$.) A tableau has several branches, each a consistent labeling of subformulas if one exists (when the branch is open), else a partial labeling (when it is closed). The tableau is the result of applying all rules to the goal. Two tableaux are equal if and only if they have the same goal. The tableau of a formula is obviously computable, since the number of branches is no greater than 2^N, where N is the number of subformulas of its goal.

We state without proof the following properties of the tableau method:

The procedure is *complete* in the sense that a formula is provable if and only if its tableau has all closed branches.

The procedure is *exhaustive* in the following sense: if X and Y are sets of formulas such that $X \subseteq Y$ and $Y \vdash_{SC} p$ but $X \nvdash_{SC} p$, then in the tableau for p, in every open branch there is some element of $Y - X$ labeled 0.

For non-monotonic logic, we need to generalize to tableau structures. If A is a statement theory, and p is a formula whose provability is to be tested, then $\langle A, p, t, X \rangle$ is an A-tableau structure if and only if t is the tableau with goal $A \supset p$, and X is the smallest set such that $t \in X$, and if $t' \in X$, then if $\mathrm{M}q$ appears labeled 0 in some branch b of t', then $t'' \in X$, where t'' is the tableau with goal $A \supset \neg q$. In this last situation, we say that t' *mentions* t'' in branch b.

In the classical procedure, a tableau is closed if all its branches are, and this can be determined unambiguously. In the case of a tableau structure, we can't tell whether a tableau is closed until we have determined the status of the tableaux it mentions, and there may be loops to contend with.

Therefore we introduce the notion of an *admissible labeling* of a tableau structure, an assignment of one label, either OPEN or CLOSED, to each tableau in the structure, such that:

(a) If the tableau with goal $A \supset \neg q$ is labeled OPEN, then every occurrence of $\mathrm{M}q$ is labeled 1 in every tableau, and

(b) A branch is labeled CLOSED if and only if some formula is labeled both 0 and 1 in that branch.

The proof procedure creates tableau structures and labels them, as follows. Given A and p, the first step is to construct the tableau with goal $A \supset p$. All other tableaux needed are then constructed. That is, if some constructed tableau has a formula $\mathrm{M}q$ labeled 0 in an open branch, then construct the tableau with goal $A \supset \neg q$ if that tableau was not previously constructed. The tableau structure is then checked for admissible labelings by examining all possible labelings of the tableaux for labelings satisfying the admissibility test. This test consists of first labeling with 1 each occurrence of $\mathrm{M}q$ in the tableau structure provided that the structure contains the tableau with goal $A \supset \neg q$ labeled OPEN. Then the labeling is admissible if all tableaux labeled OPEN have some open branch, and all tableaux labeled CLOSED have every branch closed. If in all admissible labelings the initial tableau with goal $A \supset p$ is labeled CLOSED, then p is provable, and otherwise is unprovable. We will shortly prove the correctness of this algorithm.

We first present some examples. In the theory

(26) $T11 = SC \cup \{MC \supset \neg D,\ MD \supset \neg E,\ ME \supset \neg F\}$

(see [39]) the T11-tableau structure for $\neg F$ has only one admissible labeling:

T11 =	t $\neg F$	t' $\neg E$	t'' $\neg D$	t''' $\neg C$
$MC \supset \neg D$				
1	0 1	0 1	0 1	0 1
$MD \supset \neg E$	ME	MD	MC	
1	0	0	0	
$ME \supset \neg F$				
1	CLOSED	OPEN	CLOSED	OPEN

Notice that we don't bother to copy the axioms in each tableau, but only those parts that become relevant. The tableau structure shows that $\neg F \in TH(T11)$, but $\neg C \notin TH(T11)$.

Another example is the T12-tableau structure for $\neg C$, where

(27) $T12 = SC \cup \{MC \supset \neg D,\ MD \supset \neg C\}$.

T12 =	t $\neg C$	t' $\neg D$
$MC \supset \neg D$		
1	0 1	0 1
$MD \supset \neg C$	MD	MC
1	0	0

This tableau structure has two admissible labelings. If t' is labeled OPEN, t is labeled CLOSED, and vice versa. So there is an admissible labeling in which t is labeled OPEN, and $\neg C$ is not provable.

On the other hand, the T12-tableau structure for $MC \vee MD$ looks like this:

T12 =	t $MC \vee MD$	t' $\neg C$	t'' $\neg D$
$MC \supset \neg D$			
1	0 0 0	0 1	0 1
$MD \supset \neg C$		MD	MC
1		0	0

Again, there are two admissible labelings, but in both of them t is labeled CLOSED, so $MC \vee MD$ is a theorem of T12.

(The tableau structures just given are not really complete. It is left as an exercise for the reader to show that using the axioms to split each tableau into branches will not change the outcome.)

Theorem 13. *The proof procedure always halts and finds all admissible labelings of the tableau structure for its goal.*

Proof. The theorem is easily seen true by noting that because the set of proper axioms of the theory is finite, only a finite set of tableaux can be constructed. Once this is done, there are only finitely many labelings to cycle through, with trivial checks for admissibility and provability.

The next two lemmas guarantee the correctness of the approach.

Lemma 14. *If S is a fixed point of NM_A, there is an admissible labeling of the tableau structure for $A \supset p$ such that $p \in S$ if and only if the tableau is labeled* CLOSED *in that labeling.*

Proof. Let $S \in FP(A)$. We will construct the admissible labeling. In the tableau structure for $A \supset p$, label a tableau OPEN if the goal of the tableau is $A \supset q$ and $q \notin S$. Consider one of the remaining tableaux, with goal $A \supset r$ There must be a minimal set of elements $X = \{Mq_1, \ldots, Mq_n\}$, such that $X \subseteq As_A(S)$ and $X \vdash_A r$. If $X = \emptyset$, then the tableau for $A \supset r$ is closed no matter how assumptions are labeled. Otherwise, by exhaustiveness, every branch of the tableau has some $Mq_i \in X$ labeled 0. So there will be a tableau for each such $A \supset \neg q_i$. But these tableaux will be labeled OPEN (because $\neg q_i \notin S$), so the corresponding branch of the tableau for $A \supset r$ will be CLOSED. So the whole tableau for $A \supset r$ will be CLOSED. Further, no open tableau will be labeled CLOSED, because then there would be a proof of its goal from assumptions. Thus, if the tableau for $A \supset p$ is labeled CLOSED, it can be proved from assumptions in $As_A(S)$, so $p \in S$. If it is OPEN, $p \notin S$ by construction.

Lemma 15. *If there is an admissible labeling for the tableau structure for $A \supset p$, there is a fixed point S of NM_A such that, for every tableau with goal $A \supset q$, the tableau is labeled* CLOSED *if and only if $q \in S$.*

Proof. We construct S from the labeling. Let R_0 be the set of formulas Mq such that the tableau for $A \supset \neg q$ is labeled OPEN. Let $S_0 = Th(A \cup R_0)$, and let $Mq_1, Mq_2, \ldots$ be an enumeration of all the formulas of the form Mq in $\mathscr{L} - R_0$, with the property that if Mq_i is a subexpression of Mq_j, then $i \leqslant j$. (E.g., MC is a subexpression of $M\neg MC$.)

Define R_{i+1} and S_{i+1}, for $i = 0, 1, \ldots$ as follows:

$$R_{i+1} = R_i \text{ if } \neg q_{i+1} \in S_i, \text{ else } R_i = R_i \cup \{Mq_{i+1}\}, \text{ and}$$
$$S_{i+1} = Th(A \cup R_{i+1}).$$

Now let $S = \bigcup_{i=0}^{\infty} S_i$, and $R = \bigcup_{i=0}^{\infty} R_i$. Clearly, $S_i \subseteq S_{i+1}$ and $S = Th(A \cup R)$. Since $NM_A(S) = Th(A \cup As_A(S))$, we can show that $NM_A(S) = S$ by showing that $R = As_A(S)$.

First, to show $As_A(S) \subseteq R$. Let $\neg q \notin S$. We will show $Mq \in R$. If $Mq \in R_0$, then since $R_0 \subseteq R$, $Mq \in R$. Otherwise q must be some q_i. If $\neg q \notin S$, then $\neg q \notin S_{i-1}$, so $Mq \in R_i$, so $Mq \in R$.

Second, to show $R \subseteq As_A(S)$, that is, if $Mq \in R$, then $\neg q \notin S$. There are two cases. If $Mq \in R_0$, then there is an OPEN tableau for $A \supset \neg q$. Assume that $\neg q \in S$. Then there must be a $k \geqslant 1$ such that $\neg q \in S_k$ and $\neg q \notin S_{k-1}$. So $R_k \vdash_A \neg q$ and $R_{k-1} \nvdash_A \neg q$. But then by exhaustiveness, Mq_k is labeled 0 in the tableau for $A \supset \neg q$. So there is also a tableau for $A \supset \neg q_k$. If this tableau is OPEN, then $Mq_k \in R_0$. If this tableau is CLOSED, $Mq_k \in S_0$, and hence $Mq_k \in S_{k-1}$. Either way, $R_k = R_{k-1}$, which is impossible.

In the other case, q will be some q_i, so $Mq \in R_i$, and $\neg q \notin S_{i-1}$. Assume that $\neg q \in S$, that is, $\neg q$ is an element of some S_k, $k \geqslant i$, and $\neg q \notin S_{k-1}$. Then $R_k \vdash_A \neg q$ but $R_{k-1} \nvdash_A \neg q$, so $\{ Mq_k\} \cup R_{k-1} \vdash_A \neg q$.

Now, Mq_k does not occur as a subexpression of $q = q_i$ (since $k \geqslant i$), so Mq_k must occur in the axioms A. So in some branch of the tableau for $A \supset \neg q$, Mq_k must be labeled 0. But this means that Mq_k must be labeled 0 in some branch of the tableau for $A \supset p$, for any p. So any tableau structure must have a tableau for $A \supset \neg q_k$. This tableau must be OPEN, or $\neg q_k$ would be a member of S_0, and hence a member of S_{k-1}. So $Mq_k \in R_0$, so $R_k = R_{k-1}$, which is a contradiction.

It remains to show that the labels agree with the fixed point. If the tableau for $A \supset \neg q$ is OPEN, then $Mq \in S$ by construction. If it is CLOSED, there is a proof of $\neg q$ from R_0, so $\neg q \in S_0$. But $S_0 \subseteq S$, so the final labeling agrees as well.

Theorem 16. *If A is a statement theory (a finite extension of the sentential calculus), then non-monotonic provability in A is decidable.*

Proof. Let $\langle A, p, t, X\rangle$ be the tableau structure for a formula p. If the procedure labels t CLOSED in every admissible labeling, then there is no fixed point of NM_A which does not contain p, since there then would be an OPEN labeling. So p is in all fixed points, and hence provable. If the procedure labels t OPEN in some admissible labeling, there is a fixed point of NM_A which does not contain p, so p is unprovable.

The proof procedure extends a previous procedure due to Hewitt [12], and embodied in MICRO-PLANNER [43], a computer programming language for (among other things) mechanical theorem proving. A practical implementation of this procedure would interleave the building and labeling of tableaux, and would avoid building a complete tableau structure when unnecessary. We invite you to compare this procedure with, for instance, the tableau-structure method for S5 [14]. One difference between these procedures is that the present procedure splits tableaux into branches before generating alternatives, while the S5 procedure splits the whole set of alternatives into branches.

10. The Truth Maintenance System

The only known adequate solutions to the handling of non-monotonic proofs are Doyle's [6] TMS program and its relatives [21, 23]. With our theoretical results in hand, we can present a description of what this program does. The TMS has two basic responsibilities:

(a) It maintains a data base of proofs of formulas generated by an independent proof procedure or perceptual program. In our terms its goal is to avoid the presence of both $\neg q$ and Mq in the data base simultaneously.

(b) It detects inconsistencies, and adds axioms to a theory in order to eliminate them.

The TMS keeps track, for each formula in the data base, of the formula's *justifications.* A justification of a formula p is a set $\{p_1, \ldots, p_n\}$ of formulas which entail p. Such a justification may be viewed as a fragment of the tableau for $A \supset p$; that is, for each branch of p's tableau, the justification contains a formula p_i labeled 0 in that branch.

The basic TMS algorithm searches for a labeling of formulas involved in justifications. It obeys two principles; p is labeled 1 if and only if all the formulas in some justification of p are labeled 1, and Mp is labeled 1 if and only if $\neg p$ is labeled 0. When the TMS finds a labeling satisfying these conditions, it arranges the data base so that only formulas labeled 1 are 'visible' to the higher-level proof procedure or program. Thus, from the point of view of a program using the TMS, it chooses a subset of formulas to 'believe.' These formulas are said to be *in*; the other formulas are *out.*

This is reminiscent of our proof procedure's search for admissible tableau labelings, but there are some important differences. The TMS operates on partial sets of tableau fragments, so its decisions may require revision as new fragments (justifications) are discovered. But there is a more striking difference between our proof procedure and the TMS. The TMS searches for just one admissible labeling of its tableau fragments, not all such labelings. The most it can hope to find is one fixed point (actually, a finite subset of one), not all of them. In the terminology we developed earlier, it finds some of the arguable formulas rather than the provable formulas. For example, consider its behavior on the theory T12 in (27). In this theory, MC is arguable, and so is MD, but neither is provable (only $MC \vee MD$ is provable). Nonetheless, the TMS, given the justifications $\{ MC\}$ of $\neg D$ and $\{ MD\}$ of $\neg C$, will pick one of $\{ MC, MD\}$ to be *in*, and the other to be *out.*

There are several reasons for such jumping to conclusions. One is that since all arguable formulas are also assumable, these decisions may at worst lead to later shifts in fixed points. That is, since arguable formulas might be added consistently later on, it cannot hurt much to act on the assumption that they will be added. A more pressing rationale for this behavior is that the program of proof procedure using the TMS typically depends on beliefs of certain types to decide what to do, and cannot abide by suspended judgement; even if there is a choice of possible circumstances, the program expects the TMS to decide on one so that action may be taken.

Of course, jumping to conclusions in this manner introduces the problem of having to choose between fixed points of the theory. In many cases this problem solves itself because of the way the TMS is typically used. Usually a program using the TMS is attempting to discover which fixed point of a theory corresponds to the real world. The best way to do this is to pick one model and stick with it until trouble arises, and then salvage as much information as possible by making as few changes as necessary. 'Trouble' can take the form of new information or new deductions from old information conflicting with old information or assumptions. Either way, the response is the same; to switch to a new fixed point. Programs frequently try to organize their use of the TMS so as to ensure the case of a single fixed point being the usual case. However, it is not possible to completely determine in this fashion how the TMS should decide between alternate fixed points. One way even more information of this sort might be used would be to employ Rescher's [36] suggestion of modal categories as a method for selecting among the various fixed points generated by a theory. That is, suppose the formulas of the language are segmented into $n+1$ modal categories $\mathscr{L} = \mathscr{M}_0 \cup \cdots \cup \mathscr{M}_n$. Then given fixed points of a theory A as $S_1, \ldots, S_m$, with corresponding sets of assumptions $A_1, \ldots, A_m$, we can segment the A_i into components $A_{1,0}, \ldots, A_{1,n}, \ldots, A_{m,0}, \ldots, A_{m,n}$ in concordance with the modal categories. We can then rank the fixed points by schemes involving orderings on the vectors of assumption components. Adding such devices to TMS-like systems is an interesting topic for future research.

The two goals of the TMS, to prevent both $\neg p$ and $\mathrm{M}p$ being *in*, and to prevent both p and $\neg p$ being *in*, give rise to two different types of activity. In the first case, when a new justification is discovered for some formula which then invalidates some current assumption, the TMS must reexamine the current labeling to find a new labeling consonant with the enlarged set of justifications. This process is fairly straightforward, although there are important special cases concerning circular proofs which require special care. This process thus takes on the appearance of a relaxation procedure for finding an acceptable labeling, and then determination of non-circular proofs for all formulas labeled 1.

The second type of inconsistency handled by the TMS, that of p and $\neg p$ being *in*, requires somewhat different treatment. In the first type of process just described, the TMS uses justifications in a unidirectional manner, determining labelings of formulas from the labelings of the formulas of their justifications, and not vice versa. In the second case, the TMS must traverse these justifications in the opposite direction, seeking the assumptions underlying the conflicting formulas. To resolve the inconsistency of these assumptions, the TMS converts the problem to one of the first type by producing a new justification for the denial of one of the assumptions in terms of the other assumptions. This might be viewed as the TMS sharing the weakness of our logic; it cannot rule out an assumption $\mathrm{M}p$ by deriving $\neg\,\mathrm{M}p$, but must instead produce a derivation of $\neg p$. This second process is called dependency-directed backtracking [42].

For example, the existing theory may be $\{\mathrm{M}C \supset E\}$ in which both $\mathrm{M}C$ and E are believed. Adding the axiom $\mathrm{M}D \supset \neg E$ leads to an inconsistent theory, as $\mathrm{M}D$ is assumed (there being no proof of $\neg D$), which leads to proving $\neg E$. The dependency-directed backtracking process would trace the proofs of E and $\neg E$, find that two assumptions, $\mathrm{M}C$ and $\mathrm{M}D$, were responsible. Just concluding $\neg\,\mathrm{M}C \vee \neg\,\mathrm{M}D$ does no good, since this does not rule out any assumptions, so the TMS adds the new axiom $E \supset \neg D$ which invalidates the assumption $\mathrm{M}D$ and so restores consistency. There are many subtleties involved, as discussed in [6].

Of course, in non-monotonic logic there is also another kind of inconsistency, that due to there being no fixed point at all. The TMS can loop forever in some cases when presented with a theory containing an inconsistent subtheory of this sort. Normally, however, this does not happen. [3] describes some conditions on the structure of the set of justifications under which a simplified variant of the TMS can be shown to always halt. McAllester's [23] TMS, through a different organization, apparently avoids these problems.

11. Discussion

In contrast to classical logics, the non-monotonic logics examined in this paper have the property that extending a theory does not always leave all theorems of the original theory intact. Such logics are of great practical interest in artificial intelligence research, but have suffered from foundational weakness. We have tried to repair this weakness by providing analyses of non-monotonic provability and semantics. Our definitions lead to proofs of the completeness of non-monotonic logic and the decidability of the non-monotonic sentential calculus.

The area of non-monotonic logic is ripe for further research. Some open problems have been mentioned in the preceding sections. In the following, we list some further interesting topics.

The major problem for non-monotonic logic is deciding provability for more general cases than statement theories. Unlike classical logic, it appears that the non-monotonic predicate calculus is not even semi-decidable. That is, there seems to be no procedure which will tell you when something is a theorem. If there were, then we could use it to decide whether p was a theorem of number theory by trying to prove p and $\mathrm{M}\neg p$ simultaneously, since one of these must be a theorem (as there is only one non-monotonic fixed point of number theory).

Are there special cases in which provability is decidable or semi-decidable? We conjecture that many theories of interest to artificial intelligence are *asymptotically decidable*, in the following sense: there is a procedure which is allowed to change its answer an indefinite number of times about whether a formula is provable, but changes its answer only a finite number of times on each particular formula. (See for example the problem solving procedures given in [5]. Note also that classical first-order provability is asymptotically decidable by a procedure that changes its answer only once; answer 'unprovable' and then call any complete proof procedure, changing the answer if the proof procedure succeeds.) Asymptotic decidability is a fairly weak property of a predicate, but it isn't vacuous since there are predicates (such as totality) which are not decidable even in this sense. Furthermore, a procedure of this kind could be useful in spite of the provisional nature of its outputs, since a robot always has to act on the basis of incomplete cogitation.

Unfortunately, it appears that even for some finite first-order theories, provability is not asymptotically decidable. We must look for useful special cases.

We have presented a formalization of non-monotonic logic which, although very weak, captures most of the important properties desired, especially with regard to the structure of models of non-monotonic theories and their behavior upon extension by new axioms. The logic seems to be adequate for describing the TMS, an ability following naturally from the structure and evolution properties just mentioned. The logic also admits a proof of completeness and a proof procedure for the case of statement theories.

Unfortunately, the weakness of the logic manifests itself in some disconcerting exceptional cases which, while essentially irrelevant to the structure and evolution properties, indicate that the logic fails to capture a coherent notion of consistency. For example, the theory

(28) $T13 = PC \cup \{ MC \supset D, \neg D\}$

is inconsistent in our logic because although $\neg MC$ follows from $\neg D$ and $MC \supset D$, $\neg C$ does not follow, thus allowing MC to be assumed; and so the theory fails to have a fixed point. This can be remedied by extending the theory to include $\neg C$, the approach taken by the TMS, but this extension seems arbitrary to the casual observer. As it happens, axioms like $MC \supset D$ are much less common in applications than the unproblematic $MC \supset C$, but it would be nice to get rid of this problem. Another incoherence of our logic is that consistency is not distributive; MC does not follow from $M[C \wedge D]$. Our logic tolerates axioms which force an incoherent notion of consistency, as in

(29) $T14 = PC \cup \{ MC, \neg C\}$.

A stronger logic might not allow this by forcing such theories to be inconsistent. We think that such logics are available, and will report their details in a forthcoming paper. Boolos's [2] System G gives some hints about the form of logics of provability.

There are several problems of a mathematical nature raised by non-monotonic logic. What are the details of the relationship between non-monotonic logic and the logics of incomplete information? What are the effects of different rules of inference on the construction of non-monotonic models? What are the details of the evolution of the properties of decision and provability? Are there interpretations of non-monotonic logic within classical logics? Are there connections between non-monotonic logic and logics with statements of infinite length? Is there a topological interpretation of non-monotonic logic in analogy to the topological interpretation of the intuitionistic calculus?

There are also a number of more speculative and long range topics for investigation raised by non-monotonic logic. The revision of beliefs performed by artificial intelligence programs can be viewed as a microscopic version of the process of change of scientific theories. (For a figurative description of such processes which is very close to a true description of non-monotonic logic and the TMS, see the beginning of Section 6 of Quine's *Two Dogmas of Empiricism* [32].) Can the ideas captured in non-monotonic logic be used to describe the general process of scientific discovery, or pragmatic behavior in general? How are the holistic semantics of non-monotonic logic related to changes in meanings? (Cf. particularly [7].) What are the trade-offs involved in jumping to conclusions? How costly is the suspension of judgement? Can non-monotonic logic be used to effectively describe and reason about actions, commands, conterfactuals, and causality?

ACKNOWLEDGEMENTS

We wish to thank Gerald Jay Sussman, Rohit Parikh, David Harel, Mitchell Marcus, Lucia Vaina, and Vaughan Pratt for helpful criticisms and comments. Drew McDermott acknowledges the support of a Josiah Willard Gibbs instructorship. Jon Doyle thanks the Fannie and John Hertz Foundation for supporting his research with a graduate fellowship.

REFERENCES

1. Beth, E. W., On machines which prove theorems, *Simon Stevin* (*Wis- en Natuurkundig Tijdschrift*) 32 (1958) 49.
2. Boolos, G., *The Unprovability of Consistency* (Cambridge University Press, Cambridge, 1979).
3. Charniak, E., Riesbeck, C. and McDermott, D., *Artificial Intelligence Programming* (Lawrence Erlbaum, Hillsdale, NJ, 1980).
4. de Kleer, J., Causal and teleological reasoning in circuit recognition, Ph.D. thesis, MIT Department of Electrical Engineering and Computer Science (1979).
5. de Kleer, J., Doyle, J., Steele, G. L. Jr. and Sussman, G. J., Explicit control of reasoning, MIT Artificial Intelligence Laboratory, Memo 427 (1977).
6. Doyle, J., A truth maintenance system, *Artificial Intelligence* 12 (1979), 231–272.
7. Dummett, M. A. E., The justification of deduction, *Proc. British Academy* LIX (1973).
8. Fikes, R. E. and Nilsson, N. J., STRIPS: A new approach to the application of theorem, proving to problem solving. *Artificial Intelligence* 2 (1971) 189–208.
9. Hayes, P. J., Robotologic, in Meltzer, B. and Michie, D. (Eds), *Machine Intelligence* 5 (American Elsevier, New York, 1970) 533–554.
10. Hayes, P. J., A logic of actions, in Meltzer, B. and Michie, D. (Eds), *Machine Intelligence* 6 (American Elsevier, New York, 1971), 495–520.
11. Hayes, P. J., The frame problem and related problems in artificial intelligence, in: Elithorn, A. and Jones, D. (Eds), *Artificial and Human Thinking* (Josey–Bass, San Francisco, 1973).
12. Hewitt, C. E., Description and theoretical analysis (using schemata) of PLANNER: a language for proving theorems and manipulating models in a robot, MIT Artificial Intelligence Laboratory TR–258 (1972).
13. Heyting, A., *Intuitionism: An Introduction* (North-Holland, Amsterdam, 1956).
14. Hughes, G. E. and Cresswell, M. J., *An Introduction to Model Logic* (Methuen and Co., London, 1972).
15. Joshi, A. K., Some extensions of a system for inferencing on partial information, in: Hayes-Roth, F. and Waterman, D. (Eds), *Pattern Directed Inference Systems* (Academic Press, New York, 1978).

16. Joshi, A. K. and Rosenschein, S. J., A formalism for relating lexical and pragmatic information: its relevance to recognition and generation, *Proc. Workshop on Theoretical Issues in Natural Language Processing* (Cambridge, MA, 1975) 79–83.
17. Kramosil, I., A note on deduction rules with negative premises, *Proc. Fourth International Joint Conference on Artificial Intelligence* (1975) 53–56.
18. Kripke, S. A., Semantical analysis of intuitionistic logic I, in: Crossley, J. N. and Dummett, M. A. E. (Eds), *Formal Systems and Recursive Functions* (North-Holland, Amsterdam, 1965) 92–130.
19. Kripke, S. A., Outline of a theory of truth, *J. Philosophy* **72** (19) (1975) 690–716.
20. Lipski, W. Jr., On the logic of incomplete information, in: Goos, G. and Hartmanis, J. (Eds), *Proc. Symp. on Mathematical Foundations of Computer Science 1977* (Springer, Berlin, 1977) 374–381.
21. London, P. E., Dependency networks as a representation for modelling in general problem solvers, Department of Computer Science TR–698, University of Maryland (1978).
22. Martin, R. L. and Woodruff, P. W., On representing 'True-in-*L*' in *L*, in: Kasher, A. (Ed.), *Language in Focus: Foundations, Methods and Systems* (D. Reidel, Dordrecht, 1976) 113–117.
23. McAllester, D. A., A three-valued truth maintenance system, MIT Artificial Intelligence Laboratory, Memo 473 (1978).
24. McCarthy, J. and Hayes, P. J., Some philosophical problems from the standpoint of artificial intelligence, in: Meltzer, B. and Michie, D. *Machine Intelligence* **4** (American Elsevier, New York, 1969) 463–502.
25. McCarthy, J., Epistemological problems of artificial intelligence, *Proc. Fifth International Joint Conference on Artificial Intelligence* (1977) 1038–1044.
26. McDermott, D., Assimilation of new information by a natural language-understanding System, MIT Artificial Intelligence Laboratory, AI–TR–291 (1974).
27. Mendelson, E., *Introduction to Mathematical Logic* (Van Nostrand Reinhold, New York, 1964).
28. Minsky, M., A framework for representing knowledge, MIT Artificial Intelligence Laboratory, AI Memo 306 (1974), reprinted without appendix in: Winston, P. (Ed.), *The Psychology of Computer Vision* (McGraw-Hill, New York, 1975).
29. Moore, R. C., Reasoning from incomplete knowledge in a procedural deduction system, MIT Artificial Intelligence Laboratory, AI–TR–347 (1975).
30. Nevins, A. J., A human-oriented logic for automatic theorem proving, *J. Assoc. Comput. Machinery* **21** (1974) 606–621.
31. Pratt, V. R., The competence/performance dichotomy in programming, MIT Artificial Intelligence Laboratory, Memo 400 (1977).
32. Quine, W. V., *From a Logical Point of View* (Harvard University Press, Cambridge, 1953).
33. Quine, W. V. and Ullian, J. S., *The Web of Belief*, second edition (Random House, New York, 1978).
34. Reiter, R., On closed world data bases, Department of Computer Science, University of British Columbia, TR–77–14 (1977).
35. Reiter, R., On reasoning by default, *Proc. Second Symp. on TINLAP*, Urbana, IL. (1978).
36. Rescher, N., *Hypothetical Reasoning* (North-Holland, Amsterdam, 1964).
37. Robinson, A., Formalism 64, in: Bar-Hillel, Y. (Ed.), *Logic, Methodology and Philosophy of Science* (North-Holland, Amsterdam, 1965) 228–246.
38. Robinson, J. A., A machine-oriented logic based on the resolution principle, *J. Assoc. Comput. Machinery* **12** (1965) 23–41.
39. Sandewall, E., An approach to the frame problem, and its implementation, in: Meltzer, B. and Michie, D. (Eds), *Machine Intelligence* **7** (Wiley, New York, 1972) 195–204.
40. Scriven, M., Truisms as the grounds for historical explanations, in: Gardiner, P. (Ed.), *Theories of History* (Free Press, New York, 1959).
41. Scriven, M., New issues in the logic of explanation, in: Hook, S. (Ed.), *Philosophy and History* (New York University Press, New York, 1963).
42. Stallman, R. M. and Sussman, G. J., Forward reasoning and dependency-directed backtracking in a system for computer-aided circuit analysis, *Artificial Intelligence* **9** (2) (1977) 135–196.
43. Sussman, G. J., Winograd, T. and Charniak, E., MICRO-PLANNER reference manual, MIT Artificial Intelligence Laboratory, AI Memo 203a (1971).
44. Takeuti, G., Formalization principle, in: Van Rootselaar, B. and Staal, J. F. (Eds), *Logic Methodology and Philosophy of Science III*, (North-Holland, Amsterdam, 1968) 105–118.
45. Van Frassen, B., Singular terms, truth-value gaps and free logic, *J. Phil.* **LXIII** (17) (1966) 481–495.
46. Weyhrauch, R. Prolegomena to a theory of formal reasoning, Stanford Artificial Intelligence Laboratory, Memo AIM–315 (1978).

Semantical Considerations on Nonmonotonic Logic*

Robert C. Moore
SRI International, Artificial Intelligence Center, Computer Science and Technology Division, Menlo Park, CA 94025, U.S.A.

Recommended by Drew McDermott

ABSTRACT

Commonsense reasoning is 'nonmonotonic' in the sense that we often draw, on the basis of partial information, conclusions that we later retract when we are given more complete information. Some of the most interesting products of recent attempts to formalize nonmonotonic reasoning are the nonmonotonic logics of McDermott and Doyle [1, 2]. *These logics, however, all have peculiarities that suggest they do not quite succeed in capturing the intuitions that prompted their development. In this paper we reconstruct nonmonotonic logic as a model of an ideally rational agent's reasoning about his own beliefs. For the resulting system, called* autoepistemic *logic, we define an intuitively based semantics for which we can show autoepistemic logic to be both sound and complete. We then compare autoepistemic logic with the approach of McDermott and Doyle, showing how it avoids the peculiarities of their nonmonotonic logic.*

1. Introduction

It has been generally acknowledged in recent years that one important feature of ordinary commonsense reasoning that standard logics fail to capture is its *nonmonotonicity*. An example frequently given to illustrate the point is the following. If we know that Tweety is a bird, we will normally assume, in the absence of evidence to the contrary, that Tweety can fly. If, however, we later learn that Tweety is a penguin, we will withdraw our prior assumption. If we try to model this in a formal system, we seem to have a situation in which a theorem P is derivable from a set of axioms S, but is not derivable from some set S' that is a superset of S. The set of theorems, therefore, does not increase monotonically with the set of axioms; hence this sort of reasoning is said to be 'nonmonotonic'. As Minsky [3] has pointed out, standard logics are always monotonic, because their inference rules make every axiom *permissive*. That is, the inference rules are always of the form "P is a theorem if $Q_1, \ldots, Q_n$ are theorems", so that new axioms can only make more theorems derivable; they can never invalidate a previous theorem.

Recently there have been a number of attempts to formalize this type of nonmonotonic reasoning. The general idea is to allow axioms to be restrictive as well as permissive, by employing inference rules of the form "P is a theorem if $Q_1, \ldots, Q_n$ are *not* theorems". The inference that birds can fly is handled by having, in effect, a rule that says that, for any X, "X can fly" is a theorem if "X is a bird" is a theorem and "X cannot fly" is not a theorem. If all we are told about Tweety is that he is a bird, we will not be able to derive "Tweety cannot fly"; consequently, "Tweety can fly" will be inferable. If we are told that Tweety is a penguin and we already know that no penguin can fly, we will be able to derive the fact that Tweety cannot fly, and so the inference that Tweety can fly will be blocked.

One of the most interesting embodiments of this approach to nonmonotonic reasoning is McDermott and Doyle's 'nonmonotonic logic' [1, 2]. McDermott and Doyle modify a standard first-order logic by introducing a sentential operator M, whose informal interpretation is "is consistent". Nonmonotonic inferences about birds being able to fly would be sanctioned in their system by the axiom [2, p. 33]

$$\forall X(\text{BIRD}(X) \wedge M(\text{CAN-FLY}(X)) \rightarrow \text{CAN-FLY}(X))\,.$$

This formula can be read informally as "For all X, if X is a bird and it is consistent to assert that X can fly, then X can fly". McDermott and Doyle can then have a single general nonmonotonic inference rule, whose intuitive content is "MP is derivable if $\sim P$ is not derivable".

McDermott and Doyle's approach to nonmonotonic reasoning seems more interesting and ambitious than some other approaches in two respects. First, since the principles that lead to nonmonotonic inferences are explicitly represented in the logic, those very principles can be reasoned about. That is, if P is such a principle, we could start out believing $Q \rightarrow P$ or even $MP \rightarrow P$, and come to hold P by drawing inferences, either monotonic or nonmonotonic. So, if we use McDermott and Doyle's representation of the belief that birds can fly,

*This is a revised and expanded version of a paper in *Proceedings of the Eighth International Joint Conference on Artificial Intelligence*, Karlsruhe, West Germany, August 8–12, 1983.

The research reported herein was supported by the Air Force Office of Scientific Research under Contract No. F49620-82-K-0031. The views and conclusions expressed in this document are those of the author and should not be interpreted as necessarily representing the official policies or endorsements, either expressed or implied, of the Air Force Office of Scientific Research or the U.S. Government.

we could also represent various inferences that would lead us to *adopt* that belief. Second, since they use only general inference rules, they are able to provide a formal semantic interpretation with soundness and completeness proofs for each of the logics they define. In formalisms that use content-specific nonmonotonic inference rules dealing with contingent aspects of the world (i.e., it might have been the case that birds could not fly), it is difficult to see how this could be done. The effect is that nonmonotonic inferences in McDermott and Doyle's logics are justified by the meaning of the premises of the inferences.

There are a number of problems with McDermott and Doyle's nonmonotonic logics, however. The first logic they define [1] gives such a weak notion of consistency that, as they point out, MP is not inconsistent with $\sim P$. That is, it is possible for a theory to assert simultaneously that P is consistent with the theory and that P is false. McDermott subsequently [2] tried basing nonmonotonic logics on the standard model logics T, S4, and S5. He discovered, however, that the most plausible candidate for formalizing the notion of consistency that he wanted, nonmonotonic S5, collapses to ordinary S5 and is therefore monotonic. In the rest of this paper we develop an alternative formalization of nonmonotonic logic that shows why these problems arise in McDermott and Doyle's logics and how they can be avoided.

2. Nonmonotonic Logic and Autoepistemic Reasoning

The first step in analyzing nonmonotonic logic is to determine what sort of nonmonotonic reasoning it is meant to model. After all, nonmonotonicity is a rather abstract *syntactic* property of an inference system, and there is no a priori reason to believe that all forms of nonmonotonic reasoning should have the same logical basis. In fact, McDermott and Doyle seem to confuse two quite distinct forms of nonmonotonic reasoning, which we will call *default reasoning* and *autoepistemic reasoning*. They talk as though their systems were intended to model the former, but they actually seem much better suited to modeling the latter.

By default reasoning we mean the drawing of plausible inferences from less-than-conclusive evidence in the absence of information to the contrary. The examples about birds being able to fly are of this type. If we know that Tweety is a bird, that gives us some evidence that Tweety can fly, but it is not conclusive. In the absence of information to the contrary, however, we are willing to go ahead and tentatively conclude that Tweety can fly. Now even before we do any detailed analysis of nonmonotonic logic, we can see that there will be problems in interpreting it as a model of default reasoning: In the formal semantics McDermott and Doyle provide for nonmonotonic logic, all the nonmonotonic inferences are valid. Default reasoning, however, is clearly not a form of valid inference[1].

Consider the belief that lies behind our willingness to infer that Tweety can fly from the fact that Tweety is a bird. It is probably something like most birds can fly, or almost all birds can fly, or a typical bird can fly. To model this kind of reasoning, in a theory whose *only* axioms are "Tweety is a bird" and "Most birds can fly", we ought to be able to infer (nonmonotonically) "Tweety can fly". Now if this were a form of valid inference, we would be guaranteed that the conclusion is true if the premises are true. This is manifestly not the case. The premises of this inference give us a good reason to draw the conclusion, but not the ironclad guarantee that validity demands.

Now reconsider McDermott's formula that yields nonmonotonic inferences about birds being able to fly:

$$\forall X(\text{BIRD}(X) \wedge M(\text{CAN-FLY}(X)) \rightarrow \text{CAN-FLY}(X)).$$

McDermott suggests as a gloss of this formula "Most birds can fly", which would indicate that he thinks of the inferences it sanctions as default inferences. But if we read M as "is consistent" as McDermott and Doyle repeatedly tell us to do elsewhere, the formula actually says something quite different: "For all X, if X is a bird and it is consistent to assert that X can fly, then X can fly". Since the inference rule for M is intended to convey "MP is derivable if $\sim P$ is not derivable", the notion of consistency McDermott and Doyle have in mind seems to be that it is consistent to assert P if $\sim P$ is not derivable. McDermott's formula, then, says that the *only* birds that cannot fly are the ones that can be inferred not to fly. If we have a theory whose only axioms are this one and an assertion to the effect that Tweety is a bird, then the conclusion that Tweety can fly *would* be a valid inference. That is, if it is true that Tweety is a bird, and it is true that only birds inferred not to fly are in fact unable to fly, and Tweety is not inferred not to fly, then it *must* be true that Tweety can fly.

This type of reasoning is not a form of default reasoning at all; it rather seems to be more like reasoning about one's own knowledge or belief. Hence, we will refer to it as *autoepistemic* reasoning. Autoepistemic reasoning, while different from default reasoning, is an important form of commonsense reasoning in its own right. Consider my reason for believing that I do not have an older brother. It is surely not that one of my parents once casually remarked, "You know, you don't have any older brothers", nor have I pieced

[1]In their informal exposition, McDermott and Doyle [1, pp. 44–46] emphasize that their notion of nonmonontonic inference is *not* to be taken as a form of valid inference. If this is the case, their formal semantics cannot be regarded as the 'real' semantics of their nonmonotonic logic. At best, it would provide the conditions that *would* have to hold for the inferences to be valid, but this leaves unanswered the question of what formulas of nonmonotonic logic actually *mean*.

it together by carefully sifting other evidence. I simply believe that if I did have an older brother I would know about it; therefore, since I don't know of any older brothers, I must not have any. This is quite different from a default inference based on the belief, say, that most MIT graduates are eldest sons, and that, since I am an MIT graduate, I am probably an eldest son.

Default reasoning and autoepistemic reasoning are both nonmonotonic, but for different reasons. Default reasoning is nonmonotonic because, to use a term from philosophy, it is *defeasible*: its conclusions are tentative, so, given better information, they may be withdrawn. Purely autoepistemic reasoning, however, is not defeasible. If you really believe that you already know all the instances of birds that cannot fly, you cannot consistently hold to that belief and at the same time accept new instances of birds that cannot fly.[2]

As Stalnaker [4] has observed, autoepistemic reasoning is nonmonotonic because the meaning of an autoepistemic statement is context-sensitive; it depends on the theory in which the statement is embedded.[3] If we have a theory whose only two axioms are

$$\text{BIRD(TWEETY)},$$
$$\forall X(\text{BIRD}(X) \wedge M(\text{CAN-FLY}(X)) \rightarrow \text{CAN-FLY}(X)),$$

then MP does not merely mean that P is consistent—it means that P is consistent with the nonmonotonic theory that contains only those two axioms. We would expect CAN-FLY(TWEETY) to be a theorem of this theory. If we change the theory by adding ~CAN-FLY(TWEETY) as an axiom, we then change the meaning of MP to be that P is consistent with the nonmonotonic theory that contains only the axioms

$$\sim\text{CAN-FLY(TWEETY)},$$
$$\text{BIRD(TWEETY)},$$
$$\forall X(\text{BIRD}(X) \wedge M(\text{CAN-FLY}(X)) \rightarrow \text{CAN-FLY}(X)),$$

and we would not expect CAN-FLY(TWEETY) to be a theorem. The operator M changes its meaning with context just as do indexical words in natural language, such as 'I' 'here', and 'now'. The nonmonotonicity associated with autoepistemic statements should therefore be no more puzzling than the fact that "I am hungry" can be true when uttered by a particular speaker at a particular time, but false when uttered by a different speaker at the same time or the same speaker at a different time. So we might say that, whereas default reasoning is nonmonotonic because it is defeasible, autoepistemic reasoning is nonmonotonic because it is indexical.

3. The Formalization of Autoepistemic Logic

Rather than try directly to analyze McDermott and Doyle's nonmonotonic logic as a model of autoepistemic reasoning, we will first define a logic that demonstrably does model certain aspects of autoepistemic reasoning and then compare nonmonotonic logic with that. We will call our logic, naturally enough, *autoepistemic logic.* The language will be much like McDermott and Doyle's, an ordinary logical language augmented by autoepistemic modal operators. McDermott and Doyle treat consistency as their fundamental notion, so they take M as the basic modal operator and define its dual L to be $\sim M\sim$. Our logic, however, will be based on the notion of belief, so we will take L to mean "is believed", treat it as primitive, and define M as $\sim L\sim$. In any case, this gives us the same notion of consistency as theirs: a formula is consistent if its negation is not believed. Since there are some problems with regard to the meaning of quantifying into the scope of an autoepistemic operator that are not relevant to the main point of this paper, we will limit our attention to propositional autoepistemic logic.

Autoepistemic logic is intended to model the beliefs of an agent reflecting upon his own beliefs. The primary objects of interest are sets of autoepistemic logic formulas that are interpreted as the total beliefs of such agents. We will call such a set of formulas an *autoepistemic theory.* The truth of an agent's beliefs, expressed as a propositional autoepistemic theory, will be determined by (1) which propositional constants are true in the external world and (2) which formulas the agent believes. A formula of the form LP will be true with respect to an agent if and only if P is in his set of beliefs. To formalize this, we define notions of interpretation and model as follows:

We proceed in two stages. First we define a *propositional interpretation* of an autoepistemic theory T to be an assignment of truth-values to the formulas of the language of T that is consistent with the usual truth recursion for propositional logic and with any arbitrary assignment of truth-values to propositional constants and formulas of the form LP. A *propositional model* of an autoepistemic theory T is a propositional interpretation of T in which all the formulas of T are true. The propositional interpretations and models of an autoepistemic theory are, therefore, precisely those we would get in ordinary propositional logic by treating all formulas of the form LP as propositional constants. We therefore inherit the soundness and completeness theorems of propositional logic; i.e., a formula P is true in all the propositional models of an

[2]Of course, autoepistemic reasoning can be combined with default reasoning; we might believe that we know about *most* of the birds that cannot fly. This could lead to defeasible autoepistemic inferences, but their defeasibility would be the result of their also being default inferences.

[3]Stalnaker's note, which to my knowledge remains unpublished, grew out of his comments as a respondent to McDermott at a Conference on Artificial Intelligence and Philosophy, held in March 1980 at the Center for Advanced Study in the Behavioral Sciences. N.B., the term 'autoepistemic reasoning' is ours, not his.

autoepistemic theory T if and only if it is a tautological consequence of T (i.e., derivable from T by the usual rules of propositional logic).

Next we define an ***autoepistemic interpretation*** of an autoepistemic theory T to be a propositional interpretation of T in which, for every formula P, LP is true if and only if P is in T. It should be noted that the theory T itself completely determines the truth of any formula of the form LP in all the autoepistemic interpretations of T, independently of the truth assignment to the propositional constants. Hence, for every truth assignment to the propositional constants of T, there is exactly one corresponding autoepistemic interpretation of T. Finally, an ***autoepistemic model*** of T is an autoepistemic interpretation of T in which all the formulas of T are true. So the autoepistemic interpretations and models of T are just the propositional interpretations and models of T that conform to the intended meaning of the modal operator L.

This gives us a formal semantics for autoepistemic logic that matches its intuitive interpretation. Suppose that the beliefs of the agent situated in a particular world are characterized by the autoepistemic theory T. The world in question will provide an assignment of truth-values for the propositional constants of T, and any formula of the form LP will be true relative to the agent just in case he believes P. In this way, the agent and the world in which he is situated directly determine an autoepistemic interpretation of T. That interpretation will be an autoepistemic model of T, just in case all the agent's beliefs are true in his world.

Given this semantics for autoepistemic logic, what do we want from a notion of inference for the logic? From an epistemological perspective, the problem of inference is the problem of what set of beliefs (theorems) an ideally rational agent would adopt on the basis of his initial premises (axioms). Since we are trying to model the beliefs of a rational agent, the beliefs should be sound with respect the premises; we want a guarantee that the beliefs are true provided that the premises are true. Moreover, since we assume that the agent is *ideally* rational, the beliefs should be semantically complete; we want them to contain everything that the agent would be semantically justified in concluding from his beliefs and from the knowledge that they are his beliefs. An autoepistemic logic that meets these conditions can be viewed as a competence model of reflection upon one's own beliefs. Like competence models generally, it assumes unbounded resources of time and memory, and is therefore not a plausible model of any finite agent. It is, however, the model upon which the behavior of rational agents ought to converge as their time and memory resources increase.

Formally, we will say an autoepistemic theory T is ***sound*** with respect to an initial set of premises A if and only if every autoepistemic interpretation of T in which all the formulas of A are true is an autoepistemic model of T. This notion of soundness is the weakest condition that guarantees that all of the agent's beliefs are true whenever all his premises are true. Let I be the autoepistemic interpretation of T that is determined by what is true in the actual world (including what the agent actually believes). If all the formulas of T are true in every autoepistemic interpretation of T in which all the formulas of A are true, then all the formulas of T will be true in I if all the formulas of A are true in I; hence, all the agent's beliefs will be true in the world if all the agent's premises are true in the world. However, if there is an autoepistemic interpretation of T in which all the formulas of A are true but some formulas of T are false, then it is possible that I is that interpretation, and that all the agent's premises will be true in the world, but some of his beliefs will not.

Our formal notion of completeness is that an autoepistemic theory T is ***semantically complete*** if and only if T contains every formula that is true in every autoepistemic model of T. If a formula P is true in every autoepistemic model of an agent's beliefs, then it must be true if all the agent's beliefs are true, and an ideally rational agent should be able to recognize that and infer P. On the other hand, if P is false in some autoepistemic model of the agent's beliefs, then that model, for all he can tell, might be the way the world actually is; he is therefore justified in not believing P.

The next problem is to give a syntactic characterization of the autoepistemic theories that satisfy these conditions. With a monotonic logic, the usual procedure is to define a collection of inference rules to apply to the axioms. For a nonmonotonic logic this is a nontrivial matter. Much of the technical ingenuity of McDermott and Doyle's systems lies simply in their formulation of a coherent notion of nonmonotonic derivability. The problem is that nonmonotonic inference rules do not yield a simple iterative notion of derivability the way monotonic inference rules do. We can view a monotonic inference process as applying the inference rules in all possible ways to the axioms, generating additional formulas to which the inference rules are applied in all possible ways, and so forth. Since monotonic inference rules *are* monotonic, once a formula has been generated at a given stage, it remains in the generated set of formulas at every subsequent stage. Thus the theorems of a theory in a monotonic system can be defined simply as all the formulas that are generated at any stage. The problem with attempting to follow this pattern with nonmonotonic inference rules is that we cannot draw nonmonotonic inferences reliably at any particular stage, since something inferred at a later stage may invalidate them. Lacking such an iterative structure, nonmonotonic systems often use nonconstructive 'fixed point' definitions, which do not directly yield algorithms for enumerating the 'derivable' formulas, but do define sets of formulas that respect the intent of the nonmonotonic inference rules (e.g., in McDermott and Doyle's fixed points, MP is inlcuded whenever $\sim P$ is not included.)

For our logic, it is easiest to proceed by first specifying the closure conditions that we would expect the beliefs of an ideally rational agent to possess. Viewed informally, the beliefs should include whatever the agent could infer either b ordinary logic or by reflecting on what he believes. Stalnaker [4] has put this formally by suggesting that a set of formulas T that represents the beliefs of an ideally rational agent should satisfy the following conditions:

(1) If $P_1, \ldots, P_n \in T$, and $P_1, \ldots, P_n \vdash Q$, then $Q \in T$, (where '$\vdash$' means ordinary tautological consequence).
(2) If $P \in T$, then $LP \in T$.
(3) If $P \notin T$, then $\sim LP \in T$.

Stalnaker [4, p. 6] describes the state of belief characterized by such a theory as *stable* "in the sense that no further conclusions could be drawn by an ideally rational agent in such a state". We will therefore describe the theories themselves as *stable autoepistemic theories.*

There are a number of interesting observations we can make about stable autoepistemic theories. First we note that, if a stable autoepistemic theory T is consistent, it will satisfy two more intuitively sound conditions:

(4) If $LP \in T$, then $P \in T$.
(5) If $\sim LP \in T$, then $P \notin T$.

Condition (4) holds because, if LP were in T and P were not, $\sim LP$ would be in T (by Condition (3)) and T would be inconsistent.[4] Condition (5) holds bcause, if $\sim LP$ and P were both in T, LP would be in T (by Condition (2)) and T would be inconsistent.

Conditions (2)–(5) imply that any consistent stable autoepistemic theory will be both sound and semantically complete with respect to formulas of the form LP and $\sim LP$: If T is such a theory, then LP will be in T if and only if P is in T, and $\sim LP$ will be in T if and only if P is not in T. Thus, all the propositional models of a stable autoepistemic theory are autoepistemic models. Stability implies a soundness result even stronger than this, however. We can show that the truth of any formula of a stable autoepistemic theory depends only on the truth of the formulas of the theory that contain no autoepistemic operators. (We will call these formulas 'objective'.)

Theorem 3.1. *If T is a stable autoepistemic theory, then any autoepistemic interpretation of T that is a propositional model of the objective formulas of T is an autoepistemic model of T.*

(The proofs of all theorems are given in Appendix A.)

[4]Condition (4) will, of course, also be satisfied by an inconsistent stable autoepistemic theory, since such a theory would include all formulas of autoepistemic logic.

In other words, if all the objective formulas in an autoepistemic theory are true, then all the formulas in that theory are true. Given that the objective formulas of a stable autoepistemic theory determine whether the theory is true, it is not surprising that they also determine what all the formulas of the theory are.

Theorem 3.2. *If two stable autoepistemic theories contain the same objective formulas, then they contain exactly the same formulas.*[5]

Finally, with these characterization theorems, we can prove that the syntactic property of stability is equivalent the semantic property of completeness.

Theorem 3.3. *An autoepistemic theory T is semantically complete if and only if T is stable.*

By Theorem 3.3, we know that stability of an agent's beliefs guarantees that they are semantically complete, but stability alone does not tell us whether they are sound with respect to his initial premises. That is because the stability conditions say nothing about what an agent should *not* believe. They leave open the possibility of an agent's believing propositions that are not in any way grounded in his initial premises. What we need to add is a constraint specifying that the only propositions the agent believes are his initial premises and those required by the stability conditions. To satisfy the stability conditions and include a set of premises A, an autoepistemic theory T must include all the tautological consequences of $A \cup \{LP \mid P \in T\} \cup \{\sim LP \mid P \notin T\}$. Conversely, we will say that an autoepistemic theory T is *grounded* in a set of premises A if and only if every formula of T is included in the tautological consequences of $A \cup \{LP \mid P \in T\} \cup \{\sim LP \mid P \notin T\}$. The following theorem shows that this syntactic constraint on T and A captures the semantic notion of soundness.

Theorem 3.4. *An autoepistemic theory T is sound with respect to an initial set of premises A if and only if T is grounded in A.*

From Theorems 3.3 and 3.4, we can see that the possible sets of beliefs that a rational agent might hold, given A as his premises, ought to be just the extensions of A that are grounded in A and stable. We will call these the *stable*

[5]This theorem implies that our autoepistemic logic does not contain any 'nongrounded' self-referential formulas, such as one finds in what are usually called 'syntactical' treatments of belief. If, instead of a belief operator, we had a belief predicate, Bel, there might be a term p that denotes the formula Bel(p). Whether Bel(p) is believed or not is clearly independent of any objective beliefs. The lack of such formulas constitutes a characteristic difference between sentence-operator and predicate treatments of propositional attitudes and modalities.

expansions of A. Note that we say 'sets', because there may be more than one stable expansion of a given set of premises. For example, consider $\{\sim LP \rightarrow Q, \sim LQ \rightarrow P\}$ as an initial set of premises.[6] The first formula asserts that, if P is not believed, then Q is true; the second asserts that, if Q is not believed, then P is true. In any stable autoepistemic theory that includes these premises, if P is not in the theory, Q will be, and vice versa. But if the theory is grounded in these premises, if P is in the theory there will be no basis for including Q, and vice versa. Consequently, a stable expansion of $\{\sim LP \rightarrow Q, \sim LQ \rightarrow P\}$ will contain either P or Q, but not both.

It can also happen that there are ***no*** stable expansions of a given set of premises. Consider, for instance, $\{\sim LP \rightarrow P\}$.[7] If T is a stable autoepistemic theory that contains $\sim LP \rightarrow P$, it must also contain P. If P were not in T, $\sim LP$ world have to be in T, but then P would be in T—a contradiction. On the other hand, if P is in T, then T is not grounded in $\{\sim LP \rightarrow P\}$. Therefore no stable autoepistemic theory can be grounded in $\{\sim LP \rightarrow P\}$.

This seemingly strange behavior results from the indexicality of the autoepistemic operator L. Since L is interpreted relative to an entire set of beliefs, its interpretation will change with the various ways of completing a set of beliefs. In each acceptable completion of a set of beliefs, the interpretation of L will change to make that set stable and grounded in the premises. Sometimes, though, no matter how we try to form a complete a set of beliefs, the result never coincides with the interpretation of L in a way that gives us a stable set of beliefs grounded in the premises.

This raises the question of how to view autoepistemic logic *as* a logic. If we consider a set of premises A as axioms, what do we consider the theorems of A to be? If there is a unique stable expansion of A, it seems clear that we want this expansion to be the set of theorems of A. But what if there are several stable expansion of A—or none at all? If we take the point of view of the agent, we have to say that there can be alternative sets of theorems, or no set of theorems of A. This may be a strange property for a logic to possess, but, given our semantics, it is clear why this happens. An alternative (adopted by McDermott and Doyle with regard to their fixed points) is to take the theorems of A to be the intersection of the set of all formulas of the language with all the stable expansions of A. This yields the formulas that are in all stable expansions of A if there is more than one, and it makes the theory inconsistent if there is no stable expansion of A. This too is reasonable, but it has a different interpretation. It represents what an outside observer would know, given only knowledge of the agent's premises and that he is ideally rational.

[6] McDermott and Doyle [1, p. 51] present this example as $\{MC \rightarrow \sim D, MD \rightarrow \sim C\}$.
[7] McDermott and Doyle [1, p. 51] present this example as $\{MC \rightarrow \sim C\}$.

4. Analysis of Nonmonotonic Logic

Now we are in a position to provide an analysis of nonmonotonic logic that will explain its peculiarities in terms of autoepistemic logic. Briefly, our conclusions will be that the original nonmonotonic logic of McDermott and Doyle [1] is simply too weak to capture the notions they wanted, and that McDermott's [2] attempt to strengthen the logic does so in the wrong way.

McDermott and Doyle's first logic is very similar to our autoepistemic logic with one glaring exception; its specification includes nothing corresponding to our Condition (2) (if $P \in T$, then $LP \in T$). McDermott and Doyle define the nonmonotonic *fixed points* of a set of premises A, corresponding to our stable expansions of A. In the propositional case, their definition is equivalent to the following:

> T is a fixed point of A just in case T is the set of tautological consequences of $A \cup \{\sim LP \mid P \notin T\}$.

Our definition of a stable expansion of A, on the other hand, could be stated as

> T is a stable expansion of A just in case T is the set of tautological consequences of $A \cup \{LP \mid P \in T\} \cup \{\sim LP \mid P \notin T\}$.

In nonmonotonic logic, $\{LP \mid P \in T\}$ is missing from the 'base' of the fixed points. This makes it possible for there to be nonmonotonic theories with fixed points that contain P but not LP. So, under an autoepistemic interpretation of L, McDermott and Doyle's agents are omniscient as to what they do not believe, but they may know nothing as to what they do believe.

This explains essentially all the peculiarities of McDermott and Doyle's original logic. For instance, they note [1, p. 69] that MC does not follow from $M(C \wedge D)$. Changing the modality to L, this is equivalent to saying that $\sim LP$ does not follow from $\sim L(P \vee Q)$. The problem is that, lacking the ability to infer LP from P, nonmonotonic logic permits interpretations of L that are more restricted than simple belief. Suppose we interpret L as "inferable in n or fewer steps" for some particular n. P might be inferable in exactly n steps, and $P \vee Q$ in $n+1$. According to this interpretation $\sim L(P \vee Q)$ would be true and $\sim LP$ would be false. Since this interpretation of L is consistent with McDermott and Doyle's definition of a fixed point, $\sim LP$ does not follow from $\sim L(P \vee Q)$. The other example of this kind noted by McDermott and Doyle is that $\{MC, \sim C\}$ has a consistent fixed point, which amounts to saying simultaneously that P is consistent with everything asserted and that P is false. But this set of premises is equivalent to $\{\sim LP, P\}$, which would have no consistent fixed points if LP were forced to be in every fixed point that contains P.

On the other hand, McDermott and Doyle consider it to be a problem that

$\{MC \rightarrow D, \sim D\}$ has no consistent fixed point in their theory. Restated in terms of L, this set of premises is equivalent to $\{P \rightarrow LQ, P\}$. Since a stable autoepistemic theory containing these premises will also contain LQ, it must also contain Q to be consistent. (Otherwise it would contain $\sim LQ$.) But Q is not contained in any theory grounded in the premises $\{P \rightarrow LQ, P\}$; it is possible for $P \rightarrow LQ$ and P both to be true with respect to an agent while Q is false. So there is no consistent stable expansion of $\{P \rightarrow LQ, P\}$ in autoepistemic logic; hence, this set of premises cannot be the foundation of an appropriate set of beliefs for an ideally rational agent. Thus, our analysis justifies nonmonotonic logic in this case, contrary to the intuition of McDermott and Doyle.

McDermott and Doyle recognized the weakness of the original formulation of nonmonotonic logic, and McDermott [2] has gone on to develop a group of theories that are stronger because they are based on modal rather than classical logic. McDermott's nonmonotonic modal theories alter the logic in two ways. First, the definition of fixed point is changed to be equivalent to

> T is a fixed point of A just in case T is the set of *modal* consequences of $A \cup \{\sim LP \mid P \notin T\}$,

where 'modal consequence' means that $P \vdash LP$ is used as an additional inference rule. Second, McDermott considers only theories that include as premises the axioms of one of the standard modal logics T, S4, and S5.

Merely changing the definition of fixed point brings McDermott's logic much closer to autoepistemic logic. In particular, adding $P \vdash LP$ as an inference rule means that all modal fixed points of A are stable expansions of A. However, adding $P \vdash LP$ as an inference rule, rather than adding $\{LP \mid P \in T\}$ to the base of T, has as a consequence that not all stable expansions of A are modal fixed points of A. The difference is that, in autoepistemic logic, if P can be derived from LP, then both can be in a stable expansion of the premises. whereas in McDermott's logic there must be a derivation of P that does not rely on LP. Thus, although in autoepistemic logic there is a stable expansion of $\{LP \rightarrow P\}$ that includes P, in McDermott's logic there is no modal fixed point of $\{LP \rightarrow P\}$ that includes P. It is as if, in autoepistemic logic, one can acquire the belief that P and justify it later by the premise that, if P is believed, then it is true. In nonmonotonic logic, however, the justification of P has to precede belief in LP. This makes the interpretation of L in nonmonotonic modal logic more like "justified belief" than simple belief.

Since we have already shown that autoepistemic logic requires no specific axioms to capture a competence model of autoepistemic reasoning, we might wonder what purpose is served by McDermott's second modification of nonmonotonic logic, the addition of the axioms of various modal logics. The most plausible answer is that, besides behaving in accordance with the principles of autoepistemic logic, an ideally rational agent might well be expected to know what some of those principles are. For instance, the modal logic T has all instances of the schema $L(P \rightarrow Q) \rightarrow (LP \rightarrow LQ)$ as axioms. This says that the agents beliefs are closed under modus ponens—which is true for an ideally rational agent, so he might as well believe it. S4 adds the schema $LP \rightarrow LLP$, which means that, if the agent believes P, he believes that he believes it (Condition (2)). S5 adds the schema $\sim LP \rightarrow L \sim LP$, which means that, if the agent does not believe P, he believes that he does not believe it (Condition (3)). Since all these formulas are always true with respect to any ideally rational agent, it seems plausible to expect him to adopt them as premises. Thus, S5 seems to be the most plausible candidate of the nonmonotonic logics as a model of autoepistemic reasoning.

The problem is that all of these logics also contain the schema $LP \rightarrow P$, which means that, if the agent believes P, then P is true—but this is not generally true, even for ideally rational agents.[8] It turns out that $LP \rightarrow P$ will always be contained in any stable autoepistemic theory (that is, ideally rational agents always believe that their beliefs are true), but making it a premise allows beliefs to be grounded that otherwise would not be. As a premise the schema $LP \rightarrow P$ can itself be justification for believing P, while as a 'theorem' it must be derived from $\sim LP$, in which case P is not believed, or from P, in which case P must be independently justified, or from some other grounded formulas. In any case, as a premise schema, $LP \rightarrow P$ can sanction *any* belief whatsoever in autoepistemic logic. This is not generally true in modal nonmonotonic logic, as we have also seen, but it is true in nonmonotonic S5. The S5 axiom schema $\sim LP \rightarrow L \sim LP$ embodies enough of the model theory of autoepistemic logic to allow LP to be 'self-grounding': The schema $\sim LP \rightarrow L \sim LP$ is equivalent to the schema $\sim L \sim LP \rightarrow LP$, which allows LP to be justified by the fact that its negation is not believed. This inference is never in danger of being falsified, but, from this and $LP \rightarrow P$, we obtain an unwarranted justification for believing P.

The collapse of nonmonotonic S5 into monotonic S5 follows immediately. Since $LP \rightarrow P$ can be used to justify belief in any formula at all, there are no formulas that are absent from every fixed point of theories based on nonmonotonic S5. It follows that there are no formulas of the form $\sim LP$ that are contained in every fixed point of theories based on nonmonotonic S5; hence there are no theorems of the form $\sim LP$ in any theory based on nonmonotonic S5. (Recall that the theorems are the intersection of all the fixed points.) Since these formulas are just the ones that would be produced by nonmonotonic

[8] $LP \rightarrow P$ would be an appropriate axiom schema if the interpretation of LP were "P is known" rather than "P is believed", but *that* notion is not nonmonotonic. An agent cannot, in general, know when he does not know P, because he might believe P—leading him to believe that he knows P—while P is in fact false. Since agents are unable to reflect directly on what they do not know (only on what they do not believe), an autoepistemic logic of knowledge would not be a nonmonotonic logic; rather, the appropriate logic would seem to be monotonic S4.

inference, nonmonotonic S5 collapses to monotonic S5. In more informal terms, an agent who assumes that he is infallible is liable to believe anything, so an outside observer can conclude nothing about what he does not believe.

The real problem with nonmonotonic S5, then, is not the S5 schema; therefore McDermott's rather unmotivated suggestion to drop back to nonmonotonic S4 [2, p. 45] is not the answer. The S5 schema merely makes explicit the consequences of adopting $LP \rightarrow P$ as a premise schema that are implicit in the logic's natural semantics. If we want to base nonmonotonic logic on a modal logic, the obvious solution is to drop back, not so S4, but to what Stalnaker [4] calls 'weak S5' (S5 without $LP \rightarrow P$). It is much better motivated and, moreover, has the advantage of actually being nonmonotonic.

In autoepistemic logic, however, even this much is unneccessary. Adopting any of the axioms of weak S5 as premises makes no difference to what can be derived. The key fact is the following theorem:

Theorem 4.1. *If P is true in every autoepistemic interpretation of T, then T is grounded in $A \cup \{P\}$ if and only if T is grounded in A.*

An immediate corollary of this result is:

Corollary 4.2. *If P is true in every autoepistemic interpretation of T, then T is a stable expansion of $A \cup \{P\}$ if and only if T is a stable expansion of A.*

The modal axiom schemata of weak S5,

$$L(P \rightarrow Q) \rightarrow (LP \rightarrow LQ),$$
$$LP \rightarrow LLP,$$
$$\sim LP \rightarrow L \sim LP,$$

simply state Conditions (1)–(3), so all their instances are true in every autoepistemic interpretation of any stable autoepistemic theory. The nonmodal axioms of weak S5 are just the tautologies of propositional logic, so they are true in every interpretation (autoepistemic or otherwise) of any autoepistemic theory (stable or otherwise). It immediately follows by Corollary 4.2, therefore, that a set of premises containing any of the axioms of weak S5 will have exactly the same stable expansions as the corresponding set of premises without any weak-S5 axioms.

5. Conclusion

McDermott and Doyle recognized that their original nonmonotonic logic was too weak; when McDermott tried to strengthen it, however, he misdiagnosed the problem. Because he was thinking of nonmonotonic logic as a logic of provability rather than belief, he apparently thought the problem was the lack of any connection between provability and truth. At one point he says "Even though $\sim M \sim P$ (abbreviated LP) might plausibly be expected to mean 'P is provable', there was not actually any relation between the truth values of P and LP", [2, p. 34], and later he acknowledges the questionability of the schema $LP \rightarrow P$, but says that "it is difficult to visualize any other way of relating provability and truth", [2, p. 35]. If one interprets nonmonotonic logic as a logic of belief, however, there is no reason to expect any connection between the truth of LP and the truth of P. And, as we have seen, the real problem with the original nonmonotonic logic was that the 'if' half of the semantic definition of L—that LP is true if and only if P is believed—was not expressed in the logic.

Appendix A. Proofs of Theorems

Theorem 3.1. *If T is a stable autoepistemic theory, then any autoepistemic interpretation of T that is a propositional model of the objective formulas of T is an autoepistemic model of T.*

Proof. Suppose that T is a stable autoepistemic theory and I is an autoepistemic interpretation of T that is a propositional model of the objective formulas of T. All the objective formulas of T are true in I. T must be consistent because an inconsistent stable autoepistemic theory would contain all formulas of the language, which would include many objective formulas that are not true in I. Let P be an arbitrary formula in T. Since stable autoepistemic theories are closed under tautological consequence, T must also contain a set of formulas $P_1, \ldots, P_k$ that taken together entail P, where, for each i between 1 and k, there exist n and m such that P_i is of the form

$$P_{i,1} \vee LP_{i,2} \vee \cdots \vee LP_{i,n} \vee \sim LP_{i,n+1} \vee \cdots \vee \sim LP_{i,m}$$

and $P_{i,1}$ is an objective formula. (Any formula is interderivable with a set of such formulas by propositional logic alone.) There are two cases to be considered:

(1) Suppose at least one of $LP_{i,2}, \ldots, LP_{i,n}, \sim LP_{i,n+1}, \ldots, \sim LP_{i,m}$ is in T. By Conditions (4) and (5), we know that, if any such formula is in T, it must be true in I, since T is consistent and I is an autoepistemic interpretation of T. But, since each of these formulas entails P_i, it follows that P_i is also true in I.

(2) Suppose the first case does not hold. Conditions (2) and (3) guarantee that in every stable autoepistemic theory, for every formula P, either LP or $\sim LP$ will be in the theory. Hence, if T does not contain any of $LP_{i,2}, \ldots, LP_{i,n}, \sim LP_{i,n+1}, \ldots, \sim LP_{i,m}$, it must contain all of $\sim LP_{i,2}, \ldots, \sim LP_{i,n}, LP_{i,n+1}, \ldots, LP_{i,m}$. But $P_{i,1}$ is a tautological consequence of P_i and these formulas (imagine repeated applications of the resolution principle); so $P_{i,1}$ must be in T. But $P_{i,1}$ is objective, and so, by hypothesis, must be true in I. Since $P_{i,1}$ entails P_i, it must be the case that P_i is true in I.

In either case, P_i will be true in I. All the P_i taken together entail P, so P must also be true in I. Since P was chosen arbitrarily, every formula of T must be true in I; hence I is an autoepistemic model of T.

Theorem 3.2. *If two stable autoepistemic theories contain the same objective formulas, then they contain exactly the same formulas.*

Proof. Suppose that T_1 and T_2 contain the same objective formulas and T_1 contains P. We prove by induction on the depth of nesting of autoepistemic operators in P (the 'L-depth' of P) that T_2 also contains P. If the L-depth of P is 0, the theorem is trivially true, since P will be an objective formula. Now suppose that P has an L-depth of d greater than 0, and that, if two stable autoepistemic theories contain the same objective formulas, then they contain exactly the same formulas whose L-depth is less than d.

Since stable autoepistemic theories are closed under tautological consequence, T_1 must also contain a set of formulas $P_1, \ldots, P_k$ that are interderivable with P by propositional logic, where, for each i between 1 and k, there exist n and m such that P_i is of the form

$$P_{i,1} \vee LP_{i,2} \vee \cdots \vee LP_{i,n} \vee \sim LP_{i,n+1} \vee \cdots \vee \sim LP_{i,m}$$

and $P_{i,1}$ is an objective formula. Note that, since propositional logic will treat all the formulas of the form $LP_{i,j}$ as propositional constants, it is impossible to increase the L-depth of a formula by propositional inference, so each of these formulas will have an L-depth of not more than d.

We can also assume that T_1 and T_2 are consistent. If one of these theories were inconsistent, it would contain all formulas of the language. Since, by hypothesis, the two theories contain the same objective formulas, the other theory would contain all the objective formulas of the language and, since these formulas are inconsistent, it would also contain all the formulas of the language. For each P_i, there are three cases to be considered:

(1) T_1 contains $LP_{i,j}$ for some j between 2 and n. Since T_1 is consistent, by Condition (4) it must also contain $P_{i,j}$. Since the L-depth of $P_{i,j}$ is one less than that of $LP_{i,j}$, it must be less than d; so, by hypothesis, T_2 must contain $P_{i,j}$ and, by Condition (2), it must contain $LP_{i,j}$. But P_i is a tautological consequence of $LP_{i,j}$, so T_2 contains P_i.

(2) T_1 contains $\sim LP_{i,j}$ for some j between $n+1$ and m. Since T_1 is consistent, by Condition (5) it must not contain $P_{i,j}$. Since the L-depth of $P_{i,j}$ is one less than that of $\sim LP_{i,j}$, it must be less than d; therefore, by hypothesis, T_2 must not contain $P_{i,j}$ and, by Condition (3), it must contain $\sim LP_{i,j}$. But P_i is a tautological consequence of $\sim LP_{i,j}$, so T_2 contains P_i.

(3) Suppose neither of the first two cases holds. Conditions (2) and (3) guarantee that in every stable autoepistemic theory, for every formula P, either LP or $\sim LP$ will be in the theory. Hence, if T_1 does not contain any of $LP_{i,2}, \ldots, LP_{i,n}$, $\sim LP_{i,n+1}, \ldots, \sim LP_{i,m}$, it must contain all of $\sim LP_{i,2}, \ldots, \sim LP_{i,n}$, $LP_{i,n+1}, \ldots, LP_{i,m}$. But $P_{i,1}$ is a tautological consequence of P_i and these formulas; so $P_{i,1}$ must be in T_1. $P_{i,1}$ is objective, however, so $P_{i,1}$ must also be in T_2. Since P_i is a tautological consequence of $P_{i,1}$, T_2 contains P_i.

Thus, all of $P_1, \ldots, P_k$ are in T_2. Since P is a tautological consequence of these formulas, P is also in T_2. Since P was chosen arbitrarily, every formula in T_1 is also in T_2. The same argument can be used to show that every formula in T_2 is also in T_1, so T_1 and T_2 contain exactly the same formulas.

Theorem 3.3. *An autoepistemic theory T is semantically complete if and only if T is stable.*

Proof. 'If' direction: we show that, if T is a stable autoepistemic theory, then T contains every formula that is true in every autoepistemic model of T. Let T be a stable autoepistemic theory and let P be an arbitrary formula that is not in T. We show that there is an autoepistemic model of T in which P is false.

We know from propositional logic that P is propositionally equivalent to (i.e., true in the same propositional models as) the conjunction of a set of formulas $P_1, \ldots, P_k$, where, for each i between 1 and k, there exist n and m such that P_i is of the form

$$P_{i,1} \vee LP_{i,2} \vee \cdots \vee LP_{i,n} \vee \sim LP_{i,n+1} \vee \cdots \vee \sim LP_{i,m}$$

and $P_{i,1}$ is an objective formula. Since P will be a tautological consequence of $P_1, \ldots, P_k$ and T is stable, Condition (1) guarantees that, if P is not in T, at least one of $P_1, \ldots, P_k$ must not be in T. Let P_i be such a formula. P_i is a tautological consequence of each of its disjuncts, so none of them can be in T. We show that there is an autoepistemic model of T in which all of these disjuncts are false.

Since $P_{i,1}$ is not in T, it must not be a tautological consequence of the objective formulas of T. Given this and the fact that $P_{i,1}$ is objective, it follows from the completeness theorem for propositional logic that there must be a truth assignment to the propositional constants of T in which $P_{i,1}$ is false and all the objective formulas of T are true. But, we can extend this truth assignment (or any truth assignment to the propositional constants of T—see Section 3) to an autoepistemic interpretation of T. Call this interpretation I and note that $P_{i,1}$ is false in I. I will be a propositional model of the objective formulas of T; so, by Theorem 3.1, I is an autoepistemic model of T in which $P_{i,1}$ is false.

Now consider the other disjuncts of P_i. Note that Conditions (2) and (3) require that a stable theory contain all the formulas of the form LP or $\sim LP$ that are true in the autoepistemic interpretations of the theory. Since none of $LP_{i,2}, \ldots, LP_{i,n}$, $\sim LP_{i,n+1}, \ldots, \sim LP_{i,m}$ is in T, none of $LP_{i,2}, \ldots, LP_{i,n}$,

$\sim LP_{i,n+1}, \ldots, \sim LP_{i,m}$ is true in any autoepistemic interpretation of T. In particular, none of $LP_{i,2}, \ldots, LP_{i,m}, \sim LP_{i,n+1}, \ldots, \sim LP_{i,m}$ is true in I. Therefore, I is an autoepistemic model of T in which, since all of the disjuncts of P_i are false, P_i itself is false. But P is propositionally equivalent to a conjunction that includes P_i, so I is an autoepistemic model of T in which P is false.

'Only if' direction: we show that, if T is semantically complete, then T is stable. Suppose T is semantically complete. For any formula P, if P is true in every autoepistemic model of T, then P is in T. Let I be an arbitrary autoepistemic model of T. If we can show that some formula P is true in I, P must be true in every autoepistemic model of T (since I is arbitrarily chosen) and, thus, thus, P must be in T. We now show that T satisfies Conditions (1)–(3).

(1) Suppose $P_1, \ldots, P_n$ are in T and $P_1, \ldots, P_n \vdash Q$. Since I is a model of T, $P_1, \ldots, P_n$ will be true in I. Since $P_1, \ldots, P_n$ are true in I and Q is a tautological consequence of $P_1, \ldots, P_n$, Q will also be true in I. Therefore, Q will be in T. (2) Suppose P is in T. Since I is an autoepistemic model of T, LP will be true in I. Therefore, LP will be in T. (3) Suppose P is not in T. Since I is an autoepistemic model of T, $\sim LP$ will be true in I. Therefore, $\sim LP$ will be in T.

Conditions (1)–(3) are all satisfied, so T is stable.

Theorem 3.4. *An autoepistemic theory T is sound with respect to an initial set of premises A if and only if T is grounded in A.*

Proof. 'If' direction: suppose T is grounded in A. Every formula of T is therefore included in the tautological consequences of $A \cup \{LP \mid P \in T\} \cup \{\sim LP \mid P \notin T\}$. We show that T is sound with respect to A—i.e., that every autoepistemic interpretation of T in which all the formulas of A are true is an autoepistemic model of T.

Let I be an autoepistemic interpretation of T in which all the formulas in A are true. We show that I is an autoepistemic model of T. If P is in A, then, trivially, P is true in I. If P is of the form LQ and Q is in T, or if P is of the form $\sim LQ$ and Q is not in T, then P is true in I because I is an autoepistemic interpretation of T. We have now shown that all the formulas in $A \cup \{LP \mid P \in T\} \cup \{\sim LP \mid P \notin T\}$ are true in I, so all their tautological consequences are true in I. But all the formulas of T are included in this set, so I is an autoepistemic model of T. Since I was an arbitrarily chosen autoepistemic interpretation of T in which all the formulas of A are true, every autoepistemic interpretation of T in which all the formulas of A are true is an autoepistemic model of T.

'Only if' direction: suppose T is sound with respect to A. Every autoepistemic interpretation of T in which all the formulas of A are true is therefore an autoepistemic model of T. We show that T is grounded in A—i.e., every formula of T is a tautological consequence of $A \cup \{LP \mid P \in T\} \cup \{\sim LP \mid P \notin T\}$.

Let

$$A' = A \cup \{LP \mid P \in T\} \cup \{\sim LP \mid P \notin T\}.$$

Note that, for all P, if P is in T, LP will be in A', so LP will be true in every propositional model of A'; however, if P is not in T, $\sim LP$ will be in A' and LP will not be true in any propositional model of A'. Therefore, in every propositional model of A', LP is true if and only if P is in T, so every propositional model of A' is an autoepistemic interpretation of T. Since every autoepistemic interpretation of T in which all the formulas of A are true is an autoepistemic model of T, every propositional model of A' is an autoepistemic model of T. Since every formula in T is true in every autoepistemic model of T, every formula in T is true in every propositional model of A'. By the completeness theorem for propositional logic, every formula of T is therefore a tautological consequence of A'. Hence T is grounded in A.

Theorem 4.1. *If P is true in every autoepistemic interpretation of T, then T is grounded in $A \cup \{P\}$ if and only if T is grounded in A.*

Proof. Suppose that P is true in every autoepistemic interpretation of T. For any set of premises A, the set of autoepistemic interpretations of T in which every formula of $A \cup \{P\}$ is true is therefore the same as the set of autoepistemic interpretations of T in which every formula of A is true. Thus, every autoepistemic interpretation of T in which every formula of $A \cup \{P\}$ is true is an autoepistemic model of T if and only if every autoepistemic interpretation of T in which every formula of A is true is an autoepistemic model of T. Hence, T is sound with respect to $A \cup \{P\}$ if and only if T is sound with respect to A. By Theorem 3.4, therefore, T is grounded in $A \cup \{P\}$ if and only if T is grounded in A.

REFERENCES

1. McDermott, D. and Doyle, J., Non-monotonic logic I, *Artificial Intelligence* **13** (1, 2) (1980) 41–72.
2. McDermott, D., Nonmonotonic logic II: Nonmonotonic modal theories, *J. ACM* **29** (1) (1982) 33–57.
3. Minsky, M., A framework for representing knowledge, MIT Artificial Intelligence Laboratory, AIM-306, Cambridge, MA, 1974.
4. Stalnaker, R., A note on non-monotonic modal logic, Department of Philosophy, Cornell University, Ithaca, NY, unpublished manuscript.

POSSIBLE-WORLD SEMANTICS FOR AUTOEPISTEMIC LOGIC

Robert C. Moore
Artificial Intelligence Center
SRI International, Menlo Park, CA 94025

I INTRODUCTION

In a previous paper [Moore, 1983a, 1983b], we presented a nonmonotonic logic for modeling the beliefs of ideally rational agents who reflect on their own beliefs, which we called "autoepistemic logic." We defined a simple and intuitive semantics for autoepistemic logic and proved the logic sound and complete with respect to that semantics. However, the nonconstructive character of both the logic and its semantics made it difficult to prove the existence of sets of beliefs satisfying all the constraints of autoepistemic logic. This note presents an alternative, possible-world semantics for autoepistemic logic that enables us to construct finite models for autoepistemic theories, as well as to demonstrate the existence of sound and complete autoepistemic theories based on given sets of premises.

Autoepistemic logic is nonmonotonic, because we can make statements in the logic that allow an agent to draw conclusions about the world from his own lack of information. For example, we can express the belief that "If I do not believe P, then Q is true." If an agent adopts this belief as a premise and he has no means of inferring P, he will be able to derive Q. On the other hand, if we add P to his premises, Q will no longer be derivable. Hence, the logic is nonmonotonic.

Autoepistemic logic is closely related to the nonmonotonic logics of McDermott and Doyle [1980; McDermott, 1982]. In fact, it was designed to be a reconstruction of these logics that avoids some of their peculiarities. This is discussed in detail in our earlier paper [Moore, 1983a, 1983b]. This work is also closely related to that of Halpern and Moses [1984], the chief difference being that theirs is a logic of knowledge rather than belief. Finally, Levesque [1981] has also developed a kind of autoepistemic logic, but in his system the agent's premises are restricted to a sublanguage that makes no reference to what he believes.

II SUMMARY OF AUTOEPISTEMIC LOGIC

The language of autoepistemic logic is that of ordinary propositional logic, augmented by a modal operator L. We want formulas of the form LP to receive the intuitive interpretation "P is believed" or "I believe P." For example, $P \supset LP$ could be interpreted as saying "If P is true, then I believe that P is true."

The type of object that is of primary interest in autoepistemic logic is a set of formulas that can be interpreted as a specification of the beliefs of an agent reflecting upon his own beliefs. We will call such a set of formulas an _autoepistemic theory_. The truth of an agent's beliefs, expressed as an autoepistemic theory, is determined by (1) which propositional constants are true in the external world and (2) which formulas are believed by the agent. A formula of the form LP will be true with respect to an agent if and only if P is in his set of beliefs. To formalize this, we define the notions of autoepistemic interpretation and autoepistemic model. An _autoepistemic interpretation_ I of an autoepistemic theory T is a truth assignment to the formulas of the language of T that satisfies the following conditions:

1. I conforms to the usual truth recursion for propositional logic.
2. A formula LP is true in I if and only if $P \in T$.

An _autoepistemic model_ of T is an autoepistemic interpretation of T in which all the formulas of T are true. (Any truth assignment satisfying Condition 1 in which all the formulas of T are true will be called simply a _model_ of T.)

We can readily define notions of soundness and completeness relative to this semantics. Soundness of a theory must be defined with respect to some set of premises. Intuitively speaking, an autoepistemic theory T, viewed as a set of beliefs, will be sound with respect to a set of premises A, just in case every formula in T must be true, given that all the formulas in A are true and given that T is, in fact, the set of beliefs under consideration. This is expressed formally by the following definition:

> An autoepistemic theory T is _sound_ with respect to a set of premises A if and only if every autoepistemic interpretation of T that is a model of A is also a model of T.

The definition of completeness is equally simple. A semantically complete set of beliefs will be one that contains everything that must be true, given that the entire set of beliefs is true and given that it is the set of beliefs being reasoned about. Stated formally, this becomes

> An autoepistemic theory T is _semantically complete_ if and only if T contains every formula that is true in every autoepistemic model of T.

Finally, we can give syntactic characterizations of the autoepistemic theories that conform to these definitions of soundness and completeness [Moore, 1983b, Theorems 3 and 4]. We say that an autoepistemic theory T is _stable_ if and only if (1) it is closed under ordinary tautological consequence, (2) $LP \in T$ whenever $P \in T$, and (3) $\neg LP \in T$ whenever $P \notin T$.

> Theorem: An autoepistemic theory T is semantically complete if and only if T is stable.

We say that an autoepistemic theory T is _grounded_ in a set of premises A if and only if every formula in T is a tautological consequence of $A \cup \{LP \mid P \in T\} \cup \{\neg LP \mid P \notin T\}$.

> Theorem: An autoepistemic theory T is sound with respect to a set of premises A if and only if T is grounded in A.

With these soundness and completeness theorems, we can see that the possible sets of beliefs an ideally rational agent might hold, given A as his premises, would be stable autoepistemic theories that contain A and are grounded in A. We call these theories <u>stable expansions</u> of A.

III AN ALTERNATIVE SEMANTICS FOR AUTOEPISTEMIC LOGIC

The semantics we have provided for autoepistemic logic is simple, intuitive, and allows us to prove a number of important general results, but it requires enumerating an infinite truth assignment if the theory under consideration contains infinitely many formulas. This makes it difficult to exhibit particular models and interpretations we may be interested in. The problem is that, in the general case, there need be no systematic connection between the truth of one formula of the form LP and any other. Autoepistemic logic is designed to characterize the beliefs of ideally rational agents, but we want the semantics to be broader than that. The semantics we have defined is intended to apply to arbitrary sets of beliefs, with the beliefs of ideally rational agents being a special case (just as model theory for standard logic applies to arbitrary sets of formulas, not just to those that are closed under logical consequence). Thus, our semantics makes no necessary connection between the truth of $L(P \wedge Q)$ and LP or LQ, because it is at least conceivable that an agent might be so logically deficient as to believe $P \wedge Q$ without believing P or believing Q. In such a case, there is little we can expect the truth definition for an autoepistemic theory to do, other than to list the true formulas of the form LP by brute stipulation.

If we confine our attention to ideally rational agents, however, much more structure emerges. In fact, we can show that stable autoepistemic theories can be simply characterized by Kripke-style possible-world models for modal logic [Kripke, 1971]. For our purposes, what we need to recall about a Kripke structure is that it contains a set of possible worlds and an accessibility relation between pairs of worlds. The truth of a formula is defined relative to a world, and conforms to the usual truth recursion for propositional logic. A formula of the form LP is true in a world W just in case P is true in every world accessible from W. Kripke structures in which the accessibility relation is an equivalence relation are called S5 structures, and the S5 structures that will be of interest to us are those in which every world is accessible from every world. We will call these the <u>complete</u> S5 structures. Our major result is that the sets of formulas that are true in every world of some complete S5 structure are exactly the stable autoepistemic theories. (This result has been obtained independently by Halpern and Moses [1984] and by Melvin Fitting [personal communication]).

> Theorem: T is the set of formulas that are true in every world of some complete S5 structure if and only if T is a stable autoepistemic theory.

Proof: Suppose T is the set of formulas true in every world of a complete S5 structure. By the soundness of propositional logic, T is closed under tautological consequence. By the truth rule for L, LP is true in every world just in case P is true in every world; therefore $LP \in T$ if and only if $P \in T$. Furthermore, by the truth rule for L, LP is false in every world just in case P is false in some world; so $\neg LP \in T$ if and only if $P \notin T$. Therefore T is stable. In the opposite direction, suppose that T is stable. Let T' be the set of formulas of T that contain no occurrences of L. We will call these the _objective_ formulas of T. Since T is closed under tautological consequence, T' will also be closed under tautological consequence. Consider the set of all models of T' and the complete S5 structure in which each of these models defines a possible world. T' will contain exactly the objective formulas true in every world in this model; hence, T' will contain precisely the objective formulas of the stable autoepistemic theory T'' defined by this S5 structure. But by a previous result [Moore 1983b, Theorem 2], stable theories containing the same objective formulas are identical, so T must be the same as T''. Hence, T is the set of formulas true in every world of a complete S5 structure.

Given this result, we can characterize any autoepistemic interpretation of any stable theory by an ordered pair consisting of a complete S5 structure (to specify the agent's beliefs) and a propositional truth assignment (to specify what is actually true in the world). Such a structure (K, V) defines an autoepistemic interpretation of the theory T consisting of all the formulas that are true in every world in K. A formula of T is true in (K, V) if it is true according to the standard truth recursion for propositional logic, where the propositional constants are true in (K, V) if and only if they are true in V, and the formulas of the form LP are true in (K, V) if and only if they are true in every world in K (using the truth rules for Kripke structures). We will say that (K, V) is a _possible-world interpretation_ of T and, if every formula of T is true in (K, V), we will say that (K, V) is also a _possible-world model_ of T. In view of the preceding theorem, it should be obvious that for every autoepistemic interpretation or autoepistemic model of a stable theory there is a corresponding possible-world interpretation or possible-world model, and vice versa.

> Theorem: If (K, V) is an autoepistemic interpretation of T, then (K, V) will be an autoepistemic model of T if and only if the truth assignment V is consistent with the truth assignment provided by one of the possible worlds in K (i.e., if the actual world is one of the worlds that are compatible with what the agent believes).

Proof: If V is compatible with one of the worlds in K, then any propositional constant that is true in all worlds in K will be true in V. Therefore, any formula that comes out true in all worlds in K will also come out true in (K, V), and (K, V) will be a possible-world model of T. In the opposite direction, suppose that V is not compatible with any of the worlds in K. Then, for each world W in K, there will be some propositional constant that W and V disagree on. Take that constant or its negation, whichever is true in W, plus the corresponding formulas for all other worlds in K, and form their disjunction. (This will be a finite disjunction, provided there are only finitely many propositional constants in the language.) This disjunction will be true in every world in K, so it will be a formula of T, but it will be false in V. Therefore, (K, V) will not be a possible-world model of T.

IV APPLICATIONS OF POSSIBLE-WORLD SEMANTICS

One of the problems with our original presentation of autoepistemic logic was that, since both the logic and its semantics were defined nonconstructively, we were unable to easily prove the existence of stable expansions of nontrivial sets of premises. With the finite models provided by the possible-world semantics for autoepistemic logic, this becomes quite straightforward. For instance, we claimed [Moore, 1983a, 1983b] that the set of premises {¬LP ⊃ Q, ¬LQ ⊃ P} has two stable expansions--one containing P but not Q, and the other containing Q but not P--but we were unable to do more than give a plausibility argument for that assertion. We can now demonstrate this fact quite rigorously.

Consider the stable theory T, generated by the complete S5 structure that contains exactly two worlds, {P, Q} and {P, ¬Q}. (We will represent a possible world by the set of propositional constants and negations of propositional constants that are true in it.) The possible-world interpretations of T will be the ordered pairs consisting of this S5 structure and any propositional truth assignment. Consider all the possible-world interpretations of T in which ¬LP ⊃ Q and ¬LQ ⊃ P are both true. By exaustive enumeration, it is easy to see that these are exactly

({{P, Q}, {P, ¬Q}}, {P, Q})
({{P, Q}, {P, ¬Q}}, {P, ¬Q})

Since, in each case, the actual world is one of the worlds that are compatible with everything the agent believes, each of these is a possible-world model of T. Therefore, T is sound with respect to {¬LP ⊃ Q, ¬LQ ⊃ P}. Since T is stable and includes {¬LP ⊃ Q, ¬LQ ⊃ P} (note that both these formulas are true in all worlds in the S5 structure), T is a stable expansion of A. Moreover, it is easy to see that T contains P but not Q. A similar construction yields a stable expansion of T that contains Q but not P.

On the other hand, if both P and Q are to be in a theory T, the corresponding S5 structure contains only one world, {P, Q}. But then {{{P, Q}}, {¬P, ¬Q}} is a possible-world interpretation of T in which ¬LP ⊃ Q and ¬LQ ⊃ P are both true, but some of the formulas of T are not (P and Q, for instance). Hence, if T contains both P and Q, T is not a stable expansion of {¬LP ⊃ Q, ¬LQ ⊃ P}.

ACKNOWLEDGMENTS

The research reported herein was supported by the Air Force Office of Scientific Research under Contract No. F49620-82-K-0031.

REFERENCES

Kripke, S. A. [1971] "Semantical Considerations on Modal Logic," in Reference and Modality, L. Linsky, ed., pp. 63-72 (Oxford University Press, London, England).

Halpern, J. Y. and Y. Moses [1984] "Towards a Theory of Knowledge and Ignorance," Workshop on Nonmonotonic Reasoning, Mohonk Mountain House, New Paltz, New York (October 17-19, 1984).

Levesque, H. J. [1981] "The Interaction with Incomplete Knowledge Bases: A Formal Treatment," Proceedings of the Seventh International Joint Conference on Artificial Intelligence, University of British Columbia, Vancouver, B.C., Canada, pp. 240-245 (August 24-28, 1981).

McDermott, D. and J. Doyle [1980] "Non-Monotonic Logic I," Artificial Intelligence, Vol. 13, Nos. 1, 2, pp. 41-72 (April 1980).

McDermott, D. [1982] "Nonmonotonic Logic II: Nonmonotonic Modal Theories," Journal of the Association for Computing Machinery, Vol. 29, No. 1, pp. 33-57 (January 1982).

Moore R. C. [1983a] "Semantical Considerations on Nonmonotonic Logic," Proceedings of the Eighth International Joint Conference on Artificial Intelligence, Karlsruhe, West Germany, pp. 272-279 (August 8-12, 1983).

Moore R. C. [1983b] "Semantical Considerations on Nonmonotonic Logic," SRI Artificial Intelligence Center Technical Note 284, SRI International, Menlo Park, California (June 1983).

3.3 Circumscription

This section begins with the two papers by McCarthy describing the idea of circumscription. Bear in mind, however, that the second of these papers is in part a response to technical criticisms of the idea that are raised by other papers in this section.

McCarthy's first paper, "Circumscription—A form of nonmonotonic reasoning," is the third of the three landmark papers from the 1980 special issue of *Artificial Intelligence* [Bobrow, 1980]. As with the other early papers, McCarthy spends the first part of this paper (Sections 1–3) discussing motivational material. A form of circumscription known as *predicate circumscription* is introduced and discussed in Sections 4–7; of all of the circumscriptive theories, predicate circumscription is the closest to that described in the introduction to this collection.

McCarthy raises a variety of interesting points in the final section of this first paper. First, he remarks in (1)[1] that circumscription is not a "nonmonotonic logic" but is instead a nonmonotonic augmentation of first-order logic using the circumscription axiom. In (2), he notes that the circumscriptive approach is capable of handling quantified default rules, allowing it to reason effectively with statements such as, "A block is clear if there is nothing that can be shown to be on top of it." In (7), he remarks that the result of any particular circumscription "may depend on the set of predicates used to express the facts." The choice of the language used to describe the domain may be crucial.

The key technical advance in the second paper is the introduction of a more powerful form of circumscription known as *formula* circumscription. Formula circumscription differs from predicate circumscription in that, as one attempts to minimize the extent of some particular predicate p,[2] one is permitted to vary the extents of *other* predicates. This is a crucial modification: If only abnormal birds don't fly, it is impossible to minimize the set of abnormal birds without varying the set of flying things.

There is other new material in this second paper as well. The abnormality predicate $\mathbf{ab}$ is introduced, and McCarthy discusses a "typology of uses of nonmonotonic reasoning" in Section 3. Section 12 introduces a notion of *prioritized* circumscription that Lifschitz shows **[Lifschitz, 1985b]** can be reduced to a special case of formula circumscription. An extended use of circumscription with an automatic proof checker appears in the appendix.

[1] The parenthetical numbering here matches that used by McCarthy in Section 8 of the paper itself.

[2] Formula circumscription also allows for the minimization of the extent of an arbitrary formula.

Formula circumscription was not the only modification suggested after the appearance of McCarthy's original paper in 1980. Minker and Perlis introduce a notion of *protected* circumscription [Minker, Perlis, 1984], and Lifschitz discusses *pointwise* circumscription **[Lifschitz, 1987b]**. Of these two papers, only the latter is included in this collection, since protected circumscription appears to have been generalized by the later work on formula circumscription in McCarthy's 1986 paper.

In his paper on pointwise circumscription, Lifschitz formalizes the idea of minimizing a predicate such as $\mathbf{ab}$ "one point at a time," so that we determine individually whether $\mathbf{ab}(x)$ should hold for each possible value of x.

There are many attractive features of this approach. Lifschitz shows in Section 2 of this paper that the pointwise circumscription axiom is often first-order, allowing its use with an automatic theorem prover. He goes on to show that pointwise circumscription can be used to minimize several predicates simultaneously, either in parallel (Section 4) or preferentially (as in prioritized circumscription, Section 5). Most important, perhaps, is the fact that it is possible in Lifschitz' formalism to state a "circumscription policy" within the theory itself. This circumscription policy indicates which predicates are to be minimized before others, which predicates are to be varied when others are minimized, and so on.

A possible problem with the pointwise approach appears in Example 2 of Section 2 of the paper, where Lifschitz notes that if $\mathbf{ab}(a) \equiv \mathbf{ab}(b)$, pointwise circumscription may not be able to minimize $\mathbf{ab}$ completely, since changing the value of $\mathbf{ab}$ at a alone may not be possible. Thus, if we know that Fred and Wilma are two birds of the same species, we may have difficulty concluding by default that they are not ostriches.

The various modifications to McCarthy's original formulation are a response to difficulties that were discovered with it. Probably the most compelling paper on this topic is Etherington and colleagues' "On the adequacy of predicate circumscription for closed-world reasoning." Their principal results are that:

1. There are some theories that admit no minimal models.
2. The predicate circumscription axiom can never introduce new positive instances of any predicate.

The theory they present with no minimal models is the following:

$$\begin{gathered}\exists x.p(x) \wedge [\forall y.p(y) \rightarrow x \neq s(y)] \\ \forall x.p(x) \rightarrow p(s(x)) \\ \forall xy.s(x) = s(y) \rightarrow x = y\end{gathered} \tag{3.1}$$

The axioms describe the positive integers, with $p(x)$ denoting the fact that x is a positive integer, and s the successor function. (The first axiom states that there is a least positive integer.) It is not hard to see that these axioms admit no minimal model—given a model where the extent of p is

$$\{n, n+1, n+2, \ldots\}$$

it is clear that a "smaller" model can be obtained by taking the extent of p to be[3]

$$\{n+1, n+2, \ldots\}$$

The second observation, that predicate circumscription axiom can never introduce new positive instances of any predicate, was a surprise. It says, in part, that it is not possible to use predicate circumscription to conclude that a bird can fly! The reason is that predicate circumscription does not allow noncircumscribed predicates to vary when the circumscription is attempted. Addressing this difficulty was one of the motivations behind McCarthy's introduction of the new formalism in [**McCarthy, 1986**]. Results related to those in the Etherington paper also can be found in [Lifschitz, 1986b] and [Perlis, Minker, 1986].

Finally, there has been work on making the circumscriptive approach computationally tractable. The first paper on this topic is Lifschitz' "Computing circumscription." Lifschitz gives a variety of examples where the general circumscription axiom can be replaced by a first-order one. (These ideas are extended using pointwise circumscription in the later paper [**Lifschitz, 1987b**].) As discussed in the introduction, Przymusinski develops in [Przymusinski, 1986] a resolution-like algorithm for determining whether or not a particular formula follows from the application of the circumscription axiom.

[3] Turning these informal remarks into a proof is actually rather difficult. The reason is that the axioms (3.1) are in fact quite weak, and admit models other than the integers.

Circumscription—A Form of Non-Monotonic Reasoning

John McCarthy
Stanford University, Stanford, CA, U.S.A.

Recommended by Patrick J. Hayes

ABSTRACT

Humans and intelligent computer programs must often jump to the conclusion that the objects they can determine to have certain properties or relations are the only objects that do. Circumscription *formalizes such conjectural reasoning.*

1. Introduction . The Qualification Problem

McCarthy [6] proposed a program with 'common sense' that would represent what it knows (mainly) by sentences in a suitable logical language. It would decide what to do by deducing a conclusion that it should perform a certain act. Performing the act would create a new situation, and it would again decide what to do. This requires representing both knowledge about the particular situation and general common sense knowledge as sentences of logic.

The 'qualification problem', immediately arose in representing general common sense knowledge. It seemed that in order to fully represent the conditions for the successful performance of an action, an impractical and implausible number of qualifications would have to be included in the sentences expressing them. For example, the successful use of a boat to cross a river requires, if the boat is a rowboat, that the oars and rowlocks be present and unbroken, and that they fit each other. Many other qualifications can be added, making the rules for using a rowboat almost impossible to apply, and yet anyone will still be able to think of additional requirements not yet stated.

Circumscription is a rule of conjecture that can be used by a person or program for 'jumping to certain conclusions'. Namely, *the objects that can be shown to have a certain property P by reasoning from certain facts A are all the objects that satisfy P.* More generally, circumscription can be used to conjecture that the tuples $\langle x, y, \ldots, z\rangle$ that can be shown to satisfy a relation $P(x, y, \ldots, z)$ are all the tuples satisfying this relation. Thus we *circumscribe* the set of relevant tuples.

We can postulate that a boat can be used to cross a river unless 'something' prevents it. Then circumscription may be used to conjecture that the only entities that can prevent the use of the boat are those whose existence follows from the facts at hand. If no lack of oars or other circumstance preventing boat use is deducible, then the boat is concluded to be usable. The correctness of this conclusion depends on our having 'taken into account' all relevant facts when we made the circumscription.

Circumscription formalizes several processes of human informal reasoning. For example, common sense reasoning is ordinarily ready to jump to the conclusion that a tool can be used for its intended purpose unless something prevents its use. Considered purely extensionally, such a statement conveys no information; it seems merely to assert that a tool can be used for its intended purpose unless it can't. Heuristically, the statement is not just a tautologous disjunction; it suggests forming a plan to use the tool.

Even when a program does not reach its conclusions by manipulating sentences in a formal language, we can often profitably analyze its behavior by considering it to *believe* certain sentences when it is in certain states, and we can study how these *ascribed beliefs* change with time (see [9]). When we do such analyses, we again discover that successful people and programs must jump to such conclusions.

2. The Need for Non-Monotonic Reasoning

We cannot get circumscriptive reasoning capability by adding sentences to an axiomatization or by adding an ordinary rule of inference to mathematical logic. This is because the well known systems of mathematical logic have the following *monotonicity property.* If a sentence q follows from a collection A of sentences and $A \subset B$, then q follows from B. In the notation of proof theory: if $A \vdash q$ and $A \subset B$, then $B \vdash q$. Indeed a proof from the premisses A is a sequence of sentences each of which is a either a premiss, an axiom or follows from a subset of the sentences occurring earlier in the proof by one of the rules of inference. Therefore, a proof from A can also serve as a proof from B. The semantic notion of entailment is also monotonic; we say that A entails q (written $A \models q$) if q is true in all models of A. But if $A \models q$ and $A \subset B$, then every model of B is also a model of A, which shows that $B \models q$.

Circumspection is a formalized *rule of conjecture* that can be used along with the *rules of inference* of first order logic. *Predicate circumscription* assumes that entities satisfy a given predicate only if they have to on the basis of a collection of facts. *Domain circumscription* conjectures that the 'known' entities are all there are. It turns out that domain circumscription, previously called *minimal inference*, can be subsumed under predicate circumscription.

We will argue using examples that humans use such 'non-monotonic' reasoning and that it is required for intelligent behavior. The default case reasoning of many computer programs [11] and the use of THNOT in MICROPLANNER [12] programs are also examples of non-monotonic reasoning, but possibly of a different kind from those discussed in this paper. Hewitt [5] gives the basic ideas of the PLANNER approach.

The result of applying circumscription to a collection A of facts is a sentence schema that asserts that the only tuples satisfying a predicate $P(x, \ldots, z)$ are those whose doing so follows from the sentences of A. Since adding more sentences to A might make P applicable to more tuples, circumscription is not monotonic. Conclusions derived from circumscription are conjectures that A includes all the relevant facts and that the objects whose existence follows from A are all the relevant objects.

A heuristic program might use circumscription in various ways. Suppose it circumscribes some facts and makes a plan on the basis of the conclusions reached. It might immediately carry out the plan, or be more cautious and look for additional facts that might require modifying it.

Before introducing the formalism, we informally discuss a well known problem whose solution seems to involve such non-monotonic reasoning.

3. Missionaries and Cannibals

The *Missionaries and Cannibals* puzzle, much used in AI, contains more than enough detail to illustrate many of the issues.

> "Three missionaries and three cannibals come to a river. A rowboat that seats two is available. If the cannibals ever outnumber the missionaries on either bank of the river, the missionaries will be eaten. How shall they cross the river"

Obviously the puzzler is expected to devise a strategy of rowing the boat back and forth that gets them all across and avoids the disaster.

Amarel [1] considered several representations of the problem and discussed criteria whereby the following representation is preferred for purposes of AI, because it leads to the smallest state space that must be explored to find the solution. A state is a triple comprising the numbers of missionaries, cannibals and boats on the starting bank of the river. The initial state is 331, the desired final state is 000, and one solution is given by the sequence (331, 220, 321, 300, 311, 110, 221, 020, 031, 010, 021, 000).

We are not presently concerned with the heuristics of the problem but rather with the correctness of the reasoning that goes from the English statement of the problem to Amarel's state space representation. A generally intelligent computer program should be able to carry out this reasoning. Of course, there are the well known difficulties in making computers understand English, but suppose the English sentences describing the problem have already been rather directly translated into first order logic. The correctness of Amarel's representation is not an ordinary logical consequence of these sentences for two further reasons.

First, nothing has been stated about the properties of boats or even the fact that rowing across the river doesn't change the numbers of missionaries or cannibals or the capacity of the boat. Indeed it hasn't been stated that situations change as a result of action. These facts follow from common sense knowledge, so let us imagine that common sense knowledge, or at least the relevant part of it, is also expressed in first order logic.

The second reason we can't *deduce* the propriety of Amarel's representation is deeper. Imagine giving someone the problem, and after he puzzles for a while, he suggests going upstream half a mile and crossing on a bridge. "What bridge," you say. "No bridge is mentioned in the statement of the problem." And this dunce replies, "Well, they don't say there isn't a bridge." You look at the English and even at the translation of the English into first order logic, and you must admit that "they don't say" there is no bridge. So you modify the problem to exclude bridges and pose it again, and the dunce proposes a helicopter, and after you exclude that, he proposes a winged horse or that the others hang onto the outside of the boat while two row.

You now see that while a dunce, he is an inventive dunce. Despairing of getting him to accept the problem in the proper puzzler's spirit, you tell him the solution. To your further annoyance, he attacks your solution on the grounds that the boat might have a leak or lack oars. After you rectify that omission from the statement of the problem, he suggests that a sea monster may swim up the river and may swallow the boat. Again you are frustrated, and you look for a mode of reasoning that will settle his hash once and for all.

In spite of our irritation with the dunce, it would be cheating to put into the statement of the problem that there is no other way to cross the river than using the boat and that nothing can go wrong with the boat. A human doesn't need such an ad hoc narrowing of the problem, and indeed the only watertight way to do it might amount to specifying the Amarel representation in English. Rather we want to avoid the excessive qualification and get the Amarel representation by common sense reasoning as humans ordinarily do.

Circumscription is one candidate for accomplishing this. It will allow us to conjecture that no relevant objects exist in certain categories except those whose existence follows from the statement of the problem and common sense knowledge. When we *circumscribe* the first order logic statement of the problem together with the common sense facts about boats etc., we will be able to conclude that there is no bridge or helicopter. "Aha," you say, "but there won't be any oars either." No, we get out of that as follows: It is a part of common knowledge that a boat can be used to cross a river *unless there is something wrong with it or something else prevents using it*, and if our facts do not require that there be something that prevents crossing the river, circumscription will generate the conjecture that there isn't. The price is introducing as entities in our language the 'somethings' that may prevent the use of the boat.

If the statement of the problem were extended to mention a bridge, then the circumscription of the problem statement would no longer permit showing the non-existence of a bridge, i.e., a conclusion that can be drawn from a smaller collection of facts can no longer be drawn from a larger. This non-monotonic character of circumscription is just what we want for this kind of problem. The statement, "*There is a bridge a mile upstream, and the boat has a leak.*" doesn't contradict the text of the problem, but its addition invalidates the Amarel representation.

In the usual sort of puzzle, there is a convention that there are no additional objects beyond those mentioned in the puzzle or whose existence is deducible from the puzzle and common sense knowledge. The convention can be explicated as applying circumscription to the puzzle statement and a certain part of common sense knowledge. However, if one really were sitting by a river bank and these six people came by and posed their problem, one wouldn't take the circumscription for granted, but one *would* consider the result of circumscription as a hypothesis. In puzzles, circumscription seems to be a rule of inference, while in life it is a rule of conjecture.

Some have suggested that the difficulties might be avoided by introducing probabilities. They suggest that the existence of a bridge is improbable. The whole situation involving cannibals with the postulated properties cannot be regarded as having a probability, so it is hard to take seriously the conditional probability of a bridge given the hypotheses. More to the point, we mentally propose to ourselves the normal non-bridge non-sea-monster interpretation *before* considering these extraneous possibilities, let alone their probabilities, i.e. we usually don't even introduce the sample space in which these possibilities are assigned whatever probabilities one might consider them to have. Therefore, regardless of our knowledge of probabilities, we need a way of formulating the normal situation from the statement of the facts, and non-monotonic reasoning seems to be required. The same considerations seem to apply to fuzzy logic.

Using circumscription requires that common sense knowledge be expressed in a form that says a boat can be used to cross rivers unless there is something that prevents its use. In particular, it looks like we must introduce into our *ontology* (the things that exist) a category that includes *something wrong with a boat* or a category that includes *something that may prevent its use*. Incidentally, once we have decided to admit *something wrong with the boat*, we are inclined to admit a *lack of oars* as such a something and to ask questions like, "*Is a lack of oars all that is wrong with the boat?*"

Some philosophers and scientists may be reluctant to introduce such *things*, but since ordinary language allows "*something wrong with the boat*" we shouldn't be hasty in excluding it. Making a suitable formalism is likely to be technically difficult as well as philosophically problematical, but we must try.

We challenge anyone who thinks he can avoid such entities to express in his favorite formalism, "*Besides leakiness, there is something else wrong with the boat.*" A good solution would avoid counterfactuals as this one does.

Circumscription may help understand natural language, because if the use of natural language involves something like circumscription, it is understandable that the expression of general common sense facts in natural language will be difficult without some form of non-monotonic reasoning.

4. The Formalism of Circumscription

Let A be a sentence of first order logic containing a predicate symbol $P(x_1, \ldots, x_n)$ which we will write $P(\bar{x})$. We write $A(\Phi)$ for the result of replacing all occurrences of P in A by the predicate expression Φ. (As well as predicate symbols, suitable λ-expressions are allowed as predicate expressions).

Definition *The circumscription of P in A(P)* is the sentence schema

$$A(\Phi) \wedge \forall \bar{x}.(\Phi(\bar{x}) \supset P(\bar{x})) \supset \forall \bar{x}.(P(\bar{x}) \supset \Phi(\bar{x})). \qquad (1)$$

(1) can be regarded as asserting that the only tuples $(\bar{x})$ that satisfy P are those that have to—assuming the sentence A. Namely, (1) contains a predicate parameter Φ for which we may substitute an arbitrary predicate expression. (If we were using second order logic, there would be a quantifier $\forall\Phi$ in front of (1).) Since (1) is an implication, we can assume both conjuncts on the left, and (1) lets us conclude the sentence on the right. The first conjunct $A(\Phi)$ expresses the assumption that Φ satisfies the conditions satisfied by P, and the second $\forall \bar{x}.(\Phi(\bar{x}) \supset P(\bar{x}))$ expresses the assumption that the entities satisfying Φ are a subset of those that satisfy P. The conclusion asserts the converse of the second conjunct which tells us that in this case, Φ and P must coincide.

We write $A \vdash_P q$ if the sentence q can be obtained by deduction from the result of circumscribing P in A. As we shall see $\vdash_P$ is a non-monotonic form of inference, which we shall call *circumscriptive inference*.

A slight generalization allows circumscribing several predicates jointly; thus jointly circumscribing P and Q in $A(P, Q)$ leads to

$$A(\Phi, \Psi) \wedge \forall \bar{x}.(\Phi(\bar{x}) \supset P(\bar{x})) \wedge \forall \bar{y}.(\Psi(\bar{y}) \supset Q(\bar{y}))$$
$$\supset \forall \bar{x}.(P(\bar{x}) \supset \Phi(\bar{x})) \wedge \forall \bar{y}.(Q(\bar{y}) \supset \Psi(\bar{y})) \qquad (2)$$

in which we can simultaneously substitute for Φ and Ψ. The relation $A \vdash_{P,Q} q$ is defined in a corresponding way. Although we do not give examples of joint circumscription in this paper, we believe it will be important in some AI applications.

Consider the following examples:

Example 1. In the blocks world, the sentence A may be

$$isblock\ A \wedge isblock\ B \wedge isblock\ C \qquad (3)$$

asserting that A, B and C are blocks. Circumscribing *isblock* in (3) gives the schema

$$\Phi(A) \wedge \Phi(B) \wedge \Phi(C) \wedge \forall x.(\Phi(x) \supset isblock\ x) \supset \forall x.(isblock\ x \supset \Phi(x)). \qquad (4)$$

If we now substitute

$$\Phi(x) \equiv (x = A \vee x = B \vee x = C) \qquad (5)$$

into (4) and use (3), the left side of the implication is seen to be true, and this gives

$$\forall x.(isblock\ x \supset (x = A \vee x = B \vee x = C)), \qquad (6)$$

which asserts that the only blocks are A, B and C, i.e. just those objects that (3) requires to be blocks. This example is rather trivial, because (3) provides no way of generating new blocks from old ones. However, it shows that circumscriptive inference is non-monotonic since if we adjoin *isblock D* to (3), we will no longer be able to infer (6).

Example 2. Circumscribing the disjunction

$$isblock\ A \lor isblock\ B \tag{7}$$

leads to

$$(\Phi(A) \lor \Phi(B)) \land \forall x.(\Phi(x) \supset isblock\ x) \supset \forall x.(isblock\ x \supset \Phi(x)). \tag{8}$$

We may then substitute successively $\Phi(x) \equiv (x = A)$ and $\Phi(x) \equiv (x = B)$, and these give respectively

$$(A = A \lor A = B) \land \forall x.(x = A \supset isblock\ x) \supset \forall x.(isblock\ x \supset x = A), \tag{9}$$

which simplifies to

$$isblock\ A \supset \forall x.(isblock\ x \supset x = A) \tag{10}$$

and

$$(B = A \lor B = B) \land \forall x.(x = B \supset isblock\ x) \supset \forall x.(isblock\ x \supset x = B), \tag{11}$$

which simplifies to

$$isblock\ B \supset \forall x.(isblock\ x \supset x = B). \tag{12}$$

(10), (12) and (7) yield

$$\forall x.(isblock\ x \supset x = A) \lor \forall x.(isblock\ x \supset x = B), \tag{13}$$

which asserts that either A is the only block or B is the only block.

Example 3. Consider the following algebraic axioms for natural numbers, i.e., non-negative integers, appropriate when we aren't supposing that natural numbers are the only objects.

$$isnatnum\ 0 \land \forall x.(isnatnum\ x \supset isnatnum\ succ\ x). \tag{14}$$

Circumscribing *isnatnum* in (14) yields

$$\Phi(0) \land \forall x.(\Phi(x) \supset \Phi(succ\ x)) \land \forall x.(\Phi(x) \supset isnatnum\ x) \supset \forall x.(isnatnum\ x \supset \Phi(x)). \tag{15}$$

(15) asserts that the only natural numbers are those objects that (14) forces to be natural numbers, and this is essentially the usual axiom schema of induction. We can get closer to the usual schema by substituting $\Phi(x) \equiv \Psi(x) \land isnatnum\ x$. This and (14) make the second conjunct drop out giving

$$\Psi(0) \land \forall x.(\Psi(x) \supset \Psi(succ\ x)) \supset \forall x.(isnatnum\ x \supset \Psi(x)). \tag{16}$$

Example 4. Returning to the blocks world, suppose we have a predicate $on(x, y, s)$ asserting that block x is on block y in situation s. Suppose we have another predicate $above(x, y, s)$ which asserts that block x is above block y in situation s. We may write

$$\forall x\, y\, s.(on(x, y, s) \supset above(x, y, s)) \tag{17}$$

and

$$\forall x\, y\, z\, s.(above(x, y, s) \land above(y, z, s) \supset above(x, z, s)), \tag{18}$$

i.e., *above* is a transitive relation. Circumscribing *above* in (17) and (18) gives

$$\begin{aligned} &\forall x\, y\, s.(on(x, y, s) \supset \Phi(x, y, s)) \\ &\land \forall x\, y\, z\, s.(\Phi(x, y, s) \land \Phi(y, z, s) \supset \Phi(x, z, s)) \\ &\land \forall x\, y\, s.(\Phi(x, y, s) \supset above(x, y, s)) \\ &\quad \supset \forall x\, y\, s.(above(x, y, s) \supset \Phi(x, y, s)) \end{aligned} \tag{19}$$

which tells us that *above* is the transitive closure of *on*.

In the preceding two examples, the schemas produced by circumscription play the role of axiom schemas rather than being just conjectures.

5. Domain Circumscription

The form of circumscription described in this paper generalizes an earlier version called *minimal inference*. Minimal inference has a semantic counterpart called *minimal entailment*, and both are discussed in [8] and more extensively in [3]. The general idea of minimal entailment is that a sentence q is minimally entailed by an axiom A, written $A \models_m q$, if q is true in all *minimal models* of A, where one model if is considered less than another if they agree on common elements, but the domain of the larger many contain elements not in the domain of the smaller. We shall call the earlier form *domain circumscription* to contrast it with the *predicate circumscription* discussed in this paper.

The domain circumscription of the sentence A is the sentence

$$Axiom(\Phi) \land A^{\Phi} \supset \forall x.\Phi(x). \tag{20}$$

where A^{Φ} is the relativization of A with respect to Φ and is formed by replacing each universal quantifier $\forall x.$ in A by $\forall x.\Phi(x) \supset$ and each existential quantifier $\exists x.$ by $\exists x.\Phi(x) \land$. $Axiom(\Phi)$ is the conjunction of sentences $\Phi(a)$ for each constant a and sentences $\forall x.(\Phi(x) \supset \Phi(f(x)))$ for each function symbol f and the corresponding sentences for functions of higher arities.

Domain circumscription can be reduced to predicate circumscription by relativizing A with respect to a new one place predicate called (say) *all*, then circumscribing *all* in $A^{all} \wedge Axiom(all)$, thus getting

$$Axiom(\Phi) \wedge A^{\Phi} \wedge \forall x.(\Phi(x) \supset all(x)) \supset \forall x.(all(x) \supset \Phi(x)). \tag{21}$$

Now we justify our using the name all by adding the axiom $\forall x.all(x)$ so that (21) then simplifies precisely to (20).

In the case of the natural numbers, the domain circumscription of true, the identically true sentence, again leads to the axiom schema of induction. Here *Axiom* does all the work, because it asserts that 0 is in the domain and that the domain is closed under the successor operation.

6. The Model Theory of Predicate Circumscription

This treatment is similar to Davis's [3] treatment of domain circumscription. Pat Hayes [4] pointed out that the same ideas would work.

The intuitive idea of circumscription is saying that a tuple $\bar{x}$ satisfies the predicate P only if it has to. It has to satisfy P if this follows from the sentence A. The model-theoretic counterpart of circumscription is *minimal entailment*. A sentence q is minimally entailed by A, iff q is true in all minimal models of A, where a model is minimal if as few as possible tuples $\bar{x}$ satisfy the predicate P. More formally, this works out as follows.

Definition. Let $M(A)$ and $N(A)$ be models of the sentence A. We say that *M is a submodel of N in P*, writing $M \leqslant_P N$, if M and N have the same domain, all other predicate symbols in A besides P have the same extensions in M and N, but the extension of P in M is included in its extension in N.

Definition. A model M of A is called *minimal in P* iff $M' \leqslant_P M$ only if $M' = M$. As discussed by Davis [3], minimal models do not always exist.

Definition. We say that *A minimally entails q with respect to P*, written $A \models_P q$ provided q is true in all models of A that are minimal in P.

Theorem. *Any instance of the circumscription of P in A is true in all models of A minimal in P, i.e., is minimally entailed by A in P.*

Proof. Let M be a model of A minimal in P. Let P' be a predicate satisfying the left side of (1) when substituted for Φ. By the second conjunct of the left side, P is an extension of P'. If the right side of (1) were not satisfied, P would be a proper extension of P'. In that case, we could get a proper submodel M' of M by letting M' agree with M on all predicates except P and agree with P' on P. This would contradict the assumed minimality of M.

Corollary. *If $A \vdash_P q$, then $A \models_P q$.*

While we have discussed minimal entailment in a single predicate P, the relation $<_{P,Q}$, models minimal in P and Q, and $\models_{P,Q}$ have corresponding properties and a corresponding relation to the syntactic notion $\vdash_{P,Q}$ mentioned earlier.

7. More on Blocks

The axiom

$$\forall x\, y\, s.(\forall z.\ \neg prevents(z, move(x, y), s) \supset on(x, y, result(move(x, y), s))) \tag{22}$$

states that unless something prevents it, x is on y in the situation that results from the action $move(x, y)$.

We now list various 'things' that may prevent this action.

$$\forall x\, y\, s.(\neg isblock\ x \vee \neg isblock\ y \supset prevents(NONBLOCK, move(x, y), s)) \tag{23}$$

$$\forall x\, y\, s.(\neg clear(x, s) \vee \neg clear(y, s) \supset prevents(COVERED, move(x, y), s)) \tag{24}$$

$$\forall x\, y\, s.(tooheavy\ x \supset prevents(weight\ x, move(x, y), s)). \tag{25}$$

Let us now suppose that a heuristic program would like to move block A onto block C in a situation $s0$. The program should conjecture from (22) that the action $move(A, C)$ would have the desired effect, so it must try to establish $\forall z.\neg prevents(z, move(A, C), s0)$. The predicate $\lambda z.prevents(z, move(A, C), s0)$ can be circumscribed in the conjunction of the sentences resulting from specializing (23), (24) and (25), and this gives

$$\begin{aligned}&(\neg isblock\ A \vee \neg isblock\ C \supset \Phi(NONBLOCK))\\ &\wedge (\neg clear(A, s0) \vee \neg clear(C, s0) \supset \Phi(COVERED))\\ &\wedge (tooheavy\ A \supset \Phi(weight\ A))\\ &\wedge \forall z.(\Phi(z) \supset prevents(z, move(A, C), s0))\\ &\quad \supset \forall z.(prevents(z, move(A, C), s0) \supset \Phi(z))\end{aligned} \tag{26}$$

which says that the only things that can prevent the move are the phenomena described in (23)–(25). Whether (26) is true depends on how good the program was in finding all the relevant statements. Since the program wants to show that nothing prevents the move, it must set $\forall z.(\Phi(z) \equiv false)$, after which (26) simplifies to

$$(isblock\ A \wedge isblock\ B \wedge clear(A, s0) \wedge clear(B, s0) \wedge \neg tooheavy\ A \supset \forall z.\neg prevents(z, move(A, C), s0). \tag{27}$$

We suppose that the premisses of this implication are to be obtained as follows:

(1) *isblock A* and *isblock B* are explicitly asserted.

(2) Suppose that the only *on*ness assertion explicitly given for situation $s0$ is $on(A, B, s0)$. Circumscription of $\lambda x\, y.on(x, y, s0)$ in this assertion gives

$$\Phi(A, B) \wedge \forall x\, y.(\Phi(x, y) \supset on(x, y, s0)) \supset \forall x\, y.(on(x, y, s0) \supset \Phi(x, y)), \tag{28}$$

and taking $\Phi(x, y) \equiv x = A \wedge y = B$ yields

$$\forall x\, y.(on(x, y, s0) \supset x = A \wedge y = B). \tag{29}$$

Using

$$\forall x\, s.(clear(x, s) \equiv \forall y. \neg on(y, x, s)) \tag{30}$$

as the definition of *clear* yields the second two desired premisses.

(3) $\neg$*tooheavy*(x) might be explicitly present or it might also be conjectured by a circumscription assuming that if x were too heavy, the facts would establish it.

Circumscription may also be convenient for asserting that when a block is moved, everything that cannot be proved to move stays where it was. In the simple blocks world, the effect of this can easily be achieved by an axiom that states that all blocks except the one that is moved stay put. However, if there are various sentences that say (for example) that one block is attached to another, circumscription may express the heuristic situation better than an axiom.

8. Remarks and Acknowledgments

(1) Circumscription is not a 'non-monotonic logic.' It is a form of non-monotonic reasoning augmenting ordinary first order logic. Of course, sentence schemata are not properly handled by most present general purpose resolution theorem provers. Even fixed schemata of mathematical induction when used for proving programs correct usually require human intervention or special heuristics, while here the program would have to use new schemata produced by circumscription. In [10] we treat some modalities in first order logic instead of in modal logic. In our opinion, it is better to avoid modifying the logic if at all possible, because there are many temptations to modify the logic, and it would be very difficult to keep them compatible.

(2) The default case reasoning provided in many systems is less general than circumscription. Suppose, for example, that a block x is considered to be on a block y only if this is explicitly stated, i.e., the default is that x is not on y. Then for each individual block x, we may be able to conclude that it isn't on block A, but we will not be able to conclude, as circumscription would allow, that there are no blocks on A. That would require a separate default statement that a block is clear unless something is stated to be on it.

(3) The conjunct $\forall \bar{x}.(\Phi(\bar{x}) \supset P(\bar{x}))$ in the premiss of (1) is the result of suggestions by Ashok Chandra [2] and Patrick Hayes [4] whom I thank for their help. Without it, circumscribing a disjunction, as in the second example in Section 4, would lead to a contradiction.

(4) The most direct way of using circumscription in AI is in a heuristic reasoning program that represents much of what it believes by sentences of logic. The program would sometimes apply circumscription to certain predicates in sentences. In particular, when it wants to perform an action that might be prevented by something, it circumscribes the prevention predicate in a sentence A representing the information being taken into account.

Clearly the program will have to include domain dependent heuristics for deciding what circumscriptions to make and when to take them back.

(5) In circumscription it does no harm to take irrelevant facts into account. If these facts do not contain the predicate symbol being circumscribed, they will appear as conjuncts on the left side of the implication unchanged. Therefore, the original versions of these facts can be used in proving the left side.

(6) Circumscription can be used in other formalisms than first order logic. Suppose for example that a set a satisfies a formula $A(a)$ of set theory. The circumscription of this formula can be taken to be

$$\forall x.(A(x) \wedge (x \subset a) \supset (a \subset x)). \tag{31}$$

If a occurs in $A(a)$ only in expressions of the form $z \in a$, then its mathematical properties should be analogous to those of predicate circumscription. We have not explored what happens if formulas like $a \in z$ occur.

(7) The results of circumscription depend on the set of predicates used to express the facts. For example, the same facts about the blocks world can be axiomatized using the relation *on* or the relation *above* considered in Section 4 or also in terms of the heights and horizontal positions of the blocks. Since the results of circumscription will differ according to which representation is chosen, we see that the choice of representation has epistemological consequences if circumscription is admitted as a rule of conjecture. Choosing the set of predicates in terms of which to axiomatize as set of facts, such as those about blocks, is like choosing a co-ordinate system in physics or geography. As discussed in [9], certain concepts are definable only relative to a theory. What theory admits the most useful kinds of circumscription may be an important criterion in the choice of predicates. It may also be possible to make some statements about a domain like the blocks world in a form that does not depend on the language used.

(8) This investigation was supported in part by ARPA Contract MDA-903-76-C-0206, ARPA Order No. 2494, in part by NSF Grant MCS 78-00524, in part by the IBM 1979 Distinguished Faculty Program at the T. J. Watson Research Center, and in part by the Center for Advanced Study in the Behavioral Sciences.

REFERENCES

1. Amarel, S., On representation of problems of reasoning about actions, in D. Michie (Ed.) *Machine Intelligence* 3 (Edinburgh University Press, Edinburgh, 1971), pp. 131–171.
2. Chandra, A., personal conversation (August 1979).
3. Davis, M., Notes on the mathematics of non-monotonic reasoning. *Artificial Intelligence*, this issue.

4. Hayes, P., personal conversation (September 1979).
5. Hewitt, C., Description and theoretical analysis (using schemata) of PLANNER: a language for proving theorems and manipulating models in a robot, MIT AI Laboratory TR-258 (1972).
6. McCarthy, J., Programs with common sense, in: *Proceedings of the Teddington Conference on the Mechanization of Thought Processes* (H.M. Stationery Office, London, 1960).
7. McCarthy, J., and Hayes, P., Some philosophical problems from the standpoint of Artificial Intelligence, in: D. Michie (Ed.), *Machine Intelligence* 4 (American Elsevier, New York, NY, 1969).
8. McCarthy, J., Epistemological problems of artificial intelligence, in: *Proceedings of the Fifth International Joint Conference on Artificial Intelligence* (MIT, Cambridge, MA, 1977).
9. McCarthy, J., Ascribing mental qualities to machines, in: M. Ringle (Ed.), *Philosophical Perspectives in Artificial Intelligence* (Harvester Press, July 1979).
10. McCarthy, J., First order theories of individual concepts and propositions, in: D. Michie (Ed.), *Machine Intelligence* 9 (University of Edinburgh Press, Edinburgh, 1979).
11. Reiter, R., A logic for default reasoning, *Artificial Intelligence*, this issue.
12. Sussman, G. J., Winograd, T., and Charniak, E., Micro-Planner Reference Manual, AI Memo 203, MIT AI Lab. (1971).

Addendum: Circumscription and other Non-Monotonic Formalisms

John McCarthy

Stanford University, Stanford, CA, U.S.A.

Circumscription and the non-monotonic reasoning formalisms of McDermott and Doyle (1980) and Reiter (1980) differ along two dimensions. First, circumscription is concerned with minimal models, and they are concerned with arbitrary models. It appears that these approaches solve somewhat different though overlapping classes of problems, and each has its uses. The other difference is that the reasoning of both other formalisms involves models directly, while the syntactic formulation of circumscription uses axiom schemata. Consequently, their systems are incompletely formal unless the metamathematics is also formalized, and this has not yet been done.

However, schemata are applicable to other formalisms than circumscription. Suppose, for example, that we have some axioms about trains and their presence on tracks, and we wish to express the fact that if a train may be present, it is unsafe to cross the tracks. In the McDermott–Doyle formalism, this might be expressed

$$\mathsf{M}\ on\ (train,\ tracks) \supset \neg safe\text{-}to\text{-}cross\ (tracks), \tag{1}$$

where the properties of the predicate *on* are supposed expressed in a formula that we may call *Axiom* (*on*). The M in (1) stands for 'is possible.' We propose to replace (1) and *Axiom* (*on*) by the schema

$$Axiom(\Phi) \wedge \Phi\ (train,\ tracks) \supset \neg safe\text{-}to\text{-}cross\ (tracks), \tag{2}$$

where Φ is a predicate parameter that can be replaced by any predicate expression that can be written in the language being used. If we can find a Φ that makes the left hand side of (2) provable, then we can be sure that *Axiom* (*on*) together with *on* (*train, tracks*) has a model assuming that *Axiom* (*on*) is consistent. Therefore, the schema (2) is essentially a consequence of the McDermott–Doyle formula (1). The converse is not true. A predicate symbol may have a model without there being an explicit formula realizing it. I believe, however, that the schema is usable in all cases where the McDermott–Doyle or Reiter formalisms can be practically applied, and, in particular, to all the examples in their papers.

(If one wants a counter-example to the usability of the schema, one might look at the membership relation of set theory with Gödel–Bernays set theory as the axiom. Instantiating Φ in this case would amount to giving an internal model of set theory, and this is possible only in a stronger theory).

It appears that such use of schemata amounts to importing part of the model theory of a subject into the theory itself. It looks useful and even essential for common sense reasoning, but its logical properties are not obvious.

We can also go frankly to second order logic and write

$$\exists\Phi\,.\,(\mathit{Axiom}\ (\Phi) \wedge \mathit{on}\ (\mathit{train},\ \mathit{tracks}) \supset \neg \mathit{safe\text{-}to\text{-}cross}\ (\mathit{tracks})). \qquad (3)$$

Second order reasoning, which might be in set theory or a formalism admitting concepts as objects rather than in second order logic, seems to have the advantage that some of the predicate and function symbols may be left fixed and others imitated by predicate parameters. This allows us to say something like, "For any interpretation of P and Q satisfying the axiom A, if there is an interpretation in which R and S satisfy the additional axiom A', then it is unsafe to cross the tracks." This maybe needed to express common sense non-monotonic reasoning and it seems more powerful than any of the above-mentioned non-monotonic formalisms including circumscription.

The train example is a non-normal default in Reiter's sense, because we cannot conclude that the train is on the tracks in the absence of evidence to the contrary. Indeed, suppose that we want to wait for and catch a train at a station across the tracks. If there might be a train coming we will take a bridge rather than a shortcut across the tracks, but we don't want to jump to the conclusion that there is a train, because then we would think we were too late and give up trying to catch it. The statement can be reformulated as a normal default by writing

$$\mathsf{M}\ \neg \mathit{safe\text{-}to\text{-}cross}\ (\mathit{tracks}) \supset \neg \mathit{safe\text{-}to\text{-}cross}\ (\mathit{tracks}), \qquad (4)$$

but this is unlikely to be equivalent in all cases and the non-normal expression seems to express better the common sense facts.

Like normal defaults, circumscription doesn't deal with possibility directly, and a circumscriptive treatment of the train problem would involve circumscribing *safe-to-cross* (*tracks*) in the set of axioms. It therefore might not be completely satisfactory.

ADDENDUM TO REFERENCES

1. McDermott, Drew and Jon Doyle, Non-monotonic logic I, *Artificial Intelligence*, **13** (1, 2) (1980), 41–72. (This issue.)
2. Reiter, R., A logic for default reasoning, *Artificial Intelligence*, **13** (1, 2), 81–132. (This issue.)

Applications of Circumscription to Formalizing Common-Sense Knowledge

John McCarthy
Department of Computer Science, Stanford University, Stanford, CA 94305–2095, U.S.A.

Recommended by Ray Reiter

ABSTRACT

We present a new and more symmetric version of the circumscription method of non-monotonic reasoning first described by McCarthy [9] and some applications to formalizing common-sense knowledge. The applications in this paper are mostly based on minimizing the abnormality of different aspects of various entities. Included are non-monotonic treatments of "is-a" hierarchies, the unique names hypothesis, and the frame problem. The new circumscription may be called formula circumscription *to distinguish it from the previously defined* domain circumscription *and* predicate circumscription. *A still more general formalism called* prioritized circumscription *is briefly explored.*

1. Introduction and New Definition of Circumscription

McCarthy introduced in [9], the circumscription method of non-monotonic reasoning and gave motivation, some mathematical properties and some examples of its application. The present paper is logically self-contained, but motivation may be enhanced by reading the earlier paper. We don't repeat its arguments about the importance of non-monotonic reasoning in AI, and its examples are instructive.

Here we give a more symmetric definition of circumscription and applications to the formal expression of common-sense facts. Our long-term goal (far from realized in the present paper) is to express these facts in a way that would be suitable for inclusion in a general-purpose database of common-sense knowledge. We imagine this database to be used by AI programs written after the initial preparation of the database. It would be best if the writers of these programs didn't have to be familiar with how the common-sense facts about particular phenomena are expressed. Thus common-sense knowledge must be represented in a way that is not specific to a particular application.

It turns out that many such common-sense facts can be formalized in a uniform way. A single predicate *ab*, standing for "abnormal," is circumscribed with certain other predicates and functions considered as variables that can be constrained to achieve the circumscription subject to the axioms. This also seems to cover the use of circumscription to represent default rules.

Artificial Intelligence **28** (1986) 89–116
0004-3702/86/$3.50

2. A New Version of Circumscription

Definition 2.1 Let $A(P)$ be a formula of second-order logic, where P is a tuple of some of the free predicate symbols in $A(P)$. Let $E(P, x)$ be a wff in which P and a tuple x of individual variables occur free. The circumscription of $E(P, x)$ relative to $A(P)$ is the formula $A'(P)$ defined by

$$A(P) \wedge \forall P'.[A(P') \wedge [\forall x.E(P',x) \supset E(P,x)] \supset [\forall x.E(P',X) \equiv E(P,X)]] . \tag{1}$$

[We are here writing $A(P)$ instead of $A(P_1, \ldots, P_n)$ for brevity and likewise writing $E(P, x)$ instead of $E(P_1, \ldots, P_n, x_1, \ldots, x_m)$]. Likewise the quantifier $\forall x$ stands for $\forall x_1 \ldots x_m$. $A(P)$ may have embedded quantifiers. Circumscription is a kind of minimization, and the predicate symbols in $A(P)$ that are not in P itself act as parameters in this minimization. When we wish to mention these other predicates we write $A(P; Q)$ and $E(P; Q, x)$, where Q is a vector of predicate symbols which are not allowed to be varied.

There are two differences between this paper and [9]. First, in the latter paper $E(P, x)$ had the specific form $P(x)$. Here we speak of circumscribing a wff and call the method *formula circumscription*, while there we could speak of circumscribing a predicate. We still speak of circumscribing the predicate P when $E(P, x)$ has the special form $P(x)$. Formula circumscription is more symmetric in that any of the predicate symbols in P may be regarded as variables, and a wff is minimized; the earlier form distinguishes one of the predicates themselves for minimization. However, formula circumscription is reducible to predicate circumscription provided we allow as variables predicates besides the one being minimized.

Second, in definition (1) we use an explicit quantifier for the predicate variable P' whereas in [9] the formula was a schema. One advantage of the present formalism is that now $A'(P)$ is the same kind of formula as $A(P)$ and can be used as part of the axiom for circumscribing some other wff.

In some of the literature, it has been supposed that non-monotonic reasoning involves giving all predicates their minimum extension. This mistake has led to theorems about what reasoning cannot be done that are irrelevant to AI and database theory, because their premisses are too narrow.

3. A Typology of Uses of Non-Monotonic Reasoning

Before proceeding to applications of circumscription I want to suggest a typology of the uses of non-monotonic reasoning. Each of the several papers that introduces a mode of non-monotonic reasoning seems to have a particular application in mind. Perhaps we are looking at different parts of an elephant. The orientation is towards circumscription, but I suppose the considerations apply to other formalisms as well.

Non-monotonic reasoning has several uses.

(1) As a communication convention. Suppose A tells B about a situation involving a bird. If the bird cannot fly, and this is relevant, then A must say so. Whereas if the bird can fly, there is no requirement to mention the fact. For example, if I hire you to build me a bird cage and you don't put a top on it, I can get out of paying for it even if you tell the judge that I never said my bird could fly. However, if I complain that you wasted money by putting a top on a cage I intended for a penguin, the judge will agree with you that if the bird couldn't fly I should have said so.

The proposed Common Business Communication Language (CBCL) [10] must include non-monotonic conventions about what may be inferred when a message leaves out such items as the method of delivery.

(2) As a database or information storage convention. It may be a convention of a particular database that certain predicates have their minimal extension. This generalizes the closed-world assumption. When a database makes the closed-world assumption for all predicates it is reasonable to imbed this fact in the programs that use the database. However, when only some predicates are to be minimized, we need to say which ones by appropriate sentences of the database, perhaps as a preamble to the collection of ground sentences that usually constitute the main content.

Neither (1) nor (2) requires that most birds can fly. Should it happen that most birds that are subject to the communication or about which information is requested from the database cannot fly, the convention may lead to inefficiency but not incorrectness.

(3) As a rule of conjecture. This use was emphasized in [9]. The circumscriptions may be regarded as expressions of some probabilistic notions such as "most birds can fly" or they may be expressions of standard cases. Thus it is simple to conjecture that there are no relevant present material objects other than those whose presence can be inferred. It is also a simple conjecture that a tool asserted to be present is usable for its normal function. Such conjectures sometimes conflict, but there is nothing wrong with having incompatible conjectures on hand. Besides the possibility of deciding that one is correct and the other wrong, it is possible to use one for generating possible exceptions to the other.

(4) As a representation of a policy. The example is Doyle's "The meeting will be on Wednesday unless another decision is explicitly made." Again probabilities are not involved.

(5) As a very streamlined expression of probabilistic information when numerical probabilities, especially conditional probabilities, are unobtainable. Since circumscription doesn't provide numerical probabilities, its probabilistic interpretation involves probabilities that are either infinitesimal, within an infinitesimal of one, or intermediate—without any discrimination among the intermediate values. The circumscriptions give conditional probabilities. Thus we may treat the probability that a bird can't fly as an infinitesimal. However, if the rare event occurs that the bird is a penguin, then the conditional probability that it can fly is infinitesimal, but we may hear of some rare condition that would allow it to fly after all.

Why don't we use finite probabilities combined by the usual laws? That would be fine if we had the numbers, but circumscription is usable when we can't get the numbers or find their use inconvenient. Note that the general probability that a bird can fly may be irrelevant, because we are interested in the facts that influence our opinion about whether a particular bird can fly in a particular situation.

Moreover, the use of probabilities is normally considered to require the definition of a sample space, i.e. the space of all possibilities. Circumscription allows one to conjecture that the cases we know about are all that there are. However, when additional cases are found, the axioms don't have to be changed. Thus there is no fixed space of all possibilities.

Notice also that circumscription does not provide for weighing evidence; it is appropriate when the information permits snap decisions. However, many cases nominally treated in terms of weighing information are in fact cases in which the weights are such that circumscription and other defaults work better.

(6) Auto-epistemic reasoning. "If I had an elder brother, I'd know it." This has been studied by R. Moore. Perhaps it can be handled by circumscription.

(7) Both common-sense physics and common-sense psychology use non-monotonic rules. An object will continue in a straight line if nothing interferes with it. A person will eat when hungry unless something prevents it. Such rules are open ended about what might prevent the expected behavior, and this is required, because we are always encountering unexpected phenomena that modify the operation of our rules. Science, as distinct from common sense, tries to work with exceptionless rules. However, this means that common-sense reasoning has to decide when a scientific model is applicable, i.e. that there are no important phenomena not taken into account by the theories being used and the model of the particular phenomena.

Seven different uses for non-monotonic reasoning seem too many, so perhaps we can condense later.

4. Minimizing Abnormality

Many people have proposed representing facts about what is "normally" the case. One problem is that every object is abnormal in some way, and we want to allow some aspects of the object to be abnormal and still assume the normality of the rest. We do this with a predicate *ab* standing for "abnormal." We circumscribe *ab z*. The argument of *ab* will be some aspect of the entities involved. Some aspects can be abnormal without affecting others. The aspects themselves are abstract entities, and their unintuitiveness is somewhat a blemish on the theory.

The idea is illustrated by the examples of the following sections.

5. Whether Birds Can Fly

Marvin Minsky challenged us, advocates of formal systems based on mathematical logic, to express the facts and non-monotonic reasoning concerning the ability of birds to fly.

There are many ways of non-monotonically axiomatizing the facts about which birds can fly. The following axioms using *ab* seem to me quite straightforward.

$$\forall x. \neg\, ab\ aspect1\ x \supset \neg\, flies\ x. \tag{2}$$

Unless an object is abnormal in *aspect1*, it can't fly. (We're using a convention that parentheses may be omitted for functions and predicates of one argument, so that (2) is the same as $\forall x.(\neg\, ab(aspect1(x)) \supset \neg flies(x))$.)

It wouldn't work to write *ab x* instead of *ab aspect1 x*, because we don't want a bird that is abnormal with respect to its ability to fly to be automatically abnormal in other respects. Using aspects limits the effects of proofs of abnormality.

$$\forall x. bird\ x \supset ab\ aspect1\ x. \tag{3}$$

$$\forall x. bird\ x \wedge \neg\, ab\ aspect2\ x \supset flies\ x. \tag{4}$$

Unless a bird is abnormal in *aspect2*, it can fly.

A bird is abnormal in *aspect1*, so (2) can't be used to show it can't fly. If (3) were omitted when we did the circumscription, we would only be able to infer a disjunction. Either a bird is abnormal in *aspect1* or it can fly unless it is abnormal in *aspect2*. Axiom (3) expresses our preference for inferring that a bird is abnormal in *aspect1* rather than *aspect2*. We call (3) a *cancellation of inheritance* axiom.

$$\forall x. ostrich\ x \supset ab\ aspect2\ x. \tag{5}$$

Ostriches are abnormal in *aspect2*. This doesn't say that an ostrich cannot fly—merely that (4) can't be used to infer that it does. Axiom (5) is another cancellation of inheritance axiom.

$$\forall x. penguin\ x \supset ab\ aspect2\ x. \tag{6}$$

Penguins are also abnormal in *aspect2*.

$$\forall x. ostrich\ x \wedge \neg\, ab\ aspect3\ x \supset \neg\, flies\ x. \tag{7}$$

$$\forall x. penguin\ x \wedge \neg\, ab\ aspect4\ x \supset \neg\, flies\ x. \tag{8}$$

Normally ostriches and penguins can't fly. However, there is an out. Axioms (7) and (8) provide that, under unspecified conditions, an ostrich or penguin might fly after all. If we give no such conditions, we will conclude that an ostrich or penguin can't fly. Additional objects that can fly may be specified. Each needs two axioms. The first says that it is abnormal in *aspect1* and prevents (2) from being used to say that it can't fly. The second provides that it can fly unless it is abnormal in yet another way. Additional non-flying birds can also be provided for at a cost of two axioms per kind.

We haven't yet said that ostriches and penguins are birds, so let's do that and throw in that canaries are birds also.

$$\forall x. ostrich\ x \supset bird\ x. \tag{9}$$

$$\forall x. penguin\ x \supset bird\ x. \tag{10}$$

$$\forall x. canary\ x \supset bird\ x. \tag{11}$$

Asserting that ostriches, penguins and canaries are birds will help inherit other properties from the class of birds. For example, we have

$$\forall x. bird\ x \wedge \neg\, ab\ aspect6\ x \supset feathered\ x. \tag{12}$$

So far there is nothing to prevent ostriches, penguins and canaries from overlapping. We could write disjointness axioms like

$$\forall x. \neg\, ostrich\ x \vee \neg\, penguin\ x, \tag{13}$$

but we require n^2 of them if we have n species. It is more efficient to write axioms like

$$\forall x. ostrich\ x \supset species\ x = {'ostrich}, \tag{14}$$

which makes the n species disjoint with only n axioms assuming that the distinctness of the names is apparent to the reasoner. This problem is like the unique names problem.

If these are the only facts to be taken into account, we must somehow specify that what can fly is to be determined by circumscribing the wff *ab z* using *ab* and *flies* as variables. Why exactly these? If *ab* were not taken as variable, *ab z* couldn't vary either, and the minimization problem would go away. Since the purpose of the axiom set is to describe what flies, the predicate *flies* must be varied also. Suppose we contemplate taking *bird* as variable also. In the first place, this violates an intuition that deciding what flies follows deciding what is a bird in the common-sense situations we want to cover. Secondly, if we use exactly the above axioms and admit bird as a variable, we will further conclude that the only birds are penguins, canaries and ostriches. Namely, for these entities something has to be abnormal, and therefore minimizing *ab z* will involve making as few entities as possible penguins, canaries and ostriches. If we also admit *penguin*, *ostrich*, and *canary* as variable, we will succeed in making *ab z* always false, and there will be no birds at all.

However, if the same circumscriptions are done with additional axioms like *canary Tweety* and *ostrich Joe*, we will get the expected result that Tweety can fly and Joe cannot even if all the above are variable.

While this works, it may be more straightforward, and therefore less likely to lead to subsequent trouble, to circumscribe birds, ostriches and penguins with axioms like

$$\forall x. \neg\, ab\ aspect8\ x \supset \neg\, bird\ x. \tag{15}$$

We have not yet specified how a program will know what to circumscribe. One extreme is to build it into the program, but this is contrary to the declarative spirit. However, a statement of what to circumscribe isn't just a sentence of the language because of its non-monotonic character. Another possibility is to include some sort of metamathematical statement like

$$circumscribe(ab\ z;\ ab, flies, bird, ostrich, penguin) \tag{16}$$

in a "policy" database available to the program. Axiom (16) is intended to mean that *ab z* is to be circumscribed with *ab, flies, bird, ostrich* and *penguin* taken as variable. Explicitly listing the variables makes adding new kinds awkward, since they will have to be mentioned in the *circumscribe* statement. Section 11 on *simple abnormality theories* presents yet another possibility.

6. The Unique Names Hypothesis

Raymond Reiter [12] introduced the phrase "unique names hypothesis" for the assumption that each object has a unique name, i.e. that distinct names denote distinct objects. We want to treat this non-monotonically. Namely, we want a wff that picks out those models of our initial assumptions that maximize the inequality of the denotations of constant symbols. While we're at it, we might as well try for something stronger. We want to maximize the extent to which distinct terms designate distinct objects. When there is a unique model of the axioms that maximizes distinctness, we can put it more simply; two terms denote distinct objects unless the axioms force them to denote the same. If we are even more fortunate, as we are in the examples to be given, we can say that two terms denote distinct objects unless their equality is provable.

We don't know a completely satisfactory way of doing this. Suppose that we have a language L and a theory T consisting of the consequences of a formula A. It would be most pleasant if we could just circumscribe equality, but as Etherington, Mercer and Reiter [1] point out, this doesn't work, and nothing similar works. We could hope to circumscribe some other formula of L, but this doesn't seem to work either. Failing that, we could hope for some other second-order formula taken from L that would express the unique names hypothesis, but we don't presently see how to do it.

Our solution involves extending the language by introducing the names themselves as the only objects. All assertions about objects are expressed as assertions about the names.

We suppose our theory is such that the names themselves are all provably distinct. There are several ways of doing this. Let the names be n_1, n_2, etc. The simplest solution is to have an axiom $n_i \neq n_j$ for each pair of distinct names. This requires a number of axioms proportional to the square of the number of names, which is sometimes objectionable. The next solution involves introducing an arbitrary ordering on the names. We have special axioms $n_1 < n_2$, $n_2 < n_3$, $n_3 < n_4$, etc. and the general axioms

$$\forall x\ y. x < y \supset x \neq Y \quad \text{and} \quad \forall x\ y\ z. x < y \wedge y < z \supset x < z.$$

This makes the number of axioms proportional to the number of names. A third possibility involves mapping the names onto integers with axioms like

$$index\ n_1 = 1, \qquad index\ n_2 = 2, \quad \text{etc.}$$

and using a theory of the integers that provides for their distinctness. The fourth possibility involves using string constants for the names and "attaching" to equality in the language a subroutine that computes whether two strings are equal. If our names were quoted symbols as in LISP, this amounts to having $'a \neq 'b$ and all its countable infinity of analogs as axioms. Each of these devices is useful in appropriate circumstances.

From the point of view of mathematical logic there is no harm in having an infinity of such axioms. From the computational point of view of a theorem-proving or problem-solving program, we merely suppose that we rely on the computer to generate the assertion that two names are distinct whenever this is required, since a subroutine can easily tell whether two strings are the same.

Besides axiomatizing the distinctness of the constants, we also want to axiomatize the distinctness of terms. This may be accomplished by providing for each function two axioms. Letting *foo* be a function of two arguments we postulate

$$\forall x_1 \ x_2 \ y_1 \ y_2 . foo(x_1,y_1) = foo(x_2,y_2) \supset x_1 = x_2 \land y_1 = y_2 \qquad (17)$$

and

$$\forall x \ y . fname \ foo(x,y) = {'foo}. \qquad (18)$$

The first axiom ensures that unless the arguments of *foo* are identical, its values are distinct. The second ensures that the values of *foo* are distinct from the values of any other function or any constant, assuming that we refrain from naming any constant *'foo.*

These axioms amount to making our domain isomorphic to an extension of the Herbrand universe of the language.

Now that the names are guaranteed distinct, what about the objects they denote? We introduce a predicate $e(x, y)$ and axiomatize it to be an equivalence relation. Its intended interpretation is that the names x and y denote the same object. We then formulate all our usual axioms in terms of names rather than in terms of objects. Thus $on(n_1,n_2)$ means that the object named by n_1 is on the object named by n_2, and *bird* x means that the name x denotes a bird. We add axioms of substitutivity for e with regard to those predicates and functions that are translates of predicates referring to objects rather than predicates on the names themselves. Thus for a predicate *on* and a function *foo* we may have axioms

$$\forall n_1 \ n_2 \ n_1' \ n_2' . e(n_1,n_1') \land e(n_2,n_2') \supset (on(n_1,n_2) \equiv on(n_1', n_2')) \qquad (19)$$

and

$$\forall x_1 \ x_2 \ y_1 \ y_2 . e(x_1,x_2) \land e(y_1,y_2) \supset e(foo(x_1,y_1),foo(x_2,y_2)) . \qquad (20)$$

If for some class C of names, we wish to assert the unique names hypothesis, we simply use an axiom like

$$\forall n_1 \ n_2 . n_1 \in C \land n_2 \in C \supset (e(n_1,n_2) \equiv n_1 = n_2) . \qquad (21)$$

However, we often want only to assume that distinct names denote distinct objects when this doesn't contradict our other assumptions. In general, our axioms won't permit making all names distinct simultaneously, and there will be several models with maximally distinct objects. The simplest example is obtained by circumscribing $e(x,y)$ while adhering to the axiom

$$e(n_1,n_2) \lor e(n_1,n_3) \qquad (22)$$

where n_1,n_2, and n_3 are distinct names. There will then be two models, one satisfying $e(n_1,n_2) \land \neg e(n_1,n_3)$ and the other satisfying $\neg e(n_1,n_2) \land e(n_1,n_3)$. Thus circumscribing $e(x,y)$ maximizes uniqueness of names. If we only want unique names for some class C of names, then we circumscribe the formula

$$x \in C \land y \in C \supset e(x,y) .$$

An example of such a circumscription is given in Appendix B. However, there seems to be a price. Part of the price is admitting names as objects. Another part is admitting the predicate $e(x,y)$ which is substitutive for predicates and functions of names that really are about the objects denoted by the names. $e(x,y)$ is not to be taken as substitutive for predicates on names that aren't about the objects. Of these our only present example is equality. Thus we don't have

$$\forall n_1 \ n_2 \ n_1' \ n_2' . e(n_1, n_1') \land e(n_2, n_2') \supset (n_1 = n_2 \equiv n_1' = n_2') . \qquad (*)$$

The awkward part of the price is that we must refrain from any functions whose values are the objects themselves rather than names. They would spoil the circumscription by not allowing us to infer the distinctness of the objects denoted by distinct names. Actually, we can allow them provided we don't include the axioms involving them in the circumspection. Unfortunately, this spoils the other property of circumscription that lets us take any facts into account.

The examples of the use of circumscription in AI in the rest of the paper don't interpret the variables as merely ranging over names. Therefore, they are incompatible with getting unique names by circumscription as described in this section. Presumably it wouldn't be very difficult to revise those axioms for compatibility with the present approach to unique names.

7. Two Examples of Raymond Reiter

Reiter asks about representing, "Quakers are normally pacifists and Republicans are normally non-pacifists. How about Nixon, who is both a Quaker and a Republican?" Systems of non-monotonic reasoning that use non-provability as a basis for inferring negation will infer that Nixon is neither a pacifist nor a non-pacifist. Combining these conclusions with the original premiss leads to a contradiction. We use

$$\forall x . quaker \ x \land \neg \ ab \ aspect1 \ x \supset pacifist \ x , \qquad (23)$$

$$\forall x . republican \ x \land \neg \ ab \ aspect2 \ x \supset \neg \ pacifist \ x \qquad (24)$$

and

$$\mathit{quaker}\ \mathit{Nixon} \wedge \mathit{republican}\ \mathit{Nixon}. \tag{25}$$

When we circumscribe *ab z* using these three sentences as *A*(*ab*,*pacifist*), we will only be able to conclude that Nixon is either abnormal in *aspect*1 or in *aspect*2, and we will not be able to say whether he is a pacifist. Of course, this is the same conclusion as would be reached without circumscription. The point is merely that we avoid contradiction.

Reiter's second example is that a person normally lives in the same city as his wife and in the same city as his employer. But A's wife lives in Vancouver and A's employer is in Toronto. We write

$$\forall x. \neg\, \mathit{ab}\ \mathit{aspect}1\ x \supset \mathit{city}\ x = \mathit{city}\ \mathit{wife}\ x \tag{26}$$

and

$$\forall x. \neg\, \mathit{ab}\ \mathit{aspect}2\ x \supset \mathit{city}\ x = \mathit{city}\ \mathit{employer}\ x. \tag{27}$$

If we have

$$\mathit{city}\ \mathit{wife}\ A = \mathit{Vancouver}$$
$$\wedge\, \mathit{city}\ \mathit{employer}\ A = \mathit{Toronto} \wedge \mathit{Toronto} \neq \mathit{Vancouver}, \tag{28}$$

We will again only be able to conclude that A lives either in Toronto or Vancouver. In this circumscription, the function *city* must be taken as variable. This might be considered not entirely satisfactory. If one knows that a person either doesn't live in the same city as his wife or doesn't live in the same city as his employer, then there is an increased probability that he doesn't live in the same city as either. A system that did reasoning of this kind would seem to require a larger body of facts and perhaps more explicitly metamathematical reasoning. Not knowing how to do that, we might want to use *aspect*1 *x* in both (26) and (27). Then we would conclude nothing about his city once we knew that he wasn't in the same city as both.

8. A More General Treatment of An *is-a* Hierarchy

The bird example works fine when a fixed *is-a* hierarchy is in question. However, our writing the inheritance cancellation axioms depended on knowing exactly from what higher level the properties were inherited. This doesn't correspond to my intuition of how we humans represent inheritance. It would seem rather that when we say that birds can fly, we don't necessarily have in mind that an inheritance of inability to fly from things in general is being cancelled. We can formulate inheritance of properties in a more general way provided we reify the properties. Presumably there are many ways of doing this, but here's one that seems to work.

The first-order variables of our theory range over classes of objects (denoted by *c* with numerical suffixes), properties (denoted by *p*) and objects (denoted by *x*). We don't identify our classes with sets (or with the classes of Gödel–Bernays set theory). In particular, we don't assume extensionality. We have several predicates: *ordinarily*(*c*,*p*) means that objects of class *c* ordinarily have property *p*. $c1 \leq c2$ means that class *c*1 ordinarily inherits from class *c*2. We assume that this relation is transitive. *in*(*x*,*c*) means that the object *x* is in class *c*. *ap*(*p*,*x*) means that property *p* applies to object *x*. Our axioms are

$$\forall c1\ c2\ c3. c1 \leq c2 \wedge c2 \leq c3 \supset c1 \leq c3, \tag{29}$$

$$\forall c1\ c2\ p. \mathit{ordinarily}(c2,p) \wedge c1 \leq c2 \wedge \neg\, \mathit{ab}\ \mathit{aspect}1(c1,c2,p)$$
$$\supset \mathit{ordinarily}(c1,p), \tag{30}$$

$$\forall c1\ c2\ c3\ p. c1 \leq c2 \wedge c2 \leq c3 \wedge \mathit{ordinarily}(c2,\mathit{not}\ p)$$
$$\supset \mathit{ab}\ \mathit{aspect}1(c1,c3,p), \tag{31}$$

$$\forall x\ c\ p. \mathit{in}(x,c) \wedge \mathit{ordinarily}(c,p) \wedge \neg\, \mathit{ab}\ \mathit{aspect}2(x,c,p)$$
$$\supset \mathit{ap}(p,x), \tag{32}$$

$$\forall x\ c1\ c2\ p. \mathit{in}(x,c1) \wedge c1 \leq c2 \wedge \mathit{ordinarily}(c1,\mathit{not}\ p)$$
$$\supset \mathit{ab}\ \mathit{aspect}2(x,c2,p) \tag{33}$$

Axiom (29) is the afore-mentioned transitivity of $\leq$. Axiom (30) says that properties that ordinarily hold for a class are inherited unless something is abnormal. Axiom (31) cancels the inheritance if there is an intermediate class for which the property ordinarily doesn't hold. Axiom (32) says that properties which ordinarily hold actually hold for elements of the class unless something is abnormal. Axiom (33) cancels the effect of (32) when there is an intermediate class for which the negation of the property ordinarily holds. Notice that this reification of properties seems to require imitation Boolean operators. Such operators are discussed in [8].

9. The Blocks World

The following set of "situation calculus" axioms solves the frame problem for a blocks world in which blocks can be moved and painted. Here *result*(*e*,*s*) denotes the situation that results when event *e* occurs in situation *s*. The formalism is approximately that of McCarthy and Hayes [6].

$$\forall x\ e\ s.\neg ab\ aspect1(x,e,s) \supset location(x,result(e,s)) = location(x,s)\,. \tag{34}$$

$$\forall x\ e\ s.\neg ab\ aspect2(x,e,s) \supset color(x,result(e,s)) = color(x,s)\,. \tag{35}$$

Objects change their locations and colors only for a reason.

$$\forall x\ l\ s.ab\ aspect1(x,move(x,l),s) \tag{36}$$

and

$$\forall x\ l\ s.\neg ab\ aspect3(x,l,s) \supset location(x,result(move(x,l),s)) = l\,.$$

$$\forall x\ c\ s.ab\ aspect2(x,paint(x,c),s) \tag{37}$$

and

$$\forall x\ c\ s.\neg ab\ aspect4(x,c,s) \supset color(x,result(paint(x,c),s)) = c\,.$$

Objects change their locations when moved and their colors when painted.

$$\forall x\ l\ s.\neg clear(top\ x,s) \vee \neg clear(l,s) \vee tooheavy\ x \vee l = top\ x \supset ab\ aspect3(x,move(x,l),s)\,. \tag{38}$$

This prevents the rule (36) from being used to infer than an object will move if its top isn't clear or to a destination that isn't clear or if the object is too heavy. An object also cannot be moved to its own top.

$$\forall l\ s.clear(l,s) \equiv \neg \exists x.(\neg trivial\ x \wedge location(x,s) = l)\,. \tag{39}$$

A location is clear if all the objects there are trivial, e.g. a speck of dust.

$$\forall x.\neg ab\ aspect7\ x \supset \neg trivial\ x\,. \tag{40}$$

Trivial objects are abnormal in *aspect7*).

10. An Example of Doing the Circumscription

In order to keep the example short we will take into account only the following facts from the earlier section on flying.

$$\forall x.\neg ab\ aspect1\ x \supset \neg flies\ x\,. \tag{2}$$

$$\forall x.bird\ x \supset ab\ aspect1\ x \tag{3}$$

$$\forall x.bird\ x \wedge \neg ab\ aspect2\ x \supset flies\ x\,. \tag{4}$$

$$\forall x.ostrich\ x \supset ab\ aspect2\ x\,. \tag{5}$$

$$\forall x.ostrich\ x \wedge \neg ab\ aspect3\ x \supset \neg flies\ x\,. \tag{7}$$

Their conjunction is taken as $A(ab,flies)$. This means that what entities satisfy *ab* and what entities satisfy *flies* are to be chosen so as to minimize *ab z*. Which objects are birds and ostriches are parameters rather than variables, i.e. what objects are birds is considered given.

We also need an axiom that asserts that the aspects are different. Here is a straightforward version that would be rather long were there more than three aspects.

$$\begin{aligned}
&(\forall x\ y.\neg(aspect1\ x = aspect2\ y))\\
&\wedge (\forall x\ y.\neg(aspect1\ x = aspect3\ y))\\
&\wedge (\forall x\ y.\neg(aspect2\ x = aspect3\ y))\\
&\wedge (\forall x\ y.aspect1\ x = aspect1\ y \equiv x = y)\\
&\wedge (\forall x\ y.aspect2\ x = aspect2\ y \equiv x = y)\\
&\wedge (\forall x\ y.aspect3\ x = aspect3\ y \equiv x = y)\,.
\end{aligned}$$

We could include this axiom in $A(ab,flies)$, but as we shall see, it won't matter whether we do, because it contains neither *ab* nor *flies*. The circumscription formula $A'(ab,flies)$ is then

$$A(ab,flies) \wedge \forall ab'\ flies'.[A(ab',flies') \wedge [\forall x.ab'\ x \supset ab\ x] \supset [\forall x.ab\ x \equiv ab'\ x]]\,, \tag{41}$$

which spelled out becomes

$$\begin{aligned}
&[\forall x.\neg ab\ aspect1\ x \supset \neg flies\ x]\\
&\wedge [\forall x.bird\ x \supset ab\ aspect1\ x]\\
&\wedge [\forall x.bird\ x \wedge \neg ab\ aspect2\ x \supset flies\ x]\\
&\wedge [\forall x.ostrich\ x \supset ab\ aspect2\ x]
\end{aligned}$$

$$\begin{aligned}
&\wedge [\forall x.ostrich\ x \wedge \neg ab\ aspect3\ x \supset \neg flies\ x]\\
&\wedge \forall ab'\ flies'.[[\forall x. \neg ab'\ aspect1\ x \supset \neg flies'\ x] \qquad (42)\\
&\qquad \wedge [\forall x.bird\ x \supset ab'\ aspect1\ x]\\
&\qquad \wedge [\forall x.bird\ x \wedge \neg ab'\ aspect2\ x \supset flies'\ x]\\
&\qquad \wedge [\forall x.ostrich\ x \supset ab'\ aspect2\ x]\\
&\qquad \wedge [\forall x.ostrich\ x \wedge \neg ab'\ aspect3\ x \supset \neg flies'\ x]\\
&\qquad \wedge [\forall z.ab'\ z \supset ab\ z]\\
&\qquad \supset [\forall z.ab\ z \equiv ab'\ z]] .
\end{aligned}$$

$A(ab,flies)$ is guaranteed to be true, because it is part of what is assumed in our common-sense database. Therefore (42) reduces to

$$\begin{aligned}
&\forall ab'\ flies'.[[\forall x. \neg ab'\ aspect1\ x \supset \neg flies'\ x]\\
&\qquad \wedge [\forall x.bird\ x \supset ab'\ aspect1\ x]\\
&\qquad \wedge [\forall x.bird\ x \wedge \neg ab'\ aspect2\ x \supset flies'\ x]\\
&\qquad \wedge [\forall x.ostrich\ x \supset ab'\ aspect2\ x]\\
&\qquad \wedge [\forall x.ostrich\ x \wedge \neg ab'\ aspect3\ x \supset \neg flies'\ x]\\
&\qquad \wedge [\forall z.ab'\ z \supset ab\ z]\\
&\qquad \supset [\forall z.ab\ z \equiv ab'\ z]] . \qquad (43)
\end{aligned}$$

Our objective is now to make suitable substitutions for ab' and $flies'$ so that all the terms preceding the $\supset$ in (43) will be true, and the right side will determine *ab*. The axiom $A(ab,flies)$ will then determine *flies*, i.e. we will know what the fliers are. $flies'$ is easy, because we need only apply wishful thinking; we want the fliers to be just those birds that aren't ostriches. Therefore, we put

$$flies'\ x \equiv bird\ x \wedge \neg ostrich\ x . \qquad (44)$$

ab' isn't really much more difficult, but there is a notational problem. We define

$$\begin{aligned}
ab'\ z \equiv &[\exists x.bird\ x \wedge z = aspect1\ x]\\
&\vee [\exists x.ostrich\ x \wedge z = aspect2\ x] , \qquad (45)
\end{aligned}$$

which covers the cases we want to be abnormal.

Appendix A contains a complete proof as accepted by Jussi Ketonen's [2] interactive theorem prover EKL. EKL uses the theory of types and therefore has no problem with the second-order logic required by circumscription.

11. Simple Abnormality Theories

The examples in this paper all circumscribe the predicate *ab*. However, they differ in what they take as variable in the circumscription. The declarative expression of common sense requires that we be definite about what is circumscribed and what is variable in the circumscription. We have the following objectives.

(1) The general facts of common sense are described by a collection of sentences that are not oriented in advance to particular problems.

(2) It is prescribed how to express the facts of particular situations including the goals to be achieved.

(3) The general system prescribes what is to be circumscribed and what is variable.

(4) Once the facts to be taken into account are chosen, the circumscription process proceeds in a definite way resulting in a definite theory—in general second-order.

(5) The conclusions reached taking a given set of facts into account are intuitively reasonable.

These objectives are the same as those of McCarthy [5] except that that paper used only monotonic reasoning.

The examples of this paper suggest defining a *simple abnormality formalism* used as follows.

(1) The general facts include *ab* and a variety of aspects.

(2) The specific facts do not involve *ab*.

(3) The circumscription of *ab* is done with all predicates variable. This means that the axioms must be sufficient to tie them down.

I had hoped that the simple abnormality formalism would be adequate to express common-sense knowledge. Unfortunately, this seems not to be the case. Consider the following axioms.

$$\begin{aligned}
&\neg ab\ aspect1\ x \supset \neg flies\ x ,\\
&bird\ x \supset ab\ aspect1\ x ,\\
&bird\ x \wedge \neg ab\ aspect2\ x \supset flies\ x ,\\
&canary\ x \wedge \neg ab\ aspect3\ x \supset bird\ x ,\\
&canary\ Tweety .
\end{aligned}$$

We ask whether Tweety flies. Simply circumscribing *ab* leaves this undecided, because Tweety can either be abnormal in *aspect1* or in *aspect3*.

Common sense tells us that we should conclude that Tweety flies. This can be achieved by preferring to have Tweety abnormal in *aspect*1 to having Tweety abnormal in *aspect*3. It is not yet clear whether this can be done using the *simple circumscriptive formalism.* Our approach to solving this problem is discussed in the following section on prioritized circumscription. However, simple abnormality theories may be adequate for an interesting set of common-sense axiomatizations.

12. Prioritized Circumscription

An alternate way of introducing formula circumscription is by means of an ordering on tuples of predicates satisfying an axiom. We define $P \leqslant P'$ by

$$\forall P\ P'.P \leqslant P' \equiv \forall x.E(P,x) \supset E(P',x)\,. \tag{46}$$

That $P0$ is a relative minimum in this ordering is expressed by

$$\forall P.P \leqslant P0 \supset P = P0\,, \tag{47}$$

where equality is interpreted extensionally, i.e. we have

$$\forall P\ P'.P = P' \equiv (\forall x.E(P,x) \equiv E(P',x))\,. \tag{48}$$

Assuming that we look for a minimum among predicates P satisfying $A(P)$, (46) expands to precisely to the circumscription formula (1). In some earlier expositions of circumscription this ordering approach was used, and Vladimir Lifschitz in a recent seminar advocated returning to it as a more fundamental and understandable concept.

I'm beginning to think he's right about it being more understandable, and there seems to be a more fundamental reason for using it. Namely, certain common-sense axiomatizations are easier to formalize if we use a new kind of ordering, and circumscription based on this kind of ordering doesn't seem to reduce to ordinary formula circumscription.

We call it *prioritized circumscription.*

Suppose we write some bird axioms in the form

$$\forall x. \neg\, ab\ aspect1\ x \supset \neg\, flies\ x \tag{49}$$

and

$$\forall x.bird\ x \wedge \neg\, ab\ aspect2\ x \supset ab\ aspect1\ x\,. \tag{50}$$

The intent is clear. The goal is that being a bird and not abnormal in *aspect*2 prevents the application of (49). However, circumscribing *ab z* with the conjunction of (49) and (50) as $A(ab)$ doesn't have this effect, because (50) is equivalent to

$$\forall x.bird\ x \supset ab\ aspect1\ x \vee ab\ aspect2\ x\,, \tag{51}$$

and there is no indication that one would prefer to have *aspect*1 *x* abnormal rather than to have *aspect*2 *x* abnormal. Circumscription then results in a disjunction which is not wanted in this case. The need to avoid this disjunction is why the axioms in Section 5 included cancellation of inheritance axioms.

However, by using a new kind of ordering we can leave (49) and (50) as is, and still get the desired effect.

We define two orderings on *ab* predicates, namely

$$\forall ab\ ab'.ab \leqslant_1 ab' \equiv \forall x.ab\ aspect1\ x \supset ab'\ aspect1\ x \tag{52}$$

and

$$\forall ab\ ab'.ab \leqslant_2 ab' \equiv \forall x.ab\ aspect2\ x \supset ab'\ aspect2\ x\,. \tag{53}$$

We then combine these orderings lexicographically giving $\leqslant_2$ priority over $\leqslant_1$ getting

$$\forall ab\ ab'.ab \leqslant_{1<2} ab' \equiv [ab \leqslant_2 ab' \wedge ab =_2 ab' \supset ab \leqslant_1 ab']\,. \tag{54}$$

Choosing $ab0$ so as to minimize this ordering yields the result that exactly birds can fly. However, if we add

$$\forall x.ostrich\ x \supset ab\ aspect2\ x\,, \tag{55}$$

we'll get that ostriches (whether or not ostriches are birds) don't fly without further axioms. If we use

$$\forall x.ostrich\ x \wedge \neg\, ab\ aspect3\ x \supset ab\ aspect2\ x \tag{56}$$

instead of (55), we'll have to revise our notion of ordering to put minimizing *ab aspect*3 *x* at higher priority than minimizing *aspect*2 *x* and *a fortiori* at higher priority than minimizing *aspect*1.

This suggests providing a partial ordering on aspects giving their priorities and providing axioms that permit deducing the ordering on *ab* from the sentences that describe the ordering relations. Lifschitz [4] further develops the idea of prioritized circumscription.

I expect that *prioritized circumscription* will turn out to be the most natural and powerful variant.

Simple abnormality theories seem to be inadequate also for the blocks world described in Section 11. I am indebted to Lifschitz for the following example. Consider

$$S2 = result(move(B,top\ A),result(move(A,top\ B),S0)),$$

where *S*0 is a situation with exactly blocks *A* and *B* on the table. Intuitively, the second action *move*(*B*,*top A*) is unsuccessful, because after the first action *A* is on *B*, and so *B* isn't clear. Suppose we provide by a suitable axiom that when the block to be moved is not clear or the destination place is not clear, then the situation is normally unchanged. Then *S*2 should be the same situation as $S1 = result(move(A,B),S0)$. However, simple circumscription of *ab* won't give this result, because the first move is only normally successful, and if the first move is unsuccessful for some unspecified reason, the second move may succeed after all. Therefore, circumscription of *ab* only gives a disjunction.

Clearly the priorities need to be arranged to avoid this kind of unintended "sneak disjunction." The best way to do it by imposing priorities isn't clear at the time of this writing.

13. General Considerations and Remarks

(1) Suppose we have a database of facts axiomatized by a formalism involving the predicate *ab*. In connection with a particular problem, a program takes a subcollection of these facts together with the specific facts of the problem and then circumscribes *ab z*. We get a second-order formula, and in general, as the natural number example of McCarthy [8] shows, this formula is not equivalent to any first-order formula. However, many common-sense domains are axiomatizable in such a way that the circumscription is equivalent to a first-order formula. In this case we call the circumscription collapsible. For example, Vladimir Lifschitz [4] has shown that this is true if the axioms are from a certain class he calls "separable" formulas. This can presumably be extended to other cases in which the ranges and domains of the functions are disjoint, so that there is no way of generating an infinity of elements.

Circumscription is also collapsible when the predicates are all monadic and there are no functions.

(2) We can then regard the process of deciding what facts to take into account and then circumscribing as a process of compiling from a slightly higher-level non-monotonic language into mathematical logic, especially first-order logic. We can also regard natural language as higher-level than logic. However, as I shall discuss elsewhere, natural language doesn't have an independent reasoning process, because most natural-language inferences involve suppressed premisses which are not represented in natural language in the minds of the people doing the reasoning.

Reiter has pointed out, both informally and implicitly in [13], that circumscription often translates directly into PROLOG program once it has been decided what facts to take into account.

(3) Circumscription has interesting relations to Reiter's [11] logic of defaults. In simple cases they give the same results. However, a computer program using default logic would have to establish the existence of models, perhaps by constructing them, in order to determine that the sentences mentioned in default rules were consistent. Such computations are not just selectively applying the rules of inference of logic but are metamathematical. At present this is treated entirely informally, and I am not aware of any computer program that finds models of sets of sentences or even interacts with a user to find and verify such models.

Circumscription works entirely within logic as Appendices A and B illustrate. It can do this, because it uses second-order logic to import some of the model theory of first-order formulas into the theory itself. Finding the right substitution for the predicate variables is, in the cases we have examined, the same task as finding models of a first-order theory. Putting everything into the logic itself is an advantage as long as there is neither a good theory of how to construct models nor programs that do it.

Notice, however, that finding an interpretation of a language has two parts—finding a domain and interpreting the predicate and function letters by predicates and functions on the domain. It seems that the second is easier to import into second-order logic than the first. This may be why our treatment of unique names is awkward.

(4) We are only part way to our goal of providing a formalism in which a database of common-sense knowledge can be expressed. Besides sets of axioms involving *ab*, we need ways of specifying what facts shall be taken into account and what functions and predicates are to be taken as variable.

Moreover, some of the circumscriptions have unwanted conclusions, e.g. that there are no ostriches if none are explicitly mentioned. Perhaps some of this can be fixed by introducing the notion of present situation. An axiom that ostriches exist will do no harm if what is allowed to vary includes only ostriches that are present.

(5) Non-monotonic formalisms in general, and circumscription in particular, have many as yet unrealized applications to formalizing common-sense knowledge and reasoning. Since we have to think about these matters in a new way, what the applications are and how to realize them isn't immediately obvious. Here are some suggestions.

When we are searching for the "best" object of some kind, we often jump to the conclusion that the best we have found so far is the best. This process can be represented as circumscribing *better*(*x*,*candidate*), where *candidate* is the best we have found so far. If we attempt this circumscription while including certain information in our axiom *A*(*better*,*P*), where *P* represents additional predicates being varied, we will succeed in showing that there is nothing better only if this is consistent with the information we take into account. If the attempt to circumscribe fails, we would like our reasoning program to use the failure as an aid to finding a better object. I don't know how hard this would be.

Appendix A. Circumscription in a Proof Checker

At present there are no reasoning or problem-solving programs using circumscription. A first step towards such a program involves determining what kinds of reasoning are required to use circumscription effectively. As a step towards this we include in this and the following appendix two proofs in EKL (Ketonen and Weening [2]), an interactive theorem prover for the theory of types. The first does the bird problem and the second a simple unique names problem. It will be seen that the proofs make substantial use of EKL's ability to admit arguments in second-order logic.

Each EKL step begins with a command given by the user. This is usually followed by the sentence resulting from the step in a group of lines each ending in a semicolon, but this is omitted for definitions when the information is contained in the command. We follow each step by a brief explanation. Of course, the reader may skip this proof if he is sufficiently clear about what steps are involved. However, I found that pushing the proof through EKL clarified my ideas considerably as well as turning up bugs in my axioms.

```
1. (DEFINE A
   |∀AB FLIES.A(AB,FLIES)≡
        (∀X. ¬AB(ASPECT1(X)) ⊃ ¬ FLIES(X)) ∧
        (∀X.BIRD(X) ⊃ AB(ASPECT1(X))) ∧
        (∀X.BIRD(X) ∧ ¬ AB(ASPECT2(X)) ⊃ FLIES(X)) ∧
        (∀X.OSTRICH(X) ⊃ AB(ASPECT2(X))) ∧
        (∀X.OSTRICH(X) ∧ ¬ AB(ASPECT3(X)) ⊃ ¬ FLIES(X))| NIL)
```

This defines the second-order predicate $A(ab, flies)$, where *ab* and *flies* are predicate variables. Included here are the specific facts about flying being taken into account.

```
;labels: SIMPINFO
2. (AXIOM
   |(∀X Y. ¬ ASPECT1(X) = ASPECT2(Y)) ∧
   (∀X Y. ¬ ASPECT1(X) = ASPECT3(Y)) ∧
   (∀X Y. ¬ ASPECT2(X) = ASPECT3(Y)) ∧
   (∀X Y.ASPECT1(X) = ASPECT1(Y) ≡ X = Y) ∧
   (∀X Y.ASPECT2(X) = ASPECT2(Y) ≡ X = Y) ∧
   (∀X Y.ASPECT3(X) = ASPECT3(Y) ≡ X = Y|)
```

These facts about the distinctness of aspects are used in step 20 only. Since axiom 2 is labelled SIMPINFO, the EKL simplifier used it as appropriate when it is asked to simplify a formula.

```
3. (DEFINE A1
    |∀AB FLIES.A1(AB,FLIES)≡
          A(AB,FLIES) ∧
          (∀AB1 FLIES1.A(AB1,FLIES1) ∧
                 (∀Z.AB1(Z) ⊃AB(Z)) ⊃(∀Z.AB(Z)≡ AB1(Z)))|
    NIL)
```

This is the circumscription formula itself.

```
4. (ASSUME |A1(AB,FLIES)| )
deps: (4)
```

Since EKL cannot be asked (yet) to do a circumscription, we assume the result. Most subsequent statements list line 4 as a dependency. This is appropriate since circumscription is a rule of conjecture rather than a rule of inference.

```
5. (DEFINE FLIES2 |∀X.FLIES2(X)≡BIRD(X) ∧ ¬ OSTRICH(X)| NIL)
```

This definition and the next say what we are going to substitute for the bound predicate variables.

```
6. (DEFINE AB2
    |∀Z.AB2(Z) ≡ (∃X.BIRD(X) ∧ Z = ASPECT1(X)) ∨
       (∃X.OSTRICH(X) ∧ Z = ASPECT2(X))| NIL)
```

The fact that this definition is necessarily somewhat awkward makes for some difficulty throughout the proof.

```
7. (RW 4 (OPEN A1))
A(AB,FLIES) ∧ (∀AB1 FLIES1.A(AB1,FLIES1) ∧
        (∀Z.AB1(Z) ⊃ AB(Z)) ⊃ (∀Z.AB(Z) ≡ AB1(Z)))
deps: (4)
```

This step merely expands out the circumscription formula. RW stands for "rewrite a line," in this case line 4.

```
8. (TRW |A(AB,FLIES)| (USE 7))
A(AB,FLIES)
deps: (4)
```

We separate the two conjuncts of 7 in this and the next step.

```
9. (TRW |∀AB1 FLIES1.A(AB1,FLIES1) ∧
              (∀Z.AB1(Z) ⊃ AB(Z)) ⊃ (∀Z. AB(Z) ≡ AB1(Z))| (USE 7))
∀AB1 FLIES1.A(AB1,FLIES1) ∧
         (∀Z.AB1(Z) ⊃ AB(Z)) ⊃ (∀Z.AB(Z) ≡ AB1(Z))
deps: (4)

10. (RW 8 (OPEN A))
(∀X. ¬ AB(ASPECT1(X)) ⊃ ¬ FLIES(X)) ∧ (∀X.BIRD(X) ⊃ AB(ASPECT1(X))) ∧
(∀X.BIRD(X) ∧ ¬ AB(ASPECT2(X)) ⊃ FLIES(X)) ∧
(∀X.OSTRICH(X) ⊃ AB(ASPECT2(X))) ∧
(∀X.OSTRICH(X) ∧ ¬ AB(ASPECTS3(X)) ⊃ ¬ FLIES(X))
deps: (4)
```

Expanding out the axiom using the definition A in step 1.

```
11. (ASSUME |AB2(Z)|)
deps: (11)
```

Our goal is step 15, but we need to assume its premiss and then derive its conclusion.

```
12. (RW 11 (OPEN AB2))
(∃X.BIRD(X) ∧ Z = ASPECT1(X)) ∨ (∃X.OSTRICH(X) ∧ Z = ASPECT2(X))
deps: (11)
```

We use the definition of *ab*.

```
13. (DERIVE |AB(Z)| (12 10) NIL)
AB(Z)
deps: (4 11)
```

This is our first use of EKL's DERIVE command. It is based on the notion of direct proof of Ketonen and Weyhrauch [3]. Sometimes it can do rather complicated things in one step.

```
14. (CI (11) 13 NIL)
AB2(Z) ⊃ AB(Z)
deps: (4)
```

We discharge the assumption 11 with the "conditional introduction" command.

```
15. (DERIVE |∀Z.AB2(Z) ⊃ AB(Z)| (14) NIL)
∀Z.AB2(Z) ⊃ AB(Z)
deps: (4)
```

Universal generalization.

```
16. (DERIVE
   |(∀X. ¬ AB2(ASPECT1(X)) ⊃ ¬ FLIES2(X)) ∧
   (∀X.BIRD(X) ⊃ AB2(ASPECT1(X))) ∧
   (∀X.BIRD(X) ∧ ¬ AB2(ASPECT2(X)) ⊃ FLIES2(X)) ∧
   (∀X.OSTRICH(X) ⊃ AB2(ASPECT2(X))) ∧
   (∀X.OSTRICH(X) ∧ ¬ AB2(ASPECT3(X)) ⊃ ¬ FLIES2(X))|
   () (OPEN AB2 FLIES2))
;(∀X. ¬ AB2(ASPECT1(X)) ⊃ ¬ FLIES2(X)) ∧
;(∀X.BIRD(X) ⊃ AB2(ASPECT1(X))) ∧
;(∀X.BIRD(X) ∧ ¬ AB2(ASPECT2(X)) ⊃ FLIES2(X)) ∧
;(∀X.OSTRICH(X) ⊃ AB2(ASPECT2(X))) ∧
;(∀X.OSTRICH(X) ∧ ¬ AB2(ASPECT3(X)) ⊃ ¬ FLIES2(X))
```

This is another rather lengthy computation, but it tells us that *ab*2 and *flies*2 satisfy the axioms for *ab* and *flies*.

```
17. (UE ((AB.|AB2|) (FLIES.|FLIES2|)) 1 NIL)
;A(AB2,FLIES2) ≡
;(∀X. ¬ AB2(ASPECT1(X)) ⊃ ¬ FLIES2(X)) ∧
;(∀X.BIRD(X) ⊃ AB2(ASPECT1(X))) ∧
;(∀X.BIRD(X) ∧ ¬ AB2(ASPECT2(X)) ⊃ FLIES2(X)) ∧
;(∀X.OSTRICH(X) ⊃ AB2(ASPECT2(X))) ∧
;(∀X.OSTRICH(X) ∧ ¬AB2(ASPECT3(X)) ⊃ ¬ FLIES2(X))
```

Now we substitute *ab*2 and *flies*2 in the definition of A and get a result we can compare with step 16.

```
18. (RW 17 (USE 16))
;A(AB2,FLIES2)
```

We have shown that *ab*2 and *flies*2 satisfy A.

```
19. (DERIVE |∀Z.AB(Z) ≡ AB2(Z)| (9 15 18) NIL)
:∀Z.AB(Z) ≡ AB2(Z)
;deps: (4)
```

Step 9 was the circumscription formula, and 15 and 18 are its two premisses, so we can now derive its conclusion. Now we know exactly what entities are abnormal.

```
20. (RW 8 ((USE 1 MODE: EXACT) ((USE 19 MODE: EXACT) (OPEN AB2))))
;(∀X. ¬ (∃X1.BIRD(X1) ∧ X = X1) ⊃ ¬ FLIES(X)) ∧
```

```
;(∀X.BIRD(X) ∧ ¬(∃X2.OSTRICH(X2) ∧ X = X2) ⊃ FLIES(X))
;(∀X.OSTRICH(X) ⊃ ¬FLIES(X))
;deps: (4)
```

We rewrite the axiom now that we know what's abnormal. This gives a somewhat awkward formula that nevertheless contains the desired conclusion. The occurrences of equality are left over from the elimination of the aspects that used the axiom of step 2.

```
21. (DERIVE |∀X.FLIES(X) ≡ BIRD(X) ∧ ¬OSTRICH(X)| (20) NIL)
;∀X.FLIES(X) ≡ BIRD(X) ∧ ¬OSTRICH(X)
;deps: (4)
```

DERIVE straightens out 20 to put the conclusion in the desired form. The result is still dependent on the assumption of the correctness of the circumscription made in step 4.

Clearly if circumscription is to become a practical technique, the reasoning has to become much more automatic.

Appendix B

Here is an annotated EKL proof that circumscribes the predicate $e(x,y)$ discussed in Section 6.

```
(proof unique names)
```

What the user types is indicated by the numbered statements in lower case. What EKL types is preceded by semicolons at the beginning of each line and is in upper case. We omit EKL's type-out when it merely repeats what the command asked it to do, as in the commands DERIVE, ASSUME and DEFINE.

```
1. (axiom |index a = 1 ∧ index b = 2 ∧
           index c = 3 ∧ index d = 4|)
```

Since EKL does not have attachments to determine the equivalence of names, we establish a correspondence between the names in our domain and some natural numbers.

```
2. (derive |¬(1 = 2) ∧ ¬(1 = 3) ∧ ¬(2 = 3) ∧ ¬(1 = 4) ∧ ¬(2 = 4) ∧ ¬(2 = 4)|)
```

EKL does know about the distinctness of natural numbers, so this can be derived.

```
(der-slow)
```

We have to tell EKL to use the properties of equality rather than regarding it as just another predicate symbol in order to do the next step. Sometimes this leads to combinatorial explosion.

```
3. (derive |a ≠ b| (1 2))
```

This shows that two names themselves are distinct.

```
4. (define equiv |∀e.equiv e ≡ (∀x.e(x,x)) ∧ (∀x y.e(x,y) ⊃ e(y,x)) ∧
                  (∀x y z.e(x,y) ∧ e(y,z) ⊃ e(x,z))|)
```

Here we use second-order logic to define the notion of equivalence relation. The first word after "define" is the entity being defined and included between vertical bars is the defining relation. EKL checks that an entity satisfying the relation exists.

```
5. (define ax |∀e.ax e ≡ e(a,b) ∧ equiv e|)
```

We define ax as a predicate we want our imitation equality to satisfy. We have chosen a very simple case, namely making a and b "equal" and nothing else.

```
6. (define ax1 |∀e.ax1 e ≡ ax e ∧
        ∀e1.(ax e1 ∧ (∀x y.e1(x,y) ⊃ e(x,y)) ⊃ (∀x y.e(x,y) ≡ e1(x,y)))|)
```

This defines $ax1$ as the second-order predicate specifying the circumscription of ax.

```
7. (assume |ax1(e0)|)
(label circum)
```

We now specify that $e0$ satisfies $ax1$. It takes till step 17 to determine what $e0$ actually is. When EKL includes circumscription as an operator, we may be able to write something like circumscribe $(e0,ax1)$ and make this step occur. For now it's just an ordinary assumption.

```
8. (define e2 |∀x y.e2(x,y) ≡ (x = a ∧ y = b) ∨
                   (x = b ∧ y = a) ∨ x = y|)
```

The predicate $e2$ defined here is what $e0$ will turn out to be.

```
9. (derive |equiv e2| nil (open equiv) (open e2))
```

Now EKL agrees that $e2$ is an equivalence relation. This step takes the KL-10 about 14 seconds.

```
10. (derive |ax e2| (9) (open ax) (open e2))
(label ax e2)
```

Moreover it satisfies ax.

```
11. (rw circum (open ax1))
;AX(E0) ∧ (∀E1.AX(E1) ∧ (∀X Y.E1(X,Y) ⊃ E0(X,Y)) ⊃ (∀X Y.E0(X,Y) ≡ E1(X,Y)))
;deps: (CIRCUM)
```

A trivial step of expanding the definition of $ax1$. EKL tells us that this fact depends on the assumption CIRCUM. So do many of the subsequent lines of the proof, but we omit it henceforth to save space.

```
12. (trw |ax e0| (use 11))
;AX(E0)
```

The first conjunct of the previous step.

```
13. (rw 12 (open ax equiv))
(label fact1)
;E0(A,B) ∧ (∀X.E0(X,X)) ∧ (∀X Y.E0(X,Y) ⊃ E0(Y,X) ∧
;(∀X Y Z.E0(X,Y) ∧ E0(Y,Z) ⊃ E0(X,Z))
```

We exapnd $ax\ e0$ according to the definitions of ax and $equiv$.

```
14. (derive |(∀p q r.(p ∨ q ⊃ r) ≡ (p ⊃ r) ∧ (q ⊃ r)|)
(label rewrite by cases)
```

This is a fact of propositional calculus used as a rewrite rule in the next step. A program that can use circumscription by itself will either need to generate this step or systematically avoid the need for it.

```
15. (trw |e2(x,y) ⊃ e0(x,y)|
    ((open e2) (use rewrite by cases mode: always) (use fact1)))
;E2(X,Y) ⊃ E0(X,Y)
```

This is the least obvious step, because rewrite by cases is used after some preliminary transformation of the formula.

```
16. (derive |∀x y.e0(x,y) ≡ e2(x,y)| (ax e2 11 15))
```

DERIVE is substituting $e2$ for the variable $e1$ in step 11 and using the fact $ax(e2)$ and step 15 to infer the conclusion of the implication that follows the quantifier $\forall e$.

```
17. (rw 16 (open E2))
;∀X Y.E0(X,Y) ≡ X = A ∧ Y = B ∨ X = B ∧ Y = A ∨ X = Y
;deps: (CIRCUM)
```

Expanding the definition of $e2$ tells us the final result of circumscribing $e0(x,y)$. A more complex $ax(e0)$—see step 5—would give a more complex result upon circumscription. However, it seems that the proof would be similar. Therefore, it could perhaps be made into some kind of macro.

ACKNOWLEDGMENT

I had useful discussions with Matthew Ginsberg, Benjamin Grosof, Vladimir Lifschitz and Leslie Pack. The work was partially supported by NSF and by DARPA. I also thank Jussi Ketonen for developing EKL and helping me with its use. In particular he greatly shortened the unique names proof.

REFERENCES

1. Etherington, D., Mercer, R. and Reiter, R., On the adequacy of predicate circumscription for closed-world reasoning, *Comput. Intelligence* **1** (1985) 11–15.
2. Ketonen, J. and Weening, J.S., *EKL*—an interactive proof checker, user's reference manual, Computer Science Department, Stanford University, Stanford, CA, 1984.
3. Ketonen, J. and Weyhrauch, R.W., A decidable fragment of predicate calculus, *Theoret. Comput. Sci.* **32** (1984) 297–307.
4. Lifschitz, V., Computing circumscription in: *Proceedings Ninth International Joint Conference on Artificial Intelligence*, Los Angeles, CA, 1985.
5. McCarthy, J., Programs with common sense, in: *Proceedings Teddington Conference on the Mechanization of Thought Processes* (HMSO, London, 1960).
6. McCarthy, J. and Hayes, P.J., Some philosophical problems from the standpoint of artificial intelligence, in: D. Michie (Ed.), *Machine Intelligence* **4** (American Elsevier, New York, 1969).
7. McCarthy, J., Epistemological problems of artificial intelligence, in: *Proceedings Fifth International Joint Conference on Artificial Intelligence*, Cambridge, MA, 1977.
8. McCarthy, J., First order theories of individual concepts and propositions, in: D. Michie, (Ed.), *Machine Intelligence* **9** (University of Edinburgh Press, Edinburgh, 1979).
9. McCarthy, J., Circumscription—a form of non-monotonic reasoning, *Artificial Intelligence* **13** (1980) 27–39.
10. McCarthy, J., Common Business Communication Language, in: A. Endres and J. Reetz (Eds.), *Textverarbeitung und Bürosysteme* (Oldenburg, Munich, 1982).
11. Reiter, R., A logic for default reasoning, *Artificial Intelligence* **13** (1980) 81–132.
12. Reiter, R., Equality and domain closure in first order data bases, *J.ACM* **27** (1980) 235–249.
13. Reiter, R., Circumscription implies predicate completion (sometimes), *Proceedings Second National Conference on Artificial Intelligence*, Pittsburgh, PA, 1982.

COMPUTING CIRCUMSCRIPTION

Vladimir Lifschitz

Department of Computer Science
Stanford University
Stanford, CA 94305

Abstract

Circumscription is a transformation of predicate formulas proposed by John McCarthy for the purpose of formalizing non-monotonic aspects of commonsense reasoning. Circumscription is difficult to implement because its definition involves a second-order quantifier. This paper presents metamathematical results that allow us in some cases to replace circumscription by an equivalent first-order formula.

1. Introduction

Research in the theory of commonsense reasoning has revealed a fundamental difference between how universal assertions are used in mathematics on the one hand, and in the area of commonsense knowledge on the other. In mathematics, when a proposition is claimed to be universally true, the assertion includes a complete list of conditions on the objects involved under which the proposition is asserted ("for all $x \neq 0$", "for all sufficiently large natural numbers", etc.) But in everyday life we often assert that a certain proposition is true "in general"; we know that there are exceptions, and we can list some of them, but the list of exceptions is not a part of the assertion. The "abnormality" of each item on the list is a separate piece of commonsense knowledge. We know, for instance, that birds, generally, can fly. We know, futhermore, that ostriches are exceptions. And penguins are exceptions. And dead birds are exceptions. All these assertions appear to be separate commonsense facts.

The language of predicate logic has been created primarily for the purpose of formalizing mathematics, and it does not provide any means for talking about what is "generally true" and what "exceptions" are. If we want to use that language for representing commonsense knowledge then methods for formalizing assertions about exceptions have to be developed.

The study of such methods belongs to the area of *non-monotonic logic*. Extending an axiom set can force us to retract some of the conclusions we have derived from the axioms if the new axioms include additional information about abnormal objects. The set of theorems depends on the set of axioms in a non-monotonic way.

Consider a simple example which illustrates some of the difficulties involved. Let $BI\,x$, $OS\,x$, $FL\,x$ and $AB\,x$ represent the conditions "x is a bird", "x is an ostrich", "x can fly" and "x is abnormal". We want to express these commonsense facts: birds, generally, can fly; ostriches are birds and cannot fly. Consider the formulas:

$$\forall x(BI\,x \wedge \neg AB\,x \supset FL\,x), \qquad (A_1)$$

$$\forall x(OS\,x \supset BI\,x), \qquad (A_2)$$

$$\forall x(OS\,x \supset \neg FL\,x). \qquad (A_3)$$

These formulas represent a part of what has been said about the ability of birds to fly, but they do not say one important thing: objects are considered normal if there is no evidence to the contrary. The three available facts imply that ostriches are abnormal, and they give no information about the abnormality of any other objects. We want to be able to conclude then that ostriches are the only exceptions:

$$\forall x(AB\,x \equiv OS\,x). \qquad (1)$$

But (1) does not follow from the conjunction A of A_1, A_2, A_3.

We discuss here one of the approaches to this problem, the theory of circumscription (McCarthy 1980, 1984). The process of circumscription transforms A into a stronger formula A' which says essentially that AB has a minimal possible extension under the condition A. It turns out that A' is equivalent to the conjunction of A and (1).

A' depends on A non-monotonically. In this sense, circumscription provides an interpretation of non-monotonic reasoning in the usual (monotonic) logic.

In more complex cases, we deal with several kinds of abnormality, and the extensions of several predicates $AB_1, AB_2, \ldots$ have to be minimized. These minimizations sometimes conflict with each other, and there may be a need to establish relative priorities between them (McCarthy 1984).

Currently there are no working systems of knowledge representation based on circumscription. Such a system would include a database A and a metamathematical statement describing how circumscription should be performed. (Such a description would specify, for instance, which predicates should be minimized, and what their priorities are). The system would also include a theorem prover capable of deriving logical consequences from the result A' of circumscribing A.

The design of such a system has to deal with a major difficulty: the definition of circumscription involves a second-order quantifier, so that A' is a formula of a second-order language. The purpose of this paper is to present metamathematical theorems which, in some instances, enable us to replace the result of circumscription by an equivalent first-order formula. These methods can be successfully applied to some examples of circumscription that seem to be typical for applications to the formalization of commonsense knowledge, and, hopefully, they can be used as a basis for implementing circumscription. Our main tool is a theorem which establishes the equivalence of a special case of circumscription to a modification of Clark's predicate completion (Clark 1978). Connections between these two concepts were first studied in (Reiter 1982).

Proofs of some special cases of the results stated in this paper can be found in (Lifschitz 1984). Complete proofs will be published elsewhere.

2. Second-Order Formulas

A *second order language* is defined, just as a first order language, by sets of *function constants* and *predicate constants*, each of some arity n, $n \geq 0$. In the second order language we have, besides *object variables*, also *n-ary function variables* and *n-ary predicate variables*. (Object variables and constants are identified with function variables and constants of arity 0). Both function and predicate variables can be bound by quantifiers. A *sentence* is a formula without free (function or predicate) variables.

A *structure* M for a second order language L consists of a non-empty *universe* $|M|$, functions from $|M|^n$ to M representing the function constants and subsets of $|M|^n$ representing the predicate constants. For any constant K, we denote the object (function or set) representing K in M by $M[K]$. Equality is interpreted as identity, function variables range over arbitrary functions from $|M|^n$ to M, and predicate variables range over arbitrary subsets of $|M|^n$. A *model* of a sentence A is any structure M such that A is true in M. A *implies* B if every model of A is a model of B; A is *equivalent* to B if they have the same models.

An *n-ary predicate* is an expression of the form $\lambda x A(x)$, where x is a tuple of n object variables, $A(x)$ a formula. As usual, if U is $\lambda x\, A(x)$, and t is a tuple of n terms, then Ut stands for $A(t)$. We identify a predicate constant P with the predicate $\lambda x Px$, and similarly for predicate variables.

If U, V are n-ary predicates, then $U \leq V$ stands for $\forall x(Ux \supset Vx)$. Thus $U \leq V$ expresses that the extension of U is a subset of the extension of V. We apply this notation to tuples $U = U_1, \ldots, U_m$ and $V = V_1, \ldots, V_m$ of predicates, assuming that they are similar (i.e., that U_i and V_i have the same arity): $U \leq V$ stands for

$$U_1 \leq V_1 \wedge \ldots \wedge U_m \leq V_m.$$

Furthermore, $U = V$ stands for $U \leq V \wedge V \leq U$, and $U < V$ stands for $U \leq V \wedge \neg(V \leq U)$. If $m = 1$ then $U < V$ means simply that the extension of U is a proper subset of the extension of V.

3. Parallel Circumscription

First we consider *parallel* circumscription, when no priorities between the minimized predicates are specified. Let P be a tuple of predicate constants, Z a tuple of function and/or predicate constants disjoint with P, and let $A(P, Z)$ be a sentence. The *circumscription of P in A(P, Z) with variable Z* is the sentence

$$A(P, Z) \wedge \neg\exists pz(A(p, z) \wedge p < P). \qquad (2)$$

(Here p,z are tuples of variables similar to P,Z). This formula expresses that P has a minimal possible extension under the condition $A(P, Z)$ when Z is allowed to vary in the process of minimization. We denote (2) by Circum($A(P, Z); P; Z$). When Z is empty, we write Circum($A(P); P$).

In applications to the formalization of commonsense reasoning, $A(P, Z)$ is the conjunction of the axioms, P is the list of abnormality predicates, and Z is the list of symbols that we intend to characterize by means of circumscription, as FL in the example discussed in the introduction. The circumscription we intend to perform in that case is

$$\text{Circum}(A(AB, FL); AB; FL). \qquad (3)$$

The model-theoretic meaning of circumscription can be expressed in terms of the following notation. Let P,

Z be as in the definition of circumscription. For any two structures M_1, M_2, we write $M_1 \leq^{P;Z} M_2$ if

(i) $|M_1| = |M_2|$,
(ii) $M_1[\![K]\!] = M_2[\![K]\!]$ for every constant K not in P, Z,
(iii) $M_1[\![P_i]\!] \subset M_2[\![P_i]\!]$ for every P_i in P.

Thus $M_1 \leq^{P;Z} M_2$ if M_1 and M_2 differ only in how they interpret the constants in P and Z, and the extension of each P_i in M_1 is a subset of its extension in M_2.

Clearly, $\leq^{P;Z}$ is a pre-order (i.e., a reflexive and transitive relation) on the class of all structures. It is possible, however, that $M_1 \leq^{P;Z} M_2$ and, at the same time, $M_2 \leq^{P;Z} M_1$ for two different structures M_1, M_2. This happens when M_1, M_2 differ by the interpretations of symbols in Z. In other words, $\leq^{P;Z}$ is, generally, not anti-symmetric and thus not a partial order. Still, we can speak of the minimality of structures with respect to $\leq^{P;Z}$: a structure M is *minimal* in a class S of structures if $M \in S$ and there is no structure $M' \in S$ such that $M' <^{P;Z} M$. (We write $M_1 <^{P;Z} M_2$ if $M_1 \leq^{P;Z} M_2$ but not $M_2 \leq^{P;Z} M_1$). This concept of minimality was introduced essentially in (McCarthy 1980).

The models of circumscription can be characterized now as follows:

Proposition 1. *A structure M is a model of* Circum$(A; P; Z)$ *iff M is minimal in the class of models of A with respect to $\leq^{P;Z}$.*

This equivalence follows from the fact that specifying values of p, z for which $A(p, z) \wedge p < P$ is true in M is equivalent to specifying a model M' of A such that $M' <^{P;Z} M$.

4. Examples

Before describing general methods for determining the result of circumscription, we discuss a few examples. In these examples Z is empty, and P is a single predicate constant.

Example 1. $A \equiv Pa$, a an object constant. Circumscription asserts that the extension of P is a minimal set satisfying this condition; in other words, a is its only element:

$$\text{Circum}(Pa; P) \equiv \forall x(Px \equiv x = a).$$

Example 2. $A \equiv \neg Pa$. This does not give any "positive" information about P and is true even when P is identically false. Hence

$$\text{Circum}(\neg Pa; P) \equiv \forall x \neg Px.$$

We get the same result whenever A contains no positive occurrences of P.

Example 3. $A \equiv Pa \wedge Pb$. Circumscription asserts that a and b are the only elements of P:

$$\text{Circum}(Pa \wedge Pb; P) \equiv \forall x(Px \equiv x = a \vee x = b).$$

Example 4. $A \equiv Pa \vee Pb$. In Examples 1-3, circumscription provided an explicit definition and thus a unique possible value for P. In this case, there are two minimal values:

$$\text{Circum}(Pa \vee Pb; P) \equiv \forall x(Px \equiv x = a) \vee \forall x(Px \equiv x = b).$$

Example 5. $A \equiv Pa \vee (Pb \wedge Pc)$. The previous examples suggest that the answer might be

$$\forall x(Px \equiv x = a) \vee \forall x(Px \equiv x = b \vee x = c).$$

But we should take into consideration that a may be equal to one of b, c, and then the second disjunctive term does not give a minimal P. The correct answer is

$$\text{Circum}(Pa \vee (Pb \wedge Pc); P) \equiv \forall x(Px \equiv x = a) \\ \vee [\forall x(Px \equiv x = b \vee x = c) \wedge a \neq b \wedge a \neq c].$$

Example 6. $A \equiv \forall x(Qx \supset Px)$. Clearly, circumscription simply changes implication to equivalence:

$$\text{Circum}(\forall x(Qx \supset Px); P) \equiv \forall x(Qx \equiv Px).$$

More generally, for any predicate U (without parameters) which does not contain P,

$$\text{Circum}(U \leq P; P) \equiv U = P.$$

This can be also viewed as a generalization of Examples 1 and 3, because in those examples A can be written in the form $U \leq P$:

$$Pa \equiv \lambda x(x = a) \leq P,$$

$$Pa \wedge Pb \equiv \lambda x(x = a \vee x = b) \leq P.$$

Example 7. $A \equiv \exists x Px$. Circumscription asserts that the extension of P is a "minimal non-empty" set, i.e., a singleton:

$$\text{Circum}(\exists x Px; P) \equiv \exists x \forall y(Py \equiv x = y).$$

Example 8. In all examples above, we were able to express the result of circumscription without second-order quantifiers. Let now P, Q be binary predicate constants, and A be

$$\forall xy(Qxy \supset Pxy) \wedge \forall xyz(Pxy \wedge Pyz \supset Pxz).$$

Then Circum$(A; P)$ asserts that P is the transitive closure of Q and thus is not equivalent to a first-order sentence.

Notice that the formula of this example is "good" by all logical standards: it is universal and, moreover, Horn, and it contains no function symbols. What syntactic features make it difficult for circumscription? This question will be answered in the next section.

5. Separable Formulas

In Examples 2 and 6 above we saw that there are two classes of formulas for which the result of circumscription can be easily determined: formulas without positive occurences of P, and formulas of the form $U \leq P$, where U does not contain P. What about formulas constructed from subformulas of these two types using conjunctions and disjunctions?

First let us look at conjunctions of such formulas. Let P be again a tuple of predicate constants $P_1, \ldots P_m$. We say that $A(P)$ is *solitary* with respect to P if it is a conjunction of

(i) formulas containing no positive occurences of $P_1, \ldots P_m$, and
(ii) formulas of the form $U \leq P_i$, where U is a predicate not containing $P_1, \ldots P_m$.

Using predicate calculus, we can write any solitary formula in the form

$$N(P) \wedge (U \leq P),$$

where $N(P)$ contains no positive occurences of $P_1, \ldots$, P_m, and U is a tuple of predicates not containing $P_1, \ldots P_m$. Then the result of circumscription is given by the formula

$$\text{Circum}(N(P) \wedge (U \leq P); P) \equiv N(U) \wedge (U = P). \quad (4)$$

Using this formula, we can do, in particular, the circumscriptions of Examples 1, 2, 3 and 6.

Next we want to be able to handle formulas with disjunctions, like Examples 4 and 5. If a formula is constructed from subformulas of forms (i) and (ii) using conjunctions and disjunctions, we call it *separable*. In a separable formula, positive occurences of $P_1, \ldots P_m$ are separated by conjunctions and disjunctions from negative occurences and from each other.

Any separable formula is equivalent to a disjunction of solitary formulas and consequently can be written in the form

$$\bigvee_i [N_i(P) \wedge (U^i \leq P)], \quad (5)$$

where $N_i(P)$ contains no positive occurences of $P_1, \ldots$, P_m, and each U^i is a tuple of predicates not containing $P_1, \ldots P_m$.

The following theorem generalizes (4) to separable formulas.

Theorem 1. *If $A(P)$ is equivalent to (5) then* Circum$(A(P); P)$ *is equivalent to*

$$\bigvee_i [D_i \wedge (U^i = P)], \quad (6)$$

where D_i is

$$N_i(U^i) \wedge \bigwedge_{j \neq i} \neg[N_j(U^j) \wedge (U^j < U^i)].$$

Thus the result of circumscription in a separable first-order sentence is a first-order sentence of about the same logical complexity. Circum$(A(P); P)$ asserts that P may have one of the finite number of possible values U^1, U^2, ... Hence every model of Circum$(A(P); P)$ belongs to one of a finite number of classes: there are models in which P is the same as U^1, models in which P is the same as U^2, etc. If M is a structure in which $P = U^i$ then D_i is the additional condition which, if true in M, guarantees that M is a model of Circum$(A(P); P)$.

The transformation of $U^i \leq P$ into $U^i = P$ is based on the same idea as *predicate completion* of (Clark 1978): transforming sufficient conditions into necessary and sufficient. When applied to non-separable Horn formulas, like the formula of Example 8, predicate completion often gives conditions that are weaker than the result of circumscription. On the other hand, the transformation of (5) into (6) is not restricted to Horn formulas and is in this respect more general.

Using Theorem 1, we can easily do all circumscriptions of Examples 1-6. Examples 7 and 8 are not separable.

Example 7 shows that there are non-separable formulas for which circumscription can be done in the first-order language. Here is one more example:

$$\text{Circum}(\forall x(P_1 x \vee P_2 x); P_1, P_2) \equiv \forall x(P_1 x \equiv \neg P_2 x). \quad (7)$$

The first argument can be easily written in the form separable with respect to P_1 and in the form separable with respect to P_2, but it is not equivalent to a formula separable with respect to the pair P_1, P_2.

Theorem 1 cannot be applied directly to circumscriptions with a non-empty Z, like (3). Two observations often help in such cases.

First, every circumscription with a non-empty Z can be reduced to a circumscription with the empty Z:

Proposition 2. Circum$(A(P,Z); P; Z)$ *is equivalent to*

$$A(P,Z) \wedge \text{Circum}(\exists z A(P,z); P). \tag{8}$$

For example, (3) reduces to

$$\text{Circum}(\exists fl(A_1(AB, fl) \wedge A_2 \wedge A_3(fl)); AB), \tag{9}$$

where fl is a binary predicate variable.

The problem with this trick is, of course, that the first argument of circumscription in (8), generally, contains new second-order quantifiers. In our example, we have to circumscribe AB in a formula with the quantifier $\exists fl$.

The second observation sometimes helps eliminate quantifiers like this. If q is a tuple of predicate variables, and $A(q)$ is separable with respect to q, then we can write $A(q)$ in the form

$$\bigvee_i [N_i(q) \wedge (U^i \leq q)]. \tag{5'}$$

(Separability with respect to a tuple of predicate variables is defined in the same way as separability with respect to a tuple of predicate constants). It can be easily seen that $\exists q A(q)$ is equivalent then to $\bigvee_i N_i[U^i]$. In our example, the only positive occurence of fl is in the first conjunctive term, so we write the conjunction as

$$A_2 \wedge A_3(fl) \wedge \lambda x(BI\,x \wedge \neg AB\,x) \leq fl.$$

Then the first argument of (9) is equivalent to the conjunction of A_2 and

$$\forall x(OS\,x \supset \neg(BI\,x \wedge \neg AB\,x)).$$

In the presence of A_2 this simplifies to $\forall x(OS\,x \supset AB\,x)$. Thus it remains to circumscribe AB in $A_2 \wedge OS \leq AB$. By (4), the result is $A_2 \wedge OS = AB$. The second term here is equivalent to (1).

Many other examples of circumscription arising in connection with the formalization of commonsense reasoning can be handled in the same manner.

6. General Circumscription

In some applications of circumscription we have several abnormality predicates which are assigned different priorities. For example, we may wish to minimize AB_1 and AB_2, the former at higher priority than the latter. This means that, instead of minimizing (AB_1, AB_2) with respect to the relation $\leq$ defined by

$$(p_1, p_2) \leq (q_1, q_2) \equiv p_1 \leq q_1 \wedge p_2 \leq q_2,$$

we use the relation

$$(p_1, p_2) \preceq (q_1, q_2) \equiv p_1 \leq q_1 \wedge (p_1 = q_1 \supset p_2 \leq q_2). \tag{10}$$

To prepare for the general treatment of priorities in the next section, we define now the generalization of circumscription needed for that purpose.

Let p, q be disjoint similar tuples of predicate variables, and let $p \preceq q$ be a formula which has no parameters besides p, q. We say that $p \preceq q$ *defines a regular order* in a structure M if the sentences

$$\forall pq(p \leq q \supset p \preceq q),$$

$$\forall pqr(p \preceq q \wedge q \preceq r \supset p \preceq r),$$

$$\forall pq(p \preceq q \wedge q \preceq p \supset p = q)$$

are true in M. As the name suggests, such a formula defines a (partial) order on vectors of subsets of $|M|^n$. Clearly, $p \leq q$ defines a regular order in every structure. A more interesting example is given by (10). We write $p \prec q$ for $p \preceq q \wedge p \neq q$.

As before, let P be a tuple of predicate constants, Z a tuple of constants disjoint with P, $A(P,Z)$ a sentence. Let $p \preceq q$ be a formula which does not contain P, Z, and defines a regular order in every model of $A(P,Z)$. The *circumscription of P in $A(P,Z)$ with variable Z with respect to $\preceq$*, symbolically Circum$_\preceq(A(P,Z); P; Z)$, is

$$A(P,Z) \wedge \neg\exists pz(A(p,z) \wedge p \prec P).$$

The results of Sections 3 and 5 can be extended to general circumscription as follows. We write

$$M_1 \leq^{P;Z;\preceq} M_2$$

if

(i) $|M_1| = |M_2|$,
(ii) $M_1[K] = M_2[K]$ for every constant K not in P, Z,
(iii) $p \preceq q$ is true in M_1 (or, equivalently, in M_2) for $M_1[P]$ as p and $M_2[P]$ as q.

Proposition 1′. *A structure M is a model of* $\text{Circum}_{\preceq}(A; P; Z)$ *iff M is minimal in the class of models of A with respect to* $\leq^{P;Z;\preceq}$.

Theorem 1′. *If $A(P)$ is equivalent to (5) then* $\text{Circum}_{\preceq}(A(P); P)$ *is equivalent to*

$$\bigvee_i [D_i \wedge (U^i = P)],$$

where D_i is

$$N_i(U^i) \wedge \bigwedge_{j \neq i} \neg[N_j(U^j) \wedge (U^j \prec U^i)].$$

Notice that this formula for D_i differs from the formula of Theorem 1 only when there are at least two disjunctive terms. Consequently, the effect of general circumscription on a *solitary* formula can be computed using the same formula (4) that we used for parallel circumscription. Thus we have:

Corollary. *If A is solitary then* $\text{Circum}_{\preceq}(A; P)$ *does not depend on* $\preceq$.

Proposition 2′. $\text{Circum}_{\preceq}(A(P, Z); P; Z)$ *is equivalent to*

$$A(P, Z) \wedge \text{Circum}_{\preceq}(\exists z A(P, z); P).$$

In the next section we show how this generalization of circumscription works in applications to the formalization of commonsense reasoning.

7. Priorities

The database B defined below contains these commonsense facts: things, in general, do not fly; airplanes and birds, in general, do; but ostriches and dead birds, generally, do not. B is the conjunction of these formulas:

$$\forall x(OS\,x \supset BI\,x), \qquad (B_1)$$

$$\forall x \neg(BI\,x \wedge PL\,x), \qquad (B_2)$$

$$\forall x(\neg AB_1\,x \supset \neg FL\,x), \qquad (B_3)$$

$$\forall x(PL\,x \wedge \neg AB_2\,x \supset FL\,x), \qquad (B_4)$$

$$\forall x(BI\,x \wedge \neg AB_3\,x \supset FL\,x), \qquad (B_5)$$

$$\forall x(OS\,x \wedge \neg AB_4\,x \supset \neg FL\,x), \qquad (B_6)$$

$$\forall x(BI\,x \wedge DE\,x \wedge \neg AB_5\,x \supset \neg FL\,x). \qquad (B_7)$$

We expect that circumscribing $AB_1, \ldots, AB_5$ in B should give the following result: AB_2, AB_4 and AB_5 are identically false (since there is no evidence that they are not); ostriches and dead birds are the only objects satisfying AB_3; airplanes and the birds that are alive and not ostriches are the only objects satisfying AB_1.

However, the circumscription

$$\text{Circum}(B; AB_1, \ldots, AB_5; FL)$$

does not lead to these conclusions. The reason is that the goals of minimizing our five abnormality predicates conflict with each other. For instance, minimizing the extensions of AB_2 and AB_3 conflicts with the goal of minimizing AB_1.

The solution proposed in (McCarthy 1984) is to establish priorities between different kinds of abnormality. Let a tuple P of predicate variables be broken into disjoint parts P^1, P^2, ..., P^k. We want to express the idea that the predicates in P^1 should be minimized at higher priority than the predicates in P^2, P^2 at higher priority than P^3, etc. Let p^i, q^i be tuples of predicate variables similar to P^i, and let p, q stand for $p^1, \ldots, p^k$ and $q^1, \ldots, q^k$. Define

$$p \preceq q \equiv \bigwedge_{i=1}^{k} \left(\bigwedge_{j=1}^{i-1} p^j = q^j \supset p^i \leq q^i \right). \qquad (11)$$

If $k = 1$ then (11) defines simply $p \leq q$. If $k = 2$, P^1 consists of only one predicate P_1, and P^2 consists of one predicate P_2, then (11) becomes (10).

Formula (11) defines a regular order in every structure. We denote the circumscription $\text{Circum}_{\preceq}(A; P; Z)$ with respect to this order by

$$\text{Circum}(A; P^1 > \ldots > P^k; Z)$$

and call it *prioritized circumscription.*

To see how establishing priorities affects the result of circumscription, compare (7) with the result of prioritized circumscription:

$$\begin{aligned} &\text{Circum}(\forall x(P_1 x \vee P_2 x); P_1 > P_2) \\ &\qquad \equiv \forall x \neg P_1 x \wedge \forall x P_2 x. \end{aligned} \qquad (12)$$

Minimizing P_1 at higher priority means that we minimize (P_1, P_2) with respect to (10). Without priorities, circumscription only leads to the conclusion that P_1 and P_2 do not overlap. In (12) we make the extension of P_1 as small as possible, even if it leads to making the extension of P_2 larger; that makes P_1 identically false and P_2 identically true.

In applications it is reasonable to assign higher priorities to the abnormality predicates representing exceptions to "more specific" commonsense facts. In the example above, we use the circumscription

$$\text{Circum}(B; AB_4, AB_5 > AB_2, AB_3 > AB_1; FL). \quad (13)$$

How to compute the result of a prioritized circumscription? We can try to use Theorem 1′ and Proposition 2′. It turns out, however, that in cases when priorities are essential, the axiom set is usually not separable with respect to the collection of all abnormality predicates; at best, we have separability with respect to individual ABs or small groups of ABs. Even in simple cases, doing prioritized circumscription requires an additional tool.

Such a tool is given by the fact that any prioritized circumscription can be written as a conjunction of parallel circumscriptions, as follows:

Theorem 2. Circum($A; P^1 > \ldots > P^k; Z$) *is equivalent to*

$$\bigwedge_{i=1}^{k} \text{Circum}(A; P^i; P^{i+1}, \ldots, P^k, Z).$$

According to this theorem, we can do circumscription (12) by taking the conjunction of

$$\text{Circum}(\forall x(P_1 x \lor P_2 x); P_1; P_2)$$

and

$$\text{Circum}(\forall x(P_1 x \lor P_2 x); P_2).$$

Each of the two circumscriptions can be easily evaluated using the methods of Section 5. The first of them gives $\forall x \neg P_1 x$, the second $\forall x(P_2 x \equiv \neg P_1 x)$. The conjunction of these formulas is equivalent to the right-hand side of (12).

The result of circumscription (13) can be determined along the same lines. We come up with the conclusion that (13) is equivalent to the universal formula

$$\begin{aligned} & B_1 \land B_2 \\ & \quad \land FL = AB_1 = \lambda x(PL\,x \lor (BI\,x \land \neg OS\,x \land \neg DE\,x)) \\ & \quad \land AB_3 = \lambda x(OS\,x \lor (BI\,x \land DE\,x)) \\ & \quad \land AB_2 = AB_4 = AB_5 = \lambda x{:}false. \end{aligned}$$

Acknowledgements

I am indebted to John McCarthy for introducing me to problems of non-monotonic reasoning and circumscription. I have also benefited from discussing this work with David Etherington, Michael Gelfond, Benjamin Grosof, Kurt Konolige, Nils Nilsson, Donald Perlis and Raymond Reiter.

References

Clark, K. (1978) "Negation as Failure", In: *Logic and Databases* (Gallaire, H. and Minker, J., Eds.), Plenum Press, N. Y., 1978, 293-322.

Lifschitz, V. (1984) "Some Results on Circumscription", Technical Report No. STAN-CS-84-1019, Department of Computer Science, Stanford University, 1984 (= *AAAI Workshop on Non-Monotonic Reasoning*, 1984, 151-164).

McCarthy, J. (1980) "Circumscription – A Form of Non-Monotonic Reasoning", *Artificial Intelligence 13*, 1980, 295-323.

McCarthy, J. (1984) "Applications of Circumscription to Formalizing Commonsense Knowledge", *AAAI Workshop on Non-Monotonic Reasoning*, 1984, 295-323, and to appear in *Artificial Intelligence*.

Reiter, R. (1982) "Circumscription Implies Predicate Completion (Sometimes)", *Proc. AAAI-82*, 1982, 418-420.

On the adequacy of predicate circumscription for closed-world reasoning

DAVID W. ETHERINGTON[1], ROBERT E. MERCER[2], AND RAYMOND REITER[2,3]
Department of Computer Science, University of British Columbia, Vancouver, B.C., Canada V6T 1W5

Received September 19, 1984
Revision accepted December 6, 1984

We focus on McCarthy's method of predicate circumscription in order to establish various results about its consistency, and about its ability to conjecture new information. A basic result is that predicate circumscription cannot account for the standard kinds of default reasoning. Another is that predicate circumscription yields no new information about the equality predicate. This has important consequences for the unique names and domain closure assumptions.

Nous nous concentrons sur la méthode de McCarthy de limitation des prédicats afin d'établir différents constats sur sa consistance et sur sa capacité à déduire de l'information nouvelle. Un des principaux résultats est que la limitation des prédicats ne peut rendre compte des cas ordinaires de raisonnement par défaut. D'autre part, la limitation des prédicats n'apporte aucune information nouvelle sur le prédicat d'égalité. Ceci a des conséquences importantes pour les hypothèses sur les noms uniques et la fermeture du domaine.

[Traduit par la revue]

Comput. Intell. 1, 11–15 (1985)

1. Introduction

There are many settings in artificial intelligence and in the theory of data bases where we must assume that the available information consists of all and only the relevant facts. A variety of different intuitions appears to underlie this so-called *Closed-World Assumption*. These differing intuitions have led to different formalizations of this important notion:

(1) Negation as failure to derive (Reiter 1978*a*, *b*)—If a ground atomic formula cannot be proved using the given information as premises, then assume the formula's negation.
(2) Predicate completion (Clark 1978; Kowalski 1978)—When the given information about a predicate consists of a set of sufficient conditions on that predicate, assume that these conditions are also necessary.
(3) Domain circumscription (McCarthy 1977; 1980)—Assume that the individuals required by the given information are all there are.
(4) Predicate circumscription (McCarthy 1980)—Assume those facts that are true in all models of the given theory having minimal extensions for certain predicates.

The relationships among these different formalisms are not completely understood, but some results are known. Domain circumscription can be reduced to predicate circumscription (McCarthy 1980). Under certain circumstances, predicate completion is a special case of predicate circumscription (Reiter 1982). Shepherdson (1984) provides a careful analysis of the relationships between predicate completion and negation as failure to derive.

In this paper we focus on predicate circumscription, as presented in McCarthy (1980). Our objective is to establish various results concerning the consistency of this formalism, and to describe some limitations of its ability to conjecture new information. One such limitation is that predicate circumscription cannot account for the standard kinds of default reasoning. Another limitation relates to equality; predicate circumscription yields no new information about the equality predicate for a large class of first-order theories. This has important consequences for the so-called "unique names assumption" and "domain closure assumption".

Recently, McCarthy has proposed a generalization of predicate circumscription, which minimizes arbitrary first-order expressions rather than simple predicates. Certain predicates are allowed to act as variables during this minimization (McCarthy 1984). Some of the limitations of predicate circumscription that we describe in this paper do not apply to this generalized form of circumscription, although equality appears to remain problematic.

2. Predicate circumscription: formal preliminaries

The semantic intuition underlying predicate circumscription is that closed-world reasoning about one or more predicates of a theory corresponds to truth in all models of the theory that are minimal in those predicates. Specifically, let $T(P_1, \ldots, P_n)$ be a first-order theory, some (but not necessarily all) of whose predicates are $\mathbf{P} = \{P_1, \ldots, P_n\}$. A model M of T is a **P**-*submodel* of a model M' of T iff the extension of each P_i in M is a subset of its extension in M', and M and M' are otherwise identical. M is a **P**-*minimal model of* T iff every **P**-submodel of M is identical to M.

For finite theories, $T(P_1, \ldots, P_n)$, McCarthy (1980) proposes realizing predicate circumscription syntactically by adding the following axiom schema to T:

$$\left[T(\Phi_1, \ldots, \Phi_n) \wedge \bigwedge_{i=1}^{n} [\forall x.(\Phi_i x \supset P_i x)]\right] \supset \bigwedge_{i=1}^{n} [\forall x.(P_i x \supset \Phi_i x)].$$

Here $\Phi_1, \ldots, \Phi_n$ are predicate variables with the same arities as $P_1, \ldots, P_n$, respectively. $T(\Phi_1, \ldots, \Phi_n)$ is the sentence obtained by conjoining the sentences of T, then replacing every occurrence of $P_1, \ldots, P_n$ in T by $\Phi_1, \ldots, \Phi_n$, respectively. The above schema is called *the (joint) circumscription schema of* $P_1, \ldots, P_n$ *in* T. Let $CLOSURE_{\mathbf{P}}(T)$—*the closure of* T *with respect to* **P** $= \{P_1, \ldots, P_n\}$—denote the theory consisting of T together with the above axiom schema. McCarthy formally identifies reasoning about T under the closed-world assumption with respect to the predicates **P** with first-order deductions from the theory $CLOSURE_{\mathbf{P}}(T)$.

[1]This research was supported in part by an I.W. Killam Memorial Predoctoral Fellowship and a Natural Sciences and Engineering Research Council of Canada Postgraduate Scholarship.
[2]This research was supported in part by the Natural Sciences and Engineering Research Council of Canada, grant A7462, and the U.S. National Science Foundation, grant MCS-8203954.
[3]Fellow of the Canadian Institute for Advanced Research.

McCarthy (1980) shows that any instance of the schema resulting from circumscribing a single predicate P in a sentence $T(P)$ is true in all $\{P\}$-minimal models of T. This generalizes directly to the joint circumscription of multiple predicates; we omit the proof of this. We use this generalization extensively in the proofs of the results of this paper. Because predicate circumscription is applicable only to finitely axiomatizable theories, we will restrict our attention to such theories.

3. On the consistency of predicate circumscription

The minimal model semantics of predicate circumscription suggests that certain consistent first-order theories lacking minimal models may have inconsistent closures. Indeed, this can happen, as we now show.

Example 3.1 – An inconsistent circumscription

Let T be the following consistent theory:

$$\left\{\begin{array}{l} \exists x.\, Nx \wedge \forall y.\, [Ny \supset x \neq succ(y)] \\ \forall x.\, Nx \supset Nsucc\,(x) \\ \forall xy.\, succ(x) = succ\,(y) \supset x = y \end{array}\right\}$$

In any model of T, the extension of N contains a sequence of elements isomorphic to the natural numbers. A $\{N\}$-submodel can always be constructed by deleting a finite initial segment of this sequence. Hence every model of T has at least one proper $\{N\}$-submodel, so T has no $\{N\}$-minimal models.

Circumscribing N in this theory, and letting Φx be $[Nx \wedge \exists y.x = succ(y) \wedge Ny]$ yields $\forall x.Nx \supset \exists y.[Ny \wedge x = succ(y)]$, which contradicts the first axiom. ■

In view of this example, it is natural to seek classes of first-order theories for which predicate circumscription does not introduce inconsistencies. The well-founded theories form such a class. We say that a first-order theory is *well-founded* iff each of its models has a **P**-minimal submodel for every finite set of predicates **P**. Any consistent well-founded theory obviously has at least one **P**-minimal model. Since every instance of the circumscription schema of **P** in a theory T is true in all **P**-minimal models of T, we have:

Theorem 3.1

If T is a consistent well-founded theory, then $CLOSURE_{\mathbf{P}}(T)$ is consistent for any set **P** of predicates of T, i.e., predicate circumscription preserves consistency for well-founded theories. ■

Which theories are well-founded? We know of no complete syntactic characterization, but a partial answer comes from a generalization of a result on universal theories due to Bossu and Siegel (1985). A first-order theory is *universal* iff the prenex normal form of each of its formulae contains no existential quantifiers.

Theorem 3.2

Universal theories are well-founded. ■

In view of Theorem 3.1, we know that predicate circumscription preserves consistency for universal theories:

Corollary 3.3

If T is a consistent universal theory, then $CLOSURE_{\mathbf{P}}(T)$ is consistent for any set **P** of predicates of T. ■

Notice that the class of universal theories includes the Horn theories, which have attracted considerable attention from the PROLOG, AI, and Database communities.

4. Well-founded theories and predicate circumscription

In this section we describe some limitations of predicate circumscription with respect to well-founded theories. The first such result is that predicate circumscription yields no new positive ground instances of any of the predicates being circumscribed.

Theorem 4.1

Suppose that T is a well-founded theory, $P \in \mathbf{P}$ is an n-ary predicate, and α is an n-tuple of ground terms. Then

$$CLOSURE_{\mathbf{P}}(T) \vdash P\alpha \Leftrightarrow T \vdash P\alpha. \quad ■$$

On reflection, this is not too surprising, since circumscription is intended to minimize the extensions of those predicates being circumscribed. New positive instances of such predicates should not arise from this minimization.

A more interesting result is that no new ground instances, positive or negative, of uncircumscribed predicates can be derived by predicate circumscription.

Theorem 4.2

Suppose that T is a well-founded theory, $P \notin \mathbf{P}$ is an n-ary predicate, and α is an n-tuple of ground terms. Then

(i) $CLOSURE_{\mathbf{P}}(T) \vdash P\alpha \Leftrightarrow T \vdash P\alpha$, and

(ii) $CLOSURE_{\mathbf{P}}(T) \vdash \neg P\alpha \Leftrightarrow T \vdash \neg P\alpha$. ■

In summary, Theorems 4.1 and 4.2 tell us that the only new ground literals that can be conjectured by predicate circumscription of well-founded theories are negative instances of one of the predicates being circumscribed. An unfortunate consequence of this result is that the usual kinds of default reasoning cannot be realized by predicate circumscription. To see why, consider the standard "flying birds" example. The relevant facts may be represented in various ways, two of which follow:

(1) In this representation, all of the exceptions to flight are listed explicitly in the axiom sanctioning the conclusion that birds can fly.

$$\forall x.\, Bird(x) \wedge \neg Penguin(x) \wedge \neg Ostrich(x) \wedge \neg Dead(x) \wedge \ldots \supset Can-Fly(x)$$

In addition, there are various IS-A axioms, as well as mutual exclusion axioms:

$$\forall x.\, Canary(x) \supset Bird(x)$$

$$\forall x.\, Penguin(x) \supset Bird(x)$$

etc.

$$\forall x.\, \neg(Canary(x) \wedge Penguin(x))$$

$$\forall x.\, \neg(Penguin(x) \wedge Ostrich(x))$$

etc.

(2) In this representation, due to McCarthy (1984), a new predicate, *ab*, standing for "abnormal", is introduced. One then states that "normal" birds can fly:

$$\forall x.\, Bird(x) \wedge \neg ab(x) \supset Can-Fly(x)$$

The abnormal birds are listed:

$$\forall x.\, Penguin(x) \supset ab(x)$$

$$\forall x.\, Ostrich(x) \supset ab(x)$$

etc.

Finally, one includes the IS-A and mutual exclusion axioms as in representation (1) above.

Both representations (1) and (2) are universal, and hence well-founded, theories. Therefore, if *Bird(Tweety)* is given, Theorems 4.1 and 4.2(i) tell us that the default assumption *Can* – *Fly(Tweety)* cannot be conjectured by predicate circumscription.

Careful readers of McCarthy (1980) might find Theorems 4.1 and 4.2 inconsistent with the results in Section 7 of that paper. In the blocks-world example presented there to illustrate predicate circumscription, the ground instance *on* $(A, C, \textit{result}\ (\textit{move}\ (A, C), s_0))$ can be derived by circumscribing a different predicate, $\lambda z.\ \textit{prevents}\ (z, \textit{move}\ (A, C), s_0)$. This appears to violate our Theorem 4.2(i). This discrepancy stems from the fact that in formulating the circumscription schema for this example, McCarthy uses specializations of some of the original axioms (i.e., the axioms that specify what can *prevent* a *move* from succeeding), and omits one of the axioms (i.e., the axiom that states that if nothing *prevents* a *move* from succeeding, the *move* will be successful). Thus, only part of the theory enters into the circumscription for his example, whereas our Theorems 4.1 and 4.2 suppose that the entire theory is used in proposing a circumscription schema.

A generalization of predicate circumscription has been recently formulated by McCarthy (1984). This generalization provides for the minimization of arbitrary first-order expressions rather than simple predicates. It also provides for the treatment of designated predicates as variables of the minimization. In this version of circumscription the limitations of our Theorem 4.2 no longer apply. Thus, as some of McCarthy's examples show, it is possible to circumscribe a predicate P, treating another predicate Q as variable, and derive new positive and negative ground instances of Q. In particular, McCarthy's new formalism appears adequate for the treatment of default reasoning, as his "flying birds" example shows.

5. Equality

We now consider some limitations of predicate circumscription with respect to the treatment of equality. These limitations will be seen to have consequences for two special cases of closed-world reasoning, namely deriving the "unique names assumption" and the "domain closure assumption".

5.1. The unique names assumption

When told that Tom, Dick, and Harry are friends, one naturally assumes that 'Tom', 'Dick', and 'Harry' denote distinct individuals: Tom ≠ Dick, Tom ≠ Harry, Dick ≠ Harry. For a more general example, consider a setting in which one is told that Tom's telephone number is the same as Sue's, and that Bill's number is 555-1234, which is different from Mary's number. Thus, we have:

$$\textit{tel-no}(\text{Tom}) = \textit{tel-no}\ (\text{Sue})$$

$$\textit{tel-no}(\text{Bill}) = 555\text{–}1234$$

$$\textit{tel-no}(\text{Mary}) \neq 555\text{–}1234$$

One would naturally assume from this information that *tel-no*(Tom) ≠ 555–1234, and that *tel-no*(Tom) ≠ *tel-no*(Mary).

In general, the unique names assumption is invoked whenever one can assume that all of the relevant information about the equality of individuals has been specified. All pairs of individuals not specified as identical are assumed to be different. This assumption arises in a number of settings, for example in the theory of databases (Reiter 1980), and in connection with the semantics of negation in PROLOG (Clark 1978). Virtually ever AI reasoning system, with the exception of those based on theorem-provers, implicitly makes this assumption. Because of Clark's results, we know that this is also the case for PROLOG-based AI systems.

Unique names axioms are also important for closed-world reasoning using predicate circumscription. For example, if all we know is that *Opus* is a *Penguin*, we can circumscriptively conjecture $\forall x.\ \textit{Penguin}(x) \equiv x = \textit{Opus}$. We cannot use this to deduce $\neg\textit{Penguin}(\textit{Tweety})$, however, unless we know that $\textit{Opus} \neq \textit{Tweety}$.

How then can we formalize reasoning under the unique names assumption? The natural first attempt is to circumscribe the equality predicate in the theory under consideration. To that end, we shall assume that the theory T contains the following axioms, which define the equality predicate, =, for the theory:

$$\forall x.\ x = x$$

$$\forall xy.\ x = y \supset y = x$$

$$\forall xyz.\ x = y \wedge y = z \supset x = z$$

$$\forall x_1, \ldots, x_n, y_1, \ldots, y_n\,.\ x_1 = y_1 \wedge \ldots \wedge x_n = y_n \wedge P(x_1, \ldots, x_n) \supset P(y_1, \ldots, y_n),$$

for each n-ary predicate symbol P of T.

$$\forall x_1, \ldots, x_n, y_1, \ldots, y_n\,.\ x_1 = y_1 \wedge \ldots \wedge x_n = y_n \supset f(x_1, \ldots, x_n) = f(y_1, \ldots, y_n),$$

for each n-ary function symbol f of T.

When T is finite, it is therefore possible to circumscribe the equality predicate, since the resulting schema is finite. The next result informs us that doing so yields nothing new.

Theorem 5.1

Let T be a first-order theory containing axioms that define the equality predicate, =. Then $T \vdash \textit{CLOSURE}_{\{=\}}(T)$. ■

In view of this result, one might attempt to capture the unique names assumption by jointly circumscribing several predicates of the theory, not just the equality predicate. We do not know whether there are any theories for which this might work, but it cannot succeed for well-founded theories. No new ground equalities or inequalities can be derived by circumscribing a well-founded theory, regardless of the predicates circumscribed.

Theorem 5.2

Suppose that T is a well-founded theory containing axioms that define the equality predicate, α and β are ground terms, and **P** is a set of some of the predicates of T. Then

(i) $\textit{CLOSURE}_{\mathbf{P}}(T) \vdash \alpha = \beta \Leftrightarrow T \vdash \alpha = \beta$, and

(ii) $\textit{CLOSURE}_{\mathbf{P}}(T) \vdash \alpha \neq \beta \Leftrightarrow T \vdash \alpha \neq \beta$. ■

Returning to the "Penguin" example above, we see that predicate circumscription cannot conjecture $\neg$*Penguin (Tweety)* unless it is known that *Opus* ≠ *Tweety*; otherwise we could derive *Opus* ≠ *Tweety* from *CLOSURE*({*Penguin (Opus)*}), contradicting Theorem 5.2.

In a recent paper, McCarthy (1984) proposes a circumscriptive approach to the unique names assumption by introducing two equality predicates. One of these is the standard equality predicate, but restricted to arguments that are names of objects. The other equality predicate, $e(x, y)$, means that the names x and y denote the same object. e is axiomatized as an equivalence relation, which does not, however, satisfy the full principle of substitution, in contrast to "normal" equality. This failure of full substitutivity for the predicate e prevents our Theorems 5.1 and 5.2 from applying to e. Benjamin Grosof (personal communication) has independently proposed a similar approach to the unique names assumption. He has also observed that our Theorem 5.1 applies to McCarthy's (1984) more general notion of circumscription.

5.2. The domain closure assumption

The domain closure assumption is the assumption that, in a given first-order theory T, the universe of discourse is restricted to the smallest set that contains those individuals mentioned in T, and which is closed under the application of those functions mentioned in T. Domain circumscription (McCarthy 1977, 1980) is a proposed formalization of this assumption. McCarthy (1980) shows that domain circumscription can be reduced to predicate circumscription.

The simplest setting in which the domain closure assumption can arise is for a theory with a finite Herbrand Universe $\{c_1, \ldots, c_n\}$. In this case we might want to conjecture the *domain closure axiom* for this theory: $\forall x.\ x = c_1 \vee \ldots \vee x = c_n$. Such an axiom is important for the theory of first-order databases (Reiter 1980). No such axiom can arise from predicate circumscription for well-founded theories.

Theorem 5.3

Suppose that T is a well-founded theory; $t_1, \ldots, t_n$ are ground terms; and $\mathbf{P}$ is a set of some of the predicate symbols of T. Then

$$CLOSURE_{\mathbf{P}}(T) \vdash \forall x.\ x = t_1 \vee \ldots \vee x = t_n \Leftrightarrow T \vdash \forall x.\ x = t_1 \vee \ldots \vee x = t_n. \quad \blacksquare$$

6. Discussion

One obvious problem with using circumscription in a given setting is knowing just what to circumscribe. Some of our results provide clues in this direction. Theorem 4.2 tells us that if we wish to use predicate circumscription to conjecture $\neg P(\alpha)$ in some well-founded theory then we must include P among the predicates being circumscribed. Theorems 4.1 and 4.2 tell us that predicate circumscription will not do at all if we wish to conjecture $P(\alpha)$, as is the case for most forms of default reasoning, so that we must appeal to some other mechanism, such as McCarthy's more general form of circumscription.

A natural question is the extent to which our results translate to McCarthy's generalized circumscription. Grosof (personal communication, 1984) has observed that an appropriate version of our Theorem 5.1 continues to hold. Most of the examples of McCarthy (1984) invoke the following pattern: Jointly circumscribe predicates $P_1, \ldots, P_m$ treating predicates $Q_1, \ldots, Q_n$ as variables. Our results apply only to the case with no variables. The natural question, therefore, is what role do the variables play in circumscriptively conjecturing ground instances, $P(\alpha)$ and $\neg P(\alpha)$, of some predicate P. Is there some way to determine which predicates should be taken as variable? Similarly, one might seek classes of theories for which such circumscriptions preserve consistency. Notice, however, that many of our proofs appeal to the model theory of predicate circumscription. It would seem, therefore, that a prior problem is to determine the appropriate model theory for predicate circumscription with variables.

Acknowledgments

We would like to thank Paul Gilmore, Akira Kanda, and Philippe Besnard for their insights and suggestions. Thanks also to the University of British Columbia's Laboratory for Computational Vision for access to their coveted typesetting facilities.

Bossu, G., and Siegel, P. 1985. The saturation to the rescue of the non-monotonicity. Artificial Intelligence. To be published.

Clark, K.L. 1978. Negation as failure. *In* Logic and data bases. *Edited by* H. Gallaire and J. Minker. Plenum Publishing Corporation, New York, NY. pp. 293–322.

Kowalski, R. 1978. Logic for data description. *In* Logic and data bases. *Edited by* H. Gallaire and J. Minker. Plenum Publishing Corporation, New York, NY. pp. 77–103.

McCarthy, J. 1977. Epistemological problems of artificial intelligence. Proceedings of the Fifth International Joint Conference on Artificial Intelligence, Cambridge, Mass., 1977, pp. 1038–1044.

——— 1980. Circumscription—a form of non-monotonic reasoning. Artificial Intelligence, **13**, pp. 27–39.

——— 1984. Applications of circumscription to formalizing commonsense knowledge. Department of Computer Science, Stanford University, Stanford, California, Technical Report.

Reiter, R. 1978*a*. On closed-world data bases. *In* Logic and data bases. *Edited by* H. Gallaire and J. Minker. Plenum Publishing Corporation, New York, NY. pp. 55–76.

——— 1978*b*. On reasoning by default. Proceedings of the Second Symposium on Theoretical Issues in Natural Language Processing, Urbana, Illinois, 1978, pp. 210–218.

——— 1980. Equality and domain closure in first-order data bases. Journal of the Association for Computing Machinery, **27**(2), pp. 235–249.

——— 1982. Circumscription implies predicate completion (sometimes). Proceedings of the American Association for Artificial Intelligence, Pittsburgh, PA, 1982, pp. 418–420.

Shepherdson, J.C. 1984. Negation as failure: a comparison of Clark's completed data base and Reiter's closed-world assumption. Journal of Logic Programming, **1**(1), pp. 51–79.

Appendix: Proofs of theorems

Theorem 3.2

Universal theories are well-founded.

Proof

The proof is identical to that of Proposition 4 in Bossu and Seigel (1985). The definition of submodel used there is less restrictive than that used here, but this does not alter the form of the proof. $\blacksquare$

Theorem 4.1

If T is a well-founded theory, α is an n-tuple of ground terms, and $P \in \mathbf{P}$, is an n-ary predicate, then

$$CLOSURE_{\mathbf{P}}(T) \vdash P\alpha \Leftrightarrow T \vdash P\alpha.$$

Proof

The if-half of the theorem is immediate. We prove the contrapositive of the only-if-half. Assume that $CLOSURE_{\mathbf{P}}(T) \vdash P\alpha$ and $T \nvdash P\alpha$. Then T has a model, M, in which $P\alpha$ is false. Since T is well founded, there is a $\mathbf{P}$-minimal submodel, M', of M. Furthermore, since the circumscription is true in all $\mathbf{P}$-minimal submodels, $P\alpha$ is true in M'. But then M' is not a $\mathbf{P}$-submodel of M, and this contradicts the fact that M' is a $\mathbf{P}$-minimal submodel of M. Therefore $CLOSURE_{\mathbf{P}}(T) \nvdash P\alpha$. $\blacksquare$

Theorem 4.2

If T is a well-founded theory, α is an n-tuple of ground terms, and $P \notin \mathbf{P}$ is an n-ary predicate, then

(i) $CLOSURE_{\mathbf{P}}(T) \vdash P\alpha \Leftrightarrow T \vdash P\alpha$, and

(ii) $CLOSURE_{\mathbf{P}}(T) \vdash \neg P\alpha \Leftrightarrow T \vdash \neg P\alpha$.

Proof
(i) The if-half is immediate. We prove the contrapositive of the only-if-half. Assume $T \nvdash P\alpha$. Then there is a model, M, for T in which $P\alpha$ is false. Since T is well-founded, there is a **P**-minimal submodel, M', of M. By the definition of submodel, the interpretation of P remains the same in M and M', since $P \notin \mathbf{P}$. Hence $P\alpha$ is false in M'. Since the circumscription is true in all minimal models, $CLOSURE_{\mathbf{P}}(T) \nvdash P\alpha$. The proof for (ii) is similar. ■

In the proofs of Theorems 5.1 and 5.2 we use the following notational conventions:

1. $SCHEMA(T,\mathbf{P})$ is the circumscription schema resulting from circumscribing the predicates of **P** in T.
2. $CLOSURE_{\{\,\}}(T) = T$. (The closure of T with respect to the empty set of predicates is defined to be T itself.)
3. $\bigwedge_{i=1}^{0} Q_i$, the empty conjunction, stands for any tautology.

Theorem 5.1
If T is an arbitrary theory containing axioms which define the equality predicate, =, then $T \vdash CLOSURE_{\{=\}}(T)$.

Proof
Consider the schema resulting from circumscribing = in T:

$$SCHEMA(T,\{=\}) = [T(\Phi) \wedge \forall xy.\ \Phi xy \supset x = y] \supset \forall xy.\ x = y \supset \Phi xy.$$

We show that $T \vdash SCHEMA(T, \{=\})$, whence $T \vdash CLOSURE_{\{=\}}(T)$. It is sufficient to show for any instance Ψ of the predicate parameter Φ that

$$[5.1] \quad T, T(\Psi) \vdash \forall xy.\ x = y \supset \Psi xy.$$

Now $\forall x.\ \Psi xx$ is one of the conjuncts of $T(\Psi)$, since T contains the axiom $\forall x.\ x = x$. Moreover, by basic properties of the equality axioms of the theory T,

$$T \vdash \forall xy.\ \Psi xx \wedge x = y \supset \Psi xy.$$

The result [5.1] now follows. ■

Theorem 5.2
If T is a well-founded theory containing axioms that define the equality predicate, =; α and β are ground terms; and **P** is a set of some of the predicates of T; then

(i) $CLOSURE_{\mathbf{P}}(T) \vdash \alpha = \beta \Leftrightarrow T \vdash \alpha = \beta$, and
(ii) $CLOSURE_{\mathbf{P}}(T) \vdash \alpha \neq \beta \Leftrightarrow T \vdash \alpha \neq \beta$.

Proof
(i) This is a corollary of Theorems 4.1 and 4.2(i).
(ii) The if-half is immediate. To prove the only-if-half, notice that if **P** does not include the equality predicate then the result follows directly from Theorem 4.2(ii). So assume **P** does include the equality predicate, say $\mathbf{P} = \{=, P_1, \ldots, P_n\}$. Writing Φ for $\Phi_1, \ldots, \Phi_n$; $A(\Phi)$ for $\bigwedge_{i=1}^{n} (\forall x.\ \Phi_i x \supset P_i x)$; and $B(\Phi)$ for $\bigwedge_{i=1}^{n} (\forall x.\ P_i x \supset \Phi_i x)$; we have

$$SCHEMA(T, \{P_1, \ldots, P_n\}) = T(\Phi) \wedge A(\Phi) \supset B(\Phi)$$

$$SCHEMA(T, \{=, P_1, \ldots, P_n\}) = T(\Psi, \Phi) \wedge A(\Phi) \wedge (\forall xy.\ \Psi xy \supset x = y) \supset B(\Phi) \wedge (\forall xy.\ x = y \supset \Psi xy)$$

To establish the result we seek, it is sufficient to show that

$$[5.2] \quad CLOSURE_{\{P_1, \ldots, P_n\}}(T) \vdash [\text{any instance of } SCHEMA\ (T, \{=, P_1, \ldots, P_n\})]$$

since, by hypothesis,

$$CLOSURE_{\{=, P_1, \ldots, P_n\}}(T) \vdash \alpha \neq \beta.$$

Therefore, if [5.2] holds, we would have

$$CLOSURE_{\{P_1, \ldots, P_n\}}(T) \vdash \alpha \neq \beta.$$

By Theorem 4.2(ii), $T \vdash \alpha \neq \beta$, as required, since $\{P_1, \ldots, P_n\}$ does not include the equality predicate. To show [5.2], we first establish the following result: For fixed predicates, Ψ' and Φ',

$$[5.3] \quad T, T(\Psi', \Phi'), \forall xy.\ \Psi' xy \supset x = y \vdash \forall xy.\ \Psi' xy \equiv x = y$$

Clearly, to show this, it is sufficient to show

$$T, T(\Psi', \Phi') \vdash \forall xy.\ x = y \supset \Psi' xy$$

whose proof is essentially the same as the proof of [5.1] in Theorem 5.1. Now [5.3] says that, under the stated assumptions, the predicates Ψ' and = are indistinguishable. Hence

$$[5.4] \quad T, T(\Psi', \Phi'), \forall xy.\ \Psi' xy \supset x = y \vdash T(\Psi', \Phi') \equiv T(=, \Phi')$$

Noting that $T(=, \Phi')$ is what we are denoting by $T(\Phi')$ we have, using [5.3] and [5.4]:

$$T, T(\Psi', \Phi'), \forall xy.\ \Psi' xy \supset x = y, T(\Phi') \wedge A(\Phi') \supset B(\Phi'), A(\Phi') \vdash B(\Phi') \wedge (\forall xy.\ x = y \supset \Psi' xy)$$

which is equivalent to

$$T, T(\Phi') \wedge A(\Phi') \supset B(\Phi') \vdash [T(\Psi', \Phi') \wedge A(\Phi') \wedge (\forall xy.\ \Psi' xy \supset x = y)] \supset [B(\Phi') \wedge (\forall xy.\ x = y \supset \Psi' xy)].$$

Thus we have

$$T, [\text{instance of } SCHEMA(T, \{P_1, \ldots, P_n\})] \vdash [\text{instance of } SCHEMA(T, \{=, P_1, \ldots, P_n\})]$$

from which [5.2] follows. ■

Theorem 5.3
If T is a well-founded theory; $\alpha_1, \ldots, \alpha_n$ are ground terms; and **P** is a set of some of the predicate symbols of T; then

$$CLOSURE_{\mathbf{P}}(T) \vdash \forall x.\ x = \alpha_1 \vee \ldots \vee x = \alpha_n \Leftrightarrow T \vdash \forall x.\ x = \alpha_1 \vee \ldots \vee x = \alpha_n.$$

Proof
The if-half is immediate. For the only-if-half, assume that $T \nvdash \forall x.\ x = \alpha_1 \vee \ldots \vee x = \alpha_n$. Then T has a model that falsifies $\forall x.\ x = \alpha_1 \vee \ldots \vee x = \alpha_n$. Since T is well founded, this model has a **P**-minimal submodel. But $\forall x.\ x = \alpha_1 \vee \ldots \vee x = \alpha_n$ is false in this submodel, because the extension of the equality predicate in this submodel must be a subset of its extension in the original model. Since the circumscription is true in all minimal models, $CLOSURE_{\mathbf{P}}(T) \nvdash \forall x.\ x = \alpha_1 \vee \ldots \vee x = \alpha_n$. ■

Pointwise Circumscription

Vladimir Lifschitz
Computer Science Department
Stanford University
Stanford, CA 94305

Abstract. *Circumscription is the minimization of predicates subject to restrictions expressed by predicate formulas. We propose a modified notion of circumscription so that, instead of being a single minimality condition, it becomes an "infinite conjunction" of "local" minimality conditions; each of these conditions expresses the impossibility of changing the value of a predicate from* true *to* false *at one point. We argue that this "pointwise" circumscription is conceptually simpler than the traditional "global" approach and, at the same time, leads to generalizations with the additional flexibility needed in applications to the theory of commonsense reasoning.*

1. Introduction

Circumscription (McCarthy 1980, 1986) is *logical minimization*, that is, the minimization of predicates subject to restrictions expressed by predicate formulas.

The interpretation of a predicate symbol in a model can be described in two ways. One is to represent a k-ary predicate by a subset of U^k, where U is the universe of the model. This approach identifies a predicate with its *extension*. The other possibility is to represent a predicate by a Boolean-valued function on U^k. These two approaches are, of course, mathematically equivalent; but the intuitions behind them are somewhat different, and they suggest different views on what "minimizing a predicate" might mean.

If a predicate is a set then predicates are ordered by *set inclusion*, and it is natural to understand the minimality of a predicate as minimality relative to this order. A *smaller* predicate is a *stronger* predicate. A predicate satisfying a given condition is minimal if it cannot be made stronger without violating the condition. This understanding of minimality leads to the usual definition of circumscription.

Let us accept now the view of predicates as Boolean-valued functions, or, in other words, as *families of truth values*. Each predicate is a family of elements of the ordered set $\{false, true\}$. Understanding "smaller" as "stronger" still makes sense; but another approach becomes also possible. We can think of making a predicate smaller *at a point* $\xi \in U^k$ as changing its value at that point from *true* to *false*. As far as the values at other points are concerned, we can require, in the simplest case, that they remain the same; or we can allow them to change in an arbitrary way; or some of them can be required to remain fixed, and the others allowed to vary.

The new definition of circumscription proposed in this paper expresses, intuitively, the minimality of a predicate "at every point". It can be interpreted as an "infinite conjunction" of "local" minimality conditions; each of these conditions expresses the impossibility of changing the value of a predicate from *true* to *false* at one point. (Formally, this "infinite conjunction" will be represented by a universal quantifier). This is what we call "pointwise circumscription".

We argue that the pointwise approach to circumscription is in some ways conceptually simpler than the traditional global approach and, at the same time, leads to generalizations with the additional flexibility needed in some applications to the theory of commonsense reasoning. Its power is illustrated by applying it to the problem of temporal minimization (Hanks and McDermott 1985). The pointwise approach is also used here for developing new methods for computing global circumscription.

A short version of this paper was published in the Proceedings of AAAI-86 (Lifschitz 1986).

2. The Basic Case of Pointwise Circumscription

Let us start with the simplest case of circumscribing one predicate with all other non-logical constants treated as parameters. Let $A(P)$ be a sentence containing a predicate constant P. Recall that the *(global) circumscription of* P *in* $A(P)$ is, by definition, the second-order formula

$$A(P) \wedge \forall p \neg (A(p) \wedge p < P). \tag{1}$$

Here p is a predicate variable of the same arity as P, and $p < P$ stands for

$$\forall x(px \supset Px) \wedge \neg \forall x(Px \supset px)$$

(x is a tuple of object variables). We denote (1) by Circum($A(P); P$). This formula has a simple model-theoretic meaning: a model of (1) is a model of $A(P)$ which cannot be transformed into another model of $A(P)$ by making P stronger.

The *pointwise circumscription* of P in $A(P)$ is

$$A(P) \wedge \forall x \neg [Px \wedge A(\lambda y(Py \wedge x \neq y))]. \tag{2}$$

Notice that this is a first-order formula. We denote (2) by $C_P(A(P))$; the subscript P indicates which predicate is being minimized. A model of (2) is a model of $A(P)$

which cannot be transformed into another model of $A(P)$ by changing the value of P from *true* to *false* at one point. The quantifier $\forall x$ represents the "infinite conjunction" mentioned above, and the formula following the quantifier can be viewed as a minimality condition: it asserts the minimality of the value of P at point x.

Proposition 1. Circum$(A; P)$ *implies* $C_P(A)$.

Proof. We should prove that the second term of (1) implies the second term of (2). Assume $Px \wedge A(\lambda y(Py \wedge x \neq y))$ and set $p = \lambda y(Py \wedge x \neq y)$.

There is an important special case when the two definitions are equivalent:

Proposition 2. *If all occurrences of* P *in* A *are positive then* Circum$(A; P)$ *is equivalent to* $C_P(A)$.

Proof. In view of Proposition 1, it is sufficient to prove that the second term of (2) implies the second term of (1). Assume $A(p) \wedge p < P$. Then there is an x such that Px and $\neg px$. Define $p' = \lambda y(Py \wedge x \neq y)$. Clearly, $\forall x(px \supset p'x)$. Since all occurrences of P in $A(P)$ are positive, it follows that $A(p')$, contrary to the second term of (2).

As a corollary, we get a new "collapsible" case of global circumscription:

Corollary. *If all occurrences of* P *in* A *are positive then* Circum$(A; P)$ *is equivalent to a first-order formula.*

Example 1. Let us express Circum$(\exists x Px; P)$ by a first-order formula. (The methods of (Lifschitz 1985) do not work in this case because it is not "separable"). By Proposition 2, this formula is equivalent to $C_P(\exists x Px)$, i.e.,

$$\exists x Px \wedge \forall x \neg[Px \wedge \exists y(Py \wedge x \neq y)],$$

or, equivalently,

$$\exists x Px \wedge \neg\exists xy(Px \wedge Py \wedge x \neq y).$$

The examination of standard applications of circumscription (McCarthy 1986) shows that the minimized predicates usually have no negative occurrences in the axioms. It can be expected then that pointwise circumscription with P having negative occurrences in A will not be important for applications. But, for the purpose of illustrating the definition, let us consider an example of that kind.

Example 2. Let A be $Pa \equiv Pb$. Any model with P identically false satisfies both Circum$(A; P)$ and $C_P(A)$. In addition, any model of A in which P is true at exactly two points, a and b, is a model of the pointwise version, but not of the global one.

3. A Generalization

Even in simple applications to formalizing commonsense knowledge we usually need forms of circumscription slightly more general than those defined in the previous section.

Let us start with a formula $A(P, Z)$, where Z is a tuple of predicate and/or function constants. The *(global) circumscription of P in $A(P, Z)$ with Z allowed to vary* is

$$A(P, Z) \land \forall pz \neg(A(p, z) \land p < P), \tag{3}$$

where z is a tuple of predicate and/or function variables similar to Z. This formula, denoted by Circum$(A(P, Z); P; Z)$, asserts that the extension of P cannot be made smaller even at the price of changing the interpretations of the symbols included in Z.

The corresponding form of *pointwise circumscription* is

$$A(P, Z) \land \forall xz \neg[Px \land A(\lambda y(Py \land x \neq y), z)]. \tag{4}$$

It will be denoted by $C_P(A(P, Z); Z)$. Because of the variables z, (4) is, generally, a second-order formula.

Propositions 1 and 2 and their proofs can be easily extended to this version of pointwise circumscription:

Proposition 1a. Circum$(A; P; Z)$ *implies* $C_P(A; Z)$.

Proposition 2a. *If all occurrences of P in A are positive then* Circum$(A; P; Z)$ *is equivalent to* $C_P(A; Z)$.

Since (4) may contain second-order variables, we cannot extend the corollaries to Proposition 2 to this more general case.

In applications, the minimized predicate usually has only positive occurrences in the axioms. By Proposition 2a, pointwise circumscription (4) can be used in such cases instead of (3).

To get additional information on the relative power of (3) and (4), consider the following property of global circumscription:

Proposition 3. *Let Q be a new predicate constant of the same arity as P. Then*

$$\text{Circum}(A \land \forall x(Px \supset Qx); Q; P, Z) \tag{5}$$

is equivalent to

$$\mathrm{Circum}(A; P; Z) \wedge \forall x(Px \equiv Qx). \tag{6}$$

We see that the circumscriptions in (5) and in (6) are essentially equivalent to each other; the latter is equivalent to the former plus an explicit definition of Q. But the circumscription in (6) is the general case of (3), while the only occurrence of the minimized predicate Q in the first argument of (5) is positive. In view of this remark, Proposition 2a actually shows that pointwise circumscription (4) has at least as much expressive power as global circumscription (3).

Proof of Proposition 3.

$$\begin{aligned}
&\mathrm{Circum}(A(P,Z) \wedge P \leq Q; Q; P, Z)\\
&\qquad \equiv A(P,Z) \wedge P \leq Q \wedge \forall pqz \neg(A(p,z) \wedge p \leq q \wedge q < Q)\\
&\qquad \equiv A(P,Z) \wedge P \leq Q \wedge \forall pz \neg(A(p,z) \wedge \exists q(p \leq q \wedge q < Q))\\
&\qquad \equiv A(P,Z) \wedge P \leq Q \wedge \forall pz \neg(A(p,z) \wedge p < Q)\\
&\qquad \equiv A(P,Z) \wedge P \leq Q \wedge \forall pz \neg(A(p,z) \wedge p < Q) \wedge \neg(A(P,Z) \wedge P < Q)\\
&\qquad \equiv A(P,Z) \wedge P \leq Q \wedge \forall pz \neg(A(p,z) \wedge p < Q) \wedge \neg(P < Q)\\
&\qquad \equiv A(P,Z) \wedge \forall x(Px \equiv Qx) \wedge \forall pz \neg(A(p,z) \wedge p < Q)\\
&\qquad \equiv A(P,Z) \wedge \forall x(Px \equiv Qx) \wedge \forall pz \neg(A(p,z) \wedge p < P)\\
&\qquad \equiv \mathrm{Circum}(A(P,Z); P, Z) \wedge \forall x(Px \equiv Qx).
\end{aligned}$$

4. Minimizing Several Predicates

In a further generalization of global circumscription (3), P is a *tuple* of predicate constants $P_1, \ldots, P_n$. The meaning of $\mathrm{Circum}(A; P; Z)$ is given again by (3), with p standing this time for a tuple of predicate variables $p_1, \ldots, p_n$, and $p < P$ understood as

$$\bigwedge_{i=1}^{n} \forall x(p_i x \supset P_i x) \wedge \bigvee_{i=1}^{n} \neg \forall x(P_i x \supset p_i x).$$

This form of joint minimization of several predicates is called *parallel circumscription* (to distinguish it from the case when different members of P are minimized with different priorities, which is discussed below).

What is the relationship between circumscribing $P_1, \ldots, P_n$ in parallel and circumscribing each P_i?

Proposition 4. $\mathrm{Circum}(A; P; Z)$ *implies* $\mathrm{Circum}(A; P_i; Z)$, $i = 1, \ldots, n$.

Proof. To simplify notation, assume $i = 1$. We should show that

$$\forall pz \neg(A(p, z) \wedge p < P)$$

implies

$$\neg(A(p_1, P_2, \ldots, P_n, z) \wedge p_1 < P_1).$$

Assume $A(p_1, P_2, \ldots, P_n, z) \wedge p_1 < P_1$ and set $p_2 = P_2, \ldots, p_n = P_n$.

In an important special case, the converse holds too:

Proposition 5. *If all occurrences of* $P_1, \ldots, P_n$ *in* A *are positive then* $\text{Circum}(A; P; Z)$ *is equivalent to*

$$\bigwedge_{i=1}^{n} \text{Circum}(A; P_i; Z). \tag{7}$$

Proof. In view of Proposition 4, it is sufficient to show that (7) implies the second term of (3). Assume $A(p, z) \wedge p < P$. Take an i such that $\neg\forall x(P_i x \supset p_i x)$; to simplify notation, assume that $i = 1$. Since all occurrences of $P_2, \ldots, P_n$ in $A(P, Z)$ are positive, $A(p, z)$ implies $A(p_1, P_2, \ldots, P_n, z)$, which contradicts the first term of conjunction (7).

Example 3. The methods of (Lifschitz 1985) easily give:

$$\text{Circum}(\forall x(P_1 x \vee P_2 x); P_1) \equiv \text{Circum}(\forall x(P_1 x \vee P_2 x); P_2) \equiv \forall x(P_1 x \equiv \neg P_2 x),$$

because $\forall x(P_1 x \vee P_2 x)$ is separable relative to each of P_1, P_2. But this formula is not separable relative to the pair (P_1, P_2); for this reason, we cannot use the same method to compute

$$\text{Circum}(\forall x(P_1 x \vee P_2 x); P_1, P_2).$$

Proposition 4 shows that this circumscription is equivalent to the conjunction of the two circumscriptions computed above and consequently gives $\forall x(P_1 x \equiv \neg P_2 x)$ too.

Proposition 5 shows that conjunction (7) can be used in applications instead of parallel circumscription. Perhaps, there is not much need for parallel circumscription at all.

Corollary. *If all occurrences of* $P_1, \ldots, P_n$ *in* A *are positive then* $\text{Circum}(A; P; Z)$ *is equivalent to*

$$\bigwedge_{i=1}^{n} C_{P_i}(A; Z). \tag{8}$$

Proof: Propositions 5 and 2a.

Condition (8) asserts that, whenever one value of one of the predicates $P_1, \ldots, P_n$ is changed from *true* to *false*, and the interpretation of Z is changed in an arbitrary way, the resulting structure cannot possibly be a model of A. This conjunction is the pointwise counterpart of parallel circumscription; there is no need to introduce a special definition.

Corollary to Proposition 2 generalizes to parallel circumscription. Moreover, we can prove the following:

Proposition 6. *If $P_1, \ldots, P_n$ have only positive occurrences in A and only negative occurrences in B then* Circum$(A \wedge B; P)$ *is equivalent to a first-order formula.*

So if A is the conjunction of several formulas, each containing either only positive or only negative occurrences of $P_1, \ldots, P_n$ then the circumscription of these predicates relative to A is collapsible. This is more general than the "solitary" case of circumscription, and partially overlaps the "separable" case (see (Lifschitz 1985), Section 5). Proposition 6 follows from Corollary to Proposition 5 and the following lemma:

Lemma. *If $P_1, \ldots, P_n$ have only negative occurrences in B then*

$$\text{Circum}(A \wedge B; P) \equiv \text{Circum}(A; P) \wedge B.$$

Proof. Circum$(A(P) \wedge B(P); P)$ is

$$A(P) \wedge B(P) \wedge \forall p \neg[A(p) \wedge B(p) \wedge p < P].$$

If $P_1, \ldots, P_n$ have only negative occurrences in $B(P)$ then $B(P)$ and $p < P$ imply $B(p)$. Hence the part in the brackets can be replaced by $A(p) \wedge p < P$. It remains to notice that

$$A(P) \wedge \forall p \neg[A(p) \wedge p < P]$$

is Circum$(A(P); P)$.

5. Priorities

Let us turn now to *prioritized* circumscription, and consider, for simplicity, the case of two predicates P_1, P_2. Assigning a higher priority to P_1 means interpreting $p < P$ lexicographically, as

$$\forall x(p_1 x \supset P_1 x) \wedge [\forall x(P_1 x \supset p_1 x) \supset [\forall x(p_2 x \supset P_2 x) \wedge \neg\forall x(P_2 x \supset p_2 x)]]. \quad (9)$$

Formula (3) with $p < P$ defined as (9) is denoted by Circum($A; P_1 > P_2; Z$).

The formula for computing the result of prioritized circumscription from (Lifschitz 1985), Theorem 2, gives in this case:

$$\text{Circum}(A; P_1 > P_2; Z) \equiv \text{Circum}(A; P_1; P_2, Z) \wedge \text{Circum}(A; P_2; Z). \tag{10}$$

Notice that in the right-hand side of (10) we vary P_2 when minimizing P_1, but P_1 is fixed when P_2 is minimized. This equivalence is easy to understand if we remember that there are two ways to transform a pair (P_1, P_2) into a pair which comes earlier in the lexicographic ordering: either replace P_1 by something smaller and change P_2 arbitrarily, or leave P_1 the same and replace P_2 by something smaller.

It follows from (10) and Proposition 2a that

$$\text{Circum}(A; P_1 > P_2; Z) \equiv C_{P_1}(A; P_2, Z) \wedge C_{P_2}(A; Z) \tag{11}$$

whenever P_1, P_2 have only positive occurrences in A. The right-hand side of (11) is the pointwise counterpart of prioritized circumscription.

6. Subdomain Circumscription

Our next goal is to introduce some more general forms of pointwise circumscription. We start with a motivating example.

Consider a simple version of the blocks world, in which a block can be in only one of two places: either on the table or on the floor. We want to describe the effect of one particular action, putting block B on the table. This can be done using two unary predicate constants, $ONTABLE_0$ and $ONTABLE_1$, which represent the configurations of blocks before and after the action. There are two axioms:

$$\neg AB\ x \supset (ONTABLE_0\ x \equiv ONTABLE_1\ x) \tag{12}$$

and

$$ONTABLE_1\ B. \tag{13}$$

Here AB is the "abnormality" predicate which will be circumscribed in the conjunction of (12) and (13). The first axiom expresses what John McCarthy calls the "commonsense law of inertia": normally, objects remain where they are. This formula exemplifies the use of circumscription for solving the frame problem (McCarthy 1986). The second axiom expresses the basic property of the action under consideration: in the new configuration of blocks, B is on the table.

What should be varied in the process of minimizing AB? The purpose of our axiom set is to characterize the new configuration of blocks; hence it is natural to circumscribe AB with $ONTABLE_1$ allowed to vary. According to Proposition 2a, it does not matter whether we apply global or pointwise circumscription. Using the methods of (Lifschitz 1985), we easily determine that the result of circumscription is equivalent to the conjunction of (12), (13) and

$$AB\ x \equiv (x = B \wedge \neg ONTABLE_0\ B).$$

This is exactly what we would intuitively expect; the only block which changes its location is B, and this only happens if it was not on the table prior to the event. Notice that circumscription does not lead to the same result if $ONTABLE_0$ and $ONTABLE_1$ are both varied or both fixed. (If they are both fixed then the result of circumscription is

$$\neg AB\ x \equiv (ONTABLE_0\ x \equiv ONTABLE_1\ x),$$

which is much too weak. If $ONTABLE_0$ is varied then we can conclude that AB is identically false, so that B was originally on the table, and no blocks have changed their positions; this interpretation of commonsense inertia is much too strong.) To sum up, circumscription must treat $ONTABLE_0$ and $ONTABLE_1$ in different ways.

Let us change now slightly the formal language used in this example and move closer to the formalism of the *situation calculus* of (McCarthy and Hayes 1969). In addition to variables for blocks, we introduce a second sort of variables, variables for *situations*. There are two situation constants, S_0 and S_1, which represent two situations separated by the action of placing B on the table. Instead of two unary predicates $ONTABLE_0$ and $ONTABLE_1$, we have now one binary predicate $ONTABLE$, which is supposed to have a situation term as its second argument. In the new notation, (12) and (13) become

$$\neg AB\ x \supset (ONTABLE(x, S_0) \equiv ONTABLE(x, S_1))$$

and

$$ONTABLE(B, S_1).$$

We also add the axiom $S_0 \neq S_1$.

These two axiom sets are very similar. Any model of the first set can be obtained from a model of the second set by taking two "slices" corresponding to the values S_0, S_1 of the situation argument of $ONTABLE$; any model of the second set can be obtained from a model of the first set by defining $ONTABLE$ arbitrarily for situations other than S_0, S_1.

What then corresponds to the circumscription described above in this notation? We would like to vary "one slice" of $ONTABLE$ and have "another slice" fixed. Definitions (3), (4), do not allow us to do that; for any predicate or function constant in the language, we have to either include it in list Z, and then all values of that predicate or function may vary, or not include it in Z, and then all of its values must remain fixed in the process of minimization. We would like to be able to specify, for each function and predicate in Z, the *part of its domain* on which its values must remain fixed, and allow the other values to be varied.

The following notation will be useful. If p, q, r are predicate symbols of the same arity then we write $EQ_r(p,q)$ for

$$\forall x(\neg rx \supset (px \equiv qx))$$

("p and q are equal outside r"). If f, g are function symbols of the same arity as r then $EQ_r(f,g)$ stands for

$$\forall x(\neg rx \supset (fx = gx)).$$

Assume first that Z consists of only one symbol, a predicate constant or a function constant. Consider a λ-expression V of the same arity as Z, which has no parameters and contains neither P nor Z. Intuitively, it specifies the part of the domain of Z on which Z may vary.

For global circumscription, we propose the following formula:

$$A(P,Z) \wedge \forall pz \neg[EQ_V(z,Z) \wedge A(p,z) \wedge p < P]. \tag{14}$$

If V is identically true then this *subdomain circumscription* turns into (3). Making V identically false is equivalent to treating Z as a parameter rather than varying it; (14) becomes (1). In the example from the previous section, Z is $ONTABLE$, and we can get the desired effect, for instance, by taking V to be $\lambda ys(s \neq S_0)$; $ONTABLE$ is allowed to vary in situations other than S_0.

The counterpart of (14) for pointwise circumscription is

$$A(P,Z) \wedge \forall xz \neg[Px \wedge EQ_V(z,Z) \wedge A(\lambda y(Py \wedge x \neq y), z)].$$

We can allow even more flexibility by making it possible for x to affect the choice of the part of the domain on which Z may vary when P is minimized at x. (This additional flexibility is essential for more complex applications, as we will see in Section 9). Let V be a λ-expression $\lambda xuV(x,u)$ whose arity equals the sum of the arities of P and Z. Intuitively, V represents the function which maps every value of x into the set of all values of u satisfying $V(x,u)$; accordingly, we will write Vx for $\lambda uV(x,u)$. The new form of circumscription is

$$A(P,Z) \wedge \forall xz \neg[Px \wedge EQ_{Vx}(z,Z) \wedge A(\lambda y(Py \wedge x \neq y), z)].$$

We will denote this *subdomain pointwise circumscription* by $C_P(A(P,Z); Z/V)$. Making V weaker, i.e., varying Z at a larger part of its domain, makes $C_P(A; Z/V)$ stronger. In the extreme case when V is identically true $C_P(A; Z/V)$ becomes $C_P(A; Z)$. If V is identically false then $C_P(A; Z/V)$ is equivalent to $C_P(A)$.

7. More on Priorities

Now we know how to perform circumscription with some values of Z allowed to vary. There is another interesting possibility: we may vary some values of the minimized predicate P itself. This may create the effect of assigning different priorities to the tasks of minimizing P at different points.

We start with the case when Z is empty. The new schema is

$$A(P) \wedge \forall xp \neg [Px \wedge \neg px \wedge EQ_{Vx}(p, P) \wedge A(p)]. \tag{15}$$

Here V is a λ-expression $\lambda xy V(x,y)$ which has no parameters and does not contain P. The second term of (15) expresses that it is impossible to change the values of P on $\{y : V(x,y)\}$ so that its value at x will change from *true* to *false*, without loosing the property A. We denote (15) by $C_P(A; P/V)$. It turns into the basic form of pointwise circumscription $C_P(A)$ when $V(x,y)$ is $x = y$. If V is identically false then the first three conjunctive terms in the brackets contradict each other, and (15) is equivalent to $A(P)$. If V is identically true then the third conjunctive term in the brackets can be dropped, and (15) can be written then as

$$A(P) \wedge \forall p[A(p) \supset \forall x(Px \supset px)]$$

or

$$A(P) \wedge \forall x[Px \equiv \forall p(A(p) \supset px)].$$

This case of (15) expresses that P is the "absolute minimum" of $A(P)$; see Remark 3 in Section 8 of (McCarthy 1980).

Let us look now at some other possible choices of V.

Example 4. Applying the basic forms of global circumscription (1) or pointwise circumscription (2) to $Pa \vee Pb$ gives

$$\forall x(Px \equiv x = a) \vee \forall x(Px \equiv x = b). \tag{16}$$

Using the form of pointwise circumscription introduced in this section, we can express the idea of assigning a higher priority to the task of minimizing P at b; this circumscription will lead to the stronger result

$$\forall x(Px \equiv x = a). \tag{17}$$

To this end, introduce a binary predicate constant V, and let $A(P)$ be the conjunction of $Pa \vee Pb$, $\forall x V(x,x)$ and $V(b,a)$. The third formula shows that P may be varied at point a when it is minimized at b. This condition expresses in the language of pointwise circumscription that minimizing P at b is given a higher priority. It is easy to see that, in this case, (15) implies (17). (If P is true at any point other than

a or b then its value at that point can be changed without violating the axioms. If P is true at b and $a \neq b$ then we can make P false at b and true at a).

An interesting feature of this example is that information on priorities is represented by the axiom $V(b, a)$, which is included in the database along with $Pa \vee Pb$. A circumscriptive theory is usually thought of as an axiom set along with a *circumscription policy*, a metamathematical statement describing which predicates are allowed to vary, and what the priorities are. The form of circumscription proposed here allows us to describe circumscription policies by *axioms* rather than *metamathematical expressions*.

Unlike metamathematical descriptions, axiomatic descriptions of circumscription policies do not have to be complete. For instance, in the example above we minimized P at b with a higher priority than at a, but the axioms say nothing about priorities assigned to objects other than a and b. Such incomplete descriptions of circumscription policies can be useful when some details of the policy are inessential.

Example 5. Consider the problem posed in (Hanks and McDermott 1985), Section 7.1. Let $A(P)$ be the conjunction of these axioms:

$$a_i \neq a_j \qquad (0 \leq i < j \leq 3),$$

$$S(x, y) \equiv [(x = a_1 \wedge y = a_0) \vee (x = a_2 \wedge y = a_1) \vee (x = a_3 \wedge y = a_2)],$$

$$\neg Px \wedge S(y, x) \supset Py,$$

$$\neg Pa_0.$$

We can think of $a_0, \ldots, a_3$ as instances of time, S as the successor relation, and P as an "abnormality" of some kind. Applying any of circumscriptions (1), (2) to $A(P)$ gives

$$\forall x[Px \equiv (x = a_1 \vee x = a_2)] \vee \forall x[Px \equiv (x = a_1 \vee x = a_3)]. \tag{18}$$

Hanks and McDermott ask what kind of formal non-monotonic reasoning can capture the idea of preferring "minimization at earlier moments of time", which would lead to selecting the second disjunctive term. Their analysis shows that "temporal reasoning" of this kind may be useful but apparently cannot be captured by the existing formalisms.

The problem is clearly similar to the one discussed above. Extend the theory by these "policy" axioms:

$$\forall x V(x, x), \quad V(a_i, a_j) \qquad (0 \leq i < j \leq 3).$$

The additional axioms tell us that P may be varied at the points "later than x"when minimized at x; in this way, it "gives preference to the past". If a model with $a_2 \neq a_3$ satisfies the first term of (21) then a "better" model can be constructed by making Pa_2 false and Pa_3 true.

In examples of circumscription from (McCarthy 1986), the distinction between different kinds of abnormality is expressed by means of function constants called *aspects*, so that we write

$$ab\ aspect_1\ x,\ ab\ aspect_2(y, z, u),\ \ldots$$

instead of

$$ab_1\ x,\ ab_2(y, z, u),\ \ldots .$$

When prioritized circumscription is required, priorities are established between aspects (not between minimized predicates, as we did in Section 5). The difference between these two approaches is basicaly notational. But it is interesting to notice that the possibility of assigning different priorities to the tasks of minimizing ab at different points demonstrated here enables us to express priorities between aspects as well. For instance, the axiom

$$V(aspect_2(y, z, u), aspect_1\ x),$$

expresses that $aspect_2$ has a higher priority than $aspect_1$.

8. The General Case

Now we are ready to give the most general definition of pointwise circumscription which covers the forms introduced in Sections 6 and 7.

Let $A(S_1, \ldots, S_n)$ be a sentence, where each S_i is a predicate symbol or a function symbol (in particular, it can be a 0-ary function symbol, i.e., an object constant). We want to minimize one of the predicate symbols from this list, S_{i_0}. (Thus S_{i_0} corresponds to P, and the other members of the list correspond to Z in the notation used before). The *pointwise circumscription of S_{i_0} in A with S_i allowed to vary on V_i* is, by definition,

$$A(S) \wedge \forall xs \neg [S_{i_0} x \wedge \neg s_{i_0} x \wedge \bigwedge_{i=1}^{n} EQ_{V_i x}(s_i, S_i) \wedge A(s)]. \tag{19}$$

Here S stands for $S_1, \ldots, S_n$, s is a list $s_1, \ldots, s_n$ of predicate and function variables corresponding to the predicate and function constants S; V_i $(i = 1, \ldots, n)$ is a predicate without parameters which does not contain $S_1, \ldots, S_n$ and whose arity is the arity of S_1 plus the arity of S_i.

We denote (19) by $C_{S_1}(A; S_1/V_1, \ldots, S_n/V_n)$. To simplify notation, we assumed so far that the predicate to be circumscribed is the first on the list; generally, it can be any of the symbols $S_1, \ldots, S_n$ (provided, of course, it is a predicate, not a function).

If V_i is identically true then we will drop $/V_i$ in this notation. In particular, the circumscription from Proposition 7 above can be denoted by $C_P(A; P)$.

We will consider now the model theoretic meaning of circumscription (19). As usual in model theory, we denote the object representing a symbol K in a model M by $M[\![K]\!]$. (This is an element of M if K is an object constant, a function with values in M if K is a function constant of arity > 0, and a Boolean-valued function if K is a predicate constant). For any λ-expression $\lambda u V u$ without parameters, $M[\![\lambda u V u]\!]$ is the set of those tuples of elements of M which satisfy Vu.

Let U be a non-empty set; we are interested in the models of $A(S)$ with the universe U. For any $\xi \in U^k$, where k is the arity of S_1, we will define a reflexive and transitive relation $\leq^\xi$ on the set of all such models. The minimality of a model relative to this relation will express the impossibility of changing the value of S_1 from *true* to *false* at point ξ under the conditions corresponding to circumscription (19). This relation is defined as follows: $M_1 \leq^\xi M_2$ if
(i) $M_1[\![K]\!] = M_2[\![K]\!]$ for every function or predicate constant K which is not in S,
(ii) for any $i = 1, \ldots, n$, $M_1[\![S_i]\!]$ and $M_2[\![S_i]\!]$ coincide on $\{\eta : (\xi, \eta) \notin M_1[\![V_i]\!]\}$,
(iii) $M_1[\![S_1]\!](\xi) \leq M_2[\![S_1]\!](\xi)$.

Symbol $\leq$ in part (iii) of this definition refers to the usual ordering of Boolean values ($false < true$). Notice that M_1 in the expression $\{\eta : (\xi, \eta) \notin M_1[\![V_i]\!]\}$ can be equivalently replaced by M_2, because it follows from (i) that $M_1[\![V_i]\!] = M_2[\![V_i]\!]$.

Proposition 8. *A model of A with the universe U is a model of $C_{S_1}(A; S_1/V_1, \ldots, S_n/V_n)$ iff, for each $\xi \in U^k$, it is minimal relative to $\leq^\xi$ in the set of models of A with the universe U.*

Proof. Consider a model M of $A(S)$ with the universe U. M is *not* minimal relative to $\leq^\xi$ iff one can find a model M' with the universe U such that
(i) $M[\![K]\!] = M'[\![K]\!]$ for every function or predicate constant K which is not in S,
(ii) for any $i = 1, \ldots, n$, $M[\![S_i]\!]$ and $M'[\![S_i]\!]$ coincide on $\{\eta : (\xi, \eta) \notin M[\![V_i]\!]\}$,
(iii) $M[\![S_1]\!](\xi) = true$, $M'[\![S_1]\!](\xi) = false$.
Finding values of x and s which make the condition in the brackets in (19) true is equivalent to finding a ξ and a model M' of $A(S)$ satisfying these conditions.

9. Conclusion

The pointwise approach to circumscription has the following advantages over the traditional global approach.

1. The basic case of pointwise circumscription is expressed by a first-order formula.

2. There is no need to define the circumscription of more than one predicate.

3. Circumscription policies become more "modular": a separate policy is defined for each of the minimized predicates.

4. Circumscription policies, including the selection of priorities, can be described by axioms, instead of metamathematical definitions.

5. Circumscription policies may vary from point to point, which provides additional flexibility useful in applications to formalizing reasoning about time and actions.

We hope that the form of circumscription proposed in this paper is sufficiently powerful for formalizing many relatively complex forms of commonsense reasoning. Future work will show whether this is indeed the case.

Acknowledgements

I am grateful to Michael Gelfond, Robert Givan, Benjamin Grosof, John McCarthy, Drew McDermott, Nils Nilsson, Raymond Reiter and Yoav Shoham for useful discussions. This research was partially supported by DARPA under Contract N0039-82-C-0250.

References

Hanks, S. and McDermott, D., *Temporal Reasoning and Default Logics*, Technical Report YALEU/CSD/RR#430, Yale University (1985).

Lifschitz, V., Computing circumscription, *Proc. 9th International Joint Conference on Artificial Intelligence* **1**, 1985, 121–127.

Lifschitz, V., Pointwise circumscription: Preliminary report, *Proc. 5th National Conference on Artificial Intelligence* **1**, 1986, 406–410.

McCarthy, J., Circumscription – a form of non-monotonic reasoning, *Artificial Intelligence* **13** (1980), 27–39.

McCarthy, J., Applications of circumscription to formalizing commonsense knowledge, *Artificial Intelligence* **28** (1986), 89-118.

McCarthy, J. and Hayes, P., Some philosophical problems from the standpoint of artificial intelligence, in: Meltzer, B. and Michie, D. (Eds.), *Machine Intelligence* 4 (Edinburgh University Press, Edinburgh, 1969), 463-502.

3.4 Unifications

In this section, you will find three different papers connecting the various approaches to default reasoning; the latter two attempt to provide uniform frameworks for understanding all the formalisms.

Konolige's paper, "Autoepistemic logic and default theories," is the sharpest of the three. Konolige has a precise claim to make: that the propositional version of Reiter's default logic is formally identical to Moore's autoepistemic logic. The paper presents a translation between the two.

Konolige rewrites a default rule of the form

$$\frac{\alpha : \beta_1, \ldots, \beta_n}{\omega}$$

as

$$(L\alpha \wedge \neg L\neg\beta_1 \wedge \ldots \wedge \neg L\neg\beta_n) \rightarrow \omega \qquad (3.2)$$

where L is the "necessity" or "belief" modal operator introduced in Section 1.3.2 of the introduction. Konolige shows that the stable expansions of such a theory correspond exactly to Reiter's extensions. He demonstrates the existence of a mapping in the reverse direction (from a modal theory to a default one) by noting that, if quantification into a modal expression is not allowed (i.e., there are no expressions such as $\forall x.Lp(x)$), any modal theory can be reexpressed as a list of propositions of the form (3.2).

The other two papers are both more ambitious and less precise. Shoham, in "Nonmonotonic logics," suggests that a partial order on the set of all models for a theory can be used to unify existing approaches to default inference. He shows that this approach can be applied to circumscription, a result that is not surprising in light of the general result that the circumscription axioms do indeed select minimal models among those of a given theory. (See Proposition 8 of Lifschitz' pointwise circumscription paper **[Lifschitz, 1987b]**, for example.)

Shoham goes on to consider a description of default logics in terms of minimal models. Unfortunately, he runs into trouble for two reasons:

1. As discussed in the introduction, the default approach does not "contrapose." This makes Shoham's model-based approach very awkward, and Shoham suggests salvaging it by using Lukaszewicz' modification [Lukaszewicz, 1984] to Reiter's logic.
2. Shoham translates the default rule $\alpha : \beta/\omega$ into the modal expression $\alpha \wedge \neg L\neg\beta \rightarrow \omega$. In light of Konolige's result, this translation seems not to capture adequately the sense of the default rule.

The final paper in the set is a short description of my own work on multi-valued logics. I argue that there is a need to label default conclusions as such, so that they may be conveniently retracted if they are found to be in conflict with other information in the database. The basic idea of the approach is that a pair of truth values corresponding to "true" and "false" is insufficient, and that truth values should in fact be selected from a larger set. I assume that the elements of this set can be ordered in two distinct ways; the first corresponds to how true some statement is, whereas the second indicates how much information underlies our belief in that statement.

Unfortunately, the development of this approach involves quite a bit of algebra and lattice theory, and the longer papers describing the work [Ginsberg, 1987b; Ginsberg, 1987c; Ginsberg, 1987d] did not seem suitable for inclusion in this collection. It does appear, however, that the approach unifies a variety of existing formalisms, and that it effectively addresses difficulties such as those raised by Perlis in **[Perlis, 1986]**. It also leads to the development of general-purpose algorithms that appear likely to lead to effective implementations of the formalisms being generalized; an application to the development of a circumscriptive theorem prover is discussed in [Ginsberg, 1987a].

A variety of other authors also have investigated the issue of unifications among the nonmonotonic formalisms. Bossu and Siegel develop a general theory of entailment in minimal models in [Bossu, Siegel, 1985]. Etherington discusses connections among a variety of approaches in [Etherington, 1986]. Gelfond also has investigated connections between the consistency-based methods and circumscription. In [Gelfond, Przymusinska, Prsymusinski, 1986], he considers the connection between the closed-world assumption and circumscription;[1] in [Gelfond, 1986; Gelfond, Przymusinska, 1986], he examines the connection between circumscription and autoepistemic logic. Finally, Imielinski shows in [Imielinski, 1987] that there cannot be a complete translation between the consistency-based approaches and the minimization ones.

In addition to this work relating the various nonmonotonic theories, Doyle has examined connections between nonmonotonic work and results in other disciplines. In [Doyle, 1984], he examines the relationship between circumscription and the mathematical concept of implicit definability; in [Doyle, 1985], he shows that default reasoning can be recast in terms of an economic conecpt known as *Pareto optimality*. Finally, there is recent technical work by Schlipf [Schlipf, 1986] and Jaeger [Jaeger, 1986] connecting circumscription with the mathematical notion of an *inductive definition*.

[1] Lifschitz also considers this issue in **[Lifschitz, 1985a]**. The paper is in Section 5.1 of this collection.

ON THE RELATION BETWEEN DEFAULT AND AUTOEPISTEMIC LOGIC

Kurt Konolige
Artificial Intelligence Center*
Center for the Study of Language and Information
SRI International
333 Ravenswood, Menlo Park, Ca. 94025
(415)859-2788 KONOLIGE@AI.SRI.COM

Abstract

Default logic is a formal means of reasoning about defaults: what *normally* is the case, in the absence of contradicting information. Autoepistemic logic, on the other hand, is meant to describe the consequences of reasoning about ignorance: what must be true if a certain fact is *not* known. Although the motivation and formal character of these two systems are different, a closer analysis shows that they share a common trait, which is the indexical nature of certain elements in the theory. In this paper we compare the expressive power of the two systems. First, we give an effective translation of default logic into autoepistemic logic; default theories can thus be embedded into autoepistemic logic. We also present a more suprising result: the reverse translation is also possible, so that every set of sentences in autoepistemic logic can be effectively rewritten as a default theory. The formal equivalence of these two differing systems is thus established. This analysis gives an interpretive semantics to default logic, and yields insight into the nature of defaults in autoepistemic reasoning.

[keywords: nonmonotonic reasoning, default logic, autoepistemic logic]

*This research was supported by contract N00014-85-C-0251 from the Office of Naval Research, by subcontract from Stanford University under contract N00039-84-C-0211 from the Defense Advanced Research Projects Administration, and by a gift from the System Development Foundation.

Contents

1 Introduction

Default reasoning can be informally described as the process of jumping to conclusions based on what is normally the case. To say that "power corrupts," for example, is to say that for typical x, in typical situations, x will be corrupted by the exercise of authority.

Default logic [14] is a formalization of default reasoning. An agent's knowledge base (KB), its collection of facts about the world, is taken to be a first-order theory. Default reasoning is expressed by *default rules* of the form

$$\frac{\alpha : M\beta}{\omega}, \tag{1}$$

which can be read roughly as, "If α is provable from the KB, and β is consistent with it, then assume ω as a default." Unlike ordinary first-order inference rules, default rules are *defeasible*: given a KB containing just α, for example, the rule above would allow the inference of ω, but if $\neg\beta$ is added to the KB, then the default rule is no longer applicable. Default rules are thus nonmonotonic inference rules.

In default logic, the default rules operate at a metatheoretic level, as they are not expressed in the language of the KB, and are not inference rules within the KB. Rather, they can be thought of as a means for taking a KB and transforming it into another by the addition of sentences that are not logically derivable from the original. The transformation is defined in terms of a fix-point operator.

This formulation of default reasoning leads us to ask several questions which do not have readily apparent answers. The first concerns the expressiveness of the logic. Certain simple types of defaults can be readily stated; for example, "power corrupts" could be expressed as

$$\frac{Powerful(x) : M\, Corrupt(x)}{Corrupt(x)}, \tag{2}$$

but it is not clear that more complicated constructs could be accommodated. One example is a conditional defaults, where a default rule is the conclusion of an implication; another is a default whose consequent is itself a default. Because the default rules are not part of the logical language, there is no obvious, straightforward expression of these concepts.

The second question, related to the first, concerns the semantics of default logic. Because defaults are expressed as inference rules operating in conjunction with a fixed-point construction, the *meaning* of such objects as $M\beta$ is not clear. In some recent work, there have been proposals for a semantics for a restricted class of default theories [8] and for default logic in general [3]. In both cases, the "semantics" is a reformulation of the KB-transformation induced by the defaults in terms of restrictions on the models of the KB. Although such a reformulation can provide an alternative view of the construction of default extensions, it does not provide a semantics in the sense of providing an interpretation for default rules in a model structure (an *interpretive semantics*). Indeed, because defaults are expressed as inference rules, they are not amenable to interpretation in this fashion.

Our idea in this paper is to define default reasoning within the theory of the KB itself, rather than as a transformation of the KB. If we take the sentences of a KB to be the knowledge or beliefs of an agent, then defaults can be expressed by referring to what an agent *doesn't know*. The default that "power corrupts" could be stated informally as

If x is powerful, then assume x is corrupt *if nothing known contradicts it*. (3)

It is easy to see that such reasoning is defeasible in the presence of additional information about the integrity of x. From a formal point of view, it is clear that to assert this statement, the language of the KB must be augmented by a construction that refers to the KB as a whole.

Let us call a theory containing an operator that refers to the theory itself an *indexical theory*. We will use the expression $L\phi$ within a theory to mean that the sentence ϕ is part of the theory. Now we can rephrase the default rule (1) in the following manner, using the operator L:

$$L\alpha \wedge \neg L\neg\beta \supset \omega\ . \tag{4}$$

The intent of a rule of this form is something like: "If α is in the KB, and $\neg\beta$ is *not* in the KB, then ω is true." The negation sign in $\neg\beta$ arises from the use of the provability operator L, the dual of the consistency operator M. Because L is an operator of the KB language, we have been able to express the default within the language of the KB itself, rather than as a metatheoretic construct.

The introduction of an indexical operator is an added complexity, for now we allow our initial KB to contain statements not only about the world, but also about its own contents. Indeed, even interpreting the modal operators of (4) is a problem. Fortunately, the mathematical properties of indexical theories have recently been studied by Moore [13] as a formalization for a another type of nonmonotonic reasoning, called *autoepistemic reasoning*, in which an agent reasons about the relationship of her knowledge to the world. Moore has derived an elegant and natural interpretive semantics for indexical theories incorporating the self-referential operator L. This semantics gives an interpretation to the operator L based on model structures.

We are naturally led to ask what relationship exists between default theories and their corresponding expression in AE logic. Are they essentially different, in the sense that agents using each one would have widely differing sets of beliefs? The answer, which is the main result of this paper, is *no*: default logic and AE logic sanction the same inferences on corresponding initial inputs. This fact has several important consequences. Since default rules are expressible in AE logic, both default and autoepistemic reasoning can be combined within this single formalism. Also, the formal expression of defaults gains the benefits of an interpretive semantics.

A second and more surprising consequence is that AE logic is no more expressive than default logic, even though the L operator is part of the language: there exists a translation from every set of AE logic premises into a corresponding default theory. As we shall see, it is possible by translating the appropriate AE logic statements to construct default theories with the effect of conditional defaults, defaults whose conclusion is a default, and so on. The expression of these concepts is still much more natural in terms of the L operator, but the mathematical properties of the corresponding default theories are the same.

Of independent interest are some results in the theory of AE logic, especially the characterization and equivalence of moderately-grounded and minimal extensions, the definition of strongly-grounded extensions and introspective idempotency, and the relationship of AE logic to the modal logic of weak *S5*.

2 Autoepistemic Logic

Autoepistemic (AE) logic was defined by Moore [13] as a formal account of an agent reasoning about her own beliefs. The agent's beliefs are assumed to be a set of sentences in some logical language augmented by a modal operator L. The intended meaning of $L\phi$ is that ϕ is one of the the agent's beliefs; thus the agent could have beliefs about her own beliefs. For example, consider a space shuttle flight director who believes that it is safe to launch not because of any positive information, but by reasoning that if something were wrong, she would know about it from her engineers. This belief can be expressed using sentences of the augmented language. If P stands for "It is safe to launch the shuttle," then

$$\neg L\neg P \supset P \tag{5}$$

expresses the flight director's self-knowledge. Equation (5) is a logical constraint between a belief state ($L\neg P$) and a condition on the world (P).

The primary focus of AE logic is a normative one: given an initial (or ***base***) set of beliefs A about the world, what final set T should an ideal ***introspective*** agent settle on? If we restrict ourselves for the moment to languages without the self-belief operator, then clearly an ideal agent should believe all of the logical consequences of her base beliefs, a condition sometimes referred to as *logical omniscience* [5]. More formally, let the expression $\Gamma \models \phi$ mean that the sentence ϕ is logically implied by the set of sentences Γ. Then, if the base set is A, the belief set T of an ideal agent is given by:

$$T = \{\phi \mid A \models \phi\}\,. \tag{6}$$

The presence of a self-belief operator complicates matters. Because the intended meaning of $L\phi$ depends on the belief set of the agent, the definition of the belief set itself becomes circular, which necessitates the use of a fixed-point equation to define T. In this section we will present this definition and give several alternative formulations that will prove useful.

2.1 Logical preliminaries

We begin with a language $\mathcal{L}$ for expressing self-belief, and introduce valuations of $\mathcal{L}$. The treatment generally follows and extends Moore [13], but differs in two ways. First, the base language is first-order rather than propositional; but this is a minor change, because no quantifying into a modal context is permitted. Second, ideal belief sets are defined with a fixed-point equation over valuations of the language. This definition is equivalent to Moore's original one, but leads to different insights on the nature of the ideal belief set, simpler proofs of many results, and several natural extensions.

Let $\mathcal{L}_0$ be a first-order language with functional terms and a distinguished sentence $\bot$ which is always false. The normal formation rules for formulas of first-order languages hold. A *sentence* of $\mathcal{L}_0$ is a formula with no free variables; an *atom* is a sentence of the form $P(t_1, \cdots, t_n)$. We extend $\mathcal{L}_0$ by adding a unary modal operator L; the extended language is called $\mathcal{L}$. $\mathcal{L}$ can be defined recursively as containing all the formation rules of $\mathcal{L}_0$, plus the following:

$$\text{If } \phi \text{ is a sentence of } \mathcal{L}, \text{ then so is } L\phi. \tag{7}$$

An expression $L\phi$ is a *modal atom*. Sentences and atoms of $\mathcal{L}_0$ are called *ordinary*. Note that nestings such as $LL\phi$ are modal atoms (and hence sentences) of $\mathcal{L}$. Because the argument of a modal operator never contains free variables, there is no quantifying into the scope of a modal atom, e.g., $\exists x LPx$ is not allowed. A sentence has a *modal depth n* if its modal operators are nested to a depth of n; e.g., $L(P \vee LP)$ has a modal depth of 2. We use the abbreviation $\mathcal{L}_n$ for the set of all sentences of modal depth n or less. Often we will use a subscript to indicate a subset of sentences based on modal depth; e.g., $\Gamma_n = \Gamma \cap \mathcal{L}_n$.

From the point of view of first-order valuations, the modal atoms $L\phi$ are simply nilary predicates. Our intended interpretation of these atoms is that ϕ is an element of the belief set of the agent. So we will consider valuations of $\mathcal{L}$ to be standard first-order valuations, with the addition of a belief set Γ. The atoms $L\phi$ are interpreted as true or false depending on whether ϕ is in Γ. To distinguish these valuations, we will sometimes call them ***L valuations***.

The interaction of the interpretation of L with first-order valuations is often a delicate matter in this paper, and so a perspicuous terminology for talking about L valuations is necessary. In particular, it is often useful to decouple the interpretation of modal and ordinary atoms. First-order valuations are built upon the truthvalues of atoms: for ordinary atoms, truthvalues are given by a structure $\langle U, \varphi, \mathcal{R}\rangle$, where φ is a mapping from terms to elements of the universe U, and $\mathcal{R}$ is a set of relations over U, one for each predicate. We will refer to any such structure as an *ordinary index*, and denote it with the symbol I. Modal atoms are given a truthvalue by a belief set Γ, which is called a *modal index*.

The truthvalue of any sentence in $\mathcal{L}$ can be determined by the normal rules for first-order valuations, given an ordinary and modal index. We write $\models_{I,\Gamma} \phi$ if a valuation $\langle I, \Gamma\rangle$ satisfies ϕ. The valuation rule for modal atoms can be written as

$$\models_{I,\Gamma} L\phi \quad \text{if and only if} \quad \phi \in \Gamma\,. \tag{8}$$

A valuation that makes a every member of a set of sentences true is called a *model* of the set. A sentence that is true in every member of a class of valuations is called *valid* with respect to the class. The following classes of valuations are useful:

$$\begin{array}{ll} \models_\Gamma & \text{valuations with modal index } \Gamma \\ \models & \text{all valuations} \\ \Sigma \models & \text{models of } \Sigma\,. \end{array} \tag{9}$$

A sentence ϕ is a *first-order consequence* (FOC) of a set of sentences Σ if it is true in all models of Σ. Σ is *closed under first-order consequence* if it contains all sentences that are true in all of its models.

2.2 Autoepistemic extensions

Now we return to the original question of what an ideal introspective agent should believe. Obviously, we want to use equation (6), with an appropriate choice for logical implication. Given that the intended meaning of L is *self*-belief, it becomes obvious that we should consider all models in which the interpretation of $L\phi$ is the belief set of the agent itself; that is, the valuations we consider all have a modal index that is the belief set of the agent. Following Moore, we call such valuations *autoepistemic* (or AE), and define the extension of a base set A of beliefs as follows:

DEFINITION 2.1 *Any set of sentences T which satisfies the equation*

$$T = \{\phi \mid A \models_T \phi\}$$

is an autoepistemic extension *of A.*

This is a fixed-point equation for a belief set T, and is a candidate for the belief set of an ideal introspective agent with premises A. It is similar to the belief set definition for a nonintrospective agent (Equation 6) in that it contains A and is closed under first-order consequence. As we will see in later sections, there are other conditions that we may want extensions to satisfy if they are to be considered as ideal belief sets.

Defining AE extensions in this manner gives us an alternative, compact expression of the *stable expansions* of Moore's original exposition [13]. He defines a set of sentences T of $\mathcal{L}$ as *sound* with respect to the premises A if every AE valuation of T (that is, every L valuation with modal index T) that is a model of A is also a model of T. T is *semantically complete* if T contains every sentence that is true in every AE model of T. If T is sound and complete with respect to A, it is called a stable expansion of A.

It is easy to verify from the fixed-point equation that every AE extension is sound and complete with respect to A. Further, any stable expansion of A also satisfies the fixed-point equation. Hence stable expansions are exactly AE extensions.

EXAMPLE 2.1 A base set A may give rise to one or several AE extensions, or to none. As we show below, any set of ordinary sentences has exactly one extension. The extension for the base set $A = \{P\}$ contains all the first-order consequences of P, but no other ordinary formulas. It contains modal atoms of the form $L\phi$, where ϕ is a FOC of A, and $\neg L\psi$, where ψ is not a FOC of A.

Any set of first-order inconsistent sentences gives rise to the same AE extension, containing all sentences. This is the only AE extension that contains the false sentence $\bot$.

The base set $A = \{LP\}$ has no extensions. For suppose T is such an extension; either $P \in T$ or $P \notin T$. Clearly the latter cannot be the case, for then for *any* sentence ϕ, $A \models_T \phi$ (because $\models_{I,T} A$ is false for any I). Now suppose $P \in T$. In this case, we can construct an interpretation that satisfies A but falsifies P, namely one in which I makes P false. Therefore it cannot be that $A \models_T P$, and so P is not in T, a contradiction.

The base set $\{LP \supset P\}$ has two extensions, one of which contains P, and the other of which does not.

The base set $\{\neg LP \supset Q,\ \neg LQ \supset P\}$ has two extensions; in one of them, LP is true and LQ is not, and in the other the reverse.

Suppose an agent has only ordinary sentences in her base set A. These sentences determine a unique extension for the agent. This proposition was proven independently by Marek [9]. (To make the development of this paper clearer, we include proofs of propositions in an appendix).

PROPOSITION 2.1 *If A is a set of ordinary sentences, it has exactly one AE extension T. T_0 is the first-order closure of A.*

We now consider an alternative semantic characterization of AE extensions. In Definition 2.1, an extension T is defined using the operator $\models_T$, which incorporates T itself. However, if the definition used the simple validity operator $\models$, self-reference would be eliminated, and a proof-theoretic analog for $\models$ could be used. Note that in $\models_T$, the modal index of the interpretation gives truthvalues to all atoms of the form $L\phi$, according to whether ϕ is in T or not. Let LT stand for the set of formulas $\{L\phi \mid \phi \in T\}$, and $\neg L\overline{T}$ for $\{\neg L\phi \mid \phi \notin T\}$. The sets LT and $\neg L\overline{T}$ are satisfied only by the interpretations whose modal index is T; hence $LT \cup \neg L\overline{T} \models \phi$ if and only if $\models_T \phi$. This gives the following alternative characterization of extensions:

PROPOSITION 2.2 *A set T is an AE extension of A if and only if it satisfies the equation*

$$T = \{\phi \mid A \cup LT \cup \neg L\overline{T} \models \phi\}\,.$$

Essentially, the self-referential part of the definition has been transferred from the implication operator to the set of assumptions LT and $\neg L\overline{T}$. Note that there is a trade-off between the strength of assumptions and of the implication operator: in substituting the weak operator $\models$ for $\models_T$, we were forced to introduce the strong assumptions LT and $\neg L\overline{T}$ to eliminate unwanted models.

Moore has called belief sets defined by the above equation *grounded in A*, because they are derived from A and assumptions about self-belief. This notion of groundedness is a fairly weak one, in that the allowable assumptions are very liberal — an agent is able to assume a self-belief in any proposition as a basis for the derivation of beliefs. In later sections we will define two strengthenings of groundedness; to distinguish Moore's definition, we will call extensions *weakly grounded* if they obey the equation of Proposition 2.2.

It is possible to modify the above equation by strengthening the implication operator (still avoiding self-reference) and weakening the assumptions. This gives us yet another semantic characterization of AE extensions. However, we first need to introduce and analyze a special type of belief set, called a *stable set.*

2.3 Stable sets

Following Stalnaker [16], we call a belief set Γ *stable* if it satisfies the following three properties:

1. Γ is closed under first-order consequence.[1]
2. If $\phi \in \Gamma$, then $L\phi \in \Gamma$.
3. If $\phi \notin \Gamma$, then $\neg L\phi \in \Gamma$.

Given Proposition 2.2, it is clear that AE extensions must be stable sets. They are closed under first-order consequence because they are defined using the operator $\models$; and the presence of LT and $\neg L\overline{T}$ guarantees that properties (2) and (3) above are satisfied. Thus we have:

PROPOSITION 2.3 (MOORE) *Every AE extension of A is a stable set containing A.*

The strict converse of this proposition is not true, since there can be stable sets containing A that are not AE extensions of A. The simplest example is $A = \{LP\}$, which has no AE extension (see Example 2.1). Yet there are many stable sets that contain LP.

A partial converse is available if we consider stable sets as AE extensions of their own ordinary sentences.

PROPOSITION 2.4 *Every stable set Γ is an AE extension of Γ_0.*

Stable sets are thus AE extensions of their ordinary sentences. From Proposition 2.1, we know that every such AE extension is unique; hence every stable set is uniquely determined by its ordinary sentences.

PROPOSITION 2.5 (MOORE) *If two stable sets agree on ordinary formulas, they are equal.*

The set of ordinary formulas contained in a stable set is closed under first-order consequence. Different stable sets thus have different sets of first-order (FO) closed ordinary formulas. We now show that stable sets cover the sets of FO-closed ordinary formulas; that is, every such FO-closed set is the ordinary part of some stable set.

PROPOSITION 2.6 *Let W be a set of ordinary formulas closed under first-order consequence. There is a unique stable set Γ such that $\Gamma_0 = W$. W is called the* kernel *of the stable set.*

The stable set whose kernel contains the element $\bot$ is the set of all sentences of $\mathcal{L}$. This is the unique inconsistent stable set.

We are now ready to give a third semantic characterization of AE extensions. Since AE extensions are stable, let us consider restricting the range of modal indices on the logical implication operator to just stable sets; we indicate this by $\models_{SS}$. From Proposition 2.5, we know that the ordinary formulas of a stable set uniquely determine it. As usual, let T_0 be the set of ordinary formulas of T, and $\overline{T}_0$

[1] Stalnaker considered propositional languages and so used tautological consequence.

the set of ordinary formulas *not* in T. Then, if T is stable, it must be the case that $\models_T$ is equivalent to $LT_0 \cup \neg L\overline{T}_0 \models_{SS}$, because LT_0 and $\neg L\overline{T}_0$ specify only those models in which the modal index is the unique stable set containing exactly the ordinary formulas T_0. This suggests how we can replace $\models_T$ in the definition of AE extensions.

PROPOSITION 2.7 *A set T is an AE extension of A if and only if it satisfies the equation*

$$T = \{\phi \mid A \cup LT_0 \cup \neg L\overline{T}_0 \models_{SS} \phi\}.$$

By using a stronger type of implication ($\models_{SS}$ over stable sets), we have been able to eliminate all self-referential assumptions except for those involving the ordinary formulas of T. Proposition 2.7 also hints that the nesting of L operators gives no extra expressive power to the language, since stable sets are characterized by giving the sets LT_0 and $\neg L\overline{T}_0$. Indeed this is so, and we will prove it in section 3, when we have introduced proof-theoretic analogs to the semantic fixed-point equations.

2.4 Moderately-grounded extensions

One way of evaluating the fixed-point equations in Propositions 2.2 and 2.7 is by the type of reasoning they sanction for introspective agents. So, according to Proposition (2.2), an agent is justified in believing all of the first-order consequences of her base set A and the assumptions LT and $\neg L\overline{T}$. As we have noted, this is a fairly weak groundedness condition, and we might want the belief sets of ideal reasoning agents to obey stronger constraints. Consider, for example, the base set $A = \{LP \supset P\}$. A has two AE extensions, which we call T and T' (see Example 2.1). T contains P and LP, while T' does not contain P, but has $\neg LP$. The difference between these extensions lies in whether LP is introduced as an assumption in the fixed-point equation of Proposition 2.2. For the belief set T, the agent's belief in P is grounded in her assumption that she believes P. If she chooses to believe P, she is justified in believing it precisely because she made it one of her beliefs. This certainly seems to be an anomolous situation, since the agent can, simply by choosing to assume a belief or not, be justified in either believing or not believing a fact about the real world.

We would like to define a stronger notion of groundedness to eliminate this circularity. Now consider the belief set definition given in Proposition 2.7:

$$T = \{\phi \mid A \cup LT_0 \cup \neg L\overline{T}_0 \models_{SS} \phi\}.$$

The set of ordinary sentences in the belief set is T_0. LT_0 is the assumption that the agent believes all of these sentences. There would be no circular justifications if we replace LT_0 by LA in the fixed-point definition. In this way we are assured that the derivation of facts about the world does not depend on the assumption of belief in those facts. The assumption of A is necessary because an ideally introspective agent should at least believe that her base beliefs are beliefs.

From this discussion, we can define the following notion of *moderately grounded.*

DEFINITION 2.2 *A set of sentences Γ is* moderately grounded *in A if it obeys the equation*

$$\Gamma = \{\phi \mid A \cup LA \cup \neg L\overline{\Gamma}_0 \models_{SS} \phi\}.$$

Sets that are moderately grounded in A are also AE extensions of A, as we will shortly show. However, not every AE extension is moderately grounded.

EXAMPLE 2.2 The base set $A = \{LP \supset P\}$ has two extensions, but only one of them is moderately grounded. The extension containing P cannot be moderately grounded, because P cannot be derived without the assumption of LP.

A more complicated case is the base set $A = \{LP \supset Q,\ LQ \supset P\}$. Again there are two extensions, one containing the ordinary formulas P and Q, and one without them. For the former, LP and LQ must be assumed together in order to justify P and Q. Because they cannot be derived without this assumption, this extension is not moderately grounded.

All extensions of the set of ordinary formulas A are moderately grounded, because every $\phi \in T_0$ is in the first-order closure of A and so in the stable set containing LA.

Moderately grounded sets are conservative in what they assume about the world, given the base beliefs. As shown in example 2.2, the base set $\{LP \supset P\}$ has only one moderately grounded extension, for which P is not a belief. In fact, moderate groundedness is closely related to another concept, the ***minimality*** of ordinary sentences in an extension.

DEFINITION 2.3 *An AE extension T of A is* minimal for A *if there is no other extension T' of A such that $T'_0 \subset T_0$.*

Note that there can be more than one minimal extension for a given base set, e.g., $A = \{\neg LP \supset Q,\ \neg LQ \supset P\}$ has two extensions, both of which are minimal for A. The base set $A = \{LP \supset P\}$ has a single minimal extension, the one that doesn't contain P. Minimal extensions are appealing candidates for ideal introspective belief sets, because they limit the assumptions an agent makes about the world.

We now prove that, in fact, the minimal AE extensions of A are exactly the sets moderately grounded in A. Thus we have two independent motivations for choosing moderate groundedness as a condition for ideal belief sets.

PROPOSITION 2.8 *A set of sentences is moderately grounded in A if and only if it is a minimal AE extension of A.*

There is an interesting connection between stable sets and minimal AE extensions. By analogy with Definition 2.3, we define a minimal stable set for A as follows:

DEFINITION 2.4 *A stable set S is* minimal for A *if S contains A and there is no other stable set S' containing A such that $S'_0 \subset S_0$.*

In the last part of the proof of Proposition 2.8, it is noted that, if T is a minimal AE extension of A, there cannot be any stable sets S containing A for which $S_0 \subset T_0$. Thus:

PROPOSITION 2.9 *Every minimal AE extension for A is a minimal stable set for A.*

The converse of this proposition is not true, since there are minimal stable sets for A which are not AE extensions of A (see the discussion following Proposition 2.3). However, if a minimal stable set for A *is* an AE extension, then it must be a minimal extension, since any other extension of A is also a stable set.

PROPOSITION 2.10 *If a minimal stable set for A is an AE extension of A, it is a minimal extension.*

3 Proof Theory

We now examine proof-theoretic analogs to the semantics of AE extensions. The immediate reason for this examination is to establish a normal form for base sets that will be useful in proving the correspondence between AE and default extensions. A longer-term goal, and one which we will not pursue here, is to understand how an agent can reason about and justify her own beliefs, starting from an initial set, by using rules of inference.

3.1 Proof-theoretic fixed-points

The simplest analog is to replace the logical implication operator $\models$ in Proposition 2.2 by a first-order deduction operator $\vdash$. There are sound and complete systems of first-order deduction, that is, the derivations of such systems are exactly the first-order consequences. So we have the following proposition:

PROPOSITION 3.1 (MOORE) *A set T is an AE extension of A if and only if it satisfies the equation*

$$T = \{\phi \mid A \cup LT \cup \neg L\overline{T} \vdash \phi\} .$$

Moore originally proved this theorem for the case of a propositional base language. It gives a completely proof-theoretic characterization of AE extensions. Unfortunately, it is still a fixed-point equation, and so does not yield a constructive method for finding extensions.

Finding a deductive analog to the operator $\models_{SS}$ is more difficult, because it involves logical implication over modal indices that are stable sets. The correct logic is a modal system known as *K45*. For those familiar with modal logic, *K45* is a weakening of the well-known modal system *S5*; it is appropriate for belief, as opposed to knowledge, because beliefs can be false. The development of this result is somewhat long, and involves exploring the connection between stable sets and the possible-worlds semantics for *S5*.

Possible worlds have been used as a semantical basis for a variety of epistemic logics (those dealing with knowledge or belief).[2] In this approach, an agent's beliefs are represented by a set of worlds W, those that are ***compatible with*** her beliefs. Each world is a first-order valuation.

Now suppose an agent has a base set A consisting entirely of ordinary sentences. We define the set of worlds W compatible with A as all first-order valuations that make every element of A true. Because each world is a first-order valuation, all of the first-order consequences of A will also be true. On the other hand, for every sentence ϕ which is not a first-order consequence of A, there must be some world in which $\neg\phi$ is true, or else ϕ would also be a belief.

This takes care of beliefs which are ordinary formulas; what about self-beliefs? Since we assume that the agent is ideally introspective, $L\phi$ should be a belief (and hence true in all worlds) just in case ϕ is a belief. So the semantics of belief atoms is given by:

$$L\phi \text{ is true in } w \quad \text{iff} \quad \forall w' \in W \,.\, \phi \text{ is true in } w' \,. \tag{10}$$

A structure defined by a set of possible worlds and the truth-recursion rule (10) is an *S5 interpretation*. Let us call the set of sentences true at every world in W an *S5 set*, and if W was generated by a set of ordinary sentences A, an *S5 set for A*. These sets have the following properties:

1. If W was generated by A, the ordinary formulas in the set are just the first-order consequences of A.

[2] A good overview for computer science applications is given by Halpern and Moses [4].

2. The set is closed under first-order consequence.

3. If ϕ is in the set, then $L\phi$ must also be, according to (10).

4. If ϕ is not in the set, then $\neg L\phi$ must be, because there is some world at which $\neg\phi$ is true.

These are exactly the conditions for stable sets, so every *S5* set must be stable. The converse is also true, namely, every stable set is an *S5* set. Let A be the kernel of a stable set; by the above conditions, there is an *S5* set for A, which is also the stable set whose kernel is A. Hence we have the following equivalence between stable sets and *S5* sets:

PROPOSITION 3.2 *A set is stable if and only if it is an S5 set.*

The relationship between stable sets and *S5* structures has been noted by others, and a version of this proposition was originally proven, in an independent fashion, by Moore, Halpern and Moses, and Fitting (see [11, p. 7]).

The equivalence between *S5* sets and stable sets leads to an alternative form of the $\models_{SS}$ operator. Let us define an $S5^+$ *valuation* $\langle w, W\rangle$, where w is a possible world, and W is a set of possible worlds (perhaps containing w), by the truth-recursion rules:

$$\begin{array}{lll} \models_{\langle w,W\rangle} \phi & \text{iff} & \phi \text{ is true in } w, \text{ for ordinary } \phi \\ \models_{\langle w,W\rangle} L\phi & \text{iff} & \text{for all } w' \in W, \models_{\langle w',W\rangle} \phi \end{array} \tag{11}$$

If a sentence ϕ is valid in all $S5^+$ valuations, we write $\models_{S5^+} \phi$.[3]

PROPOSITION 3.3 *For any* $\phi \in \mathcal{L}$, $\models_{S5^+} \phi$ *if and only if* $\models_{SS} \phi$.

We now have equivalence between validity in possible-worlds structures, and validity in stable-set L valuations. There is a large body of literature about possible-worlds structures which we can draw on to derive the correct proof theory of $S5^+$ valuations. First, we must relate $S5^+$ valuations to the usual form of possible-worlds semantics, Kripke stuctures.

A Kripke structure $\langle w, W, R\rangle$ consists of a distinguished possible world, a set of possible worlds (containing w), and a binary relation R among the elements of W (the *accessibility relation*). The truth-recursion rule is:

$$\begin{array}{lll} \models_{\langle w,W,R\rangle} \phi & \text{iff} & \phi \text{ is true in } w, \text{ for ordinary } \phi \\ \models_{\langle w,W,R\rangle} L\phi & \text{iff} & \text{for all } w' \text{ such that } wRw', \models_{\langle w',W,R\rangle} \phi \end{array} \tag{12}$$

Different classes of Kripke structures are generated by restrictions on the form of the accessibility relation. The condition which corresponds to $S5^+$ valuations is that R be transitive and euclidean (aRb and aRc implies bRc); let us call these TE valuations. We now prove that TE and $S5^+$ valuations are isomorphic.

LEMMA 3.4 *Let R be an equivalence relation on W, and let every element of W be the only immediate successors of w. Then the Kripke valuation $\langle w, W, R\rangle$ is equivalent to the $S5^+$ valuation $\langle w, W\rangle$.*

PROPOSITION 3.5 *$S5^+$ valuations are isomorphic to TE valuations.*

[3] $S5^+$ valuations are closely related to the model descriptions of Levesque [7]. The only significant difference appears to be that he assumes W is always nonempty; this corresponds to eliminating the inconsistent *S5* set.

The correct proof theory for Kripke models whose accessibility relation is transitive and euclidean is a system called *K45*, or ***weak** S5* (see Chellas [2]). Here is the axiomatization for propositional $\mathcal{L}_0$.

DEFINITION 3.1 *By the system propositional K45 we mean the following set of axioms and inference rules:*

all tautologies	
$L(\phi \supset \psi) \supset (L\phi \supset L\psi)$	*Dist*
$L\phi \supset LL\phi$	4
$\neg L\phi \supset L\neg L\phi$	5
$\dfrac{\phi \quad \phi \supset \psi}{\psi}$	*MP*
$\dfrac{\phi}{L\phi}$	*Nec*

The distribution schema (*Dist*) says that *K45*-theorems are closed under modus ponens. Axiom 4 states that if ϕ is true at every world, then so is $L\phi$; and Axiom 5 that if ϕ isn't true at some world, $\neg L\phi$ must be true at every world. Modus ponens and necessitation are the rules of inference. Necessitation and the distribution schema ensure that all worlds are closed under tautologous consequence.

For a first-order base language, we would modify the provision of all tautologies to a suitable generator of first-order valid sentences. We write $\Gamma \vdash_{K45} \phi$ if $(\gamma_1 \wedge \gamma_2 \wedge \cdots \wedge \gamma_n) \supset \phi$ is a theorem of *K45*, for some finite subset $\{\gamma_1 \ldots \gamma_n\}$ of Γ. It is known that *K45* is sound, complete, and compact with respect to TE valuations; hence $\Gamma \models_{\mathrm{TE}} \phi$ if and only if $\Gamma \vdash_{K45} \phi$.

Now we can give the proof-theoretic analogs to Propositions 2.7 and 2.8.

PROPOSITION 3.6 *A set T is an AE extension of A if and only if it satisfies the equation*

$$T = \{\phi \mid A \cup LT_0 \cup \neg L\overline{T}_0 \vdash_{K45} \phi\}\ .$$

It is a minimal (moderately-grounded) extension of A if and only if it satisfies the equation

$$T = \{\phi \mid A \cup LA \cup \neg L\overline{T}_0 \vdash_{K45} \phi\}\ .$$

3.2 Normal form

Normal form significantly reduces the conceptual complexity of AE sentences, since we need not be concerned with nested modal operators. It is essential to the notion of *strong groundedness* in the next subsection, and to the translation of AE logic into default logic.

The following two facts about *K45* theories are useful in establishing a normal form:

1. Every AE sentence is equivalent to a sentence containing modal atoms only of the form $L\phi$ or $\neg L\phi$, where ϕ is an ordinary sentence.

2. $L\phi \wedge L\psi$ is equivalent to $L(\phi \wedge \psi)$.

The first of these facts enables us to consider only base sets A drawn from $\mathcal{L}_1$. As we hinted in the last section, the nesting of L operators lends no extra expressive power to the language, since they can always be re-expressed in terms of $\mathcal{L}_1$.

In deriving a normal form for a set of sentences A, we first show that every sentence from $\mathcal{L}_1$ has an equivalent form in which no modal operator appears in the scope of a quantifier, i.e., it is a boolean combination of modal atoms and ordinary sentences.

Proposition 3.7 *Every sentence of $\mathcal{L}_1$ is equivalent to a sentence of the form*

$$\begin{array}{l} (L_1 \vee \omega_1) \ \wedge \\ (L_2 \vee \omega_2) \ \wedge \\ \cdots \qquad\quad \wedge \\ (L_n \vee \omega_n) \end{array}$$

where each L_i is a disjunction of modal literals on ordinary sentences, and each ω_i is ordinary.

Next, we show that any modal atom with nested modal operators is equivalent to a sentence from $\mathcal{L}_1$.

Proposition 3.8 *Every modal atom $L\phi$, where ϕ is from $\mathcal{L}_1$, is equivalent to a sentence of $\mathcal{L}_1$.*

Example 3.1 Let us reduce the following sentence to one from $\mathcal{L}_1$.

$$P \wedge \neg L(L\neg Q \vee LQ) \supset \neg L\neg Q \wedge \neg LQ$$

Concentrating on the second part of the antecedent, we have:

$$\begin{array}{l} \neg L(L\neg Q \vee LQ) \equiv_{K45} \\ \neg(L\neg Q \vee LQ) \equiv_{K45} \\ \neg L\neg Q \wedge \neg LQ \end{array}$$

Substituting into the original sentence, we get:

$$P \wedge \neg L\neg Q \wedge \neg LQ \supset \neg L\neg Q \wedge \neg LQ \quad ,$$

which is just a tautology.

We are now ready to define normal form for sets of AE sentences. By successively applying Proposition 3.8 to a sentence of $\mathcal{L}$, all nested modal operators can be eliminated. Using Proposition 3.7 and the fact that $L\phi \wedge L\psi \equiv L(\phi \wedge \psi)$, any sentence of $\mathcal{L}_1$ can be converted into a set of simple disjunctive sentences.

Proposition 3.9 *Every set A of $\mathcal{L}$-sentences has a K45-equivalent set in which each sentence is of the form*

$$\neg L\alpha \vee L\beta_1 \vee \cdots \vee L\beta_n \vee \omega \ , \tag{13}$$

with α, β_i, and ω all being ordinary sentences. Any of the disjuncts, except for ω, may be absent.

3.3 Strong groundedness

Consider the following base set:[4]

$$\begin{array}{l} \neg LP \supset Q \\ LP \supset P \end{array} \tag{14}$$

This base set has *two* moderately grounded extensions, which we call T and T'. T contains Q and $\neg LP$, while T' has P and $\neg LQ$. It is easy to see how T is grounded: assuming $\neg LP$, Q is derivable from the base set. On the other hand, it is not clear how, in T', P can be derived from the base

[4]This example was suggested by Michael Gelfond and Halina Przymusinska in a private communication.

set and $\neg LQ$. But recall that in the definition of moderately grounded (2.2), both the base set A and LA are present. In *K45*, $L(\neg LP \supset Q)$ is equivalent to $\neg LQ \supset LP$; from $\neg LQ$, it is possible to derive LP; and from $LP \supset P$, we arrive at P.

There is something curious about this reasoning, because LP is derived before P is. It is as if an agent, in the course of reasoning, arrives first at the point of believing "I believe that P," without first having come to believe P itself. In defining moderately-grounded extensions, we eliminated one possible way that this could occur, namely using the *assumption* of LP to justify belief in P. But there are other means by which an agent might arrive at a belief in LP before P, as the above example shows. Here it is the assumption of $\neg LQ$ that leads to the derivation of LP, without having derived P.

So we seek a further notion of groundedness, which we call *strong groundedness*, in which every ordinary sentence ϕ has a derivation that does not depend on $L\phi$. The most straightforward approach would be to exclude sentences such as $LP \supset P$ above, which clearly expresses the derivation. The problem here is that $LP \supset P$ may not be explicitly represented: we could replace it, for example, by the chain $LP \supset Q_1$, $LQ_1 \supset Q_2$, ..., $LQ_n \supset P$, or even more complicated constructions, so just ruling out sentences of the form $LP \supset P$ will not suffice.

The solution is to break the derivation of ϕ from $L\phi$ by never allowing $L\phi$ to be derived, except as a consequence of the derivation of ϕ. There is a simple way to accomplish this. Note that in the above example, T' does not contain Q. Hence the first sentence of the base set, $\neg LP \supset Q$, is not used to derive Q. Rather, given $\neg LQ$, it can be used (via $L(\neg LP \supset Q) \equiv \neg LQ \supset LP$) to derive LP. Now suppose a base set A is in normal form, so all sentences are of the form $\neg L\alpha \vee L\beta_1 \vee \cdots \vee L\beta_n \vee \omega$. We want this sentence to be used only for the derivation of ω, the ordinary formula. We will call an extension *strongly grounded* if all of its base sentences are used in this way.

DEFINITION 3.2 *Let A be a set of AE sentences in normal form, and let T be an extension of A. Let A' be the set of sentences of A whose ordinary part is contained in T. Then T is* strongly grounded *in A if and only if*

$$T = \{\phi \mid A' \cup LA' \cup \neg L\overline{T}_0 \models_{SS} \phi\} .$$

Strongly grounded extensions have some curious properties. First, we show that every strongly grounded extension is moderately grounded (and hence minimal).

PROPOSITION 3.10 *If T is a strongly grounded extension of A, it is moderately grounded in A.*

Not every moderately-grounded extension is strongly-grounded; the minimal extension T' in the example above is not strongly-grounded.

One of the nice properties of moderate groundedness is that it is insensitive to the syntactic form of the base set. If two base sets A and A' are *K45*-equivalent, then they have the same moderately-grounded extensions. However, they do not necessarily have the same strongly-grounded extensions. For example, consider the following two equivalent normal-form base sets:

$$\begin{aligned} A &= \left\{ \begin{array}{c} P \\ LP \vee \bot \end{array} \right\} \\ A' &= \left\{ \begin{array}{c} \neg LP \vee P \\ LP \vee \bot \end{array} \right\} \end{aligned} \tag{15}$$

They both have one extension, which is moderately grounded ($LP \vee \bot$ is equivalent to LP). This extension is strongly grounded for A, but not for A', since eliminating $LP \vee \bot$ leaves no way to derive P.

So strong groundedness is at least partially a *syntactic* property of AE base sets, depending on the exact form of the sentences. This seems inevitable if we want to formalize the notion that ϕ be derived independently of $L\phi$, since the notion of derivation itself is a syntactic one. This idea — that the *form* of the sentences in a KB is important for the derivation of answers from the KB — is neither unfamiliar nor undesirable, and in fact has been at the center of the earliest uses of specialized deductive mechanisms in AI. There is even a name for systems of this sort: *procedural deductive system* (see Moore [12]). The main characteristic of such systems is the presence of several syntactic varieties of implication, all of which have the same semantics, but different procedural interpretations in derivations: forward chaining, backward chaining, and the like. The form in which an implication is expressed has a great influence on the derivational behavior of the system. In like manner, the exact expression of self-belief in AE sentences can have an effect on whether an extension is strongly grounded or not.

Strongly grounded extensions enjoy one useful property that moderately grounded ones do not: they are insensitive to the addition of the schema $L\phi \supset \phi$ to the base set. The only way $L\phi$ could be derived in a strongly-grounded extension is if ϕ is derived independently; hence $L\phi \supset \phi$ will never be used to derive ϕ, and cannot cause the derivation of any new ordinary sentences. Thus T is a strongly-grounded extension of A if and only if it is a strongly grounded extension of $A \cup L\phi \supset \phi$. We call this property *introspective idempotency.*

3.4 Summary of groundedness results

There are three notions of groundedness for AE extensions. Every AE extension T of a base set A is weakly grounded, that is, it satisfies the equation

$$T = \{\phi \mid A \cup LT \cup \neg L\overline{T} \models \phi\} .$$

Moderately-grounded extensions eliminate all assumptions of positive modal atoms, and use a stronger notion of logical consequence:

$$T = \{\phi \mid A \cup LA \cup \neg L\overline{T}_0 \models_{SS} \phi\} .$$

All moderately-grounded extensions are weakly grounded, but the converse is not necessarily true. An alternate characterization of moderate groundedness is provided by a minimality condition: the moderately-grounded extensions of A are just those extensions which are minimal in their kernels (see Proposition 2.8).

Strong groundedness is partially a syntactic concept, based on the normal form for AE sentences. Let A' be all sentences of A in normal form whose ordinary sentence is contained in T. Then T is strongly grounded if

$$T = \{\phi \mid A' \cup LA' \cup \neg L\overline{T}_0 \models_{SS} \phi\} .$$

All strongly-grounded extensions are moderately grounded, but the converse is not necessarily true.

4 Default Logic

We briefly review the logic of default theories. As defined by Reiter [14], a default theory is a pair $\langle W, D\rangle$, where W is a set of first-order sentences and D is a set of defaults, each of which has the form

$$\frac{\alpha : M\beta_1, M\beta_2, \ldots M\beta_n}{\omega} .$$

A default d is satisfied by a set of sentences Γ if either (1) α is not in Γ or some $\neg\beta_i$ is in Γ (the premisses of the rule are not satisfied), or (2) ω is in Γ (the conclusion is satisfied). A default extension of $\langle W, D\rangle$, informally, is a minimal set of sentences containing W, closed under first-order consequence and satisfying all the defaults D.

If none of α, β_i, or ω contain free variables, then the default is called *closed.* An open default is treated as a schema for the set of closed defaults that are its substitution instances. We thus need consider only closed defaults, as long as we allow default theories to contain a denumerably infinite set of them.

Default extensions share many of the properties of AE extensions. There may be one or many extensions of a default theory, or none. The following examples are analogous to the AE extensions in Example 2.1.

EXAMPLE 4.1 The default extension for the theory $\langle\{P\}, \emptyset\rangle$ (no defaults) is exactly the first-order consequences of P.

The theory $\langle\emptyset, P : /P\rangle$ has one extension, the set of all first-order valid sentences. P is *not* an element of this extension. This differs from the AE base set $\{LP \supset P\}$ which has an extension containing P.

The theory $\langle\emptyset, \{M\neg P/Q,\ M\neg Q/P\}\rangle$ has two extensions; in one of them, P is true and Q is not, and in the other the reverse.

These examples are instructive by comparison to AE extensions. If the theory $\langle W, D\rangle$ contains no defaults (D empty), then there is exactly one extension, which is the first-order part of the AE extension of W. In general, a default of the form $\alpha : M\beta/\omega$ corresponds to the AE sentence $L\alpha \wedge \neg L\neg\beta \supset \omega$; thus, in the third default theory of the example, there are two default extensions, corresponding to the first-order parts of the two AE extensions of $\{\neg LP \supset Q,\ \neg LQ \supset P\}$. However, note the difference in the case of the second default theory of this example. The default $P : /P$ has only one extension, in which P does not appear. The AE set $\{LP \supset P\}$ has *two* extensions; the one in which P appears arises from the ability of AE extensions to support circular justifications (assuming LP, the sentence $LP \supset P$ gives a derivation of P). So although it appears that default extensions have corresponding AE extensions for a suitable transformation of the defaults, not all AE extensions will have corresponding default extensions. In fact, as we show below, default extensions correspond to *strongly grounded* AE extensions.

Default extensions are the fixed points of an operator $\Gamma(V)$. This operator is meant to formalize the informal criteria given above for the extensions of $\langle W, D\rangle$, namely, it should contain W, be closed under first-order consequence, and satisfy all of D. Let V be an arbitrary set of first-order sentences. Then $\Gamma(V)$ is the smallest set satisfying the following properties:

D1. $W \subseteq \Gamma(V)$

D2. $\Gamma(V)$ is closed under first-order consequence.[5]

D3. If $\alpha : M\beta/\omega \in D$, $\alpha \in \Gamma(V)$, and $\neg\beta \notin V$, then $\omega \in \Gamma(V)$.

Extensions are fixed-points of Γ, i.e., any set E satisfying $E = \Gamma(E)$. As a fixed-point definition, it is similar to the fixed-point account of minimal AE extensions (Proposition 2.8). The parameter of $\Gamma(V)$ essentially fills the role of the assumptions $\neg L\overline{T}_0$, since $\neg\beta$ must *not* be present in order for the default to be satisfied. Minimality is part of the definition of $\Gamma(V)$ (the *least set* satisfying the conditions D1–D3); if it were excluded, then default extensions corresponding to nonminimal AE extensions would be present.

[5] In the original definition, this is stated in terms of deduction rather than logical consequence.

5 Default and AE Extensions

In this section we explore the relationship between default and AE extensions.

5.1 Translations

In standard mathematical reasoning, to compare a formal systems Q_1 to another system Q_2 it is necessary to provide a sentence-to-sentence translation from the language of Q_1 to the language of Q_2 (see Boolos [1, p. 46]) The difficulty here is that the *language* of the two formalisms is different: default theories are first-order but contain inference rules with a metatheoretic operator M, while AE logic has a modal operator L in the language itself. How do we go about comparing the two?

Both formalisms have in common the notion of an *extension*. In AE logic, an extension is a set of sentences in a modal language. We have shown that AE extensions are always stable sets, and so are uniquely determined by their kernel, the set of ordinary formulas of the extension (see Propositions 2.5 and 2.6); further, this kernel is closed under first-order consequence. In default logic, an extension is also a set of first-order sentences closed under FO-consequence. If we choose the first-order language of default logic to be the same as the base langauge $\mathcal{L}_0$ of AE logic, then there is a natural notion of equivalence between the two: we will say that an AE extension is the same as a default extension if the latter is the kernel of the former.

There are now two questions that we wish to answer.

- Is an arbitrary default theory expressible in AE logic?
- Is an arbitrary AE base set expressible as a default theory?

To show that default theories are expressible in AE logic, we must provide a translation from an arbitrary default theory U to an AE base set A, such that U and A have equivalent extensions. For AE logic, we have three choices for the class of extensions, depending on the groundedness condition — weak, moderate, or strong. The best fit with default logic occurs for strong groundedness, and we define equivalence of base sets accordingly: U and A are equivalent if every extension of U is the same as some strongly-grounded extension of A, and every strongly-grounded extension of A is the same as some extension of U. Obviously, U and A must have the same number of extensions if they are equivalent.

We may want to impose some restrictions on the translation from U to A. The strongest and most natural condition is that it be effectively computable, one-to-one, and context-independent:— every sentence or default rule of U is effectively translated into exactly one sentence of A, independent of any other sentences or defaults in U. Let us call a translation of this sort *local.*[6] The translation that we propose, which follows from our reasoning in section 1 about the relationship between default rules and AE sentences, is a local one. The main result of this paper is that this translation yields an equivalent AE base set.

What about expressing AE base sets as default theories? Here we might expect more difficulty because the structure of default rules is fixed, while the modal operator of AE logic can be arbitrarily embedded in a sentence. However, by reducing a base set A to the normal form developed in section 3.2, we can find a local translation for it into an equivalent default theory U. So if we restrict our attention to the strongly-grounded extensions, AE logic and default logic turn out to be essentially the same, although their formal structure is very different.

[6] Imielinski [6] defines the notion of a *modular* translation: the translation of a default rule in $\langle W, D\rangle$ cannot depend on W, but can depend on the presence of other defaults in D. All local translations are modular.

5.2 Defaults as self-belief

We now define a local transformation from a default theory $\langle W, D\rangle$ to a set of AE sentences A, such that the default extensions of $\langle W, D\rangle$ are exactly the kernels (the first-order part) of the strongly-grounded AE extensions of A. Thus (as we prove), there is an exact correspondence between default extensions for $\langle W, D\rangle$ and strongly-grounded AE extensions for A.

The transformation is:

$$\frac{\alpha : M\beta_1 \ldots M\beta_n}{\omega} \quad \mapsto \quad (L\alpha \wedge \neg L\neg\beta_1 \wedge \cdots \wedge \neg L\neg\beta_n) \supset \omega\,. \tag{16}$$

As we mentioned in the introduction, this is the natural interpretation of defaults in terms of introspective knowledge. A paraphrase of the AE sentence for agent might be: "If I know that α is true, *and I have no knowledge that any of the β_i are false*, then ω must be true." The key phrase has been emphasized; it is in reasoning about what is not known that the nonmonotonic character of AE logic appears. However, the role of the other parts of the sentence ($L\alpha$ and ω) also deserves closer scrutiny; for example, why does w appear as the consequent, and not $L\omega$? As it stands, this is the transformation that yields the correspondence between default and AE extensions. We will comment more extensively on the form transformation later, after the basic results are presented.

For most of the rest of this section, we assume that there is at most a single operator $M\beta$ in the antecedent of rules. The proofs can be stated much more simply, and the needed modifications for the general case are obvious. In a default, we allow either α or $M\beta$ to be missing; the corresponding AE sentence just deletes the appropriate conjunct in the antecedent. The conclusion of the default must always be present (defaults with no conclusion are senseless). Let D' be the set of sentences formed by taking the transforms of defaults D; we call the set $\{W, D'\}$ the *AE transform of* $\langle W, D\rangle$.

Now consider a particular default theory $\langle W, D\}$ and an associated extension $E = \Gamma(E)$. E is closed under first-order consequence, and hence is the kernel of a unique stable set. This stable set is closely related to the AE transform of $\langle W, D\rangle$: it is a minimal stable set containing the AE transform. We prove this result as the following proposition.

PROPOSITION 5.1 *Let $\langle W, D\rangle$ be a default theory, with $A = \{W, D'\}$ its AE transform. Suppose E is an extension of the default theory. Then E is the kernel of a minimal stable set containing A and $\neg L\overline{E}$.*

The minimal stable set of the above proposition is also an AE extension of A (recall that a stable set must be (weakly) grounded in A if it is to be an extension of A).

PROPOSITION 5.2 *Same conditions as the previous proposition. The set E is the kernel of a minimal AE extension of A.*

The minimal stable set is also strongly grounded in A, if we consider the obvious normal form for A (that is, the translation of a default rule given by Equation (16) is $\neg L\alpha \vee L\neg\beta_1 \vee \cdots \vee L\neg\beta_n \vee \omega$).

PROPOSITION 5.3 *Same conditions as the previous proposition. The set E is the kernel of a strongly-grounded AE extension of A.*

The converse of this proposition is also true.

PROPOSITION 5.4 *Let A be the AE transform of a default theory $\langle W, D\rangle$. If E is the kernel of a strongly-grounded AE extension of A, then $E = \Gamma(E)$.*

We collect the preceding two propositions into the following theorem, the main result connecting AE and default extensions.

THEOREM 5.5 *Let A be the AE transform of a default theory Δ. A set E is a default extension of Δ if and only if it is the kernel of a strongly-grounded AE extension of A.*

Thus every default theory can be translated into an equivalent AE base set. The extensions of the default theory correspond to the AE belief sets with the strongest groundedness conditions.

5.3 Semantics

The semantics of AE sentences is an interpretive semantics, in the sense that a sentence ϕ is true or false in an interpretation $\models_{I,\Gamma}$. The interpretation of modal atoms is given by the modal index Γ, according to Equation (8). The interpretations themselves are straightforward augmentations of standard first-order interpretations. The troublesome characteristics of AE logic, from a semantical point of view, occur in the fixed-point definition of extensions (Definition 2.1), in which only interpretations containing a certain modal index are considered. So, although it is hard to construct and analyze extensions, all of our ordinary intuitions about the meaning of the language $\mathcal{L}$ and its semantics with respect to individual interpretations is still available.

As an example, consider the difference between the two default sentences

$$L\mathit{Bird}(\mathit{Tweety}) \wedge \neg L\neg \mathit{Fly}(\mathit{Tweety}) \supset \mathit{Fly}(\mathit{Tweety}) \tag{17}$$

and

$$\mathit{Bird}(\mathit{Tweety}) \wedge \neg L\neg \mathit{Fly}(\mathit{Tweety}) \supset \mathit{Fly}(\mathit{Tweety})\,. \tag{18}$$

The first sentence states that in any interpretation in which *Bird*(*Tweety*) is a belief and $\neg$*Fly*(*Tweety*) is not a belief, *Fly*(*Tweety*) will be true. In default logic, the rule which translates to this sentence is *Bird*(*Tweety*) : *M Fly*(*Tweety*) / *Fly*(*Tweety*). The antecedent of the second default is less strict: it states only that *Bird*(*Tweety*) must be true. The second default permits case analysis of a type not sanctioned by the first. For example, suppose it is known that either Tweety is a bird, or Tweety is housebroken (*Houseb*(*Tweety*)). In every interpretation in which $\neg$*Fly*(*Tweety*) is not a belief and the second default sentence is true, *Houseb*(*Tweety*) $\vee$ *Fly*(*Tweety*) is true. On the other hand, nothing can be concluded by assuming the first default sentence is true, because *Bird*(*Tweety*) itself may not be a belief. As Etherington [3, p. 34] has noted, the second sentence seems more in accord with our intuitions about the way defaults should work.

The distinction between (17) and (18) makes clear the reason why $L\alpha$ must be used to translate default rules. We can also answer a question posed earlier: why does ω appear in the antecedent of the AE translation, instead of $L\omega$? The reason is that, from the agent's point of view, the conclusion ω is the simple belief that ω is true of the world. Using $L\omega$ would mean that the agent concludes she has a self-belief $L\omega$, and she would have to reason further from that to the simple belief in ω. As we have pointed out in the discussions on moderate and strong groundedness, such reasoning can lead to ungrounded justification of beliefs, and is to be avoided.

Another instance of the utility of interpretive semantics is in the concepts of equivalence and substitution. Two formulas ϕ and ϕ' of $\mathcal{L}$ are equivalent if they have the same truthvalue in all models. Because the definition of AE extensions is framed in terms of the interpretive semantics, ϕ' can be substituted wherever ϕ occurs in a base set A, without changing the AE extensions of A. We used this fact extensively in arriving at the normal form for AE sentences in section 3.2.

For a final example of the use of equivalence, we turn to the literature of inheritance networks. These networks are meant to express class/subclass relationships, and the inheritance of properties by default from a class to its subclasses. Touretzky (in [17, p. 34]) has offered a translation from his particular type of inheritance networks into AE logic. To formally express the intent of the statement "P implies that typically Q is unknown," he uses:

$$P \wedge \neg L(L\neg Q \vee LQ) \supset \neg L\neg Q \wedge \neg LQ \tag{19}$$

However, from Example 3.1 we know that this is equivalent to a tautology, and thus not a very satisfying translation.

5.4 Expressiveness

The question of expressiveness can be phrased as follows: Is it the case that default sentences of the type (18), or perhaps other AE sentences involving complicated constructions such as embedded L operators, have no counterpart in default theories? On the face of it this would seem a plausible conjecture, since the L operator is part of the language, while default rules are not. However, it turns out that AE logic is no more expressive than default logic: there is an effective transformation of any base set of AE sentences into a default theory, such that the default extensions are exactly the kernels of the strongly-grounded AE extensions. To show this, we rely on the fact (see Proposition 3.9) that every set of sentences of $\mathcal{L}$ has an equivalent normal form in which every sentence looks like:

$$\neg L\alpha \vee L\beta_1 \vee \cdots \vee L\beta_n \vee \omega\ , \tag{20}$$

where all of α, β_i, and ω are ordinary sentences. Any of the modal atoms may be missing, but ω is always present.

Given any set of $\mathcal{L}$-sentences A in normal form, it is possible to effectively construct a corresponding default theory $\langle W, D\rangle$, in the following way. Any ω that appears without other disjuncts is put into W. All other sentences are transformed into defaults, in the manner indicated by Equation 16.

$$\neg L\alpha \vee L\beta_1 \vee \cdots \vee L\beta_n \vee \omega \quad \mapsto \quad \frac{\alpha : M\neg\beta_1 \ldots M\neg\beta_n}{\omega} \tag{21}$$

It is easy to see that A is the AE transform of $\langle W, D\rangle$; by Theorem 5.5, these two have essentially the same extensions. More precisely, we have proven the following theorem:

THEOREM 5.6 *For any set of sentences A of $\mathcal{L}$ in normal form, there is an effectively constructable default theory $\langle W, D\rangle$ such that E is a default extension of $\langle W, D\rangle$ if and only if it is the kernel of a strongly-grounded extension of A.*

So, suprisingly, default theories have the same expressiveness as AE logic over the modal language $\mathcal{L}$. However, some caveats should be noted. The extensions are the same only if we restrict ourselves to strongly-grounded ones on the AE side. If we wish to use, say, moderate groundedness as our condition on ideal belief sets, then the translation into default logic is lacking in that some of the AE extensions may not have corresponding default extensions.

A second caveat is that if we extend $\mathcal{L}$ by allowing quantifying-in (i.e., expressions such as $\exists x.L\phi(x)$), in all likelihood Theorem 5.6 will no longer hold. There are a number of reasons to think this; perhaps the most compelling is Levesque's observation [7] that in the presence of quantifying-in, there are sentences of modal depth greater than 1 with no equivalents in $\mathcal{L}_1$.

Given that AE logic can be embedded in default logic, we can translate various types of defaults that have a natural expression in AE logic. The default rules corresponding to the two types of defaults (17) and (18) are

$$\frac{Bird(Tweety) : M Fly(Tweety)}{Fly(Tweety)} \tag{22}$$

and

$$\frac{M Fly(Tweety)}{Bird(Tweety) \supset Fly(Tweety)} . \tag{23}$$

Note that the second type of default (Equation 18), when translated into the default rule (23), causes the atom *Bird*(*Tweety*) to appear not in the antecedent of the default, but in the consequent.

Conditional defaults are expressed in $\mathcal{L}$ by sentences of the form:

$$C \supset (L\alpha \wedge \neg L \neg \beta \supset \omega) \tag{24}$$

By simple propositional manipulations, this is equivalent to:

$$\neg L\alpha \vee L\neg\beta \vee (C \supset \omega) , \tag{25}$$

which translates into the default rule

$$\frac{\alpha : M\beta}{C \supset \omega} . \tag{26}$$

The condition is expressed in the consequent of the default rule.

A default whose conclusion is a default can be expressed by:

$$L\alpha \wedge \neg L \neg \beta \supset (L\alpha' \wedge \neg L \neg \beta' \supset \omega') \tag{27}$$

Again, by propositional manipulations this can be put into the form

$$\neg L\alpha \vee \neg L\alpha' \vee L\neg\beta \vee L\neg\beta' \vee \omega' . \tag{28}$$

The first two disjuncts can be combined into the *K45*-equivalent literal $\neg L(\alpha \wedge \alpha')$. The resulting default rule translation is

$$\frac{\alpha \wedge \alpha' : M\beta, M\beta'}{\omega} . \tag{29}$$

6 Conclusion

Given the current proliferation of nonmonotonic formalisms, it seems wise to establish comparisons among them, especially regarding expressiveness. The results presented here show that there is an exact correspondence between AE logic over $\mathcal{L}$ and default theories. There is a general, effective translation between the two that is *local*: each sentence (or default rule) can be translated in isolation from the others. The translation preserves theoremhood, in that the default extensions are the first-order part of the strongly-grounded AE extensions.

The relationship between default logic and various forms of circumscription [10] has been investigated by a number of researchers. Etherington [3] collects a number of comparability results, and notes that there is a fundamental difference between the minimal-model semantics of circumscription and the fixed-point semantics of default theories. In particular, he cites the following points:

1. Default logic is *brave* in the sense that in the presence of competing defaults, individual extensions will satisfy a maximally consistent set of defaults; in contrast, a natural corresponding circumscriptive theory for defaults would be *cautious*, inferring only what the competing extensions have in common.

2. Default logic can make nonmonotonic inferences about equality, and circumscription cannot.

3. Circumscriptive statements can apply to all individuals, whereas default rules are restricted to those individuals with names in the language.

4. In default logic, there seems to be no way to capture the distinction between *fixed* and *variable* predicates in circumscription.

These results suggest that circumscription and default logic are incomparable, in the sense that there is no local translation of one into the other that preserves theoremhood.

What about the relationship between AE logic and circumscription? Because AE logic is "brave," and can make nonmonotonic inferences about equality (if we allow an equality predicate in $\mathcal{L}$), there is no local translation of AE theories into circumscription. And as long as the language of AE logic is $\mathcal{L}$, it will have the same expressiveness as default logic, and the last two items seem to preclude any general translation of circumscription into AE logic. By allowing quantifying-in in the language, it is possible to construct AE statements applying to all individuals, and so the third item may not present a problem. The fourth item remains, however, and creates pessimism about the existence of a translation from circumscription with fixed predicates.

7 Acknowledgements

This paper is a rewritten and expanded version of a preliminary report that appeared in IJCAI87 in Milan. I would like to thank Michael Gelfond, Hector Levesque, W. Marek, Karen Myers, Donald Perlis, Halina Przymusinska, and Ray Reiter for their careful reading and comments on the paper. In particular, Michael Gelfond and Halina Przymusinski found a counterexample to the original "proof" of the equivalence of minimal AE extensions and default theories, which led me to formulate the concept of strongly-grounded extensions.

References

[1] Boolos, G. *The Unprovability of Consistency.* Cambridge University Press, Cambridge, England, 1979.

[2] Chellas, B. F. *Modal Logic: An Introduction.* Cambridge University Press, 1980.

[3] Etherington, D. W. *Reasoning with Incomplete Information: Investigations of Non-Monotonic Reasoning.* PhD thesis, University of British Columbia, Vancouver, British Columbia, 1986.

[4] Halpern, J. Y. and Moses, Y. O. A guide to the modal logics of knowledge and belief. In *Proceedings of the International Joint Conference on Artificial Intelligence*, pages 50–61, Los Angeles, 1985.

[5] Hintikka, J. Impossible possible worlds vindicated. *Journal of Philosophical Logic*, 4:475–484, 1975.

[6] Imielinski, T. Results on translating defaults to circumscription. *Artificial Intelligence*, 32(1):131–146, April 1987.

[7] Levesque, H. J. *A Formal Treatment of Incomplete Knowledge Bases.* Technical Report 614, Fairchild Artificial Intelligence Laboratory, Palo Alto, California, 1982.

[8] Łukaszewicz, W. Two results on default logic. In *Proceedings of the American Association of Artificial Intelligence*, pages 459–461, University of California at Los Angeles, 1985.

[9] Marek, W. Stable theories in autoepistemic logic. 1986. Unpublished Note, Department of Computer Science, University of Kentucky.

[10] McCarthy, J. Circumscription — a form of nonmonotonic reasoning. *Artificial Intelligence*, 13(1–2), 1980.

[11] Moore, R. C. *Possible-world Semantics for Autoepistemic Logic.* Technical Note 337, SRI Artificial Intelligence Center, Menlo Park, California, 1984.

[12] Moore, R. C. *Reasoning from Incomplete Knowledge in a Procedural Deduction System.* Technical Report AI–TR–347, MIT Artificial Intelligence Laboratory, 1975.

[13] Moore, R. C. Semantical considerations on nonmonotonic logic. *Artificial Intelligence*, 25(1), 1985.

[14] Reiter, R. A logic for default reasoning. *Artificial Intelligence*, 13(1–2), 1980.

[15] Robinson, J. A. *Logic: Form and Function.* Elsevier North Holland, New York, 1979.

[16] Stalnaker, R. C. A note on nonmonotonic modal logic. 1980. Department of Philosophy, Cornell University.

[17] Touretzky, D. S. *The Mathematics of Inheritance Systems.* Morgan Kaufmann Publishers, Inc., Los Altos, California, 1986.

Appendix: Propositions and Proofs

This appendix contains all theorems, propositions, lemmas, and their proofs. Some informal proofs have already been given in the main body of this paper, and are not repeated here.

PROPOSITION 2.1 *If A is a set of ordinary sentences, it has exactly one AE extension T. T_0 is the first-order closure of A.*

Proof. We define the sets $S(n)$ in the following iterative fashion:

$$\begin{aligned} S(0) &= \{\phi \in \mathcal{L}_0 \mid A \models \phi\} \\ S(n) &= \{\phi \in \mathcal{L}_n \mid A \models_{S(n-1)} \phi\} \end{aligned}$$

Let T_n be the set of sentences of T from $\mathcal{L}_n$, and let S be the infinite union of all $S(i)$. We will show that if T is an AE extension of A, $T_n = S(n)$; there is thus at most one AE extension T, with $T_0 = S(0)$, the first-order closure of A. We prove existence by showing that S is always an AE extension of A.

Let T be an AE extension of A. Obviously, $T_0 = S(0)$. Assume that $T_{n-1} = S(n-1)$. We have:

$$\begin{aligned} T_n &= \{\phi \in \mathcal{L}_n \mid A \models_T \phi\} \\ &= \{\phi \in \mathcal{L}_n \mid A \models_{T_{n-1}} \phi\} \\ &= \{\phi \in \mathcal{L}_n \mid A \models_{S(n-1)} \phi\} \end{aligned}$$

The second equality holds because the truthvalue of any sentence in $\mathcal{L}_n$ depends only on the subset of the modal index in $\mathcal{L}_{n-1}$.

Let us define S' by:

$$S' = \{\phi \mid A \models_S \phi\} .$$

To show that S is an AE extension of A, we will show by induction that $S = S'$. Let us assume for the moment that $S_n = S(n)$, that is, S restricted to $\mathcal{L}_n$ is just the set $S(n)$. For the base step, it is obvious that $S'_0 = S(0) = S_0$. Now assume that $S'_{n-1} = S_{n-1}$. Then we have:

$$\begin{aligned} S'_n &= \{\phi \in \mathcal{L}_n \mid A \models_S \phi\} \\ &= \{\phi \in \mathcal{L}_n \mid A \models_{S_{n-1}} \phi\} \\ &= \{\phi \in \mathcal{L}_n \mid A \models_{S(n-1)} \phi\} \\ &= S(n) \\ &= S_n \end{aligned}$$

Now we show that $S_n = S(n)$. As preliminary facts, observe that:

$$\begin{aligned} S(k) &= \{\phi \in \mathcal{L}_k \mid A \models_{S(k-1)} \phi\} \\ &= \{\phi \in \mathcal{L}_k \mid A \models_{S(k)} \phi\} \\ &= S(k+1)_k , \end{aligned}$$

and hence, by simple induction, for any k and $j > 0$, $S(k) = S(k+j)_k$.

We already know that $S(n) \subseteq S_n$. Assume that S_n is larger than $S(n)$, so there is a sentence ϕ such that $\phi \in S_n$ and $\phi \notin S(n)$. Let the modal depth of ϕ be k, where $k \leq n$. For all $j > 0$, $S(k+j)_k = S(k)$, and so ϕ must be in $S(n)$, a contradiction. Therefore S_n cannot be larger than $S(n)$, and must be equal to it.

PROPOSITION 2.2 *A set T is an AE extension of A if and only if it satisfies the equation*

$$T = \{\phi \mid A \cup LT \cup \neg L\overline{T} \models \phi\} .$$

PROPOSITION 2.3 (MOORE)

Every AE extension of A is a stable set containing A.

PROPOSITION 2.4 *Every stable set Γ is an AE extension of Γ_0.*

Proof. For any set Γ, it must be the case that

$$\Gamma = \{\phi \mid \Gamma \models \phi\} .$$

If Γ is stable, then both $L\Gamma \subset \Gamma$ and $\neg L\overline{\Gamma} \subset \Gamma$, so we have

$$\Gamma = \{\phi \mid \Gamma \cup L\Gamma \cup \neg L\overline{\Gamma} \models \phi\} .$$

By the argument preceding proposition 2.2, we know from this that

$$\Gamma = \{\phi \mid \Gamma \models_\Gamma \phi\} .$$

Finally, only the ordinary sentences of Γ are important in determining whether $\models_{I,\Gamma} \Gamma$ is true, and so

$$\Gamma = \{\phi \mid \Gamma_0 \models_\Gamma \phi\} .$$

PROPOSITION 2.5 (MOORE)

If two stable sets agree on ordinary formulas, they are equal.

PROPOSITION 2.6 *Let W be a set of ordinary formulas closed under first-order consequence. There is a unique stable set Γ such that $\Gamma_0 = W$. W is called the* kernel *of the stable set.*

Proof. By Proposition 2.1, there is a unique AE extension T of W. T is a stable set (Proposition 2.3), and by the discussion preceding Proposition 2.1, T_0 is the set of ordinary sentences logically implied by W. Since W is FO-closed, $T_0 = W$.

PROPOSITION 2.7 *A set T is an AE extension of A if and only if it satisfies the equation*

$$T = \{\phi \mid A \cup LT_0 \cup \neg L\overline{T}_0 \models_{SS} \phi\} .$$

Proof. If T is an AE extension, then by Proposition 2.3 it must be stable, and from the above discussion the fixed-point equation reduces to

$$T = \{\phi \mid A \models_T \phi\} ,$$

which is just the definition of an AE extension of A.

On the other hand, suppose T satisfies the fixed-point equation. T_0 is a set of ordinary formulas closed under first-order consequence; hence by Proposition 2.6 they are exactly the ordinary formulas of a unique stable set; so LT_0 and $\neg L\overline{T}_0$ determine a unique stable set, which we call T'. The fixed-point equation reduces to

$$T = \{\phi \mid A \models_{T'} \phi\} .$$

T will be an AE extension of A if we can show that $T = T'$. Having fixed the modal index as T', we note that $\models_{(I,T')} A$ if and only if $\models_{(I,T')} T_0$, and thus, since $T_0 = T'_0$,

$$T = \{\phi \mid T'_0 \models_{T'} \phi\} .$$

By Proposition 2.4, the right-hand side defines the stable set T', and so $T = T'$.

PROPOSITION 2.8 *A set of sentences is moderately grounded in A if and only if it is a minimal AE extension of A.*

Proof. Assume that T is a minimal AE extension of A. By definition, it obeys the equation

$$T = \{\phi \mid A \models_T \phi\}\ .$$

Because T is minimal for A, there is no other stable set containing A which does not contain some element of $\overline{T}_0$. Hence $LA \cup L\overline{T}_0$ determine the unique stable set T, and the above equation can be rewritten as

$$T = \{\phi \mid A \cup LA \cup \neg L\overline{T}_0 \models_{SS} \phi\}\ .$$

Assume that Γ is moderately grounded in A. First we show that if $\phi \in T$, where ϕ is ordinary, then $L\phi \in T$. Consider any modal index Γ that satisfies $A \cup LA \cup \neg L\overline{T}_0$. By the properties of stable sets, $A \cup LA \cup \neg L\overline{T}_0 \subset \Gamma$. By Propositions 2.4 and 2.7, we have

$$\begin{aligned} \Gamma &= \{\phi \mid \Gamma_0 \models_\Gamma \phi\} \\ &= \{\phi \mid \Gamma_0 \cup L\Gamma_0 \cup \neg L\overline{\Gamma}_0 \models_{SS} \phi\}\ , \end{aligned}$$

so we must have $\Gamma_0 \cup L\Gamma_0 \cup \neg L\overline{\Gamma}_0 \models_{SS} A \cup LA \cup \neg L\overline{T}_0$; and since we know that $A \cup LA \cup \neg L\overline{T}_0 \models_{SS} \phi$, it must be that $\phi \in \Gamma$. Since Γ was arbitrarily chosen, $A \cup LA \cup \neg L\overline{T}_0 \models_{SS} L\phi$.

Now the proof proceeds along the lines of Proposition 2.7. We have

$$T = \{\phi \mid A \cup LA \cup LT_0 \cup \neg L\overline{T}_0 \models_{SS} \phi\}\ ,$$

and because T_0 is closed under first-order consequence, by Proposition 2.6 it determines a unique stable set T' with $T'_0 = T_0$. We rewrite the above equation as

$$T = \{\phi \mid A \cup LA \models_{T'} \phi\}\ .$$

The assumption LA is irrelevant, because $A \subset T'$; hence, by the reasoning in the proof of Proposition 2.7,

$$T = \{\phi \mid T'_0 \models_{T'} \phi\}\ ,$$

which just defines the stable set T', and $T = T'$. T is thus an AE extension of A, since

$$T = \{\phi \mid A \models_T \phi\}\ .$$

T must also be minimal for A; if it weren't, then there would be another stable set containing A (and hence LA) and not containing any of $\overline{T}_0$; hence $A \cup LA \cup \neg L\overline{T}_0$ would not determine a unique stable set, which we have shown to be the case.

PROPOSITION 2.9 *Every minimal AE extension for A is a minimal stable set for A.*

PROPOSITION 2.10 *If a minimal stable set for A is an AE extension of A, it is a minimal extension.*

PROPOSITION 3.1 (MOORE)

A set T is an AE extension of A if and only if it satisfies the equation

$$T = \{\phi \mid A \cup LT \cup \neg L\overline{T} \vdash \phi\}\ .$$

PROPOSITION 3.2 *A set is stable if and only if it is an S5 set.*

PROPOSITION 3.3 *For any $\phi \in \mathcal{L}$, $\models_{S5^+} \phi$ if and only if $\models_{SS} \phi$.*

Proof. This proposition is true if every $S5^+$ valuation has an equivalent L valuation whose modal index is a stable set, and *vice versa*. Let $\langle w, W\rangle$ be an $S5^+$ valuation, and Γ the $S5$ set defined by W. By the truth-recursion definition (11), $\models_{S5^+} L\phi$ if and only if $\phi \in \Gamma$. Hence $\langle w, W\rangle$ is equivalent to the L valuation $\langle w, \Gamma\rangle$. By Proposition 3.2, Γ is a stable set.

On the other hand, let $\langle I, \Gamma\rangle$ be an L valuation with Γ stable. Γ is also an $S5$ set; let W be a set of possible worlds such that Γ_0 are exactly the ordinary sentences true at every world in the set. Then $\models_{\langle I,W\rangle} L\phi$ if and only if $\models_{\langle I,\Gamma\rangle} L\phi$, and these are equivalent valuations.

LEMMA 3.4 *Let R be an equivalence relation on W, and let every element of W be the only immediate successors of w. Then the Kripke valuation $\langle w, W, R\rangle$ is equivalent to the $S5^+$ valuation $\langle w, W\rangle$.*

Proof. Because R is an equivalence relation, every world in W is accessible from every other world. Thus the second Kripke truth-recursion rule (12) on W is equivalent to the second $S5^+$ recursion rule (11) on W. The first rules are also equivalent the elements of W are exactly the successors of w.

PROPOSITION 3.5 *$S5^+$ valuations are isomorphic to TE valuations.*

Proof. Let $\langle w, W, R\rangle$ be a TE valuation. Let W' be all successors of w, that is, the set of w' such that wRw'. Because R is euclidean, it is an equivalence relation on W' (any two elements a and b of W' have wRa and wRb, and by the euclidean condition aRb is true). By the lemma above, $\langle w, W, R\rangle$ is equivalent to the $S5^+$ valuation $\langle w, W'\rangle$.

Let $\langle w, W\rangle$ be an $S5^+$ valuation. Let R be a relation that is an equivalence on W, and also for any element $a \in W$, wRa. By the lemma above, $\langle w, W\rangle$ is equivalent to the Kripke valuation $\langle w, W, R\rangle$. We must now show that R is transitive and euclidean.

Let aRb and bRc. If $a \in W$, then aRc because R is an equivalence on W. If $a \notin W$, it must be w, so that $b \in W$ and $c \in W$, and bRc by the equivalence of R on W.

Let aRb and aRc. If $a \in W$, then $b \in W$ and $c \in W$ by the equivalence property of R, and hence bRc. If $a \notin W$, it must be w, and again $b \in W$ and $c \in W$.

PROPOSITION 3.6 *A set T is an AE extension of A if and only if it satisfies the equation*

$$T = \{\phi \mid A \cup LT_0 \cup \neg L\overline{T}_0 \vdash_{K45} \phi\}\ .$$

It is a minimal (moderately-grounded) extension of A if and only if it satisfies the equation

$$T = \{\phi \mid A \cup LA \cup \neg L\overline{T}_0 \vdash_{K45} \phi\}\ .$$

PROPOSITION 3.7 *Every sentence of $\mathcal{L}_1$ is equivalent to a sentence of the form*

$$\begin{array}{ll} (L_1 \vee \omega_1) & \wedge \\ (L_2 \vee \omega_2) & \wedge \\ \cdots & \wedge \\ (L_n \vee \omega_n) & \end{array}$$

where each L_i is a disjunction of modal literals on ordinary sentences, and each ω_i is ordinary.

Proof. Using only first-order valid operations, a sentence of $\mathcal{L}_1$ is put into prenex normal form:

$$Q_1 x_1 \ldots Q_n x_n \; M \; , \tag{30}$$

where Q_i is either $\forall$ or $\exists$, and M is a propositional matrix containing modal and ordinary atoms. Note that the modal atoms themselves may contain embedded quantifiers, e.g., $L\exists x P(x)$.

We will use the following equivalences:

$$\begin{aligned} Qx([\neg]L\phi \vee \psi) &\equiv [\neg]L\phi \vee Qx\psi \\ Qx([\neg]L\phi \wedge \psi) &\equiv [\neg]L\phi \wedge Qx\psi \\ \exists x(\phi \vee \psi) &\equiv \exists x\phi \vee \exists x\psi \\ \forall x(\phi \wedge \psi) &\equiv \forall x\phi \wedge \forall x\psi \end{aligned}$$

where $[\neg]L\phi$ is either $L\phi$ or $\neg L\phi$. The first two are consequences of the fact that $L\phi$ contains no free variables. The second two are first-order consequences (see Robinson [15]).

Returning to the prenex form (30): suppose Q_n is an existential quantifier. Then put M into disjunctive normal form, and using the equivalence for $\exists x$, distribute $\exists x$ onto each of the disjuncts. The matrix now looks like

$$\begin{array}{r} \exists x(L_1 \wedge \omega_1) \vee \\ \exists x(L_2 \wedge \omega_2) \vee \\ \ldots \quad \vee \end{array} \tag{31}$$

where L_i are conjunctions of modal literals and ω_i are ordinary. By using the first two equivalences, the quantifiers can be pushed through the modal literals (modal atoms or their negations), giving:

$$\begin{array}{r} L_1 \wedge \exists x\, \omega_1 \vee \\ L_2 \wedge \exists x\, \omega_2 \vee \\ \ldots \quad \vee \end{array} \tag{32}$$

If Q_n is a universal quantifier, then the same operations can take place, except that the matrix is put into conjunctive normal form.

The same process can be repeated for Q_{n-1}, where we now consider expressions of the form $Q_n x_n \omega_i$ to be atomic for the purposes of putting M into conjunctive or disjunctive normal form. In this way all quantifiers can be pushed around the modal atoms, and the end result is a sentence of the form

$$\begin{array}{l} (L_1 \vee \omega_1) \;\wedge \\ (L_2 \vee \omega_2) \;\wedge \\ \ldots \qquad\quad \wedge \\ (L_n \vee \omega_n) \end{array} \tag{33}$$

where each L_i is a disjunct of modal literals and each ω_i is ordinary.

PROPOSITION 3.8 *Every modal atom $L\phi$, where ϕ is from $\mathcal{L}_1$, is equivalent to a sentence of $\mathcal{L}_1$.*

Proof. We will use the following equivalences:

$$\begin{aligned} L(\phi \wedge \psi) &\equiv L\phi \wedge L\psi \\ LL\phi &\equiv L\phi \\ L\neg L\phi &\equiv \neg L\phi \vee L\bot \\ L(L\phi \vee \psi) &\equiv L\phi \vee L\psi \\ L(\neg L\phi \vee \psi) &\equiv \neg L\phi \vee L\bot \vee L\psi \end{aligned}$$

All of these are theorems of *K45*.

By Proposition 3.7 and the first equivalence above, a modal atom $L\phi$, where ϕ is in $\mathcal{L}_1$, can be put into the equivalent form

$$\begin{array}{ll} L(L_1 \vee \omega_1) & \wedge \\ L(L_2 \vee \omega_2) & \wedge \\ \cdots & \wedge \\ L(L_n \vee \omega_n) & \end{array}$$

where each L_i is a disjunction of modal literals on ordinary sentences, and each ω_i is ordinary. By applying the equivalences repeatedly, this can be reduced to a sentence in $\mathcal{L}_1$.

PROPOSITION 3.9 *Every set A of $\mathcal{L}$-sentences has a K45-equivalent set in which each sentence is of the form*

$$\neg L\alpha \vee L\beta_1 \vee \cdots \vee L\beta_n \vee \omega\ , \tag{34}$$

with α, β_i, and ω all being ordinary sentences. Any of the disjuncts, except for ω, may be absent.

PROPOSITION 3.10 *If T is a strongly grounded extension of A, it is moderately grounded in A.*

Proof. Since T contains A and LA, we can add these as premises to the fixed-point equation for strongly-grounded T:

$$T = \{\phi \mid A \cup LA \cup A' \cup LA' \cup \neg L\overline{T}_0 \models_{SS} \phi\}\ .$$

Since A subsumes A' and LA subsumes LA', this reduces to the equation for a moderately-grounded extension.

PROPOSITION 5.1 *Let $\langle W, D\rangle$ be a default theory, with $A = \{W, D'\}$ its AE transform. Suppose E is an extension of the default theory. Then E is the kernel of a minimal stable set containing A and $\neg L\overline{E}$.*

Proof. The stable set S whose kernel is E contains W. Consider the AE transform $L\alpha \wedge \neg L\neg\beta \supset \omega$ of an arbitrary member d of D, and suppose it is not in S. Then ω is not in E, α is in E, and $\neg\beta$ is not in E. But this means that d is not satisfied by $\Gamma(E)$, a contradiction. Hence S contains all of D', the AE transform of D. Because its kernel is E, it also contains $\neg L\overline{E}$.

To show that S is minimal, assume that there is some other set $V \subset E$ that is the kernel of a stable set containing A and $\neg L\overline{E}$. Consider an arbitrary member $L\alpha\wedge\neg L\neg\beta \supset \omega$ of D'; because this is a member of the stable set, either α is not V, $\neg\beta$ is in V (and hence E), or ω is in V. If this is the case, then all defaults D of the default theory are satisfied in V, and so $\Gamma(E) \subseteq V$ by the minimality of Γ. But this contradicts $\Gamma(E) = E$.

PROPOSITION 5.2 *Let $\langle W, D\rangle$ be a default theory, with $A = \{W, D'\}$ its AE transform. Suppose E is an extension of the default theory. Then E is the kernel of a minimal AE extension of A.*

Proof. By Proposition 5.1, E is the kernel of a minimal stable set S containing A and $\neg L\overline{E}$. Now consider the set

$$\{\phi | A \cup LA \cup \neg L\overline{E} \models_{SS} \phi\}\ .$$

We want to show that this set is equal to S. By the preceding proposition, S is a minimal stable set containing A and $\neg L\overline{E}$. In fact, it is the only stable set with this property, because the kernel of any other stable set containing them must be a subset of E, and hence S would not be minimal. Thus LA and $\neg L\overline{E}$ pick out the unique stable set S. We can rewrite the above set as

$$\{\phi | A \models_S \phi\} .$$

Let us call this set T. The modal index, S, is fixed, so we can rewrite it as

$$\{\phi | T_0 \models_S \phi\} .$$

If we can show that $T_0 = E$, then by Proposition 2.4 it must be the case that $T = S$, and S is an AE extension of A. Since it is a minimal stable set containing A, it is also a minimal AE extension, by Proposition 2.10.

But T_0 must be the same as E, since it is just the first-order closure of W and the consequents ω of all AE transforms whose antecedents are satisfied by the modal index S. This is exactly the same as $\Gamma(E)$, which by hypothesis is equal to E.

PROPOSITION 5.3 *Same conditions as the previous proposition. E is the kernel of a strongly-grounded AE extension of A.*

Proof. Consider the subset of defaults $D_1 \subseteq D$ whose conclusions are in E. E is still a default extension of $\langle W, D_1 \rangle$. Therefore, by Proposition 5.2, the AE transform $A_1 = \langle W, D'_1 \rangle$ has a minimal extension T' whose kernel is E. Since AE extensions are uniquely determined by their kernels, $T' = T$. Thus we have:

$$T = \{\phi \mid A_1 \cup LA_1 \cup \neg L\overline{T}_0 \models_{SS} \phi\} .$$

Since A_1 are all of A whose ordinary part is contained in T, T must be strongly grounded.

PROPOSITION 5.4 *Let A be the AE transform of a default theory $\langle W, D \rangle$. If E is the kernel of a strongly-grounded AE extension of A, then $E = \Gamma(E)$.*

Proof. By Proposition 2.8, a strongly-grounded extension T of A obeys the equation

$$T = \{\phi \mid A_1 \cup LA_1 \cup \neg L\overline{T}_0 \models_{SS} \phi\} ,$$

where A_1 are all of A whose ordinary part is contained in T.

We now show that $\Gamma(T_0)$ cannot be a proper subset of T_0. Assume that this is so. By definition, $\Gamma(T_0)$ satisfies all defaults D. Let $D_1 \subseteq D$ be those defaults whose transform is A_1. Consider the transform $L\alpha \wedge \neg L \neg \beta \supset \omega$ of any member of D_1. Because the default is satisfied, either ω is in $\Gamma(T_0)$ or α is not in $\Gamma(T_0)$ (we already know that $\neg\beta$ is not in T_0). Hence every member of D'_1 (and $A_1 = D'_1 \cup W$) is in the stable set S whose kernel is $\Gamma(T_0)$. But by Proposition 2.9, T is a minimal stable set containing A_1, a contradiction. Thus $\Gamma(T_0)$ is equal to or a superset of T_0.

T_0 is closed under first-order consequence and contains W. It also satisfies all of the defaults D. Consider a default $\alpha : M\beta/\omega$; because its AE transform is in T, and so either ω is in T_0, α is not in T_0, or $\neg\beta$ is in T_0. These are precisely the conditions for the satisfaction of the default.

Since $\Gamma(T_0)$ is the least first-order-closed set containing W and satisfying D, and since it must at least contain T_0, it is equal to T_0. Thus T_0 is a fixed point of Γ and a default extension of $\langle W, D \rangle$.

THEOREM 5.5 *Let A be the AE transform of a default theory Δ. A set E is a default extension of Δ if and only if it is the kernel of a strongly-grounded AE extension of A.*

THEOREM 5.6 *For any set of sentences A of $\mathcal{L}$ in normal form, there is an effectively constructable default theory $\langle W, D\rangle$ such that E is a default extension of $\langle W, D\rangle$ if and only if it is the kernel of a strongly-grounded extension of A.*

A Semantical Approach to Nonmonotonic Logics

Yoav Shoham
Computer Science Department
Stanford University

Abstract

Recent years have seen a proliferation of so-called *nonmonotonic logics*, including several versions of circumscription, default logic, and autoepistemic logic. The different systems that have been proposed have strong surface dissimilarities, and comparison between them has proven challenging.

In this paper we propose a uniform approach to constructing and understanding nonmonotonic logics. This framework subsumes many existing nonmonotonic formalisms, and yet is remarkably simple, adding almost no extra baggage to traditional logic. In the new framework we redefine classical notions such as satisfiability and entailment, and look at what happens to some standard results from classical logic, such as the deduction theorem. We also discuss briefly the informal motivation for using nonmonotonic logics, and argue against the proposed distinction between different sorts of nonmonotonic inferences.

1 Introduction

The last decade or so has seen many logical systems which support so-called *nonmonotonic inferences.* In these formalisms one is allowed not only traditional inferences of classical logic, but also more "speculative" ones. It is often said that in those systems one may "jump to a conclusion" in the absence of evidence to the contrary, or that one may assign formulas a "default value," or that one may make a "defeasible inference." The prototypical example is inferring that a particular individual can fly from the fact that it is a bird, but retracting that inference when an additional fact is added, that the individual is a penguin. This is why such formalisms are called nonmonotonic: a fact entailed by a theory might no longer be entailed by a larger theory. Of course, classical logic is monotonic.

The original and best-known nonmonotonic logics are McCarthy's *circumscription* [17], Reiter's *default logic* [22], McDermott and Doyle's *nonmonotonic logic I* [20], McDermott's *nonmonotonic logic II* [19], and Clark's *predicate completion* [2]. In recent years several other systems have been suggested, and the old ones were further explored. Lifschitz provided new results on circumscription [12]. Further investigations of default logic include Etherington's work [5] and Lukaszewicz' [14]. Moore's *autoepistemic logic* [21] is an adaptation of McDermott's NML II, and a version of it was further investigated by Halpern and Moses [7].

These various formalisms are very different superficially. For example, circumscription amounts to adding a second-order axiom to a given first-order theory. A default theory, on the other hand, contains a collection of *default rules*, a notion quite outside classical logic, and its meaning is defined using a fixed-point construction which relies on those default rules. McDermott's and Moore's logics are still different, and formulas in those logics contain modal operators, which are meant to capture the notions of consistency and belief, respectively. The nonstandard nature of the various systems and their diversity has made it hard to gain a good understanding of them and to compare among them.

Another problem with existing nonmonotonic formalisms, beside their overwhelming complexity, is their limited expressiveness. In particular, they were all shown to fail to capture nonmonotonic *temporal* inferences. The problems were first reported by Hanks and McDermott [9], in response to which several solutions were offered. One such solution was proposed by Lifschitz, and it was to generalize circumscription to so-called *pointwise circumscription* [13]. My approach has been to construct the logic of *chronological ignorance* [23], and in doing so I defined a very general framework for nonmonotonic logics. The purpose of this article is to present this general framework. The main contributions of this paper are twofold: On the one hand I offer a simple framework to which most existing nonmonotonic logics can be reduced (and thus more easily understood and compared to one another), and on the other hand this general framework suggests radically new nonmonotonic logics.

The basic idea behind the construction is the following. In traditional logic, the meaning of a formula is the set of interpretations that satisfy it, or its set of models (where "interpretation" means truth assignment for PC, a first-order interpretation for FOPC, and a ⟨Kripke interpretation, world⟩-pair for modal logic). One gets a nonmonotonic logic by changing the rules of the game, and focusing on only a subset of those models, those that are "preferable" in a certain respect (these preferred models are sometimes called "minimal models," a term introduced by McCarthy in connection with circumscription, although by an unfortunate, and, by now, irreversible, choice of terminology I will call them "maximal"). The reason this transition makes the logic nonmonotonic is as follows. In classical logic $A \models C$ if C is true in all models of A. Since all models of $A \wedge B$ are also models of A, it follows that $A \wedge B \models C$, and hence that the logic is monotonic. In the new scheme we have that $A \models C$ if C is true in all *preferred* models of A, but $A \wedge B$ may have preferred models that are not preferred models of A. In fact, the class of preferred models of $A \wedge B$ and the class of preferred models of A may be completely disjoint.

Many different preference criteria are possible, all resulting in different nonmonotonic logics. All of those, however, have the same basic properties. In the remainder of this article I look at the general case of nonmonotonic logics in more detail. I first provide new definitions of nonmonotonic logic and of notions such as nonmonotonic satisfiability and nonmonotonic entailment. I then discuss the intuitive idea behind nonmonotonic inferences, and in the process address the question of whether it is meaningful to distinguish, as has been suggested, between nonmonotonic inferences that are *default inferences* and those that are *autoepistemic inferences.* In the last section I briefly show how previous nonmonotonic systems fit in with the new definitions.

2 Formal construction of nonmonotonic logics

This first section is devoted to defining the notion of nonmonotonic logics in the most general sense. At the time this work was carried out I was unaware of related work done previously by Bossu and Siegel [1], otherwise I would have made an effort to use their terminology where possible. I compare my treatment of nonmonotonic logic to theirs in the comparison section at the end of this article.

The discussion in this section will be most general, and when I talk of a "standard logic" I allow in principle any logic with the usual compositional, model-theoretic semantics. Rather than give a precise definition of this condition, however, let me in the following assume that by a "standard logic" one means the propositional calculus or first-order predicate logic, either classical or modal (i.e., one of four logics); extension to other cases (such as higher-order logic) will be obvious.[1]

In order to have the following discussion apply uniformly to the classical and modal logics, let me misuse the terminology slightly by calling anything which goes to the left of the $\models$ an *interpretation*. In the classical cases this is what is indeed usually called an interpretation. In the modal cases it is a pair ⟨Kripke structure,world⟩.

The transition to nonmonotonic logic puts into question notions that are well understood in logic, such as satisfaction, entailment, satisfiability, validity, and proof theory. To see what these might mean in the context of nonmonotonic logic, it will be helpful to make some precise definitions. We first recall some definitions in the standard case.

Definition 1 (Reminder)
Let $\mathcal{L}$ be a standard logic, and A and B two sentences in $\mathcal{L}$.

The fact that an interpretation M satisfies A is denoted by $M \models A$. In this case we say that M is a model of A.

A is satisfiable if A has a model.

A is valid if A is satisfied by all interpretations. Clearly A is satisfiable iff $\neg A$ is not valid.

A entails B (written $A \models B$) if B is satisfied by all models of A, or, equivalently, if all models of A are also models of B.

[1] When I say 'a modal logic' I deliberately do not commit myself to a particular modal system; that too is not essential here. Again, rather than define the class of all modal systems to which the following applies, let me in the following assume an S5 system whenever a modal logic is mentioned, and leave it to the reader to extend it to other systems.

From these definitions, the deduction theorem follows very easily[2]:

Theorem 1 (Reminder)
Let $\mathcal{L}$ be a standard logic, and A, B and C sentences in $\mathcal{L}$. Then $A \wedge B \models C$ iff $A \models B \supset C$.

Nonmonotonic logics are the result of associating with a standard logic a preference relation on models. More specifically, we make the following definitions. Let $\mathcal{L}$ be a standard logic and A a sentence in it, and let $\sqsubset$ be a strict partial order on interpretations for $\mathcal{L}$. Intuitively, $M_1 \sqsubset M_2$ will mean that the interpretation M_2 is *preferred over* the interpretation M_1. $\mathcal{L}$ and $\sqsubset$ define a new logic $\mathcal{L}_\sqsubset$. I will call such logics *preference logics.* The syntax of $\mathcal{L}_\sqsubset$ is identical to that of $\mathcal{L}$. The semantics of $\mathcal{L}_\sqsubset$ are as follows.

Definition 2 *An interpretation M preferentially satisfies A (written $M \models_\sqsubset A$) if $M \models A$, and if there is no other interpretation M' such that $M \sqsubset M'$ and $M' \models A$. In this case we say that M is a preferred model of A.*

Clearly, if $M \models_\sqsubset A$ then also $M \models A$. Next I define the notions of satisfiability and validity in $\mathcal{L}_\sqsubset$. These can be defined in more than one way, none of them entirely satisfactory. The definition of satisfiability is the more intuitive of the two.

Definition 3 *A is preferentially satisfiable if there exists an M such that $M \models_\sqsubset A$.*

Clearly, all preferentially satisfiable formulas are also satisfiable, though the converse is not necessarily true. The definition of preferential validity is much less intuitive. In fact, I have no intuition at all on what preferential validity should mean. Since that is the case, I will define it simply as the dual relation to preferential satisfiability:

Definition 4 *A is preferentially valid (written $\models_\sqsubset A$) iff $\neg A$ is not preferentially satisfiable.*

Lemma 2 *A is preferentially valid if for any M, either*

1. *$M \models A$, or else*

2. *there is an M' such that $M \sqsubset M'$ and $M' \not\models A$.*

[2]This is misuse of terminology on my part, since the the deduction theorem really refers to deducibility and not to entailment. I'm appropriating it for my purposes since, as far as I can tell, there is no other name for the following true fact.

(The proof follows immediately from the definitions.) Again, it is easy to see that all valid formulas are also preferentially valid, although the converse is not true. Indeed, preferential validity has some strange properties. For example, depending on $\sqsubset$, both a formula and its negation can be preferentially valid. Or, as a more concrete example, for $\sqsubset$ that is *unbounded* (that is, if for any M there is an M' such that $M \sqsubset M'$), if φ is valid then, not only is φ preferentially valid, but so is $\neg\varphi$.

Perhaps it makes no sense to define the notion of validity in this general context. There are, however, restricted cases where the above definition of preferential validity is very well behaved:

Definition 5 *A partial order $\sqsubset$ on models is said to be* <u>*bounded*</u> *if there does not exist an infinite sequence of models $M_1, M_2, M_3 \ldots$ such that $M_1 \sqsubset M_2 \sqsubset M_3 \sqsubset \ldots$*

Theorem 3 *Let $\mathcal{L}$ be a preferential logic, $\sqsubset$ a bounded partial order on its models, and A a formula in $\mathcal{L}$ (and therefore also in $\mathcal{L}_\sqsubset$). Then A is satisfiable in $\mathcal{L}$ iff A is preferentially satisfiable in $\mathcal{L}_\sqsubset$.*

Proof:

$\Leftarrow$: Trivial.

$\Rightarrow$: Suppose $M_0 \models A$. Define an A-sequence to be any sequence of models $\langle M_0, M_1, M_2, \ldots\rangle$ such that for every element M_i in the sequence, a) $M_i \models A$, and b) if there exists an M_{i+1} in the A-sequence then $M_i \sqsubset M_{i+1}$. Clearly at least one A-sequence exists, the sequence $\langle M_0\rangle$. From the boundedness of $\sqsubset$ it follows that no infinite A-sequences exist. Therefore there is at least one maximal A-sequence $\langle M_0, M_1, M_2, \ldots, M_n\rangle$, one that cannot be extended to a longer one. Then by definition $M_n \models_\sqsubset A$. ■

Corollary 4 *Under the same conditions, A is valid in $\mathcal{L}$ iff A is preferentially valid in $\mathcal{L}_\sqsubset$.*

<u>Observation</u>. $\mathcal{L}$ can be viewed as a special case of $\mathcal{L}_\phi$, where ϕ is the empty relation. Note that ϕ is bounded.

As was said before, despite these well-behaved properties, preferential satisfiability and validity are somewhat strange notions. Fortunately, neither is central to understanding nonmonotonic reasoning. What is crucial is the notion of preferential entailment, and that has a very intuitive definition:

Definition 6 *A preferentially entails B (written $A \models_{\sqsubset} B$) if for any M, if $M \models_{\sqsubset} A$ then $M \models B$, or equivalently, if the models of B (preferred and otherwise) are a superset of the preferred models of A.*

Definition 7 *$\mathcal{L}_{\sqsubset}$ is monotonic if for all $A,B,C \in \mathcal{L}$, if $A \models_{\sqsubset} C$ then also $A \wedge B \models_{\sqsubset} C$.*

Observation. The above definition is equivalent to saying that a logic is monotonic if all preferred models of $A \wedge B$ are also preferred models of A. Again viewing $\mathcal{L}$ as the special case $\mathcal{L}_{\phi}$, we note that $\mathcal{L}_{\phi}$ is monotonic.

Observation. If $\mathcal{L}$ is a preferential logic, it may contain sentences A and B such that both $A \models_{\sqsubset} B$ and $A \models_{\sqsubset} \neg B$. Furthermore, A need not be inconsistent for this to be the case – it is sufficient that it have no preferred models. Indeed, in preferential logic the role played by preferential satisfiability is exactly analogous to that played by satisfiability in standard logics, witness the following obvious lemma:

Lemma 5 *Let $\mathcal{L}_{\sqsubset}$ be a preferential logic, and A a sentence in it. Then A is preferentially satisfiable iff there does not exists a sentence B in $\mathcal{L}_{\sqsubset}$ such that both $A \models_{\sqsubset} B$ and $A \models_{\sqsubset} \neg B$.*

It is interesting to see what happens to the deduction theorem in light of the new definition of entailment. It turns out that while the theorem is false in general, a weaker version of it still holds, in which the 'iff' is changed to an 'if'. First we give a lemma whose truth follows obviously from the definitions.

Lemma 6 *Let $\mathcal{L}_{\sqsubset}$ be a preferential logic, A and B two sentences in it, and M a model. Then if $M \models B$ and $M \models_{\sqsubset} A$, then $M \models_{\sqsubset} A \wedge B$.*

Theorem 7 (The weak deduction theorem) *Let $\mathcal{L}_{\sqsubset}$ be a preferential logic, and A, B and C three sentences in it. Then, if $A \wedge B \models_{\sqsubset} C$, then also $A \models_{\sqsubset} B \supset C$.*

Proof:

1. $A \wedge B \models_{\sqsubset} C$ (assumption).

2. $A \not\models_{\sqsubset} B \supset C$ (assumption).

3. There exists an M_0 such that $M_0 \models_{\sqsubset} A$, but $M_0 \not\models B \supset C$ (from 2).

4. $M_0 \models_{\sqsubset} A$, $M_0 \models B$, and $M_0 \not\models C$ (from 3).

5. $M_0 \not\models_{\sqsubset} A \wedge B$ (from 1).

6. If $M_0 \models_{\sqsubset} A$ and $M_0 \models B$ then $M_0 \models_{\sqsubset} A \wedge B$ (Lemma 6).

7. Contradiction (from 4, 5 and 6). ■

The converse to this theorem does not hold: if $A \models_{\sqsubset} B \supset C$ then it does not necessarily follow that $A \wedge B \models_{\sqsubset} C$. It is not hard to construct a counterexample, for example one in which C is identically false, $A \wedge B$ is *not* identically false, and B is false in all preferred models of A. In fact, it is easy to show that if the converse to the theorem holds then the logic is necessarily monotonic:

Theorem 8 *Let $\mathcal{L}_{\sqsubset}$ be a preferential logic. Then the following two statements are equivalent:*

1. *For all $A,B,C \in \mathcal{L}_{\sqsubset}$, if $A \models_{\sqsubset} B \supset C$ then also $A \wedge B \models_{\sqsubset} C$.*

2. *$\mathcal{L}_{\sqsubset}$ is monotonic.*

Proof:
The $(2 \Rightarrow 1)$ direction is trivial. For the $(1 \Rightarrow 2)$ direction, assume that $A \models_{\sqsubset} C$. Therefore by definition $A \models_{\sqsubset} B \supset C$ for any B. Then by the assumption in the statement of the theorem $A \wedge B \models_{\sqsubset} C$. ■

Notice that so far the discussion has been entirely model-theoretic, and I have made no mention of syntactical considerations (such as proof theory). Indeed, many of the notions that are quite clear in monotonic logic, such as complete axiomatization, cease to make sense in the context of nonmonotonic logic. The whole motivation behind nonmonotonic logics is the desire to be able to "jump to conclusions," inferring new facts not only from what is already known but also from what is not known. This seems to imply that traditional inference rules, which are rules for deriving new sentences from old ones, are inadequate.

What is the alternative? I'm not at all sure that there is one. The natural approach is to replace derivation rules in which the l.h.s. refers only to previously derived sentences with rule whose l.h.s. refers also to sentences *not* previously derived. Indeed, this is close to what both Reiter and McDermott do in their systems (see last section). However, it turns out that referring merely to sentences that were not explicitly derived is insufficient, and one ends up with rules of the form "if α has been derived, and if β is consistent with what has been derived, then derive

γ." But rules that demand checking consistency no longer have the computational advantages of traditional inference rules.

Perhaps something else is possible, along the lines of what are known as systems for *truth maintenance* (or *belief maintenance*, or *reason maintenance* or *data dependency*) [4,15,18,3], in which the entities manipulated by programs are not sentences, but rather beliefs and records of justifications for each belief. For these programs to be elevated to the level of a proof procedures, however, much more needs to be said about the meaning of the justifications, about consistency, about soundness and completeness, and so on.

I do not pursue this line of enquiry here. The main point to remember is that such syntactical considerations are entirely secondary. What is important is to have clear semantics, which determine what sentences follow from one another. Reasoning about sentences can then proceed without any proof theory, and indeed that is what I do in [24].

3 A look at past nonmonotonic logics

I have so far refrained from discussing any details of previous nonmonotonic formalisms. I have done so deliberately in order to present the concept of nonmonotonic logic to the reader in what I believe is its "pure form," and in a way which does not obscure the essence of the concept by inessential considerations. Nevertheless, my formulation was strongly influenced by previous nonmonotonic systems, although the precise connection to past work is yet to be investigated: while it is clear how some previous systems are special cases of the general framework just presented, the connection to others is not completely understood at the moment. In this section I will very briefly survey some of the better known formulations, and indicate how they fit in with the general scheme which I defined above.

3.1 Circumscription

The formalism which is closest in spirit to the definitions given in the previous section is the logic of *circumscription*. It is actually a family of logics, starting with John McCarthy's original formulation in [17], and continuing with later formulations by McCarthy himself [16] and more recently by Vladimir Lifschitz [12,13].

The property common to all versions of circumscription is the existence of a *circumscription axiom*. It is essentially a second-order axiom that is assumed to implicitly accompany any first-order theory (by a theory I mean a collection of sentences that are implicitly conjoined). In McCarthy's original formulation, the circumscription axiom (and I am using Lifschitz' recent reconstruction of it) was:

$$\mathtt{A(P)} \wedge \forall \mathtt{p}\ \neg(\mathtt{A(p)} \wedge \mathtt{p<P})$$

where p is a predicate variable with free variables x, and p<P stands for

$$\forall \mathtt{x(px} \supset \mathtt{Px)} \wedge \neg\forall \mathtt{x(Px} \supset \mathtt{px)}$$

Intuitively, what this means is that if x are the free variables of a wff P, then the effect of circumscribing P in a theory A is to limit the instances of x which satisfy P to only those that are necessary in light of A. For example, the result of circumscribing CANFLY(x) in $\{\forall$b (BIRD(b) $\supset$ CANFLY(b)), BIRD(POLLY)$\}$ has the effect that the *only* object that can fly is POLLY.[3]

[3]One has to be careful here. The inference that the only object that can fly is POLLY is certainly the intended one, but, as shown by Etherington, Mercer and Reiter in [6], the original formulation did not have this property. The discussion here refers to the formulation which allows varying some predicates in the process of minimizing others.

Notice that this is exactly a way of preferring some models to others. The sentence $\forall$b (BIRD(b) $\supset$ CANFLY(b)) $\wedge$ BIRD(POLLY) has many models, but circumscribing CANFLY is a way of preferring models in which only POLLY can fly.

In the terminology used earlier, circumscribing P(x) defines a preference criterion according to which $M_1 \sqsubset M_2$ if

1. For all x, M_1 and M_2 agree on the interpretation of function symbols and all relation symbols other than P,
2. for all x, if $M_2 \models$ P(x) then also $M_1 \models$ P(x), and
3. there exists a y such that $M_1 \models$ P(y) but $M_2 \not\models$ P(y).

Thus the original version of circumscription is simply a special case of nonmonotonic logic, as I defined it earlier. The same is true of the more sophisticated versions of circumscription which have appeared since then. For example, the axiom of *parameterized circumscription* is the following generalization of original axiom (again, I am using Lifschitz' reconstruction of it):

$$A(P,Z) \wedge \forall pz\ \neg(A(p,z) \wedge p<P)$$

where Z is a tuple of predicates or function symbols. Here, the preference criterion embodied in the axiom requires minimizing the extension of P, possibly by varying the denotation of the symbols appearing in Z. In other words, according to this new criterion, $M_1 \sqsubset M_2$ if

1. M_1 and M_2 agree on the interpretation of all function symbols and all relation symbols other than P and those appearing in Z,
2. for all x, if $M_2 \models$ P(x) then also $M_1 \models$ P(x), and
3. there exists a y such that $M_1 \models$ P(y) but $M_2 \not\models$ P(y).

Several other circumscription schemes have been suggested, such as *joint circumscription* and *prioritized circumscription*. Most recently, Vladimir Lifschitz has suggested a family of circumscription axioms called *pointwise circumscription* [13]. Without going into the details, these new schemes allow one to express preference criteria that were not expressible in previous circumsciption schemes.

To avoid giving the wrong impression, it must be said that the notion of preferred models was implicit in McCarthy's work from the start. In fact, in his original paper he gave precisely the first minimality criterion that was stated above, although in subsequent publications the model-theoretic discussion seemed to play a diminishing role. Other researchers too have addressed the model theory of nonmonotonic logics, such as Lifschitz in [13] and Etherington in [5].

My formulation can be viewed as a suggestion to generalize McCarthy's approach in three ways:

I. Start with any standard logic, not necessarily FOPC. In another article in this volume, I base my formulations on a standard modal logic.

II. Allow any partial order on interpretations, not only the one implied by a particular circumscription axiom. For example, in that same article I will suggest a preference criterion that relies on temporal precedence.

III. Shift the emphasis to the semantics, stressing the partial order on models and not the particular way of defining that partial order. The various circumscription axioms, either McCarthy's original ones or Lifschitz's more recent ones, are one way of doing so, and they are most elegant. In my own formulations I choose other means of defining preference criteria.

3.2 Bossu and Siegel

I mentioned earlier that, unaware of Bossu and Siegel's work reported in [1], I rediscovered some of their ideas and renamed some of their terms, and by now I am too fond of my definitions to let go of them. I will now compare the two formulations. The summary of the relation between the two treatments is that the they share the basic semantical approach, although there are some minor technical differences between the two, but that Bossu and Siegel thoroughly investigated what turns out to be a very special case of my general formulation. In a little more detail the connection is as follows.

The main part common to both Bossu and Siegel's treatment and my own is the model-theoretic approach, which posits a partial order on interpretations. There are some minor differences in the precise definitions. For example, whereas I defined φ to be preferentially satisfiable (or, in their terminology, *minimally modelable*) if φ has a preferred model, Bossu and Siegel require in addition that *any* nonpreferred model of φ have a better model than it which is preferred. Or, as another example, they explicitly reject the definition I chose for preferential entailment (which they call *subimplication* and denote by $]\!\models$), since if φ is not preferentially satisfiable (i.e., it has no maximally preferred models) then it entails both ϑ and $\neg\vartheta$. I don't view that as a disadvantage, since preferential satisfiability plays a role that is completely analogous to satisfiability. Thus by the same argument one should object to the regular notion of entailment, since inconsistent (i.e., unsatisfiable) theories entail both ϑ and $\neg\vartheta$.

These are fairly minor differences, and they are overwhelmed by the similarity in the semantical approach to nonmonotonic logics. There is, however, a big difference between the two treatments, and that is in their generality. Whereas I allow starting with arbitrary standard logics as a basis, Bossu and Siegel require starting with FOPC. More crucially, whereas I allow *any* partial order on interpretations, Bossu and Siegel assume one fixed such partial order. As they themselves say,

> The difference between [John McCarthy's] definition and ours is that McCarthy 'minimizes' on some literals only, whereas we 'minimize' on every literal.

Circumscription was discussed in the previous subsection. As we have seen, in the simplest version of the logic, preferred models are those in which $P_1(x_1), \ldots, P_n(x_n)$ are true for as few x_i's as possible, where the P_i's are predicate symbols specified separately, and x_i are the arguments to P_i. What Bossu and Siegel do is fix the P_i's to be all the predicate symbols that appear in the theory that is being modeled.

Bossu and Siegel seem to imply that from their perspective, that of maintaining certain kinds of data bases, there is justification for choosing this particular partial order on interpretations. As I discuss in another article in this volume, for the temporal reasoning domain a radically different preference criterion is called for.

3.3 Modal nonmonotonic logics

It would be natural to discuss next Reiter's *default logic* [22], which since its publication has gained as much popularity as circumscription. However, the embedding of default logic in the "preferred models" setting will require talking about a modal logic, which at first might seem a bit radical. Let me then first address various nonmonotonic systems that are modal to begin with.

Along with circumscription and default logic, a series of somewhat more ambitious logics has appeared in the literature, which tried to represent in the logic itself notions such as consistency, belief or knowledge. The first construction was *Nonmonotonic Logic I* by Drew McDermott and Jon Doyle [20]. Problems in the logic later prompted McDermott to propose *Nonmonotonic Logic II* [19]. Later, drawing on previous work by Stalnaker [25] and Konolige [10], Robert Moore proposed an alternative, epistemic view of McDermott's logic, and a reformulation of it called *Autoepistemic Logic* [21]. Moore's formulation was changed slightly and further investigated by

Halpern and Moses in [7] (they prefer to talk of self-knowledge rather than self-belief, which is what underlies the difference between the two logics). In the following I will refer directly to Halpern and Moses' formulation.

The formulas of their logic are simply those of modal logic, with $\Box$ serving as the necessity operator.[4] The intuitive interpretation of the modal operator is epistemic, and so $\Box\varphi$ reads "φ is known."[5]

The question Halpern and Moses consider, which is also the one considered explicitly by Moore and implicitly by McDermott, is what it means for a theory to be a "complete" description of what is known. Moore views the theory as a data base, so that if an assertion is not in the database and does not follow from it deductively, then the assertion is not known. Similarly, Halpern and Moses ask what it means to say "I know α" and imply that that is *all* I know. So, if the data base contains the assertions $\mathtt{p}$ and $\mathtt{q}$ (or, if $\alpha = \mathtt{p} \land \mathtt{q}$), then all the base facts (those containing no modal operator) that are known are $\mathtt{p}$, $\mathtt{q}$, and their tautological consequences. In addition many nonbase facts are known, such as the fact $\neg\Box\mathtt{r}$. Notice that this is a nonmonotonic property: if $\mathtt{r}$ is added to the data base then $\Box\mathtt{r}$ is true, and therefore $\neg\Box\mathtt{r}$ is no longer known.

Halpern and Moses conclude that the statement "all I know is α" is meaningful only under certain conditions. They actually give four different conditions for it to be meaningful, and show all four to be equivalent. For the first one, they borrow from Moore (and, through him, from Stalnaker) the notion of a *stable set.* A collection of formulas T is called *stable* if it has the following properties:

1. T contains all instances of tautologies.
2. If $p \in T$ and $p \supset q \in T$ then $q \in T$.
3. $p \in T$ iff $\Box p \in T$.
4. $p \notin T$ iff $\neg\Box p \in T$.

Let us call the subset of a stable set T consisting of all the base formulas (again, those containing no modal operator) the *kernel* of T (although this is not a definition that any of the above authors make).

[4] They actually use the operator $\mathtt{K}$, but I adopt $\Box$ since later I will want to use the $\Diamond$ operator, and there is no widely accepted convention as to the dual of $\mathtt{K}$. Moore uses $\mathtt{L}$ rather than $\mathtt{K}$, and suggests that the $\mathtt{M}$ operator in NML II be viewed as the dual to $\mathtt{L}$.

[5] For an overview of current epistemic interpretations of modal logic in computer science see, e.g., [8]. Halpern and Moses choose the model in which the agent has total introspective capabilities, which is the S_5 system (I am ignoring the extension to many knowers here).

According to Halpern and Moses' first definition, the statement "all I know is α" is meaningful only if there is a stable set T containing α whose kernel is T', such that for any stable set $S \neq T$ with kernel S', T' is a proper subset of S'. In that case T is exactly all that is known.

The same definition can be couched in terms of preferred models. In fact, the following definition of preferred models is almost identical to one of the other three offered by Moses and Halpern. Let us define a preference criterion on Kripke interpretations according to which $M_1 \sqsubset M_2$ if

1. for all base wffs φ, if $M_2 \models \Box\varphi$ then also $M_1 \models \Box\varphi$, and

2. there exists a base wff φ such that $M_1 \models \Box\varphi$ but $M_2 \not\models \Box\varphi$.

Let us also say that M_1 and M_2 are *equiignorant* if for all base wffs φ, $M_1 \models \Box\varphi$ iff $M_2 \models \Box\varphi$.

We are now in a position to couch the analysis of "all I know is α" in our terms (I assume that α is a single formula). "All I know is α" is meaningful just in case all preferred models of $\Box\alpha$ are equiignorant, and in that case all I know is all that is known in those preferred models. I think this second definition is more intuitive that the first one.

3.4 Default logic

The nonmonotonic logic cited most often, perhaps other than circumscription, is Raymond Reiter's *default logic* [22]. It is also the logic that is the least natural to fit into the general framework of preference logics. In fact, as we shall see, I will be able to capture only variants of Reiter's original logic in this framework.

A *default theory* is a pair ⟨W,D⟩, where W is a set of ordinary sentences, and D is a set of *default rules.* Default rules are inference rules which have the form

$$\alpha\text{:M}\beta_1, \ldots, \text{M}\beta_n \;/\; \gamma$$

In fact, Reiter allows for default rule schemes, so α, β_i and γ may have and share free variables. Informally, such an inference rule reads "if you know α, and for all i β_i is consistent with all you know, then infer γ - but in the future make sure that the β_i's remain a consistent assumption." An example of a default rule is `:M(¬CANFLY(x)) / ¬CANFLY(x)`, whose informal meaning is that for any object, if it is consistent to assume that it cannot fly, assume so.

More precisely, Reiter defines the notion of an *extension.* Intuitively, an extension is reached by adding as many of the default inferences as possible, but making sure that when a default inference is made, the assumptions on which it is based are never violated. Reiter provides several equivalent formal definitions of an extension, possibly the most intuitive one being the following (it is restricted to the case of closed wffs):

> Let E be a set of closed wffs, and let $\Delta = \langle W, D \rangle$ be a closed default theory. Define $E_0 = W$, and for all $i \geq 0$
>
> $$E_{i+1} = Th(E_i) \cup \{\gamma : (\alpha{:}\mathrm{M}\beta_1, \ldots, \mathrm{M}\beta_n \ / \ \gamma) \in \mathrm{D},\ \alpha \in E_i, \text{ and for all } i,\ \neg\beta_i \notin E\}$$
>
> where $Th(X)$ are all the monotonic consequences of X (note the occurrence of E in the definition of E_{i+1}). E is an *extension* of Δ if
>
> $$E = \cup_{i=0}^{\infty} E_i$$

For example, the (open) default theory

W = {BIRD(POLLY),BIRD(x)⊃CANFLY(x),PROFESSOR(MCCARTHY)},
D = {:M(¬CANFLY(x)) / ¬CANFLY(x)}

has a single extension, which includes the sentence ¬CANFLY(MCCARTHY). In general, a default theory may have many extensions or none at all.

The first thing to notice about the definition is that it is hard to grasp intuitively. The general motivation behind the definition seems clear, but not all of the actual details are as obviously motivated. For example, in [14] Lukaszewicz suggests an alternative definition of an extension, which leads to a very different default logic. It is hard to choose among such alternatives without a model-theory for the logic, since in its absence all one has to go by is a gut-level feeling.

In light of the discussion in the previous subsection, the reader will not be surprised to learn that I propose translating any default theory into a modal one, interpreting the modal operator epistemically, and identifying an appropriate preference criterion on Kripke structures.

To simplify the discussion, in the following I will discuss only default theories in which default rules contain a single default assumption (that is, all rules have the form α:M(β) / γ). A default theory ⟨W,D⟩ will be translated into the modal theory

$$\{\Box w : w \in \mathrm{W}\} \cup \{\Box\alpha \wedge \Diamond\beta \supset \Box\gamma : (\alpha{:}\mathrm{M}(\beta)/\gamma) \in \mathrm{D}\}$$

For example, consider the first example given in [22]:

$$\mathrm{W} = \{B \supset \neg A \wedge \neg C\}\ ,\ \mathrm{D} = \{{:}\mathrm{M}(A)/A,\ {:}\mathrm{M}(B)/B,\ {:}\mathrm{M}(C)/C\}$$

This default theory is translated into the modal theory:

$$\{\Box(B \supset \neg A \wedge \neg C), \Diamond A \supset \Box A, \Diamond B \supset \Box B, \Diamond C \supset \Box C\}$$

The default theory has two extensions: $Th(\mathrm{W} \cup \{A,C\})$ and $Th(\mathrm{W} \cup \{B\})$. The modal theory has many models, including those in which *nothing* is known, and those in which much more is known than only A and C, or B. However, we will identify a definition of "preferred models" according to which in all preferred models either $Th(\{B\})$ are all the propositional sentences that are known, or else $Th(\{A, C\})$ are.

Define the *biases* of a default theory $\langle \mathrm{W,D} \rangle$ to be $\{\beta\text{: } (\alpha\text{:M}(\beta) \ / \ \gamma) \in \mathrm{D}\}$. For each default theory with a set of biases S, we define a preference criterion $\sqsubset_S$ on models, as follows. Let M_1 and M_2 be two models, and $S_i = \{s\text{: } s \in S \text{ and } M_i \models \Diamond s\}$, $(i = 1,2)$. $M_1 \sqsubset_S M_2$ if

1. $S_1 \subsetneq S_2$, or

2. $S_1 = S_2$, and $\{\varphi\text{: } M_2 \models \Box\varphi\} \subsetneq \{\varphi\text{: } M_1 \models \Box\varphi\}$.

Intuitively, we prefer models with minimal sets of biases whose negation is known (the set of "violated biases"), and among those we prefer models in which as little as possible is known (that is, among those we assume the preference criterion which was discussed in the previous subsection). One can verify that this two-layered preference criterion allows only models in which all that is known is B and its tautological consequences, or else all that are known are A, C and their tautological consequences.

As was said earlier, this preference criterion does not reflect Reiter's original formulation. Consider, for example, the second example given in [22]:

$$\mathrm{W} = \phi \text{ , } \mathrm{D} = \{\text{:M}(C)/\neg D, \text{:M}(D)/\neg E, \text{:M}(E)/\neg F\}$$

In Reiter's system this theory has a unique extension, $Th(\{\neg D,\neg F\})$, but if we translate this theory to the modal one and assume the preference criterion just defined, we end up with two classes of minimal models: those in which $\neg D$ and $\neg F$ are known and $\neg E$ is not (which correspond to the "correct" extension), but also those in which $\neg E$ is known and $\neg D$ and $\neg F$ are not. It turns out that in Lukaszewicz' formulation the latter *is* a legal extension, which suggests that indeed the preference criterion captures his modification of Reiter's system (as I have said, I will not give a formal proof of this connection).

Intuitively, the reason $Th(\{\neg E\})$ is not an extension in Reiter's system is because there is nothing to "block" the application of the default rule (:M$(C)/\neg D$); the application of a default rule cannot be blocked by the rule's own consequence. Therefore $\neg D$ is always in the extension, precluding the possibility of ever applying the second default rule. This suggests a modification of the previous preference criterion, a modification which takes into account the fact that sets of default rules may "dominate" one another. For example, $\{$:M$(C)/\neg D\}$ dominates $\{$:M$(D)/\neg E\}$, since the consequent $\neg D$ implies the dissatisfaction of the precondition : $M(D)$, and nothing in the second set implies the dissatisfaction of the precondition : $M(C)$. As another example, neither of the two sets $\{$:M$(C)/\neg D\}$ and $\{$:M$(D)/\neg C\}$ dominates the other, since each implies the dissatisfaction of the preconditions in the other set.

I will not give the precise definition of this modified preference critetion. Let me only remark that this partial order too doesn't quite capture Reiter's original definition. The interested reader is referred to [24] for further discussion of this issue, but the bottom line is that more work needs to be done before definite conclusions about this issue can be drawn.

4 The meaning and utility of nonmonotonic inferences

My treatment of nonmonotonic logics so far has been purely technical. As with all formalisms, giving the technical details is only part of the effort, and clarifying the connection between the formal system and its practical usage can be no less demanding. This last section is devoted to discussing very briefly the intuition behind nonmonotonic inferences. My limited goal here is to argue against the suggestion that there are two fundamentally different sorts of nonmonotonic inferences.

The distinction I am alluding to was suggested by Robert Moore in [21]. He contrasts *default inferences*, which are based on biases that are manifested in the world (e.g., that most birds can fly), with *autoepistemic inferences*, which are based on the lack of some particular knowledge. Says Moore,

> Consider my reason for believing that I do not have an older brother. It is surely not that one of my parents once casually remarked, "you know, you don't have any older brothers," nor have I pieced it together by carefully sifting other evidence. I simply believe that if I had an older brother I would surely know about it ... This is quite different from a default inference based on the belief, say, that most MIT graduates are oldest sons ...

On the face of it this distinction is quite appealing (certainly I was convinced for a while), but upon closer examination it seems to break down completely.

To begin with, one may note that Moore applies his own logic, labelled an autoepistemic one, to the flying birds example, which he himself characterizes as a default case.[6] (In this connection, see K. Konolige's article in this volume, relating default logic to autoepistemic logic.) Furthermore, consider Moore's own older-brother example. If one accepts the statement "if I had an older brother then I'd know it," surely one must also accept the statement "if I *didn't* have an older brother then I'd know it." Yet if we adopt this latter sentence rather than the first one, the opposite inference will follow, namely that I have an older brother. On what basis does one prefer the first sentence to the second one, if at all? Notice that if you adopt *both* sentences, then you end up with two distinct preferred models – one in which you have an older brother and know it, and another in which you don't have an older brother and know it – which isn't much help.

Let me suggest a different distinction than the one made by Moore. Rather than distinguish between different kinds of default inferences, one should distinguish between the *meaning* of

[6] A fact pointed out to me by Ray Perrault.

sentences on the one hand, and the (extra logical) *reason* for adopting that meaning on the other. The meaning, I argue, can be viewed epistemically, while the reason for adopting that meaning is computational economy.

Consider the flying birds example. The *meaning* of "birds fly by default" is that if I don't know that a particular bird cannot fly, then it can. The computational *reason* for adopting this meaning is that now whenever a bird can indeed fly, we need not mention the fact explicitly – either in external communication with other reasoners, or in "internal communication," i.e., thought – it will follow automatically. Of course, if we happen to be talking about a penguin, we had better add the knowledge that penguins cannot fly, or else we will make wrong inferences. In the long run, however, we win: the overwhelming percentage of birds about which we are likely to speak can indeed fly, and so on average this default rule saves us work. If this gain seems small, consider a realistic situation in which we apply thousands and thousands of such rules.

I am not at all arguing that one makes φ true by default just in case φ is true most of the time. As I have said, the flipside of making a default assumption is the danger of making faulty inferences. For example, the default inference "people you'll meet on the street will not stab you in the back" seems inappropriate in a city where only 5% of the population are back stabbers. There is a more complicated "expected utility" consideration that goes into selecting a nonmonotonic logic, but, as I have said, further discussion of this is beyond the scope intended for this article. All I want here is to separate the two issues, that of defining the meanings of nonmonotonic logics, and that of selecting one.

The reader may still be bothered by the fact that circumscription involves only classical sentences, and it is not clear how epistemic notions enter into it. It is not hard, however, to convert circumscription into a logic of minimal knowledge. The basic idea is instead of circumscribing a formula $\varphi(\mathtt{x})$, to add the axiom $\forall \mathtt{x}\ \varphi(\mathtt{x}) \supset \Box\varphi(\mathtt{x})$. (For example, in the flying birds case we add the axiom $\forall \mathtt{x}\ \mathtt{BIRD(x)} \supset (\neg\mathtt{CANFLY(x)} \supset \Box\neg\mathtt{CANFLY(x)})$.) Since we prefer models in which as few propositional formulas as possible are known, the effect is to have φ true of as few $\mathtt{x}$'s as possible. The natural reading of the axiom $\varphi \supset \Box\varphi$ is indeed "if φ were true then I'd know it." However, if we take the contrapositive form of the axiom, we get the familiar "default rule": $\Diamond\neg\varphi \supset \neg\varphi$, or "if it is possible that φ is false then it is."

As a final clincher in the argument for the meaning/utility distinction, let me show how this distinction resolves the Lottery Paradox, discussed, for example, in [19]. The paradox is as follows:

> A lottery is held with 1 million participants, including our friend John. The odds of John's winning are so low that we infer by default that he won't. Yet by the

same token we can infer that none of the other 999,999 members will win, which contradicts our knowledge that at least one person must win.

In the logic of minimal knowledge we describe the situation by

$$[\mathtt{WIN(JOHN)} \vee \mathtt{WIN}(P_1) \vee \mathtt{WIN}(P_2) \vee \ldots \vee \mathtt{WIN}(P_{999,999})] \wedge$$
$$\forall x\ \mathtt{WIN}(x) \supset \Box\mathtt{WIN}(x)$$

The most ignorant models are ones in which one of the million people wins and we know that he won it, but the identity of that person varies among models. We are therefore not justified in concluding that any particular individual will not win, since there are models in which he does. True, those models are vastly outnumbered by those in which he does not win, but nonmonotonic logics do not let us express the property of a proposition being true in "most" models.

So in the above formulation we cannot conclude that John will not win, nor should we want to. If one claims that such a conclusion *is* one that corresponds to default reasoning people use, one must agree to the conclusion that no rational person would ever buy lottery tickets, a prediction that obviously isn't borne out in reality.[7] However, the above formulation is not as useless as it might appear. We can still make inferences involving the possibility of people winning, in which rather than condition an inference on their not winning, we condition it on the *possibility* of their not winning. For example, we may add the sentence

$$\Diamond\neg\mathtt{WIN(ME)} \supset \neg\mathtt{SHOULD\text{-}RESIGN\text{-}JOB(ME)}$$

The rationale here is again clear. Although there is a model in which I win the lottery and therefore needn't bother teaching a course on AI, it would be foolish for me to resign on that basis.

[7]The argument that indeed no rational person should, given that in all lotteries the expected winning amount is negative, is irrelevant. The example would still hold if some bored millionaire organized the lottery, charging each participant one dollar and giving the winner one million and one dollars.

5 Summary

I have presented a uniform approach to constructing and understanding nonmonotonic logics. The value of the formulation has not been its mathematical sophistication, but rather the opposite: the only notion added to traditional logic was that of a partial order on interpretations. The simplicity of the formulations makes transparent what in other systems is less immediate. The formulation is not only simple but also very general. In particular, I indicated how several previous nonmonotonic logics are special cases of the new framework. I also addressed the intuition behind nonmonotonic logics, and suggested abolishing the proposed distinction between default inferences and autoepistemic ones.

Several intriguing issues remain to be explored. One that was discussed in the previous section is the precise relation to Reiter's original default logic, a relation which is not completely clear at the moment. Another has to do with the relation to other nonstandard logical formulations. In particular, Johan van Benthem has drawn my attention to the close parallels between my formulations and formulations in Conditional Logic, as pioneered by D. Lewis [11,26]. In CL one has, instead of a partial order on interpretations, a similarity measure on possible worlds, and the notion of counterfactual entailment is similar to my notion of preferential entailment.

Another open question is which particular instances of the general framework I have outlined are interesting from the practical point of view, in that they they pick out models that are intuitively correct. As I have said, the general treatment of nonmonotonic logics offered here grew out of limitations of existing systems. It is still the case, however, that very few concrete preference criteria on models have been investigated. The most common ones are those embodied in the various circumscription axioms and in some default theories. One preference criterion transcending those is that of chronological ignorance, presented in [24]. Lifschitz too has investigated an instance of pointwise circumscription that does not collapse into "old" circumscription. All these, however, are still a drop in the bucket, and we have yet to understand which of the many possible partial orders on models are of practical importance.

Acknowledgements. Among the people who contributed to the form and content of this paper are Drew McDermott, Johan van Benthem, Matt Ginsberg, David Etherington, Steve Hanks, Kurt Konolige, and Vladimir Lifschitz.

References

[1] G. Bossu and P. Siegel. Saturation, nonmonotonic reasoning, and the closed-world assumption. *Artificial Intelligence*, 25(1):13–65, January 1985.

[2] K. L. Clark. Negation as failure. In *Logic and Databases*, pages 293–322, Plenum Press, New York, 1978.

[3] T. Dean. *Temporal Imagery: An Approach to Reasoning about Time for Planning and Problem Solving.* PhD thesis, Yale University, Computer Science Department, 1986.

[4] J. Doyle. A truth maintenance system. *Artificial Intelligence*, 12:231–272, 1979.

[5] D. W. Etherington. *Reasoning with Incomplete Information: Investigations of Non-Monotonic Reasoning.* PhD thesis, Computer Science department, University of British Columbia, 1986.

[6] D. W. Etherington, R. Mercer, and R. Reiter. On the adequacy of predicate circumscription for closed-world reasoning. *Computational Intelligence*, 1(1), 1985.

[7] J. Halpern and Y. Moses. *Towards a Theory of Knowledge and Ignorance: Preliminary Report.* Technical Report RJ 4448 48136, IBM Research Laboratory, San Jose, October 1984.

[8] J. Y. Halpern and Y. Moses. A guide to the modal logics of knowledge and belief: preliminary draft. In *Proc. IJCAI-85*, pages 480–490, 1985.

[9] S. Hanks and D. V. McDermott. *Temporal Reasoning and Default Logics.* Technical Report YALEU/CSD/RR 430, Yale University, October 1985.

[10] K. Konolige. Circumscriptive ignorance. In *Proc. 2nd AAAI*, Pittsburgh, PA, 1982.

[11] D. Lewis. Causation. *Journal of Philosophy*, 70:556–567, 1973.

[12] V. Lifschitz. Computing circumscription. In *Proc. 9th IJCAI*, August 1985.

[13] V. Lifschitz. Pointwise circumscription. In *Proceedings of AAAI*, Philadelphia, PA, August 1986.

[14] V. Lukaszewicz. Considerations on default logic. In *Proceedings of the Workshop on Non-monotonic Reasoning*, pages 165–193, AAAI, 1984.

[15] D. A. McAllester. *Reasoning Utility Package User's Manual.* Technical Report 667, M.I.T. AI Lab memo, 1982.

[16] J. M. McCarthy. Applications of circumscription to formalizing common sense knowledge. In *Proceedings of the Nonmonotonic Reasoning Workshop*, pages 295–324, AAAI, October 1984.

[17] J. M. McCarthy. Circumscription - a form of non monotonic reasoning. *Artificial Intelligence*, 13:27–39, 1980.

[18] D. V. McDermott. Contexts and data dependencies: a synthesis. *IEEE Trans. on Pattern Analysis and Machine Intelligence*, 5(3):237–246, 1983.

[19] D. V. McDermott. Nonmonotonic logic ii: nonmonotonic modal theories. *JACM*, 29(1):33–57, 1982.

[20] D. V. McDermott and J. Doyle. Nonmonotonic logic i. *Artificial Intelligence*, 13:41–72, 1980.

[21] R. C. Moore. Semantical considerations on nonmonotonic logic. In *Proc. 8th IJCAI*, Germany, 1983.

[22] R. Reiter. A logic for default reasoning. *Artificial Intelligence*, 13:81–132, 1980.

[23] Y. Shoham. Chronological ignorance: time, nonmonotonicity and necessity. In *Proc. AAAI*, Philadelphia, PA, August 1986.

[24] Y. Shoham. *Reasoning about Change.* MIT Press, Boston, MA, 1987.

[25] R. Stalnaker. A note on nonmonotonic modal logic. 1982. Cornell University, Department of Philosophy, unpublished manuscript.

[26] J. F. A. K. van Benthem. *The Logic of Time.* D. Reidel, 1983.

Multi-valued logics

Matthew L. Ginsberg*

THE LOGIC GROUP
KNOWLEDGE SYSTEMS LABORATORY
Department of Computer Science
Stanford University
Stanford, California 94305

ABSTRACT

A great deal of recent theoretical work in inference has involved extending classical logic in some way. I argue that these extensions share two properties: firstly, the formal addition of truth values encoding intermediate levels of validity between true (i.e., valid) and false (i.e., invalid) and, secondly, the addition of truth values encoding intermediate levels of certainty between true or false on the one hand (complete information) and unknown (no information) on the other. Each of these properties can be described by associating lattice structures to the collection of truth values involved; this observation lead us to describe a general framework of which both default logics and truth maintenance systems are special cases.

1 Introduction

There has been increasing interest in AI generally in inference methods which are extensions of the description provided by first order logic. Circumscription [9], default logic [10] and probabilistic inference schemes such as that discussed in [7] are examples.

Research in truth maintenance systems [4] has involved recording information concerning not only the truth or falsity of a given conclusion, but also justifications for that truth or falsity. This is useful in providing explanations, and also in the revision of inferences drawn using non-monotonic inference rules. Assumption-based truth maintenance systems [3] provide an interesting extension of this idea, taking the truth value of a given proposition to be the set of contexts in which it will hold.

My intention in this paper is to show that these different approaches can be subsumed under a uniform framework. Hopefully, such a framework will lead to a greater understanding of the natures of the individual approaches. In addition, an implementation of the general approach should facilitate the implementation of any of the individual approaches mentioned earlier, in addition to combinations of them (such as probabilistic truth maintenance systems) or new ones yet to be devised.

The ideas presented in this paper should not be taken as supporting any specific multi-valued logic, but as supporting a multi-valued approach to inference generally. The specific logic selected in any given application can be expected to depend upon the domain being explored.

2 A motivating example

Let me motivate the approach I am proposing with a rather tired example. Suppose that Tweety is a bird, and that birds fly by default.

*This work supported by the Office of Naval Research.

Any of the standard formalizations of default reasoning (such as [9] or [10]) will allow us to conclude that Tweety can fly; suppose that we do so, adding this conclusion to our knowledge base. Only now do we learn that Tweety is in fact a penguin.

The difficulty is that this new fact is in contradiction with the information just added to our knowledge base. Having incorporated the fact the Tweety can fly into this knowledge base, we are unable to withdraw it gracefully.

Truth maintenance systems [4] provide a way around this difficulty. The idea is to mark a statement not as merely "true" or "false", but as true or false *for a reason*. Thus Tweety's flying may depend on Tweety's being a penguin *not* being in the knowledge base; having recorded this, it is straightforward to adjust our knowledge base to record the consequences of the new information.

The truth maintenance approach, however, provides us with a great deal more power than is needed to solve this particular problem. We drew a default conclusion which was subsequently overturned by the arrival of new information. Surely we should be able to deal with this without recording the justification for the inference involved; it should be necessary merely to record the fact that the conclusion never achieved more than default status.

In this particular example, we would like to be able to label the conclusion that Tweety can fly not as true, but as true by default. The default value explicitly admits to the possibility of new information overturning the tentative conclusion it represents.

3 Truth values

3.1 Lattices

This approach is not a new one. There is an extensive literature discussing the ramifications of choosing the truth value assigned to a given statement from a continuum of possibilities instead of simply the two-point set $\{t, f\}$. Typical examples are a suggestion of Scott's in 1982 [12] and one of Sandewall's in 1985 [11].

Scott notices that we can partially order statements by their truth or falsity, and looks at this as corresponding to an assignment to these statements of truth values chosen from some set L which is partially ordered by some relation $\leq_t$ (the reason for the subscript will be apparent shortly).

He goes on to note that if we can associate to the partial order $\leq_t$ greatest lower bound and least upper bound operations, the set L is what is known to mathematicians as a *lattice* [8]. Essentially, a lattice is a triple $\{L, \wedge, \vee\}$ where $\wedge$ and $\vee$ are binary operations from $L \times L$ to L which are *idempotent, commutative and associative:*

$$a \wedge a = a \vee a = a$$

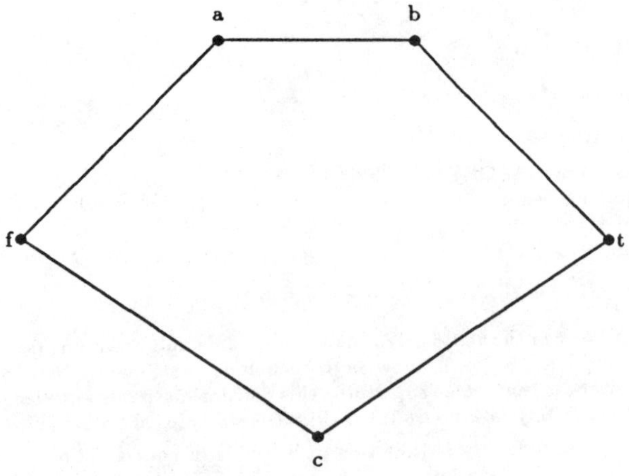

Figure 1: A lattice

Figure 2: The two-point lattice

$$a \wedge b = b \wedge a; \quad a \vee b = b \vee a$$

$$(a \wedge b) \wedge c = a \wedge (b \wedge c); \quad (a \vee b) \vee c = a \vee (b \vee c).$$

In terms of the partial order mentioned earlier, we have $a \wedge b = \text{glb}(a, b)$ and $a \vee b = \text{lub}(a, b)$. $\wedge$ is called the *meet* operation of the lattice; $\vee$ is called the *join*. We also require that if $a \leq b$, then $a \wedge b = \text{glb}(a, b) = a$ and $a \vee b = \text{lub}(a, b) = b$. This is captured by the *absorption identities*:

$$a \wedge (a \vee b) = a; \quad a \vee (a \wedge b) = a.$$

Lattices can be represented graphically. Given such a representation, we will take the view that $p \leq_t q$ if a path can be drawn on the graph from p to q which moves uniformly from left to right on the page.

In the lattice in figure 1, f is the minimal element of the lattice, and t is the maximal element. We also have $a \leq_t b$; a and c are incomparable since there is no unidirectional path connecting them.

Up to isomorphism, there is a unique two-point lattice, shown in figure 2. The truth values in first order logic are chosen from this lattice; all we are saying here is that $f \leq_t t$; "true" is more true than "false".

3.2 Uncertainty

Sandewall's proposal, although also based on lattices, is a different one. Instead of ordering truth values based on truth or falsity, he orders them based on the completeness of the information they represent. Specifically, Sandewall suggests that the truth values be subsets of the unit interval $[0, 1]$, the truth value

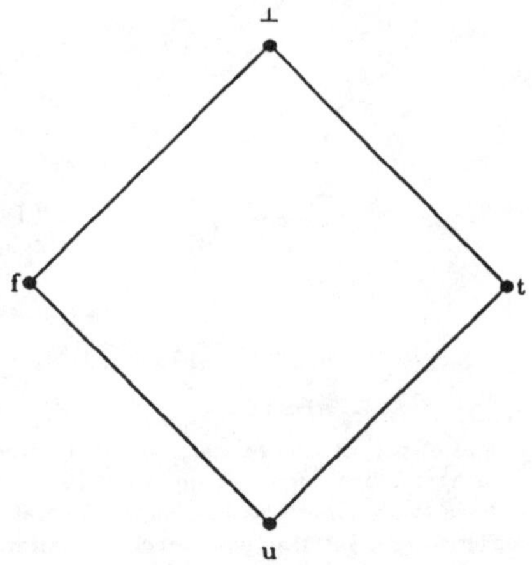

Figure 3: The smallest non-trivial bilattice

indicating that the probability of the statement in question is known to lie somewhere in the associated probability interval. This proposal also appears in [7] and [5].

The lattice operation used is that of set inclusion. Thus true, corresponding to the singleton set $\{1\}$, is *incomparable* to false, which corresponds to the singleton $\{0\}$. (And each is in turn incomparable with any other point probability, such as $\{0.4\}$.) Instead, the inclusion of one truth value in another relates to our acquiring more information about the statement in question. The minimal element of the lattice is the full unit interval $[0, 1]$; the fact that the probability of some statement lies in this interval contains no real information at all.

This is in sharp contrast with knowing, for example, that the probability of the statement in question is .5. If the probability of a coin's coming up heads is .5, the coin is fair; if nothing is known about the probability, it may well not be.

It is clear that the partial order corresponding to Sandewall's notion is conceptually separate from that in Scott's construction. To capture it, we introduce a second partial order $\leq_k$ onto our lattice of truth values, interpreting $p \leq_k q$ to mean loosely that the evidence underlying an assignment of the truth value p is subsumed by the evidence underlying an assignment of the truth value q. Informally, more is known about a statement whose truth value is q than is known about one whose truth value is p.

Since f and t in the two-point lattice corresponding to first order logic should be incomparable with respect to this second partial order, there is no way to introduce this second lattice structure onto the lattice in figure 2. Instead, we need to introduce two additional truth values $\text{glb}_k(t, f)$ and $\text{lub}_k(t, f)$, as shown in figure 3. Just as $p \leq_t q$ if p is to the left of q in a graphical representation, we will adopt the convention that $p \leq_k q$ if p is *below* q on the page.

The two new values are given by u (unknown) and $\perp$ (contradictory). The latter indicates a truth value subsuming both true *and* false; this truth value will be assigned to a given statement just in case it is possible to prove it true using one method and false using another.

We will denote the two lattice operations corresponding to $\leq_k$ by $+$ (lub_k) and $\cdot$ (glb_k) respectively. In general, we define a *bilattice* to be a quintuple $(B, \wedge, \vee, \cdot, +)$ such that:

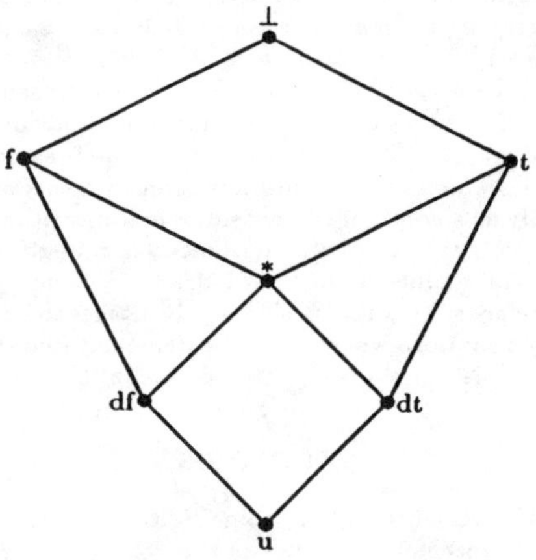

Figure 4: D, the bilattice for default logic

1. $(B, \wedge, \vee)$ and $(B, \cdot, +)$ are both lattices, and
2. Each operation respects the lattice relations in the alternate lattice. For example, we require that if $p \leq_k q$ and $r \leq_k s$, then $p \wedge r \leq_k q \wedge s$. Equivalently, $\wedge$ must be a lattice homomorphism from the product lattice $(B \times B, \cdot, +)$ into $(B, \cdot, +)$ (and similarly for $\vee$, $\cdot$ and $+$).

Just as figure 2 depicts the smallest non-trivial lattice, figure 3 depicts the smallest bilattice which is non-trivial in each lattice direction. Belnap [1,2] has considered the possibility of selecting truth values from this bilattice.

Another bilattice is shown in figure 4; this is the bilattice of truth values in default logic. In addition to the old values of t, f, u and $\perp$, a sentence can also be labelled as dt (true by default) or df (false by default). The additional value $* = dt + df$ labels statements which are both true *and* false by default. This is of course distinct from u (indicating that no information at all is available) or $\perp$ (indicating the presence of a proven contradiction). We will discuss this bilattice in greater detail in a subsequent section.

Before proceeding, however, note that this bilattice shares the elements t, f, $\perp$ and u with the previous one. In fact, *any* bilattice will have four distinguished elements, corresponding to the maximal and minimal elements under the two partial orders. We will denote these distinguished elements in this fashion throughout the paper.

4 Logical operations

In order to apply these ideas, it is insufficient merely to give a framework in which to describe the truth values associated to the sentences of our language. We must also be able to perform inference using these truth values. We now turn to the issue of describing logical operations in a multi-valued setting.

4.1 Extensions and logical connectives

Let L be the set of all well-formed formulae in our language. We will define a *truth function* to be any mapping

$$\phi : L \rightarrow B,$$

corresponding to an assignment of some truth value in the bilattice B to each formula in L.

In first order logic, consistency is defined for truth functions ϕ that are models, so that for each well-formed formula p, $\phi(p) = t$ or $\phi(p) = f$. We will continue to use this definition in the case of multi-valued logics, calling ϕ a *model* if ϕ maps L into the two-point set $\{t, f\}$.

If ϕ and ψ are two truth functions with $\phi(p) \leq_k \psi(p)$ for all $p \in L$, we will write $\phi \leq_k \psi$ and say that ψ is an *extension* of ϕ. If the inequality is strict for at least one $p \in L$, we will write $\phi <_k \psi$ and say that the extension is *proper*. If ψ is a model, we will say that it is a *complete* extension of ϕ.

Informally, an extension of a truth function is what is obtained upon the acquisition of more information about some sentence or sentences in L. The extension will be proper if and only if the new information was not already implicit in the existing truth values.

The usual logical operators of negation, conjunction, disjunction and implication can be described in terms of natural operations on the bilattice structure of our truth values. Conjunction and disjunction are the most easily described, since they are essentially captured by the lattice operators $\wedge$ and $\vee$. In order for a model to be consistent, we therefore require:

$$\phi(p \wedge q) = \phi(p) \wedge \phi(q) \tag{1}$$

$$\phi(p \vee q) = \phi(p) \vee \phi(q). \tag{2}$$

Negation is rather different. Clearly we want to have in general that $\phi(\neg p) \leq_t \phi(\neg q)$ if and only if $\phi(p) \geq_t \phi(q)$. Somewhat less transparent is that we should have $\phi(\neg p) \leq_k \phi(\neg q)$ if and only if $\phi(p) \leq_k \phi(q)$: if we know less about p than about q, we also know less about the negation of p than about that of q. Additionally, we require that $\phi(\neg\neg p) = \phi(p)$.

This leads us to define negation in terms of a map $\neg$ from B to itself such that:

1. $\neg$ is a bilattice isomorphism from $(B, \wedge, \vee, \cdot, +)$ to $(B, \vee, \wedge, \cdot, +)$, and
2. $\neg^2 = 1$.

Note that in the first condition, we have reversed the order of $\wedge$ and $\vee$ between the two bilattices while retaining the order of $\cdot$ and $+$. This corresponds to the observations of the previous paragraph.

For a model, we require:

$$\phi(\neg p) = \neg\phi(p). \tag{3}$$

We handle implication by retaining the usual identification

$$(p \rightarrow q) \equiv (\neg p \vee q).$$

This gives us

$$\phi(p \rightarrow q) = \neg\phi(p) \vee \phi(q). \tag{4}$$

We deal with quantification by noting that $\forall x.p \rightarrow p_x^t$, where t is substitutable for x in p and p_x^t is the result of replacing some (but not necessarily all) of the occurrences of x in p with t. This leads us to assume:

$$\phi(\forall x.p) = \text{glb}_t\{\phi(p_x^t) | t \text{ is substitutable for } x \text{ in } p\}. \tag{5}$$

The existential operator is similar:

$$\phi(\exists x.p) = \text{lub}_t\{\phi(p_x^t) | t \text{ is substitutable for } x \text{ in } p\}. \tag{6}$$

In general, we will call a truth function ϕ *consistent* if it has a complete extension satisfying (1)–(6).

Here are some predicate calculus examples:

x	$\phi(x)$	$\psi(x)$	$\phi(x)$	$\psi(x)$	$\phi(x)$	$\psi(x)$
A	t	t	f	f	f	f
B	f	f	u	t (or f)	u	?
$A \wedge B$	f	f	u	f	t	t

In the first two cases, ψ is a consistent complete extension of ϕ. Since ϕ in the third case has no consistent complete extension, it is itself inconsistent.

Suppose that ϕ is consistent, and let $\{\psi_i\}$ be the set of its consistent complete extensions. We define $\overline{\phi}$ to be the greatest lower bound of the ψ_i:

$$\overline{\phi} = \text{glb}_k\{\psi|\psi \text{ is a consistent complete extension of } \phi\}.$$

In the following two examples, ϕ has two consistent complete extensions given by ϕ_1 and ϕ_2, and $\overline{\phi}$ is the greatest lower bound of these.

	$\phi(x)$	$\phi_1(x)$	$\phi_2(x)$	$\overline{\phi}(x)$
A	t	t	t	t
B	u	t	f	u
$A \vee B$	u	t	t	t

	$\phi(x)$	$\phi_1(x)$	$\phi_2(x)$	$\overline{\phi}(x)$
A	u	t	f	u
$\neg A$	u	f	t	u
$A \vee \neg A$	u	t	t	t

The above construction is closely related to the usual notion of logical inference. In fact, if we denote by ϕ_p the truth function given by

$$\phi_p(q) = \begin{cases} t, & \text{if } q = p; \\ u, & \text{otherwise,} \end{cases}$$

we have:

Theorem 4.1 *$p \models q$ if and only if $\overline{\phi_p} \geq_k \phi_q$.*

Proof. All proofs can be found in [6].

If p is consistent, ϕ_p is the k-minimal truth function in which p is true; the point of the theorem is that q will be true in $\overline{\phi_p}$ if and only if $p \models q$.

4.2 Closure

It might seem that $\overline{\phi}$ is a natural choice for the closure of a truth function in general, but it suffers the drawback of having $\overline{\phi}(p) \geq_k \text{glb}_k\{t, f\}$ for all p. As our bilattice of truth values becomes more complex, such a closure will be insensitive to some of the information contained in ϕ. In the default bilattice D, for example, we have $\overline{\phi}(p) \geq_k *$. Contrast this with theorem 5.1, where the closure of ϕ can also take the values dt, df or u.

The general construction is somewhat more involved; the reader is referred to [6] for details. If we denote the closure of some truth function ϕ by cl(ϕ), the key features of the construction are the following:

1. It can be described completely in terms of the bilattice structure of the truth values.
2. Logical inference always "adds" information to a truth function, so that $\phi \leq_k \text{cl}(\phi)$ in all cases.
3. The construction is non-monotonic, so that it is possible to have $\phi <_k \psi$ without $\text{cl}(\phi) \leq_k \text{cl}(\psi)$. An example of this is given in the next section.

The final remark above refers only to a portion of what is generally referred to as "non-monotonic" behavior. Consider a truth function with $\phi(p) = dt$ but $\text{cl}(\phi)(p) = f$, for example; here inference is behaving "non-monotonically" in the sense that $\phi(p) >_t u$ but $\text{cl}(\phi)(p) <_t u$. It is behaving monotonically, however, in that $\phi(p) <_k \text{cl}(\phi)(p)$. It turns out that the computational difficulties which plague non-monotonic inference systems arise principally as a result of the potential non-monotonicity in the k sense; loosely speaking, k-monotonicity is enough to guarantee that we can maintain our knowledge base using updates. There are therefore substantial practical advantages to be gained by recognizing situations where it can be demonstrated that the closure operation is k-monotonic. Details are in [6].

5 Examples

Let me end by very briefly describing Reiter's default reasoning and truth maintenance in terms of this sort of construction. The second of these is extremely straightforward, essentially requiring us merely to identify those statements that support some fixed one. Default reasoning is a bit more intricate, since the philosophy underlying Reiter's approach is very different from that of the one we have been presenting.

5.1 Default logic

Reiter defines default reasoning in terms of a *default theory* (R, T) where T is a collection of first order sentences, and R is a collection of *defaults*, each of the form

$$\frac{\alpha : \beta_1, \ldots, \beta_m}{w},$$

indicating that if α holds and all of the β's are possible, then w holds. If every default rule is of the form

$$\frac{\alpha : w}{w},$$

so that we infer w from α in the absence of information to the contrary, the default theory is called *normal*.

Reiter goes on to define an *extension* of a default theory (R, T), and shows that these extensions correspond to the collections of facts derivable from such a theory. Since there may be conflicting default rules, it is possible that a given default theory have more than one extension.

The bilattice for default logic appeared in figure 4.

Theorem 5.1 *Let (R, T) be a normal default theory, with default rules*

$$\frac{\alpha_i : w_i}{w_i},$$

where i indexes the elements in R. Associate to (R, T) a truth function ϕ given by

$$\phi(p) = \begin{cases} t, & \text{if } p \in T; \\ dt, & \text{if } p \text{ is } \alpha_i \to w_i \text{ for some } i \text{ but } p \notin T; \\ u, & \text{otherwise.} \end{cases}$$

Then:

$$\text{cl}(\phi)(p) = \begin{cases} t, & \text{iff } T \models p; \\ f, & \text{iff } T \models \neg p; \\ *, & \text{iff } p \text{ is true in some extensions of } (R,T) \text{ and false in others;} \\ dt, & \text{iff } T \not\models p \text{ but } p \text{ is true in some of the extensions and false in none;} \\ df, & \text{iff } T \not\models \neg p \text{ but } p \text{ is false in some of the extensions and true in none;} \\ u, & \text{iff } p \text{ is undecided in all extensions of } (R,T). \end{cases}$$

Theorem 5.2 *The closure operation is potentially non-monotonic.*

Suppose that we have two default rules, one of which indicates that birds can fly, and the other that flying things are stupid. Consider the following two truth functions:

p	$\phi(p)$	$\psi(p)$
bird(Tweety)	t	t
penguin(Tweety)	u	t
flies(Tweety)	u	u
dumb(Tweety)	u	u

Clearly $\phi <_k \psi$. But in light of the previous theorem, the closures of ϕ and ψ are given by:

p	$\phi(p)$	$\psi(p)$
bird(Tweety)	t	t
penguin(Tweety)	df	t
flies(Tweety)	dt	f
dumb(Tweety)	dt	u

We do not have $\text{cl}(\phi) \leq_k \text{cl}(\psi)$. The point is that the fact that Tweety is now known not to fly keeps the default rule about stupidity from firing. □

5.2 Truth maintenance

In a truth maintenance system, the truth values assigned to propositions contain information concerning the reasons for their truth or falsity. We can capture this using a multi-valued logic in which the truth values consist of pairs $[\ a\ .\ b\ ]$ where a and b are respectively justifications for the truth and falsity of the statement in question. We can assume that these justifications are themselves in disjunctive normal form, consisting of a list of parallel conjunctive justifications.

An example will make this clearer. Suppose that p is the statement $q \vee (r \wedge s)$. Then if q, r and s are all in the knowledge base, the truth value of p will be

$$[\ (\{q\}\{r,s\})\ .\ \text{nil}\ ]$$

Either q or the $\{r, s\}$ pair provides independent justification for p, and there is no justification for $\neg p$. We will assume in general that if the truth value of p is $[\ a\ .\ b\ ]$, either a or b is empty; in other words, that either p or $\neg p$ is unjustified.

Given two justifications j_1 and j_2 expressed in disjunctive normal form, we write $j_1 \leq j_2$ if every conjunctive subclause in j_1 contains some subclause in j_2 as a subset:

$$(a_1 \dots a_n) \leq (b_1 \dots b_m)$$

if for each a_i, there is some b_j with $b_j \subseteq a_i$. It is not hard to see that the empty justification (containing no information) is a minimal element under this partial order, while the justification $(\{\})$ consisting of a single empty conjunct (a justification needing no premises) is maximal.

If $j_1 \leq j_2$, we now define:

$$[\ j_1\ .\ \text{nil}\ ] \leq_t [\ j_2\ .\ \text{nil}\ ] \qquad [\ j_1\ .\ \text{nil}\ ] \leq_k [\ j_2\ .\ \text{nil}\ ] \qquad (7)$$

and

$$[\ \text{nil}\ .\ j_1\ ] \geq_t [\ \text{nil}\ .\ j_2\ ] \qquad [\ \text{nil}\ .\ j_1\ ] \leq_k [\ \text{nil}\ .\ j_2\ ] \qquad (8)$$

The k-join $t \cdot f$ is of course $\perp$ as usual. Note the sense of the first inequality in (8).

The analog to theorem 5.1 is now:

Theorem 5.3 *Let $p_1, \dots, p_n$ be possible assumptions in our knowledge base; and suppose that ϕ is given by*

$$\phi(q) = \begin{cases} [\ (\{p_i\})\ .\ \text{nil}\ ], & \textit{if } q = p_i \textit{ for some } i; \\ u, & \textit{otherwise.} \end{cases}$$

Then if $q_1, \dots, q_m$ form a subset of the p_i's and x is an arbitrary sentence,

$$[\ (\{q_1, \dots, q_m\})\ .\ \text{nil}\ ] \leq_k \text{cl}(\phi)(x)$$

if and only if the q_j's form a justification of x.

6 Future work

It is painfully clear that the work presented in this paper only scratches the surface of the approach being discussed.

Both theoretical and engineering issues need to be explored. There are many other non-standard approaches to inference; can they be captured in this framework? Circumscription and probabilistic schemes seem especially important candidates.

Equally important is an implementation of the ideas we have discussed. Ideally, a general-purpose inference engine can be constructed which accepts as input four functions giving the two glb and two lub operations in the bilattice, and which then performs suitable multi-valued inference. The key issue is the determination of what price must be paid in terms of efficiency for the increased generality of the approach we are proposing.

Work in each of these areas is currently under way at Stanford.

REFERENCES

[1] N. D. Belnap. How a computer should think. In *Proceedings of the Oxford International Symposium on Contemporary Aspects of Philosophy*, pages 30–56, 1975.

[2] N. D. Belnap. A useful four-valued logic. In G. Epstein and J. Dumm, editors, *Modern Uses of Multiple-valued Logic*, pages 8–37, D. Reidel Publishing Company, Boston, 1977.

[3] J. de Kleer. An assumption-based truth maintenance system. *Artificial Intelligence*, 28:127–162, 1986.

[4] J. Doyle. A truth maintenance system. *Artificial Intelligence*, 12:231–272, 1979.

[5] M. L. Ginsberg. *Analyzing Incomplete Information.* Technical Report 84-17, KSL, Stanford University, 1984.

[6] M. L. Ginsberg. *Multi-valued Logics.* Technical Report 86-29, KSL, Stanford University, 1986.

[7] M. L. Ginsberg. Non-monotonic reasoning using Dempster's rule. In *Proceedings of the American Association for Artificial Intelligence*, pages 126–129, 1984.

[8] G. Grätzer. *General Lattice Theory.* Birkhäuser Verlag, Basel, 1978.

[9] J. McCarthy. Applications of circumscription to formalizing common sense knowledge. *Artificial Intelligence*, 89–116, 1986.

[10] R. Reiter. A logic for default reasoning. *Artificial Intelligence*, 13:81–132, 1980.

[11] E. Sandewall. A functional approach to non-monotonic logic. In *Proceedings of the Ninth International Joint Conference on Artificial Intelligence*, pages 100–106, 1985.

[12] D. S. Scott. Some ordered sets in computer science. In I. Rival, editor, *Ordered Sets*, pages 677–718, D. Reidel Publishing Company, Boston, 1982.

Chapter 4

Truth Maintenance

The work on truth maintenance has a strange relationship to research in nonmonotonic reasoning. In the original paper describing the idea, Doyle's "A truth maintenance system," it is made clear from the start that Doyle is attempting to provide an effective computational framework for default reasoning. He stresses this in Section 1.1.1; the whole approach is founded on the idea of a sentence's becoming "in" (i.e., believed) if another sentence is "out" (i.e., not believed). Doyle goes on to suggest that, "The reasoned retraction of assumptions helps in formulating a class of backtracking procedures which revise the set of current assumptions when inconsistencies are discovered." As discussed in the introduction, a variety of authors have noticed that such a facility is crucial to the implementation of any nonmonotonic formalism. The connection is drawn quite sharply by Doyle himself in Section 10 of the paper on truth maintenance.

The multiple-extension problem also appears in the work on truth maintenance, although Doyle restricts his attention to problems arising from what he calls circular arguments in Section 3.1. One of his examples involves the pair of conflicting default rules

$$M\neg g \rightarrow f$$
$$M\neg f \rightarrow g$$

In spite of this, work on truth maintenance appears to have become disconnected from progress on default reasoning. The reason appears to be that Doyle's paper presents an algorithm, as opposed to a declarative description of nonmonotonic reasoning. He goes to great efforts to present a detailed description of the workings of a TMS, but nowhere is there a satisfactory explanation of the semantics of the approach. His paper with McDermott [**McDermott, Doyle, 1980**] was an attempt to rectify this, but suffered from other difficulties. Other attempts at formalizing the truth maintenance process can be found in [Reiter, de Kleer, 1987; Doyle, 1983; Doyle, 1982].

Two papers on truth maintenance have nevertheless been included in this collection. As described in the introduction, the reason is that there remains a general consensus that Doyle's ideas must be better understood if nonmonotonic inference is ever to become a practical technique. Although the problem of finding a suitably formal connection between Doyle's work and the other results in nonmonotonic logic remains unsolved, this collection would not have been complete without the papers in this section.

The other paper that has been included is Johan de Kleer's "An assumption-based TMS," which describes a variant of Doyle's work. De Kleer suggests that an effective way to store justification information is by labelling the propositions being considered with the sets of premises needed to derive them. He refers to such a collection of premises as a *context*; for each proposition, de Kleer maintains a list of the minimal contexts (i.e., the contexts with the fewest assumptions) in which it holds.

Once again, the work is algorithmic rather than declarative. De Kleer argues that the ATMS architecture is capable of solving some of the problems that appear when implementing conventional TMSs (including the problem of circular justifications mentioned earlier). In spite of the algorithmic nature of the presentation, however, it seems that the ATMS approach can be concisely formalized [Reiter, de Kleer, 1987; Ginsberg, 1987b], and also that the use of *minimal* contexts is closely related to the uses of minimization elsewhere in the nonmonotonic literature (compare the two papers on diagnostic applications in Section 5.2).

A preliminary version of the ATMS paper appeared at in the proceedings of the Fourth National Conference on Artificial Intelligence [de Kleer, 1984], in which de Kleer indicated that similar ideas had been investigated earlier by Martins and Shapiro [Martins, Shapiro, 1984; Martins, Shapiro, 1983]. The ATMS approach is described further in [de Kleer, 1986b] and [de Kleer, 1986c].

A Truth Maintenance System*

Jon Doyle

Massachusetts Institute of Technology, Artificial Intelligence Laboratory, Cambridge, MA, U.S.A.

Recommended by Patrick J. Hayes

ABSTRACT

To choose their actions, reasoning programs must be able to make assumptions and subsequently revise their beliefs when discoveries contradict these assumptions. The Truth Maintenance System (TMS) *is a problem solver subsystem for performing these functions by recording and maintaining the reasons for program beliefs. Such recorded reasons are useful in constructing explanations of program actions and in guiding the course of action of a problem solver. This paper describes (1) the representations and structure of the* TMS, *(2) the mechanisms used to revise the current set of beliefs, (3) how dependency-directed backtracking changes the current set of assumptions, (4) techniques for summarizing explanations of beliefs, (5) how to organize problem solvers into "dialectically arguing" modules, (6) how to revise models of the belief systems of others, and (7) methods for embedding control structures in patterns of assumptions. We stress the need of problem solvers to choose between alternative systems of beliefs, and outline a mechanism by which a problem solver can employ rules guiding choices of what to believe, what to want, and what to do.*

In memory of **John Sheridan Mac Nerney**

1. Introduction

Computer reasoning programs usually construct computational models of situations. To keep these models consistent with new information and changes in the situations being modelled, the reasoning programs frequently need to remove or change portions of their models. These changes sometimes lead to further changes, for the reasoner often constructs some parts of the model by making inferences from other parts of the model. This paper studies both the problem of how to make changes in computational models, and the underlying problem of how the models should be constructed in order to make making changes convenient. Our approach is to record the reasons for believing or using each program belief, inference rule, or procedure. To allow new information to displace previous conclusions, we employ "non-monotonic" reasons for beliefs, in which one belief depends on a lack of belief in some other statement. We use a program called the *Truth Maintenance System*[1] (TMS) to determine the current set of beliefs from the current set of reasons, and to update the current set of beliefs in accord with new reasons in a (usually) incremental fashion. To perform these revisions, the TMS traces the reasons for beliefs to find the consequences of changes in the set of assumptions.

1.1. The essence of the theory

Many treatments of formal and informal reasoning in mathematical logic and artificial intelligence have been shaped in large part by a seldom acknowledged view: the view that the process of reasoning is the process of deriving new knowledge from old, the process of discovering new truths contained in known truths. This view, as it is simply understood, has several severe difficulties as a theory of reasoning. In this section, I propose another, quite different view about the nature of reasoning. I incorporate some new concepts into this view, and the combination overcomes the problems exhibited by the conventional view.

Briefly put, the problems with the conventional view of reasoning stem from the *monotonicity* of the sequence of states of the reasoner's beliefs: his beliefs are true, and truths never change, so the only action of reasoning is to augment the current set of beliefs with more beliefs. This monotonicity leads to three closely related problems involving commonsense reasoning, the frame problem, and control. To some extent, my criticisms here of the conventional view of reasoning will be amplifications of Minsky's [36] criticisms of the logistic approach to problem solving.

One readily recalls examples of the ease with which we resolve apparent contradictions involving our commonsense beliefs about the world. For example, we routinely make assumptions about the permanence of objects and the typical features or properties of objects, yet we smoothly accommodate corrections to the assumptions and can quickly explain our errors away. In such cases, we discard old conclusions in favor of new evidence. Thus, the set of our commonsense beliefs changes non-monotonically.

Our beliefs of what is current also change non-monotonically. If we divide the trajectory of the temporally evolving set of beliefs into discrete temporal situations, then at each instant the most recent situation is the set of current beliefs, and the preceding situations are past sets of beliefs. Adjacent sets of beliefs in this trajectory are usually closely related, as most of our actions have only a relatively small set of effects. The important point is that the trajectory does not form a sequence of monotonically increasing sets of beliefs, since many actions change what we expect is true in the world. Since we base our actions on what we currently believe, we must continually update our current set of beliefs. The problem of describing and performing this updating efficiently is sometimes called the *frame problem*. In

* This research was conducted at the Artificial Intelligence Laboratory of the Massachusetts Institute of Technology. Support for the Laboratory's artificial intelligence research is provided in part by the Advanced Research Projects Agency of the Department of Defense under Office of Naval Research contract number N00014-75-C-0643, and in part by NSF grant MCS77-04828.

[1] As we shall see, this term not only sounds like Orwellian Newspeak, but also is probably a misnomer. The name stems from historical accident, and rather than change it here, I retain it to avoid confusion in the literature.

connection with the frame problem, the conventional view suffers not only from monotonicity, but also from *atomicity*, as it encourages viewing each belief as an isolated statement, related to other beliefs only through its semantics. Since the semantics of beliefs are usually not explicitly represented in the system, if they occur there at all, atomicity means that these incremental changes in the set of current beliefs are difficult to compute.

The third problem with the conventional view actually subsumes the problem of commonsense reasoning and the frame problem. The problem of control is the problem of deciding what to do next. Rather than make this choice blindly, many have suggested that we might apply the reasoner to this task as well, to make inferences about which inferences to make. This approach to the problem of control has not been explored much, in part because such control inferences are useless in monotonic systems. In these systems, adding more inference rules or axioms just increases the number of inferences possible, rather than preventing some inferences from being made. One gets the unwanted inferences together with new conclusions confirming their undesirability.

Rather than give it up, we pursue this otherwise attractive approach, and make the deliberation required to choose actions a form of reasoning as well. For our purposes, we take the desires and intentions of the reasoner to be represented in his set of current beliefs as beliefs about his own desires and intention. We also take the set of inference rules by which the reasoning process occurs to be represented as beliefs about the reasoner's own computational structure. By using this self-referential, reflexive representation of the reasoner, the inference rules become rules for self-modification of the reasoner's set of beliefs (and hence his desires and intentions as well). The control problem of choosing which inference rule to follow takes the form "Look at yourself as an object (as a set of beliefs), and choose what (new set of beliefs) you would like to become."

The language of such inference rules, and the language for evaluating which self-change to make, are for the most part outside the language of inference rules encouraged by the conventional view of reasoning. For example, when the current set of beliefs is inconsistent, one uses rules like "Reject the smallest set of beliefs possible to restore consistency" and "Reject those beliefs which represent the simplest explanation of the inconsistency." These sorts of rules are all we have, since we cannot infallibly analyze errors or predict the future, yet these rules are non-monotonic, since they lead to removing beliefs from the set of current beliefs.

To repeat, one source of each of these problems is the monotonicity inherent in the conventional view of reasoning. I now propose a different view, and some new concepts which have far reaching consequences for these issues.

Rational thought is the process of finding reasons for attitudes.

To say that some attitude (such as belief, desire, intent, or action) is rational is to say that there is some acceptable reason for holding that attitude. Rational thought is the process of finding such acceptable reasons. Whatever purposes the reasoner may have, such as solving problems, finding answers, or taking action, it operates by constructing reasons for believing things, desiring things, intending things, or doing or willing things. The actual attitude in the reasoner occurs only as a by-product of constructing reasons. The current set of beliefs and desires arises from the current set of reasons for beliefs and desires, reasons phrased in terms of other beliefs and desires. When action is taken, it is because some reason for the action can be found in terms of the beliefs and desires of the actor. I stress again, the only *real* component of thought is the current set of reasons—the attitudes such as beliefs and desires arise from the set of reasons, and have no independent existence.

One consequence of this view is that to study rational thought, we should study justified belief or reasoned argument, and ignore questions of truth. Truth enters into the study of extra-psychological rationality and into what commonsense truisms we decide to supply to our programs, but truth does not enter into the narrowly psychological rationality by which our programs operate.

Of course, this sort of basic rationality is simpler to realize than human belief. Humans exhibit "burn-in" phenomena in which long-standing beliefs come to be believed independently of their reasons, and humans sometimes undertake "leaps of faith" which vault them into self-justifying sets of beliefs, but we will not study these issues here. Instead, we restrict ourselves to the more modest goal of making rational programs in this simpler sense.

The view stated above entails that for each statement or proposition P just one of two states obtains: Either

(a) P has at least one currently acceptable (*valid*) reason, and is thus a member of the current set of beliefs, or

(b) P has no currently acceptable reasons (either no reasons at all, or only unacceptable ones), and is thus not a member of the current set of beliefs.

If P falls in state (a), we say that P is *in* (the current set of beliefs), and otherwise, that P is *out* (of the current set of beliefs). These states are not symmetric, for while reasons can be constructed to make P *in*, no reason can make P *out*. (At most, it can make $\neg$P *in* as well.)

This shows that the proposed view also succumbs to monotonicity problems, for the set of reasons grows monotonically, which (with the normal sense of "reason") leads to only monotonic increases in the set of current beliefs. To solve the problem of monotonicity, we introduce novel meanings for the terms "a reason" and "an assumption".

Traditionally, a reason for a belief consists of a set of other beliefs, such that if each of these basis beliefs is held, so also is the reasoned belief. To get off the ground, this analysis of reasons requires either circular arguments between beliefs (and the appropriate initial state of belief) or some fundamental type of belief which grounds all other arguments. The traditional view takes these fundamental beliefs, often called assumptions (or premises), as believed without reason. On this view, the reasoner makes changes in the current set of beliefs by removing some of the current assumptions and adding some new ones.

To conform with the proposed view, we introduce meanings for "reason" and "assumption" such that assumptions also have reasons. A *reason* (or justification) for a belief consists of an ordered pair of sets of other beliefs, such that the reasoned belief is *in* by virtue of this reason only if each belief in the first set is *in*, and each belief in the second set is *out*. An *assumption* is a current belief one of whose valid reasons depends on a non-current belief, that is, has a non-empty second set of antecedent beliefs. With these notions we can create "ungrounded" yet reasoned beliefs by making assumptions. (E.g. give P the reason $(\{\ \}, \{\neg P\})$.) We can also effect non-monotonic changes in the set of current beliefs by giving reasons for some of the *out* statements used in the reasons for current assumptions. (E.g. to get rid of P, justify $\neg P$.) We somewhat loosely say that when we justify some *out* belief supporting an assumption, (e.g. $\neg P$), we are *denying* or *retracting* the assumption (P).

These new notions solve the monotonicity problem. Following from this solution we find ways of treating the commonsense reasoning, frame, and control problems plaguing the conventional view of reasoning. Commonsense default expectations we represent as new-style assumptions. Part of the frame problem, namely how to non-monotonically change the set of current beliefs, follows from this non-monotonic notion of reason. However, much of the frame problem (e.g. how to give the "laws of motion" and how to retrieve them efficiently) lies outside the scope of this discussion. The control problem can be dealt with partially by embedding the sequence of procedural states of the reasoner in patterns of assumptions. We will treat this idea, and the rest of the control problem, in more detail later.

Other advantages over the conventional view also follow. One of these advantages involves how the reasoner retracts assumptions. With the traditional notion of assumption, retracting assumptions was unreasoned. If the reasoner removed an assumption from the current set of beliefs, the assumption remained out until the reasoner specifically put it back into the set of current beliefs, even if changing circumstances obviated the value of removing this belief. The new notions introduce instead the *reasoned retraction of assumptions*. This means that the reasoner retracts an assumption only by giving a reason for why it should be retracted. If later this reason becomes invalid, then the retraction is no longer effective and the assumption is restored to the current set of beliefs.

The reasoned retraction of assumptions helps in formulating a class of backtracking procedures which revise the set of current assumptions when inconsistencies are discovered. The paradigm procedure of this sort we call dependency-directed backtracking after Stallman and Sussman [53]. It is the least specialized procedure for revising the current set of assumptions in the sense that it only operates on the reasons for beliefs, not on the form or content of the beliefs. In short, it traces backwards through the reasons for the conflicting beliefs, finds the set of assumptions reached in this way, and then retracts one of the assumptions with a reason involving the other assumptions. (We describe the procedure in detail later.) Dependency-directed backtracking serves as a template for more specialized revision procedures. These specialized procedures are necessary in almost all practical applications, and go beyond the general procedure by taking the form of the beliefs they examine into account when choosing which assumption to reject.

1.2. Basic terminology

The TMS records and maintains arguments for potential program beliefs, so as to distinguish, at all times, the current set of program beliefs. It manipulates two data structures: *nodes*, which represent beliefs, and *justifications*, which represent reasons for beliefs. We write St(N) to denote the statement of the potential belief represented by the node N. We say the TMS believes in (the potential belief represented by) a node if it has an argument for the node and believes in the nodes involved in the argument. This may seem circular, but some nodes will have arguments which involve no other believed nodes, and so form the base step for the definition.

As its fundamental actions,

(1) the TMS can create a new node, to which the problem solving program using the TMS can attach the statement of a belief (or inference rule, or procedure, or data structure). The TMS leaves all manipulation of the statements of nodes (for inference, representation, etc.) to the program using the TMS.

(2) It can add (or retract) a new justification for a node, to represent a step of an argument for the belief represented by the node. This argument step usually represents the application of some rule or procedure in the problem solving program. Usually, the rules or procedures also have TMS nodes, which they include in the justifications they create.

(3) Finally, the TMS can mark a node as a *contradiction*, to represent the inconsistency of any set of beliefs which enter into an argument for the node.

A new justification for a node may lead the TMS to believe in the node. If the TMS did not believe in the node previously, this may in turn allow other nodes to be believed by previously existing but incomplete arguments. In this case, the TMS invokes the *truth maintenance* procedure to make any necessary revisions in the set of beliefs. The TMS revises the current set of beliefs by using the recorded justifications to compute non-circular arguments for nodes from premises and other special nodes, as described later. These non-circular arguments distinguish one justification as the *well-founded supporting justification* of each node representing a current belief. The TMS locates the set of nodes to update by finding those nodes whose well-founded arguments depend on changed nodes.

The program using the TMS can indicate the inconsistency of the beliefs represented by certain currently believed nodes by using these nodes in an argument for a new node, and by then marking the new node as a contradiction. When this happens, another process of the TMS, *dependency-directed backtracking*, analyzes the well-founded argument of the contradiction node to locate the *assumptions* (special types of nodes defined later) occurring in the argument. It then makes a record of the inconsistency of this set of assumptions, and uses this record to change one of the assumptions. After this change, the contradiction node is no longer believed. We explain this process in Section 4.

The TMS employs a special type of justification, called a *non-monotonic justification*, to make tentative guesses. A non-monotonic justification bases an argument for a node not only on current belief in other nodes, as occurs in the most familiar forms of deduction and reasoning, but also on lack of current belief in other nodes. For example, one might justify a node N–1 representing a statement P on the basis of lack of belief in node N–2 representing the statement ¬P. In this case, the TMS would hold N–1 as a current belief as long as N–2 was not among the current beliefs, and we would say that it had assumed belief in N–1. More generally, by an *assumption* we mean any node whose well-founded support is a non-monotonic justification.

As a small example of the use of the TMS, suppose that a hypothetical office scheduling program considers holding a meeting on Wednesday. To do this, the program assumes that the meeting is on Wednesday. The inference system of the program includes a rule which draws the conclusion that due to regular commitments, any meeting on Wednesday must occur at 1:00 P.M. However, the fragment of the schedule for the week constructed so far has some activity scheduled for that time already, and so another rule concludes the meeting cannot be on Wednesday. We write these nodes and rule-constructed justifications as follows:

Node	*Statement*	*Justification*	*Comment*
N–1	DAY (*M*) = WEDNESDAY	(SL ( ) (N–2))	*an assumption*
N–2	DAY (*M*) ≠ WEDNESDAY		*no justification yet*
N–3	TIME (*M*) = 13:00	(SL (R–37 N–1) ( ))	

The above notation for the justifications indicates that they belong to the class of *support-list* (SL) justifications. Each of these justifications consists of two lists of nodes. A SL-justification is a *valid* reason for belief if and only if each of the nodes in the first list is believed and each of the nodes in the second list is not believed. In the example, if the two justifications listed above are the only existing justifications, then N–2 is not a current belief since it has no justifications at all. N–1 is believed since the justification for N–1 specifies that this node depends on the lack of belief in N–2. The justification for N–3 shows that N–3 depends on a (presumably believed) node R–37. In this case, R–37 represents a rule acting on (the statement represented by) N–1.

Subsequently another rule (represented by a node R–9) acts on beliefs about the day and time of some other engagement (represented by the nodes N–7 and N–8) to reject the assumption N–1.

N–2 DAY (*M*) ≠ WEDNESDAY (SL (R–9 N–7 N–8) ( ))

To accommodate this new justification, the TMS will revise the current set of beliefs so that N–2 is believed, and N–1 and N–3 are not believed. It does this by tracing "upwards" from the node to be changed, N–2, to see that N–1 and N–3 ultimately depend on N–2. It then carefully examines the justifications of each of these nodes to see that N–2's justification is valid (so that N–2 s *in*). From this it follows that N–1's justification is invalid (so N–1 is *out*), and hence that N–3's justification is invalid (so N–3 is *out*).

2. Representation of Reasons for Beliefs

2.1. States of belief

A node may have several justifications, each justification representing a different reason for believing the node. These several justifications comprise the node's *justification-set*. The node is believed if and only if at least one of its justifications is *valid*. We described the conditions for validity of SL-justifications above, and shortly will introduce and explain the other type of justification used in the TMS. We say that a node which has at least one valid justification is *in* (the current set of beliefs), and that a node with no valid justifications is *out* (of the current set of beliefs). We will alternatively say that each node has a *support-status* of either *in* or *out*. The distinction between *in* and *out* is not that between *true* and *false*. The former classification refers to current possession of valid reasons for belief. *True* and *false*, on the other hand, classify statements according to truth value independent of any reasons for belief.

In the TMS, each potential belief to be used as a hypothesis or conclusion of an argument must be given its own distinct node. When uncertainty about some statement (e.g. P) exists, one must (eventually) provide nodes for both the statement and its negation. Either of these nodes can have or lack well-founded arguments, leading to a four-element belief set (similar to the belief set urged by Belnap [2]) of neither P nor ¬P believed, exactly one believed, or both believed.

The literature contains many proposals for using three-element belief sets of *true*, *false*, and *unknown*. With no notion of justified belief, these proposals have some attraction. I urge, however, that systems based on a notion of justified belief should forego three-valued logics in favor of the four-valued system presented here, or risk a confusion of truth with justified belief. Users of justification-based three-valued systems can avoid problems if they take care to interpret their systems in terms of justifications rather than truth-values, but the danger of confusion seems greater when the belief set hides this distinction. One might argue that holding contradictory beliefs is just a transient situation, and that any stable situation uses only three belief states: *true*—only P believed, *false*—only ¬P believed, and *unknown*—neither believed. But the need for the four-element system cannot be dismissed so easily. Since we make the process of revising beliefs our main interest, we concern ourselves with those processes which operate during the transient situation. For hard problems and tough decisions, these "transient" states can be quite long-lived.

2.2. Justifications

Justifications, as recorded in the TMS, have two parts; the external form of the justification with significance to the problem solver, and the internal form of significance to the TMS. For example, a justification might have the external form (Modus Ponens A $A \supset B$) and have the internal form (SL (N–1 N–2 N–3) ( )), supposing that N–1 represents the rule Modus Ponens, N–2 represents A, and N–3 represents $A \supset B$. The TMS never uses or examines the external forms of justifications, but merely records them for use by the problem solver in constructing externally meaningful explanations. Henceforth, we will ignore these external forms of justifications.

Although natural arguments may use a wealth of types of argument steps or justifications, the TMS forces one to fit all these into a common mold. The TMS employs only two (internal) forms for justifications, called *support-list* (SL) and *conditional-proof* (CP) justifications. These are inspired by the typical forms of arguments in natural deduction inference systems, which either add or subtract dependencies from the support of a proof line. A proof in such a system might run as follows:

Line	*Statement*	*Justification*	*Dependencies*
1.	$A \supset B$	Premise	{1}
2.	$B \supset C$	Premise	{2}
3.	A	Hypothesis	{3}
4.	B	MP 1, 3	{1, 3}
5.	C	MP 2, 4	{1, 2, 3}
6.	$A \supset C$	Discharge 3, 5	{1, 2}

Each step of the proof has a line number, a statement, a justification, and a set of line numbers on which the statement depends. Premises and hypotheses depend on themselves, and other lines depend on the set of premises and hypotheses derived from their justifications. The above proof proves $A \supset C$ from the premises $A \supset B$ and $B \supset C$ by hypothesizing A and concluding C via two applications of Modus Ponens. The proof of $A \supset C$ ends by discharging the assumption A, which frees the conclusion of dependence on the hypothesis but leaves its dependence on the premises.

This example displays justifications which sum the dependencies of some of the referenced lines (as in line 4) and subtract the dependencies of some lines from those of other lines (as in line 6). The two types of justifications used in the TMS account for these effects on dependencies. A support-list justification says that the justified node depends on each node in a set of other nodes, and in effect sums the dependencies of the referenced nodes. A conditional-proof justification says that the node it justifies depends on the validity of a certain hypothetical argument. As in the example above, it subtracts the dependencies of some nodes (the hypotheses of the hypothetical argument) from the dependencies of others (the conclusion of the hypothetical argument). Thus we might rewrite the example in terms of TMS justifications as follows (here ignoring the difference between premises and hypotheses, and ignoring the inference rule MP):

N–1	$A \supset B$	(SL ( ) ( ))	*Premise*
N–2	$B \supset C$	(SL ( ) ( ))	*Premise*
N–3	A	(SL ( ) ( ))	*Premise*
N–4	B	(SL (N–1 N–3) ( ))	*MP*
N–5	C	(SL (N–2 N–4) ( ))	*MP*
N–6	$A \supset C$	(CP N–5 (N–3) ( ))	*Discharge*

CP-justifications, which will be explained in greater detail below, differ from ordinary hypothetical arguments in that they use two lists of nodes as hypotheses, the *in*hypotheses and the *out*hypotheses. In the above justification for N–6, the list of *in*hypotheses contains just N–3, and the list of *out*hypotheses is empty. This difference results from our use of non-monotonic justifications, in which arguments for nodes can be based both on *in* and *out* nodes.

2.3. Support-list justifications

To repeat the definition scattered throughout the previous discussion, the support-list justification has the form

(SL ⟨*in*list⟩ ⟨*out*list⟩),

and is valid if and only if each node in its *in*list is *in*, and each node in its *out*list is *out*. The SL-justification form can represent several types of deductions. With empty *in*list and empty *out*list, we say the justification forms a *premise* justification. A premise justification is always valid, and so the node it justifies will always be *in*. SL-justifications with nonempty *in*lists and empty *out*lists represent normal deductions. Each such justification represents a monotonic argument for the node it justifies from the nodes of its *in*list. We define *assumptions* to be nodes whose supporting-justification has a nonempty *out*list. These assumption justifications can be interpreted by viewing the nodes of the *in*list as comprising the reasons for wanting to assume the justified node; the nodes of the *out*list represent the specific criteria authorizing this assumption. For example, the reason for wanting to assume "The weather will be nice" might be "Be optimistic about the weather"; and the assumption might be authorized by having no reason to believe "The weather will be bad." We occasionally interpret the nodes of the *out*list as "denials" of the justified node, beliefs which imply the negation of the belief represented by the justified node.

2.4. Terminology of dependency relationships

I must pause to present some terminology before explaining CP-justifications. The definitions of dependency relationships introduced in this section are numerous, and the reader should consult Tables 1, 2 and Fig. 1 for examples of the definitions.

TABLE 1. A sample system of six nodes and seven justifications.

Node	Justification	Justification name
1	(SL (3) ( ))	J1
2	(SL ( ) (1))	J2
3	(SL (1) ( ))	J3
4	(SL (2) ( ))	J4a
4	(SL (3) ( ))	J4b
5	(SL ( ) ( ))	J5
6	(SL (3 5) ( ))	J6

TABLE. 2. All the dependency relationships implicit in the system of Table 1. Dashed entries are empty. All other entries are lists of nodes in the dependency relationship to the node given at the top of the column.

Dependency	Node 1	Node 2	Node 3	Node 4	Node 5	Node 6
Support-status	out	in	out	in	in	out
Supporting-justification	—	J2	—	J4a	J5	—
Supporting-nodes	3	1	1	2	—	3
Antecedents	—	1	—	2	—	—
Foundations	—	1	—	1, 2	—	—
Ancestors	1, 3	1, 3	1, 3	1, 2, 3	—	1, 3
Consequences	2, 3	4	1, 4, 6	—	6	—
Affected-consequences	2, 3	4	1, 6	—	—	—
Believed-consequences	2	4	—	—	—	—
Repercussions	1, 2, 3, 4, 6	4	1, 2, 3, 4, 6	—	—	—
Believed-repercussions	2, 4	4	—	—	—	—

As mentioned previously, the TMS singles out one justification, called the *supporting-justification*, in the justification-set of each *in* node to form part of the noncircular argument for the node. For reasons explained shortly, all nodes have only SL-justifications as their supporting-justifications, never CP-justifications. The set of *supporting-nodes* of a node is the set of nodes which the TMS used to determine the support-status of the node. For *in* nodes, the supporting-nodes are just the nodes listed in the *in*list and *out*list of its supporting-justification, and in this case we also call the supporting-nodes the *antecedents* of the node. For the supporting-nodes of *out* nodes, the TMS picks one node from each justification in the justification-set. From SL-justifications, it picks either an *out* node from the *in*list or an *in* node from the *out*list. From CP-justifications, it picks either an *out* node from the *in*hypotheses or consequent or an *in* from the *out*hypotheses. We define the supporting-nodes of *out* nodes in this way so that the support-status of the node in question cannot change without either a change in the support-status of one of the supporting nodes, or without the addition of a new valid justification. We say that an *out* node has no antecedents. The TMS keeps the supporting-nodes of each node as part of the node data-structure, and computes the antecedents of the node from this list.

The set of *foundations* of a node is the transitive closure of the antecedents of the node, that is, the antecedents of the node, their antecedents, and so on. This set is the set of nodes involved in the well-founded argument for belief in the node. The

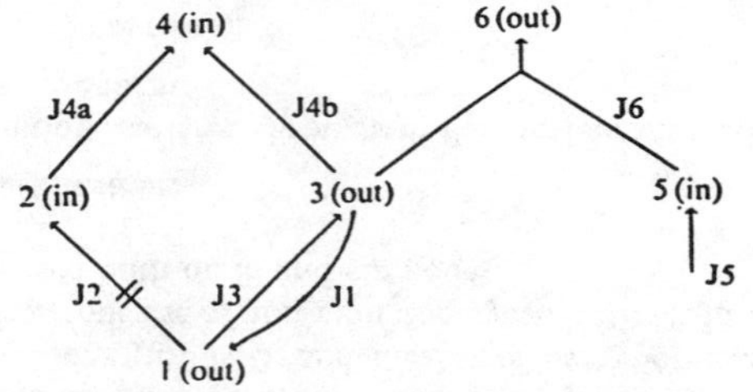

FIG. 1. A depiction of the system of Table 1. All arrows represent justifications. The uncrossed arrows represent *in*lists, and only the crossed line of J2 represents an *out* list. We always visualize support relationships as pointing upwards.

set of *ancestors* of a node, analogously, is the transitive closure of the supporting-nodes of the node, that is, the supporting-nodes of the node, their supporting-nodes, and so on. This set is the set of nodes which might possibly affect the support-status of the node. The ancestors of a node may include the node itself, for the closure of the supporting-nodes relation need not be well-founded. The TMS computes these dependency relationships from the supporting-nodes and antecedents of nodes.

In the other direction, the set of *consequences* of a node is the set of all nodes which mention the node in one of the justifications in their justification-set. The *affected-consequences* of a node are just those consequences of the node which contain the node in their set of supporting-nodes. The *believed-consequences* of a node are just those *in* consequences of the node which contain the node in their set of antecedents. The TMS keeps the consequences of each node as part of the node data-structure, and computes the affected- and believed-consequences from the consequences.

The set of *repercussions* of a node is the transitive closure of the affected-consequences of the node, that is, the affected-consequences of the node, their affected-consequences, and so on. The set of *believed-repercussions* of a node is the transitive closure of the believed-consequences of the node, that is, the believed-consequences of the node, their believed-consequences, and so on. The TMS computes all these relationships from the consequences of the node.

In all of the following, I visualize the lines of support for nodes as directed upwards, so that I look up to see repercussions, and down to see foundations. I say that one node is of lower level than another if its believed-repercussions include the other node.

2.5. Conditional-proof justifications

With this terminology, we can now begin to explain conditional-proof justifications. The exact meaning of these justifications in the TMS is complex and difficult to describe, so the reader may find this section hard going, and may benefit by referring back to it while reading Sections 3.3, 4, and 5. CP-justifications take the form

(CP ⟨consequent⟩ ⟨*in*hypotheses⟩ ⟨*out*hypotheses⟩).

A CP-justification is valid if the consequent node is *in* whenever

(a) each node of the *in*hypotheses is *in* and

(b) each node of the *out*hypotheses is *out*. Except in a few esoteric uses described later, the set of *out*hypotheses is empty, so normally a node justified with a CP-justification represents the implication whose antecedents are the *in*hypotheses and whose consequent is the consequent of the CP-justification. Standard conditional-proofs in natural deduction systems typically specify a single set of hypotheses, which corresponds to the *in*hypotheses of a CP-justification. In the present case, the set of hypotheses must be divided into two disjoint subsets, since nodes may be derived both from some nodes being *in* and other nodes being *out*. Some deduction systems also employ multiple-consequent conditional-proofs. We forego these for reasons of implementation efficiency.

The TMS handles CP-justifications in special ways. It can easily determine the validity of a CP-justification only when the justification's consequent and *in*hypotheses are *in* and the *out*hypotheses are *out*, since determining the justification's validity with other support-statuses for these nodes may require switching the support-statuses of the hypothesis nodes and their repercussions to set up the hypothetical situation in which the validity of the conditional-proof can be evaluated. This may require truth maintenance processing, which in turn may require validity checking of further CP-justifications, and so the whole process becomes extremely complex. Instead of attempting such a detailed analysis (for which I know no algorithms), the TMS uses the opportunistic and approximate strategy of computing SL-justifications currently equivalent to CP-justifications. At the time of their creation, these new SL-justifications are equivalent to the CP-justifications in terms of the dependencies they specify, and are easily checked for validity. Whenever the TMS finds a CP-justification valid, it computes an equivalent SL-justification by analyzing the well-founded argument for the consequent node of the CP-justification to find those nodes which are not themselves supported by any of the *in*hypotheses or *out*hypotheses but which directly enter into the argument for the consequent node along with the hypotheses. Precisely, the TMS finds all nodes N in the foundations of the consequent such that N is not one of the hypotheses or one of their repercussions, and N is either an antecedent of the consequent or an antecedent of some other node in the repercussions of the hypotheses. The *in* nodes in this set form the *in*list of the equivalent SL-justification, and the *out* nodes of the set form the *out*list of the equivalent SL-justification. The TMS attaches the list of SL-justifications computed in this way to their parent CP-justifications, and always prefers to use these SL-justifications in its processing. The TMS checks the derived SL-justifications first in determining the support-status of a node, and uses them in explanations. It uses only SL-justifications (derived or otherwise) as supporting-justifications of nodes.

2.6. Other types of justifications

My experience with the TMS indicates that yet more forms of justifications would be useful. A *general-form* (GF) justification merges the above two forms into one in which the nodes in an *in*list and an *out*list are added to the result of a conditional-proof. We might notate this as

(GF ⟨*in*list⟩ ⟨*out*list⟩ ⟨consequent⟩ ⟨*in*hypotheses⟩ ⟨*out*hypotheses⟩).

I also suggest a *summarization* (SUM) justification form,

(SUM ⟨consequent⟩ ⟨*in*hypotheses⟩ ⟨*out*hypotheses⟩),

which abbreviates

(GF ⟨*in*hypotheses⟩ ⟨*out*hypotheses⟩ ⟨consequent⟩ ⟨*in*hypotheses⟩ ⟨*out*hypotheses⟩).

This form adds the hypotheses of a conditional-proof back into the result of the conditional-proof, thus summarizing the argument for the consequent by excising the intermediate part of the argument. Section 5 explains this technique in detail. I use SUM-justifications there for expository convenience, although I have not implemented them in the TMS.

3. Truth Maintenance Mechanisms

3.1. Circular arguments

Suppose a program manipulates three nodes as follows:

F	(= (+ *X Y*) 4)	. . .	*omitted*
G	(= *X* 1)	(SL (*J*) ( ))	
H	(= *Y* 3)	(SL (*K*) ( )).	

(We sometimes leave statements and justifications of nodes unspecified when they are not directly relevant to the presentation. We assume that all such omitted justifications are valid.) If *J* is *in* and *K* is *out*, then the TMS will make *F* and *G in*, and *H out*. If the program then justifies *H* with

(SL (*F G*) ( )),

the TMS will bring *H in*. Suppose now that the TMS makes *J out* and *K in*, leading to *G* becoming *out* and *H* remaining *in*. The program might then justify *G* with

(SL (*F H*) ( )).

If the TMS now takes *K out*, the original justification supporting belief in *H* becomes invalid, leading the TMS to reassess the grounds for belief in *H*. If it makes its decision to believe a node on the basis of a simple evaluation of each of the justifications of the node, then it will leave both *G* and *H in*, since the two most recently added justifications form circular arguments for *G* and *H* in terms of each other.

These circular arguments supporting belief in nodes motivate the use of well-founded supporting justifications, since nodes imprudently believed on tenuous circular bases can lead to ill-considered actions, wasted data base searches, and illusory inconsistencies which might never have occurred without the misleading, circularly supported beliefs. In view of this problem, the algorithms of the TMS must ensure that it believes no node for circular reasons.

Purported arguments for nodes can contain essentially three different kinds of circularities. The first and most common type of circularity involves only nodes which can be taken to be *out* consistently with their justifications. Such circularities arise routinely through equivalent or conditionally equivalent beliefs and mutually constraining beliefs. The above algebra example falls into this class of circularity.

The second type of circularity includes at least one node which must be *in*. Consider, for example

F TO–BE (SL ( ) (*G*))
G ¬TO–BE (SL ( ) (*F*)).

In the absence of other justifications, these justifications force the TMS either to make *F in* and *G out*, or *G in* and *F out*. This type of circularity can arise in certain types of sets of alternatives.

In unsatisfiable circularities, the third type, no assignment of *in* or *out* to nodes is consistent with their justifications. Consider

F ... (SL ( ) (*F*)).

With no other justifications for *F*, the TMS must make *F in* if and only if it makes *F out*, an impossible task. Unsatisfiable circularities sometimes indicate real inconsistencies in the beliefs of the program using the truth maintenance system, and can be manifest, for example, when prolonged backtracking rules out all possibilities. The current version of the TMS does not handle unsatisfiable circularities (it goes into a loop), as I removed the occasionally costly check for the presence of such circularities to increase the normal-case efficiency of the program. A robust implementation would reinstate this check. Step 5 in Section 3.2 discusses this problem in more detail.

3.2. The truth maintenance process

The truth maintenance process makes any necessary revisions in the current set of beliefs when the user adds to or subtracts from the justification-set of a node. Retracting justifications presents no important problems beyond those of adding justifications, so we ignore retractions to simplify the discussion. We first outline the procedure, and then present it in greater detail. The details will not be crucial in the following, so the casual reader should read the overview and then skip to Section 4.

In outline, the truth maintenance process starts when a new justification is added to a node. Only minor bookkeeping is required if the new justification is invalid, or if it is valid but the node is already *in*. If the justification is valid and the node is *out*, then the node and its repercussions must be updated. The TMS makes a list containing the node and its repercussions, and marks each of these nodes to indicate that they have not been given well-founded support. The TMS then examines the justifications of these nodes to see if any are valid purely on the basis of unmarked nodes, that is, purely on the basis of nodes which do have well-founded support. If it finds any, these nodes are brought *in* (or *out* if all their justifications are invalid purely on the basis of well-founded nodes). Then the marked consequences of the nodes are examined to see if they too can now be given well-founded support. Sometimes, after all of the marked nodes have been examined in this way, well-founded support-statuses will have been found for all nodes. Sometimes, however, some nodes will remain marked due to circularities. The TMS then initiates a constraint-relaxation process which assigns support-statuses to the remaining nodes. Finally, after all this, the TMS checks for contradictions and CP-justifications, performs dependency-directed backtracking and CP-justification processing if necessary, and then signals the user program of the changes in support-statuses of the nodes involved in truth maintenance.

In detail, the steps of the algorithm are as follows. We enclose comments in bracket-asterisk pairs (E.g. [*This is a comment.*])

Step 1 (*Adding a new justification*). Add the new justification to the node's justification-set and add the node to the set of consequences of each of the nodes mentioned in the justification. If the justification is a CP-justification, add the node to the *CP-consequent-list* of the consequent of the CP-justification, for use in Step 6. If the node is *in*, we are done. If the node is *out*, check the justification for validity. If invalid, add to the supporting-nodes either an *out* node from the *in*list, or an *in* node from the *outlist*. If valid, proceed to Step 2.

Step 2 (*Updating beliefs required*). Check the affected-consequences of the node. If there are none, change the support-status to *in*, and make the supporting-nodes the sum of the *in*list and *out*list; then stop. Otherwise, make a list L containing the node and its repercussions, record the support-status of each of these nodes, and proceed to Step 3. [*We must collect all the repercussions of the node to avoid constructing circular arguments which use repercussions of a node in its supposedly well-founded supporting argument.*]

Step 3 (*Marking the nodes*). Mark each node in L with a support-status of *nil*, and proceed to Step 4. [*Nodes can have a support-status of *nil* only during truth maintenance. This mark distinguishes those nodes with well-founded support from those for which well-founded support has not been determined.*]

Step 4 (*Evaluating the nodes' justifications*). For each node in L, execute the following subprocedure. When all are done, proceed to Step 5.

Step 4(*a*) (*Evaluating the justification-set*). If the node is either *in* or *out*, do nothing. Otherwise, keep picking justifications from the justification-set, first the SL-justifications and then the CP-justifications, checking them for well-founded validity or invalidity (to be defined shortly) until either a valid one is found or the justification-set is exhausted. [*The TMS tries justifications in chronological order, oldest first.*] If a valid justification is found, then (1) install it as the supporting-justification (first converting it to SL form if it is a CP-justification), (2) install the supporting-nodes as in Step 2, (3) mark the node *in*, and (4) recursively perform Step 4(a) for all consequences of the node which have a support-status of *nil*. If only well-founded invalid justifications are found, mark the node *out*, install its supporting-nodes as in Step 1, and recursively perform Step 4(a) for all *nil*-marked consequences of the node. Otherwise, the processing of the node is temporarily deferred; the subprocedure is finished. [*An SL-justification is *well-founded valid* if each node in the *in*list is *in* and each node of the *out*list is *out*; it is *well-founded invalid* if some node of the *in*list is *out* or some node of the *out*list is *in*. CP-justifications are well-founded valid if all *in*hypotheses are *in*, all *out*hypotheses are *out*, and the consequent is *in*; they are well-founded invalid if all *in*hypotheses are *in*, all *out*hypotheses are *out*, and the consequent is *out*.*]

[* This step may find well-founded supporting-justifications for some nodes in L, but may leave the support-status of some nodes undetermined due to circularities in potential arguments. These leftover nodes are handled by Step 5 below. If it were not for CP-justifications, Step 4 could be dispensed with entirely, as Step 5 effectively subsumes it. However, we include Step 4 both to handle CP-justifications and to improve (we hope) the efficiency of the algorithm by getting the solidly supported nodes out of the way first. *]

Step 5 (*Relaxing circularities*). For each node in L, execute the following subprocedure. On completion, proceed to Step 6.

Step 5(*a*) (*Evaluating the justification-set*). If the node is either *in* or *out*, do nothing. Otherwise, continue to select justifications from the SL-justifications (ignoring the CP-justifications) and to check them for not-well-founded validity or invalidity [* which assumes that all nodes currently marked *nil* will eventually be marked *out*, as explained shortly *] until either a valid justification is found or the justification-set is exhausted. If all justifications are invalid, mark the node *out*, install its supporting-nodes as in Step 1, and recursively perform Step 5(a) for all *nil*-marked consequences of the node. If a valid justification is found, then a special check must be made to see if the node already has affected-consequences. If the node does have affected-consequences, then all of them, and the node as well, must be re-marked with *nil* and re-examined by the loop of Step 5. [* We do this because the procedure may have previously determined the support-status of some other node on the assumption that this node was *out*. *] If there are no affected-consequences, then install the valid justification as the supporting-justification, install the supporting-nodes as in Step 2, mark the node *in*, and then recursively perform Step 5(a) for all consequences of the node which have a support-status of *nil*. [* All justifications will be either not-well-founded valid or invalid; there is no third case. An SL-justification is *not-well-founded valid* if each node in the *in*list is *in* and no node of the *out*list is *in*; otherwise, it is *not-well-founded invalid*. This evaluation of nodes assumes that a support-status of *nil* is the same as *out*, i.e. that all currently unassigned nodes will eventually be marked *out*. *]

[* If step 5 terminates, it finds well-founded support for all nodes in L. It will not terminate if unsatisfiable circularities exist. These circularities can be detected by checking to see if a node is its own ancestor after finding a not-well-founded valid justification for it in Step 5(a). If the node is its own ancestor, an unsatisfiable circularity exists in which the argument for belief in the node depends on lack of belief in the node. Unfortunately, this sort of non-termination can also occur with a satisfiable set of nodes and justifications which requires making changes to nodes not in the list L to find this satisfiable assignment of support-statuses. For example, if *F* is *in* but not in L, and if *G* has only the justification (SL (*F*) (*G*)) and is in L, then the procedure will not be able to assign a well-founded support-status to *G* without going outside L to change the support-status of *F*. In consequence, if truth maintenance is done properly it must be non-incremental in such cases.

This relaxation procedure finds one assignment of support-statuses to nodes, but there may be several such assignments possible. A more sophisticated system would incorporate some way in which to choose between these alternatives, since guidance in what the program believes will typically produce guidance in what the program does. Some versions of the TMS (e.g. [14]) incorporated rudimentary analysis facilities, but the current version lacks any such ability. It appears that this relaxation step must be fairly blind in choosing what revision to make. Methods for choosing between alternate revision must have some idea of what all the alternate revisions are, and these are very hard to determine accurately. One can approximate the set of alternate revisions by revisions including some particular belief, but after several such approximations this adds up to just trying some partial revision and seeing if it works out. *]

Step 6 (*Checking for CP-justifications and contradictions*). Call each of the following subprocedures for each of the nodes in L, and then proceed to Step 7. [* This step attempts to derive new SL-justifications from CP-justifications, and to resolve any inconsistencies appearing in the new set of beliefs. Since Step 5 leaves all nodes in L either *in* or *out*, it may now be possible to evaluate some CP-justifications which were previously unevaluable, and to resolve newly apparent contradictions. *]

Step 6(a) (*Check for CP-justifications*). Do nothing if the node is *out* or has an empty CP-consequent list. Otherwise, for each node in the CP-consequent-list, check its CP-justifications for validity, and if any are valid, derive their currently equivalent SL-justifications and justify the node with the resulting justification. If this justification is new and causes truth maintenance (Steps 1 through 5), start Step 6 over, otherwise return.

Step 6(b) (*Check for contradiction*). Ignore the node unless it is *in* and is marked as a contradiction, in which case call the dependency-directed backtracking system on the node. If truth maintenance (Steps 1 through 5) occurs during backtracking, start Step 6 over, otherwise return.

[* This step halts only when no new SL-justifications can be computed from CP-justifications, and no contradictions exist or can be resolved. *]

Step 7 (*Signalling changes*). Compare the current support-status of each node in L with the initial status recorded in Step 2, and call the user supplied *signal-recalling functions* and *signal-forgetting functions* to signal changes from *out* to *in* and from *in* to *out*, respectively. [* The user must supply two global functions which, if not overridden by a local function that the user might attach to the changed node, are called with the changed node as the argument. However, if the user has attached local function to the changed node, the TMS will call that function instead. *]

End of the truth maintenance procedure.

For more detail, I recommend the chapter on data dependencies in [4], which presents a simplified LISP implementation of a TMS-like program along with a proof of its correctness. McAllester [30] presents an alternative implementation of a truth maintenance system with a cleaner organization than the above. Doyle [15] presents a program listing of one version of the TMS in an appendix.

3.3. Analyzing conditional-proofs

The *Find Independent Support* (FIS) procedure computes SL-justifications from valid CP-justifications by finding those nodes supporting the consequent which do not depend on the hypotheses. Repeating our earlier explanation of what this means, FIS finds all nodes N in the foundations of the consequent of the conditional-proof justification such that

(1) N is not one of the hypotheses or one of their repercussions, and

(2) N is either an antecedent of the consequent or an antecedent of some node in the repercussions of the hypotheses. The *in* nodes in this set form the *in*list of the equivalent SL-justification, and the *out* nodes of the set form the *out*list of the equivalent SL-justification.

Let (CP C IH OH) be a valid CP-justification, where C is the consequent node, IH is the list of *in*hypotheses, and OH is the list of *out*hypotheses. The steps of FIS are as follows:

Step 1 (*Mark the hypotheses*). Mark each of the nodes in IH and OH with both an E (*examined*) mark and a S (*subordinates*) mark, then proceed to Step 2. [* The E mark means that the node has been examined by the procedure. We use it to make the search through the foundations of C efficient. The S mark means that the node is either one of the hypotheses or a repercussion of one of the hypotheses. *]

Step 2 (*Mark the foundations*). Call the following subprocedure on C, and proceed to Step 3.

Step 2(a) (*Mark the repercussions of the hypotheses*). If the node has an E mark, return. If the node has no E mark, mark it with the E mark, and call Step 2(a) on each of the antecedents of the node. If any of the antecedent nodes is marked with an S mark, mark the current node with an S mark. Finally, return. [* This step marks those nodes in both the foundations of C and the repercussions of the hypotheses. *]

Step 3 (*Unmark the foundations*). Using a recursive scan, similar to Step 2(a), remove the E marks from the foundations of C and proceed to Step 4.

Step 4 (*Remark the hypotheses*). As in Step 1, mark the hypotheses with E marks, this time ignoring their S marks. Proceed to Step 5.

Step 5 (*Collect the net support*). Call the following subprocedure on C and proceed to Step 6.

Step 5(a) (*Skip repercussions and collect support*). If the node has an E mark, return. Otherwise, mark the node with an E mark. If the node has no S mark, add it to IS if it is *in*, and to OS if it is *out*, then return. If the node has an S mark, execute Step 5(a) on each of its antecedents, then return. [* This step collects just those nodes in the foundations of C which are not hypotheses or their repercussions, and which directly support (are antecedents of) repercussions of the hypotheses. These nodes are exactly the nodes necessary to make the argument go through for C from the hypotheses. *]

Step 6 (*Clean up and return the result*). Repeat Step 3, removing both E and S marks, remove all marks from the nodes in IH and OH, and return the justification (SL IS OS).

End of the Find Independent Support procedure.

4. Dependency-Directed Backtracking

When the TMS makes a contradiction node *in*, it invokes dependency-directed backtracking to find and remove at least one of the current assumptions in order to make the contradiction node *out*. The steps of this process follow. As above, we enclose commentary in bracket-asterisk pairs ([*, *]).

Step 1 (*Find the maximal assumptions*). Trace through the foundations of the contradiction node C to find the set $S = \{A_1, \ldots, A_n\}$, which contains an assumption A if and only if A is in C's foundations and there is no other assumption B in the foundations of C such that A is in the foundations of B. [* We call S the set of the *maximal* assumptions underlying C. *]

[* Just as the TMS relies on the problem solving program to point out inconsistencies by marking certain nodes as contradictions, it also relies on the problem solver to use non-monotonic assumptions for any beliefs to which backtracking might apply. Because the TMS does not inspect the statements represented by its nodes, it foregoes the ability, for example, to retract premise justifications of nodes. *]

Step 2 (*Summarize the cause of the inconsistency*). If no previous backtracking attempt on C discovered S to be the set of maximal assumptions, create a new node NG, called a *nogood*, to represent the inconsistency of S. [* We call S the *nogood-set*. *] If S was encountered earlier as a nogood-set of a contradiction, use the previously created nogood node. [* Since C represents a false statement, NG represents

$$\mathrm{St}(A_1) \wedge \cdots \wedge \mathrm{St}(A_n) \supset \mathit{false},$$

or

$$\neg(\mathrm{St}(A_1) \wedge \cdots \wedge \mathrm{St}(A_n)) \tag{1}$$

by a simple rewriting. *]

Justify NG with

$$(\mathrm{CP}\ C\ S\ (\,)). \tag{2}$$

[* With this justification, NG will remain *in* even after Step 3 makes one of the assumptions *out*, since the CP-justification means that NG does not depend on any of the assumptions. *]

Step 3 (*Select and reject a culprit*). Select some A_i, the *culprit*, from S. Let $D_1, \ldots, D_k$ be the *out* nodes in the *out*list of A_i's supporting-justification. Select D_j from this set and justify it with

$$(\mathrm{SL}\ (NG\ A_1 \cdots A_{i-1}\ A_{i+1} \cdots A_n)\ (D_1 \cdots D_{j-1}\ D_{j+1} \cdots D_k)). \tag{3}$$

[* If one takes these underlying D nodes as "denials" of the selected assumption, this step recalls *reductio ad absurdum*. The backtracker attempts to force the culprit *out* by invalidating its supporting-justification with the new justification, which is valid whenever the nogood and the other assumptions are *in* and the other denials of the culprit are *out*. If the backtracker erred in choosing the culprit or denial, presumably a future contradiction will involve D_j and the remaining assumptions in its foundations. However, if the *out*list of the justification (3) is nonempty, D_j will be an assumption, of higher level than the remaining assumptions, and so will be the first to be denied.

The current implementation picks the culprit and denial randomly from the alternatives, and so relies on blind search. Blind search is inadequate for all but the simplest sorts of problems, for typically one needs to make a guided choice among the alternative revisions of beliefs. I will return to this problem in Section 8. *]

Step 4 (*Repeat if necessary*). If the TMS finds other arguments so that the contradiction node C remains *in* after the addition of the new justification for D_j, repeat this backtracking procedure. [* Presumably the previous culprit A_i will no longer be an assumption. *] Finally, if the contradiction becomes *out*, then halt; or if no assumptions can be found in C's foundations, notify the problem solving program of an unanalyzable contradiction, then halt.

End of the dependency-directed backtracking procedure.

As an example, consider a program scheduling a meeting, to be held preferably at 10 A.M. in either room 813 or 801.

N-1	TIME(M) = 1000	(SL ( ) (N-2))
N-2	TIME(M) ≠ 1000	
N-3	ROOM(M) = 813	(SL ( ) (N-4)
N-4	ROOM(M) = 801	

With only these justifications, the TMS makes N-1 and N-3 *in* and the other two nodes *out*. Now suppose a previously scheduled meeting rules out this combination of time and room for the meeting by supporting a new node with N-1 and N-3 and then declaring this new node to be a contradiction.

N-5	CONTRADICTION	(SL (N-1 N-3) ( ))

The dependency-directed backtracking system traces the foundations of N-5 to find two assumptions, N-1 and N-3, both maximal.

N-6	NOGOOD N-1 N-3	(CP N-5 (N-1 N-3) ( ))	*here* ≡ (SL ( ) ( ))
N-4	ROOM(M) = 801	(SL (N-6 N-1) ( ))	

The backtracker creates N-6 which means, in accordance with form (1) of Step 2,

$$\neg(\mathrm{TIME}(M) = 1000 \wedge \mathrm{ROOM}(M) = 813)$$

and justifies N-6 according to form (2) above. It arbitrarily selects N-3 as the culprit, and justifies N-3's only *out* antecedent, N-4, according to form (3) above. Following this, the TMS makes N-1, N-4 and N-6 *in*, and N-2, N-3 and N-5 *out*. N-6 has a CP-justification equivalent to a premise SL-justification, since N-5 depends directly on the two assumptions N-1 and N-3 without any additional intervening nodes.

A further rule now determines that room 801 cannot be used after all, and creates another contradiction node to force a different choice of room.

N–7	CONTRADICTION	(SL (N–4) ( ))	
N–8	NOGOOD N–1	(CP N–7 (N–1) ( ))	*here*≡(SL (N–6) ( ))
N–2	TIME(M) ≠ 1000	(SL (N–8) ( ))	

Tracing backwards from N–7 through N–4, N–6 and N–1, the backtracker finds that the contradiction depends on only one assumption, N–1. It creates the nogood node N–8, justifies it with a CP-justification, in this case equivalent to the SL-justification (SL (N–6) ( )), since N–7's foundations contain N–6 and N–1's repercussions do not. The loss of belief in N–1 carried N–5 away as well, for the TMS makes N–2, N–3, N–6 and N–8 *in*, and N–1, N–4, N–5 and N–7 *out*.

5. Summarizing Arguments

Long or extremely detailed arguments are usually unintelligible. When possible, able expositors make their explanations intelligible by structuring them into clearly separated levels of detail, in which explanations of major points consist of several almost-major points, and so on, with each item explained in terms of the level of detail proper to the item. Structuring arguments in this way serves much the same purpose as structuring plans of action into levels of detail and abstraction. Users of the TMS, or any other means for recording explanations, must take care to convert raw explanations into structured one, if the explanations lack structure initially. Consider, as an exaggerated example, a centralized polling machine for use in national elections. At the end of Election Day, the machine reports that John F. Kennedy has won the election, and when pressed for an explanation of this decision, explains that Kennedy won because Joe Smith voted for him, and Fannie Jones voted for him, and Bert Brown voted for him, et cetera, continuing in this way for many millions of voters, pro and con. The desired explanation consists of a summary total of the votes cast for Kennedy, Nixon, and the other candidates. If pressed for further explanations, breakdowns of these totals into state totals follow. The next level of explanation expands into city totals, and only if utterly pressed should the machine break the results into precincts or individual voters for some place, say Cook County.

One can summarize the arguments and explanations recorded in the TMS by using conditional-proofs to subtract nodes representing "low-level" details from arguments. Summarizations can be performed on demand by creating a new node, and justifying this node with a CP-justification mentioning the node to be explained as its consequent, and the set of nodes representing the unwanted low-level beliefs as its *in* and *out*hypotheses. The effective explanation for the new node, via a SL-justification computed from the CP-justification, will consist solely of those high-level nodes present in the well-founded argument being summarized.

Explanations can be generalized or made more abstract by this device as well, by justifying the original node in terms of the new node, or by justifying the original node with the new SL-justification computed for the new node. This new justification will not mention any of the low-level details subtracted from the original argument, and so will support the conclusion as a general result, independent of the particular low-level details used to derive it. For example, an electronic circuit analysis program might compute the voltage gain of an amplifier by assuming a typical input voltage, using this voltage to compute the other circuit voltages including the output voltage, computing the voltage gain as the ratio of the output voltage to the input voltage, and finally justifying the resulting value for the gain using a conditional-proof of the output voltage value given the hypothesized input voltage value. This would leave the gain value depending only on characteristics of the circuit, not on the particular input voltage value used in the computation.

Returning to the election example above, summarizing the election result by subtracting out all the individual voter's ballots leaves the argument empty, for presumably the intermediate results were computed solely in terms of the ballots. In order to summarize an explanation, one must know the form of the desired summarization. While this analytical knowledge is frequently unavoidable, we typically can reduce its scope by introducing structure into arguments during their creation. To illustrate this point, we explain how one simple structuring technique works smoothly with so-called structured descriptions to easily produce perspicuous explanations.

For this discussion, we take a structured description to consist of a description-item (sometimes termed a "node" in the knowledge-representation literature; but we reserve this term for TMS nodes), a set of roles-items representing the parts of the description, and a set of local inference rules. These roles frequently represent entities associated with the description. For example, a PERSON description may have a MOTHER role, and an ADDER description may have roles for ADDEND, AUGEND, and SUM.

To structure explanations, we draw an analogy between the parts of a description and the calling sequence of a procedure. We associate one TMS node with each description-item and two TMS nodes with each role-item. We will use the node associated with a description-item to mark the arguments internal to the description, as explained shortly. We separate the nodes for role-items into two sets, corresponding to the external "calling sequence" and the internal "formal parameters" of the procedure. We use one of the nodes associated with each role-item to represent the external system's view of that "argument" to the procedure call, and the other node associated with the role-item to represent the procedure's view of that "formal parameter" of the procedure. Then we organize the problem solving program so that only the procedure and its internal rules use or justify the internal set of nodes, and that all other descriptions and procedures use or justify only the external set of nodes. The motivation for this separation of the users and justifiers of two sets of nodes into internal users and external users is that we can structure arguments by transmitting information between these two sets of nodes in a special way, as we now describe.

Let D be the node associated with the description, and let E_i and I_i be corresponding external and internal role-item nodes. We justify D to indicate the reason for the validity of the description. To distinguish internal arguments from external arguments, we justify I_i with

(SL (DE_i) ( )).

This makes all portions of arguments internal to the description depend on D. With the internal arguments marked in this way, we can separate them from other arguments when transmitting information from the internal nodes to the external nodes. We justify E_i with

(SUM I_i(D) ( )).

This justification subtracts all internal arguments from the explanation of E_i, and replaces them with the single node D.

For example, suppose the hypothetical voting program above computed the vote total for Somewhere, Illinois by summing the totals from the three precincts A, B, and C. The program isolates this level of the computation from the precinct computations by using an ADDER description to sum these subtotals.

N–1	ADDER DESCRIPTION AD	···	*Somewhere, IL*
N–2	EXTERNAL A OF AD = 500	···	*Precinct A*
N–3	EXTERNAL B OF AD = 200	···	*Precinct B*
N–4	EXTERNAL C OF AD = 700	···	*Precinct C*

Here the computations for the precinct totals justify the three precinct totals. The program then transmits these values to nodes representing the internal components of the adder description, and a local rule of the description computes the value of the sum component.

N–5	INTERNAL A OF AD = 500	(SL (N–1 N–2) ( ))
N–6	INTERNAL B OF AD = 200	(SL (N–1 N–3) ( ))
N–7	INTERNAL C OF AD = 700	(SL (N–1 N–4) ( ))
N–8	A+B OF AD = 700	(SL (N–5 N–6) ( )) *intermediate result*
N–9	INTERNAL SUM OF AD = 1400	(SL (N–7 N–8) ( ))

The program transmits this value for the sum to the node representing the external form of the result.

N–10	EXTERNAL SUM OF AC = 1400	(SUM N–9 (N–1) ( )) *here* ≡ (SL (N–1 N–2 N–3 N–4) ( ))

The SUM-justification for N–10 subtracts all dependence on any internal computations made by the adder, N–1. The resulting explanation for N–10 includes only N–1, N–2, N–3 and N–4. In cases involving more complex procedures than adders, with large numbers of internal nodes and computations of no interest to the external system, the use of this technique for structuring explanations into levels of detail might make the difference between an intelligible explanation and an unintelligible one.

6. Dialectical Arguments

Quine [41] has stressed that we can reject any of our beliefs at the expense of making suitable changes in our other beliefs. For example, we either can change our beliefs to accommodate new observations, or can reject the new observations as hallucinations or mistakes. Notoriously, philosophical arguments have argued almost every philosophical conclusion at the expense of other propositions. Philosophers conduct these arguments in a discipline called dialectial argumentation, in which one argues for a conclusion in two steps; first producing an argument for the conclusion, then producing arguments against the arguments for the opposing conclusion. In this discipline, each debater continually challenges those proposed arguments which he does not like by producing new arguments which either challenge one or more of the premises of the challenged arguments, or which challenge one or more steps of the challenged argument. We can view each debater as following this simplified procedure:

Step 1 (*Make an argument*). Put forward an argument A for a conclusion based on premises thought to be shared between debaters.

Step 2 (*Reply to challenges*). When some debater challenges either a premise or a step of A with an argument B, either (1) make a new argument for the conclusion of A, or (2) make an argument for the challenged premise or step of A challenging one of the premises or steps of B.

Step 3 (*Repeat*). Continue to reply to challenges, or make new arguments.

In this section we show how to organize a problem solving program's use of the TMS into the form of dialectical argumentation. Several important advantages and consequences motivate this. As the first consequence, we can reject any belief in a uniform fashion, simply by producing a new, as yet unchallenged, argument against some step or premise of the argument for the belief. We were powerless to do this with the basic TMS mechanisms in any way other than physically removing justifications from the belief system. This ability entails the second consequence, that we must explicitly provide ways to choose what to believe, to select which of the many possible revisions of our beliefs we will take when confronting new information. Quine has urged the fundamentally pragmatic nature of this question, and we must find mechanisms for stating and using pragmatic belief revision rules. As the third consequence of adopting this dialectial program organization, the belief system becomes additive. The system never discards arguments, but accumulates them and uses them whenever possible. This guides future debates by keeping them from repeating past debates. But the arguments alone comprise the belief system, since we derive the current set of beliefs from these arguments. Hence all changes to beliefs occur by adding new arguments to a monotonically growing store of arguments. Finally, as the fourth consequence, the inference system employed by the program becomes modular. We charge each component of the inference system with arguing for its conclusion and against opposing conclusions. On this view, we make each module be a debater rather than an inference rule.

We implement dialectial argumentation in the TMS by representing steps of arguments both by justifications and by beliefs. To allow us to argue against argument steps, we make these beliefs assumptions.

Suppose some module wants to justify node N with the justification (SL I O). Instead of doing this directly, the module creates a new node, J, representing the statement that I and O SL-justify N; in other words, that belief in each node of I and lack of belief in each node of O constitute a reason for believing in N. The module justifies N with the justification (SL $J+I$ O), where $J+I$ represents the list I augmented by J. The TMS will make N *in* by reason of this justification only if J is *in*. The nodule then creates another new node, $\neg J$, representing the statement that J represents a challenged justification. Finally, the module justifies J with the justification (SL ( ) ($\neg J$)). In this way, the module makes a new node to represent the justification as an explicit belief, and then assumes that the justification has not been challenged.

For example, suppose a module wishes to conclude that $X = 3$ from $X+Y = 4$ and $Y = 1$. In the dialectical use of the TMS, it proceeds as follows:

N–1	$X+Y = 4$	. . .
N–2	$Y = 1$	. . .
N–3	$X = 3$	(SL (N–4 N–1 N–2) ( ))
N–4	(N–1) AND (N–2) SL–JUSTIFY N–3	(SL ( ) (N–5))
N–5	N–4 IS CHALLENGED	*no justifications yet*

Since N–5 has no justifications, it is *out*, so N–4, and hence N–3, are *in*.

In this discipline, conflicts can be resolved either by challenging premises of arguments, or by challenging those justifications which represent arguments steps. Actually, premise justifications for nodes now become assumptions, for the explicit form of the premise justification is itself assumed. In either case, replies to arguments invalidate certain justifications by justifying the nodes representing the challenges. The proponent of the challenged argument can reply by challenging some justification in the challenging argument.

This way of using the TMS clearly makes blind dependency-directed backtracking useless, since the number of assumptions supporting a node becomes very large. Instead, we must use more refined procedures for identifying certain nodes as the causes of inconsistencies. I will return to this issue in Section 8.

7. Models of Others' Beliefs

Many problem solving tasks require us to reason about the beliefs of some agent. For example, according to the speech act theory of purposeful communication, I must reason about your beliefs and wants, and about your beliefs about my beliefs and wants [5, 49]. This requirement entails the ability to reason about embedded belief and want spaces, so called because these are sets of beliefs reported as compound or embedded statements of belief, for example, "I believe that you believe that it is raining." In fact, I must frequently reason about my own system of beliefs and wants. In planning, I must determine what I will believe and want after performing some actions, and this requires my determining how the actions affect my beliefs and wants. In explaining my actions, I must determine what I believed and wanted at some time in the past, before performing the intervening actions. And when choosing what to do, want or believe, I must reason about what I now am doing, wanting, or believing.

In making a problem solver which uses such models of belief systems, we face the problem of how to describe how additions to these models affect the beliefs contained in them, how belief revision proceeds within a model of a belief system. It would be extremely convenient if the same mechanism by which the program revises its own beliefs, namely the TMS, could be applied to revising these models as well. Fortuitously, the mechanism of representing justifications as explicit beliefs introduced in Section 6 lets us do just that.

To represent a belief system within our own, we use beliefs in our own system about the beliefs and justifications in the other system. We then mirror the other system's justifications of its beliefs by making corresponding justifications in our system's TMS of our beliefs about the other system's beliefs. For each node N in an agent U's belief system, we make two nodes, UB[N] and $\neg$UB[N], one representing that U believes in N, and the other representing that U doesn't believe in N. We justify $\neg$UB[N] with

(SL ( ) (UB[N])),

thus assuming that all nodes in U's system are *out* until given valid justifications. For each SL-justification J (= (SL I O)) for N in U's belief system, we make a node UB[J] representing that U's belief system contains J. We then justify UB[N] with the justification (SL L ( )), where L contains the node UB[J], the nodes UB[M] for each node M in I, and the nodes $\neg$UB[M] for each node M in O.

We might view this technique as embodying an observation of traditional modal logics of belief. Most of these logics include an axiom schema about the belief modality Bel of the form

$$\mathrm{Bel}(p \supset q) \supset (\mathrm{Bel}(p) \supset \mathrm{Bel}(q)).$$

When we mirror embedded justifications with TMS justifications, we are making an inference analogous to the one licensed by this axiom.

For example, suppose the program believes than an agent U believes A, that U does not believe B, and that U believes C because he believes A and does not believe B. If we looked into U's TMS we might see the following nodes and justifications.

A	· · ·	· · ·
B	· · ·	· · ·
C	· · ·	(SL (A) (B))

Our program represents this fragment of U's belief system as follows:

N–1	UB[A]	· · ·	*UB means "U believes"*
N–2	¬UB[B]	(SL ( ) (N–3))	
N–3	UB[B]		*no justification yet*
N–4	UB[(A) AND (B) SL–JUSTIFY C]	· · ·	
N–5	UB[C]	(SL (N–4 N–1 N–2) ( ))	

In this case, N–1, N–2, N–4 and N–5 are *in*, and N–3 is *out*. If the program revises its beliefs so that N–2 is *out*, say by the addition of a new justification in U's belief system,

N–5	UB[· · · SL–JUSTIFY B]	· · ·
N–2	UB[B]	(SL (N–5 · · ·) ( ))

then the TMS will make N–5 *out* as well. In this way, changes made in particular beliefs in the belief system lead automatically to other changes in beliefs which represent the implied changes occurring within the belief system.

Of course, we can repeat this technique at each level of embedded belief spaces. To use this technique we must require the inference rules which draw conclusions inside a belief space to assert the corresponding beliefs about justifications for those conclusions. One frequently assumes that others have the same set of inference rules as oneself, that they can draw the same set of inferences from the same set of hypotheses. This assumption amounts to that of assuming that everyone operates under the same basic "program" but has different data or initial beliefs. I am currently exploring a formalization of this assumption in an "introspective" problem solver which has a description of itself as a program, and which uses this self-description as the basis of its models of the behavior of others [16].

8. Assumptions and the Problem of Control

How a problem solver revises its beliefs influences how it acts. Problem solvers typically revise their beliefs when new information (such as the expected effect of an action just taken or an observation just made) contradicts previous beliefs. These inconsistencies may be met by rejecting the belief that the action occurred or that the observation occurred. This might be thought of as the program deciding it was hallucinating. Sometimes, however, we choose to reject the previous belief and say that the action made a change in the world, or that we had made some inappropriate assumption which was corrected by observation. Either of these ways of revising beliefs may be warranted in different circumstances. For example, if during planning we encounter a contradiction by thinking through a proposed sequence of actions, we might decide to reject one of the proposed actions and try another action. On the other hand, if while carrying out a sequence of actions we encounter a contradiction in our beliefs, we might decide that some assumption we had about the world was wrong, rather than believe that we never took the last action. As this example suggests, we might choose to revise our beliefs in several different ways. Since we decide what to do based on what we believe and what we want, our choice of what to believe affects what we choose to do.

How can we guide the problem solver in its choice of what to believe? It must make its choice by approximating the set of possible revisions by the set of assumptions it can change directly, for it cannot see beforehand all the consequences of a change without actually making that change and seeing what happens. We have studied two means by which the problem solver can decide what to believe, the technique of encoding control information into the set of justifications for beliefs, and the technique of using explicit choice rules. Both of these approaches amount to having the reasoner deliberate about what to do. In the first case, the reasoning is "canned." In the second, the reasoning is performed on demand.

We encode some control information into the set of justifications for beliefs by using patterns of non-monotonic justifications. We can think of a non-monotonic justification (SL ( ) (N–2 N–3)) for N–1 as suggesting the order in which these nodes should be believed, N–1 first, then N–2 or N–3 second. On this view, each non-monotonic justification contributes a fragment of control information which guides how the problem solver revises its beliefs. In Sections 8.1, 8.2 and 8.3, we illustrate how to encode several standard control structures in patterns of justifications, namely default assumptions, sequences of alternatives, and a way of choosing representatives of equivalence classes useful in controlling propagation of constraints (a deduction technique presented by [53]). These examples should suggest how other control structures such as decision trees or graphs might be encoded.

Even with these fragments of control information, many alternative revisions may appear possible to the problem solver. In such cases, we may wish to provide the problem solver with rules or advice about how to choose which revision to make. If we are clever (or lazy), we might structure the problem solver so that it uses the same language and mechanisms for these revision rules as for rules for making other choices, such as what action to perform next, how to carry out an action, or which goal to pursue next. In [11] my colleagues and I incorporated this suggestion into a general methodology which we call *explicit control of reasoning*, and implemented AMORD, a language of pattern-invoked procedures controlled by the TMS. I am currently studying a problem solver architecture, called a *reflexive interpreter*, in which the problem solver's structure and behavior are themselves domains for reasoning and action by the problem solver [16]. This sort of interpreter represents its own control state to itself explicitly among its beliefs as a *task network* similar to that used in McDermott's [34] NASL, in which problems or intentions are represented as *tasks*. The interpreter also represents to itself its own structure as a program by means of a set of *plans*, abstract fragments of task network. It represents the important control state of having to make a choice by creating a *choice task*, whose carrying out involves making a choice. The interpreter can then treat this choice task as a problem for solution like any other task. In this framework, we formulate rules for guiding belief revision as plans for carrying out choice tasks. We index these revision plans by aspects of the problem solver state, for example, by the historical state, by the control state, by the state of the problem solution, by the domain, by the action just executed, and by other circumstances. Each revision plan might be viewed as a specialization of the general dependency-directed backtracking procedure. Such refinements of the general backtracking procedure take the form of the beliefs (and thus the problem solver state) into account when deciding which assumptions should be rejected. I will report the details of my investigation in my forthcoming thesis.

8.1. Default assumptions

Problem solving programs frequently make specifications of default values for the quantities they manipulate, with the intention either of allowing specific reasons for using other values to override the current values, or of rejecting the default if it leads to an inconsistency. (See [45] for a lucid exposition of some applications.) The example in Section 1.2 includes such a default assumption for the day of the week of a meeting.

To pick the default value from only two alternatives, we justify the default node non-monotonically on the grounds that the alternative node is *out*. We generalize this binary case to choose a default from a larger set of alternatives. Take $S = \{A_1, \ldots, A_n\}$ to be the set of alternative nodes, and if desired, let G be a node which represents the reason for making an assumption to choose the default. To make A_i the default, justify it with

$$(\mathrm{SL}\,(G)\,(A_1 \cdots A_{i-1}\, A_{i+1} \cdots A_n)).$$

If no additional information about the value exists, none of the alternative nodes except A_i will have a valid justification, so A_i will be *in* and each of the other alternative nodes will be *out*. Adding a valid justification to some other alternative node causes that alternative to become *in*, and invalidates the support of A_i, so A_i goes *out*. When analyzing a contradiction derived from A_i, the dependency-directed backtracking mechanism recognizes A_i as an assumption because it depends on the other alternative nodes being *out*. The backtracker may then justify one of the other alternative nodes, say A_j, causing A_i to go *out*. This backtracker-produced justification for A_j will have the form

(SL ⟨various nodes⟩ ⟨remainder nodes⟩)

where ⟨remainder nodes⟩ is the set of A_k's remaining in S after A_i and A_j are taken away. In effect, the backtracker removes the default node from the set of alternatives, and makes a new default assumption from the remaining alternatives. As a concrete example, our scheduling program might default a meeting day as follows:

N–1	PREFER W. TO M. OR F.	· · ·
N–2	DAY(M) = MONDAY	
N–3	DAY(M) = WEDNESDAY	(SL (N–1) (N–2 N–4))
N–4	DAY(M) = FRIDAY	

The program assumes Wednesday to be the day of the meeting M, with Monday and Friday as alternatives. The TMS will make Wednesday the chosen day until the program gives a valid reason for taking Monday or Friday instead.

We use a slightly different set of justifications if the complete set of alternatives cannot be known in advance but must be discovered piecemeal. This ability to extend the set of alternatives is necessary, for example, when the default is a number, due to the large set of possible alternatives. Retaining the above notation, we represent the negation of $\mathrm{St}(A_i)$ with a new node, $\neg A_i$. We arrange for A_i to be believed if $\neg A_i$ is *out*, and set up justifications so that if A_j is distinct from A_i, A_j supports $\neg A_i$. We justify A_i with

$$(\mathrm{SL}\,(G)\,(\neg A_i)),$$

and justify $\neg A_i$ with a justification of the form

$$(\mathrm{SL}\,(A_j)\,(\;))$$

for each alternative A_j distinct from A_i. As before, A_i will be assumed if no reasons for using any other alternative exist. Furthermore, new alternatives can be added to the set S simply by giving $\neg A_i$ a new justification corresponding to the new alternative. As before, if the problem solving program justifies an unselected alternative, the TMS will make the default node *out*. Backtracking, however, has a new effect. If A_i supports a contradiction, the backtracker may justify $\neg A_i$ so as to make A_i become *out*. When this happens, the TMS has no way to select an alternative to take the place of the default assumption. The extensible structure requires an external mechanism to construct a new default assumption whenever the current default is ruled out. For example, a family planning program might make assumptions about the number of children in a family as follows:

N–1	PREFER 2 CHILDREN	· · ·
N–2	#-CHILDREN(F) = 2	(SL (N–1) (N–3))
N–3	#-CHILDREN(F) ≠ 2	(SL (N–4) ( ))
		(SL (N–5) ( ))
□		(SL (N–6) ( ))
		(SL (N–7) ( ))
N–4	#-CHILDREN(F) = 0	
N–5	#-CHILDREN(F) = 1	
N–6	#-CHILDREN(F) = 3	
N–7	#-CHILDREN(F) = 4	

With this system of justifications, the TMS would make N–2 *in*. If the planning program finds some compelling reason for having 5 children, it would have to create a new node to represent this fact, along with a new justification for N–3 in terms of this new node.

8.2. Sequences of alternatives

Linearly ordered sets of alternatives add still more control information to a default assumption structure, namely the order in which the alternatives should be tried. This extra heuristic information might be used, for example, to order selections of the day of the week for a meeting, of a planning strategy, or of the state of a transistor in a proposed circuit analysis.

We represent a sequence of alternatives by a controlled progression of default assumptions. Take $\{A_1, \ldots, A_n\}$ to be the heuristically-ordered sequence of alternative nodes, and let G be a node which represents the reason for this heuristic ordering. We justify each A_i with

$$(\mathrm{SL}\,(G\ \neg A_{i-1})\,(\neg A_i)).$$

A_1 will be selected initially, and as the problem solver rejects successive alternatives by justifying their negations, the TMS will believe the successive alternatives in turn. For example, our scheduling program might have:

N–1	SEQUENCE N–2 N–4 N–6	...
N–2	DAY(M) = WEDNESDAY	(SL (N–1) (N–3))
N–3	DAY(M) ≠ WEDNESDAY	
N–4	DAY(M) = THURSDAY	(SL (N–1 N–3) (N–5))
N–5	DAY(M) ≠ THURSDAY	
N–6	DAY(M) = TUESDAY	(SL (N–1 N–5) ( ))

This would guide the choice of day for the meeting M to Wednesday, Thursday and Tuesday, in that order.

Note that this way of sequencing through alternatives allows no direct way for the problem solving program to reconsider previously rejected alternatives. If, say, we wish to use special case rules to correct imprudent choices of culprits made by the backtracking system, we need a more complicated structure to represent linearly ordered alternatives. We create three new nodes for each alternative A_i: PA_i, which means that A_i is a possible alternative, NSA_i, which means that A_i is not the currently selected alternative, and ROA_i, which means that A_i is a ruled-out alternative. We suggest members for the set of alternatives by justifying each PA_i with the reason for including A_i in the set of alternatives. We leave ROA_i unjustified, and justify each A_i and NSA_i with

A_i: (SL (PA_i $NSA_1 \cdots NSA_{i-1}$) (ROA_i))
NSA_i: (SL ( ) (PA_i))
(SL (ROA_i) ( )).

Here the justification for A_i is valid if and only if A_i is an alternative, no better alternative is currently selected, and A_i is not ruled out. The two justifications for NSA_i mean that either A_i is not a valid alternative, or that A_i is ruled out. With this structure, different parts of the problem solver can independently rule in or rule out an alternative by justifying the appropriate A or ROA node. In addition, we can add new alternatives to the end of such a linear order by constructing justifications as specified above for the new nodes representing the new alternative.

8.3. Equivalence class representatives

Problem solvers organized to encourage modularity and additivity frequently contain several different methods or rules which compute values for the same quantity or descriptions for the same object. We call these multiple results *coincidences*, after [9, 59]. If the several methods compute several values, we can often derive valuable information by checking these competing values for consistency. With polynomials as values, for example, this consistency checking sometimes allows solving for the values of one or more variables. After checking the coincidence for consistency and new information, prudent programs normally use only one of the suggested values in further computation, and retain the other values for future reference. The various values form an *equivalence class* with respect to the propagation of the value in other computations, and one of the values in this class must be chosen as the representative for propagation. We could choose the representative with a default assumption, but this would lead to undesirable backtracking behavior. For instance, if the backtracking system finds the equivalence class representative involved in an inconsistency, then it should find some way of rejecting the representative as a proper value, rather than letting it stand and selecting a new representative. This means the backtracker should find the choice of representative invisible, and this requirement rules out using either the default assumption or sequence of alternatives representations.

We select equivalence class representatives by using conditional-proof justifications to hide the choice mechanism from the backtracking system. For each node R_i representing an equivalence class member, we create two new nodes: PR_i, which means that R_i is a possible representative, and SR_i, which means that R_i is the selected representative. Rather than the program deriving justifications for the R nodes directly, it should instead suggest these values as possible representatives by justifying the corresponding PR nodes instead. With this stipulation we justify each R_i and SR_i as follows:

SR_i: (SL (PR_i) ($SR_1 \cdots SR_{i-1}$))
R_i: (CP SR_i ( ) ($SR_1 \cdots SR_{i-1}$))

Here the justification for SR_i means that R_i has been suggested as a member of the equivalence class, and that no other member of the class has been selected as the representative. This justification constitutes a default assumption of R_i as the selected representative. However, the justification for R_i means that the reason for believing R_i will be the reason for both suggesting and selecting R_i (the argument for SR_i), minus the reason for selecting it (the default assumption), thus leaving only the reason for which R_i was suggested, namely the antecedents of PR_i. In this way the equivalence class selector picks alternatives as the representative in the order in which they were added to the set of alternatives, while hiding this selection from the backtracking system.

For example, suppose a commodity analysis program derives two values for the predicted number of tons of wheat grown this year and notices this coincidence.

N–1	SUGGEST WHEAT (1979) = $5X+3000$	(SL (R–57 · · ·) ( ))
N–2	SUGGEST WHEAT (1979) = $7Y$	(SL (R–60 · · ·) ( ))
N–3	$Y = (5X+3000)/7$	(SL (N–1 N–2) ( ))

These suggested values correspond to possible equivalence class representatives. To avoid using both values in further computations, the program chooses one.

N–4	N–1 SELECTED	(SL (N–1) ( ))
N–5	WHEAT (1979) = $5X+3000$	(CP N–4 ( ) ( ))
		here=(SL (N–1) ( ))
N–6	N–2 SELECTED	(SL (N–2) (N–4))
N–7	WHEAT (1979) = $7Y$	(CP N–6 ( ) (N–4))

Since N–1 is *in* and it is the first in the ordering imposed by the selection justifications, it is selected to be the value propagated, and the TMS makes N–4 and N–5 *in*. Suppose now that some contradiction occurs and has N–5 in its foundations, and that the dependency-directed backtracker denies some assumption in N–1's foundations. Consequently, the TMS makes N–1 (and N–3) *out*, and N–6 and N–7 *in*, with N–7's CP-justification equivalent in this case to (SL(N–2)( )). Thus the pattern of justifications leads to selecting the second suggested value. If the program then finds a third value,

N–8	SUGGEST WHEAT (1979) = $4X+100$	. . .
N–9	$Y = (4X+100)/7$	(SL (N–2 N–8) ( ))
N–10	N–8 SELECTED	(SL (N–8) (N–4 N–6))
N–11	WHEAT (1979) = $4X+100$	(CP N–10 ( ) (N–4 N–6))

it will derive any new information possible from the new value, then add the new value to the list of waiting alternative values for propagation. In this case, N–8 and N–9 are *in*, and N–10 and N–11 are *out*.

9. Experience and Extensions

We have experience with the TMS in a number of programs and applications. I implemented the first version of the TMS in September 1976, as an extension (in several ways) of the "fact garbage collector" of Stallman and Sussman's [53] ARS electronic circuit analysis program. After that, I took the program through many different versions. Howard Shrobe and James Stansfield also made improvements in the program. Truth maintenance techniques have been applied in several other circuit analysis and synthesis programs, including SYN [12] and QUAL [10], and in Steele and Sussman's [56] constraint language. We organized our rule-based problem solving system AMORD [11] around the TMS, and used AMORD in developing a large number of experimental programs, ranging from blocks world problem solvers to circuit analysis programs and compilers. McAllester [31] uses his own truth maintenance system in a program for symbolic algebra, electronic circuit analysis, and programming. In addition, Weiner [62] of UCLA used AMORD to implement an explanation system in studying the structure of natural explanations, and Shrobe [50] uses AMORD in a program-understanding system.

Several researchers have extended the basic belief-revision techniques of the TMS by embedding them in larger frameworks which incorporate time, certainty measures, and other problem solving concepts and processes. Friedman [19] and Stansfield [54] merge representations of continuous degrees of belief with truth maintenance techniques. London [29] and Thompson [60] add chronological contexts to a dependency-based framework. London also presents many detailed examples of the use of dependency networks in the modelling component of a problem solving program.

Improvements in the basic truth maintenance process have also been suggested. McAllester [30] describes a relative of the TMS based on a three-valued belief set, with multi-directional clauses as justifications. Thompson [60] generalizes the node-justification structure of the TMS to non-clausal arguments and justifications. Shrobe (in [50] and in personal communications) has suggested several ways in which the problem solver can profit by reasoning about the structure of arguments, particularly in revising its set of goals after solving some particular goal. These ideas suggest other improvements including (1) modification of the TMS to make use of multiple supporting-justifications whenever several well-founded arguments can be found for a node, (2) use of the TMS to signal the problem solver whenever the argument for some node changes, and (3) development of a language for describing and efficiently recognizing patterns in arguments for nodes, well-founded or otherwise. How to incorporate truth maintenance techniques into "virtual-copy" representational systems [17] also seems worth study.

The TMS continually checks CP-justifications for validity, in hopes of deriving new equivalent SL-justifications. This makes the implementation considerably more complex than one might imagine. I expect that a simpler facility would be more generally useful, namely the TMS without CP-justifications, but with the Find Independent Support procedure isolated as a separate, user invoked facility. Practical experience shows that in most cases, one only expects the CP-justification to be valid in the situation in which it is created, so it seems reasonable to make the user responsible for calling FIS directly rather than letting the TMS do it.

Finally, a cluster of problems center about incrementality. The TMS normally avoids examining the entire data base when revising beliefs, and instead examines only the repercussions of the changed nodes. However, apparently unsatisfiable circularities can occur which require examining nodes not included in these repercussions. In another sense of incrementality, some circumstances can force the TMS to examine large numbers of nodes, only to leave most of them in their original state after finding alternate non-circular arguments for the supposedly changed nodes. Latombe [27] has investigated ways of avoiding this, but these difficulties deserve further study. One particularly enticing possibility is that of adapting the ideas of Baker's [1] real-time list garbage-collection algorithms to the case of truth maintenance.

10. Discussion

The TMS solves part of the belief revision problem, and provides a mechanism for making non-monotonic assumptions. Artificial intelligence researchers recognized early on that AI systems must make assumptions, and many of their systems employed some mechanism for this purpose. Unfortunately, the related problem of belief revision received somewhat less study. Hayes [21] emphasized the importance of the belief revision problem, but with the exception of Colby [6], who employed a belief system with reasons for some beliefs, as well as measures of credibility and emotional importance for beliefs, most work on revising beliefs appears to have been restricted to the study of backtracking algorithms operating on rather simple systems of states and actions. The more general problem of revising beliefs based on records of inferences has only been examined in more recent work, including Cox's [7] graphical deduction system, Crocker's [8] verification system, de Kleer's [9] electronic circuit analysis program, Fikes' [18] deductive modelling system, Hayes' [22] travel planning system, Katz and Manna's [24] program modification system, Latombe's [26, 27] design program, London's [29] planning and modelling system, McDermott's [32, 33, 34] language understanding, data base, and design programs, Moriconi's [39] verification system, Nevins' [40] theorem prover, Shrobe's [50] program understanding system, the MDS/AIMDS/BELIEVER programs [47, 51, 52], and Sussman and Stallman's [53, 59] electronic circuit analysis programs. Berliner's [3] chess program employed "lemmas" for recording interesting facts about partial board analyses of conditional-proofs, but the program derives these lemmas through a perturbation technique rather than through analysis of arguments and justifications.

In addition, the philosophical literature includes many treatments of belief revision and related problems. Many writers study evaluative criteria for judging which belief revisions are best, based on the connections between beliefs. Quine and Ullian [43] survey this area. Other writers study the problems of explanations, laws, and counterfactual conditions. Rescher [44] builds on Goodman's [20] exposition of these problems to present a framework for belief revision motivated by Quine's [41, 42] "minimum mutilation" principle. Lewis [28] and Turner [61] propose means for filling in this framework. Scriven [48] relates these questions to the problem of historical explanation in a way quite reminiscent of our non-monotonic arguments for beliefs. Suppes [57] surveys work on learning and rational changes of belief. The view of reasoning proposed in Section 1.1 is connected with many topics in the theories of belief, action, and practical reasoning. Minsky [37] presents a theory of memory which includes a more general view of reasoning.

Kramosil [25] initiated the mathematical study of non-monotonic inference rules, but reached pessimistic conclusions. More recently, McDermott and I [35] attempt to formalize the logic underlying the TMS with what we call *non-monotonic logic*. We also survey the history of such reasoning techniques. Weyhrauch [63] presents a framework for meta-theoretic reasoning in which these reasoning techniques and others can be expressed. Hintikka [23] presents a form of possible-world semantics for modal logics of knowledge and belief. Moore [38] combines this semantics for knowledge with a modal logic of action, but ignores belief and belief revision.

One might hope to find clues about how to organize the TMS's analysis of potential arguments for beliefs by studying what types of arguments humans find easy or difficult to understand. Statman [55] indicates that humans have difficulty following arguments which have many back-references to distant statements. He attempts to formalize some notions of the complexity of proofs using measures based on the topology of the proof graph. Wiener [62] catalogues and analyzes a corpus of human explanations, and finds that most exhibit a fairly simple structure. De Kleer [10] studies causal explanations of the sort produced by engineers, and discovers that a few simple principles govern a large number of these explanations.

I have used the term "belief" freely in this paper, so much so that one might think the title "Belief Revision System" more appropriate, if no less ambitious, than "Truth Maintenance System." Belief, however, for many people carries with it a concept of grading, yet the TMS has no non-trivial grading of beliefs. (Section 9 mentioned some extensions which do.) Perhaps a more accurate label would be "opinion revision system," where I follow Dennett [13] in distinguishing between binary judgemental assertions (opinions) and graded underlying feelings (beliefs). As Dennett explains, this distinction permits description of those circumstances in which reasoned arguments force one to assert a conclusion, even though one does not believe the conclusion. Hesitation, self-deception, and other complex states of belief and opinion can be described in this way. I feel it particularly apt to characterize the TMS as revising opinions rather than beliefs. Choosing what to "believe" in the TMS involves making judgements, rather than continuously accreting strengths or confidences. A single new piece of information may lead to sizable changes in the set of opinions, where new beliefs typically change old ones only slightly.

I also find this distinction between binary judgements and graded approximations useful in distinguishing non-monotonic reasoning from imprecise reasoning, such as that modelled by Zadeh's [64] fuzzy logic. I view the non-monotonic capabilities of the TMS as capabilities for dealing with incomplete information, but here the incompleteness is "exact": it makes binary statements about (typically) precise statements. Any approximation in the logic enters only when one views the set of current beliefs as a whole. In the logics of imprecise reasoning, the incompleteness is "inexact": the statements themselves are vague, and the vagueness need not be a property of the entire system of beliefs. While both approaches appear to be concerned with related issues, they seem to be orthogonal in their current development, which suggests studies of their combination. (Cf. [19].)

One final note: the overhead required to record justifications for every program belief might seem excessive. Some of this burden might be eliminated by using the summarization techniques of Section 5 to replace certain arguments with smaller ones, or by adopting some (hopefully well-understood) discipline of retaining only essential records from which all discarded information can be easily recomputed. However, the pressing issue is not the expense cf keeping records of the sources of beliefs. Rather, we must consider the expense of *not* keeping these records. If we throw away information about derivations, we may be condemning ourselves to continually rederiving information in large searches caused by changing irrelevant assumptions. This original criticism of MICRO-PLANNER (in [58]) applies to the context mechanisms of CONNIVER and QA4 as well. If we discard the sources of beliefs, we may make impossible the correction of errors in large, evolving data bases. We will find such techniques not just desirable, but necessary, when we attempt to build truly complex programs and systems. Lest we follow the tradition of huge, incomprehensible systems which spawned Software Engineering, we must, in Gerald Sussman's term, make "responsible" programs which can explain their actions and conclusions to a user. (Cf. [46].)

ACKNOWLEDGEMENTS

This paper is based on a thesis submitted in partial fulfillment of the degree of Master of Science to the department of Electrical Engineering and Computer Science of the Massachusetts Institute of Technology on May 12, 1977. Sections 6 and 7 contain material not reported in that thesis. Although I have held the views expressed in Section 1.1 for several years, I found my prior attempts at explaining them unsatisfactory, so these views appear here for the first time as well. I thank Gerald Jay Sussman (thesis advisor), Johan de Kleer, Scott Fahlman, Philip London, David McAllester, Drew McDermott, Marvin Minsky, Howard Shrobe, Richard M. Stallman, Guy L. Steele, Jr., and Alan Thompson for ideas and comments. de Kleer, Steele, Marilyn Matz, Richard Fikes, Randall Davis, Shrobe, and the referees of the Journal *Artificial Intelligence* gave me valuable editorial advice. I thank the Fannie and John Hertz Foundation for supporting my research with a graduate fellowship.

REFERENCES

1. Baker, H. G. Jr., List processing in real time on a serial computer, *C. ACM*, **21** (4) (April 1978) 280–294.
2. Belnap, N. D., How a computer should think, in: Gilbert Ryle (Ed.), *Contfempoorary Aspects Philosophy* (Oriel, Stocksfield, 1976).
3. Berliner, H. J., Chess as problem solving: The development of a tactics analyzer, CMU Computer Science Department (1974).
4. Charniak, E., Riesbeck, C. and McDermott, D., *Artificial Intelligence Programming* (Lawrence Erlbaum, Hillsdale, New Jersey, 1979).
5. Cohen, P. R., On knowing what to say: Planning speech acts, Department of Computer Science, University of Toronto, TR-118 (1978).
6. Colby, K. M., Simulations of belief systems, in: R. C. Schank and K. M. Colby (Eds.) *Computer Models of Thought and Language* (W. H. Freeman, San Francisco, 1973) pp. 251–286.
7. Cox, P. T., Deduction plans: A graphical proof procedure for the first-order predicate calculus, Department of Computer Science, University of Waterloo, Research Report CS-77-28 (1977).
8. Crocker, S. D., State deltas: A formalism for representing segments of computation, University of Southern California, Information Sciences Institute, RR–77–61 (1977).
9. De Kleer, J., Local methods for localization of failures in electronic circuits, MIT AI Lab, Memo 394 (November 1976).
10. De Kleer, J., Causal and teleological reasoning in circuit recognition, Ph.D. Thesis, MIT Department of Electrical Engineering and Computer Science (1979).
11. De Kleer, J., Doyle, J., Steele, G. L. Jr., and Sussman, G. J., Explicit control of reasoning, *Proc. ACM Symp. on Artificial Intelligence and Programming Languages* (Rochester, New York, 1977), also MIT AI Lab, Memo 427 (1977).
12. De Kleer, J. and Sussman, G. J., Propagation of constraints applied to circuit synthesis, MIT AI Lab, Memo 485 (1978).
13. Dennett, D. C., How to change your mind, in: *Brainstorms* (Bradford, Montgomery, VT, 1978), pp. 300–309.
14. Doyle, J., The use of dependency relationships in the control of reasoning, MIT AI Lab, Working Paper 133 (1976).
15. Doyle, J., Truth maintenance systems for problem solving, MIT AI Lab, TR–419 (1978).
16. Doyle, J., Reflexive interpreters, MIT Department of Electrical Engineering and Computer Science, Ph.D. proposal (1978).
17. Fahlman, S. E., NETL: *A System for Representing and Using Real World Knowledge* (MIT Press, Cambridge, 1979).
18. Fikes, R. E., Deductive retrieval mechanisms for state description models, *Proc. Fourth International Joint Conference on Artificial Intelligence* (1975) pp. 99–106.
19. Friedman, L., Plausible inference: A multi-valued logic for problem solving, Jet Propulsion Laboratory, Pasadena, CA, Report 79–11 (1979).
20. Goodman, N., The problem of counterfactual conditionals, in: *Fact, Fiction, and Forecast* (Bobbs-Merrill, NY, 1973) pp. 3–27.
21. Hayes, P. J., The frame problem and related problems in artificial intelligence, in: A. Elithorn and D. Jones (Eds.), *Artificial and Human Thinking* (Josey-Bass, San Francisco, 1973).
22. Hayes, P. J., A representation for robot plans, *Proc. Fourth IJCAI* (1975), pp. 181–188.
23. Hintikka, J., *Knowledge and Belief* (Cornell University Press, Ithica, 1962).
24. Katz, S. and Manna, Z., Logical analysis of programs, C. *ACM* 19 (4) (1976) 188–206.
25. Kramosil, I., A note on deduction rules with negative premises, *Proc. Fourth IJCAI* (1975) 53–56.
26. Latombe, J.-C., Une application de l'intelligence artificielle a la conception assistée par ordinateur (TROPIC), Université Scientifique et Médicale de Grenôble, Thesis D.Sc. Mathematiques (1977).
27. Latombe, J.-C., Failure processing in a system for designing complex assemblies, *Proc. Sixth IJCAI* (1979).
28. Lewis, D., *Counterfactuals* (Basil Blackwell, London, 1973).
29. London, P. E., Dependency networks as a representation for modelling in general problem solvers, Department of Computer Science University of Maryland, TR–698 (1978).

30. McAllester, D. A., A three-valued truth maintenance system, MIT AI Lab., Memo 473 (1978).
31. McAllester, D. A., The use of equality in deduction and knowledge representation, MIT Department of Electrical Engineering and Computer Science, M.S. Thesis (1979).
32. McDermott, D., Assimilation of new information by a natural language understanding system, MIT AI Lab., AI–TR–291 (1974).
33. McDermott, D., Very large PLANNER-type data bases, MIT AI Lab. AI Memo 339 (1975).
34. McDermott, D., Planning and acting, *Cognitive Science* 2 (1978) 71–109.
35. McDermott, D. and Doyle, J., Non-monotonic logic I, MIT AI Lab., Memo 486 (1978).
36. Minsky, M., A framework for representing knowledge, MIT AI Lab., Memo 306 (1974).
37. Minsky, M., *K*-lines: A theory of memory, MIT AI Lab., Memo 516 (1979).
38. Moore, R. C., Reasoning about knowledge and action, Ph.D. Thesis MIT, Department of Electrical Engineering and Computer Science (1979).
39. Moriconi, M., A system for incrementally designing and verifying programs, University of Southern California, Information Sciences Institute, RR–77–65 (1977).
40. Nevins, A. J., A human-oriented logic for automatic theorem proving, *J. ACM* **21** (4) (October 1974) 606–621.
41. Quine, W. V., Two dogmas of empiricism, in: *From a Logical Point of View* (Harvard University Press, Cambridge, 1953).
42. Quine, W. V., *Philosophy of Logic* (Prentice-Hall, Englewood Cliffs, 1970).
43. Quine, W. V. and Ullian, J. S., *The Web of Belief* (Random House, NY, 1978).
44. Rescher, N., *Hypothetical Reasoning* (North-Holland, Amsterdam, 1964).
45. Reiter, R., On reasoning by default, *Proc. Second Symp. on Theoretical Issues in Natural Language Processing* (Urbana, IL, 1978).
46. Rich, C., Shrobe, H. E., and Waters, R. C., Computer aided evolutionary design for software engineering, MIT AI Lab., Memo 506 (1979).
47. Schmidt, C. F. and Sridharan, N. S., Plan recognition using a hypothesize and revise paradigm: An example, *Proc. Fifth IJCAI* (1977) 480–486.
48. Scriven, M., Truisms as the grounds for historical explanations, in: P. Gardiner (Ed.) *Theories of History* (Free Press, New York, 1959).
49. Searle, J. R., *Speech Acts* (Cambridge University Press, 1969).
50. Shrobe, H. E., Dependency directed reasoning for complex program understanding, MIT AI Lab., TR–503 (1979).
51. Sridharan, N. S. and Hawrusik, F., Representation of actions that have side-effects, *Proc. Fifth IJCAI* (1977) 265–266.
52. Srinivasan, C. V., The architecture of coherent information system: A general problem solving system, *IEEE Trans. Computers* C–25 (4) (April 1976) 390–402.
53. Stallman, R. M. and Sussman, G. J., Forward reasoning and dependency-directed backtracking in a system for computer-aided circuit analysis, *Artificial Intelligence* **9** (2) (October 1977) 135–196.
54. Stansfield, J. L., Integrating truth maintenance systems with propagation of strength of belief as a means of addressing the fusion problem, MIT AI Lab., draft proposal (1978).
55. Statman, R., Structural complexity of proofs, Stanford University Department of Mathematics, Ph.D. Thesis (1974).
56. Steele, G. L. Jr. and Sussman, G. J., Constraints, MIT AI Lab., Memo 502 (1978).
57. Suppes, P., A survey of contemporary learning theories, in: R. E. Butts and J. Hintikka (Eds.), *Foundational Problems in the Special Sciences* (D. Reidel, Dordrecht, 1977).
58. Sussman, G. J. and McDermott, D., From PLANNER to CONNIVER—A genetic approach, *Proc. AFIPS FJCC* (1972) 1171–1179.
59. Sussman, G. J. and Stallman, R. M., Heuristic techniques in computer-aided circuit analysis, *IEEE Trans. Circuits and Systems* CAS–22 (11) (November 1975) 857–865.
60. Thompson, A., Network truth maintenance for deduction and modelling. *Proc. Sixth IJCAI* (1979).
61. Turner, R., Counterfactuals without possible worlds, University of Essex (1978).
62. Weiner, J., The structure of natural explanations: Theory and applications, Ph.D. Thesis, University of California, Los Angeles (1979).
63. Weyhrauch, R. W., Prolegomena to a theory of formal reasoning, Stanford AI Lab., AIM–315 (1978).
64. Zadeh, L., Fuzzy logic and approximate reasoning, *Synthese* **30** (1975) 407–428.

An Assumption-based TMS

Johan de Kleer

Intelligent Systems Laboratory, XEROX Palo Alto Research Center, 3333 Coyote Hill Road, Palo Alto, CA 94304, U.S.A.

Recommended by Daniel G. Bobrow

ABSTRACT

This paper presents a new view of problem solving motivated by a new kind of truth maintenance system. Unlike previous truth maintenance systems which were based on manipulating justifications, this truth maintenance system is, in addition, based on manipulating assumption sets. As a consequence it is possible to work effectively and efficiently with inconsistent information, context switching is free, and most backtracking (and all retraction) is avoided. These capabilities motivate a different kind of problem-solving architecture in which multiple potential solutions are explored simultaneously. This architecture is particularly well-suited for tasks where a reasonable fraction of the potential solutions must be explored.

1. Introduction

Most problem solvers search. If it were otherwise, a direct algorithm would solve the task. Problem solvers are constantly confronted with the necessity to select among equally plausible alternatives. These may concern the selection of which goal to try to achieve next, which plausible inference to draw from incomplete data, which hypothetical world to explore next, which action to perform, etc. Ultimately most, and often all, of these alternatives will be demonstrated to be incorrect. However, at the point the problem solver first encounters them, the alternatives appear equally likely. In this view, the problem solver is searching a space where each dimension is defined by a set of alternatives it has encountered. This view raises two questions to which the body of this paper is an answer: "How can this space be searched efficiently, or how can maximum information be transferred from one point in the space to another?" and "How, conceptually, should the problem solver be organized?"

One method for exploring the space, generate-and-test, simply enumerates every point in the search space and tests to see whether it satisfies the goal. This method, although extremely inefficient, is guaranteed to find a solution if there is one (for infinite spaces the enumeration must be appropriately ordered for this to be true). If each point of the search space is dissimilar this is the best that can be achieved. However, for most tasks there is a great deal of similarity among the points of the search space. As a consequence efficiency can be gained by carrying results obtained in one region of the search space into other regions. This is not an easy task. Unless the problem solver is carefully designed, the increased efficiency is achieved at the cost of coherency and exhaustivity.

Often the efficiency is gained by incorporating special case routines which detect similarities for the particular task domain at hand. The resulting problem solver is incoherent as the presence of the special case routines confuse content rules referring to the search space with control rules looking for similarities. Even more devastating, the complexities of the resulting system make it impossible to guarantee that a solution will be found in all the cases where one exists (i.e., exhaustivity is lost).

These concerns helped prompt the development of truth maintenance systems [12] (also called belief revision or reason maintenance systems). These systems forced a clean division within the problem solver between a component solely concerned with the rules of the domain and a component solely concerned with recording the current state of the search (i.e., the TMS). These TMSs allow designers to increase the efficiency of problem solvers without giving up coherency or exhaustivity. This paper presents a new *assumption-based* TMS (ATMS) which, for many tasks, is more efficient than previous TMSs and has a more coherent interface between the TMS and the problem solver without giving up exhaustivity. In addition, the assumption-based TMS avoids the usual restriction that only one point of the search space can be examined at a time.

This introduction concludes with a discussion of the basic intuitions underlying the ATMS. The following section analyzes search and the role a conventional TMS can play. In particular, chronological backtracking is contrasted with dependency-directed backtracking. Good as they are, all conventional TMSs suffer, to some extent, from shortcomings which, for many problem-solving tasks, are avoidable. The ATMS, which overcomes these shortcomings, is then presented in detail. The paper concludes with an overall discussion of the ATMS algorithms plus implementation details which significantly affect efficiency.

De Kleer shows in [7] how the basic ATMS framework supports a variety of styles of default reasoning. It also extends the basic ATMS to correctly deal with arbitrary propositional expressions. In [8], de Kleer presents a protocol for problem-solver-TMS interaction which assures that the advantages of the TMS are not accidentally lost. It includes an extensive comparison of the ATMS with other TMSs.

1.1. Basic results developed in this paper

Consider a conventional, *justification-based*, TMS such as presented in [12]. The basic architectural presupposition is that the overall reasoning system consists of two components: A problem solver which draws inferences and a TMS which records these inferences (called justifications). The TMS serves three roles in this overall system. First, it functions as a cache for all the inferences ever made. Thus inferences, once made, need not be repeated, and contradictions, once discovered, are avoided in the future. Second, the TMS allows the problem solver to make nonmonotonic inferences (e.g., "Unless there is evidence to the contrary infer A"). The presence of nonmonotonic justifications requires that the TMS use a constraint satisfaction procedure (called truth maintenance) to determine what data is to be believed. Third, the TMS ensures that the database is contradiction-free. Contradictions are removed by identifying absent justification(s) whose addition to the database would remove the contradiction. The added justifications are attached to the antecedents of the nonmonotonic justifications. The procedure of identifying and adding justifications to remove contradictions is called dependency-directed backtracking. The ATMS extends the cache idea, simplifies truth maintenance and avoids most dependency-directed backtracking. The ATMS can be viewed as an intelligent cache, or a very primitive learning scheme.

In a justification-based TMS a status of *in* (believed) or *out* (not believed)[1] is associated with every problem-solver datum. The entire set of in data define the current context. Therefore, the contexts under which a particular datum is believed are implicit. This requires that the database always be kept consistent, makes it impossible to refer to problem-solving contexts explicitly and requires truth maintenance and dependency-directed backtracking to move to a different point in the search space.

On the other hand, in an ATMS each datum is labeled with the sets of assumptions (representing the contexts) under which it holds. These assumption sets are computed by the ATMS from the problem-solver-supplied justifications. The idea is that the assumptions are the primitive data from which all other data are derived. These assumption sets can be manipulated far more conveniently than the datum sets they represent. There is no necessity that the overall database be consistent; it is easy to refer to contexts and moving to a different point in the search space requires very little work.

The actions of the ATMS are best understood in terms of a spatial metaphor. The assumptions are the dimensions of the search space. A solution corresponds to a point in the space and a context, characterized by a set of assumptions, depending on its generality, defines a point, line, plane, volume, etc., in the space. When a derivation is made, the ATMS records it in the most general way so that it covers as large a region of the space as possible. Conversely when a contradiction is recorded the ATMS finds its most general form in order to rule out as much of the search space as possible. Much of the work of the ATMS is determining the most general and parsimonious ways to record data and contradictions. All this is to facilitate what must happen when the problem solver shifts contexts. The problem is: how much of what was believed in previous contexts can be believed in the new one. This is yet another instance of the frame problem. The new context includes all the derivations of the preceding contexts which depend solely on the assumptions of the current context. Determining the next context and its contents is expensive in a justification-based TMS. Context membership is a simple subset test in the ATMS.

We can carry over many of the data to the new context, but where should the problem solver start working? This is not a simple task because the next context is only partially filled out and we want to start the problem solver precisely at this boundary. Certainly if there are pending problem-solving inferences which remain applicable in the new context these should be done. However, this is still not sufficient because there may have been rules which were attempted and failed or only partially attempted in old contexts. In the current context these rules may now succeed or run further. If we ignored these rules, then the problem solver would miss solutions. If we were to rerun these rules, then we would make redundant inferences. It is difficult to identify rules that failed in this way, so most problem solvers using TMSs usually take the conservative approach and rerun rules.

This problem is not intrinsic to the TMS but rather to the boundary between the TMS and the problem solver. De Kleer, in [8], outlines an interface protocol which solves the preceding problem. The difficulties arise when the problem solver is permitted to make a control decision based on the statuses, assumptions and justifications of nodes *without informing the TMS*. In this new interface the problem solver may only refer to the *content* of the datum, and all control decisions must be communicated explicitly to the TMS. It is important to note that this protocol is not intended to restrict the capabilities of the problem solver, but rather to move the boundary between the problem solver and the TMS to a more natural place in which each need only be concerned with issues relevant to it. The result is a slightly more complex TMS and a far simpler problem solver. Nevertheless, this protocol could be applied to any TMS—it does not intrinsically depend on an assumption-based TMS.

This protocol views problem solving as a continuous process of compiling rules. The problem solver compiles the rules and the TMS runs them to determine the solutions. A rule examined by the problem solver, i.e. compiled, need *never* be examined again on the same data because it is already compiled within the TMS as a justification.

[1] It is important to distinguish lack of belief in a datum from belief in the negation of a datum.

The ATMS and its interface protocol share a great deal of intellectual territory with RUP [14–16]. Our views of what an assumption is, what a solution is, and what a rule language should be like are very similar. However, RUP is oriented to problem solving using a single consistent context which is constantly changed and updated as problem solving progresses. The ATMS, on the other hand, is oriented towards problem solving in multiple contexts simultaneously. This is efficiently achieved by labeling each datum with the assumptions upon which it ultimately depends. This idea and its ramifications radically alters the conception and technology of problem solving.

1.2. Reasoning with inconsistency

Conventional TMSs insist on consistency: the subset of the database currently believed must be consistent. There are two basic reasons for this. The first, originating from procedurally encoding knowledge, insists that the problem solver has a single controlled focus. The second, originating from classical logic, insists that the presence of inconsistency renders all deductions meaningless. Both of these reasons can be defeated, thereby retracting the insistence on consistency.

A consistent database ensures that the problem solver is working on only one part of the search space at a time. Consistency is a poor method for achieving control. The task of selecting the part of the search space to examine is the problem solver's, the TMS should only record the state of the search so far.

In classical logic, the presence of an inconsistency allows one to prove (and disprove) all assertions. However, few problem solvers using a TMS would deduce all things if a contradiction were allowed to persist. Assertions derived from data unaffected by the contradiction remain useful. Only assertions directly affected by the contradiction should be retracted. The fundamental difficulty is that it is costly to determine which data are affected. Thus the insistence on a single consistent state. In an assumption-based TMS, one can tell directly whether an assertion is affected or not, so demanding consistency is unnecessary.

This is best illustrated by an example. Suppose we had the theory consisting of:

$$a, \qquad c,$$
$$a \rightarrow b, \qquad c \rightarrow d,$$
$$a \wedge c \rightarrow e, \qquad b \wedge d \rightarrow \bot .$$

$\bot$, $\rightarrow$, and $\wedge$ designate falsity, material implication, and conjunction. This theory is inconsistent as it allows the derivation of $\bot$. As there is no way to remove the contradiction, in a sense, everything is affected by the contradiction. Suppose the example were reformulated:

$$:MA/A, \qquad :MC/C,$$
$$A \rightarrow b, \qquad C \rightarrow d, \qquad A \wedge C \rightarrow e,$$

where $:M$ is Reiter's [18] default operator. $:MA/A$ indicates A (by convention capital letters represent defaults) is believed unless there is evidence to the contrary. This default theory has exactly one *extension* containing the atoms:

$$\{A,b,C,d,e\} .$$

The addition of the final axiom has a very different effect than in the preceding formulation.

$$b \wedge d \rightarrow \bot .$$

This introduces a contradiction, but this contradiction only directly affects e, not anything else. Both defaults cannot hold simultaneously. The theory now has two extensions containing the atoms:

$$\{A,b\}, \qquad \{C,d\}.$$

Intuitively, the addition of the final axiom forced the extension to split into two.

The ATMS operates as suggested by this example. Each datum is labeled with the consistent sets of defaults (represented by ATMS assumptions) actually used to derive it:

$$\langle b,\{\{A\}\},\rangle , \qquad \langle d,\{\{C\}\},\rangle , \qquad \langle e,\{\ \},\rangle .$$

Before adding the final axiom, e was represented:

$$\langle e,\{\{A,C\}\},\rangle .$$

A contradiction merely indicates that a specific set of assumptions is inconsistent, and that data depending on them are affected. In this sense the ATMS is similar to systems of Martins [13] and Williams [22].

1.3. The history of the ATMS idea

The ATMS was born out of frustration. Qualitative reasoning and constraint languages, the primary topics of my research, both involve choosing among alternatives. Various packages for dealing with alternatives have been proposed, primarily derived from [12]. These systems have proven to be inadequate for even simple qualitative reasoning tasks. The reasons for this are twofold. First, they are intrinsically incapable of working with multiple contradictory assumptions at once—something one needs to do all the time in qualitative reasoning. Second, they are inefficient.

LOCAL [3] is a program for troubleshooting electronic circuits which was incorporated in SOPHIE III [1]. It uses propagation of constraints to make predictions about device behavior from component models and circuit measurements. As the circuit is faulted, some component is not operating as intended. Thus, at some point, as the correct component model does not describe the actual faulty component, the predictions will become inconsistent. The assumptions are that individual components are functioning correctly. A contradiction implies that some assumption is violated, hence the fault is localized to a particular component set. The best measurement to make next is the one that provides maximal information about the validity of the yet unverified assumptions, This program requires that the assumptions of an inference be explicitly available and that multiple contradictory propagations be simultaneously present in the database. Hence, for this task the assumption-based approach is better.

QUAL [4, 6] and ENVISION [9] produce causal accounts for device behavior. QUAL can determine the function of a circuit solely from its schematic. Qualitative analysis is inherently ambiguous, and thus multiple solutions are produced. However, for any particular situation a device has only one function. QUAL selects the correct one by explicitly comparing different solutions—something that is only possible using assumption-based schemes.

By clarifying the ATMS ideas as reported in this paper, it is now possible to reexamine this earlier research. For example, [11] presents a new trouble-shooter based on the ATMS which handles multiple faults.

2. Search

This section discusses the various approaches for controlling search leading to the idea of a conventional TMS. Many of these examples are artificial and pathological. I have tried to reduce real problem-solving issues to the simplest possible examples so that the difficulties can be seen in their clearest form. De Kleer [5] presents these same issues in the abstract.

2.1. A simple constraint language

In order to explicate the ideas I define a simple constraint language to be used as a source of convenient examples. Each variable may have one of a fixed number of values, e.g.,

$$y \in \{-1,0,1\} .$$

Constraints utilize variables (single lower-case letters), integers, =, ≠, +, −, × (usually expressed as juxtaposition), and ! operators, e.g.,

$$x + y = z .$$

Inclusive disjunction is indicated by ∨, e.g.,

$$(x + y = z) \vee (z = 3) .$$

A very useful specialization of inclusive disjunction adds the stipulation that no two of the disjuncts hold simultaneously. I term this *oneof* disjunction as it is equivalent to specifying a disjunction in which exactly one of the disjuncts hold. In the binary case, oneof disjunction is equivalent to conventional exclusive disjunction. Oneof disjunction is notated by ⊕, e.g.,

$$(x + y = z) \oplus (z = 3) .$$

Note that,

$$x \in \{-1,0,1\} ,$$

is thus equivalent to,

$$(x = -1) \oplus (x = 0) \oplus (x = 1) .$$

The functions $e_i(x)$ require expensive computation: $e_i(x) = (x + 100000)!$. The goal of the problem solving is to discover all assignments of values to variables that satisfy the constraints. Values are always rational numbers, and usually integers.

2.2. Approaches to efficient search

Consider the following (admittedly pathological problem):

(1) $x \in \{0,1\}$, (2) $a = e_1(x)$,

(3) $y \in \{0,1\}$, (4) $b = e_2(y)$,

(5) $z \in \{0,1\}$, (6) $c = e_3(z)$,

(7) $b \neq c$, (8) $a \neq b$.

The simplest and most often used search strategy is exponential: Enumerate all the possibilities and try each one until a solution is found (or all solutions are found). In the example, there are 3 binary selections giving $2^3 = 8$ tentative solutions to test ('*' indicates a valid solution and '•' indicates a contradiction):

$x = 0, \quad y = 0, \quad z = 0, \ldots \bullet$

$x = 0, \quad y = 0, \quad z = 1, \ldots \bullet$

$x = 0, \quad y = 1, \quad z = 0, \ldots *$

$x = 0, \quad y = 1, \quad z = 1, \ldots \bullet$

$x = 1, \quad y = 0, \quad z = 0, \ldots \bullet$

$x = 1, \quad y = 0, \quad z = 1, \ldots *$

$x = 1, \quad y = 1, \quad z = 0, \ldots \bullet$

$x = 1, \quad y = 1, \quad z = 1, \ldots \bullet$

As each solution requires 3 expensive computations, 24 expensive computations are required total.

Chronological backtracking, which only requires the additional machinery of a stack of variable bindings, improves efficiency. This depth-first problem solver processes the expressions in the order presented. If the expression is a selection, then try the first one, otherwise evaluate the equation. If the expression is inconsistent, back up to the most recent selection with a remaining alternative and resume processing expressions from that point. In this example, the search space of assumptions is:

(1) $x = 0$

(2) $x = 0, \quad y = 0$

(3) $x = 0, \quad y = 0, \quad z = 0 \bullet$

(4) $x = 0, \quad y = 0, \quad z = 1 \bullet$

(5) $x = 0, \quad y = 1$

(6) $x = 0, \quad y = 1, \quad z = 0 *$

(7) $x = 0, \quad y = 1, \quad z = 1 \bullet$

(8) $x = 1$

(9) $x = 1, \quad y = 0$

(10) $x = 1, \quad y = 0, \quad z = 0 \bullet$

(11) $x = 1, \quad y = 0, \quad z = 1 *$

(12) $x = 1, \quad y = 1$

(13) $x = 1, \quad y = 1, \quad z = 0 \bullet$

(14) $x = 1, \quad y = 1, \quad z = 1 \bullet$

The extra machinery (a stack) for controlling the search is well worth it. Only 14 expensive computations are required, while the brute-force technique requires 24. One early application of chronological backtracking was QA4 [19]. It is the central control mechanism of PROLOG [2].

Examining the actions of the problem solver we observe that eight of the expensive computations are easily avoided[2]:

Futile backtracking. Steps (4) and (14) are futile. The selection $z \in \{0,1\}$ has no effect on the contradiction in steps (3) or (13), so steps (4) and (14) could have been safely ignored. When a contradiction is discovered the search should backtrack to an assumption which contributed to the contradiction, not to the most recent assumption made.

Rediscovering contradictions. Steps (10) and (14) are futile. When step (3) contradicted, it could have been determined that the contradiction only depended on $y = 0$ and $z = 0$, and that x's value was irrelevant. Thus step (10), which has the same values for y and z should never have been attempted. By a similar argument, step (14) is shown to be futile.

Rediscovering inferences. The factorial computations of steps (6), (7), and (9)–(14) are unnecessary. For example, step (6) repeats the factorial computation evoked by $z = 1$ of step (4). Backtracking erased the earlier factorial, but if the previous results could somehow be cached each factorial would only need to be computed once.

Incorrect ordering. Steps (3), (4), (13), and (14) are futile. If the test $a \neq b$ were moved just after the computation of b, 4 expensive computations would be eliminated.

These four problems are not independent. For example, carefully ordering the equations eliminates step (3), but step (3) computed a value for c which could have been used to eliminate step (6). In this example, careful ordering avoids futile backtracking, but this is not true in general.

TMSs, by exploiting dependencies, completely solve the first three defects and partially resolve the ordering problems. In the preceding example, solving the first three defects leaves only one futile step, (3), due to incorrect ordering. The scheduling strategy proposed in [8] for the problem-solver-TMS eliminates step (3) as well.

A solution to the defects is enabled by maintaining records of the dependence of each inference on earlier ones. When a contradiction is encountered these dependency records are consulted to determine which selection to backtrack to. Consider step (3). The dependency records indicate that $x = 0$ and $y = 0$ contribute to the contradiction, but $z = 0$ does not. Then the

[2] Mathematical analysis of the equations would reduce this set even further. Each e_i is the same function, so the number of expensive computations could be reduced to two. Furthermore, $e_i(x)$ is a one-to-one function, thus the solutions can be determined for x, y, z without performing a single expensive computation.

problem solver can backtrack to the most recent selection which actually contributed the contradiction. This technique is called dependency-directed backtracking [20].

The assumption set (e.g., $\{x = 0, y = 0\}$) which caused the contradiction is recorded so that the set can be avoided in the future. These are called the ***nogood*** sets [21] as they represent assumptions which are mutually contradictory.

Dependency records are bidirectional, linking antecedents to consequents as well as consequents to antecedents, thus the problem of rediscovering inferences is also avoided. Thus, if $x = 1$ is believed, the previously derived a = 'A big number' is as well. Whenever some assumption is included in the current set, the dependency records are consulted to reinstate the previously derived consequents of that assumption. This can be effected quite directly within the database. Entries are marked as temporarily unavailable (i.e., out) if they are not derivable from the set of assumptions currently being explored. In addition, each new assumption set is checked to see whether it contains some known contradiction (i.e., has a subset in the nogood database).

These techniques are the basis of all the TMSs. In the more general TMS strategies it is not necessary to specify the overall ordering of the search space (so far we have been presuming some simple-minded enumeration algorithm). They, in effect, choose their own enumeration but this ordering can be controlled somewhat by specifying which parts of the search space to explore first.

It is important to note that all these strategies are ultimately equivalent. The most sophisticated TMS will find as many consistent solutions as pure enumeration. The goal is to enhance efficiency without sacrificing exhaustivity.

3. Limitations of Current TMSs

Truth maintenance systems are the best general-purpose mechanisms for dealing with assumptions. However, when designing a TMS mechanism one must be careful to avoid certain pitfalls. All previous TMS mechanisms which are known to the author suffer from one or more of the limitations listed in Section 3.2. However, the ATMS presented in this paper provides a simultaneous solution to all of these problems. De Kleer, in [8], analyzes the systems of Doyle [12], Martins [13], McAllester [15], McDermott [17], and Williams [22] and points out how these TMSs have addressed or failed to address these problems. He also discusses in [8] some of the costs associated with using the ATMS. The ATMS is not a panacea and is not suited to all tasks. Conventional TMSs are oriented to finding one solution, and extra cost is incurred to control the TMS to find many solutions. The ATMS is oriented to finding all solutions, and extra cost is incurred to control the ATMS to find fewer solutions.

3.1. Doyle's TMS

This paper adopts much of Doyle's nomenclature, so this section presents a thumbnail (and somewhat simplistic) sketch of his TMS.

The TMS associates a special data structure, called a node, with each problem-solver datum (which includes database entries, inference rules, and procedures). Although the node is a complex data structure from the TMS' point of view, as far as the problem solver using the TMS is concerned, it is just a convenient way of referring to the belief in a datum. Justifications represent inference steps from combinations of nodes to another node. The simplest kind of justification, an SL-justification, consists of an inlist and an outlist. A node is believed, or in, if it has a valid justification. A justification is valid, if each of the nodes of its inlist are in and each of the nodes of its outlist are out. The problem solver can add nodes, justifications and mark nodes as contradictory at any time.

The TMS provides two services: truth maintenance and dependency-directed backtracking. Truth maintenance finds an assignment of belief statuses (i.e., in or out) for every node such that every justification is satisfied. However, each node must have well-founded support, so circular supports which may satisfy the justifications locally are outlawed. Although a node may have many justifications, only a few may hold, and one of these is chosen as the current supporting justification. A contradiction is encountered when a node, marked as contradictory, is assigned belief. Dependency-directed backtracking searches for the assumptions contributing to the contradiction. An assumption is a node with a current supporting justification with a nonempty outlist. The contradiction is removed by picking one assumption, the culprit, and adding a justification for one of the nodes of its outlist by a conjunction of the culprit's inlist and the remaining assumptions (see [8] for more details).

3.2. TMS limitations

The single-state problem. Given a set of assumptions which admits multiple solutions, the TMS algorithms only allow one solution to be considered at a time. This makes it extremely difficult to compare two equally plausible solutions. For example, $\{x = 0, y = 1, z = 0\}$ and $\{x = 1, y = 0, z = 1\}$ are both solutions to the preceding problem. It is impossible to examine both of these solutions together. However, this is often exactly what one wants to do in problem solving—differential diagnosis to determine the best solution.

Overzealous contradiction avoidance. Suppose A and B are contradictory. The TMS will guarantee that either A or B will be worked on, but not both. This is not necessarily the best problem-solving tactic. All a contradiction between A and B indicates is that inferences dependent on both A and B be avoided. But it is still important to draw inferences from A and B independently.

Switching states is difficult. Suppose that the problem solver decides to temporarily change an assumption (i.e., not in response to a contradiction). There is no efficient mechanism to facilitate this. The only direct way to change assumptions is to introduce a contradiction, but once added it cannot be removed so the knowledge state of the problem solver is irreconcilably altered. Suppose a change out of the current state was somehow achieved; there is no way to specify the target state. All a TMS can guarantee is that the database state is contradiction-free. So, in particular, there is no way to go back to a previous state. The reason for these oddities is that a TMS has no useful notion of global state. One inelegant mechanism that is sometimes utilized to manipulate states is to take snapshots of the status and justifications of each datum then later reset the entire database from the snapshot. This approach is antithetical to the spirit of TMS for it reintroduces chronological backtracking. Information garnered within one snapshot is not readily transferred to another.

The dominance of justifications. What Doyle [12] calls an assumption is context-dependent: an assumption is any node whose current supporting justification depends on some other node being out. As problem solving proceeds, the underlying support justifications and hence the set of nodes considered assumptions changes. This is problematic for problem solvers which frequently consult the assumptions and justifications for data.

The machinery is cumbersome. The TMS algorithm can spend a surprising amount of resources finding a solution that satisfies all the justifications. Determining the well-founded support for a node requires a global constraint satisfaction process. Detecting loops of odd numbers of nonmonotonic justifications (which provoke infinite computation loops) is expensive. The dependency-directed backtracking in response to a contradiction may require extensive search, and the resolution of the contradiction often results in other contradictions. Eventually, all contradictions are resolved, but only after much backtracking. During this time the status of some datum may have changed between in (believed) and out (not believed) many times.

Unouting. As problem solving progresses a datum can be derived, retracted when a contradiction occurs, and then reasserted when a second contradiction causes the current context to switch again (a common occurrence in problem solving). The process of determining which retracted, previously derived, data can be reasserted is called unouting. The maintenance of dependency records avoids having to rediscover these inferences. Unfortunately, unless great care is taken at the problem-solver-TMS interface, some previously discovered data will be rederived.

Consider the following simple (again pathological) example:

(1) $x \in \{1,2\}$

(2) $y \in \{1,2)$

(3) $x \neq y \oplus x = y$

(4) $z = (1000xy)!$

(5) $r = (100xy)!$

Lines (1), (2), and (3) each represent a binary selection. The problem solver starts with the first assumption[3] of each selection: $\{\Gamma_{x=1}, \Gamma_{y=1}, \Gamma_{x\neq y}\}$. The first two equations immediately assign values to x and y leaving the three equations $x \neq y$, $z = (1000xy)!$, and $r = (100xy)!$. None of these equations depends on the result of a previous one, thus each of them can be done first. The problem solver could first compute $z = 1000!$, then $r = 100!$, and finally notice that $x \neq y$ provoked a contradiction. The computation of $z = 1000!$ is recorded with a dependency record indicating that it depends on $\{\Gamma_{x=1}, \Gamma_{y=1}\}$. Later when the assumption set $\{\Gamma_{x=1}, \Gamma_{y=1}, \Gamma_{x=y}\}$ is explored, these dependency records are consulted and $z = 1000!$ is reasserted without having to recompute it.

The difficult case occurs if the original order were, instead, $z = (1000xy)!$, $x \neq y$, and $r = (100xy)!$. As a result $z = 1000!$ is computed, the contradiction is detected, but $r = 100!$ is *not* computed. Sometime later the assumption set $\{\Gamma_{x=1}, \Gamma_{y=1}, \Gamma_{x=y}\}$ is examined. The previously derived $z = 1000!$ is unouted, but $r = 100!$ is not because it was never derived. We have a dilemma: If we do nothing $r = 100!$ is not computed, but if we restart the problem solver on $\{\Gamma_{x=1}, \Gamma_{y=1}, \Gamma_{x=y}\}$ we derive $z = 1000!$ twice. This is the unouting problem. Put abstractly, if the same datum is reexamined in a new context, it is insufficient to just reexamine its previous consequents to see if they hold in the new context because there may be consequents not derivable in the old context, which are derivable in the new. The difficult task is how to fill the "gaps" of the consequents without redoing the entire computation.

There have been four styles of solutions to this task, none completely satisfactory.

(1) Even though a contradiction occurs during analysis of $\{\Gamma_{x=1}, \Gamma_{y=1}, \Gamma_{x\neq y}\}$ this computation could be allowed to go on. The difficulty here is that a great deal of effort may be spent working on a set of assumptions that may be irrelevant to an overall solution.

(2) Another technique is to store a snapshot of the problem solver's state (its pending task queue) which can be reactivated at a later time.

(3) It is also possible to restart the computation from $\{\Gamma_{x=1}, \Gamma_{y=1}\}$, taking advantage of the previous result by examining existing consequents to determine ones are missing.

[3] For perspicuity, when there is no ambiguity, Γ_n is used to represent the assumption n.

(4) The easiest technique is just to restart the computation from $\{\Gamma_{x=1}, \Gamma_{y=1}\}$ without taking any effort to see which consequents should be unouted. All expensive problem-solving steps are memoized so no time-consuming steps are repeated. For example, de Kleer and Sussman, [10], use this technique to cache all symbolic GCD computations.

None of these four solutions is completely general or optimal. De Kleer, [8], presents a problem-solver-TMS protocol which, if followed, allows the TMS to control the problem solver so that no inference is ever done twice.

4. The Basic ATMS

Most of the preceding TMS problems result from the inability to refer directly to the contexts in which a datum holds. As a consequence the database must be kept contradiction-free, describe one context at a time, and cannot be labeled so that it can be reexamined later. The fundamental reason for this is that a datum is solely marked with a set of justifications which specify how it derives from other data, but which only implicitly describe the contexts in which it holds. The solution proposed here augments the justifications of a conventional TMS with a label which explicitly describes the contexts under which the datum holds. This label is updated and manipulated along with the justifications.

4.1. Problem-solver architecture

The ATMS adopts the same view of problem solving as a conventional TMS. The reasoning system (or *overall* problem solver) consists of two components: a problem solver and a TMS (Fig. 1). The problem solver is usually at least first order and includes all domain knowledge and inference procedures. Every inference made is communicated to the TMS. The TMS' job is to determine what data are believed and disbelieved given the justifications recorded thus far. The TMS performs this task through propositional inference using the justifications as propositional axioms.

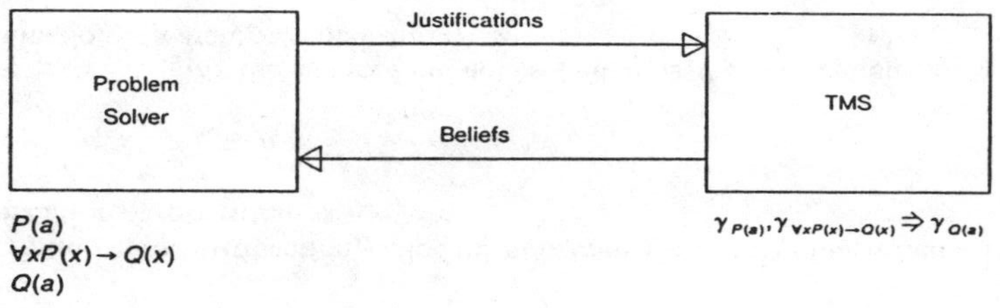

FIG. 1. Reasoning system.

Fig. 1 highlights two properties which are crucial to understanding the use of TMSs in reasoning systems. First, the same expressions have internal structure to the problem solver but are atomic to the TMS. For example, the inference $Q(a)$ is made by matching the structure of $P(a)$ with $\forall x P(x) \rightarrow Q(x)$. When this inference is recorded as a justification, the TMS treats the expressions as uninterpreted symbols or propositional atoms. The TMS task is solely to determine what symbols follow from what given the propositional axioms (the justifications). Thus there are two inference procedures in the reasoning system both operating on the same expressions but treating them entirely differently. Second, problem solving is a process of accumulating justifications and changing beliefs until some goal is satisfied. The TMS determines belief *given the justifications encountered thus far* and *not with respect to the logic of the problem solver*. The addition of a justification may cause any belief to change. Problem solving is a continual process of consulting the current beliefs to decide what inference to make next, recording the inference as a justification, and redetermining the current set of beliefs. The task of the problem-solver designer is to ensure that this process converges to a solution which satisfies the problem-solving goals.

4.2. Basic definitions

Crucial to the ATMS architecture is a subtle distinction that, to this point in the paper, has been left implicit. It is critical to distinguish the thing assumed from the decision to assume. Thus far, the word "assumption" has been used to designate both of these concepts. An *assumption* is restricted to designate a decision to assume without any commitment as to what is assumed. An *assumed* datum is the problem-solver datum that has been assumed to hold. Assumptions are connected to assumed data via justifications as discussed in the next section.

Assumptions form the foundation to which every datum's support can be ultimately traced. Intuitively, it thus makes little sense to allow assumptions themselves to be derived. This point of view has provoked considerable controversy. Therefore, the ATMS permits assumptions to be derived if need be, although this paper avoids utilizing this feature.

If an assumption is uniquely associated with a particular datum x, then, for purposes of perspicuity, this assumption is written Γ_x. Not all assumptions can be so represented, the same assumption may justify multiple data or one datum may be justified by multiple assumptions.

An ATMS *node* corresponds to a problem-solver datum. An assumption is a special kind of node.

An ATMS *justification* describes how a node is derivable from other nodes. A justification has three parts: the node being justified, called the *consequent*; a list of nodes, called the *antecedents*, and the problem solver's description of the justification, called the *informant* (its utility is illustrated in [8]). Justifications are written as:

$$x_1, x_2, \ldots \Rightarrow n\,.$$

Here $x_1, x_2, \ldots$ are the antecedent nodes and n is the consequent node. A justification is a material implication,

$$x_1 \wedge x_2 \wedge \cdots \rightarrow n,$$

where $x_1, x_2, \ldots, n$ are atoms. Thus, the justifications are propositional Horn clauses. The nonlogical notation "$\Rightarrow$" is used because the ATMS does not allow negated literals and treats implication unconventionally.

An ATMS *environment* is a set of assumptions. Logically, an environment is a conjunction of assumptions.

A node n is said to hold in environment E if n can be derived from E and the current set of justifications J. Derivability is defined in terms of the usual propositional calculus,

$$E, J \vdash n\,,$$

where E is viewed as a conjunction of atoms and J is viewed as a set of implications.

An environment is inconsistent if false (notated $\perp$) is derivable propositionally:

$$E, J \vdash \perp\,.$$

An ATMS *context* is the set formed by the assumptions of a consistent environment combined with all nodes derivable from those assumptions.

A *characterizing environment* for a context is a set of assumptions from which every node of the context can be derived. Every context has at least one characterizing environment. Usually (when assumptions have no justifications) every context has exactly one characterizing environment.

Given these basic definitions, the goals of the ATMS can be conceptually outlined. The ATMS is provided with a set of assumptions and justifications. The task of the ATMS is to efficiently determine the contexts. Efficiency is achieved by taking advantage of two important observations about TMS use. First, the problem solver is supplying the ATMS with justifications and assumptions one at a time. Therefore, the ATMS is incremental, updating only the changed contexts. Second, it is extremely rare for a problem solver to ask for the contents of a context. Problem solvers usually only require to be able to tell when a context becomes inconsistent and whether a node holds in a particular context. Therefore, instead of explicitly determining the contexts, the ATMS constructs an intermediate data structure which makes context-consistency checking and node inclusion very fast.

The ATMS constructs this data structure by associating descriptions of contexts with data, instead of the usual association of data with contexts. The ATMS associates with every datum a parsimonious description of every context in which the datum holds. This organization has the advantage that it is extremely convenient for the problem solver to work in all contexts at once (this is discussed further in [8]).

4.3. Labels

An ATMS *label* is a set of environments associated with every node. Every environment E of n's label is consistent and has the property that:

$$E, J \vdash n\,.$$

More intuitively,

$$J \vdash E \rightarrow n\,.$$

The label describes the assumptions the datum ultimately depends on and, unlike the justification, is constructed by the ATMS itself. While a justification describes how the datum is derived from immediately preceding antecedents, a label environment describes how the datum ultimately depends on assumptions. These sets of assumptions can be computed from the justifications, but computing them each time would destroy the efficiency advantages of this ATMS.

The task of the ATMS is to guarantee that each label of each node is consistent, sound, complete and minimal with respect to the justifications. A label is consistent if all of its environments are consistent. A label for node n is sound if n is derivable from each E of the label:

$$J \vdash E \rightarrow n\,.$$

The label for node n is complete if every consistent environment E for which,

$$J \vdash E \rightarrow n\,,$$

is a superset of some environment E' of n's label (viewing environments as sets):

$$E' \subset E\,.$$

The label is minimal if no environment of the label is a superset of any other. For any label environment E there should not exist any other label environment E' such that:

$$E' \subset E .$$

As a consequence of these definitions, node n is derivable from environment E in exactly those cases that E is a superset of any environment of the label. This property has an important consequence for the problem solver manipulating the data. It can directly tell whether a node holds in some environment or not. A node has an empty label iff it is not derivable from a consistent set of assumptions. A node has a nonempty label iff it is derivable from a consistent set of assumptions.

A node is a member of a context if it can be derived from the assumptions of an environment characterizing the context. The representation makes it easy to determine this: A node is in the context if it has at least one environment which is a subset of an environment characterizing the context. Thus a node implicitly specifies all the contexts it can be a member of: namely, those contexts having a characterizing environment which are a superset of one of its label's environments. One of the basic advantages of this ATMS is that membership within a context can be checked by a direct subset test which itself can be implemented efficiently.

Each context implicitly separates all the nodes into three categories: nodes necessarily present, nodes necessarily absent, and nodes currently absent but which may be become necessarily present or absent with subsequent justifications. A node is necessarily absent if its addition would cause the derivation of $\perp$. Assumptions necessarily absent are easily identified. If a nogood is a superset of a context's assumptions, then those assumptions of the nogood not mentioned by the context form a conjunction of assumptions which cannot consistently extend the context. It is harder to identify other necessarily absent nodes, however, if a necessarily absent assumption has only a single consequent, then that assumed datum is necessarily absent.

Consequently, the set of nodes can be separated into four nonoverlapping sets (membership is easily computable). The *true* set contains nodes which hold in the empty environment. These nodes must hold in every consistent context which has or will be found. This set grows monotonically. The *in* set contains nodes whose label has at least one nonempty environment. These nodes hold in at least one nonuniversal consistent context. However, as problem solving proceeds these contexts may be discovered to be inconsistent. Thus, this set grows nonmonotonically. The *out* set contains nodes whose label is empty. These nodes hold in no known consistent context. Subsequent problem solving may discover a new context for a node moving the node to the in set, or discover a context is inconsistent moving some in node to the out set. The *false* set corresponds to nodes which do not hold in any context which has or will be found. This set grows monotonically.

The flow of nodes between these sets is straightforward. Every new node is created with an empty label and thus as a member of the out set. Problem solving may move out and in nodes to any other set, but no problem solving can remove nodes from the true or false set.

4.4. Basic data structures

The basic data structure is an ATMS node. It contains the problem-solver datum with which it is associated, the justifications the problem solver has created for it, and a label computed for it by the ATMS:

$$\gamma_{\text{datum}}: \langle \text{datum,label,justifications} \rangle .$$

γ_x designates the node with datum x. However, in cases where it makes little difference the same designation is used to represent both the node and its datum. The label is computed by the ATMS and must not be changed by the problem solver. The datum is supplied by the problem solver, and is never examined by the ATMS. The justifications are supplied by the problem solver and are examined but never modified by the ATMS.

All nodes are treated identically, and are distinguished only by their individual pattern of label environments and justifications. There are four types of nodes: *premises, assumptions, assumed nodes,* and *derived nodes.*

A premise has a justification with no antecedents, i.e., it holds universally. The node,

$$\langle p, \{\{\,\}\}, \{(\,)\}\rangle$$

represents the premise p. Although new justifications can be added to a premise, this will not affect the label unless the empty environment becomes inconsistent.

An assumption is a node whose label contains a singleton environment mentioning itself. The node,

$$\langle A, \{\{A\}\}, \{(A)\}\rangle ,$$

represents the assumption A (lower-case letters and γ_x represent any node and upper-case letters and Γ_x represent assumptions). Assumptions may be justified:

$$\langle A, \{\{A\}, \{B, C\}\}, \{(A), (d)\}\rangle .$$

An assumed node is neither a premise nor an assumption and has a justification mentioning an assumption. The assumed datum a which holds under assumption A is represented,

$$\langle a,\{\{A\}\},\{(A)\}\rangle .$$

Preferably, defeasible problem-solving nodes should be created by assumption-assumed-node pairs. This technique avoids having to ever justify assumptions and makes it convenient to remove unnecessary assumptions if need be (i.e., by contradicting the assumption, not the assumed node).

All other nodes are derived. The derived node,

$$\langle w = 1,\{\{A,B\},\{C\},\{E\}\},\{(b),(c,d)\}\rangle$$

represents the fact that $w = 1$ is derived from either the node b or the nodes c and d. In addition, the node holds in environments $\{A, B\}$ and $\{C\}$ and $\{E\}$.

Justifications can be added to any type of node, conceivably changing its type. However, purely for efficiency, as assumptions require a more elaborate data structure, nonassumptions cannot become assumptions, or assumptions cannot become another type of node. If that capability is needed, the assumption-assumed-node technique should be used.

Logically, the label represents a material implication. The label of

$$\langle n, \{\{A_1, A_2, \ldots\}, \{B_1, B_2, \ldots\}, \ldots\}, \{(z_1, z_2, \ldots)(y_1, y_2, \ldots)\ldots\}\rangle$$

represents the implication,

$$(A_1 \wedge A_2 \wedge \cdots) \vee (B_1 \wedge B_2 \wedge \cdots) \vee \cdots \rightarrow n .$$

Similarly, the justifications represent the implication,

$$(z_1 \wedge z_2 \wedge \cdots) \vee (y_1 \wedge y_2 \wedge \cdots) \vee \cdots \rightarrow n .$$

An out set node may have justifications if no justification holds in a consistent environment. Such a node must not be removed from the database because future ATMS processing (in response to new justifications) may produce a consistent environment for it.

The distinguished node,

$$\gamma_{\perp}: \langle \perp, \{\}, \{\ldots\}\rangle ,$$

represents falsity. The inconsistent environments are called *nogoods* because they represent inconsistent conjunctions of assumptions. Note that the nogoods are the label $\gamma_{\perp}$ would have if inconsistent environments were not excluded from node labels.

4.5. The environment lattice

Every consistent environment characterizes a context. If there are n assumptions, then there are potentially 2^n contexts. There are $\binom{n}{k}$ environments having k assumptions. Fig. 2 illustrates the environment lattice for assumptions $\{A, B, C, D, E\}$. The nodes represent environments. The upward edges from an environment represent subset relationships with environments one larger in size. Conversely, the downward edges from an environment represent superset relationships with environments one smaller. All the supersets of an environment can be found by tracing upward through the lattice, and all the subsets of an environment can be found by tracing downwards through the lattice. Thus, all environments are subsets of the top-most node $\{A, B, C, D, E\}$, and all environments are supersets of the bottom-most node $\{\}$.

Any environment which allows the derivation of $\perp$ is nogood and removed from the lattice. On figures, the crossed-out nodes correspond to nogoods. If an environment is nogood, then all of its superset environments are nogood as well. The nogoods of Fig. 2 are the result of the single nogood $\{A, B, E\}$.

The ATMS associates every datum with its contexts. If a datum is in a context, then it is in every superset as well (the inconsistent supersets are ignored). For example, the circled nodes of Fig. 2 indicate all the contexts of $\gamma_{x+y=1}$. The label of a node is the set of greatest lower bounds of the circled nodes:

$$\gamma_{x+y=1}: \langle x + y = 1, \{\{A, B\}, \{B, C, D\}\}, \{\ldots\}\rangle .$$

The square nodes of Fig. 2 correspond the contexts of $\gamma_{x=1}$:

$$\gamma_{x=1}: \langle x = 1, \{\{A, C\}, \{D, E\}\}, \{\ldots\}\rangle .$$

Suppose nothing is known about y, and the problem solver infers $y = 0$ from $x + y = 1$ and $x = 1$:

$$\gamma_{x+y=1}, \gamma_{x=1} \Rightarrow \gamma_{y=0} .$$

The contexts of $\gamma_{y=0}$ are the intersection of the contexts of $\gamma_{x+y=1}$ and $\gamma_{x=1}$. The label for $\gamma_{y=0}$ is the set of greatest lower bounds of the intersection:

$$\gamma_{y=0}: \langle y = 0, \{\{A, B, C\}, \{B, C, D, E\}\}, \{(\gamma_{x+y=1}, \gamma_{x=1})\}\rangle .$$

4.6. Basic operations

The three basic ATMS actions are creating an ATMS node for a problem-solver datum, creating an assumption, and adding a justification to a node. The

ATMS is incremental. The algorithms ensure that, after every primitive operation, every label of every node is consistent, sound, complete and minimal. All ATMS operations can be built out of the three primitive operations.

Associating ATMS nodes with data is preliminary to any ATMS actions. It is crucial that two data which are the "same" be associated with the same ATMS node. This can only be achieved by some indexing scheme within the problem solver such that all forms of the same datum are associated with the same node. If this is not done, and each new derived datum is automatically associated with a new node, then many of the advantages of the ATMS disappear. Creating an assumption, like creating a node, requires little ATMS work. Identifying what assumptions should be created, however, can be a difficult task for the problem solver or its designer. The only primitive operation which can cause significant processing for the ATMS and the problem solver is adding a justification.

A node n is assumed by giving it a justification which includes an assumption, e.g.,

$$A \Rightarrow n .$$

Premises are represented as justifications with no antecedent nodes (hence their labels consist of the empty environment). The justification,

$$\Rightarrow p .$$

results in the node,

$$\langle p, \{\{\}\}, \{(), \ldots\}\rangle .$$

justifications for $\gamma_\perp$ indicate inconsistent conjunctions of nodes (i.e., $(n_1 \wedge n_2 \wedge \cdots \wedge n_k \rightarrow \gamma_\perp) \equiv \neg(n_1 \wedge n_2 \wedge \cdots \wedge n_k)$).

It is important to note that node labels are completely insensitive to the order in which the assumptions, nodes, and justifications are introduced.

4.7. Basic algorithms

The ATMS must ensure that for every justification the intersection of the contexts of the antecedents are equal to the contexts of the consequent. As the ATMS represents a context by its greatest lower bound, this computation is involved. Consider the example just discussed:

$$\gamma_{x+y=1}: \langle x + y = 1, \{\{A, B\}, \{B, C, D\}\}, \{\ldots\}\rangle ,$$

$$\gamma_{x=1}: \langle x = 1, \{\{A, C\}, \{D, E\}\}, \{\ldots\}\rangle ,$$

$$\gamma_{y=0}: \langle y = 0, \{\}, \{\}\rangle ,$$

$$nogood\{A, B, E\} .$$

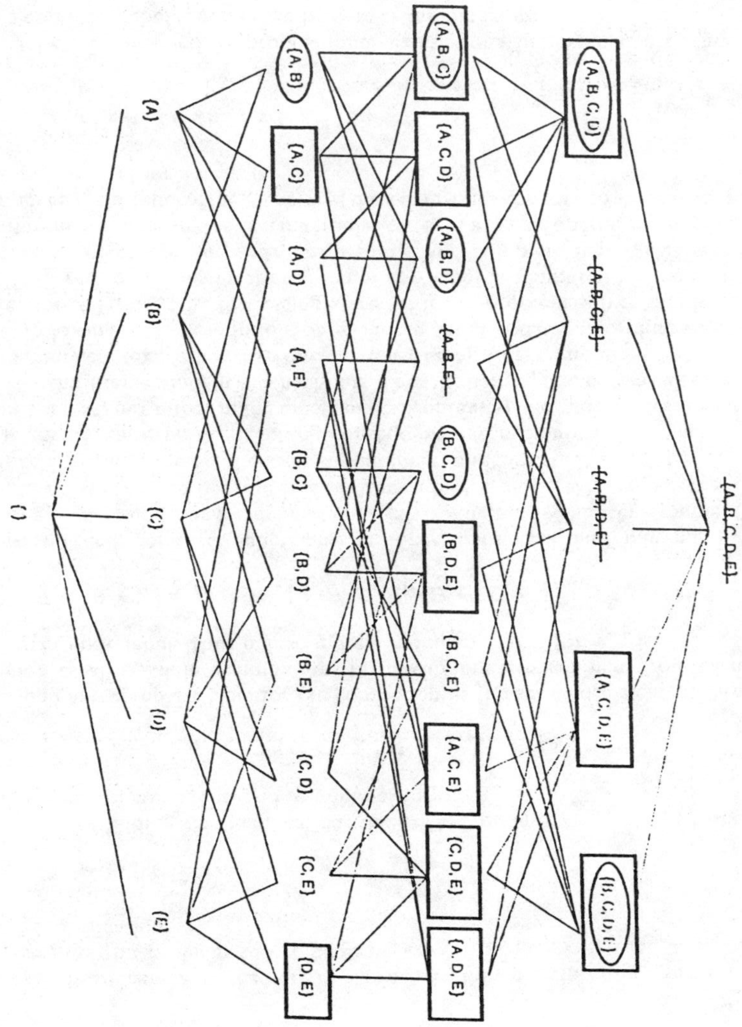

FIG. 2. Environment lattice.

(As nogoods are central to the ATMS algorithms, they are stored in a separate database.) As the problem solver deduces $y = 0$ from $x + y = 1$ and $x = 1$ it adds the justification:

$$\gamma_{x+y=1}, \gamma_{x=1} \Rightarrow \gamma_{y=0} .$$

As a result of adding this justification, the ATMS updates $\gamma_{y=0}$'s label to be sound, complete, consistent, and in minimal form:

$$\gamma_{y=0}: \langle y = 0, \{\{A, B, C\}, \{B, C, D, E\}\}, \{(\gamma_{x+y=1}, \gamma_{x=1})\}\rangle .$$

One sound and complete label for the consequent is the set whose elements are the union of all possible combinations of picking one environment from each antecedent node label. Thus one sound and complete label for $\gamma_{y=0}$ is

$$\{\{A, B, C\}, \{A, B, C, D\}, \{A, B, D, E\}, \{B, C, D, E\}\} .$$

Any sound and complete label can be made consistent and minimal by removing subsumed and inconsistent environments. The environment $\{A, B, C, D\}$ is removed because it is subsumed by $\{A, B, C\}$. The environment $\{A, B, D, E\}$ is not included because it contains the inconsistent $\{A, B, E\}$.

In terms of contexts, the resulting consequent datum is not inserted into a current context, but rather in the most general context(s) (i.e. the greatest lower bounds of the intersection) in which it holds. Thus the consequent datum will carry over to many contexts other than one currently being worked upon.

The following is a description of a simple label-update algorithm which satisfies the ATMS goals. Processing starts with the problem solver supplying the ATMS with a new justification. First, a new label is computed for the node assuming every antecedent node has a sound and complete label. This label computation can be viewed as a set manipulation, or as a logical operation. In terms of sets, given j_{ik} the label of the ith node of the kth justification for consequent node n, a complete label for node n is:

$$\bigcup_k \left\{ x \mid x = \bigcup_i x_i \text{ where } x_i \in j_{ik} \right\} .$$

If the labels are viewed as propositional expressions in disjunctive normal form, a complete label is computed by converting the expression,

$$\bigvee_k \bigwedge_i j_{ik} ,$$

into disjunctive normal form. After removing inconsistent and subsumed environments, the label is sound and minimal. Second, if the newly computed label is the same as the old label, then we are finished with the node. Third, if the node is $\gamma_\perp$, each environment of the label is added to a nogood database and all inconsistent environments (i.e., it and all its supersets) are removed from every node label. Fourth, if the node is not $\gamma_\perp$, then the updating process recurs updating the labels of all the consequent nodes (i.e., other nodes having justifications which mention the node whose label changed). Although this simple process may update the same node label more than once, the process must terminate because there are a finite number of assumptions. Note that labels are not guaranteed to be consistent and complete until the algorithm terminates.

There are many optimizations to this algorithm. The LISP implementation of this propagator takes more advantage of the fact that node labels are sound, consistent, complete and minimal to start with. It is not necessary to recompute the entire node label for each node update. It is sufficient to compute the incremental change in the label contributed by the new justifications. If a node has only one justification which mentions only one node with a nonempty label, then the label can just be copied forward.

In the design of the basic algorithm, each node has five slots:
- Datum: The problem solvers' representation of the fact.
- Label: A set of environments.
- Justifications: A list of the derivations of the datum.
- Consequents: A list of justifications in which the node is an antecedent.
- Contradictory: A single bit indicating whether the datum is contradictory.

In addition an environment has three slots:
- Assumptions: The set of assumptions defining it.
- Nodes: The set of nodes whose label mentions it.
- Contradictory: A single bit indicating whether the environment is contradictory.

A justification has three slots:
- Informant: A problem-solver-supplied description of the inference.
- Consequent: The node justified.
- Antecedents: A list of nodes upon which the inference depends.

4.8. Complexity considerations

The architecture of the ATMS is such that it is practical to use even when n is very large (e.g., 1000). The ATMS is then exploring a space of size 2^{1000}. To clarify how the ATMS can efficiently explore such large spaces consider the environment lattice. The efficiency of the ATMS arises from two important observations about this lattice. First, due to the fact that a node is in every superset context as well, it is only necessary to record the greatest lower bound environments in which a node holds (the label). Similarly, it is only necessary to record the greatest lower bounds of the inconsistent environments. Second, in cases where most of the environments are inconsistent, these inconsistencies are identifiable in small subsets of assumptions. Therefore, large parts of the environment lattice need never be explicitly checked for consistency.

The efficiency of the ATMS is thus directly proportional to the number of environments it is forced to consider (thus actually constructing the environment lattice is always a bad idea). Ultimately, the observed efficiency of the ATMS is a result of the fact that it is not that easy to create a problem which forces the TMS to consider all 2^n environments without either doing work of order 2^n to set up the problem or creating a problem with 2^n solutions. To construct such a pathological case, one has to cleverly create a set of justifications such that every possible environment is a minimal nogood or a minimal environment for some node at some point in the process. De Kleer, in [8], considers these issues in more detail.

4.9. Retracting justifications

To make a justification retractable, it is conjoined with an extra assumption which represents its defeasability. To retract the justification, the problem solver contradicts the conjoined assumption. This is the only reasonable way to retract a justification.

Although some TMSs permit direct retraction, few implement it correctly (correct means that all the labels of the datum will be as if the removed justification never existed). Retraction is inherently inefficient for all TMSs. (Direct justification retraction is isomorphic to LISP garbage collection.) The ATMS incorporates a correct but very inefficient direct retraction algorithm. Removing a justification from a node requires invalidating the labels of all the consequents (recursively) and recomputing them from correct labels. That part is easy and is akin to conventional garbage collection. The inefficiency arises if any of those recursive consequents is $\perp$. If so, an environment may have to be removed from the nogood database, and that can provoke an enormous amount of work. If a nogood has to be removed, the more specific nogoods which it subsumed have to be put back and every label of every node is potentially affected. For these reasons, directly removing a justifications is a bad idea.

4.10. Classes

It is often convenient to group nodes together into sets and treat each member identically. The architecture incorporates a notion of node set, or *class*. The node-class framework is not logically necessary, but it is a minor extension which greatly simplifies problem-solver-ATMS interactions. De Kleer, in [8], utilizes this framework to encode complex inference rules.

The node-class organization is intended to be very general. A node can be a member of any number of classes (possibly none), and a class can have any number of members (possibly none). The membership of a node in a class has no relation to whether it holds in any environment. Unless a class has been specifically closed, nodes can be added to it at any time. It is not possible to remove a node from a class.

In many applications a node can be a member of at most one class. In such cases, the class is viewed as a variable and its nodes as values. The node $\gamma_{x=n}$ represents the fact that class x has value n, and is distinguished from the node $\gamma_{x=n}$ which represents the equation $x = n$. Such classes are used to represent the usual notion of variable in programming or constraint languages. In the usual constraint-language terminology [21], a cell is represented as a class and a value by a node. Unlike conventional constraint languages, a cell can simultaneously have many values. In most applications differing values for the same variable are inconsistent.

Suppose $X \in \{1, 2, 3\}$. A closed class is constructed for x, and is given three nodes: $\gamma_{x=1}$, $\gamma_{x=2}$ and $\gamma_{x=3}$. Each pair of these nodes are marked inconsistent, e.g., $\gamma_{x=1}, \gamma_{x=2} \Rightarrow \gamma_{\perp}$. $\Gamma_{x=n}$ refers to the assumption which justifies $\gamma_{x=n}$:

$$\Gamma_{x=n} \Rightarrow \gamma_{x=n} .$$

Classes are also used to represent patterns in assertional languages. A pattern represents the collection of its instances (i.e., nodes). Every assertion is a node, and every rule antecedent pattern is a class. Unlike constraint languages, a node can be a member of an arbitrary number of classes, as the same assertion match multiple-antecedent patterns. (See [8] for more details.)

5. Limitations Removed

The single-state problem. As the assumption-based approach does not require a notion of current global context, multiple, mutually contradictory, solutions may coexist. Thus, it is simple to compare two solutions.

Overzealous contradiction avoidance. The presence of two contradictory data does not terminate work on the overall knowledge state, rather only other data which depend on both contradicting data are removed. This is exactly the result desired from a contradiction—no more, no less. The nogood database guarantees that mutually contradictory data will never be combined. Said differently, the nogood database, in effect, provides the partitioning of the database into the consistent solutions.

Switching states is difficult. Changing state is now trivial or irrelevant. A state is completely specified by a set of assumptions. Problem solving can be restricted to a current context (i.e., a set of assumptions) or all states can be explored simultaneously. In either case, data obtained in one state are "automatically" transferred to another. For example, if $\langle x = 1, \{\{E, G\}\}, \{\ldots\}\rangle$ is deduced while exploring $\{B, C, E, G\}$, then $x = 1$ will still be present while exploring $\{B, D, E, G\}$.

The dominance of justifications. As assumptions, not justifications, are the dominant representational mode it is easy to compare sets of assumptions underlying data. For example, it is easy to find the datum with the most assumptions or the least; it is easy to determine whether the presence of one datum implies the presence of another (a implies b if every environment of a is a superset of one of the environments of b). Also, the justifications underlying a datum never change.

The machinery is cumbersome. The underlying mechanism is simple. There is no backtracking of any kind within the ATMS—let alone dependency-directed backtracking. The assumptions underlying a contradiction are directly identifiable. It is not necessary to explicitly mark data as believed or disbelieved, or signal the problem solver when the statuses of data change.

Checking for circular supporting justifications is unnecessary. Although it is simple to construct circular justifications, the basic ATMS mechanism will never mistakenly use it as a basis for support. Consider a database consisting of only two justifications: $a \Rightarrow b$ and $b \Rightarrow a$. This is represented by two nodes: $\langle a, \{\}, \{(b)\}\rangle$ and $\langle b, \{\}, \{(a)\}\rangle$. The circular justification has no effect as both nodes have empty labels. Suppose a receives an environment. This label propagates to b, and back to a, but the second update leaves the label unchanged terminating the propagation. Notice that even if the loop back to a were longer, any environment added by b to a would have to be a superset of one of a's. The point is that circularities cause no special difficulties for the ATMS label propagation mechanism.

Unouting. For those tasks requiring all solutions (or where there is only one solution), the ATMS completely finesses the earlier unouting problem. Unlike with a conventional TMS, the ATMS allows the problem solver to explore all solutions at once. There is no backtracking, no retraction, and no context switching. Thus, the previous unouting example is handled trivially:

(1) $x \in \{1, 2\}$

(2) $y \in \{1, 2\}$

(3) $x \neq y \oplus x = y$

(4) $z = (1000xy)!$

(5) $r = (100xy)!$

Consider the problematic ordering in which z is computed before the contradiction is detected. In this simple architecture, a contradiction within $\{\Gamma_{x=1}, \Gamma_{y=1}, \Gamma_{x\neq y}\}$ merely implies that any exploration of that state ceases, i.e., any inferences involving environments which contain $\{\Gamma_{x=1}, \Gamma_{y=1}, \Gamma_{x\neq y}\}$ are avoided. Work on environment $\{\Gamma_{x=1}, \Gamma_{y=1}, \Gamma_{x=y}\}$ continues as if the contradiction never occurred. Data derived from $\{\Gamma_{x=1}, \Gamma_{y=1}\}$ alone are automatically part of every superset, and hence are also part of $\{\Gamma_{x=1}, \Gamma_{y=1}, \Gamma_{x=y}\}$. There is never any question of rerunning rules.

Unouting problems also arise due to *implicit* context switches caused by alternative justifications for previously derived data. Consider a new example. The problem solver has proceeded until the following database state is reached:

$$\gamma_{x=1}\colon \langle x = 1, \{\{A\}\}, \{\ldots\}\rangle,$$

$$\gamma_{y=-x}\colon \langle y = -x, \{\{B\}\}, \{\ldots\}\rangle,$$

$$\gamma_{z=x}\colon \langle z = x, \{\{C\}\}, \{\ldots\}\rangle,$$

$$nogood\{A, B\}.$$

The problem solver immediately notices that it has a value for x which it could substitute into the equation $y = -x$, however the value would be computed under $\{A, B\}$ which is a nogood set so the substitution is not permitted. Now suppose the problem solver discovers the premise

$$\gamma_{z=1}\colon \langle z = 1, \{\{\ \}\}, \{\ldots\}\rangle.$$

The equation $z = x$ provides a different way of computing x:

$$\gamma_{x=1}\colon \langle x = 1, \{\{C\}, \{A\}\}, \{(\gamma_{z=x}, \gamma_{z=1})\ldots\}\rangle.$$

Now $\langle y = -1, \{\{B, C\}\}, \{(\gamma_{x=1}, \gamma_{y=-x})\}\rangle$ is derivable. Thus, $\gamma_{x=1}$ has no believed consequents under its original label $\{\{A\}\}$ and has consequent $y = -1$ under its new label $\{\{C\}, \{A\}\}$. The unouting problem is whether to work on $x = 1$ again after the second derivation is found for it.

De Kleer [5] and Williams [22] suggest an inelegant scheme for dealing with multiple justifications for the same datum. Suppose a second derivation for the same datum is discovered, the old environment being E_{old} and the new one E_{new}. There are four possible cases. If E_{old} is the same as E_{new}, then the new derivation holds in exactly those contexts where the old one was, so no new information can be gained by having the problem solver reexamine the datum. If E_{old} is a proper subset of E_{new}, then the new datum is a more specific instance which holds in a subset of the contexts where the old one did so the datum can also be ignored. On the other hand if E_{new} is a proper subset of E_{old}, the new instance is a more general and might hold in *more* contexts than the old one. If the two environments are incomparable the new instance might hold in other contexts than the old one. In both these latter cases the problem solver is reinvoked on the datum, deriving all of its consequents, rederiving the old consequents and in addition deriving the consequents which could not be derived in the old environment. This process recurs. Note that this recursion might descend many levels before a genuinely new piece of problem-solving work is done (if ever). ART handles this problem in an equivalent, and thus problematic, manner by creating multiple copies of the datum if necessary. De Kleer presents a problem-solver-TMS protocol in which no piece of problem solving need ever be done twice in [8].

6. Implementation Issues

To avoid the ATMS being the dominant consumer of resources of the overall problem solver, great care must be taken in the choice of the representations and algorithms. The following is a description of the basic design choices and some of their alternatives.

Implemented straightforwardly, the ATMS would be too slow, spending all of its time performing set unions and subset tests. The implementation employs two representation ideas to minimize both the cost and the number of set operations. Sets are represented by bit-vectors: each assumption is assigned a unique position so that a one bit in a position indicates the presence of the corresponding assumption in the set. The union of two sets is computed by or'ing the bit-vectors. Set1 is a subset of set2 if the result of and'ing the bit-vector of set1 with the complement of set2 is zero.

As every environment has to be checked whether it contains a contradiction, the nogood database is kept as small as possible. Therefore, whenever a contradiction is discovered, its more specific instances (i.e., its supersets), if any, are removed from the nogood database.

Most subset tests occur when checking whether environments contain nogoods. Almost all such subset tests can be avoided by having a unique data structure for each environment. Whenever a union operation produces a new environment it must still be checked to see whether it contains a contradiction. However, this unique data structure ensures that this test be done once per environment, not once per union operation. This is implemented with a hash table using bit-vectors as keys (here we see another advantage of the bit-vector representation—it is very easy to compute the hash for a bit-vector). The only expensive operations thus are the creation of a new environment and the discovery of a new contradiction. Note that as supersets of nogoods have few interesting properties it is unnecessary to create a full environment structure for them.

Contradictions involving less than three assumptions are common and are best handled with special case mechanisms. A contradiction of the empty environment indicates an error which should be reported to the user without performing any ATMS operations. A contradiction of length one indicates an individual assumption has become inconsistent. Each environment containing this assumption becomes inconsistent. Furthermore, every ATMS operation on assumptions first checks to see whether any of the supplied assumptions are inconsistent. If so, the operation is ignored. The efficient handling of binary contradictions requires a more specialized representation. Each assumption is associated with the set of assumptions it is inconsistent with. Like label environments, these sets are represented by bit-vectors. Every ATMS operation which attempts to create an environment first checks whether its results would violate a binary contradiction. If so, the operation fails, and the environment is not created. Although this mechanism slows down all environment creation operations, the reduction in the number of nogoods and environments greatly improves overall efficiency.

As a side-effect of the representation of binary nogoods, oneof disjunctions are represented at no cost. Without this efficient representation, n^2 nogoods would have been required to represent a oneof disjunction of size n.

In most ATMS applications most of the environment unions involve one environment of length one. Such union operations can be highly optimized. The optimization is based on viewing the union as adding a single assumption to the environment. This optimization uses three caches. The first cache, associated with each assumption, is the set of minimal nogoods of size three or larger in which the assumption appears. When an assumption is added to an environment, the consistency check of the resulting environment need only be checked against this set. The second cache, associated with each environment, is the set of assumptions it is inconsistent with, represented as a bit-vector. The third cache, also associated with each environment, associates each added assumption with the resulting consistent environment. These three caches, combined with the environment hash table and the binary contradiction optimization, make adding an assumption to an environment very fast.

The set of all environments and the set of all nogoods should be organized by length. A new environment needs only be tested against every nogood smaller than it. Likewise every new contradiction needs only be tested against every environment larger than it.

The label-update algorithm should not be applied to true (having an empty environment) or false (marked contradictory) nodes. Instead, label updates of true nodes should be ignored, and updates of false nodes should be computed incrementally and added directly to the nogood database.

Nodes can be inferred to be contradictory. If all but one of the antecedents of a contradictory node are true, then that one antecedent is necessarily false as well. This requires a second, but extremely simple propagator which follows antecedent links of justifications.

Assumptions consume two valuable resources: bit-vector positions and environment hash-table positions (that contain the assumption). Therefore it is worthwhile garbage collecting assumptions. An assumption can be garbage collected if either all its consequent nodes are true (i.e., hold universally) or false (i.e., is contradictory), or if the singleton environment containing the assumption is contradictory. In my experience, typically 30% of the assumptions can be garbage collected. When the assumption is garbage collected, all environments which include it are removed from the environment hash table and nogood database, and the bit-vector position representing it is recycled. The garbage collector is run whenever the environment hash table is grown and rehashed. Some care must be taken that assumptions which have not yet been integrated into all their justifications are not accidentally garbage collected. The problem solver must indicate when an assumption becomes garbage collectible.

Bit-vectors are only worth using because operations on them are efficiently executed by computer hardware. The environments could also be represented as ordered lists. Union and intersection would then take linear time of order of the size of the environments. With bit-vectors the time is linear but each test is of order of all the assumptions ever considered and thus is potentially exponential.

Caching the results of all subset tests and union operations is not worth it. The bit-vector representation combined with the hash table is so efficient that the overhead of maintaining the cache is more expensive than the operation itself.

Representing all the subset relations in a dag (directed acyclic graph) is not worth it. Even with the dag it is not worth using the dag for a subset test because bit-vector operations are so fast. Sweeping out all superset good environments or sweeping out all subset nogood environments, however, is much faster. Unfortunately, the time and space resources of maintaining the dag overwhelms this advantage.

The following are untried possibilities.

A dag consisting only of unions. Instead of caching all subset tests, one can only cache the subset links implied by union operations actually required in the problem solving. To determine whether a new environment contains a contradiction one can look at the supersets of the antecedents which are contradictory. This type of scheme is used in ART [22, 23].

A discrimination net for nogoods. In my experience, relatively few of the environments actually encountered are nogood, thus it makes sense to optimize the subset test at the expense of a complex representation.

All the set operations are a result of updating the labels of nodes. However, unless the node is examined for some reason, there is no reason to update its label. Thus node labels could be updated only if needed. This requires a second propagator which propagates 'update' messages backwards along justification links. However, the labels for contradictory nodes must always be updated otherwise contradictions will be missed.

Introducing these efficiency techniques extends the data structures required for assumptions and environments (no changes are necessary to nonassumption nodes): In addition to the slots for a basic node, an assumption has three additional slots.

- Position: Bit-vector position corresponding to this assumption.
- Contras: Bit-vector of other assumptions it is inconsistent with.
- Nogoods: Minimal nogoods of length three or greater in which it appears.

An environment has three additional slots:

- Contras: Bit-vector of other assumptions it is inconsistent with.
- Cache: A cache of the results of adding assumptions to this environment.
- Count: Number of assumptions.

7. Summary

The ATMS is given a set of assumptions A, a set of nodes N ($N \supset A$), and a set of justifications J in terms of N (which includes A). The triple $\langle A, N, J\rangle$ implicitly defines a set of contexts where a context is defined as a consistent (i.e., not admitting $\gamma_\perp$) set of assumptions ($A' \subset A$) and nodes ($N' \subset N$) derivable from A' using J. Given k assumptions there are conceivably 2^k contexts. The ATMS never explicitly computes these contexts. The contexts provide a convenient concept with which to define what the ATMS actually does. A node's label is a minimal description of the characterizing environments of the contexts within which it appears. A node is a member of every context having a characterizing environment which is a superset of one of the label's environments.

As a consequence the ATMS has four important properties. These properties are worth highlighting because they both illustrate the utility of the ATMS to problem solving and because care must be taken to preserve them when more complex axioms are permitted as in J (in [7]).

Most fundamentally, *label consistency* ensures all inconsistent environments are identified and defined not to have contexts and do not appear in node labels.

Label soundness ensures that no context will contain a datum it should not. Thus, nodes which hold in no context will have empty labels. This property is important to problem solving because it ensures that the problem solver will not mistakenly work on irrelevant nodes which do not hold in any context.

Label completeness guarantees that every context will contain every datum it should. Thus, all nodes which hold in any context have nonempty labels. This property is important to problem solving because it ensures that the problem solver can easily identify all relevant nodes (i.e., those which hold in at least one context).

Label minimality states that each node label has the fewest disjuncts and that each disjunct has the fewest assumptions. This property is important to the problem solver because it ensures that changing any label assumption affects the node's status. This property is true by definition for the basic ATMS, but becomes an important consideration for dealing with disjunction axioms.

Label consistency and minimality are also important for ATMS efficiency.

Although label soundness allows the problem solver to ignore irrelevant nodes, this does not guarantee that these nodes will ultimately be irrelevant. Conversely, although label completeness enables the problem solver to identify all relevant nodes, this does not guarantee that these nodes will ultimately be relevant. If the problem solver could be guaranteed to work only on ultimately relevant nodes, the entire problem-solving process should be written as an efficient straightforward algorithm. All the ATMS can ensure is, given the justifications and assumptions *so far*, that these properties hold. With the addition of every justification, the set of contexts may change and nodes that were irrelevant become relevant and vice versa.

ACKNOWLEDGMENT

I have received tremendous technical help and encouragement from Daniel Bobrow, Ken Forbus, Brian Williams, and Benjamin Grosof. David McAllester helped clarify the differences between the ATMS and conventional TMSs. Greg Clemenson, Randy Davis, David Etherington, Richard Fikes, Jeff Finger, Matthew Ginsberg, Kris Halvorsen, Ken Kahn, Paul Morris, Ray Reiter, Peter Struss, Chuck Williams, provided valuable discussions. Many of their ideas appear throughout this paper. Lenore Johnson drew the figures. I cannot thank them all enough.

REFERENCES

1. Brown, J.S., Burton R.R. and de Kleer, J., Pedagogical, natural language and knowledge engineering techniques in SOPHIE I, II and III, in: D. Sleeman and J.S. Brown (Eds.), *Intelligent Tutoring Systems* (Academic Press, New York, 1983) 227–282.
2. Clocksin, W.F. and Mellish, C.S., *Programming in Prolog* (Springer, Berlin, 1981).
3. de Kleer, J., Local methods of localizing faults in electronic circuits, Artificial Intelligence Laboratory, AIM-394, MIT, Cambridge, MA, 1976.
4. de Kleer, J., Causal and teleological reasoning in circuit recognition, Artificial Intelligence Laboratory, TR-529, MIT, Cambridge, MA, 1979.
5. de Kleer, J., Choices without backtracking, in: *Proceedings Fourth National Conference on Artificial Intelligence*, Austin, TX (1984) 79–85.
6. de Kleer, J., How circuits work, *Artificial Intelligence* **24** (1984) 205–280.
7. de Kleer, J., Extending the ATMS, *Artificial Intelligence* **28** (1986) 163–196 (this issue).
8. de Kleer, J., Problem solving with the ATMS, *Artificial Intelligence* **28** (1986) 197–224 (this issue).
9. de Kleer, J. and Brown, J.S., A qualitative physics based on confluences, *Artificial Intelligence* **24** (1984) 7–83.
10. de Kleer, J. and Sussman, G.J., Propagation of constraints applied to circuit synthesis, *Circuit Theory and Applications* **8** (1980).
11. de Kleer, J. and Williams, B.C., Diagnosing multiple faults, *Artificial Intelligence*, submitted.
12. Doyle, J., A truth maintenance system, *Artificial Intelligence* **12** (1979), 231–272.
13. Martins, J.P., Reasoning in multiple belief spaces, Department of Computer Science, Tech. Rept. No. 203, State University of New York, Buffalo, NY, 1983.
14. McAllester, D., A three-valued truth maintenance system, S.B. Thesis, Department of Electrical Engineering, MIT, Cambridge, MA, 1978.
15. McAllester, D., An outlook on truth maintenance, Artificial Intelligence Laboratory, AIM-551, MIT, Cambridge, MA, 1980.
16. McAllester, D., Reasoning utility package user's manual, Artificial Intelligence Laboratory, AIM-667, MIT, Cambridge, MA 1982.
17. McDermott D., Contexts and data dependencies: a synthesis, *IEEE Trans. Pattern Anal. Machine Intelligence* **5** (3) (1983).
18. Reiter, R., A logic for default reasoning, *Artificial Intelligence* **13** (1980) 81–132.
19. Rulifson, J.F., Derkson, J.A. and Waldinger, R.J., QA4: a procedural calculus for intuitive reasoning, Artificial Intelligence Center, Tech. Note 73, SRI, Menlo Park, CA, 1972.
20. Stallman, R.M. and Sussman, G.J., Forward reasoning and dependency-directed backtracking in a system for computer-aided circuit analysis, *Artificial Intelligence* **9** (1977) 135–196.
21. Steele, G.L., The definition and implementation of a computer programming language based on constraints, Artificial Intelligence Laboratory, TR-595, MIT, Cambridge, MA 1979.
22. Williams, C., ART the advanced reasoning tool—conceptual overview, Inference Corporation, 1984.
23. Williams, C., Managing search in a knowledge-based system, unpublished, 1985.

Chapter 5

Applications of Nonmonotonic Reasoning

5.1 Logic Programming

Applications to logic programming are the oldest and best investigated of the uses for nonmonotonic reasoning. Negation as failure is commonly used by PROLOG programs; the direct application of nonmonotonic inference methods to understanding the technique dates to Reiter's paper, "On closed world data bases."

In this important paper, Reiter defines the closed-world assumption (CWA) for relational databases, using as a motivating example one similar to the airline database that appeared in the introduction. The closed-world assumption will be consistent if and only if there is a unique extension for the default theory in question; Reiter shows (Theorem 6) that this is the case for Horn databases.

The CWA is investigated more formally by Lifschitz in "Closed world databases and circumscription." Lifschitz shows there (Theorem 3.1) that if applying the CWA to some predicate A is consistent, then it is equivalent to circumscribing A.

The CWA is generalized by Minker in "On indefinite databases and the closed world assumption." Minker notices that it is possible to split non-Horn databases into disjunctions of Horn databases, and that the CWA can then be applied to each of the resulting disjuncts. Minker defines the generalized closed-world assumption (GCWA) as entailing those sentences that are entailed by *all* the individual applications of the CWA. We see from this that the GCWA is cautious, in the sense of Section 1.4.3 of the introduction. Minker's ideas are pushed still further by Gelfond and Przymusinska in [Gelfond, 1987]; Yahya and Henschen also discuss the GCWA in [Yahya, Henschen, 1985].

The other two papers in this section deal with the related issue of negation as failure. The first of the papers is Clark's original "Negation as failure," which introduces the ideas. The problem is that Clark is interpreting negation as the failure of a specific inference procedure (a resolution algorithm, in this case), and this makes it difficult to interpret the results formally.[1] The principal result of the paper (which applies to Horn databases only) is that, if the proof procedure being used does not prove some sentence p, then p does not follow from the database, so $\neg p$ can be consistently assumed.

A similarly procedural approach is taken by many of the other papers describing negation as failure, and they have for this reason been omitted from this collection. Shepherdson describes negation as failure via an implementation [Shepherdson, 1984], and in terms of intuitionistic logic [Shepherdson, 1985].

More satisfactory from a formal point of view is Lifschitz' paper, "On the declarative semantics of logic programs with negation." Lifschitz begins by showing that, if a logic program is *stratified* (this term is defined in Section 1.4.2 of the introduction), its semantics can be uniquely described using the notion of minimal models (Theorem 2). He then goes on to show (Theorem 3) that this minimization leads to a semantics identical to that obtained independently by Apt and colleagues [Apt, Blair, Walker, 1986] and by Van Gelder [Van Gelder, 1986].

[1] Clark argues, in fact, that this sort of an interpretation is necessary, because it potentially avoids the non-semidecidability of the problem.

ON CLOSED WORLD DATA BASES

Raymond Reiter

The University of British Columbia

Vancouver, British Columbia

ABSTRACT

Deductive question-answering systems generally evaluate queries under one of two possible assumptions which we in this paper refer to as the open and closed world assumptions. The open world assumption corresponds to the usual first order approach to query evaluation: Given a data base DB and a query Q, the only answers to Q are those which obtain from proofs of Q given DB as hypotheses. Under the closed world assumption, certain answers are admitted as a result of failure to find a proof. More specifically, if no proof of a positive ground literal exists, then the negation of that literal is assumed true.

In this paper, we show that closed world evaluation of an arbitrary query may be reduced to open world evaluation of so-called atomic queries. We then show that the closed world assumption can lead to inconsistencies, but for Horn data bases no such inconsistencies can arise. Finally, we show how for Horn data bases under the closed world assumption purely negative clauses are irrelevant for deductive retrieval and function instead as integrity constraints.

INTRODUCTION

Deductive question-answering systems generally evaluate queries under one of two possible assumptions which we in this paper refer to as the open and closed world assumptions. The open world assumption corresponds to the usual first order approach to query evaluation: Given a data base DB and a query Q, the only answers to Q are those which obtain from proofs of Q given DB as hypotheses. Under the closed world assumption, certain answers are admitted as a result of <u>failure</u> to find a proof. More specifically, if no proof of a positive ground literal exists, then the negation of that literal is assumed true. This can be viewed as equivalent to implicitly augmenting the given data base with all such negated literals.

For many domains of application, closed world query evaluation is appropriate since, in such domains, it is natural to explicitly represent only positive knowledge and to assume the truth of negative facts by default. For example, in an airline data base, all flights and the cities which they connect will be explicitly represented. Failure to find an entry indicating that Air Canada flight 103 connects Vancouver with Toulouse permits one to conclude that it does not.

This paper is concerned with closed world query evaluation and its relationship to open world evaluation. In the section, Data Bases and Queries, we define a query language and the notion of an open world answer to a query. The section called The Closed World Assumption formally defines the notion of a closed world answer. The section, Query Evaluation Under the CWA, shows how closed world query evaluation may be decomposed into open world evaluation of so-called "atomic queries" in conjunction with the set operations of intersection, union and difference, and the relational algebra operation of projection. In the section, On Data Bases Consistent with the CWA, we show that the closed world assumption can lead to inconsistencies. We prove, moreover, that for Horn data bases no such inconsistencies can arise. Also, for Horn data bases, the occurrence of purely negative clauses is irrelevant to closed world query evaluation. By removing such negative clauses one is left with so-called definite data bases which are then consistent under both the open and closed world assumptions. Finally, in the section, The CWA and Data Base Integrity, we show that these purely negative clauses, although irrelevant to deductive retrieval, have a function in maintaining data base integrity.

In order to preserve continuity we have relegated all proofs of the results in the main body of this paper to an appendix.

DATA BASES AND QUERIES

The query language of this paper is set oriented, i.e. we seek all objects (or tuples of objects) having a given property. For example, in an airline data base the request "Give all flights and their carriers which fly from Boston to England" might be represented in our query language by:

$$< x/Flight,\ y/Airline \mid (Ez/City) Connect\ x,Boston,z \wedge Owns\ y,x \wedge City\text{-}of\ z,England >$$

which denotes the set of all ordered pairs (x,y) such that x is a flight, y is an airline and

$$(Ez/City) Connect\ x,Boston,z \wedge Owns\ y,x \wedge City\text{-}of\ z,England$$

is true. The syntactic objects Flight, Airline and City are called types and serve to restrict the variables associated with them to range over objects of that type. Thus, (Ez/City) may be read as "There is a z which is a city".

Formally, all queries have the form

$$< x_1/\tau_1,\ldots,x_n/\tau_n \mid (Ey_1/\theta_1)\ldots(Ey_m/\theta_m) W(x_1,\ldots,x_n,y_1,\ldots,y_m) >$$

where $W(x_1,\ldots,x_n,y_1,\ldots,y_m)$ is a quantifier-free formula with free variables $x_1,\ldots,x_n,y_1,\ldots,y_m$ and moreover W contains no function signs. For brevity we shall often denote a typical such query by $< \vec{x}/\vec{\tau} \mid (E\vec{y}/\vec{\theta})W >$. The τ's and θ's are called <u>types</u>. We assume that with each type τ is associated a set of constant signs which we denote by $|\tau|$. For example, in an airline data base, |City| might be {Toronto, Boston, Paris,...,}. If $\vec{\tau} = \tau_1,\ldots,\tau_n$ is a sequence of types we denote by $|\vec{\tau}|$ the set $|\tau_1| \times \ldots \times |\tau_n|$.

A <u>data base</u> (DB) is a set of clauses containing no function signs. For an airline data base, DB might contain such information as:

"Air Canada flight 203 connects Toronto and Vancouver."

Connect AC203, Toronto, Vancouver

"All flights from Boston to Los Angeles serve meals."

$$(x/Flight) Connect\ x,Boston,LA \supset Meal\text{-}serve\ x$$

Let $Q = < \vec{x}/\vec{\tau} \mid (E\vec{y}/\vec{\theta})W(\vec{x},\vec{y}) >$ and let DB be a data base. A set of n-tuples of constant signs $\{\vec{c}^{(1)},\ldots,\vec{c}^{(r)}\}$ is an <u>answer</u> to Q (with respect to DB) iff

1. $\vec{c}^{(i)} \in |\vec{\tau}|$ $i = 1,\ldots,r$ and

2. $DB \vdash \bigvee_{i \le r} (E\vec{y}/\vec{\theta})W(\vec{c}^{(i)},\vec{y})$

Notice that if $\{\vec{c}^{(1)},\ldots,\vec{c}^{(r)}\}$ is an answer to Q, and $\vec{c}$ is any n-tuple of constant signs satisfying 1. then so also is $\{\vec{c}^{(1)},\ldots,\vec{c}^{(r)},\vec{c}\}$ an answer to Q. This suggests the need for the following definitions:

An answer A to Q is <u>minimal</u> iff no proper subset of A is an answer to Q. If A is a minimal answer to Q, then if A consists of a single n-tuple, A is a <u>definite</u> answer to Q. Otherwise, A is an <u>indefinite</u> answer to Q. Finally define $\|Q\|_{OWA}$ to be the set of minimal answers to Q. (For reasons which will become apparent later, the subscript OWA stands for "Open World Assumption".) Notice the interpretation assigned to an indefinite answer $\{\vec{c}^{(1)},\ldots,\vec{c}^{(r)}\}$ to Q: $\vec{x}$ is either $\vec{c}^{(1)}$ or $\vec{c}^{(2)}$ or...or $\vec{c}^{(r)}$ but there is no way, given the information in DB, of determining which. Instead of denoting an answer as a set of tuples $\{\vec{c}^{(1)},\ldots,\vec{c}^{(r)}\}$ we prefer the more suggestive notation $\vec{c}^{(1)} + \ldots + \vec{c}^{(r)}$, a notation we shall use in the remainder of this paper.

<u>Example 1.</u>

Suppose DB knows of 4 humans and 2 cities:

$$|Human| = \{a,b,c,d\} \quad |City| = \{B,V\}$$

Suppose further that everyone is either in B or in V:

$$(x/Human) Loc\ x,B \vee Loc\ x,V$$

and moreover, a is in B and b is in V:

$$Loc\ a,B \quad Loc\ b,V$$

Then for the query "Where is everybody?"

$$Q = < x/Human, y/City \mid Loc\ x,y >$$

we have

$$\|Q\|_{OWA} = \{(a,B),(b,V),(c,B) + (c,V),(d,B) + (d,V)\}$$

i.e. a is in B, b is in V, c is either in B or V and d is either in B or V.

Since it is beyond the scope of this paper, the reader is referred to Reiter [1977] or Reiter [1978] for an approach to query evaluation which returns $\|Q\|_{OWA}$ given any query Q.

THE CLOSED WORLD ASSUMPTION

In order to illustrate the central concept of this paper, we consider the following purely extensional data base (i.e., a data base consisting of ground literals only):

$|Teacher| = \{a,b,c,d\}$

$|Student| = \{A,B,C\}$

Teach	
a	A
b	B
c	C
a	B

Now consider the query: Who does not teach B?

$Q = < x/Teacher \mid \overline{Teach}\ x,B >$

By the definition of the previous section, we conclude, counter-intuitively, that

$\|Q\|_{OWA} = \phi$.

Intuitively, we want $\{c,d\}$ i.e. $|Teacher| - \| < x/Teacher|Teach\ x,B > \|_{OWA}$. The reason for the counterintuitive result is that first order logic interprets the DB literally; all the logic knows for certain is what is explicitly represented in the DB. Just because $\overline{Teach}\ c,B$ is not present in the DB is no reason to conclude that $\overline{Teach}\ c,B$ is true. Rather, as far as the logic is concerned, the truth of Teach c,B is unknown! Thus, we would also have to include the following facts about Teach:

$\overline{Teach}$	
a	C
b	A
b	C
c	A
c	B
d	A
d	B
d	C

Unfortunately, the number of negative facts about a given domain will, in general, far exceed the number of positive ones so that the requirement that all facts, both positive and negative, be explicitly represented may well be unfeasible. In the case of purely extensional data bases there is a ready solution to this problem. Merely explicitly represent positive facts. A negative fact is implicitly present provided its positive counterpart is not explicitly present. Notice, however, that by adopting this convention, we are making an assumption about our knowledge about the domain, namely, that we know everything about each predicate of the domain. There are no gaps in our knowledge. For example, if we were ignorant as to whether or not a teaches C, we could not permit the above implicit representation of negative facts. This is an important point. The implicit representation of negative facts presumes total knolwedge about the domain being represented. Fortunately, in most applications, such an assumption is warranted. We shall refer to this as the closed world assumption (CWA). Its opposite, the open world assumption (OWA), assumes only the information given in the data base and hence requires all facts, both positive and negative, to be explicitly represented. Under the OWA, "gaps" in one's knowledge about the domain are permitted.

Formally, we can define the notion of an answer to a query under the CWA as follows:

Let DB be an extensional data base and let $\overline{EDB} = \{\overline{P\vec{c}} \mid P$ is a predicate sign, $\vec{c}$ a tuple of constant signs and $P\vec{c} \notin DB\}$
Then $\vec{c}$ is a CWA answer to $< \vec{x}/\vec{\tau} \mid (E\vec{y}/\vec{\theta})W(\vec{x},\vec{y}) >$ (with respect to DB) iff

1. $\vec{c} \in |\vec{\tau}|$ and

2, $DB \cup \overline{EDB} \vdash (E\vec{y}/\vec{\theta})W(\vec{c},\vec{y})$

For purely extensional data bases, the CWA poses no difficulties. One merely imagines the DB to contain all negative facts each of which has no positive version in the DB. This conceptual view of the DB fails in the presence of non ground clauses. For if $P\vec{c} \notin DB$, it may nevertheless be possible to infer $P\vec{c}$ from the DB, so that we cannot, with impunity, imagine $\overline{P\vec{c}} \in DB$. The obvious generalization is to assume that the DB implicitly contains $\overline{P\vec{c}}$ whenever it is not the case that $DB \vdash P\vec{c}$.

Formally, we can define the notion of an answer to a query under the CWA for an arbitrary data base DB as follows:

Let

$\overline{EDB} = \{\overline{P\vec{c}} \mid P$ is a predicate sign, $\vec{c}$ a tuple of constant signs and $DB \nvdash P\vec{c}\ \}$

Then $\vec{c}^{(1)} + \ldots + \vec{c}^{(r)}$ is a CWA answer to

$< \vec{x}/\vec{\tau} \mid (E\vec{y}/\vec{\theta})W(\vec{x},\vec{y}) >$ (with respect to DB) iff

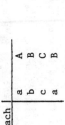

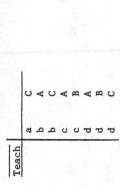

1. $\vec{c}^{(i)} \in |\vec{\tau}|$ i=1,...,r and

2. $DB \cup \overline{EDB} \vdash \bigvee_{i \le r} (E\vec{y}/\vec{\theta})W(\vec{c}^{(i)},\vec{y})$

This definition should be compared with the definition of an answer in the previous section. We shall refer to this latter notion as an OWA answer. As under the OWA, we shall require the notions of minimal, indefinite and definite CWA answers. If Q is a query, we shall denote the set of minimal CWA answers to Q by $||Q||_{CWA}$.

Example 2.

We consider a fragment of an inventory data base.

1. Every supplier of a part supplies all its subparts.

   (x/Supplier)(yz/Part)Supplies x,y ∧ Subpart z,y ⊃ Supplies x,z

2. Foobar Inc. supplies all widgets.

   (x/Widget)Supplies Foobar,x

3. The subpart relation is transitive.

   (xyz/Part)Subpart z,y ∧ Subpart y,x ⊃ Subpart z,x

Assume the following type extensions:

$|Supplier|$ = {Acme, Foobar, AAA}

$|Widget| = \{w_1, w_2, w_3, w_4\}$

$|Part| = \{p_1, p_2, p_3, w_1, w_2, w_3, w_4\}$

Finally, assume the following extensional data base:

Supplies	x	y
	Acme	p_1
	AAA	w_3
	AAA	w_4

Subpart	x	y
	p_2	p_1
	p_3	p_2
	w_1	p_1
	w_2	w_1

Then $\overline{EDB}$ is:

$\overline{Supplies}$	x	y
	Acme	w_3
	Acme	w_4
	AAA	p_1
	AAA	p_2
	AAA	p_3
	AAA	w_1
	AAA	w_2
	Foobar	p_1
	Foobar	p_2
	Foobar	p_3
	p_1	Acme
	p_1	AAA
	p_1	Foobar
	p_1	p_1
	p_1	p_2
	p_1	p_3
	p_1	w_1
	etc.	

$\overline{Subpart}$	x	y
	p_1	p_1
	p_1	p_2
	p_1	p_3
	p_1	w_1
	p_1	w_2
	p_1	w_3
	p_1	w_4
	p_2	p_2
	p_2	p_3
	p_2	w_1
	p_2	w_2
	p_2	w_3
	p_2	w_4
	p_3	p_3
	p_3	w_1
	p_3	w_2
	p_3	w_3
	p_3	w_4
	etc.	

The notion of a CWA answer is obviously intimately related to the negation operators of PLANNER (Hewitt [1972]) and PROLOG (Roussel [1975]) since in these languages, negation means "not provable" and the definition of $\overline{EDB}$ critically depends upon this notion. Clark [1978] investigates the relation between this notion of negation as failure and its truth functional semantics. The need for the CWA in deductive question-answering systems has been articulated in Nicolas and Syre [1974].

Notice that under the CWA, there can be no "gaps" in our knowledge about the domain. More formally, for each predicate sign P and each tuple of constant signs $\vec{c}$, either $DB \vdash P\vec{c}$ or $\overline{EDB} \vdash \overline{P\vec{c}}$ and since, under the CWA the data base is taken to be $DB \cup \overline{EDB}$, we can always infer either $P\vec{c}$ or $\overline{P\vec{c}}$ from $DB \cup \overline{EDB}$. Since there are no "knowledge gaps" under the CWA, it should be intuitively clear that indefinite CWA answers cannot arise, i.e. each minimal CWA answer to a query is of the form $\vec{c}$. The following result confirms this intuition.

Theorem 1.

Let $Q = < \vec{x}/\vec{\tau} | (E\vec{y}/\vec{\theta})W(\vec{x},\vec{y})>$. Then every minimal CWA answer to Q is definite.

There is one obvious difficulty in directly applying the definition of a CWA answer to the evaluation of queries. The definition requires that we explicitly know $\overline{EDB}$ and, as Example 2 demonstrates, the determination of $\overline{EDB}$ is generally non trivial.

In any event, for non toy domains, $\overline{EDB}$ would be so large that its explicit representation would be totally unfeasible. Fortunately, as we shall <u>see</u> in the next section, there is no need to know the elements of $\overline{EDB}$ i.e. it is possible to determine the set of closed world answers to an arbitrary query Q by appealing only to the given data base DB.

QUERY EVALUATION UNDER THE CWA

It turns out that the CWA admits a number of significant simplifications in the query evaluation process. The simplest of these permits the elimination of the logical connectives $\wedge$ and $\vee$ in favour of set intersection and union respectively, as follows:

<u>Theorem 2.</u>

1. $\| < \vec{x}/\vec{\tau} \,|\, (E\vec{y}/\vec{\theta})(W_1 \vee W_2) > \|_{CWA} = \| < \vec{x}/\vec{\tau} \,|\, (E\vec{y}/\vec{\theta})W_1 > \|_{CWA} \cup \| < \vec{x}/\vec{\tau} \,|\, (E\vec{y}/\vec{\theta})W_2 > \|_{CWA}$

2. $\| < \vec{x}/\vec{\tau} \,|\, W_1 \wedge W_2 > \|_{CWA} = \| < \vec{x}/\vec{\tau} \,|\, W_1 > \|_{CWA} \cap \| < \vec{x}/\vec{\tau} \,|\, W_2 > \|_{CWA}$

Notice that in the identity 2, the query must be quantifier free. Notice also that the identities of Theorem 2 fail under the OWA. To see why, consider the following:

<u>Example 3</u>

$|\tau| = \{a\}$

DB: Pa $\vee$ Ra

$Q = < x/\tau \,|\, Px \vee Rx >$

$\|Q\|_{OWA} = \{a\}$

but

$\| < x/\tau \,|\, Px > \|_{OWA} = \| < x/\tau \,|\, Rx > \|_{OWA} = \phi$

<u>Example 4</u> .

$|\tau| = \{a,b\}$

DB: Pa $\vee$ Pb, Ra, Rb

$Q = < x/\tau \,|\, Px \wedge Rx >$

$\|Q\|_{OWA} = \{a+b\}$

but

$\| < x/\tau \,|\, Px > \|_{OWA} = \{a+b\}$

$\| < x/\tau \,|\, Rx > \|_{OWA} = \{a,b\}$

One might also expect that all occurrences of negation can be eliminated in favour of set difference for CWA query evaluation. This is indeed the case, but only for quantifier free queries and then only when DB $\cup$ $\overline{EDB}$ is consistent.

<u>Theorem 3.</u>

If W, W_1 and W_2 are quantifier free, and DB $\cup$ $\overline{EDB}$ is consistent, then

1. $\| < \vec{x}/\vec{\tau} \,|\, \overline{W} > \|_{CWA} = |\vec{\tau}| - \| < \vec{x}/\vec{\tau} \,|\, W > \|_{CWA}$

2. $\| < \vec{x}/\vec{\tau} \,|\, W_1 \wedge \overline{W}_2 > \|_{CWA} = \| < \vec{x}/\vec{\tau} \,|\, W_1 > \|_{CWA} - \| < \vec{x}/\vec{\tau} \,|\, W_2 > \|_{CWA}$

To see why Theorem 3 fails for quantified queries, consider the following:

<u>Example 5</u>

$|\tau| = \{a,b\}$

DB: Pa,a

Then $\overline{EDB} = \{\overline{P}a,b,\ \overline{P}b,a,\ \overline{P}b,b\}$

Let $Q(P) = < x/\tau \,|\, (Ey/\tau)Px,y >$

$Q(\overline{P}) = < x/\tau \,|\, (Ey/\tau)\overline{P}x,y >$

Then $\| Q(P) \|_{CWA} = \{a\}$

$\| Q(\overline{P}) \|_{CWA} = \{a,b\} \neq |\tau| - \|Q(P)\|_{CWA}$

Notice also that Theorem 3 fails under the OWA.

By an <u>atomic query</u> we mean any query of the form $< \vec{x}/\vec{\tau} \,|\, (E\vec{y}/\vec{\theta})Pt_1,\ldots,t_n >$ where P is a predicate sign and each t is a constant sign, an x, or a y.

Theorems 2 and 3 assure us that for quantifier free queries, CWA query evaluation can be reduced to the Boolean operations of set intersection union and difference applied to atomic queries. However, we can deal with quantified queries by introducing the following projection operator (Codd [1972]):

Let $Q = \langle \vec{x}/\vec{\tau}, z/\psi | W \rangle$ where W is a possibly existentially quantified formula, and $\vec{x}$ is the n-tuple $x_1, \ldots, x_n$. Then $\|Q\|_{CWA}$ is a set of (n+1)-tuples, and the projection of $\|Q\|_{CWA}$ with respect to z, $\pi_z \|Q\|_{CWA}$, is the set of n-tuples obtained from $\|Q\|_{CWA}$ by deleting the (n+1)st component from each (n+1)-tuple of $\|Q\|_{CWA}$. For example, if $Q = \langle x_1/\tau_1, x_2/\tau_2, z/\psi | W \rangle$ and if

$$\|Q\|_{CWA} = \{(a,b,c),(a,b,d),(c,a,b)\}$$

then

$$\pi_z \|Q\|_{CWA} = \{(a,b),(c,a)\}$$

Theorem 4.

$$\|\langle \vec{x}/\vec{\tau} | (E\vec{y}/\vec{\theta})W \rangle\|_{CWA} = \pi_{\vec{y}} \|\langle \vec{x}/\vec{\tau}, \vec{y}/\vec{\theta} | W \rangle\|_{CWA}$$

where $\pi_{\vec{y}}$ denotes $\pi_{y_1}\pi_{y_2}\cdots\pi_{y_m}$

Corollary 4.1

1. $\|\langle \vec{x}/\vec{\tau} | (E\vec{y}/\vec{\theta})\overline{W} \rangle\|_{CWA} = \pi_{\vec{y}} \|\langle \vec{x}/\vec{\tau}, \vec{y}/\vec{\theta} | \overline{W} \rangle\|_{CWA}$

   $= \pi_{\vec{y}}(|\vec{\tau}| \times |\vec{\theta}| - \|\langle \vec{x}/\vec{\tau}, \vec{y}/\vec{\theta} | W \rangle\|_{CWA})$

2. $\|\langle \vec{x}/\vec{\tau} | (E\vec{y}/\vec{\theta})W_1 \wedge W_2 \rangle\|_{CWA} = \pi_{\vec{y}}(\|\langle \vec{x}/\vec{\tau}, \vec{y}/\vec{\theta} | W_1 \rangle\|_{CWA}$

   $\cap \|\langle \vec{x}/\vec{\tau}, \vec{y}/\vec{\theta} | W_2 \rangle\|_{CWA})$

Thus, in all cases, an existentially quantified query may be decomposed into atomic queries each of which is evaluated under the CWA. The resulting sets of answers are combined under set union, intersection and difference, but only after the projection operator is applied, if necessary.

Example 6.

$$\|\langle x/\tau | (Ey/\theta)Px,y \vee Qx,y\ \overline{R}x,y \rangle\|_{CWA}$$

$$= \|\langle x/\tau | (Ey/\theta)Px,y \rangle\|_{CWA} \cup \pi_y(\|\langle x/\tau, y/\theta | Qx,y \rangle\|_{CWA}$$

$$\cap \|\langle x/\tau, y/\theta | Rx,y \rangle\|_{CWA})$$

$$\|\langle x/\tau | PxQx \vee \overline{R}x \rangle\|_{CWA} = \|\langle x/\tau | Px \rangle\|_{CWA}$$

$$\cap \|\langle x/\tau | Qx \rangle\|_{CWA} \cup [|\tau| - \|\langle x/\tau | Rx \rangle\|_{CWA}]$$

$$\|\langle x/\tau | (Ey/\theta)Px,y \vee Qx,y\ \overline{R}x,y \rangle\|_{CWA}$$

$$= \|\langle x/\tau | (Ey/\theta)Px,y \rangle\|_{CWA} \cup \pi_y(\|\langle x/\tau, y/\theta | Qx,y \rangle\|_{CWA}$$

$$- \|\langle x/\tau, y/\theta | Rx,y \rangle\|_{CWA})$$

In view of the above results, we need consider CWA query evaluation only for atomic queries.

We shall say that DB is consistent with the CWA iff DB $\cup$ $\overline{EDB}$ is consistent.

Theorem 5.

Let Q be an atomic query. Then if DB is consistent with the CWA, $\|Q\|_{CWA} = \|Q\|_{OWA}$.

Theorem 5 is the principal result of this section. When coupled with Theorems 2 and 3 and the remarks following Corollary 4.1 it provides us with a complete characterization of the CWA answers to an arbitrary existential query Q in terms of the application of the operations of projection, set union, intersection and difference as applied to the OWA answers to atomic queries. In other words, CWA query evaluation has been reduced to OWA atomic query evaluation. A consequence of this result is that we need never know the elements of $\overline{EDB}$. CWA query evaluation appeals only to the given data base DB.

Example 7.

We consider the inventory data base of Example 2. Suppose the following query:

$$Q = \langle x/Supplier | (Ey/Widget)Supplies\ x,y \wedge Subpart\ y,p_1 \wedge \overline{Supplies}\ x,p_3 \rangle$$

Then

$$\|Q\|_{CWA} = \pi_y(\|Q_1\|_{OWA} \cap \|Q_2\|_{OWA}) \cap (|Supplier| - \|Q_3\|_{OWA})$$

where

$$Q_1 = \langle x/Supplier, y/Widget | Supplies\ x,y \rangle$$

$Q_2 = < x/\text{Supplier},\ y/\text{Widget} \mid \text{Subpart } y, p_1 >$

$Q_3 = < x/\text{Supplier} \mid \text{Supplies } x, p_3 >$

It is easy to see that

$$\|Q_1\|_{OWA} = \{(\text{Foobar},w_1),\ (\text{Foobar},w_2),\ (\text{Foobar},w_3),\ (\text{Foobar},w_4),\ (\text{AAA},w_3),\ (\text{AAA},w_4),\ (\text{Acme},w_1),\ (\text{Acme},w_2)\}$$

$$\|Q_2\|_{OWA} = \{(\text{Acme},w_1),\ (\text{Acme},w_2),\ (\text{AAA},w_1),\ (\text{AAA},w_2),\ (\text{Foobar},w_1),\ (\text{Foobar},w_2)\}$$

$$\|Q_3\|_{OWA} = \{\text{Acme}\}$$

whence

$$\pi_y(\|Q_1\|_{OWA} \cap \|Q_2\|_{OWA}) = \{\text{Foobar},\text{Acme}\}$$

and

$$|\text{Supplier}| - \|Q_3\|_{OWA} = \{\text{Foobar},\text{AAA}\}$$

Hence

$$\|Q\|_{CWA} = \{\text{Foobar}\}.$$

ON DATA BASES CONSISTENT WITH THE CWA

Not every consistent data base remains consistent under the CWA.

<u>Example 8.</u>

DB: Pa $\vee$ Pb

Then, since DB $\nvdash$ Pa and Db $\nvdash$ Pb , $\overline{EDB} = \{\overline{Pa}, \overline{Pb}\}$ so that DB $\cup$ $\overline{EDB}$ is inconsistent.

Given this observation, it is natural to seek a characterization of those data bases which remain consistent under the CWA. Although we know of no such characterization, it is possible to give a sufficient condition for CWA consistency which encompasses a large natural class of data bases, namely the Horn data bases. (A data base is <u>Horn</u> iff every clause is Horn i.e. contains at most one positive literal. The data base of Example 2 is Horn.)

<u>Theorem 6</u>

Suppose DB is Horn, and consistent. Then DB $\cup$ $\overline{EDB}$ is consistent i.e., DB is consistent with the CWA.

Following van Emden [1977] we shall refer to a Horn clause with exactly one positive literal as a <u>definite clause</u>. If DB is Horn, let Δ(DB) be obtained from DB by removing all non definite clauses i.e., all negative clauses. The following Theorem demonstrates the central importance of these concepts:

<u>Theorem 7</u>

If $Q = < \vec{x}/\vec{\tau} \mid (E\vec{y}/\vec{\theta})W >$ and DB is Horn and consistent, then $\|Q\|_{CWA}$ when evaluated with respect to DB yields the same set of answers as when evaluated with respect to Δ(DB). In other words, negative clauses in DB have no influence on CWA query evaluation.

Theorem 7 allows us, when given a consistent Horn DB, to discard all its negative clauses without affecting CWA query evaluation. Theorem 7 fails for non Horn DBs, as the following example demonstrates:

<u>Example 9</u>

DB: $\overline{Pa} \vee \overline{Ra}$, Ra $\vee$ Sa, Pa

Then DB $\vdash$ Sa

But Δ(DB) = {Ra $\vee$ Sa, Pa} and Δ(DB) $\nvdash$ Sa.

Let us call a data base for which all clauses are definite a <u>definite data base</u>.

<u>Theorem 8</u>

If DB is definite then DB is consistent.

<u>Corollary 8.1</u>

If DB is definite then

(i) DB is consistent

(ii) DB is consistent with the CWA.

Corollary 8.1 is a central result. It guarantees data base and CWA consistency for a large and natural class of data bases. Since the data base of Example 2 is definite we are assured that it is consistent with the CWA.

In van Emden [1977], he addresses, from a semantic point of view, the issues of data base consistency under the CWA. He defines the notion of a "minimal model" for a data base as the intersection of all its models. If this minimal model is itself a model of the data base, then the data base is consistent with the CWA. Van Emden goes on to point out some intriguing connections between minimal models and Scott's minimal fixpoint approach to the theory of computation, results which are elaborated in van Emden and Kowalski [1976].

THE CWA AND DATA BASE INTEGRITY

Theorem 7 has an interesting consequence with respect to data base integrity. In a first order data base, both intensional and extensional facts may serve a dual purpose. They can be used for deductive retrieval, or they can function as integrity constraints. In this latter capacity they are used to detect inconsistencies whenever the data base is modified. For example, if the data base is updated with a new fact then logical consequences of this fact can be derived using the entire data base. If these consequences lead to an inconsistency, the update will be rejected.

In general, it is not clear whether a given fact in a data base functions exclusively as an integrity constraint, or for deductive retrieval, or both (Nicolas and Gallaire [1978]). However, if the data base is both Horn and closed world, Theorem 7 tells us that purely negative clauses can function only as integrity constraints. Thus the CWA induces a partition of a Horn data base into negative and non-negative clauses. The latter are used only for deductive retrieval. Both are used for enforcing integrity.

SUMMARY

We have introduced the notion of the closed world assumption for deductive question-answering. This says, in effect, "Every positive statement that you don't know to be true may be assumed false". We have then shown how query evaluation under the closed world assumption reduces to the usual first order proof theoretic approach to query evaluation as applied to atomic queries. Finally, we have shown that consistent Horn data bases remain consistent under the closed world assumption and that definite data bases are consistent with the closed world assumption.

ACKNOWLEDGMENT

This paper was written with the financial support of the National Research Council of Canada under grant A7642. Much of this research was done while the author was visiting at Bolt, Beranek and Newman, Inc., Cambridge, Mass. I wish to thank Craig Bishop for his careful criticism of an earlier draft of this paper.

APPENDIX

Proofs of Theorems

Theorem 1.

Let $Q = < \vec{x}/\vec{\tau} \mid (E\vec{y}/\vec{\theta})W(\vec{x},\vec{y}) >$. Then every minimal CWA to Q is definite.

The proof requires the following two lemmas:

Lemma 1

Let $W_1,\ldots,W_r$ be propositional formulae. Then

$DB \cup \overline{EDB} \vdash W_1 \vee \ldots \vee W_r$

iff $DB \cup \overline{EDB} \vdash W_i$ for some i.

Proof: The "only if" half is immediate.

With no loss in generality, assume that the set of W's is minimal, i.e., for no i do we have

$$DB \cup \overline{EDB} \vdash W_1 \vee \ldots \vee W_{i-1} \vee W_{i+1} \vee \ldots \vee W_r .$$

Suppose W_1 is represented in conjunctive normal form, i.e. as a conjunct of clauses. Let $C = L_1 \vee \ldots \vee L_m$ be a typical such clause. Then $DB \cup \overline{EDB} \vdash L_i$ or $DB \cup \overline{EDB} \vdash \overline{L}_i$, $i=1,\ldots,m$. Suppose the latter is the case for each i, $1 \le i \le m$. Then $DB \cup \overline{EDB} \vdash \overline{C}$ so that $DB \cup \overline{EDB} \vdash \overline{W}_1$. Since also $DB \cup \overline{EDB} \vdash W_1 \vee \ldots \vee W_r$, then $DB \cup \overline{EDB} \vdash W_2 \vee \ldots \vee W_r$ contradicting the assumption that the set of W's is minimal. Hence, for some i, $1 \le i \le m$, $DB \cup \overline{EDB} \vdash L_i$ so that $DB \cup \overline{EDB} \vdash C$. Since C was an arbitrary clause of W_1, $DB \cup \overline{EDB} \vdash W_1$ which establishes the lemma.

Lemma 2

$DB \cup \overline{EDB} \vdash (E\vec{y}/\vec{\theta})W(\vec{y})$ iff there is a tuple $\vec{d} \in |\vec{\theta}|$ such that $DB \cup \overline{EDB} \vdash W(\vec{d})$.

Proof: The "only if" half is immediate.

Since $DB \cup \overline{EDB} \vdash (E\vec{y}/\vec{\theta})W(\vec{y})$ then for tuples $\vec{d}^{(1)},\ldots,\vec{d}^{(r)} \in |\vec{\theta}|$

$$DB \cup \overline{EDB} \vdash \bigvee_{i \le r} W(\vec{d}^{(i)})$$

The result now follows by Lemma 1.

Proof of Theorem 1:

Suppose, to the contrary, that for $m \geq 2$, $\vec{c}^{(1)} + \ldots + \vec{c}^{(m)}$ is a minimal CWA answer to Q. Then

$$DB \cup \overline{EDB} \vdash \bigvee_{i \leq m} (E\vec{y}/\vec{\theta}) W(\vec{c}^{(i)}, \vec{y})$$

i.e.,

$$DB \cup \overline{EDB} \vdash (E\vec{y}/\vec{\theta}) \bigvee_{i \leq m} W(\vec{c}^{(i)}, \vec{y})$$

so by Lemma 2 there is a tuple $\vec{d} \in |\vec{\theta}|$ such that

$$DB \cup \overline{EDB} \vdash \bigvee_{i \leq m} W(\vec{c}^{(i)}, \vec{d})$$

By Lemma 1, $DB \cup \overline{EDB} \vdash W(\vec{c}^{(i)}, \vec{d})$ for some i whence $\vec{c}^{(i)}$ is an answer to Q, contradicting the assumed indefiniteness of $\vec{c}^{(1)} + \ldots + \vec{c}^{(m)}$.

<u>Theorem 2.</u>

1. $\| < \vec{x}/\vec{\tau} \,|\, (E\vec{y}/\vec{\theta})(W_1 \vee W_2) > \|_{CWA} = \| < \vec{x}/\vec{\tau} \,|\, (E\vec{y}/\vec{\theta}) W_1 > \|_{CWA} \cup \| < \vec{x}/\vec{\tau} \,|\, (E\vec{y}/\vec{\theta}) W_2 > \|_{CWA}$

2. $\| < \vec{x}/\vec{\tau} \,|\, W_1 \wedge W_2 > \|_{CWA} = \| < \vec{x}/\vec{\tau} \,|\, W_1 > \|_{CWA} \cap \| < x/\tau \,|\, W_2 > \|_{CWA}$

Proof: 1. follows from Lemmas 1 and 2 and Theorem 1. The proof of 2. is immediate from Theorem 1.

<u>Theorem 3.</u>

If W, W_1 and W_2 are quantifier free, and $DB \cup \overline{EDB}$ is consistent, then

1. $\| < \vec{x}/\vec{\tau} \,|\, \overline{W} > \|_{CWA} = |\vec{\tau}| - \| < \vec{x}/\vec{\tau} \,|\, W > \|_{CWA}$
2. $\| < \vec{x}/\vec{\tau} \,|\, W_1 \wedge \overline{W}_2 > \|_{CWA} = \| < \vec{x}/\vec{\tau} \,|\, W_1 > \|_{CWA} - \| < \vec{x}/\vec{\tau} \,|\, W_2 > \|_{CWA}$

Proof: 1. The proof is by structural induction on W. Denote $\| < \vec{x}/\vec{\tau} \,|\, W > \|_{CWA}$ by Q(W).

We must prove

$$Q(\overline{W}) = |\vec{\tau}| - Q(W).$$

<u>Case 1:</u> W is $Pt_1, \ldots, t_m$ where P is a predicate sign and $t_1, \ldots, t_m$ are terms.

Suppose $\vec{c} \in Q(\overline{W})$. Let $\Pi(\vec{c})$ be $Pt_1, \ldots, t_m$ with all occurrences of x_i replaced by c_i. Then $DB \cup \overline{EDB} \vdash \overline{\Pi}(\vec{c})$. Since $DB \cup \overline{EDB}$ is consistent, $DB \cup \overline{EDB} \nvdash \Pi(\vec{c})$, i.e. $\vec{c} \notin Q(W)$. Since $\vec{c} \in |\vec{\tau}|$, then $\vec{c} \in |\vec{\tau}| - Q(W)$, so that $Q(\overline{W}) \subseteq |\vec{\tau}| - Q(W)$. Now suppose $\vec{c} \in |\vec{\tau}| - Q(W)$. Then $\vec{c} \notin Q(W)$ so $DB \cup \overline{EDB} \nvdash \Pi(\vec{c})$. But then $DB \cup \overline{EDB} \vdash \overline{\Pi}(\vec{c})$, and since $\vec{c} \in |\vec{\tau}|$, then $\vec{c} \in Q(\overline{W})$, so that $|\vec{\tau}| - Q(W) \subseteq Q(\overline{W})$.

<u>Case 2:</u> W is $U_1 \wedge U_2$.

Assume, for i=1,2 that $Q(\overline{U}_i) = |\vec{\tau}| - Q(U_i)$.

Then
$$\begin{aligned} Q(\overline{W}) &= Q(\overline{U_1 \wedge U_2}) \\ &= Q(\overline{U}_1 \vee \overline{U}_2) \\ &= Q(\overline{U}_1) \cup Q(\overline{U}_2) \quad \text{by Theorem 2} \\ &= [|\vec{\tau}| - Q(U_1)] \cup [|\vec{\tau}| - Q(U_2)] \\ &= |\vec{\tau}| - [Q(U_1) \cap Q(U_2)] \\ &= |\vec{\tau}| - Q(U_1 \wedge U_2) \quad \text{by Theorem 2} \\ &= |\vec{\tau}| - Q(W) \end{aligned}$$

<u>Case 3:</u> W is $U_1 \vee U_2$.

The proof is the dual of Case 2.

<u>Case 4:</u> W is $\overline{U}$.

Assume that $Q(\overline{U}) = |\vec{\tau}| - Q(U)$. Since $Q(U) \subseteq |\vec{\tau}|$, it follows that $Q(U) = |\vec{\tau}| - Q(\overline{U})$. i.e. $Q(\overline{W}) = |\vec{\tau}| - Q(W)$.

$$\begin{aligned} Q(W_1 \wedge \overline{W}_2) &= Q(W_1) \cap Q(\overline{W}_2) \quad \text{by Theorem 2} \\ &= Q(W_1) \cap [|\vec{\tau}| - Q(W_2)] \text{ by 1.} \\ &= Q(W_1) - Q(W_2) \quad \text{since } Q(W_1) \subseteq |\vec{\tau}|. \end{aligned}$$

<u>Theorem 4.</u>

$$\| < \vec{x}/\vec{\tau} \,|\, (E\vec{y}/\vec{\theta}) W(\vec{x}, \vec{y}) > \|_{CWA} = \pi_{\vec{y}} \| < \vec{x}/\vec{\tau}, \vec{y}/\vec{\theta} \,|\, W(\vec{x}, \vec{y}) > \|_{CWA}$$

where $\pi_{\vec{y}}$ denotes $\pi_{y_1} \pi_{y_2} \ldots \pi_{y_m}$

Proof:

Suppose $\vec{c} \in \| < \vec{x}/\vec{\tau} | (E\vec{y}/\vec{\theta}) W(\vec{x},\vec{y}) > \|_{CWA}$

Then by definition

$DB \cup \overline{EDB} \vdash (E\vec{y}/\vec{\theta}) W(\vec{c},\vec{y})$

whence by Lemma 2 there is a tuple $\vec{d} \in |\vec{\theta}|$ such that

$DB \cup \overline{EDB} \vdash W(\vec{c},\vec{d})$

i.e., $\vec{c},\vec{d} \in \| < \vec{x}/\vec{\tau}, \vec{y}/\vec{\theta} | W(\vec{x},\vec{y}) > \|_{CWA}$

i.e., $\vec{c} \in \Pi_{\vec{y}} \| < \vec{x}/\vec{\tau}, \vec{y}/\vec{\theta} | W(\vec{x},\vec{y}) > \|_{CWA}$

Now Suppose $\vec{c} \in \Pi_{\vec{y}} \| < \vec{x}/\vec{\tau}, \vec{y}/\vec{\theta} | W(\vec{x},\vec{y}) > \|_{CWA}$

Then for some tuple $\vec{d} \in |\vec{\theta}|$

$\vec{c},\vec{d} \in \| < \vec{x}/\vec{\tau}, \vec{y}/\vec{\theta} | W(\vec{x},\vec{y}) > \|_{CWA}$

so that $DB \cup \overline{EDB} \vdash W(\vec{c},\vec{d})$

i.e., $DB \cup \overline{EDB} \vdash (E\vec{y}/\vec{\theta}) W(\vec{c},\vec{y})$

i.e. $\vec{c} \in \| < \vec{x}/\vec{\tau} | (E\vec{y}/\vec{\theta}) W(\vec{x},\vec{y}) > \|_{CWA}$

Theorem 5.

Let Q be an atomic query. Then if DB is consistent with the CWA, $\|Q\|_{CWA} = \|Q\|_{OWA}$

Proof: The proof requires the following:

Lemma 3

If DB is consistent with the CWA then every atomic query has only definite OWA answers.

Proof:

Let $Q = < \vec{x}/\vec{\tau} | (E\vec{y}/\vec{\theta}) P(\vec{x},\vec{y}) >$ be an atomic query where $P(\vec{x},\vec{y})$ is a positive literal. Suppose, on the contrary, that Q has an indefinite OWA answer $\vec{c}^{(1)} + \ldots + \vec{c}^{(m)}$ for $m \geq 2$. Then

$$DB \vdash \bigvee_{i \leq m} (E\vec{y}/\vec{\theta}) P(\vec{c}^{(i)},\vec{y}) \qquad (1)$$

and for no i, $1 \leq i \leq m$, is it the case that $DB \vdash (E\vec{y}/\vec{\theta}) P(\vec{c}^{(i)},\vec{y})$.

Hence, for all $\vec{d} \in |\vec{\theta}|$, $DB \not\vdash P(\vec{c}^{(i)},\vec{d})$ i=1,...,m.

Thus $\overline{P}(\vec{c}^{(i)},\vec{d}) \in \overline{EDB}$ for all $\vec{d} \in |\vec{\theta}|$, i=1,...,m.

Hence, $DB \cup \overline{EDB} \vdash \overline{P}(\vec{c}^{(i)},\vec{d})$ for all $\vec{d} \in |\vec{\theta}|$, i=1,...,m and from (1), $DB \cup \overline{EDB} \vdash \bigvee_{i \leq m} (E\vec{y}/\vec{\theta}) P(\vec{c}^{(i)},\vec{y})$

i.e. $DB \cup \overline{EDB}$ is inconsistent, contradiction.

Proof of Theorem 5:

Let $Q = < \vec{x}/\vec{\tau} | (E\vec{y}/\vec{\theta}) P(\vec{x},\vec{y}) >$ where $P(\vec{x},\vec{y})$ is a positive literal. By Lemma 3 $\|Q\|_{OWA}$ consists only of definite answers. Now

$\vec{c} \in \|Q\|_{OWA}$ iff $\vec{c} \in |\vec{\tau}|$ and $DB \vdash (E\vec{y}/\vec{\theta}) P(\vec{c},\vec{y})$
$\vec{c} \in \|Q\|_{CWA}$ iff $\vec{c} \in |\vec{\tau}|$ and $DB \cup \overline{EDB} \vdash (E\vec{y}/\vec{\theta}) P(\vec{c},\vec{y})$

Hence $\|Q\|_{OWA} \subseteq \|Q\|_{CWA}$.

We prove $\|Q\|_{CWA} \subseteq \|Q\|_{OWA}$. To that end, let $\vec{c} \in \|Q\|_{CWA}$. Then $DB \cup \overline{EDB} \vdash P(\vec{c},\vec{d})$ for some $\vec{d} \in |\vec{\theta}|$.

If $DB \vdash P(\vec{c},\vec{d})$, then $\vec{c} \in \|Q\|_{CWA}$ and we are done.

Otherwise, $DB \not\vdash P(\vec{c},\vec{d})$ so that $\overline{P}(\vec{c},\vec{d}) \in \overline{EDB}$

i.e. $DB \cup \overline{EDB} \vdash P(\vec{c},\vec{d})$ and $DB \cup \overline{EDB} \vdash \overline{P}(\vec{c},\vec{d})$

i.e. DB is inconsistent with the CWA, contradiction.

Theorem 6.

Suppose DB is Horn, and consistent. Then $DB \cup \overline{EDB}$ is consistent, i.e. DB is consistent with the CWA.

Proof: Suppose, on the contrary, that $DB \cup \overline{EDB}$ is inconsistent. Now a theorem of Henschen and Wos [1974] assures us that any inconsistent set of Horn clauses has a positive unit refutation by binary resolution in which one parent of each resolution operation is a positive unit. We shall assume this result, without proof, for typed resolution*. Then since $DB \cup \overline{EDB}$ is an inconsistent

*Because all variables are typed, the usual unification algorithm (Robinson [1965]) must be modified to enforce consistency of types. Resolvents are then formed using typed unification. For details, see (Reiter [1977]).

Horn set, it has such a (typed) positive unit refutation. Since all clauses of $\overline{EDB}$ are negative units, the only occurrence of a negative unit of $\overline{EDB}$ in this refutation can be as one of the parents in the final resolution operation yielding the empty clause. There must be such an occurrence of some $\overline{U} \in \overline{EDB}$, for otherwise $\overline{EDB}$ does not enter into the refutation in which case DB must be inconsistent. Hence, $DB \cup \{\overline{U}\}$ is unsatisfiable, i.e. $DB \vdash U$. But then $\overline{U}$ cannot be a member of $\overline{EDB}$, contradiction.

Theorem 7.

If $Q = \langle \vec{x}/\vec{\tau} \mid (E\vec{y}/\vec{\theta})W \rangle$ and DB is Horn and consistent, then $\|Q\|_{CWA}$ when evaluated with respect to DB yields the same set of answers as when evaluated with respect to $\Delta(DB)$. In other words, negative clauses in PB have no influence on CWA query evaluation.

Proof: By Theorems 2, 3, and 4 CWA query evaluation is reducible to OWA evaluation of atomic queries whenever DB is consistent. Hence, with no loss in generality, we can take Q to be an atomic query. Suppose then that $Q = \langle \vec{x}/\vec{\tau} \mid (E\vec{y}/\vec{\theta})P(\vec{x},\vec{y}) \rangle$, where $P(\vec{x},\vec{y})$ is a positive literal. Denote the value of $\|Q\|_{CWA}$ with respect to DB by $\|Q\|^{DB}_{CWA}$. Similarly, $\|Q\|^{\Delta(DB)}_{CWA}$, $\|Q\|^{DB}_{OWA}$, $\|Q\|^{\Delta(DB)}_{OWA}$. We must prove $\|Q\|^{DB}_{CWA} = \|Q\|^{\Delta(DB)}_{CWA}$. Since DB is consistent and Horn, so also is $\Delta(DB)$ so by Theorem 6, both DB and $\Delta(DB)$ are consistent with the CWA. Hence, by Theorem 5, it is sufficient to prove $\|Q\|^{DB}_{OWA} = \|Q\|^{\Delta(DB)}_{OWA}$. Clearly $\|Q\|^{\Delta(DB)}_{OWA} \subseteq \|Q\|^{DB}_{OWA}$ since $\Delta(DB) \subseteq DB$. We prove $\|Q\|^{DB}_{OWA} \subseteq \|Q\|^{\Delta(DB)}_{OWA}$. To that end, let $\vec{c} \in \|Q\|^{DB}_{OWA}$. Then $DB \vdash (E\vec{y}/\vec{\theta})P(\vec{c},\vec{y})$. Hence, as in the proof of Theorem 6, there is a (typed) positive unit refutation of $DB \cup \{\overline{P}(\vec{c},\vec{y})\}$. Since DB is Horn and consistent, $\overline{P}(\vec{c},\vec{y})$ enters into this refutation, and then only in the final resolution operation which yields the empty clause. Clearly, no negative clause other than $\overline{P}(\vec{c},\vec{y})$ can take part in this refutation i.e. only definite clauses of DB enter into the refutation. Hence we can construct the same refutation from $\Delta(DB) \cup \{\overline{P}(\vec{x},\vec{y})\}$ so that $\Delta(DB) \vdash P(\vec{c},\vec{y})$ i.e. $\vec{c} \in \|Q\|^{\Delta(DB)}_{OWA}$.

Theorem 8.

If DB is definite, then DB is consistent.

Proof: Every inconsistent set of clauses contains at least one negative clause.

REFERENCES

1. Clark, K.L. [1978] Negation as Failure, In *Logic and Data Bases* (H. Gallaire and J. Minker, Eds.), Plenum Press, New York, N.Y., 1978, 293-322.

2. Codd, E.F. [1972] Relational Completeness of Data Base Sublanguages, In *Data Base Systems* (R. Rustin, Ed.), Prentice-Hall, Englewood Cliffs, N.J., 1972, 65-98.

3. Henschen, L. and Wos, L. [1974] Unit Refutations and Horn Sets, *JACM 21*, 4 (October 1974), 590-605.

4. Hewitt, C. [1972] Description and Theoretical Analysis (Using Schemata) of PLANNER: A Language for Proving Theorems and Manipulating Models in a Robot, *AI Memo No. 251*, MIT Project MAC, Cambridge, Mass., April 1972.

5. Nicolas, J.M. and Gallaire, H. [1978] Data Bases: Theory vs. Interpretation, In *Logic and Data Bases* (H. Gallaire and J. Minker, Eds.), Plenum Press, New York, 1978, 33-54.

6. Nicolas, J. M. and Syre, J.C. [1974] Natural Question Answering and Automatic Deduction in the System Syntex, *Proceedings IFIP Congress 1974*, Stockholm, Sweden, August, 1974.

7. Reiter, R. [1977] An Approach to Deductive Question-Answering, *BBN Report No. 3649*, Bolt, Beranek and Newman, Inc., Cambridge, Mass., Sept. 1977.

8. Reiter, R. [1978] Deductive Question-Answering on Relational Data Bases, In *Logic and Data Bases* (H. Gallaire and J. Minker, Eds.), Plenum Press, New York, N.Y., 1978, 149-177.

9. Robinson, J. A. [1965] A Machine Oriented Logic Based on the Resolution Principle, *JACM 12*, (January 1965), 25-41.

10. Roussel, P. [1975] PROLOG: Manuel de Reference et d'Utilisation, Groupe d'Intelligence Artificielle, U.E.R. de Luminy, Universite d'Aix-Marseille, Sept. 1975.

11. van Emden, M. H. [1977] Computation and Deductive Information Retrieval, Dept. of Computer Science, University of Waterloo, Ont., Research Report CS-77-16, May 1977.

12. van Emden, M.H. and Kowalski, R.A. [1976] The Semantics of Predicate Logic as a Programming Language, *JACM 23*, (Oct. 1976), 733-742.

NEGATION AS FAILURE

Keith L. Clark

Department of Computer Science & Statistics

Queen Mary College, London, England

ABSTRACT

A query evaluation process for a logic data base comprising a set of clauses is described. It is essentially a Horn clause theorem prover augmented with a special inference rule for dealing with negation. This is the <u>negation as failure</u> inference rule whereby ~ P can be inferred if every possible proof of P <u>fails</u>. The chief advantage of the query evaluator described is the effeciency with which it can be implemented. Moreover, we show that the negation as failure rule only allows us to conclude negated facts that could be inferred from the axioms of the completed data base, a data base of relation definitions and equality schemas that we consider is implicitly given by the data base of clauses. We also show that when the clause data base and the queries satisfy certain constraints, which still leaves us with a data base more general than a conventional relational data base, the query evaluation process will find every answer that is a logical consequence of the completed data base.

INTRODUCTION

Following Kowalski [1978] and van Emden [1978] we consider a logic data base to comprise a set of clauses. The ground unit clauses are the extensional component of the data base. They provide us with a set of instances of the data base relations. The remaining clauses constitute the intensional component, they are the general rules of the data base. The general rules as well as the explicit 'data' are to be used in the deductive retrieval of information.

The shortcoming of such a data base is that, like a more conventional relational data base (Codd [1970]), it only contains information about <u>true</u> instances of relations. Even so, quite straightforward queries make use of negation, and can be answered only by showing that certain relation instances are <u>false</u>. Thus, to answer a request for the name of a student not taking a particular course, C, we need to find a student, S, such that Takes(S,C) is false. For his relational calculus (Codd [1972]), Codd's solution to the problem is to assume that a tuple is in the complement of the relation if it is not a given instance of the relation. For a logic data base, where a relation instance which is not explicitly given may still be implied by a general rule, the analogous assumption is that a relation instance is false if we <u>fail</u> to prove that it is true. The great advantage of such a 'solution to negation' is the ease with which it can be implemented. To show that P is <u>false</u> we do an exhaustive search for a proof of P. If every possible proof fails, ~ P is 'inferred'. This is the way that both PLANNER (Hewitt [1972]) and PROLOG (Roussel [1975], Warren et al. [1977]) handle negation.

What we have here is a proof rule:

$$\vdash \sim \vdash P \quad \text{infer} \quad \vdash \sim P$$

where the proof that P is not provable is always the exhaustive but unsuccessful search for a proof of P. Let us call it the <u>negation as failure</u> inference rule. For pragmatic reasons this is adopted as the sole inference rule for negated formulae. Is the consequence that we have given "~" a new meaning as "fail to prove", or can we perhaps reconcile negation, operationally understood as "fail to prove", with its truth functional semantics? In other words, can we interpret a failure proof of ~ P as a valid first order inference that P is false.

Note that to assume that a relation instance is false if it is not implied, is to assume that the data base gives <u>complete</u> information about the true instances of its relations. This is the closed world assumption referred to by Reiter [1978] and Nicolas and Gallaire [1978]. More precisely, it is the assumption that a relation instance is true <u>only if</u> it is given explicitly or else is implied by one of the <u>general</u> rules for the relation. Thus, let us suppose that the data base contains just two instances of the unary relation, Maths-course:

$$\begin{array}{l}\text{Maths-course(C101)}\leftarrow \\ \text{Maths-course(C301)}\leftarrow\end{array} \qquad (1)$$

and no general rules about this relation. For any course name C, different from C101 and C301, Maths-course(C) is not provable. But to conclude, in consequence, that Maths-course(C) is false, is to assume that C101 and C301 are the only Maths-courses, and that C is not an alternative name for either course. If we were to make these assumptions explicit we would need to add to our data base the completion law:

$$(\forall x)[\text{Maths-course}(x) \rightarrow x{=}C101 \lor x{=}C301] \quad (2)$$

and the inequality schemas:

$C101 \neq C$ for all names C different from C101
$C301 \neq C$ for all names C different from C301

Note that (1) and (2) are together equivalent to a definition

$$(\forall x)[\text{Maths-course}(x) \leftrightarrow x{=}C101 \lor x{=}C301]$$

of the Maths-course relation.

As we might expect, every negated fact ~ Maths-course(C) that we can 'infer' by showing that Maths-course(C) is not given, can now be proved by a first order deduction using the completion law and inequality schemas. More than that, the failure proof of Maths-course(C) and the first order deduction are structurally almost identical (see Figure 1). The alternatives of the failed proof space become explicit disjunctions in the first order deduction, match failures of the former become <u>false</u> equalities of the latter. Thus the failure proof is essentially a structural representation of a natural deduction style proof:

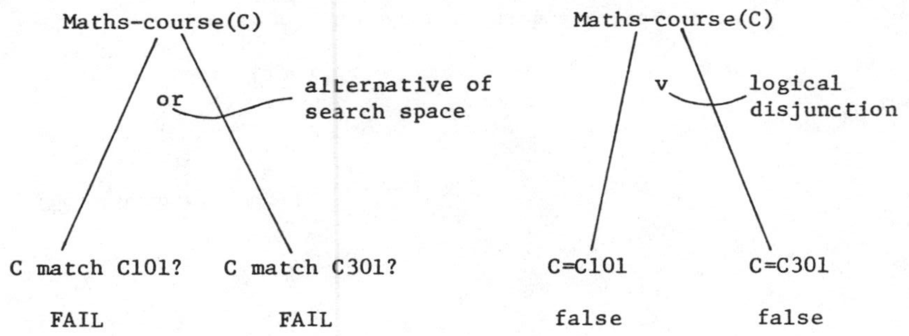

Figure 1. First Order Deduction

$$\text{Maths-course}(C) \leftrightarrow C{=}C101 \lor C{=}C301$$
$$\leftrightarrow \text{false} \lor \text{false}$$
$$\leftrightarrow \text{false}$$
$$\therefore \sim \text{Maths-course}(C)$$

This suggests a way of reconciling negation as failure with its truth functional semantics. We can assume that the clauses that appear in a logic data base B comprise just the if-halves of a set of if-and-only-if definitions of the data base relations, the only-if half of each definition being a completion law for the relation. The <u>completed</u> data base C(B), implicitly given by the clauses of B, comprises this set of definitions together with a set of equality schemas which make explicit the convention that different object names denote different objects. If we can show that every <u>failed</u> attempt to prove P using just the data base of clauses B, is in effect a proof of ~ P using the completed data base C(B), then 'negation as failure' is just a derived inference rule for deductions from C(B).

In this paper we present just such a validation of the negation as failure inference rule. The structure of the paper is as follows. In the next section, Query Evaluation for a Data Base of Clauses, we make precise what constitutes a data base of clauses, a data base query, and the deduction process of query evaluation. As we describe it, query evaluation is a non-deterministic process for which every evaluation path either succeeds, or fails, or does not terminate. A negated literal ~ P is evaluated by recursively entering the query evaluator with the query P. If every possible evaluation path for P ends in failure, we return with ~ P evaluated as true. These recursively constructed failure proofs can be nested to any depth.

In the section, Data Base Completion, we define the completion of a data base of clauses. Then in the section, Correctness of Query Evaluation, we give the formal results validating the use of the negation as failure inference rule. We prove that a query evaluation will only produce results that are implied by the completed data base. The proof is constructive. It gives us a method for reformulating a query evaluation from the data base of clauses as a deduction from the completed data base. In the last section, Completeness of Query Evaluation, we address the issue of the deductive completeness of the query evaluation process. That is, we deal with the issue of whether or not there are answers to a query implied by the completed data base which are not the answer of any evaluation of the query.

As a final word of introduction we should say something about the relationship between the negation as failure inference rule treated here and the deduction rules considered by Kramosil [1975]. Kramosil shows that the adoption of sound deduction rules of the form

$$\text{from} \quad \vdash A, \ \sim\vdash B \quad \text{infer} \quad \vdash C$$

which contain preconditions such as $\sim\vdash B$ about unprovability of certain formula, cannot extend the class of theorems that are derivable in a first order theory. There are two differences between the negation as failure rule

$$\text{from} \ \vdash \sim\vdash P \quad \text{infer} \ \vdash \sim P$$

and the rules to which Kramosil's result applies.

The first difference, which is not the major difference, is that the single rule that we consider has a definite and proscribed method for proving unprovability. It is, in fact, a relatively weak rule, for the unprovability condition is so strong. Kramosil leaves unspecified the means by which the unprovability of a formula would be determined.

The second, and crucial difference, is that his formal result applies only to inference rules that sit on top of a complete inference system for first order logic. However, the negation as failure inference rule sits on top of a resolution inference procedure which, without the rule, can only cope with Horn clause refutations. In other words, it is used to extend the deduction power of inference system that is <u>not</u> a complete deductive system for first order logic. We show that the enrichment of a Horn clause theorem prover with this inference rule is, at least when seeking answers to a query logically implied by the axioms of a completed data base, somewhat of an alternative to using a more conventional deductive system which is not restricted to Horn clauses.

QUERY EVALUATION FOR A DATA BASE OF CLAUSES

We assume a familiarity with the terminology of resolution logic (but see Chang and Lee [1973] for an introduction). The statements of the data base are a set of clauses each of which contains a distinguished positive literal. The relation of this literal is the relation that the clause is <u>about</u>. Using the notation of Kowalski [1978], the clauses are written as implications of the form

$$R(t_1,..,t_n) \leftarrow L_1 \& L_2 \& \ldots \& L_m \ , \ m \geq 0 \qquad (3)$$

Here, $R(t_1,\ldots,t_n)$ is the distinguished positive literal (so the clause is <u>about</u> the relation R), the $L_1,\ldots,L_m$ are all literals, and each free variable is implicitly universally quantified over the entire implication. In more conventional clause notation this would be written as the disjunction

$$R(t_1,\ldots,t_n) \vee \sim L_1 \vee \sim L_2 \vee .. \vee \sim L_m \qquad (4)$$

Note that any other positive literal of the disjunctive form (4) will appear as a negated precondition of the implication (3). When m=0, we have a unit clause.

Example Data Base

Table 1 gives the clauses of a micro logic data base. The unit clauses, which are all ground, are the explicitly given relation instances. The single non-unit clause is a general rule for the relation Non-maths-major. Since the variable y appears only in the antecedent of this clause we can read it as

> Anything x is a Non-maths-major if there is a Maths-course y which x does not take.

The functor "." is simply a data constructor, constructing a compound name "J.Brown" from the initial "J" and the surname "Brown". Every functor of a logic data base has this data constructor role. In logic parlance, the functors implicitly have their free or Herbrand interpretation. In our example data base, if we required to refer to the surname or initial of a name separately, we would include the general rules:

Initial(x.y,x)←
Surname(x.y,y)←

Table 1. Micro Data Base

Student(J.Brown)←	
	Takes(J.Brown,C101)←
Student(D.Smith)←	
	Takes(D.Smith,C101)←
	Takes(D.Smith,C301)←
Maths-course(C101)←	
Maths-course(C301)←	
Non-maths-major(x) ← Maths-course(y) & ~ Takes(x,y)	

Queries

A query is a conjunction of literals written as

$\leftarrow L_1 \& \ldots \& L_n$

If $x_1, \ldots, x_k$ are the variables appearing in the query we interpret this as a request for a constructive proof that

$(\exists x_1, \ldots, x_k)\ L_1 \& \ldots \& L_n$;

constructive in the sense that the proof should find a substitution

$\theta = \{x_1/e_1, x_2/e_2, \ldots, x_k/e_k\}$

such that

$(L_1 \& \ldots \& L_n)\theta$

is a logical consequence of the completed data base. θ is an answer to the query. For the time being we ignore the more general query which asks for the set of all answers.

Example Queries

The following are queries for the logic data base of Table 1.

(i) ←Student(x) & Takes(x,C101)

(ii) ←Student(x) & Non-maths-major(x)

(iii) ←Student(x) & ~ Non-maths-major(x)

The first is a request for the name of a student who takes course C101; the second is a request for a student who is a non-maths-major, for a student who does not take all the maths courses; in contrast the third is a request for a student who is <u>not</u> a non-maths-major, for a student who <u>does</u> take all the maths courses. In the relational calculus, or a more elaborate query notation, such a condition on the data to be retrieved would be expressed by the formula

(iv) ←Student(x) & ∀y[Maths-course(y) → Takes(x,y)]

in which the free variable x refers to the data to be retrieved. There is no reason why the user query language should not allow such general form queries. For, by the simple expedient of introducing clauses about auxiliary relations, we can translate such a query into our standard form of a conjunction of literals. Thus, the expression of query (iv) is equivalent to

←Student(x) & ~∃y [Maths-course(y) & ~ Takes(x,y)]

which is equivalent to

←Student(x) & ~ Non-maths-major(x)

where

Non-maths-major(x) ↔ ∃y[Maths-course(y) & ~ Takes(x,y)]

The if-halve of the definition of Non-maths-major is the clause about the relation that we included in the micro data base of Table 1. It was because of this that we were able to express query (iv) directly as the standard form query (iii). As we shall see, the presence of this single clause about Non-maths-major is tantamount to giving it to the above definition in the completed data base.

The Query Evaluation Process

The query evaluation process is essentially a linear resolution proof procedure with negated literals 'evaluated' by a failure proof. However we shall view the alternate derivations of the search space as different paths of a non-deterministic evaluation which can SUCCEED, FAIL or not terminate. A path terminates with SUCCESS if its terminal query is the empty query. The binding of the variables of the initial query induced by a successful evaluation is an answer to the query. A path terminates with FAILURE if the selected literal of its terminal query does not unify with the consequent literal of the selected data base clause. The literal is selected using a prescribed selection rule, but the subsequent selection of a data base clause, and the attempted unification, is a non-deterministic step of the evaluation. Finally, a non-terminating evaluation path comprises an infinite sequence of queries each of which is derived from the initial query as described below.

Evaluation Algorithm

Until an empty query is derived, and the evaluation succeeds, proceed as follows:

Using the selection rule, select a literal L_i from the current query $\leftarrow L_1 \& \ldots \& L_n$. The selection rule is constrained so that a negative literal is only selected if it contains no variables.

<u>Case 1</u>

L_i is a positive literal $R(t_1, \ldots, t_n)$

Non-deterministically choose a database clause

$$R(t'_1,\ldots,t'_n) \leftarrow L'_1\&\ldots\&L'_m$$

about R and try to unify L_i, with $R(t'_1,\ldots,t'_n)$. If there are several data base clauses about R, the selection of a clause together with the attempted unification is a non-deterministic step in the evaluation. Each of the other clauses offer an alternative evaluation path. If L_i does not unify with $R(t'_1,\ldots,t'_n)$, FAIL (this path). If L_i does unify, with most general unifier θ, replace the current query with the derived query

$$\leftarrow\{L_1\&\ldots\&L_{i-1} \;\&\; L'_1\&\ldots\&L'_m \;\&\; L_{i+1}\&\ldots\&L_n\}\theta$$

Should there be no data base clauses about the relation of the selected literal, we consider that there is just one next step to the evaluation of the query

$$\leftarrow L_1\&\ldots\&L_n$$

which immediately FAILS.

<u>Case 2</u>

L_i is a negative ground literal $\sim P$. There is just one next step for the evaluation. This is the attempt to discover whether $\sim P$ can be assumed as a lemma. To do this we recursively enter the query evaluation process with $\leftarrow P$ as a query.

If the evaluation of $\leftarrow P$ SUCCEEDS, FAIL.

If the evaluation of $\leftarrow P$ FAILS for every path of its nondeterministic evaluation, assume $\sim P$ as a lemma. Hence replace the current query by

$$L_1\&\ldots\&L_{i-1} \;\&L_{i+1}\&\ldots\&L_n \;.$$

Remarks

(1) Note that in the special case that no negative literals appear in the query evaluation what we have described is essentially LUSH resolution (Hill [1974]), a linear resolution inference procedure for Horn clauses.

(2) Only the distinguished positive literal of each clause of the data base is a candidate for unification with a query literal. Other positive literals of the clause (that appear as negated preconditions of the implication) are never resolved upon; they can only be deleted after a failure proof.

(3) The different possible selections of a literal in a query <u>do not</u> provide alternatives for the evaluation process. However any rule for selecting the literal can be used. The PROLOG selection rule is - always choose the leftmost literal in a query.

(4) The constraint that a negative literal should only be selected if it is ground is not a significant restriction. It just means that every variable appearing in a negated condition should have its 'range' specified by some unnegated condition. This is just the constraint that Codd imposes on the use of negation in his relational calculus.

(5) Let $\theta_1,\ldots,\theta_n$ be the sequence of unifying substitutions of a successful evaluation of some query Q. Let θ be the composition

$$\theta_1 \circ \theta_2 \circ\ldots\circ \theta_n$$

of these unifying substitutions. The subset of θ which gives the substitutions for variables of the query Q, augmented with the identity substitution for any variables of Q not bound by θ, is the answer given by the evaluation. If Q has no variables, the answer is <u>true</u>. On the other hand, if every evaluation path of the query Q ends with FAIL, the answer is <u>false</u>.

(6) Suppose that for some selection rule every branch of the evaluation tree rooted at a query Q terminates with a SUCCESS or FAIL. By König's Lemma (see Knuth [1968]), the evaluation tree contains a finite number of queries. Hence, by back-tracking when the non-deterministic evaluation succeeds or fails, we can find every answer of the evaluation tree. In the section, Completeness of Query Evaluation, we shall consider constraints which guarantee finite evaluation trees.

(7) Using Boyer and Moore [1972] structure sharing methods a back-tracking search for a successful evaluation can be achieved by manipulating a stack of activation records as in a more conventional computation. Broadly speaking, the currently derived query is represented by the entire stack. The i'th activation record on the stack records the subset of literals that were introduced at the i'th resolution step but which have not yet been deleted by a subsequent resolution. These literals are represented implicitly by a pointer to the data base clause that was used and a tuple of substitutions - the binding environment for this activation of the data base clause. The activation record also contains information about the data base clauses that have not yet been used to resolve on its literals. This information is used for back-tracking. Should one of these literals have a relation R that is extensionally characterised by a large set of unit clauses, the back-tracking information might be a pointer into a file of R-records. In which case a back-tracking search for a clause that matches the literal is just a search through the file. We can of course index the file to speed up the search. This is a very brief and slightly simpli-

fied description of the implementation possibilities. For more details the reader can consult Warren et al. [1977]. However, with the query evaluation process implemented using such techniques we can justly claim that its execution is a computational retrieval of information.

DATA BASE COMPLETION

Remember we are going to validate the query evaluation process as an inference not from the data base of clauses, but from the completed data base, the data base of definitions and equality schemas implicitly given by the set of clauses.

Suppose that

$$R(t_1,\ldots,t_n) \leftarrow L_1\&\ldots\&L_m \qquad (5)$$

is a data base clause about relation R. Where = is the equality relation, and $x_1,\ldots,x_n$ are variables not appearing in the clause, it is equivalent to the clause

$$R(x_1,\ldots,x_n) \leftarrow x_1=t_1\&\ldots\&x_n=t_n\&L_1\&\ldots\&L_m$$

Finally, if $y_1,\ldots,y_p$ are the variables of (5), this is itself equivalent to

$$R(x_1,\ldots,x_n) \leftarrow (\exists y_1,\ldots,y_p)[x_1=t_1\&x_2=t_2\&\ldots\&x_n=t_n\&L_1\&\ldots\&L_m] \qquad (6)$$

We call this the general form of the clause.

Suppose there are exactly k clauses, $k>0$, in the data base about the relation R. Let

$$\begin{array}{l} R(x_1,\ldots,x_n) \leftarrow E_1 \\ \vdots \\ R(x_1,\ldots,x_n) \leftarrow E_k \end{array} \qquad (7)$$

be the k general forms of these clauses. Each of the E_i will be an existentially quantified conjunction of literals as in (6). The definition of R, implicitly given by the data base, is

$$(\forall x_1,\ldots,x_n)[R(x_1,\ldots,x_n) \leftrightarrow E_1 \vee E_2 \vee \ldots \vee E_k]$$

The if-half of this definition is just the k general form clauses (7) grouped as a single implication. The only-if half is the completion law for R.

Should there be no data base clauses for R, the definition implicitly given by the data base, is

$$(\forall x_1,\ldots,x_n)[R(x_1,\ldots,x_n) \leftrightarrow \text{false}]$$

Example

Suppose

$P(a)\leftarrow$

$P(b)\leftarrow$

$P(f(y)) \leftarrow P(y)$

are all the clauses about a unary relation P. Its disjunctive definition is

$$(\forall x)[P(x) \leftrightarrow x=a \vee x=b \vee \exists y[x=f(y)\&P(y)]] \blacksquare$$

In moving to the disjunctive definitions from the original clauses we have been forced to introduce equalities. Thus the onus is upon us to say something about the equality relation for the objects of the data base. That is we need to state explicitly that the constants and functors have their free interpretation. The following schemas suffice. Each schema is implicitly universally quantified with respect to its variables.

$c \neq c'$ c,c' any pair of distinct constants (8)

$f(x_1,\ldots,x_n) \neq g(y_1,\ldots,y_m)$ f,g any pair of distinct functors (9)

$f(x_1,\ldots,x_n) = f(y_1,\ldots,y_n) \rightarrow x_1=y_1\&\ldots\&x_n=y_n$ f any functor (10)

$f(x_1,\ldots,x_n) \neq c$ f any functor, c any constant (11)

$\tau(x) \neq x$ $\tau(x)$ any term structure in which x is free (12)

Schema (8) tells us that different constants denote different objects. Schema (9) tells us that different functors are different data constructors, and (10) tells us that constructed objects are equal only if they are constructed from equal components. Axioms (11) and (12) together tell us that the data constructors always generate new objects.

The above axioms, together with the following general axioms for equality:

$$x = x$$

$$x = y \rightarrow y = x$$

$$x = y \ \& \ y = z \rightarrow x = z$$

Substitution schema:

$$x = y \rightarrow [W(x) \leftrightarrow W(y)], \ W \text{ any wff}$$

we call the identity theory for a completed data base.

The identity theory, together with the set of relation definitions implicitly given by a logic data base, constitute the completed data base.

Example

The definitions and axioms of Table 2 are the completed data base of Table 1. In the definitions each free variable is implicitly universally quantified.

CORRECTNESS OF QUERY EVALUATION

In this section we give the formal results that validate query evaluation from a data base of clauses as a first order inference from the completed form of the data base. The main results are Theorems 2 and 3. Theorem 2 is the validation of negation as failure. It is the proof that whenever for some selection rule every branch of the query evaluation tree ends in a failure, then the

Table 2. Completed Data Base of Table 1

Student(x) ↔ x=J.Brown V x=D.Smith

Maths-course(x) ↔ x=C101 V x=X301

Takes(x,y) ↔ x=J.Brown & y=C101 V x=D.Smith & y=C101
V x=D.Smith & y=C301

Non-maths-major(x) ↔ (∃y)[Maths-course(y) & ~ Takes(x,y)]

For any other relation, a definition that it is always false.

The identity theory

construction of the tree is in effect a proof that there are no answers to the query. Theorem 3 is a generalisation of this result for an evaluation tree every branch of which terminates with a failure or a success. It tells us that the set of answers given by the success branches are provably the only answers to the query. Each of these theorems relies on Theorem 1. Roughly speaking, this tells us that a query Q is equivalent to the disjunction of the queries derivable from Q by resolving on any positive literal. This, in turn, relies on the fact that by using the identity theory we can emulate unification by inference about equalities:

Lemma

(1) If $R(t_1,\ldots,t_n)$ unifies with $R(t'_1,\ldots,t'_n)$ with m.g.u.

$$\theta = \{x_1/e_1,\ldots,x_k/e_k\}$$

then, using the identity theory of the completed data base, the conjunction of equalities

$$t_1=t'_1 \ \&\ldots\& \ t_n=t'_n$$

is provably equivalent to

$$x_1=e_k \ \&\ldots\& \ x_k=e_k$$

(2) If $R(t_1,\ldots,t_n)$ does not unify with $R(t'_1,\ldots,t'_n)$ then, using the identity theory,

$$t_1=t'_1 \ \&\ldots\& \ t_n=t'_n$$

is provably equivalent to false.

Proof

For brevity we simply sketch the proof. What is needed is an induction on the number of steps of an attempt to unify the two literals. Schema (10) of the identity theory is used to infer e=e' where e and e' are corresponding sub-terms which differ. If e is a variable and e' a term in which the variable does not appear, we use the substitution schema for equality to 'apply' the substitution {e/e'}. Otherwise, one of the inequalities (8), (9), (11) or (12) gives us the contradiction. ■

Our first theorem is a direct application of this lemma and the fact that the completed data base defines a relation as the disjunction of antecedents of its general form clauses. To state it we need the concept of the general form of a derived query.

Definition

Let Q' be the query derived from some query Q by selecting a positive literal $R(t_1,\ldots,t_n)$ and resolving with a data base clause C. The general form of the resolvent Q' is

$$(\exists y_1,\ldots,y_p)[z_1=e_1\&\ldots\&z_k=e_k \;\&\; Q']$$

Where $\{z_1/e_1,\ldots,z_k/e_k\}$ is the subset of the m.g.u. θ which applies to variables of Q, and $y_1,\ldots,y_p$ are the variables of data base clause C that remain in $e_1,\ldots,e_k$ or Q'. ■

Theorem 1

Let Q be a query which contains the positive literal $R(t_1,\ldots,t_n)$. Suppose $Q_1,\ldots,Q_j$ are all the alternative queries that are derivable from Q by resolving on $R(t_1,\ldots,t_n)$ with some data base clause about R. If $G_1,\ldots,G_j$ are the general forms of these derived queries

$$Q \leftrightarrow G_1 \vee G_2 \vee \ldots \vee G_j$$

is a theorem of the completed data base. If j=0, i.e., there are no queries derivable from Q by resolving on $R(t_1,\ldots,t_n)$, then

$$Q \leftrightarrow \text{false}$$

is a theorem of the completed data base. ■

The proof of this theorem is quite straightforward. We are now in a position to establish our first main result. We want to show that the construction of a failure evaluation tree - an evaluation tree every branch of which terminates with a failure - is tantamount to a first order proof that the root query has no solutions.

Figure 2 gives the structure of such a failure evaluation tree. Every branch of the tree, every evaluation path, ends at a terminal query Q' whose off-springs are all failure nodes. We want to prove that whenever some query Q is the root of a failed evaluation tree

$$Q \leftrightarrow \text{false}$$

or, equivalently

$$\sim (\exists z_1,\ldots,z_n)Q$$

where $z_1,\ldots,z_n$ are the free variables of Q, is a theorem of the completed data base.

As a special case let us consider a failure tree T which records the top-level structure of a failure proof that does not depend on any subsidiary failure proofs. For such a failure tree the selected literal of the root query Q must be a positive literal $R(t_1,\ldots,t_n)$, with $Q_1,\ldots,Q_j$ the set of resolvents with the data base clauses about R. But Theorem 1 tells us that

$$Q \leftrightarrow G_1 \vee \ldots \vee G_j$$

where $G_1,\ldots,G_j$ are the general forms of $Q_1,\ldots,Q_j$. Clearly, if each of the Q_i is provably equivalent to false so is its general form. What we need therefore is an induction of the structure of T.

The above use of Theorem 1 is our induction step. The base case of the induction is established by considering the two single query failure trees of Figure 3 and Figure 4.

Theorem 1 again covers the case of Figure 3. When T is as depicted in Figure 4 it records a failure proof of the root query because the recursively entered evaluation of ←P has succeeded. But in this case the successful evaluation of ←P will be a resolution proof of P. It would be other than a straightforward resolution proof only if it involved the failure proof of some negated literal. However we have discounted this possibility by our assumption that the failure tree records a failure proof that does not

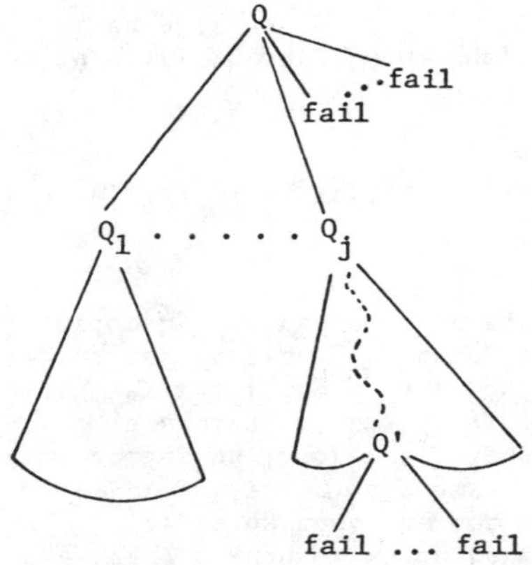

Figure 2. Failure Evaluation Tree

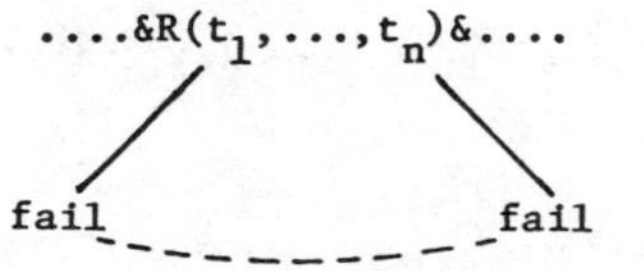

$R(t_1,...,t_n)$ fails to unify with any data base clause about R.

Figure 3. Single Failure Tree

depend on any subsidiary failure proofs. Moreover, a resolution proof of P from the data base of clauses is also a proof that

$$\sim P \leftrightarrow \text{false}$$

from the completed data base. Hence the root query is again provable equivalent to false.

We now need to establish the result for a failure tree T whose construction may depend on auxiliary failure proofs. Since the number of such auxiliary proofs must be finite, we do this by an induction on the number, n, of these auxiliary failure proofs.

The above argument establishes the base case, n=0, of this induction. Let us now assume that the root query of a failure tree whose construction depends on less than n subsidiary failure proofs is provably equivalent to false. Let T be a failure tree whose construction depends on at most n failure proofs $n > 0$.

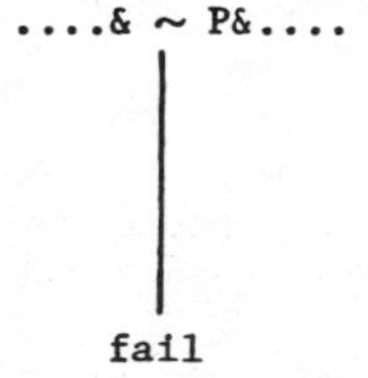

A query evaluation for ←P succeeds.

P is a ground literal

Figure 4. Single Failure Tree

As above, we show that the root query of T is provably equivalent to false by a secondary induction of the structure of T. Again the base cases of this structural induction are as depicted in Figures 3 and 4. As before, Theorem 1 covers the case of Figure 3. However, this time the single query tree of Figure 4 records a successful evaluation of ←P which may depend on a failure proof of some negated literal ~ L, this failure proof being the construction of a failure tree rooted at L. But such a failure proof can itself make use of at most n-1 subsidiary failure proofs. By the induction hypothesis

$$L \leftrightarrow \text{false}$$

and hence

$$\sim L$$

is a theorem of the completed data base. This applies to any failure proved negated literal selected in the evaluation of ←P. The deletion of such a negated literal can therefore be regarded as a resolution step which uses a lemma ~ L of the completed data base. Since every other step in the evaluation of ←P is just a resolution with a data base clause, we have again that

$$\sim P \leftrightarrow \text{false}.$$

is a thoerem of the completed data base.

The induction step of our structural induction on T is just a slight elaboration of the argument for the special case failure tree that required no subsidiary failure proofs. This time we must also consider the failure tree structure depicted in Figure 5. Here the root query has a single off-spring derived by deleting a negated literal ~ L, which has been failure proved. But again the failure proof of ~ L

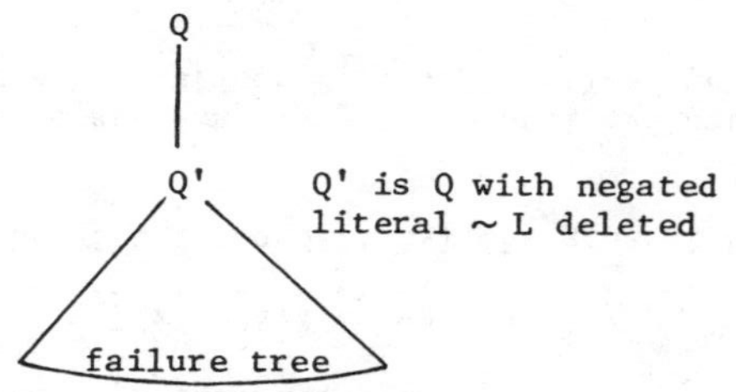

Figure 5. Failure Trees

can itself depend on at most n-1 failure proofs, so $\sim L$ is a theorem of the completed data base. Therefore

$$Q \leftrightarrow Q'$$

is also a theorem. But Q' is the root of a sub-tree which is a failure tree, so

$$Q' \leftrightarrow \text{false}$$

and hence

$$Q \leftrightarrow \text{false}$$

as required. We have proved:

Theorem 2

If for some literal selection rule every branch of the evaluation tree of a query $\leftarrow Q$ terminates with failure, then

$$\sim(\exists x_1,\dots,x_k)Q$$

where $x_1,\dots,x_k$ are the free variables of Q, is a theorem of the completed data base. ■

Let us now look at the case of a successful query evaluation. By the above theorem, any failure evaluation of a negated literal $\sim L$ that it might use can be viewed as the derivation from the completed data base of a lemma $\sim L$. Thus the whole evaluation can be viewed as a linear resolution proof using the data base clauses (the if-halves of the relation definitions) and a set of negated ground literal lemmas. Suppose that the answer given by the successful evaluation is

$$\theta = \{x_1/e_1,\dots,x_i/e_i,x_{i+1}/x_{i+1},\dots,x_k/x_k\}$$

$x_1,\dots,x_i$ being the subset of the free variables $x_1,\dots,x_k$ of the query Q that are bound by the evaluation. By the soundness of resolution

$$(\forall x_{i+1},\dots,x_k)(\forall y_1,\dots,y_n)Q\theta \;,$$

where $y_1,\dots,y_n$ are the extra free variables of $Q\theta$ introduced by the substitution θ , is a theorem of the completed data base.

It follows that

$$(\forall x_1,\dots,x_i,x_{i+1},..,x_k)(\forall y_1,\dots,y_n)[x_1=e_1\&\dots\&x_i=e_i \rightarrow Q]$$

is also a theorem. Finally, since $y_1,..,y_n$ were introduced by θ and do not appear in Q, this is equivalent to

$$(\forall x_1,\dots,x_k)[(\exists y_1,\dots,y_n)(x_1=e_1\&\dots\&x_i=e_i) \rightarrow Q]$$

Let us call the antecedent of this conditional the general form of the answer θ, and denote it by $\hat{\theta}$.

Suppose now that there are exactly j successful evaluations of the query $\leftarrow Q$ with answer substitutions $\theta_1,\dots,\theta_j$. Then we know that

$$(\forall x_1,\dots,x_k)\ [\hat{\theta}_1 \rightarrow Q]$$
$$\vdots$$
$$(\forall x_1,\dots,x_k)\ [\hat{\theta}_j \rightarrow Q]$$

are all theorems of the completed data base. Suppose further that every other branch of the evaluation tree (constructed using some particular selection rule) ends in a failure node. By an exhaustive search we can discover that there are no other solutions given by this evaluation tree. We should like to know no other evaluation tree would provide us with an extra solution. Assuming that the completed data base is consistent, this is guaranteed by:

Theorem 3

If for some literal selection rule every branch of the evaluation tree of a query $\leftarrow Q$ ends with a success or failure, and $\theta_1,\dots,\theta_j$ are all the answers given by the evaluation paths that end in success, then

$$(\forall x_1,\dots,x_k)[Q \leftrightarrow \hat{\theta}_1 \vee \hat{\theta}_2 \vee..\vee \hat{\theta}_j]$$

is a theorem of the completed data base. Here, $x_1,\dots,x_k$ are the free variables of Q and $\hat{\theta}_1,\dots,\hat{\theta}_j$ are the general forms of the answers. ■

The proof is a straightforward induction on the structure of the evaluation tree.

Example Application of Theorem 2

Figure 6 is the failure tree generated by the PROLOG selection rule for the query ←Non-maths-major(D.Smith). The proof of Theorem 2 gives us a method for lifting this failure tree into a first order proof of

$\sim$ Non-maths-major(D.Smith).

We simply climb down the tree substituting for each query the disjunction of general forms of its immediate descendents. By Theorem 2 each substitution preserves equivalence. For FAIL we substitute false. This deduction, with some intermediary steps inserted, is :-

Non-maths-major(D.Smith)

$\leftrightarrow$ $\exists$y[Maths-course(y)& ~Takes(D.Smith,y)] by definition of Non-maths-major

$\leftrightarrow$ $\exists$y[(y=C101 V y=C301)& ~Takes(D.Smith,y)] by definition of Maths-course

$\leftrightarrow$ $\exists$y[y=C101& ~Takes(D.Smith,y) V y=C301& ~Takes(D.Smith,y)]

$\leftrightarrow$ ~ Takes(D.Smith,C101) V ~ Takes(D.Smith,C301)

$\leftrightarrow$ ~ true V ~ true

$\leftrightarrow$ false

$\therefore$ ~ Non-maths-major(D.Smith) ■

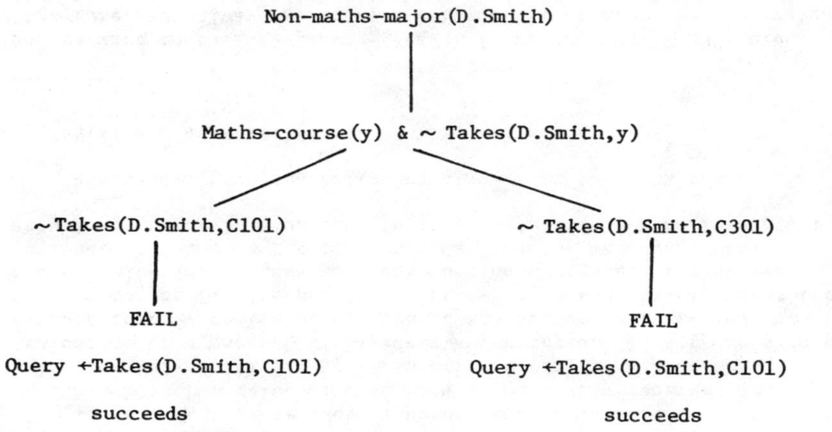

Figure 6. Failure Tree Generated by PROLOG Selection Rule

COMPLETENESS OF QUERY EVALUATION

We have argued that the evaluation of a query can and should be viewed as a deduction from the completed data base. However, when we evaluate a query, that is try to discover whether or not some instance is implied by the completed data base, we ignore the completion laws and inequality schemas. As a substitute we augment a Horn clause theorem prover for the remaining if-halves of the relation definitions - the data base clauses - with our negation as failure inference rule. Is this an adequate substitute? Will we still be able to infer every answer to the query implied by the completed data base? With certain restrictions on the data base and its queries, yes. In general, no.

Let us look at the ways in which query evaluation falls short of a complete inference system. To begin with there is the restriction that our failure inference rule should only be applied to a ground literal. With this restriction we cannot even begin to answer a query

$\leftarrow$ ~ R(x,a)

which is a request for any x not related to a by R. We could relax this restriction on failure proofs. Let us suppose that the recursively entered evaluation of ←R(x,a) constructs a failure tree rooted at R(x,a). By Theorem 2 we can infer (x)~ R(x,a), giving as an answer to the query the identity substitution x/x. We can also give an answer when the evaluation of ←R(x,a) succeeds, providing the answer is the identity substitution x/x. For in this case the evaluation is a proof of (x)R(x,a), i.e. ~ $\exists$x ~R(x,a). So false is the answer to the query ←~ R(x,a). However, should we have a successful evaluation of ←R(x,a) with an answer other than the identity substitution we cannot conclude anything about the query ← ~ R(x,a). To patch our query evaluation process in this circumstance, we would need to resort to a systematic search for a ground instance of ~R(x,a) that can be failure proved. But of course, just such a systematic search will be invoked by the modified query,

$\leftarrow$ Q(x)& ~ R(x,a)

providing Q(x) only has ground solutions. Our insistence that queries must have this form is a requirement that the querier must implicitly constrain the search.

The second limitation associated with failure proofs is much more serious. It is the fact that we search for a failure proof by constructing just one evaluation tree.

For a query that has a successful evaluation we do not have to search alternative evaluation trees, at least not for the top-level deduction. This is because at the top-level we can view each deletion of a negated literal as a resolution step. Thus, the evaluation is in essential respects a Horn clause refutation. In the search for such a refutation we know we need only consider one selection rule (Hill [1974]). In other words, if a successful evaluation of a query Q with answer substitution θ appears on one evaluation tree rooted at Q, then it appears on every evaluation tree rooted at Q. The problem arises when we recursively enter the query evaluation process to check that some negated literal $\sim P$ is indeed a lemma of the completed data base. When we do this, to grow just one evaluation tree is to risk 'missing' a failure proof.

Suppose we have the following clauses in the data base,

$P(x) \leftarrow Q(y) \,\&\, R(y)$
$Q(h(y)) \leftarrow Q(y)$
$R(g(y)) \leftarrow$

and we want to failure prove $\sim P(a)$. If we use the PROLOG selection rule, and always select the leftmost literal, we get an evaluation tree with a single infinite branch (see Figure 7a). Using another selection rule, in fact any other rule in this instance, we get a finite failure tree (see Figure 7b).

A complete search for a failure proof should therefore search over the space of alternative evaluation trees. That is the different selections of a literal in a query should be treated as alternatives when we search for a failure proof. Interestingly, the different ways of resolving on the selected literal are not alternatives for a failure proof. Every one of them must eventually be investigated and shown to FAIL. This gives us a nice duality between search for a successful evaluation, and search for a failure proof.

```
(a)
P(a)
 |
Q(y) & R(y)
 |
Q(y') & R(h(y'))
 |
Q(y") & R(h(h(y")))
 :

(b)
P(a)
 |
Q(y) & R(y)
 |
Q(y') & R(h(y'))
          |
         FAIL
```

Figure 7. Incompleteness of PROLOG Selection Rule

We have seen that we might miss the failure proof of some negated literal $\sim P$ by restricting ourselves to the construction of just one evaluation tree rooted at P. In consequence, we may not be able to successfully complete a query evaluation that depends on the lemma $\sim P$. However, this very insistence that all negated literals should be inferred as lemmas; and the consequent neglect of a case analysis proof - check if the same answer is given on the assumption that P is true, and on the assumption that P is false - is another hole in the query evaluation process.

The following clauses give an example of this:

$$\begin{aligned} &R(x,y) \leftarrow P(x) \,\&\, Q(x,y)\\ &R(x,y) \leftarrow \sim P(x) \,\&\, T(x,y)\\ &P(x) \leftarrow P(f(x))\\ &Q(a,b) \leftarrow\\ &T(a,b) \leftarrow \end{aligned} \tag{13}$$

$R(a,b)$ is implied by these clauses. This is because

$$R(x,y) \leftarrow Q(x,y) \,\&\, T(x,y) \tag{14}$$

is a consequence of the two clauses for R. If we resolve these two clauses on the 'test' literal $P(x)$ we get

$$R(x,y) \vee R(x,y') \leftarrow Q(x,y) \,\&\, T(x,y'),$$

which we can factor to give (14). Clause (14) tells us that no matter whether $P(x)$ is true or false we can conclude $R(x,y)$ if only Q and T can 'agree' on y. $R(a,b)$ is now an immediate consequence of (14) and the ground clauses for Q and T. However, no evaluation of the query

$$\leftarrow R(a,b)$$

which uses only the given clauses (13) can terminate. This is because the single clause for P, which amounts to a definition

$$\forall x[P(x) \leftrightarrow P(f(x))]$$

in the completed data base, does not allow us to prove or disprove $P(a)$, and the query evaluator insists on the proven truth or falsity of every literal encountered in the evaluation. Like intuitionist logic, the query evaluator does not countenance the law of the excluded middle

$$P \vee \sim P .$$

Put another way, it treats

$$P \vee Q$$

as a statement that is true only when $\vdash P$ or $\vdash Q$.

There is also an interesting analogy with the two different interpretations that can be given to the conditional expression

if P(x) then q(x) else t(x)

in a more conventional programming formalism. For any x, the value is g(x) if P(x) is true, and t(x) if P(x) is false. But what if P(x) is undefined, i.e., its evaluation for some argument x does not terminate, just as our evaluation of ←P(a) does not terminate. The 'sequential' semantics for the conditional says that the conditional is undefined. The 'parallel' semantics says that it is undefined except in the special case that g(x) and t(x) agree, i.e. return the same value. In this case the value of the conditional is this common value. This is precisely what derived clause (15) asserts. First order logic, then, insists on the 'parallel' semantics. Our query evaluation gives us the 'sequential'.

Finally, let us note that an SL refutation (Kowalski and Kuehner [1971]) used to evaluate the query would cope with the case analysis allowed by classical logic by an ancestor resolution.

Where does that leave us? In the light of the above shortcomings is query evaluation as we have described it worth considering? It is, because as we have already remarked, coupled with a back-tracking search strategy it can be most efficiently implemented. Can we perhaps side-step its inadequacies?

Firstly, the constraint that every variable in a negated literal should have its range specified by an unnegated literal that will generate a candidate set of ground substitutions is perfectly acceptable. Let us call this an <u>allowed query</u>. For an allowed query no evaluation can flounder because it encounters a query with only unground negative literals. (Remember the literal selection rule is constrained so that it can only select a negative literal if it is ground.) Now suppose that for some given data base we can define a literal selection rule such that the evaluation tree for every allowed query is finite. Providing the completed data base is consistent (and I think that the finiteness of every evaluation tree guarantees this, although I have not checked it out) query evaluation is complete. This is because the back-tracking traversal of the finite evaluation tree will find each and every answer given by a successful evaluation path, and Theorem 3 tells us that these are the only answers. Note that a proof that a data base + selection rule has a finite evaluation tree for each and every query is a termination proof for the data base viewed as a non-deterministic program, each posed query being a 'call' of the program.

With regards providing such a termination proof for a data base I have no ready suggestions, although I think it is an interesting area to explore. Typically we might have to modify the selection rule and perhaps further restrict the legitimate queries as a data base evolves. We can however lay down a strong but quite general condition for a logic data base which ensures termination of every allowed query evaluation for <u>any</u> selection rule. It is that each relation R of the data base, whether it be explicitly or implicitly defined, should have finite extension that can be computed by constructing any evaluation tree for the query

$$\leftarrow R(x_1,\ldots,x_k)$$

Let us call this the condition of <u>computable finite extensions</u>.

It is quite easy to show that for a data base which only has computable finite extensions the evaluation tree for an allowed query

$$\leftarrow L_1 \ \& \ L_2 \ \&\ldots\& \ L_n$$

is finite no matter what selection rule is used. Remember that any variable in a negative literal appears in some positive literal for which there are only computable ground solutions. So negative literals present no problem, all selection rules being constrained to select a negative literal only after it has become ground. We leave the reader to provide the termination proof for a query comprising only positive literals. There is a slight complication due to the fact that we can, in effect, coroutine between the evaluations of

$$\leftarrow L_1, \leftarrow L_2, \ldots, \leftarrow L_n$$

We can now come back on ourselves and use this result to specify a hierarchical data base in which each relation does have a computable finite extent, hence a data base with the termination property for any selection rule. The clauses of the data base must be such that they can be grouped into disjoint sequence of sets

$$S_0, S_1, \ldots, S_n$$

which satisfy the following condition.

Let us call a relation R of the data base in i-level relation if it is completely specified by the clauses in

$$S_0 \cup S_1 \cup \ldots \cup S_i$$

That is, there are no clauses about R, or any relation referred to directly or indirectly by the clauses for R, that are outside this set. The data base of clauses satisfies the hierarchical constraint if:

(i) S_0 is the set of all unit clauses which all ground

(ii) S_{i+1} only contains clauses of the form

$$L \leftarrow L_1 \;\&\; .. \;\&\; L_n$$

where the antecedent $L_1 \&..\& L_n$ is an allowed query using only j-level relations, $j \leq i$.

Note that this rules out recursive or mutually recursive definitions of relations. It is, unfortunately, a very strong constraint. It derives from the data base structuring proposals of Reiter [1977].

By an induction on i, it is easy to show that each i-level relation has a computable finite extent. Each 0-level relation is a relation completely defined by a set of ground instances. The induction step makes use of the fact that each i+1 level relation that is not also an i-level relation is defined by a set of clause each of which has a precondition

$$\leftarrow L_1 \;\&\; .. \;\&\; L_n$$

which is an allowed query about j-level relations, $j \leq i$, i.e. relations with computable finite extents. The details are quite straightforward. Another induction on i can be used to prove the consistency of the completed data base. The induction step is a proof that we can extend the model for the completion of $S_0 \cup .. \cup S_i$ to a model for the completion of $S_0 \cup \ldots \cup S_i \cup S_{i+1}$. We can conclude:

Theorem 4

For a data base satisfying the hierarchical constraint the evaluation process for allowed queries is complete. ■

The hierarchical constraint guarantees that our query evaluation process will be find each and every answer to a query. Is it too restrictive? Perhaps, but it still characterizes a data base which generalizes a conventional relational data base in the following respects:

(1) We can define the computable finite extensions of the relations by a set of instances, or by general rules, or by a mixture of both.

(2) The components of a relation are not restricted to strings and numbers. They can be quite general data structures (terms of the logic program).

(3) The clausal notation fills the role of data description language, query language and host programming language. Indeed, a data base is just a logic program with a large number of ground clauses. This multi-role aspect of logic programs is more fully explored by van Emden [1978] and Kowalski [1978].

(4) Finally, the retrieval of information is not just a search over a set of files. It genuinely involves a computational deduction.

FINAL REMARKS

We have shown that the negation as failure inference rule applied to a data base of clauses is a sound rule for deductions from the completed data base. As a generalization of this, we have shown that an exhaustive search for solutions to a query, if it returns a finite set of solutions, is a proof that these are exactly the set of solutions. We have described a query evaluation process for a data base of clauses which uses negation as failure as its sole proof rule for negated literals. Although it is in general not complete, its chief advantage is the efficiency of its implementation. Using it the deductive retrieval of information can be regarded as a computation. However, by imposing constraints on the logic data base and its queries, which generalise the constraints of a relational data base, the query evaluation process is guaranteed to find each and every solution to a query.

ACKNOWLEDGMENTS

I have benefited much from discussions with Bob Kowalski and Maarten van Emden. The research was supported by the Science Research Council.

REFERENCES

1. Boyer, R.S. and Moore, J.S. [1972] The Sharing of Structure in Theorem Proving Programs. In *Machine Intelligence 7* (B. Meltzer and D. Michie, Eds.), Edinburgh University Press, 101-116.

2. Chang, C. L. and Lee, R.C.T. [1973] *Symbolic Logic and Mechanical Theorem Proving*, Academic Press, New York, 1973.

3. Codd, E. F. [1970] A Relational Model for Large Shared Data Banks, *CACM 13*, 6 (June, 1970), 377-387.

4. Codd, E. F. [1972] Relational Completeness of Data Base Sublanguages, In *Data Base Systems* (R. Rustin, Ed.), Prentice-Hall, 65-98.

5. Hewitt, C. [1972] Description and Theoretical Analysis (Using Schemata) of PLANNER: A Language for Proving Theorems and Manipulating Models in a Robot, *A. I. Memo No. 251*, MIT Project MAC, 1972.

6. Hill, R. [1974] Lush-Resolution and Its Completeness, *DCL Memo No. 78*, Department of Artificial Intelligence, Edinburgh University, 1974.

7. Knuth, D. [1968] *Fundamental Algorithms, The Art of Computer Programming, Vol. 1*, Addison-Wesley, Reading, Mass, 1968.

8. Kowalski, R. and Kuehner, D. [1971] Linear Resolution with Selection Function, *Artificial Intelligence 2*, 3/4 (1971), 221-260.

9. Kowalski, R. [1978] Logic for Data Description, In *Logic and Data Bases* (H. Gallaire and J. Minker, Eds.), Plenum Press, New York, N.Y., 77-103.

10. Kramosil, I. [1975] A Note on Deduction Rules with Negative Premises, *Proceedings IJCAI 4*, Tbilisi, USSR, 1975, 53-56.

11. Nicolas, J. M. and Gallaire, H. [1978] Data Bases: Theory vs. Interpretation, In *Logic and Data Bases* (H. Gallaire and J. Minker, Eds.), Plenum Press, New York, N.Y., 1978, 33-54.

12. Reiter, R. [1978] On Closed World Data Bases, In *Logic and Data Bases* (H. Gallaire and J. Minker, Eds.), Plenum Press, New York, N.Y., 1978, 55-76.

13. Reiter, R. [1977] An Approach to Deductive Question-Answering, *BBN Report No. 3649*, Bolt, Beranek and Newman, Cambridge, Mass., 1977.

14. Roussel, P. [1975] PROLOG: Manual d'Utilisation, *Rapport Interne, G.I.A., UER de LUMINY*, Universite d'Aix-Marseille, 1975.

15. van Emden, M. [1978] Computation and Deductive Information Retrieval, In *Formal Description of Programming Concepts*, (E. Neuhold, Ed.), North-Holland, 1978.

16. Warren, D., Pereira, L. and Pereira, F. [1977] PROLOG - The Language and Its Implementation Compared with LISP, *Proceedings of SIGART/SIGPLAN Conference on Programming Languages*, Rochester, New York, 1977.

On Indefinite Databases and the Closed World Assumption

Jack Minker
University of Maryland
College Park, Maryland 20742

Abstract

A database is said to be indefinite if there is an answer to a query of the form $Pa \vee Pb$ where neither Pa nor Pb can be derived from the database. Indefinite databases arise where, in general, the data consists of non-Horn clauses. A clause is non-Horn if it is a disjunction of literals in which more than one literal in the clause is positive.

Horn databases, which comprise most databases in existence, do not admit answers of the form $Pa \vee Pb$ where neither Pa nor Pb are derivable from the database. It has been shown by Reiter that in such databases one can make an assumption, termed the Closed World Assumption (CWA), that to prove that $\overline{P}a$ is true, one can try to prove Pa, and if the proof for Pa fails, one can assume $\overline{P}a$ is true.

When a database consists of Horn and non-Horn clauses, Reiter has shown that it is not possible to make the CWA. In this paper we investigate databases that consist of Horn and non-Horn clauses. We extend the definition of CWA to apply to such databases. The assumption needed for such databases is termed the Generalized Closed World Assumption (GCWA). Syntactic and semantic definitions of generalized closed worlds are given. It is shown that the two definitions are equivalent. In addition, given a class of null values it is shown that the GCWA gives a correct interpretation for null values.

1. Introduction

We consider a relational database to consist of a set of *extensional data*, and a set of *intensional data*. The extensional data consists of data as stored in any relational database. The intensional data consists of a set of axioms, or views, from which new relations can be derived using both the axioms and the extensional data.

Databases which are exclusively extensional, or whose axioms are all Horn are of greatest interest as they arise frequently. An axiom is said to be Horn if it consists of a conjunction which implies a single atomic formula. That is, if it is of the form $R_1 \wedge \ldots \wedge R_n \rightarrow R_{n+1}$, where R_i, $i=1,\ldots,n+1$ are positive literals. Alternatively, it may be considered to be a disjunctive form, in which there is at most one positive literal, i.e., $\overline{R}_1 \vee \ldots \vee \overline{R}_n \vee R_{n+1}$. Each R_i is an n_i-ary expression of the form $R_i(t_1,\ldots,t_{n_i})$, where the t_i are terms. A term is a constant or a variable. We do not permit function symbols or Skolem constants (zero-ary function symbols). An axiom is assumed to be universally quantified and hence the universal quantifier symbol over the variables in an axiom are omitted.

Reiter [1978a,1978b] has considered databases in which one has both an extensional and an intensional database and has shown that Horn data bases always have definite answers. That is, there can be no answers to questions where the answers are of the form $Pa \vee Pb$ and neither Pa nor Pb can be derived from the database.

Clearly there are databases (DB) which have indefinite data. The trivial DB given by DB : $\{Pa \vee Pb\}$, and consists of no other data either extensional or intensional has no definite answers. The indefiniteness arises because the only data in the database is non-Horn. Not all databases that have non-Horn axioms result in indefinite answers. Consider the following : DB : $\{Pa \vee Pb, \overline{P}a\}$. The answer to the question of whether Pb is true is "yes". That is, although $Pa \vee Pb$ is in the data base, Pb can be derived since $\overline{P}a$ is true and $Pa \vee Pb$ is true, then Pb must be true. Hence, there are no indefinite answers in this database. This database has, in fact, an equivalent Horn database, Horn DB : $\{\overline{P}a, Pb\}$.

Our focus in this paper is that of indefinite databases. Before addressing indefinite databases some background is necessary.

1.1 Open and Closed World Data Bases

The terms open and closed world databases were introduced by Reiter [1978a,1978b]. An *open world* is associated with a first-order theory. That is, first-order predicate logic. Data is represented by clauses, and negative data is listed explicitly in the database. Answers to queries may be either looked-up or derived from the data and the axioms. In an open world, negative data must be listed explicitly. When the database complies with this assumption concerning negative data, the database is said to satisfy the *open world assumption* (OWA). A problem arises in that negative data may overwhelm a system.

An alternative to an open world is a closed world database that arises from an assumption concerning negative data. That is, the data base contains no negative data and, to determine whether one can derive a negative fact from the data base, one attempts to prove the positive fact true. If one fails to prove the positive fact, then the negative data is assumed to be true. That is, under the *closed world assumption* (CWA) certain answers are admitted as a result of *failure* to find a proof. The need for a closed world assumption in deductive databases was described first, perhaps, by Nicolas and Syre [1974]. It is also related to the negative operators of PLANNER (Hewitt [1972]) and PROLOG (Roussel [1975]) where, in these languages, negative means "not provable". For a description of negation as failure and its truth function semantics see Clark [1978].

Given a DB, one can associate an extended data base $\overline{EDB}$ which consists of negative data whose positive counterparts cannot be proved from DB. More formally,
$\overline{EDB} = \{\overline{P}\vec{c} \mid P$ is a predicate letter, $\vec{c}$ a tuple of constants and $P\vec{c} \notin DB$ or $P\vec{c}$ cannot be proved from DB, (written $DB \nvdash P\vec{c}$). This statement can be simplified to :
$\overline{EDB} = \{\overline{P}\vec{c} \mid P$ is a predicate letter, $\vec{c}$ a tuple of constants, and $DB \nvdash P\vec{c}\}$.

By a DB we assume a finite set of constants which belong to a single universe. We do this for simplicity and note that Reiter assumes a universe that is subdivided into types, and variables belong to types. The work described in this paper also encompasses types.

An answer to a query under the CWA, as defined by Reiter, is given as follows. Let EDB be given as above, then $\vec{c}^{(1)} + \dots + \vec{c}^{(r)}$ is a *CWA* answer to $<\vec{x} \mid (\exists \vec{y}) W(\vec{x},\vec{y})>$ (with respect to DB), and W is a well-formed formula if and only if $DB \cup \overline{EDB} \vdash \bigvee_{i \leq r} (\exists \vec{y}) W(\vec{c}^{(i)}, \vec{y})$. Reiter has shown that in Horn databases it is not necessary to have explicit knowledge of $\overline{EDB}$ to find answers to queries. Furthermore, since either $P\vec{c}$ or $\overline{P}\vec{c}$ can be derived as an answer, there is no indefiniteness possible in answers under the CWA. Additionally, Reiter has shown that queries of the form given above can be transformed into the union and intersection of queries on atomic formulae. Horn data bases are shown to comply with the CWA.

The concept of a CWA has been addressed from a semantic point of view by van Emden [1977] who considers the issue of database consistency under the CWA. A model of a set of clauses is a set of ground atomic formulae (atomic formulae that only contain constants) that make all formuale true. A "minimal model" of a data base as defined by van Emden is the intersection of all its models. If this minimal model is itself a model of the database, then the database is consistent with the CWA. It has been shown by van Emden and Kowalski [1976] that Horn databases have a minimal model.

We note that DB : $Pa \vee Pb$ does not have a minimal model. Consider all of the models : M_1 : {Pa}

M_2 : {Pb}

M_3 : {Pa, Pb}

$M = M_1 \cap M_2 \cap M_3 = \{\emptyset\}$.

This can be seen as follows. M_1 consists of only Pa since Pa "true" is a model of DB. Similarly M_2 consists of Pb and M_3 consists of both Pa and Pb. The intersection of the three sets is empty. This denotes that $\overline{P}a$ and $\overline{P}b$ must be "true". But Pa and Pb "true" cause the DB to be false. Hence it has no model. The DB is clearly not consistent with the CWA since we cannot prove Pa then $\overline{P}a$ is assumed "true" and since we cannot prove Pb, $\overline{P}b$ is assumed "true". Hence, $\overline{EDB} = \{\overline{P}a, \overline{P}b\}$. But, $DB \cup \overline{EDB} = \{Pa \vee Pb, \overline{P}a, \overline{P}b\}$ is always false and the database is not consistent with the CWA.

A database DB is termed *mixed world* if part of the data complies with the closed world assumption, and part with the open world assumption.

1.2 Approaches To Handling Indefinite Data

We describe three approaches to handle DBs with non-Horn clauses that have been proposed in the literature. These are : (1) Viewing the perceived world as a first order theory as discussed by Nicolas and Gallaire [1978]. (2) Mixing the OWA and CWA by the use of if-and-only-if definitions as described by Clark [1978] and Kowalski [1978]. (3) Splitting the DB into a disjunction of DBs each of which contains only Horn clauses, as proposed by Loveland [1978]. In Section 2 we provide a definition for a GCWA which applies to mixed worlds and serves to extend the concept of the CWA applicable only to Horn databases.

1.2.1 The Perceived World As A First-Order Theory

In the perceived world as a first-order theory as discussed by Nicolas and Gallaire [1978], a DB is formalized in terms of first-order logic where the elementary facts (relational database) and the general axioms are considered as the proper axioms of a first-order theory with equality. The theory is defined as follows:

- its set of constants (respectively predicate names) is the set of elements (relations) appearing within information;
- its set of proper axioms is the set of well-formed formulae (wff) associated with information in the following way : if the statement is known to be true, then the wff is an axiom, and if it is known to be false then the negation of the wff is an axiom.

Viewing the world as a set of wffs extends the concept of relational databases in several ways. First, it permits negative data to be represented explicitly in the database. Second it allows indefinite data to be represented, which is not possible in a relational data base. Third, it allows general axioms as part of the database, which corresponds to the concept of a "view" in database terminology. Whereas "views" generally are not recursive, general axioms have no such restriction.

The above advantages of a first-order theory for databases must be tempered by its disadvantages. First, whereas in a relational database negative data is implicitly stored and corresponds to the CWA, all negative data must be stored explicitly in the DB. The amount of negative data that needs to be stored may be overwhelming as it is generally an order of magnitude larger than the positive data. Consider, for example, a large university with 30,000 students and a course in which 30 students are enrolled. To determine who is not in the course, either 29,970 facts must exist explicitly listing those not in the course or if and only if definitions are used as explained in the following section.

A DB which contains indefinite data becomes more complex than one which does not contain such information. In general, one is forced to include negative data to answer questions, and cannot rely upon the CWA. Furthermore, a general purpose inference mechanism must be used. If one did not have indefinite data, then a straightforward inference mechanism termed LUSH resolution (Hill [1974]), complete and sound only for the Horn clauses can be used. Indefinite data requires a general purpose inference mechanism that is complete and sound for arbitrary clauses. Useful inference mechanisms are linear resolution with selection function (SL) as developed independently by Kowalski and Kuehner [1971], Loveland [1968], and Reiter [1971] or a variant of these approaches that allows somewhat greater flexibility, linear resolution with selection function based on trees (LUST), developed by Minker and Zanon

[1979]. A discussion of why a general purpose inference mechanism is needed can be found in Loveland and Stickel [1973]. In contrast to LUSH resolution, the other inference systems mentioned above require two added operations - ancestry resolution and factoring.

1.2.2 <u>The Use of If-And-Only-If Definitions</u>

It has been noted by Clark [1978] and Kowalski [1978] that Horn clauses express only the if-half of definitions which are otherwise expressed completely by using the full intended if-and-only-if definition. For example, the clauses (or facts, or assertions)

(1) TEACHES (A,PROGRAMMING)

(2) TEACHES (B,PROGRAMMING)

state that A and B teach programming. They could have been written equivalently as "if" statements :

(1') $E(x,A) \rightarrow$ TEACHES (x,PROGRAMMING)

(2') $E(x,B) \rightarrow$ TEACHES (x,PROGRAMMING),

where E denotes the equality predicate. That is, x teaches programming if x equals A. If the intent is to mean that "only A and B teach programming", then the "if" statements do not capture the intent. Under the CWA, the meaning is assumed to be that A and B are the only ones. In first order logic, by including the intended "only-if" part of the definition, both Clark and Kowalski note that one makes the statement explicit. Thus, one would write

(3) $E(x,A) \vee E(x,B) \leftrightarrow$ TEACHES (x,PROGRAMMING).

Whereas (1) and (2) (or (1') and (2')) are sufficient to find all instances of the TEACHES relation, they are inadequate to conclude that some individual "C" does not teach programming (unless some assumption is made) when "C" is not found among the instances of the relation. However, (3) does capture this relationship.

While Reiter captures negative data implicitly through the CWA, Clark and Kowalski capture the same information explicitly through if-and-only-if definitions. Using such definitions precludes the necessity for listing all negative information. Thus, (3) is sufficient to prove that C does not teach programming and does not require that $\overline{\text{TEACHES}}$ (C,PROGRAMMING) be stored explicitly.

While not having to store negative data, the introduction of if-and-only-if definitions precludes the use of LUSH resolution for the clauses are now non-Horn. Derivations now become more complex than when Horn clauses exist to evaluate queries.

1.2.3 <u>Splitting a Non-Horn DB into a Disjunction of Horn DBs</u>.

We have noted the desirability of working with a Horn DB above. It would be of interest to determine if a DB could be factored in some way so as to become a Horn DB. Loveland [1978] (cf. pp. 100-102) shows how this may be accomplished. As an example of his method consider a DB which consists of only Horn clauses to which we add the non-Horn clause $D = (a_1 \vee a_2 \vee C)$, where C is a disjunction of negative atomic formulae. Then $DB \wedge D \equiv DB \wedge (a_1 \vee a_2 \vee C) \equiv (DB \wedge (a_1 \vee C)) \vee (DB \wedge (a_2 \vee C))$ is a tautology. Thus, a negated query, $\overline{Q}$, together with $DB \wedge D$ is unsatisfiable if-and-only-if $\overline{Q}$ taken individually with $DB \wedge (a_1 \vee C)$, and with $DB \wedge (a_2 \vee C)$ are both unsatisfiable. The test for unsatisfiability in each of the two DBs is not independent. Specifically, variables from a split clause in each DB must be identical. Notice what happens if they are not independent. Consider the DB as follows :

DB: $Ra \wedge Rb \wedge (Px \vee Qx \vee \overline{R}x)$.

Split DB (DBS) : $(Ra \wedge Rb \wedge (Px \vee \overline{R}x)) \vee (Ra \wedge Rb \wedge (Qx \vee \overline{R}x))$.

Let the query be

Q : $Pa \vee Qb$.

Now,

$$DB \wedge \overline{Q} = Ra \wedge Rb \wedge (Px \vee Qx \vee \overline{R}x) \wedge \overline{P}a \wedge \overline{Q}b$$

is satisfiable since $\{\overline{P}a, Pb, Qa, \overline{Q}b, Ra, Rb\}$ all true constitutes a model. However,

$DBS \wedge \overline{Q}$ yields a split into

$DBS_1 \wedge \overline{Q} = Ra \wedge Rb \wedge (Px \vee \overline{R}x) \wedge \overline{P}a \wedge \overline{Q}b$ and

$DBS_2 \wedge \overline{Q} = Ra \wedge Rb \wedge (Qx \vee \overline{R}x) \wedge \overline{P}a \wedge \overline{Q}b$

both of which are unsatisfiable when viewed independently. One must first prove $DBS_1 \wedge \overline{Q}$ unsatisfiable. Once this is done, bindings tu variables in DBS_2 that arise from clauses that were split must be made identical. Thus, in $DBS_2 \wedge \overline{Q}$ a derivation can be found with x = a. If $DBS_2 \wedge \overline{Q}$ has x bound to a before the proof, we find $DBS_2 \wedge \overline{Q}$ to be satisfiable. If we back up to find an alternative proof in $DBS_1 \wedge \overline{Q}$ to be the case when x = b, binding x to b in $DBS_2 \wedge \overline{Q}$ now leads to a derivation of the null clause.

The above illustrates the care that must be used in performing splits. The splitting process is easily generalized to having n non-Horn clauses with n_i positive literals in the ith non-Horn clause. For a single non-Horn clause with n positive literals $D = a_1 \vee \ldots \vee a_n \vee C$, a_i are positive literals and C_i a clause with all negative literals $DB \wedge D \equiv (DB \wedge (a_1 \vee C_1)) \vee \ldots \vee (DB \wedge (a_n \vee C_1))$. For n non-Horn clauses we have a split into $\prod_{i=1}^{n} n_i$ different databases. It should be clear from the above that splitting becomes extremely cumbersome even for small values of n and n_i. For example if $n_i = 2$ for i = 1,...,n, there are 2^n different spaces in which a query must be solved.

1.2.4 <u>The Non Monotonic Character of Closed World Definitions</u>

An important property of first order logic is that it is *monotonic*, i.e., if P and Q are sets of first order formulae and $P \vdash w$ then $P \cup Q \vdash w$. Formulae valid with respect to the formulae in P remain valid when additional information is added. The closed world assumption is *non-monotonic*. This may be seen as follows :

Let $DB = \{p \vee q\}$. Then we may assume $\overline{p}$ and $\overline{q}$ by the closed world assumption. Thus, $DB \vdash \overline{p}$. Now, if to DB we add q, then $DB \cup \{q\} = \{p \vee q, q\}$ and $DB \cup \{q\} \vdash p$. Hence when dealing with a closed world assumption one is dealing with a non-monotonic logic. The generalization of the closed world assumption as described in subsequent sections of this paper is also a non-monotonic logic. We shall show this later.

Some interesting descriptions of non-monotonic logics are given by McCarthy [1980],

Mc Dermott and Doyle [1980], Davis [1980], Reiter [1980], and Weyhrauch [1980] in a special issue of the *Artificial Intelligence Journal* of April 1980 devoted to this subject.

2. Indefinite Databases and the Closed World Assumption

2.1 Need for an Extended Closed World Assumption Definition

Consider the simple database

$$(2.1 - 1) \qquad \begin{Bmatrix} Pa \vee Pb \\ Pc \vee \overline{P}d \end{Bmatrix}.$$

We have seen previously that the closed world assumption does not apply to this database and leads to an inconsistent database if applied. However, (2.1 - 1) does admit a definition of atoms whose negations can be assumed to be true. In particular, there is no loss if we assume $\overline{P}c$ and $\overline{P}d$ to be true. Notice that if we add $\overline{P}c$ and $\overline{P}d$ to (2.1 - 1) to obtain

$$(2.1 - 2) \qquad \begin{Bmatrix} Pa \vee Pb \\ Pc \vee \overline{P}d \\ \overline{P}c \\ \overline{P}d \end{Bmatrix},$$

that this set of clauses is consistent. In a sense this is a maximally consistent set of clauses since if $\overline{P}a$ is added we can prove Pb from (2.1 - 2) and Pb cannot be proven from (2.1 - 1). Similarly if we add $\overline{P}b$ (but not $\overline{P}a$) we can prove Pa. If both $\overline{P}a$ and $\overline{P}b$ are added to (2.1 - 2), then the set is inconsistent.

We shall, in the following sections, make precise our definitions of a closed world assumption that encompasses both Horn and non-Horn databases.

2.2 Semantic Definition for a Closed World Definition of Databases

We shall first give a definition of a closed world assumption which applies to all databases. We shall refer to this as the GCWA in contrast to the CWA which applies only to Horn databases. The semantic definition will be a suitable generalization of the definition given by van Emden and Kowalski. We first need some preliminaries.

The database to which we shall refer is function-free and therefore contains no Skolem constants. An expression (term, literal, set of clauses) is *ground* if it contains no variables. We refer to the database as DB, where DB is a set of clauses. The set of all *ground atomic formulas* $P(t_1,\ldots,t_n)$ where P occurs in the set of clauses DB and $t_1,\ldots,t_n$ belong to the Herbrand universe H of DB is called the Herbrand base, $\hat{H}$, of DB. A Herbrand interpretation simulataneously associates, with every n-ary predicate symbol in DB a unique n-ary relation over H. The relation $\{(t_1,\ldots,t_n) : P(t_1,\ldots,t_n) \in I\}$ is *associated* by I with the predicate symbol P in DB.

(1) A ground atomic formula A is *true* in a Herbrand interpretation I iff $A \in I$.

(2) A ground negative literal $\overline{A}$ is *true* in I iff $A \notin I$.

(3) A ground clause $L_1 \ \ldots \ L_n$ is *true* in I iff at least one literal L_i is true in I.

(4) In general a clause C is *true* in I iff every ground instance $C\sigma$ is true in I. ($C\sigma$ is obtained by replacing every occurrence of a variable in C by a term in H. Different occurrences of the same variable are replaced by the same term).

(5) A set of clauses is *true* in I if and only if each clause in DB is true in I.

Given a Horn database van Emden and Kowalski have shown that the intersection of all models is a model. This is referred to as the model intersection property. As shown in Section 1.1, non-Horn data bases do not have a corresponding intersection property. The *model intersection* property of Horn clauses results in a unique minimal model. We generalize this concept for non-Horn databases.

A *model* of a set of clauses DB is an interpretation I such that every clause in DB is true in I. The set of Herbrand interpretations that are models of DB are denoted by $M(DB)$. A Herbrand interpretation I that forms a model for DB, i.e., $I \in M(DB)$ such that no smaller subset of I is a model is termed a *minimal mouel Herbrand interpretation* or simply a *minimal model*. The set of *minimal models of DB* is denoted by $MM(DB)$.

We illustrate the minimal model concept by the following examples.

Example 1.

$$\text{Let } DB = \begin{Bmatrix} Pa \vee Pb \\ Pc \vee \overline{P}d \end{Bmatrix}.$$

the following constitute $M(DB)$.

$$\begin{Bmatrix} \{Pa\}, \\ \{Pb\}, \\ \{Pa, Pb\}, \\ \{Pa, Pc\}, \\ \{Pb, Pc\}, \\ \{Pa, Pb, Pc\}, \\ \{Pa, Pc, Pd\}, \\ \{Pb, Pc, Pd\}, \\ \{Pa, Pb, Pc, Pd\} \end{Bmatrix}.$$

The set of minimal models is given by :

$$MM(DB) = \begin{Bmatrix} \{Pa\}, \\ \{Pb\} \end{Bmatrix}.$$

Note that there are two minimal models. Note that $\overline{P}c$ and $\overline{P}d$ are in both minimal models since the positive atoms Pc and Pd do not appear in the minimal models.

Example 2.

Consider the following database :

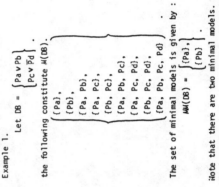

$$DB = \left\{\begin{array}{l} Qa, \\ Pa \vee Pb, \\ Pc \vee Pd, \\ Rx \vee Qx \vee \overline{P}x \end{array}\right\}$$

It is clear that DB can be replaced by an equivalent set of clauses :

$$DB_1 = \left\{\begin{array}{l} Qa, \\ Pa \vee Pb, \\ Pc \vee Pd, \\ Ra \vee Qa \vee \overline{P}a, \\ Rb \vee Qb \vee \overline{P}b, \\ Rc \vee Qc \vee \overline{P}c, \\ Rd \vee Qd \vee \overline{P}d \end{array}\right\} = \left\{\begin{array}{l} Qa, \\ Pa \vee Pb, \\ Pc \vee Pd, \\ Rb \vee Qb \vee \overline{P}b, \\ Rc \vee Qc \vee \overline{P}c, \\ Rd \vee Qd \vee \overline{P}d \end{array}\right\}$$

where the clause $Qa \vee Ra \vee \overline{P}a$ is subsumed by the clause Qa and is therefore deleted.

It can be seen that there are twelve minimal models of DB.

Γ_1 = {Qa, Pa, Pc, Rc},
Γ_2 = {Qa, Pa, Pc, Qc},
Γ_3 = {Qa, Pa, Pd, Rd},
Γ_4 = {Qa, Pa, Pd, Qd},
Γ_5 = {Qa, Pb, Pc, Rb, Rc},
Γ_6 = {Qa, Pb, Pc, Rb, Qc},
Γ_7 = {Qa, Pb, Pc, Qb, Qc},
Γ_8 = {Qa, Pb, Pc, Qb, Rc},
Γ_9 = {Qa, Pb, Pd, Rb, Rd},
Γ_{10} = {Qa, Pb, Pd, Qb, Rd},
Γ_{11} = {Qa, Pb, Pd, Rb, Qd},
Γ_{12} = {Qa, Pb, Pd, Qb, Pd}.

We note that Qa is in every minimal model, and $\overline{R}a$ is in every minimal model.

Let DB be a database whose Herbrand base is $\hat{H}_{DB}$. Let $MM(DB) = \{\Gamma_1\}$, i=1,...,n. be the set of minimal models of DB. Let $\Gamma = \left\{\bigcap_{i=1}^{n} \Gamma_i\right\}$, and let $\tilde{\Gamma}$ be the set of ground atomic formulae not in any minimal model of DB. Thus, $\tilde{\Gamma} = \left\{\bigcap_{i=1}^{n} (\hat{H}_{DB} - \Gamma_i)\right\}$. Let $\widetilde{\Gamma D} = \Gamma \cup \tilde{\Gamma}$. Every atomic formula in $\widetilde{\Gamma D}$ is said to be definite. Let ΓI be the set of atomic formulae not in $\widetilde{\Gamma D}$. Thus, $\Gamma I = \hat{H}_{DB} - \widetilde{\Gamma D}$. Then every atomic formula in ΓI is said to be indefinite. An atomic formula in $\tilde{\Gamma}$ is interpreted to be false and hence its negation is interpreted to be true. The atomic formulae in $\tilde{\Gamma}$ are said to form the *generalized closed world assumption for databases* (GCWA). If we let $\overline{\Gamma} = \{\vec{\overline{Pc}} \mid \vec{Pc} \in \tilde{\Gamma}\}$, then $\overline{\Gamma}$ represents the negative formulae true in the database. Similarly, if we let $\Gamma D = \Gamma \cup \overline{\Gamma}$, then ΓD represents the atomic formulae and negation of atomic formulae that can be assumed true in the DB.

It should be clear that the above definition is consistent with the CWA for Horn databases. In this case Γ represents the set of all atomic formulae that can be proven from DB since there is a unique minimal model. The set $\tilde{\Gamma}$ then contains all atomic formulae that cannot be proven from DB. Thus, the definition for CWA is contained within the definition for GCWA.

Example 3.

DB = {Pa ∨ Pb}

Γ_1 = {Pa}
Γ_2 = {Pb}   only minimal model interpretations of DB.

$\Gamma = \tilde{\Gamma} = \{\emptyset\}$, $\Gamma D = \{\emptyset\}$, ΓI = {Pa,Pb}

Example 4.

DB = {Qa, Pa ∨ Pb}

Γ_1 = {Qa, Pa}
Γ_2 = {Qa, Pb}   only minimal model interpretations of DB.

Γ = {Qa}, $\tilde{\Gamma}$ = {Qb}, $\widetilde{\Gamma D}$ = {Qa, Qb}, ΓI = {Pa, Pb}.

There are two definite atomic formulae Qa and Qb, and two indefinite formulae. We can assume $\overline{Q}b$ since it is a member of both minimal models.

Given a consistent set of Horn clauses in a DB, then by van Emden and Kowalski there is a unique minimal model, the intersection of all models. If an atomic formula does not appear in the intersection, its negation is true. Thus, Γ corresponds to the set of positive atomic formulae that are true in every model, while $\tilde{\Gamma}$ corresponds to the set of positive atomic formulae whose negations are true. $\Gamma \cup \tilde{\Gamma}$ then corresponds to the set of all atomic formulae in the Herbrand base. In Horn databases every atomic formula is definite.

When one has indefinite data, $\Gamma \cup \tilde{\Gamma}$ contains the atomic formulae that are definite while the remaining atomic formulae are indefinite. If we have two indefinite formulae, say Pa and Qb, and we want to determine whether or not Pa∨Qb is true, it suffices to find in every minimal model if either Pa or Qb is true. If this is the case, then Pa∨Qb is true. The above definition of a GCWA thereby generalizes the concept of a CWA to be applicable to Horn databases, non-Horn databases, or mixed databases.

2.3 <u>Syntactic Definition for a Closed World Definition of Databases</u>

In Horn databases if from DB $\nvdash$ Pc, then $\overline{P}c$ can be assumed to be true. We seek a suitable definition that corresponds here.

Let DB be a consistent set of clauses. Let $E = \{\vec{Pc} \mid DB \vdash \vec{Pc} \vee K$, and K is either the null clause, or K is a positive clause such that $DB \nvdash K\}$. That is, $\widetilde{E}$ corresponds to the set of atoms that appear in positive clauses derivable from DB. Let $\widetilde{EDB} = \hat{H}_{DB} - E$, where $\hat{H}_{DB}$ is the Herbrand base of DB. We claim that $\widetilde{EDB}$ corresponds to the set of atoms whose negation may be assumed to be true in DB. Hence $\widetilde{EDB}$ corresponds to the syntactic definition of the GCWA assumption. Let $\overline{EDB} = \{\overline{\vec{Pc}} \mid \vec{Pc} \in \widetilde{EDB}\}$, then $\overline{EDB}$ consists of the negated atoms assumed to be true in the DB. We must show that the syntactic and the semantic definitions are equivalent.

For Horn databases Reiter has defined $\overline{EDB} = \{\overline{\vec{Pc}} \mid DB \nvdash \vec{Pc}\}$ to be the definition of the closed world assumption (CWA). As shown by Reiter, if DB is a consistent database consisting only of Horn clauses, then we can derive only definite answers. Hence, E reduces to $E = \{P\vec{c} \mid DB \vdash P\vec{c}\}$, and since $\widetilde{\widetilde{EDB}} = \hat{H}_{DB} - E = \{P\vec{c} \mid DB \nvdash P\vec{c}\}$, and $\overline{EDB} = \{P\vec{c} \mid P\vec{c} \in \widetilde{\widetilde{EDB}}\}$, $\overline{\overline{EDB}} = \overline{EDB}$. Hence, for Horn databases $\overline{\overline{EDB}}$ encompasses $\overline{EDB}$.

We can show the following.

Theorem 1

Let DB be a consistent database, and K a clause.

If $DB \vdash K$, then every minimal model of DB contains a literal of K.

Proof : If $DB \vdash K$, then K is true in every model of DB. Hence, K is true in every minimal model of DB.

3. Equivalence of Generalized Closed World Assumption (GCWA) Syntactic and Semantic Definitions for Databases

3.1 Proof of Equivalence

We now show that the semantic and syntactic definitions of the GCWA are equivalent. The proof will be based on the following lemma.

Lemma 1

Let DB be a consistent set of clauses C, and $C = CP \cup CNP$ where CP consists of all positive clauses provable from DB, and CNP is the set of all clauses provable from DB that contain at least one negated atom. Then, every minimal model of C is a minimal model of CP.

Proof :

Let M be a minimal model of C. Let M_{CP} be a minimal model of M restricted to the clauses in CP. If $M = M_{CP}$, we are done. Hence, assume $M_{CP} \subset M$. There must be a non empty minimal mode M_{CP} of M restricted to the positive clauses in C since M is a model of CP.

There must be a clause in CNP such that every positive atom in the clause is not in M_{CP} and every negated atom in the clause is in M_{CP}. If this were not the case, then M_{CP} would be a model of every clause in CNP. But then M_{CP} would be a model of C. Since $M_{CP} \subset M$, it contradicts the assumption that M is minimal. Let a clause having this property be :

(1) $L \vee \bar{B}_1 \vee \ldots \vee \bar{B}_n$,

where L is a positive clause all of whose atoms are not in M_{CP}, and the B_i, $i=1,\ldots,n$ are positive atoms such that $B_i \in M_{CP}$.

Let the clauses in CP containing the B_i be of the following forms :

(2) $\{\bigwedge_{i_1=1}^{K_1} \mathcal{D}_{1i_1} \vee B_1,\ \bigwedge_{i_2=1}^{K_2} \mathcal{D}_{2i_2} \vee B_2, \ldots, \bigwedge_{i_n=1}^{K_n} \mathcal{D}_{ni_n} \vee B_n\}$

where the $\mathcal{D}_{ji_j}$ are positive clauses that contain no B_t for $t \neq j$, and

(3) {clauses containing two or more B_i, $i = 1,\ldots,n$}.

Assume that (2) does not contain any clauses of the form $\bigwedge_{i_j=1}^{K_j} \mathcal{D}_{ji_j} \vee B_j$ for some j. Then, the only clauses in which B_j appear in CP are in (3). But B_j always appears with some other atom $B_i \in M_{CP}$. Hence, $M_{CP} - \{B_j\}$ is a model of CP. But M_{CP} was assumed to be minimal and we have a contradiction.

Now assume that B_j must appear in a clause in (1) for $i = 1,\ldots,n$. That is, there must be at least one clause in CP of the form $\mathcal{D}_{ji_j} \in B_j$ for $j = 1,\ldots,n$. Resolving clauses in (1) with clauses in (2) yields the following set of clauses in CP:

(4) $\{\bigwedge_{i_1=1}^{K_1} \ldots \bigwedge_{i_n=1}^{K_n} L \vee \mathcal{D}_{1i_1} \vee \ldots \vee \mathcal{D}_{ni_n}\}$.

Since L is false in M_{CP}, and every clause in (4) is in CP, an atom in each of the clauses (4), coming from the $\mathcal{D}_{ti_t}$ must be in M_{CP}. Now, there must be at least one B_j such that there is an atom for each $\mathcal{D}_{ji_j}$, $i_j = 1,\ldots,k_j$ that is true in M_{CP}. If this were not the case, i.e. each B_j has a $\mathcal{D}_{ji_j}$ all of whose atoms are falsified in M_{CP}, we would have constructed a clause (4) in CP (or a clause in CP that subsumes a clause in (4)) that is falsified in M_{CP}, which is clearly not possible since M_{CP} is a minimal model of CP. Since there is an atom in every $\mathcal{D}_{ji_j}$, $i_j=1,\ldots,k_j$ that is true in M_{CP}, then every clause in (2) of the form $\mathcal{D}_{ji_j} \vee B_j$ is true in $M_{CP}-\{B_j\}$ and furthermore, every clause in (3) is true in $M_{CP}-\{B_j\}$, and these are the only clauses in CP that contain B_j, $M_{CP}-\{B_j\}$ is a model of CP and M_{CP} cannot be a minimal model of CP. Hence, we have a contradiction. The above argument applies for every clause in CNP. Hence, we must have $M_{CP}=M$ which was to be proven.

Theorem 2

Let DB be a consistent database. An atom L is in $\tilde{\Gamma}$ iff L is in EDB. That is, $\widetilde{\widetilde{EDB}} = \tilde{\Gamma}$.

Proof : We show first that $\tilde{\Gamma} \subseteq \widetilde{\widetilde{EDB}}$ and then that $\widetilde{\widetilde{EDB}} \subseteq \tilde{\Gamma}$.

Proof that $\tilde{\Gamma} \subseteq \widetilde{\widetilde{EDB}}$. To show that if $L \in \tilde{\Gamma}$, then $L \in \widetilde{\widetilde{EDB}}$ is equivalent to showing that if $L \in \tilde{\Gamma}$, then $L \notin E$. Assume that $L \in \tilde{\Gamma}$ and $L \in E$. Since we assume $L \in E$, by definition $DB \vdash L \vee K$ where K is either the null clause or a positive clause such that $DB \nvdash K$. If $DB \vdash L$, then L is in every minimal model and hence, L cannot be in Γ which is a contradiction. In the case $DB \vdash L \vee K$, every minimal model must contain an atom of $L \vee K$. But, since $DB \nvdash K$, there is a minimal model that contains no atom of K (for otherwise $DB \vdash K$). This minimal model must contain L since $DB \vdash L \vee K$. Hence L appears in some minimal model and hence L cannot be in $\tilde{\Gamma}$ which is a contradiction.

Proof that $\widetilde{\widetilde{EDB}} \subseteq \tilde{\Gamma}$. Let $L \in \widetilde{\widetilde{EDB}}$. Then, $DB \nvdash L \vee K$, where K is either null or a positive clause such that $DB \nvdash K$. Now, L cannot appear in any positive clause in CP (the set of all positive clauses derivable from DB). For, if it did then it would not be in $\widetilde{\widetilde{EDB}}$. Hence, $L \notin CP$ and since every minimal model of DB is a minimal model of CP as shown by the above lemma, L is in no minimal model of DB. But then

$L \in \tilde{\Gamma}$. Hence, $\widetilde{\widetilde{EDB}} \subseteq \tilde{\Gamma}$.

Since we have shown that $\widetilde{\widetilde{EDB}} \subseteq \tilde{\Gamma}$ and $\tilde{\Gamma} \subseteq \widetilde{\widetilde{EDB}}$, we have $\tilde{\Gamma} = \widetilde{\widetilde{EDB}}$.

<u>Corollary 2.1</u> :

$\overline{\overline{EDB}} = \overline{\Gamma}$.

<u>Proof</u> : The corollary is obvious from the definitions of $\overline{\overline{EDB}}$, $\overline{\Gamma}$ and the equivalence of $\widetilde{\widetilde{EDB}}$ and $\tilde{\Gamma}$.

3.2 <u>Properties of GCWA</u>

We derive some consequences of the above. Let $\overline{\overline{EDB}}$ be the negated atoms of $\widetilde{\widetilde{EDB}}$ defined previously.

<u>Theorem 3</u>

Let DB be a consistent database, then $DB \cup \overline{\overline{EDB}}$ is consistent.

Proof : Every minimal model of DB is free of atoms of $\widetilde{\widetilde{EDB}}$ since $\tilde{\Gamma} = \widetilde{\widetilde{EDB}}$. Hence, every minimal model of DB is a minimal model of $DB \cup \overline{\overline{EDB}}$. Hence $DB \cup \overline{\overline{EDB}}$ is consistent.

<u>Theorem 4</u>

Let DB be a consistent database and let K be a positive clause. If $DB \nvdash K$, then $DB \cup \overline{\overline{EDB}} \nvdash K$.

Proof : The previous theorem states that not only is $DB \cup \overline{\overline{EDB}}$ consistent, but every minimal model of DB is a minimal model of $DB \cup \overline{\overline{EDB}}$. If $DB \cup \overline{\overline{EDB}} \vdash K$ an atom of K must appear in every minimal model of DB. However, this means that $DB \vdash K$ which is a contradiction.

The above theorem states that we cannot prove any more positive clauses from $DB \cup \overline{\overline{EDB}}$ than we can prove from DB. However, there are some non-positive clauses that can be proven from $DB \cup \overline{\overline{EDB}}$ that cannot be proven from DB aside from the unit clauses in $\overline{\overline{EDB}}$.

<u>Example 5.</u>

Let $DB = \{P \vee Q \vee \overline{R}\}$.

Then, $\Gamma_1 = \{\emptyset\}$ is the only minimal model. Hence $\Gamma = \{\emptyset\}$ and $\tilde{\Gamma} = \{P,Q,R\}$. Hence $\widetilde{\widetilde{EDB}} = \{P,Q,R\}$, and $\overline{\overline{EDB}} = \{\overline{P},\overline{Q},\overline{R}\}$. Now, $DB \cup \overline{\overline{EDB}} = \{P \vee Q \vee \overline{R}, \overline{P}, \overline{Q}, \overline{R}\}$. $DB \cup \overline{\overline{EDB}} \vdash P \vee \overline{R}$ and $DB \nvdash P \vee \overline{R}$.

The set of clauses $\overline{\overline{EDB}}$ when added to DB forms a maximal set of clauses in the following sense. A set of clauses *DB is maximally consistent with the closed world assumption for databases* if the addition of a negative atom to DB, where the atom, say Pa, is taken from the Herbrand base of DB and is not subsumed by DB satisfies the following conditions.

(1) $DB \cup \{\overline{P}a\}$ is inconsistent or

(2) $DB \cup \{\overline{P}a\} \vdash C$, where C is a positive clause and $DB \nvdash C$.

<u>Theorem 5</u>

Let DB be a consistent database, then $DB \cup \overline{\overline{EDB}}$ is maximally consistent.

Proof : Assume that $DB \cup \overline{\overline{EDB}}$ is not maximally consistent. From Theorem 3, $DB \cup \overline{\overline{EDB}}$ is consistent. If $Pa \in \widetilde{\widetilde{EDB}}$, then $\overline{P}a \in \overline{\overline{EDB}}$ and the addition of $\overline{P}a$ does not change the status of $DB \cup \overline{\overline{EDB}}$. Now, let Pa be an atom in a positive clause in CP. Consider $DB \cup \overline{\overline{EDB}} \cup \{\overline{P}a\}$. Since $DB \vdash Pa \vee K$, where K is null or positive and $DB \nvdash Pa$, $DB \nvdash K$, then every minimal model for $DB \cup \overline{\overline{EDB}}$ that contains Pa cannot be a model of $DB \cup \overline{\overline{EDB}} \cup \{\overline{P}a\}$. If every model of $DB \cup \overline{\overline{EDB}}$ contains Pa, then the addition of $\overline{P}a$ causes the set of clauses to be inconsistent. The remaining minimal models of $DB \cup \overline{\overline{EDB}}$ must be minimal models of $DB \cup \overline{\overline{EDB}} \cup \{\overline{P}a\}$. Hence, since every minimal model of $DB \cup \overline{\overline{EDB}}$ contains either an atom of Pa or an atom of K, the minimal models of $DB \cup \overline{\overline{EDB}} \cup \{\overline{P}a\}$ must contain atoms of K. Hence $DB \cup \overline{\overline{EDB}} \cup \{\overline{P}a\} \vdash K$ and therefore $DB \cup \overline{\overline{EDB}}$ is maximally consistent with the GCWA.

The concept of maximally consistent is useful. However, it may be possible to make a weaker assumption about databases that might prove computationally efficient. For example let the database be $DB \cup \{Pa \vee Pb, Pc\}$, where DB is Horn and contains no predicate letter of the form P. We may define every atom of P to be indefinite. Using a Horn theorem prover, failure to prove Pa would not permit us to assume $\overline{P}a$, which is correct. We could also prove Pc which is again correct. However, if we could not find Pd we could not assume $\overline{P}d$ which is not correct according to the GCWA. We could only conclude that Pd could be proven with another atom which would not be correct. However, this might be satisfactory for some database applications. With the GCWA we obtain a maximally complete set so that there would be no ambiguity concerning the status of Pd. That is, $\overline{P}d$ could be assumed to be true.

In Section 1.2.4 we noted that the GCWA had the non-monotonicity property. This can be seen easily as follows. Let, $DB = \{p \vee q \vee \overline{r}\}$. Then, assuming the GCWA, $DB \vdash \overline{r}$. Consider now $DB \cup \{r\}$. Then, $DB \cup \{r\} \nvdash \overline{r}$. Hence the GCWA has the non-monotonicity property. Thus, when adding new information to DB, we must *revise our concept of* $\overline{\overline{EDB}}$. That is our belief about what negative data holds true must be modified.

3.3 <u>Null Values and the GCWA</u>

The concept of a null value in database systems has many connotations. It may denote, "value at present unknown, but one of some finite set of known possible values", or "value at present unknown, but it is not necessarily one of some finite set of known possible values".

We shall consider the case where the unknown value must be among the finite set of constants that define the database. An unknown value such as in $P(a,\omega)$, where a is a constant and ω a special symbol denoting unknown is, in fact, a logical statement $(\exists x)P(a,x)$. When the logical statement is transformed to clause form, a Skolem constant is introduced.

The statement $(\exists x)P(a,x)$ can be replaced by an equivalent statement, $P(a,a_1) \vee \ldots \vee P(a,a_n)$, where the a_i, $i = 1,\ldots,n$ are all of the finite number of constants in the database. Hence, a null value corresponds to an indefinite statement in the database.

Assume now that the only data in some database that contains constants a and b is $P(a,\omega)$, where ω is a Skolem constant. Since the database appears to be Horn, if one attempts to prove P(a,b), one cannot do so and one is led, under the closed world assumption (CWA) to assume $\overline{P}(a,b)$. For the same reason one is led to assume $\overline{P}(a,a)$. But, then $P(a,\omega) \wedge \overline{P}(a,a) \wedge \overline{P}(a,b)$ is not consistent since ω is either a or b. However, using the generalized closed world assumption (GCWA), and recognizing that $P(a,\omega)$ is equivalent to $P(a,a) \vee P(a,b)$, we cannot conclude $\overline{P}(a,a)$ or $\overline{P}(a,b)$

The GCWA is compatible, then, with null values in a database where the null value must be among the constants in the database. Null values in a formula such as $(\exists x)(P(a,x) \wedge Q(x,b))$ may be written as $P(a,\omega) \wedge Q(\omega,b)$. The Skolem constant ω must be the same in the two clauses which result from this formula, namely, $\{P(a,\omega), Q(\omega,b)\}$. However, given that null values arise from different formulae, the Skolem constants must be written as $R(\omega_1,b)$, where ω and ω_1 are distinct Skolem constants.

4. Summary

An extended definition has been given to the concept of a closed world assumption that applies to function-free clauses. Semantic and syntactic definitions have been provided for the GCWA that serves to generalize the CWA described by Reiter. It was shown that the syntactic and semantic definitions are equivalent. The generalization reduces to the CWA when one has Horn DBs. The concept of an open world assumption (OWA) makes no assumption about failure by negation and hence remains the same. We have also defined the concept of maximally complete, and have shown that $DB \cup \overline{\overline{EDB}}$ is maximally complete, where DB is the database and EDB the negated atoms defined by the GCWA. The GCWA was also shown to handle the concept of null values correctly.

What remains to be addressed is how the concept can be used in a practical sense.

Acknowledgements

I wish to express my appreciation to John Grant and Michael Hudak for stimulating discussions on this work. I also wish to express my appreciation to Jorges Vidart and the Universidad Simon Bolivar who provided support to me for a visit where collaborative work was performed with Phillipe Roussel. The concept of minimal models for non Horn databases as used in this paper is due to Phillipe Roussel. I also gratefully acknowledge support from the National Science Foundation under grant number SK-CRC6. Thanks are also due to Liz Bassett for her careful typing of this paper.

References

1. Clark, K.L. 1978 , "Negation as Failure" In Logic and Data Bases (H. Gallaire and J. Minker, Eds.), Plenum Press, New York, N.Y., 1978, 293-322.

2. Davis, M. 1980 , "The Mathematics of Non-Monotonic Reasoning", Artificial Intelligence Journal, 13, 2 (April 1980), 73-80.

3. Hewitt, C. 1972 , "Description and Theoretical Analysis (Using Schemata) of PLANNER : A Language for Proving Theorems and Manipulating Models in a Robot", AI Memo No. 251, MIT Project MAC, Cambridge, Mass., April 1980.

4. Hill, R. 1974 , "LUSH Resolution and its Completeness" DCL Memo No. 78, University of Edinburg School of Artificial Intelligence, August 1974.

5. Kowalski, R.A. and Kuehner, D. 1971 , "Linear Resolution with Selection Function" Artificial Intelligence Vol. 2, 1971, 227-260.

6. Kowalski, R.A. 1978 , "Logic for Data Description", In Logic and Data Bases (H. Gallaire and J. Minker, Eds.), Plenum Press, New York, N.Y., 1978, 77-103.

7. Loveland, D.W. 1968 , "Mechanical Theorem Proving by Model Elimination", JACM 15, (April 1968) 236-251.

8. Loveland, D.W., Stickel, M.E. 1973 , "A Hole in Goal Trees : Some Guidance from Resolution Theory", Reproduced in IEEE Transactions on Computers, C-25, April 1976, 335-341.

9. Loveland, D.W. 1978 , Automated Theorem Proving : A Logical Basis, North Holland Publishing Co., New York, 1978.

10. McCarthy, J. 1980 , "Circumscription - A Form of Non-Monotonic Reasoning", Artificial Intelligence Journal, 13, 2 (April 1980), 27-39.

11. McDermott, D. and J. Doyle 1980 , "Non-Monotonic Logic I", Artificial Intelligence Journal, 13, 2 (Apirl 1980), 41-72.

12. McCarthy, J. 1980 , "Addendum : Circumscription and other Non-Montonic Formalisms", Artificial Intelligence Journal, 13,2 (April 1980), 171-172.

13. Minker, J. and Zanon, G. 1979 , "LUST Resolution : Resolution with Arbitrary Selection Function", University of Maryland Technical Report TR-736, February 1979.

14. Nicolas, J.M. and Syre, J.C. 1974 , "Natural Question Answering and Automatic Deduction in the System Syntex", Proceedings IFIP Congress 1974, Stockholm, Sweden, August 1974.

15. Nicolas, J.M. and Gallaire, H. 1978 , "Data Bases : Theory vs. Interpretation", In Logic and Data Bases (H. Gallaire and J. Minker, Eds.), Plenum Press, New York, N.Y. 1978, 33-54.

16. Reiter, R. 1971 , "Two Results on Ordering for Resolution with Merging and Linear Format", JACM 18, (October 1971), 630-646.

17. Reiter, R. 1978a , "Deductive Question-Answering on Relational Data Bases", In Logic and Data Bases (H. Gallaire and J. Minker, Eds.), Plenum Press, New York, N.Y. 1978, 149-177.

18. Reiter, R. 1978b , "On Closed World Data Bases", In Logic and Data Bases (H. Gallaire and J. Minker, Eds.), Plenum Press, New York, N.Y., 1978, 55-76.

19. Reiter, R. 1980 , "A Logic for Default Reasoning", Artificial Intelligence Journal, 13, 2 (April 1980), 81-132.

20. Roussel, P. 1975 , PROLOG - Manuel de Reference et de Utilisation, Groupe d' Intelligence Artificielle, Universite d' Air Marseilles, Luminy, September 1975.

21. van Emden, M.H. 1977 , "Computation and Deductive Information Retrieval", Department of Computer Science, University of Waterloo, Ont., Research Report CS-77-16, May 1977.

22. van Emden, M.H. and Kowalski, R.A. 1976 , "The Semantics of Predicate Logic as a Programming Language" JACM 23, 4 (October 1976), 723-742.

23. Weyhrauch, R. W. 1980 , "Prologomena to a Theory of Mechanized Formal Reasoning" Artificial Intelligence Journal, 13, 2 (April 1980), 133-170.

Closed-World Databases and Circumscription*

Vladimir Lifschitz
Department of Mathematics and Computer Science, San Jose State University, San Jose, CA 95192, U.S.A. and Department of Computer Science Stanford University, Stanford, CA 93405, U.S.A.

Recommended by Ray Reiter

ABSTRACT

We compare two forms of non-monotonic reasoning: closed-world evaluation of queries in databases and circumscription. For closed E-saturated databases we show that the closed-world assumption, if consistent, is equivalent to circumscribing all predicates in the database.

1. Introduction

Reiter's closed-world evaluation of queries in databases [1] and McCarthy's circumscription [2, 3] are two forms of non-monotonic reasoning discussed in recent AI literature.

Under the closed-world assumption (CWA), the negation of a positive ground literal F is assumed true if F cannot be derived from the facts in the database. This mechanism makes it possible to include only 'positive knowledge' in the database and assume the truth of 'negative' facts by default.

The result of circumscribing a predicate symbol P in a predicate formula A is the formula asserting that no predicate which is stronger than P satisfies A. For instance, circumscribing P in $Pc_1 \wedge Pc_2$ gives $\forall x(Px \equiv (x = c_1 \vee x = c_2))$. More generally, we can jointly circumscribe several predicates $P_1, \ldots, P_m$.

Clearly, there is a similarity between the CWA and circumscribing *all* predicate symbols in a predicate formula: in both cases we 'minimize' the predicates represented by the symbols. At the same time, these two procedures are technically quite different from each other. The CWA extends the database by very simple formulas, negated ground atoms, but uses the concept of derivability to decide which formulas should be added. Circumscription, on the other hand, is a purely syntactic translation, but its result is expressed by a formula of second-order logic.

The purpose of this paper is to investigate under what conditions the closed-world assumption and the result of circumscribing all predicates are equivalent.

Relation between closed-world reasoning and circumscription is discussed also by Doyle [4] and Etherington et al. [5]. Shepherdson [6] studies the relation between the CWA and the concept of predicate completion introduced by Clark [7].

Recall the definitions. Consider a first-order language without equality or functions symbols, with a finite number of constant symbols $c_1, \ldots, c_n$ and a finite number of predicate symbols $P_1, \ldots, P_m$. Let A be a closed universal formula in this language. We will sometimes write A as $A(P)$, where P stands for $P_1, \ldots, P_m$.

Let G_0 be the set of atomic formulas formed from $P_1, \ldots, P_m$ and $c_1, \ldots, c_n$, and

$$G(A) = \{F \in G_0 : A \models F\}.$$

We define

$$CWA(A) \equiv A \wedge \bigwedge_{F \in G_0 \setminus G(A)} \neg F.$$

The result of circumscribing all predicate symbols in A is expressed by the second-order formula

$$CIRC(A) \equiv A(P) \wedge \neg \exists P'(A(P') \wedge P' < P),$$

where P' stands for $P'_1, \ldots, P'_m$, and $P' < P$ means

$$\bigwedge_{i=1}^{m} \forall x(P'_i x \supset P_i x) \wedge \bigvee_{i=1}^{m} \exists x(P_i x \wedge \neg P'_i x)$$

(x is a tuple of variables).

We would like to know when, and in what sense, $CWA(A)$ is equivalent to $CIRC(A)$.

2. Domain Closure and the Uniqueness of Names

The following example shows that even in simple cases we cannot expect any of the formulas $CWA(A)$ and $CIRC(A)$ to imply the other in predicate calculus. Let A be $P_1 c_1 \wedge P_2 c_2$. Then

$$CWA(A) \equiv P_1 c_1 \wedge P_2 c_2 \wedge \neg P_1 c_2 \wedge \neg P_2 c_1,$$

$$CIRC(A) \equiv \forall x(P_1 x \equiv x = c_1) \wedge \forall x(P_2 x \equiv x = c_2).$$

To derive $CIRC(A)$ from $CWA(A)$ we have to assume that the objects denoted by c_1 and c_2 are the only objects in the universe: $\forall x(x = c_1 \vee x = c_2)$. In the general case, we need the 'domain-closure assumption' of Reiter [8]: every object in the universe of the theory is represented by a constant available in the language. This assumption is expressed by the formula

$$D \equiv \forall x \bigvee_{i=1}^{n} x = c_i .$$

To derive $CIRC(A)$ from $CWA(A)$, we have to assume that the objects denoted by c_1 and c_2 are different: $c_1 \neq c_2$. In the general case, we need the 'uniqueness of names':

$$U \equiv \bigwedge_{1 \leq i < j \leq n} c_i \neq c_j .$$

These two assumptions, D and U, characterize the important class of *closed E-saturated* databases studied by Reiter [8]. The domain-closure assumption D is quite strong: it implies that quantifiers can be replaced by finite conjunctions and disjunctions, so that any formula is equivalent to a propositional combination of atoms. In many applications of logic to AI, there is no reason to accept the assumption that all objects are represented by constants (or even constant terms). This especially clear when the universe of the theory contains arbitrary situations. (A *situation* is defined by McCarthy and Hayes [9] as "the complete state of the universe at an instant of time").

For some A the equivalence $CWA(A) \equiv CIRC(A)$ cannot be proved even assuming D and U. This is clear from the fact that the CWA is sometimes contradictory (Reiter [1]), whereas the result of circumscription in a universal formula never leads to a contradiction, according to Etherington et al. [5]. The simplest example is $Pc_1 \vee Pc_2$. The CWA gives $\neg Pc_1$ and $\neg Pc_2$, which contradict the given formula; circumscribing P gives only

$$\forall x(Px \equiv x = c_1) \vee \forall x(Px \equiv x = c_2) .$$

Theorem 3.1 shows, however, that in all other cases the CWA is equivalent to the result of circumscription.

3. The Equivalence of the CWA and Circumscription

We write $A_1, \ldots, A_k \models B$ if $A_1, \ldots, A_k$ *semantically imply* B, i.e., if B is true in every model of $A_1, \ldots, A_k$.

Theorem 3.1. *If $CWA(A)$ is consistent then*

$$D, U \models CWA(A) \equiv CIRC(A) .$$

In the proof of the theorem we use the notation:

$$A^+ \equiv \bigwedge_{F \in G(A)} F, \quad A^- \equiv \bigwedge_{F \in G_0 \setminus G(A)} \neg F.$$

In this notation,

$$CWA(A) \equiv A \wedge A^- . \tag{1}$$

Clearly,

$$A \models A^+ . \tag{2}$$

Lemma 3.2. *If $CWA(A)$ is consistent then*

$$D, A^+, A^- \models A.$$

Proof. In the presence of D, every closed formula is equivalent to a propositional combination of closed atomic formulas. Hence every closed formula can be either proved or refuted from D, A^+, A^-. Thus it suffices to show that D, A^+, A^- and A are consistent. By (1) and (2), the last three formulas are derivable from $CWA(A)$; hence it suffices to show that $CWA(A)$ is consistent with D. But every consistent universal formula F is consistent with D, because D holds in the minimal model of F.

Proof of Theorem 3.1. To derive circumscription from the CWA, assume D, $A \wedge A^-$, and $P' < P$. From D and the second conjunctive term of $P' < P$,

$$\bigvee_i \bigvee_C (P_i C \wedge \neg P'_i C) ,$$

where C ranges over the tuples of constants. A^- implies $\neg P_i C$ for all i, C such that $P_i C \notin G(A)$. Hence

$$\bigvee_i \bigvee_{C : P_i C \in G(A)} \neg P'_i C .$$

Then $\neg A^+(P')$ and, by (1), $\neg A(P')$.

To prove the other half of the equivalence, consider the predicates

$$P'_i \equiv \lambda x \bigvee_{P_i C \in G(A)} x = C .$$

(For tuples x, C, we write $x = C$ for $x_1 = C_1 \wedge x_2 = C_2 \wedge \cdots$). Clearly, $\models P'_i C$ for all $C \in G(A)$; consequently,

$$\models A^+(P') . \tag{3}$$

Furthermore, $U \models \neg P'_i C$ for all $C \in G_0 \setminus G(A)$; consequently,

$$U \models A^-(P'). \tag{4}$$

From (3), (4) and Lemma 3.2,

$$D, U \models A(P'). \tag{5}$$

We also need one other property of P', which follows immediately from the definitions of P' and A^+:

$$A^+ \models \forall x(P'_i x \supset P_i x). \tag{6}$$

Assume now D, U, and $CIRC(A)$. From (5) and the second conjunctive term of $CIRC(A)$ we conclude that $\neg(P' < P)$. On the other hand, the first conjunctive term of $CIRC(A)$, (2) and (6) imply the first conjunctive term of $P' < P$. Then, for all i,

$$\forall x(P_i x \equiv P'_i x).$$

Consequently (4) implies A^-.

The theorem is proved.

It is interesting to notice that our original justification for assuming the domain-closure condition D and the uniqueness of names U was that the former is needed for deriving circumscription from the CWA, and the latter for deriving the CWA from circumscription; however, D is used in both parts of the proof and thus seems essential for both implications. The following example shows that this is indeed the case. Let A be the conjunction of the formulas:

$$\forall x P_1 xx,$$

$$\forall xy(P_1 xy \supset P_1 yx),$$

$$\forall xyz(P_1 xy \wedge P_1 yz \supset P_1 xz),$$

$$\forall x(P_1 c_1 x \vee P_1 c_2 x) \wedge P_2.$$

Thus A asserts that P_1 is an equivalence relation and, if P_2 is false, every object is equivalent either to c_1 or to c_2. $CWA(A)$ is

$$A \wedge \neg P_1 c_1 c_2 \wedge \neg P_1 c_2 c_1 \wedge \neg P_2$$

and is, of course, consistent. The model in which the universe consists of three objects, c_1 and c_2 are different, P_1 is equality, and P_2 is true satisfies $CIRC(A)$ and U, but not $CWA(A)$.

4. Conclusion

It should be emphasized that the closed-world assumption is equivalent not to general circumscription, but to its very special case, and in rather special circumstances. There are several reasons to view circumscription as a substantially more powerful form of non-monotonic reasoning:

(1) The characterization of the minimized predicates given by circumscription is expressed by universal formulas, not just by the negations of ground atoms. This is essential when the domain-closure assumption is not applicable.

(2) Circumscription often leads to non-trivial conditions on the minimized predicates when the closed-world assumption is contradictory.

(3) Circumscription can be applied to arbitrary finitely axiomatized first-order theories (or even second-order theories), not only to universal theories without function symbols.

(4) Circumscription allows us to minimize a *subset* of the predicates, not necessarily all represented in the language. As to the predicates that are not minimized, we are free to decide which of them are allowed to vary in the process of minimization.

(5) On the other hand, with circumscription we can minimize predicates that do not correspond to any predicate symbols, but are defined by λ-expressions.

(6) If the goals of minimizing several predicates conflict with each other, circumscription provides an opportunity to assign relative priorities of these goals.

ACKNOWLEDGMENT

I would like to thank Michael Gelfond and John McCarthy for fruitful discussions.

REFERENCES

1. Reiter, R., On closed world data bases, in: H. Gallaire and J. Minker. (Eds.), *Logic and Data Bases* (Plenum Press, New York, 1978) 55–76.
2. McCarthy, J., Circumscription—a form of non-monotonic reasoning, *Artificial Intelligence* **13** (1980) 295–323.
3. McCarthy, J., Applications of circumscription to formalizing commonsense knowledge, *AAAI Workshop on Non-Monotonic Reasoning* (1984) 295–323.
4. Doyle, J., Circumscription and implicit definability, *AAAI Workshop on Non-Monotonic Reasoning* (1984) 57–68.
5. Etherington, D., Mercer, R. and Reiter, R., On the adequacy of predicate circumscription for closed-world reasoning, *Computational Intelligence* **1** (1985) 11–15.
6. Shepherdson, J., Negation as failure: a comparison of Clark's completed data base and Reiter's closed-world assumption, *Logic Programming* **1** (1984) 51–79.
7. Clark, K., Negation as failure; in: H. Gallaire and J. Minker (Eds.), *Logic and Data Bases* (Plenum Press, New York, 1978) 293–322.
8. Reiter, R., Equality and domain closure in first order data bases, *J. ACM* **27** (1980) 235–249.
9. McCarthy, J. and Hayes, P., Some philosophical problems from the stand-point of artificial intelligence, in: B. Meltzer and D. Michie (Eds.), *Machine Intelligence* **4** (Edinburgh University Press, Edinburgh, 1969) 463–502.

ON THE DECLARATIVE SEMANTICS OF LOGIC PROGRAMS WITH NEGATION

Vladimir Lifschitz*

ABSTRACT

A logic program can be viewed as a set of predicate formulas, and its declarative meaning can be defined by specifying a certain Herbrand model of that set. For programs without negation, this model is defined either as the Herbrand model with the minimal set of positive ground atoms, or, equivalently, as the minimal fixed point of a certain operator associated with the program (van Emden and Kowalski). These solutions do not apply to general logic programs, because a program with negation may have many minimal Herbrand models, and the corresponding operator may have many minimal fixed points. Apt, Blair and Walker and, independently, Van Gelder, introduced a class of *stratified* programs which disallow certain combinations of recursion and negation, and showed how to use the fixed point approach to define a declarative semantics for such programs. Using the concept of circumscription, we extend the minimal model approach to stratified programs and show that it leads to the same semantics.

INTRODUCTION

Logic programming is based on the idea that substantial subsets of predicate calculus can be used as programming languages. A logic program is essentially a collection of predicate formulas, so that we can talk about the *models* of a logic program, about formulas that can be *derived* from it in predicate logic, and so forth. This is the *declarative* aspect of logic programming. On the other hand, we can accept the *procedural* view and, by specifying a logic programming interpreter, define *the process of computation* associated with a given program.

The investigation of the semantics of logic programs includes defining their declarative semantics and their procedural semantics and studying the relation between the two. In this paper we are interested primarily in the declarative interpretation of logic programs. But it should be remembered that a declarative semantics is useful only as long as it allows us to justify the correctness of the computational procedures employed in logic programming interpreters.

* Computer Science Department, Stanford University, Stanford, CA 94305.

Given a logic program P and a query F without variables, what do we consider to be the right answer to the query? According to one possible definition, the answer is *yes* if F is a *logical consequence* of P, and *no* otherwise. This simple characterization provides a satisfactory declarative semantics for logic programming with Horn clauses (i.e., for programs without negation, as in pure Prolog.) Consider, for instance, the program

$$\begin{aligned} &p(1), \\ &q(2), \\ &r(x) \leftarrow q(x). \end{aligned} \tag{1}$$

The answer to each of the queries $p(1)$, $q(2)$ and $r(2)$ is *yes*, because they follow from (1) in predicate calculus; the answer to each of the queries $p(2)$, $q(1)$ and $r(1)$ is *no*, because they do not follow from (1).

In view of Gödel's completeness theorem, this semantics can be equivalenly expressed in terms of models: the answer to a query is *yes* iff the query is true in every model of the program. For a query with variables we can say that the answer is the set of tuples of values for the variables which make the query true in every model of the program.

On the other hand, we can take a somewhat different path and, instead of referring to *arbitrary* models of the program P, consider just *one* of them, the *canonical* model M_P. The answer to a query is the set of tuples of values for the variables which make the query true in that particular model. For program (1), for example, the canonical model has the universe $\{1,2\}$, with $p(x)$ true for $x = 1$, and $q(x)$ and $r(x)$ true for $x = 2$.

A general description of how the canonical model is constructed for logic programs without negation was given by van Emden and Kowalski [1976]. M_P is selected among the *Herbrand* models of P, i.e., among the models whose universe is the set of ground terms in the language of P, and whose object and function constants are interpreted in such a way that every ground term denotes itself. An Herbrand model is completely characterized by the set of ground atoms which are true in the model, and it is sometimes identified with this set. For instance, the model which defines the meaning of program (1) is represented by the set

$$\{p(1), q(2), r(2)\}. \tag{2}$$

Another Herbrand model of (1) can be written as

$$\{p(1), p(2), q(1), q(2), r(1), r(2)\}. \tag{3}$$

How do we select M_P among the Herbrand models of P? Herbrand models, viewed as sets of ground atoms, can be compared using set inclusion. For example, we can say that (2) is less than (3). A program P without negation has exactly one *minimal* Herbrand model, which is the intersection of all Herbrand models of P; in other words, a ground atom is true in that model iff it is true in every Herbrand model of P. According to van Emden and Kowalski, the meaning of P is represented by this minimal model. This description of the canonical model provides another declarative semantics for logic programming with Horn clauses, equivalent to the logical consequence semantics.

An equivalent description of the canonical model M_P is given by van Emden and Kowalski in the same paper, again for programs without negation, in terms of an operator T_P associated with P. When applied to a set M of ground atoms in the language of P, T_P produces the set $T_P(M)$ of ground atoms which follow from the facts in M by "one application" of one of the rules in P. The operator corresponding to program (1), for instance, transforms $\{q(1)\}$ into

$$\{p(1), q(2), r(1)\}.$$

The canonical model M_P can be characterized as the minimal fixed point of T_P:

$$M_P = T_P(\emptyset) \cup T_P(T_P(\emptyset)) \cup \ldots$$

In case of program (1),

$$T_P(\emptyset) = \{p(1), q(2)\},$$
$$T_P(T_P(\emptyset)) = \{p(1), q(2), r(2)\},$$

and further applications of T_P do not add new elements. (In this example, the infinite union defining M_P can be replaced by its finite segment. But this is not necessarily so for programs with function symbols, when the Herbrand universe is infinite, and M_P may be infinite also.) Apt and van Emden [1982] prove other important properties of the fixed points of T_P.

We are interested in extending these ideas to logic programs with negation. Consider the program

$$\begin{aligned} &p(1), \\ &q(2), \\ &r(x) \leftarrow \neg q(x). \end{aligned} \tag{4}$$

The procedural intepretation of this program based on the familiar "negation as failure" principle suggests that the query $q(1)$ should be answered *no*, and then the query $r(1)$ should be answered *yes*. Let us see whether any of the declarative approaches outlined above can provide a justification for this.

1. *The Logical Consequence Semantics.* The formula $r(1)$ is *not* a logical consequence of (4). It is true in some models of (1), but certainly not in all of them. For instance, it is true in the Herbrand model

$$\{p(1), q(2), r(1)\}, \tag{5}$$

but false in

$$\{p(1), q(1), q(2)\}. \tag{6}$$

It appears then that the answer to the query $r(1)$ should have been negative.

2. *The Minimal Model Semantics.* Program (4) has *two* different minimal Herbrand models, (5) and (6). The "negation as failure" interpretation suggests that the meaning of (4) is correctly repesented by the former. But how can we define in general terms why (5) is the "right" model? What complicates the matter is that the choice of M_P is apparently not invariant relative to logically equivalent transformations of P. The program

$$\begin{aligned} &p(1), \\ &q(2), \\ &q(x) \leftarrow \neg r(x), \end{aligned} \tag{7}$$

viewed as a set of formulas, is equivalent to (4), so that it has the same minimal models (5) and (6); but now (6) seems to correctly represent the meaning of the program.

3. *The Fixed Point Semantics.* The operator T_P corresponding to program (4) has *two* different minimal fixed ponts, (5) and (6). How can we define in general terms why (5) is the "right" fixed point?

We have to conclude that the approaches which worked so well for logic programming with Horn clauses do not immediately provide a satisfactory declarative semantics for programs with negation.

An extension of the fixed point semantics applicable to some programs with negation was proposed recently by Apt, Blair and Walker [1987] and independently by Van Gelder [1987]. (The extension is based on an idea discussed informally by Chandra and Harel [1985].) These authors introduce a class of general logic programs, called "stratified", or "free from recursive negation", and assign a unique Herbrand model M_P to every such program P using "iterated" fixed points. (The definitions will be reproduced below.) Programs (4) and (7) are stratified, and the iterated fixed point semantics assigns model (5) to (4) and model (6) to (7), as suggested by the procedural interpretation.

Here is an example of a program which is *not* stratified:

$$\begin{aligned} &p(1,2), \\ &p(2,1), \\ &q(x) \leftarrow p(x,y), \neg q(y). \end{aligned} \tag{8}$$

Its minimal Herbrand models are

$$\{p(1,2), p(2,1), q(1)\}$$

and

$$\{p(1,2), p(2,1), q(2)\}.$$

There seems to be no reasonable way to select one of them as canonical. Perhaps, one should not try to define a declarative meaning for (8) and other programs of this kind (at least as long as the meaning is to be conveyed by selecting a single model). When writing a stratified program, the programmer indicates what the declarative meaning of the program is by deciding whether a given atom should be placed in the head of a rule or, negated, in its body. Programs like (8) do not contain such "signals"; this is why it is not clear how to define a declarative semantics for arbitrary logic programs with negation. It is interesting to notice that the NAIL! system, currently under development at Stanford University (Morris, Ullman and Van Gelder [1986]), explicitly prohibits non-stratified programs.

The iterated fixed pont construction allows us to single out the canonical model M_P from among the minimal models of P; by itself, the minimality condition is not suffucient for defining the canonical model.

The purpose of this paper is to show that the situation becomes quite different if we take into account some recent work in the theory of circumscription (McCarthy [1986], Lifschitz [1986]). Applications of the idea of logical minimization to formalizing non-monotonic aspects of commonsense reasoning have led to introducing some forms of minimization more general than the simple minimality condition used above. We will employ these more general forms of minimization to give a simple description of M_P in terms of minimality. This result can be viewed as an additional argument in favor of the declarative semantics of stratified programs proposed by Apt, Blair, Walker and Van Gelder. It suggests, on the other hand, that the ideas of logic programming can be useful for implementing some special forms of circumscription.

LOGIC PROGRAMS AND CIRCUMSCRIPTION

Consider a finite set of object, function and predicate symbols which contains at least one object symbol and at least one predicate symbol. An *atom* is any atomic formula formed from these symbols and object variables. A *literal* is an atom A or its negation $\neg A$. A *clause* is a formula of the form

$$A \leftarrow L_1 \wedge \ldots \wedge L_m, \tag{9}$$

where A is an atom and $L_1, \ldots, L_m$ are literals, $m \geq 0$. A *program* is a finite set of clauses. We consider only programs that contain occurrences of all object, function and predicate symbols. We identify a program P with the conjunction of the universal closures of its clauses.

In this paper we use the pointwise version of circumscription (Lifschitz [1986]) and define only a special case of this concept sufficient for our present purposes. Let

$p_1, \ldots, p_l$ be distinct predicate symbols. The *(pointwise) circumscription of* one of these predicates, p_i, *relative to* $P(p_1, \ldots, p_l)$ *with* $p_1, \ldots, p_l$ *allowed to vary* is the second-order formula

$$P(p_1, \ldots, p_l) \wedge \forall x p'_1 \ldots p'_l \neg [p_i(x) \wedge \neg p'_i(x) \wedge P(p'_1, \ldots, p'_l)], \tag{10}$$

where x is a tuple of distinct object variables, and $p'_1, \ldots, p'_l$ are distinct predicate variables of the same arities as $p_1, \ldots, p_l$. This formula expresses that it is impossible to change the value of p_i at any point x from *true* to *false* without losing the property P, even if we are allowed to make arbitrary additional changes in the values of $p_1, \ldots, p_l$. In this sense, all values of p_i are "minimal". We denote (10) by $C_{p_i}(P; p_1, \ldots, p_l)$.

The definition of circumscription applies, of course, to arbitrary sentences; but here we are interested only in the case when P is a program.

Example 1. Let P be program (1). The result of circumscribing p with all three predicates p, q and r allowed to vary

$$C_p(P; p, q, r) \tag{11}$$

is equivalent to the conjunction of P and $\forall x(p(x) \equiv x = 1)$. To prove this fact, consider a model M of P. If the value of p at any point in the universe of M other than (the point representing) 1 is *true* then it can be changed to *false* without losing properties (1). On the other hand, the first of formulas (1) shows that the value of p at 1 cannot be changed to *false*. In a similar way we check that circumscribing q,

$$C_q(P; p, q, r), \tag{12}$$

gives the conjunction of P and $\forall x(q(x) \equiv x = 2)$. The circumscription

$$C_r(P; p, q, r), \tag{13}$$

is equivalent to the conjunction of P and $\forall x(r(x) \equiv x = 2)$. (If the value of r at a point other than 2 is *true* then we change the values of *both* r and q at that point to *false*, and it is clear that the new model will satisfy P). It follows that the conjunction of all three circumscriptions (11), (12) and (13) is equivalent to

$$\forall x(p(x) \equiv x = 1) \wedge \forall x(q(x) \equiv x = 2) \wedge \forall x(r(x) \equiv x = 2).$$

This formula has exactly one Herbrand model, and that model is (2). Thus we have a characterization of M_P as *the only Herbrand model* of a certain *set of circumscriptions*, one for each predicate symbol in the language of P.

By changing the set of predicates allowed to vary we can sometimes affect the result of circumscription. Removing predicates from this set, generally, makes the circumscription weaker, because circumscription becomes the expression of minimality among a smaller number of alternatives. We will see that the possibility of deciding, for each predicate p, which other predicates are allowed to vary when p is minimized gives the additional flexibility needed for describing the semantics of programs with negation in terms of minimality.

Example 2. Let us compare circumscriptions (11), (12) and (13) with

$$C_p(P;p), \tag{14}$$

$$C_q(P;q), \tag{15}$$

$$C_r(P;r). \tag{16}$$

It is easy to verify that (14) is equivalent to (11) and (15) to (12); but (16) gives the conjunction of P and $\forall x(r(x) \equiv q(x))$ and thus is weaker than (13). The Herbrand model

$$\{p(1), q(1), q(2), r(1), r(2)\}$$

satisfies (16), but not (13): it can be transformed into a model with a stronger r (namely, (2)), but only at the price of changing the interpretation of q as well. In spite of this difference, circumscriptions (14), (15) and (16) can be used instead of (11), (12), (13) to characterize model (2).

The characterization of M_P as the only Herbrand model of a set of circumscriptions in Example 1 can be extended to arbitrary programs without negation. Generally (in the presence of mutually recursive predicates), it may be essential that the list $p_1, \ldots, p_l$ of predicates allowed to vary in the circumscriptions contain not only the minimized predicate, as in Example 2, but also other predicates used in the program.

Let us turn now to the case when P may contain negation. Then the set of circumscription formulas constructed as in Example 1 may have no Herbrand models.

Example 3. Let P be program (4). Then circumscriptions (11) and (12) give again $\forall x(p(x) \equiv x = 1)$ and $\forall x(q(x) \equiv x = 2)$. The result of (13) is $\forall x \neg r(x)$. (Any value of r can be changed to *false* if the value of q at the same point is simultaneously changed to *true*). Hence the only possible Herbrand model of (11), (12) and (13) is in this case

$$\{p(1), q(2)\}.$$

But the third clause of (4) is false in this model. It follows that no Herbrand model satisfies all three circumscriptions. (In fact, in the only model of (11), (12) and (13) for this program P we have 1=2).

It is easy to understand the source of this difficulty. The universal closure of the last clause of (4) is logically equivalent to $\forall x(q(x) \vee r(x))$. This sentence tells us that q and r cover the whole universe of the model. There is a conflict between the tasks of minimizing q and r.

In what sense then does model (5) minimize both q and r? The form of the last clause of (4) suggests that its intention is to use information about q for defining r. Among the possible interpretations of r, we want the one which is minimal, but minimal only under the assumption that q is given, i.e., minimal in the class of models *with the same* q. On the contrary, when q is minimized, we require that it be impossible to change any of its values to *false* even at the price of changing r arbitrarily.

In the language of circumscription, this kind of minimization can be expressed by formulas

$$C_p(P;p), \quad C_q(P;q,r), \quad C_r(P;r). \tag{17}$$

If P is (4) then circumscriptions (17) hold in exactly one Herbrand model, and this model is (5).

This idea can be also expressed in terms of "priorities". When there is a conflict between the tasks of minimizing two predicates, like q and r in Example 3, we may wish to specify which minimization should be given a higher priority, i.e., whether we are ready to change values of q to *false* at the price of changing values of r to *true*, or the other way around. Model (5) corresponds to the first alternative, model (6) to the second. According to (17), predicate r is allowed to vary when q is minimized, but q must remain fixed when we minimize r. Thus we are willing to change r in order to make q stronger; in this sense, q is minimized at a higher priority than r.

For program (7), we would use the circumscriptions

$$C_p(P;p), \quad C_q(P;q), \quad C_r(P;q,r).$$

Model (6) is the only Herbrand model of P satisfying these three formulas.

In the general case, this idea can be expressed in terms of the *dependency graph* of P. Its nodes are the predicate symbols in the language of P, and it contains an edge (p,q) whenever there is a clause (9) in P which contains q in its head A and p in its body $L_1 \wedge \ldots \wedge L_m$. For instance, the dependency graph of program (4) has three nodes p, q and r and one edge, (q,r).

We denote by S the set of predicate symbols in P, i.e., the set of nodes of its dependency graph. By $\preceq$ we denote the pre-order on S defined by the dependency graph of P. In other words, we write $p \preceq q$ if there is a path from p to q in the graph ($p,q \in S$).

The model M_P will be defined by the circumscriptions which assign "higher priorities" to the predicates which are "smaller" with respect to this pre-order:

$$C_p(P;\{q : p \preceq q\}) \qquad (p \in S). \tag{18}$$

In a model satisfying these circumscriptions, each predicate p is minimal at each point x in the sense that the value of $p(x)$ cannot be changed from *true* to *false*, even if we are allowed to simultaneously change any other values of p or any values of any predicates that follow p in the dependency graph of the program.

Theorem 1. *Any program P has at most one Herbrand model satisfying (18).*

An edge (p, q) in the dependency graph of P is *negative* if, for some clause (9) in P, its head contains q and its body contains negated p. For instance, the edge (q, r) in the dependency graph of (4) is negative. P is *stratified* if in its dependency graph there are no cycles containing a negative edge (Apt, Blair and Walker [1986]).

Theorem 2. *Any stratified program P has exactly one Herbrand model satisfying (18).*

Theorem 1 is proved at the end of the paper. Theorem 2 follows from Theorem 1 and from Theorem 3 below.

Our minimal model semantics for stratified programs defines M_P to be the Herbrand model of (18). Theorem 2 expresses the correctness of this definition.

It is easy to see that the assertion of Theorem 2 does not hold for arbitrary programs. If P is (8) then (18) becomes the pair of formulas

$$C_p(P; p, q),\ C_q(P; q).$$

The second circumscription is false in all Herbrand models of (8).

ITERATED FIXED POINTS

We will review now the iterated fixed point semantics of stratified programs according to Apt, Blair and Walker [1986].

Let P be represented as the union of disjoint sets of clauses

$$P_1, \ldots, P_n, \tag{19}$$

with P_1 possibly empty. We say that (19) is a *stratification* of P if the following two conditions hold for $i = 1, \ldots, n$:

(i) if a predicate p occurs in P_i then its definition is contained within $\bigcup_{j \leq i} P_j$;

(ii) if a predicate p occurs in P_i under $\neg$ then its definition is contained within $\bigcup_{j<i} P_j$.

(The *definition* of p is the subset of P consisting of all clauses containing p on the left). A program has a stratification iff it is stratified (Apt, Blair and Walker [1986], Lemma 3.5).

Consider now a stratification (19) of a program P. For every $i = 1, \ldots, n$, let T_i be the operator on Herbrand models (i.e., on sets of ground atoms) defined as follows: for every Herbrand model M and every ground atom A, $A \in T_i(M)$ iff $A \in M$ or, for some clause $A_1 \leftarrow L_1 \wedge \ldots \wedge L_m$ in P_i and some substitution θ of ground terms for variables, $L_1\theta, \ldots, L_m\theta$ are true in M and $A = A_1\theta$.

The sets $M_0, \ldots, M_n$ of ground atoms are defined by the equations:

$$M_0 = \emptyset,$$
$$M_i = \bigcup_{j \geq 0} T_i^j(M_{i-1}) \qquad (i = 1, \ldots, n).$$

(T^j is T applied j times). Apt, Blair and Walker [1986] show that M_n is a model of P (Theorem 6.8), and that it does not depend on the choice of stratification (18) (Theorem 6.17). They propose to take this model M_n to be the denotation M_P of P.

The following theorem tells us that this semantics is equivalent to the circumscriptive semantics defined above.

Theorem 3. *For any stratification (19) of a program P, M_n satisfies circumscriptions (18).*

By Theorem 1, M_n is the only Herbrand model of P satisfying (18). Thus the results of this paper give an alternative proof of the fact that M_n does not depend on the stratification.

PROOF OF THEOREM 1

An Herbrand model of P is completely defined by the interpretations of all predicate constants in it. Consequently, we will prove Theorem 1 if we show that circumscriptions (18) allow us to derive an explicit definition of each predicate constant:

Lemma. *Let p be an n-ary predicate constant, x an n-tuple of distinct object variables. There exists a formula $A(x)$ (possibly second-order), which has no parameters other than the members of x and contains no predicate constants other than equality, such that circumscriptions (18) imply $\forall x(p(x) \equiv A(x))$.*

Proof. The lemma is proved by induction on the pre-order $\preceq$ (which is well-founded, as is any pre-order on a finite set). Thus it is sufficient to find $A(x)$ which has all the required properties except that it may contain predicate constants which are $\prec p$ (i.e., constants q such that $q \preceq p$ but not $p \preceq q$); it will remain then to replace these constants in $A(x)$ by their explicit definitions.

Circumscription $C_p(P; \{q : p \preceq q\})$ is

$$P(p_1, \ldots, p_l) \wedge \forall x p'_1 \ldots p'_l \neg [p_1 x \wedge \neg p'_1 x \wedge P(p'_1, \ldots, p'_l)],$$

where $p_1, \ldots, p_l$ are all predicates q such that $p \preceq q$; to simplify notation, we assume that p is p_1. This formula can be written as

$$P(p_1, \ldots, p_l) \wedge \forall x [p_1(x) \supset \forall p'_1 \ldots p'_l (P(p'_1, \ldots, p'_l) \supset p'_1(x))]. \tag{20}$$

The first term of (20) implies the converse of the conditional in the brackets, i.e.,

$$\forall x [\forall p'_1 \ldots p'_l (P(p'_1, \ldots, p'_l) \supset p'_1(x)) \supset p_1(x)]$$

(substitute $p_1, \ldots, p_l$ for $p'_1, \ldots, p'_l$). Hence (20) can be rewritten in the form

$$P(p_1, \ldots, p_l) \wedge \forall x [p_1(x) \equiv \forall p'_1 \ldots p'_l (P(p'_1, \ldots, p'_l) \supset p'_1(x))]. \tag{21}$$

The second term of (21) has the required form, except that its right-hand side possibly contains predicate constants which are not $\prec p_1$. Let $p_1, \ldots, p_k$ $(k \leq l)$ be the predicate constants from the same strongly connected component of the dependency graph as p_1, so that we have

$$p_1 \preceq p_i, \; p_i \preceq p_1 \qquad (i = 1, \ldots, k),$$

$$p_1 \prec p_i \qquad (i = k+1, \ldots, l).$$

Divide program P into three parts: P^1, consisting of the definitions of $p_1, \ldots, p_k$; P^2, consisting of the definitions of $p_{k+1}, \ldots, p_l$; P^3, consisting of the definitions of all the other predicate symbols. It is clear that P^1 does not contain $p_{k+1}, \ldots, p_l$, and P^3 does not contain $p_1, \ldots, p_l$; to emphasize this fact, we will write $P^1(p_1, \ldots, p_k)$, $P^2(p_1, \ldots, p_l)$ and P^3. Then the right-hand side of the equivalence in (21) can be written as

$$\forall p'_1 \ldots p'_l [(P^1(p'_1, \ldots, p'_k) \wedge P^2(p'_1, \ldots, p'_l) \wedge P^3) \supset p'_1(x)]. \tag{22}$$

P^3 follows from the first term of (21) and thus can be dropped. Furthermore, P^2 is the only part of the formula containing $p'_{k+1}, \ldots, p'_l$, so that we can rewrite (22) as

$$\forall p'_1 \ldots p'_k [(P^1(p'_1, \ldots, p'_k) \wedge \exists p'_{k+1} \ldots p'_l P^2(p'_1, \ldots, p'_l)) \supset p'_1(x)]. \tag{23}$$

To further simplify this formula, recall that P^2 consists of the definitions of $p_{k+1}, \ldots, p_l$. It follows that $\exists p'_{k+1} \ldots p'_l P^2(p'_1, \ldots, p'_l)$ is identically true (by taking each of $p'_{k+1}, \ldots, p'_l$ identically true we can make head of each clause in $P^2(p'_1, \ldots, p'_l)$ true). Hence (23) can be replaced by

$$\forall p'_1 \ldots p'_k [P^1(p'_1, \ldots, p'_k) \supset p'_1(x)],$$

so that the second term of (21) becomes

$$\forall x[p_1(x) \equiv \forall p'_1 \ldots p'_k(P^1(p'_1, \ldots, p'_k) \supset p'_1(x))].$$

It remains to notice that all predicate constants in $P^1(p_1, \ldots, p_k)$ are $\preceq p_1$, so that all predicate constants in $P^1(p'_1, \ldots, p'_k)$ are $\prec p_1$.

PROOF OF THEOREM 3

Let $p_1, \ldots, p_l$ be all elements of $\{q : p \preceq q\}$. As in the previous proof, we will assume that p is p_1. We know that M_n is a model of $P(p_1, \ldots, p_l)$; our goal is to show that this model satisfies the second term of the circumscription:

$$\forall x p'_1 \ldots p'_l \neg[p_1(x) \wedge \neg p'_1(x) \wedge P(p'_1, \ldots, p'_l)].$$

Assume that this is not the case. Then M_n satisfies

$$\exists x p'_1 \ldots p'_l[p_1(x) \wedge \neg p'_1(x) \wedge P(p'_1, \ldots, p'_l)]. \tag{24}$$

This assumption can be stated in terms of models as follows. As usual in model theory, we write $M[\![q]\!]$ for the extension of a predicate q in a model M. Finding values of $p'_1, \ldots, p'_l$ which satisfy $P(p'_1, \ldots, p'_l)$ in M_n is equivalent to constructing a model of P which differs from M_n only by the interpretations of $p_1, \ldots, p_l$. Hence assumption (24) means that there exists a Herbrand model M' of P such that
(i) $M'[\![q]\!] = M_n[\![q]\!]$ for each $q \neq p_1, \ldots, p_l$,
(ii) $M_n[\![p_1]\!] \setminus M'[\![p_1]\!] \neq \emptyset$.

The definition of each predicate constant is contained in some P_i. For each $i = 1, \ldots, n$, let D_i be the set of predicate constants whose definitions are contained in P_i. The description of the operators $T_1, T_2, \ldots$ shows then that, for any Herbrand model M and any predicate constant $q \in D_i$, $T_{i'}(M)[\![q]\!]$ may differ from $M[\![q]\!]$ only if $i' = i$. Hence

$$M_0[\![q]\!] = \ldots = M_{i-1}[\![q]\!] \qquad (q \in D_i), \tag{25}$$

$$M_i[\![q]\!] = \ldots = M_n[\![q]\!] \qquad (q \in D_i). \tag{26}$$

Since $M_0 = \emptyset$, (25) implies

$$M_{i-1}[\![q]\!] = \emptyset \qquad (q \in D_i). \tag{27}$$

Let i_1 be such that $p_1 \in D_{i_1}$. If $q \in D_i$ for some $i < i_1$ then both property (i) of M' and formula (26) apply; it follows that

$$M_{i_1-1}[\![q]\!] = M'[\![q]\!] \qquad (q \in \bigcup_{i<i_1} D_i). \tag{28}$$

Let us prove, by induction on j, that

$$T_{i_1}^j(M_{i_1-1})[\![q]\!] \subset M'[\![q]\!] \qquad (q \in D_{i_1}). \tag{29}$$

For $j = 0$ this assertion follows from (27). Assume that (29) holds for some j and that, for some $q \in D_{i_1}$ and some tuple t of ground terms, $t \in T_{i_1}^{j+1}(M_{i_1-1})[\![q]\!]$, i.e.,

$$q(t) \in T_{i_1}^{j+1}(M_{i_1-1}) = T_{i_1}(T_{i_1}^j(M_{i_1-1})).$$

Then, by the definition of T_{i_1}, either $q(t) \in T_{i_1}^j(M_{i_1-1})$ or, for some clause

$$A_1 \leftarrow L_1 \wedge \ldots \wedge L_m$$

from P_{i_1}, and some substitution θ, $A_1\theta$ is $q(t)$ and all literals $L_1\theta, \ldots, L_m\theta$ are true in $T_{i_1}^j(M_{i_1-1})$. In the first case, by the induction hypothesis, $t \in M'[\![q]\!]$. In the second case, let us show that all literals $L_1\theta, \ldots, L_m\theta$ are true in M'. Each of these literals has the form $q^*(t^*)$, possibly preceded by a negation, where q^* is a predicate constant and t^* is a tuple of ground terms. If

$$q^* \in \bigcup_{i<i_1} D_i$$

then, by (28), the literal is true in M'. If not then, by the definition of a stratification, the literal must be positive. Hence $q^*(t^*)$ is true in $T_{i_1}^j(M_{i_1-1})$, and it follows, by the induction hypothesis, that it is also true in M'. Thus all literals $L_1\theta, \ldots, L_m\theta$ are true in M'. Since M' is a model of P, it follows that $A_1\theta$, i.e., $q(t)$, is true in M' as well, so that again $t \in M'[\![q]\!]$. This completes the proof of (29). In particular,

$$T_{i_1}^j(M_{i_1-1})[\![p_1]\!] \subset M'[\![p_1]\!]. \tag{30}$$

Since

$$M_{i_1}[\![p_1]\!] = \bigcup_{j\geq 0} T_{i_1}^j(M_{i_1-1})[\![p_1]\!],$$

it follows from (30) that $M_{i_1}[\![p_1]\!] \subset M'[\![p_1]\!]$. Then, by (26), $M_n[\![p]\!] \subset M'[\![p]\!]$, in contradiction with property (ii) of M'.

ACKNOWLEDGEMENTS

I would like to thank Michael Gelfond and Allen Van Gelder for the discussions in which they called my attention to connections between circumscription and logic programming. In particular, Allen's observation that the dependency graph of a program contains an encoding of priorities has directly led me to the results presented in this paper. I am also grateful to Krzysztof Apt, John McCarthy and Jack Minker for their comments on earlier drafts. This research was partially supported by DARPA under Contract N0039-82-C-0250.

REFERENCES

1. Apt, K. R., H. Blair and A. Walker, *Towards a Theory of Declarative Knowledge*, 1987 (this volume).
2. Apt, K. R. and van Emden M. H., Contributions to the theory of logic programming, *JACM 29*, 3 (1982), 841-862.
3. Chandra, A. and Harel, D., Horn clause queries and generalizations, *The Journal of Logic Programming 1* (1985), 1-15.
4. Lifschitz, V., Pointwise circumscription: preliminary report, *Proceedings AAAI-86* **1**, 1986, 406-410.
5. McCarthy, J., Applications of circumscription to formalizing commonsense knowledge, *Artificial Intelligence* **28** (1986), 89-118.
6. Morris, K., J. D. Ullman and A. Van Gelder, Design overview of the NAIL! system, in: G. Goos and J. Hartmanis (eds.), *Third International Conference on Logic Programming* (Lecture Notes in Computer Science 225), Springer-Verlag, 1986, pp. 554-568.
7. Van Emden, M. H. and R. A. Kowalski, The semantics of predicate logic as a programming language, *Journal ACM*, **23**(4) (1976), 733-742.
8. Van Gelder, A., Negation as failure using tight derivations for general logic programs, 1987 (this volume).

5.2 Diagnosis

The suggestion that nonmonotonic techniques could be profitably applied to diagnostic problems appears to be due to Ginsberg [Ginsberg, 1986a], with an independent and approximately simultaneous observation by Poole and colleagues [Poole, Aleliunas, Goebel, 1985]. We have already described the use of nonmonotonic inference in automated diagnosis in the introduction; the two papers in this section expand on these ideas.

The first is Reiter's "A theory of diagnosis from first principles." Reiter describes in detail the general use of nonmonotonic inference in diagnosis in the first three sections of the paper; in Section 4, he presents a nonmonotonic algorithm designed specifically for the diagnostic task.

The key observation underlying the application of nonmonotonic techniques to diagnostic problems is that the diagnostic task is that of finding a minimal set of components the collective failure of which can explain an observed malfunction. In "Diagnosing multiple faults," de Kleer and Williams show that an assumption-based truth maintenance system can be used for the same purpose.[1] The minimal assumption sets used by the ATMS correspond to the minimal failure sets appearing in the explicitly nonmonotonic approaches.

As with the other work on truth maintenance, de Kleer and Williams' paper is less formal than the other material in this collection. They also go on to show that the ATMS can be used to determine an effective strategy for deciding among diagnoses (i.e., choosing among competing extensions). They make the assumption here that it is possible to test any of the suspect components directly; this may not be possible in a realistic diagnosis problem. The idea is nonetheless an interesting one, and it also bears on the problem of updating nonmonotonic conclusions.

[1] Goodwin also discusses the use of a TMS and nonmonotonic reasoning for diagnostic purposes in his thesis [Goodwin, 1987].

A Theory of Diagnosis from First Principles

Raymond Reiter

Department of Computer Science, University of Toronto, Toronto, Ontario, Canada M5S 1A4; The Canadian Institute for Advanced Research

Recommended by Johan de Kleer and Daniel G. Bobrow

ABSTRACT

Suppose one is given a description of a system, together with an observation of the system's behaviour which conflicts with the way the system is meant to behave. The diagnostic problem is to determine those components of the system which, when assumed to be functioning abnormally, will explain the discrepancy between the observed and correct system behaviour.

We propose a general theory for this problem. The theory requires only that the system be described in a suitable logic. Moreover, there are many such suitable logics, e.g. first-order, temporal, dynamic, etc. As a result, the theory accommodates diagnostic reasoning in a wide variety of practical settings, including digital and analogue circuits, medicine, and database updates. The theory leads to an algorithm for computing all diagnoses, and to various results concerning principles of measurement for discriminating among competing diagnoses. Finally, the theory reveals close connections between diagnostic reasoning and nonmonotonic reasoning.

1. Introduction

In the theory and design of diagnostic reasoning systems there appear to be two quite different approaches in the literature.

In the first approach, often referred to as diagnosis from first principles, one begins with a description of some system—a physical device or real world setting of interest, say—together with an observation of the system's behaviour. If this observation conflicts with the way the system is meant to behave, one is confronted with a diagnostic problem, namely, to determine those system components which, when assumed to be functioning abnormally, will explain the discrepancy between the observed and correct system behaviour. For solving this diagnostic problem from first principles, the only available information is the system description, i.e. its design or structure, together with the observation(s) of the system behaviour. In particular, no heuristic information about system failures is available, for example, of the kind "When the system exhibits such and such aberrant behaviour, then in 90% of these cases, such and such components have failed." Notable examples of approaches to diagnostic reasoning from first principles are [4–7, 15, 16].

Under the second approach to diagnostic reasoning, which might be described as the experiential approach, heuristic information plays a dominant role. The corresponding diagnostic reasoning systems attempt to codify the rules of thumb, statistical intuitions, and past experience of human diagnosticians considered experts in some particular task domain. The structure or design of the corresponding real world system being diagnosed is only weakly represented, if at all. Successful diagnoses stem from the codified experience of the human expert being modeled, rather than from what is often referred to as "deep" knowledge of the system being diagnosed. A notable example of such an approach to diagnosis from experience is the MYCIN system [3].

As one will gather from its title, the current paper deals exclusively with the problem of diagnosis from first principles. Without in any way denying the importance of expert experience in diagnostic reasoning, we believe that a precise theoretical foundation for diagnosis from first principles will be a necessary ingredient in any general theory of diagnostic reasoning. The purpose of this paper is to provide such a theoretical foundation for diagnosis from first principles. Our theory primarily builds upon, and generalizes, the work of de Kleer [5] and Genesereth [7].

We begin by abstractly defining the concept of a system of interacting components. Initially, we choose first-order logic as a language for representing such systems, but as we shall eventually see, many different logics will lead to the same theory of diagnosis presented in this paper. Whatever one's choice of representation logic, the description within it of a system will specify how that system normally behaves on the assumption that all its components are functioning correctly. If we have available an observation of the system's actual behaviour and if this observation conflicts with (i.e. is logically inconsistent with) the way the system is meant to behave, then we have a diagnostic problem. The problem is to determine those system components which, when assumed to be functioning abnormally, will explain the discrepancy between the observed and correct system behaviour. These intuitions, coupled with our appeal to a logical system representation language, will allow us in Section 2 to formally define the concept of a diagnosis, including multiple fault diagnoses. Diagnoses need not be unique; there may be several competing explanations for the same faulty system.

The computational problem, then, is to determine all possible diagnoses for a given faulty system. After proving some preliminary results in Section 3, we derive an "algorithm"[1] in Section 4 for computing all diagnoses for a given

[1] The reason for the scare quotes will become evident later.

faulty system. This algorithm has a number of virtues, not the least of which is its relative independence of the particular logic representing the system being diagnosed. By "relative independence" here we mean that the algorithm assumes the availability of a sound and complete theorem prover for the logic being used, but in all other respects is unconcerned with the underlying logic. A nice consequence of this decomposition is that special purpose theorem provers can be designed for particular diagnostic applications, for example, Boolean equation solvers for switching circuits. Such a special purpose theorem prover can then "hook into" the general purpose algorithm to yield a domain specific diagnostic algorithm.

As we remarked above, multiple, competing diagnoses can arise for a given faulty system. The normal approach to discriminating among competing diagnoses is to make system measurements, for example inserting probes into a circuit, or performing laboratory tests on a patient. In Section 5 we prove a variety of results about the conclusions which can legitimately be drawn from the results of certain system measurements.

Diagnostic reasoning turns out to be a form of nonmonotonic reasoning. In Section 6 we explore this connection, and show how the theory of diagnosis of this paper is related to default logic [17].

In Section 7 we consider the relationship of our theory of diagnosis to other research in this area. Finally, we summarize what we take to be the principal contributions of this work in Section 8.

2. Problem Formulation

2.1. Systems

We seek a very general theory of diagnosis, one which will account for diagnostic reasoning in a wide variety of task domains such as medicine, digital and analogue circuits, etc. To achieve the necessary generality, we appeal to first-order logic with equality as a language for representing task specific information.[2] Also in the interest of generality, we define the domain-independent concept of a system which is designed to formalize as abstractly as possible the concept of a component, and the concept of a collection of interacting components.

Definition 2.1. A *system* is a pair (SD, COMPONENTS) where:
(1) SD, the *system description*, is a set of first-order sentences;
(2) COMPONENTS, the *system components*, is a finite set of constants.

[2] Actually, all of the results of this paper continue to hold for a wide variety of logics, not just first-order. However, in order to provide a concrete development of the theory, we shall initially appeal only to first-order logic. In Section 6.1, we shall indicate how the results so obtained generalize to other logics.

In all intended applications, the system description will mention a distinguished unary predicate $\text{AB}(\cdot)$, interpreted to mean "abnormal."

Example 2.2. Figure 1 depicts the binary full adder used extensively by Genesereth [7] as an example. This adder may be represented by a system with components $\{A_1, A_2, X_1, X_2, O_1\}$ and the following system description:

$$\text{ANDG}(x) \wedge \neg\text{AB}(x) \supset \text{out}(x) = \text{and}(\text{in1}(x), \text{in2}(x))\,,$$
$$\text{XORG}(x) \wedge \neg\text{AB}(x) \supset \text{out}(x) = \text{xor}(\text{in1}(x), \text{in2}(x))\,,$$
$$\text{ORG}(x) \wedge \neg\text{AB}(x) \supset \text{out}(x) = \text{or}(\text{in1}(x), \text{in2}(x))\,,$$
$$\text{ANDG}(A_1), \quad \text{ANDG}(A_2)\,,$$
$$\text{XORG}(X_1)\,, \quad \text{XORG}(X_2) \quad \text{ORG}(O_1)\,,$$

$$\text{out}(X_1) = \text{in2}(A_2)\,,$$
$$\text{out}(X_1) = \text{in1}(X_2)\,,$$
$$\text{out}(A_2) = \text{in1}(O_1)\,,$$
$$\text{in1}(A_2) = \text{in2}(X_2)\,,$$
$$\text{in1}(X_1) = \text{in1}(A_1)\,,$$
$$\text{in2}(X_1) = \text{in2}(A_1)\,,$$
$$\text{out}(A_1) = \text{in2}(O_1)\,.$$

In addition, the system description contains axioms specifying that the circuit inputs are binary valued:

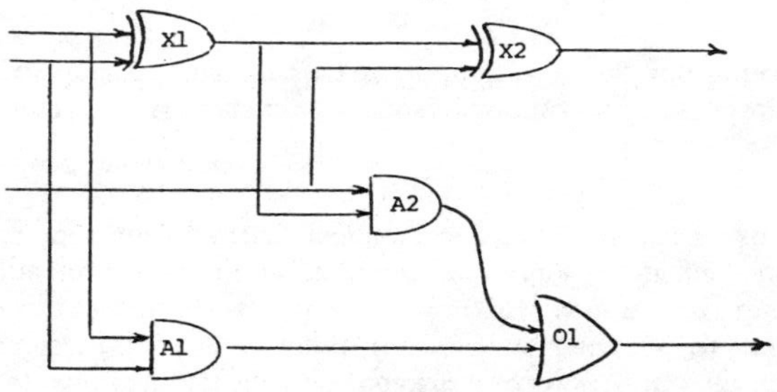

FIG. 1. A full adder. A_1 and A_2 are and gates; X_1 and X_2 are exclusive-or gates; O_1 is an or gate.

$$\text{in1}(X_1) = 0 \lor \text{in1}(X_1) = 1\,,$$
$$\text{in2}(X_1) = 0 \lor \text{in2}(X_1) = 1\,,$$
$$\text{in1}(A_1) = 0 \lor \text{in1}(A_1) = 1\,.$$

Finally there are axioms for a Boolean algebra over $\{0, 1\}$, which we do not specify here.

Typically, a system description describes how the system components *normally* behave by appealing to the distinguished predicate AB whose intended meaning is "abnormal." Thus, the first axiom in the example system description states that a normal (i.e. not ABnormal) and gate's output is the Boolean and function of its two inputs. Many other kinds of component descriptions are possible, e.g. "Normally an adult human's heart rate is between 70 and 90 beats per minute."

$$\text{ADULT}(x) \land \text{HEART-OF}(x, h) \land \neg\text{AB}(h) \supset \text{rate}(h) \geq 70 \land \text{rate}(h) \leq 90.$$

"Normally, if the voltage across a zener diode is positive and less than its breakdown voltage, the current through it must be zero."

$$\text{ZENER-DIODE}(z) \land \neg\text{AB}(z) \land$$
$$\text{voltage}(z) > 0 \land \text{voltage}(z) < \text{break-voltage}(z)$$
$$\supset \text{current}(z) = 0\,.$$

We can represent the fact that a fault in component c_1 will cause a fault in component c_2:

$$\text{AB}(c_1) \supset \text{AB}(c_2)\,.$$

If we know all the ways components of a certain type can be faulted, we can express this by an axiom of the form:

$$\text{TYPE}(x) \land \text{AB}(x) \supset \text{FAULT}_1(x) \lor \cdots \lor \text{FAULT}_n(x)\,.$$

By introducing several kinds of AB predicates, we can represent more general component properties, e.g. "Normally, a faulty resistor is either open or shorted."

$$\text{RESISTOR}(r) \land \text{AB}(r) \land \neg\text{AB}'(r)$$
$$\supset \text{OPEN}(r) \lor \text{SHORTED}(r)\,.$$

The use of an AB predicate for system descriptions is borrowed from McCarthy [11] who exploits such a predicate in conjunction with his formalization of circumscription to account for various patterns of nonmonotonic common-sense reasoning. As we shall see in Section 6.2, this seemingly tenuous connection with nonmonotonic reasoning is in fact fundamental. Diagnosis provides an important example of nonmonotonic reasoning.

2.2. Observations of systems

Real world diagnostic settings involve observations. Without observations, we have no way of determining whether something is wrong and hence whether a diagnosis is called for.

Definition 2.3. An *observation* of a system is a finite set of first-order sentences. We shall write (SD, COMPONENTS, OBS) for a system (SD, COMPONENTS) with observation OBS.

Example 2.2 (continued). Suppose a physical full adder is given the inputs 1, 0, 1 and it outputs 1, 0 in response. Then this observation can be represented by:

$$\text{in1}(X_1) = 1\,,$$
$$\text{in2}(X_1) = 0\,,$$
$$\text{in1}(A_2) = 1\,,$$
$$\text{out}(X_2) = 1\,,$$
$$\text{out}(O_1) = 0\,.$$

Notice that this observation indicates that the physical circuit is faulty; both circuit outputs are wrong for the given inputs.

Notice also that distinguished inputs and outputs are features of digital circuits (and many man-made artifacts) not of the general theory we are proposing.

2.3. Diagnoses

Suppose we have determined that a system (SD, $\{c_1, \ldots, c_n\}$) is faulty, by which we mean informally that we have made an observation OBS which conflicts with what the system description predicts should happen if all its components were behaving correctly. Now $\{\neg\text{AB}(c_1), \ldots, \neg\text{AB}(c_n)\}$ represents the assumption that all system components are behaving correctly, so that $\text{SD} \cup \{\neg\text{AB}(c_1), \ldots, \neg\text{AB}(c_n)\}$ represents the system behaviour on the assumption that all its components are working properly. Hence the fact that the observation OBS conflicts with what the system should do were all its components behaving correctly can be formalized by:

$$\text{SD} \cup \{\neg\text{AB}(c_1), \ldots, \neg\text{AB}(c_n)\} \cup \text{OBS} \tag{2.1}$$

is inconsistent.

Intuitively, a diagnosis is a *conjecture* that certain of the components are faulty (ABnormal) and the rest normal. The problem is to specify which components we conjecture to be faulty. Now our objective is to explain the inconsistency (2.1), an inconsistency which stems from the assumptions $\neg\text{AB}(c_1), \ldots, \neg\text{AB}(c_n)$, i.e. that all components are behaving correctly. The natural way to explain this inconsistency is to retract enough of the assumptions $\neg\text{AB}(c_1), \ldots, \neg\text{AB}(c_n)$, so as to restore consistency to (2.1). But we should not be overzealous in this; retracting all of $\neg\text{AB}(c_1), \ldots, \neg\text{AB}(c_n)$ will restore consistency to (2.1), corresponding to the diagnosis that all components are faulty. We should appeal to:

The Principle of Parsimony. A diagnosis is a conjecture that some minimal set of components are faulty.

This leads us to the following:

Definition 2.4. A *diagnosis* for (SD, COMPONENTS, OBS) is a minimal set $\Delta \subseteq$ COMPONENTS such that

$$\text{SD} \cup \text{OBS} \cup \{\text{AB}(c) \mid c \in \Delta\} \cup \{\neg\text{AB}(c) \mid c \in \text{COMPONENTS} - \Delta\}$$

is consistent.

In other words, a diagnosis is determined by a smallest set of components with the following property: The assumption that each of these components is faulty (ABnormal), together with the assumption that all other components are behaving correctly (not ABnormal), is consistent with the system description and the observation.

Example 2.2 (continued). For the full adder, there are three diagnoses: $\{X_1\}$, $\{X_2, O_1\}$, $\{X_2, A_2\}$.

2.4. Computing diagnoses: Decidability

The definition of a diagnosis appeals to a consistency test for arbitrary first-order formulae. Since there is no decision procedure for determining the consistency of first-order formulae, we cannot hope to compute diagnoses in the most general case. Nevertheless, there are many practical settings where consistency is decidable, hence diagnoses are computable.

For example, in the case of switching circuits like that of the full adder, it is sufficient, for the purpose of computing diagnoses, to determine whether a system of Boolean equations is consistent, i.e. has a solution, and this is decidable. Similarly, in the case of linear electronic circuits, we need only have the capacity to determine whether a system of linear equations has a solution. As we shall see in Section 7, at least one established model for medical diagnosis leads to a computable theory. The point is: we should not allow the undecidability of the general problem to prevent us from developing a theory of diagnosis because there are many practical settings in which the theory does provide effective computations.

This means that for any given application it will be necessary first to establish decidability of its diagnostic problem. If the problem turns out to be undecidable, heuristic techniques will be necessary. It is an interesting question to characterize classes of systems whose diagnostic problems are decidable, but we shall not pursue that question in this paper.

3. Some Consequences of the Definition

The first two results are simple consequences of the definition of a diagnosis (Definition 2.4); we omit their proofs.

Proposition 3.1. *A diagnosis exists for* (SD, COMPONENTS, OBS) *iff* SD $\cup$ OBS *is consistent.*

Proposition 3.2. { } *is a diagnosis (and the only diagnosis) for* (SD, COMPONENTS, OBS) *iff*

$$\text{SD} \cup \text{OBS} \cup \{\neg\text{AB}(c) \mid c \in \text{COMPONENTS}\}$$

is consistent, i.e. iff the observation does not conflict with what the system should do if all its components were behaving correctly.

This is as it should be; we observe nothing wrong, so there is no reason to conjecture a faulty component.

Proposition 3.3. *If* Δ *is a diagnosis for* (SD, COMPONENTS, OBS), *then for each* $c_i \in \Delta$,

$$\text{SD} \cup \text{OBS} \cup \{\neg\text{AB}(c) \mid c \in \text{COMPONENTS} - \Delta\} \models \text{AB}(c_i).$$

Proof. If Δ is the empty set, then the result is true vacuously. Suppose then that $\Delta = \{c_1, \ldots, c_k\}$, and that the proposition is false, so that

$$\textsc{sd} \cup \textsc{obs} \cup \{\neg\textsc{ab}(c) \mid c \in \textsc{components} - \Delta\}$$
$$\cup \{\neg\textsc{ab}(c_1) \vee \cdots \vee \neg\textsc{ab}(c_k)\}$$

is consistent. Now $\neg\textsc{ab}(c_1) \vee \cdots \vee \neg\textsc{ab}(c_k)$ is logically equivalent to

$$\bigvee [\textsc{ab}(c_1)^{i_1} \wedge \cdots \wedge \textsc{ab}(c_k)^{i_k}]$$

where the disjunction is over all $i_1, \ldots, i_k \in \{0, 1\}$ such that at least one $i_j = 0$, and where

$$\textsc{ab}(c_j)^{i_j} = \begin{cases} \textsc{ab}(c_j), & \text{if } i_j = 1, \\ \neg\textsc{ab}(c_j), & \text{if } i_j = 0. \end{cases}$$

So we have that

$$\textsc{sd} \cup \textsc{obs} \cup \{\neg\textsc{ab}(c) \mid c \in \textsc{components} - \Delta\}$$
$$\cup \{\bigvee [\textsc{ab}(c_1)^{i_1} \wedge \cdots \wedge \textsc{ab}(c_k)^{i_k}]\}$$

is consistent, in which case, for some choice of $i_1, \ldots, i_k \in \{0, 1\}$ with at least one $i_j = 0$, we have that

$$\textsc{sd} \cup \textsc{obs} \cup \{\neg\textsc{ab}(c) \mid c \in \textsc{components} - \Delta\}$$
$$\cup \{\textsc{ab}(c_1)^{i_1} \wedge \cdots \wedge \textsc{ab}(c_k)^{i_k}\}$$

is consistent. But this says that Δ has a strict subset Δ' with the property that

$$\textsc{sd} \cup \textsc{obs} \cup \{\neg\textsc{ab}(c) \mid c \in \textsc{components} - \Delta\}$$
$$\cup \{\textsc{ab}(c) \mid c \in \Delta\}$$

is consistent, contradicting the fact that Δ is a diagnosis for (SD, COMPONENTS, OBS). □

Proposition 3.3 is rather interesting. It says that the faulty components Δ are logically determined by the normal components COMPONENTS $- \Delta$.

The next result provides a simpler characterization of a diagnosis than does the original Definition 2.4.

Proposition 3.4. *$\Delta \subseteq$ COMPONENTS is a diagnosis for* (SD, COMPONENTS, OBS) *iff Δ is a minimal set such that*

$$\textsc{sd} \cup \textsc{obs} \cup \{\neg\textsc{ab}(c) \mid c \in \textsc{components} - \Delta\}$$

is consistent.

Proof. ($\Rightarrow$) since Δ is a diagnosis,

$$\textsc{sd} \cup \textsc{obs} \cup \{\textsc{ab}(c) \mid c \in \Delta\}$$
$$\cup \{\neg\textsc{ab}(c) \mid c \in \textsc{components} - \Delta\}$$

is consistent, so that

$$\textsc{sd} \cup \textsc{obs} \cup \{\neg\textsc{ab}(c) \mid c \in \textsc{components} - \Delta\}$$

is consistent. Moreover, by Proposition 3.3, for each $c_i \in \Delta$

$$\textsc{sd} \cup \textsc{obs} \cup \{\neg\textsc{ab}(c) \mid c \in \textsc{components} - \Delta\} \cup \{\neg\textsc{ab}(c_i)\}$$

is inconsistent. The result now follows.

($\Leftarrow$) By the minimality of Δ, we must have, for each $c_i \in \Delta$, that

$$\textsc{sd} \cup \textsc{obs} \cup \{\neg\textsc{ab}(c) \mid c \in \textsc{components} - \Delta\} \cup \{\neg\textsc{ab}(c_i)\}$$

is inconsistent, i.e. for each $c_i \in \Delta$,

$$\textsc{sd} \cup \textsc{obs} \cup \{\neg\textsc{ab}(c) \mid c \in \textsc{components} - \Delta\} \models \textsc{ab}(c_i).$$

Moreover, by hypothesis,

$$\textsc{sd} \cup \textsc{obs} \cup \{\neg\textsc{ab}(c) \mid c \in \textsc{components} - \Delta\}$$

is consistent. Hence

$$\textsc{sd} \cup \textsc{obs} \cup \{\textsc{ab}(c) \mid c \in \Delta\}$$
$$\cup \{\neg\textsc{ab}(c) \mid c \in \textsc{components} - \Delta\}$$

is consistent. It remains only to show that Δ is a minimal set with this property in order to establish that Δ is a diagnosis. But this is easy, for if Δ had a strict subset Δ' with this property, then

$$\textsc{sd} \cup \textsc{obs} \cup \{\neg\textsc{ab}(c) \mid c \in \textsc{components} - \Delta'\}$$

would be consistent, contradicting the hypothesis of this proposition. □

4. Computing Diagnoses

Our objective in this section is to show how to determine all diagnoses for (SD, COMPONENTS, OBS). There is a direct generate-and-test mechanism based upon Proposition 3.4: Systematically generate subsets Δ of COMPONENTS, generating Δs with minimal cardinality first, and test the consistency of

$$\text{SD} \cup \text{OBS} \cup \{\neg\text{AB}(c) \mid c \in \text{COMPONENTS} - \Delta\} .$$

The obvious problem with this approach is that it is too inefficient for systems with large numbers of components. Instead, we propose a method based upon a suitable formalization of the concept of a conflict set, a concept due originally to de Kleer [5].

4.1. Conflict sets and diagnoses

Definition 4.1. A *conflict set* for (SD, COMPONENTS, OBS) is a set $\{c_1, \ldots, c_k\} \subseteq$ COMPONENTS such that

$$\text{SD} \cup \text{OBS} \cup \{\neg\text{AB}(c_1), \ldots, \neg\text{AB}(c_k)\}$$

is inconsistent.

A conflict set for (SD, COMPONENTS, OBS) is *minimal* iff no proper subset of it is a conflict set for (SD, COMPONENTS, OBS).

Proposition 3.4 can be reformulated in terms of conflict sets as follows:

Proposition 4.2. *$\Delta \subseteq$ COMPONENTS is a diagnosis for (SD, COMPONENTS, OBS) iff Δ is a minimal set such that COMPONENTS $- \Delta$ is not a conflict set for (SD, COMPONENTS, OBS).*

Definition 4.3. Suppose C is a collection of sets. A *hitting set* for C is a set $H \subseteq \bigcup_{S \in C} S$ such that $H \cap S \neq \{\ \}$ for each $S \in C$. A hitting set for C is *minimal* iff no proper subset of it is a hitting set for C.

The following is our principal characterization of diagnoses, and will provide the basis for computing diagnoses:

Theorem 4.4. *$\Delta \subseteq$ COMPONENTS is a diagnosis for (SD, COMPONENTS, OBS) iff Δ is a minimal hitting set for the collection of conflict sets for (SD, COMPONENTS, OBS).*

Proof. ($\Rightarrow$) By Proposition 4.2, COMPONENTS $- \Delta$ is not a conflict set for (SD, COMPONENTS, OBS). Hence, every conflict set contains an element of Δ, so that Δ is a hitting set for the collection of conflict sets for (SD, COMPONENTS, OBS). We must prove Δ is a minimal such hitting set. Now by Proposition 4.2, Δ is a minimal set such that COMPONENTS $- \Delta$ is not a conflict set. This means for each $c \in \Delta$ that $\{c\} \cup$ (COMPONENTS $- \Delta$) is a conflict set. From this it follows that Δ is a minimal hitting set for the conflict sets for (SD, COMPONENTS, OBS).

($\Leftarrow$) We use Proposition 4.2 to prove that Δ is a diagnosis for (SD, COMPONENTS, OBS) by showing that:

(1) COMPONENTS $- \Delta$ is not a conflict set for (SD, COMPONENTS, OBS),

(2) Δ is a minimal set with property (1) by proving, for each $c \in \Delta$, that $\{c\} \cup$ (COMPONENTS $- \Delta$) is a conflict set for (SD, COMPONENTS, OBS).

Proof of (1): If, on the contrary, COMPONENTS $- \Delta$ were a conflict set, then Δ would not hit it, contradicting the fact that Δ is a hitting set for all conflict sets.

Proof of (2): Every conflict set has the form $\Delta' \cup K$ where $\Delta' \subseteq \Delta$ and $K \subseteq$ COMPONENTS $- \Delta$. Moreover, for each $c \in \Delta$, some conflict set must contain c, for otherwise Δ would not be a minimal hitting set. We prove that some conflict set containing c is of the form $\{c\} \cup K$. For if not, then every conflict set containing c must have the form $\{c, c', \ldots\} \cup K$ where $c' \in \Delta$ and $c' \neq c$. But then $\Delta - \{c\}$ is a smaller hitting set than Δ, a contradiction. Hence, for each $c \in \Delta$ there is a conflict set of the form $\{c\} \cup K$ where $K \subseteq$ COMPONENTS $- \Delta$. But then $\{c\} \cup$ (COMPONENTS $- \Delta$) is also a conflict set. □

Notice that every superset of a conflict set for (SD, COMPONENTS, OBS) is also a conflict set. Because of this, we can easily prove the following:

> H is a minimal hitting set for the collection of all conflict sets for (SD, COMPONENTS, OBS) iff H is a minimal hitting set for the collection of all minimal conflict sets for (SD, COMPONENTS, OBS).

Combining this result with Theorem 4.4 we obtain an alternative characterization of diagnoses:

Corollary 4.5. *$\Delta \subseteq$ COMPONENTS is a diagnosis for (SD, COMPONENTS, OBS) iff Δ is a minimal hitting set for the collection of minimal conflict sets for (SD, COMPONENTS, OBS).*

Example 2.2 (continued). The full adder has two minimal conflict sets $\{X_1, X_2\}$ and $\{X_1, A_2, O_1\}$ corresponding, respectively, to the inconsistency of

$$\text{SD} \cup \text{OBS} \cup \{\neg\text{AB}(X_1), \neg\text{AB}(X_2)\}$$

and

$$\text{SD} \cup \text{OBS} \cup \{\neg\text{AB}(X_1), \neg\text{AB}(A_2), \neg\text{AB}(O_1)\} .$$

There are three diagnoses, given by the minimal hitting sets for $\{X_1, X_2\}$ and $\{X_1, A_2, O_1\}$: $\{X_1\}$, $\{X_2, A_2\}$, $\{X_2, O_1\}$.

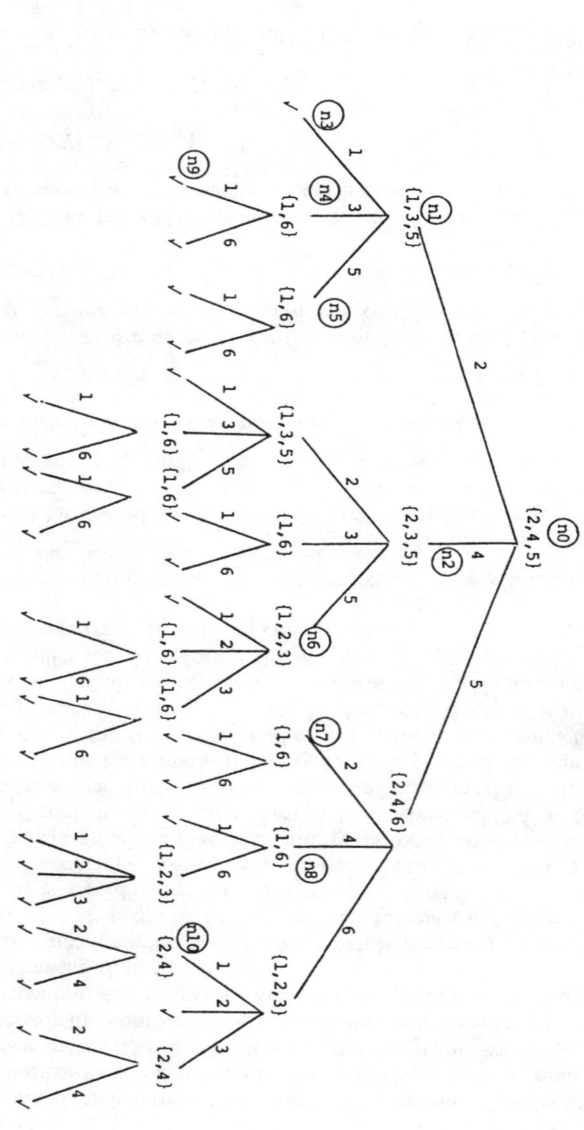

FIG. 2. An *HS*-tree for $F = \{\{2,4,5\}, \{1,2,3\}, \{1,3,5\}, \{2,4,6\}, \{2,4\}, \{2,3,5\}, \{1,6\}\}$.

De Kleer and Williams [6] have independently proposed a characterization of diagnoses which corresponds to our Corollary 4.5. However, the major difference between their result and ours is that, while theirs derives from sound intuitions, it is based upon an unformalized approach to diagnosis, while our results have been derived from initial formal definitions.

4.2. Computing hitting sets

Our approach to computing diagnoses is based upon Theorem 4.4 and therefore requires computing all minimal hitting sets for the collection of conflict sets for (SD, COMPONENTS, OBS). Accordingly, in this section, we focus on computing the minimal hitting sets for an arbitrary collection of sets. The approach we shall propose will be particularly appropriate in a diagnostic setting.

Definition 4.6. Suppose F is a collection of sets. An edge-labeled and node-labeled tree T is an *HS-tree* for F iff it is a smallest tree with the following properties:

(1) Its root is labeled by "$\surd$" if F is empty. Otherwise, its root is labeled by a set of F.

(2) If n is a node of T, define $H(n)$ to be the set of edge labels on the path in T from the root node to n. If n is labeled by $\surd$, it has no successor nodes in T. If n is labeled by a set Σ of F, then for each $\sigma \in \Sigma$, n has a successor node n_σ joined to n by an edge labeled by σ. The label for n_σ is a set $S \in F$ such that $S \cap H(n_\sigma) = \{\ \}$ if such a set S exists. Otherwise, n_σ is labeled by $\surd$.

Example 4.7. Figure 2 is an *HS*-tree for $F = \{\{2,4,5\}, \{1,2,3\}, \{1,3,5\}, \{2,4,6\}, \{2,4\}, \{2,3,5\}, \{1,6\}\}$.

The following results are obvious for any *HS*-tree for a collection F of sets:
(1) If n is a node of the tree labeled by $\surd$, then $H(n)$ is a hitting set for F.
(2) Each minimal hitting set for F is $H(n)$ for some node n of the tree labeled by $\surd$.

Notice that the sets of the form $H(n)$ for nodes labeled by $\surd$ do not include all hitting sets for F. The important point for our purpose is that they do include all minimal hitting sets for F. Our objective is to determine various tree pruning techniques to allow us to generate as small a subtree of an *HS*-tree as is possible, while preserving the property that the subtree so generated will give us all minimal hitting sets for F. In addition, we wish to minimize the number of accesses to F required to generate this subtree, where by an access to F we mean the computation required to determine the label of a node in this subtree. Such a computation of a label for node n is determined (at least conceptually) by searching F for a set S such that $S \cap H(n) = \{\ \}$. If such an S

is found, node n is labeled by S, else it is labeled by $\surd$. For our purposes, this computation requiring an access to F must be treated as extremely expensive. This is so because for us, F will be the set of all conflict sets for (SD, COMPONENTS, OBS). Moreover, F will not be explicitly available, but will instead be implicitly defined. An access to F will be the computation of a conflict set, and this will require a call to a theorem prover. Clearly, we will want as few such accesses to F as possible.

The natural way to reduce accesses to F in generating an *HS*-tree is to reuse node labels which have already been computed. For example, if the *HS*-tree of Fig. 2 was generated breadth-first, generating nodes at any fixed level in the tree in left-to-right order, then node n_2 could have been assigned the same label as n_1, namely, $\{1,3,5\}$, since $H(n_2) \cap \{1,3,5\} = \{\ \}$. For the same reason, all of the nodes labeled $\{1,6\}$ other than node n_4 require no access to F; their labels can be determined from the tree itself as the previously computed label for n_4.

Next, we consider three tree pruning devices for *HS*-trees which preserve the property that the resulting pruned *HS*-tree will include all minimal hitting sets for F.

(1) Notice that in Fig. 2 $H(n_6) = H(n_8)$. Moreover, we could have reused the label of n_6 for n_8. This means that the subtrees rooted at n_6 and n_8 respectively could be identically generated had we chosen the reused label for n_8. Thus, n_8's subtree is redundant, and we can close node n_8. Similarly, $H(n_7) = H(n_5)$ so we can close node n_7.

(2) In Fig. 2, $H(n_3) = \{1,2\}$ is a hitting set for F. Therefore, any other node n of the tree for which $H(n_3) \subseteq H(n)$ cannot possibly define a smaller hitting set than $H(n_3)$. Since we are only interested in minimal hitting sets, such a node n can be closed. In Fig. 2, node n_9 is an example of such a node which we can close. The computational advantage of recognizing that node n_9 can be closed is that we need not access F to determine that n_9's label is $\surd$.

(3) The following is a simple result about minimal hitting sets: If F is a collection of sets, and if $S \in F$ and $S' \in F$ with S a proper subset of S', then $F - \{S'\}$ has the same minimal hitting sets as F.

We can use this result to prune the *HS*-tree of Fig. 2. Notice that the label $\{2,4\}$ of node n_{10} is a proper subset of $\{2,4,5\}$, the label of the previously generated node n_0. This means that, in generating the label of n_{10} we have discovered that F contains a strict subset $\{2,4\}$ of $\{2,4,5\}$, another set of F. Thus, in generating the *HS*-tree, we could have labeled n_0 by the smaller set $\{2,4\}$, instead of $\{2,4,5\}$. In other words, the edge from n_0 labeled 5 and the entire subtree beneath this edge are redundant; they can be removed from the tree while preserving the property that the resulting pruned tree will yield all minimal hitting sets.

Notice that this tree pruning device appears unnecessarily clumsy. We waited until node n_{10} was generated and labeled by $\{2,4\}$ before noticing that F therefore contains a set $\{2,4\}$ which is a proper subset of another set $\{2,4,5\}$ of F. Why not simply prescan F, remove from F all supersets of sets in F, and use the resulting trimmed F to generate an *HS*-tree? In the example of Fig. 2 we could first have removed $\{2,4,5\}$ and $\{2,4,6\}$ from F before generating its *HS*-tree. The reason we did not do this is, as we have already remarked, for our purposes F will be *implicitly* defined as the set of all conflict sets for (SD, COMPONENTS, OBS). Since we will not have available an explicit enumeration of these conflict sets, we cannot perform a preliminary subset test on them.

We summarize our method for generating a pruned *HS*-tree for F as follows:

(1) Generate the *HS*-tree breadth-first, generating nodes at any fixed level in the tree in left-to-right order.

(2) Reusing node labels: If node n is labeled by the set $S \in F$, and if n' is a node such that $H(n') \cap S = \{\ \}$, label n' by S. (We indicate that the label of n' is a reused label by underlining it in the tree.) Such a node n' requires no access to F.

(3) Tree pruning:

(i) If node n is labeled by $\surd$ and node n' is such that $H(n) \subseteq H(n')$, close n', i.e. do not compute a label for n'; do not generate any successors of n'.

(ii) If node n has been generated and node n' is such that $H(n') = H(n)$, then close n'. (We indicate a closed node in the tree by marking it with "×".)

(iii) If nodes n and n' have been respectively labeled by sets S and S' of F, and if S' is a proper subset of S, then for each $\alpha \in S - S'$ mark as redundant the edge from node n labeled by α. A redundant edge, together with the subtree beneath it, may be removed from the *HS*-tree while preserving the property that the resulting pruned *HS*-tree will yield all minimal hitting sets for F. (We indicate a redundant edge in a pruned *HS*-tree by cutting it with ")(".)

Figure 3 depicts such a pruned *HS*-tree for the example of Fig. 2.

In view of the preceding discussion, the following result should be clear:

Theorem 4.8. *Let F be a collection of sets, and T a pruned HS-tree for F, as previously described. Then $\{H(n) \mid n$ is a node of T labeled by $\surd\}$ is the collection of minimal hitting sets for F.*

Example 4.7 (continued). For the set F of Fig. 3, the minimal hitting sets are:

$$\{1,2\}\,,\quad \{2,3,6\}\,,\quad \{2,5,6\}\,,\quad \{4,1,3\}\,,\quad \{4,1,5\}\,,\quad \{4,3,6\}\,.$$

The computation of these hitting sets required 13 accesses to F.

4.3. Computing all diagnoses

A conceptually simple approach to computing diagnoses can be based upon Theorems 4.4 and 4.8 as follows: First compute the collection F of all conflict sets for (SD, COMPONENTS, OBS), then use the method of pruned *HS*-trees to compute the minimal hitting sets for *F*. These minimal hitting sets will be the diagnoses.

The problem, then, is to systematically compute all conflict sets for (SD, COMPONENTS, OBS). Recall that $\{c_1, \ldots, c_k\} \subseteq$ COMPONENTS is a conflict set iff SD $\cup$ OBS $\cup$ $\{\neg$AB$(c_1), \ldots, \neg$AB$(c_k)\}$ is inconsistent. Now if SD $\cup$ OBS $\cup$ $\{\neg$AB$(c_1), \ldots, \neg$AB$(c_k)\}$ is inconsistent, so is SD $\cup$ OBS $\cup$ $\{\neg$AB$(c) \mid c \in$ COMPONENTS$\}$. So, using a sound and complete theorem prover, compute all refutations of SD $\cup$ OBS $\cup$ $\{\neg$AB$(c) \mid c \in$ COMPONENTS$\}$ and for each such refutation, record the AB instances entering into the refutation. If $\{\neg$AB$(c_1), \ldots, \neg$AB$(c_k)\}$ is the set of AB instances used in such a refutation, then $\{c_1, \ldots, c_k\}$ is a conflict set.

For example, Fig. 4 gives a stylized resolution style refutation tree for SD $\cup$ OBS $\cup$ $\{\neg$AB$(c) \mid c \in$ COMPONENTS$\}$ in which the AB instances entering into the refutation are explicitly indicated. This refutation yields the conflict set $\{c_1, c_5, c_7\}$.

Therefore, one approach to computing all conflict sets for (SD, COMPONENTS, OBS) is to invoke a sound and complete theorem prover which computes all refutations of SD $\cup$ OBS $\cup$ $\{\neg$AB$(c) \mid c \in$ COMPONENTS$\}$, and which, for each such refutation, records the AB instances entering into the refutation in order to determine the corresponding conflict set.

Unfortunately, there is a serious problem with this approach: the conflict sets do not stand in a 1-1 relationship with the refutations of SD $\cup$ OBS $\cup$ $\{\neg$AB$(c) \mid c \in$ COMPONENTS$\}$. There will be refutations which are inessential variants of each other. Figure 5 illustrates two resolution refutations which, although different refutations, involve the same AB instances. A refutation-based approach to the computation of conflict sets ought not compute such

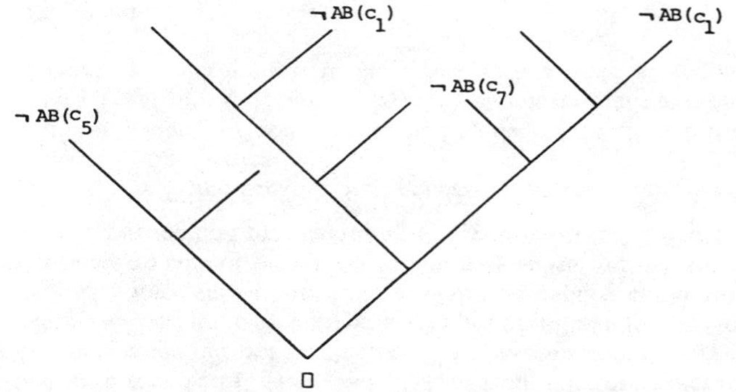

FIG. 4. Resolution style refutation tree for SD $\cup$ OBS $\cup$ $\{\neg$AB$(c) \mid c \in$ COMPONENTS$\}$.

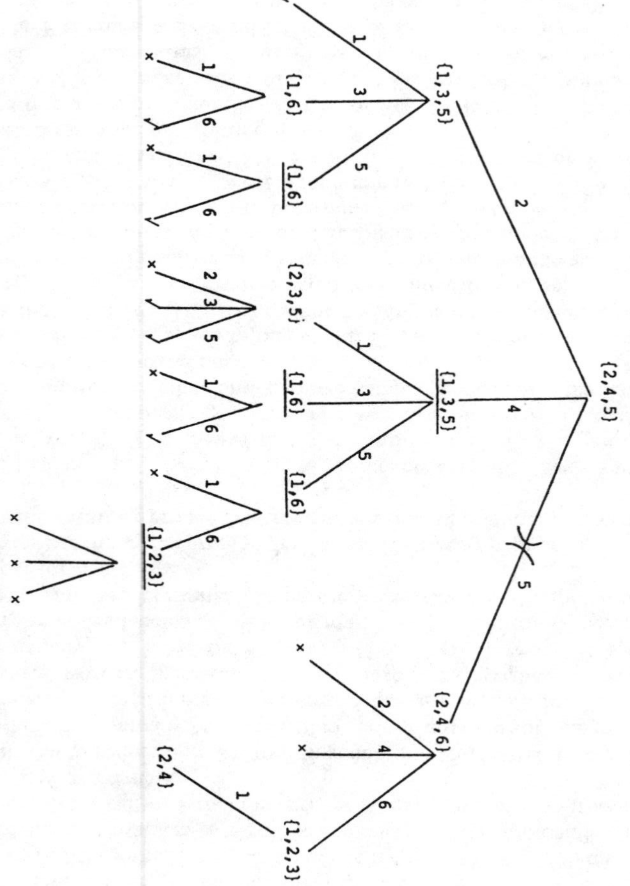

FIG. 3. A pruned *HS*-tree for $F = \{\{2,4,5\}, \{1,2,3\}, \{1,3,5\}, \{2,4,6\}, \{2,4\}, \{2,3,5\}, \{1,6\}\}$.

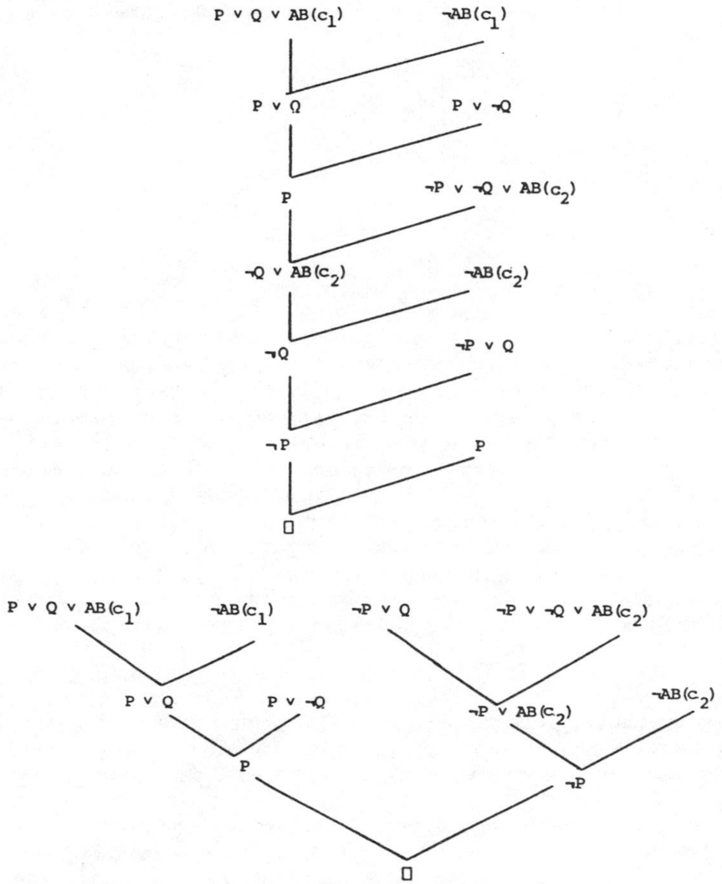

FIG. 5. Two resolution refutations involving the same AB instances.

inessential variants. If we were relying on a resolution theorem prover for computing refutations, then fixing on some particular resolution strategy (e.g. linear resolution, resolution with literal ordering, etc.) might help with this problem. Depending upon a particular style of theorem prover would not be a good idea, however. We should not restrict the underlying theorem proving system since particular applications might benefit from special purpose theorem provers, e.g. constraint propagation techniques for diagnosis, as used by Davis [4] and de Kleer and Williams [6], or specialized Boolean equation solvers. So our problem is to prevent the computation of inessential variants of refutations, without imposing any constraints on the nature of the underlying theorem proving system. As we shall see, our algorithm for computing minimal hitting sets handles this problem very nicely. In fact, the underlying theorem prover is relieved of all responsibility for the systematic generation of all conflict sets; this responsibility for determining the order in which conflict sets are computed, and when they have all been determined, is assumed by our algorithm for computing minimal hitting sets. The role of the theorem prover is simply to return a suitable conflict set when so requested by the algorithm for generating pruned *HS*-trees.

We now develop our "algorithm"[3] for computing all diagnoses for (SD, COMPONENTS, OBS). Our approach is based upon Theorem 4.4 and therefore requires all minimal hitting sets for the collection F of conflict sets for (SD, COMPONENTS, OBS). The minimal hitting set calculation will involve generating a pruned *HS*-tree for F, as per Theorem 4.8, but with one significant difference: F will not be given explicitly. Instead, suitable elements of F will be computed, as required, while the *HS*-tree is being generated.

Recall that in generating a pruned *HS*-tree for a collection, F, of sets, a node n of the tree can be assigned a label in one of two ways:

(1) By reusing a label S previously determined for some other node n' whenever $H(n) \cap S = \{\ \}$; in this case, no access to F is required since n's label is obtained from that part of the pruned *HS*-tree generated thus far.

(2) By searching F for a set S such that $H(n) \cap S = \{\ \}$. If such a set S can be found in F, n is labeled by S, otherwise by $\surd$. In this case the set F must be accessed; n's label cannot be determined without F.

Now it should be clear that the set F need not be given explicitly. The only time that F is needed is in case (2) above. Therefore, to generate a pruned *HS*-tree for F, we only require a function which, when given $H(n)$, returns a set S such that $H(n) \cap S = \{\ \}$ if such a set S exists in F, and $\surd$ otherwise. We now exhibit such a function when F is the collection of conflict sets for (SD, COMPONENTS, OBS). Let TP(SD COMPONENTS, OBS) be a function with the property that whenever (SD, COMPONENTS) is a system and OBS an observation for that system, TP(SD, COMPONENTS, OBS) returns a conflict set for (SD, COMPONENTS, OBS) if one exists, i.e. if SD $\cup$ OBS $\cup$ $\{\neg$AB$(c) \mid c \in$ COMPONENTS$\}$ is inconsistent, and returns $\surd$ otherwise. It is easy to see that any such function TP has the following property: If $C \subseteq$ COMPONENTS, then TP(SD, COMPONENTS $- C$, OBS) returns a conflict set S for (SD, COMPONENTS, OBS) such that $C \cap S = \{\ \}$ if such a set S exists, and $\surd$ otherwise. It follows that we can generate a pruned *HS*-tree for F, the collection of conflict sets for (SD, COMPONENTS, OBS) as described in Section 4.2 except that whenever a node n of this tree needs an

[3] The scare quotes serve as a reminder that the general problem is undecidable.

access to F to compute its label, we label n by TP(SD, COMPONENTS $- H(n)$, OBS). From this pruned *HS*-tree T we can extract the set of all minimal hitting sets for F, namely $\{H(n) \mid n$ is a node of T labeled by $\surd\}$. By Theorem 4.4, this is the set of diagnoses for (SD, COMPONENTS, OBS).

We have proved the correctness of the following "algorithm":

Algorithm. DIAGNOSE(SD, COMPONENTS, OBS).

{COMMENT: (SD, COMPONENTS) is a system and OBS is an observation of the system. TP is any function with the property that TP(SD, COMPONENTS, OBS) returns a conflict set for (SD, COMPONENTS, OBS) if one exists, i.e. if SD $\cup$ OBS $\cup$ $\{\neg$AB$(c) \mid c \in$ COMPONENTS$\}$ is inconsistent, and returns $\surd$ otherwise. DIAGNOSE(SD, COMPONENTS, OBS) returns the set of all diagnoses for (SD, COMPONENTS, OBS).}

Step 1. Generate a pruned *HS*-tree T for the collection F of conflict sets for (SD, COMPONENTS, OBS) as described in Section 4.2 except that whenever, in the process of generating T a node n of T needs an access to F to compute its label, label that node by TP(SD, COMPONENTS $- H(n)$, OBS).

Step 2. Return $\{H(n) \mid n$ is a node of T labeled by $\surd\}$.

Example 2.2 (continued). *The full adder.* Figure 6 shows a possible pruned *HS*-tree for the full adder example, as computed by DIAGNOSE(SD, $\{X_1, X_2, A_1, A_2, O_1\}$, OBS) where SD and OBS are the system description and observation described earlier for the full adder. Recall that $\{X_1, X_2, A_1, A_2, O_1\}$ are the components of this system. The root node of Fig. 6 is labeled by a call to TP(SD, $\{X_1, X_2, A_1, A_2, O_1\}$, OBS) which we are supposing returns $\{X_1, X_2\}$. Node n_1 is labeled by a call to TP(SD, $\{X_2, A_1, A_2, O_1\}$, OBS). Since SD $\cup$ OBS $\cup$ $\{\neg$AB(X_2), $\neg$AB(A_1), $\neg$AB(A_2), $\neg$AB$(O_1)\}$ is consistent, this call returns $\surd$. Node n_2 is labeled by a call to TP(SD, $\{X_1, A_1, A_2, O_1\}$, OBS) which we are supposing returns $\{X_1, A_2, O_1\}$. Node n_3 is marked closed by an *HS*-tree pruning rule. Node n_4 is labeled by a call to TP(SD, $\{X_1, A_1, O_1\}$, OBS) which returns $\surd$ since SD $\cup$ OBS $\cup$ $\{\neg$AB(X_1), $\neg$AB(A_1), $\neg$AB$(O_1)\}$ is consistent. Similarly, node n_5 is labeled $\surd$ by a call to TP(SD, $\{X_1, A_1, A_2\}$, OBS). The set of all diagnoses can now be read from the tree of Fig. 6: $\{\{X_1\}, \{X_2, A_2\}, \{X_2, O_1\}\}$. Five calls to TP were required. Figure 6 is, of course, not the only possible computation of the diagnoses for the full adder. The particular trees one obtains depend upon what the function TP returns. Figure 7 shows a different possible pruned *HS*-tree for the full adder, corresponding to a different function TP. Notice that in this case the root node is labeled by a nonminimal conflict set returned by TP(SD, $\{X_1, X_2, A_1, A_2, O_1\}$, OBS). Notice also that the *HS*-tree pruning algorithm marks one of the edges (labeled A_1) redundant after TP returns a strict subset $\{X_1, A_2, O_1\}$ of the roots node's label. Six calls to TP were required for this example.

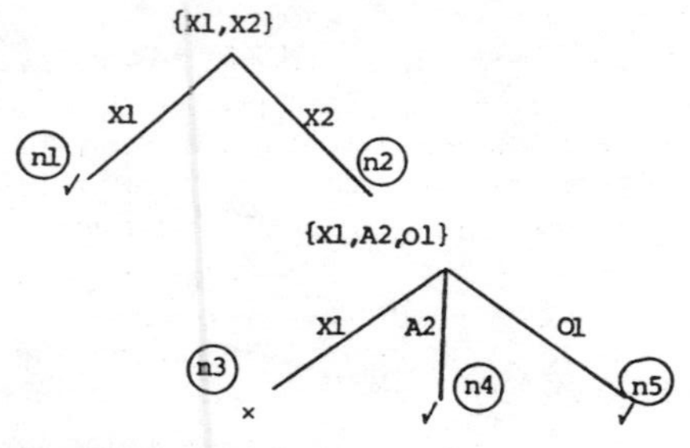

FIG. 6. Computing all diagnoses for the full adder.

We make several remarks about algorithm DIAGNOSE:

(1) No two calls by DIAGNOSE to TP will ever return the same conflict set. This a simple consequence of the way node labels are determined in generating a pruned *HS*-tree. As a result, the theorem prover underlying TP need not compute the same conflict set in two inessentially different ways, as was the case for example in Fig. 5. Moreover, for any two calls by DIAGNOSE to TP, the later call will never return a superset of the earlier call. A consequence of this is that normally DIAGNOSE will explicitly compute only a small subset of all possible conflict sets for (SD, COMPONENTS, OBS). For example, in Fig. 6, DIAGNOSE computes only two of the possible 12 conflict sets, while in Fig. 7 it computes three. This is important because the computation of a conflict set requires an expensive call to a theorem prover.

(2) The function TP may be realized computationally in many different ways. One way, as we remarked earlier, is to use a complete refutation based theorem prover which records the AB instances entering into the refutations it computes. Another way to compute a conflict set is to use a theorem prover to directly derive, from SD $\cup$ OBS as premises, a disjunction of AB instances, i.e. a

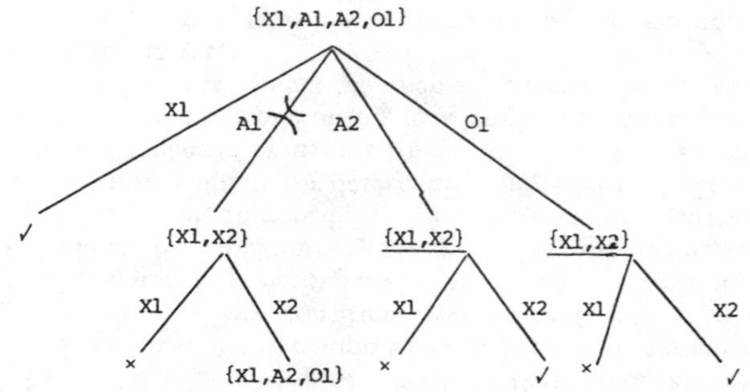

FIG. 7. A different computation of diagnoses for the full adder.

formula of the form $\text{AB}(c_1) \vee \cdots \vee \text{AB}(c_k)$, for then, since $\text{SD} \cup \text{OBS} \vdash \text{AB}(c_1) \vee \cdots \vee \text{AB}(c_k)$, we have $\text{SD} \cup \text{OBS} \cup \{\neg\text{AB}(c_1), \ldots, \neg\text{AB}(c_k)\}$ inconsistent, whence $\{c_1, \ldots, c_k\}$ is a conflict set. This appears to be the basis for computing suspects used by Genesereth's DART program [7].

In particular applications TP might profitably be realized by special purpose theorem provers, e.g. constraint propagation techniques for solving systems of equations, as used by Davis [4] and de Kleer and Williams [6].

Whatever the theorem proving techniques used by TP, it should probably be implemented in such a way that intermediate computations obtained while computing a conflict set are cached for possible use in subsequent calls to TP.

(3) If the function TP can be realized so that it returns only minimal conflict sets, then in the generation of a pruned *HS*-tree, no edge will ever be marked redundant so that in this circumstance we can simplify the tree generation algorithm.

(4) Because pruned *HS*-trees are generated breadth-first, diagnoses are computed in order of increasing cardinality. Thus, all of the diagnoses involving just a single component are determined by those nodes labeled by $\surd$ at level 1[4] in the tree, and these are computed before the level-2 nodes which determine the diagnoses involving two components, etc. If, for some reason, we believe that diagnoses of cardinality greater than k are highly improbable, or if we are interested only in diagnoses of cardinality k or less, then DIAGNOSE can stop growing the *HS*-tree at level k.

Example 4.9. Figure 8 illustrates a device first introduced by Davis [4], and subsequently extensively analyzed by de Kleer and Williams [6]. The device has 5 components, M_1, M_2, M_3, A_1, and A_2. The observation is given by:

$$\text{in1}(M_1) = 3\,, \quad \text{in2}(M_1) = 2\,, \quad \text{in1}(M_2) = 3\,, \quad \text{in2}(M_2) = 2\,,$$
$$\text{in1}(M_3) = 3\,, \quad \text{in2}(M_3) = 2\,, \quad \text{out}(A_1) = 10\,, \quad \text{out}(A_2) = 12\,.$$

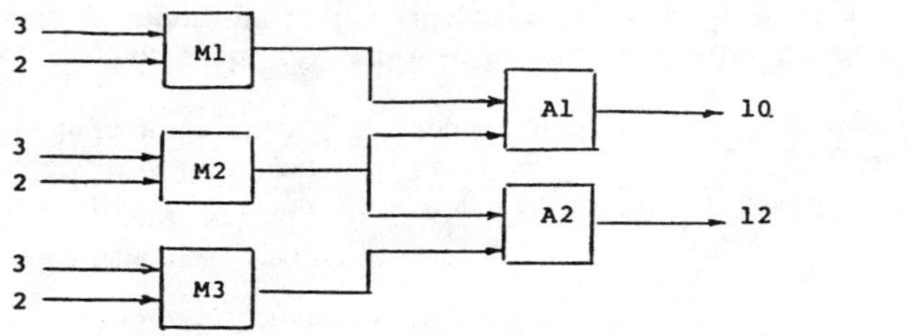

FIG. 8. A device with observed inputs and outputs. M_1, M_2, and M_3 are multipliers; A_1 and A_2 are adders.

[4] The root node is at level 0.

We omit a full specification of the system description; it will involve axioms specifying how the components normally behave, together with axioms about addition and multiplication of integers.

For example, the normal behaviour of a multiplier will be specified by:

$$\text{MULTIPLIER}(m) \wedge \neg\text{AB}(m) \supset \text{out}(m) = \text{in1}(m) * \text{in2}(m)\,.$$

The system description will also contain axioms describing how the components are interconnected, e.g.

$$\text{out}(M_1) = \text{in1}(A_1)\,, \quad \text{out}(M_2) = \text{in2}(A_1)\,,$$
$$\text{out}(M_2) = \text{in1}(A_2)\,, \quad \text{etc.}$$

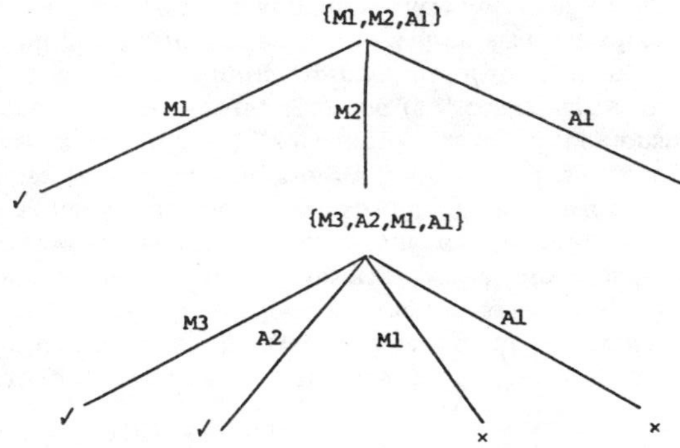

FIG. 9. A pruned *HS*-tree for Example 4.9.

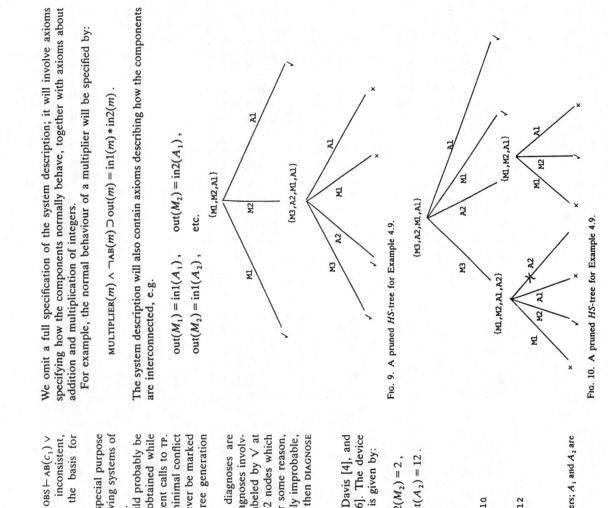

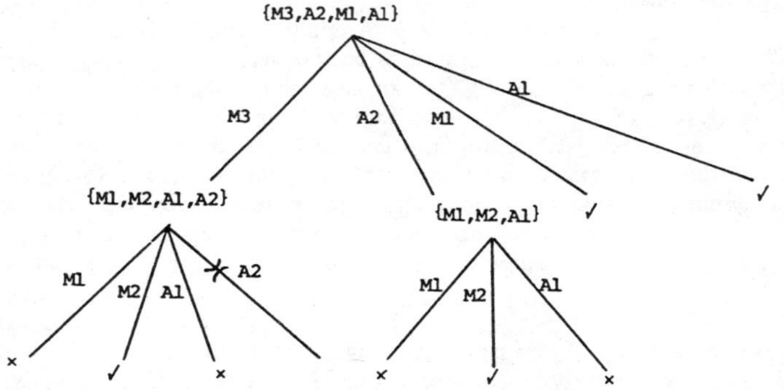

FIG. 10. A pruned *HS*-tree for Example 4.9.

Since the observation $\text{out}(A_1) = 10$ conflicts with the predicted value $\text{out}(A_1) = 12$ the device is faulty. Figures 9 and 10 give two possible pruned *HS*-trees which algorithm DIAGNOSE might compute. From either of these we obtain the four diagnoses for this device: $\{M_1\}$, $\{A_1\}$, $\{M_2, M_3\}$, $\{A_2, M_2\}$.

4.4. Single fault diagnoses

A diagnosis is a *single fault* diagnosis iff it is a singleton. If it contains two or more components, it is a *multiple fault* diagnosis. For the full adder example, there is one single fault diagnosis, $\{X_1\}$, and two multiple fault diagnoses, $\{X_2, A_2\}$ and $\{X_2, O_1\}$.

Single fault diagnoses are of particular interest, primarily because one normally expects components to fail independently of each another. As a result, single fault diagnoses are judged more likely to be correct than any of their companion multiple fault diagnoses. Thus, in the case of the full adder, the single fault diagnosis $\{X_1\}$ is to be preferred over the other two multiple fault diagnoses.

Theorem 4.4 (Corollary 4.5) provides the following characterization of single fault diagnoses:

Corollary 4.10. *$\{c\}$ is a single fault diagnosis for* (SD, COMPONENTS, OBS) *iff c is an element of every (minimal) conflict set for* (SD, COMPONENTS, OBS).

If our concern is only to compute all single fault diagnoses, we can do so by allowing algorithm DIAGNOSE to generate a pruned *HS*-tree only to level 1 of the tree, returning $H(n)$ for each level-1 node labeled by $\surd$. In fact, the following result is a simple consequence of the correctness of algorithm DIAGNOSE.

Theorem 4.11 (Determining all single fault diagnoses from one conflict set). *Suppose C is a conflict set for* (SD, COMPONENTS, OBS). *Then $\{c\}$ is a diagnosis for* (SD, COMPONENTS, OBS) *iff $c \in C$ and* $\mathrm{SD} \cup \mathrm{OBS} \cup \{\neg\mathrm{AB}(k) \mid k \in \mathrm{COMPONENTS} - \{c\}\}$ *is consistent.*

Theorem 4.11 generalizes in the natural way to the case where we have several, but not necessarily all, conflict sets.

Theorem 4.12 (Determining all single fault diagnoses from several conflict sets). *Suppose for $n \geq 1$ that $C_1, C_2, \ldots, C_n$ are conflict sets for* (SD, COMPONENTS, OBS), *and that $C = \bigcap_{i=1}^{n} C_i$. Then $\{c\}$ is a diagnosis for* (SD, COMPONENTS, OBS) *iff $c \in C$ and* $\mathrm{SD} \cup \mathrm{OBS} \cup \{\neg\mathrm{AB}(k) \mid k \in \mathrm{COMPONENTS} - \{c\}\}$ *is consistent.*

Proof. ($\Rightarrow$) By Corollary 4.10, $c \in C$. The rest follows by Proposition 3.4.

($\Leftarrow$) Since (SD, COMPONENTS, OBS) has a conflict set, then $\mathrm{SD} \cup \mathrm{OBS} \cup \{\neg\mathrm{AB}(k) \mid k \in \mathrm{COMPONENTS}\}$ is inconsistent. Since $\mathrm{SD} \cup \mathrm{OBS} \cup \{\neg\mathrm{AB}(k) \mid k \in \mathrm{COMPONENTS} - \{c\}\}$ is consistent, then by Proposition 3.4, $\{c\}$ is a diagnosis for (SD, COMPONENTS, OBS). □

Theorem 4.12 is a generalization of the candidate generation procedure of Davis [4], and provides a formal justification for Davis' procedure. Davis' concern was the determination of single fault diagnoses for digital circuits represented by constraint networks. His candidate generation procedure computes some (not necessarily all) conflict sets, intersects these to obtain a set C of possible single fault candidates, then for each $c \in C$ performs a candidate consistency test by suspending (turning off) the constraint modeling c's behaviour. This consistency test via the suspension of c's constraint corresponds to the consistency test, called for by Theorem 4.12, of $\mathrm{SD} \cup \mathrm{OBS} \cup \{\neg\mathrm{AB}(k) \mid k \in \mathrm{COMPONENTS} - \{c\}\}$. The exclusion of c from COMPONENTS amounts to "turning off" component c while performing the consistency test.

5. Measurements

Suppose that (SD, COMPONENTS, OBS) has more than one diagnosis. Without further information about the system, one cannot conjecture a unique diagnosis. One way to obtain further information about a system is to perform measurements of some kind e.g. insert a probe into a circuit, or perform a laboratory test on a patient. In this section, we study how such measurements can affect diagnoses. Specifically, we shall define a *measurement* MEAS to be an additional observation (and therefore a finite set of first-order sentences), and we shall consider the following question: What is the relationship between the diagnoses for (SD, COMPONENTS, OBS) and (SD, COMPONENTS, OBS $\cup$ MEAS)?

Typically, OBS will be an initial observation of the system (SD, COMPONENTS), leading to multiple diagnoses, and MEAS will be a measurement (an additional observation) of the system taken in an attempt to discriminate among the original multiple diagnoses.

Definition 5.1. A diagnosis Δ for (SD, COMPONENTS, OBS) *predicts Π* (a first-order sentence) iff

$$\mathrm{SD} \cup \mathrm{OBS} \cup \{\mathrm{AB}(c) \mid c \in \Delta\}$$
$$\cup \{\neg\mathrm{AB}(c) \mid c \in \mathrm{COMPONENTS} - \Delta\} \models \Pi ,$$

i.e. on the assumption that the components of Δ are all faulty, and the remaining components are all functioning normally, system behaviour Π must hold.

Example 5.2. For the device of Fig. 8 (Example 4.9), diagnosis $\{M_1\}$ predicts $\text{out}(M_2) = 6$ and $\text{out}(M_1) = 4$; diagnosis $\{M_2, M_3\}$ predicts $\text{out}(M_2) = 4$ and $\text{out}(M_3) = 8$.

Proposition 3.3 immediately provides a simpler version of Definition 5.1.

Proposition 5.3. *A diagnosis* Δ *for* (SD, COMPONENTS, OBS) *predicts* Π *iff*

$$\text{SD} \cup \text{OBS} \cup \{\neg \text{AB}(c) \mid c \in \text{COMPONENTS} - \Delta\} \models \Pi .$$

The following two results are immediate consequences of Definition 2.4.

Proposition 5.4. *If no diagnosis for* (SD, COMPONENTS, OBS) *predicts* $\neg\Pi$, *then* (SD, COMPONENTS, OBS $\cup \{\Pi\}$) *has the same diagnoses as* (SD, COMPONENTS, OBS).

In other words, a measurement which disconfirms no diagnosis provides no new information.

Proposition 5.5.

(1) *Every diagnosis for* (SD, COMPONENTS, OBS) *which predicts* Π *is a diagnosis for* (SD, COMPONENTS, OBS $\cup \{\Pi\}$), *i.e. diagnoses are preserved under confirming measurements.*

(2) *No diagnosis for* (SD, COMPONENTS, OBS} *which predicts* $\neg\Pi$ *is a diagnosis for* (SD, COMPONENTS, OBS $\cup \{\Pi\}$), *i.e. a measurement rejects the diagnoses which it disconfirms.*

A simple consequence of Proposition 5.5 is that whenever each diagnosis for (SD, COMPONENTS, OBS) predicts one of Π, $\neg\Pi$, then measuring Π retains all diagnoses predicting Π, and rejects all diagnoses predicting $\neg\Pi$. It is therefore tempting to conjecture that whenever every diagnosis predicts Π or $\neg\Pi$, then the diagnoses which remain after measuring Π are precisely those which predicted Π i.e. that the diagnoses for (SD, COMPONENTS, OBS $\cup \{\Pi\}$) are precisely those for (SD, COMPONENTS, OBS) which predict Π. Unfortunately, as the next example shows, this conjecture is false.

Example 5.6. Consider the device of Fig. 8, with the indicated inputs and outputs. Recall that this had four diagnoses: $\{M_1\}$, $\{A_1\}$, $\{M_2, M_3\}$, $\{A_2, M_3\}$.

$$\{M_1\} \text{ predicts } \text{out}(M_2) = 6 ,$$
$$\{A_1\} \text{ predicts } \text{out}(M_2) = 6 ,$$
$$\{M_2, M_3\} \text{ predicts } \text{out}(M_2) = 4 ,$$
$$\{M_2, A_2\} \text{ predicts } \text{out}(M_2) = 4 .$$

Suppose we now measure $\text{out}(M_2)$ and obtain $\text{out}(M_2) = 5$. All four diagnoses predict $\text{out}(M_2) \neq 5$, so that if the above conjecture were correct, this measurement should reject all four diagnoses, and *no new diagnoses should arise*. But in fact the four old diagnoses are replaced by four new ones: $\{M_1, M_2, M_3\}$, $\{M_1, M_2, A_2\}$, $\{M_2, M_3, A_1\}$, $\{M_2, A_1, A_2\}$.

Notice that each new diagnosis resulting from the measurement $\text{out}(M_2) = 5$ is a strict superset of some old diagnosis predicting $\text{out}(M_2) \neq 5$. This is no accident, as the following result shows:

Theorem 5.7. *Suppose every diagnosis for* (SD, COMPONENTS, OBS) *predicts one of* Π, $\neg\Pi$. *Then:*

(1) *Every diagnosis for* (SD, COMPONENTS, OBS) *which predicts* Π *is a diagnosis for* (SD, COMPONENTS, OBS $\cup \Pi\}$).

(2) *No diagnosis for* (SD, COMPONENTS, OBS) *which predicts* $\neg\Pi$ *is a diagnosis for* (SD, COMPONENTS, OBS $\cup \{\Pi\}$).

(3) *Any diagnosis for* (SD, COMPONENTS, OBS $\cup \{\Pi\}$) *which is not a diagnosis for* (SD, COMPONENTS, OBS) *is a strict superset of some diagnosis for* (SD, COMPONENTS, OBS) *which predicts* $\neg\Pi$. *In other words, any new diagnosis resulting from the new measurement* Π *will be a strict superset of some old diagnosis which predicted* $\neg\Pi$.

Proof. Claims (1) and (2) are simply Proposition 5.5. To prove claim (3) suppose that Δ_Π is a diagnosis satisfying the hypothesis of this claim. Because Δ_Π is a diagnosis for (SD, COMPONENTS, OBS $\cup \{\Pi\}$),

$$\text{SD} \cup \text{OBS} \cup \{\Pi\}$$
$$\cup \{\neg \text{AB}(c) \mid c \in \text{COMPONENTS} - \Delta_\Pi\}$$

is consistent. Therefore

$$\text{SD} \cup \text{OBS} \cup \{\neg \text{AB}(c) \mid c \in \text{COMPONENTS} - \Delta_\Pi\}$$

is consistent. Let Δ be a minimal subset of Δ_Π such that

$$\text{SD} \cup \text{OBS} \cup \{\neg \text{AB}(c) \mid c \in \text{COMPONENTS} - \Delta\}$$

is consistent. By Proposition 3.4, Δ is a diagnosis for (SD, COMPONENTS, OBS). Since, by the hypothesis of claim (3), Δ_Π is not a diagnosis for (SD, COMPONENTS, OBS), Δ must be a strict subset of Δ_Π. It remains only to prove that Δ predicts $\neg\Pi$. By hypothesis of the theorem, Δ predicts one of Π, $\neg\Pi$, so assume to the contrary that Δ predicts Π, i.e. that

$$\text{SD} \cup \text{OBS} \cup \{\neg \text{AB}(c) \mid c \in \text{COMPONENTS} - \Delta\} \models \Pi .$$

Therefore

$$\text{SD} \cup \text{OBS} \cup \{\Pi\} \cup \{\neg\text{AB}(c) \mid c \in \text{COMPONENTS} - \Delta\}$$

is consistent. But by Proposition 3.4, this together with the fact that Δ is a proper subset of Δ_Π implies that Δ_Π cannot be a diagnosis for (SD, COMPONENTS, OBS $\cup \{\Pi\}$), contradiction. □

In general, Theorem 5.7 precludes a divide-and-conquer approach to discriminating among competing diagnoses on the basis of additional system measurements. While it is true that measuring Π preserves the old diagnoses predicting Π, and rejects the old diagnoses predicting $\neg\Pi$, new diagnoses can arise.

Corollary 5.8. *Suppose that* { } *is not a diagnosis for* (SD, COMPONENTS, OBS). *Then under the assumptions of Theorem* 5.7, *any new diagnosis arising from the new measurement* Π *will be a multiple fault diagnosis.*

Thus, in the nontrivial case where the system is truly faulty, the new diagnoses (if any) resulting from a new measurement will be multiple fault diagnoses. This provides the following characterization of the single fault diagnoses which survive a new measurement:

Corollary 5.9. *Suppose that* { } *is not a diagnosis for* (SD, COMPONENT, OBS). *Then under the assumptions of Theorem* 5.7, *the single fault diagnoses for* (SD, COMPONENTS, OBS $\cup \{\Pi\}$) *are precisely those of* (SD, COMPONENTS, OBS) *which predict* Π.

Corollary 5.9 justifies a divide-and-conquer strategy for discriminating among competing single fault diagnoses on the basis of system measurements.

Example 5.10. Consider the device of Fig. 8, with the indicated inputs and outputs. Recall that this had two single fault diagnoses: $\{M_1\}$ and $\{A_1\}$. We can discriminate between these single fault diagnoses by measuring out(M_1) because $\{M_1\}$ predicts out(M_1) = 4 while $\{A_1\}$ predicts out(M_1) = 6. Suppose we measure out(M_1) and obtain out(M_1) = 6. Then by Corollary 5.9, we now know that $\{A_1\}$ is the only possible single fault diagnosis. Of course, there may still be other remaining multiple fault diagnoses, including new multiple fault diagnoses. In fact, no new diagnoses arise, and the remaining diagnoses after the measurement are: $\{A_1\}$, $\{M_2, M_3\}$, and $\{M_2, A_2\}$.

Many interesting problems remain to be explored for a theory of measurement. Can we characterize situations in which measurements do not lead to new diagnoses but simply filter old ones? When new diagnoses do arise as a result of system measurements, can we determine these new diagnoses in a reasonable way from the pruned *HS*-tree already computed in determining the old diagnoses? Genesereth [8] describes a method for automatically generating certain system measurements. Are there other approaches to this test generation problem?

6. Generalizations and Relationship to Nonmonotonic Reasoning

Thus far our development of a theory of diagnosis has relied upon first-order logic as the underlying representation language for system descriptions. A close inspection of the preceding definitions, theorems, and proofs reveals that very few special features of first-order logic were actually required in developing the theory, so that the logical representation language may be generalized. In this section, we shall consider such generalizations. We shall also observe that diagnostic reasoning is nonmonotonic, and relate the theory of this paper to default logic [17].

6.1. Beyond first-order logic

In order to provide a concrete development of a theory of diagnoses, we have been assuming first-order logic with equality as the underlying representation language. In actual fact, Definition 2.4 of a diagnosis, the subsequent results of Section 3 leading to the algorithm DIAGNOSE of Section 4, and the results of Section 5 on measurements require very weak assumptions on the nature of the logic used. Specifically, suppose that L is any logic with the following properties:

(1) Its semantics is binary i.e. every sentence of L has value true or false in a given structure.

(2) L has $\{\wedge, \vee, \neg\}$ among its logical connectives, and these have their usual interpretations.

Then we can generalize the concept of a system so that a system description and its observation can be any set of sentences of L. The definition of a diagnosis remains the same in this generalized setting as in Definition 2.4. It is a simple matter to inspect the proofs of all results in Section 3 to see that they continue to hold, provided $\models$ is understood to denote the semantic entailment relation for the logic L. The "algorithm" DIAGNOSE of Section 4.3 for computing all diagnoses for a system remains the same and is correct for L. Of course, for DIAGNOSE really to be an algorithm, we need a sound, complete and decidable theorem prover for L at the core of the function TP which DIAGNOSE calls. It is also easy to see that our results of Section 4.4 on single fault diagnoses remain the same when L is the underlying logic. Finally, inspection of the proofs of Section 5 reveals that all of our results on measurements continue to hold for L.

Since our theory of diagnosis imposes such weak constraints on the system representation logic, the theory can accomodate a wide range of diagnostic tasks. For example, time varying digital hardware have natural representations in a temporal logic [12] and this might form the basis for a diagnostic reasoning system for such devices. Similarly, time varying physiological properties are central to certain kinds of medical diagnosis tasks [18]. Database logic has been proposed for representing many forms of databases [9] so that violation of database integrity constraints might profitably be viewed as a diagnostic reasoning problem with database logic providing the system description language.

These examples, and others like them, require a proper investigation with respect to problems of representation and computation. The fact that they all conform to a common theory of diagnosis is an encouraging and unifying observation.

6.2. Diagnosis and default logic[5]

As we have seen in Section 5, diagnostic reasoning is nonmonotonic in the sense that it can happen that none of a system's diagnoses survive a new observation of that system. In fact, as we now show, there is an intimate connection between diagnostic reasoning when the underlying logic is first-order and default logic [17].

To show the connection, we consider a system (SD, COMPONENTS) under observation OBS, and the corresponding default theory D whose first-order axioms are SD $\cup$ OBS, and whose default rules are

$$\left\{\frac{:\neg\mathrm{AB}(c)}{\neg\mathrm{AB}(c)} \mid c \in \mathrm{COMPONENTS}\right\}.^{6}$$

The following theorem shows that there is a 1-1 correspondence between the diagnoses for (SD, COMPONENTS, OBS) and the extensions for the above default theory, and that these extensions are precisely the sentences predicted by the corresponding diagnoses.

Theorem 6.1. *Consider a system* (SD, COMPONENTS) *under observation* OBS *where* SD *and* OBS *are sets of first-order sentences. Then E is an extension for the default theory*

$$\mathrm{DT} = \left(\left\{\frac{:\neg\mathrm{AB}(c)}{\neg\mathrm{AB}(c)} \mid c \in \mathrm{COMPONENTS}\right\}, \mathrm{SD} \cup \mathrm{OBS}\right)$$

iff for some diagnosis Δ for (SD, COMPONENTS, OBS), $E = \{\Pi \mid \Delta \text{ predicts } \Pi\}$.

Proof. The proof relies upon the following proposition which follows easily from the results of [17]:

Proposition. *Suppose R is a set of default rules, each of the form $:\alpha/\alpha$ for α a first-order sentence. Then E is an extension for the default theory (R, W) iff $E = \mathrm{Th}(W \cup \{\beta \mid :\beta/\beta \in D\})$*[7] *where D is a maximal subset of R such that $W \cup \{\beta \mid :\beta/\beta \in D\}$ is consistent.*

We now proceed with the proof of the main theorem.

($\Rightarrow$) Suppose E is an extension for DT. By the above proposition,

$$E = \mathrm{Th}\left(\mathrm{SD} \cup \mathrm{OBS} \cup \left\{\neg\mathrm{AB}(c) \mid \frac{:\neg\mathrm{AB}(c)}{\neg\mathrm{AB}(c)} \in D\right\}\right), \tag{6.1}$$

where D is a maximal subset of the default rules of DT such that

$$\mathrm{SD} \cup \mathrm{OBS} \cup \left\{\neg\mathrm{AB}(c) \mid \frac{:\neg\mathrm{AB}(c)}{\neg\mathrm{AB}(c)} \in D\right\} \text{ is consistent}. \tag{6.2}$$

Let

$$\Delta = \left\{c \mid c \in \mathrm{COMPONENTS} \text{ and } \frac{:\neg\mathrm{AB}(c)}{\neg\mathrm{AB}(c)} \notin D\right\}.$$

Then

$$\left\{\neg\mathrm{AB}(c) \mid \frac{:\neg\mathrm{AB}(c)}{\neg\mathrm{AB}(c)} \in D\right\} = \{\neg\mathrm{AB}(c) \mid c \in \mathrm{COMPONENTS} - \Delta\}, \tag{6.3}$$

so that by (6.2), SD $\cup$ OBS $\cup \{\neg\mathrm{AB}(c) \mid c \in \mathrm{COMPONENTS} - \Delta\}$ is consistent. Moreover, Δ is a minimal subset of COMPONENTS with this property because D is a maximal subset of the default rules of DT with property (6.2). Hence, by Proposition 3.4, Δ is a diagnosis for (SD, COMPONENTS, OBS). Finally, by (6.1) and (6.3),

$$E = \mathrm{Th}(\mathrm{SD} \cup \mathrm{OBS} \cup \{\neg\mathrm{AB}(c) \mid c \in \mathrm{COMPONENTS} - \Delta\}),$$

so that by Proposition 5.3, $E = \{\Pi \mid \Delta \text{ predicts } \Pi\}$.

[5] This section assumes that the reader is familiar with the literature on nonmonotonic reasoning (e.g. [1]), and specifically with default logic as described in [17].

[6] In [17] the notation $\alpha : M\beta/\gamma$ was used for default rules. The "M" was an unfortunate choice of notation meant to suggest "consistent" although it is in no way a sentential operator. As a piece of notation it was entirely spurious and we omit it from this paper.

[7] If S is a set of first-order sentences, Th(S) denotes the logical closure of S.

($\Leftarrow$) Suppose Δ is a diagnosis for (SD, COMPONENTS, OBS) and let $E = \{\Pi \mid \Delta$ predicts $\Pi\}$. By Proposition 5.3,

$$E = \mathrm{Th}(\mathrm{SD} \cup \mathrm{OBS} \cup \{\neg\mathrm{AB}(c) \mid c \in \mathrm{COMPONENTS} - \Delta\}) . \tag{6.4}$$

Since Δ is a diagnosis, then by Proposition 3.4 it is a minimal subset of COMPONENTS such that

$$\mathrm{SD} \cup \mathrm{OBS} \cup \{\neg\mathrm{AB}(c) \mid c \in \mathrm{COMPONENTS} - \Delta\} \text{ is consistent} . \tag{6.5}$$

Let

$$D = \left\{ \frac{:\neg\mathrm{AB}(c)}{\neg\mathrm{AB}(c)} \mid c \notin \Delta \right\} .$$

Then (6.3) holds. Hence, by (6.4),

$$E = \mathrm{Th}\left(\mathrm{SD} \cup \mathrm{OBS} \cup \left\{\neg\mathrm{AB}(c) \mid \frac{:\neg\mathrm{AB}(c)}{\neg\mathrm{AB}(c)} \in D\right\}\right)$$

and by (6.5),

$$\mathrm{SD} \cup \mathrm{OBS} \cup \left\{\neg\mathrm{AB}(c) \mid \frac{:\neg\mathrm{AB}(c)}{\neg\mathrm{AB}(c)} \in D\right\}$$

is consistent. Finally, D is a maximal subset of the default rules of DT with this consistency property since Δ is a minimal subset of COMPONENTS with property (6.5). Hence, by the above proposition, E is an extension for DT. □

7. Relationship to Other Research

The primary influences on this paper have been the work of de Kleer [5] and Genesereth [7].

De Kleer's research, while restricted to troubleshooting electronic circuits, appears to be among the earliest approaches in the literature to diagnosis from first principles. In his 1976 paper, de Kleer introduces the important concept of a conflict set, a concept which we have appropriated for our diagnostic algorithm. De Kleer's LOCAL system provided the diagnostic component for the SOPHIE III electronic computer aided instruction system [2]. In a recent paper de Kleer and Williams [6] have independently proposed a characterization of diagnoses, including multiple fault diagnoses, which corresponds to our Theorem 4.4. Their work differs from ours, however, in lacking a formalization of their diagnostic theory. On the other hand, de Kleer and Williams go beyond our theory of diagnosis by providing a method for computing the probabilities of the different diagnoses that arise in a given setting, and for using these probabilities to identify appropriate system measurements to make next.

One of the first uses of logic as a representation language for diagnosis from first principles is due to Genesereth [7], who uses first-order logic for representing systems, and a resolution style theorem prover for computing candidate faults as well as for generating tests to discriminate among competing diagnoses. Our work extends and generalizes some of his results in a number of ways, the most fundamental of which are:

(1) Our theory applies equally well to a wide variety of logics, not just first-order.

(2) We provide a formal analysis of multiple fault diagnoses.

(3) We give an algorithm for computing all diagnoses, including multiple fault diagnoses.

(4) We prove various results about the effects of system measurements on diagnoses.

Davis [4] has proposed an approach to diagnosis from first principles, but oriented towards devices simulatable by constraint propogation techniques. Moreover, he addresses single fault diagnoses only. Unfortunately, Davis does not formalize his approach, so that comparisons between our theory and his are difficult to make. Nevertheless, Davis does describe a "Candidate Generation Procedure" for computing potential single fault diagnoses. As we remarked in Section 4.4, our Theorem 4.12 can be interpreted as a formal justification for Davis' procedure. On the other hand, his analysis of bridge faults in digital circuits is beyond the capabilities of our theory because our theory requires a fixed, a priori enumeration of the system components which might fail.

There are two other approaches to diagnosis from first principles, similar in spirit to ours in that they are logically based. One, by David Poole and his colleagues [10, 13] has independently observed the connection of diagnostic reasoning with default logic. Both references describe how a default logic theorem prover can be used to compute diagnoses, but the focus of these papers is on mechanisms for such computations, and hence is quite different than ours. The other logically based approach to diagnosis is by Ginsberg [8], who adopts a logic of counterfactual implication as a foundation for diagnostic reasoning. Following Genesereth [7] Ginsberg assumes a first-order representation of the system being diagnosed. His departure from Genesereth is to define diagnoses in terms of counterfactual consequences of the system observation. As an illustration of Ginsberg's theory, consider the full adder of Example 2.2. Recall that the diagnoses of this adder under the observation that it outputs 1, 0 in response to inputs 1, 0, 1 are $\{X_1\}$, $\{X_2, O_1\}$, $\{X_2, A_2\}$. If we denote by SD and OBS the adder's system description and observation, then the following formula is a counterfactual consequence of OBS with respect to the theory

$\text{SD} \cup \{\neg\text{AB}(X_1), \neg\text{AB}(X_2), \neg\text{AB}(A_1), \neg\text{AB}(A_2), \neg\text{AB}(O_1)\}$:[8]

$$\text{AB}(X_1) \vee \text{AB}(X_2) \wedge \text{AB}(O_1) \vee \text{AB}(X_2) \wedge \text{AB}(A_2)$$

This, of course, represents the above three diagnoses for the adder. Obviously there is a close relationship between our consistency based definition of a diagnosis, and Ginsberg's counterfactual based definition. In fact, it is a simple matter to show that in the case of first-order logic there is a 1-1 correspondence between the diagnoses, in our sense, of (SD, COMPONENTS, OBS), and Ginsberg's possible worlds for OBS in $\text{SD} \cup \{\neg\text{AB}(c) \mid c \in \text{COMPONENTS})$, provided all formulae in SD are protected. From this it follows that our two definitions of a diagnosis are essentially equivalent in the first-order case.

7.1. The GSC diagnostic model

A recent theory of diagnosis is the GSC (generalized set covering) model of Reggia, Nau and Wang [15, 16]. This provides a formal model of what they call "abductive diagnostic inference" and has been applied to problems of medical diagnosis [15]. In this section we describe the GSC model, show how it may be represented within our formalism, and using our formalism derive a characterization of its diagnoses which conforms (almost) to that defined by Reggia et al. A nice side effect of our logical reconstruction of the GSC model is the scope for generalizing the model which the logical representation provides.

In the GSC model, a *diagnostic problem* (D, M, C, M^+) is defined by four sets:

D—a finite set of *disorders* (e.g. in a medical setting D might represent all the known diseases).

M—a finite set of *manifestations* (e.g. in a medical setting M might represent all possible symptoms, laboratory results, etc. that can be caused by diseases in D).

$C \subseteq D \times M$. The relation C is meant to capture the notion of causation: $(d, m) \in C$ means "d can cause m."

$M^+ \subseteq M$. M^+ is the set of manifestations which have been observed to occur in the current diagnostic setting.

Within our formalism, we interpret a GSC model's diagnostic problem (D, M, C, M^+) as follows:

(1) Define a system (SD, D) whose components are the disorders of D, and whose system description SD is given by the following:

(i) For each disorder $d \in D$, SD contains the axiom $\text{DISORDER}(d)$.

(ii) For each $m \in M$, if $(d_1, m), \ldots, (d_n, m)$ are all the elements of C with second component m, then SD contains the axiom

$$\text{OBSERVED}(m) \supset \text{PRESENT}(d_1) \vee \cdots \vee \text{PRESENT}(d_n)\,. \tag{7.1}$$

This says that an observed manifestation m must be "caused" by the presence of at least one of the disorders $d_1, \ldots, d_n$.

(iii) SD contains the axiom

$$(\forall d).\text{DISORDER}(d) \wedge \neg\text{AB}(d) \supset \neg\text{PRESENT}(d)\,,$$

i.e. normally, a disorder is not present.

(2) The observation of the above system is given by an axiom $\text{OBSERVED}(m)$ for each $m \in M^+$.

This completes our logical reconstruction of the GSC diagnostic problem. We consider next the definition of a diagnosis (called an explanation by Reggia et al.) in the GSC model. If (D, M, C, M^+) is a diagnostic problem, then $E \subseteq D$ is a *cover* of M^+ iff for each $m \in M^+$ there exists $d \in E$ such that $(d, m) \in C$. E is a *minimum cardinality* cover[9] of M^+ iff $|E| \leq |E'|$ for every cover E' of M^+. E is a *minimal* cover[10] of M^+ iff no proper subset of E is a cover of M^+. According to Reggia et al., an *explanation* for a diagnostic problem (D, M, C, M^+) is defined to be a minimum cardinality cover for M^+. As we shall now see, it is the minimum cardinality property of an explanation, as distinct from the property of being minimal with respect to set inclusion, which will distinguish the concept of an explanation in the GSC model from the concept of a diagnosis in our logical reconstruction of the GSC model.

Theorem 7.1. *Suppose (D, M, C, M^+) is a diagnostic problem in the* GSC *model, and* (SD, D, OBS) *is the logical representation of this diagnostic problem as described above. Then Δ is a diagnosis for* (SD, D, OBS) *iff Δ is a minimal cover of M^+.*

Proof. Suppose $M^+ = \{m_1, \ldots, m_k\}$, so that all the axioms of SD of the form (7.1) are:

$$\text{OBSERVED}(m_1) \supset \text{PRESENT}(d_1^{(1)}) \vee \cdots \vee \text{PRESENT}(d_{n_1}^{(1)})\,,$$
$$\vdots$$
$$\text{OBSERVED}(m_k) \supset \text{PRESENT}(d_1^{(k)}) \vee \cdots \vee \text{PRESENT}(d_{n_k}^{(k)})\,.$$

It is easy to see that each of $\{d_1^{(1)}, \ldots, d_{n_1}^{(1)}\}, \ldots, \{d_1^{(k)}, \ldots, d_{n_k}^{(k)}\}$ is a conflict

[8] Assuming that all the formulae of SD are protected. See [8] for details.

[9] Note that what we here call a minimum cardinality cover, Reggia et al. call a minimal cover.

[10] Not to be confused with what Reggia et al. call a minimal cover. See Footnote 9.

set for (SD, D, OBS) since clearly, for $i = 1, \ldots, k$, SD $\cup$ OBS $\cup$ $\{\neg AB(d_1^{(i)}), \ldots, \neg AB(d_{n_i}^{(i)})\}$ is inconsistent. We shall prove that any minimal conflict set for (SD, D, OBS) is one of the sets $\{d_1^{(i)}, \ldots, d_{n_i}^{(i)}\}$. To that end let K be a minimal conflict set for (SD, D, OBS), and suppose on the contrary that K is not one of the sets $\{d_1^{(i)}, \ldots, d_{n_i}^{(i)}\}$. Since K is a minimal conflict set and since each $\{d_1^{(i)}, \ldots, d_{n_i}^{(i)}\}$ is a conflict set, K cannot be a superset of $\{d_1^{(i)}, \ldots, d_{n_i}^{(i)}\}$. Hence, for $i = 1, \ldots, k$, each set $\{d_1^{(i)}, \ldots, d_{n_i}^{(i)}\}$ contains an element, say $d_1^{(i)}$, not contained in K. We shall show how to construct a model M of SD $\cup$ OBS $\cup$ $\{\neg AB(d) \mid d \in K\}$. From this it will follow that K cannot be a conflict set for (SD, D, OBS)—a contradiction.

To construct M, take $M \cup D$ as its domain. Take DISORDER(d) to be true for each $d \in D$, false otherwise. Let OBSERVED(m) be true for each $m \in M^+$, false otherwise. Finally, let AB(d) and PRESENT(d) both be false for each $d \in K$, true otherwise. Notice that PRESENT($d_1^{(i)}$) is true in M for $i = 1, \ldots, k$, since $d_1^{(i)} \notin K$. It follows that M is a model of SD $\cup$ OBS $\cup$ $\{\neg AB(d) \mid d \in K\}$.

To sum up, we have proved that every set of $\{\{d_1^{(1)}, \ldots, d_{n_1}^{(1)}\}, \ldots, \{d_1^{(k)}, \ldots, d_{n_k}^{(k)}\}\}$ is a conflict set for (SD, D, OBS) and that every minimal conflict set for (SD, D, OBS) is contained in $\{d_1^{(1)}, \ldots, d_{n_1}^{(1)}\}, \ldots, \{d_1^{(k)}, \ldots, d_{n_k}^{(k)}\}\}$.

Now it is simple to prove that $\Delta \subseteq D$ is a minimal cover of M^+ iff Δ is a minimal hitting set for $\{\{d_1^{(1)}, \ldots, d_{n_1}^{(1)}\}, \ldots, \{d_1^{(k)}, \ldots, d_{n_k}^{(k)}\}\}$. Since every member of this last set is a conflict set for (SD, D, OBS) and since every minimal conflict set for (SD, D, OBS) is a member of this last set, the theorem now follows by Corollary 4.5. □

Theorem 7.1 allows us to compare our concept of a diagnosis for the GSC model with the concept of an explanation of Reggia et al. For us, a diagnosis is a minimal cover of M^+, while for Reggia et al. it is a minimum cardinality cover of M^+. Now every minimum cardinality cover of M^+ is also a minimal cover of M^+, but not conversely. Thus every explanation as defined by Reggia et al. will be a diagnosis according to our theory, but not conversely. In fact, it is easy to see that the explanations for a GSC diagnostic problem are precisely the minimum cardinality diagnoses for our logical version of the diagnostic problem. This suggests that the concept of an explanation as a minimum cardinality cover of M^+ is inappropriate, that the appropriate concept should be based upon minimal covers as we have done.

In general, a theory of diagnosis could be based on minimal cardinality principles, as in the GSC model, but in our opinion such a theory would lead to unintuitive results. For example, in the case of the full adder, it would correctly yield the single fault diagnosis $\{X_1\}$, but overlook the two intuitively plausible double faults $\{X_2, A_2\}$ and $\{X_2, O_1\}$. Recently, Reggia and his colleagues have independently adopted this point of view, and their current investigations of the GSC model and its extensions are based upon minimal covers of M^+, rather than minimal cardinality covers [14].

8. Summary

We summarize what we take to be the main contributions of this paper to a theory of diagnosis from first principles:

(1) The definition of the concept of a diagnosis, including multiple fault diagnoses, based upon the preservation of the consistency of the system description and its observation.

(2) The explicit use of the AB predicate for representing faults and possible relationships between faults.

(3) The ability of the theory to accommodate a wide variety of logics.

(4) The algorithm DIAGNOSE for computing all diagnoses.

(5) Characterizations of single fault diagnoses and their computation.

(6) Various results about the affects of system measurements on diagnoses.

(7) The nonmonotonic character of diagnosis, specifically its relationship to default logic.

ACKNOWLEDGMENT

I owe a special debt to Johan de Kleer for his encouragement, and for his ready responses to my many questions about diagnosis, especially during the initial phases of this research. Many thanks to David Etherington for acting as an insightful sounding board during the development of these ideas. My thanks also to Teresa Miao for her careful and patient preparation of this manuscript.

This research was done with the financial support of the National Sciences and Engineering Research Council of Canada, under operating grant A7642.

REFERENCES

1. Bobrow, D.G. (Ed.), Special Issue on Non-Monotonic Logic, *Artificial Intelligence* **13** (1, 2) (1980).
2. Brown, J.S., Burton, D. and de Kleer, J., Pedagogical natural language and knowledge engineering techniques in SOPHIE I, II and III, in: D. Sleeman and J.S. Brown (Eds.), *Intelligent Tutoring Systems* (Academic Press, New York, 1982) 227–282.
3. Buchanan, B.G. and Shortliffe E.H. (Eds.), *Rule-based Expert Systems: The MYCIN Experiments of the Stanford Heuristic Programming Project* (Addison-Wesley, Reading, MA, 1984).
4. Davis, R., Diagnostic reasoning based on structure and behavior, *Artificial Intelligence* **24** (1984) 347–410.
5. de Kleer, J., Local methods for localizing faults in electronic circuits, MIT AI Memo 394, Cambridge, MA, 1976.
6. de Kleer, J. and Williams, B.C., Diagnosing multiple faults, *Artificial Intelligence* **32** (1987) 97–130 (this issue).
7. Genesereth, M.R., The use of design descriptions in automated diagnosis, *Artificial Intelligence* **24** (1984) 411–436.
8. Ginsberg, M.L., Counterfactuals, *Artificial Intelligence* **30** (1986) 35–79.

9. Jacobs, B.E., On database logic, *J. ACM* **29** (2) (1982) 310–332.
10. Jones, M. and Poole, D., An expert system for educational diagnosis based on default logic, in: *Proceedings Fifth International Workshop on Expert Systems and their Applications* **II**, Avignon, France (1985) 673–683.
11. McCarthy, J., Applications of circumscription to formalizing common-sense knowledge, *Artificial Intelligence* **28** (1986) 89–116.
12. Moszkowski, B., A temporal logic for multilevel reasoning about hardware, *IEEE Computer* **18** (2) (1985) 10–19.
13. Poole, D., Aleliunas, R. and Goebel, R., Theorist: A logical reasoning system for defaults and diagnosis, Tech. Rept., Logic Programming and Artificial Intelligence Group, Department of Computer Science, University of Waterloo, Waterloo, Ont., 1985.
14. Reggia, J.A., Personal communication.
15. Reggia, J.A., Nau, D.S. and Wang, Y., Diagnostic expert systems based on a set covering model, *Int. J. Man-Mach. Stud.* **19** (1983) 437–460.
16. Reggia, J.A., Nau, D.S. and Wang, Y., A formal model of diagnostic inference I. Problem formulation and decomposition, *Inf. Sci.* **37** (1985) 227–256.
17. Reiter, R., A logic for default reasoning, *Artificial Intelligence* **13** (1, 2) (1980) 81–132.
18. Tsotsos, J.K., Knowledge organization and its role in representation and interpretation for time-varying data: The ALVEN system, *Comput. Intell.* **1** (1985) 16–32.

Diagnosing Multiple Faults

Johan de Kleer
Intelligent Systems Laboratory, XEROX Palo Alto Research Center, Palo Alto, CA 94304, U.S.A.

Brian C. Williams
Artificial Intelligence Laboratory, MIT, Cambridge, MA 02139, U.S.A.

Recommended by Judea Pearl

ABSTRACT

Diagnostic tasks require determining the differences between a model of an artifact and the artifact itself. The differences between the manifested behavior of the artifact and the predicted behavior of the model guide the search for the differences between the artifact and its model. The diagnostic procedure presented in this paper is model-based, inferring the behavior of the composite device from knowledge of the structure and function of the individual components comprising the device. The system (GDE—general diagnostic engine) has been implemented and tested on many examples in the domain of troubleshooting digital circuits.

This research makes several novel contributions: First, the system diagnoses failures due to multiple faults. Second, failure candidates are represented and manipulated in terms of minimal sets of violated assumptions, resulting in an efficient diagnostic procedure. Third, the diagnostic procedure is incremental, exploiting the iterative nature of diagnosis. Fourth, a clear separation is drawn between diagnosis and behavior prediction, resulting in a domain (and inference procedure) independent diagnostic procedure. Fifth, GDE combines model-based prediction with sequential diagnosis to propose measurements to localize the faults. The normally required conditional probabilities are computed from the structure of the device and models of its components. This capability results from a novel way of incorporating probabilities and information theory into the context mechanism provided by assumption-based truth maintenance.

1. Introduction

Engineers and scientists constantly strive to understand the differences between physical systems and their models. Engineers troubleshoot mechanical systems or electrical circuits to find broken parts. Scientists successively refine a model based on empirical data during the process of theory formation. Many everyday common-sense reasoning tasks involve finding the difference between models and reality.

Diagnostic reasoning requires a means of assigning credit or blame to parts of the model based on observed behavioral discrepancies. If the task is troubleshooting, then the model is presumed to be correct and all model-artifact differences indicate part malfunctions. If the task is theory formation, then the artifact is presumed to be correct and all model-artifact differences indicate required changes in the model (Fig. 1).

Usually the evidence does not admit a unique model-artifact difference. Thus, the diagnostic task requires two phases. The first, mentioned above, identifies the set of possible model-artifact differences. The second proposes evidence-gathering tests to refine the set of possible model-artifact differences until they accurately reflect the actual differences.

This view of diagnosis is very general, encompassing troubleshooting mechanical devices and analog and digital circuits, debugging programs, and modeling physical or biological systems. Our approach to diagnosis is also independent of the inference strategy employed to derive predictions from observations.

Earlier research work (see Section 6) on model-based diagnosis concentrated on determining a single faulty component that explains all the symptoms. This paper extends that research by diagnosing systems with multiple failed components, and by proposing a sequence of measurements which efficiently localize the failing components.

When one entertains the possibility of multiple faults, the space of potential candidates grows exponentially with the number of faults under consideration. This work is aimed specifically at developing an efficient general method, referred to as the general diagnostic engine (GDE), for diagnosing failures due to any number of simultaneous faults. To achieve the needed efficiency, GDE exploits the features of assumption-based truth maintenance (ATMS) [8]. This is the topic of the first half of the paper.

Usually, additional measurements are necessary to isolate the set of components which are actually faulted. The best next measurement is the one which will, on average, lead to the discovery of the faulted set of components in a minimum number of measurements. Unlike other probabilistic techniques which require a vast number of conditional probabilities, GDE need only be provided with the a priori probabilities of individual component failure. Using an ATMS, this probabilistic information can be incorporated into GDE such that it is straightforward to compute the conditional probabilities of the candidates, as well as the probabilities of the possible outcomes of measurements, based on the faulty device's model. This combination of probabilistic inference and assumption-based truth maintenance enables GDE to apply a minimum entropy method [1] to determine what measurement to make next: the best measurement is the one which minimizes the expected entropy of candidate prob-

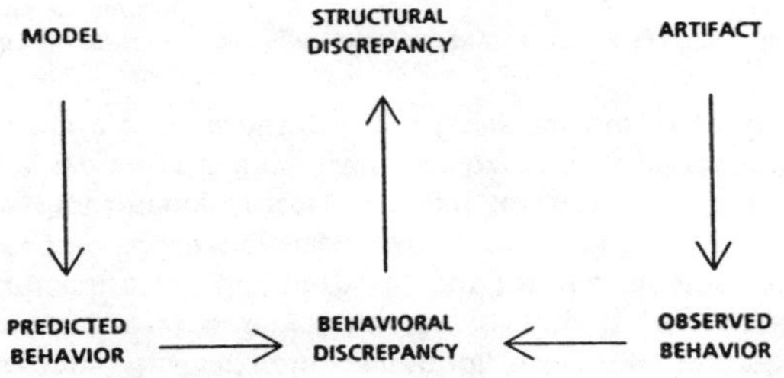

FIG. 1. Model-artifact difference.

abilities resulting from the measurement. This is the topic of the second half of the paper.

1.1. Troubleshooting circuits

For troubleshooting circuits, the diagnostic task is to determine why a correctly designed piece of equipment is not functioning as it was intended; the explanation for the faulty behavior being that the particular piece of equipment under consideration is at variance in some way with its design (e.g., a set of components is not working correctly or a set of connections is broken). To troubleshoot a system, a sequence of measurements must be proposed, executed and then analyzed to localize this point of variance, or fault. The task for the diagnostician is to use the results of measurements to identify the cause of the variance when possible, and otherwise to determine which additional measurements must be taken.

For example, consider the circuit in Fig. 2, consisting of three multipliers, M_1, M_2, and M_3, and two adders, A_1 and A_2. The inputs are $A = 3$, $B = 2$, $C = 2$, $D = 3$, and $E = 3$, and the outputs are measured showing that $F = 10$ and $G = 12$.[1] From these measurements it is possible to deduce that at least one of the following sets of components is faulty (each set is referred to as a candidate and is designated by $[\cdot]$): $[A_1]$, $[M_1]$, $[A_2, M_2]$, or $[M_2, M_3]$. Furthermore, measuring X is likely to produce the most useful information in further isolating the faults. Intuitively, X is optimal because it is the only measurement that can differentiate between two highly probable singleton candidates: $[A_1]$ and $[M_1]$.

Next the value of X is measured and the result is used to reduce the size of the candidate set. The candidate generation-measurement process continues until a single high-probability candidate remains.

[1]This circuit is also used by both [5] and [12] in explaining their systems.

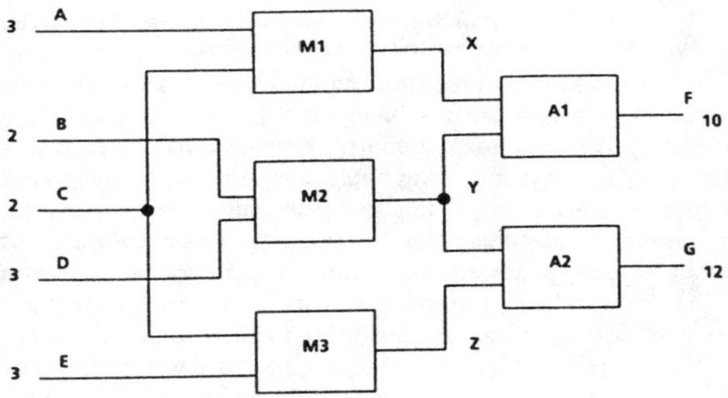

FIG. 2. A familiar circuit.

1.2. Some basic presuppositions

Although GDE considers multiple faults and probabilistic information, it shares many of the basic presuppositions of other model-based research. We presume that the act of taking a measurement (i.e., making an observation) has no affect on the faulty device. We presume that once a quantity is measured to be a certain value, that the quantity remains at the value. This is equivalent to assuming that no component's (correct or faulty) functioning depends on the passage of time. For example, this rules out flip-flops as well as intermittent components which spontaneously change their behavior. We presume that if a component is faulty, the distribution of input-output values becomes random (i.e., contains no information). We do not presume that if a component is faulty, that it must be exhibiting this faulty behavior—it may exhibit faulty behavior on some other set of inputs. These presuppositions suggest future directions for research, and we are extending GDE in these directions.

2. A Theory of Diagnosis

The remainder of this paper presents a general, domain-independent, diagnostic engine (GDE) which, when coupled with a predictive inference component provides a powerful diagnostic procedure for dealing with multiple faults. In addition the approach is demonstrated in the domain of digital electronics, using propagation as the predictive inference engine.

2.1. Model-artifact differences

The model of the artifact describes the physical structure of the device in terms of its constituents. Each type of constituent obeys certain behavioral rules. For example, a simple electrical circuit consists of wires, resistors and so forth, where wires obey Kirchhoff's Current Law, resistors obey Ohm's Law, and so on. In diagnosis, it is given that the behavior of the artifact differs from its model. It is then the task of the diagnostician to determine what these differences are.

The model for the artifact is a description of its physical structure, plus models for each of its constituents. A constituent is a very general concept, including components, processes and even steps in a logical inference. In addition, each constituent has associated with it a set of one or more possible model-artifact differences which establishes the grain size of the diagnosis.

Diagnosis takes (1) the physical structure, (2) models for each constituent, (3) a set of possible model-artifact differences, and (4) a set of measurements, and produces a set of candidates, each of which is a set of differences which explains the observations.

Our diagnostic approach is based on characterizing model-artifact differences as assumption violations. A constituent is guaranteed to behave according to its model only if none of its associated differences are manifested, i.e., all the constituent's assumptions hold. If any of these assumptions are false, then the artifact deviates from its model, thus, the model may no longer apply. An important ramification of this approach [4,5,10,12,29] is that we need only specify correct models for constituents—explicit fault models are not needed.

Reasoning about model-artifact differences in terms of assumption violations is very general. For example, in electronics an assumption might be the correct functioning of each component and the absence of any short circuits; in a scientific domain a faulty hypothesis; in a commonsense domain an assumption such as persistence, defaults or Occam's razor.

2.2. Detection of symptoms

We presume (as is usually the case) that the model-artifact differences are not directly observable.[2] Instead, all assumption violations must be inferred indirectly from behavioral observations. In Section 2.7 we present a general inference architecture for this purpose, but for the moment we presume an inference procedure which makes behavioral predictions from observations and assumptions without being concerned about the procedure's details.

Intuitively, a *symptom* is any difference between a prediction made by the inference procedure and an observation. Consider our example circuit. Given the inputs, $A = 3$, $B = 2$, $C = 2$, $D = 3$, and $E = 3$, by simple calculation (i.e., the inference procedure), $F = X \times Y = A \times C + B \times D = 12$. However, F is measured to be 10. Thus "F is observed to be 10, not 12" is a symptom. More generally, a symptom is *any* inconsistency detected by the inference procedure and may occur between two predictions (inferred from distinct measurements) as well as a measurement and a prediction (inferred from some other measurements).

[2] In practice the diagnostician can sometimes directly observe a malfunctioning component by looking for a crack or burn mark.

2.3. Conflicts

The diagnostic procedure is guided by the symptoms. Each symptom tells us about one or more assumptions that are possibly violated (e.g., component that may be faulty). Intuitively, a *conflict* is a set of assumptions which support a symptom, and thus leads to an inconsistency. In this electronics example, a conflict is a set of components which cannot all be functioning correctly. Consider the example symptom "F is observed to be 10, not 12." The prediction that $F = 12$ depends on the correct operation of A_1, M_1, and M_2, i.e., if A_1, M_1, and M_2 were correctly functioning, then $F = 12$. Since F is not 12, at least one of A_1, M_1, and M_2 is faulted. Thus the set $\langle A_1, M_1, M_2\rangle$ is a conflict for the symptom (conflicts are indicated by $\langle \cdot \rangle$). Because the inference is monotonic with the set of assumptions, the set $\langle A_1, A_2, M_1, M_2\rangle$, and any other superset of $\langle A_1, M_1, M_2\rangle$ are conflicts as well; however, no subsets of $\langle A_1, M_1, M_2\rangle$ are necessarily conflicts since all the components in the conflict were needed to predict the value at F.

A measurement might agree with one prediction and yet disagree with another, resulting in a symptom. For example, starting with the inputs $B = 2$, $C = 2$, $D = 3$, and $E = 3$, and assuming A_2, M_2, and M_3 are correctly functioning we calculate G to be 12. However, starting with the observation $F = 10$, the inputs $A = 3$, $C = 2$, and $E = 3$, and assuming that A_1, A_2, M_1, and M_3, (i.e., ignoring M_2) are correctly functioning we calculate $G = 10$. Thus, when G is measured to be 12, even though it agrees with the first prediction, it still produces a conflict based on the second: $\langle A_1, A_2, M_1, M_3\rangle$.

For complex domains any single symptom can give rise to a large set of conflicts, including the set of all components in the circuit. To reduce the combinatorics of diagnosis it is essential that the set of conflicts be represented and manipulated concisely. If a set of components is a conflict, then every superset of that set must also be a conflict. Thus the set of conflicts can be represented concisely by only identifying the minimal conflicts, where a conflict is minimal if it has no proper subset which is also a conflict. This observation is central to the performance of our diagnostic procedure. The goal of *conflict recognition* is to identify the complete set of minimal conflicts.[3]

[3] Representing the conflict space in terms of minimal conflicts is analogous to the idea of version spaces for representing plausible hypotheses in single concept learning [19].

2.4. Candidates

A *candidate* is a particular hypothesis for how the actual artifact differs from the model. For example "A_2 and M_2 are broken" is a candidate for the two symptoms observed for our example circuit. Ultimately, the goal of diagnosis is to identify, and refine, the set of candidates consistent with the observations thus far.

A candidate is represented by a set of assumptions (indicated by [·]). The assumptions explicitly mentioned are false, while the ones not mentioned are true. A candidate which explains the current set of symptoms is a set of assumptions such that if every assumption fails to hold, then every known symptom is explained. Thus each set representing a candidate must have a nonempty intersection with every conflict.

For electronics, a candidate is a set of failed components, where any components not mentioned are guaranteed to be working. Before any measurements have been taken we know nothing about the circuit. The candidate space is the set of candidates consistent with the observations. The size of the initial candidate space grows exponentially with the number of components. Any component could be working or faulty, thus the candidate space for Fig. 2 initially consists of $2^5 = 32$ candidates.

It is essential that candidates be represented concisely as well. Notice that, like conflicts, candidates have the property that any superset of a possible candidate for a set of symptoms must be a possible candidate as well. Thus the candidate space can be represented by the *minimal candidates*. Representing and manipulating the candidate space in terms of minimal candidates is crucial to our diagnostic approach. Although the candidate space grows exponentially with the number of potentially faulted components, it is usually the case that the symptoms can be explained by relatively few minimal candidates.

The goal of *candidate generation* is to identify the complete set of minimal candidates. The space of candidates can be visualized in terms of a subset-superset lattice (Fig. 3). The minimal candidates then define a boundary such that everything from the boundary up is a valid candidate, while everything below is not.

Given no measurements every component might be working correctly, thus the single minimal candidate is the empty set, [ ], which is the root of the lattice at the bottom of Fig. 3.

To summarize, the set of candidates is constructed in two stages: conflict recognition and candidate generation. Conflict recognition uses the observations made along with a model of the device to construct a complete set of minimal conflicts. Next, candidate generation uses the set of minimal conflicts to construct a complete set of minimal candidates. Candidate generation is the topic of the next section, while conflict recognition is discussed in Section 2.6.

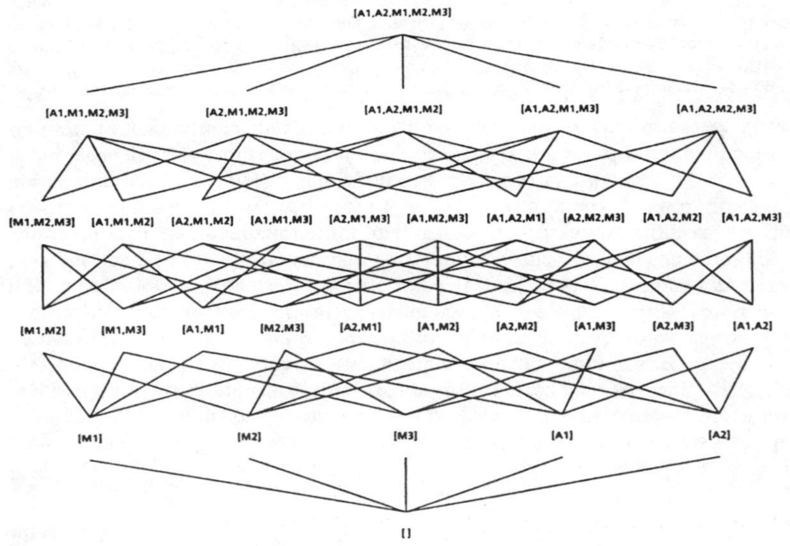

FIG. 3. Initial candidate space for the circuit example.

2.5. Candidate generation

Diagnosis is an incremental process; as the diagnostician takes measurements he continually refines the candidate space and then uses this to guide further measurements. Within a single diagnostic session the total set of candidates must decrease monotonically. This corresponds to having the minimal candidates move monotonically up through the candidate superset lattice towards the candidate containing all components. Similarly, the total set of conflicts must increase monotonically. This corresponds to having the minimal conflicts move monotonically down through a conflict superset lattice towards the conflict represented by the empty set. Candidates are generated incrementally, using the new minimal conflict(s) and the old minimal candidate(s) to generate the new minimal candidate(s).

The set of minimal candidates is incrementally modified as follows. Whenever a new minimal conflict is discovered, any previous minimal candidate which does not explain the new conflict is replaced by one or more superset candidates which are minimal based on this new information. This is accomplished by replacing the old minimal candidate with a set of new tentative minimal candidates each of which contains the old candidate plus one assumption from the new conflict. Any tentative new candidate which is subsumed or duplicated by another is eliminated; the remaining candidates are added to the set of new minimal candidates.

Consider our example. Initially there are no conflicts, thus the minimal candidate [ ] (i.e., everything is working) explains all observations. We have already seen that the single symptom "$F = 10$ not 12" produces one conflict $\langle A_1, M_1, M_2 \rangle$. This rules out the single minimal candidate [ ]. Thus, its immediate supersets containing one assumption of the conflict $[A_1]$, $[M_1]$, and $[M_2]$ are considered. None of these are duplicated or subsumed as there were no other old minimal candidates. The new minimal candidates are $[A_1]$, $[M_1]$, and $[M_2]$. This situation is depicted with the lattice in Fig. 4. All candidates above the line labeled by the conflict "C1: $\langle A_1, M_1, M_2 \rangle$" are valid candidates.

The second conflict (inferred from observation $G = 12$), $\langle A_1, A_2, M_1, M_3 \rangle$, only eliminates minimal candidate $[M_2]$; the unaffected minimal candidates

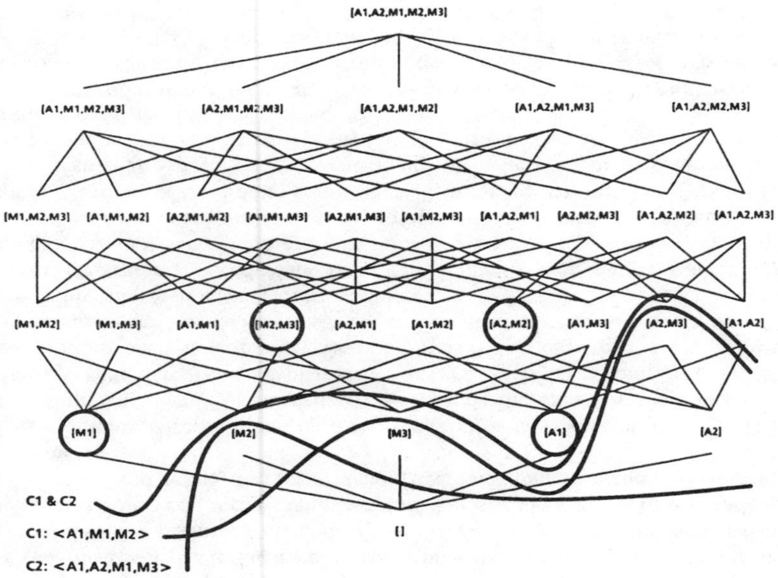

FIG. 4. Candidate space after measurements.

$[M_1]$, and $[A_1]$ remain. However, to complete the set of minimal candidates we must consider the immediate supersets of $[M_2]$ which cover the new conflict: $[A_1, M_2]$, $[A_2, M_2]$, $[M_1, M_2]$, and $[M_2, M_3]$. Each of these candidates explains the new conflict, however, $[A_1, M_2]$ and $[M_1, M_2]$ are supersets of the minimal candidates $[A_1]$ and $[M_1]$, respectively. Thus the new minimal candidates are $[A_2, M_2]$, and $[M_2, M_3]$, resulting in the minimal candidate set: $[A_1]$, $[M_1]$, $[A_2, M_2]$, and $[M_2, M_3]$. The line labeled by conflict "C2: $\langle A_1, A_2, M_1, M_3 \rangle$" in Fig. 4 shows the candidates eliminated by the observation $G = 12$ alone, and the line labeled "C1 & C2" shows the candidates eliminated as a result of both measurements ($F = 10$ and $G = 12$). The minimal candidate which split the lattice into valid and eliminated candidates are circled.

Candidate generation has several interesting properties. First, the set of minimal candidates may increase or decrease in size as a result of a measurement; however, a candidate, once eliminated can never reappear. As measurements accumulate eliminated minimal candidates are replaced by larger candidates. Second, if an assumption appears in every minimal candidate (and thus every candidate), then that assumption is necessarily false. Third, the presupposition that there is only a single fault (exploited in all previous model-based troubleshooting strategies), is equivalent to assuming all candidates are singletons. In this case, the set of candidates can be obtained by intersecting all the conflicts.

2.6. Conflict recognition strategy

The remaining task involves incrementally constructing the conflicts used by candidate generation. In this section we first present a simple model of conflict recognition. This approach is then refined into an efficient strategy.

A conflict can be identified by selecting a set of assumptions, referred to as an *environment*, and testing if they are inconsistent with the observations.[4] If they are, then the inconsistent environment is a conflict. This requires an inference strategy C(OBS, ENV) which given the set of observations OBS made thus far, and the environment ENV, determines whether the combination is consistent. In our example, after measuring $F = 10$, and before measuring $G = 12$, $C(\{F = 10\}, \{A_1, M_1, M_2\})$ (leaving off the inputs) is false indicating the conflict $\langle A_1, M_1, M_2 \rangle$. This approach is refined as follows:

Refinement 1: *Exploiting minimality*. To identify the set of minimal inconsistent environments (and thus the minimal conflicts), we begin our search at the

[4] An environment should not be confused with a candidate or conflict. An environment is a set of assumptions all of which are assumed to be true (e.g., M_1 and M_2 are assumed to be working correctly), a candidate is a set of assumptions all of which are assumed to be false (e.g., components M_1 and M_2 are not functioning correctly). A conflict is a set of assumptions, at least one of which is false. Intuitively an environment is the set of assumptions that define a "context" in a deductive inference engine, in this case the engine is used for prediction and the assumptions are about the lack of particular model-artifact differences.

empty environment, moving up along its parents. This is similar to the search pattern used during candidate generation. At each environment we apply C(OBS, ENV) to determine whether or not ENV is a conflict. Before a new environment is explored, all other environments which are a subset of the new environment must be explored first. If the environment is inconsistent, then it is a minimal conflict and its supersets are not explored. If an environment has already been explored or is a superset of a conflict, then C is not run on the environment and its supersets are not explored.

We presume the inference strategy operates entirely by inferring hypothetical predictions (e.g., values for variables in environments given the observations made). Let P(OBS, ENV) be all behavioral predictions which follow from the observations OBS given the assumptions ENV. For example, $P(\{A=3, B=2, C=2, D=3\}, \{A_1, M_1, M_2\})$ produces $\{A=3, B=2, C=2, D=3, X=6, Y=6, F=12\}$.

C can now be implemented in terms of P. If P computes two distinct values for a quantity (or more simply both x and $\neg x$), then a symptom is manifested and ENV is a conflict.

Refinement 2: *Monotonicity of measurements*. If input values are kept constant, measurements are cumulative and our knowledge of the circuit's structure grows monotonically. Given a new measurement M, $P(\text{OBS} \cup \{M\}, \text{ENV})$ is always a superset of P(OBS, ENV). Thus if we cache the values of every P, when a new measurement is made we need only infer the incremental addition to the set of predictions.

Refinement 3: *Monotonicity for assumptions*. Analogous to Refinement 2, the set of predictions grows monotonically with the environment. If a set of predictions follows from the environment, then the addition of any assumption to that environment only expands this set. Therefore P(OBS, ENV) contains $P(\text{OBS}, E)$ for every subset E of ENV. This makes the computation of P(OBS, ENV) very simple if all its subsets have already been analyzed.

Refinement 4: *Redundant inferences*. P must be run on a large number of (overlapping) environments. Thus, the same rule will be executed over and over again on the same facts. All of this overlap can be avoided by utilizing ideas of truth maintenance such that every inference is recorded as a dependency and no inference is ever performed twice [11].

Refinement 5: *Exploiting the sparseness of the search space*. The four refinements allow the strategy to ignore (i.e., to the extent of not even generating its name) any environment which doesn't contain some interesting inferences absent in every one of its subsets. If every environment contained a new unique inference, then we would still be faced computationally with an exponential in the number of potential model-artifact differences. However, in practice, as the components are weakly connected, the inference rules are weakly connected. Therefore, it is more efficient to associate environments with rules than vice versa. Our strategy depends on this empirical property. For example, in electronics the only assumption sets of interest will be sets of components which are connected and whose signals interact—typically circuits are explicitly designed so that component interactions are limited.

2.7. Inference procedure architecture

To completely exploit the ideas discussed in the preceding section we need to modify and augment the implementation of P. We presume that P meets (or can be modified to) the two basic criteria for utilizing truth maintenance: (1) a dependency (i.e., justification) can be constructed for each inference, and (2) belief or disbelief in a datum is completely determined by these dependencies. In addition, we presume that, during processing, whenever more than one inference is simultaneously permissible, that the actual order in which these inferences are performed is irrelevant and that this order can be externally controlled (i.e., by our architecture). Finally, we presume that the inference procedure is monotonic. Most AI inference procedures meet these four general criteria. For example, many expert rule-based systems, constraint propagation, demon invocation, taxonomic reasoning, qualitative simulations, natural deduction systems, and many forms of resolution theorem proving fit this general framework.

We associate with every prediction, V, the set of environments, ENVS(V), from which it follows (i.e., $\text{ENVS}(V) \equiv \{\text{env} \mid V \in P(\text{OBS}, \text{env})\}$). We call this set the *supporting environments of the prediction*. Exploiting the monotonicity property, it is only necessary to represent the minimal (under subset) supporting environments.

Consider our example after the measurements $F=10$ and $G=12$. In this case we can calculate $X=6$ in two different ways. First, $Y=B \times D=6$ assuming M_2 is functioning correctly. Thus, one of its supporting environments is $\{M_2\}$. Second, $Y=G-Z=G-(C \times E)=6$ assuming A_2 and M_3 are working. Therefore the supporting environments of $Y=6$ are $\{\{M_2\}\{A_2, M_3\}\}$. Any set of assumptions used to derive $Y=6$ is a superset of one of these two.

By exploiting dependencies no inference is ever done twice. If the supporting environments of prediction change, then the supporting environments of its consequents are updated automatically by tracing the dependencies created when the rule was first run. This achieves the consequence of a deduction without rerunning the rule.

We control the inference process such that whenever more than one rule is runnable, the one producing a prediction in the smaller supporting environment is performed first. A simple agenda mechanism suffices for this. Whenever a symptom is recognized, the environment is marked a conflict and all rule execution stops on that environment. Using this control scheme predictions are always deduced in their minimal environment, achieving the desired property that only minimal conflicts (i.e., inconsistent environments) are generated.

In this architecture P can be incomplete (in practice it usually is). The only consequence of incompleteness is that fewer conflicts will be detected and thus fewer candidates will be eliminated than the ideal—no candidate will be mistakenly eliminated.

3. Circuit Diagnosis

Thus far we have described a very general diagnostic strategy for handling multiple faults, whose application to a specific domain depends only on the selection of the function P. In this section, we demonstrate the power of this approach, by applying it to the problem of circuit diagnosis.

For our example we make a number of simplifying presuppositions. First, we assume that the model of a circuit is described in terms of a circuit topology plus a behavioral description of each of its components. Second, that the only type of model-artifact difference considered is whether or not a particular component is working correctly. Finally, all observations are made in terms of measurements at a component's terminals.

Measurements are expensive, thus not every value at every terminal is known. Instead, some values must be inferred from other values and the component models. Intuitively, symptoms are recognized by propagating out locally through components from the measurement points, using the component models to deduce new values. The application of each model is based on the assumption that its corresponding component is working correctly. If two values are deduced for the same quantity in different ways, then a coincidence has occurred. If the two values differ then the coincidence is a symptom. The conflict then consists of every component propagated through from the measurement points to the point of coincidence (i.e., the symptom implies that at least one of the components used to deduce the two values is inconsistent). Note however, if the two coinciding values are the same, then it is not necessarily the case that the components involved in the predictions are functioning correctly. Instead, it may be that the symptom simply does not manifest itself at that point. Also, it might be that one of these components is faulty, but does not manifest its fault, given the current set of inputs. (For example, an inverter with an output stuck at one will not manifest a symptom given an input of zero.) Thus if the coinciding values are in agreement then no information is gained.

3.1. Constraint propagation

Constraint propagation [33, 34] operates on cells, values, and constraints. Cells represent state variables such as voltages, logic levels, or fluid flows. A constraint stipulates a condition that the cells must satisfy. For example, Ohm's law, $v = iR$, is represented as a constraint among the three cells v, i, and R. Given a set of initial values, constraint propagation assigns each cell a value that satisfies the constraints. The basic inference step is to find a constraint that allows it to determine a value for a previously unknown cell. For example, if it has discovered values $v = 2$ and $i = 1$, then it uses the constraint $v = iR$ to calculate the value $R = 2$. In addition, the propagator records R's dependency on v, i and the constraint $v = iR$. The newly recorded value may cause other constraints to trigger and more values to be deduced. Thus, constraints may be viewed as a set of conduits along which values can be propagated out locally from the inputs to other cells in the system. The recorded dependencies trace out a particular path through the constraints that the inputs have taken. A symptom is manifested when two different values are deduced for the same cell (i.e., a logical inconsistency is identified). In this event dependencies are used to construct the conflict.

Sometimes the constraint propagation process terminates leaving some constraints unused and some cells unassigned. This usually arises as a consequence of insufficient information about device inputs. However, this can also arise as the consequence of logical incompleteness in the propagator.

In the circuit domain, the behavior of each component is modeled as a set of constraints. For example, in analyzing analog circuits the cells represent circuit voltages and currents, the values are numbers, and the constraints are mathematical equations. In digital circuits, the cells represent logic levels, the values are 0 and 1, and the constraints are Boolean equations.

Consider the constraint model for the circuit of Fig. 2. There are ten cells: A, B, C, D, E, X, Y, Z, F, and G, five of which are provided the observed values: $A = 3$, $B = 2$, $C = 2$, $D = 3$, and $E = 3$. There are three multipliers and two adders each of which is modeled by a single constraint: $M_1 : X = A \times C$, $M_2 : Y = B \times D$, $M_3 : Z = C \times E$, $A_1 : F = X + Y$, and $A_2 : G = Y + Z$. The following is a list of deductions and dependencies that the constraint propagator generates (a dependency is indicated by (component : antecedents)):

$$X = 6 \quad (M_1 : A = 3, C = 2)\,,$$
$$Y = 6 \quad (M_2 : B = 2, D = 3)\,,$$
$$Z = 6 \quad (M_3 : C = 2, E = 3)\,,$$
$$F = 12 \quad (A_1 : X = 6, Y = 6)\,,$$
$$G = 12 \quad (A_2 : Y = 6, Z = 6)\,.$$

A symptom is indicated when two values are determined for the same cell (e.g., measuring F to be 10 not 12). Each symptom leads to new conflict(s) (e.g., in this example the symptom indicates a conflict $\langle A_1, M_1, M_2 \rangle$).

This approach has some important properties. First, it is not necessary for the starting points of these paths to be inputs or outputs of the circuit. A path may begin at any point in the circuit where a measurement has been taken.

Second, it is not necessary to make any assumptions about the direction that signals flow through components. In most digital circuits a signal can only flow from inputs to outputs. For example, a subtractor cannot be constructed by simply reversing an input and the output of an adder since it violates the directionality of signal flow. However, the directionality of a component's signal flow is irrelevant to our diagnostic technique; a component places a constraint between the values of its terminals which can be used in any way desired. To detect discrepancies, information can flow along a path through a component in any direction. For example, although the subtractor does not function in reverse, when we observe its outputs we can infer what its inputs must have been.

3.2. Generalized constraint propagation

Each step of constraint propagation takes a set of antecedent values and computes a consequent. We have built a constraint propagator within our inference architecture which explores minimal environments first. This guides each step during propagation in an efficient manner to incrementally construct minimal conflicts and candidates for multiple faults.

Consider our example. We ensure that propagations in subset environments are performed first, thereby guaranteeing that the resulting supporting environments and conflicts are minimal. We use $\llbracket x, e_1, e_2, \ldots \rrbracket$ to represent the assertion x with its associated supporting environments. Before any measurements or propagations take place, given only the inputs, the database consists of: $\llbracket A=3, \{\ \} \rrbracket$, $\llbracket B=2, \{\ \} \rrbracket$, $\llbracket C=2, \{\ \} \rrbracket$, $\llbracket D=3, \{\ \} \rrbracket$, and $\llbracket E=3, \{\ \} \rrbracket$. Observe that when propagating values through a component, the assumption for that component is added to the dependency, and thus to the supporting environment(s) of the propagated value. Propagating A and C through M_1 we obtain: $\llbracket X=6, \{M_1\} \rrbracket$. The remaining propagations produce: $\llbracket Y=6, \{M_2\} \rrbracket$, $\llbracket Z=6, \{M_3\} \rrbracket$, $\llbracket F=12, \{A_1, M_1, M_2\} \rrbracket$, and $\llbracket G=12, \{A_2, M_2, M_3\} \rrbracket$.

Suppose we measure F to be 10. This adds $\llbracket F=10, \{\ \} \rrbracket$ to the database. Analysis proceeds as follows (starting with the smaller environments first): $\llbracket X=4, \{A_1, M_2\} \rrbracket$, and $\llbracket Y=4, \{A_1, M_1\} \rrbracket$. Now the symptom between $\llbracket F=10, \{\ \} \rrbracket$ and $\llbracket F=12, \{A_1, M_1, M_2\} \rrbracket$ is recognized indicating a new minimal conflict: $\langle A_1, M_1, M_2 \rangle$. Thus the inference architecture prevents further propagation in the environment $\{A_1, M_1, M_2\}$ and its supersets. The propagation goes one more step: $\llbracket G=10, \{A_1, A_2, M_1, M_3\} \rrbracket$. There are no more inferences to be made.

Next, suppose we measure G to be 12. Propagation gives: $\llbracket Z=6, \{A_2, M_2\} \rrbracket$, $\llbracket Y=6, \{A_2, M_3\} \rrbracket$, $\llbracket Z=8, \{A_1, A_2, M_1\} \rrbracket$, and $\llbracket X=4, \{A_1, A_2, M_3\} \rrbracket$. The symptom "$G=12$ not 10" produces the conflict $\langle A_1, A_2, M_1, M_3 \rangle$. The final database state is shown below.[5]

[5]The justifications are not shown but are the same as those in Section 3.1.

$$
\begin{aligned}
&\llbracket A=3, \{\ \} \rrbracket, \\
&\llbracket B=2, \{\ \} \rrbracket, \\
&\llbracket C=2, \{\ \} \rrbracket, \\
&\llbracket D=3, \{\ \} \rrbracket, \\
&\llbracket E=3, \{\ \} \rrbracket, \\
&\llbracket F=10, \{\ \} \rrbracket, \\
&\llbracket G=12, \{\ \} \rrbracket, \\
&\llbracket X=4, \{A_1, M_2\}\ \{A_1, A_2, M_3\} \rrbracket, \\
&\llbracket X=6, \{M_1\} \rrbracket, \\
&\llbracket Y=4, \{A_1, M_1\} \rrbracket, \\
&\llbracket Y=6, \{M_2\}\ \{A_2, M_3\} \rrbracket, \\
&\llbracket Z=8, \{A_1, A_2, M_1\} \rrbracket, \\
&\llbracket Z=6, \{M_3\}\ \{A_2, M_2\} \rrbracket .
\end{aligned}
\tag{1}
$$

This results in two minimal conflicts:

$$\langle A_1, M_1, M_2 \rangle, \qquad \langle A_1, A_2, M_1, M_3 \rangle .$$

The algorithm discussed in Section 2.5 uses the two minimal conflicts to incrementally construct the set of minimal candidates. Given new measurements the propagation/candidate generation cycle continues until the candidate space has been sufficiently constrained.

4. Sequential Diagnosis

In order to reduce the set of remaining candidates the diagnostician must perform measurements [14] which differentiate among the remaining candidates. This section presents a method for choosing a next measurement which best distinguishes the candidates, i.e., that measurement which will, on average, lead to the discovery of the actual candidate in a minimum number of subsequent measurements.

4.1. Possible measurements

The conflict recognition strategy (via P(OBS, ENV)) identifies all predictions for each environment. The results of this analysis provides the basis for a differential diagnosis procedure, allowing GDE to identify possible measurements and their consequences.

Consider how measuring quantity x_i could reduce the candidate space. GDE's database (e.g., (1)) explicitly represents x_i's values and their supporting environments:

$$\llbracket x_i = v_{ik}, e_{ik1}, \ldots, e_{ikm} \rrbracket .$$

If x_i is measured to be v_{ik}, then the supporting environments of any value distinct from the measurement are necessarily conflicts. If v_{ik} is not equal to any of x_i's predicted values, then every supporting environment for each predicted value of x_i is a conflict. Given GDE's database, it is simple to identify useful measurements, their possible outcomes, and the conflicts resulting from each outcome. Furthermore, the resulting reduction of the candidate space is easily computed for each outcome.

Consider the example of the previous section. $X = 4$ in environments $\{A_1, M_2\}$ and $\{A_1, A_2, M_3\}$, while $X = 6$ in environment $\{M_1\}$. Measuring X has three possible outcomes: (1) $X = 4$ in which case $\langle M_1 \rangle$ is a conflict and the new minimal candidate is $[M_1]$, (2) $X = 6$ in which case $\langle A_1, M_2 \rangle$ and $\langle A_1, A_2, M_3 \rangle$ are conflicts and the new minimal candidates are $[A_1]$, $[M_2, M_3]$ and $[A_2, M_2]$, or (3) $X \neq 4$ and $X \neq 6$ in which case $\langle M_1 \rangle$, $\langle A_1, M_2 \rangle$ and $\langle A_1, A_2, M_3 \rangle$ are conflicts and $[A_1, M_1]$, $[M_1, M_2, M_3]$, and $[A_2, M_1, M_2]$ are minimal candidates.

The minimal candidates are a computational convenience for representing the entire candidate set. For presentation purposes, in the following we dispense with the idea of minimal candidates and consider all candidates.

The diagnostic process described in the subsequent sections depends critically on manipulating three sets: (1) R_{ik} is the set of (called remaining) candidates that would remain if x_i were measured to be v_{ik}, (2) S_{ik} is the set of (called selected) candidates in which x_i *must* be v_{ik} (equivalently, the candidates necessarily eliminated if x_i is measured not to be v_{ik}), and (3) U_i is the set of (called uncommitted) candidates which do not predict a value for x_i (equivalently, the candidates which would not be eliminated independent of the value measured for x_i). This set R_{ik} is covered by the sets S_{ik} and U_i:

$$R_{ik} = S_{ik} \cup U_i , \qquad S_{ik} \cap U_i = \phi .$$

4.2. Lookahead versus myopic strategies

Section 4.1 describes how to evaluate the consequences of a hypothetical measurement. By cascading this procedure, we could evaluate the consequences of any sequence of measurements to determine the optimal next measurement (i.e., the one which is expected to eliminate the candidates in the shortest sequence of measurement). This can be implemented as a classic decision tree analysis, but the computational cost of this analysis is prohibitive. Instead we use a one-step lookahead strategy based on Shannon entropy [1, 20, 26]. Given a particular stage in the diagnostic process we analyze the consequences of each single measurement to determine which one to perform next. To accomplish this we need an evaluation function to determine for each possible outcome of a measurement how difficult it is (i.e., how many additional measurements are necessary) to identify the actual candidate. From decision and information theory we know that a very good cost function is the entropy (H) of the candidate probabilities:

$$H = -\sum p_i \log p_i ,$$

where p_i is the probability that candidate C_i is the actual candidate given the hypothesized measurement outcome.

Entropy has several important properties (see a reference on information theory [30] for a more rigorous account). If every candidate is equally likely, we have little information to provide discrimination—H is at a maximum. As one candidate becomes much more likely than the rest H approaches a minimum. H estimates the expected cost of identifying the actual candidate as follows. The cost of locating a candidate of probability p_i is proportional to $\log p_i^{-1}$ (cf. binary search through p_i^{-1} objects). The expected cost of identifying the actual candidate is thus proportional to the sum of the product of the probability of each candidate being the actual candidate and the cost of identifying that candidate i.e., $\Sigma\, p_i \log p_i^{-1} = -\Sigma\, p_i \log p_i$. Unlikely candidates, although expensive to find, occur infrequently so they contribute little to the cost: $p_i \log p_i^{-1}$ approaches 0 as p_i approaches 0. Conversely, likely candidates, although they occur frequently, are easy to find so contribute little to the cost: $p_i \log p_i^{-1}$ approaches 0 as p_i approaches 1. Locating candidates in between these two extremes is more costly because they occur with significant frequency and the cost of finding them is significant.

4.3. Minimum entropy

Under the assumption that every measurement is of equal cost, the objective of diagnosis is to identify the actual candidate in a minimum number of measurements. This section shows how the entropy cost function presented in the previous section is utilized to choose the best next measurement. As the diagnosis process is sequential, these formulas describe the changes in quantities as a consequence of making a single measurement.

The best measurement is the one which minimizes the expected entropy of candidate probabilities resulting from the measurement. Assuming that the process of taking a measurement doesn't influence the value measured, the expected entropy $H_e(x_i)$ after measuring quantity x_i is given by:

$$H_e(x_i) = \sum_{k=1}^{m} p(x_i = v_{ik}) H(x_i = v_{ik}) .$$

Where $v_{i1}, \ldots, v_{im}$ are all possible values[6] for x_i, and $H(x_i = v_{ik})$ is the

[6] These results are easily generalized to account for an infinite number of possible values since, although a quantity may take on an infinite number of possible values, only a finite number of these will be predicted as the consequences of other quantities measured. Further the entropy resulting from the measurement of a value not predicted is independent of that value. Thus the system never has to deal with more than a finite set of expected entropies.

entropy resulting if x_i is measured to be v_{ik}. $H(x_i = v_{ik})$ can be computed from the information available.

At each step, we compute $H(x_i = v_{ik})$ by determining the new candidate probabilities, p'_l from the current probabilities p_l and the hypothesized result $x_i = v_{ik}$. The initial probabilities are computed from empirical data (see Section 4.4). When x_i is measured to be v_{ik}, the probabilities of the candidates shift. Some candidates will be eliminated, reducing their posterior probability to zero. The remaining candidates R_{ik} shift their probabilities according to (see Section 4.5):

$$p'_l = \begin{cases} \dfrac{p_l}{p(x_i = v_{ik})}, & l \in S_{ik}, \\[2ex] \dfrac{p_l/m}{p(x_i = v_{ik})}, & l \in U_i. \end{cases}$$

If every candidate predicts a value for x_i, then $p(x_i = v_{ik})$ is the combined probabilities of all the candidates predicting $x_i = v_{ik}$. To the extent that U_i is not empty, the probability $p(x_i = v_{ik})$ can only be approximated with error ε_{ik}:

$$p(x_i = v_{ik}) = p(S_{ik}) + \varepsilon_{ik}, \quad 0 < \varepsilon_{ik} < p(U_i),$$

$$\sum_{k=1}^{m} \varepsilon_{ik} = p(U_i).$$

where,

$$p(S_{ik}) = \sum_{C_l \in S_{ik}} p_l, \qquad p(U_i) = \sum_{C_l \in U_i} p_l.$$

At any stage of the diagnostic process only some (say the first n of the m possible) of the v_{ik} are actually predicted (i.e., those with nonempty S_{ik}) for x_i. If a candidate does not predict a value for a particular x_i, we assume each possible v_{ik} is equally likely[7]:

$$\varepsilon_{ik} = p(U_i)/m.$$

So,

$$p(x_i = v_{ik}) = p(S_{ik}) + p(U_i)/m.$$

Notice that for unpredicted values S_{ik} is empty, so $p(x_i = v_{ik}) = p(U_i)/m$.

[7]We could assume that if a component were faulted (i.e., a member of the actual candidate), then its current observed inputs and outputs would be inconsistent with its model. Under such an assumption, the distribution would be skewed away from those v_{ik} predicted from the set of assumptions of the candidate (i.e., viewing a candidate as an environment). We do not make this assumption because a component may appear to be functioning correctly, but actually be faulted producing incorrect outputs for a different set of inputs.

The expected entropy can be computed from predicted quantities:

$$H_e(x_i) = \sum_{k=1}^{n} \big(p(x_i = v_{ik}) + \varepsilon_{ik}\big)H(x_i = v_{ik}) + \sum_{k=n+1}^{m} \varepsilon_{ik} H_{U_i},$$

where H_{U_i} is the expected entropy if x_i is measured to have an unpredicted value (i.e., all but the candidates U_i are eliminated):

$$H_{U_i} = -\sum_{C_l \in U_i} p'_l \log p'_l.$$

H_{U_i} and ε_{ik} are independent of the unpredicted value measured, thus, rewriting we obtain:

$$H_e(x_i) = \sum_{k=1}^{n} \big(p(x_i = v_{ik}) + \varepsilon_{ik}\big)H(x_i = v_{ik}) + \frac{(m-n)}{m} p(U_i) H_{U_i}.$$

Substituting and simplifying gives:

$$H_e(x_i) = H + \Delta H_e(x_i).$$

Where H is the current entropy, and $\Delta H_e(x_i)$ is:

$$\sum_{k=1}^{n} p(x_i = v_{ik}) \log p(x_i = v_{ik}) + p(U_i) \log p(U_i) - \frac{np(U_i)}{m} \log \frac{p(U_i)}{m}.$$

The expected entropy can be calculated from the current candidate probability distribution—there is no necessity to explicitly construct the possible posterior probability distributions and compute their entropies. Thus the best, on average, measurement is the one that minimizes $\Delta H_e(x_i)$.

The choice of base for the logarithm does not affect the relative order of costs. Purely for convenience GDE computes base e (this corresponds to measurements, on average, having e known outcomes). To obtain a positive cost, GDE adds one to this equation. This cost indicates the quality of a hypothesized measurement. The cost is the expected increase in total (i.e., in the entire diagnostic session) number of measurements that need to be made to identify the candidate after making the measurement. A cost of 1 indicates that no information at all is obtained. A cost of 0 is ideal as it indicates perfect information gain.

4.4. Independence of faults

The initial probabilities of candidates are computed from the initial probabilities of component failure (obtained from their manufacturer or by observation). We make the assumption that components fail independently. (This approach could be extended to dependent faults except that voluminous data is required.) The initial probability that a particular candidate C_i is the actual candidate C_a is given by:

$$p_i = \prod_{c \in C_i} p(c \in C_a) \prod_{c \notin C_i} (1 - p(c \in C_a)) .$$

4.5. The conditional probability of a candidate

Given measurement outcome $x_i = v_{ik}$, the probability of a candidate is computed via Bayes' rule (see Section 6.6.):

$$p(C_l | x_i = v_{ik}) = \frac{p(x_i = v_{ik} | C_l) p(C_l)}{p(x_i = v_{ik})} .$$

Where $p_l = p(C_l)$ where $p_l' = p(C_l | x_i = v_{ik})$. There are three cases for evaluating $p(x_i = v_{ik} | C_l)$. If C_l predicts $x_i = w_{ik}$ where $w_{ik} \neq v_{ik}$, then the conditional probability is 0:

$$p(x_i = v_{ik} | C_l) = 0, \quad \text{if } C_l \not\in R_{ik} .$$

If $w_{ik} = v_{ik}$, then the conditional probability is 1:

$$p(x_i = v_{ik} | C_l) = 1, \quad \text{if } C_l \in S_{ik} .$$

In the third case, C_l predicts no value for x_i. We assume that every possible value for x_i (there are m of them) is equally likely:

$$p(x_i = v_{ik} | C_l) = 1/m, \quad \text{if } C_l \in U_i .$$

Substituting these probabilities into Bayes' rule we obtain:

$$P(C_l | x_i = v_{ik}) = \begin{cases} 0, & \text{if } C_l \not\in R_{ik}, \\[2mm] \dfrac{p(C_l)}{p(x_i = v_{ik})}, & \text{if } C_l \in S_{ik}, \\[3mm] \dfrac{p(C_l)/m}{p(x_i = v_{ik})}, & \text{if } C_l \in U_i, \end{cases}$$

where

$$p(x_i = v_{ik}) = p(S_{ik}) + p(U_i)/m .$$

The estimate $p(x_i = v_{ik} | C_l) = 1/m$ is suspect and introduces various computational complexities. Fortunately, U_i contains primarily low probability candidates and thus any error tends to be minor. On average, the candidates in U_i are nonminimal (because minimal candidates tend to assign values to most of the device's variables) and as nonminimal candidates have lower probability than minimal candidates, the candidates in U_i have relatively lower probability. In practice, using $P(x_i = v_{ik} | C_l) = 1$ for $C_l \in R_{ik}$ greatly simplifies the computations and rarely affects the number of measurements required.

4.6. Examples

This section presents a series of examples to illustrate some of the intuitions behind our technique.

4.6.1. Cascaded inverters: $a = 1$

Consider circuit of Fig. 5. Assume the initial probability of component failure is 0.01 and input $a = 1$ is given. As initially no symptom has been detected on average, little is gained by making any measurement—all costs are nearly 1. Compare the advantages and disadvantages of measuring b or e. If the value measured differs from the value predicted, then measuring closer to the input (or any previously measured value) produces as a smaller conflict, and thus more information. For example, if we measure b to be 1, then we learn that A must be faulted, where measuring $e = 0$ tell us only that some component is faulted. On the other hand, measuring further away from the input is more likely to produce a discrepant value. That is, as there is a large number of intervening components, it is more likely that one will be faulted and thus produce an incorrect value. These two effects tend to cancel each other, however, the probability of finding a particular value outweighs the expected cost of isolating the candidate from a set. In terms of entropy, every possible outcome contributes $p_i \log p_i^{-1}$ but p_i dominates $\log p_i^{-1}$. In general for any cascaded sequence of components for which only the input is known, the best next measurement is the output of the sequence. This is illustrated in Table 1.

4.6.2. Cascaded inverters: $a = 1, e = 0$

Suppose e is measured to be 0, violating the prediction and thus telling us that at least one of the components is faulted. The best next measurement is the one that is equidistant from the previous two measurements, c (Table 2).

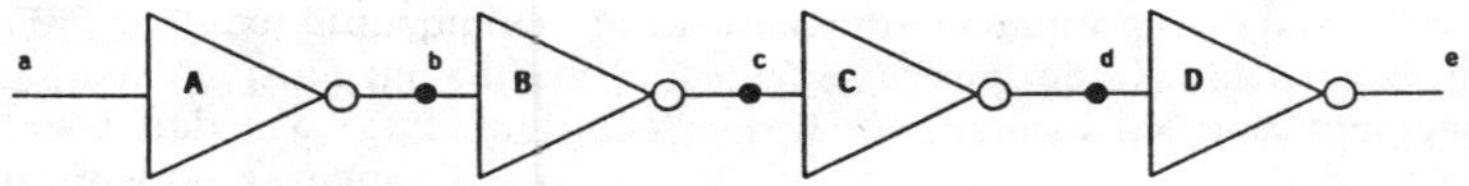

Fig. 5. Cascaded inverters.

TABLE 1. Expected costs after $a = 1$ with $p = 0.01$

a	1
b	0.98
c	0.96
d	0.94
e	0.93

TABLE 2. Expected costs after $a = 1$, $e = 0$ with $p = 0.01$

a	1
b	0.45
c	0.31
d	0.44
e	1

TABLE 3. Expected costs after $a = 1$, $e = 1$ with $p = 0.01$

a	1
b	0.999
c	0.999
d	0.999
e	1

TABLE 4. Expected costs after $a = 1$, $e = 0$ with $p(a) = 0.025$

a	1
b	0.33
c	0.36
d	0.53
e	1

TABLE 5. Initial expected costs

F	0.88
G	0.88
X	0.95
Y	0.95
Z	0.95

TABLE 6. Costs after $F = 10$

F	1
G	0.28
X	0.34
Y	0.34
Z	0.95

4.6.3. *Cascaded inverters*: $a = 1$, $e = 1$

Suppose that instead of measuring e to be 0 it was measured 1 as predicted. The circuit must have a relatively unlikely double fault (if it has any fault at all) where one fault shadows the effect of the other. Nevertheless the best measurement to identify a possible double fault is still c (Table 3).

4.6.4. *Cascaded inverters*: $a = 1$, $e = 0$, $p(a) = 0.025$

If we are given that the first inverter A is more likely to be faulted, then the best measurement point is no longer equidistant from the previous observations. The advantage of measuring b first instead of c is that we might identify that inverter A is faulted immediately. As A is far more likely to be faulted, it is better to measure b first (Table 4).

4.6.5. *Diagnosing a fault*

Consider the circuit of Fig. 2. Suppose that M_2 is faulted exhibiting behavior $Y = B \times C - 2$ and A_2 is faulted with behavior $G = Y \times Z + 2$. The inputs are the same as earlier. The following illustrates GDE's strategy to localize this fault. Note that this is an unusual fault in that the effect of the two faults cancel, producing the value predicted for G. Thus, several measurements are necessary to identify the fault. We assume that components fail with initial probability 0.01 and that $m = 16$.

Initially the most probable candidate is [ ], $p([\ ] = C_a) = 0.951$. The expected cost associated with each hypothetical measurement is shown in Table 5. All the costs are nearly one, indicating that little is to be gained by any of the measurements, this is because on average components are not faulted, and there is yet no evidence that anything is malfunctioning. Not surprisingly, F and G as well as X, Y, Z are treated symmetrically. F and G have slightly lower cost because their predicted values depend on three components functioning correctly, while X, Y, and Z depend on two (i.e., F and G are more likely to have discrepant values).

Suppose F is measured with result $F = 10$ (Table 6). The most probable candidates are now $[A_1]$, $[M_1]$, and $[M_2]$, all having probability 0.323. G, X and Y are all good measurements because each one differentiates among the high-probability single-fault candidates. Each high-probability candidate predicts $Z = 6$ so measuring Z provides little new information. G is a slightly better point to measure because the candidates are more balanced between G's two predicted outcomes (the best measurement is one whose predicted outcomes all have equal probability and which cover all the candidates).

Next, suppose G is measured with result $G = 12$ (Table 7). The most probable candidates are now $[A_1]$ and $[M_1]$ both with probability 0.478. At this point X is the best measurement because it splits the two high-probability candidates.

Next, suppose X is measured with result $X = 6$ (Table 8). This results in a single high-probability candidate $[A_1]$ with probability 0.942. The next seven most likely candidates are: $[A_1, M_3]$, $[A_1, M_2]$, $[A_1, M_1]$, $[A_1, A_2]$, $[A_2, M_2]$, and $[M_2, M_3]$, all with probability 0.00951.

Next, suppose Y is measured with result $Y = 4$. M_2 is now necessarily faulted and at least one other fault exists. The costs are now as shown in Table 9.

Finally, suppose Z is measured with result $Z = 6$. There are six remaining candidates: $[A_2, M_2]$ with probability 0.970, $[A_2, M_1, M_2]$, $[A_1, A_2, M_2]$, $[A_2, M_2, M_3]$, with probabilities 0.0098, $[A_1, A_2, M_1, M_2]$, $[A_1, A_2, M_2, M_3]$, $[A_2, M_1, M_2, M_3]$, with probabilities 0.0001, and $[A_1, A_2, M_1, M_2, M_3]$ with probability 0.000001. Components M_2 and A_2 are necessarily faulted, and A_1, M_1, and M_3 are possibly faulted, each with probability 0.01. No measurement points remain in the circuit, so no further information can be obtained.

TABLE 7. Costs after $F = 10$, $G = 12$

F	1
G	1
X	0.28
Y	0.94
Z	0.97

TABLE 8. Costs after $F = 10$, $G = 12$, and $X = 6$

F	1
G	1
X	1
Y	0.90
Z	0.94

TABLE 9. Costs after $F = 10$, $G = 12$, $X = 6$, and $Y = 4$

F	1
G	1
X	1
Y	1
Z	0.141

4.7. Logical incompleteness

In practice, for diverse reasons, the underlying inference process is usually incomplete. One of the consequences of this incompleteness is that it becomes more difficult to evaluate the results of hypothetical measurements—the U_i are larger than ideal. As any incompleteness degrades GDE's performance, it is instructive to examine the sources and types of this incompleteness.

An often avoidable form of incompleteness occurs when the conflict recognition strategy misses some conflicts. This was discussed earlier. Here we assume the conflict recognition strategy is complete. U_i will be larger than ideal only if the prediction process is incomplete. This incompleteness manifests itself in two ways. First, an incomplete inference process may result in missing predicted values and missing supporting environments. As a consequence, the hypothesized conflicts resulting from measuring a quantity will be incomplete. For example, consider an inverter which is incompletely modeled by a rule which predicts its output from its input, but not its input from its output. Even though the inverter's output is measured to be one, the prediction that its input is zero is not made. Thus, GDE does not consider measuring its input. A second source of incompleteness is inherent in the $x_i = v_{ik}$ representation—there may be many additional properties that could be inferred about x_i, but as there is no way to represent them they cannot be used by our strategy. For example, it cannot represent $x \neq 1$. Thus, although $x \neq 1$ might be derivable from an environment, GDE cannot foresee the resulting conflict when considering, say, $x = 2$.

Assuming the basic conflict recognition strategy is complete, both these sources of incompleteness can be avoided at prohibitive computational costs. The first source of incompleteness can be avoided with a complete inference process. The second source of incompleteness can be avoided with a more general representation.[8]

5. Pragmatics

5.1. Most probable candidates

Computing all candidates is computationally prohibitive. In practice it is only necessary to compute the more probable candidates. There is no way to tell whether a single candidate *actually* has a high probability without knowing the overall normalization factor. This suggests using a best-first search of the lattice to find candidates in increasing order of probability. This search is arbitrarily stopped for candidates below some threshold fraction (e.g., $\frac{1}{10}$ of the highest probability candidate). Although the most probable candidate is a minimal candidate, the remaining minimal candidates need not be very probable.

[8] Assuming the number of possible values for quantities are finite, GDE could hypothesize each possible measurement outcome, run its complete inference procedure and precisely compute the R_{ik} from which the S_{ik} could then be computed.

5.2. When to stop making measurements

If there are many points in a device that could be measured choosing the best point to measure can be computationally expensive. A heuristic is to make the first reasonable measurement whose cost is computed to be less than $1 - \log 0.5 = 0.7$ as this measurement on average, splits the candidate space in half.

The point at which measurement should stop depends greatly on the seriousness of a misdiagnosis as well as on the a priori probabilities of component failure. When a candidate is found whose probability approaches some threshold (e.g., 0.9), diagnosis can stop. If the cost of misdiagnosis is high, then the threshold should be increased.

6. Comparison to Other Work

6.1. Circuit diagnosis based on structure and behavior

Work in the AI community on model-based hardware diagnosis has grown out of a desire to move away from the domain and device specific fault models used in traditional circuit diagnosis.[9] Instead, during candidate generation the model-based approach reasons from a small set of component behavior models plus the structure of the device. The requirement for device specific fault models is eliminated by basing the diagnostic approach solely on the knowledge that, if a component's behavior is inconsistent with its model, then it must be faulty. This results in a domain independent diagnostic technique. A number of systems have followed this approach for diagnosing both analog (e.g., LOCAL [10] and SOPHIE [4]) and digital circuits (e.g., HT [5] and DART [12]).

Our work naturally extends this approach along a number of dimensions. First, unlike earlier approaches, our work is aimed specifically at coping with the problem of diagnosing multiple faults. Earlier work focused primarily on the case where all symptoms could be explained by a single component being faulty. As Davis points out, the obvious extension to his work to handle multiple faults results in an algorithm which is exponential in the number of potential faults. As our approach represents the candidate space implicitly in terms of the minimal candidates, we need only be concerned with the growth of this smaller set. Typically the size of each minimal candidate is relatively small (i.e., the symptom can usually be explained by one, two or three

[9] See Davis' [5], Sections 5.1., 12.1. and 13 for a discussion of traditional circuit diagnosis and the advantages of the model-based approach. Also see [16].

components being simultaneously faulty), thus in practice our approach tends to grow with the square or cube of the number of potential faults.

Second, our approach to diagnosis is inference procedure independent, as well as domain independent. LOCAL, SOPHIE, and Davis' system all represent circuit knowledge as constraints and then use some form of constraint propagation to infer circuit quantities and their dependencies. The motivation behind this approach is that constraints naturally reflect the local interaction of behavior in the real world. These are similar (although not identical) to the constraint propagation technique used to demonstrate GDE in this paper.

On the other hand, DART expresses circuit knowledge as logical propositions and uses an inference system based on resolution residue to infer circuit properties. This same general inference procedure allows DART to deduce which components are suspect and how to change circuit inputs to reduce the suspect set to a singleton. Such a resolution-based inference strategy can be incorporated into the candidate generation and conflict recognition portion of GDE by recording, for each resolution step, the dependence of the resolvent on the formulas used to perform the resolution. Then, as in the case for constraint propagation, GDE can guide the inference process in identifying minimal candidates first.

Resolution is highlighted as having an advantage over constraint propagation in that it is logically complete with respect to a first-order theory, where most constraint propagators are not. However, this can be misleading. A significant computational cost is incurred using a logically complete inference strategy, such as resolution. Yet a logically complete inference strategy does not guarantee that the set of predictions will also be complete. For example in an analog domain, producing exact predictions often involves solving systems of higher-order nonlinear differential equations. As this type of equation is not generally solvable with known techniques, completeness in the predictor is currently beyond our reach. In practice propagation of constraints (without symbolic algebra) provides a good compromise between completeness and computational expense.

Third, our approach is incremental. This is crucial as diagnosis is an iterative process of making observations, refining hypotheses, and then using this new knowledge to guide further observations.

Finally, our approach is unique in that it combines model-based reasoning with probabilistic information in a sequential probing strategy. SOPHIE also proposes measurements to localize the failing component, but is based on an ad hoc half-split method. Its design is based on the presupposition that the circuit contains a single fault. Thus, candidate generation is trivial (set intersection), and identifying good measurements is easy.

6.1.1. *Possible extensions*

Representing and manipulating candidates in terms of minimal candidates gives us a significant computational advantage over previous approaches; however, even this representation can grow exponentially in the worst case. To effectively cope with very large devices, additional techniques must be incorporated.

One approach involves grouping components into larger modules and modifying the candidate generation strategy to deal with hierarchical decompositions. Although we have not implemented this, the strategies proposed by Davis and Genesereth, as they are model-based, apply. Their basic idea is to troubleshoot at the most abstract level in the hierarchy first and only analyze the contents of a module when there is reasonable evidence to suspect it. If there is no conflict involving the module, then there is no reason to suspect it.

Complexity is directly related to the number of hypothetical faults entertained. Thus another approach, proposed by Davis, involves enumerating and layering categories of failures based on their likelihood. Troubleshooting begins by considering faults in the most likely category first, moving to less likely categories if these fail to explain the symptoms. GDE uses a variation on this approach whereby candidates can be enumerated based on their likelihood. However, no theory has been developed about failure categories.

LOCAL and SOPHIE also address a number of issues which GDE does not. LOCAL and SOPHIE use corroborations as well as conflicts to eliminate candidates. To take advantage of corroborations, SOPHIE includes an *exhaustive* set of fault modes for each component. As a consequence, SOPHIE can identify a component as being unfaulted by determining that it is not operating in any of its fault modes (i.e., none of the components fault modes can explain the failure, and we know all the component's modes of failure, so the component must be working). Thus, SOPHIE reduces the candidate space from both sides: conflicts eliminate candidates that do not explain a conflict, and corroborations eliminate candidates which include known working components.

In addition, SOPHIE and LOCAL dealt with the problem of imprecise models and values as well. This makes constraint propagation very difficult because it is hard to tell whether two differing values corroborate or conflict within the precision of the analysis.

GDE proposes optimal measurements given a fixed set of inputs. Both Shirley's system [31] and DART generate test vectors to localize circuit faults. This approach is useful in cases where it is both difficult to make internal measurements, and easy to change circuit inputs. Both approaches produce tests which are likely to give useful information; however, no serious attempt is made at selecting the optimal tests. A fairly simple extension can be made to our cost function to account for tests, by taking into consideration, for example the cost of modifying the inputs.

In Shirley's approach, each test isolates a single potentially faulted component by using known good components to guide the input signals to the faulty component and the output of that component to a point which can be measured. However, it is not always possible to route the test signals such that all other suspects are avoided. Using the information constructed by GDE, this approach can be modified, so that tests are constructed first for components which are most likely to be faulted, while propagating the signal along a path with the lowest probability of having a faulty component.

6.2. Counterfactuals

Ginsberg [13] points out how David Lewis' possible world semantics could be applied to diagnosis. Each component is modeled by a counterfactual, a statement such as "if p, then q," where p is expected to be false. Thus A_1 is modeled by the counterfactual "if A_1 fails, then $F = X + Y$ need not hold." Counterfactuals are evaluated by considering a "possible world" that is as similar as possible to the real world where p is true. The counterfactual is true if q holds in such a possible world. In this framework the most similar worlds (i.e., those closest to the one in which the circuit functions correctly) correspond directly to our minimal candidates. A most similar world is one in which as few of the p's (e.g., "A_1 fails") as possible become true. Thus, in this instance Ginsberg uses counterfactuals for hypotheticals.

Ginsberg's approaches handles multiple faults, but he does not discuss measurement strategies or probabilities. Both could be integrated into his approach.

6.3. Reiter

Reiter [29] has been independently exploring many of the ideas incorporated in GDE. His theory of diagnosis provides a formal account of our "intuitive" techniques for conflict recognition and candidate generation. However, his theory does not include a theory of measurements nor how to exploit probabilistic information.

Reiter's theory uses McCarthy's [18] AB predicate. Reiter writes $\neg$AB(A_1) (i.e., adder A_1 is not ABnormal), while we write A_1 (i.e., the assumption that adder A_1 is working correctly). Under this mapping, Reiter's definition of diagnosis is equivalent to our definition of minimal candidate, and his definition of conflict set is equivalent to our definition of conflict.

Reiter proposes (unimplemented) a diagnostic algorithm based on his theory. This architecture is quite different from GDE's. The theorem prover of his architecture corresponds roughly to our inference engine. While GDE's procedure first computes all minimal conflicts resulting from a new measurement before updating the candidate space, Reiter's algorithm intermingles conflict recognition with candidate generation to guide the theorem proving to "prevent the computation of inessential variants of refutations, without imposing any constraints on the nature of the underlying theorem proving system." Given GDE's inference architecture (and the necessity to choose the best next measurement), GDE avoids almost all these inessential variants and also avoids much of the computation Reiter's architecture demands.

6.4. SNEPS

SNEPS [17] incorporates a belief revision system SNEBR which reasons about the consistency of hypotheses. This belief revision system has been [6] applied to fault detection in circuits. Some of the basic concepts used in the SNEPS approach are similar to those used in GDE—both use an assumption-based belief revision system (see [9] for a comparison). As described in [6] SNEPS is weaker than either GDE or Reiter's approach. In GDE's terminology, SNEPS operates in a single environment, detecting symptoms (and hence conflicts) for only those variables about which a user query is made. The system provides no mechanisms to detect all symptoms (and thus all conflicts), to identify candidates, to propose measurements, or to exploit probabilistic information. However, there seems no reason, in principle that the methods of GDE cannot be incorporated into their system.

6.5. IN-ATE and FIS

IN-ATE [7] and FIS [24] are expert system shells specifically designed for fault diagnosis. Although neither is purely model-based (i.e., not purely within the structure-function paradigm), they are the only other electronic diagnosis systems we are aware of that propose measurements, and thus it is instructive to compare them with GDE.

IN-ATE incorporates two formal criteria to determine the best next measurement: minimum entropy (as in GDE) and gamma miniaverage heuristic search [32]. We chose minimum entropy (as FIS does) in GDE because it was the best evaluation function which is efficiently computable (i.e., it is based on one-step lookahead). The gamma miniaverage heuristic search is a multi-step lookahead procedure and hence computationally expensive to apply. Nevertheless, there is no reason, in principle, it could not be incorporated into GDE.

Unlike GDE, IN-ATE and FIS can exploit a variety of kinds of knowledge (e.g., fault trees, expert-supplied rules, hierarchy) in the diagnostic process. However, viewed from the pure model-based approach, they are limited in predictive power and as a consequence can only estimate the probabilities for their predictions.

As IN-ATE is not model-based, it does not construct explicit value predictions as does GDE. Instead, it predicts whether a particular measurement outcome will be "good" or "bad." (This, in itself, presents difficulties because a measurement being "good" or "bad" is relative to the observations being compared to. However, IN-ATE takes "good" and "bad" as absolute.) These predictions are computed by analyzing expert-supplied empirical associations based on "good" and "bad." IN-ATE incorporates a heuristic rule generator which exploits connectivity information, but it, at a minimum, must be provided with the definitions of "good" and "bad" for the test points. In this approach, the number of test points is limited to those explicitly mentioned in rules (or for which "good" and "bad" are externally defined). With this limited set of test points full search (i.e., gamma miniaverage search) becomes plausible. FIS exploits more model knowledge, propagating qualitative values such as {hi, ok, lo} through the circuit topology via expert-supplied causal rules. The propagated values are always relative to fixed expert-supplied values. Thus neither FIS nor IN-ATE can analyze hypothetical faults.

All three systems must compute probabilities for their predictions. GDE directly computes the probability of the predictions from the probabilities of the candidates involved. IN-ATE has a much more difficult time determining good/bad probabilities because it cannot determine the candidate space and their associated probabilities. Instead it uses the expert-supplied rules to propagate probabilities (much like MYCIN) and Dempster–Shafer to combine the resulting evidence. FIS' definition of candidate probability is similar to GDE's, however, as it cannot perform hypothetical reasoning it can only estimate the probabilities of its predictions.

6.6. Medical diagnosis

There has been extensive research on the diagnostic task in the medical decision making community. Although most of this research is not model-based, its concern with identifying the diseases causing symptoms and subsequently proposing information-gathering queries is analogous to ours.

Like Gorry and Barnett [14] GDE solves a sequential diagnostic task. The fundamental equation (Bayes' rule) [35, formula (2)] states that the posterior probability of hypothesis H_i being the true state H_T given evidence Q_i is:

$$p(H_j|Q_i) = \frac{p(Q_i|H_j)p(H_j)}{\sum_{k=1}^{n} p(Q_i|H_k)p(H_k)},$$

where $p(Q_i|H_j)$ is the conditional probability of evidence Q_i while $p(H_j)$ is the a priori probability of H_j. Given these probabilities it is possible to determine the posterior probability distribution, and, in addition, to determine the hypothetical probability distribution resulting from proposed tests. Thus, this provides complete information to evaluate the expected gain of a test [14] and to select the best test to make next.

The practical obstacle to employing Bayes' rule is the unavailability of the conditional probabilities. These probabilities are both hard to estimate and extremely numerous. For even small numbers of possible symptoms and diseases the number of probabilities required is extremely large (given just 10 hypotheses and 5 possible binary tests, 2420 conditional probabilities are required [35]).

The engineering domain differs from the medical domain in that very accurate models exist based on the structure of the (faulty) system. Thus, exploiting model-based reasoning, GDE computes these conditional probabilities directly rather than depending on empirical results. Another advantage of the model-based approach for engineering is that the potential tests are computed in the course of the analysis instead of having them supplied a priori.

Early research [14] presumed that the patient had only one disease. This is analogous to the single-fault assumption in circuit diagnosis. More recent research allows for multiple simultaneous diseases. Bayes' rule can also be applied to this multimembership classification problem [2, 3] but the number of conditional probabilities required becomes exponentially larger than the single-disease case (which already is a large number). Again, GDE computes these conditional probabilities by model-based reasoning.

The concept of set covering used in [21, 22, 23, 25, 27, 28] is similar to the candidate generation phase of our diagnostic approach. The irredundant set cover of the general set covering theory (GSC) of Reggia corresponds directly to our notion of minimal candidates. The primary difference is that we consider, in theory, every possible cover to be an explanation for the symptoms while GSC considers only the minimal candidates as explanations. Although GSC incorporates a crude heuristic strategy for proposing new measurements, as the conditional probabilities are available to GDE, the preferred approach, minimum entropy, can be applied.

ACKNOWLEDGMENT

Daniel G. Bobrow, Randy Davis, Kenneth Forbus, Matthew Ginsberg, Frank Halasz, Walter Hamscher, Tad Hogg, Ramesh Patil, Leah Ruby, Mark Shirley and Jeff Van Baalen, provided useful insights. We especially thank Ray Reiter for his clear perspective and many productive interactions. Lenore Johnson and Denise Pawson helped edit drafts and prepare figures.

REFERENCES

1. Ben-Bassat, M., Myopic policies in sequential classification, *IEEE Trans. Comput.* **27** (1978) 170–178.
2. Ben-Bassat, M., Multimembership and multiperspective classification: Introduction, applications, and a Bayesian model, *IEEE Trans. Syst. Man Cybern.* **6** (1980) 331–336.
3. Ben-Bassat, M. Campbell, D.B., Macneil A.R. and Weil, M.H., Pattern-based interactive diagnosis of multiple disorders: The MEDAS system, *IEEE Trans. Pattern Anal. Mach. Intell.* **2** (1980) 148–160.
4. Brown, J.S., Burton, R.R. and de Kleer, J., Pedagogical, natural language and knowledge engineering techniques in SOPHIE I, II and III, in: D. Sleeman and J.S. Brown (Eds.), *Intelligent Tutoring Systems* (Academic Press, New York, 1982) 227–282.
5. Davis, R., Diagnostic reasoning based on structure and behavior, *Artifical Intelligence* **24** (1984) 347–410.
6. Campbell, S.S. and Shapiro, S.C., Using belief revision to detect faults in circuits, SNeRG Tech. Note No. 15, Department of Computer Science, SUNY at Buffalo, NY, 1986.

7. Cantone, R.R., Lander, W.B., Marrone, M.P. and Gaynor, M.W., IN-ATE: Fault diagnosis as expert system guided search, in: L. Bolc and M.J. Coombs (Eds.), *Computer Expert Systems* (Springer, New York, 1986).
8. de Kleer, J., An assumption-based TMS, *Artifical Intelligence* **28** (1986) 127–162.
9. de Kleer, J., Problem solving with the ATMS, *Artifical Intelligence* **28** (1986) 197–224.
10. de Kleer, J., Local methods of localizing faults in electronic circuits, Artificial Intelligence Laboratory, AI Memo 394, MIT, Cambridge, MA, 1976.
11. Doyle, J., A truth maintenance system, *Artificial Intelligence* **12** (1979) 231–272.
12. Genesereth, M.R., The use of design descriptions in automated diagnosis, *Artificial Intelligence* **24** (1984) 411–436.
13. Ginsberg, M.L., Counterfactuals, *Artificial Intelligence* **30** (1986) 35–79.
14. Gorry, G.A. and Barnett, G.O., Experience with a model of sequential diagnosis, *Comput. Biomedical Res.* **1** (1968) 490–507.
15. Hamscher, W. and Davis, R., Diagnosing circuits with state: An inherently underconstrained problem, in: *Proceedings AAAI-84*, Austin, TX (1984) 142–147.
16. Hamscher, W. and Davis, R., Issues in diagnosis from first principles, Artificial Intelligence Laboratory, AI Memo 394, MIT, Cambridge, MA, 1986.
17. Martins, J.P. and Shapiro, S.C., Reasoning in multiple belief spaces, in: *Proceedings IJCAI-83*, Karlsruhe, F.R.G., 1983.
18. McCarthy, J., Applications of circumscription to formalizing common-sense knowledge, *Artificial Intelligence* **28** (1986) 89–116.
19. Mitchell, T., Version spaces: An approach to concept learning, Computer Science Department, STAN-CA-78-711, Stanford University, Palo Alto, CA, 1970.
20. Pearl, J., Entropy, information and rational decision, *Policy Anal. Inf. Syst.* **3** (1979) 93–109.
21. Peng, Y.P. and Reggia, J.A., Plausibility of diagnostic hypotheses: the nature of simplicity, in: *Proceedings AAAI-86*, Philadelphia, PA (1986) 140–145.
22. Peng, Y.P. and Reggia, J.A., A probabilistic causal model for diagnostic problem-solving; Part 1: Integrating symbolic causal inference with numeric probabilistic inference, Department of Computer Science, University of Maryland, College Park, MD, 1986.
23. Peng, Y.P. and Reggia, J.A., A probabilistic causal model for diagnostic problem-solving; Part 2: Diagnostic strategy, Department of Computer Science, University of Maryland, College Park, MD, 1986.
24. Pipitone, F., The FIS electronics troubleshooting system, *IEEE Computer* (1986) 68–75.
25. Pople, H., The formation of composite hypotheses in diagnostic problem solving: An exercise in synthetic reasoning, in: *Proceedings IJCAI-77*, Cambridge, MA (1977) 1030–1037.
26. Quinlan, J.R., Learning efficient classification procedures and their application to chess end games, in: R.S. Michalski, J.G. Carbonell and T.M. Mitchell, (Eds.), *Machine Learning* (Tioga, Palo Alto, CA, 1983) 463–482.
27. Reggia, J.A. and Nau, D.S., An abductive non-monotonic logic, in: *Workshop on Non-monotonic Reasoning*, New Paltz, NY, 1984.
28. J.A. Reggia, Nau, D.S., and Wang, P.Y., Diagnostic expert systems based on a set covering model, *Int. J. Man-Mach. Stud.* **19** (1983) 437–460.
29. Reiter, R., A theory of diagnosis from first principles, *Artificial Intelligence* **32** (1987) 57–95 (this issue).
30. Shannon, C.E., A mathematical theory of communication, *Bell Syst. Tech. J.* **27** (1948) 379–623.
31. Shirley, M.H. and Davis R., Generating distinguishing tests based on hierarchical models and symptom information, in: *Proceedings IEEE International Conference on Computer Design*, Rye, NY, 1983.
32. Slagle, J.R. and Lee, R.C.T., Application of game tree searching techniques to sequential pattern recognition, *Commun. ACM* **14** (1971) 103–110.
33. Steele, G.L., The definition and implementation of a computer programming language based on constraints, AI Tech. Rept. 595, MIT, Cambridge, MA, 1979.
34. Sussman, G.J. and Steele, G.L., CONSTRAINTS: A language for expressing almost-hierarchical descriptions, *Artificial Intelligence* **14** (1980) 1–39.
35. Szolovitz, P. and Pauker, S.G., Categorical and probabilistic reasoning in medical diagnosis, *Artificial Intelligence* **11** (1978) 115–144.
36. Williams, B.C., Doing time: Putting qualitative reasoning on firmer ground, in: *Proceedings AAAI-86*, Philadelphia, PA (1986) 105–112.

5.3 Reasoning about Action

The papers in this final section of the collection represent the most active research area in nonmonotonic reasoning.

The research was sparked by Hanks and McDermott's paper, "Default reasoning, nonmonotonic logics, and the frame problem." In it, Hanks and McDermott present the temporal projection problem, and show that none of the conventional formulations of nonmonotonic inference is capable of dealing with it.

The other three papers propose remedies. Unfortunately, none of the proposed solutions is completely satisfactory, and more work remains to be done.

Shoham, with his theory of chronological ignorance, suggests solving the Hanks-McDermott problem by temporally ordering the conflicting extensions that underlie it. The Hanks-McDermott problem arises because we need to distinguish between an extension that violates a default rule at time t and one that violates a default rule at a later time t'; Shoham formalizes the notion that we prefer violations of the default rule at time t', since there is no reason to violate the earlier default.

The difficulty with this approach is that, although it is capable of dealing with the Hanks-McDermott problem, Shoham has yet to show that it can deal with the other nonmonotonic problems arising in reasoning about action. The frame problem is unaddressed and, although Shoham does consider some aspects of the qualification problem, the approach cannot deal with the examples to be found in [Ginsberg, Smith, 1987b]. Additional technical difficulties are discussed in [Haugh, 1987].

Other authors also have suggested solving the temporal projection problem by introducing a temporal order. Lifschitz makes this proposal in the paper on pointwise circumscription **[Lifschitz, 1987b]**, and Kautz makes a similar, although less general, suggestion in [Kautz, 1986].

Another approach is suggested by Lifschitz in "Formal theories of action." Lifschitz shows that the prioritization introduced by Shoham to solve the temporal projection problem is not necessary. By formalizing the notion of causality directly, Lifschitz solves the Hanks-McDermott problem without introducing a new nonmonotonic formalism. A similar approach is taken by Haugh [Haugh, 1987].

Once again, there are drawbacks to this approach. The Lifschitz and Haugh solution deals with the frame and temporal projection problems, but the qualification problem is only partially addressed and the ramification problem described in Section 1.6.1 of the introduction and in [Finger, 1987] is not dealt with at all. Finally, McDermott argues [McDermott, 1987a] that this approach is invalidated by what he considers to be its nonintuitive nature—recall that one of the principal arguments for a nonmonotonic solution to the frame problem (and related difficulties) was that this approach would make formal sense of an intuitively satisfying description of action.

The final approach is the one suggested in my paper with Smith, "Reasoning about action I: A possible worlds approach." This work is based on the idea of using the notion of possible worlds[1] to determine the consequences of an action. The approach taken here is quite like that of STRIPS [Fikes, Nilsson, 1971], where a single copy of the world description is maintained and modified to reflect the execution of any particular action.

This approach leads to an effective solution to the frame and ramification problems, and to the qualification problem as well [Ginsberg, Smith, 1987b]. It sidesteps the temporal projection problem, since the actions are considered one at a time, with the effects of any particular action being evaluated before the next action is even considered. The principal thrust of the paper is to show that the approach has clear computational advantages over other suggestions.

The difficulty with this approach is that, since actions are being described in terms of their effects on a particular database, the semantics of the approach are not nearly so clear as are those of the others. It is not clear whether the attractive features of the possible worlds idea will be retained when the semantics are sharpened.

[1] The possible worlds here are those described by Lewis [Lewis, 1973]. Kripke's notion of possible worlds is a different one.

Default Reasoning, Nonmonotonic Logics, and the Frame Problem

Steve Hanks and Drew McDermott[1]

Department of Computer Science, Yale University
Box 2158 Yale Station
New Haven, CT 06520

Abstract

Nonmonotonic formal systems have been proposed as an extension to classical first-order logic that will capture the process of human "default reasoning" or "plausible inference" through their inference mechanisms just as *modus ponens* provides a model for deductive reasoning. But although the technical properties of these logics have been studied in detail and many examples of human default reasoning have been identified, for the most part these logics have not actually been applied to practical problems to see whether they produce the expected results.

We provide axioms for a simple problem in temporal reasoning which has long been identified as a case of default reasoning, thus presumably amenable to representation in nonmonotonic logic. Upon examining the resulting nonmonotonic theories, however, we find that the inferences permitted by the logics are *not* those we had intended when we wrote the axioms, and in fact are much weaker. This problem is shown to be independent of the logic used; nor does it depend on any particular temporal representation. Upon analyzing the failure we find that the nonmonotonic logics we considered are inherently incapable of representing this kind of default reasoning. Finally we discuss two recent proposals for solving this problem.

1 Introduction

Logic as a representation language for AI theories has always held a particular appeal in the research community (or in some parts of it, anyway): its rigid syntax forces one to be precise about what one is saying, and its semantics provide an agreed-upon and well-understood way of assigning meaning to the symbols. But if logic is to be more than just a concise and convenient notation that helps us in the task of writing programs, we somehow have to validate the axioms we write: are the conclusions we can draw from our representation (*i.e.*, the inferences the logic allows) the same as the ones characteristic of the reasoning process we are trying to model? If so, we've gone a long way toward validating our theory.

The limitation of classical logic as a representation for human knowledge and reasoning is that its inference rule, *modus ponens*, is the analogue to human *deductive* reasoning, but for the most part everyday human reasoning seems to have significant non-deductive components. But while certain aspects of human reasoning (*e.g.* inductive generalization and abductive explanation) seem to be substantially different from deduction, a certain class of reasoning, dubbed "default reasoning," resembles deduction more closely. Thus it was thought that extensions to first-order logic might result in formal systems capable of representing the process of default reasoning.

While it is still not clear *exactly* what constitutes default reasoning, the phenomenon commonly manifests itself when we know what conclusions should be drawn about *typical* situations or objects, but we must jump to the conclusion that an observed situation or object *is* typical. For example, I may know that I typically meet with my advisor on Thursday afternoons, but I can't deduce that I will actually have a meeting *next* Thursday because I don't know whether next Thursday is typical. While certain facts may allow me to deduce that next Thursday is *not* typical (*e.g.* if I learn he will be out of town all next week), in general there will be no way for me to deduce that it *is*. What we want to do in cases like this is to jump to the conclusion that next Thursday is typical based on two pieces of information: first that most Thursdays *are* typical, and second that we have no reason to believe that this one is not. Another way to express the same notion is to say that I know that I have meetings on typical Thursdays, and that the only *atypical* Thursdays are the ones that I *know* (can deduce) are atypical.

Research on nonmonotonic logics[2], most notably by McCarthy (in [8] and [9]), McDermott and Doyle (in [12]) and Reiter (in [14]) attacked the problem of extending first-order logic in a way that captured the intuitive meaning of statements of the form "lacking evidence to the contrary, infer α" or more generally "infer β from the inability to infer α."[3] But since that first flurry of research the area has developed in a strange way. On one hand the logics have been subjected to intense technical scrutiny (in the papers cited above, and also, for example, in Davis [2]) and have been shown to produce counterintuitive results under certain circumstances. At the same time we see in the literature practical representation problems such as story understanding (Charniak [1]), social convention in conversation (Joshi, Webber, and Weischedel [6]), and temporal reasoning (McDermott [11] and McCarthy [9]), in which default rules would *seem* to be of use, but in these cases technical details of the formal systems are for the most part ignored.

The middle ground—whether the technical workings of the logics correctly bear out one's intentions in representing practical default-reasoning problems—is for the most part empty, though the work of Reiter, Etherington, and Criscuolo, in [3], [4], and elsewhere, is a notable exception. Logicians have for the most part ignored practical problems to focus on technical details, and "practitioners" have used the default rules intuitively, with the hope (most often unstated) that the proof theory or semantics of the logics can eventually be shown to support those intuitions.

We explore that middle ground by presenting a problem in temporal reasoning that involves default inference, writing axioms in nonmonotonic logics intended to represent that reasoning process,

[1]This work was supported in part by ONR grant N00014-85-K-0301. Many thanks to Alex Kass and Yoav Shoham for discussing this work with us, and for reading drafts of the paper.

[2]So called because of the property that inferences allowed by the logic may be *disallowed* as axioms are added. For example I may jump to the conclusion that next Thursday is typical, thus deduce that I will have a meeting. If I later come to find out that it is *atypical*, I will have to *retract* that conclusion. In first-order logic the addition of new knowledge (axioms) to a theory can never diminish the deductions one can make from that theory, thus it is never necessary to retract conclusions.

[3]This sounds much more straightforward than it is: consider that the theorems of a logic are defined in terms of its inference rules, yet here we are trying to define an inference rule in terms of what is or is not a theorem.

then analyzing the resulting theory. Reasoning about time is an interesting application for a couple of reasons. First of all, the problem of representing the tendency of facts to endure over time (the "frame problem" of McCarthy and Hayes [10] or the notion of "persistence" in McDermott [11]) has long been assumed to be one of those practical reasoning problems that nonmonotonic logics would solve. Second, one has strong intuitions about how the problem *should* be formalized in the three logics, and even stronger intuitions about what inferences should then follow, so it will be clear whether the logics have succeeded or failed to represent the domain correctly.

In the rest of the paper we discuss briefly some technical aspects of nonmonotonic logics, then go on to pose formally the problem of temporal projection. We then analyze the inferences allowed by the resulting theory and show that they do *not* correspond to what we intended when we wrote the axioms. Finally we point out the (unexpected) characteristics of the domain that the logics were unable to capture, and discuss proposed solutions to the problem.

2 Nonmonotonic inference

Since we are considering the question of what inferences can be drawn from a nonmonotonic theory, we should look briefly at how inference is defined in these logics. We will concentrate on Reiter's default logic and on circumscription, but the discussion and subsequent results hold for McDermott's nonmonotonic logic as well.

2.1 Inference in default logic

Reiter in [14] defines a *default theory* as two sets of rules. The first consists of sentences in first-order logic (and is usually referred to as **W**), and the second is a set of *default rules* (referred to as **D**). Default rules are supposed to indicate what conclusions to jump to, and are of the form

$$\frac{\alpha \ : \ \mathbf{M}\,\beta}{\gamma}$$

where α, β, and γ are first-order sentences. The intended interpretation of this rule is "if you believe α, and it's consistent to believe β, then believe γ," or, to phrase the idea more like an inference rule, "from α and the *inability* to prove $\neg\beta$, infer γ." (But recall our note above about the futility of trying to define inference in terms of inference.)

In order to discuss default inference we must introduce the concept of an *extension*—a set of sentences that "extend" the sentences in **W** according to the dictates of the default rules. A default theory defines zero or more extensions, each of which has the following properties: (1) any extension **E** contains **W**, (2) **E** is closed under (monotonic) deduction, and (3) **E** is faithful to the default rules. By the last we mean that if there's a default rule in the theory of the form $\frac{\alpha\,:\,M\,\beta}{\gamma}$, and if $\alpha \in \mathbf{E}$, and $(\neg\beta) \notin \mathbf{E}$, then $\gamma \in \mathbf{E}$. The extensions of a default theory are all the minimal sets **E** that satisfy these three properties. Extensions can be looked upon as internally consistent and coherent states of the world, though the union of two extensions may be inconsistent.

Finding a satisfying definition of default inference—what sentences can be said to follow from a default theory—is tricky. Reiter avoids the problem altogether, focusing on the task of defining extensions and exploring their properties. He expresses the view that default reasoning is really a process of selecting *one* extension of a theory, then reasoning "within" this extension until new information forces a revision of one's beliefs and hence the selection of a new extension.

This view of default reasoning, while intuitively appealing, is infeasible from a practical standpoint: there is no way of "isolating" a single extension of a theory, thus no procedure for enumerating or testing theoremhood within an extension. So any definition of default reasoning based on discriminating among extensions is actually beyond the expressive power of default logic. Reiter does provide a proof procedure for asking whether a sentence is a member of *any* extension, but, as he points out, this is not a satisfying definition of inference since both a sentence and its negation may appear in different extensions.

Our view in this paper is that *some* notion of inference is necessary to judge the representational power of the logic. A logic that generates one intuitive extension and one unintuitive extension does not provide an adequate representation of the problem, since there is no way to distinguish between the two interpretations. For that reason we will define inference in the manner of McDermott's logic: a sentence δ can be inferred from a default theory just in case δ is in *every* extension of that theory. (This definition is also consistent with circumscriptive inference as described in the next section.)

While there is no general procedure for determining how many extensions a given theory has, as a practical matter it has been noted that theories with "conflicting" default rules tend to generate multiple extensions. For example, the following default theory

$$\mathbf{W} = \{Q(N), R(N)\}, \quad \mathbf{D} = \{\frac{Q(x) \ : \ \mathbf{M}\,P(x)}{P(x)}, \frac{R(x) \ : \ \mathbf{M}\,\neg P(x)}{\neg P(x)}\}$$

has two rules that would have us jump to contradictory conclusions. But note that applying one of the rules means that the other cannot be applied, since its precondition is not met. This default theory has two extensions: $\mathbf{E}_1 = \{Q(N), R(N), P(N)\}$ and $\mathbf{E}_2 = \{Q(N), R(N), \neg P(N)\}$ that correspond to the two choices one has in applying the default rules. (One interpretation of this theory reads Q as "Quaker," R as "Republican," P as "Pacifist," and N as "Nixon.") Thus the above theory entails only the sentences in **W**, plus tautologies (for example $P(N) \vee \neg P(N)$).

We are not claiming that this admission of multiple extensions is a fault or deficiency of the logic—in this particular example it's hard to imagine how the logic could license any *other* conclusions. Our point is that when a theory generates multiple extensions it's generally going to be the case that only weak inferences can be drawn. Further, if one extension captures the *intended* interpretation but there are other different extensions, it will not be possible to make only the intended inferences.

2.2 Inference in circumscription

To describe inference in circumscribed theories we will have to be rather vague: there are several versions of the logic, defined in [8], [9] and elsewhere, and we will not spend time discussing these differences.

We will speak generally of *predicate circumscription*, in which the intent is to minimize the extension of a predicate (say P) in a set of first-order axioms. Using terms like those we used in describing default logic, we might say that when we circumscribe axioms over P we intend that "the only individuals for which P holds are those individuals for which P *must* hold," or alternatively we might phrase it as "believe '*not P*' by default."

To circumscribe a set of axioms **A** over a predicate P one adds to **A** an axiom (the exact form of which is not important for our discussion) that says something like this: "any predicate P' that satisfies the axioms **A**, and is at least as strong as P, is *exactly* as strong as P." The intended effect is (roughly) that for any individual x,

if $\mathbf{A} \not\vdash P(x)$ then
$\mathrm{Circum}(\mathbf{A}, P) \vdash \neg P(x)$

where Circum($\mathbf{A}$, P) refers to the axioms $\mathbf{A}$ augmented by the circumscription axiom for P.

To talk about circumscriptive inference, we should first note that since Circum($\mathbf{A}$, P) is a first-order theory we want to know what ***deductively*** follows, but we are interested in characterizing these deductions in terms of the original axioms $\mathbf{A}$. In brief, the results are these: if a formula φ is a theorem of Circum($\mathbf{A}$, P) then φ is true in all models of $\mathbf{A}$ ***minimal in*** P (this property is called ***soundness***), and if a formula φ is true in all models of $\mathbf{A}$ minimal in P then φ is a theorem of Circum($\mathbf{A}$, P) (this property is called ***completeness***). Completeness does not hold for all circumscribed theories, but it does hold in certain special cases—see Minker and Perlis [13].

Minimal models, the model-theoretic analogue to default-logic extensions, are defined as follows: a model $\mathcal{M}$ is minimal in P just in case there is no model $\mathcal{M}'$ that agrees with $\mathcal{M}$ on all predicates ***except*** for P, but whose extension of P is a ***subset*** of $\mathcal{M}$'s extension of P.

As with default logic, there is no effective procedure for determining how many minimal models a theory has. And note that the converse of the soundness property says that if φ is ***not*** true in all models minimal in P it does ***not*** follow from Circum($\mathbf{A}$, P). So once again, if we have multiple minimal models, what we can deduce are only those formulas true in all of them. Because of the obvious parallels between extensions and minimal models (and "NM fixed points" in McDermott's logic, which we will not discuss here), we will use the terms interchangeably when the exact logic or object doesn't matter.

3 The temporal projection problem

The problem we want to represent is this: given an initial description of the world (some facts that are true), the occurence of some events, and some notion of causality (that an event occuring can cause a fact to become true), what facts are true once all the events have occured?

We obviously need some temporal representation to express these concepts, and we will use the ***situation calculus*** [10]. We will thus speak about ***facts*** holding true in ***situations***. A fact syntactically has the form of a first-order sentence, and is intended to be an assertion about the world, such as *SUNNY*, *LOADED(GUN-35)*, or $\forall$ *x.HAPPY(x)*. Situations are individuals denoting intervals of time over which facts hold or do not hold, but over which ***no*** fact changes its truth value. This latter property allows us to speak unambiguously about what facts are true or false in a situation. To say that a fact f is true in a situation s we assert $T(f, s)$, where T is a predicate and f and s are terms.

Events are things that happen in the world, and the occurence of an event may have the effect of changing the truth value of a fact. So we think of an event occuring in a situation and causing a transition to another situation—one in which the event's effects on the world are reflected. The function *RESULT* maps a situation and an event into another situation, so if S_0 is a situation and *WAKEUP(JOHN)* is an event, then *RESULT(WAKEUP(JOHN),* S_0*)* is also a situation—presumably the one resulting from *JOHN* waking up in situation S_0. We might then want to state that *JOHN* is awake in this situation:

$$T(\mathit{AWAKE(JOHN)},\ \mathit{RESULT}(\mathit{WAKEUP(JOHN)},\ S_0))$$

or more generally we might state that

$$\forall\ p,\ s.\ T(\mathit{AWAKE}(p),\ \mathit{RESULT}(\mathit{WAKEUP}(p),\ s)).$$

A problem arises when we try to express the notion that facts tend to ***stay*** true from situation to situation as irrelevant events occur. For example, is *JOHN* still awake in the state S_2, where

$$S_2 = \mathit{RESULT}(\mathit{EAT\text{-}BREAKFAST(JOHN)},\ \mathit{RESULT}(\mathit{WAKEUP(JOHN)},\ S_0))?$$

Intuitively we would like to assume so, because it's typically the case that eating breakfast does not cause one to fall asleep. But given the above axioms there is no way to deduce

$$T(\mathit{AWAKE(JOHN)},\ S_2).$$

We could add an axiom to the effect that if one is awake in a situation then one is still awake after eating breakfast, but this seems somewhat arbitrary (and will occasionally be false). And in any reasonable description of what one might do in the course of a morning there would have to be a staggering number of axioms expressing something like "if fact f is true in a situation s, and e is an event, then f is still true in the situation *RESULT(e, s)*." McCarthy and Hayes (in [10]) call axioms of this kind "frame axioms," and identified the "frame problem" as that of having to explicitly state many such axioms. Deductive logic forces us into the position of assuming that an event occurence may potentially change the truth value of all facts, thus if it does ***not*** change the value of a particular fact in a particular situation we must explicitly say so. What we would like to do is assume just the opposite: that most events do ***not*** affect the truth of most facts under most circumstances.

Intuitively we want to solve the frame problem by assuming that in general an event happening in a situation is ***irrelevant*** to a fact's truth value in the resulting situation. Or, to make the notion a little more precise, we want to assume "by default" that

$$T(f,\ s) \supset T(f,\ \mathit{RESULT}(e,\ s))$$

for all facts, situations, and events. But note the quotes: the point of this paper is that formalizing this assumption is not as straightforward as the phrase might lead one to believe.

McCarthy's proposed solution to the frame problem (described in [9]) involves extending the situation calculus a little, to make it what he calls a "simple abnormality theory." We state that all "normal" facts persist across occurences of "normal" events:

$$\forall\ f,\ e,\ s.\ T(f,\ s) \land \neg\ \mathit{AB}(f,\ e,\ s) \supset T(f,\ \mathit{RESULT}(e,\ s))$$

where *AB(f, e, s)* is taken to mean "fact f is abnormal with respect to event e occuring in state s," or, "there's something about event e occuring in state s that causes fact f to stop being true in *RESULT(e,s)*." We would expect, for example, that it would be true that

$$\forall\ p,\ s.\ \mathit{AB}(\mathit{AWAKE}(p),\ \mathit{GOTOSLEEP}(p),\ s)$$

and we would have to add a specific axiom to that effect.

Of course we still haven't solved the frame problem, since we haven't provided any way to deduce $\neg$ *AB(f,e,s)* for most facts, events, and situations. As an alternative to providing myriad frame axioms of this form, McCarthy proposes that we circumscribe over the predicate *AB*, thus "minimizing" the abnormal temporal individuals. The question is whether this indeed represents what we intuitively mean by saying that we should "assume the persistence of facts by default," or "once true, facts tend to stay true over time."

As an illustration of what we ***can*** infer from a very simple situation-calculus abnormality theory, consider the axioms of Figure 1. For simplicity we have restricted the syntactic form of facts and events to be propositional symbols, so the axioms can be interpreted as referring to a single individual who at any point in time (situation) can be either *ALIVE* or *DEAD* and a gun that can be either *LOADED* or *UNLOADED*. At some known situation S_0 the person is alive (Axiom 1), and the gun becomes loaded any time a *LOAD* event happens (Axiom 2). Axiom 3 says that any time the person is shot with a loaded gun he becomes dead, and furthermore that being shot with a loaded gun is abnormal with respect to staying alive. Or to use our definition from above: there is something about a *SHOOT* event occuring in a situation in which the gun is loaded that causes the fact *ALIVE* to stop being true in the situation resulting from the shot. Axiom 4 is just the assertion we made above that "normal" facts persist across the occurence of "normal" events.

(1) $T(ALIVE, S_0)$
(2) $\forall s.\ T(LOADED, RESULT(LOAD, s))$
(3) $\forall s.\ T(LOADED, s) \supset AB(ALIVE, SHOOT, s) \wedge T(DEAD, RESULT(SHOOT, s))$
(4) $\forall f, e, s.\ T(f, s) \wedge \neg AB(f, e, s) \supset T(f, RESULT(e, s))$

Figure 1: Simple situation-calculus axioms

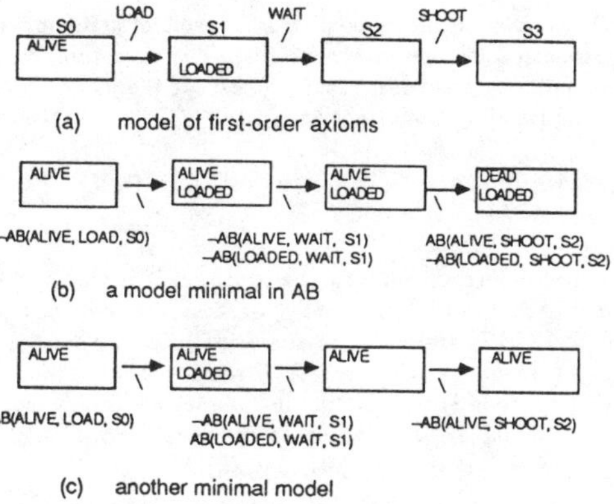

Figure 2: Three models of the Figure 1 axioms

Then we circumscribe Axioms 1–4 over AB, recalling that the deducible formulas will be those that are true in all models minimal in AB. As above we will refer to Axioms 1–4 as **A**, and to the circumscribed axioms as Circum(**A**, AB).

Now consider the problem of projecting what facts will be true in the following situations:

$$S_0$$
$$S_1 = RESULT(LOAD, S_0),$$
$$S_2 = RESULT(WAIT, S_1), \quad \text{and}$$
$$S_3 = RESULT(SHOOT, S_2)$$
$$= RESULT(SHOOT, RESULT(WAIT, RESULT(LOAD, S_0))).$$

In other words, our individual is initially known to be alive, then the gun is loaded, then he waits for a while, then he is shot with the gun. The projection problem is to determine what facts are true at the situations S_i. The event *WAIT* is supposed to signify a period of time when nothing of interest happens. Since according to the axioms no fact is abnormal with respect to a *WAIT* event occuring, we intend that every fact true before the event happens should also be true *after* it happens.

One interpretation of the Figure 1 axioms is shown in Figure 2a. This first picture represents facts true in all models of **A** (thus what we can deduce if we *don't* circumscribe). From Axioms 1 and 2 we can make the following deductions:

$$T(ALIVE, S_0), \qquad T(LOADED, S_1),$$

but we can deduce nothing about what is true in S_2 or in S_3. We also cannot deduce any "abnormalities" nor their negations. But this is pretty much as expected: the *ALIVE* fact did not persist because we could not deduce that it was "not *AB*" with respect to loading the gun, and the gun being loaded did not persist through the *WAIT* event because we could not deduce that it was "not *AB*" with respect to waiting.

Intuitively we would like to reason about "minimizing abnormalities" like this: we know *ALIVE* must be true in S_0, and nothing compels us to believe $AB(ALIVE, LOAD, S_0)$, so we assume its negation. From this assumption and from Axiom 4 we deduce $T(ALIVE, S_1)$. Reasoning along the same lines, we can deduce $T(LOADED, S_1)$ and we are free to make the assumptions $\neg AB(ALIVE, WAIT, S_1)$ and $\neg AB(LOADED, WAIT, S_1)$ so we do so and go on to deduce $T(ALIVE, S_2)$ and $T(LOADED, S_2)$. Again moving forward in time, we can deduce from Axiom 3 that $AB(ALIVE, SHOOT, S_2)$ so we can't assume its negation, but we *can* assume $\neg AB(LOADED, SHOOT, S_2)$. At that point we have $T(DEAD, S_3)$ and $T(LOADED, S_3)$.

This line of reasoning leads us to the interpretation of Figure 2b. We can easily verify that this interpretation is indeed a model of **A** (that Axioms 1 through 4 are satisfied). Furthermore, this model is minimal in AB: any submodel would have to have an empty extension for AB, which cannot be the case.[5]

The interesting question now is whether the model of Figure 2b—our *intended* model of **A**—is the *only* minimal model, or, more to the point, whether $T(DEAD, S_3)$ and $T(LOADED, S_2)$ are true in all minimal models. Because if they're not true in all minimal models they can't be deduced from Circum(**A**, AB).

Consider the situation in Figure 2c. The picture describes a state of affairs in which the gun ceases to be loaded "as a result of" waiting. Then the individual *does not* die as a result of the shot, since the gun is not loaded. Of course this state of affairs directly contradicts our stated intention that since nothing is explicitly "*AB*" with respect to waiting everything should be "not *AB*" with respect to waiting. Does this interpretation describe a minimal model? First recall that there can be no models having a null extension for AB, so if this interpretation is a model at all it must be minimal in AB.

One can "build" this model in much the same way we constructed the model of Figure 2b, except this time instead of starting at S_0 and working forward in time, we will start at S_3 and work backward. In other words, we will start by noting that $T(ALIVE, S_2)$ must be true, then consider what must have been true at S_2 and in earlier situations for that to have been the case.

The first abnormality decision to make is whether $AB(ALIVE, SHOOT, S_2)$ is true. Since we haven't made a decision to the contrary, we will assume its negation. But then from the contrapositive of Axiom 3, we we can deduce $\neg T(LOADED, S_2)$. But if that is the case, and since it must also be the case that $T(LOADED, S_1)$, we can deduce from Axiom 4 that $AB(LOADED, WAIT, S_1)$. The rest of Figure 2c follows directly, since we can assume that *ALIVE* is "not AB" with respect to *LOAD* and *WAIT*, thus deduce that it is true in both S_1 and S_2.

What, then, can be deduced from the (circumscribed) abnormality theory? It's fairly easy to verify that the two models we have presented are the only two minimal in AB, so the theorems of Circum(**A**, AB) are those common to those two models. So we can deduce that *ALIVE* and *LOADED* are true in S_1, that *ALIVE* is true in S_2, but we can say nothing about what is true in S_3 except for statements like $T(ALIVE, S_3) \vee T(DEAD, S_3)$. What we can deduce from Circum(**A**, AB) is therefore considerably weaker than what we had intended.

4 How general is this problem?

The question now arises: how dependent is this result on the specific problem and formulation we just presented? Does the same problem arise if we use a different default logic or a different temporal formalism?

[5] To see why this is true, consider that in any model of **A** either $T(ALIVE, S_2)$ is true, or it's false. If it's true we can immediately deduce an abnormality from Axiom 3. But if it's false then either $AB(ALIVE, LOAD, S_0)$ or $AB(ALIVE, WAIT, S_1)$ would have to be true. In either case we must have at least one abnormality.

We can easily express the theory above in Reiter's logic: we use the same first-order axioms from Figure 1, but instead of circumscribing over *AB* we represent "minimizing abnormal individuals" with a class of (normal) default rules of the form

$$D = \{\frac{: \mathbf{M} \neg AB(f, e, s)}{\neg AB(f, e, s)}\}$$

(where any individual may be substituted for *f*, *e*, and *s*). Recall that extensions are defined proof-theoretically instead of in terms of models, so we must translate the minimal models shown in Figure 2 (b and c) into sets of sentences; the question becomes whether the following sets are default-logic extensions:

$\mathbf{E_a}$	$\mathbf{E_b}$
$T(ALIVE, S_0)$	$T(ALIVE, S_0)$
$\neg AB(ALIVE, LOAD, S_0)$	$\neg AB(ALIVE, LOAD, S_0)$
$T(ALIVE, S_1)$	$T(ALIVE, S_1)$
$T(LOADED, S_1)$	$T(LOADED, S_1)$
$\neg AB(ALIVE, WAIT, S_1)$	$\neg AB(ALIVE, WAIT, S_1)$
$\neg AB(LOADED, WAIT, S_1)$	$AB(LOADED, WAIT, S_1)$
$T(ALIVE, S_2)$	$T(ALIVE, S_2)$
$T(LOADED, S_2)$	
$AB(ALIVE, SHOOT, S_2)$	$\neg AB(ALIVE, SHOOT, S_2)$
$\neg AB(LOADED, SHOOT, S_2)$	
$T(DEAD, S_3)$	$T(ALIVE, S_3)$
$T(LOADED, S_3)$	

Of course these are partial descriptions of extensions. Each set also contains **A** and all tautologies, and in $\mathbf{E_a}$, for example, we also include all sentences of the form $\neg AB(f, e, s)$ for all individuals (f, e, s) *except* $(ALIVE, SHOOT, S_2)$.

We will omit the proof that both $\mathbf{E_a}$ and $\mathbf{E_b}$ are extensions, though in our longer paper, [5], we carry it out in some detail. It should be easy to convince oneself that both sets satisfy the three conditions we set down in Section 2: they contain **A**, they are closed under deduction, and they are faithful to the default rule in the sense defined previously. To verify that they are both minimal, note that in both cases all the sentences except the default-rule assumptions indeed follow from the default assumptions and the axioms in **A**.

So circumscription is not the culprit here—Reiter's proof-theoretic default logic has the same problem. We can also express the same problem in McDermott's nonmonotonic logic and show that the theory has the same two fixed points.

Nor is the situation calculus to blame: in a previous paper [5] we use a simplified version of McDermott's temporal logic and show that the same problem arises, again for all three default logics. In the next section we will show what characteristics of temporal projection lead to the multiple-extension problem, and why it appears that the three default logics are inherently unable to represent the domain correctly.

5 A minimality criterion for temporal reasoning

We noted above that default-logic theories often generate multiple extensions. But characteristic of all the usual examples, like the one we used in Section 2, is the fact that the default rules of these theories were mutually exclusive: the application of one rule rendered other rules inapplicable by blocking their preconditions.

Thus it comes as somewhat of a surprise that the temporal projection problem should exhibit several extensions. How can there be conflicting rules in the same way we saw above when our theory has only a single default rule? It turns out that conflict between rules arises in our domain in a different, more subtle, manner. To see how, recall how we built the first minimal model (that of Figure 2b). The idea was that we assumed one "normality," then went on to make all possible deductions, then assumed another "normality," and so on. The picture looks something like this:

$$\neg AB(LOADED, WAIT, S_1) \Rightarrow T(LOADED, S_2) \Rightarrow \ldots \Rightarrow AB(ALIVE, SHOOT, S_2)$$

where the conflict to notice is that as a result of assuming a "normality" we could deduce an ***abnormality***. The same thing happened when we build the model in Figure 2c, except the picture looks like this instead (reading from right to left):

$$AB(LOADED, WAIT, S_1) \Leftarrow \ldots \Leftarrow \neg T(LOADED, S_2) \Leftarrow \neg AB(ALIVE, SHOOT, S_2).$$

The only difference between the two models is that in the first case we started at the (temporally) earliest situation and worked our way forward in time, and in the second case we started at the latest point and worked our way backward in time. Another way to express the idea is that in the first model we always picked the "earliest possible" (f, e, s) triple to assume "normal" and in the second model we always picked the latest.

So the class of models we want our logic to select is not the "minimal models" in the set-inclusion sense of circumscription, but the "chronologically minimal" models (a term due to Yoav Shoham): those in which normality assumptions are made in chronological order, from earliest to latest, or, equivalently, those in which abnormality occurs as late as possible.

(In a richer temporal formalism the criterion chronological minimality might not be the right one. If several years had lapsed between the *WAIT* and the *SHOT*, for example, it would be reasonable to assume that the gun was no longer loaded. But chronological minimality ***does*** correctly represent our simple notion of persistence: that facts tend to stay true (forever) unless they are "clipped" by a contradictory fact.)

There appears to be no way represent this criterion, either in published versions of circumscription[6] or in the logics of Reiter or McDermott. The concept of minimality in circumscription is intimately bound up with the notion of set inclusion, and chronological minimality cannot be expressed in those terms. As far as Reiter and McDermott's logics go, what we need is some way to mediate ***application*** of default rules in building extensions or fixed points, which is beyond the expressive power of (Reiter's) default rules or of NML sentences involving the ***M*** operator.

6 Potential solutions

Two lines of work have been proposed as solutions to this problem. Yoav Shoham in [15] presents a logic that directly addresses the problem of representing causation in terms of "time flowing forward." Rather than trying to extend existing nonmonotonic logics so that they capture this new minimality criterion, he instead starts with a precise description of the chronologically minimal models. He then demonstrates that when a certain restricted class of first-order theories are minimized with respect to how much is ***known*** about each situation (instead of minimizing what is ***true*** in each situation) the resulting theory has a unique chronologically minimal model. While Shoham's logic handles the specific case of causal or temporal

[6]These include predicate circumscription and joint circumscription [8], formula circumscription and prioritized circumscription [9]. But see the note on pointwise circumscription below.

reasoning, his solution is obviously not an answer to the question we pose about the general relationship between default reasoning and nonmonotonic logics.

A second proposal, due to Vladimir Lifschitz in [7], involves a reformulation of and extension to predicate circumscription called *pointwise circumscription*, in which one minimizes a predicate one point at a time (in our example a point would be a *(fact, event, situation)* triple). The order in which points are minimized is specified by an object-language formula that can express the concept of "temporally earlier" and "temporally later." Thus one is able to say something to the effect "minimize abnormalities, but favoring chronologically earlier ones." Pointwise circumscription contains predicate circumscription as a special case, and has been shown to solve a simple example of interacting defaults that we presented in [5].

But what benefits do we realize from these new, more expressive, more complex versions of circumscription? The problem is that the original idea behind circumscription, that a simple, problem-independent extension to a first-order theory would "minimize" predicates in just the right way, has been lost along the way. Instead, a complex, problem-specific axiom must be found to rationalize a set of inferences which must themselves be justified *on completely separate grounds*. The real theory of reasoning is the minimality criterion. In this example it was Shoham's chronological minimality; for other cases of default reasoning there will be other criteria for adding deductively unwarranted conclusions to a theory. It contributes little to our understanding of the problem that these criteria can be expressed as a second-order circumscription axiom; the criteria are justifying the axiom rather than the other way around.

The situation might be different if the second-order axiom were "productive," that is, if further, perhaps unforeseen conclusions could be drawn from it, mechanically or otherwise. But it can be very hard to characterize the consequences of the circumscription axioms for a reasonably large and complex theory, and when the consequences *are* understood, they may not be at all what we intended. The upshot is that no one really wants to know what follows from circumscription axioms; they usually wind up as hopefully harmless decorations to the actual theory.

7 Conclusion

We have presented a problem in temporal reasoning—causal or temporal projection—that involves defeasible inference of the sort normally associated with nonmonotonic logics. But upon writing axioms that describe temporal projection in an intuitive way, we found that the inferences licensed by the logics did not correspond to our intentions in writing the axioms. There seem to be two reasons for this: that conflicting default rule *instances* lead to unexpected multiple fixed points (minimal models), and that our preference of one extension over another (our criterion for minimality) depends on an ordering of individuals that cannot be expressed by circumscribing over any predicate or set of predicates, or by the default rules in the other nonmonotonic logics.

At this point we need to re-evaluate the relationship between nonmonotonic logics and human default reasoning. We can no longer engage in the logical "wishful thinking" that led us to claim that circumscription solves the frame problem [9], or that "'consistent' is to be understood in the normal way it is construed in nonmonotonic logic.[1]" From a technical standpoint, there *is* no "normal way" to understand the *M* operator, or the Reiter default rules, or a theory circumscribed over some predicate, apart from the proof- or model theory of the chosen logic.

The term "consistent," has too often used informally by researchers (*e.g.* in [6]) as if it had an intuitive and domain-independent meaning. We have shown that in at least one case a precise definition of the term is much more complex than intuition would have us believe, and that the definition is tightly bound up with the problem domain. As such, the claim implicit in the development of nonmonotonic logics—that a simple extension to classical logic would result in the power to express an important class of human nondeductive reasoning—is certainly called into question by our result.

References

[1] Charniak, Eugene "Motivation Analysis, Abductive Unification, and Non-Monotonic Equality", *Cognitive Science*, to appear.

[2] Davis, Martin, "The Mathematics of Non-Monotonic Reasoning", *Artificial Intelligence*, vol. 13 (1980), pp. 73–80.

[3] Etherington, David W., "Formalizing Non-Monotonic Reasoning Systems", Computer Science Technical Report No. 83-1, University of British Columbia.

[4] Etherington, David W. and Raymond Reiter, "On Inheritance Hierarchies with Exceptions", *Proceedings AAAI-83*, pp. 104–108.

[5] Hanks, Steven and Drew McDermott, "Temporal Reasoning and Default Logics", Computer Science Research Report No. 430, Yale University, October 1985.

[6] Joshi, Aravind, Bonnie Webber and Ralph Weischedel, "Default Reasoning in Interaction", *Proceedings of the Non-Monotonic Reasoning Workshop*, AAAI, October 1984, pp. 151–164.

[7] Lifschitz, Vladimir "Pointwise Circumscription", unpublished, draft of March 11, 1986.

[8] McCarthy, John, "Circumscription – A Form of Non-Monotonic Reasoning", *Artificial Intelligence*, vol. 13 (1980), pp. 27–39.

[9] McCarthy, John, "Applications of Circumscription to Formalizing Common Sense Knowledge", *Proceedings of the Non-Monotonic Reasoning Workshop*, AAAI, October 1984, pp. 295–324.

[10] McCarthy, John, and P. J. Hayes, "Some Philosophical Problems from the Standpoint of Artificial Intelligence", in: B. Meltzer and D. Michie (eds.), *Machine Intelligence 4*, Edinburgh University Press, 1969, pp. 463–502.

[11] McDermott, Drew V., "A Temporal Logic for Reasoning About Processes and Plans", *Cognitive Science*, vol. 6 (1982), pp. 101–155.

[12] McDermott, Drew V. and Jon Doyle, "Non-Monotonic Logic I", *Artificial Intelligence*, vol. 13 (1980), pp. 41–72.

[13] Perlis, Donald, and Jack Minker, "Completeness Results for Circumscription", Computer Science Technical Report TR-1517, University of Maryland.

[14] Reiter, Raymond, "A Logic for Default Reasoning", *Artificial Intelligence*, vol. 13 (1980), pp. 81–132.

[15] Shoham, Yoav, "Time and Causation from the Standpoint of Aritificial Intelligence", Computer Science Research Report, Yale University, forthcoming (1986).

Chronological Ignorance:

An Experiment in Nonmonotonic Temporal Reasoning

Yoav Shoham
Computer Science Department
Stanford University

Abstract

We illustrate the use of our approach to constructing nonmonotonic logics by applying it to problems in formal temporal reasoning. We introduce a new nonmonotonic logic, called *chronological ignorance*, which combines elements of temporal logic and the modal logic of knowledge. We illustrate the usefulness of the logic with an example, and identify a class of theories in the logic which have elegant model-theoretic and computational properties.

1 Introduction: problems in temporal reasoning

In a previous article in this collection I presented an approach to constructing and understanding nonmonotonic logics. In this short article I will illustrate the use of that approach by constructing a new nonmonotonic logic which is useful for certain kinds of temporal reasoning. This is a very abridged discussion, summarizing the content of four chapters in [3].

The context of the work described here is formal temporal reasoning. The particular task with which I'm concerned is *prediction*, and the fundamental problem is that, practically speaking, we not only have to make predictions while still missing much potentially relevant information, but that we can't even afford to explicitly reason about everything that we *do* know; there's simply too much of it.

In [3] I discuss this at some length. Here let me just illustrate things with an example. Consider a simple scenario in which a gun is loaded at time $t = 1$ and fired at time $t = 5$. Assume that we have realistic knowledge about guns, so that we know that whenever a loaded gun is fired a loud noise follows (at the "next" point in time, if we view time as discrete), provided no strange circumstances obtain, such as the gun having no firing pin, there being no air to carry the sound, and so on. Given this information, are we justified in concluding that a loud noise will occur at time $t = 6$?

The answer is of course no, and there are two reasons for that. First, there is the question of whether the gun is loaded at time $t = 5$. It was loaded at $t = 1$, but how long did that last? We would like to say that it lasted until the firing, or, more generally, that it lasted "for as long as possible" (that is, the interval of the gun being loaded cannot be extended without introducing an inconsistency). How do we capture in a logic the property of persisting "for as long as possible"? Second, even if we managed to show that the gun was loaded at time $t = 5$, we would still not be able to show that none of the "weird" circumstances hold at $t = 5$; that is not entailed by our statements.

The first problem, that of assigning inertia to propositions, is an instance of what I have called the *extended-prediction problem*, which subsumes the infamous *frame problem* [2]. The second problem, that of having to explicitly state that none of many unlikely conditions hold, has been called the *qualification problem*. I discuss these two problems at some length in [3]. Here I will not give a more formal description of these problems, and will rely on the reader's intuition.

In the remainder of this paper I will outline a solution to the qualification problem, and will hint at a solution to the extended-prediction problem. The basic idea is to make nonmonotonic inferences. For example, from the fact that a loaded gun is fired, one would like to conclude that a loud noise follows, but to retract that if additional information is supplied (for example, that the gun has a silencer). Similarly, when a gun is loaded, one infers that it will remain loaded potentially forever, but shortens the scope of that prediction if it leads to an inconsistency. The question is which nonmonotonic logic is appropriate here. In [1], Hanks and McDermott pointed out serious problems encountered when using the three best known nonmonotonic systems. The following logic avoids those problems.

2 Chronological ignorance

As I explained in a previous article in this collection, I will define a nonmonotonic logic by first defining a standard logic, and then adding a partial order on its models.

2.1 *TK*: a monotonic logic of temporal knowledge

The logic of *temporal knowledge* (or the logic *TK*) is a logic of knowledge of temporal information. By this I mean that what is known has a temporal aspect to it, rather than the fact that knowledge changes over time. The logic is defined as follows.

Syntax. Given `P`: a set of primitive propositions, `TV`: a set of variables, `TC`: the set $\{\ldots,-3,-2,-1,0,1,2,\ldots\}$ (i.e., the standard representation of the integers), and `U`: $\mathtt{TC} \cup \mathtt{TV}$, the set of well-formed formulas of *TK* is defined inductively as follows:

1. If $u_1 \in U$ and $u_2 \in U$ then $u_1 = u_2$ and $u_1 \preceq u_2$ are wffs.
2. If $u_1 \in U$, $u_2 \in U$, and $p \in P$ then $\mathtt{TRUE}(u_1, u_2, p)$ is a wff.
3. If φ_1 and φ_2 are wffs then so are $\varphi_1 \wedge \varphi_2$, $\neg\varphi_1$, and $\Box\varphi_1$.
4. If φ is a wff and $v \in \mathtt{TV}$, then $\forall v\ \varphi$ is also a wff.

We assume the usual definitions of $\vee$, $\supset$, $\equiv$, $\exists$, and so on. As usual, $\Diamond$ is defined by $\Diamond\varphi \equiv \neg\Box\neg\varphi$. I will also use some convenient abbreviations. I will replace $\Box\mathtt{TRUE}(t_1,t_2,p)$ by $\Box(t_1,t_2,p)$, and $\Box\neg\mathtt{TRUE}(t_1,t_2,p)$ by $\Box(t_1,t_2,\neg p)$. Similarly, $\Diamond\mathtt{TRUE}(t_1,t_2,p)$ will be replaced by $\Diamond(t_1,t_2,p)$, and $\Diamond\neg\mathtt{TRUE}(t_1,t_2,p)$ by $\Diamond(t_1,t_2,\neg p)$. Also, I will use $\mathtt{TRUE}(t,p)$ to abbreviate $\mathtt{TRUE}(t,t,p)$. Correspondingly, I will use $\Box(t,p)$ and $\Diamond(t,p)$ with the obvious intended meaning.

Semantics. In TK, a *Kripke interpretation* is a set of infinite "parallel" time lines, all sharing the same interpretation of time: a "synchronized" copy of the integers. Each world describes an entire possible course of the universe, and so over the same time interval, but in different worlds, different facts are true.

More formally, we make the following definitions ($\mathcal{N}$ is used to denote the integers with $\leq$). A *Kripke interpretation* is a pair $\langle W,M \rangle$ where W is a nonempty universe of *(possible) worlds*, and M is a meaning function M: $\mathtt{P} \rightarrow 2^{W \times \mathcal{N} \times \mathcal{N}}$. We also require that $\langle w, t_1, t_2 \rangle \in M(\mathtt{p})$ iff $\langle w, t_2, t_1 \rangle \in M(\mathtt{p})$, reflecting the intuition that a pair of time points denotes a single interval.

(The reader familiar with standard modal logics will notice that no accessibility relation is mentioned. The explanation for this is that I will want to assume an S_5 structure (with a fixed interpretation of time across worlds). Therefore the possible worlds form a single equivalence class, and since the set of all worlds can thus be equated with the set of accessible ones, explicit mention of an accessibility relation is unnecessary.)

A *variable assignment* is a function VA: $\mathtt{TV} \rightarrow \mathcal{N}$. Also, we if $\mathtt{u} \in \mathtt{U}$ then define $VAL(\mathtt{u})$ to be $VA(\mathtt{u})$ if $\mathtt{u} \in \mathtt{TV}$, and the standard interpretation of $\mathtt{u}$ if $\mathtt{u} \in \mathtt{TC}$.

A Kripke interpretation $KI = \langle W, M \rangle$ and a world $w \in W$ satisfy a formula φ under the variable assignment VA (written $KI, w \models \varphi[VA]$) under the following conditions.

- $KI, w \models \mathtt{u}_1 \mathtt{=} \mathtt{u}_2[VA]$ iff $VAL(\mathtt{u}_1) = VAL(\mathtt{u}_2)$.
- $KI, w \models \mathtt{u}_1 \preceq \mathtt{u}_2[VA]$ iff $VAL(\mathtt{u}_1) \leq VAL(\mathtt{u}_2)$.
- $KI, w \models \mathtt{TRUE(u_1,u_2,p)}[VA]$ iff $\langle w, VAL(\mathtt{u}_1), VAL(\mathtt{u}_2) \rangle \in M(\mathtt{p})$.
- $KI, w \models (\varphi_1 \wedge \varphi_2)[VA]$ iff $KI, w \models \varphi_1[VA]$ and $KI, w \models \varphi_2[VA]$.
- $KI, w \models (\neg\varphi)[VA]$ iff $KI, w \not\models \varphi[VA]$.
- $KI, w \models (\forall \mathtt{v}\ \varphi)[VA]$ iff $KI, w \models \varphi[VA']$ for all VA' that agree with VA everywhere except possibly on $\mathtt{v}$.
- $KI, w \models \Box\varphi[VA]$ iff $KI, w' \models \varphi[VA]$ for all $w' \in W$.
  (Therefore we will be able to write $KI \models \Box\varphi[VA]$ and $KI \not\models \Box\varphi[VA]$ without fear of ambiguity.)

(The reader familiar with modal logic will note that from the identity of time across worlds follows the validity of the "Barcan formula," $\Box\forall \mathtt{v}\ \varphi \equiv \forall \mathtt{v}\ \Box\varphi$.)

Definition 1

A Kripke interpretation $KI = \langle W, M \rangle$ and a world $w \in W$ are a model for a formula φ (written $KI, w \models \varphi$) if $KI, w \models \varphi[VA]$ for any variable assignment VA. (As in the classical case, it is easy to see that if φ is a sentence, and $KI, w \models \varphi[VA]$ for some *VA, then KI and w are a model for φ.)*

A wff is satisfiable if it has a model, and valid if its negation has no model.

φ_1 entails φ_2 (written $\varphi_1 \models \varphi_2$) iff φ_2 is satisfied by all models of φ_1.

So far the definitions have been ordinary ones of modal logic. Indeed, TK is an ordinary modal logic, except for the special temporal nature of the classical propositional logic on which it is based. We now deviate more significantly from standard constructions by making the logic nonmonotonic.

2.2 CI: a nonmonotonic logic of temporal knowledge

The logic of chronological ignorance (or the logic CI) is a nonmonotonic version of the logic of temporal knowledge TK. As usual, the syntax of the two is identical, and CI is obtained by associating with TK a preference criterion on Kripke structures. We begin with a few preliminary definitions.

Definition 2 *Base wffs are those containing no occurrence of the modal operator.*

Definition 3 *The latest time point (l.t.p) of a base formula is the latest time point mentioned in it (that is, the latest chronologically, not the last syntactically). Formally, it is defined as follows.*

1. *The l.t.p. of* `TRUE(t1,t2,p)` *is the latest (w.r.t. the standard interpretation of time) between* t_1 *and* t_2.

2. *The l.t.p. of $\varphi_1 \wedge \varphi_2$ is the latest between the l.t.p. of φ_1 and the l.t.p. of φ_2.*

3. *The l.t.p. of $\neg\varphi$ is the l.t.p. of φ.*

4. *The l.t.p. of $\forall$v φ is the earliest among the l.t.p.'s of all $\varphi\prime$ which result from substituting in φ a time-point symbol for all free occurrences of* v*, or $-\infty$ if there is no such earliest l.t.p.*

This last case requires some explanation, since one might have intuitively expected "latest" and "∞" rather than "earliest" and "$-\infty$." It turns out, however, that we will be interested in formulas with the *earliest* l.t.p.'s. But $\forall \mathtt{v}\ \varphi$ entails $\varphi\prime$ for any $\varphi\prime$ which result from the above substitution, and hence the definition.

Definition 4 *A Kripke interpretation M_2 is chronologically more ignorant than a Kripke interpretation M_1 (written $M_1 \sqsubset_{ci} M_2$) if there exists a time $\mathtt{t}_0$ such that*

1. *for any base sentence φ whose l.t.p. $\leq \mathtt{t}_0$, if $M_2 \models \Box\varphi$ then also $M_1 \models \Box\varphi$, and*
2. *there exists some base sentence φ whose l.t.p. is $\mathtt{t}_0$ such that $M_1 \models \Box\varphi$ but $M_2 \not\models \Box\varphi$.*

Definition 5 *M is said to be a chronologically maximally ignorant (c.m.i.) model of φ if $M \models_{\sqsubset_{ci}} \varphi$, that is, if $M \models \varphi$ and there is no other $M\prime$ such that $M\prime \models \varphi$ and $M \sqsubset_{ci} M\prime$.*

Definition 6 *The logic of chronological ignorance, CI, is the nonmonotonic logic $TK_{\sqsubset_{ci}}$.*

2.3 The shooting scenario revisited

We now return to the example discussed in the introduction. There is more than one way that the shooting scenario can be represented in the logic of chronological ignorance; I choose the following axioms and axiom schemas for reasons that will become clear soon.

1. `□(1,loaded)`
2. `□(5,fire)`
3. `□(t,loaded) ∧ ◇(t,¬fire) ∧ ◇(t,¬emptied-manually) ⊃ □(t+1,loaded)`,
   for all `t`
4. `□(t,loaded) ∧ □(t,fire) ∧`
   `◇(t,air) ∧`
   `◇(t,firingpin) ∧`
   `...◇ ...other mundane conditions`
   `⊃`
   `□(t+1,noise)`,   for all `t`

Axioms 1 and 2 can be thought of as the *boundary conditions* of the scenario. Axiom schema 3 is a frame axiom propagating the property of the gun being loaded. This axiom really succumbs to the extended-prediction problem. I will later indicate how one can do without it, making a slightly more sophisticated use of the logic. Axiom schema 4 represents "physics," in this case consisting of a single *causal rule.* It says that firing a loaded gun causes a noise, unless certain conditions obtain which "disable" this particular rule.

What do c.m.i. models of this theory look like? There are many different such models, but they have one thing in common: in all of them exactly the same base sentences are known. These are `TRUE(1,loaded)`, `...`, `TRUE(5,loaded)`, `TRUE(5,fire)` `TRUE(6,noise)`, and their tautological consequences — exactly the ones we would have liked.

In fact, this model-theoretic property is no coincidence, and in the next section I identify an entire class of theories that share it. Furthermore, while I have so far said nothing about algorithms for computing valid wffs, I will show that while the general problem of determining the consequences of a theory in CI is very hard, determining the consequences of any theory in this particular class is easy.

3 Causal theories

In the previous section I offered a representation of the shooting scenario whose formal properties were "exactly right": the theory had one class of c.m.i. models, in all of which what is known is precisely what one would expect (the persistence of the gun being loaded, the firing, and the subsequent noise). Shortly I will discuss the intuition behind the construction, but first let me define a class of theories which share the properties of the shooting scenario example.

3.1 Technicalities

Returning to the theory describing the shooting scenario, we notice that it consists of two kinds of statements. The first two axioms had the structure "it is known that this fact is true at this time," that is, knowledge of an atomic sentence. The last two axioms embodied an implication from knowledge of past atomic sentences and ignorance of past atomic sentences to knowledge of future atomic sentences: "if it is known that these facts are true at these times, and it is not known that these other facts are true at these other times, then it is also known that that fact is true at that *later* time." In fact, the first kind of sentence can be viewed as a special case of the second kind, in which the antecedent is identically true. It turns out that *any* theory consisting of sentences which fit this mold has the same attractive model-theoretic property: in all its c.m.i. models the same base sentences are known. In the following definition, Φ will denote the conjunction of those atomic sentences that must be known in order for the prediction to hold (such as the gun being loaded and fired), and Θ will denote the conjunction of the conditions such that prediction depends only on not knowing their negation (such as there being air, the gun being in good working order, and so on).

Definition 7 *A <u>causal theory</u> Ψ is a theory in CI, in which all sentences have the form*

$$\Phi \wedge \Theta \supset \Box\varphi$$

where (in the following, $[\neg]$ means that the negation sign may or may not appear)

1. *φ is a (positive or negative) atomic base sentence,*
2. *Φ is a conjunction of sentences $\Box\varphi_i$, where φ_i is a (positive or negative) atomic base sentence whose l.t.p. $<$ the l.t.p. of φ,*
3. *Θ is a conjunction of sentences $\Diamond\varphi_j$, where φ_j is a (positive or negative) atomic base sentence whose l.t.p. $<$ the l.t.p. of φ,*

4. *Either or both Φ and Θ may be empty (that is, identically true). A sentence in which Φ is empty is called a* <u>*boundary condition*</u>*. Other sentences are called* <u>*causal rules*</u>*.*

5. *There is a time point $t_0 \neq -\infty$ preceding the l.t.p. of the r.h.s. in all boundary conditions (that is, if $\Theta \supset \Box\varphi$ is a boundary condition, then $t_0 <$ the l.t.p. of φ).*

6. *For any p, t_1 and t_2, there do not exist two sentences in Ψ such that one contains $\Diamond(t_1,t_2,p)$ on its l.h.s. and the other contains $\Diamond(t_1,t_2,\neg p)$ in its l.h.s.*

7. *If $\Phi_1 \wedge \Theta_1 \supset \Box(t_1,t_2,p)$ and $\Phi_2 \wedge \Theta_2 \supset \Box(t_1,t_2,\neg p)$ are two sentences in Ψ, then $\Phi_1 \wedge \Theta_1 \wedge \Phi_2 \wedge \Theta_2$ is inconsistent.*

The discussion here will be purely technical. Let me, however, digress for a moment, and in two paragraphs motivate the terms "causal rules" and "boundary conditions." In [3] I propose a new account of the concept of causation. In a nutshell, causation is viewed as implication from knowledge and ignorance about the past and present to knowledge about the future. I suggest that when we say "A causes B" then A and B have the form TRUE(t_1,t_2,[$\neg$]p), and the statement means that we believe in the validity of the implication $\Box A \wedge \Diamond C \supset \Box B$, for some C. Boundary conditions are those items of knowledge that come into being "for no reason," simply because one posits their truth. All other knowledge must be "justified" by causal rules, as it will turn out in the logic.

At this point the structure of causal rules may seem too restrictive, since it prohibits simultaneous or overlapping cause and effect. For example, one cannot say that pushing the box at a time instant (or over a period of time) causes it to move at that time instant (or over that period). In [3] I discuss generalizations that permit simultaneity and overlapping between causes and effects.

Let us now continue with the technical analysis of causal theories, ignoring for now the intuitive motivation behind them. Informally, the properties of causal theories can be summarized as follows. Not only are causal theories are always consistent, but they also have c.m.i. models. In fact, in all c.m.i. models of a given causal theory the same base sentences are known. Furthermore, these known base sentences can be computed efficiently. The basic argument is very simple: since all we have are implications from knowledge and ignorance about the past to knowledge about the future, and since we'd like to know as little as possible for as long as we can, we can always build a c.m.i. model of a causal theory by going forward in time and adding only knowledge that is implied by what is already known and what is not known about the prior times.

More precisely, we have the following results.

Theorem 1

If Ψ is any causal theory, then

1. *Ψ has a c.m.i. model,*

2. *if M_1 and M_2 are both c.m.i. models of Ψ, and φ any base sentence, then $M_1 \models \Box\varphi$ iff $M_2 \models \Box\varphi$, and*

3. *if M is a c.m.i. of Ψ, then the set of known base sentences consists of the tautological consequences of the (positive and negative) known* atomic *base sentences.*

Theorem 2

Let Ψ be a finite causal theory of size n, and let S be the (unique) set of (positive and negative) atomic base sentences that are known in any c.m.i. model of Ψ. Then $|S| \leq n$, and furthermore S can be computed in time $O(n \log n)$.[1]

3.2 Intuition

Let me end this section by abstracting away from technicalities, and discussing the intuition behind causal theories. In [3] I discuss the general intuition behind nonmonotonic logics, calling the principle underlying any nonmonotonic logic *the ostrich principle*, or the *what-you-don't-know-won't-hurt-you* principle. According to it, when we bias the models of our theories in a certain way (here, by preferring chronologically most ignorant models), we do so in order to save computational resources in the long run. To use the standard example from the literature, when we prefer models in which birds can fly to those in which they cannot, we do not have to specify the flying capabilities of most birds; their ability to fly will follow "automatically." The price we pay is when reasoning about "abnormal" birds such as penguins: if we do not specify their (nonexistent) flying capabilities then we will erroneously infer that they can fly (whereas in an ordinary monotonic logic, in the absence of explicit information about it, we would neither infer that they can fly nor that they cannot). When the frequency of flying birds overwhelms the expected danger of making wrong predictions about penguins, we assume that birds fly by default.

The same tradeoff underlies causal theories. For example, the last causal rule in the theory describing the shooting scenario was the formula:

[1] Although this is a vast improvement on the undecidability of the full logic, the reader should note that when calculating the "size" of a theory, one should include all the instances of the axiom schemas contained in it. For example, in the case of Axiom schema 4 of the shooting scenario, we must count 5 instances, corresponding to $t = 1, \ldots 5$.

$$\begin{array}{l} \Box(\texttt{t,loaded}) \wedge \Box(\texttt{t,fire}) \wedge \\ \quad \Diamond(\texttt{t,air}) \wedge \\ \quad \Diamond(\texttt{t,firingpin}) \wedge \\ \quad \ldots\Diamond\ldots\text{other mundane conditions} \\ \quad \supset \\ \quad \Box(\texttt{t+1,noise}), \qquad \text{for all } \texttt{t} \end{array}$$

Consider the conjunct $\Diamond$(t,air). We could replace this expression by $\Box$(t,air), but the result would be slightly different. In the theory as we have it above, we need not say anything about there being air in order to be able to infer that there will be a noise after the firing (since $\Diamond$(t,air) $\equiv$ $\neg\Box$(t,$\neg$air), and we minimize knowledge). On the other hand, if there is *no* air we had better state that fact explicitly in the initial conditions, otherwise we will erroneously conclude that there will be a loud noise. If we changed the $\Diamond$ to a $\Box$, we would be in the exact opposite situation: although we would never conclude that a loud noise took place in a vacuum, we would fail to predict a noise if we neglected to state explicitly that air was present. Which alternative is better depends on a variety of factors, such as what atmospheric conditions are more common, and what is the price we will pay for making wrong predictions. If shooting scenarios rarely take place in a vacuum, as indeed is the case in everyday life, then we are better off sticking with the original theory. One can imagine other circumstances, say of creatures living in outer space, in which it would be more economical to adopt the alternative formulation, since then you would have to explicitly describe the atmospheric conditions only in those rare cases in which air were present.

The explanation just given of the role played by causal rules relied on the principle of minimal knowledge, and thus on the contrapositive reading $\neg\Box$(t,$\neg$p) of the conjunct on the l.h.s. of causal rules ($\neg\Box$(t,$\neg$air) in the particular causal rule used as an example). Another way to understand causal rules is by their relation to "real" rules of lawful change, and this relies on the original form of the causal rules (in the particular example, $\Diamond$(t,air)).

Rules of lawful change are believed to be universally true, and therefore one could expect them to hold in every possible world. Correspondingly, the causal rule under discussion might have been expected to be:

```
□ [
    TRUE(t,loaded) ∧ TRUE(t,fire) ∧
    TRUE(t,air) ∧
    TRUE(t,firingpin) ∧
    ...TRUE ...other mundane conditions
   ⊃
   TRUE(t+1,noise)
   ]
```

As defined, causal rules have a different structure. Indeed, according to the particular causal rule being discussed, there is a possible world in which a loaded a gun is fired in a vacuum, and nevertheless a loud noise follows. Does that mean that the physics embodied in the causal rule is unsound?

The answer is no, and the trick is to make sure that such a world which violates true physics is not the "real world."

Definition 8 *The soundness conditions of a causal theory* Ψ *are the set of sentences* $\Diamond(\mathtt{t_1,t_2,p}) \supset \mathtt{TRUE(t_1,t_2,p)}$ *such that* $\Diamond(\mathtt{t_1,t_2,p})$ *appears on the l.h.s. of some sentence in* Ψ.

Notice that from the restriction on causal theories, namely that there do not exist two sentences in a causal theory such that one contains $\Diamond(\mathtt{t_1,t_2,p})$ on its l.h.s. and the other includes $\Diamond(\mathtt{t_1,t_2,\neg p})$ on its l.h.s., it follows that the soundness conditions introduce no inconsistency into the c.m.i. models.

We now assume that the soundness conditions are implicitly part of the causal theory itself, and are omitted simply for reasons of economy of expression. In our particular example, we get (among other sentences) the sentence $\Diamond(\mathtt{t,air}) \supset \mathtt{TRUE(t,air)}$, which reads "if there exists a world in which `TRUE(t,air)` holds, then `TRUE(t,air)` is true in our world." This means that if we ever use this causal rule, we might be making wrong predictions about *some* possible worlds, but never about the "real" one. This is why "what you don't know won't hurt you": anything potentially harmful is guaranteed to happen in a different world from your own.

4 Discussion

This article has provided one application of the approach to nonmonotonic reasoning proposed in my earlier article in this collection. In the first section I gave a loose description of two problems in temporal reasoning, the qualification problem and the extended-prediction problem. I then proposed a solution to the qualification problem in the form of the logic of chronological ignorance. I also identified a class of theories in that logic, causal theories, which have advantageous properties.

In the discussion here I have had to suppress many issues which are discussed in [3]. First, I have not addressed the extended-prediction problem (or, in its special form, the frame problem). In particular, I needed to supply a "frame axiom" in the theory which was proposed as a solution to the qualification problem in the shooting example (axiom schema 3). It turns out, however, that a slightly more sophisticated use of the logic of chronological ignorance allows us to get rid of this unfortunate axiom (unfortunate, since in a real application most of our axioms would be frame axioms; see in Chapter 1 of [3]). A full discussion of the details would be impossible here, but let me give the intuition behind them. The basic intuitive concept is that of a *potential history*, which is the way part of the world tends to behave in the absence of interference, or the "natural course of events." One then assumes that each such part indeed behaves in this fashion, but that behavior is assumed to cease as soon as it leads to a contradiction. To use the shooting example again, instead of having the boundary condition of the gun being loaded at time $t = 1$, we have as a boundary condition the gun being loaded from $t = 1$ until, potentially, $t = \infty$.

This modification takes us outside the class of causal theories, but the resulting theory still has the "unique"-model and easy computability properties. As it turns out, there is an extension of causal theories, the class of *inertial theories*, which retains these properties, and which includes the modified shooting scenario. For the details, again, the reader is referred to Chapter 5 of [3].

Another issue which I had to sidestep here is my use of terms such as 'causal theories,' which I did not motivate except in passing. I'm sure the reader can by now imagine the gist of my account of the concept of causation. The basic idea is to say that A causes B just in case we believe in the causal rule $\Box A \wedge \Diamond C \supset \Box B$, for some C. In our shooting scenario, for example, we would have by this account that firing a loaded gun causes a loud noise to follow. The details of this proposal, and comparison to the philosophical literature on causation, appear in Chapter 6 of [3].

Although the referenced work provides many more details, there is much more that is yet to be done. More than it has settled existing questions, this work has helped ask new ones. These include questions about the applicability of the results to other models of time (chiefly, that of the reals), about more sophisticated algorithms than the $O(n \log n)$ one I hinted at, and about theories that lie outside the class of inertial (and therefore also causal) theories. Among these the most prominent are theories which call for *explanation*, rather than mere prediction. An example of this is the theory resulting from augmenting the shooting scenario by an assertion that a noise did not take place at time $t = 6$ after all. As it stands right now, the logic will give us an answer that is intuitively wrong.[2]

Finally, there has been much recent work by others on solving the qualification and extended-prediction problems (although I am alone in using the latter term, most researchers sticking to the original 'frame problem,' but understanding it in a general sense). Reviewing this work here would have been hard, given its diverse and fluid nature. Thus I have not discussed nonmonotonic systems similar to mine proposed by V. Lifschitz (this collection) and H. Kautz, nor more radical proposals on so-called *causal minimization* proposed independently by V. Lifschitz and B. Haugh, nor more computation-oriented proposals, such as the ones by M. Ginsberg and D. Smith (this collection), P. Morris, D. Poole, R. Goebel, and R. Kowalski.

The overall situation in this research area, then, is that we have tangible results behind us, and also good hard problems to sink our teeth into. This seems to be a common view, and the areas of temporal reasoning and nonmonotonic reasoning are enjoying unprecedented popularity in AI nowadays. If this trend continues, and especially if it makes contact with other areas such as robotics, we can expect exciting times ahead.

References

[1] S. Hanks and D. V. McDermott. *Temporal Reasoning and Default Logics.* Technical Report YALEU/CSD/RR 430, Yale University, October 1985.

[2] J. M. McCarthy and P. J. Hayes. Some philosophical problems from the standpoint of artificial intelligence. In *Readings in Artificial Intelligence*, pages 431–450, Tioga Publishing Co., Palo Alto, CA, 1981.

[3] Y. Shoham. *Reasoning about Change.* MIT Press, Boston, MA, 1987.

[2] V. Lifschitz and M. Ginsberg pointed this out early on.

FORMAL THEORIES OF ACTION

Vladimir Lifschitz

Computer Science Department
Stanford University
Stanford, CA 94305

ABSTRACT

We apply circumscription to formalizing reasoning about the effects of actions in the framework of the situation calculus. An axiomatic description of causal connections between actions and changes allows us to solve the qualification problem and the frame problem using only simple forms of circumscription. The method is applied to the Hanks—McDermott shooting problem and to a blocks world in which blocks can be moved and painted.

1. Introduction

We consider the problem of formalizing reasoning about action in the framework of the *situation calculus* of McCarthy and Hayes (1969). A *situation* is the complete state of the universe at an instant of time. A *fluent* is a function defined on situations. For instance, in the blocks world, the location of a given block x is a fluent whose values are the possible locations of blocks. In the language of the situation calculus, the value of this fluent at s for a block x is denoted by $location(x, s)$. If s is a situation and a an *action* then $result(a, s)$ stands for the situation that results when the action a is carried out starting in the situation s. Here is a typical situation calculus formula:

$$location(A, result(move(A, Table), S0)) = Table.$$

Formulas of the situation calculus may also contain variables and logical symbols and thus can express general facts about the effects of actions.

We are primarily interested in the form of reasoning which Hanks and McDermott (1986) call "temporal projection": given some description of the current situation, some description of the effects of possible actions, and a sequence of actions to be performed, predict the properties of the world in the resulting situation.

A number of difficulties arise in attempts to describe the effects of actions in the situation calculus and in similar formalisms. One of them, known as the *qualification problem*, is related to the fact that the successful performance of an action may depend on a large number of qualifications. As a consequence, the axiom describing the effect of such an action has to include a long list of assumptions. It is desirable to treat each qualification as a separate fact and describe it by a separate axiom.

Another difficulty is that, in addition to the axioms describing how the properties of the current situation change when an action is performed, we need a large number of axioms listing the properties which are *not* affected by a given action. This is called the *frame problem*. For instance, when a robot is moving a block, appropriate "frame axioms" must guarantee that all the properties of the situation which are not related to the positions of the robot and the block (for instance, the positions of all other objects) remain the same.

John McCarthy proposed approaching the qualification problem and the frame problem using *circumscription* (McCarthy 1980, 1986). We assume that the reader has some familiarity with this concept. (For the definition, see (McCarthy 1986) or (Lifschitz 1985). Here we apply circumscription to many-sorted languages; this generalization is straightforward.) With regard to the qualification problem, the idea is, instead of listing all the qualifications in the antecedent of one axiom, to condition the axiom on the fact that (a certain aspect of) the action is not "abnormal" in the situation in which the action is performed. For instance, the effect of moving a block x to a location l is described in (McCarthy 1986) by

$$\neg ab\ aspect3(x, l, s) \supset location(x, result(move(x, l), s)) = l.$$

For each qualifying condition, a separate axiom postulates that the condition implies the abnormality of this aspect of the action, for instance:

$$\neg clear(top\ x, s) \supset ab\ aspect3(x, l, s).$$

By circumscribing ab, we "minimize abnormality", which should ensure that the action has its expected effect whenever we are not in any of those exceptional situations which, according to the axioms, make the action abnormal.

For the frame problem, similarly, McCarthy proposes an axiom which guarantees that the location of x in the situation $result(a, s)$ is the same as its location in the situation s unless a certain aspect of a is abnormal. Then minimizing ab should allow us to prove that x does not change its position if the action consists of moving a block other than x, or in painting a block, etc., so that all "frame axioms" should become provable.

Further analysis has shown, however, that the result of minimizing abnormality relative to McCarthy's axiom set is not quite as strong as necessary for the successful formalization of the blocks world. The difficulty can be illustrated by the following example (McCarthy 1986). Consider the situations

$$S1 = result(move(A, top\ B), S0)$$

and

$$S2 = result(move(B, top\ A), S1),$$

where $S0$ is a situation with exactly blocks A and B on the table. We expect circumscription to guarantee that the first action, $move(A, top\ B)$, is "normal", so that A is on top of B in situation $S1$. In view of that, the second action is "abnormal" (so that the positions of the blocks in situation $S2$ will be impossible to predict on the basis of McCarthy's axioms). However, if the first move is "abnormal" (for some unspecified reason), the positions of the blocks after the first action may remain unchanged, so that the second move may succeed after all. This observation shows that the intended model of McCarthy's axioms is not the only one in which the extension of ab is minimal. In the intended model, the first action is normal, and the second is not; in the other model, it is the other way around. Using circumscription, we can only prove the common properties of all minimal models; minimizing *ab* will only give a disjunction.

Another example of such an "overweak disjunction", for an even simpler system of actions, is discussed in (Hanks and McDermott 1986). (See also (Hanks and McDermott 1985) and (McDermott 1986), where formulations not based on the situation calculus are given.) There are three possible actions: *load* (a gun), *wait*, and *shoot* (an individual, whose name, according to some accounts, is Fred). Normally, waiting does not cause any changes in the world, but shooting leads to Fred's death, provided, of course, that the gun is loaded. Assume that all three actions are performed, in the given order. An axiom set similar to McCarthy's axioms for the blocks world is shown to have an unintended minimal model, in which the gun mysteriously gets unloaded on the waiting stage, so that the shooting does not kill Fred. In the intended model, *wait* does not change the world, but *shoot* does; in the unintended model, it is the other way around. In either case, *ab* is minimal. Here again, the result of circumscription is too weak.

It is easy to notice that, in both examples, there is a conflict between minimizing abnormality at two instants of time. In the intended model, minimization at the earlier instant is preferred. But circumscription knows nothing about time; it interprets minimality of a predicate as the minimality of its extension relative to set inclusion. This, according to Hanks and McDermott, is the reason why circumscription does not live up to our expectations in application to temporal reasoning: "... the class of models we want our logic to select is not the "minimal models" in the set-inclusion sense of circumscription, but the "chronologically minimal" (a term due to Yoav Shoham): those in which normality assumptions are made in chronological order, from earliest to latest, or, equivalently, those in which abnormality occurs as late as possible" (Hanks and McDermott 1986).

The paper by Hanks and McDermott was presented at the AAAI conference in 1986, and three more talks given at the same conference, (Kautz 1986), (Lifschitz 1986) and (Shoham 1986), met their challenge by formalizing, in somewhat different contexts, the idea of chronological minimization. As could be expected, all of them had to use forms of logical minimization other than circumscription in the sense of (McCarthy 1986).

In this paper we argue that formalizing chronological minimization is not the easiest way to solve the temporal projection problem. We start with another view on the difference between the intended and the unintended models of the axioms for actions: in the intended model, *all changes in the values of fluents are caused by actions*, whereas in other models this is not the case. To express this distinction formally, we add new primitive predicates to the language. With this different choice of primitive concepts, the effects of actions can be characterized by simple axioms in the language of the situation calculus plus traditional circumscription. The axiomatic treatment of causality is the main distinctive feature of our approach.

The method is illustrated by formalizing two examples: the shooting problem and the blocks world. All fluents dealt with in these examples are truth-valued, but the method can be easily extended to fluents of other kinds. Metamathematical theorems are presented demonstrating that the formalizations are consistent and reasonably complete. We also show that the result of circumscription in these applications can be determined by simple syntactic methods, such as predicate completion. This allows us, in each case, to prove the correctness of a natural procedure for determining the effect of a given sequence of actions.

2. The Yale Shooting Problem

To formalize the shooting story from the Hanks—McDermott papers, we use object variables of four sorts: for truth values (v), for actions (a), for situations (s), and for truth-valued fluents (f). The object constants are: truth values *false* and *true*, actions *load*, *wait* and *shoot*, situation $S0$ and fluents *loaded* and *alive*. The binary situation-valued function *result* must have an action term and a situation term as arguments. Finally, there are three predicate constants: $holds(f, s)$ expresses that f is true in the situation s; $causes(a, f, v)$ expresses that a causes the fluent f to take on the value v; $precond(f, a)$ expresses that f is a precondition for the successful execution of a.*

Our axioms for the shooting problem can be classified into three groups. The first group describes the initial situation:

$$holds(alive, S0), \tag{Y1.1}$$

$$\neg holds(loaded, S0). \tag{Y1.2}$$

The second group tells us how the fluents are affected by actions:

$$causes(load, loaded, true), \tag{Y2.1}$$

* Notice that, syntactically, the variables for actions are *object* variables, not function variables, even though each action a has a function associated with it: the situational fluent $s \mapsto result(a, s)$. Similarly, the variables for truth-valued fluents are object variables, not predicate variables. The value of f at s is represented by $holds(f, s)$.

$$causes(shoot, loaded, false), \qquad (Y2.2)$$

$$causes(shoot, alive, false). \qquad (Y2.3)$$

These axioms describe the effects of *successfully performed* actions; they do not say *when* an action can be successful. This information is supplied separately:

$$precond(loaded, shoot). \qquad (Y2.4)$$

The last group consists of two axioms of a more general nature. We use the abbreviations:

$$success(a, s) \equiv \forall f (precond(f, a) \supset holds(f, s)),$$

$$affects(a, f, s) \equiv success(a, s) \wedge \exists v \; causes(a, f, v).$$

One axiom describes how the value of a fluent changes after an action affecting this fluent is carried out:

$$success(a, s) \wedge causes(a, f, v) \supset (holds(f, result(a, s)) \equiv v = true). \qquad (Y3.1)$$

(Recall that v can take on two values here, $true$ and $false$; the equivalence in $Y3.1$ reduces to $holds(f, result(a, s))$ in the first case and to the negation of this formula in the second.) If the fluent is not affected then its value remains the same:

$$\neg affects(a, f, s) \supset (holds(f, result(a, s)) \equiv holds(f, s)). \qquad (Y3.2)$$

This axiom set obviously does not include a number of assumptions that may be essential. The axioms do not tell us, for instance, whether $false$ and $true$ are different from each other and whether there are any truth values other than these two; we do not know whether *load*, *shoot* and *wait* are three different actions, etc. In this preliminary discussion, instead of making all these assumptions explicit, we limit our attention to the *term models* of the axioms, in which every element of the universe is represented by a ground term of the language, and different terms represent different objects. (Such models are also called *Herbrand models* in case of universal theories). We will identify the universe of a term model with the set of ground terms.

It remains to specify how circumscription is used. We circumscribe $causes$ and *precond*, with the remaining predicate *holds* allowed to vary, relative to the conjunction Y of the axioms $Y1.1$—$Y3.2$. This will lead us to the conclusion that $causes$ and *precond* are true only when this is required by the axioms of the second group, $Y2$. The minimization of $causes$ will imply, in view of axiom $Y3.2$, that the only changes taking place in the world are those corresponding to axioms $Y2.1$—$Y2.3$. This solves the frame problem. The minimization of *precond*, in view of the definition of *success*, will imply that the only unsuccessful actions are those in which precondition $Y2.4$ is violated. This solves the qualification problem.

To illustrate this last point, assume for a moment that we would like to make the problem one step closer to the reality of assassination attempts as we know them in our everyday life and take into account that one has to have bullets available in order to load a gun. To introduce this qualification, we would simply add the axiom

$$precond(bulletsavailable, load)$$

to group $Y2$, where *bulletsavailable* is a new fluent. (We may also wish to introduce an initial condition for this fluent and actions affecting its value, such as *stealbullets*, *losebullets*, etc.)

We will show in the next section that there is exactly one term model of the circumscription described, and that in this model the formula

$$holds(alive, result(shoot, result(wait, result(load, S0))))$$

is false.

The main technical difference between this formulation and other attempts to apply circumscription to the situation calculus is that the predicates which we circumscribe, *causes* and *precond*, are *not fluents*, they do not have situation arguments. The predicate *success*, which does have a situation argument, is *defined* in terms of the minimized primitive *precond*. Since the minimized predicates have no situation arguments, the conflict between minimizing in earlier and later instants of time simply cannot arise.

3. The Minimal Model of Y

In this section, by a *model* we understand a term model of Y; a model is *minimal* if it satisfies the result of circumscribing *causes* and *precond* in Y with *holds* allowed to vary. The universe of any model consists of the ground terms of the language of Y, which include:

(i) truth values *false* and *true*,

(ii) actions *load*, *wait* and *shoot*,

(iii) fluents *loaded* and *alive*,

(iv) infinitely many situations, which can be visualized as the nodes of a finitely branching tree:

		$result(load, result(load, S0))$	...
	$result(load, S0)$	$result(wait, result(load, S0))$	...
		$result(shoot, result(load, S0))$	...
		$result(load, result(wait, S0))$	...
$S0$	$result(wait, S0)$	$result(wait, result(wait, S0))$	...
		$result(shoot, result(wait, S0))$	...
		$result(load, result(shoot, S0))$	...
	$result(shoot, S0)$	$result(wait, result(shoot, S0))$	...
		$result(shoot, result(shoot, S0))$	...

We use the letters **v**, **a**, **f**, **s** as metavariables for ground terms of types (i)—(iv), respectively.

A model is defined by interpreting the predicate constants *causes*, *precond* and *holds* on this universe, or, equivalently, by assigning a truth value to each ground atom.

Consider the Boolean function $\mathcal{T}$ defined on the set of ground atoms by the following recursive equations:

$$\begin{aligned}
\mathcal{T}[causes(\mathbf{a},\mathbf{f},\mathbf{v})] = {} & (\mathbf{a} = load \wedge \mathbf{f} = loaded \wedge \mathbf{v} = true) \\
& \vee(\mathbf{a} = shoot \wedge \mathbf{f} = loaded \wedge \mathbf{v} = false) \qquad (1)\\
& \vee(\mathbf{a} = shoot \wedge \mathbf{f} = alive \wedge \mathbf{v} = false),
\end{aligned}$$

$$\mathcal{T}[precond(\mathbf{f},\mathbf{a})] = \mathbf{f} = loaded \wedge \mathbf{a} = shoot, \qquad (2)$$

$$\mathcal{T}[holds(loaded, S0)] = false, \qquad (3)$$

$$\mathcal{T}[holds(alive, S0)] = true, \qquad (4)$$

$$\mathcal{T}[holds(\mathbf{f}, result(\mathbf{a},\mathbf{s}))] = \begin{cases} \mathbf{v}, & \text{if } \mathcal{S}[\mathbf{a},\mathbf{s}] \wedge \mathcal{T}[causes(\mathbf{a},\mathbf{f},\mathbf{v})], \\ \mathcal{T}[holds(\mathbf{f},\mathbf{s})], & \text{otherwise,} \end{cases} \qquad (5)$$

where

$$\mathcal{S}[\mathbf{a},\mathbf{s}] = \bigwedge_{\mathbf{f}:\mathcal{T}[precond(\mathbf{f},\mathbf{a})]} \mathcal{T}[holds(\mathbf{f},\mathbf{s})]. \qquad (6)$$

The correctness of clause (5) follows from the fact that $causes(\mathbf{a},\mathbf{f},\mathbf{v})$ is never satisfied for more than one value of **v**.

Define M_0 as the model in which every ground atom **A** has the truth value $\mathcal{T}[\mathbf{A}]$. It is clear from the definitions of *success* and $\mathcal{S}$ that $\mathcal{S}[\mathbf{a},\mathbf{s}] = true$ if and only if the formula $success(\mathbf{a},\mathbf{s})$ is true in M_0. It is easy to check using this fact that each axiom of Y is indeed true in M_0. Furthermore, axioms $Y2$ show that the extension of each of the predicates *causes* and *precond* in any model is a superset of its extension in M_0. This means that M_0 is minimal, and in any other minimal model *causes* and *precond* are interpreted in the same way as in M_0. It remains to notice that, in view of axioms $Y1$ and $Y3$, equations (3)—(5), which define T on atoms of the form $holds(\mathbf{f}, \mathbf{s})$, are satisfied for any function which computes the truth values of these atoms in some model of Y; consequently, *holds* also has to be interpreted in any minimal model as in M_0. We have proved that M_0 is the only minimal model.

Equations (1)—(5) give an algorithm for evaluating any ground atom in the model M_0.

According to (1) and (2), the predicates *causes* and *prccond* can be described in M_0 by these explicit definitions:

$$\begin{aligned} causes(a,p,f) \equiv\ & (a = load \wedge p = loaded \wedge f = true) \\ & \vee(a = shoot \wedge p = loaded \wedge f = false) \\ & \vee(a = shoot \wedge p = alive \wedge f = false), \\ precond(f,a) \equiv\ & (f = loaded \wedge a = shoot). \end{aligned} \tag{7}$$

These definitions can be obtained by applying the "predicate completion" procedure (Clark 1978) to axioms $Y2$. They can be also characterized as the result of circumscribing the predicates *causes* and *precond* relative to $Y2$. These predicates occur both in $Y2$ and in $Y3$, but we see that axioms $Y3$ can be ignored when the result of circumscription is determined.

Equations (3)—(5) can be interpreted as the description of a deterministic finite automaton $\mathcal{A}$ with 4 internal states, corresponding to all possible combinations of values of the fluents *loaded* and *alive*. The input symbols of $\mathcal{A}$ are *load*, *wait*, *shoot*. Formulas (3) and (4) define the initial state of $\mathcal{A}$ to be $(false, true)$, and (5) defines its transition function. Strings of input symbols are "plans", and the goal condition of a planning problem would define a set of final states. For example, the goal $\neg alive$ corresponds to selecting $(false, false)$ and $(true, false)$ as the final states; the plan *load*, *wait*, *shoot* is accepted by $\mathcal{A}$ with the set of final states defined in this way.

Each state of $\mathcal{A}$ corresponds to a set of situations which are indistinguishable in terms of fluents (iii). The states of $\mathcal{A}$ can be identified with the equivalence classes of the space of situations relative to the relation

$$\bigwedge_{\mathbf{f}} holds(\mathbf{f}, s) \equiv holds(\mathbf{f}, s'),$$

where **f** ranges over the set of fluent constants $\{loaded, alive\}$. These fluents form a "coordinate frame" in the quotient set of the space of situations relative to this equivalence relation.

4. An Alternative Formulation

The formalization of the Yale shooting problem proposed above has two defects. First, we were only able to show that actions lead to the expected results in *term models* of the circumscription, not in arbitrary models. Second, we exploited some special features of the problem that are not present in more complex problems of this kind. Now we will consider an improved, though somewhat less economical, formalization of the shooting story. Here are the main differences between the two versions.

1. Since it is essential in the first solution that, in a term model, different ground terms have different values, we will need some *uniqueness of names* axioms, expressing this property. The following notation will be useful: If $c_1, \ldots, c_n$ are constants of the same type then $U[c_1, \ldots, c_n]$ stands for the set of axioms $c_i \neq c_j$ $(1 \leq i < j \leq n)$. For instance, $U[load, wait, shoot]$ is

$$load \neq wait, \; load \neq shoot, \; wait \neq shoot.$$

2. It is also essential in the first solution that every situation in a term model is "in the future" of the situation $S0$, i.e., is the result of executing a sequence of actions in $S0$.* We see several ways to deal with this problem, all of them, admittedly, somewhat unintuitive. In the new solution we choose to restrict axioms $Y3$ to a subclass of *relevant* situations; we will postulate that $S0$ is relevant and that the result of executing an action in a relevant situation is relevant also.

3. The only precondition in the Yale shooting problem (given by axiom $Y2.4$) is extremely simple: *loaded* is one of the "coordinate fluents" defining the state of the corresponding automaton (see the end of Section 3). Even in the blocks world, we need preconditions of a more complex nature, such as *clear l* and *clear top b* for the action $move(b, l)$, where *clear* is explicitly defined in terms of primitive fluents. Accordingly, in the second solution we explicitly distinguish between fluents in the general sense and primitive fluents. Only a primitive fluent can occur as the second argument of *causes*, but preconditions do not have to be primitive.

---

* This fact was used to define the interpretation of *holds* in M_0 by recursion on the second argument.

4. The value which a causes f to take on may depend on the situation in which a is executed. For instance, toggling a switch may cause its status to change in two different ways, depending on its current status.* Similarly, an assignment statement which has variables in the right-hand side causes the value of the left-hand side to change in different ways depending on the current state of computation. Accordingly, we will allow a truth-valued fluent (not necessarily primitive), rather than a truth value, to be the last argument of *causes*; the value of that fluent in the situation s is the value that f will take on in the situation $result(a, s)$, provided a is successful. The effect of toggling a switch can be described then by an axiom such as

$$causes(toggle, on, not\ on)$$

(*not* is the function which transforms a fluent into its negation), and the effect of an assignment by

$$causes(var := exp, var, exp).$$

In the new formalization of the Yale shooting we have an additional sort of variables, primitive fluents. On the other hand, we do not need variables for truth values any more. Thus the language has variables for actions (a), for situations (s), for truth-valued fluents (f), and for primitive truth-valued fluents (p). This last sort is considered a subtype of fluents, so that a term representing a primitive fluent can be used wherever the syntax requires a fluent. (Accordingly, in a structure for the language the domain of primitive fluents must be a subset of the domain of fluents).

The object constants are the same as in the language of Section 2. As before, *load*, *wait* and *shoot* are action constants and $S0$ a situation constant; *loaded* and *alive* are primitive fluents and *false* and *true* are fluents (intuitively, the identically false fluent and the identically true fluent). The only function constant, *result*, and the predicate constants *holds* and *precond* are used as in the first formulation. The arguments of *causes* must be an action, a primitive fluent and a fluent. In addition, we need the unary predicate *relevant*, whose argument must be a situation term.

The axioms of the first two groups, $Y1$ and $Y2$ (Section 2) are included in the new formulation without change. (It is easy to see that all of them are well-formed formulas of the new language.) The definitions of *success* and *affects* remain the same, except that variables of different sorts are required now in the definition of *affects*:

$$affects(a, p, s) \equiv success(a, s) \land \exists f\ causes(a, p, f).$$

The counterpart of $Y3.1$ is the following *Law of Change:*

$$relevant\ s \land success(a, s) \land causes(a, p, f) \supset (holds(p, result(a, s)) \equiv holds(f, s)). \qquad (LC)$$

* This generalization was suggested by Michael Georgeff.

$Y3.2$ becomes the *Commonsense Law of Inertia:*

$$relevant\ s \wedge \neg affects(a,p,s) \supset (holds(p, result(a,s)) \equiv holds(p,s)). \qquad (LI)$$

In addition, we need a few axioms which have no counterparts in the first version. Let *Act* be the list of actions *load*, *wait*, *shoot*, and let *Fl* be the list of fluents

$$loaded, alive, false, true.$$

We need the following uniqueness of names axioms:

$$U[Act], \qquad (U1)$$

$$U[Fl], \qquad (U2)$$

$$result(a1, s1) = result(a2, s2) \supset a1 = a2 \wedge s1 = s2. \qquad (U3)$$

The formula $loaded \neq alive$, for instance, one of the axioms $U2$, means that there exists a situation in which the fluents *loaded* and *alive* have different values. Alternatively, we can accept the "intensional" view and think that fluent variables range over the "names" of fluents. (Then, of course, it is not true that $\forall s(holds(f1, s) \equiv holds(f2, s))$ implies $f1 = f2$, and indeed we have no such axiom.) The same applies to other axioms in $U2$. Axiom $U3$ represents the assumption that a situation includes a complete description of its history, i.e., uniquely defines what action has led to it and in what situation the action was performed.

We also need to assume that the non-primitive fluent constants

$$false, true$$

denote objects which do not belong to the subdomain of primitive fluents. If this list is denoted by NPF then this assumption can be expressed by

$$p \neq \mathbf{t} \qquad (\mathbf{t} \in NPF). \qquad (U4)$$

The next group of axioms consists of the *fluent definitions* for the non-primitive fluents:

$$holds(true, s), \qquad (FD.true)$$

$$\neg holds(false, s). \qquad (FD.false)$$

Finally, there are 3 axioms for the new predicate *relevant*:

$$relevant\ S0, \qquad (R1)$$

$$relevant\ s \supset relevant\ result(a, s), \tag{R2}$$

$$result(a, s) = S0 \supset \neg relevant\ s. \tag{R3}$$

Axioms $R1$, $R2$ imply

$$relevant\ \mathbf{s} \tag{8}$$

for any situation term **s** without variables.

By Y' we denote the conjunction of the axioms $Y1$, $Y2$, LC, LI, U, FD, R. The predicates *causes* and *precond* are circumscribed now relative to Y', with the remaining predicates *holds* and *relevant* allowed to vary. By a *minimal model* of Y' we understand any model satisfying this circumscription.

Proposition 1. *Y' has minimal models.*

In fact, Y' has many non-isomorphic minimal models. But in all of them the predicates *causes* and *precond* can be characterized by the same explicit definitions (essentially identical to their definitions (7) in the minimal model of Y):

Proposition 2. *Each minimal model of Y' satisfies the conditions*

$$\begin{aligned} causes(a, p, f) \equiv\ & (a = load \wedge p = loaded \wedge f = true) \\ & \vee(a = shoot \wedge p = loaded \wedge f = false) \\ & \vee(a = shoot \wedge p = alive \wedge f = false), \\ precond(f, a) \equiv\ & (f = loaded \wedge a = shoot). \end{aligned} \tag{7'}$$

Let us adapt the definition of $\mathcal{T}$ (Section 3) to the new language in the following way:

$$\begin{aligned} \mathcal{T}[causes(\mathbf{a}, \mathbf{p}, \mathbf{f})] =\ & (\mathbf{a} = load \wedge \mathbf{p} = loaded \wedge \mathbf{f} = true) \\ & \vee (\mathbf{a} = shoot \wedge \mathbf{p} = loaded \wedge \mathbf{f} = false) \\ & \vee (\mathbf{a} = shoot \wedge \mathbf{p} = alive \wedge \mathbf{f} = false), \end{aligned} \tag{1'}$$

$$\mathcal{T}[precond(\mathbf{f}, \mathbf{a})] = \mathbf{f} = loaded \wedge \mathbf{a} = shoot, \tag{2}$$

$$\mathcal{T}[holds(loaded, S0)] = false, \tag{3}$$

$$\mathcal{T}[holds(alive, S0)] = true, \tag{4}$$

$$\mathcal{T}[holds(\mathbf{p}, result(\mathbf{a}, \mathbf{s}))] = \begin{cases} \mathcal{T}[holds(\mathbf{f}, \mathbf{s})], & \text{if } \mathcal{S}[\mathbf{a}, \mathbf{s}], \mathcal{T}[causes(\mathbf{a}, \mathbf{p}, \mathbf{f})], \\ \mathcal{T}[holds(\mathbf{p}, \mathbf{s})], & \text{otherwise}, \end{cases} \tag{8'}$$

$$\mathcal{T}[holds(false, \mathbf{s})] = false, \tag{9}$$

$$\mathcal{T}[holds(true, \mathbf{s})] = true, \tag{10}$$

$$\mathcal{T}[relevant\ \mathbf{s}] = true. \tag{11}$$

Here **p** is a metavariable for the ground terms representing primitive fluents; as before, $\mathcal{S}$ is defined by (6). Notice that equations (3), (4), (8′) define *holds* for the case when the second argument is primitive, and (9), (10) for the opposite case.

Proposition 3. *For any ground atom* **A** *and any minimal model* M *of* Y', *the truth value of* **A** *in* M *is* $T[\mathbf{A}]$.

We see that any ground atom is either true in all minimal models of Y' simultaneously, or false in all of them, so that our "circumscriptive theory" is sufficiently strong to decide any sentence without variables.

Proofs of Propositions 1—3 are given in the appendix.

5. The Blocks World

Now we are ready to consider a slightly larger example: a blocks world in which blocks can be moved and painted, as in (McCarthy 1986). Even though the object domain is now entirely different, the primitive concepts *result*, *holds*, *causes* and *precond* will be used again, and some axioms (notably, the law of change and the law of inertia) will be included in the axiom set for the blocks world in exactly the same form. These axioms represent the general properties of actions which are likely to be useful for constructing axiomatic descriptions of many different object domains.

As before, we have variables for actions (a), for situations (s), for truth-valued fluents (f), and for primitive truth-valued fluents (p), the last sort being again a subtype of fluents. In addition, there are 3 "domain-specific" sorts: blocks (b), locations (l) and colors (c). Object constants: S_0, *true*, *false*, blocks $Block_1$, ..., $Block_N$ (where N is a fixed positive integer), location *Table*, and, finally, colors *Red*, *White* and *Blue*. Here is the list of function constants, along with the sorts of their arguments and values:

top	$(b \to l)$,
at	$(b, l \to p)$,
color	$(b, c \to p)$,
clear	$(l \to f)$,
move	$(b, l \to a)$,
paint	$(b, c \to a)$,
result	$(a, s \to s)$.

The predicate constants are the same as in Section 4: *holds*, *causes*, *precond* and *relevant*.

Notice that in this language actions can be represented by ground terms containing function symbols, such as $move(Block_1, top\ Block_2)$ or $paint(Block_1, Blue)$, and not merely by object constants, as in the Yale shooting problem. Still there are only finitely many ground terms representing actions, so that only finitely many actions have individual names. The same applies to primitive fluents. As a result, we will be able to transform the theory of the blocks world into a description of this world in terms of a finite automaton, as was done for the shooting problem in Section 3.

The first group of axioms contains some general facts about blocks, their locations and colors:

$$b = Block_1 \vee \ldots \vee b = Block_N, \tag{B0.1}$$

$$holds(at(b, l1), s) \wedge holds(at(b, l2), s) \supset l1 = l2, \tag{B0.2}$$

$$holds(color(b, c1), s) \wedge holds(color(b, c2), s) \supset c1 = c2. \tag{B0.3}$$

Initially, all blocks are white and on the table:

$$holds(at(b, Table), S0), \tag{B1.1}$$

$$holds(color(b, White), S0). \tag{B1.2}$$

The effects of actions:

$$causes(move(b, l), at(b, l), true), \tag{B2.1}$$

$$l \neq l1 \supset causes(move(b, l), at(b, l1), false), \tag{B2.2}$$

$$causes(paint(b, c), color(b, c), true), \tag{B2.3}$$

$$c \neq c1 \supset causes(paint(b, c), color(b, c1), false), \tag{B2.4}$$

$$l \neq Table \supset precond(clear\ l, move(b, l)), \tag{B2.5}$$

$$precond(clear\ top\ b, move(b, l)), \tag{B2.6}$$

$$precond(false, move(b, top\ b)). \tag{B2.7}$$

(It is impossible to move a block on its own top). Axioms $B2.2$ and $B2.4$ may seem redundant: we already know from axioms $B0.2$ and $B0.3$ that a block cannot possibly be at two places or have two colors simultaneously. But our method requires that all changes of all primitive fluents caused by an action be described explicitly. It does not solve the "ramification problem" in the sense of (Finger 1986) and (Ginsberg and Smith 1986).*

* This fact was pointed out by Matthew Ginsberg.

The laws of change and inertia LC and LI are formulated as in Y' above. To state the counterparts of the uniqueness of names axioms from Y', we define *Act* and Fl for the blocks world language as follows:

$$Act = (move, paint),$$

$$Fl = (at, color, true, false, clear).$$

Now the list *Act* consists of the symbols for *functions* returning actions, not of object constants, as in Y'. Fl contains both object constants and function constants. We will extend the definition of $U[\ldots]$ to the case when some or all of its arguments are functions. We can treat constants as 0-ary functions and thus define the meaning of $U[f_1, \ldots, f_n]$, where f_1, ..., f_n are functions returning values of the same sort. By definition, this stands for the following set of axioms:

$$f_i x_1 \ldots x_k \neq f_j y_1 \ldots y_l$$

for all $i < j$, and

$$f_i x_1 \ldots x_k = f_i y_1 \ldots y_k \supset (x_1 = y_1 \wedge \ldots x_k = y_k),$$

for all f_i of arity $k > 0$, where x_1, ..., y_1, ... are variables of appropriate sorts. These axioms express that f_1, ..., f_n are injections with disjoint ranges. If each f_i is an object constant then we get the special case defined in Section 4 above. Example: Axiom $U3$ can be written in this notation as $U[result]$.

NPF is defined as the list of terms

$$false,\ true,\ clear\ l.$$

Now axioms $U1$—$U4$ are expressed exactly as in Section 4. In addition, we have 3 domain-specific uniqueness axioms:

$$U[B_1, \ldots, B_N], \qquad (U.block)$$

$$U[Table, top], \qquad (U.location)$$

$$U[Red, White, Blue]. \qquad (U.color).$$

The fluent definitions include, in addition to $FD.true$ and $FD.false$, the definition of $clear$:

$$holds(clear\ l, s) \equiv \forall b \neg holds(at(b, l), s). \qquad (FD.clear)$$

Finally, the axioms R are formulated as in Y'.

By B we denote the conjunction of all these axioms. A *minimal* model of B is a model of the circumscription of *causes* and *precond* relative to B with *holds* and *relevant* allowed to vary. Properties of these models are similar to properties of the minimal models of Y': Every ground atom has the same truth value in all minimal models of B, and the values of the atoms of the form $holds(\mathbf{p}, \mathbf{s})$ can be found by a recursive process describing the work of a deterministic finite automaton. More specifically, we can prove the following counterparts of Propositions 1—3.

Proposition 4. *B has minimal models.*

Proposition 5. *Each minimal model of B satisfies the conditions*

$$\begin{aligned} causes(a,p,f) \equiv \exists b,l,l1,c,c1[&(a = move(b,l) \wedge p = at(b,l) \wedge f = true) \\ &\vee(a = move(b,l) \wedge move(b,l1) \wedge l \neq l1 \wedge f = false) \\ &\vee(a = paint(b,c) \wedge p = color(b,c2) \wedge f = true) \\ &\vee(a = paint(b,c) \wedge move(b,c1) \wedge c \neq c1 \wedge f = false)], \quad (12) \\ precond(f,a) \equiv \exists b,l[a = move(b,l) \wedge (&(f = clear\ l \wedge l \neq Table) \\ &\vee f = clear\ top\ b \\ &\vee (l = top\ b \wedge f = false))]. \end{aligned}$$

Notice that here, as in the Yale shooting problem, the explicit definitions of *causes* and *precond* are obtained simply by applying predicate completion to a subset of axioms (or, equivalently, by circumscribing *causes* and *precond* relative to that subset).

To state the analogue of Proposition 3, we define the operator $\mathcal{T}$ for the blocks world by the equations

$$\mathcal{T}[causes(move(\mathbf{b},\mathbf{l}),\mathbf{p},\mathbf{f})] = \begin{cases} \mathbf{f} = true, & \text{if } \mathbf{p} = at(\mathbf{b},\mathbf{l}), \\ \mathbf{f} = false, & \text{if } \mathbf{p} = at(\mathbf{b},\mathbf{l1}),\ \mathbf{l} \neq \mathbf{l1}, \\ false, & \text{otherwise,} \end{cases} \qquad (13)$$

$$\mathcal{T}[causes(paint(\mathbf{b},\mathbf{c}),\mathbf{p},\mathbf{f})] = \begin{cases} \mathbf{f} = true, & \text{if } \mathbf{p} = color(\mathbf{b},\mathbf{c}), \\ \mathbf{f} = false, & \text{if } \mathbf{p} = color(\mathbf{b},\mathbf{c1}),\ \mathbf{c} \neq \mathbf{c1}, \\ false, & \text{otherwise,} \end{cases} \qquad (14)$$

$$\mathcal{T}[precond(\mathbf{f}, move(\mathbf{b}, \mathbf{l}))] = ((\mathbf{f} = clear\ \mathbf{l} \land \mathbf{l} \neq Table) \lor \mathbf{f} = clear\ top\ \mathbf{b} \lor (\mathbf{l} = top\ \mathbf{b} \land \mathbf{f} = false)), \tag{15}$$

$$\mathcal{T}[precond(\mathbf{f}, paint(\mathbf{b}, \mathbf{c}))] = false, \tag{16}$$

$$\mathcal{T}[holds(at(\mathbf{b}, \mathbf{l}), S0)] = \mathbf{l} = Table, \tag{17}$$

$$\mathcal{T}[holds(color(\mathbf{b}, \mathbf{c}), S0)] = \mathbf{c} = White, \tag{18}$$

$$\mathcal{T}[holds(\mathbf{p}, result(\mathbf{a}, \mathbf{s}))] = \begin{cases} \mathcal{T}[holds(\mathbf{f}, \mathbf{s})], & \text{if } \mathcal{S}[\mathbf{a}, \mathbf{s}], \mathcal{T}[causes(\mathbf{a}, \mathbf{p}, \mathbf{f})], \\ \mathcal{T}[holds(\mathbf{p}, \mathbf{s})], & \text{otherwise,} \end{cases} \tag{8'}$$

$$\mathcal{T}[holds(false, \mathbf{s})] = false, \tag{9}$$

$$\mathcal{T}[holds(true, \mathbf{s})] = true, \tag{10}$$

$$\mathcal{T}[holds(clear\ \mathbf{l}, \mathbf{s})] = \bigwedge_{\mathbf{b}} \neg\mathcal{T}[holds(at(\mathbf{b}, \mathbf{l}), \mathbf{s})], \tag{19}$$

$$\mathcal{T}[relevant\ \mathbf{s}] = true. \tag{11}$$

Proposition 6. *For any ground atom* $\mathbf{A}$ *and any minimal model* M *of* B, *the truth value of* $\mathbf{A}$ *in* M *is* $\mathcal{T}[\mathbf{A}]$.

Proofs of Propositions 4—6 are given in the appendix.

The finite automaton described by the equations for T has N^2+4N input symbols (the ground terms representing actions) and 2^{N^2+4N} states (Boolean vectors whose components correspond to the ground terms representing primitive fluents). In view of the restrictions $B0.2$, $B0.3$, only few of these states are accessible. The accessible states correspond to the equivalence classes of the situation space relative to the relation

$$\bigwedge_{\mathbf{p}} holds(\mathbf{p}, s) \equiv holds(\mathbf{p}, s'),$$

where $\mathbf{p}$ ranges over the ground terms representing primitive fluents.

Appendix. Proofs of Theorems

Proposition 1. *Y' has minimal models.*

Proof. A minimal model M of Y' can be constructed as follows. M is defined as a term model, so it has 4 fluents (*loaded*, *alive*, *false* and *true*), the first 2 of them primitive; actions and situations are the same as in M_0 (Section 3). A ground atom $\mathbf{A}$ is true in M if $\mathcal{T}[\mathbf{A}] = true$, where $\mathcal{T}$ is defined as at the end of Section 4.

In the proof of Proposition 2 we use the following sequence of formulas $F_n(s)$, $n \geq 0$:

$$F_0(s) \equiv s = S_0,$$
$$F_{n+1}(s) \equiv \exists s' a(F_n(s') \wedge s = result(a, s')).$$

$F_n(s)$ expresses that s is the result of executing a sequence of n actions, starting in S_0. Here are some simple properties of these formulas.

Lemma 1. *Y' implies $F_n(s) \supset relevant\ s$.*

Proof: By induction on n, using axioms $R1$ and $R2$.

Lemma 2. *Y' implies $\neg F_n(S_0)$ for $n \neq 0$.*

Proof. Assume $F_n(S_0)$, $n \neq 0$. Take s' and a such that $F_{n-1}(s')$ and $S_0 = result(a, s')$. By Lemma 1, $relevant\ s'$, contrary to axiom $R3$.

Lemma 3. *Y' implies $\neg(F_m(s) \wedge F_n(s))$ for $m \neq n$.*

Proof. We use induction on the smallest of the numbers m, n. Assume for definiteness that $m < n$. If $m = 0$ then the assertion of the lemma follows from Lemma 2. Otherwise take s' and s'' such that

$$F_{m-1}(s'), \quad \exists a(s = result(a, s')), \quad F_{n-1}(s''), \quad \exists a(s = result(a, s'')).$$

Axiom $U3$ implies $s' = s''$, so that $F_{m-1}(s') \wedge F_{n-1}(s')$, contrary to the induction hypothesis.

Proposition 2. *Each minimal model of Y' satisfies the conditions*

$$\begin{aligned} causes(a, p, f) \equiv\ & (a = load \wedge p = loaded \wedge f = true) \\ & \vee(a = shoot \wedge p = loaded \wedge f = false) \\ & \vee(a = shoot \wedge p = alive \wedge f = false), \\ precond(f, a) \equiv\ & (f = loaded \wedge a = shoot). \end{aligned} \tag{7'}$$

Proof. Take a minimal model M of Y'. We will construct a model M^* of Y' which differs from M only by the interpretations of predicate symbols and which satisfies conditions (7′). The interpretations of *causes* and *precond* in M^* are defined by (7′). The extension of *relevant* in M^* is the union of the extensions of all F_n, $n \geq 0$. The value of $holds(f, s)$ in M^* is the same as its value in M unless s satisfies one of the conditions $F_n(s)$, $n > 0$, in which case it is defined by induction on n so that the following be true for all $n > 0$:

$$\begin{aligned} &F_n(s) \wedge s = result(a, s') \\ &\qquad \supset [(success(a, s') \wedge causes(a, p, f) \supset (holds(p, s) \equiv holds(f, s'))) \\ &\qquad \wedge(\neg affects(a, p, s') \supset (holds(p, s) \equiv holds(p, s'))) \\ &\qquad \wedge holds(true, s) \wedge \neg holds(false, s)]. \end{aligned}$$

To check that this condition can be satisfied, notice that

(i) for any given value of s, $F_n(s)$ may be true for only one value of n (Lemma 3),

(ii) $s = result(a, s')$ may be true for only one pair of values a, s' (axiom $U3$),

(iii) this s' satisfies $F_{n-1}(s')$ (the definition of F_n),

(iv) for any given values of a and p, $causes(a, p, f)$ may be true for only one value of f (the definition of *causes* in M^* and axioms $U1$, $U2$),

(v) the last two conjunctive terms do not conflict with the other terms and with each other in view of axioms $U2$ and $U4$.

Let us check that all axioms Y' are true in M^*. $Y1$ and U are true in M^* because they are true in M. The axioms $Y2$ follow from the definitions of *causes* and *precond* in M^*. LC and LI are guaranteed by the definitions of *relevant* and *holds*. To show that the fluent definitions FD are true in M^*, observe that, for the values of s satisfying some $F_n(s)$ $(n > 0)$, the values of $holds(true, s)$ and $holds(false, s)$ are defined in accordance with the fluent definitions, and for other values of s the interpretations of *holds* in M and M^* coincide. $R1$ and $R2$ follow from the definition of *relevant*. $R3$ is true because it is true in M and the extension of *relevant* in M^* is a subset of its extension in M^*.

The construction of M^* is completed. It is clear from axioms $Y2$ and the definitions of *causes* and *precond* in M^* that the extension of each of these two predicates in M^* is a superset of its extension in M. Since M is minimal, it follows that each of the predicates has the same extension is both models. Consequently formulas $(7')$ are true in M.

The next proposition refers to the operator $\mathcal{T}$ defined at the end of Section 4.

Proposition 3. *For any ground atom* $\mathbf{A}$ *and any minimal model* M *of* Y', *the truth value of* $\mathbf{A}$ *in* M *is* $\mathcal{T}[\mathbf{A}]$.

Proof. Consider several cases, depending on which equation in the definition of $\mathcal{T}$ applies. For equations $(4')$ and (5), we use Proposition 2 and axioms $U1$, $U2$; for equations (3) and (4), axioms $Y1$; for (8'), axioms LC and LI; for (9) and (10), axioms FD; for (11), formula (8).

Proposition 4. *B has minimal models.*

Proof. As in the proof of Proposition 1, a minimal term model can be constructed by assigning $\mathcal{T}(\mathbf{A})$ to every ground atom $\mathbf{A}$ as its truth value (with $\mathcal{T}$ defined as at the end of Section 5). Checking axioms $B0.2$ and $B0.3$ requires some additional work. We should verify that for all $\mathbf{b}$, $\mathbf{s}$ there is at most one $\mathbf{l}$ such that $\mathcal{T}[holds(at(\mathbf{b},\mathbf{l})] = true$ and at most one $\mathbf{c}$ such that $\mathcal{T}[holds(color(\mathbf{b},\mathbf{c})] = true$. This can be easily done by induction on $\mathbf{s}$.

Proposition 5. *Each minimal model of B satisfies the conditions*

$$\begin{aligned} causes(a,p,f) \equiv \exists b,l,l1,c,c1[&(a = move(b,l) \wedge p = at(b,l) \wedge f = true) \\ &\vee(a = move(b,l) \wedge move(b,l1) \wedge l \neq l1 \wedge f = false) \\ &\vee(a = paint(b,c) \wedge p = color(b,c2) \wedge f = true) \\ &\vee(a = paint(b,c) \wedge move(b,c1) \wedge c \neq c1 \wedge f = false), \quad (12) \\ precond(f,a) \equiv \exists b,l[a = move(b,l) \wedge ((&f = clear\ l \wedge l \neq Table) \\ &\vee f = clear\ top\ b \\ &\vee (l = top\ b \wedge f = false))]. \end{aligned}$$

Proof. The proof is similar to the proof of Proposition 2. It is clear that the statements and proofs of Lemmas 1—3 can be extended to B. Take a minimal model M of B. We will construct a model M^* of B which differs from M only by the interpretations of predicate symbols and which satisfies conditions (15). The extension of *relevant* in M^* is the union of the extensions of all F_n, $n \geq 0$. The value of $holds(f,s)$ in M^* is the same as its value in M unless s satisfies one of the conditions $F_n(s)$, $n > 0$, in which case it is defined by induction on n so that the following be true for all $n > 0$:

$$\begin{aligned} &F_n(s) \wedge s = result(a,s') \\ &\qquad \supset [(success(a,s') \wedge causes(a,p,f) \supset (holds(p,s) \equiv holds(f,s'))) \\ &\qquad \wedge(\neg affects(a,p,s') \supset (holds(p,s) \equiv holds(p,s'))) \\ &\qquad \wedge holds(true,s) \wedge \neg holds(false,s) \\ &\qquad \wedge(holds(clear\ l,s) \equiv \forall b \neg holds(at(b,l),s)]. \end{aligned}$$

The verification of the correctness of this definition and of the axioms of B is similar to the corresponding part of the proof of Proposition 2, except for the group $B0$, which has no counterpart in Y'. The axiom $B0.1$ is true in M^* because it is true in M, and the same can be said about $B0.2$ and $B0.3$ in the case when s does not satisfy $F_n(s)$ for any $n > 0$. For the values of s satisfying $F_n(s)$, the axioms $B0.2$ and $B0.3$ can be verified by induction on n.

Now it follows, as in the proof of Proposition 2, that the extension of each of the predicates *causes*, *precond* in M^* is the same as its extension in M. Consequently formulas (15) are true in M.

The next proposition refers to the operator $\mathcal{T}$ defined at the end of Section 5.

Proposition 6. *For any ground atom* **A** *and any minimal model* M *of* B, *the truth value of* **A** *in* M *is* $\mathcal{T}[\mathbf{A}]$.

Proof: Similar to the proof of Proposition 3. The axioms $B0.2$, $B0.3$ are required in the cases corresonding to equations (17) and (18), and $B0.1$ is used in the case of equation (19).

Acknowledgements

This paper is an outgrowth of ideas developed by John McCarthy in his research on commonsense and non-monotonic reasoning, and I am grateful for the opportunity to discuss my work with him. I have also benefitted from discussions with David Etherington, Michael Gelfond, Michael Georgeff, Matthew Ginsberg, Robert Givan, Patrick Hayes, Robert Kowalski, Drew McDermott, Nils Nilsson, Donald Perlis, Raymond Reiter and Yoav Shoham. This research was partially supported by DARPA under Contract N0039-82-C-0250.

References

Finger, J., *Exploiting Constraints in Design Synthesis*, PhD thesis, Stanford University, Stanford, CA, 1986.

Ginsberg, M., and Smith, D., *Reasoning About Action I: A Possible World Approach*" (1986), forthcoming.

Hanks, S. and McDermott, D., *Temporal Reasoning and Default Logics*, Technical Report YALEU/CSD/RR#430, Yale University (1985).

Hanks, S. and McDermott, D., Default reasoning, nonmonotonic logics, and the frame problem, *Proc. AAAI-86* **1**, 1986, 328-333.

Kautz, H., The logic of persistence, *Proc. AAAI-86* **1**, 1986, 401-405.

Lifschitz, V., Computing circumscription, *Proc. IJCAI-85* **1**, 1985, 121-127.

Lifschitz, V., Pointwise circumscription: Preliminary report, *Proc. AAAI-86* **1**, 1986, 406-410.

McCarthy, J., Circumscription – a form of non-monotonic reasoning, *Artificial Intelligence* **13** (1980) 27–39.

McCarthy, J., Applications of circumscription to formalizing commonsense knowledge, *Artificial Intelligence* **28** (1986), 89-118.

McCarthy, J. and Hayes, P., Some philosophical problems from the standpoint of artificial intelligence, in: Meltzer, B. and Michie, D. (Eds.), *Machine Intelligence* 4 (Edinburgh University Press, Edinburgh, 1969), 463-502.

McDermott, D., *Critique of Pure Reason*, forthcoming, 1987.

Shoham, Y., Chronological ignorance: Time, nonmonotonicity, necessity and causal theories, *Proc. AAAI-86* **1**, 1986, 389-393.

Reasoning About Action I: A Possible Worlds Approach

Matthew L. Ginsberg
David E. Smith

Department of Computer Science
Stanford University
Stanford, California 94305

Reasoning About Action I: A Possible Worlds Approach

Abstract

Reasoning about change is an important aspect of commonsense reasoning and planning. In this paper we describe an approach to reasoning about change for rich domains where it is not possible to anticipate all situations that might occur. The approach provides a solution to the frame problem, and to the related problem that it is not always reasonable to explicitly specify all of the consequences of actions. The approach involves keeping a single model of the world that is updated when actions are performed. The update procedure involves constructing the nearest world to the current one in which the consequences of the actions under consideration hold. The way we find the nearest world is to construct proofs of the negation of the explicit consequences of the expected action, and to remove a premise in each proof from the current world. Computationally, this construction procedure appears to be tractable for worlds like our own where few things tend to change with each action, or where change is regular.

1 Introduction

1.1 The problem

An important aspect of commonsense reasoning is the ability to reason about change. For example, imagine a robot responsible for various household chores. It must be able to infer that if it moves the lamp, the shade and cord move, too. But when it tries to move the bookcase, with the lamp on top, the cord will come tight, and the lamp will fall off and break. On the other hand, a napkin, or piece of paper on top of the bookcase might flutter off, but probably wouldn't cause any harm. Then too, the robot must know where to find things, like the vacuum, the carpet, the closet, or the bookcase. This requires the ability to infer that furniture and appliances stay in the same place unless specifically moved, and that these objects don't change their shape or color unless someone deliberately modifies them. There are effectively an infinite number of such reasoning situations that a household robot might come up against. It is therefore essential to its function that the robot be able to reason about actions and their effects on the world. Such abilities are also essential in somewhat more specialized domains, such as reasoning about mechanical devices and processes, and reasoning about analog circuits. For these applications a reasoner must be able to infer what will happen when various adjustments or stimuli are applied, or when parts malfunction.

Reasoning about action gives rise to three classical problems. The first is the *frame problem*, recognized and so named by McCarthy and Hayes [23]. The difficulty is that of indicating and inferring all those things that do not change when actions are performed and time passes. For example, when the lamp is moved from the bookcase to the endtable, we need to determine that the vacuum cleaner and the carpet remain stationary, and do not change shape or color.

The second, and closely related problem, is the *ramification problem* (so named by Finger [6]). The difficulty is that it is unreasonable to explicitly record all of the consequences of actions. For example, if we move the bookcase, all of the books inside move along with it. The papers and doilies on top move also. The arrangement of furniture is changed, and certain parts of the carpet become covered or uncovered. Some of the heating ducts and pictures may also be blocked. For any given action there are essentially an infinite number of possible consequences that might occur, depending upon the details of the situation in which the action occurs.

The third problem is called the *qualification problem*, also named by McCarthy [21]. The problem is that the number of preconditions for each action is immense. Imagine all of the things that could prevent the robot from moving the bookcase: it could be too heavy with all of the books in it, it could be too fragile to survive the move, it could be fastened to the floor, the floor where we might want to put it might be too weak to hold it, the door might be too small, the house might catch on fire, or there might be a nuclear war. Computationally, we cannot afford to check all of these unlikely possibilities explicitly.

In this paper we focus on the frame and ramification problems—specifically, our objective is to provide a formal mechanism for reasoning about action that provides 1) an epistemologically convenient way of expressing information about the domain, and 2) a computationally effective means of reasoning about the consequences of actions. In doing so, we will assume that not all of the consequences of actions are explicitly described. We will, however, ignore the qualification problem, assuming that all of the qualifications for the actions being considered are explicitly provided. In [10,12] we show how the same techniques can be used to advantage in solving the qualification problem.

1.2 Classical approaches

1.2.1 The monotonic approach

The earliest proposal for formalizing reasoning about change is due to McCarthy [22, 23]. The approach involves providing explicit axioms for inferring what propositions hold following each possible action. These axioms are of two sorts: 1) *action axioms* indicating the things that change when each action takes place, and 2) *frame axioms* indicating the things that remain unaffected by each action.

As an example, consider a simple move operation for our household robot. If an object, x, and destination, l, are both clear, moving x to l will result in x being at l following the action. Formally, we can express this as:

$$\texttt{clear}(x)_s \wedge \texttt{clear}(l)_s \rightarrow \texttt{on}(x,l)_{\texttt{do}(\texttt{move}(x,l),s)},$$

where the notation p_s means that the proposition p holds in the situation (or at the time) s, and the expression $\texttt{do}(a,s)$ refers to the situation (or time) when the action a is completed.[1]

In addition to this action axiom, we need frame axioms indicating the facts that are unaffected when a move action takes place. For example, we need a frame axiom stating that all other objects don't move. This can be expressed as:

$$\texttt{on}(y,l')_s \wedge y \neq x \rightarrow \texttt{on}(y,l')_{\texttt{do}(\texttt{move}(x,l),s)}.$$

Similarly, we need frame axioms stating that moving does not change the color or shape of objects:

$$\texttt{color}(x,c)_s \rightarrow \texttt{color}(x,c)_{\texttt{do}(\texttt{move}(u,v),s)},$$
$$\texttt{shape}(x,c)_s \rightarrow \texttt{shape}(x,c)_{\texttt{do}(\texttt{move}(u,v),s)},$$

and so forth.

There are two basic problems with the monotonic approach — an epistemological one, and a computational one. The epistemological difficulty is that we must provide explicit frame axioms for every action and every relation of interest, stating under what circumstances facts involving the relation don't change when the action is performed. In general, if there are a different possible actions, and r different relations, on the order of ar frame axioms are required in order to determine which facts persist from one time to the next.[2] To make matters worse, these axioms may be very complex. Witness the case of the on relation for a move operation: If the object being considered is a piece of paper on a bookcase, the paper will stay when the bookcase is moved, but if the object is a lamp, it will stay if the bookcase is not moved far, but will fall off if the lamp is plugged in and the bookcase is moved beyond the reach of the cord. In short, the monotonic approach is cumbersome at best because the set of frame axioms required is large and complex, and must be constantly augmented as additional relations or actions are added.

The second problem with the monotonic approach is that it is computationally intractable if there are many facts in the database. To determine what is true after some action or event has taken place, the reasoner must examine every fact in its world model, and prove that it still holds. If the database contains n facts and each action only changes one fact, $n-1$ deductions will have to be performed for each action or event that takes place.

---

[1] We are being deliberately vague about whether we are using situation calculus, or a temporal logic such as that of Allen [1]. Although the monotonic approach was originally conceived in the situation calculus, the approach is equally applicable to temporal logics.

[2] Yoav Shoham has pointed out that frame axioms are also needed for compound sentences. We are assuming here that the database consists of only atomic facts and their negations.

1.2.2 The default approach

The basic problem with the monotonic approach is that we need to state all of the things that don't change explicitly. What we want to do is provide axioms only for the things that change and write a single *default* axiom stating that everything else persists. There are many different nonmonotonic formalisms that could be used for this purpose [25,20,19,24]. The basic idea in all of these formalizations is to write an axiom stating that facts persist in the absence of information to the contrary. Using Reiter's default rules [25] we could express this as:

$$\frac{p_s : p_{\mathrm{do}(a,s)}}{p_{\mathrm{do}(a,s)}} \tag{1}$$

which states that if p is true in situation (or time) s and p is still consistent after the action a then we can infer p after the action.[3]

The default approach does not suffer from the epistemological difficulties inherent in the monotonic approach because only a single default rule is required, independent of the number of relations and actions appearing in the domain. However, the default approach still suffers from serious computational problems; to determine what is true about the world after an action has been performed, the default frame axiom must be examined once for every fact of interest.

1.2.3 The STRIPS approach

An entirely different approach to reasoning about change is the STRIPS approach [5]. The basic insight in STRIPS is that the world does not change much from one instant to the next. Thus STRIPS keeps a single model of the world that is updated to reflect the result of any action that takes place. The STRIPS approach describes actions in terms of preconditions, add lists and delete lists. The intention is that a given action can be executed if all of its preconditions are satisfied. The result of the execution is to add the facts in the add list to the world description while removing the facts in the delete list.

While this approach provides an effective solution to the frame problem, it cannot handle inferred consequences, and thus fails to solve the ramification problem. All consequences of actions must be explicitly listed in the add and delete lists, and the system designer is responsible for maintaining satisfactory descriptions of the actions. As the domain becomes more complex, this becomes an increasingly difficult task. Consider our robot/furniture example; if the bookcase is moved from one location to another, where it obscures vents or pictures, all of these consequences must be explicitly provided in the add and delete lists. In addition, the absolute locations of the television, bird and birdcage

[3]Hanks and McDermott [14] have pointed out a serious technical difficulty with representing default frame axioms using nonmonotonic formalisms. The basic problem is that these formalisms allow unintended extensions in addition to those one would expect. Much recent work in nonmonotonic logic has been aimed at solving this problem [18,17,15,28]. Although the attempts differ considerably in terms of specifics, the basic default approach remains unchanged. Since this issue is not the primary concern of this paper, we will continue to characterize these approaches in terms of the straightforward default rule given above.

change. If there were a lamp on top, moving the bookcase would cause the cord to tighten, and the lamp would fall off and break. All of these consequences would have to be specified explicitly in the add and delete lists for the action. This makes the descriptions of actions cumbersome and difficult for complex domains. Furthermore, if new facts are ever added to the database, such as the weight on various locations of the floor, all actions that can potentially affect those facts must be updated. This is also a cumbersome task.

These problems with STRIPS are actually a reflection of a more general problem. It is remarked in [7] that the problem of maintaining consistency of a database in the presence of new information is at best semi-decidable. It is therefore not theoretically possible for STRIPS to achieve this consistency maintenance via the simple mechanism of delete lists.

The STRIPS designers were aware of this. They got around the problem by requiring that the knowledge base contain only facts of a very specific nature, essentially guaranteeing through this that their description retains consistency. It is not clear how to maintain the validity of the restrictions on the knowledge base (essentially that it contain only atomic propositions) in more complex domains. Lifschitz [16] has also discussed this issue, and concludes that the approach used in STRIPS is viable when the facts used to describe the world can be guaranteed to be chosen from some predetermined set. Lifschitz calls the sentences in this predetermined set *essential.*

As our example illustrates, this is an increasingly restrictive assumption as the domain becomes more complex. The reason is that our domain information may increasingly be non-atomic (e.g., "all of the books are in the bookcase"), and it will be difficult to specify the form of this information in advance.

1.3 The Possible Worlds Approach

Suppose that we are given an action and a situation. Our approach to reasoning about action is to take the result of the action to be the nearest world to the given one in which the consequences of the action hold. For example, if our robot were considering moving the bookcase from one location to another, the expected result would be the nearest world to the current one in which the bookcase was at its new location. In this world, the bookcase would no longer be at its old location, and everything on or in it would also be at the new location. Furthermore, heating ducts and pictures might be covered in this new world as a result of the new position of the bookcase.

The way we find the nearest world is to construct proofs of the negation of the explicit consequences of the expected action, and remove a premise in each proof from the current world. In the case of the robot, one proof that the bookcase cannot be at its new location is based on the fact that it is at its old location, and that an object cannot be in two places at once. One of these two statements must therefore be removed, and the latter has the status of a *domain constraint* or *protected* law. Another proof that the bookcase cannot be in its new location stems from the fact that the heating duct is not obscured, and the bookcase would obscure it. Therefore the former fact must also go, and so forth. Computationally, this construction procedure appears to be tractable for worlds like our own where very few things tend to change with each action, or where change is regular.

We will refer to the nearest world for an action in a situation as a *possible world*, and will refer to our approach as the possible worlds approach. Formally, this approach is very similar to the default approach; we will show in Section 4 that, given the same set of axioms and domain constraints, the two approaches normally yield the same result. Computationally, however, the approaches differ, in that a clear and effective implementation exists for the possible worlds approach, but not for the default approach.

The computational mechanism used by the possible worlds approach is, in many respects, similar to the STRIPS approach. Like STRIPS, the result of an action is characterized as an update to a single model of the world corresponding to the sentences that are true at the time the action is performed.[4]

However, unlike the STRIPS approach, the possible worlds approach does not require a complete description of the consequences of each action. Instead, the world model is updated inferentially from the explicitly stated consequences of the action, and *domain constraints*. The domain constraints specify the relationships of different things in the world, such as the relationship between one object being on another object, and the locations of the two objects.

1.4 Conventions

Standard first-order predicate calculus will be used throughout this paper to represent sentences about the world. Variables are written in italics; free variables are assumed to be universally quantified. We will also use standard mathematical notation for dealing with sets; the symbol $\subset$ will be used to mean *strict* set inclusion.

For simplicity, we will use the situation calculus throughout the remainder of the paper. As mentioned earlier, the notation p_s will mean that the proposition p holds in the situation s, and the expression $\mathsf{do}(a, s)$ refers to the situation when the action a is completed.

The restriction to situation calculus does not appear to be a fundamental limitation. Historical information or information about the future could still be maintained using a temporal logic such as that of Allen [1]. In such a case, the situation in which an action or event takes place is just considered to be the collection of sentences that hold at the time at which the action or event begins.

1.5 Organization

The following section (Section 2) describes the basic possible world construction. This formalization is also discussed in somewhat greater detail in [7]. Section 3 presents a formalization of actions and of reasoning about actions that naturally incorporates an implicit description of the necessary frame axioms.

[4]Both the STRIPS approach and the possible worlds approach avoid the Hanks-McDermott problem [14], since actions are described by incremental changes to a database as opposed to being described by formulae that are universally quantified over time or situations.

The bulk of the paper (Section 4) consists of comparisons of the computational characteristics of our approach with other approaches to reasoning about action. First, in Section 4.1, we examine the space requirements of the various approaches. In particular we consider the relationship between the number of frame axioms required for the monotonic approach, and the number of domain constraints required for the default and possible worlds approaches. We also consider the space requirements of an equivalent STRIPS add and delete list representation for those cases where it is possible. In Section 4.2 we go on to consider the time requirements of the different approaches, both for investigating a single proposition and for deriving the entire world state resulting from a sequence of n actions. For the monotonic approach, this involves considering the number of frame axioms that must be examined; for the default and possible worlds approaches, this involves considering the number of domain constraints that must be examined.

2 Possible worlds

2.1 Theoretical construction

We first define a *partial world* to be any consistent collection of sentences describing the domain in question. There will in general be many specific sentences that are logically independent of the domain description; these will be left undetermined in the partial world being considered.

Now, suppose that we have some partial world S describing the current situation, and wish to add the facts in some new set C. The problem is that we cannot simply take the union of the two sets, $S \cup C$, because C may be inconsistent with S.

Instead, we will consider consistent subsets of $S \cup C$ that contain C. In considering these subsets, there will also be other facts in S that we want to preserve. Domain constraints often have this property; consider a blocks world fact such as

$$\mathrm{on}(x, y) \land y \neq z \rightarrow \neg\mathrm{on}(x, z), \tag{2}$$

indicating that a block can be in only one place at a time. This constraint can be expected to hold independent of the modifications we might make to our world description. We cater to this formally by supposing that we have identified some set P containing all of those sentences in our language having this "protected" or preferred status.

Definition 2.1 *Given a set S of logical formulae, a set P of protected sentences, and an additional set of formulae C,* a potential world for C in S *is defined to be any subset $T \subseteq S \cup C$ such that:*

1. *$C \subseteq T$. T contains the formulae in C that are explicitly to be added in constructing the new partial world.*

2. $P \cap S \subseteq T$. *Any protected sentence in* S *is preserved when the partial world is constructed.*[5]

3. T *is consistent.*

Note that the "nearness" of a potential world for C in S to the original world S is reflected by how large the subset is. Thus, if T_1 and T_2 are both potential worlds for C in S, and $T_1 \subseteq T_2$, T_2 is at least as close to S as T_1 is. This leads us to define a *nearest potential world* or *possible world* for C in S as any potential world for C in S that is not a subset of any other potential world for C in S.[6]

Definition 2.2 *Given a set* S *of logical formulae, a set* P *of protected sentences, and an additional set of formulae* C, *a* possible world for C in S *is defined to be any subset* $T \subseteq S \cup C$ *such that:*

1. $C \subseteq T$,
2. $P \cap S \subseteq T$,
3. T *is consistent,*
4. T *is maximal subject to these constraints.*

This definition closely follows that of [7] and, as mentioned there, is similar to notions developed by Fagin et. al. [4] in considering the semantics of database updates.

We will denote the collection of all possible worlds for C in S by $W(C, S)$.

2.2 An example

In order to illustrate this construction, let us introduce an example similar to that described in Section 1. The example is shown in Figure 1.

The domain in question contains a table, a chest, a plant, a piece of fine art and a bookcase (which itself contains a bird and a television). Ventilation for the room is provided by a pair of ducts under the floor; if both of these are blocked, the room becomes stuffy. Putting an object on the table will obscure the picture.

[5]It might seem more natural to assume that $P \subseteq S$, so that S already contains all protected formulae, and this is in fact done in [7]. The formulation used here is needed for the treatment of the qualification problem in [10,12].

[6]Note that both potential worlds and possible worlds are only partial. The phrase "possible partial world" seems rather unwieldy, however.

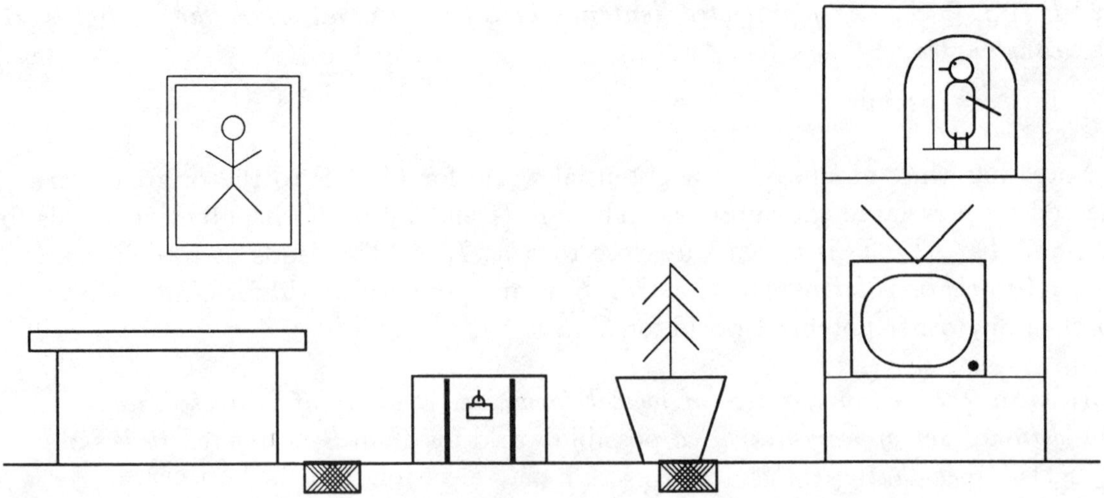

Figure 1: A household domain

Formally, the initial situation shown in the figure can be described as follows (the * and # symbols should be ignored for the moment):

	on(bird,top-shelf)	rounded(bird)
*#	on(tv,bottom-shelf)	rounded(plant)
	on(chest,floor)	
*	on(plant,duct2)	duct(duct1)
	on(bookcase,floor)	duct(duct2) (3)
*	blocked(duct2)	in(bottom-shelf,bookcase)
	¬obscured(picture)	in(top-shelf,bookcase)
#	¬stuffy(room)	

There are also the associated domain constraints:

$$\texttt{on}(x,y) \wedge y \neq z \rightarrow \neg\texttt{on}(x,z) \tag{4}$$
$$\texttt{on}(x,y) \wedge z \neq x \wedge y \neq \texttt{floor} \rightarrow \neg\texttt{on}(z,y) \tag{5}$$
$$\texttt{rounded}(x) \rightarrow \neg\texttt{on}(y,x) \tag{6}$$
$$\texttt{duct}(d) \wedge \exists x.\texttt{on}(x,d) \rightarrow \texttt{blocked}(d) \tag{7}$$
$$\exists x.\texttt{on}(x,\texttt{table}) \leftrightarrow \texttt{obscured(picture)} \tag{8}$$
$$\texttt{blocked(duct1)} \wedge \texttt{blocked(duct2)} \leftrightarrow \texttt{stuffy(room)} \tag{9}$$

The first domain constraint indicates that an object can be in only one place at any given time; the second that two different objects cannot be in the same place. The third indicates that no object can be on top of a rounded object; the bird (more accurately, the bird cage) and the plant both fit this description. Domain constraint (7) indicates that anything on a duct blocks it. The final two domain constraints define the conditions under which the portrait will be obscured or the room will be stuffy.

Assuming that we are not prepared to drop the domain constraints appearing at the end of the above description or any of the "structural" facts appearing on the right hand side of (3), there is a unique possible world corresponding to the new fact `on(tv, chest)`. This possible world corresponds to the removal of the fact indicating that the television is on the bottom shelf of the bookcase. It is necessary to remove this fact since, in light of the domain constraint indicating that an object can be in only one place at any given time, it is inconsistent with the new location of the television.

There is also a unique world corresponding to the television moving to the table. As before, we must remove the fact stating that the television is in the bookcase, but we must also remove the fact that the picture is not obscured. Each of these facts is inconsistent with the new location.

2.3 Automatic generation of possible worlds

One possible implementation of the ideas presented in Section 2.1 involves constructing the possible worlds for a set C by examining proofs of $\neg q$ for the various sentences $q \in C$. Suppose that our theorem prover generates n such proofs $\pi_1, \ldots, \pi_n$, and that these proofs depend upon the (possibly overlapping) sets of unprotected database facts $S_1, \ldots, S_n$ respectively.[7] The intention here is that *all* of the facts in S_i must hold in order for the proof given by π_i to be valid.

To construct a world where the facts in C are consistent, we must remove from our original scenario enough to ensure that each of these proofs of some $\neg q$ now fails. Removing any fact in S_i is enough to invalidate the corresponding proof π_i, so that a subset T of $S \cup C$ with $(P \cap S) \cup C \subseteq T$ will be consistent (in the sense that our theorem prover will not derive inconsistencies from it) if and only if $(S - T) \cap S_i \neq \emptyset$ for each $i \in 1, \ldots, n$. Since non-maximal subsets of $S \cup C$ do not correspond to possible worlds for C in S, we need only select one member from each of the S_i's for deletion from the state description of the possible world, and we have:

Algorithm 2.1 *Let C be as above. Then every possible world for C in S is of the form*

$$S \cup C - \{s_1, \ldots, s_n\} \tag{10}$$

for some choice of $s_1, \ldots, s_n$ with $s_i \in S_i$.

It follows that we can generate all of the possible worlds for C in S by considering each expression of the form (10) and testing it for maximality. Assuming that $|S_1| \cdots |S_n|$ (the

[7] In theory, there will be an infinite number of proofs of the various $\neg q$ if there are any, since one can always add irrelevant steps to any proof. The following algorithms can take the S_i to be the minimal subsets of S from which some $\neg q$ follows.

product of the cardinalities of the various S_i's) is manageably small, this will provide us with an effective means for enumerating these possible worlds.

For most actions in domains of interest to AI, this seems to be a reasonable assumption.[8] Returning to our usual example, suppose that our set C is

$$\{\texttt{on(tv,table)}\}.$$

There are two proofs of ¬on(tv, table). One uses the facts that on(tv, bottom-shelf) and that the television can only be in one place at a time. The other uses the domain fact ¬obscured(picture) together with the domain constraint (8). This gives us:

$$\begin{aligned} S_1 &= \{\texttt{on(tv,bottom-shelf)}\} \\ S_2 &= \{\neg\texttt{obscured(picture)}\} \end{aligned}$$

Each of these sets is of cardinality 1, and we therefore conclude immediately that the unique possible world for on(tv, table) is as described in Section 2.2.

We will assume throughout this paper that the computational effort involved in constructing possible worlds for C in S from proofs of negations of elements of C is small compared to the effort involved in enumerating the proofs themselves. Essentially, this amounts to the assumption that any particular domain fact appears in only a small number of the proofs being considered.

The possibility of modifying the approach we have presented to deal with a situation where this assumption fails is discussed in [7]. The basic idea presented there is to work through the various proofs of $\neg q$ for $q \in C$ in a "breadth-first" fashion, attempting to construct a single possible world for C in S before beginning the construction of another. This has the advantage that the single world so constructed can then be used to eliminate *potential* worlds constructed later that are included in it; further work on these partial worlds is thus avoided. For problems with a great deal of internal correlation (such as the diagnostic problems discussed in [7] and [26]), this appears to be a more satisfactory approach than a straightforward implementation of the ideas presented in this section, with the result that, once again, the time needed to generate the possible worlds is on a par with that needed to enumerate the proofs of the negations of facts in C.

The approach we have outlined instead works "depth-first" through the proofs of the various $\neg q$, constructing the possible worlds for C in parallel [7]. The effect of this will be to generate many *potential* worlds early in the construction process, and this will allow us to obtain lower bounds on the distance to the nearest world for C in S even before all of the proofs of the $\neg q$ have been examined. It is argued in [9] that this has substantial impact on the control of planning search.

2.4 Multiple worlds

Suppose we return to the example in Figure 1, but instead of moving the television onto the chest or the table, we move it to duct 1. Here, there are *two* possible worlds that result.

[8]This need not always be the case, however. Consider the action of starting a nuclear war.

As usual, we must remove the fact giving the original location of the television from both.

Where the two worlds differ is in their handling of the stated domain fact indicating that the room is not stuffy, which is inconsistent with the plant being located on duct 2. One possibility is to simply remove the fact indicating that the room is not stuffy; the two facts that must be removed are those marked with a # in (3).

The other possibility is to remove the fact that duct 2 is blocked by the plant. In order to do this, we must remove the fact that the plant is located on duct 2, resulting in the possible world where the facts marked with an asterisk have been removed.

More precisely we note that there are essentially three proofs of ¬on(tv,duct1). One uses the fact that the television is in the bookcase. Another uses the facts that the room is not stuffy and duct 2 is blocked. The third uses the facts that the room is not stuffy and the plant is on duct 2 (from which it *follows* that duct 2 is blocked):

$$\begin{aligned} S_1 &= \{\texttt{on(tv,bottom-shelf)}\} \\ S_2 &= \{\neg\texttt{stuffy(room)},\texttt{blocked(duct2)}\} \\ S_3 &= \{\neg\texttt{stuffy(room)},\texttt{on(plant,duct2)}\} \end{aligned}$$

This leads us to consider the four potential worlds:

$$\begin{aligned} W_1 &= S \cup C - \{\texttt{on(tv,bottom-shelf)},\neg\texttt{stuffy(room)}\} \\ W_2 &= S \cup C - \{\texttt{on(tv,bottom-shelf)},\neg\texttt{stuffy(room)},\texttt{on(plant,duct2)}\} \\ W_3 &= S \cup C - \{\texttt{on(tv,bottom-shelf)},\texttt{blocked(duct2)},\neg\texttt{stuffy(room)}\} \\ W_4 &= S \cup C - \{\texttt{on(tv,bottom-shelf)},\texttt{blocked(duct2)},\texttt{on(plant,duct2)}\} \end{aligned}$$

The worlds W_2 and W_3 are non-maximal (W_1 is a superset of each) and need not be considered further.

The two remaining worlds, W_1 and W_4, correspond to legitimate but distinct possibilities in light of our limited knowledge of the world. In W_1, the television blocks the duct and the room becomes stuffy; in W_4, the plant is dislodged from duct 2 (presumably because of the power of the ventilation system), and air continues to circulate.

In this particular example, it seems reasonable to assume that moving the television to a position where it blocks duct 1 will cause the room to become stuffy (W_1) rather than one where the plant has moved (W_4). But this is a consequence of facts not recorded in the database: that the plant is heavy, for example. If it were only a piece of paper blocking the second duct, we might well prefer a result where the paper had moved to one where the room became stuffy.

Our formal construction is unable to select between these two possible worlds because neither of them is a subset of the other. This is to be expected: the information in our database is insufficient to determine, in and of itself, which of the two possible worlds will be the consequence of moving the television to duct 1. Resolving the ambiguity will require the introduction of additional information about the television, plant and ventilation system.

There are several ways we might capture this; unfortunately, none of the approaches we are about to suggest is completely satisfactory at this point, and the remainder of this section should be viewed as preliminary.

One approach is to restrict the possible worlds considered as results of the action by incorporating domain-dependent information in the possible worlds construction. We do this by thinking of the subsets of $S \cup C$ as ordered not by set inclusion, but by some other partial order $\leq$ that extends it[9] (so that $T_1 \subseteq T_2 \Rightarrow T_1 \leq T_2$). We now repeat the definition exactly, defining possible worlds to correspond to subsets that are maximal not merely in a set-theoretic sense, but that are maximal with respect to $\leq$ as well.

One possible partial order involves prioritizing the facts in the database in some way, perhaps preferring the removal of facts involving certain predicates over the removal of facts involving others. For example, we might prefer removing facts involving the relation `stuffy` over removing facts involving `on`.

The simplest formalization of this requires that we identify some subset T of our initial world description that contains the preferred facts in S. We now define a partial order on S by saying that $U < V$ if either $U \subset V$ or $U \cap T \subset V \cap T$, so that we attempt not to remove preferred facts from our database. (This partial order is clearly an extension of set inclusion.)

In our living room example, we might take T to be the collection of facts of the form on(x, y). When considering moving the television to duct 1, this leads us to select W_1 in our example, since this world reverses fewer on facts than W_4 does. (W_1 is the world in which the room becomes stuffy.) Unfortunately, it is not clear how to establish a partial order on the facts in a database, or even that a single partial order will suffice for a wide range of actions.

A second approach to the original ambiguity involves the incorporation of reason maintenance information [2,3] into our database, and to then remove any sentence that becomes unsupported when a new possible world is constructed.

As an example, we could record the fact that the room's being not stuffy is a consequence of duct 1's being unblocked. Since the result of moving the television to duct 1 is to block it, `¬stuffy(room)` will become unsupported and will therefore be removed from the database independent of the status of the fact `on(plant,duct2)`. The new database (where the stuffiness of the room is undetermined, but the plant stays where it was) is consistent, and we once again conclude that the room becomes stuffy (since both ducts are blocked).

The advantage of this approach is that it does not depend on the use of domain dependent information (such as an identification of the set of preferred sentences). The disadvantages are that it depends upon more powerful theoretical mechanisms, including some formal understanding of the reason maintenance process. Although progress is being made in this area [8,27], difficult problems remain. It also appears that the simple approach proposed here may remove more facts than necessary in more complex examples.

A final approach resolves the ambiguity between W_1 and W_4 by appealing to a more detailed description of the domain under consideration. In the example we are considering, we might include precise information about the workings of the ventilation system, the

[9] In [7], only partial orders on subsets of S were considered. The advantage of the present scheme is that it allows the partial order to depend upon the set C.

weight of the plant, and basic physical knowledge about air pressure, forces, and so on.

Unfortunately, this sort of a redescription may not always be available, and the computational impact of such an ontological shift is likely to be substantial. This idea is also discussed in [7].

3 Formalizing actions

Suppose that we are given some initial world description S, together with some collection A of actions. Each action $a \in A$ will be defined using a precondition $p(a)$ and a consequence set $C(a)$. Informally, the precondition must hold if the action is to be possible, and the result of the action is to add the facts in $C(a)$ to the world description. We will assume throughout this paper that the precondition $p(a)$ is complete, in the sense that the action can definitely be performed if the precondition is satisfied.[10] The consequence of the action, however, will *not* be assumed complete, since there may be many ramifications of an action in any particular situation. Not all of these need be explicitly included in the consequence set.

Given a world description and an action, we would like to define the result of the action to be the world obtained by adding to the existing description the consequences of the action. The difficulty, of course, is that this world may be inconsistent for a variety of reasons, and we therefore take the result of the action to be the possible world corresponding to its consequences.

Specifically, suppose we are given some world description S and some action a having consequences $C(a)$, and $W(C(a), S)$ is nonempty. We define the *result* of a in S, to be denoted $r(a, S)$, as the intersection of all of the possible worlds for $C(a)$ in S. We adopt this conservative definition in order to ensure that any sentence in $r(a, S)$ is valid in *all* of the possible worlds for $C(a)$ in S.[11] If $W(C(a), S) = \emptyset$, we take $r(a, S) = S$. (We include this for completeness only; an action whose consequences have *no* possible world is effectively impossible.)

It is straightforward to extend this definition to an action *sequence*; if $a_1, \ldots, a_n$ is a sequence of actions, we can define a corresponding sequence of situations recursively by:

$$s_i = \begin{cases} S, & \text{if } i = 0, \\ r(a_i, s_{i-1}), & \text{if } 0 < i \leq n. \end{cases} \tag{11}$$

We will say that a sequence of actions is *viable* if $s_{i-1} \models p(a_i)$ for all $i \in 1, \ldots, n$.

As an example, consider once again the scenario of Figure 1. In this domain, there is a single action $\texttt{move}(x, y)$, which moves the object x to the location y. The preconditions

[10]Generally, of course, actions have a variety of preconditions. All of these can be conjoined to obtain the single formula $p(a)$.

[11]The converse need not hold, since a fact may follow from a disjunction of the facts characterizing the individual worlds. This can be handled by saying that some sentence p is valid after performing an action a whenever p is counterfactually implied by the consequences of the action [7].

for the action are that x and y both be clear (or that x is clear and y is the floor), and that y not be rounded, and the consequence is that x is on y:

$$\begin{aligned} p(\texttt{move}(x,y)) &= \texttt{clear}(x) \wedge [\texttt{clear}(y) \vee y = \texttt{floor}] \wedge \neg\texttt{rounded}(y) \\ C(\texttt{move}(x,y)) &= \{\texttt{on}(x,y)\}. \end{aligned}$$

Consider now the action sequence ⟨move(tv, duct1), move(chest, table)⟩ where we move the television to duct 1 and then move the chest to the table.

We have already discussed the first of these actions in some detail; certainly this action is possible in the initial situation. In the absence of domain-specific information as discussed in Section 2.4, the result of this action will be to remove from the domain description all of the facts that are marked *either* with a * or with a # in the domain description.

Even in the face of our inability to select between the possible worlds describing the consequences of the first action, the precondition to the second remains provable. We therefore conclude that the entire action sequence is viable.

This would not have been the case had the first action been to move the television to the chest. Now, clear(chest) fails in the (unique) possible world obtained by adjoining on(tv, chest) to our initial world description, so that the precondition to the second action fails.

4 Comparison with other approaches

In Section 1.2 we gave brief descriptions of the monotonic approach, the default approach, and the STRIPS approach to reasoning about action. Our objective in this section is to provide a more rigorous comparison of the computational properties of these approaches with those of the possible worlds approach.

We will assume we are given some initial state and some sequence of actions, and are interested in the complexity of 1) determining whether or not some specific formula holds after the actions are executed (for example, the precondition to a hypothetical next action), and 2) in constructing the entire final state reflecting the execution of the action sequence. The symbol α will be used to refer to the number of action types in the domain, and r will be used to refer to the number of relation symbols appearing in the database. For simplicity, we will assume that the database contains only atomic facts and their negations. (Note that neither the default approach nor the possible worlds approach requires this assumption.)

4.1 Space requirements

In order to properly compare the efficiencies of the different approaches, we need to know the relationship between the sets of axioms required for each. We therefore start by considering the relationship between the number of frame axioms required for the monotonic approach and the number of domain constraints required for the default and possible worlds approaches.

4.1.1 Frame axioms

In general, for each relation symbol in our domain and each possible action, we will need one frame axiom, indicating the conditions under which that relation is preserved when the action takes place. We will also generally need a second rule indicating the conditions under which the negation of the relation is preserved when the action takes place. Thus for the on relation and move action we would need the two frame axioms:

$$\begin{aligned} \mathtt{on}(y,l')_s \wedge y \neq x &\rightarrow \mathtt{on}(y,l')_{\mathtt{do}(\mathtt{move}(x,l),s)} \\ \neg\mathtt{on}(y,l')_s \wedge l' \neq l &\rightarrow \neg\mathtt{on}(y,l')_{\mathtt{do}(\mathtt{move}(x,l),s)} \end{aligned}$$

In general, if there are α different possible actions, and r different relations, $2\alpha r$ frame axioms are required in order to determine which facts persist from one time to the next.

It might seem that some of these $2\alpha r$ frame axioms may be unnecessary in certain domains. For example, if we know that an object's being blue persists through a move action, why should we need to know that its being non-red also persists? Of course, the fact that an object can only be one color at a time is a domain constraint; the possibility of replacing a set of frame axioms with a smaller set of domain constraints is the subject of the following section.

4.1.2 Domain Constraints

In order to investigate the relationship between frame axioms and domain constraints, we will take a collection of frame axioms and derive domain constraints from them. The form of the derived domain constraints will enable us to make the comparison.

Suppose, then, that we have some frame axiom stating that if some condition π_+ holds, then q will persist through an action a. In other words, if q holds in s and the preconditions to a hold in s, then $\pi_+ \rightarrow q_{\mathtt{do}(a,s)}$:

$$q_s \wedge p(a)_s \rightarrow [\pi_+ \rightarrow q_{\mathtt{do}(a,s)}].$$

We assume in addition that π_+ is a minimal persistence requirement, so that q persists *only* if π_+ holds. This allows us to strengthen the above expression to:

$$q_s \wedge p(a)_s \rightarrow [\pi_+ \leftrightarrow q_{\mathtt{do}(a,s)}]. \tag{12}$$

Related to the persistence of q is the persistence of $\neg q$, and we assume that π_- is a persistence condition for it (we only need to examine persistence conditions for q and $\neg q$ because of our assumption that the database consists entirely of atomic facts and negations of atomic facts):

$$\neg q_s \wedge p(a)_s \wedge \pi_- \rightarrow \neg q_{\mathtt{do}(a,s)}. \tag{13}$$

Note that we do not need to require π_- to be minimal.

We will call any π_+ satisfying (12) a *positive persistence condition* for q and a, and any π_- satisfying (13) a *negative persistence condition* for q and a.[12]

If we denote by $c(a)$ an arbitrary element of the consequence set $C(a)$, we now have the following:

Theorem 4.1 *Let π_+ and π_- be positive and negative persistence conditions for q and a, and set $\lambda = \neg\pi_+ \wedge \pi_-$. Then if $p(a)$ is a negative persistence condition for λ,*

$$p(a)_s \rightarrow [\lambda \wedge c(a) \rightarrow \neg q]_{\mathsf{do}(a,s)}. \tag{14}$$

Proof. We first show that

$$p(a)_s \wedge \lambda_s \rightarrow [c(a) \wedge \neg q]_{\mathsf{do}(a,s)}. \tag{15}$$

It is clear that

$$p(a)_s \rightarrow c(a)_{\mathsf{do}(a,s)}.$$

With regard to q, we note that if $\neg q$ holds before the action a, it will hold afterwards by virtue of λ's implying the negative persistence condition π_-. Alternatively, if q holds before the action, $\neg q$ will once again hold afterwards due to the failure of the positive persistence condition π_+, together with (12).

We rewrite (15) as

$$p(a)_s \rightarrow [\lambda_s \rightarrow (c(a) \wedge \neg q)_{\mathsf{do}(a,s)}]. \tag{16}$$

If $p(a)$ is a negative persistence condition for λ, we have from (13) that

$$\neg\lambda_s \wedge p(a)_s \rightarrow \neg\lambda_{\mathsf{do}(a,s)},$$

or

$$p(a)_s \rightarrow [\lambda_{\mathsf{do}(a,s)} \rightarrow \lambda_s].$$

Combining this with (16) gives us

$$p(a)_s \rightarrow \{[\lambda_{\mathsf{do}(a,s)} \rightarrow \lambda_s] \wedge [\lambda_s \rightarrow (c(a) \wedge \neg q)_{\mathsf{do}(a,s)}]\},$$

so that

$$p(a)_s \rightarrow [\lambda \rightarrow (c(a) \wedge \neg q)]_{\mathsf{do}(a,s)}, \tag{17}$$

or

$$p(a)_s \rightarrow [\lambda \wedge c(a) \rightarrow \neg q]_{\mathsf{do}(a,s)}. \quad \square \tag{18}$$

Given this result, it seems appropriate to treat

$$\lambda \wedge c(a) \rightarrow \neg q$$

[12] Because of the bidirectional implication appearing in (12), it follows that a positive persistence condition for q is a negative persistence condition for $\neg q$, but not necessarily vice versa. In actuality, it is only the reverse arrow in (12) that we need, and Theorem 4.1 could be strengthened to reflect this.

as a domain constraint for the domain in question, since this constraint holds in any state that can be reached by performing the action a.[13]

As an example, consider a simple blocks world situation where $q = \mathtt{on}(x, y)$ is the domain fact, and $a = \mathtt{move}(u, v)$ is the action. The frame axiom is given by:

$$\mathtt{on}(x, y)_s \wedge u \neq x \rightarrow \mathtt{on}(x, y)_{\mathtt{do}(\mathtt{move}(u,v),s)},$$

so the positive persistence condition π_+ is $u \neq x$.

A negative persistence condition must satisfy

$$\neg\mathtt{on}(x, y)_s \wedge \pi_- \rightarrow \neg\mathtt{on}(x, y)_{\mathtt{do}(\mathtt{move}(u,v),s)}.$$

Since

$$\neg\mathtt{on}(x, y)_s \wedge v \neq y \rightarrow \neg\mathtt{on}(x, y)_{\mathtt{do}(\mathtt{move}(u,v),s)},$$

we take $\pi_- = v \neq y$. Setting $\lambda = (v \neq y \wedge u = x)$, the calculated domain constraint is:

$$v \neq y \wedge u = x \wedge \mathtt{on}(u, v) \rightarrow \neg\mathtt{on}(x, y),$$

which we rewrite as:

$$v \neq y \wedge \mathtt{on}(x, v) \rightarrow \neg\mathtt{on}(x, y).$$

This is precisely the usual constraint indicating that a block can be in only one place at a time.

If our persistence conditions are such that some quality *always* persists through a certain action type (as with `color` and `shape` for the `move` operation), an examination of (12) makes it clear that we can take π_+ to be $\pi_+ = t$ (truth). Then we obtain $\lambda = f$, and the associated domain constraint, $\lambda \wedge c(a) \rightarrow \neg q$, will be vacuous.

Here is another example, where λ is in fact state-dependent: Again in a blocks world domain, suppose that if we move a blue block onto another blue block, the block being moved changes color. Thus, blueness persists if and only if either the block being considered is not the one being moved, or if the target block is itself non-blue:

$$\mathtt{blue}(x)_s \rightarrow [\mathtt{blue}(x)_{\mathtt{do}(\mathtt{move}(u,v),s)} \leftrightarrow x \neq u \vee \neg\mathtt{blue}(v)].$$

We see from this that we can take the positive persistence condition π_+ to be $x \neq u \vee \neg\mathtt{blue}(v)$. Since non-blueness persists through any motion, we take π_- to be t, so that $\lambda = [x = u \wedge \mathtt{blue}(v)]$.

To see that $\neg\lambda$ persists, we must check that

$$x \neq u \vee \neg\mathtt{blue}(v)_s \rightarrow x \neq u \vee \neg\mathtt{blue}(v)_{\mathtt{do}(\mathtt{move}(u,v),s)},$$

or that

$$\neg\mathtt{blue}(v)_s \rightarrow \neg\mathtt{blue}(v)_{\mathtt{do}(\mathtt{move}(u,v),s)}.$$

[13] It was in order to treat the result in this fashion that we moved $c(a)$ to the premise of the implication, taking the result of the theorem to be (18) rather than the stronger (17).

Since non-blueness always persists, we conclude that

$$x = u \wedge \texttt{blue}(v) \wedge \texttt{on}(u, v) \rightarrow \neg\texttt{blue}(x)$$

holds after moving u to v. The associated domain constraint is:

$$\texttt{blue}(v) \wedge \texttt{on}(u, v) \rightarrow \neg\texttt{blue}(u), \tag{19}$$

indicating that one blue block cannot be on top of another.

This example is one in which the domain constraint posited as a result of an expression such as that in (14) may *not* be valid for the domain in question. We might, for example, be working in a domain where one blue block could be (initially) on top of another, but we are incapable of *moving* a blue block onto another.

This can be captured by adding to the consequences of the move operator a marker of the form $\texttt{moved}(u, v)$, indicating that u has been moved to v. Having done this, (19) becomes:

$$\texttt{blue}(v) \wedge \texttt{moved}(u, v) \wedge \texttt{on}(u, v) \rightarrow \neg\texttt{blue}(u),$$

capturing exactly the fact that blue blocks cannot be moved to other blue blocks. In general, similar dummy consequences can be introduced to enable domain constraints to adequately describe any set of positive and negative persistence conditions. This guarantees the epistemological adequacy of using domain constraints.

We will call a domain *persistence-constrained* if all of the domain constraints can be obtained from the frame axioms without having to insert an additional clause like $\texttt{moved}(u, v)$. In general, if there are $2ar$ frame axioms these will lead to at most ar domain constraints. However, this is far too conservative for a persistence-constrained domain with many relation and action types. In this case we can expect many relations to persist through many of the actions, and the result will be that the number of domain constraints will frequently be much smaller than the number of frame axioms. It also seems likely that many of the frame axioms in large domains will generate identical domain constraints, further decreasing the number of domain constraints relative to the number of frame axioms.

Theorem 4.2 *In a persistence-constrained domain having $2ar$ frame axioms the number of domain constraints is κar, where κ is generally much less than one for large domains.* □

4.1.3 Explicit consequences

In Section 1.2 we remarked on the fact that the STRIPS, or *explicit consequences* approach is not epistemologically adequate for general reasoning about action where non-atomic facts are allowed. However, this is not a concern for many applications. Assuming that we can represent all of the effects of every action explicitly using STRIPS add and delete lists, what is the complexity of the resulting descriptions for a domain having κar domain constraints?

To derive this we consider a single action that, in the possible worlds formulation, adds a single consequence c to the database. On the average, there will be $\kappa\alpha$ domain constraints involving the relation symbol appearing in c, and the validity of any subset of these may require the deletion of some domain fact when the action is executed.

In order to handle the fact that the delete list for some action may vary depending upon the circumstances in which the action is executed, we will need to split the original action into a variety of special cases, specifying preconditions, add lists and delete lists for each. Since there are potentially $2^{\kappa\alpha}$ distinct action subtypes, we get

Theorem 4.3 *The space required to describe a domain containing $\kappa\alpha r$ domain constraints using explicit consequences may grow as rapidly as $\alpha 2^{\kappa\alpha}$.* □

As an example of this, consider the `move` operator in the example we have been considering. STRIPS will certainly need to distinguish among situations where the target of the motion is the table (blocking the picture), where it is a duct (potentially making the room stuffy) and where it is a location of another type.

Given that the target of the motion is one of the two ducts, STRIPS must also distinguish between situations where the other duct is blocked (so that the room does indeed become stuffy) and where the other duct is not blocked. But even this is insufficient, since moving an object from one duct to the other will not make the room stuffy. Additionally, we need to consider the possibility that the location we are moving *from* is either the table (making the picture visible) or a duct (clearing the room).

The following table summarizes the possibilities. We have described the possible motions in terms of their starting and ending locations, with "other" indicating a location which is not the table or a duct. Motions to a duct also indicate whether the other duct is clear or blocked. We also indicate which of the four potential database facts needs to be deleted (in addition, of course, to deleting the fact giving the object's initial location).

	Deleted fact(s)			
Motion type	obscured	¬obscured	stuffy	¬stuffy
other–other				
other–table		x		
other–duct (clear)				
other–duct (blocked)				x
table–other	x			
table–duct (clear)	x			
table–duct (blocked)	x			x
duct–other			x	
duct–table		x	x	
duct–duct				

Instead of a single move operator, we have eleven. Since there are only seven distinct possibilities for the delete lists, it is possible to reduce this to a set of seven move operators;

the preconditions to each will be fairly complex, as they will need to determine which of the eleven cases above applies for any particular motion.

The example with which we have been working is fairly simple, but seems typical of the exponential difficulties that will be suffered by any approach that must explicitly list all consequences of all actions.

4.2 Time

Using the information about space requirements derived in the previous sections, we can now consider the time complexity of the various approaches.

4.2.1 The monotonic approach

Let us suppose that in order to investigate some proposition q after performing an action, we need to examine an average of l domain facts to determine whether or not they held before the action was executed. Determining the color of a block after moving it, for example, involves simply discovering its color before the motion, so that $l = 1$ in this case.

To investigate q after a sequence of n actions, we will therefore need to examine l database facts after $n - 1$ actions, l^2 after $n - 2$ actions, and so on.

There will, of course, be some overlap among the many facts investigated at early times, and it will be effective to cache these facts as we consider them. In general, if we suppose that we are working in a domain containing d facts in the state description, a random collection of x of these facts (possibly with repetition) will involve, on average,

$$d\left[1 - \left(1 - \frac{1}{d}\right)^x\right]$$

distinct domain facts. (A proof of this can be found in the appendix.) The time spent investigating q will be spent investigating each of these domain facts at various times; if t is the time required to investigate each of them, the total time required will be:

$$\sum_{i=1}^{n} t\left\{d\left[1 - \left(1 - \frac{1}{d}\right)^{(l^i)}\right]\right\}.$$

A Taylor expansion of this result leads to:

Lemma 4.4 *The time taken to investigate the query q after a sequence of n actions in the monotonic approach is approximately given by:*

$$t(q) = \begin{cases} td(n-1), & \text{if } l^n \gg d, \\ \frac{tl(l^n-1)}{l-1}, & \text{if } l^n \ll d. \end{cases} \tag{20}$$

If we are constructing the entire final state, we should clearly cache all of the intermediate results. This gives us the following:

Theorem 4.5 *In a domain described by a large number d of domain facts, the time needed to investigate the validity of a single proposition q after a sequence of n actions is*

$$\frac{tl(l^n - 1)}{l - 1},$$

where t and l are as described above. The time needed to construct the entire state resulting from the action sequence is

$$ntd. \quad \square$$

4.2.2 The possible worlds approach

The possible worlds approach is somewhat simpler to analyze. Suppose that the result of an action is to add x new facts $q_1, \ldots, q_x$ to the database, that r_i is the relation symbol appearing in q_i, and that there are $c(r_i)$ domain constraints involving r_i. The possible worlds construction requires that we investigate the $c(r_i)$ domain constraints for each consequence q_i to determine whether or not they lead to proofs of $\neg q_i$. If it takes time t' to examine each domain constraint, the total time spent will therefore be approximately $\sum_1^x t'c(r_i)$.[14] Assuming that the constraints are distributed uniformly among the relation symbols, the time spent constructing the state corresponding to the consequences of the action will be $xt'c/r$, where c is the number of constraints on the domain in its entirety, and r is the number of relation symbols.

Lemma 4.6 *The time spent analyzing a sequence of n actions using the possible worlds approach is given by*

$$\frac{nxt'c}{r}. \quad \square$$

Note that this result is independent of whether we are interested in only a single proposition q, or are interested in constructing the entire state resulting from the action sequence. This is because there is a basic computational difference between the monotonic approach and the possible worlds approach. The possible worlds approach proceeds by constructing the final state *in its entirety*, while the monotonic approach work by considering the validity of specific formulae in the final state. (We will see in Section 4.2.3 that similar remarks hold for the default approach.)

We will assume that the time t' needed to investigate each domain constraint is comparable to the sum of the time t needed to examine a persistence condition such as π_+ and the time t_c needed to examine a consequence $c(a)$ of the (now hypothetical) action a. Using this, together with the result from Theorem 4.2 that $c = \kappa\alpha r$ we get:

[14] Note that if several domain constraints appear in some proof, t' will become larger. This has an analog in the monotonic approach, where it may be necessary to derive information about some domain fact instead of simply looking for the fact in the database. This would be reflected in an increase of the t appearing in Theorem 4.5.

Theorem 4.7 *In a persistence-constrained domain, the time spent analyzing a sequence of n actions using the possible worlds approach is given by*

$$\kappa n x(t + t_c)\alpha. \quad \square \tag{21}$$

The relative magnitudes of t and t_c may vary depending upon the fashion in which the domain is being described. In most monotonic approaches, for example, t will be fairly small, since little inference needs to be done in order to determine if some specific domain fact or persistence condition holds. In the absence of substantial interaction or "chaining" between the derived domain constraints, we can expect t_c to be comparably small, but this need not always be the case.

4.2.3 The default approach

In [25], Reiter gives a proof procedure for default logics. Defining PREREQUISITES and CONSEQUENCES in the obvious fashion for a collection of default rules and denoting by W the facts known to hold in the default theory, he notes that a formula β will be a member of *some* extension of the default theory if we can find

> ... a subset D_0 of the defaults such that $W \cup \texttt{CONSEQUENCES}(D_0) \vdash \beta$. For $i \geq 1$, if D_{i-1} has been determined, then determine a subset D_i of the defaults such that $W \cup \texttt{CONSEQUENCES}(D_i) \vdash \texttt{PREREQUISITES}(D_{i-1})$. If, for some k, $W \vdash \texttt{PREREQUISITES}(D_{k-1})$ and if $W \cup_{i=0}^{k-1} \texttt{CONSEQUENCES}(D_i)$ is satisfiable, then a proof of β has been found.

Even in the best case where $k = 1$, we will have to investigate the satisfiability of $W \cup \texttt{CONSEQUENCES}(D_0)$. Since β is entailed by D_0, this can be no easier than investigating the satisfiability of $W \cup \{\beta\}$.

Any practical implementation will assume W itself to be consistent, so that the satisfiability of $W \cup \{\beta\}$ can be determined simply by attempting to prove $\neg\beta$ from W. This will involve investigating each of the c/r domain constraints; if the time needed to investigate each is comparable to the time t' needed to investigate a single domain constraint in the possible worlds approach, we conclude that it will take time $\frac{t'c}{r}$ to examine all of them. Substituting $t' = t + t_c$ and $c = \kappa\alpha r$, we obtain:

Theorem 4.8 *The time spent analyzing a sequence of n actions using the default approach is as given by Theorem 4.5, with t replaced with*

$$(t + t_c)\kappa\alpha. \quad \square$$

We should also remark at this point that there are instances where the default and possible worlds approaches will generate different situations corresponding to the results of some specific action. In order to make this point precise, we need the following result:

Theorem 4.9 *Let S be some collection of sentences, and P the protected sentences in our language. Now consider a default theory in which the default rules are given by*

$$\frac{: w}{w}$$

for each $w \in S - P$, so that w holds in the absence of information proving it false. The facts in the default theory consist of q, together with the sentences in P.

The possible worlds for q in S are in natural correspondence with the extensions of the above default theory.

A proof of this result can be found in [7].

This correspondence is also discussed in [26]; Reiter goes on to show how it is possible to capture some sorts of domain-dependent information in this framework, although it does not appear that possible worlds generated using arbitrary partial orders will always correspond naturally to results obtained using some default theory.

It follows from Theorem 4.9 that if there is a *unique* possible world corresponding to the consequences of an action, a statement will be true in that possible world if and only if it follows from the default rule given by (1). But if there are multiple extensions or possible worlds (corresponding perhaps to an action such as `move(tv,duct1)` whose consequences are only partially known), the proof procedure given by Reiter will accept any statement that is true in *any* of these possible worlds, while the construction we have given, based as it is upon the intersection of the possible worlds, will require a potential plan to achieve its goal for *any* of the possible outcomes of the action or actions in question. In realistic planning situations, this seems likely to be the more effective approach, since it requires the planning agent to consider all possible outcomes of his actions, as opposed to hoping optimistically that they will result in his achieving his goal. Unfortunately, Reiter gives no method for determining whether or not a formula holds in every extension of a default theory.

4.2.4 STRIPS

Because STRIPS modifies its database directly using add and delete lists, the principal computational cost involved in this approach is simply that of finding which of the $\alpha 2^{\kappa\alpha}$ possible add and delete lists should be used when a particular action is executed. Locating any particular add and delete list will take time at best logarithmic in the number of possibilities, so we can expect the time taken by the STRIPS approach to be on the order of $t\kappa\alpha$ (the t appears as an approximation to the time needed to determine if some particular add-delete pair is appropriate in any given situation). Analyzing a sequence of n actions can therefore be expected to take time $nt\kappa\alpha$.

4.3 Comparisons

We can summarize the results of the previous sections in the following:

Theorem 4.10 *In a persistence-constrained domain with α action types, r relations, and a large number d of domain facts, the space and time required by the various approaches is:*

	possible worlds	monotonic	default	STRIPS
space	$\kappa\alpha r$	$2\alpha r$	$\kappa\alpha r$	$\alpha 2^{\kappa\alpha}$
time				
single query	$nx(t+t_c)\kappa\alpha$	$\frac{tl(l^n-1)}{l-1}$	$\frac{(t+t_c)\kappa\alpha l(l^n-1)}{l-1}$	$nt\kappa\alpha$
entire state	$nx(t+t_c)\kappa\alpha$	ntd	$n(t+t_c)\kappa\alpha d$	$nt\kappa\alpha$

One can expect x, t, t_c, l and α to all be approximately independent of the size of the domain being investigated. If we assume additionally that $d \gg x$ (few facts change with each action), and that κ is sufficiently small that $d \gg \kappa\alpha x$ as well, we can conclude that the possible worlds approach will be more efficient than the monotonic approach when either:

1. $l > 1$ and n is large, or

2. The entire final state needs to be constructed.

The first condition corresponds to a case where a great many facts need to be investigated at early times in order to determine the validity of even a single one at a later time.

If $x = 1$, so that each action has a single consequence, some simple algebraic manipulation shows that the possible worlds approach is uniformly more efficient than the default one. Informally, the reason for this is that both the default approach and the possible worlds approach involve a complete search through the proof tree for some proposition. In the default case, the proposition being considered is the negation of the consequence of the default rule; a complete search is necessary because the default rule is generally valid. In the possible worlds approach, we must explicitly examine all proofs of the negations of the consequences of the action being considered. These tasks are of comparable computational complexity; the difference between the approaches is that the possible worlds approach requires only x such proof attempts, while the default approach will in general require many.

Finally, we see that the STRIPS approach is exponentially expensive in terms of the space used to describe a particular domain; although this approach needs less time than the others to evaluate the results of any particular action, the times needed by the STRIPS and possible worlds approaches are roughly comparable. (This is true even though the activities performed by the two approaches are completely different: The possible worlds approach is inferentially investigating domain constraints, while the STRIPS approach is searching through an extensive collection of add and delete lists.)

5 Conclusion

In this paper we have described an approach to reasoning about action using possible worlds. The approach involves keeping a single model of the world that is updated when actions are performed. The update procedure involves constructing the nearest world to the current one in which the consequences of the actions under consideration hold. The way we find the nearest world is to construct proofs of the negation of the explicit consequences of the expected action, and remove a premise in each proof from the current world. Computationally, this construction procedure appears to be tractable for worlds like our own where very few things tend to change with each action, or where change is regular.

The approach developed here is in some sense a formalized extension of the STRIPS approach; in both cases, a single model of the world is maintained, which is updated to reflect the result of any particular action. The difference is that in STRIPS, consistency is maintained after the execution of an action via the delete lists; in our approach, it is maintained inferentially using the constraints describing the domain in question. In some sense, the STRIPS descriptions of the actions "compile" the interactions between these actions and the domain constraints into the delete list.

In this paper we have focussed specifically on the frame and ramification problems, but have ignored the qualification problem. As mentioned earlier, we have applied the possible worlds construction described here to the qualification problem as well. In these cases one is forced to decide among different possible worlds: worlds in which the action is prevented by hidden qualifications, and worlds in which the consequences of the action overcome the qualifications. This work is described in detail in [10,12].

We have also applied the possible worlds approach described here to the construction of a working planning system. For planning problems we construct the closest possible world to the initial state for which the desired goal holds. The procedure for constructing this state is the same as that described in Section 3. The planning process is guided by seeking those actions that will lead to the nearest possible world from the initial one where a goal or subgoal holds. This planning system and the control procedure based on nearness of possible worlds are described in detail in [9,11].

Appendix

Proposition A.1. *Suppose we have an urn containing d distinct items. Then if we make x selections from the urn, replacing each item selected, the number of different items selected will be, on average,*

$$d\left[1-\left(1-\frac{1}{d}\right)^x\right].$$

Proof. Suppose that we fix d, and denote by $p(n, x)$ the probability of drawing n different items in x drawings, and by $f(x)$ the expected number of items selected. We are therefore trying to show that

$$f(x) = d\left[1 - \left(1 - \frac{1}{d}\right)^x\right].$$

If we are to select n items in $x+1$ drawings, then we must either select $n-1$ items in the first x drawings, followed by selecting a new item in the last drawing, or select n items in the first x drawings, followed by selecting an old item in the last one. Thus

$$p(n, x+1) = p(n, x)\frac{n}{d} + p(n-1, x)\left[1 - \frac{n-1}{d}\right].$$

We also have that

$$f(x) = \sum_1^d ip(i, x),$$

so that

$$\begin{aligned}
f(x+1) &= \sum_1^d ip(i, x+1) \\
&= \sum_1^d ip(i, x)\frac{i}{d} + \sum_1^d ip(i-1, x)\left(1 - \frac{i-1}{d}\right) \\
&= \sum_1^d p(i, x)\frac{i^2}{d} + \sum_0^{d-1} jp(j, x)\left(1 - \frac{j}{d}\right) + \sum_0^{d-1} p(j, x)\left(1 - \frac{j}{d}\right) \\
&= dp(d, x) + \sum_0^d jp(j, x) - dp(d, x) + \sum_0^d p(j, x) - \frac{1}{d}\sum_0^d jp(j, x) \\
&= \left(1 - \frac{1}{d}\right) f(x) + 1.
\end{aligned}$$

We also know that $f(0) = 0$.

For $x = 0$, the expression in the statement of the theorem does indeed reduce to 0; we must therefore show that it satisfies the recursion relation appearing above. But we have:

$$\begin{aligned}
f(x+1) &= d\left[1 - \left(1 - \frac{1}{d}\right)^{x+1}\right] \\
&= d\left[1 - \left(1 - \frac{1}{d}\right)^x \left(1 - \frac{1}{d}\right)\right] \\
&= d - d\left(1 - \frac{1}{d}\right)^x + \left(1 - \frac{1}{d}\right)^x \\
&= f(x) + \left[1 - \frac{f(x)}{d}\right] \\
&= \left(1 - \frac{1}{d}\right) f(x) + 1. \qquad \square
\end{aligned}$$

Acknowledgement

This work has been supported by DARPA under grant number N00039-86-C-0033 and by ONR under grant number N00014-81-K-0004. We would like to thank the Logic Group for providing, as ever, a cooperative and stimulating — and demanding — environment in which to work. We would also like to thank Mike Genesereth, Vladimir Lifschitz, Drew McDermott, Yoav Shoham, Narinder Singh and Marianne Winslett for their comments on various drafts of this paper.

References

[1] J. F. Allen. Towards a general theory of action and time. *Artificial Intelligence*, 23:123–154, 1984.

[2] J. de Kleer. An assumption-based truth maintenance system. *Artificial Intelligence*, 28:127–162, 1986.

[3] J. Doyle. A truth maintenance system. *Artificial Intelligence*, 12:231–272, 1979.

[4] R. Fagin, J. Ullman, and M. Vardi. On the semantics of updates in databases. In *Proceedings Second ACM Symposium on Principles of Database Systems*, pages 352–365, Atlanta, Georgia, 1983.

[5] R. Fikes and N. J. Nilsson. STRIPS: a new approach to the application of theorem proving to problem solving. *Artificial Intelligence*, 2:189–208, 1971.

[6] J. J. Finger. *Exploiting Constraints in Design Synthesis.* PhD thesis, Stanford University, Stanford, CA, 1987.

[7] M. L. Ginsberg. Counterfactuals. *Artificial Intelligence*, 30:35–79, 1986.

[8] M. L. Ginsberg. Multi-valued logics. In *Proceedings of the Fifth National Conference on Artificial Intelligence*, pages 243–247, 1986.

[9] M. L. Ginsberg. Possible worlds planning. In *Proceedings of the 1986 Workshop on Planning and Reasoning about Action*, pages 213–243, Morgan Kaufmann, Timberline, Oregon, 1986.

[10] M. L. Ginsberg and D. E. Smith. Possible worlds and the qualification problem. In *Proceedings of the Sixth National Conference on Artificial Intelligence*, pages 212–217, 1987.

[11] M. L. Ginsberg and D. E. Smith. Possible worlds planning. In preparation.

[12] M. L. Ginsberg and D. E. Smith. Reasoning about action II: The qualification problem. In *Proceedings of the 1987 Workshop on the Frame Problem in Artificial Intelligence*, Morgan Kaufmann, Lawrence, Kansas, 1987. To appear in *Artificial Intelligence.*

[13] C. C. Green. Theorem proving by resolution as a basis for question-answering systems. In B. Meltzer and D. Mitchie, editors, *Machine Intelligence 4*, pages 183–205, American Elsevier, New York, 1969.

[14] S. Hanks and D. McDermott. Default reasoning, nonmonotonic logics and the frame problem. In *Proceedings of the Fifth National Conference on Artificial Intelligence*, pages 328–333, 1986.

[15] V. Lifschitz. Formal theories of action. In *Proceedings of the 1987 Workshop on the Frame Problem in Artificial Intelligence*, Lawrence, Kansas, 1987.

[16] V. Lifschitz. On the semantics of STRIPS. In *Proceedings of the 1986 Workshop on Planning and Reasoning about Action*, Timberline, Oregon, 1986.

[17] V. Lifschitz. Pointwise circumscription. In M. L. Ginsberg, editor, *Readings in Non-Monotonic Reasoning*, Morgan Kaufmann, Los Altos, CA, 1987.

[18] V. Lifschitz. Pointwise circumscripton: preliminary report. In *Proceedings of the Fifth National Conference on Artificial Intelligence*, pages 406–410, 1986.

[19] J. McCarthy. Applications of circumscription to formalizing common sense knowledge. *Artificial Intelligence*, 28:89–116, 1986.

[20] J. McCarthy. Circumscription – a form of non-monotonic reasoning. *Artificial Intelligence*, 13:27–39, 1980.

[21] J. McCarthy. Epistemological problems of artificial intelligence. In *Proceedings of the Fifth International Joint Conference on Artificial Intelligence*, pages 1038–1044, Cambridge, MA, 1977.

[22] J. McCarthy. Programs with commmon sense. In M. Minsky, editor, *Semantic Information Processing*, pages 403–418, MIT, Cambridge, 1960.

[23] J. McCarthy and P. J. Hayes. Some philosophical problems from the standpoint of artificial intelligence. In B. Meltzer and D. Mitchie, editors, *Machine Intelligence 4*, pages 463–502, American Elsevier, New York, 1969.

[24] R. Moore. Semantical considerations on nonmonotonic logic. *Artificial Intelligence*, 25:75–94, 1985.

[25] R. Reiter. A logic for default reasoning. *Artificial Intelligence*, 13:81–132, 1980.

[26] R. Reiter. A theory of diagnosis from first principles. *Artificial Intelligence*, 32:57–95, 1987.

[27] R. Reiter and J. de Kleer. Foundations of assumption-based truth maintenance systems: Preliminary report. In *Proceedings of the Sixth National Conference on Artificial Intelligence*, pages 183–188, 1987.

[28] Y. Shoham. Chronological ignorance. In *Proceedings of the Fifth National Conference on Artificial Intelligence*, pages 389–393, 1986.

Appendix

Bibliography of Nonmonotonic Reasoning

A BIBLIOGRAPHY OF LITERATURE ON NON-MONOTONIC REASONING

Donald Perlis

Computer Science Department
and
Institute for Advanced Computer Studies

University of Maryland
College Park, MD 20742

Akama, S. [1987] Presupposition and frame problem in knowledge bases. In Proceedings of the 1987 Workshop on the Frame Problem in Artificial Intelligence, Lawrence, KS, pp 193-203.

Allen, J. [1984] Towards a general theory of action and time, Artificial Intelligence 23 (2), 1984, pp 123-154.

Apt, K., Blair, H. and Walker, A. [1986] Towards a theory of declarative knowledge. In Proceedings of the 1986 Workshop on Foundations of Deductive Databases and Logic Programming, 1986. Also to appear in Foundations of Deductive Databases and Logic Programming, J. Minker (ed.), Morgan Kaufmann, Los Altos, 1987.

Asher, N. [1984] Linguistic understanding and non-monotonic reasoning. In Proceedings 1984 Nonmonotonic Reasoning Workshop, pp 1-20, American Association for Artificial Intelligence, New Paltz, NY.

Besnard, Ph., Quiniou, R., and Quinton, P. [1983] A theorem-prover for a decidable subset of default logic. Proc. AAAI-83, pp. 27-30.

Bobrow, D. G. and Hayes, P. J. [1985] Artificial intelligence - where are we? Artificial Intelligence, 24, pp 375-415, 1985.

Borgida, A. and Imielinski, T. [1984] Decision making in committees--A framework for dealing with inconsistency and non-monotonicity. In Proceedings 1984 Nonmonotonic Reasoning Workshop, pp 21-32, American Association for Artificial Intelligence, New Paltz, NY.

Bossu, G. and Siegel, P. [1985] Saturation, nonmonotonic reasoning and the closed-world assumption. Artificial Intelligence, 25, pp 13-63, 1985.

Brachman, R. [1982] What 'IS-A' is and isn't, Proc. Canadian Soc. for Computational Studies of Intelligence-82, Saskatoon, Sask., May 17-19, pp 212-220. Also in IEEE Computer, 16(10), pp 30-36, 1983.

Brachman, R. [1985] I lied about the trees or, defaults and definitions in knowledge representation. AI Magazine, 6(3), pp 80-93, 1985.

Brewka, G. [1987] The logic of frames with exceptions. In Proceedings of the 1987 Workshop on the Frame Problem in Artificial Intelligence, Lawrence, KS, pp 77-87.

Brown, F. M. [1987] A modal logic for the representation of knowledge. In Proceedings of the 1987 Workshop on the Frame Problem in Artificial Intelligence, Lawrence, KS, pp 135-157.

Brown, F. M., and Park, S. S. [1987] Action, reflective possibility, and the frame problem. In Proceedings of the 1987 Workshop on the Frame Problem in Artificial Intelligence, Lawrence, KS, pp 159-174.

de Champeaux, D. [1987] Unframing the frame problem. In Proceedings of the 1987 Workshop on the Frame Problem in Artificial Intelligence, Lawrence, KS, pp 311-318.

Clark, K. [1978] Negation as failure. In: Logic and Databases, Gallaire, H. and Minker, J. (eds.). Plenum Press, New York, pp. 293-322.

Cottrell, G. [1984] Re: Inheritance hierarchies with exceptions. In Proceedings 1984 Nonmonotonic Reasoning Workshop, pp 33-56, American Association for Artificial Intelligence, New Paltz, NY.

Cottrell, G. [1985]. Parallelism in inheritance hierarchies with exceptions, Proc. Ninth International Joint Conference on Artificial Intelligence, Los Angeles, CA, Aug. 18-23, 1985, pp 194-202.

Davis, M. [1980] The mathematics of non-monotonic reasoning. Artificial Intelligence, 13 (1,2), pp. 73-80.

Doyle, J. [1977] Truth maintenance systems for problem solving. Proc. 5th IJCAI, p. 247.

Doyle, J. [1979] A glimpse of truth maintenance. Proc. 6th IJCAI, pp. 232-237.

Doyle, J. [1979] A truth maintenance system. Artificial Intelligence, 12, pp 231-272.

Doyle, J. [1982] Some theories of reasoned assumptions: An essay in rational psychology. Technical Report, Department of Computer Science, Carnegie-Mellon University.

Doyle, J. [1983] The ins and outs of reason maintenance. Proc. 8th IJCAI, pp. 349-351.

Doyle, J. [1984] Circumscription and implicit definability. In Proceedings 1984 Nonmonotonic Reasoning Workshop, pp 57-69, American Association for Artificial Intelligence, New Paltz, NY. Also in J. of Automated Reasoning, 1, pp 391-405, 1985.

Doyle, J. [1985] Reasoned assumptions and Pareto optimality. In Proceedings of the Ninth International Joint Conference on Artificial Intelligence, pp 87-90.

Doyle, J., and London, P. [1980] A selected descriptor-indexed bibliography to the literature on belief revision, AI Memo 568, MIT, Cambridge, Mass.

Drapkin, J. and Perlis, D. [1986] Step-logics: An alternative approach to limited reasoning. Proc. European Conference on Artificial Intelligence, Brighton, 1986.

Drapkin, J. and Perlis, D. [1986] Preliminary excursion into step-logics. Proceedings, International Symposium on Methodologies for Intelligent Systems, Knoxville, KY.

Elgot-Drapkin, J., Miller, M. and Perlis, D. [1987] The two frame problems. In Proceedings of the 1987 Workshop on the Frame Problem in Artificial Intelligence, Lawrence, KS, pp 23-28.

Elgot-Drapkin, J., Miller, M. and Perlis, D. [1987] Life on a desert island: Ongoing work on a real-time reasoning. In Proceedings of the 1987 Workshop on the Frame Problem in Artificial Intelligence, Lawrence, KS, pp 349-357.

Etherington, D. W [1982] Finite default theories. MSc Thesis, University of British Columbia.

Etherington, D. W. [1986] Reasoning with incomplete information: Investigations of non-monotonic reasoning. PhD thesis, University of British Columbia, Vancouver, Canada, 1986.

Etherington, D.W. [1987] Relating default logic and circumscription, IJCAI-87 , Milan.

Etherington, D.W. [1987] A semantics for default logic, IJCAI-87, Milan.

Etherington, D.W. [1987] On inheritance hierarchies with exceptions: Default theories and inferential distance, AAAI-87, Seattle.

Etherington, D. W. [1987] Formalizing nonmonotonic reasoning systems. Artificial Intelligence, 31, pp 41-85, 1987.

Etherington, D.W. and Mercer, R.E. [1986] Domain circumscription revisited, Proc. Canadian Society for Computational Studies of Intelligence-86, Montreal, May 1986.

Etherington, D.W. and Mercer, R.E. [1987] Domain circumscription: a re-evaluation, Computational Intelligence 3.

Etherington, D. W., Mercer, R. E., and Reiter, R. [1985] On the adequacy of predicate circumscription for closed-world reasoning. Comp. Intelligence, 1, pp 11-15.

Etherington, D. W. and Reiter, R. [1983] On inheritance hierarchies with exceptions. Proc. AAAI-83, pp. 104-108.

Fahlman, S., Touretzky, D., and Van Roggen, W. [1981] Cancellation in a parallel semantic network. Proc. 7th IJCAI, pp. 257-263.

Finger, J. J. [1987] Exploiting constraints in design synthesis. PhD thesis, Stanford University, Stanford, CA, 1987.

Fischler, M. and Firschein, O. [1984] Computational vision as a (non-monotonic) reasoning process. In Proceedings 1984 Nonmonotonic Reasoning Workshop, pp 82-92, American Association for Artificial Intelligence, New Paltz, NY.

Gabbay, D. [1982] Intuitionistic basis for non-monotonic logic. Lecture Notes in Computer Science, Vol. 139, Springer.

Gelfond, M. [1986] On stratified autoepistemic theories. Technical Report, University of Texas at El Paso, 1986.

Gelfond, M. and Przymusinska, H. [1986] On the relationship between autoepistemic logic and parallel circumscription. Technical Report, University of Texas at El Paso, 1986.

Gelfond, M. and Przymusinska, H. [1986] Negation as failure: Careful closure procedure. Artificial Intelligence, 30, pp 273-287, 1986.

Gelfond, M., Przymusinska, H. and Przymusinsk, T. [1986] The extended closed world assumption and its relationship to parallel circumscription. In Proceedings of ACM SIGACT-SIGMOD Symposium on Principles of Database Systems, pp 133-139, 1986.

Georgeff, M. P. [1987] Many agents are better than one. In Proceedings of the 1987 Workshop on the Frame Problem in Artificial Intelligence, Lawrence, KS, pp 59-75.

Ginsberg, M. L. [1984] Non-monotonic reasoning using Dempster's rule. In Proceedings of the Fourth National Conference on Artificial Intelligence, pp 126-129, 1984.

Ginsberg, M. L. [1985] Does probability have a place in non-monotonic reasoning? In Proceedings of the Ninth International Joint Conference on Artificial Intelligence, pp 107-110, 1985.

Ginsberg, M. L. [1986] Counterfactuals. Artificial Intelligence, 30, pp 35-80, 1986.

Ginsberg, M. L. [1986] Multi-valued Inference. Technical Report 86-73, KSL, Stanford University, 1986.

Ginsberg, M. L. [1986] Multi-valued Logics. Technical Report 86-29, KSL, Stanford University, 1986.

Ginsberg, M. L. [1986] Multi-valued logics. In Proceedings of the Fifth National Conference on Artificial Intelligence, pp 243-247, 1986.

Ginsberg, M. L. and Smith, D. E. [1987] Reasoning about action I: A possible worlds approach. In Proceedings of the 1987 Workshop on the Frame Problem in Artificial Intelligence, Lawrence, KS, pp 233-258.

Ginsberg, M. L. and Smith, D. E. [1987] Reasoning about action II: The qualification problem. In Proceedings of the 1987 Workshop on the Frame Problem in Artificial Intelligence, Lawrence, KS, pp 259-287.

Glymour, C. and Thomason, R. [1984] Default reasoning and the logic of theory perturbation. In Proceedings 1984 Nonmonotonic Reasoning Workshop, pp 93-102, American Association for Artificial Intelligence, New Paltz, NY.

Goebel, R. G., and Goodwin, S. D. [1987] Applying theory formation to the planning problem. In Proceedings of the 1987 Workshop on the Frame Problem in Artificial Intelligence, Lawrence, KS, pp 207-232.

Goodwin, J. [1984] WATSON: A dependency directed inference system. In Proceedings 1984 Nonmonotonic Reasoning Workshop, pp 103-114, American Association for Artificial Intelligence, New Paltz, NY.

Grant, J. and Minker, J. [1984] Answering queries in indefinite databases and the null value problem. Tech. Report 1374, University of Maryland.

Grosof, B. [1984] Default reasoning as circumscription. Workshop on Nonmonotonic Reasoning, New Paltz, NY, sponsored by AAAI, Oct. 17-19, 1984.

Grosof, B. [1986] Non-monotonicity in probabilistic reasoning. In Proceedings 1986 Workshop on Uncertainty in Artificial Intelligence, pp 91-98, Philadelphia, PA, 1986.

Haas, A. R. [1987] The case for domain-specific frame axioms. In Proceedings of the 1987 Workshop on the Frame Problem in Artificial Intelligence, Lawrence, KS, pp 343-348.

Hallnas, L. [1987] A note on non-monotonic reasoning. In Proceedings of the 1987 Workshop on the Frame Problem in Artificial Intelligence, Lawrence, KS, pp 89-104.

Halpern, J. Y. and Moses, Y. [1984] Towards a theory of knowledge and ignorance. In Proceedings 1984 Non-monotonic Reasoning Workshop, pp 165-193, American Association for Artificial Intelligence, New Paltz, NY, 1984.

Hanks, S. and McDermott, D. [1986] Default reasoning, nonmonotonic logics and the frame problem. In Proceedings of the Fifth National Conference on Artificial Intelligence, pp 328-333, 1986.

Haugh, B. [1987] Simple causal minimizations for temporal persistence and projection. AAAI-87 to appear.

Hayes, P. [1973] The frame problem and related problems in artificial intelligence, in Artificial and Human Thinking, A. Elithorn and D. Jones (eds.), Jossey-Bass Inc., San Francisco.

Hayes, P. [1987] The frame problem in histories. In Proceedings of the 1987 Workshop on the Frame Problem in Artificial Intelligence, Lawrence, KS, p 31.

Henschen, L. and Park, H.-S. [1986] In Proceedings of the 1986 Workshop on Foundations of Deductive Databases and Logic Programming, 1986. Also to appear in Foundations of Deductive Databases and Logic Programming, J. Minker (ed.), Morgan Kaufmann, Los Altos, 1987.

Imielinski, T. [1987] Results on translating defaults to circumscription. Artificial Intelligence, 32, pp 131-146.

Israel, D. [1980] What's wrong with non-monotonic logic? In Proceedings of the First National Conference on Artificial Intelligence, pp 99-101, 1980.

Joshi, A., Webber, B., and Weischedel, R. [1984] Default reasoning in interaction. In Proceedings 1984 Nonmonotonic Reasoning Workshop, pp 144-150, American Association for Artificial Intelligence, New Paltz, NY.

Kautz, H. A. [1986] The logic of persistence. In Proceedings of the Fifth National Conference on Artificial Intelligence, pp 401-405, 1986.

de Kleer, J. [1984] Choices without backtracking. In Proceedings of the Fourth National Conference on Artificial Intelligence, pp 79-85, 1984.

de Kleer, J. [1986] An assumption-based truth maintenance system. Artificial Intelligence, 28, pp 127-162, 1986.

de Kleer, J. [1986] Extending the ATMS. Artificial Intelligence, 28, pp 163-196, 1986.

de Kleer, J. [1986] Problem solving with the ATMS. Artificial Intelligence, 28, pp 197-224, 1986.

de Kleer, J. and Williams, B. C. [1987] Diagnosing multiple faults. Artificial Intelligence, 32, pp 97-130, 1987.

Konolige, K. [1982] Circumscriptive ignorance. Proc. AAAI-82, pp. 202-204.

Konolige, K. [1984] Belief and incompleteness. SRI Tech. Note 319.

Konolige, K. [1987] On the relation between default theories and autoepistemic logic. In Ginsberg, M. L., editor, Readings in Non-Monotonic Reasoning, Morgan Kaufmann, Los Altos, CA, 1987. Also in Proceedings, IJCAI-87.

Konolige, K. and Myers, K. L. [1987] Representing defaults with epistemic concepts. Draft, SRI International.

Kowalski, R. [1978] Logic for data description. In: Logic and Databases, Gallaire, H. and Minker, J. (eds.). Plenum Press, New York, pp. 77-103.

Kowalski, R. [1979] Logic for Problem Solving. North-Holland, New York.

Kowalski, R. and Sergot, M. [1986] A logic-based calculus of events. New Generation Computing, 4, pp 67-95, 1986.

Kramosil, I. [1975] A note on deduction rules with negative premises. In Proceedings of the Fourth International Joint Conference on Artificial Intelligence, pp 53-56, 1975.

Kueker, D. [1984] Another failure of completeness for circumscription. Week on Logic and Artificial Intelligence, Univ. of Maryland, Oct. 22-26, 1984.

Levesque, H. [1981] Incompleteness in knowledge bases. SIGART Newsletter 74, p. 150ff.

Levesque, H. [1981] The interaction with incomplete knowledge bases: a formal treatment. Proc. 7th IJCAI, pp. 240-245.

Levesque, H. [1982] A formal treatment of incomplete knowledge. Fairchild Lab for AI Research, Tech. Report 3.

Lifschitz, V. [1984] Some results on circumscription. Workshop on Nonmonotonic Reasoning, New Paltz, NY, sponsored by AAAI, Oct. 17-19, 1984.

Lifschitz, V. [1985] Closed-world databases and circumscription. Artificial Intelligence, 27, pp 229-235, 1985.

Lifschitz, V. [1985] Computing circumscription. In Proceedings of the Ninth International Joint Conference on Artificial Intelligence, pp 121-127, 1985.

Lifschitz, V. [1986] On the declarative semantics of logic programs with negation. In Proceedings of the 1986 Workshop on Foundations of Deductive Databases and Logic Programming, 1986. Also to appear in Foundations of Deductive Databases and Logic Programming, J. Minker (ed.), Morgan Kaufmann, Los Altos, 1987.

Lifschitz, V. [1986] On the satisfiability of circumscription. Artificial Intelligence, 28, pp 17-27, 1986.

Lifschitz, V. [1987] Pointwise circumscription. In Ginsberg, M. L., editor, Readings in Non-Monotonic Reasoning, Morgan Kaufmann, Los Altos, CA, 1987.

Lifschitz, V. [1986] Pointwise circumscription: preliminary report. In Proceedings of the Fifth National Conference on Artificial Intelligence, pp 406-410, 1986.

Lifschitz, V. [1987] Formal theories of action. IJCAI-87, to appear.

Lifschitz, V. [1987] Formal theories of action. In Proceedings of the 1987 Workshop on the Frame Problem in Artificial Intelligence, Lawrence, KS, pp 35-57.

Lipski, W. [1977] On the logic of incomplete information. Lecture Notes in Computer Science, v.53, Springer, pp. 374-381. (6th Symposium on Mathematical Foundations of Computer Science.)

Lipski, W. [1979] On semantic issues connected with incomplete information databases, ACM Transactions on Database Systems 4 (3), Sept. 1979, pp 262-296.

Lukaszewicz, W. [1984] Considerations on default logic. In Proceedings 1984 Non-monotonic Reasoning Workshop, pp 165-193, American Association for Artificial Intelligence, New Paltz, NY, 1984.

Lukaszewicz, W. [1983] General approach to nonmonotonic logics. Proc. 8th IJCAI, pp. 352-354.

Marek, W. [1984] A natural semantics for modal logic over databases and model-theoretic forcing I. In Proceedings 1984 Nonmonotonic Reasoning Workshop, pp 194-240, American Association for Artificial Intelligence, New Paltz, NY.

Martins, J. [1983] Reasoning in multiple belief spaces, PhD thesis, SUNY at Buffalo, Computer Science Technical Report 203.

Martins, J. P. and Shapiro, S. C. [1983] Reasoning in multiple belief spaces. In Proceedings of the Eighth International Joint Conference on Artificial Intelligence, pp 370-373, 1983.

Martins, J. and Shapiro, S. [1984] A model for belief revision. In Proceedings 1984 Nonmonotonic Reasoning Workshop, pp 241-294, American Association for Artificial Intelligence, New Paltz, NY.

McAllester, D.A. [1978] A three-valued truth maintenance system, AI Memo 473, MIT, Cambridge, Mass.

McAllester, D.A. [1980] An outlook on truth maintenance, AI Memo 551, MIT, Cambridge, Mass.

McCarthy, J. [1977] Epistemological problems of artificial intelligence. In Proceedings of the Fifth International Joint Conference on Artificial Intelligence, pp 1038-1044, Cambridge, MA, 1977.

McCarthy, J. [1980] Circumscription--a form of non-monotonic reasoning. Artificial Intelligence, 13 (1,2), pp. 27-39.

McCarthy, J. [1980] Addendum: circumscription and other non-monotonic formalisms. Artificial Intelligence, 13 (1,2), pp. 171-172.

McCarthy, J. [1984] Applications of circumscription to formalizing common sense knowledge. Workshop on Nonmonotonic Reasoning, New Paltz, NY, sponsored by AAAI, Oct. 17-19, 1984.

McCarthy, J. [1986] Applications of circumscription to formalizing common sense knowledge. Artificial Intelligence, 28, pp 89-116, 1986.

McCarthy, J. [1987] The frame problem today. In Proceedings of the 1987 Workshop on the Frame Problem in Artificial Intelligence, Lawrence, KS, p 3.

McCarthy, J. and Hayes, P. [1969] Some philosophical problems from the standpoint of artificial intelligence. In Machine Intelligence 4, Meltzer, B. and Michie, D. (eds.), Edinburgh University Press.

McCarty, T. [1984] Programming directly in a non monotonic logic. In Proceedings 1984 Non-monotonic Reasoning Workshop, pp 325-336, American Association for Artificial Intelligence, New Paltz, NY.

McDermott, D. [1982] Non-monotonic logic II: non-monotonic modal theories. Journal of the ACM, 29 (1), pp. 33-57.

McDermott, D. [1982] A temporal logic for reasoning about processes and plans. Cognitive Science, 6, pp 101-155.

McDermott, D. [1987] AI, logic, and the frame problem. In Proceedings of the 1987 Workshop on the Frame Problem in Artificial Intelligence, Lawrence, KS, pp 105-118.

McDermott, D. [1987] A critique of pure reason. Computational Intelligence. To appear.

McDermott, D. and Doyle, J. [1980] Non-monotonic logic I. Artificial Intelligence, 13 (1,2), pp. 41-72.

Mercer, R.E. and Reiter, R. [1982] The representation of presuppositions using defaults. Proc. 4th Nat. Conf. Can. Soc. for Computational Studies of Intelligence, Saskatoon, May 17-19,1982, pp.103-107.

Mercer, R. and Rosenberg, R.S. [1984] Generating corrective answers by computing presuppositions of answers, not questions, or Mind your P's, not Q's. Proc CSCSI-84, pp16-18.

Minker, J. [1982] On indefinite databases and the closed-world assumption. Lecture Notes in Computer Science, v. 138, pp. 292-308, Springer. (6th Conference on Automated Deduction).

Minker, J. and Perlis, D. [1984] Protected circumscription. In Proceedings 1984 Non-monotonic Reasoning Workshop, pp 337-343, American Association for Artificial Intelligence, New Paltz, NY, 1984.

Minker, J. and Perlis, D. [1984] Applications of protected circumscription. Lecture Notes in Computer Science, v. 170, pp. 414-425, Springer. (7th Conference on Automated Deduction).

Minker, J. and Perlis, D. [1985] Computing protected circumscription. Logic Programming Journal, 4, 235-249.

Minsky, M. [1975] A framework for representing knowledge. In P. Winston, editor, The Psychology of Computer Vision, pp 211-277, McGraw-Hill, 1975.

Moore, R. [1975] Reasoning from incomplete knowledge in a procedural deduction system. MIT AI Lab Memo 347.

Moore, R. [1983] Semantical considerations on non-monotonic logic. Proc. 8th IJCAI, pp. 272-279.

Moore. R. [1984] Possible-world semantics for autoepistemic logic. In Proceedings 1984 Nonmonotonic Reasoning Workshop, pp 344-354, American Association for Artificial Intelligence, New Paltz, NY.

Moore, R. [1985] Semantical considerations on nonmonotonic logic. Artificial Intelligence, 25, pp 75-94, 1985.

Morris, P. [1987] A truth maintenance based approach to the frame problem. In Proceedings of the 1987 Workshop on the Frame Problem in Artificial Intelligence, Lawrence, KS, pp 297-307.

Mott, P. L. [1987] A theorem on the consistency of circumscription. Artificial Intelligence, 31, 87-98.

Nutter, J. [1983] Default reasoning using monotonic logic: A modest proposal. In Proceedings of the Third National Conference on Artificial Intelligence, pp 297-300, 1983.

Nutter, J. [1983] Default reasoning in AI systems. MSc Thesis, SUNY at Buffalo, Computer Science Tech. Report 204.

Nutter, J. [1983] What else is wrong with nonmonotonic logics? Representational and informational shortcomings. Proc. 5th Cognitive Science Conference, Rochester.

Papalaskaris, M. A. and Bundy, A. [1984] Topics for circumscription. In Proceedings 1984 Nonmonotonic Reasoning Workshop, pp 355-362, American Association for Artificial Intelligence, New Paltz, NY.

Park, S. S. [1987] Doubting Thomas: Action and belief revision. In Proceedings of the 1987 Workshop on the Frame Problem in Artificial Intelligence, Lawrence, KS, pp 175-191.

Pena, L. [1980] The philosophical relevance of a contradictorial system of logic. Proc. 10th Int'l Symposium on Multiple-valued Logic, pp. 238-252.

Perlis, D. [1984] Non-monotonicity and real-time reasoning. In Proceedings 1984 Nonmonotonic Reasoning Workshop, pp 363-372, American Association for Artificial Intelligence, New Paltz, NY.

Perlis, D. [1987] On the consistency of commonsense reasoning. Computational Intelligence, 2, 1987, 180-190.

Perlis, D. [1987] Circumscribing with sets. Artificial Intelligence, 31, 201-211.

Perlis, D. [1987] Languages with self-reference II: Knowledge, belief, and modality. Technical Report, University of Maryland.

Perlis, D. [1987] Circumscription as introspection. Technical Report, University of Maryland.

Perlis, D. and Minker, J. [1986] Completeness results for circumscription. Artificial Intelligence, 28, pp 29-42, 1986.

Perrault, R. [1987] An application of default logic to speech act theory. Technical Report, SRI International, 1987.

Poole, D. [1984] A logical system for default reasoning. In Proceedings 1984 Nonmonotonic Reasoning Workshop, pp 373-384, American Association for Artificial Intelligence, New Paltz, NY.

Przymusinski, T. [1986] Query-answering in circumscriptive and closed-world theories. In Proceedings of the Fifth National Conference on Artificial Intelligence, pp 186-190, 1986.

Przymusinski, T. [1986] On the semantics of stratified deductive databases. In Proceedings of the 1986 Workshop on Foundations of Deductive Databases and Logic Programming, 1986. Also to appear in Foundations of Deductive Databases and Logic Programming, J. Minker (ed.), Morgan Kaufmann, Los Altos, 1987.

Raphael, B. [1971] The frame problem in problem-Solving, in Artificial Intelligence and Heuristic Programming, N.V. Findler and B. Meltzer (eds.), Edinburgh University Press, Edinburgh.

Reinfrank, M. [1987] Multiple extensions, where is the problem? In Proceedings of the 1987 Workshop on the Frame Problem in Artificial Intelligence, Lawrence, KS, pp 291-295.

Reggia, J. and Nau, D. [1984] An abductive non-monotonic logic. In Proceedings 1984 Nonmonotonic Reasoning Workshop, pp 385-395, American Association for Artificial Intelligence, New Paltz, NY.

Reiter, R. [1978] On closed world data bases. In H. Gallaire and J. Minker, editors, Logic and Data Bases, pp 119-140, Plenum, New York, 1978.

Reiter, R. [1978] On closed world databases. In: Logic and Databases, Gallaire, H. and Minker, J. (eds.), Plenum, pp. 55-76.

Reiter, R. [1978] On reasoning by default. Proceedings TINLAP-2 (Theoretical Issues in Natural Language Processing-2), Urbana, Ill.

Reiter, R. [1980] Equality and domain closure in first-order databases. Journal of the ACM 27 (2), pp. 235-249.

Reiter, R. [1980] A logic for default reasoning, Artificial Intelligence 13 (1,2), pp. 81-132.

Reiter, R. [1982] Circumscription implies predicate completion (sometimes). Proc. AAAI-82, pp. 418-420.

Reiter, R. [1987] A theory of diagnosis from first principles. Artificial Intelligence, 32, pp 57-95.

Reiter, R. [1987] Nonmonotonic reasoning. Annual Reviews of Computer Science, 1987.

Reiter, R. and Criscuolo, G. [1981] On interacting defaults. In Proceedings of the Seventh International Joint Conference on Artificial Intelligence, pp 270-276, 1981.

Reiter, R. and Criscuolo, G. [1983] Some representational issues in default reasoning. Int. J. Computers and Mathematics (special issue on computational linguistics).

Reiter, R. and de Kleer, J. [1987] Formal foundations for assumption-based truth maintenance systems: preliminary report. Proc. AAAI-87, Amer. Assoc. for Art. Intell. Nat. Conf., Seattle, to appear.

Rescher, N. [1976] Plausible Inference. Van Gorcum, Assen, The Netherlands.

Rich, E. [1983] Default reasoning as likelihood reasoning. In Proceedings of the Third National Conference on Artificial Intelligence, pp 348-351, 1983.

Rolston, D. W. [1987] Toward a tense-logic-based mitigation of the frame problem. In Proceedings of the 1987 Workshop on the Frame Problem in Artificial Intelligence, Lawrence, KS, pp 319-341.

Sandewall, E. [1972] An approach to the frame problem and its implementation. Machine Intelligence 7, University of Edinburgh Press.

Sandewall, E. [1983] Partial models, attribute propogation systems, and non-monotonic semantics. Linkoping University. LITH-IDA-R-83-01.

Sandewall, E. [1987] The frame problem in AI. In Proceedings of the 1987 Workshop on the Frame Problem in Artificial Intelligence, Lawrence, KS, p 29.

Schwind, C. B. [1987] Action theory and the frame problem. In Proceedings of the 1987 Workshop on the Frame Problem in Artificial Intelligence, Lawrence, KS, pp 121-134.

Shepherdson, J. C. [1984] Negation as failure: A comparison of Clark's completed data base and Reiter's closed world assumption. J. Logic Programming, 1, pp 51-79, 1984.

Shepherdson, J. C. [1985] Negation as failure II. J. Logic Programming, 3, pp 185- 202, 1985.

Shepherdson, J. C. [1986] Negation in logic programming. In Proceedings of the 1986 Workshop on Foundations of Deductive Databases and Logic Programming, 1986. Also to appear in Foundations of Deductive Databases and Logic Programming, J. Minker (ed.), Morgan Kaufmann, Los Altos, 1987.

Shoham,Y. [1986] Chronological ignorance. In Proceedings of the Fifth National Conference on Artificial Intelligence, pp 389-393, 1986.

Shoham, Y. [1987] Non-monotonic logics. In Ginsberg, M. L., editor, Readings in Non-Monotonic Reasoning, Morgan Kaufmann, Los Altos, CA, 1987.

Shoham, Y. [1987] What is the frame problem? In Proceedings of the 1987 Workshop on the Frame Problem in Artificial Intelligence, Lawrence, KS, pp 5-21.

Stalnaker, R. [1980] A note on non-monotonic modal logic. Dept. of Philosophy, Cornell University.

Topor, R. and Sonenberg, E. A. [1986] On domain independent databases. In Proceedings of the 1986 Workshop on Foundations of Deductive Databases and Logic Programming, 1986. Also to appear in Foundations of Deductive Databases and Logic Programming, J. Minker (ed.), Morgan Kaufmann, Los Altos, 1987.

Touretzky, D. [1984] The mathematics of inheritance systems. Ph.D. Thesis, Carnegie-Mellon University.

Touretzky, D. [1984] Implicit ordering of defaults in inheritance systems. In Proceedings of the Fifth National Conference on Artificial Intelligence, pp 322-325, 1984.

Van Gelder, A. [1986] Negation as failure using tight derivations for general logic programs. In Proceedings of the 1986 Workshop on Foundations of Deductive Databases and Logic Programming, 1986. Also to appear in Foundations of Deductive Databases and Logic Programming, J. Minker (ed.), Morgan Kaufmann, Los Altos, 1987.

Vere, S. [1980] Multi-level counterfactuals for generalizations of relational concepts and productions. Artificial Intelligence, 14 (2), pp. 139-164.

Weyhrauch, R. [1980] Prolegomena to a theory of mechanized formal reasoning Artificial Intelligence, 13 (1,2), pp. 133-170.

Winograd, T. [1980] Extended inference modes in reasoning by computer systems. Artificial Intelligence 13 (1,2), pp. 5-26.

Yahya, A. and Henschen, L. J. [1985] Deduction in non-Horn databases. Journal of Automated Reasoning, 1, pp 141-160.

1984 Workshop on Non-Monotonic Reasoning, New Paltz, NY, 1984.

1985 Workshop on Uncertainty and Probability in Artificial Intelligence, UCLA, Los Angeles, California, 1985.

1986 Workshop on Uncertainty in Artificial Intelligence, University of Pennsylvania, Philadelphia, PA, 1986.

1986 Workshop on Foundations of Deductive Databases and Logic Programming, Washington, D.C., 1986.

1987 Workshop on the Frame Problem in Artificial Intelligence, Lawrence, KS, 1987.

Index

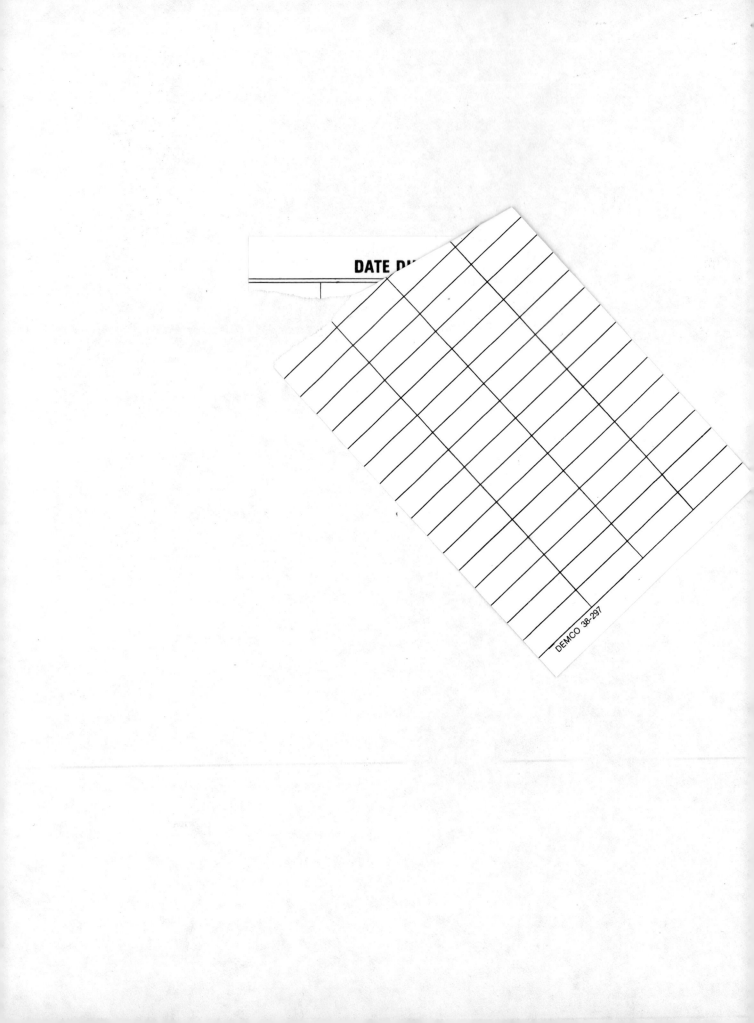